THE ICE PAGES

1997-98 MINOR-PROFESSIONAL HOCKEY GUIDE

TOM SCHETTINO

Athletic Guide Publishing

The Ice Pages 1997-98 Minor Professional Hockey Guide

Copyright 1997 by the TS Hockey Publication Company

Compiled by Thomas Schettino, Jr.

This book may not be reproduced in whole or in part in any form or by any means, electronic or mechanical, including photocopying, recording, or by any information storage and retrieval system now known or hereafter invented, without written permission by the TS Hockey Publications.

Acknowledgments:

The challenges of putting this book together for the second season were different from the first season. Many of the challenges came from the readers of the first book who suggested some changes in the format. The changes will be explained a bit later in the introduction.

The first people I would like to thank this season are the people who read the inaugural copy of The Ice Pages. If not for your creative comments, encouragement and support I would not have spent yet another summer in front of the computer terminal making this season's book. The second group of people I would like to thank is the group of people that form the In The Crease website. I found this group of people in early September of last year and I have had a blast meeting them and working with them to put together a pretty darned good website.

A special thanks goes out to Phil Komarny and Joe Levandosky who run the site for letting me create what I consider one of the better minor-pro sites on the net out there. We call it Meet the Minors and while it is a lot of work it is quite fun. Kit Amundson also gets a boatload of thanks for her work in making the site known to all the mover and shakers in the hockey world.

As always I would like to thank my friends and family, at work, at home and at play.

Of course this book would not have been accomplished without the statistics from Howe Sports Data in Boston. Many of these guys are up until 2 am getting the stats ready for us the following day. Thanks goes out to the artistic and entertainment talents of some folks that I don't know personally. However, their works of art made the long nights go by. That group includes Art Bell (Coast to Coast and Dreamland), The Connells, Uncle Tupelo and his offspring Wilco and Son Volt, January's Little Joke, Steve Wynn, Scott Miller (The Loud Family) and the Toadies. You may not know who they are, but they are good, go buy their stuff!

Finally this season I would like to dedicate this book to Tim and Mary Beth Schettino. Tim is the little brother that all of us would love to have and it is fun watching him and his adventures. Mary Beth had her own personal struggles this year and came out with flying colors. She is preparing to write a book about her ordeals that will kick the butt of this book in a second! Thanks to MJ for the time allowed to do this publication.

Until next season, Tom

The Ice Pages 1997-98 Minor Professional Hockey Guide
Published by
Athletic Guide Publishing
P. O. Box 1050
Flagler Beach, FL 32136
800-255-1050

Table Of Contents

Introduction	4
The Players	
A	7
B	18
C	66
D	98
E	127
F	137
G	153
H	175
I	201
J	203
K	211
L	230
M	261
N	316
O	325
P	331
Q	353
R	355
S	380
T and U	426
V	443
W	452
X and Y	468
Z	472
Reduced Role Players	
Skaters	475
Goalies	483
Directories and Statistics	485

Welcome to the Second Annual *Ice Pages* Minor Hockey League Guide produced in conjecture with the In the Crease's Meet the Minors Webpages

WWW.inthecrease.com

The idea seemed simple at the time, simply move from a system that had players with their 1995-96 teams to an alphabetical system. I didn't quite work out that way, we are using the alphabetical system, but it sure wasn't easy!

But I am done with this season's edition and I am very pleased with the way it turned out. As I mentioned above; the players are now in alphabetical order for easier location. I also tightened the margins a bit in order to reduce the size of the book for easier use. Another improvement was to make all of the player's team names to be printed in full. You will no longer need to know that CDI equals the Capital District Islanders or that PEI equals Prince Edward Island.

This season's guide will contain complete career records of every player who appeared in at least 20 games last season or in the playoffs. Sometimes exceptions will be made, if a player appeared in say 19 games he's likely be included. Players who didn't appear in 20 games because of injury may also be included.

We will also note if a player was part of a championship team. In order to qualify to have that notation a player must have competed in a playoff game for that club. That rule will likely effect backup goaltenders and injured players. For example, Mark Karpen will not be credited with a championship season with the Wichita Thunder during the 1994-95 season. I personally know that Karpen was not part of the playoff roster for the Thunder because of injury, but I can't possibly know that information for all leagues and all teams.

I will use abbreviations in this book, they are all standard abbreviations, but there will be a list of all abbreviations on the next page for those of you who aren't quite sure what the abbreviations mean.

My bottom line with this guide is accuracy. If you believe that I have omitted something or have made an error please help me out. I will appreciate any comment or correction that you can make. Please send those comments or corrections to:
TS Hockey Publications
949 East Manor Drive
Chandler, AZ 85525
In order for me to make final resolution of the issue in question, please include your source showing your correction along too.

Thank you very much.

Abbreviations and Terms

Player Abbreviations
League: The league that the player appeared in
GP: Games played
G: Goals
A: Assists
PTS: Points
PIM: Penalties in minutes (aka: penalty minutes)

Goaltender Abbreviations
League: The league the player appeared in.
GP: Games played
W: Wins
L: Losses
T: Ties (known as (OTL) overtime losses in every league except the American League and the NHL.
MP: Minutes played
SO: shutouts
GAVG: Goals against average. Value is determined by dividing MP (minutes played) by 60 and the number of goals against.

League Abbreviations:
NHL: National Hockey League   World's premier hockey league.

AHL: American Hockey League   Serves as the main farm league for NHL. Marketing is starting to take it's hold in the league. There is a new interest in catchy logos and entertainment to go along with solid hockey.

IHL: International Hockey League   This league put a premium on defense last season. Probably the toughest league for the players to do well in with the exception of the NHL. The IHL has teams in big cities and has an older corps of players.

ECHL: East Coast Hockey League   Feeder league provides talent to mainly the AHL, but the IHL also signs many of the ECHL's players. Happy 10th anniversary to the league that started the minor-pro hockey boom.

CeHL: Central Hockey League-   Few of the Central League's players are promoted during the season. The league is trying to establish more ties to the IHL to change that and become another "feeder" league. Climate and fan involvement are the primary attractions for the players in this league.

CoHL: Colonial Hockey League   Now known as the United Hockey League (UHL). Once the poor sister to the other leagues this loop has an aggressive commissioner who is attempting to bring the league into a boom cycle. While the UHL is a feeder league mainly to the IHL, many players also spend time in AHL lineups. Liberal veteran rules and proximity to many players' hometowns are huge plusses for the league.

WCHL: West Coast Hockey League   This league's talent pool is on a tremendous upswing. The loop's expansion into the Idaho area especially looks like a winner. The league is not quite on par with ECHL and CoHL, but advancement possibilities do exist. The western based IHL club's will be using the WCHL to place players who can't quite crack their rosters.

WPHL: Western Professional Hockey League   In a word this league is "aggressive" off the ice and on the ice. The WPHL has placed teams in areas such as Little Rock and Albuquerque that were coveted by other leagues. On the ice the WPHL has some excellent players although the depth isn't quite on par with the UHL. Part of that reason is the fact that unlike the UHL which is located near to player's hometowns, there aren't too many players from Texas, Louisiana and the like. The liberalized veteran rule in this league gives them a good shot at many experienced players.

Terms:

Entry Draft: Annual Draft held each summer to allocate 18 year old (+) players to NHL organizations.

Re-Entry: Player did not sign with team that drafted him and re-entered Entry Draft.

Supplemental Draft: Draft of players graduating unsigned from college hockey. Supplemental draft was put in place to avoid high-priced free agencies by graduating unsigned players. It has since been discontinued.

Traded: Sent to another team for a player or cash.

Sold: "Traded for cash".

Released: Team who holds players contracted rights decides to release player from all obligations.

Signed as free agent: Player with no obligations to another club signed to a contract.

Meet The Minors

The Meet the Minors section of the In The Crease website (www.inthecrease.com) is a great place to keep updated on all of the players in this book. Each and every league has a column that is updated at least once a week and also features interviews with players and coaches. We also held a logo contest which wound up attracting over 5,000 votes.

The playoffs are our crowning jewel. We had an update on each and every playoff game from the first game of the post season until the final game in the final league was completed.

We are always looking for contributors, so drop on by the site and see how you can get your own words into "cyperspace".

Congratulations

We would like to congratulate last season's champions. It takes a lot of hard work to win in these highly competitive leagues and you can bet that everyone will be gunning at these teams in the upcoming season.

NHL: Detroit Red Wings   AHL: Hershey Bears   IHL: Detroit Vipers
ECHL: South Carolina Stingrays CeHL: Fort Worth Fire   CoHL: Quad City Mallards
WCHL: San Diego Gulls   WPHL: El Paso Buzzards

Tobias Ablad — Defenseman

Season	Team	League	GP	G	A	PTS	PIM	GP	G	A	PTS	PIM
96-97	Jacksonville	ECHL	70	11	26	37	86	—	—	—	—	—

Born: 04/02/71, Stockholm, Sweden. 5-11, 207

Chad Ackerman — Defenseman

Season	Team	League	GP	G	A	PTS	PIM	GP	G	A	PTS	PIM
96-97	Portland	AHL	2	1	0	1	0	—	—	—	—	—
96-97	Hampton Roads	ECHL	65	9	11	20	50	5	2	1	3	8

Born: 06/15/73, Rochester, Michigan. 5-8, 190. Last amateur club: Bowling Green State (CCHA).

Akil Adams — Defenseman

Season	Team	League	GP	G	A	PTS	PIM	GP	G	A	PTS	PIM
95-96	Carolina	AHL	61	8	17	25	42	—	—	—	—	—
96-97	Port Huron	CoHL	6	1	1	2	6	—	—	—	—	—

Born: 8/13/74, Detroit, Michigan. 5-10, 200. Last amateur club: Ottawa 67's (OHL)

Jamie Adams — Left Wing

Season	Team	League	GP	G	A	PTS	PIM	GP	G	A	PTS	PIM
93-94	Johnstown	ECHL	43	16	21	37	16	—	—	—	—	—
93-94	Nashville	ECHL	17	8	11	19	6	2	0	0	0	2
94-95	Dallas	CeHL	65	17	30	47	24	—	—	—	—	—
95-96	Reno	WCHL	56	20	40	60	38	3	1	2	3	0
96-97	Reno	WCHL	60	21	32	53	66	—	—	—	—	—
	WCHL	Totals	116	41	72	113	104	3	1	2	3	0
	ECHL	Totals	60	24	32	56	22	2	0	0	0	2

Born: 11/24/71, Pittsburgh, Pennsylvania. 6-1, 175

Kevyn Adams — Center

Season	Team	League	GP	G	A	PTS	PIM	GP	G	A	PTS	PIM
96-97	Grand Rapids	IHL	82	22	25	47	47	5	1	1	2	4

Born: 10/8/74, Washington, District of Columbia. 6-1, 182. First choice, 25th overall by Boston Bruins in 1993 Entry Draft. Signed as a free agent by Grand Rapids Griffins. Solid defensive player who should play in the NHL someday.

Steve Adams — Defenseman

Season	Team	League	GP	G	A	PTS	PIM	GP	G	A	PTS	PIM
96-97	Austin	WPHL	5	0	0	0	0	—	—	—	—	—
96-97	Mississippi	ECHL	2	0	0	0	0	—	—	—	—	—
96-97	Nashville	CeHL	28	1	1	2	158	—	—	—	—	—

Born: 4/11/75, Edmonton, Alberta. 6-1, 215

Bernie Adlys — Center

Season	Team	League	GP	G	A	PTS	PIM	GP	G	A	PTS	PIM
96-97	Nashville	CeHL	56	10	19	29	61	—	—	—	—	—

Born: 3/4/72, Waterloo, Ontario. 5-8, 170.

Micah Aivazoff — Center

Season	Team	League	GP	G	A	PTS	PIM	GP	G	A	PTS	PIM
89-90	New Haven	AHL	77	20	39	59	71	—	—	—	—	—
90-91	New Haven	AHL	79	11	29	40	84	—	—	—	—	—

Season	Team	League	GP	G	A	PTS	PIM	GP	G	A	PTS	PIM
91-92	Adirondack	AHL	61	9	20	29	50	19	2	8	10	25
92-93	Adirondack	AHL	79	32	53	85	100	11	8	6	14	10
93-94	Detroit	NHL	59	4	4	8	38	—	—	—	—	—
94-95	Edmonton	NHL	21	0	1	1	2	—	—	—	—	—
95-96	New York Islanders	NHL	12	0	1	1	6	—	—	—	—	—
95-96	Utah	IHL	59	14	21	35	58	22	3	5	8	33
96-97	Binghamton	AHL	75	12	36	48	70	4	1	1	2	0
	NHL	Totals	92	4	6	10	46	—	—	—	—	—
	AHL	Totals	371	84	177	261	375	34	11	15	26	35

Born: 5/4/69, Powell River, British Columbia. 6-0, 195. Last amateur club: Victoria, (WHL). Signed as a free agent by Detroit Red Wings (3/18/93). Claimed by Pittsburgh Penguins from Detroit in NHL Waiver Draft (1/18/95). Claimed by Edmonton Oilers from Pittsburgh (1/18/95). Signed as a free agent by New York Islanders (8/10/95). Member of 1991-92 AHL champion Adirondack Red Wings. Member of 1995-96 IHL champion Utah Grizzlies.

Peter Akiwenzie — Defenseman

Season	Team	League	GP	G	A	PTS	PIM	GP	G	A	PTS	PIM
96-97	Columbus	CeHL	9	1	3	4	6	—	—	—	—	—
96-97	Brantford	CoHL	8	0	0	0	12	1	0	0	0	0

Born: 2/18/75, Owen Sound, Ontario. 6-0, 200

Chris Albert — Left Wing

Season	Team	League	GP	G	A	PTS	PIM	GP	G	A	PTS	PIM
95-96	San Antonio	CeHL	37	8	12	20	54	13	3	1	4	35
96-97	San Antonio	CeHL	55	19	29	48	48	—	—	—	—	—
	CeHL	Totals	92	27	41	68	102	13	3	1	4	35

Born: 10/12/72, Ottawa, Ontario. 5-11, 197

Rod Aldoff — Defenseman

Season	Team	League	GP	G	A	PTS	PIM	GP	G	A	PTS	PIM
95-96	Tallahassee	ECHL	70	13	44	57	74	12	1	4	5	10
96-97	Utah	IHL	24	1	4	5	10	—	—	—	—	—

Born: 1/30/71, Lethbridge, Alberta. 5-10, 190.

Keith Aldridge — Defenseman

Season	Team	League	GP	G	A	PTS	PIM	GP	G	A	PTS	PIM
95-96	Baltimore	AHL	7	0	2	2	2	—	—	—	—	—
96-97	Baltimore	AHL	51	4	9	13	92	3	0	0	0	4
	AHL	Totals	58	4	11	15	94	3	0	0	0	4

Born: 7/20/73, Detroit, Michigan. 5-11, 185.

Alexei Alepin — Defenseman

Season	Team	League	GP	G	A	PTS	PIM	GP	G	A	PTS	PIM
96-97	Pensacola	ECHL	3	0	0	0	14	—	—	—	—	—
96-97	Huntington	ECHL	43	1	5	6	94	—	—	—	—	—
	ECHL	Totals	46	1	5	6	108	—	—	—	—	—

Born: 09/18/75, Montreal, Quebec. 5-11, 205.

Alexander Alexeev — Defenseman

Season	Team	League	GP	G	A	PTS	PIM	GP	G	A	PTS	PIM
94-95	Portland	AHL	2	0	2	2	4	—	—	—	—	—
95-96	Portland	AHL	34	3	10	13	30	1	0	0	0	0
96-97	Portland	AHL	8	0	0	0	8	—	—	—	—	—

Season	Team	League	GP	G	A	PTS	PIM	GP	G	A	PTS	PIM
96-97	Hampton Roads	ECHL	63	6	26	32	124	9	1	6	7	18
	AHL	Totals	44	3	12	15	42	1	0	0	0	0

Born: 3/21/74, Kiev, Russia. 6-0, 216. Drafted by Winnipeg Jets (5th choice, 132nd overall) in 1992 Entry Draft. Signed as a free agent by Washington Capitals (4/8/95).

Chad Allan — Defenseman

			Regular Season					Playoffs				
Season	Team	League	GP	G	A	PTS	PIM	GP	G	A	PTS	PIM
96-97	Syracuse	AHL	73	3	10	13	83	3	0	1	1	0

Born: 7/12/76, Saskatoon, Saskatchewan. 6-1, 192. Selected by Vancouver Canucks, 4th choice, 65th overall in 1994 Entry Draft.

Jamie Allan — Forward

			Regular Season					Playoffs				
Season	Team	League	GP	G	A	PTS	PIM	GP	G	A	PTS	PIM
91-92	St. Thomas	CoHL	58	8	18	26	124	9	4	1	5	59
92-93	St. Thomas	CoHL	46	15	35	50	12	13	2	9	11	28
93-94	St. Thomas	CoHL	18	10	12	22	87	—	—	—	—	—
93-94	Chatham	CoHL	48	26	45	71	206	15	3	7	10	*95
94-95	Detroit	CoHL	65	24	41	65	239	7	2	0	2	20
95-96	Utica	CoHL	18	4	6	10	45	—	—	—	—	—
95-96	Winston-Salem	SHL	46	20	35	55	233	9	3	2	5	30
96-97	Wichita	CeHL	9	4	2	6	36	—	—	—	—	—
96-97	New Mexico	WPHL	28	10	17	27	110	—	—	—	—	—
	CoHL	Totals	253	87	157	244	713	44	11	17	28	202

Born: 3/18/70, Ottawa, Ontario. 6-0, 195.

Sandy Allan — Goaltender

			Regular Season							Playoffs					
Season	Team	League	GP	W	L	T	MIN	SO	GAVG	GP	W	L	MIN	SO	GAVG
95-96	Springfield	AHL	1	0	0	0	31	0	0.00	—	—	—	—	—	—
95-96	Richmond	ECHL	30	18	4	7	1682	0	3.25	—	—	—	—	—	—
96-97	Saint John	AHL	2	0	2	0	119	0	7.04	—	—	—	—	—	—
96-97	Richmond	ECHL	3	2	0	0	140	1	2.57	—	—	—	—	—	—
96-97	Louisville	ECHL	37	19	13	4	2104	1	3.48	—	—	—	—	—	—
	AHL	Totals	3	0	2	0	150	0	5.60	—	—	—	—	—	—
	ECHL	Totals	70	39	17	11	3926	2	3.35	—	—	—	—	—	—

Born: 1/22/74, Nassau, Bahamas. 5-11, 180. Drafted by Los Angeles Kings (2nd choice, 63rd overall) in 1992 Entry Draft.

Chris Allen — Defenseman

			Regular Season					Playoffs				
Season	Team	League	GP	G	A	PTS	PIM	GP	G	A	PTS	PIM
97-98	Carolina	AHL	9	0	0	0	2	—	—	—	—	—

Born: 5/8/78, Chatham, Ontario. 6-2, 193. Last amateur club: Kingston Frontenacs (OHL). Drafted by Florida Panthers (2nd choice, 60th overall) in 1996 Entry Draft.

Peter Allen — Defenseman

			Regular Season					Playoffs				
Season	Team	League	GP	G	A	PTS	PIM	GP	G	A	PTS	PIM
93-94	Prince Edward Island	AHL	6	0	1	1	6	—	—	—	—	—
93-94	Richmond	ECHL	52	2	16	18	62	—	—	—	—	—
94-95	Canadian	National	52	5	15	20	36	—	—	—	—	—
95-96	Pittsburgh	NHL	8	0	0	0	8	—	—	—	—	—
95-96	Cleveland	IHL	65	3	45	48	55	3	0	0	0	2
96-97	Cleveland	IHL	81	14	31	45	75	14	0	6	6	24
	IHL	Totals	146	17	76	93	130	17	0	6	6	26

Born: 3/6/70, Calgary, Alberta. 6-2, 185. Drafted by Boston Bruins (1st choice, 24th overall) in 1991 Supplemental Draft. Signed as a free agent by Pittsburgh Penguins (8/10/95).

Jamie Allison — Defenseman

Season	Team	League	GP	G	A	PTS	PIM	GP	G	A	PTS	PIM
			Regular Season					Playoffs				
94-95	Calgary	NHL	1	0	0	0	0	—	—	—	—	—
95-96	Saint John	AHL	71	3	16	19	223	14	0	2	2	16
96-97	Calgary	NHL	20	0	0	0	35	—	—	—	—	—
96-97	Saint John	AHL	46	3	6	9	139	5	0	1	1	4
	NHL	Totals	21	0	0	0	35	—	—	—	—	—
	AHL	Totals	117	6	22	28	362	19	0	3	3	20

Born: 5/13/75, Lindsay, Ontario. 6-1, 190. Last amateur club: Detroit Jr. Red Wings (OHL). Drafted by Calgary Flames (2nd choice, 44th overall) in 1993 Entry Draft. Up and coming rearguard who could see regular NHL duty next season.

Scott Allison — Left Wing

Season	Team	League	GP	G	A	PTS	PIM	GP	G	A	PTS	PIM
			Regular Season					Playoffs				
92-93	Cape Breton	AHL	49	3	5	8	34	—	—	—	—	—
92-93	Wheeling	ECHL	6	3	3	6	8	—	—	—	—	—
93-94	Cape Breton	AHL	75	19	14	33	202	3	0	1	1	2
94-95	Cape Breton	AHL	58	6	14	20	104	—	—	—	—	—
95-96	Prince Edward Island	AHL	63	11	16	27	133	4	1	0	1	15
96-97	Manitoba	IHL	42	4	12	16	140	—	—	—	—	—
96-97	Grand Rapids	IHL	12	2	1	3	41	4	0	0	0	21
96-97	Pensacola	ECHL	12	4	5	9	104	—	—	—	—	—
	AHL	Totals	245	39	49	88	473	7	1	0	1	17
	IHL	Totals	54	6	13	19	181	4	0	0	0	21
	ECHL	Totals	18	7	8	15	112	—	—	—	—	—

Born: 4/22/72, St. Boniface, Manitoba. 6-4, 205. Drafted by Edmonton Oilers (1st choice, 17th overall) in 1990 Entry Draft.

Patrick Allvin — Defenseman

Season	Team	League	GP	G	A	PTS	PIM	GP	G	A	PTS	PIM
			Regular Season					Playoffs				
95-96	Atlanta	IHL	3	0	0	0	4	—	—	—	—	—
95-96	Nashville	ECHL	59	4	13	17	93	5	0	0	0	28
96-97	Quebec	IHL	2	0	0	0	2	—	—	—	—	—
96-97	Pensacola	ECHL	51	0	3	3	104	12	0	0	0	26
	IHL	Totals	5	0	0	0	6	—	—	—	—	—
	ECHL	Totals	110	4	16	20	197	17	0	0	0	54

Born: 10/10/74, Sweden. 6-2, 195.

Matt Alvey — Right Wing

Season	Team	League	GP	G	A	PTS	PIM	GP	G	A	PTS	PIM
			Regular Season					Playoffs				
96-97	Pensacola	ECHL	7	1	2	3	0	3	0	0	0	4

Born, 5/15/75, Troy, New York. 6-5, 208. Last amateur club: Lake Superior State (CCHA). Drafted by Boston Bruins (2nd choice, 51st overall) in 1993 Entry Draft.

Peter Ambroziak — Left Wing

Season	Team	League	GP	G	A	PTS	PIM	GP	G	A	PTS	PIM
			Regular Season					Playoffs				
91-92	Rochester	AHL	2	0	1	1	0	—	—	—	—	—
92-93	Rochester	AHL	50	8	10	18	37	12	4	3	7	16
93-94	Rochester	AHL	22	3	4	7	53	—	—	—	—	—
94-95	Buffalo	NHL	12	0	1	1	0	—	—	—	—	—
94-95	Rochester	AHL	46	14	11	25	35	4	0	0	0	6
95-96	Albany	AHL	8	2	1	3	25	—	—	—	—	—
95-96	Cornwall	AHL	50	9	15	24	42	8	1	1	2	4
96-97	Fort Wayne	IHL	57	15	5	20	28	—	—	—	—	—

| | AHL | Totals | 178 | 36 | 42 | 78 | 192 | 24 | 5 | 4 | 9 | 26 |

Born: 9/15/71, Toronto, Ontario. 6-0, 200. Drafted by Buffalo Sabres (4th choice, 72nd overall) in 1991 Entry Draft.

Bujar Amidovski — Goaltender

			Regular Season						Playoffs				
Season	Team	League	GP	W	L	T	MIN	SO	GAVG	GP	W	L	MIN	SO	GAVG
96-97	Dayton	ECHL	3	1	1	0	91	0	3.31	2	0	2	118	0	4.56

Born; 2/19/77, Toronto, Ontario. 5-11, 173. Last amateur club: Kingston Frontenacs.

Wayne Anchikoski — Center

			Regular Season					Playoffs				
Season	Team	League	GP	G	A	PTS	PIM	GP	G	A	PTS	PIM
92-93	Dallas	CeHL	57	35	37	72	74	7	3	5	8	6
93-94	Dallas	CeHL	60	35	39	74	78	7	6	2	8	8
94-95	Dallas	CeHL	53	32	50	82	36	—	—	—	—	—
95-96	Reno	WCHL	50	28	34	62	40	3	3	2	5	0
96-97	Knoxville	ECHL	50	16	20	36	43	—	—	—	—	—
	CeHL	Totals	170	102	126	228	188	14	9	7	16	14

Born; 1/27/71, Salmon Arm, British Columbia. 6-4, 210.

Dave Anderson — Defenseman

			Regular Season					Playoffs				
Season	Team	League	GP	G	A	PTS	PIM	GP	G	A	PTS	PIM
96-97	Waco	WPHL	50	4	6	10	33	—	—	—	—	—

Born: Georgetown, Ontario. 5-10, 205.

Evan Anderson — Center

			Regular Season					Playoffs				
Season	Team	League	GP	G	A	PTS	PIM	GP	G	A	PTS	PIM
96-97	Johnstown	WCHL	12	2	0	2	6	—	—	—	—	—
96-97	Brantford	CoHL	7	1	2	3	0	—	—	—	—	—
96-97	Utica	CoHL	7	0	2	2	4	—	—	—	—	—
	CoHL	Totals	14	1	4	5	4	—	—	—	—	—

Born; 1/5/72, Regina, Saskatchewan. 5-9, 190.

Ryan Anderson — Right Wing

			Regular Season					Playoffs				
Season	Team	League	GP	G	A	PTS	PIM	GP	G	A	PTS	PIM
96-97	Austin	WPHL	59	2	7	9	222	6	0	1	1	30

Born; 2/27/75, Dowsman, Alberta. 6-2, 190.

Shawn Anderson — Defenseman

			Regular Season					Playoffs				
Season	Team	League	GP	G	A	PTS	PIM	GP	G	A	PTS	PIM
86-87	Buffalo	NHL	41	2	11	13	23	—	—	—	—	—
86-87	Rochester	AHL	15	2	5	7	11	—	—	—	—	—
87-88	Buffalo	NHL	23	1	2	3	17	—	—	—	—	—
87-88	Rochester	AHL	22	5	16	21	19	6	0	0	0	0
88-89	Buffalo	NHL	33	2	10	12	18	5	0	1	1	4
88-89	Rochester	AHL	31	5	14	19	24	—	—	—	—	—
89-90	Buffalo	NHL	16	1	3	4	8	—	—	—	—	—
89-90	Rochester	AHL	39	2	16	18	41	9	1	0	1	4
90-91	Quebec	NHL	31	3	10	13	21	—	—	—	—	—
90-91	Halifax	AHL	4	0	1	1	2	—	—	—	—	—
91-92	Weiswasser	Germany	38	7	15	22	83	—	—	—	—	—
92-93	Washington	NHL	60	2	6	8	18	6	0	0	0	0
92-93	Baltimore	AHL	10	1	5	6	8	—	—	—	—	—
93-94	Washington	NHL	50	0	9	9	12	8	1	0	1	12

Season	Team	League	GP	G	A	PTS	PIM	GP	G	A	PTS	PIM
94-95	Philadelphia	NHL	1	0	0	0	0	—	—	—	—	—
94-95	Hershey	AHL	31	9	21	30	18	6	2	3	5	19
95-96	Milwaukee	IHL	79	22	39	61	68	5	0	7	7	0
96-97	Utah	IHL	31	2	12	14	21	—	—	—	—	—
96-97	Manitoba	IHL	17	2	7	9	5	—	—	—	—	—
	NHL	Totals	255	11	51	62	117	19	1	1	2	16
	AHL	Totals	152	24	78	102	123	21	3	3	6	23
	IHL	Totals	127	26	58	84	94	5	0	7	7	0

Born: 2/7/68, Montreal, Quebec. 6-1, 200. Drafted by Buffalo Sabres (1st choice, 5th overall) in 1986 Entry Draft. Traded to Washington Capitals by Buffalo for Bill Houlder (9/30/90). Claimed by Quebec Nordiques from Washington in NHL Waiver Draft (10/1/90). Traded to Winnipeg Jets by Quebec for Sergei Kharin (10/22/91). Traded to Washington by Winnipeg for future considerations (10/23/91). Signed as a free agent by Philadelphia Flyers (8/16/94). Hampered by hand injury during 1996-97 season.

David Andre — Right Wing

Season	Team	League	GP	G	A	PTS	PIM	GP	G	A	PTS	PIM
96-97	Thunder Bay	CoHL	39	14	10	24	46	—	—	—	—	—

Born; 7/28/72, Ottawa, Ontario. 6-5, 215.

Mel Angelstad — Defenseman

Season	Team	League	GP	G	A	PTS	PIM	GP	G	A	PTS	PIM
92-93	Nashville	ECHL	1	0	0	0	14	—	—	—	—	—
92-93	Thunder Bay	CoHL	45	2	5	7	256	5	0	0	0	10
93-94	Prince Edward Island	AHL	1	0	0	0	5	—	—	—	—	—
93-94	Thunder Bay	CoHL	58	1	20	21	374	9	1	2	3	65
94-95	Prince Edward Island	AHL	3	0	0	0	16	—	—	—	—	—
94-95	Thunder Bay	CoHL	46	0	8	8	317	7	0	3	3	62
95-96	Phoenix	IHL	5	0	0	0	43	—	—	—	—	—
95-96	Thunder Bay	CoHL	51	3	3	6	335	16	0	6	6	94
96-97	Thunder Bay	CoHL	66	10	21	31	422	7	0	1	1	21
	AHL	Totals	4	0	0	0	21	—	—	—	—	—
	CoHL	Totals	266	16	57	73	1704	44	1	12	13	252

Born; 10/31/71, Saskatoon, Saskatchewan. 6-2, 210. Member of 1993-94 CoHL champion Thunder Bay Senators. Member of 1994-95 CoHL champion Thunder Bay Senators.

Chad Antonisyhn — Defenseman

Season	Team	League	GP	G	A	PTS	PIM	GP	G	A	PTS	PIM
96-97	Central Texas	WPHL	33	0	1	1	46	—	—	—	—	—
96-97	Waco	WPHL	15	1	0	1	30	—	—	—	—	—
	WPHL	Totals	48	1	1	2	76	—	—	—	—	—

Born; 5/25/74, Regina, Saskatchewan. 6-2, 210.

Jeff Antonovich — Center

Season	Team	League	GP	G	A	PTS	PIM	GP	G	A	PTS	PIM
95-96	Minnesota	IHL	1	0	0	0	2	—	—	—	—	—
95-96	Quad City	CoHL	66	20	34	54	32	4	1	1	2	0
96-97	Bakersfield	WCHL	44	22	31	53	35	—	—	—	—	—
96-97	Reno	WCHL	6	1	2	3	6	—	—	—	—	—
	WCHL	Totals	50	23	33	56	41	—	—	—	—	—

Born; 2/5/74, Greenway, Minnesota. 5-8, 170.

Bill C. Armstrong — Defenseman

Season	Team	League	GP	G	A	PTS	PIM	GP	G	A	PTS	PIM
90-91	Hershey	AHL	56	1	9	10	115	—	—	—	—	—
91-92	Hershey	AHL	80	2	14	16	159	3	0	0	0	2
92-93	Hershey	AHL	80	2	10	12	205	—	—	—	—	—
93-94	Providence	AHL	66	0	7	7	200	—	—	—	—	—
94-95	Providence	AHL	75	3	10	13	244	13	0	2	2	8
95-96	Cleveland	IHL	63	1	3	4	183	3	0	0	0	2
96-97	Cleveland	IHL	41	0	6	6	91	—	—	—	—	—
96-97	Providence	AHL	13	1	1	2	71	10	0	1	1	26
	AHL	Totals	370	9	51	60	996	26	0	3	3	36
	IHL	Totals	104	1	9	10	274	3	0	0	0	2

Born; 5/18/70, Richmond Hill, Ontario. 6-5, 220. Drafted by Philadelphia Flyers (6th choice, 46th overall) in 1990 Entry Draft. Signed as a free agent by Boston Bruins (7/22/93). Acquired from Cleveland Lumberjacks for Mark Cornforth, 1997.

Bill H. Armstrong — Left Wing

Season	Team	League	GP	G	A	PTS	PIM	GP	G	A	PTS	PIM
89-90	Hershey	AHL	58	10	6	16	99	—	—	—	—	—
90-91	Philadelphia	NHL	1	0	1	1	0	—	—	—	—	—
90-91	Hershey	AHL	70	36	27	63	150	6	2	8	10	19
91-92	Hershey	AHL	64	26	22	48	186	6	2	2	4	6
92-93	Cincinnati	IHL	42	14	11	25	99	—	—	—	—	—
92-93	Utica	AHL	32	18	21	39	60	—	—	—	—	—
93-94	Albany	AHL	74	32	50	82	188	—	—	—	—	—
94-95	Albany	AHL	76	32	47	79	115	13	6	5	11	20
95-96	Albany	AHL	10	3	4	7	22	—	—	—	—	—
95-96	Indianapolis	IHL	12	4	5	9	13	—	—	—	—	—
95-96	Detroit	IHL	54	34	25	59	66	12	6	2	8	15
96-97	Grand Rapids	IHL	35	1	8	9	39	—	—	—	—	—
96-97	Orlando	IHL	34	4	25	29	55	10	3	6	9	29
	AHL	Totals	384	137	177	314	820	25	10	15	25	45
	IHL	Totals	177	57	74	131	272	22	9	8	17	44

Born; 6/25/66, London, Ontario. 6-2, 195. Signed as a free agent by Philadelphia Flyers (5/16/89). Signed as a free agent by New Jersey (3/21/93). Traded to Chicago Blackhawks by New Jersey with Mike Vukonich for Darin Kimble (11/1/95). Member of 1994-95 AHL champion Albany RiverRats.

Chris Armstrong — Defenseman

Season	Team	League	GP	G	A	PTS	PIM	GP	G	A	PTS	PIM
93-94	CIN	IHL	1	0	0	0	0	10	1	3	4	2
94-95	CIN	IHL	—	—	—	—	—	9	1	3	4	10
95-96	CAR	AHL	78	9	33	42	65	—	—	—	—	—
96-97	Carolina	AHL	66	9	23	32	38	—	—	—	—	—
	AHL	Totals	144	18	56	74	103	—	—	—	—	—
	IHL	Totals	1	0	0	0	0	19	1	6	8	12

Born; 6/26/75, Regina, Saskatechewan. 6-0, 198. Last amateur club; Moose Jaw Warriors (WHL). Drafted by Florida Panthers (3rd choice, 57th overall) in 1993 Entry Draft.

Derek Armstrong — Center

Season	Team	League	GP	G	A	PTS	PIM	GP	G	A	PTS	PIM
93-94	Islanders	NHL	1	0	0	0	0	—	—	—	—	—
93-94	Salt Lake City	IHL	76	23	35	58	61	—	—	—	—	—
94-95	Denver	IHL	59	13	18	31	65	6	0	2	2	0
95-96	Islanders	NHL	19	1	3	4	14	—	—	—	—	—

Season	Team	League	GP	G	A	PTS	PIM	GP	G	A	PTS	PIM
95-96	Worcester	AHL	51	11	15	26	33	—	—	—	—	—
96-97	Islanders	NHL	50	6	7	13	33	—	—	—	—	—
96-97	Utah	IHL	17	4	8	12	10	6	0	4	4	4
	NHL	Totals	70	7	10	17	47	—	—	—	—	—
	IHL	Totals	152	40	61	101	136	12	0	6	6	4

Born; 4/23/73, Ottawa, Ontario. 5-11, 188. Last amateur club; Sudbury Wolves (OHL). Drafted by New York Islanders (5th choice, 128th overall) in 1992 Entry Draft. Member of 1994-95 IHL champion Denver Grizzlies.

Scott Arniel — Left Wing

Season	Team	League	GP	G	A	PTS	PIM	GP	G	A	PTS	PIM
81-82	Winnipeg	NHL	17	1	8	9	14	3	0	0	0	0
82-83	Winnipeg	NHL	75	13	5	18	46	2	0	0	0	0
83-84	Winnipeg	NHL	80	21	35	56	68	2	0	0	0	5
84-85	Winnipeg	NHL	79	22	22	44	81	8	1	2	3	9
85-86	Winnipeg	NHL	80	18	25	43	40	3	0	0	0	12
86-87	Buffalo	NHL	63	11	14	25	59	—	—	—	—	—
87-88	Buffalo	NHL	73	17	23	40	61	6	0	1	1	5
88-89	Buffalo	NHL	80	18	23	41	46	5	1	0	1	4
89-90	Buffalo	NHL	79	18	14	32	77	5	1	0	1	4
90-91	Winnipeg	NHL	75	5	17	22	87	—	—	—	—	—
91-92	Boston	NHL	29	5	3	8	20	—	—	—	—	—
91-92	New Haven	AHL	11	3	3	6	10	—	—	—	—	—
91-92	Maine	AHL	14	4	4	8	8	—	—	—	—	—
92-93	San Diego	IHL	79	35	48	83	116	14	6	5	11	16
93-94	San Diego	IHL	79	34	43	77	121	7	6	3	9	24
94-95	Houston	IHL	72	37	40	77	102	4	1	0	1	10
95-96	Houston	IHL	64	18	28	46	94	—	—	—	—	—
95-96	Utah	IHL	14	3	3	6	29	22	10	7	17	28
96-97	Manitoba	IHL	73	23	27	50	16	—	—	—	—	—
	NHL	Totals	730	149	189	338	599	34	3	3	6	39
	IHL	Totals	381	115	189	304	478	47	23	15	38	78
	AHL	Totals	25	7	7	14	18	—	—	—	—	—

Born; 9/17/62, Kingston, Ontario. 6-1, 190. Last amateur club; Cornwall Royals (OHL). Drafted by Winnipeg Jets (2nd choice, 22nd overall) in 1981 Entry Draft. Traded to Buffalo Sabres by Winnipeg for Gilles Hamel (6/21/86). Traded to Winnipeg by Buffalo with Phil Housley, Jeff Parker and first round choice (Keith Tkachuk) in 1990 Entry Draft for Dale Hawerchuk, first round choice (Brad May) in 1990 Entry Draft and future considerations (6/16/90). Greg Paslawski sent to Buffalo to complete deal (2/5/91). Traded to Boston Bruins by Winnipeg for future considerations (11/22/91). Signed as a free agent by San Diego Gulls (10/7/92). Member of 1995-96 IHL champion Utah Grizzlies.

Peter Arvantis — Center

Season	Team	League	GP	G	A	PTS	PIM	GP	G	A	PTS	PIM
96-97	Nashville	CeHL	36	5	10	15	50	—	—	—	—	—

Born; 4/29/74, Montreal, Quebec. 5-10, 185.

Thomas Ashe — Defenseman

Season	Team	League	GP	G	A	PTS	PIM	GP	G	A	PTS	PIM
96-97	Baton Rouge	ECHL	30	2	10	12	26	—	—	—	—	—

Last amateur club; Boston College.

Tom Askey — Goaltender

Season	Team	League	GP	W	L	T	MIN	SO	GAVG	GP	W	L	MIN	SO	GAVG
96-97	Baltimore	AHL	40	17	18	2	2239	1	3.75	3	0	3	138	0	4.79

Born; 10/4/74, Kenmore, New York. 6-2, 185. Last amateur club; Ohio State (CCHA). Drafted by Anaheim Mighty Ducks (8th choice, 186th overall) in 1993 Entry Draft.

Carlos Assayag — Right Wing

Season	Team	League	Regular Season GP	G	A	PTS	PIM	Playoffs GP	G	A	PTS	PIM
96-97	El Paso	WPHL	2	1	0	1	0	—	—	—	—	—
96-97	Fort Worth	CeHL	13	7	5	12	10	—	—	—	—	—
96-97	San Antonio	CeHL	21	7	7	14	14	—	—	—	—	—
	CeHL	Totals	34	14	12	26	24	—	—	—	—	—

Born; 2/11/72, Ste. Foy, Quebec. 5-10, 205.

Doug Ast — Center

Season	Team	League	Regular Season GP	G	A	PTS	PIM	Playoffs GP	G	A	PTS	PIM
96-97	Syracuse	AHL	61	6	14	20	19	—	—	—	—	—
96-97	Wheeling	ECHL	4	1	2	3	2	—	—	—	—	—

Born; 4/17/73, Chilliwack, British Columbia. 5-11, 177. Last amateur club; British Columbia (CWUAA).

Mark Astley — Defenseman

Season	Team	League	Regular Season GP	G	A	PTS	PIM	Playoffs GP	G	A	PTS	PIM
93-94	Ambri	Switzerland	23	5	9	14	17	—	—	—	—	—
93-94	Canada	National	13	4	8	12	6	—	—	—	—	—
93-94	Canada	Olympic	8	0	1	1	4	—	—	—	—	—
93-94	Buffalo	NHL	1	0	0	0	0	—	—	—	—	—
94-95	Buffalo	NHL	14	2	1	3	12	2	0	0	0	0
94-95	Rochester	AHL	46	5	24	29	49	3	0	2	2	2
95-96	Buffalo	NHL	60	2	18	20	80	—	—	—	—	—
96-97	Phoenix	IHL	52	6	11	17	43	—	—	—	—	—
	NHL	Totals	75	4	19	23	92	2	0	0	0	0

Born; 3/30/69, Calgary, Alberta. 5-11, 185. Last amateur club; Canadian Olympic Team. Drafted by Buffalo Sabres (9th choice, 194th overall) in 1989 Entry Draft. Signed as a free agent by Phoenix Roadrunners 1996.

Blair Atcheynum — Right Wing

Season	Team	League	Regular Season GP	G	A	PTS	PIM	Playoffs GP	G	A	PTS	PIM
89-90	Binghamton	AHL	78	20	21	41	45	—	—	—	—	—
90-91	Springfield	AHL	72	25	27	52	42	13	0	6	6	6
91-92	Springfield	AHL	62	16	21	37	64	6	1	1	2	2
92-93	Ottawa	NHL	4	0	1	1	0	—	—	—	—	—
92-93	New Haven	AHL	51	16	18	34	47	—	—	—	—	—
93-94	Portland	AHL	2	0	0	0	0	—	—	—	—	—
93-94	Springfield	AHL	40	18	22	40	13	6	0	2	2	0
93-94	Columbus	ECHL	16	15	12	27	10	—	—	—	—	—
94-95	Minnesota	IHL	17	4	6	10	7	—	—	—	—	—
94-95	Worcester	AHL	55	17	29	46	26	—	—	—	—	—
95-96	Cape Breton	AHL	79	30	42	72	65	—	—	—	—	—
96-97	Hershey	AHL	77	42	45	87	57	13	6	11	17	6
	AHL	Totals	516	184	219	403	359	38	7	20	27	14

Born; 4/20/69, Estevan, Saskatchewan. 6-2, 210. Drafted by Hartford Whalers (2nd choice, 52nd overall) in 1989 Entry Draft. Selected by Ottawa Senators in NHL Expansion Draft (6/18/92). 1996-97 AHL First Team All-Star. Member of 1990-91 AHL Champion Springfield Indians. Member of 1996-97 AHL Champion Hershey Bears.

Rob Atkinson — Center

Season	Team	League	Regular Season GP	G	A	PTS	PIM	Playoffs GP	G	A	PTS	PIM
95-96	Mobile	ECHL	61	28	31	59	44	—	—	—	—	—
96-97	Mobile	ECHL	67	26	35	61	61	3	1	1	2	2
	ECHL	Totals	128	54	66	120	105	3	1	1	2	2

Born; 1/20/70, Moncton, New Brunswick. 6-0, 180.

J.F. Aube — Right Wing

			Regular Season					Playoffs				
Season	Team	League	GP	G	A	PTS	PIM	GP	G	A	PTS	PIM
95-96	Charlotte	ECHL	50	18	41	59	12	—	—	—	—	—
96-97	Charlotte	ECHL	66	34	49	83	24	1	0	0	0	0
	ECHL	Totals	116	52	90	142	36	1	0	0	0	0

Born; 4/5/73, Montreal, Quebec. 6-0, 182.

Serge Aubin — Center

			Regular Season					Playoffs				
Season	Team	League	GP	G	A	PTS	PIM	GP	G	A	PTS	PIM
95-96	Cleveland	IHL	2	0	0	0	0	2	0	0	0	0
95-96	Hampton Roads	ECHL	62	24	62	86	74	3	1	4	5	10
96-97	Cleveland	IHL	57	9	16	25	38	2	0	0	0	0
	IHL	Totals	59	9	16	25	0	4	0	0	0	0

Born; 2/15/75, Val D'Or, Quebec. 6-0, 189. Last amateur club; Granby (QMJHL). Drafted by Pittsburgh Penguins (9th choice, 161st overall) in 1994 Entry Draft.

Philippe Audet — Left Wing

			Regular Season					Playoffs				
Season	Team	League	GP	G	A	PTS	PIM	GP	G	A	PTS	PIM
96-97	Adirondack	AHL	3	1	1	2	0	1	1	0	1	0

Born; 6/4/77, Ottawa, Ontario. 6-2, 175. Last amateur club; Granby (QMJHL). Drafted by Detroit Red Wings (2nd choice, 52nd overall) in 1995 Entry Draft.

Patrick Augusta — Left Wing

			Regular Season					Playoffs				
Season	Team	League	GP	G	A	PTS	PIM	GP	G	A	PTS	PIM
92-93	St. John's	AHL	75	32	45	77	74	8	3	3	6	23
93-94	Toronto	NHL	2	0	0	0	0	—	—	—	—	—
93-94	St. John's	AHL	77	*53	43	96	105	11	4	8	12	4
94-95	St. John's	AHL	71	37	32	69	98	4	2	0	2	7
95-96	Los Angeles	IHL	79	34	51	85	83	—	—	—	—	—
96-97	Long Beach	IHL	82	45	42	87	96	18	4	4	8	33
	AHL	Totals	223	122	120	242	277	23	9	11	20	34
	IHL	Totals	161	79	93	172	179	18	4	4	8	33

Born; Jihlava, Czechoslovakia. 5-10, 169. Drafted by Toronto Maple Leafs (8th choice, 149th overall) in 1992 Entry Draft. 1993-94 AHL Second Team All-Star. 1996-97 IHL Second Team All-Star. Re-signed for two season with Ice Dogs (6/9/97).

Dave Aussum — Right Wing

			Regular Season					Playoffs				
Season	Team	League	GP	G	A	PTS	PIM	GP	G	A	PTS	PIM
96-97	Brantford	CoHL	32	2	5	7	17	8	0	0	0	4

Born; 7/26/75, 5-9, 180.

Jesse Austin — Defenseman

			Regular Season					Playoffs				
Season	Team	League	GP	G	A	PTS	PIM	GP	G	A	PTS	PIM
95-96	Muskegon	CoHL	13	0	0	0	26	—	—	—	—	—
95-96	Brantford	CoHL	8	0	0	0	26	—	—	—	—	—
96-97	Brantford	CoHL	21	0	1	1	171	—	—	—	—	—
96-97	Dayton	CoHL	22	0	3	3	120	—	—	—	—	—
	CoHL	Totals	64	0	4	4	343	—	—	—	—	—

Born; 1/12/75, Hamilton, Ontario. 6-3, 220.

Jeffrey Azar — Right Wing

Regular Season / Playoffs

Season	Team	League	GP	G	A	PTS	PIM	GP	G	A	PTS	PIM
96-97	Adirondack	AHL	2	0	0	0	0	—	—	—	—	—
96-97	Utica	CoHL	70	28	36	64	53	3	0	0	0	0

Born; 9/7/73, Quincy, Massachusetts. 5-10, 175. Member of 1996-97 CoHL Rookie Team. Last amateur club; Plattsburgh (SUNYAC).

Jarrett Deuling sports the Kentucky Thoroughblades logo that won last season's Meet the Minors logo contest.   Photo courtesy of team

Ryan Bach — Goaltender

Regular Season / Playoffs

Season	Team	League	GP	W	L	T	MIN	SO	GAVG	GP	W	L	MIN	SO	GAVG
96-97	Adirondack	AHL	13	2	3	1	451	0	3.86	1	0	0	46	0	3.92
96-97	Toledo	ECHL	20	5	11	3	1169	0	3.80	—	—	—	—	—	—
96-97	Utica	CoHL	2	0	1	1	119	0	4.03	—	—	—	—	—	—

Born; 10/21/73, Sherwood Park, Alberta. 6-1, 180. Last amateur club; Colorado (WCHA). Drafted by Detroit Red Wings (11th choice, 262nd overall) in 1992 Entry Draft.

Andrew Backen — Defenseman

Regular Season / Playoffs

Season	Team	League	GP	G	A	PTS	PIM	GP	G	A	PTS	PIM
96-97	Memphis	CeHL	66	6	13	19	124	18	3	4	7	27

Born; 1/2/72, Thunder Bay, Ontario. 5-7, 175. Last amateur club; Miami of Ohio (CCHA).

John Badduke — Right Wing

Regular Season / Playoffs

Season	Team	League	GP	G	A	PTS	PIM	GP	G	A	PTS	PIM
93-94	Hamilton	AHL	55	6	8	14	*356	4	0	1	1	18
93-94	Columbus	ECHL	7	0	3	3	60	—	—	—	—	—
93-94	Brantford	CoHL	1	1	0	1	7	—	—	—	—	—
94-95	Syracuse	AHL	44	6	0	6	334	—	—	—	—	—
95-96	Syracuse	AHL	46	2	2	4	245	—	—	—	—	—
95-96	Wheeling	ECHL	4	1	2	3	15	—	—	—	—	—
96-97	Syracuse	AHL	24	0	0	0	70	—	—	—	—	—
96-97	Wheeling	ECHL	12	2	1	3	51	—	—	—	—	—
AHL	Totals		169	14	10	24	1005	4	0	1	1	18
ECHL	Totals		23	3	6	9	126	—	—	—	—	—

Born; 6/21/72, Calgary, Alberta. 6-2, 217. Signed as a free agent by Vancouver Canucks (2/2/94).

Greg Bailey — Defenseman

Regular Season / Playoffs

Season	Team	League	GP	G	A	PTS	PIM	GP	G	A	PTS	PIM
93-94	Huntington	ECHL	52	0	3	3	257	—	—	—	—	—
94-95	Birmingham	ECHL	18	0	2	2	149	—	—	—	—	—
94-95	Brantford	CoHL	2	1	0	1	2	—	—	—	—	—
94-95	Flint	CoHL	15	0	1	1	20	—	—	—	—	—
95-96	Utica	CoHL	2	0	0	0	8	—	—	—	—	—
95-96	Detroit	CoHL	2	0	0	0	2	—	—	—	—	—
95-96	Wichita	CeHL	8	0	0	0	38	—	—	—	—	—
95-96	San Antonio	CeHL	9	0	2	2	45	—	—	—	—	—
95-96	Tulsa	CeHL	5	0	1	1	48	—	—	—	—	—
96-97	Roanoke	ECHL	3	0	0	0	0	—	—	—	—	—
96-97	Nashville	CeHL	11	0	3	3	71	—	—	—	—	—
96-97	San Antonio	CeHL	10	2	2	4	45	—	—	—	—	—
96-97	Brantford	CoHL	16	0	2	2	15	—	—	—	—	—
96-97	Madison	CoHL	7	0	0	0	7	5	0	0	0	20
ECHL	Totals		73	0	5	5	406	—	—	—	—	—
CeHL	Totals		43	2	8	10	247	—	—	—	—	—
CoHL	Totals		44	1	3	4	54	5	0	0	0	20

Born; 10/3/73, St. Thomas, Ontario. 6-4, 227.

Scott Bailey — Goaltender

Regular Season / Playoffs

Season	Team	League	GP	W	L	T	MIN	SO	GAVG	GP	W	L	MIN	SO	GAVG
92-93	Johnstown	ECHL	36	13	15	3	1750	1	3.84	—	—	—	—	—	—
93-94	Providence	AHL	7	2	2	2	377	0	3.82	—	—	—	—	—	—

Season	Team	League	GP	W	L	T	MIN	SO	GAVG	GP	W	L	MIN	SO	GAVG
93-94	Charlotte	ECHL	36	22	11	3	2180	1	3.58	3	1	2	187	0	3.83
94-95	Providence	AHL	52	25	16	9	2936	2	3.00	9	4	4	504	*2	3.69
95-96	Boston	NHL	11	5	1	2	571	0	3.26	—	—	—	—	—	—
95-96	Providence	AHL	37	15	19	3	2209	1	3.26	2	1	1	119	0	3.03
96-97	Boston	NHL	8	1	5	0	394	0	3.65	—	—	—	—	—	—
96-97	Providence	AHL	31	11	17	2	1735	0	3.87	7	3	4	453	0	3.05
	NHL	Totals	19	6	6	2	965	0	3.42	—	—	—	—	—	—
	AHL	Totals	127	53	54	16	7257	3	3.32	18	8	9	1076	2	3.34
	ECHL	Totals	72	35	26	6	3930	2	3.69	3	1	2	187	0	3.83

Born; 5/2/72, Calgary, Alberta. 6-0, 195. Last amateur club; Spokane (WHL). Drafted by Boston Bruins (3rd choice, 112th overall) in 1992 Entry Draft. Bailey has come a long way from the ECHL to earn some starts with the Boston Bruins.

Mike Bajurny — Left Wing

			Regular Season					Playoffs				
Season	Team	League	GP	G	A	PTS	PIM	GP	G	A	PTS	PIM
94-95	Wheeling	ECHL	1	0	0	0	0	—	—	—	—	—
95-96	Brantford	CoHL	48	0	2	2	176	—	—	—	—	—
95-96	Utica	CoHL	18	0	2	2	63	—	—	—	—	—
96-97	Brantford	CoHL	30	2	4	6	95	—	—	—	—	—
96-97	Dayton	CoHL	42	3	4	7	167	—	—	—	—	—
	CoHL	Totals	138	5	12	17	501	—	—	—	—	—

Born; 9/28/74, Walkerton, Ontario. 6-2, 212.

Mike Bales — Goaltender

			Regular Season							Playoffs					
Season	Team	League	GP	W	L	T	MIN	SO	GAVG	GP	W	L	MIN	SO	GAVG
92-93	Boston	NHL	1	0	0	0	25	0	2.40	—	—	—	—	—	—
92-93	Providence	AHL	44	22	17	0	2363	1	4.21	2	0	2	118	0	4.07
93-94	Providence	AHL	33	9	15	4	1757	0	4.44	—	—	—	—	—	—
94-95	Ottawa	NHL	1	0	0	0	3	0	0.00	—	—	—	—	—	—
94-95	Prince Edward Island	AHL	45	25	16	3	2649	2	3.62	9	6	3	530	*2	2.72
95-96	Ottawa	NHL	20	2	14	1	1040	0	4.15	—	—	—	—	—	—
95-96	Prince Edward Island	AHL	2	0	2	0	118	0	5.58	—	—	—	—	—	—
96-97	Ottawa	NHL	1	0	1	0	52	0	4.62	—	—	—	—	—	—
96-97	Baltimore	AHL	46	13	21	8	2544	3	3.07	—	—	—	—	—	—
	NHL	Totals	23	2	15	1	1120	0	4.12	—	—	—	—	—	—
	AHL	Totals	170	69	71	15	9431	6	3.80	11	6	5	648	2	2.96

Born; 8/6/71, Prince Albert, Saskatchewan. 6-1, 180. Last amateur club; Ohio State (CCHA). Drafted by Boston Bruins (4th choice, 105th overall) in 1990 Entry Draft. Signed as a free agent by Ottawa Senators, 7/4/94. Loaned to Baltimore by Ottawa, 1996.

Maco Balkovec — Defenseman

			Regular Season					Playoffs				
Season	Team	League	GP	G	A	PTS	PIM	GP	G	A	PTS	PIM
95-96	Jacksonville	ECHL	21	4	8	12	40	—	—	—	—	—
95-96	Raleigh	ECHL	50	8	18	26	70	4	0	2	2	10
96-97	Raleigh	ECHL	28	2	6	8	20	—	—	—	—	—
	ECHL	Totals	99	14	32	46	130	4	0	2	2	10

Born; 1/17/71, New Westminster, British Columbia. 6-2, 200.

Martin Balleux — Left Wing

			Regular Season					Playoffs				
Season	Team	League	GP	G	A	PTS	PIM	GP	G	A	PTS	PIM
96-97	El Paso	WPHL	35	12	15	27	67	11	5	2	7	20

Member of 1996-97 WPHL champion El Paso Buzzards.

Steve Bancroft — Defenseman

Season	Team	League	GP	G	A	PTS	PIM	GP	G	A	PTS	PIM
90-91	Newmarket	AHL	9	0	3	3	22	—	—	—	—	—
90-91	Maine	AHL	53	2	12	14	46	2	0	0	0	2
91-92	Maine	AHL	26	1	3	4	45	—	—	—	—	—
91-92	Indianapolis	IHL	36	8	23	31	49	—	—	—	—	—
92-93	Chicago	NHL	1	0	0	0	0	—	—	—	—	—
92-93	Indianapolis	IHL	53	10	35	45	138	—	—	—	—	—
92-93	Moncton	AHL	21	3	13	16	16	5	0	0	0	16
93-94	Cleveland	IHL	33	2	12	14	58	—	—	—	—	—
94-95	Detroit	IHL	6	1	3	4	0	—	—	—	—	—
94-95	Ft. Wayne	IHL	50	7	17	24	100	—	—	—	—	—
94-95	St. John's	AHL	4	2	0	2	2	5	0	3	3	8
95-96	Los Angeles	IHL	15	3	10	13	22	—	—	—	—	—
95-96	Chicago	IHL	64	9	41	50	91	9	1	7	8	22
96-97	Chicago	IHL	39	6	10	16	66	—	—	—	—	—
96-97	Las Vegas	IHL	36	9	28	37	64	3	0	0	0	2
	IHL	Totals	332	55	179	234	588	12	1	7	8	24
	AHL	Totals	113	8	31	39	131	12	0	3	3	26

Born; 10/6/70, Toronto, Ontario. 6-1, 214. Last amateur team; Belleville (OHL). Drafted by Toronto Maple Leafs (3rd choice, 21st overall) in 1989 Entry Draft. Traded to Boston Bruins by Toronto for Rob Cimetta (11/9/90). Traded to Chicago Blackhawks by Boston with Boston's 11th round choice (later traded to Winnipeg, Winnipeg selected Russell Hewson) in 1993 Entry Draft for Chicago's eleventh round choice (Eugene Pavlov) in 1993 Entry Draft. (1/9/92). Traded to Winnipeg Jets by Chicago with future considerations for Troy Murray (2/21/93). Claimed by Florida Panthers from Winnipeg in Expansion Draft (6/24/93). Signed as a free agent by Pittsburgh Penguins (8/2/93). Traded to Las Vegas by Chicago, 1996.

Frank Banham — Forward

Season	Team	League	GP	G	A	PTS	PIM	GP	G	A	PTS	PIM
95-96	Baltimore	AHL	9	1	4	5	0	7	1	1	2	2
96-97	Anaheim	NHL	3	0	0	0	0	—	—	—	—	—
96-97	Baltimore	AHL	21	11	13	24	4	—	—	—	—	—
	AHL	Totals	30	12	17	29	4	7	1	1	2	2

Born; 4/14/75, Calahoo, Alberta. 6-0, 185. Last amateur club; Saskatoon (WHL). Drafted by Washington Capitals (4th choice, 147th overall) in 1993 Entry Draft. Signed as a free agent by Anaheim (1/27/96).

Cory Banika — Right Wing

Season	Team	League	GP	G	A	PTS	PIM	GP	G	A	PTS	PIM
90-91	Hampton Roads	ECHL	15	4	2	6	56	—	—	—	—	—
91-92	St. John's	AHL	2	1	0	1	2	—	—	—	—	—
91-92	Brantford	CoHL	53	10	22	32	247	6	0	1	1	27
92-93	Brantford	CoHL	56	24	26	50	318	15	4	5	9	79
93-94	Hershey	AHL	2	0	0	0	2	—	—	—	—	—
93-94	Rochester	AHL	7	1	0	1	12	3	0	0	0	0
93-94	Johnstown	ECHL	48	16	14	30	262	—	—	—	—	—
93-94	Brantford	CoHL	8	7	9	16	30	7	0	3	3	63
94-95	Cornwall	AHL	56	3	11	14	225	7	1	0	1	47
95-96	Cornwall	AHL	5	1	0	1	15	—	—	—	—	—
95-96	Muskegon	CoHL	2	0	0	0	10	5	4	1	5	14
96-97	Hershey	AHL	43	7	5	12	232	23	5	3	8	47
	AHL	Totals	115	13	16	29	488	33	6	3	9	94
	CoHL	Totals	119	41	57	98	605	33	8	10	18	183
	ECHL	Totals	63	20	16	36	318	—	—	—	—	—

Born; 4/9/70, Oshawa, Ontario. 5-10, 190. Last amateur team; Cornwall (OHL). Member of 1992-93 Colonial League champion Brantford Smoke. Member of 1996-97 AHL Champion Hershey Bears.

Darren Banks — Left Wing

Regular Season / **Playoffs**

Season	Team	League	GP	G	A	PTS	PIM	GP	G	A	PTS	PIM
89-90	Salt Lake City	IHL	6	0	0	0	11	1	0	0	0	10
89-90	Fort Wayne	IHL	2	0	1	1	0	—	—	—	—	—
89-90	Knoxville	ECHL	52	25	22	47	258	—	—	—	—	—
90-91	Salt Lake City	IHL	56	9	7	16	286	3	0	1	1	6
91-92	Salt Lake City	IHL	55	5	5	10	303	—	—	—	—	—
92-93	Boston	NHL	16	2	1	3	64	—	—	—	—	—
92-93	Providence	IHL	43	9	5	14	199	1	0	0	0	0
93-94	Boston	NHL	4	0	1	1	9	—	—	—	—	—
93-94	Providence	AHL	41	6	3	9	189	—	—	—	—	—
94-95	Detroit	CoHL	22	9	10	19	51	12	3	5	8	59
94-95	Adirondack	AHL	20	3	2	5	65	—	—	—	—	—
94-95	Portland	AHL	12	1	2	3	38	—	—	—	—	—
94-95	Las Vegas	IHL	2	0	0	0	19	—	—	—	—	—
95-96	Las Vegas	IHL	5	0	2	2	10	10	0	0	0	54
95-96	Detroit	CoHL	38	11	17	28	290	—	—	—	—	—
95-96	Utica	CoHL	6	1	2	3	22	—	—	—	—	—
96-97	Detoit	IHL	64	10	13	23	306	20	4	5	9	40
NHL	Totals		20	2	2	4	73	—	—	—	—	—
IHL	Totals		190	24	28	52	935	34	4	6	10	110
AHL	Totals		116	19	12	31	491	1	0	0	0	0
CoHL	Totals		66	21	29	50	363	12	3	5	8	59

Born; 3/18/66, Toronto, Ontario. 6-2, 228. Signed as a free agent by Calgary Flames (12/12/90). Signed as a free agent by Boston Bruins (7/16/92). Member of 1996-97 IHL Champion Detroit Vipers.

Frederic Barbeau — Defenseman

Regular Season / **Playoffs**

Season	Team	League	GP	G	A	PTS	PIM	GP	G	A	PTS	PIM
95-96	Cape Breton	AHL	28	1	0	1	33	—	—	—	—	—
95-96	Indianapolis	IHL	4	0	0	0	8	—	—	—	—	—
95-96	Wheeling	ECHL	6	0	4	4	15	5	0	0	0	2
95-96	Wheeling	ECHL	60	2	13	15	88	2	0	1	1	0
ECHL	Totals		66	2	17	19	103	7	0	1	1	2

Born; 4/24/75, Victoriaville, Quebec. 6-3, 205.

Scott Barber — Goaltender

Regular Season / **Playoffs**

Season	Team	League	GP	W	L	T	MIN	SO	GAVG	GP	W	L	MIN	SO	GAVG
95-96	Lakeland	SHL	31	20	7	3	1783	0	3.60	3	0	3	174	0	4.14
96-97	Columbus	CeHL	23	9	9	3	1261	0	4.19	—	—	—	—	—	—

Born; 6/29/72, Troy, New York. 5-10, 175.

David Barrozino — Defenseman

Regular Season / **Playoffs**

Season	Team	League	GP	G	A	PTS	PIM	GP	G	A	PTS	PIM
96-97	Quebec	IHL	11	0	4	4	8	—	—	—	—	—
96-97	Pensacola	ECHL	57	16	27	43	121	12	2	4	6	24

Born; 1/4/73, Toronto, Ontario. 6-2, 203. Last amateur club; Lowell University (Hockey East). Traded to San Antonio Dragons (8/97).

Dave Barr — Right Wing

Regular Season / **Playoffs**

Season	Team	League	GP	G	A	PTS	PIM	GP	G	A	PTS	PIM
81-82	Boston	NHL	2	0	0	0	0	5	1	0	1	0
81-82	Erie	AHL	76	18	48	66	29	—	—	—	—	—
82-83	Boston	NHL	10	1	1	2	7	10	0	0	0	2
82-83	Baltimore	AHL	72	27	51	78	67	—	—	—	—	—

Season	Team	League	GP	G	A	PTS	PIM	GP	G	A	PTS	PIM
83-84	Rangers	NHL	6	0	0	0	2	—	—	—	—	—
83-84	St. Louis	NHL	1	0	0	0	0	—	—	—	—	—
83-84	Tulsa	CHL	50	28	37	65	24	—	—	—	—	—
84-85	St. Louis	NHL	75	16	18	34	32	2	0	0	0	2
85-86	St. Louis	NHL	72	13	38	51	70	11	1	1	2	14
86-87	St. Louis	NHL	2	0	0	0	0	—	—	—	—	—
86-87	Hartford	NHL	30	2	4	6	19	—	—	—	—	—
86-87	Detroit	NHL	37	13	13	26	49	13	1	0	1	14
87-88	Detroit	NHL	51	14	26	40	58	16	5	7	12	22
88-89	Detroit	NHL	73	27	32	59	69	6	3	1	4	6
89-90	Detroit	NHL	62	10	25	35	45	—	—	—	—	—
89-90	Adirondack	AHL	9	1	14	15	17	—	—	—	—	—
90-91	Detroit	NHL	70	18	22	40	55	—	—	—	—	—
91-92	New Jersey	NHL	41	6	12	18	32	—	—	—	—	—
91-92	Utica	AHL	1	0	0	0	7	—	—	—	—	—
92-93	New Jersey	NHL	62	6	8	14	61	5	1	0	1	6
93-94	Dallas	NHL	20	2	5	7	21	3	0	1	1	4
93-94	Kalamazoo	IHL	4	3	2	5	5	—	—	—	—	—
94-95	Kalamazoo	IHL	66	18	41	59	77	16	1	4	5	8
95-96	Orlando	IHL	82	38	62	100	87	23	8	13	21	14
96-97	Orlando	IHL	50	15	29	44	29	9	2	3	5	8
	NHL	Totals	614	128	204	332	520	71	12	10	22	70
	IHL	Totals	202	74	134	208	198	48	11	20	31	30
	AHL	Totals	158	46	113	159	120	—	—	—	—	—

Born; 11/30/60, Toronto, Ontario. 6-1, 195. Signed as a free agent by Boston Bruins (9/28/81). Traded to New York Rangers by Boston for Dave Silk (10/5/83). Traded to St. Louis Blues by Rangers with third round choice (Alan Perry) in the 1984 Entry Draft for Larry Patey and Bob Brooke (3/5/84). Traded to Hartford Whalers by St. Louis for Tim Bothwell (10/21/86). Traded to Detroit Red Wings by Hartford for Randy Ladouceur (1/12/87). Acquired by New Jersey Devils from Detroit with Randy McKay as compensation for Detroit's signing of Troy Crowder (9/9/91). Signed as a free agent by Dallas Stars (8/28/93).

Doug Barrault — Right Wing

Season	Team	League	GP	G	A	PTS	PIM	GP	G	A	PTS	PIM
91-92	Kalamazoo	IHL	60	5	14	19	26	—	—	—	—	—
92-93	Minnesota	NHL	2	0	0	0	2	—	—	—	—	—
92-93	Kalamazoo	IHL	78	32	34	66	74	—	—	—	—	—
93-94	Florida	NHL	2	0	0	0	0	—	—	—	—	—
93-94	Cincinnati	IHL	75	36	28	64	59	9	8	2	10	0
94-95	Cincinnati	IHL	74	20	40	60	57	10	2	6	8	20
95-96	Atlanta	IHL	19	5	9	14	16	—	—	—	—	—
95-96	Chicago	IHL	54	12	18	30	39	9	2	3	5	6
96-97	Chicago	IHL	16	3	5	8	12	—	—	—	—	—
	NHL	Totals	4	0	0	0	2	—	—	—	—	—
	IHL	Totals	376	113	148	261	283	28	12	11	23	26

Born; 4/21/70, Golden, British Columbia. Drafted by Minnesota North Stars (8th choice, 155th overall) in 1990 Entry Draft. Claimed by Florida Panthers from Dallas in Expansion Draft (6/24/93).

Kevin Barrett — Defenseman

Season	Team	League	GP	G	A	PTS	PIM	GP	G	A	PTS	PIM
93-94	Muskegon	CoHL	61	11	14	25	307	3	0	1	1	8
94-95	Flint	COHL	71	16	14	30	254	6	0	0	0	27
95-96	Oklahoma City	CeHL	58	8	18	26	286	13	2	1	3	42
96-97	Bakersfield	WCHL	61	5	25	30	271	3	0	0	0	32
	CoHL	Totals	132	27	28	55	561	9	0	1	1	35

Born; 11/3/70, Winnipeg, Manitoba. 6-3, 220. Member of 1995-96 CeHL champion Oklahoma City Blazers.

Len Barrie — Center

			Regular Season					Playoffs				
Season	Team	League	GP	G	A	PTS	PIM	GP	G	A	PTS	PIM
89-90	Philadelphia	NHL	1	0	0	0	0	—	—	—	—	—
90-91	Hershey	AHL	63	26	32	58	60	7	4	0	4	12
91-92	Hershey	AHL	75	42	43	85	78	3	0	2	2	32
92-93	Philadelphia	NHL	8	2	2	4	9	—	—	—	—	—
92-93	Hershey	AHL	61	31	45	76	162	—	—	—	—	—
93-94	Florida	NHL	2	0	0	0	0	—	—	—	—	—
93-94	Cincinnati	IHL	77	45	71	116	246	11	8	13	21	60
94-95	Pittsburgh	NHL	48	3	11	14	66	4	1	0	1	8
94-95	Cleveland	IHL	28	13	30	45	137	—	—	—	—	—
95-96	Pittsburgh	NHL	5	0	0	0	18	—	—	—	—	—
95-96	Cleveland	IHL	55	29	43	72	178	3	3	2	5	6
96-97	San Antonio	IHL	57	26	40	66	196	9	5	5	10	20
	NHL	Totals	64	5	13	18	93	4	1	0	1	8
	IHL	Totals	217	113	184	297	757	27	17	18	35	94
	AHL	Totals	199	99	120	219	300	10	4	2	6	44

Born; 6/4/69, Kimberly, British Columbia. 6-0, 200. Drafted by Edmonton Oilers (7th choice, 124th overall) in 1988 Entry Draft. Signed as a free agent by Philadelphia Flyers (2/28/90). Signed as a free agent by Florida Panthers 7/20/93). Signed as a free agent by Pittsburgh Penguins (8/15/94). 1993-94 IHL Second Team All-Star.

Mike Barrie — Center

			Regular Season					Playoffs				
Season	Team	League	GP	G	A	PTS	PIM	GP	G	A	PTS	PIM
93-94	Rochester	AHL	—	—	—	—	—	3	0	1	1	0
94-95	Rochester	AHL	16	1	3	4	40	—	—	—	—	—
94-95	South Carolina	ECHL	39	8	14	22	122	—	—	—	—	—
95-96	South Carolina	ECHL	41	13	6	19	72	—	—	—	—	—
95-96	Hampton Roads	ECHL	12	2	6	8	42	—	—	—	—	—
96-97	Peoria	ECHL	51	17	34	51	70	—	—	—	—	—
96-97	Birmingham	ECHL	15	10	4	14	45	8	2	3	5	31
	AHL	Totals	16	1	3	4	40	3	0	1	1	0
	ECHL	Totals	158	50	64	114	351	8	2	3	5	31

Born; 3/16/74, Kelowna, British Columbia. 6-1, 170. Last amateur club; Seattle (WHL). Drafted by Buffalo Sabres (6th choice, 194th overall) in 1993 Entry Draft. Traded to Birmingham by Peoria for Max Williams and Brendan Creagh, 1997.

Wade Bartley — Defenseman

			Regular Season					Playoffs				
Season	Team	League	GP	G	A	PTS	PIM	GP	G	A	PTS	PIM
90-91	Baltimore	AHL	2	0	0	0	0	—	—	—	—	—
91-92	Baltimore	AHL	20	0	7	7	25	—	—	—	—	—
91-92	Hampton Roads	ECHL	43	8	26	34	75	14	4	8	12	38
92-93	Toledo	ECHL	13	0	10	10	21	16	5	8	13	22
93-94	N/A											
94-95	Raleigh	ECHL	41	6	17	23	47	—	—	—	—	—
94-95	Tallahassee	ECHL	23	0	16	16	31	—	—	—	—	—
95-96	Toledo	ECHL	32	5	15	20	36	6	1	3	4	12
96-97	Nashville	CeHL	27	5	16	21	58	—	—	—	—	—
	AHL	Totals	22	0	7	7	25	—	—	—	—	—
	ECHL	Totals	152	19	91	110	225	36	10	19	29	72

Born; 10/3/73, Killarney, Manitoba. 6-0, 190. Drafted by Washington Capitals (3rd choice, 41st overall) in 1988 Entry Draft. Member of 1991-92 ECHL champion Hampton Roads Admirals. Member of 1992-93 ECHL champion Toledo Storm. Sereved as coach of the Nashville Nighthawks at various times during the 1996-97 season while on injured reserve.

Brad Barton — Defenseman

			Regular Season					Playoffs				
Season	Team	League	GP	G	A	PTS	PIM	GP	G	A	PTS	PIM
93-94	Chatham	CoHL	38	1	10	11	125	15	0	4	4	41
94-95	Brantford	CoHL	65	5	15	20	122	—	—	—	—	—
95-96	Brantford	CoHL	5	0	1	1	20	—	—	—	—	—
95-96	Quad City	CoHL	61	2	18	20	116	2	0	0	0	0
96-97	Chicago	IHL	3	0	0	0	0	—	—	—	—	—
96-97	Quad City	CoHL	70	5	26	31	139	15	3	4	7	27
	CoHL	Totals	239	13	70	83	522	32	3	8	11	68

Born; 5/15/72, Uxbridge, Ontario. 6-2, 215. Drafted by Vancouver Canucks (9th choice, 205th overall) in 1991 Entry Draft. Member of 1996-97 Colonial League champion Quad City Mallards.

Egor Bashkatov — Center

			Regular Season					Playoffs				
Season	Team	League	GP	G	A	PTS	PIM	GP	G	A	PTS	PIM
94-95	Detroit	CoHL	69	49	43	92	36	12	2	6	8	2
94-95	Denver	IHL	2	0	2	2	0	—	—	—	—	—
94-95	Detroit	IHL	2	0	0	0	2	—	—	—	—	—
95-96	Detroit	CoHL	6	5	2	7	6	—	—	—	—	—
95-96	Utah	IHL	42	14	19	33	30	—	—	—	—	—
95-96	Houston	IHL	14	6	4	10	2	—	—	—	—	—
96-97	Las Vegas	IHL	71	23	38	61	26	3	0	0	0	2
	IHL	Totals	131	43	63	106	60	3	0	0	0	2
	CoHL	Totals	75	63	45	108	42	12	2	6	8	2

Born; 4/23/71, Moscow, Russia. 5-10, 182. 1994-95 CoHL Second Team All-Star.

Andrei Bashkirov — Right Wing

			Regular Season					Playoffs				
Season	Team	League	GP	G	A	PTS	PIM	GP	G	A	PTS	PIM
93-94	Providence	AHL	1	0	0	0	2	—	—	—	—	—
93-94	Charlotte	ECHL	62	28	42	70	25	3	1	0	1	0
94-95	Charlotte	ECHL	61	19	27	46	20	3	0	0	0	0
95-96	Huntington	ECHL	55	19	39	58	35	—	—	—	—	—
96-97	Detroit	IHL	2	0	0	0	0	—	—	—	—	—
96-97	Las Vegas	IHL	27	10	12	22	0	2	0	0	0	0
96-97	Huntington	ECHL	47	29	41	70	12	—	—	—	—	—
	IHL	Totals	29	10	12	22	0	2	0	0	0	0
	ECHL	Totals	225	95	149	244	92	6	1	0	1	0

Born; 6/22/70, Omsk, CIS. Signed as a free agent by Las Vegas Thunder, 1997.

Dave Bassegio

			Regular Season					Playoffs				
Season	Team	League	GP	G	A	PTS	PIM	GP	G	A	PTS	PIM
89-90	Indianapolis	IHL	10	1	7	8	2	10	2	4	6	6
89-90	Rochester	AHL	41	3	15	18	41	—	—	—	—	—
90-91	Rochester	AHL	35	3	13	16	32	1	0	0	0	0
91-92	Rochester	AHL	29	5	11	16	14	—	—	—	—	—
91-92	New Haven	AHL	31	3	19	22	8	3	0	0	0	2
92-93	93-94	N/A										
94-95	Detroit	IHL	1	0	0	0	0	—	—	—	—	—
94-95	Worcester	AHL	72	10	28	38	38	—	—	—	—	—
95-96	Cleveland	IHL	76	8	33	41	100	3	0	2	2	6
96-97	Cleveland	IHL	4	0	0	0	6	—	—	—	—	—
96-97	Houston	IHL	76	13	33	46	44	13	3	7	10	8
	AHL	Totals	208	24	86	110	133	4	0	0	0	2
	IHL	Totals	167	22	73	95	146	26	5	13	18	20

Born; 10/28/67, Niagra Falls, Ontario. 6-0, 195. Drafted by Buffalo Sabres (5th choice, 68th overall) in 1986. Member of 1989-90 IHL champion Indianapolis Ice.

Ryan Bast — Defenseman

Season	Team	League	GP	G	A	PTS	PIM	GP	G	A	PTS	PIM
96-97	Saint John	AHL	12	0	0	0	21	5	0	0	0	4
96-97	Las Vegas	IHL	49	2	3	5	266	—	—	—	—	—
96-97	Toledo	ECHL	12	2	2	4	75	—	—	—	—	—

Born; 8/27/75, Regina, Saskatchewan. 6-3, 193. Last amateur club; Swift Current (WHL).

Norm Batherson — Center

Season	Team	League	GP	G	A	PTS	PIM	GP	G	A	PTS	PIM
93-94	Prince Edward Island	AHL	67	14	23	37	85	—	—	—	—	—
93-94	Thunder Bay	CoHL	3	1	2	3	2	—	—	—	—	—
94-95	Portland	AHL	77	27	34	61	64	7	3	4	7	4
95-96	Portland	AHL	45	6	21	27	72	24	11	8	19	16
96-97	Portland	AHL	53	15	28	43	43	5	2	1	3	0
	AHL	Totals	242	62	106	168	264	36	16	13	29	20

Born; 3/27/69, Sydney, Nova Scotia. 6-1, 195.

Ruslan Batyrshin — Defenseman

Season	Team	League	GP	G	A	PTS	PIM	GP	G	A	PTS	PIM
95-96	Los Angeles	NHL	2	0	0	0	6	—	—	—	—	—
95-96	Phoenix	IHL	71	1	9	10	144	2	0	0	0	2
96-97	Phoenix	IHL	59	3	4	7	123	—	—	—	—	—
	IHL	Totals	130	4	13	17	267	2	0	0	0	2

Born; 2/19/75, Moscow, Russia. 6-1, 180. Drafted by Winnipeg Jets (4th choice, 79th overall) in 1993 Entry Draft. Rights traded to Los Angeles Kings by Winnipeg with Phoenix's second round choice (Marian Cisar) for Brent Thompson and future considerations (8/8/94).

John Batten — Defenseman

Season	Team	League	GP	G	A	PTS	PIM	GP	G	A	PTS	PIM
91-92	Erie	ECHL	15	4	2	6	49	—	—	—	—	—
92-93	Memphis	CeHL	29	11	15	26	210	—	—	—	—	—
93-94	Brantford	CoHL	29	11	20	31	155	—	—	—	—	—
93-94	St. Thomas	CoHL	28	16	18	34	133	3	1	2	3	10
94-95	London	CoHL	9	7	10	17	46	—	—	—	—	—
94-95	Utica	CoHL	1	0	0	0	2	—	—	—	—	—
95-96	Houston	IHL	1	0	0	0	0	—	—	—	—	—
95-96	Flint	CoHL	44	15	31	46	165	10	2	7	9	41
95-96	Jacksonville	SHL	8	3	9	12	54	—	—	—	—	—
96-97	Quad City	CoHL	52	29	39	68	191	10	3	5	8	52
	CoHL	Totals	163	78	118	196	692	23	6	14	20	103

Born; 2/1/70, Toronto, Ontario. 6-3, 225. Member of 1995-96 Colonial Cup Champion Flint Generals. Member of 1996-97 Colonial League champion Quad City Mallards. 1996-97 Second Team CoHL All-Star.

Collin Bauer — Defenseman

Season	Team	League	GP	G	A	PTS	PIM	GP	G	A	PTS	PIM
90-91	Cape Breton	AHL	40	4	14	18	18	4	1	1	2	4
91-92	Cape Breton	AHL	55	7	15	22	36	3	0	0	0	7
92-93	Kalamazoo	IHL	32	4	14	18	31	—	—	—	—	—
93-94	Kalamazoo	IHL	66	3	19	22	56	5	0	1	1	6
94-95	Kalamazoo	IHL	70	6	19	25	51	16	1	9	10	8

Season	Team	League	GP	G	A	PTS	PIM	GP	G	A	PTS	PIM
95-96	Michigan	IHL	70	5	25	30	62	4	0	2	2	0
96-97	Michigan	IHL	49	2	7	9	15	1	0	0	0	0
	IHL	Totals	287	20	84	109	215	26	1	12	13	14
	AHL	Totals	95	11	29	40	54	7	1	1	2	11

Born; 6/9/70, Edmonton, Alberta 6-1, 190. Drafted by Edmonton Oilers (4th choice, 61st overall) of NHL Entry Draft. Traded to Minnesota North Stars by Edmonton for cash (8/4/92).

Nolan Baumgartner — Defenseman

Season	Team	League	GP	G	A	PTS	PIM	GP	G	A	PTS	PIM
95-96	Washington	NHL	1	0	0	0	0	1	0	0	0	10
96-97	Portland	AHL	8	2	2	4	4	—	—	—	—	—

Born; 3/23/76, Calgary, Alberta. 6-1, 200. Last amateur club; Kamloops (WHL). Drafted by Washington Capitals (1st choice, 10th overall) in 1994 Entry Draft. An injury slowed Baumgartner's development. He should be in the NHL or AHL full-time next season.

Colin Baustad — Defenseman

Season	Team	League	GP	G	A	PTS	PIM	GP	G	A	PTS	PIM
94-95	Tulsa	CeHL	66	12	26	38	27	7	1	2	3	2
95-96	Tulsa	CeHL	64	17	49	66	18	6	3	4	7	2
96-97	Tulsa	CeHL	66	20	47	67	18	5	2	5	7	0
	CeHL	Totals	196	49	122	171	63	18	6	11	17	4

Born; 8/31/69, Calgary, Alberta. 5-10, 200. 1995-96 Second Team Central League All-Star.

Robin Bawa — Right Wing

Season	Team	League	GP	G	A	PTS	PIM	GP	G	A	PTS	PIM
87-88	Fort Wayne	IHL	55	12	27	39	239	6	1	3	4	24
88-89	Baltimore	AHL	75	23	24	47	205	—	—	—	—	—
89-90	Washington	NHL	5	1	0	1	6	—	—	—	—	—
89-90	Baltimore	AHL	61	7	18	25	189	11	1	2	3	49
90-91	Fort Wayne	IHL	72	21	26	47	381	18	4	4	8	87
91-92	Vancouver	NHL	2	0	0	0	0	1	0	0	0	0
91-92	Milwaukee	IHL	70	27	14	41	238	5	2	2	4	8
92-93	San Jose	NHL	42	5	0	5	47	—	—	—	—	—
92-93	Hamilton	AHL	23	3	4	7	58	—	—	—	—	—
92-93	Kansas City	IHL	5	2	0	2	20	—	—	—	—	—
93-94	Anaheim	NHL	12	0	1	1	7	—	—	—	—	—
93-94	San Diego	IHL	25	6	15	21	54	6	0	0	0	52
94-95	Kalamazoo	IHL	71	22	12	34	184	—	—	—	—	—
94-95	Milwaukee	IHL	4	1	1	2	19	15	1	5	6	48
95-96	San Fransisco	IHL	77	23	25	48	234	4	0	2	2	4
96-97	Fort Wayne	IHL	54	10	23	33	181	—	—	—	—	—
	NHL	Totals	61	6	1	7	60	1	0	0	0	0
	IHL	Totals	433	124	143	267	1550	54	8	16	24	223
	AHL	Totals	159	33	46	79	452	11	1	2	3	49

Born; 3/26/66, Duncan, British Columbia. 6-2, 210. Signed as a free agent by Washington Capitals (5/22/87). Traded to Vancouver Canucks by Washington for cash (7/31/91). Traded to San Jose Sharks by Vancouver for Rick Lessard (12/5/82). Claimed by Anahiem Mighty Ducks from San Jose in Expansion Draft (6/24/93). Signed as a free agent by Dallas Stars (7/22/94).

Steve Beadle — Defenseman

Season	Team	League	GP	G	A	PTS	PIM	GP	G	A	PTS	PIM
90-91	Hershey	AHL	24	1	12	13	8	—	—	—	—	—
91-92	Hershey	AHL	6	0	2	2	0	—	—	—	—	—
91-92	Johnstown	ECHL	4	1	1	2	4	—	—	—	—	—
91-92	Michigan	CoHL	41	12	27	39	14	5	1	5	6	8
92-93	Capital District	AHL	4	0	1	1	0	—	—	—	—	—

Season	Team	League	GP	G	A	PTS	PIM	GP	G	A	PTS	PIM
92-93	Detroit	CoHL	57	16	36	52	48	6	4	4	8	4
93-94	Huntsville	ECHL	42	7	18	25	67	—	—	—	—	—
93-94	Detroit	CoHL	15	7	12	19	8	3	1	2	3	0
94-95	Detroit	IHL	4	0	0	0	2	—	—	—	—	—
94-95	Detroit	CoHL	75	5	40	45	61	12	1	7	8	4
95-96	Flint	CoHL	74	8	27	35	62	15	1	7	8	10
96-97	Flint	CoHL	64	9	24	33	42	14	1	1	2	20
	CoHL	Totals	326	57	166	223	235	55	9	26	35	46
	ECHL	Totals	46	8	19	27	71	—	—	—	—	—
	AHL	Totals	34	2	15	17	8	—	—	—	—	—

Born; 5/30/68, Lansing, Michigan. 5-11, 195. Member of 1995-96 Colonial Cup Champion Flint Generals.

Frederic Beaubien — Goaltender

Season	Team	League	GP	W	L	T	MIN	SO	GAVG	GP	W	L	MIN	SO	GAVG
95-96	Phoenix	IHL	36	13	9	7	1831	1	3.28	2	0	2	119	0	4.52
96-97	Mississippi	ECHL	40	13	19	4	2217	2	3.52	3	0	3	189	0	4.45

Drafted by Los Angeles Kings (4th choice, 105th overall) in 1993 Entry Draft.

Nic Beaudoin — Left Wing

Season	Team	League	GP	G	A	PTS	PIM	GP	G	A	PTS	PIM
96-97	Hershey	AHL	34	4	3	7	51	—	—	—	—	—

Born; 12/25/76, Ottawa, Ontario. 6-3, 205. Drafted by Colorado (2nd choice, 51st overall) in 1995 Entry Draft.

Mark Beaufait — Center

Season	Team	League	GP	G	A	PTS	PIM	GP	G	A	PTS	PIM
92-93	San Jose	NHL	5	1	0	1	0	—	—	—	—	—
92-93	Kansas City	IHL	66	19	40	59	22	9	1	1	2	8
93-94	Kansas City	IHL	21	12	9	21	18	—	—	—	—	—
93-94	United States	National	N/A									
94-95	San Diego	IHL	68	24	39	63	22	5	2	2	4	2
95-96	Orlando	IHL	77	30	79	109	87	22	9	19	28	22
96-97	Orlando	IHL	80	26	65	91	63	10	5	8	13	18
	IHL	Totals	312	111	232	343	212	46	17	30	47	50

Born; 5/13/70, Hamilton, Ontario. 5-7, 155. Drafted by San Jose Sharks (2nd choice, 7th overall) in 1991 Supplemental Draft. 1996-97 IHL Second Team All-Star.

Don Beaupre — Goaltender

Season	Team	League	GP	W	L	T	MIN	SO	GAVG	GP	W	L	MIN	SO	GAVG
80-81	Minnesota	NHL	44	18	14	11	2585	0	3.20	6	4	2	360	0	4.33
81-82	Minnesota	NHL	29	11	8	9	1634	0	3.71	2	0	1	60	0	4.00
81-82	Nashville	CHL	5	2	3	0	299	0	5.02	—	—	—	—	—	—
82-83	Minnesota	NHL	36	19	10	5	2011	0	3.58	4	2	2	245	0	4.90
82-83	Birmingham	CHL	10	8	2	0	599	0	3.11	—	—	—	—	—	—
83-84	Minnesota	NHL	33	16	13	2	1791	0	4.12	13	6	7	782	1	3.07
83-84	Salt Lake City	CHL	7	2	5	0	419	0	4.30	—	—	—	—	—	—
84-85	Minnesota	NHL	31	10	17	3	1770	1	3.69	4	1	1	184	0	3.91
85-86	Minnesota	NHL	52	25	20	6	3073	1	3.55	5	2	3	300	0	3.40
86-87	Minnesota	NHL	47	17	20	6	2622	1	3.98	—	—	—	—	—	—
87-88	Minnesota	NHL	43	10	22	3	2288	0	4.22	—	—	—	—	—	—
88-89	Minnesota	NHL	1	0	1	0	59	0	3.05	—	—	—	—	—	—
88-89	Washington	NHL	11	5	4	0	578	1	2.91	—	—	—	—	—	—
88-89	Kalamazoo	IHL	3	1	2	0	179	1	3.02	—	—	—	—	—	—
88-89	Baltimore	AHL	30	14	12	2	1715	0	3.57	—	—	—	—	—	—
89-90	Washington	NHL	48	23	18	5	2793	2	3.22	8	4	3	401	0	2.69
90-91	Washington	NHL	45	20	18	3	2572	*5	2.64	11	5	5	624	*1	2.79

Season	Team	League	GP	W	L	T	MIN	SO	GAVG	GP	W	L	MIN	SO	GAVG
90-91	Baltimore	AHL	2	2	0	0	120	0	1.50	—	—	—	—	—	—
91-92	Washington	NHL	54	29	17	6	3108	1	3.20	7	3	4	419	0	3.15
91-92	Baltimore	AHL	3	1	1	1	184	0	3.26	—	—	—	—	—	—
92-93	Washington	NHL	58	27	23	5	3282	1	3.31	2	1	1	119	0	4.54
93-94	Washington	NHL	53	24	16	8	2853	2	2.84	8	5	2	429	1	2.94
94-95	Ottawa	NHL	38	8	25	3	2161	1	3.36	—	—	—	—	—	—
95-96	Ottawa	NHL	33	6	23	0	1170	1	3.73	—	—	—	—	—	—
95-96	Toronto	NHL	8	0	5	0	336	0	4.64	2	0	0	20	0	6.00
96-97	Toronto	NHL	3	0	3	0	110	0	5.45	—	—	—	—	—	—
96-97	St. John's	AHL	47	24	16	4	2623	3	2.93	—	—	—	—	—	—
96-97	Utah	IHL	4	2	2	0	239	0	3.27	7	3	4	439	1	2.32
	NHL	Totals	667	268	277	75	37396	17	3.45	72	33	31	3943	3	3.35
	AHL	Totals	82	41	29	5	4642	3	3.14	—	—	—	—	—	—
	IHL	Totals	7	3	4	0	418	2	3.16	7	3	4	439	1	2.32
	CHL	Totals	22	12	10	0	1317	0	3.92	—	—	—	—	—	—

Born; 9/19/61, Waterloo, Ontario. 5-10, 172. Drafted by Minnesota North Stars (2nd choice, 37th overall) in 1980 Entry Draft. Traded to Washington Capitals by Minnesota for rights to Claudio Scremin, 11/1/88. Traded to Ottawa Senators by Washington for Ottawa's fifth round choice (Benoit Gratton) in 1995 Entry Draft, 1/18/95. Traded to New York Islanders by Ottawa with Martin Straka and Bryan Berard for Damian Rhodes and Wade Redden, 1/23/96. Traded to Toronto Maple Leafs by Islanders with Kirk Muller for future considerations, 1/23/96. Loaned to Utah Grizzlies, 1997. Has announced plans to retire after 1996-97 season.

Stephane Beauregard — Goaltender
Regular Season / Playoffs

Season	Team	League	GP	W	L	T	MIN	SO	GAVG	GP	W	L	MIN	SO	GAVG
88-89	Moncton	AHL	15	4	8	2	824	0	4.51	—	—	—	—	—	—
88-89	Fort Wayne	IHL	16	9	5	0	830	0	3.10	9	4	4	484	*1	*2.60
89-90	Winnipeg	NHL	19	7	8	3	1079	0	3.28	4	1	3	238	0	3.03
89-90	Fort Wayne	IHL	33	20	8	3	1949	0	3.54	—	—	—	—	—	—
90-91	Winnipeg	NHL	16	3	10	1	836	0	3.95	—	—	—	—	—	—
90-91	Moncton	AHL	9	3	4	1	504	1	2.38	1	1	0	60	0	1.00
90-91	Fort Wayne	IHL	32	14	13	2	1761	0	3.71	*19	*10	9	*1158	0	2.95
91-92	Winnipeg	NHL	26	6	8	6	1267	2	2.89	—	—	—	—	—	—
92-93	Philadelphia	NHL	16	3	9	0	802	0	4.41	—	—	—	—	—	—
92-93	Hershey	AHL	13	5	5	3	794	0	3.63	—	—	—	—	—	—
93-94	Winnipeg	NHL	13	0	4	1	418	0	4.48	—	—	—	—	—	—
93-94	Moncton	AHL	37	18	11	6	2082	1	3.49	*21	*12	9	*1305	*2	2.62
94-95	Springfield	AHL	24	10	11	3	1381	2	3.17	—	—	—	—	—	—
95-96	San Francisco	IHL	*69	*36	24	8	*4022	1	3.09	4	1	3	241	0	2.49
96-97	Quebec	IHL	67	35	20	11	3946	4	2.65	9	5	3	498	0	2.29
	NHL	Totals	90	19	39	11	4402	2	3.65	4	1	3	238	0	3.03
	IHL	Totals	150	79	50	13	8562	1	3.32	41	20	19	2381	1	2.70
	AHL	Totals	98	40	39	15	5585	4	3.48	22	13	9	1365	2	2.55

Born; Cowansville, Quebec, 1/10/68. 5-11, 190. Drafted by Winnipeg Jets (3rd choice, 52nd overall) in 1988 Entry Draft. Traded to Buffalo Sabres by Winnipeg for Christian Ruuttu and future considerations (6/15/92). Traded to Chicago Blackhawks by Buffalo with Buffalo's fourth round choice (Eric Daze) in 1993 Entry Draft for Dominik Hasek (8/7/92). Traded to Winnipeg by Chicago for Christian Ruuttu (8/10/92). Traded to Philadelphia Flyers by Winnipeg for future considerations (10/1/92). Traded to Winnipeg by Philadelphia for future considerations (6/11/93). Aquired by Quebec Rafales after San Francisco disbanded, 1996. 1995-96 IHL MVP. 1995-96 IHL First Team All-Star.

Luc Beausoleil — Right Wing
Regular Season / Playoffs

Season	Team	League	GP	G	A	PTS	PIM	GP	G	A	PTS	PIM
92-93	Tulsa	CeHL	16	7	9	16	6	11	5	8	13	12
93-94	Tulsa	CeHL	60	64	50	114	110	7	4	4	8	20
94-95	Tulsa	CeHL	41	27	26	53	26	7	3	2	5	2
95-96	Reno	WCHL	15	14	8	22	40	—	—	—	—	—
96-97	Tulsa	CeHL	62	60	35	95	57	5	6	7	13	6
	CeHL	Totals	179	158	120	278	199	30	18	21	39	40

Born; 10/8/67, Montreal, Quebec. 5-8, 165. Member of 1993 CeHL Champion Tulsa Oilers. 1996-97 CeHL Second Team All-Star.

Jerome Bechard — Left Wing

			Regular Season					Playoffs				
Season	Team	League	GP	G	A	PTS	PIM	GP	G	A	PTS	PIM
90-91	New Haven	AHL	59	8	11	19	131	—	—	—	—	—
90-91	Phoenix	IHL	15	0	0	0	11	—	—	—	—	—
91-92	New Haven	AHL	62	8	11	19	129	5	0	3	3	7
92-93	Cincinnati	IHL	1	0	0	0	2	—	—	—	—	—
92-93	Birmingham	ECHL	64	24	41	65	216	—	—	—	—	—
93-94	Birmingham	ECHL	68	26	32	58	345	9	4	4	8	54
94-95	Birmingham	ECHL	67	22	26	48	427	7	1	3	4	14
95-96	Birmingham	ECHL	67	9	22	31	373	—	—	—	—	—
96-97	Columbus	CeHL	59	20	43	63	297	2	1	0	1	23
	AHL	Totals	121	16	22	38	260	5	0	3	3	7
	IHL	Totals	16	0	0	0	13	—	—	—	—	—
	ECHL	Totals	266	81	121	202	1361	16	5	7	12	68

Born; 3/30/69, Regina, Saskatchewan. 5-11, 190. Drafted by Hartford Whalers (5th choice, 115th overall) in 1989 Entry Draft.

Louis Bedard — Right Wing

			Regular Season					Playoffs				
Season	Team	League	GP	G	A	PTS	PIM	GP	G	A	PTS	PIM
96-97	Tallahassee	ECHL	58	7	10	17	358	3	1	0	1	11

Born; Montreal, Quebec. 5-10, 210. Last amateur club; Sherbrooke (QMJHL).

Clayton Beddoes — Center

			Regular Season					Playoffs				
Season	Team	League	GP	G	A	PTS	PIM	GP	G	A	PTS	PIM
94-95	Providence	AHL	65	16	20	36	39	13	3	1	4	18
95-96	Boston	NHL	39	1	6	7	44	—	—	—	—	—
95-96	Providence	AHL	32	10	15	25	24	4	2	3	5	0
96-97	Boston	NHL	21	1	2	3	13	—	—	—	—	—
96-97	Providence	AHL	36	11	23	34	60	7	2	0	2	4
	NHL	Totals	60	2	8	10	57	—	—	—	—	—
	AHL	Totals	133	37	58	95	123	24	7	4	11	22

Born; 11/10/70, Bentley, Alberta. 5-11, 190. Signed as a free agent by Boston Bruins (6/2/94).

Jared Bednar — Defenseman

			Regular Season					Playoffs				
Season	Team	League	GP	G	A	PTS	PIM	GP	G	A	PTS	PIM
93-94	Huntington	ECHL	66	8	11	19	115	—	—	—	—	—
94-95	Huntington	ECHL	64	9	36	45	211	2	0	2	2	4
95-96	Huntington	ECHL	25	4	10	14	90	—	—	—	—	—
95-96	South Carolina	ECHL	39	2	22	24	126	8	0	0	0	26
96-97	St. John's	AHL	55	1	2	3	151	—	—	—	—	—
96-97	South Carolina	ECHL	15	1	2	3	28	15	1	4	5	59
	ECHL	Totals	209	24	81	105	570	25	1	6	7	89

Born; 2/28/72, Yorktown, Saskatchewan. 6-3, 200. Member of 1997 ECHL Champion South Carolina Stingrays.

Bob Beers — Defenseman

			Regular Season					Playoffs				
Season	Team	League	GP	G	A	PTS	PIM	GP	G	A	PTS	PIM
89-90	Boston	NHL	3	0	1	1	6	14	1	1	2	18
89-90	Maine	AHL	74	7	36	43	63	—	—	—	—	—
90-91	Boston	NHL	16	0	1	1	10	6	0	0	0	4
90-91	Maine	AHL	36	2	16	18	21	—	—	—	—	—
91-92	Boston	NHL	31	0	5	5	29	1	0	0	0	0
91-92	Maine	AHL	33	6	23	29	24	—	—	—	—	—
92-93	Tampa Bay	NHL	64	12	24	36	70	—	—	—	—	—
92-93	Providence	AHL	6	1	2	3	10	—	—	—	—	—

Season	Team	League	GP	G	A	PTS	PIM	GP	G	A	PTS	PIM
92-93	Atlanta	IHL	1	0	0	0	0	—	—	—	—	—
93-94	Tampa Bay	NHL	16	1	5	6	12	—	—	—	—	—
93-94	Edmonton	NHL	66	10	27	37	74	—	—	—	—	—
94-95	Islanders	NHL	22	2	7	9	6	—	—	—	—	—
95-96	Islanders	NHL	13	0	5	5	6	—	—	—	—	—
95-96	Utah	IHL	65	6	36	42	54	22	1	12	13	16
96-97	Boston	NHL	27	3	4	7	8	—	—	—	—	—
96-97	Providence	AHL	45	10	12	22	18	—	—	—	—	—
	NHL	Totals	258	28	79	107	221	21	1	1	2	22
	AHL	Totals	194	26	89	115	136	—	—	—	—	—
	IHL	Totals	66	6	36	42	54	22	1	12	13	16

Born; 5/20/67, Pittsburgh, Pennsylvania. 6-2, 200. Drafted by Boston Bruins (10th choice, 210th overall) in 1985 Entry Draft. Traded to Tampa Bay by Boston for Stephane Richer (10/28/92). Traded to Edmonton Oilers by Tampa Bay for Chris Joseph (11/11/93). Signed as a free agent by New York Islanders (8/29/94). Signed as a free agent by Boston, (8/5/96). Member of 1995-96 IHL champion Utah Grizzlies.

Steve Begin — Center

			Regular Season					Playoffs				
Season	Team	League	GP	G	A	PTS	PIM	GP	G	A	PTS	PIM
96-97	Saint John	AHL	—	—	—	—	—	4	0	2	2	6

Born; 6/14/78, Trois-Rivieres, Quebec. 5-11, 180. Drafted by Calgary Flames (3rd choice, 40th overall) in 1996 Entry Draft.

Wade Belak — Defenseman

			Regular Season					Playoffs				
Season	Team	League	GP	G	A	PTS	PIM	GP	G	A	PTS	PIM
94-95	Cornwall	AHL	—	—	—	—	—	11	1	2	3	40
95-96	Cornwall	AHL	5	0	0	0	18	2	0	0	0	2
96-97	Colorado	NHL	5	0	0	0	11	—	—	—	—	—
96-97	Hershey	AHL	65	1	7	8	320	16	0	1	1	61
	AHL	Totals	70	1	7	8	338	29	1	3	4	103

Born; 3/7/75, Saskatoon, Saskatchewan. 6-4, 203. Drafted by Quebec Nordiques (1st choice, 12th overall) in 1994 Entry Draft. Member of 1996-97 AHL Champion Hershey Bears.

Hugo Belanger — Center

			Regular Season					Playoffs				
Season	Team	League	GP	G	A	PTS	PIM	GP	G	A	PTS	PIM
95-96	Birmingham	ECHL	6	3	5	8	0	—	—	—	—	—
96-97	Birmingham	ECHL	70	23	54	77	34	8	2	7	9	4
	ECHL	Totals	76	26	59	85	34	8	2	5	7	4

Born; 3/27/75, Mascouche, Quebec. 6-0, 172. Last amateur club; Laval (QMJHL).

Hugo P. Belanger — Left Wing

			Regular Season					Playoffs				
Season	Team	League	GP	G	A	PTS	PIM	GP	G	A	PTS	PIM
93-94	Indianapolis	IHL	75	23	15	38	8	—	—	—	—	—
94-95	Indianapolis	IHL	66	20	25	45	8	—	—	—	—	—
95-96	Atlanta	IHL	4	0	0	0	4	—	—	—	—	—
95-96	Nashville	ECHL	67	54	*90	*144	49	5	3	4	7	2
96-97	Phoenix	IHL	3	0	0	0	0	—	—	—	—	—
96-97	Pensacola	ECHL	53	22	40	62	14	12	6	9	15	0
	IHL	Totals	148	43	40	83	20	—	—	—	—	—
	ECHL	Totals	120	76	130	206	63	17	9	13	22	2

Born; 5/28/70, St. Hubert, Quebec. 6-1, 190. Drafted by Chicago Blackhawks (6th choice, 163rd overall) in 1990 Entry Draft. 1995-96 ECHL MVP. 1995-96 ECHL First Team All-Star.

Jesse Belanger — Center

			Regular Season					Playoffs				
Season	Team	League	GP	G	A	PTS	PIM	GP	G	A	PTS	PIM
90-91	Fredericton	AHL	75	40	58	98	30	6	2	4	6	0

Season	Team	League	GP	G	A	PTS	PIM	GP	G	A	PTS	PIM
91-92	Montreal	NHL	4	0	0	0	0	—	—	—	—	—
91-92	Fredericton	AHL	65	30	41	71	26	7	3	3	6	2
92-93	Montreal	NHL	19	4	2	6	4	9	0	1	1	0
92-93	Fredericton	AHL	39	19	32	51	24	—	—	—	—	—
93-94	Florida	NHL	70	17	33	50	16	—	—	—	—	—
94-95	Florida	NHL	47	15	14	29	18	—	—	—	—	—
95-96	Florida	NHL	63	17	21	38	10	—	—	—	—	—
95-96	Vancouver	NHL	9	3	0	3	4	3	0	2	2	2
96-97	Edmonton	NHL	6	0	0	0	0	—	—	—	—	—
96-97	Hamilton	AHL	6	4	3	7	0	—	—	—	—	—
96-97	Quebec	IHL	47	34	28	62	18	9	3	5	8	13
	NHL	Totals	218	56	70	126	52	12	0	3	3	2
	AHL	Totals	185	93	134	227	80	13	5	7	12	2

Born; 6/15/69, St. Georges de Beauce, Quebec. 6-1, 190. Last amateur club; Granby (QMJHL). Signed as a free agent by Montreal Canadiens, 10/3/90. Claimed by Florida Panthers from Montreal in Expansion Draft, 6/24/93. Traded to Vancouver Canukcs by Florida for Vancouver's third round choice (Oleg Kvasha) in 1996 Entry Draft and future considerations, 3/30/96. Signed as a free agent by Edmonton, 8/28/96. Member of 1992-93 Stanley Cup Champion Montreal Canadiens.

Ken Belanger — Left Wing

			Regular Season					Playoffs				
Season	Team	League	GP	G	A	PTS	PIM	GP	G	A	PTS	PIM
94-95	Toronto	NHL	3	0	0	0	9	—	—	—	—	—
94-95	St. John's	AHL	47	5	5	10	246	4	0	0	0	30
95-96	Islanders	NHL	7	0	0	0	27	—	—	—	—	—
95-96	St. John's	AHL	40	16	14	30	222	—	—	—	—	—
96-97	Islanders	NHL	18	0	2	2	102	—	—	—	—	—
96-97	Kentucky	AHL	38	10	12	22	164	4	0	1	1	27
	NHL	Totals	28	0	2	2	138	—	—	—	—	—
	AHL	Totals	125	31	31	62	632	8	0	1	1	57

Born; 5/14/74, Sault Ste. Marie, Ontario. 6-4, 220. Drafted by Hartford Whalers (7th choice,153rd overall) in 1992 Entry Draft. traded to Toronto Maple Leafs by Hartford for Toronto's ninth round choice (Matt Ball) in 1994 Entry Draft (3/18/94). Traded to New York Islanders by Toronto with Damian Rhodes for future considerations.

Martin Belanger — Defenseman

			Regular Season					Playoffs				
Season	Team	League	GP	G	A	PTS	PIM	GP	G	A	PTS	PIM
96-97	Macon	CeHL	57	5	24	29	43	5	0	0	0	6

Born; 2/3/76, LaSalle, Quebec. 6-0, 205. Last amateur club; St-Hyacinthe, QMJHL. Drafted by Montreal Canadiens, (5th choice, 74th overall) in 1994 Entry Draft.

Pascal Belanger — Defenseman

			Regular Season					Playoffs				
Season	Team	League	GP	G	A	PTS	PIM	GP	G	A	PTS	PIM
96-97	Flint	CoHL	15	0	0	0	52	—	—	—	—	—
96-97	Quad City	CoHL	12	0	0	0	45	—	—	—	—	—
96-97	Utica	CoHL	1	0	0	0	0	—	—	—	—	—
96-97	Madison	CoHL	35	1	3	4	92	4	0	0	0	7
	CoHL	Totals	63	1	3	4	189	4	0	0	0	7

Born; 7/8/75, Lapocatiere, Quebec. 6-0, 190.

Bob Bell — Goaltender

			Regular Season							Playoffs					
Season	Team	League	GP	W	L	T	MIN	SO	GAVG	GP	W	L	MIN	SO	GAVG
95-96	Adirondack	AHL	1	0	0	0	29	0	2.03	—	—	—	—	—	—
95-96	Tallahassee	ECHL	13	5	5	0	666	0	4.05	—	—	—	—	—	—
95-96	Toledo	ECHL	3	1	0	2	161	0	4.10	1	0	0	17	0	3.42
96-97	Thunder Bay	CoHL	41	22	11	4	2340	0	3.49	2	0	2	63	0	7.60
	ECHL	Totals	16	6	5	2	827	0	4.06	1	0	0	17	0	3.42

Born; 5/28/71, New Westminster, British Columbia, 5-10, 185. Last amateur club; Providence (Hockey East).

Mark Bell — Left Wing

			Regular Season					Playoffs				
Season	Team	League	GP	G	A	PTS	PIM	GP	G	A	PTS	PIM
96-97	Thunder Bay	CoHL	56	1	4	5	118	—	—	—	—	—
96-97	Utica	CoHL	7	2	0	2	0	3	0	0	0	2
	CoHL	Totals	63	3	4	7	118	3	0	0	0	2

Born; 2/3/75, New Westminster, British Columbia.

Scot Bell — Right Wing

			Regular Season					Playoffs				
Season	Team	League	GP	G	A	PTS	PIM	GP	G	A	PTS	PIM
96-97	Birmingham	ECHL	14	2	1	3	4	—	—	—	—	—
96-97	Dayton	ECHL	13	2	2	4	0	—	—	—	—	—
96-97	Raleigh	ECHL	5	0	3	3	0	—	—	—	—	—
	ECHL	Totals	32	4	6	10	4	—	—	—	—	—

Born; 4/18/72, Winchester, Ontario. 5-10, 180. Last amateur club; Ferris State (CCHA).

Scott Bell — Right Wing

			Regular Season					Playoffs				
Season	Team	League	GP	G	A	PTS	PIM	GP	G	A	PTS	PIM
94-95	Minnestoa	IHL	3	2	1	3	2	3	0	1	1	15
95-96	Providence	AHL	30	5	4	9	35	4	0	1	1	0
95-96	Indianapolis	IHL	2	1	0	1	2	—	—	—	—	—
95-96	Columbus	ECHL	37	23	20	43	75	—	—	—	—	—
96-97	Quad City	CoHL	17	3	5	8	9	14	5	4	9	13
	IHL	Totals	5	3	1	4	4	3	0	1	1	15

Born; 7/29/71, Inver Grove Heights, Minnesota. 5-11 195.

Brad Belland — Center

			Regular Season					Playoffs				
Season	Team	League	GP	G	A	PTS	PIM	GP	G	A	PTS	PIM
91-92	Michigan	CoHL	23	7	13	20	21	5	2	4	6	26
92-93	Birmingham	ECHL	27	10	14	24	31	—	—	—	—	—
95-96	San Diego	WCHL	51	30	*72	102	117	9	5	*13	*18	10
96-97	Utah	IHL	1	0	0	0	0	—	—	—	—	—
96-97	San Diego	WCHL	54	22	68	90	132	8	5	*12	*17	18
	WCHL	Totals	105	52	140	192	249	17	10	25	35	28

Born; 1/4/67, Belle River, Ontario. 6-1, 180. Last amateur club; Cornwall (OHL). Drafted by Chicago Blackhawks (5th choice, 95th overall) in 1985 Entry Draft. Did not play professional hockey in North America between the 1992-93 and 1995-96 seasons. Member of 1995-96 WCHL champion San Diego Gulls. Member of 1996-97 WCHL champion San Diego Gulls. 1995-96 First Team WCHL All-Star.

Rick Bennett — Left Wing

			Regular Season					Playoffs				
Season	Team	League	GP	G	A	PTS	PIM	GP	G	A	PTS	PIM
89-90	Rangers	NHL	6	1	0	1	5	—	—	—	—	—
90-91	Binghamton	AHL	71	27	32	59	206	10	2	1	3	27
90-91	Rangers	NHL	6	0	0	0	6	—	—	—	—	—
91-92	Binghamton	AHL	69	19	23	42	112	11	0	1	1	23
91-92	Rangers	NHL	3	0	1	1	2	—	—	—	—	—
92-93	Binghamton	AHL	76	15	22	37	114	10	0	0	0	30
93-94	Springfield	AHL	67	9	19	28	82	6	1	0	1	31
94-95	Springfield	AHL	34	3	5	8	74	—	—	—	—	—
94-95	Hershey	AHL	30	3	4	7	40	3	2	1	3	14
95-96	Cincinnati	IHL	4	0	1	1	0	1	0	0	0	2
95-96	Jacksonville	ECHL	67	28	34	62	182	18	5	10	15	30
96-97	Albany	AHL	4	0	0	0	0	—	—	—	—	—

96-97	Jacksonville	ECHL	64	23	33	56	120	—	—	—	—	—
	NHL	Totals	15	1	1	2	13	—	—	—	—	—
	AHL	Totals	351	76	105	181	628	40	5	3	8	125
	ECHL	Totals	131	51	67	118	302	18	5	10	15	30

Born; 7/24/67, Springfield, Massachusetts. 6-4, 215. Drafted by Minnesota North Stars (4th choice, 54th overall) in 1986 Entry Draft. Rights traded by Minnesota with Brian Lawton and Igor Liba to New York Rangers for Mark Tinordi, Paul Jerrard, Mike Sullivan, Brett Barnett and Los Angeles Kings third round pick (Murray Garbutt) in 1989 draft. Signed as a free agent by Hartford Whalers (8/93).

Drake Berehowsky — Defenseman

			Regular Season					Playoffs				
Season	Team	League	GP	G	A	PTS	PIM	GP	G	A	PTS	PIM
90-91	Toronto	NHL	8	0	1	1	25	—	—	—	—	—
91-92	Toronto	NHL	1	0	0	0	0	—	—	—	—	—
91-92	St. John's	AHL	—	—	—	—	—	6	0	5	5	21
92-93	Toronto	NHL	41	4	15	19	61	—	—	—	—	—
92-93	St. John's	AHL	28	10	17	27	38	—	—	—	—	—
93-94	Toronto	NHL	49	2	8	10	63	—	—	—	—	—
93-94	St. John's	AHL	18	3	12	15	40	—	—	—	—	—
94-95	Toronto	NHL	25	0	2	2	15	—	—	—	—	—
94-95	Pittsburgh	NHL	4	0	0	0	13	1	0	0	0	0
95-96	Pittsburgh	NHL	1	0	0	0	0	—	—	—	—	—
95-96	Cleveland	IHL	74	6	28	34	141	3	0	3	3	6
96-97	San Antonio	IHL	16	3	4	7	36	—	—	—	—	—
96-97	Carolina	AHL	49	2	15	17	55	—	—	—	—	—
	NHL	Totals	129	6	26	32	177	1	0	0	0	0
	AHL	Totals	95	15	44	59	133	6	0	5	5	21
	IHL	Totals	90	9	32	41	177	3	0	3	3	6

Born; 1/3/72, Toronto, Ontario. 6-1, 211. Last amateur club; North Bay (OHL). Drafted by Toronto Maple Leafs (1st choice, 10th overall) in 1990 Entry Draft. Traded to Pittsburgh Penguins by Toronto for Grant Jennings (4/7/95).

Aki Berg — Defenseman

			Regular Season					Playoffs				
Season	Team	League	GP	G	A	PTS	PIM	GP	G	A	PTS	PIM
95-96	Los Angeles	NHL	51	0	7	7	29	—	—	—	—	—
95-96	Phoenix	IHL	20	0	3	3	18	2	0	0	0	4
96-97	Los Angeles	NHL	41	2	6	8	24	—	—	—	—	—
96-97	Phoenix	IHL	23	1	3	4	21	—	—	—	—	—
	NHL	Totals	92	2	13	15	53	—	—	—	—	—
	IHL	Totals	43	1	6	7	39	2	0	0	0	4

Born; 7/28/77, Turku, Finland. 6-3, 200. Drafted by Los Angeles Kings (1st choice, 3rd overall) in 1995 Entry Draft.

Bob Berg — Left Wing

			Regular Season					Playoffs				
Season	Team	League	GP	G	A	PTS	PIM	GP	G	A	PTS	PIM
90-91	New Haven	AHL	19	0	1	1	8	—	—	—	—	—
91-92	Phoenix	IHL	24	2	8	10	18	—	—	—	—	—
91-92	Richmond	ECHL	37	19	14	33	65	6	2	1	3	0
92-93	Phoenix	IHL	1	0	0	0	0	—	—	—	—	—
92-93	Muskegon	CoHL	49	19	24	43	87	6	1	1	2	5
93-94	Wichita	CeHL	64	43	58	101	141	10	9	8	17	17
94-95	Wichita	CeHL	66	55	46	101	122	11	6	17	23	21
95-96	Houston	IHL	2	0	0	0	0	—	—	—	—	—
95-96	Louisiana	ECHL	68	59	50	109	127	5	3	5	8	6
96-97	Wichita	CeHL	56	36	49	85	105	9	5	5	10	29
	IHL	Totals	27	2	8	10	18	—	—	—	—	—
	CeHL	Totals	186	134	153	287	368	30	20	30	50	67
	ECHL	Totals	105	78	64	142	192	11	5	6	11	6

Born; 7/2/70, Beamsville, Ontario. 6-2, 190. Drafted by Los Angeles Kings (3rd choice, 49th overall) in 1990 Entry Draft. 1993-94 CeHL Second Team All-Star. 1994-95 CeHL First Team All-Star. 1995-96 ECHL Second Team All-Star. 1996-97 CeHL Second Team All-Star. Member of 1993-94 CeHL champion Wichita Thunder. Member of 1994-95 CeHL champion Wichita Thunder.

Mike Berger — Defenseman

Season	Team	League	Regular Season GP	G	A	PTS	PIM	Playoffs GP	G	A	PTS	PIM
86-87	Indianapolis	IHL	4	0	3	3	4	6	0	1	1	13
87-88	Minnesota	NHL	29	3	1	4	65	—	—	—	—	—
87-88	Kalamazoo	IHL	36	5	10	15	94	6	2	0	2	8
88-89	Minnesota	NHL	1	0	0	0	2	—	—	—	—	—
88-89	Kalamazoo	IHL	67	9	16	25	96	6	0	2	2	8
89-90	Binghamton	AHL	10	0	4	4	10	—	—	—	—	—
89-90	Phoenix	IHL	51	5	12	17	75	—	—	—	—	—
90-91	Kansas City	IHL	46	7	14	21	43	—	—	—	—	—
90-91	Knoxville	ECHL	7	1	7	8	31	—	—	—	—	—
91-92	Thunder Bay	CoHL	54	17	27	44	127	10	6	7	13	16
92-93	Thunder Bay	CoHL	8	3	5	8	20	—	—	—	—	—
92-93	Tulsa	CeHL	47	16	26	42	116	7	2	3	5	4
93-94	Tulsa	CeHL	58	15	19	34	134	11	7	4	11	22
94-95	Tulsa	CeHL	46	10	20	30	64	6	2	3	5	54
95-96	Tulsa	CeHL	45	9	18	27	110	6	0	1	1	22
96-97	Tulsa	CeHL	64	9	33	42	68	5	0	3	3	10
NHL	Totals		30	3	1	4	67	—	—	—	—	—
IHL	Totals		204	26	55	81	312	18	2	3	5	29
CeHL	Totals		260	59	116	175	492	34	11	14	25	112
CoHL	Totals		62	20	32	52	147	10	6	7	13	16

Born; 6/2/67, Edmonton, Alberta. 6-0, 230. Drafted by Minnesota North Stars (2nd choice, 69th overall) in 1985 Entry Draft. Traded to Hartford Whalers by Minnesota for Kevin Sullivan (10/7/89). 1992-93 CeHL Second Team All-Star. Member of 1991-92 CoHL champion Thunder Bay Senators. Member of 1992-93 CeHL champion Tulsa Oilers.

Phil Berger — Right Wing

Season	Team	League	Regular Season GP	G	A	PTS	PIM	Playoffs GP	G	A	PTS	PIM
89-90	Fort Wayne	IHL	3	2	2	4	2	—	—	—	—	—
89-90	Greensboro	ECHL	46	38	44	82	119	10	*11	3	14	32
90-91	Halifax	AHL	4	1	0	1	0	—	—	—	—	—
90-91	Greensboro	ECHL	44	22	34	56	112	13	11	11	22	17
91-92	Greensboro	ECHL	60	60	70	*130	158	11	8	13	21	56
92-93	Fort Wayne	IHL	8	2	5	7	14	—	—	—	—	—
92-93	Greensboro	ECHL	45	33	42	75	135	1	1	1	2	26
92-93	Muskegon	CoHL	4	4	7	11	2	—	—	—	—	—
93-94	Cornwall	AHL	2	2	1	3	0	—	—	—	—	—
93-94	Greensboro	ECHL	68	56	*83	*139	118	8	3	5	8	12
94-95	Detroit	CoHL	15	11	15	26	29	—	—	—	—	—
94-95	Greensboro	ECHL	40	23	27	50	114	17	6	17	23	46
95-96	Charlotte	ECHL	23	10	14	24	80	16	*10	*17	*27	32
96-97	San Antonio	IHL	4	0	0	0	0	—	—	—	—	—
96-97	Charlotte	ECHL	12	5	13	18	24	—	—	—	—	—
96-97	Raleigh	ECHL	20	3	19	22	20	—	—	—	—	—
96-97	Hampton Roads	ECHL	2	1	2	3	2	—	—	—	—	—
96-97	El Paso	WPHL	4	4	5	9	6	9	8	7	15	18
IHL	Totals		15	4	7	11	16	—	—	—	—	—
AHL	Totals		6	3	1	4	0	—	—	—	—	—
ECHL	Totals		360	251	348	599	882	49	50	67	117	221
CoHL	Totals		19	15	22	37	31	—	—	—	—	—

Born; 12/3/66, Dearborn, Michigan. 6-0, 190. Drafted by Quebec Nordiques in 1988 Supplemental Draft (6/88). 1991-92 ECHL MVP. 1991-92 ECHL Second Team All-Star. 1993-94 ECHL First Team All-Star. Member of 1989-90 ECHL champion Greensboro Monarchs. Member of 1995-96 ECHL champion Chralotte Checkers. Member of 1996-97 WPHL Champion El Paso Buzzards.

Chris Bergeron — Center

Season	Team	League	GP	G	A	PTS	PIM	GP	G	A	PTS	PIM
93-94	Adirondack	AHL	41	6	5	11	37	1	0	0	0	0
93-94	Toledo	ECHL	18	10	10	20	26	5	7	3	10	2
94-95	Cincinnati	IHL	14	1	3	4	2	2	0	0	0	0
94-95	Birmingham	ECHL	53	27	55	82	128	7	4	8	12	2
95-96	Cincinnati	IHL	25	3	2	5	8	1	0	0	0	0
95-96	Carolina	AHL	2	0	1	1	2	—	—	—	—	—
95-96	Birmingham	ECHL	33	21	38	59	85	—	—	—	—	—
95-96	Toledo	ECHL	6	3	2	5	2	10	3	8	11	4
96-97	Las Vegas	IHL	3	0	1	1	2	—	—	—	—	—
96-97	Cincinnati	IHL	62	7	18	25	68	1	0	1	1	0
96-97	Toledo	ECHL	9	6	9	15	8	—	—	—	—	—
	AHL	Totals	43	6	6	12	39	1	0	0	0	0
	IHL	Totals	104	11	24	35	80	4	0	1	1	0
	ECHL	Totals	119	67	114	181	249	22	14	19	33	8

Born; 11/28/70, Wallaceburg, Ontario. 5-11, 190. Member of 1993-94 ECHL champion Toledo Storm.

J.C. Bergeron — Goaltender

Season	Team	League	GP	W	L	T	MIN	SO	GAVG	GP	W	L	MIN	SO	GAVG
88-89	Sherbrooke	AHL	5	4	1	0	302	0	3.58	—	—	—	—	—	—
89-90	Sherbrooke	AHL	40	21	8	7	2254	2	*2.74	9	6	2	497	0	3.38
90-91	Montreal	NHL	18	7	6	2	941	0	3.76	—	—	—	—	—	—
90-91	Fredericton	AHL	18	12	6	0	1083	1	3.27	10	5	5	546	0	3.52
91-92	Fredericton	AHL	13	5	7	1	791	0	4.32	—	—	—	—	—	—
91-92	Peoria	IHL	27	14	9	3	1632	1	3.53	6	3	3	352	0	4.09
92-93	Tampa Bay	NHL	21	8	10	1	1163	0	3.66	—	—	—	—	—	—
92-93	Atlanta	IHL	31	21	7	1	1722	1	3.21	6	3	3	368	0	3.10
93-94	Tampa Bay	NHL	3	1	1	1	134	0	3.13	—	—	—	—	—	—
93-94	Atlanta	IHL	48	27	11	7	2755	0	3.097	2	1	1	153	0	2.34
94-95	Tampa Bay	NHL	17	3	9	1	883	1	3.33	—	—	—	—	—	—
94-95	Atlanta	IHL	6	3	3	0	324	0	4.44	—	—	—	—	—	—
95-96	Tampa Bay	NHL	12	2	6	2	595	0	4.24	—	—	—	—	—	—
95-96	Atlanta	IHL	25	9	10	4	1325	0	4.16	—	—	—	—	—	—
96-97	Los Angeles	NHL	1	0	1	0	56	0	4.29	—	—	—	—	—	—
96-97	Phoenix	IHL	42	11	19	7	2296	0	3.32	—	—	—	—	—	—
	NHL	Totals	72	21	33	7	3772	1	3.69	—	—	—	—	—	—
	IHL	Totals	179	85	59	21	10054	2	3.41	14	7	7	873	0	3.37
	AHL	Totals	76	42	22	8	4430	3	3.21	19	11	7	1043	0	3.45

Born; 10/14/68, Hauterive, Quebec. 6-2, 195. Drafted by Montreal Canadiens (5th choice, 104th overall) in 1988 Entry Draft. Traded to Tampa Bay Lightning by Montreal for Frederic Chabot (6/19/92). Signed as a free agent by Los Angeles King, (8/28/96). 1989-90 AHL First Team All-Star. Shared Harry "Hap" Holmes Trophy (fewest goals against, AHL) with Andre Racicot 1989-90. 1989-90 AHL Top Goaltender. 1993-94 Shared James Norris Memorial Trophy (fewest goals against, IHL) with Mike Greenlay. Member of 1993-94 IHL champion Atlanta Knights. Very talkative on the ice.

Stefan Bergkvist — Defenseman

Season	Team	League	GP	G	A	PTS	PIM	GP	G	A	PTS	PIM
95-96	Pittsburgh	NHL	2	0	0	0	2	4	0	0	0	2
95-96	Cleveland	IHL	61	2	8	10	58	3	0	0	0	14
96-97	Pittsburgh	NHL	5	0	0	0	7	—	—	—	—	—
96-97	Cleveland	IHL	33	0	1	1	54	4	0	0	0	0

	NHL	Totals	5	0	0	0	9	4	0	0	0	2
	IHL	Totals	94	2	9	11	112	4	0	0	0	0

Born; 3/10/75, Leksand, Sweden. 6-3, 216. Drafted by Pittsburgh Penguins (1st choice, 26th overall) in 1993 Entry Draft. Missed part of season while fighting cancer.

Tim Bergland — Right Wing

			Regular Season					Playoffs				
Season	Team	League	GP	G	A	PTS	PIM	GP	G	A	PTS	PIM
87-88	Fort Wayne	IHL	13	2	1	3	9	—	—	—	—	—
87-88	Binghamton	AHL	63	21	26	47	31	4	0	0	0	0
88-89	Baltimore	AHL	78	24	29	53	39	—	—	—	—	—
89-90	Washington	NHL	32	2	5	7	31	15	1	1	2	10
89-90	Baltimore	AHL	47	12	19	31	55	—	—	—	—	—
90-91	Washington	NHL	47	5	9	14	21	11	1	1	2	12
90-91	Baltimore	AHL	15	8	9	17	16	—	—	—	—	—
91-92	Washington	NHL	22	1	4	5	2	—	—	—	—	—
91-92	Baltimore	AHL	11	6	10	16	5	—	—	—	—	—
92-93	Tampa Bay	NHL	27	3	3	6	11	—	—	—	—	—
92-93	Atlanta	IHL	49	18	21	39	26	9	3	3	6	10
93-94	Tampa Bay	NHL	51	6	5	11	6	—	—	—	—	—
93-94	Washington	NHL	3	0	0	0	4	—	—	—	—	—
93-94	Atlanta	IHL	19	6	7	13	6	—	—	—	—	—
94-95	Chicago	IHL	81	12	21	33	70	3	1	2	3	4
95-96	Chicago	IHL	81	9	19	28	45	9	0	1	1	4
96-97	Chicago	IHL	82	20	22	42	26	4	1	1	2	0
	NHL	Totals	182	17	26	43	75	26	2	2	4	22
	IHL	Totals	325	67	91	158	182	25	5	7	12	18
	AHL	Totals	214	71	93	164	146	4	0	0	0	0

Born; 1/11/65, Crookston, Minnesota. 6-3, 194. Drafted by Washington Capitals (1st choice, 75th overall) in 1983 Entry Draft. Claimed by Tampa Bay Lightning from Washington in Expansion Draft (6/18/92). Claimed on waivers by Washington Capitals from Tampa Bay (3/19/94). Has appeared in all but one regular season game in the history of the Wolves.

Jim Bermingham — Center

			Regular Season					Playoffs				
Season	Team	League	GP	G	A	PTS	PIM	GP	G	A	PTS	PIM
92-93	ADK	AHL	21	0	2	2	8	—	—	—	—	—
92-93	TOL	ECHL	18	8	9	17	21	—	—	—	—	—
93-94	WHL	ECHL	66	33	28	61	54	6	1	2	3	4
94-95	WOR	AHL	10	3	4	7	4	—	—	—	—	—
94-95	HGN	ECHL	43	29	36	65	96	4	3	1	4	4
95-96	WOR	AHL	4	0	0	0	2	—	—	—	—	—
95-96	HGN	ECHL	60	35	50	85	115	—	—	—	—	—
96-97	Huntington	ECHL	52	28	38	66	63	—	—	—	—	—
96-97	Fredericton	AHL	27	4	2	6	40	—	—	—	—	—
	AHL	Totals	62	7	8	15	54	—	—	—	—	—
	ECHL	Totals	239	133	161	294	349	10	4	3	7	8

Born; 12/11/71, Montreal, Quebec. 6-4, 220. Drafted by Detroit Red Wings (7th choice, 186th overall) in 1991 Entry Draft.

Louis Bernard — Defenseman

			Regular Season					Playoffs				
Season	Team	League	GP	G	A	PTS	PIM	GP	G	A	PTS	PIM
94-95	Fredericton	AHL	31	2	1	3	34	1	0	0	0	0
94-95	Wheeling	ECHL	20	1	5	6	26	—	—	—	—	—
95-96	Fredericton	AHL	28	1	2	3	60	—	—	—	—	—
95-96	Wheeling	ECHL	29	4	5	9	30	3	0	1	1	2
96-97	Raleigh	ECHL	41	3	12	15	28	—	—	—	—	—
96-97	Toledo	ECHL	27	5	9	14	20	5	0	3	3	0

| | AHL | Totals | 59 | 3 | 3 | 6 | 94 | 1 | 0 | 0 | 0 | 0 |
| | ECHL | Totals | 117 | 13 | 31 | 44 | 104 | 8 | 0 | 4 | 4 | 2 |

Born; 7/10/74, Victoriaville, Quebec. 6-2, 205. Drafted by Montreal Canadiens (5th choice, 82nd overall) in 1992 Entry Draft.

Brad Berry — Defenseman

			Regular Season					Playoffs				
Season	Team	League	GP	G	A	PTS	PIM	GP	G	A	PTS	PIM
85-86	Winnipeg	NHL	13	1	0	1	10	3	0	0	0	0
86-87	Winnipeg	NHL	52	2	8	10	60	7	0	1	1	14
87-88	Winnipeg	NHL	48	0	6	6	75	—	—	—	—	—
87-88	Moncton	AHL	10	1	3	4	14	—	—	—	—	—
88-89	Winnipeg	NHL	38	0	9	9	45	—	—	—	—	—
88-89	Moncton	AHL	38	3	16	19	39	—	—	—	—	—
89-90	Winnipeg	NHL	12	1	2	3	6	1	0	0	0	0
89-90	Moncton	AHL	38	1	9	10	58	—	—	—	—	—
90-91	Brynas	Sweden	38	3	1	4	38	—	—	—	—	—
90-91	Canada	National	4	0	1	1	0	—	—	—	—	—
91-92	Minnestoa	NHL	7	0	0	0	6	2	0	0	0	2
91-92	Kalamazoo	IHL	65	5	18	23	90	5	2	0	2	6
92-93	Minnesota	NHL	63	0	3	3	109	—	—	—	—	—
93-94	Dallas	NHL	8	0	0	0	12	—	—	—	—	—
94-95	Kalamazoo	IHL	65	4	11	15	146	1	0	0	0	0
95-96	Michigan	IHL	80	4	13	17	73	10	0	5	5	12
96-97	Michigan	IHL	77	4	7	11	68	4	0	0	0	4
	NHL	Totals	241	4	28	32	323	13	0	1	1	16
	IHL	Totals	287	17	49	66	377	20	2	5	7	22
	AHL	Totals	86	5	28	33	111	—	—	—	—	—

Born; 1/1/65, Bashaw, Alberta. 6-2, 190. Drafted by Winnipeg Jets (3rd choice, 29th overall) in 1983 Entry Draft. Signed as a free agent by Minnesota North Stars (10/4/91).

Daniel Berthiaume — Goaltender

			Regular Season							Playoffs					
Season	Team	League	GP	W	L	T	MIN	SO	GAVG	GP	W	L	MIN	SO	GAVG
85-86	Winnipeg	NHL	—	—	—	—	—	—	—	1	0	1	68	0	3.53
86-87	Winnipeg	NHL	31	18	7	3	1758	1	3.17	8	4	4	439	0	2.87
86-87	Sherbrooke	AHL	7	4	3	0	420	0	3.29	—	—	—	—	—	—
87-88	Winnipeg	NHL	56	22	19	7	3010	2	3.51	5	1	4	300	0	5.00
88-89	Winnipeg	NHL	9	0	8	0	443	0	5.96	—	—	—	—	—	—
88-89	Moncton	AHL	21	6	9	2	1083	0	4.21	3	1	2	180	0	3.67
89-90	Winnipeg	NHL	24	10	11	3	1387	1	3.72	—	—	—	—	—	—
89-90	Minnesota	NHL	5	1	3	0	240	0	3.50	—	—	—	—	—	—
90-91	Los Angeles	NHL	37	20	11	4	2119	1	3.31	—	—	—	—	—	—
91-92	Los Angeles	NHL	19	7	10	1	979	0	4.04	—	—	—	—	—	—
91-92	Boston	NHL	8	1	4	2	399	0	3.16	—	—	—	—	—	—
92-93	Graz	ALP	28	—	—	—	—	0	4.07	—	—	—	—	—	—
92-93	Ottawa	NHL	25	2	17	1	1326	0	4.30	—	—	—	—	—	—
93-94	Ottawa	NHL	1	0	0	0	1	0	120.00	—	—	—	—	—	—
93-94	Prince Edward Island	AHL	30	8	16	3	1640	0	4.76	—	—	—	—	—	—
93-94	Adirondack	AHL	11	7	2	0	552	0	3.80	11	6	4	632	0	2.85
94-95	Providence	AHL	2	0	1	1	126	0	3.32	—	—	—	—	—	—
94-95	Wheeling	ECHL	10	6	1	1	599	0	4.10	—	—	—	—	—	—
94-95	Roanoke	ECHL	21	15	4	2	1196	0	2.36	8	4	4	464	1	2.97
94-95	Detroit	IHL	—	—	—	—	—	—	—	5	2	3	331	0	2.53
95-96	Detroit	IHL	7	4	3	0	401	2	2.84	—	—	—	—	—	—
95-96	Roanoke	ECHL	39	22	13	3	2109	*2	3.19	2	0	2	116	0	3.09
96-97	Central Texas	WPHL	*54	30	20	0	*3033	*2	*3.38	*11	5	*6	*678	*1	3.80

	NHL	Totals	215	81	90	21	11662	5	3.67	14	5	9	807	0	3.72
	AHL	Totals	71	25	31	6	3821	0	4.26	14	7	6	812	0	3.03
	IHL	Totals	7	4	3	0	401	2	2.84	5	2	3	331	0	2.53
	ECHL	Totals	70	43	18	6	3904	2	3.07	10	4	6	580	1	3.00

Born; 1/26/66, Longueuil, Quebec. 5-9, 155. Drafted by Winnipeg Jets (3rd choice, 60th overall) in 1985 Entry Draft. Traded to Minnesota North Stars by Winnipeg for future considerations (1/22/90). Traded to Los Angeles Kings by Minnesota for Craig Duncanson (9/6/90). Traded to Boston Bruins by Los Angeles for future considerations (1/18/92). Traded to Winnipeg by Boston for Doug Evans (6/10/92). Signed as a free agent by Ottawa Senators (12/15/92). Traded to Detroit Red Wings by Ottawa for Steve Konroyd (3/21/94). 1996-97 WPHL Goaltneder of the Year.

Eric Bertrand — Left Wing

Season	Team	League	Regular Season					Playoffs				
			GP	G	A	PTS	PIM	GP	G	A	PTS	PIM
95-96	Albany	AHL	70	16	13	29	199	4	0	0	0	6
96-97	Albany	AHL	77	16	27	43	204	8	3	3	6	15
	AHL	Totals	147	32	40	72	403	12	3	3	6	21

Born; 4/16/75, St. Ephrem, Quebec. 6-1, 195. Drafted by New Jersey Devils (9th choice, 207th overall) in 1994 Entry Draft.

Ron Bertrand — Goaltender

Season	Team	League	Regular Season							Playoffs				
			GP	W	L	OTL	MIN	SO	GAVG	GP	W	L	MIN	SO	GAVG
92-93	Chatham	CoHL	18	8	7	0	861	0	4.46	—	—	—	—	—	—
93-94	St. Thomas	CoHL	53	16	23	5	2537	0	5.09	3	0	3	159	0	6.77
94-95	Columbus	ECHL	1	1	0	0	65	0	4.62	—	—	—	—	—	—
94-95	Utica	CoHL	11	5	5	0	636	0	4.53	—	—	—	—	—	—
95-96	Utica	CoHL	41	16	17	3	2169	1	4.09	—	—	—	—	—	—
95-96	Quad City	CoHL	—	—	—	—	—	—	—	1	0	1	60	0	4.01
96-97	Port Huron	CoHL	2	0	1	0	72	0	2.49	—	—	—	—	—	—
96-97	Utica	CoHL	31	9	21	0	1619	1	5.23	—	—	—	—	—	—
96-97	Madison	CoHL	10	6	2	1	525	0	3.20	1	0	0	20	0	3.00
	CoHL	Totals	166	60	76	9	8419	2	4.61	5	0	4	239	0	5.78

Born; 1/13/72, Ottawa, Ontario. 5-11, 185.

Allan Bester — Goaltender

Season	Team	League	Regular Season							Playoffs					
			GP	W	L	T	MIN	SO	GAVG	GP	W	L	MIN	SO	GAVG
83-84	Toronto	NHL	32	11	16	4	1848	0	4.35	—	—	—	—	—	—
84-85	Toronto	NHL	15	3	9	1	767	1	4.22	—	—	—	—	—	—
84-85	St. Catharines	AHL	30	9	18	1	1669	0	4.78	—	—	—	—	—	—
85-86	Toronto	NHL	1	0	0	0	20	0	6.00	—	—	—	—	—	—
85-86	St. Catharines	AHL	50	23	23	3	2855	1	3.64	11	7	3	637	0	2.54
86-87	Toronto	NHL	36	10	14	3	1808	2	3.65	1	0	0	39	0	1.54
86-87	Newmarket	AHL	3	1	0	0	0	0	1.89	—	—	—	—	—	—
87-88	Toronto	NHL	30	8	12	5	1607	2	3.81	5	2	3	253	0	4.98
88-89	Toronto	NHL	43	17	20	3	2460	2	3.80	—	—	—	—	—	—
89-90	Toronto	NHL	42	20	16	0	2206	0	4.49	4	0	3	196	0	4.29
89-90	Newmarket	AHL	5	2	1	1	264	0	4.09	—	—	—	—	—	—
90-91	Toronto	NHL	6	0	4	0	247	0	4.37	—	—	—	—	—	—
90-91	Detroit	NHL	3	0	3	0	178	0	4.38	1	0	0	20	0	3.00
90-91	Newmarket	AHL	19	7	8	4	1157	1	3.01	—	—	—	—	—	—
91-92	Detroit	NHL	1	0	0	0	31	0	3.87	—	—	—	—	—	—
91-92	Adirondack	AHL	22	13	8	0	1268	0	3.69	*19	*14	5	1174	*1	*2.56
92-93	Adirondack	AHL	41	16	15	5	2268	1	3.52	10	7	3	633	*1	2.46
93-94	San Diego	IHL	46	22	14	6	2543	1	3.54	8	4	4	419	0	4.00
94-95	San Diego	IHL	58	28	23	5	3250	1	3.38	4	2	2	272	0	2.86
95-96	Dallas	NHL	10	4	5	1	601	0	3.00	—	—	—	—	—	—
95-96	Orlando	IHL	51	32	16	2	2947	1	3.58	23	11	12	1342	2	2.90
96-97	Orlando	IHL	61	37	13	3	3115	2	2.54	10	4	4	513	0	3.16

			GP	G	A		PIM	GP	G	A		PIM
	NHL	Totals	219	73	99	17	11773	7	4.01	11	2	6	508	0	4.37
	IHL	Totals	216	119	66	16	11855	5	3.24	45	21	22	2546	2	3.13
	AHL	Totals	170	71	73	14	9671	3	3.72	40	28	11	2444	2	2.53

Born; 3/26/64, Hamilton, Ontario. 5-7, 155. Drafted by Toronto Maple Leafs (3rd choice, 48th overall) in 1983 Entry Draft. Traded to Detroit Red Wings by Toronto for Detroit's sixth round choice (Alexander Kuzminsky) in 1991 Entry Draft (3/5/91). Signed as a free agent by Anaheim Mighty Ducks (9/9/93). Signed as a free agent by Dallas Stars, 1/21/96. AHL Playoff MVP 1991-92. Member of 1991-92 AHL champion Adirondack Red Wings.

Andy Bezeau — Left Wing

Season	Team	League	GP	G	A	PTS	PIM	GP	G	A	PTS	PIM
91-92	Richmond	ECHL	12	1	1	2	71	—	—	—	—	—
91-92	Johnstown	ECHL	28	11	10	21	142	—	—	—	—	—
92-93	Brantford	CoHL	38	18	13	31	278	14	2	4	6	*132
92-93	Moncton	AHL	2	0	0	0	4	—	—	—	—	—
93-94	Brantford	CoHL	22	18	16	34	240	—	—	—	—	—
93-94	St. Thomas	CoHL	1	2	0	2	12	—	—	—	—	—
93-94	South Carolina	ECHL	36	10	10	20	352	2	0	0	0	23
94-95	Phoenix	IHL	6	0	0	0	23	—	—	—	—	—
94-95	Fort Wayne	IHL	3	0	1	1	26	—	—	—	—	—
94-95	Brantford	CoHL	17	8	10	18	185	—	—	—	—	—
94-95	Muskegon	CoHL	46	14	17	31	357	17	9	7	16	88
95-96	Fort Wayne	IHL	74	10	11	21	590	5	0	2	2	28
96-97	Fort Wayne	IHL	45	4	5	9	320	—	—	—	—	—
	IHL	Totals	128	14	17	31	959	5	0	2	2	28
	CoHL	Totals	124	60	56	116	1072	31	11	11	22	220
	ECHL	Totals	76	22	21	43	565	2	0	0	0	23

Born; 3/30/70, St. John, New Brunswick. 5-9, 185. Drafted by Boston Bruins (10th choice, 231st overall) in 1990 Entry Draft.

Frank Bialowas — Defenseman

Season	Team	League	GP	G	A	PTS	PIM	GP	G	A	PTS	PIM
91-92	Roanoke	ECHL	23	4	2	6	150	3	0	0	0	4
92-93	St. John's	AHL	7	1	0	1	28	1	0	0	0	0
92-93	Richmond	ECHL	60	3	18	21	261	1	0	0	0	2
93-94	Toronto	NHL	3	0	0	0	12	—	—	—	—	—
93-94	St. John's	AHL	69	2	8	10	352	7	0	3	3	25
94-95	St. John's	AHL	51	2	3	5	277	4	0	0	0	12
95-96	Portland	AHL	65	4	3	7	211	7	0	0	0	42
96-97	Philadelphia	AHL	67	7	6	13	254	6	0	2	2	41
	AHL	Totals	259	16	20	36	1122	25	0	5	5	124
	ECHL	Totals	83	7	20	27	411	4	0	0	0	6

Born; 9/25/70, Winnipeg, Manitoba. 6-0, 235. Signed as a free agent by Toronto Maple Leafs (3/20/94). Signed as a free agent by Washington Capitals (8/10/95). Traded to Philadelphia Flyers by Washington for future considerations (7/18/96).

Radim Bicanek — Defenseman

Season	Team	League	GP	G	A	PTS	PIM	GP	G	A	PTS	PIM
94-95	Ottawa	NHL	6	0	0	0	0	—	—	—	—	—
94-95	Prince Edward Island	AHL	—	—	—	—	—	3	0	1	1	0
95-96	Prince Edward Island	AHL	74	7	19	26	87	5	0	2	2	6
96-97	Ottawa	NHL	21	0	1	1	8	7	0	0	0	8
96-97	Worcester	AHL	44	1	15	16	22	—	—	—	—	—
	NHL	Totals	27	0	1	1	22	7	0	0	0	8
	AHL	Totals	118	8	34	42	109	8	0	3	3	6

Born; 1/18/75, Uherske Hradiste, Czechoslovakia. 6-1, 195. Drafted by Ottawa Senators (2nd choice, 27th overall) in 1993 Entry Draft.

Don Biggs — Center

			Regular Season					Playoffs				
Season	Team	League	GP	G	A	PTS	PIM	GP	G	A	PTS	PIM
84-85	Minnesota	NHL	1	0	0	0	0	—	—	—	—	—
84-85	Springfield	AHL	6	0	3	3	0	2	1	0	1	0
85-86	Springfield	AHL	28	15	16	31	46	—	—	—	—	—
85-86	Nova Scotia	AHL	47	6	23	29	36	—	—	—	—	—
86-87	Nova Scotia	AHL	80	22	25	47	165	5	1	2	3	4
87-88	Hershey	AHL	77	38	41	79	151	12	5	*11	*16	22
88-89	Hershey	AHL	76	36	67	103	158	11	5	9	14	30
89-90	Philadelphia	NHL	11	2	0	2	8	—	—	—	—	—
89-90	Hershey	AHL	66	39	53	92	125	—	—	—	—	—
90-91	Rochester	AHL	65	31	57	88	115	15	9	*14	*23	14
91-92	Binghamton	AHL	74	32	50	82	122	11	2	7	10	8
92-93	Binghamton	AHL	78	54	*84	138	112	14	3	9	12	32
93-94	Cincinnati	IHL	80	30	59	89	128	11	8	9	17	29
94-95	Cincinnati	IHL	77	27	49	76	152	10	1	9	10	29
95-96	Cincinnati	IHL	82	27	57	84	160	17	9	19	19	24
96-97	Cincinnati	IHL	82	25	41	66	128	3	1	2	3	19
	NHL	Totals	12	2	0	2	8	—	—	—	—	—
	AHL	Totals	597	273	419	692	1030	70	26	52	78	110
	IHL	Totals	321	109	206	315	568	61	19	39	58	101

Born; 4/7/65, Mississauga, Ontario. 5-8, 180. Drafted by Minnesota North Stars (9th choice, 156th overall) in 1983 Entry Draft. Traded to Edmonton Oilers by Minnesota with Gord Sherven for Marc Habscheid, Don Barber and Emanuel Viveiros (12/20/85). Signed as a free agent by Philadelphia Flyers (7/17/87). Traded to New York Rangers by Philadelphia Flyers for future considerations. 1992-93 AHL MVP. 1992-93 AHL First Team All-Star. Member of 1987-88 AHL champion Hershey Bears.

Beau Bilek — Defenseman

			Regular Season					Playoffs				
Season	Team	League	GP	G	A	PTS	PIM	GP	G	A	PTS	PIM
95-96	Indianapolis	IHL	5	0	0	0	4	—	—	—	—	—
95-96	Columbus	ECHL	64	6	25	31	78	3	0	0	0	6
96-97	Indianapolis	IHL	2	0	1	1	0	—	—	—	—	—
96-97	Columbus	ECHL	68	10	35	45	83	8	1	1	2	4
	IHL	Totals	7	0	1	1	4	—	—	—	—	—
	ECHL	Totals	132	16	60	76	161	11	1	1	2	4

Born; 5/3/73, Des Moines, Iowa. 6-1, 200.

Brent Bilodeau — Defenseman

			Regular Season					Playoffs				
Season	Team	League	GP	G	A	PTS	PIM	GP	G	A	PTS	PIM
93-94	Fredericton	AHL	72	2	5	7	89	—	—	—	—	—
94-95	Fredericton	AHL	50	4	8	12	146	12	3	3	6	28
95-96	San Fransisco	IHL	65	3	14	17	123	4	1	0	1	2
96-97	Saint John	NHL	24	2	1	3	29	—	—	—	—	—
96-97	San Antonio	IHL	48	4	7	11	178	—	—	—	—	—
96-97	Las Vegas	IHL	3	0	0	0	0	—	—	—	—	—
	AHL	Totals	146	8	14	22	264	12	3	3	6	28
	IHL	Totals	116	7	21	28	301	4	1	0	1	2

Born; 3/27/73, Dallas, Texas. 6-3, 217. Drafted by Montreal Canadiens (1st choice, 17th overall) in 1991 Entry Draft.

Troy Binnie — Left Wing

			Regular Season					Playoffs				
Season	Team	League	GP	G	A	PTS	PIM	GP	G	A	PTS	PIM
92-93	Dallas	CeHL	43	22	28	50	44	7	7	3	10	6
93-94	Cape Breton	AHL	2	0	1	1	0	—	—	—	—	—
93-94	Dallas	CeHL	56	54	42	96	96	7	5	4	9	2
94-95	Dallas	CeHL	58	28	29	57	92	—	—	—	—	—

Season	Team	League	GP	G	A	PTS	PIM	GP	G	A	PTS	PIM
95-96	Knoxville	ECHL	15	4	6	10	48	—	—	—	—	—
95-96	Reno	WCHL	24	16	15	31	12	2	0	1	1	0
96-97	Detroit	IHL	1	0	0	0	0	—	—	—	—	—
96-97	Saginaw	CoHL	13	10	8	18	6	—	—	—	—	—
96-97	Austin	WPHL	47	33	31	64	30	6	5	4	9	26
	CeHL	Totals	157	104	99	203	232	14	12	7	19	8

Born; 9/22/70, Ottawa, Ontario. 6-1, 200. Drafted by Minnesota North Stars (10th choice, 197th overall) in 1990 Entry Draft.

Craig Binns — Defenseman

			Regular Season					Playoffs				
Season	Team	League	GP	G	A	PTS	PIM	GP	G	A	PTS	PIM
94-95	Columbus	ECHL	48	7	10	17	110	3	0	1	1	4
95-96	Columbus	ECHL	3	0	1	1	2	—	—	—	—	—
95-96	Mobile	ECHL	41	1	18	19	99	—	—	—	—	—
96-97	Mobile	ECHL	65	1	10	11	217	—	—	—	—	—
	ECHL	Totals	157	9	39	48	428	3	0	1	1	4

Born; 7/18/74, Ottawa, Ontario. 6-4, 225.

Jamie Bird — Defenseman

			Regular Season					Playoffs				
Season	Team	League	GP	G	A	PTS	PIM	GP	G	A	PTS	PIM
95-96	San Antonio	CeHL	25	3	12	15	22	—	—	—	—	—
95-96	Fort Worth	CeHL	35	5	12	17	30	—	—	—	—	—
96-97	Knoxville	ECHL	44	3	10	13	26	—	—	—	—	—
	CeHL	Totals	60	8	24	32	52	—	—	—	—	—

Born; 3/7/74, Rochester, New York. 5-11, 189.

Clint Black — Center

			Regular Season					Playoffs				
Season	Team	League	GP	G	A	PTS	PIM	GP	G	A	PTS	PIM
95-96	Wichita	CeHL	64	33	35	68	51	—	—	—	—	—
96-97	Wichita	CeHL	54	16	25	41	70	9	2	2	4	18
	CeHL	Totals	118	49	60	109	121	9	2	2	4	18

Born; 9/17/72, Duncan, British Columbia. 5-9, 175.

Ryan Black — Center

			Regular Season					Playoffs				
Season	Team	League	GP	G	A	PTS	PIM	GP	G	A	PTS	PIM
95-96	Hampton Roads	ECHL	5	1	1	2	0	3	1	2	3	0
96-97	Fort Worth	CeHL	52	27	20	47	44	17	5	6	11	10

Born; 10/25/73, Elmira, Ontario. 6-1, 195. Drafted by New Jersey Devils (6th choice, 114th overall) in 1992 Entry Draft. Member of 1996-97 CeHL Champion Fort Worth Fire.

Brant Blackned — Left Wing

			Regular Season					Playoffs				
Season	Team	League	GP	G	A	PTS	PIM	GP	G	A	PTS	PIM
95-96	Erie	ECHL	15	1	4	5	34	—	—	—	—	—
95-96	Thunder Bay	CoHL	15	4	10	14	17	5	0	0	0	0
96-97	Thunder Bay	CoHL	70	49	51	100	79	11	3	6	9	12
	CoHL	Totals	85	53	61	114	96	16	3	6	9	12

Born; 4/4/74, Weminji, Quebec. 6-0, 200.

Brian Blad — Defenseman

			Regular Season					Playoffs				
Season	Team	League	GP	G	A	PTS	PIM	GP	G	A	PTS	PIM
87-88	Newmarket	AHL	39	0	4	4	74	—	—	—	—	—
87-88	Milwaukee	IHL	28	1	6	7	45	—	—	—	—	—
88-89	Newmarket	AHL	59	2	4	6	149	5	0	1	1	5

Season	Team	League	GP	G	A	PTS	PIM	GP	G	A	PTS	PIM
89-90	Newmarket	AHL	58	2	4	6	216	—	—	—	—	—
90-91	Newmarket	AHL	28	0	0	0	100	—	—	—	—	—
90-91	Milwaukee	IHL	37	1	2	3	98	6	0	2	2	8
91-92	Milwaukee	IHL	58	1	3	4	162	5	0	0	0	0
92-93	Peoria	IHL	12	0	0	0	14	4	0	0	0	17
92-93	Dayton	ECHL	19	1	5	6	90	1	0	0	0	0
93-94	Rochester	AHL	3	0	0	0	0	—	—	—	—	—
93-94	South Carolina	ECHL	43	0	8	8	104	—	—	—	—	—
94-95	Brantford	CoHL	51	1	2	3	62	—	—	—	—	—
95-96	Louisville	ECHL	66	1	15	16	83	3	0	0	0	0
96-97	Toledo	ECHL	35	1	5	6	43	5	0	1	1	4
	AHL	Totals	187	4	12	16	539	5	0	1	1	5
	IHL	Totals	135	3	11	14	319	15	0	2	2	25
	ECHL	Totals	163	3	33	36	320	9	0	1	1	4

Born; 7/22/67, Brockville, Ontario. 6-0, 200. Drafted by Toronto Maple Leafs (9th choice, 175th overall) in 1987 Entry Draft. Traded to Vancouver Canucks by Toronto for Todd Hawkins (1/22/91).

Scott Blair — Center

			Regular Season					Playoffs				
Season	Team	League	GP	G	A	PTS	PIM	GP	G	A	PTS	PIM
96-97	Utica	CoHL	40	13	27	40	76	—	—	—	—	—
96-97	Madison	CoHL	24	8	8	16	52	5	1	2	3	0
	CoHL	Totals	64	21	35	56	128	5	1	2	3	0

Born; 11/1/78, Detroit, Michigan. 5-11, 170.

John Blessman — Defenseman

			Regular Season					Playoffs				
Season	Team	League	GP	G	A	PTS	PIM	GP	G	A	PTS	PIM
87-88	Utica	AHL	24	0	2	2	50	—	—	—	—	—
88-89	Utica	AHL	26	2	3	5	46	—	—	—	—	—
88-89	Indianapolis	IHL	31	2	5	7	60	—	—	—	—	—
89-90	Hershey	AHL	1	0	0	0	0	—	—	—	—	—
89-90	Winston-Salem	ECHL	17	1	6	7	108	—	—	—	—	—
89-90	Greensboro	ECHL	19	0	7	7	81	11	3	6	9	50
90-91	Greensboro	ECHL	29	7	14	21	131	13	1	9	10	36
91-92	Kansas City	IHL	25	0	2	2	24	—	—	—	—	—
91-92	Cape Breton	AHL	27	2	8	10	16	5	0	1	1	2
92-93	Baltimore	AHL	6	0	0	0	4	—	—	—	—	—
92-93	Greensboro	ECHL	5	3	1	4	16	—	—	—	—	—
94-95	Toledo	ECHL	16	1	2	3	33	—	—	—	—	—
94-95	Raleigh	ECHL	31	4	14	18	109	—	—	—	—	—
94-95	San Antonio	CeHL	16	2	10	12	13	13	4	*17	21	12
95-96	Syracuse	AHL	1	0	1	1	0	—	—	—	—	—
95-96	Wheeling	ECHL	67	8	18	26	176	7	1	3	4	2
96-97	Syracuse	AHL	23	4	4	8	9	—	—	—	—	—
96-97	Wheeling	ECHL	31	14	9	23	64	3	2	0	2	8
	AHL	Totals	108	8	18	26	125	5	0	1	1	2
	IHL	Totals	56	2	7	9	84	—	—	—	—	—
	ECHL	Totals	210	38	71	109	718	34	7	18	25	96

Born; 4/27/67, Agincourt, Ontario. 6-3, 220. Drafted by New Jersey Devils (8th choice, 170th overall) in 1987 Entry Draft. Member of 1989-90 ECHL champion Greensboro Monarchs.

Jeff Bloemberg — Defense

			Regular Season					Playoffs				
Season	Team	League	GP	G	A	PTS	PIM	GP	G	A	PTS	PIM
87-88	Colorado	IHL	5	0	0	0	0	11	1	0	1	8
88-89	Rangers	NHL	9	0	0	0	0	—	—	—	—	—

Season	Team	League	GP	G	A	PTS	PIM	GP	G	A	PTS	PIM
88-89	Denver	IHL	64	7	22	29	55	1	0	0	0	0
89-90	Rangers	NHL	28	3	3	6	25	7	0	3	3	5
89-90	Flint	IHL	41	7	14	21	24	—	—	—	—	—
90-91	Rangers	NHL	3	0	2	2	0	—	—	—	—	—
90-91	Binghamton	AHL	77	16	46	62	28	10	0	6	6	10
91-92	Rangers	NHL	3	0	1	1	0	—	—	—	—	—
91-92	Binghamton	AHL	66	6	41	47	22	11	1	10	11	10
92-93	Cape Breton	AHL	76	6	45	51	34	16	5	10	15	10
93-94	Springfield	AHL	78	8	28	36	36	6	0	3	3	8
94-95	Adirondack	AHL	44	5	19	24	10	4	0	0	0	0
95-96	Adirondack	AHL	72	10	28	38	32	3	0	1	1	4
96-97	Adirondack	AHL	69	5	31	36	24	4	0	3	3	2
	NHL	Totals	43	3	6	9	25	7	0	3	3	5
	AHL	Totals	482	56	238	294	186	54	6	33	39	44
	IHL	Totals	110	14	36	50	79	12	1	0	1	8

Born; 1/31/68, Listowel, Ontario. 6-2, 205. Drafted by New York Rangers (5th choice, 93rd overall) 1986 Entry Draft. Claimed by Tampa Bay Lightning from Rangers in Expansion draft 6/18/92. Traded by Tampa Bay to Edmonton Oilers for future considerations 9/25/92. Signed as a free agent by Hartford 8/9/93. Signed as a free agent by Detroit 5/9/95. AHL Second Team All-Star 1991. Member of 1992-93 AHL champion Cape Breton Oilers.

Dan Bloom — Defenseman

			Regular Season					Playoffs				
Season	Team	League	GP	G	A	PTS	PIM	GP	G	A	PTS	PIM
96-97	Birmingham	ECHL	19	2	1	3	16	—	—	—	—	—

Born; 2/21/73, Waterloo, Iowa.

Jean Blouin — Right Wing

			Regular Season					Playoffs				
Season	Team	League	GP	G	A	PTS	PIM	GP	G	A	PTS	PIM
91-92	Muskegon	IHL	19	4	5	9	12	—	—	—	—	—
92-93	Louisville	ECHL	2	3	1	4	0	—	—	—	—	—
92-93	Atlanta	IHL	61	11	11	22	69	—	—	—	—	—
93-94	Prince Edward Island	AHL	8	2	0	2	7	—	—	—	—	—
93-94	Thunder Bay	CoHL	23	22	12	34	31	7	0	4	4	11
94-95	Prince Edward Island	AHL	1	0	0	0	0	—	—	—	—	—
94-95	Thunder Bay	CoHL	66	70	39	109	60	11	*16	11	27	38
95-96	Thunder Bay	CoHL	13	8	7	15	27	19	*23	8	31	20
96-97	Carolina	AHL	1	0	1	1	0	—	—	—	—	—
96-97	Grand Rapids	IHL	1	0	0	0	0	—	—	—	—	—
96-97	Port Huron	CoHL	39	32	22	54	23	5	2	6	8	2
	IHL	Totals	81	15	16	31	81	—	—	—	—	—
	AHL	Totals	10	2	1	3	7	—	—	—	—	—
	CoHL	Totals	141	132	80	212	141	42	41	29	70	71

Born; 2/26/71, Beauport, Quebec. 6-1, 205. 1994-95 CoHL First Team All-Star. Member of 1993-94 CoHL champion Thunder Bay Senators. Member of 1994-95 CoHL champion Thunder Bay Senators.

Sylvain Blouin — Right Wing/Defenseman

			Regular Season					Playoffs				
Season	Team	League	GP	G	A	PTS	PIM	GP	G	A	PTS	PIM
94-95	Binghamton	AHL	10	1	0	1	46	2	0	0	0	24
94-95	Chicago	IHL	1	0	0	0	2	—	—	—	—	—
94-95	Charlotte	ECHL	50	5	7	12	280	3	0	0	0	6
95-96	Binghamton	AHL	71	5	8	13	352	4	0	3	3	4
96-97	Rangers	NHL	6	0	0	0	18	—	—	—	—	—
96-97	Binghamton	AHL	62	13	17	30	301	4	2	1	3	16
	AHL	Totals	143	19	25	44	699	10	2	4	6	44

Born; 5/21/74, Montreal, Quebec. 6-2, 216. Drafted by New York Rangers (5th choice, 104th overall) in 1994 Entry Draft.

John Blue — Goaltender

Regular Season / Playoffs

Season	Team	League	GP	W	L	T	MIN	SO	GAVG	GP	W	L	MIN	SO	GAVG
87-88	Kalamazoo	IHL	15	3	8	4	847	0	4.60	1	0	1	40	0	9.00
87-88	United States	National													
88-89	Kalamazoo	IHL	17	8	6	0	970	0	4.27	—	—	—	—	—	—
88-89	Virginia	ECHL	10				570	0	4.00	—	—	—	—	—	—
89-90	Phoenix	IHL	19	5	10	3	986	0	5.65	—	—	—	—	—	—
89-90	Kalamazoo	IHL	4	2	1	1	232	0	4.65	—	—	—	—	—	—
89-90	Knoxville	ECHL	19	6	10	1	1000	0	5.15	—	—	—	—	—	—
90-91	Maine	AHL	10	3	4	2	545	0	2.42	1	0	1	40	0	10.50
90-91	Albany	IHL	19	11	6	0	1077	0	3.96	—	—	—	—	—	—
90-91	Kalamazoo	IHL	1	1	0	0	64	0	1.88	—	—	—	—	—	—
90-91	Peoria	IHL	4	4	0	0	240	0	3.00	—	—	—	—	—	—
90-91	Knoxville	ECHL	3	1	1	0	149	0	5.23	—	—	—	—	—	—
91-92	Maine	AHL	43	11	23	6	2168	1	4.57	—	—	—	—	—	—
92-93	Boston	NHL	23	9	8	4	1322	1	2.90	2	0	1	96	0	3.13
92-93	Providence	AHL	19	14	4	1	1159	0	3.47	—	—	—	—	—	—
93-94	Boston	NHL	18	5	8	3	944	0	2.99	—	—	—	—	—	—
93-94	Providence	AHL	24	7	11	4	1298	1	3.51	—	—	—	—	—	—
94-95	Providence	AHL	10	6	3	0	577	0	3.11	4	1	3	219	0	5.19
95-96	Buffalo	NHL	5	2	2	0	255	0	3.53	—	—	—	—	—	—
95-96	Phoenix	IHL	8	1	5	0	309	0	4.07	—	—	—	—	—	—
95-96	Fort Wayne	IHL	5	1	2	2	249	0	4.58	—	—	—	—	—	—
95-96	Rochester	AHL	14	4	6	1	672	0	3.66	1	0	1	27	0	2.24
96-97	Austin	WPHL	33	17	11	5	1955	1	3.47	2	0	2	97	0	6.82
	NHL	Totals	46	16	18	7	2521	1	3.00	2	0	1	96	0	3.13
	AHL	Totals	120	45	51	14	6419	2	3.75	6	1	5	286	0	5.66
	IHL	Totals	92	36	37	10	4981	0	4.46	1	0	1	40	0	9.00
@	ECHL	Totals	32				1719	0	4.75	—	—	—	—	—	—

Born; 2/19/66, Huntington Beach, California. 5-10, 185. Drafted by Winnipeg Jets (9th choice, 197th overall) in 1986 Entry Draft. Traded to Minnesota North Stars by Winnipeg for Winnipeg's seventh round choice (Markus Akerblom) in 1988 Entry Draft. Signed as a free agent by Boston Bruins. Member of 1995-96 AHL champion Rochester Americans. @ ECHL goaltending record not complete.

Jeff Blum — Defenseman

Season	Team	League	GP	G	A	PTS	PIM	GP	G	A	PTS	PIM
95-96	Detroit	CoHL	71	6	30	36	137	10	2	5	7	14
96-97	Port Huron	CoHL	71	11	22	33	111	5	0	0	0	4
	CoHL	Totals	142	17	52	69	248	15	2	5	7	18

Born; 4/24/72, Detroit, Michigan. 6-1, 195.

Ken Blum — Left Wing

Season	Team	League	GP	G	A	PTS	PIM	GP	G	A	PTS	PIM
91-92	Toledo	ECHL	8	0	2	2	2	—	—	—	—	—
91-92	Winston-Salem	ECHL	8	0	1	1	14	—	—	—	—	—
91-92	Roanoke	ECHL	30	3	2	5	64	7	0	1	1	19
92-93	Roanoke	ECHL	63	16	21	37	132	—	—	—	—	—
93-94	Richmond	ECHL	61	11	25	36	215	—	—	—	—	—
94-95	Flint	CoHL	54	6	23	29	164	5	1	0	1	10
95-96	Carolina	AHL	1	0	0	0	0	—	—	—	—	—
95-96	Detroit	CoHL	59	22	13	35	154	10	4	1	5	26
96-97	Saginaw	CoHL	59	24	33	57	165	—	—	—	—	—
	CoHL	Totals	172	52	69	121	483	15	5	1	6	36
	ECHL	Totals	170	30	51	81	427	7	0	1	1	19

Born; 6/8/71, Hackensack, New Jersey. Selected by Minnesota North Stars (10th choice, 175th overall) 6/17/89.

Aaron Boh — Defenseman

			Regular Season					Playoffs				
Season	Team	League	GP	G	A	PTS	PIM	GP	G	A	PTS	PIM
93-94	Columbus	ECHL	10	1	9	10	31	—	—	—	—	—
94-95	Atlanta	IHL	20	2	6	8	15	—	—	—	—	—
94-95	Columbus	ECHL	58	5	25	30	186	—	—	—	—	—
95-96	Rochester	AHL	12	0	4	4	10	—	—	—	—	—
95-96	Minnesota	IHL	3	0	0	0	2	—	—	—	—	—
95-96	Columbus	ECHL	37	17	31	48	136	—	—	—	—	—
95-96	Louisiana	ECHL	17	5	8	13	58	5	1	7	8	10
96-97	Houston	IHL	3	0	0	0	2	—	—	—	—	—
96-97	Louisiana	ECHL	52	11	54	65	193	17	4	17	21	93
	IHL	Totals	26	2	6	8	19	—	—	—	—	—
	ECHL	Totals	174	39	127	166	604	22	5	24	29	103

Born; 4/4/74, Lethbridge, Alberta. 6-2, 185. Drafted by Vancouver Canucks (12th choice, 261st overall) in 1992 Entry Draft. 1995-96 ECHL Second Team All-Star.

Lonny Bohonos — Right Wing

			Regular Season					Playoffs				
Season	Team	League	GP	G	A	PTS	PIM	GP	G	A	PTS	PIM
94-95	Syracuse	AHL	67	30	45	75	71	—	—	—	—	—
95-96	Vancouver	NHL	3	0	1	1	0	—	—	—	—	—
95-96	Syracuse	AHL	74	40	39	79	82	16	14	8	22	16
96-97	Vancouver	NHL	33	11	11	22	10	—	—	—	—	—
96-97	Syracuse	AHL	41	22	30	52	28	3	2	2	4	4
	NHL	Totals	36	11	12	23	10	—	—	—	—	—
	AHL	Totals	182	92	114	206	181	19	16	10	26	20

Born; 3/26/70, Winnipeg, Manitoba. 5-11, 190. Signed as a free agent by Vancouver Canucks (5/31/94).

Alexander Boikov — Defenseman

			Regular Season					Playoffs				
Season	Team	League	GP	G	A	PTS	PIM	GP	G	A	PTS	PIM
96-97	Kentucky	AHL	61	1	19	20	182	4	0	1	1	4

Born; 2/7/75, Chelyabinsk, USSR. 6-0, 180. Signed as a free agent by San Jose Sharks (4/22/96).

Patrick Boileau — Defenseman

			Regular Season					Playoffs				
Season	Team	League	GP	G	A	PTS	PIM	GP	G	A	PTS	PIM
95-96	Portland	AHL	78	10	28	38	41	19	1	3	4	12
96-97	Washington	NHL	1	0	0	0	0	—	—	—	—	—
96-97	Portland	AHL	67	16	28	44	63	5	1	1	2	4
	AHL	Totals	145	26	56	82	104	24	2	4	6	16

Born; 2/22/75, Montreal, Quebec. 6-0, 190. Drafted by Washington Capitals (3rd choice, 69th overall) in 1993 Entry Draft.

Brad Bombardir — Defense

			Regular Season					Playoffs				
Season	Team	League	GP	G	A	PTS	PIM	GP	G	A	PTS	PIM
94-95	Albany	AHL	77	5	22	27	22	14	0	3	3	6
95-96	Albany	AHL	80	6	25	31	63	3	0	1	1	4
96-97	Albany	AHL	32	0	8	8	6	16	1	3	4	8
	AHL	Totals	189	11	55	66	91	33	1	7	8	18

Born; 5/5/72, Powell River, British Columbia. 6-2, 190. Drafted by New Jersey Devils (5th choice, 56th overall) in 1990 Entry Draft. Member of 1994-95 Calder Cup champion Albany RiverRats.

Igor Bonderev — Defenseman

Season	Team	League	GP	G	A	PTS	PIM	GP	G	A	PTS	PIM
94-95	Birmingham	ECHL	3	0	1	1	0	—	—	—	—	—
94-95	Dallas	CeHL	9	1	9	10	12	—	—	—	—	—
94-95	Fort Worth	CeHL	41	5	19	24	32	—	—	—	—	—
95-96	Huntsville	SHL	54	16	28	44	32	10	3	8	11	2
96-97	Huntsville	CeHL	60	38	53	91	26	9	1	12	13	0
	CeHL	Totals	110	44	81	125	70	9	1	12	13	0

Born; 2/9/74, Riga, Latvia. 6-0, 195. Member of 1995-96 SHL Champion Huntsville Channel Cats. 1996-97 CeHL First Team All-Star.

Brian Bonin — Center

Season	Team	League	GP	G	A	PTS	PIM	GP	G	A	PTS	PIM
96-97	Cleveland	IHL	60	13	26	39	18	1	1	0	1	0

Born; 11/28/73, White Bear Lake, Minnesota. 5-10, 185. Drafted by Pittsburgh Penguins (9th choice, 211th overall) in 1992 Entry Draft.

Doug Bonner — Goaltender

Season	Team	League	GP	W	L	T	MIN	SO	GAVG	GP	W	L	MIN	SO	GAVG
96-97	St. John's	AHL	11	0	4	1	366	0	4.27	—	—	—	—	—	—
96-97	Peoria	ECHL	23	13	8	1	1315	1	2.87	10	6	3	541	0	3.10

Born; 10/15/76, Tacoma, Washington. 5-10, 175. Drafted by Toronto Maple Leafs (3rd choice, 139th overall) in 1995 Entry Draft.

Jason Bonsignore — Center

Season	Team	League	GP	G	A	PTS	PIM	GP	G	A	PTS	PIM
94-95	Edmonton	NHL	1	1	0	1	0	—	—	—	—	—
95-96	Edmonton	NHL	20	0	2	2	4	—	—	—	—	—
95-96	Cape Breton	AHL	12	1	4	5	12	—	—	—	—	—
96-97	Hamilton	AHL	78	21	33	54	78	7	0	0	0	4
	NHL	Totals	21	1	2	3	4	—	—	—	—	—
	AHL	Totals	90	22	37	59	90	7	0	0	0	4

Born; 4/15/76, Rochester, New York. 6-4, 208. Drafted by Edmonton Oilers (1st choice, 4rth overall) in 1994 Entry Draft.

Dennis Bonvie — Defenseman

Season	Team	League	GP	G	A	PTS	PIM	GP	G	A	PTS	PIM
93-94	Cape Breton	AHL	63	1	10	11	278	4	0	0	0	11
94-95	Edmonton	NHL	2	0	0	0	0	—	—	—	—	—
94-95	Cape Breton	AHL	74	5	15	20	422	—	—	—	—	—
95-96	Edmonton	NHL	8	0	0	0	47	—	—	—	—	—
95-96	Cape Breton	AHL	38	13	14	27	269	—	—	—	—	—
96-97	Hamilton	AHL	73	9	20	29	*522	22	3	11	14	*91
	NHL	Totals	10	0	0	0	47	—	—	—	—	—
	AHL	Totals	248	28	59	87	1491	26	3	11	14	102

Born; 7/23/73, Antigosh, Nova Scotia. 5-11, 210. Signed as a free agent by Edmonton Oilers (8/25/94). Set AHL record for most penalty minutes during the regular season 1996-97.

Joe Bonvie — Goaltender

Season	Team	League	GP	MIN	GAVG	W	L	OTL	SO	GP	MIN	GAVG	W	L	SO
94-95	Indianapolis	IHL	3	118	6.60	1	1	0	0	—	—	—	—	—	—
94-95	Columbus	ECHL	10	495	5.34	2	5	1	0	—	—	—	—	—	—
94-95	Flint	CoHL	8	389	3.69	4	2	0	0	4	218	3.57	1	3	0
95-96	Madison	CoHL	36	1953	4.09	14	15	4	1	1	10	0.00	0	0	0
96-97	Alaska	WCHL	9	460	6.14	2	5	1	0	—	—	—	—	—	—
96-97	Jacksonville	ECHL	14	737	4.23	5	6	2	0	—	—	—	—	—	—

	CoHL	Totals	44	2342	4.02	18	17	4	1	5	228	3.42	1	3	0
	ECHL	Totals	24	1232	4.67	7	7	3	0	—	—	—	—	—	—

Born; 12/27/71, Stephenville, Newfoundland. 6-3, 200.

Sebastian Bordeleau — Center

			Regular Season					Playoffs				
Season	Team	League	GP	G	A	PTS	PIM	GP	G	A	PTS	PIM
95-96	Montreal	NHL	4	0	0	0	0	—	—	—	—	—
95-96	Fredericton	AHL	43	17	29	46	68	7	0	2	2	8
96-97	Montreal	NHL	28	2	9	11	2	—	—	—	—	—
96-97	Fredericton	AHL	33	17	21	38	50	—	—	—	—	—
	NHL	Totals	32	2	9	11	2	—	—	—	—	—
	AHL	Totals	76	34	50	84	118	7	0	2	2	8

Born; 2/15/75, Vancouver, British Columbia, 5-10, 180. Drafted by Montreal Canadiens (3rd choice, 73rd overall) in 1993 Entry Draft.

Scott Boston — Defenseman

			Regular Season					Playoffs				
Season	Team	League	GP	G	A	PTS	PIM	GP	G	A	PTS	PIM
92-93	Atlanta	IHL	76	2	17	19	75	2	0	0	0	0
93-94	Atlanta	IHL	7	0	0	0	2	—	—	—	—	—
93-94	Knoxville	ECHL	64	9	30	39	213	—	—	—	—	—
94-95	Rochester	AHL	16	1	1	2	6	—	—	—	—	—
94-95	South Carolina	ECHL	48	18	33	51	137	9	2	8	10	33
95-96	South Carolina	ECHL	67	12	46	58	163	8	3	10	13	18
96-97	St. John's	AHL	6	0	1	1	0	—	—	—	—	—
96-97	South Carolina	ECHL	42	12	30	42	85	—	—	—	—	—
96-97	Louisville	ECHL	18	2	6	8	28	—	—	—	—	—
	IHL	Totals	83	2	17	19	77	2	0	0	0	0
	AHL	Totals	22	1	2	3	6	—	—	—	—	—
	ECHL	Totals	239	53	145	198	806	17	5	18	23	51

Born; 7/13/71, Ottawa, Ontario. 6-2, 180. Signed as a free agent by Tampa Bay Lightning (8/13/92). Traded to Louisville RiverFrogs with Kyle Ferguson by South Carolina for Chris Rowland (1997). 1994-95 ECHL Second Team All-Star.

Jean-Francois Bouchard — Left Wing

			Regular Season					Playoffs				
Season	Team	League	GP	G	A	PTS	PIM	GP	G	A	PTS	PIM
96-97	Macon	CeHL	61	15	43	58	63	—	—	—	—	—

Born; 2/24/75, St. Jean, Quebec. 6-0, 192.

Robin Bouchard — Left Wing

			Regular Season					Playoffs				
Season	Team	League	GP	G	A	PTS	PIM	GP	G	A	PTS	PIM
94-95	Columbus	ECHL	46	30	33	63	188	3	0	3	3	38
94-95	Roanoke	ECHL	10	1	0	1	25	—	—	—	—	—
95-96	Flint	CoHL	73	56	51	107	247	15	8	9	17	52
96-97	Fort Wayne	IHL	2	1	0	1	2	—	—	—	—	—
96-97	Flint	CoHL	16	6	12	18	60	—	—	—	—	—
96-97	Muskegon	CoHL	52	34	23	57	220	3	2	1	3	6
	CoHL	Totals	141	96	86	182	527	18	10	10	20	58
	ECHL	Totals	56	31	33	64	213	3	0	3	3	38

Born; 10/22/73, Jomquiere, Quebec. 5-11, 185. Traded to Muskegon Fury for CoHL rights to Steve Walker by Flint (1996). Member of 1995-96 Colonial Cup Champion Flint Generals

Tyler Boucher — Center

			Regular Season					Playoffs				
Season	Team	League	GP	G	A	PTS	PIM	GP	G	A	PTS	PIM
96-97	Utah	IHL	5	0	0	0	17	—	—	—	—	—
96-97	New Mexico	WPHL	48	9	17	26	263	6	1	1	2	12

Born; 4/27/72, The Pas, Manitoba. 5-8, 165.

Jason Boudrais — Forward

			Regular Season					Playoffs				
Season	Team	League	GP	G	A	PTS	PIM	GP	G	A	PTS	PIM
96-97	Columbus	CeHL	21	8	15	23	16	1	0	0	0	2

Drafted by Florida Panthers (8th choice, 183rd overall) in 1994 Entry Draft.

Carl Boudreau — Center

			Regular Season					Playoffs				
Season	Team	League	GP	G	A	PTS	PIM	GP	G	A	PTS	PIM
92-93	Oklahoma City	CeHL	48	27	44	71	109	11	8	5	13	20
93-94	Oklahoma City	CeHL	64	40	67	107	93	7	5	4	9	14
94-95	France											
95-96	Oklahoma City	CeHL	59	22	49	71	98	12	5	7	12	16
96-97	Reno	WCHL	55	32	53	85	57	—	—	—	—	—
	CeHL	Totals	171	89	160	249	300	30	18	16	34	50

Born; 8/31/71, Victoriaville, Quebec. 5-11, 180. 1992-93 CeHL First Team All-Star. Member of 1995-96 CeHL champion Oklahoma City Blazers.

Francis Bouillon — Defenseman

			Regualr Season					Playoffs				
Season	Team	League	GP	G	A	PTS	PIM	GP	G	A	PTS	PIM
96-97	Wheeling	ECHL	69	10	32	42	77	3	0	2	2	10

Born; 10/17/75, Quebec City, Quebec. 5-9, 160.

Jude Boulianne — Defenseman

			Regular Season					Playoffs				
Season	Team	League	GP	G	A	PTS	PIM	GP	G	A	PTS	PIM
95-96	Quad City	CoHL	39	4	15	19	16	—	—	—	—	—
95-96	Saginaw	CoHL	18	2	1	3	10	5	0	1	1	4
96-97	Saginaw	CoHL	6	1	2	3	2	—	—	—	—	—
96-97	Columbus	CeHL	31	9	18	27	16	—	—	—	—	—
96-97	Wichita	CeHL	18	5	11	16	4	9	2	7	9	6
	CoHL	Totals	63	7	18	25	28	5	0	1	1	4
	CeHL	Totals	49	14	29	43	20	9	2	7	9	6

Born; 5/10/71, St. Anne, Manitoba. 5-11, 205

Vladislav Boulin — Defenseman

			Regular Season					Playoffs				
Season	Team	League	GP	G	A	PTS	PIM	GP	G	A	PTS	PIM
94-95	Hershey	AHL	52	1	7	8	30	—	—	—	—	—
95-96	Hershey	AHL	32	1	2	3	30	2	0	0	0	0
96-97	Philadelphia	AHL	51	1	4	5	35	—	—	—	—	—
	AHL	Totals	135	3	13	16	95	2	0	0	0	0

Born; 5/18/72, Penza, Russia. 6-4, 196. Drafted by Philadelphia Flyers (5th choice, 103rd overall) in 1992 Entry Draft.

Eric Boulton — Left Wing

			Regular Season					Playoffs				
Season	Team	League	GP	G	A	PTS	PIM	GP	G	A	PTS	PIM
96-97	Binghamton	AHL	23	2	3	5	67	3	0	0	0	4
96-97	Charlotte	ECHL	44	14	11	25	325	3	0	1	1	6

Born; 8/17/76, Halifax, Nova Scotia. Drafted by New York Rangers (12th choice, 234th overall) in 1994 Entry Draft.

Phil Bourque — Defenseman

Season	Team	League	GP	G	A	PTS	PIM	GP	G	A	PTS	PIM
82-83	Baltimore	AHL	65	1	15	16	93	—	—	—	—	—
83-84	Pittsburgh	NHL	5	0	1	1	12	—	—	—	—	—
83-84	Baltimore	AHL	58	5	17	22	96	—	—	—	—	—
84-85	Baltinore	AHL	79	6	15	21	164	13	2	5	7	23
85-86	Pittsbugh	NHL	4	0	0	0	2	—	—	—	—	—
85-86	Baltimore	AHL	74	8	18	26	226	—	—	—	—	—
86-87	Pittsburgh	NHL	22	2	3	5	32	—	—	—	—	—
86-87	Baltimore	AHL	49	15	16	31	183	—	—	—	—	—
87-88	Pittsburgh	NHL	21	4	12	16	20	—	—	—	—	—
87-88	Muskegon	IHL	52	16	36	52	66	6	1	2	3	16
88-89	Pittsburgh	NHL	80	17	26	43	97	11	4	1	5	66
89-90	Pittsburgh	NHL	76	22	17	39	108	—	—	—	—	—
90-91	Pittsburgh	NHL	78	20	14	34	106	24	6	7	13	16
91-92	Pittsburgh	NHL	58	10	16	26	58	21	3	4	7	25
92-93	Rangers	NHL	55	6	14	20	39	—	—	—	—	—
93-94	Rangers	NHL	16	0	1	1	8	—	—	—	—	—
93-94	Ottawa	NHL	11	2	3	5	0	—	—	—	—	—
94-95	Ottawa	NHL	38	4	3	7	20	—	—	—	—	—
95-96	Ottawa	NHL	13	1	1	2	14	—	—	—	—	—
95-96	Detroit	IHL	36	4	13	17	70	10	1	3	4	10
96-97	Chicago	IHL	77	7	14	21	50	4	0	2	2	2
	NHL	Totals	477	88	111	199	516	56	13	12	25	107
	AHL	Totals	325	35	81	116	762	13	2	5	7	23
	IHL	Totals	165	27	63	90	186	20	2	7	9	2

Born; 6/8/62, Chelmsford, Massachusetts. 6-1, 196. Signed as a free agent by Pittsburgh Penguins (10/4/82). Signed as a free agent by New York Rangers (8/31/92). Traded to Ottawa Senators by Rangers for future considerations (3/21/94). 1987-88 IHL Outstanding Defenseman. 1987-88 IHL First Team All-Star. Member of 1990-91 Stanley Cup champion Pittsburgh Penguins. Member of of 1991-92 Stanley Cup champion Pittsburgh Penguins.

Dany Bousquet — Center

Season	Team	League	GP	G	A	PTS	PIM	GP	G	A	PTS	PIM
95-96	Hamton Roads	ECHL	5	2	0	2	12	3	3	1	4	0
96-97	Birmingham	ECHL	68	54	53	107	39	8	6	7	13	12
	ECHL	Totals	73	56	53	109	51	11	9	8	17	12

Born; 4/3/73, Montreal, Quebec. 5-11, 165. Drafted by Washington Capitals (10th choice, 277th overall) in 1993 Entry Draft. 1996-97 ECHL Rookie of the Year. 1996-97 ECHL Second Team All-Star.

Matt Bowden — Goaltender

Season	Team	League	GP	W	L	T	MIN	SO	GAVG	GP	W	L	MIN	SO	GAVG
95-96	San Antonio	CeHL	27	12	7	3	1350	0	3.60	2	0	0	44	0	2.76
96-97	San Antonio	CeHL	22	7	9	2	1048	0	4.87	—	—	—	—	—	—
	CeHL	Totals	49	19	16	5	2398	0	4.15	2	0	0	44	0	2.76

Born; 2/20/73, Warwick, Rhode Island. 6-0, 165.

Curt Bowen — Left Wing

Season	Team	League	GP	G	A	PTS	PIM	GP	G	A	PTS	PIM
94-95	Adirondack	AHL	64	6	11	17	71	4	0	2	2	4
95-96	Adirondack	AHL	3	0	0	0	0	—	—	—	—	—
96-97	Adirondack	AHL	78	11	11	22	110	4	0	0	0	2
	AHL	Totals	145	17	22	39	181	8	0	2	2	6

Drafted by Detroit Red Wings (1st choice, 22nd overall) 1992 Entry Draft.

Jason Bowen — Defenseman

			Regular Season					Playoffs				
Season	Team	League	GP	G	A	PTS	PIM	GP	G	A	PTS	PIM
92-93	Philadelphia	NHL	7	1	0	1	2	—	—	—	—	—
93-94	Philadelphia	NHL	56	1	5	6	87	—	—	—	—	—
94-95	Philadelphia	NHL	4	0	0	0	0	—	—	—	—	—
94-95	Hershey	AHL	55	5	5	10	116	6	0	0	0	46
95-96	Philadelphia	NHL	2	0	0	0	2	—	—	—	—	—
95-96	Hershey	AHL	72	6	7	13	128	4	2	0	2	13
96-97	Philadelphia	NHL	4	0	1	1	8	—	—	—	—	—
96-97	Philadelphia	AHL	61	10	12	22	160	6	0	1	1	10
	NHL	Totals	73	2	6	8	9\9	—	—	—	—	—
	AHL	Totals	188	21	24	45	404	16	2	1	3	69

Born; 11/9/73, Port ALice, British Columbia. 6-4, 208. Drafted by Philadelphia Flyers (2nd choice, 15th overall) in 1992 Entry Draft.

Bill Bowler — Center

			Regular Season					Playoffs				
Season	Team	League	GP	G	A	PTS	PIM	GP	G	A	PTS	PIM
94-95	Las Vegas	IHL	—	—	—	—	—	1	0	0	0	0
95-96	Las Vegas	IHL	75	31	55	86	26	14	3	5	8	22
96-97	Houston	IHL	78	22	43	65	79	13	2	5	7	6
	IHL	Totals	153	53	98	151	105	28	5	10	15	28

Born; 9/25/74, Toronto, Ontario. 5-9, 180. Traded to Houston Aeros by Las Vegas Thunder to complete earlier trade (7/96).

Marc Boxer — Left Wing

			Regular Season					Playoffs				
Season	Team	League	GP	G	A	PTS	PIM	GP	G	A	PTS	PIM
95-96	Louisville	ECHL	62	7	27	34	66	3	0	1	1	2
96-97	Memphis	CeHL	64	20	33	53	120	14	4	7	11	18

Born; 1/27/71, Fort Worth, Texas. 5-10, 185.

Ian Boyce — Left Wing

			Regular Season					Playoffs				
Season	Team	League	GP	G	A	PTS	PIM	GP	G	A	PTS	PIM
90-91	Fort Wayne	IHL	39	10	12	22	11	19	5	4	9	0
90-91	Rochester	AHL	12	1	2	3	2	—	—	—	—	—
91-92	Fort Wayne	IHL	38	12	15	27	29	—	—	—	—	—
91-92	Rochester	AHL	20	5	8	13	4	16	3	1	4	0
92-93	Fort Wayne	IHL	69	19	34	53	63	12	3	1	4	6
93-94	Fort Wayne	IHL	55	12	16	28	26	18	3	6	9	2
94-95	Fort Wayne	IHL	76	26	22	48	20	4	2	1	3	4
95-96	San Fransisco	IHL	77	25	22	47	60	4	0	1	1	10
96-97	Kansas City	IHL	68	16	26	42	43	3	1	0	1	0
	IHL	Totals	422	120	147	267	252	60	14	13	27	22
	AHL	Totals	32	6	10	16	6	16	3	1	4	0

Born; 1/24/68, St. Laurent, Quebec. 5-9, 177. Member of 1992-93 IHL champion Ft. Wayne Komets.

James Boyd — Center

			Regular Season					Playoffs				
Season	Team	League	GP	G	A	PTS	PIM	GP	G	A	PTS	PIM
96-97	Fort Worth	CeHL	—	—	—	—	—	2	0	1	1	9

Member of 1996-97 CeHL champion Fort Worth Fire. Last amateur club; Belleville (OHL).

Rick Boyd — Right Wing

			Regular Season					Playoffs				
Season	Team	League	GP	G	A	PTS	PIM	GP	G	A	PTS	PIM
88-89	Indianapolis	IHL	27	2	1	3	113	—	—	—	—	—
88-89	Flint	IHL	27	4	0	4	73	—	—	—	—	—

Season	Team	League	GP	G	A	PTS	PIM	GP	G	A	PTS	PIM
89-90	Binghamton	AHL	3	0	0	0	7	—	—	—	—	—
89-90	Maine	AHL	11	0	2	2	29	—	—	—	—	—
89-90	Johnstown	ECHL	45	5	12	17	284	—	—	—	—	—
90-91	Hampton Roads	ECHL	23	0	12	12	108	13	3	2	5	63
90-91	Knoxville	ECHL	1	0	0	0	0	—	—	—	—	—
90-91	Johnstown	ECHL	26	5	10	15	128	—	—	—	—	—
95-96	Johnstown	ECHL	50	3	15	18	253	—	—	—	—	—
96-97	Johnstown	ECHL	23	3	4	7	141	—	—	—	—	—
	IHL	Totals	54	6	1	7	186	—	—	—	—	—
	ECHL	Totals	168	16	53	69	914	13	3	2	5	63

Born; 12/30/64, Fort St. John, British Columbia. 6-2, 210. Member of 1990-91 ECHL champion Hampton Roads Admirals.

Zac Boyer — Right Wing

Season	Team	League	GP	G	A	PTS	PIM	GP	G	A	PTS	PIM
92-93	Indianapolis	IHL	59	7	14	21	26	—	—	—	—	—
93-94	Indianapolis	IHL	54	13	12	25	67	—	—	—	—	—
94-95	Dallas	NHL	1	0	0	0	0	2	0	0	0	0
94-95	Kalamazoo	IHL	22	9	7	16	22	15	3	9	12	8
95-96	Dallas	NHL	2	0	0	0	0	—	—	—	—	—
95-96	Michigan	IHL	67	24	27	51	27	10	4	8	12	2
96-97	Orlando	IHL	80	25	49	74	63	3	0	1	1	2
	NHL	Totals	3	0	0	0	0	2	0	0	0	0
	IHL	Totals	282	78	109	187	205	28	7	18	25	12

Born; 10/25/71, Inuvik, Northwest Territories. 6-2, 200. Drafted by Chicago Blackhawks (4th choice, 88th overall) in 1991 Entry Draft. Signed as a free agent by Dallas Stars (7/25/94).

Lance Brady — Defenseman

Season	Team	League	GP	G	A	PTS	PIM	GP	G	A	PTS	PIM
93-94	Columbus	ECHL	56	5	22	27	130	6	0	2	2	10
94-95	Worcester	AHL	4	0	1	1	0	—	—	—	—	—
94-95	Cleveland	IHL	3	0	0	0	5	—	—	—	—	—
94-95	Columbus	ECHL	66	6	25	31	151	3	0	5	5	15
95-96	Cincinnati	IHL	27	0	2	2	12	1	0	0	0	0
95-96	Birmingham	ECHL	47	17	27	44	77	—	—	—	—	—
96-97	Las Vegas	IHL	5	0	2	2	9	—	—	—	—	—
96-97	Baltimore	AHL	2	0	0	0	9	—	—	—	—	—
96-97	Birmingham	ECHL	61	13	43	56	79	8	1	5	6	8
	IHL	Totals	30	0	2	2	17	1	0	0	0	0
	AHL	Totals	6	0	1	1	9	—	—	—	—	—
	ECHL	Totals	230	41	117	158	439	17	1	12	13	33

Born; 11/30/70, Sandwich, Massachusetts. 6-2, 205.

Neil Brady — Center

Season	Team	League	GP	G	A	PTS	PIM	GP	G	A	PTS	PIM
88-89	Utica	AHL	75	16	21	37	56	4	0	3	3	0
89-90	New Jersey	NHL	19	1	4	5	13	—	—	—	—	—
89-90	Utica	AHL	38	10	13	23	21	5	0	1	1	10
90-91	New Jersey	NHL	3	0	0	0	0	—	—	—	—	—
90-91	Utica	AHL	77	33	63	96	91	—	—	—	—	—
91-92	New Jersey	NHL	7	1	0	1	4	—	—	—	—	—
91-92	Utica	AHL	33	12	30	42	28	—	—	—	—	—
92-93	Ottawa	NHL	55	7	17	24	57	—	—	—	—	—
92-93	New Haven	AHL	8	6	3	9	2	—	—	—	—	—
93-94	Dallas	NHL	5	0	1	1	21	—	—	—	—	—
93-94	Kalamazoo	IHL	43	10	16	26	188	5	1	1	2	10

94-95	Kalamazoo	IHL	70	13	45	58	140	15	5	14	19	22
95-96	Michigan	IHL	61	14	20	34	127	10	1	4	5	8
96-97	Michigan	IHL	76	13	20	33	62	4	1	0	1	0
	NHL	Totals	89	9	22	31	95	—	—	—	—	—
	IHL	Totals	250	50	101	151	517	34	8	19	27	40
	AHL	Totals	231	77	130	207	198	9	0	4	4	10

Born; 4/12/68, Montreal, Quebec. 6-3, 205. Drafted by New Jersey Devils (1st choice, 3rd overall) in 1986 Entry Draft. Traded to Ottawa Senators by New Jersey for future considerations (9/3/92). Signed as a free agent by Dallas Stars (12/3/93).

Sean Brady — Center

		Regular Season						Playoffs				
Season	Team	League	GP	G	A	PTS	PIM	GP	G	A	PTS	PIM
96-97	Waco	WPHL	62	20	37	57	31	—	—	—	—	—

Born; Napanee, Ontario. 6-1, 190.

Rod Branch — Goaltender

		Regular Season								Playoffs					
Season	Team	League	GP	W	L	T	MIN	SO	GAVG	GP	W	L	MIN	SO	GAVG
96-97	New Mexico	WPHL	10	7	3	0	517	0	3.94	—	—	—	—	—	—
96-97	Tulsa	CeHL	18	10	7	1	1054	0	3.76	5	2	3	291	0	3.51

Born; 4/14/75, Fort St. John, British Columbia. 5-8, 160.

Aaron Brand — Center

		Regular Season						Playoffs				
Season	Team	League	GP	G	A	PTS	PIM	GP	G	A	PTS	PIM
95-96	St. John's	AHL	1	0	1	1	0	4	0	0	0	4
96-97	St. John's	AHL	75	15	25	40	80	11	3	2	5	2
	AHL	Totals	76	15	26	41	80	15	3	2	5	6

Born; 6/14/75, Toronto, Ontario. 6-0, 190.

Dampy Brar — Center

		Regular Season						Playoffs				
Season	Team	League	GP	G	A	PTS	PIM	GP	G	A	PTS	PIM
96-97	Toledo	ECHL	8	0	2	2	8	—	—	—	—	—
96-97	Nashville	CeHL	7	4	3	7	6	—	—	—	—	—
96-97	San Antonio	CeHL	40	21	19	40	48	—	—	—	—	—
	CeHL	Totals	47	25	22	47	54	—	—	—	—	—

Born; 5/22/76, Sparwood, British Columbia. 6-3, 205. Selected by Wichita in San Antonio dispersal draft (6/10/97).

Fred Brathwaite — Goaltender

		Regular Season								Playoffs					
Season	Team	League	GP	W	L	T	MIN	SO	GAVG	GP	W	L	MIN	SO	GAVG
93-94	Edmonton	NHL	19	3	10	3	982	0	3.54	—	—	—	—	—	—
93-94	Cape Breton	AHL	2	1	1	0	119	0	3.04	—	—	—	—	—	—
94-95	EDM	NHL	14	2	5	1	601	0	3.99	—	—	—	—	—	—
95-96	EDM	NHL	7	0	2	0	293	0	2.46	—	—	—	—	—	—
95-96	CPB	AHL	31	12	16	0	1699	1	3.88	—	—	—	—	—	—
96-97	Manitoba	IHL	58	22	22	5	2946	1	3.40	—	—	—	—	—	—
	NHL	Totals	40	5	17	4	1876	0	3.52	—	—	—	—	—	—
	AHL	Totals	33	13	17	0	1818	1	3.83	—	—	—	—	—	—

Signed as a free agent by Edmonton Oilers (10/6/93).

Mike Brault — Left Wing

		Regular Season						Playoffs				
Season	Team	League	GP	G	A	PTS	PIM	GP	G	A	PTS	PIM
96-97	El Paso	WPHL	5	0	0	0	10	5	0	0	0	10

Member of 1996-97 WPHL champion El Paso Buzzards.

Lindsay Braun — Defenseman

Season	Team	League	GP	G	A	PTS	PIM	GP	G	A	PTS	PIM
96-97	Toledo	ECHL	1	0	0	0	0	—	—	—	—	—
96-97	Nashville	CeHL	15	0	0	0	27	—	—	—	—	—

Born; 3/21/73, Calgary, Alberta. 5-10, 190.

George Breen — Right Wing

Season	Team	League	GP	G	A	PTS	PIM	GP	G	A	PTS	PIM
95-96	Cape Breton	AHL	50	11	12	23	20	—	—	—	—	—
96-97	Hamilton	AHL	1	0	0	0	0	—	—	—	—	—
96-97	Portland	AHL	5	0	0	0	0	—	—	—	—	—
	AHL	Totals	56	11	12	23	20	—	—	—	—	—

Born; 8/3/73, Webster, Massachusetts. 6-2, 200. Drafted by Edmonton Oilers (4rth choice, 56th overall) in 1991 Entry Draft.

Rich Brennan — Defenseman

Season	Team	League	GP	G	A	PTS	PIM	GP	G	A	PTS	PIM
95-96	Cornwall	AHL	36	4	8	12	61	7	0	0	0	6
95-96	Brantford	CoHL	5	1	2	3	2	—	—	—	—	—
96-97	Colorado	NHL	2	0	0	0	0	—	—	—	—	—
96-97	Hershey	AHL	74	11	45	56	88	23	2	*16	18	22
	AHL	Totals	110	15	53	68	149	30	2	16	18	28

Born; 11/26/72, Schenectady, New York. 6-2, 200. Drafted by Quebec Nordiques (3rd choice, 46th overall) in 1991 Entry Draft. Member of 1996-97 AHL Champion Hershey Bears.

Matt Brenner — Defenseman

Season	Team	League	GP	G	A	PTS	PIM	GP	G	A	PTS	PIM
96-97	Central Texas	WPHL	64	3	14	17	39	11	2	4	6	25

Born; 6/22/72, Helena, Montana. 5-10, 200.

Tim Breslin — Left Wing

Season	Team	League	GP	G	A	PTS	PIM	GP	G	A	PTS	PIM
91-92	Phoenix	IHL	45	8	21	29	12	—	—	—	—	—
92-93	Phoenix	IHL	79	14	30	44	55	—	—	—	—	—
93-94	South Carolina	ECHL	9	3	3	6	4	—	—	—	—	—
93-94	Phoenix	IHL	50	9	18	27	29	—	—	—	—	—
94-95	Chicago	IHL	71	7	21	28	62	3	1	1	2	0
95-96	Chicago	IHL	62	11	11	22	56	9	2	2	4	12
96-97	Chicago	IHL	44	2	10	12	18	4	0	2	2	4
	IHL	Totals	351	51	111	162	232	16	3	5	7	16

Born; 12/8/67, Downers Grove, Illinois. 6-0, 180.

Cory Bricknell — Defenseman

Season	Team	League	GP	G	A	PTS	PIM	GP	G	A	PTS	PIM
95-96	Huntington	ECHL	2	0	0	0	2	—	—	—	—	—
95-96	Columbus	ECHL	17	0	5	5	76	—	—	—	—	—
96-97	Columbus	ECHL	62	3	15	18	331	8	0	2	2	43
	ECHL	Totals	81	3	20	23	409	8	0	2	2	43

Born; 10/16/75, Port Perry, Ontario. 6-2, 185.

Dan Brierley — Defenseman

Season	Team	League	GP	G	A	PTS	PIM	GP	G	A	PTS	PIM
96-97	Phoenix	IHL	10	0	0	0	4	—	—	—	—	—
96-97	Jacksonville	ECHL	60	8	14	22	76	—	—	—	—	—

Born; 1/23/74, Brewster, New York. 6-3, 205. Drafted by New York Rangers (9th choice, 216th overall) in 1992 Entry Draft.

Aris Brimanis — Defenseman

Season	Team	League	GP	G	A	PTS	PIM	GP	G	A	PTS	PIM
93-94	Philadelphia	NHL	1	0	0	0	0	—	—	—	—	—
93-94	Hershey	AHL	75	8	15	23	65	11	2	3	5	12
94-95	Hershey	AHL	76	8	17	25	68	6	1	1	2	14
95-96	Philadelphia	NHL	17	0	2	2	12	—	—	—	—	—
95-96	Hershey	AHL	54	9	22	31	64	5	1	2	3	4
96-97	Philadelphia	NHL	3	0	1	1	0	—	—	—	—	—
96-97	Philadelphia	AHL	65	14	18	32	69	10	2	2	4	13
	NHL	Totals	21	0	3	3	12	—	—	—	—	—
	AHL	Totals	270	39	72	111	266	32	6	8	14	43

Born; 3/14/72, Cleveland, Ohio. 6-3, 210. Drafted by Philadelphia Flyers (4th choice, 86th overall) in 1991 Entry Draft.

Michel Brind'Amour — Left Wing

Season	Team	League	GP	G	A	PTS	PIM	GP	G	A	PTS	PIM
95-96	Alaska	WCHL	21	2	5	7	46	4	0	1	1	5
96-97	Columbus	CeHL	3	0	0	0	7	—	—	—	—	—
96-97	Nashville	CeHL	30	7	6	13	117	—	—	—	—	—
	CeHL	Totals	33	7	6	13	124	—	—	—	—	—

Born; 8/15/74, Campbell River, British Columbia. 6-3, 225.

Byron Briske — Defenseman

Season	Team	League	GP	G	A	PTS	PIM	GP	G	A	PTS	PIM
96-97	Baltimore	AHL	69	0	6	6	131	1	0	0	0	0

Born; 1/23/76, Humboldt, Saskatchewan. 6-2, 194. Drafted by Anaheim Mighty Ducks (4th choice, 80th overall) in 1994 Entry Draft.

Martin Brochu — Goaltender

Season	Team	League	GP	W	L	T	MIN	SO	GAVG	GP	W	L	MIN	SO	GAVG
93-94	Fredericton	AHL	32	10	11	3	1505	2	3.03	—	—	—	—	—	—
94-95	Fredericton	AHL	44	18	18	4	2475	0	3.51	—	—	—	—	—	—
95-96	Fredericton	AHL	17	6	8	2	986	0	4.26	—	—	—	—	—	—
95-96	Portland	AHL	5	2	2	1	287	0	3.14	12	7	4	700	2	2.40
95-96	Wheeling	ECHL	19	10	6	2	1060	1	2.89	—	—	—	—	—	—
96-97	Portland	AHL	55	23	17	7	2962	2	3.04	5	2	3	324	0	2.41
	AHL	Totals	153	59	56	17	8215	4	3.33	17	9	7	1024	2	2.40

Born; 3/10/73, Anjou, Quebec. 5-10, 200. Signed as a free agent by Montreal Canadiens (10/22/92). Traded to Washington Capitals by Montreal for future considerations (3/15/96).

Stephan Brochu — Defenseman

Season	Team	League	GP	G	A	PTS	PIM	GP	G	A	PTS	PIM
87-88	Colorado	IHL	52	4	10	14	70	12	3	3	6	13
88-89	Rangers	NHL	1	0	0	0	0	—	—	—	—	—
88-89	Denver	IHL	67	5	14	19	109	3	0	0	0	0
89-90	Flint	IHL	5	0	0	0	2	—	—	—	—	—
89-90	Fort Wayne	IHL	63	9	19	28	98	5	0	2	2	6

Season	Team	League	GP	G	A	PTS	PIM	GP	G	A	PTS	PIM
90-91	Fort Wayne	IHL	73	14	29	43	49	14	1	3	4	31
91-92	Kansas City	IHL	3	0	0	0	2	—	—	—	—	—
91-92	Flint	CoHL	52	13	27	40	80	—	—	—	—	—
92-93	Flint	CoHL	44	6	28	34	77	6	4	8	12	22
93-94	Flint	CoHL	54	8	32	40	116	10	1	4	5	2
94-95	Flint	CoHL	60	12	37	49	39	6	0	9	9	8
95-96	Flint	CoHL	68	4	41	45	68	15	5	12	17	18
96-97	Adirondack	AHL	18	0	8	8	12	—	—	—	—	—
96-97	Detroit	IHL	1	0	0	0	2	—	—	—	—	—
96-97	Flint	CoHL	42	8	45	53	32	14	5	*20	*25	14
	IHL	Totals	264	32	72	104	332	34	4	8	12	50
	CoHL	Totals	320	51	210	261	412	51	15	53	68	64

Born; 8/15/67, Sherbrooke, Quebec. 6-2, 195. Drafted by New York Rangers (9th round, 175th overall) 6/15/85. Member of 1995-96 Colonial League Champions Flint Generals.

Ritchie Bronilla — Defenseman

Season	Team	League	GP	G	A	PTS	PIM	GP	G	A	PTS	PIM
95-96	Hampton Roads	ECHL	29	2	0	2	36	—	—	—	—	—
96-97	Huntington	ECHL	67	6	21	27	40	—	—	—	—	—
	ECHL	Totals	96	8	21	29	76	—	—	—	—	—

Born; 7/15/75, Toronto, Ontario. 6-1, 215.

Chris Brooks — Center

Season	Team	League	GP	G	A	PTS	PIM	GP	G	A	PTS	PIM
96-97	Amarillo	WPHL	64	45	*65	*110	34	—	—	—	—	—

Born; 9/19/72, Stratford, Ontario. 5-8, 170. 1996-97 WPHL Most Valuable Player.

David Brosseau — Right Wing

Season	Team	League	GP	G	A	PTS	PIM	GP	G	A	PTS	PIM
96-97	Binghamton	AHL	2	0	0	0	0	1	0	0	0	0
96-97	Charlotte	ECHL	68	37	18	55	65	3	1	3	4	12

Born; 1/16/76, Montreal, Quebec. 6-2, 189. Drafted by New York Rangers (8th choice, 156th overall) in 1994 Entry Draft.

Paul Broten — Right Wing

Season	Team	League	GP	G	A	PTS	PIM	GP	G	A	PTS	PIM
88-89	Denver	IHL	77	28	31	59	133	4	0	2	2	6
89-90	Rangers	NHL	32	5	3	8	26	6	1	1	2	2
89-90	Flint	IHL	28	17	9	26	55	—	—	—	—	—
90-91	Rangers	AHL	28	4	6	10	18	5	0	0	0	2
90-91	Binghamton	AHL	8	2	2	4	4	—	—	—	—	—
91-92	Rangers	NHL	74	13	15	28	102	13	1	2	3	10
92-93	Rangers	NHL	60	5	9	14	48	—	—	—	—	—
93-94	Dallas	NHL	64	12	12	24	30	9	1	1	2	2
94-95	Dallas	NHL	47	7	9	16	36	5	1	2	3	2
95-96	St. Louis	NHL	17	0	1	1	4	—	—	—	—	—
95-96	Worcester	AHL	50	22	21	43	42	3	0	0	0	0
96-97	Fort Wayne	IHL	59	19	28	47	82	—	—	—	—	—
	NHL	Totals	322	46	55	101	264	38	4	6	10	18
	IHL	Totals	164	38	39	77	141	—	—	—	—	—
	AHL	Totals	58	24	23	47	46	3	0	0	0	0

Born; 10/27/65, Roseau, Minnesota. 5-11, 190. Drafted by New York Rangers (3rd choice, 77th overall) in 1984 Entry Draft. Claimed by Dallas Stars from Rangers in NHL Waiver Draft (10/3/93). Traded to St. Louis Blues by Dallas for Guy Carbonneau (10/2/95).

Jason Brousseau — Left Wing

			Regular Season					Playoffs				
Season	Team	League	GP	G	A	PTS	PIM	GP	G	A	PTS	PIM
91-92	Erie	ECHL	11	2	1	3	9	—	—	—	—	—
92-93	Flint	CoHL	19	2	7	9	15	—	—	—	—	—
92-93	Fort Worth	CeHL	38	19	16	35	36	—	—	—	—	—
93-94	Fort Worth	CeHL	36	16	17	33	47	—	—	—	—	—
93-94	Memphis	CeHL	16	4	7	11	2	—	—	—	—	—
94-95	Johnstown	ECHL	57	35	26	61	74	5	1	2	3	6
95-96	Brantford	CoHL	44	11	20	31	128	11	0	1	1	15
96-97	Brantford	CoHL	16	6	7	13	35	—	—	—	—	—
	CeHL	Totals	90	39	40	79	85	—	—	—	—	—
	CoHL	Totals	79	19	34	53	178	11	0	1	1	15
	ECHL	Totals	68	37	27	64	83	5	1	2	3	6

Born; 8/9/71, Montreal, Quebec. 6-2, 214.

Paul Brousseau — Right Wing

			Regular Season					Playoffs				
Season	Team	League	GP	G	A	PTS	PIM	GP	G	A	PTS	PIM
93-94	Cornwall	AHL	69	18	26	44	35	1	0	0	0	0
94-95	Cornwall	AHL	57	19	17	36	29	7	2	1	3	10
95-96	Colorado	NHL	8	1	1	2	2	—	—	—	—	—
95-96	Cornwall	AHL	63	21	22	43	60	8	4	0	4	2
96-97	Tampa Bay	NHL	6	0	0	0	0	—	—	—	—	—
96-97	Adirondack	AHL	66	35	31	66	25	4	1	2	3	0
	NHL	Totals	14	1	1	2	2	—	—	—	—	—
	AHL	Totals	255	93	96	189	149	20	7	3	10	12

Born; 9/18/73, Pierrefonds, Quebec. 6-2, 212. Drafted by Quebec Nordiques (2nd choice, 28th overall) in 1992 Entry Draft.

Bobby Brown — Center

			Regular Season					Playoffs				
Season	Team	League	GP	G	A	PTS	PIM	GP	G	A	PTS	PIM
96-97	Roanoke	ECHL	39	9	14	23	61	—	—	—	—	—
96-97	Baton Rouge	ECHL	24	7	8	15	26	—	—	—	—	—
	ECHL	Totals	63	16	22	38	87	—	—	—	—	—

Born; 9/26/75, 6-0, 200.

Brad Brown — Defenseman

			Regular Season					Playoffs				
Season	Team	League	GP	G	A	PTS	PIM	GP	G	A	PTS	PIM
95-96	Fredericton	AHL	38	0	3	3	148	10	2	1	3	6
96-97	Montreal	NHL	8	0	0	0	22	—	—	—	—	—
96-97	Fredericton	AHL	64	3	7	10	368	—	—	—	—	—
	AHL	Totals	102	3	10	13	516	10	2	1	3	6

Born; 12/27/75, Baie Verte, Newfoundland. 6-3, 218. Drafted by Montreal Canadiens (1st choice, 18th overall) in 1994 Entry Draft.

Cam Brown — Defenseman

			Regular Season					Playoffs				
Season	Team	League	GP	G	A	PTS	PIM	GP	G	A	PTS	PIM
90-91	Vancouver	NHL	1	0	0	0	7	—	—	—	—	—
90-91	Milwaukee	IHL	74	11	13	24	218	3	0	0	0	0
91-92	Milwaukee	IHL	51	6	8	14	179	1	0	0	0	0
91-92	Columbus	ECHL	10	11	6	17	64	—	—	—	—	—
92-93	Rochester	AHL	4	0	0	0	26	—	—	—	—	—
92-93	Hamilton	AHL	1	0	0	0	2	—	—	—	—	—
92-93	Columbus	ECHL	36	13	18	31	218	—	—	—	—	—
92-93	Erie	ECHL	15	4	3	7	50	5	0	1	1	62
93-94	N/A											

Season	Team	League	GP	G	A	PTS	PIM	GP	G	A	PTS	PIM
94-95	Adirondack	AHL	10	0	1	1	30	4	0	0	0	24
94-95	Erie	ECHL	60	14	28	42	341	—	—	—	—	—
95-96	Erie	ECHL	64	18	26	44	307	—	—	—	—	—
96-97	Baton Rouge	ECHL	57	10	13	23	220	—	—	—	—	—
	IHL	Totals	125	17	21	38	397	4	0	0	0	0
	AHL	Totals	15	0	1	1	78	4	0	0	0	24
	ECHL	Totals	242	70	94	164	1200	5	0	1	1	62

Born; 5/15/69, Saskatchewan, Saskatoon. 6-1, 210. Signed as a free agent by Vancouver Canucks (4/6/90).

Craig Brown — Goaltender

			Regular Season							Playoffs				
Season	Team	League	GP	W	L	T	MIN	SO	GAVG	GP	W	L	MIN	SO	GAVG
94-95	Nashville	ECHL	52	24	20	3	2848	2	3.48	13	8	4	731	0	3.04
95-96	Atlanta	IHL	2	1	1	0	119	0	3.03	—	—	—	—	—	—
95-96	Nashville	ECHL	*53	*32	14	4	*2934	0	4.05	3	2	3	251	0	5.26
96-97	Pensacola	ECHL	21	11	7	2	1217	0	4.09	—	—	—	—	—	—
	ECHL	Totals	126	67	41	9	6999	2	3.82	16	10	7	982	0	3.60

Born; 2/29/72, Scarborough, Ontario. 5-11, 175.

Curtis Brown — Center

Season	Team	League	GP	G	A	PTS	PIM	GP	G	A	PTS	PIM
94-95	Buffalo	NHL	1	1	1	2	2	—	—	—	—	—
95-96	Buffalo	NHL	4	0	0	0	0	—	—	—	—	—
95-96	Rochester	AHL	—	—	—	—	—	12	0	1	1	2
96-97	Buffalo	NHL	28	4	3	7	18	—	—	—	—	—
96-97	Rochester	AHL	51	22	21	43	30	10	4	6	10	4
	NHL	Totals	33	5	4	9	20	—	—	—	—	—
	AHL	Totals	51	22	21	43	30	22	4	7	11	6

Born; 2/12/76, Unity, Saskatchewan. 6-0, 182. Drafted by Buffalo Sabres (2nd choice, 43rd overall) in 1994 Entry Draft. Member of 1995-96 AHL champion Rochester Americans.

Dan Brown — Defenseman

Season	Team	League	GP	G	A	PTS	PIM	GP	G	A	PTS	PIM
94-95	Prince Edward Island	AHL	1	0	1	1	0	—	—	—	—	—
94-95	Memphis	CeHL	62	10	24	34	112	—	—	—	—	—
95-96	Memphis	CeHL	59	13	46	59	223	6	1	3	4	50
96-97	Memphis	CeHL	54	12	47	59	144	16	3	6	9	84
	CeHL	Totals	175	35	117	152	479	22	4	9	13	134

Born; 9/13/70, Milton, Ontario. 5-11, 195. 1995-96 CeHL First Team All-Star. 1995-96 CeHL Defenseman of the Year. 1996-97 CeHL Second Team All-Star.

Jim Brown — Center

Season	Team	League	GP	G	A	PTS	PIM	GP	G	A	PTS	PIM
93-94	Hampton Roads	ECHL	1	2	0	2	0	7	6	7	13	4
94-95	Hampton Roads	ECHL	49	24	21	45	50	—	—	—	—	—
94-95	Knoxville	ECHL	15	7	5	12	42	4	3	2	4	8
95-96	Knoxville	ECHL	69	50	70	120	80	8	4	7	11	4
96-97	Knoxville	ECHL	64	44	48	92	66	—	—	—	—	—
	ECHL	Totals	198	127	144	271	238	19	13	16	29	16

Born; 6/17/73, Scarborough, Ontario. 5-11, 185. 1995-96 ECHL First Team All-Star.

Kevin Brown — Right Wing

Season	Team	League	GP	G	A	PTS	PIM	GP	G	A	PTS	PIM
94-95	Dayton	ECHL	66	29	42	71	34	8	5	4	9	2

Season	Team	League	GP	G	A	PTS	PIM	GP	G	A	PTS	PIM
95-96	Peoria	IHL	3	2	1	3	0	—	—	—	—	—
95-96	Cornwall	AHL	2	0	0	0	0	—	—	—	—	—
95-96	Dayton	ECHL	55	26	35	61	30	3	1	1	2	6
96-97	Dayton	ECHL	31	9	12	21	8	—	—	—	—	—
96-97	Toledo	ECHL	16	7	12	19	6	5	1	3	4	2
	ECHL	Totals	168	71	101	172	78	16	7	8	15	10

Born; 4/1/70, Scarborough, Ontario. 5-11, 180. Traded to Toledo Storm by Dayton Bombers for Norm Dezainde (1997).

Kevin J. Brown — Right Wing

			Regular Season					Playoffs				
Season	Team	League	GP	G	A	PTS	PIM	GP	G	A	PTS	PIM
94-95	Los Angeles	NHL	23	2	3	5	18	—	—	—	—	—
94-95	Phoenix	IHL	48	19	31	50	64	—	—	—	—	—
95-96	Los Angeles	NHL	7	1	0	1	4	—	—	—	—	—
95-96	Phoenix	IHL	45	10	16	26	39	—	—	—	—	—
95-96	Prince Edward Island	AHL	8	3	6	9	2	3	1	3	4	0
96-97	Hartford	NHL	11	0	4	4	6	—	—	—	—	—
96-97	Springfield	AHL	48	32	16	48	45	15	*11	6	17	24
	NHL	Totals	41	3	7	10	28	—	—	—	—	—
	IHL	Totals	93	29	47	76	103	—	—	—	—	—
	AHL	Totals	56	35	22	57	47	18	12	9	21	24

Born; 5/11/74, Birmingham, England. 6-1, 212. Drafted by Los Angeles Kings (3rd choice, 87th overall) in 1992 Entry Draft. Traded to Ottawa Senators by Los Angeles for Jaroslav Modry and Ottawa's 8th round pick (Kai Nurminen) in 1996 Entry Draft. Traded to Anaheim Mighty Ducks by Ottawa for Mike Maneluk (7/1/96).

Kurt Brown — Goaltender

			Regular Season						Playoffs				
Season	Team	League	GP	W	L	T	MIN	SO	GAVG	GP	W	L	MIN	SO	GAVG
96-97	Birmingham	ECHL	19	4	8	3	936	1	4.23	—	—	—	—	—	—

Born; 7/20/72, Barrington, Illinois. 6-1, 185. Last amateur club; Ohio State (CCHA).

Rob Brown — Right Wing

			Regular Season					Playoffs				
Season	Team	League	GP	G	A	PTS	PIM	GP	G	A	PTS	PIM
87-88	Pittsburgh	NHL	51	24	20	44	56	—	—	—	—	—
88-89	Pittsburgh	NHL	68	49	66	115	118	11	5	3	8	22
89-90	Pittsburgh	NHL	80	33	47	80	102	—	—	—	—	—
90-91	Pittsburgh	NHL	25	6	10	16	31	—	—	—	—	—
90-91	Hartford	NHL	44	18	24	42	101	5	1	0	1	7
91-92	Hartford	NHL	42	16	15	31	39	—	—	—	—	—
91-92	Chicago	NHL	25	5	11	16	34	8	2	4	6	4
92-93	Chicago	NHL	15	1	6	7	33	—	—	—	—	—
92-93	Indianapolis	IHL	19	14	19	33	32	2	0	1	1	2
93-94	Dallas	NHL	1	0	0	0	0	—	—	—	—	—
93-94	Kalamazoo	IHL	79	42	*113	*155	188	5	1	3	4	6
94-95	Los Angeles	NHL	2	0	0	0	0	—	—	—	—	—
94-95	Phoenix	IHL	69	34	73	107	135	9	4	12	16	0
95-96	Chicago	IHL	79	52	*91	*143	100	9	4	11	15	6
96-97	Chicago	IHL	76	37	*80	*117	98	4	2	4	6	16
	NHL	Totals	353	152	199	351	514	24	8	7	15	33
	IHL	Totals	322	179	376	555	553	29	11	31	42	30

Born; 4/10/68, Kingston, Ontario. 5-11, 185. Drafted by Pittsburgh Penguins (4th choice, 67th overall) in 1986 Entry Draft. Traded to Hatford Whalers by Pittsburgh for Scott Young (12/21/90). Traded to Chicago Blackhawks by Hartford for Steve Konroyd (1/24/92). Signed as a free agent by Dallas Stars (8/12/93). Signed as a free agent by Los Angeles Kings (6/14/94). 1993-94 IHL First Team All-Star. 1993-94 IHL MVP. 1994-95 IHL Second Team All-Star. 1995-96 IHL First Team All-Star. 1996-97 IHL First Team All-Star.

Ryan Brown — Defenseman

Season	Team	League	GP	G	A	PTS	PIM	GP	G	A	PTS	PIM
95-96	Atlanta	IHL	16	0	0	0	66	—	—	—	—	—
95-96	Nashville	ECHL	18	1	0	1	64	4	1	1	2	9
96-97	Adirondack	AHL	6	0	0	0	39	—	—	—	—	—
96-97	Raleigh	ECHL	43	7	3	10	122	—	—	—	—	—
	ECHL	Totals	61	8	3	11	186	4	1	1	2	9

Born; 9/19/74, Boyle, Alberta. 6-4, 220. Drafted by Tampa Bay Lightning (5th choice, 107th overall) in 1993 Entry Draft.

Sean Brown — Right Wing

Season	Team	League	GP	G	A	PTS	PIM	GP	G	A	PTS	PIM
94-95	Phoenix	IHL	3	0	1	1	0	—	—	—	—	—
94-95	Knoxville	ECHL	62	14	21	35	243	—	—	—	—	—
95-96	Knoxville	ECHL	67	13	23	36	251	8	1	0	1	20
96-97	Roanoke	ECHL	68	8	10	18	148	4	1	0	1	4
	ECHL	Totals	197	35	54	89	642	12	2	0	2	24

Born; 3/30/70, Oshawa, Ontario. 6-3, 215.

Sean Brown — Defenseman

Season	Team	League	GP	G	A	PTS	PIM	GP	G	A	PTS	PIM
96-97	Edmonton	NHL	5	0	0	0	4	—	—	—	—	—
96-97	Hamilton	AHL	61	1	7	8	238	19	1	0	1	47

Born; 11/5/76, Oshawa, Ontario. 6-2, 205. Drafted by Boston Bruins (2nd choice, 21st overall) in 1995 Entry Draft. Traded to Edmonton Oilers by Boston with Mariusz Czerkawski and Boston's first round choice (Matthieu Descoteaux) in 1996 Entry Draft for Bill Ranford (1/11/96).

David Bruce — Left Wing

Season	Team	League	GP	G	A	PTS	PIM	GP	G	A	PTS	PIM
84-85	Fredericton	AHL	56	14	11	25	104	5	0	0	0	37
85-86	Vancouver	NHL	12	0	1	1	14	1	0	0	0	0
85-86	Fredericton	AHL	66	25	16	41	151	2	0	1	1	12
86-87	Vancouver	NHL	50	9	7	16	109	—	—	—	—	—
86-87	Fredericton	AHL	17	7	6	13	73	—	—	—	—	—
87-88	Vancouver	NHL	28	7	3	10	57	—	—	—	—	—
87-88	Fredericton	AHL	30	27	18	45	115	—	—	—	—	—
88-89	Vancouver	NHL	53	7	7	14	65	—	—	—	—	—
89-90	Milwaukee	IHL	68	40	35	75	148	6	5	3	8	0
90-91	St. Louis	NHL	12	1	2	3	14	2	0	0	0	2
90-91	Peoria	IHL	60	*64	52	116	78	18	*18	11	*29	40
91-92	San Jose	NHL	60	22	16	38	46	—	—	—	—	—
91-92	Kansas City	IHL	7	5	5	10	6	—	—	—	—	—
92-93	San Jose	NHL	17	2	3	5	33	—	—	—	—	—
93-94	San Jose	NHL	2	0	0	0	0	—	—	—	—	—
93-94	Kansas City	IHL	72	40	24	64	115	—	—	—	—	—
94-95	Kansas City	IHL	63	33	25	58	80	—	—	—	—	—
95-96	Kansas City	IHL	62	27	26	53	84	1	0	0	0	8
96-97	Kansas City	IHL	79	45	24	69	90	3	0	0	0	2
	NHL	Totals	234	48	39	87	338	3	0	0	0	2
	IHL	Totals	411	254	191	445	601	28	23	14	37	50
	AHL	Totals	169	73	51	124	443	7	0	1	1	49

Born; 10/7/64, Thunder Bay, Ontario. 5-11, 190. Drafted by Vancouver Canucks (2nd choice, 30th overall) in 1983 Entry Draft. Signed as a free agent by St. Louis (7/6/90). Claimed by San Jose Sharks from St. Louis in Expansion Draft (5/30/91). 1989-90 IHL First Team All-Star. 1990-91 IHL First Team All-Star. 1990-91 IHL MVP. Member of 1990-91 IHL champion Peoria Rivermen.

Brett Bruininks — Right Wing

Season	Team	League	GP	G	A	PTS	PIM	GP	G	A	PTS	PIM
96-97	Philadelphia	AHL	45	3	2	5	54	4	1	1	2	2

Born; 3/10/72, Minneapolis, Minnesota. 6-4, 230. Last amateur club: Notre Dame (CCHA).

Steve Brule — Center

Season	Team	League	GP	G	A	PTS	PIM	GP	G	A	PTS	PIM
94-95	ALB	AHL	3	1	4	5	0	14	9	5	14	4
95-96	ALB	AHL	80	30	21	51	37	4	0	0	0	17
96-97	Albany	AHL	79	28	48	76	27	15	7	7	14	12
	AHL	Totals	162	59	73	132	64	33	16	12	26	33

Born; 1/15/75, Montreal, Quebec. 5-11, 185. Drafted by New Jersey Devils (6th choice, 143rd overall) in 1993 Entry Draft. Member of 1994-95 Calder Cup champion Albany RiverRats.

David Brumby — Goaltender

Season	Team	League	GP	W	L	T	MIN	SO	GAVG	GP	W	L	MIN	SO	GAVG
96-97	Baltimore	AHL	2	0	1	0	60	0	7.00	—	—	—	—	—	—
96-97	Columbus	ECHL	18	9	5	2	997	0	4.09	1	0	0	10	0	0.00

Born; 5/21/75, Victoria, British Columbia. 6-1, 190. Drafted by Toronto Maple Leafs (6th choice, 201st overall) in 1993 Entry Draft.

Andrew Brunette — Left Wing

Season	Team	League	GP	G	A	PTS	PIM	GP	G	A	PTS	PIM
93-94	Portland	AHL	23	9	11	20	10	2	0	1	1	0
93-94	Hampton Roads	ECHL	20	12	18	30	32	7	7	6	13	18
94-95	Portland	AHL	79	30	50	80	53	7	3	3	6	10
95-96	Washington	NHL	11	3	3	6	0	6	1	3	4	0
95-96	Portland	AHL	69	28	66	94	125	20	11	18	29	15
96-97	Washington	NHL	23	4	7	11	12	—	—	—	—	—
96-97	Portland	AHL	50	22	51	73	48	5	1	2	3	0
	NHL	Totals	34	7	10	17	12	6	1	3	4	0
	AHL	Totals	221	89	178	277	236	34	15	24	39	25

Born; 8/24/73, Sudbury, Ontario. 6-0, 212. Drafted by Washington Capitals (6th choice, 174th overall) in 1993 Entry Draft. 1994-95 AHL Second Team All-Star. Member of 1993-94 AHL champion Portland Pirates.

Sergei Brylin — Center

Season	Team	League	GP	G	A	PTS	PIM	GP	G	A	PTS	PIM
93-94	Russian	IHL	13	4	5	9	18	—	—	—	—	—
94-95	New Jersey	NHL	26	6	8	14	8	12	1	2	3	4
94-95	Albany	AHL	63	19	35	54	78	—	—	—	—	—
95-96	New Jersey	NHL	50	4	5	9	26	—	—	—	—	—
96-97	New Jersey	NHL	29	2	2	4	20	—	—	—	—	—
96-97	Albany	AHL	43	17	24	41	38	15	3	8	11	10
	NHL	Totals	105	12	15	27	54	12	1	2	3	4
	AHL	Totals	106	36	59	95	116	15	3	8	11	10

Born; 1/13/74, Moscow, Russia. 5-9, 175. Drafted by New Jersey Devils (2nd choice, 42nd overall) in 1992 Entry Draft. Member of 1994-95 Stanley Cup Champion New Jersey Devils.

Jeff Buchanan — Defenseman

Season	Team	League	GP	G	A	PTS	PIM	GP	G	A	PTS	PIM
92-93	Atlanta	IHL	68	4	18	22	282	9	0	0	0	26
93-94	Atlanta	IHL	76	5	24	29	253	14	0	1	1	20

Season	Team	League	GP	G	A	PTS	PIM	GP	G	A	PTS	PIM
94-95	Atlanta	IHL	4	0	1	1	9	—	—	—	—	—
94-95	Indianapolis	IHL	25	3	9	12	63	—	—	—	—	—
95-96	Indianapolis	IHL	77	4	14	18	277	5	0	1	1	9
96-97	Orlando	IHL	81	11	27	38	246	—	—	—	—	—
	IHL	Totals	331	27	93	120	1130	28	0	2	2	55

Born; 5/23/71, Swift Current, Saskatchewan. 5-10, 165. Signed as a free agent by Tampa Bay Lightning (7/13/92). Traded to Chicago Blackhawks by Tampa Bay with Jim Cummins and Tom Tilley for Paul Ysebaert and Rich Sutter (2/22/95). Member of 1993-94 IHL champion Atlanta Knights.

Trevor Buchanan — Left Wing

Season	Team	League	GP	G	A	PTS	PIM	GP	G	A	PTS	PIM
91-92	Louisville	ECHL	62	38	28	66	259	13	3	4	7	77
92-93	Louisville	ECHL	64	23	38	61	270	—	—	—	—	—
93-94	Louisville	ECHL	65	26	26	52	422	6	3	3	6	52
94-95	Houston	IHL	9	1	0	1	18	—	—	—	—	—
94-95	San Antonio	CeHL	48	30	27	57	268	2	0	1	1	19
95-96	San Antonio	CeHL	63	34	27	61	336	13	6	4	10	*83
96-97	Louisville	ECHL	23	4	5	9	96	—	—	—	—	—
96-97	Pensacola	ECHL	34	4	7	11	64	—	—	—	—	—
	ECHL	Totals	248	95	104	199	1111	19	6	7	13	148
	CeHL	Totals	111	64	54	118	604	15	6	5	11	102

Born, 6/7/69, Thompson, Manitoba. 6-1, 190. Drafted by Hartford Whalers (9th choice, 199th overall) in 1989 Entry Draft.

Ashley Buckberger — Right Wing

Season	Team	League	GP	G	A	PTS	PIM	GP	G	A	PTS	PIM
95-96	Carolina	AHL	67	8	9	17	25	—	—	—	—	—
96-97	Carolina	AHL	69	8	10	18	24	—	—	—	—	—
	AHL	Totals	136	16	19	35	49	—	—	—	—	—

Born; 2/19/75, Esterhazy, Saskatchewan. 6-2, 206. Drafted by Quebec Nordiques (3rd choice, 49th overall) in 1993 Entry Draft. Signed as a free agent by Florida Panthers (8/3/95).

Tom Buckley — Center

Season	Team	League	GP	G	A	PTS	PIM	GP	G	A	PTS	PIM
96-97	Springfield	AHL	62	7	12	19	39	2	0	0	0	4
96-97	Richmond	ECHL	3	0	0	0	14	—	—	—	—	—

Born; 5/26/76, Buffalo, New York. 6-1, 204. Drafted by Hartford Whalers (4th choice, 187th overall) in 1994 Entry Draft.

Alexei Budayev — Center

Season	Team	League	GP	G	A	PTS	PIM	GP	G	A	PTS	PIM
96-97	Mississippi	ECHL	46	3	15	18	24	—	—	—	—	—

Born; 4/24/75, Pavlov Posad, Russia. 6-2, 183. Drafted by Winnipeg Jets (3rd choice, 43rd overall) in 1993 Entry Draft.

Greg Bullock — Center

Season	Team	League	GP	G	A	PTS	PIM	GP	G	A	PTS	PIM
95-96	San Francisco	IHL	79	15	32	47	62	3	0	0	0	2
96-97	St. John's	AHL	75	21	52	73	65	11	2	6	8	17

Born; 2/10/73, Cambridge, Ontario. 5-11, 180.

Mark Bultje — Center

Season	Team	League	GP	G	A	PTS	PIM	GP	G	A	PTS	PIM
93-94	Huntsville	ECHL	12	4	3	7	10	—	—	—	—	—
93-94	Erie	ECHL	15	1	5	6	19	—	—	—	—	—

Season	Team	League	GP	G	A	PTS	PIM	GP	G	A	PTS	PIM
94-95	N/A											
95-96	Jacksonville	SHL	50	30	40	70	90	—	—	—	—	—
96-97	Jacksonville	ECHL	16	4	3	7	6	—	—	—	—	—
	ECHL	Totals	43	9	11	20	35	—	—	—	—	—

Born; 6/8/73, Etobicoke, Ontario. 5-10, 185.

Geoff Bumstead — Right Wing

			Regular Season					Playoffs				
Season	Team	League	GP	G	A	PTS	PIM	GP	G	A	PTS	PIM
95-96	Alaska	WCHL	58	31	36	67	170	5	0	0	0	*34
96-97	New Mexico	WPHL	5	2	0	2	62	3	0	2	2	28

Born; 6/8/72, Winnipeg, Manitoba. 5-10, 205.

Scott Burfoot — Center

			Regular Season					Playoffs				
Season	Team	League	GP	G	A	PTS	PIM	GP	G	A	PTS	PIM
91-92	Erie	ECHL	1	2	1	3	0	—	—	—	—	—
92-93	Roanoke	ECHL	48	28	32	60	22	—	—	—	—	—
93-94	Peoria	IHL	4	0	0	0	0	—	—	—	—	—
93-94	Huntsville	ECHL	62	31	65	96	80	3	4	5	9	4
94-95	Fort Wayne	IHL	10	4	2	6	6	—	—	—	—	—
94-95	Erie	ECHL	56	29	*68	*97	66	—	—	—	—	—
95-96	Flint	CoHL	52	21	54	75	30	14	12	19	31	8
96-97	Richmond	ECHL	62	32	62	94	37	8	5	10	15	8
	IHL	Totals	14	4	2	6	6	—	—	—	—	—
	ECHL	Totals	229	122	228	350	205	11	9	15	24	12

Born; 9/23/67, Winnipeg, Manitoba. 5-9, 170. 1994-95 Second Team ECHL All-Star. 1995-96 CoHL Most Sportsmanlike Player and Playoff MVP. Member of 1995-96 Colonial Cup Champion Flint Generals.

Van Burgess — Left Wing

			Regular Season					Playoffs				
Season	Team	League	GP	G	A	PTS	PIM	GP	G	A	PTS	PIM
95-96	Huntington	ECHL	69	20	35	55	108	—	—	—	—	—
96-97	Huntington	ECHL	70	47	47	94	50	—	—	—	—	—
	ECHL	Totals	139	67	82	149	158	—	—	—	—	—

Born; 7/5/73, Lahr, Germany. 5-11, 190.

Ryan Burgoyne — Forward

			Regular Season					Playoffs				
Season	Team	League	GP	G	A	PTS	PIM	GP	G	A	PTS	PIM
96-97	Port Huron	CoHL	6	1	1	2	0	5	3	2	5	2

Last amateur club; London (OHL).

Garrett Burnett — Defenseman

			Regular Season					Playoffs				
Season	Team	League	GP	G	A	PTS	PIM	GP	G	A	PTS	PIM
95-96	Utica	CoHL	15	0	1	1	78	—	—	—	—	—
95-96	Oklahoma City	CeHL	3	0	0	0	20	—	—	—	—	—
95-96	Tulsa	CeHL	6	1	0	1	94	—	—	—	—	—
95-96	Nashville	ECHL	3	0	0	0	22	—	—	—	—	—
95-96	Jacksonville	ECHL	8	0	1	1	38	1	0	0	0	0
96-97	Knoxville	ECHL	50	5	11	16	321	—	—	—	—	—
	ECHL	Totals	61	5	12	17	381	1	0	0	0	0
	CeHL	Totals	9	1	0	1	114	—	—	—	—	—

Born; 9/23/75, Coquitlim, British Columbia. 6-3, 220.

Jim Burton — Defenseman

			Regular Season					Playoffs				
Season	Team	League	GP	G	A	PTS	PIM	GP	G	A	PTS	PIM
81-82	Fort Wayne	IHL	77	8	54	62	126	N/A				
82-83	Fort Wayne	IHL	79	17	70	87	114	10	2	11	13	23
83-84	Hershey	AHL	75	10	33	43	50	—	—	—	—	—
84-85	Fort Wayne	IHL	74	15	50	65	60	13	0	6	6	12
85-86	Fort Wayne	IHL	82	30	64	94	47	15	6	10	16	34
86-87	Fort Wayne	IHL	58	19	52	71	50	11	2	11	13	25
86-87	Rochester	AHL	10	0	2	2	4	—	—	—	—	—
87-88	Fort Wayne	IHL	80	13	74	87	72	5	0	1	1	0
88-89	Fort Wayne	IHL	21	3	13	16	8	11	2	4	6	8
95-96	Phoenix	IHL	9	1	3	4	10	—	—	—	—	—
96-97	Austin	WPHL	52	21	47	68	65	5	0	4	4	12
	*IHL	Totals	480	106	380	486	487	65	12	43	55	102
	AHL	Totals	85	10	35	45	54	—	—	—	—	—

Born; 11/13/61, Brantford, Ontario. 6-0, 188. 1982-83 IHL First Team All-Star. 1982-83 Shared IHL Governor's Trophy (Top Defenseman) with Milwaukee's Kevin Willison. 1985-86 IHL First Team All-Star. 1985-86 IHL Governor's Trophy. 1987-88 IHL Forst Team All-Star. Served as player/assistant coach with Phoenix Roadrunners (95-96). Did not play professionally in North America (89-90/95-96). IHL Playoff totals not complete, missing 1981-82 stats. Named as coach of Austin Ice Bats beginning with 1997 season.

Joe Burton — Right Wing

			Regular Season					Playoffs				
Season	Team	League	GP	G	A	PTS	PIM	GP	G	A	PTS	PIM
92-93	Oklahoma City	CeHL	55	35	26	61	25	11	8	7	15	4
93-94	Oklahoma City	CeHL	54	32	24	56	28	7	4	3	7	4
94-95	Oklahoma City	CeHL	66	*59	38	97	20	5	3	4	7	4
95-96	Oklahoma City	CeHL	64	66	32	98	53	13	6	3	9	2
96-97	Oklahoma City	CeHL	66	53	41	94	39	4	2	5	7	14
	CeHL	Totals	305	245	161	406	165	40	23	22	45	28

Born; 4/23/67, Garden City, Michigan. 5-9, 170. 1994-95 CeHL First Team All-Star. 1995-96 CeHL Second Team All-Star. 1996-97 CeHL First Team All-Star. Member of 1995-96 CeHL champion Oklahoma City Blazers.

Fran Bussey — Left Wing

			Regular Season					Playoffs				
Season	Team	League	GP	G	A	PTS	PIM	GP	G	A	PTS	PIM
95-96	Hampton Roads	ECHL	18	3	3	6	6	—	—	—	—	—
96-97	Nashville	CeHL	3	0	0	0	4	—	—	—	—	—
96-97	Fort Worth	CeHL	2	0	0	0	0	—	—	—	—	—
96-97	Amarillo	WPHL	5	0	1	1	2	—	—	—	—	—
96-97	Reno	WCHL	4	1	3	4	2	—	—	—	—	—
96-97	Utica	CoHL	1	0	0	0	0	—	—	—	—	—
	CeHL	Totals	5	0	0	0	4	—	—	—	—	—

Born; 7/9/74, Duluth, Minnesota. 6-3, 190. Drafted by Pittsburgh Penguins (8th choice, 187th overall) in 1992 Entry Draft.

Sven Butenschon — Defenseman

			Regular Season					Playoffs				
Season	Team	League	GP	G	A	PTS	PIM	GP	G	A	PTS	PIM
96-97	Cleveland	IHL	75	3	12	15	68	10	0	1	1	4

Born; 3/22/76, Itzehoe, West Germany. 6-5, 201. Drafted by Pittsburgh Penguins (3rd choice, 57th overall) in 1994 Entry Draft.

Rob Butler — Left Wing

			Regular Season					Playoffs				
Season	Team	League	GP	G	A	PTS	PIM	GP	G	A	PTS	PIM
96-97	South Carolina	ECHL	41	7	13	20	141	2	0	0	0	6

Born; 3/31/76, St. Louis, Missouri. 6-2, 180. Drafted by Toronto Maple Leafs (7th choice, 204th overall) in 1994 Entry Draft. Member of 1996-97 ECHL Champion South Carolina Stingrays.

Rod Butler — Right Wing

			Regular Season					Playoffs				
Season	Team	League	GP	G	A	PTS	PIM	GP	G	A	PTS	PIM
95-96	Mobile	ECHL	42	5	4	9	46	—	—	—	—	—
96-97	Macon	CeHL	2	0	0	0	17	—	—	—	—	—
96-97	Nashville	CeHL	22	9	13	22	26	—	—	—	—	—
	CeHL	Totals	24	9	13	22	43	—	—	—	—	—

Born; 2/27/75, Los Angeles, California. 6-3, 200.

Kevin Butt — Goaltender

			Regular Season							Playoffs				
Season	Team	League	GP	MIN	GAVG	W	L	T	SO	GP	MIN	GAVG	W	L	SO
90-91	Greensboro	ECHL	1	18	6.66	—	—	—	0	—	—	—	—	—	—
91-92	St. Thomas	CoHL	30	1606	4.22	13	10	3	1	12	744	4.11	7	5	0
92-93	St. Thomas	CoHL	41	2199	4.94	17	16	3	0	14	854	3.44	8	6	1
93-94	Knoxville	ECHL	1	60	4.00	1	0	0	0	—	—	—	—	—	—
93-94	Chatham	CoHL	43	2376	4.37	28	11	2	0	15	888	4.05	8	6	0
94-95	Saginaw	CoHL	45	2412	3.95	21	15	4	1	10	542	4.31	5	3	0
95-96	Quad City	CoHL	37	2075	4.16	15	8	2	0	—	—	—	—	—	—
95-96	Detroit	CoHL	7	406	5.17	4	2	1	0	5	233	4.90	1	3	0
96-97	Port Huron	CoHL	46	2451	3.72	25	15	3	0	3	136	3.96	1	1	0
	CoHL	Totals	249	13525	4.25	123	77	18	2	59	3397	4.01	30	24	1
	ECHL	Totals	2	78	4.62	1	0	0	0						

Born; 6/16/70, Oshawa, Ontario. 5-8, 181.

Rob Butz — Left Wing

			Regular Season					Playoffs				
Season	Team	League	GP	G	A	PTS	PIM	GP	G	A	PTS	PIM
93-94	St. John's	AHL	5	0	0	0	26	—	—	—	—	—
95-96	St. John's	AHL	74	10	20	30	127	4	1	0	1	4
96-97	St. John's	AHL	60	16	21	37	131	8	2	1	3	15
	AHL	Totals	139	26	41	67	284	12	3	1	4	19

Born; 2/24/75, Delubury, Alberta. 6-2, 195. Signed as a free agent by Toronto Maple Leafs (4/1/93).

Mike Buzak — Goaltender

			Regular Season							Playoffs				
Season	Team	League	GP	W	L	T	MIN	SO	GAVG	GP	W	L	MIN	SO	GAVG
95-96	Worcester	AHL	30	9	10	5	1671	0	3.05	—	—	—	—	—	—
96-97	Wprcester	AHL	19	9	4	3	973	1	2.53	1	0	1	59	3	3.06
96-97	Baton Rouge	ECHL	3	0	2	0	109	0	3.87	—	—	—	—	—	—
	AHL	Totals	49	18	14	8	2644	1	2.86	1	0	1	59	3	3.06

Born; 2/10/73, Edson, Alberta. 6-3, 183. Drafted by St. Louis Blues (5th choice, 167th overall) in 1993 Entry Draft.

Peter Buzek — Defenseman

			Regular Season					Playoffs				
Season	Team	League	GP	G	A	PTS	PIM	GP	G	A	PTS	PIM
96-97	Michigan	IHL	67	4	6	10	48	—	—	—	—	—

Born; 4/26/77, Jihlava, Czechoslovakia. 6-0, 205. Drafted by Dallas Stars (3rd choice, 63rd overall) in 1995 Entry Draft.

John Byce — Right Wing

			Regular Season					Playoffs				
Season	Team	League	GP	G	A	PTS	PIM	GP	G	A	PTS	PIM
89-90	Boston	NHL	—	—	—	—	—	8	2	0	2	2
90-91	Maine	AHL	53	19	29	48	20	—	—	—	—	—
90-91	Boston	NHL	18	1	3	4	6	—	—	—	—	—
91-92	Maine	AHL	55	29	21	50	41	—	—	—	—	—
91-92	Baltimore	AHL	20	9	5	14	4	—	—	—	—	—

Season	Team	League	GP	G	A	PTS	PIM	GP	G	A	PTS	PIM
91-92	Boston	NHL	3	1	0	1	0	—	—	—	—	—
92-93	Baltimore	AHL	62	35	44	79	26	7	4	5	9	4
93-94	Milwaukee	IHL	28	7	4	11	10	3	2	1	3	0
94-95	Portland	AHL	6	1	1	2	2	—	—	—	—	—
94-95	San Diego	IHL	5	2	3	5	2	—	—	—	—	—
94-95	Milwaukee	IHL	30	9	11	20	10	15	4	5	9	4
95-96	Los Angeles	IHL	82	39	46	85	40	—	—	—	—	—
96-97	Long Beach	IHL	80	29	29	58	14	18	6	7	13	4
	NHL	Totals	21	2	3	5	6	8	2	0	2	2
	IHL	Totals	225	86	93	179	76	36	12	13	25	8
	AHL	Totals	196	93	100	193	93	7	4	5	9	4

Born; 8/9/67, Madison, Wisconsin. 6-1, 180. Drafted by Boston Bruins (11th choice, 220th overall) in 1985 Entry Draft. Traded to Washington Capitals by Boston Bruins with Dennis Smith for Brent Hughes and future considerations (2/24/92).

Shawn Byram — Left Wing

			Regular Season					Playoffs				
Season	Team	League	GP	G	A	PTS	PIM	GP	G	A	PTS	PIM
88-89	Springfield	AHL	45	5	11	16	195	—	—	—	—	—
88-89	Indianapolis	IHL	1	0	0	0	2	—	—	—	—	—
89-90	Springfield	AHL	31	4	4	8	30	—	—	—	—	—
89-90	Johnstown	ECHL	8	5	5	10	35	—	—	—	—	—
90-91	Islanders	NHL	4	0	0	0	14	—	—	—	—	—
90-91	Capital District	AHL	62	28	35	63	162	—	—	—	—	—
91-92	Chicago	NHL	1	0	0	0	0	—	—	—	—	—
92-93	Indianapolis	IHL	41	2	13	15	123	5	1	2	3	8
93-94	Indianapolis	IHL	77	23	24	47	170	—	—	—	—	—
96-97	Fresno	WCHL	6	3	5	8	13	5	2	5	7	67
	NHL	Totals	5	0	0	0	14	—	—	—	—	—
	AHL	Totals	138	37	50	87	387	—	—	—	—	—
	IHL	Totals	119	25	37	62	295	5	1	2	3	8

Born; 9/12/68, Neepawa, Manitoba. 6-2, 204. Drafted by New York Islanders (4rth pick, 80th overall) in 1986 Entry Draft. Signed as a free agent by Chicago Blackhawks (8/2/91).

Jean Blouin is one of the finest playoff performers in UHL history.   Photo courtesy of Border Cats

Chad Cabana — Left Wing

			Regular Season					Playoffs				
Season	Team	League	GP	G	A	PTS	PIM	GP	G	A	PTS	PIM
95-96	Carolina	AHL	59	4	9	13	159	—	—	—	—	—
96-97	Carolina	AHL	55	8	5	13	221	—	—	—	—	—
96-97	Port Huron	CoHL	14	7	9	16	49	—	—	—	—	—
	AHL	Totals	114	12	14	26	380	—	—	—	—	—

Born; 10/1/74, Bonnyville, Alberta. 6-1, 200. Drafted by Florida Panthers (11th choice, 213th overall) in 1993 Entry Draft

Cory Cadden — Goaltender

			Regular Season							Playoffs					
Season	Team	League	GP	W	L	T	MIN	SO	GAVG	GP	W	L	MIN	SO	GAVG
92-93	Knoxville	ECHL	42	15	23	3	2413	0	4.70	—	—	—	—	—	—
93-94	Knoxville	ECHL	40	26	8	4	2349	*2	3.09	3	1	2	179	0	4.68
94-95	Knoxville	ECHL	46	19	20	5	2688	0	3.44	4	1	3	247	0	3.89
95-96	Knoxville	ECHL	17	6	9	1	915	0	4.39	—	—	—	—	—	—
95-96	Dayton	ECHL	14	7	6	0	765	0	3.61	3	0	2	160	0	3.74
96-97	Peoria	ECHL	5	2	2	1	278	0	3.89	—	—	—	—	—	—
96-97	South Carolina	ECHL	18	8	4	2	921	0	3.91	—	—	—	—	—	—
	ECHL	Totals	182	83	72	16	10329	2	3.80	10	2	7	586	0	4.09

Born; 2/21/69, Edmonton, Alberta. 6-2, 195. 1993-94 ECHL Top Goaltender. 1993-94 ECHL First Team All-Star.

Shane Calder — Right Wing

			Regular Season					Playoffs				
Season	Team	League	GP	G	A	PTS	PIM	GP	G	A	PTS	PIM
95-96	Columbus	ECHL	28	5	5	10	124	—	—	—	—	—
95-96	Nashville	ECHL	26	7	7	14	115	5	0	4	4	12
96-97	Pensacola	ECHL	64	18	19	37	221	10	1	1	2	77
	ECHL	Totals	118	30	31	61	460	15	1	5	6	89

Born; 8/28/74, Portage la Praire, Quebec. 5-11, 180.

Ryan Caley — Goaltender

			Regular Season							Playoffs					
Season	Team	League	GP	W	L	T	MIN	SO	GAVG	GP	W	L	MIN	SO	GAVG
96-97	Muskegon	CoHL	23	10	8	2	1284	0	3.55	2	0	2	119	0	*2.53

Born; 12/12/75, Owen Sound, Ontario. 6-2, 205.

Greg Callahan — Defenseman

			Regular Season					Playoffs				
Season	Team	League	GP	G	A	PTS	PIM	GP	G	A	PTS	PIM
96-97	Wheeling	ECHL	11	0	1	1	11	—	—	—	—	—
96-97	Johnstown	ECHL	47	2	10	12	156	—	—	—	—	—
	ECHL	Totals	58	2	11	13	167	—	—	—	—	—

Born; 4/25/73, Chestnut Hill, Massachusetts. 6-1, 210.

Jock Callander — Center

			Regular Season					Playoffs				
Season	Team	League	GP	G	A	PTS	PIM	GP	G	A	PTS	PIM
82-83	Salt Lake City	IHL	68	20	27	47	26	6	0	1	1	9
83-84	Montana	CHL	72	27	32	59	69	—	—	—	—	—
83-84	Toledo	IHL	2	0	0	0	0	—	—	—	—	—
84-85	Muskegon	IHL	82	39	68	107	86	17	8	13	21	33
85-86	Muskegon	IHL	82	39	72	111	121	14	*12	11	*23	12
86-87	Muskegon	IHL	82	54	82	*136	110	15	13	7	20	23
87-88	Pittsburgh	NHL	41	11	16	27	45	—	—	—	—	—
87-88	Muskegon	IHL	31	20	36	56	49	6	2	3	5	25
88-89	Pittsburgh	NHL	30	6	5	11	20	10	2	5	7	10

Season	Team	League	GP	G	A	PTS	PIM	GP	G	A	PTS	PIM
88-89	Muskegon	IHL	48	25	39	64	40	7	5	5	10	30
89-90	Pittsburgh	NHL	30	4	7	11	49	—	—	—	—	—
89-90	Muskegon	IHL	46	29	49	78	118	15	6	*14	20	54
90-91	Muskegon	IHL	30	14	20	34	102	—	—	—	—	—
91-92	Pittsburgh	NHL	—	—	—	—	—	12	1	3	4	2
91-92	Muskegon	IHL	81	42	70	112	160	10	4	10	14	13
92-93	Tampa Bay	NHL	8	1	1	2	2	—	—	—	—	—
92-93	Atlanta	IHL	69	34	50	84	172	9	*7	5	12	25
93-94	Cleveland	IHL	81	31	70	101	126	—	—	—	—	—
94-95	Cleveland	IHL	61	24	36	60	90	4	2	2	4	6
95-96	Cleveland	IHL	81	42	53	95	150	3	1	0	1	8
96-97	Cleveland	IHL	61	20	34	54	56	14	7	6	13	10
	NHL	Totals	109	22	29	51	116	22	3	8	11	12
	IHL	Totals	905	433	706	1139	1406	120	67	77	144	248

Born; 4/23/61, Regina, Saskatchewan. 6-1, 188. Signed as a free agent by St. Louis Blues (9/28/81). Signed as a free agent by Pittsburgh Penguins (7/31/87). Signed as a free agent by Tampa Bay Lightning (7/29/92). Signed by Cleveland Lumberjacks as a free agent (8/12/93). 1985-86 IHL Playoff MVP. 1986-87 Shared IHL MVP Award with Jeff Pyle. 1986-87 IHL First Team All-Star. 1991-92 IHL First Team All-Star. Member of 1990-91 Stanley Cup champion Pittsburgh Penguins. Member of 1985-86 IHL champion Muskegon Lumberjacks. Member of 1988-89 IHL champion Muskegon Lumberjacks.

Jan Caloun — Right Wing

Season	Team	League	GP	G	A	PTS	PIM	GP	G	A	PTS	PIM
94-95	Kansas City	IHL	76	34	39	73	50	21	13	10	23	18
95-96	San Jose	NHL	11	8	3	11	0	—	—	—	—	—
95-96	Kansas City	IHL	61	38	30	68	58	5	0	1	1	6
96-97	San Jose	NHL	2	0	0	0	2	—	—	—	—	—
96-97	Kentucky	AHL	66	43	43	86	68	4	0	1	1	4
	NHL	Totals	13	8	3	11	2	—	—	—	—	—
	IHL	Totals	137	72	69	141	108	26	13	11	24	24

Born; 12/20/72, Usti-ned-laben, Czechoslovakia. 5-10, 175. Drafted by San Jose Sharks (4th choice, 75th overall) in 1992 Entry Draft. 1996-97 AHL Second Team All-Star.

Malcolm Cameron — Right Wing

Season	Team	League	GP	G	A	PTS	PIM	GP	G	A	PTS	PIM
93-94	Huntington	ECHL	68	9	20	29	50	—	—	—	—	—
94-95	Saginaw	CoHL	5	0	1	1	7	—	—	—	—	—
94-95	San Antonio	CeHL	4	0	1	1	0	—	—	—	—	—
95-96	Johnstown	ECHL	20	2	5	7	25	—	—	—	—	—
95-96	Fort Worth	CeHL	32	5	11	16	16	—	—	—	—	—
96-97	Fort Worth	CeHL	26	5	11	16	10	—	—	—	—	—
96-97	Nashville	CeHL	32	7	12	19	20	—	—	—	—	—
	CeHL	Totals	94	17	35	52	46	—	—	—	—	—
	ECHL	Totals	88	11	25	36	75	—	—	—	—	—

Born; 8/30/69, Halifax, Nova Scotia. 5-11, 190.

Ed Campbell — Defenseman

Season	Team	League	GP	G	A	PTS	PIM	GP	G	A	PTS	PIM
96-97	Binghamton	AHL	74	5	17	22	108	4	0	0	0	2

Born; 11/26/74, Westboro, Massachusetts. 6-2, 202. Drafted by New York Rangers (9th choice, 190th overall) in 1993 Entry Draft.

Christian Campeau — Right Wing

Season	Team	League	GP	G	A	PTS	PIM	GP	G	A	PTS	PIM
92-93	Atlanta	IHL	66	3	5	8	40	3	0	0	0	2
93-94	Atlanta	IHL	65	8	9	17	74	14	1	0	1	2

Season	Team	League	GP	G	A	PTS	PIM	GP	G	A	PTS	PIM
94-95	Atlanta	IHL	76	10	13	23	96	5	1	0	1	11
95-96	Atlanta	IHL	75	3	19	22	95	3	1	0	1	4
96-97	Quebec	IHL	81	14	13	27	71	9	0	1	1	2
	IHL	Totals	363	38	59	97	376	34	3	1	4	21

Born; 6/2/71, Verdun, Quebec. 5-10, 180. Signed as a free agent by Tampa Bay Lightning (7/10/92). Member of 1993-94 IHL champion Atlanta Knights.

Nicolas Cantin — Defenseman

			Regular Season					Playoffs				
Season	Team	League	GP	G	A	PTS	PIM	GP	G	A	PTS	PIM
96-97	Thunder Bay	CoHL	9	1	1	2	8	10	0	1	1	2

Born;

Greg Capson — Defenseman

			Regular Season					Playoffs				
Season	Team	League	GP	G	A	PTS	PIM	GP	G	A	PTS	PIM
92-93	Binghamton	AHL	7	1	0	1	4	—	—	—	—	—
92-93	Greensboro	ECHL	54	1	8	9	258	1	0	0	0	2
93-94	Rochester	AHL	10	0	0	0	29	1	0	0	0	2
93-94	Greensboro	ECHL	50	8	14	22	277	8	3	1	4	43
94-95	N/A											
95-96	Jacksonville	ECHL	70	14	19	33	163	18	1	4	5	61
96-97	Jacksonville	ECHL	20	2	2	4	56	—	—	—	—	—
	AHL	Totals	17	1	0	1	33	1	0	0	0	2
	ECHL	Totals	194	25	43	68	754	27	4	5	9	106

Born; 8/18/69, Nanaimo, British Columbia. 6-2, 215.

Jason Carey — Goaltender

			Regular Season						Playoffs				
Season	Team	League	GP	W	L	T	MIN	SO	GAVG	GP	W	L	MIN	SO	GAVG
96-97	Saginaw	CoHL	36	9	16	1	1585	0	5.34	—	—	—	—	—	—

Born; 3/31/73, Winnipeg, Manitoba. 5-10, 190.

Matt Carmichael — Goaltender

Season	Team	League	GP	W	L	T	MIN	SO	GAVG	GP	W	L	MIN	SO	GAVG
96-97	Roanoke	ECHL	4	1	1	0	144	0	4.18	2	0	1	59	0	4.05

Born; 7/26/77, Shawville, Quebec. 5-9, 160.

Dan Carney — Forward

			Regular Season					Playoffs				
Season	Team	League	GP	G	A	PTS	PIM	GP	G	A	PTS	PIM
94-95	Nashville	ECHL	58	7	17	24	36	13	2	3	5	8
95-96	Nashville	ECHL	33	5	12	17	30	—	—	—	—	—
95-96	Erie	ECHL	15	1	3	4	8	—	—	—	—	—
96-97	Amarillo	WPHL	15	2	1	3	16	—	—	—	—	—
96-97	Jacksonville	ECHL	50	5	12	17	36	—	—	—	—	—
	ECHL	Totals	156	18	44	62	110	13	2	3	5	8

Born; 12/23/71, Brooklyn, New York. 5-10, 170.

Steve Carpenter — Defenseman

			Regular Season					Playoffs				
Season	Team	League	GP	G	A	PTS	PIM	GP	G	A	PTS	PIM
95-96	Richmond	ECHL	43	9	29	38	100	—	—	—	—	—
96-97	Fresno	WCHL	6	2	4	6	10	5	1	1	2	30

Born; 3/30/71, Prince George, British Columbia. 5-11, 181.

Brandon Carper — Defenseman

Season	Team	League	GP	G	A	PTS	PIM	GP	G	A	PTS	PIM
95-96	Toledo	ECHL	58	10	24	34	44	11	1	4	5	22
96-97	Fresno	WCHL	56	10	27	37	46	—	—	—	—	—
96-97	Reno	WCHL	7	1	2	3	0	—	—	—	—	—
	WCHL	Totals	63	11	29	40	46	—	—	—	—	—

Born; 4/2/72, Highland Park, Illinois. 6-2, 200. Drafted by Calgary Flames (10th choice, 198th overall) in 1992 Entry Draft.

Mike Carr — Right Wing

Season	Team	League	GP	G	A	PTS	PIM	GP	G	A	PTS	PIM
96-97	Tulsa	CeHL	33	1	4	5	99	—	—	—	—	—

Born;

Jimmy Carson — Center

Season	Team	League	GP	G	A	PTS	PIM	GP	G	A	PTS	PIM
86-87	Los Angeles	NHL	80	37	42	79	22	5	1	2	3	6
87-88	Los Angeles	NHL	80	55	52	107	45	5	5	3	8	4
88-89	Edmonton	NHL	80	49	51	100	36	7	2	1	3	6
89-90	Edmonton	NHL	4	1	2	3	0	—	—	—	—	—
89-90	Detroit	NHL	44	20	16	36	8	—	—	—	—	—
90-91	Detroit	NHL	64	21	25	46	28	7	2	1	3	4
91-92	Detroit	NHL	80	34	35	69	30	11	2	3	5	0
92-93	Detroit	NHL	52	25	26	51	18	—	—	—	—	—
92-93	Los Angeles	NHL	34	12	10	22	14	18	5	4	9	2
93-94	Los Angeles	NHL	25	4	7	11	2	—	—	—	—	—
93-94	Vancouver	NHL	34	7	10	17	22	2	0	1	1	0
94-95	Hartford	NHL	38	9	10	19	29	—	—	—	—	—
95-96	Hartford	NHL	11	1	0	1	0	—	—	—	—	—
95-96	Lausanne	Switzerland	13	3	4	7	14	—	—	—	—	—
96-97	Detroit	IHL	18	7	16	23	4	13	4	6	10	12
	NHL	Totals	626	275	286	561	254	55	17	15	32	22

Born; 7/20/68, Southfield, Michigan. 6-0, 200. Drafted by Los Angeles Kings (1st choice, 2nd overall) in 1986 Entry Draft. Traded to Edmonton Oilers by Los Angeles with Martin Gelinas, Los Angeles' first round choices in 1989 (later traded to New Jersey-New Jersey selected Jason Miller), 1991 (Martin Rucinsky) and 1993 (Nick Stadkuhar) Entry Drafts and cash for Wayne Gretzky, Mike Krushelnyski and Marty McSorley, 8/9/88. Traded to Detroit Red Wings by Edmonton with Kevin McClelland and Edmonton's fifth round choice (later dealt to Montreal-Montreal selected Brad Layzell) in 1991 Entry Draft for Petr Klima, Joe Murphy, Adam Graves and Jeff Sharples, 11/2/89. Traded to Los Angeles Kings with Marc Potvin and Gary Shuchuk for Paul Coffey, Sylvain Couturier and Jim Hiller, 1/29/93. Traded to Vancouver Canucks by Los Angeles for Dixon Ward and a conditional draft choice in the 1995 Entry Draft, 1/8/94. Signed as a free agent by Hartford, 7/15/94. Signed as a free agent by Detroit Vipers. Member of 1996-97 IHL Champion Detroit Vipers.

Anson Carter — Center

Season	Team	League	GP	G	A	PTS	PIM	GP	G	A	PTS	PIM
96-97	Portland	AHL	27	19	19	38	11	—	—	—	—	—
96-97	Washington	NHL	19	3	2	5	7	—	—	—	—	—
96-97	Boston	NHL	19	8	5	13	2	—	—	—	—	—
	NHL	Totals	38	11	7	18	9	—	—	—	—	—

Born; 6/6/74, 6-1, 175. Drafted by Quebec Nordiques (10th choice, 220th overall) in 1992 Entry Draft. Traded to Washington Capitals by Quebec for Washington's fourth round choice (Ben Storey) in 1996 Entry Draft. Traded to Boston Bruins by Washington with Jason Aliison, Jim Carey, third round draft pick in 1997 and conditional second round pick in 1998 for Rick Tocchet, Adam Oates and Bill Ranford, 3/1/97.

Dan Carter — Left Wing

Season	Team	League	GP	G	A	PTS	PIM	GP	G	A	PTS	PIM
95-96	Toledo	ECHL	44	7	11	18	59	10	2	1	3	29

Season	Team	League	GP	G	A	PTS	PIM	GP	G	A	PTS	PIM
96-97	Dayton	CoHL	55	27	24	41	76	—	—	—	—	—
96-97	Huntsville	CeHL	5	2	8	10	20	7	0	1	1	20

Born; 6/25/72, Mount Clemens, Michigan. 5-11, 195.

Shawn Carter — Center
Regular Season / Playoffs

Season	Team	League	GP	G	A	PTS	PIM	GP	G	A	PTS	PIM
96-97	Orlando	IHL	53	22	25	47	40	—	—	—	—	—
96-97	St. John's	AHL	18	5	6	11	15	7	1	2	3	6

Born; 4/16/73, Eagle River, Wisconsin. 6-2, 210. Traded from Orlando Solar Bears to Toronto Maple Leafs for Kelly Fairchild, 1997.

Steve Carter — Defenseman
Regular Season / Playoffs

Season	Team	League	GP	G	A	PTS	PIM	GP	G	A	PTS	PIM
96-97	Fort Worth	CeHL	64	5	18	23	95	17	0	5	5	18

Born; 3/8/75, Kingston, Ontario. 6-1, 201. Member of 1996-97 CeHL Champion Fort Worth Fire.

Brian Caruso — Left Wing
Regular Season / Playoffs

Season	Team	League	GP	G	A	PTS	PIM	GP	G	A	PTS	PIM
94-95	Saint John	AHL	1	0	0	0	2	—	—	—	—	—
94-95	Greensboro	ECHL	7	0	0	0	13	—	—	—	—	—
94-95	Erie	ECHL	12	1	2	3	36	—	—	—	—	—
95-96	Fort Worth	CeHL	63	18	14	32	59	—	—	—	—	—
96-97	Fort Worth	CeHL	59	8	29	37	117	17	6	7	13	6
	CeHL	Totals	122	26	43	69	176	17	6	7	13	6
	ECHL	Totals	19	1	2	3	49	—	—	—	—	—

Born; 9/20/72, Thunder Bay, Ontario. 6-2, 230. Drafted by Calgary Flames (4th choice, 63rd overall) in 1991 Entry Draft. Member of 1996-97 CeHL Champion Fort Worth Fire.

Mike Casselman — Center
Regular Season / Playoffs

Season	Team	League	GP	G	A	PTS	PIM	GP	G	A	PTS	PIM
91-92	Adirondack	AHL	1	0	0	0	0	—	—	—	—	—
91-92	Toledo	ECHL	61	39	60	99	83	5	0	1	1	6
92-93	Adirondack	AHL	60	12	19	31	27	8	3	3	6	0
92-93	Toledo	ECHL	3	0	1	1	2	—	—	—	—	—
93-94	Adirondack	AHL	77	17	38	55	34	12	2	4	6	10
94-95	Adirondack	AHL	60	17	43	60	42	4	0	0	0	2
95-96	Florida	NHL	3	0	0	0	0	—	—	—	—	—
95-96	Carolina	AHL	70	34	68	102	46	—	—	—	—	—
96-97	Cincinnati	IHL	68	30	34	64	54	3	1	0	1	2
	AHL	Totals	268	80	168	248	149	24	5	7	12	12
	ECHL	Totals	64	39	61	100	85	5	0	1	1	6

Born; 8/23/68, Morrisburg, Ontaio. 5-11, 185. Drafted by Detroit Red Wings (1st choice, 3rd overall) in 1990 Supplemental Draft. 1992 ECHL Second Team All-Star.

Frederic Cassivi — Goaltender
Regular Season / Playoffs

Season	Team	League	GP	W	L	T	MIN	SO	GAVG	GP	W	L	MIN	SO	GAVG
95-96	Prince Edward Island	AHL	41	20	14	3	2346	1	3.27	5	2	3	317	0	4.54
96-97	Syracuse	AHL	55	23	22	8	3069	2	3.21	1	0	1	60	0	3.01
	AHL	Totals	96	43	36	11	5415	3		6	2	4	377	0	

Born; 6/12/75, Sorel, Quebec. 6-4, 205. Drafted by Ottawa Senators (7th choice, 210th overall) in 1994 Entry Draft.

Trent Cavicchi — Goaltender

Regular Season / **Playoffs**

Season	Team	League	GP	W	L	T	MIN	SO	GAVG	GP	W	L	MIN	SO	GAVG
96-97	Knoxville	ECHL	11	2	7	1	616	0	5.45	—	—	—	—	—	—
96-97	Raleigh	ECHL	8	3	3	1	448	0	2.95	—	—	—	—	—	—
	ECHL	Totals	19	5	10	2	1064	0	4.40	—	—	—	—	—	—

Born; 8/11/74, Halifax, Nova Scotia. 6-3, 180. Drafted by Montreal Canadiens (12th choice, 236th overall) in 1992 Entry Draft.

Dan Ceman — Center

Regular Season / **Playoffs**

Season	Team	League	GP	G	A	PTS	PIM	GP	G	A	PTS	PIM
96-97	Kentucky	AHL	11	1	4	5	23	—	—	—	—	—

Born; 7/25/73, Windsor, Ontario. 6-1, 195.

Peter Cermak — Left Wing

Regular Season / **Playoffs**

Season	Team	League	GP	G	A	PTS	PIM	GP	G	A	PTS	PIM
96-97	Jacksonville	ECHL	2	0	0	0	0	—	—	—	—	—
96-97	Johnstown	ECHL	3	0	0	0	0	—	—	—	—	—
96-97	Madison	CoHL	28	8	7	15	14	—	—	—	—	—
	ECHL	Totals	5	0	0	0	0	—	—	—	—	—

Born; 4/16/76, Bratislava, Czechoslovakia. 6-0, 180.

Kord Cernich — Defenseman

Regular Season / **Playoffs**

Season	Team	League	GP	G	A	PTS	PIM	GP	G	A	PTS	PIM
90-91	Binghamton	AHL	52	5	10	15	36	—	—	—	—	—
91-92	San Diego	IHL	64	5	18	23	53	3	1	0	1	0
91-92	Binghamton	AHL	5	1	3	4	6	—	—	—	—	—
92-93	Capital District	AHL	6	0	0	0	4	—	—	—	—	—
92-93	Rochester	AHL	4	0	0	0	2	—	—	—	—	—
92-93	Flint	CoHL	31	5	12	17	18	6	3	3	6	4
92-93	San Diego	IHL	17	1	5	6	4	3	0	0	0	2
93-94	Fort Wayne	IHL	3	0	0	0	4	—	—	—	—	—
93-94	Dayton	ECHL	21	4	13	17	14	3	1	2	3	4
94-95	N/A											
95-96	Anchorage	WCHL	57	4	24	28	57	—	—	—	—	—
96-97	Anchorage	WCHL	54	8	12	20	24	9	1	2	3	2
	IHL	Totals	84	6	23	29	61	6	1	0	1	2
	AHL	Totals	67	6	13	19	48	—	—	—	—	—
	WCHL	Totals	111	12	36	48	81	9	1	2	3	2

Born; 10/20/66, Ketchikan, Alaska. 5-11, 194.

Frederic Chabot — Goaltender

Regular Season / **Playoffs**

Season	Team	League	GP	W	L	T	MIN	SO	GAVG	GP	W	L	MIN	SO	GAVG
89-90	Fort Wayne	IHL	23	6	13	3	1208	1	4.32	—	—	—	—	—	—
89-90	Sherbrooke	AHL	2	1	1	0	119	0	4.03	—	—	—	—	—	—
90-91	Montreal	NHL	3	0	0	1	108	0	3.33	—	—	—	—	—	—
90-91	Fredericton	AHL	35	9	15	5	1800	0	4.07	—	—	—	—	—	—
91-92	Fredericton	AHL	30	17	9	4	1761	2	*2.69	7	3	4	457	0	2.63
91-92	Winston-Salem	ECHL	24	15	7	2	1449	0	*2.94	—	—	—	—	—	—
92-93	Montreal	NHL	1	0	0	0	40	0	1.50	—	—	—	—	—	—
92-93	Fredericton	AHL	45	22	17	4	2544	0	3.33	4	1	3	261	0	3.68
93-94	Montreal	NHL	1	0	1	0	60	0	5.00	—	—	—	—	—	—
93-94	Philadelphia	NHL	4	0	1	1	70	0	4.29	—	—	—	—	—	—
93-94	Fredericton	AHL	3	0	1	1	143	0	5.03	—	—	—	—	—	—

93-94	Hershey	AHL	28	13	5	6	1464	2	*2.58	11	7	4	665	0	2.89
93-94	Las Vegas	IHL	2	1	1	0	110	0	2.72	—	—	—	—	—	—
94-95	Cincinnati	IHL	48	25	12	7	2622	1	2.93	5	3	2	326	0	2.94
95-96	Cincinnati	IHL	38	23	9	4	2147	3	2.46	14	9	5	853	1	2.60
96-97	Houston	IHL	*72	*39	26	7	*4265	*7	2.53	13	8	5	777	*1	2.63
	NHL	Totals	9	0	2	2	278	0	3.67	—	—	—	—	—	—
	IHL	Totals	183	94	61	21	10352	12	2.83	32	20	12	1956	2	2.67
	AHL	Totals	143	62	48	20	7831	4	3.26	22	11	11	1383	0	2.95

Born; 2/12/68, Herbertville, Quebec. 5-11, 177. Drafted by New Jersey Devils (10th choice, 192nd overall) in 1986 Entry Draft. Signed as a free agent by Montreal Canadiens (1/16/90). Claimed by Tampa Bay Lightning from Montreal in Expansion Draft (6/18/92). Traded to Montreal by Tampa Bay for J.C. Bergeron (6/19/92). Traded to Philadelphia Flyers by Montreal for cash (2/21/94). Signed as a free agent by Florida Panthers (8/11/94). Signed as a free agent by Houston Aeros (1996). Won Baz Bastien Award (best goaltender as selected by AHL coaches) 1993-94. 1995-96 IHL Second Team All-Star. 1996-97 IHL First Team All-Star. 1996-97 IHL Most Valuable Player.

Rene Chapdelaine — Right Wing

			Regular Season					Playoffs				
Season	Team	League	GP	G	A	PTS	PIM	GP	G	A	PTS	PIM
89-90	New Haven	AHL	41	0	1	1	35	—	—	—	—	—
90-91	Los Angeles	NHL	3	0	1	1	10	—	—	—	—	—
90-91	Phoenix	IHL	17	0	2	2	10	11	0	0	0	8
90-91	New Haven	AHL	65	3	11	14	49	—	—	—	—	—
91-92	Los Angeles	NHL	16	0	1	1	10	—	—	—	—	—
91-92	Phoenix	IHL	62	4	22	26	87	—	—	—	—	—
91-92	New Haven	AHL	—	—	—	—	—	4	0	2	2	0
92-93	Los Angeles	NHL	13	0	0	0	12	—	—	—	—	—
92-93	Phoenix	IHL	44	1	17	18	54	—	—	—	—	—
92-93	San Diego	IHL	9	1	1	2	8	14	0	1	1	27
93-94	Peoria	IHL	80	8	9	17	100	6	1	3	4	10
94-95	Peoria	IHL	45	3	2	5	62	9	0	2	2	12
95-96	Peoria	IHL	70	2	10	12	135	12	1	0	1	8
96-97	San Antonio	IHL	69	7	11	18	125	9	2	3	5	10
	NHL	Totals	32	0	2	2	32	—	—	—	—	—
	IHL	Totals	396	26	74	100	581	61	4	9	13	75
	AHL	Totals	106	3	12	15	84	4	0	2	2	0

Born; 9/27/66, Weyburn, Saskatchewan. 6-1, 195. Drafted by Los Angeles Kings (7th choice, 149th overall) in 1986 Entry Draft.

Brian Chapman — Defenseman

			Regular Season					Playoffs				
Season	Team	League	GP	G	A	PTS	PIM	GP	G	A	PTS	PIM
86-87	Binghamton	AHL	—	—	—	—	—	1	0	0	0	0
88-89	Binghamton	AHL	71	5	25	30	216	—	—	—	—	—
89-90	Binghamton	AHL	68	2	15	17	180	—	—	—	—	—
90-91	Binghamton	NHL	3	0	0	0	29	—	—	—	—	—
90-91	Springfield	AHL	60	4	23	27	200	18	1	4	5	62
91-92	Springfield	AHL	73	3	26	29	245	10	2	2	4	25
92-93	Springfield	AHL	72	17	34	51	212	15	2	5	7	43
93-94	Phoenix	IHL	78	6	35	41	280	—	—	—	—	—
94-95	Phoenix	IHL	60	2	23	25	181	9	1	5	6	31
95-96	Phoenix	IHL	66	8	11	19	187	4	0	1	1	14
96-97	Phoenix	IHL	69	9	16	25	109	—	—	—	—	—
96-97	Long Beach	IHL	14	1	7	8	67	—	—	—	—	—
	AHL	Totals	344	31	123	154	1053	44	5	11	16	130
	IHL	Totals	287	26	92	118	824	13	1	6	7	45

Born; 2/10/68, Brockville, Ontario. 6-0, 195. Drafted by Hartford Whalers (3rd choice, 74th overall) in 1986 Entry Draft. Signed as a free agent by Phoenix Roadrunners (7/16/93). Traded to Long Beach Ice Dogs by Phoenix to complete trade for Todd Gillingham. Rights due to return to Phoenix franchise after 1996-97 season. Member of 1990-91 AHL champion Springfield Indians.

Craig Chapman — Center

			Regular Season					Playoffs				
Season	Team	League	GP	G	A	PTS	PIM	GP	G	A	PTS	PIM
95-96	Fresno	WCHL	57	21	38	59	49	7	1	4	5	6
96-97	Fresno	WCHL	57	21	30	51	100	5	2	2	4	14
	WCHL	Totals	114	42	68	110	149	12	3	6	9	20

Born; 2/12/71, Williams Lake, British Columbia. 5-10, 190.

Daniel Chaput — Defenseman

			Regular Season					Playoffs				
Season	Team	League	GP	G	A	PTS	PIM	GP	G	A	PTS	PIM
92-93	Hampton Roads	ECHL	—	—	—	—	—	1	0	1	1	2
93-94	Hamton Roads	ECHL	68	10	36	46	95	7	2	8	10	15
94-95	Richmond	ECHL	39	8	13	21	122	—	—	—	—	—
95-96	N/A											
96-97	Knoxville	ECHL	45	2	18	20	85	—	—	—	—	—
96-97	Richmond	ECHL	22	2	10	12	55	8	1	4	5	14
	ECHL	Totals	174	22	77	99	357	16	3	13	16	31

Born; 1/2/71, St. Anne, Manitoba. 6-1, 195.

Francois Chaput — Defenseman

			Regular Season					Playoffs				
Season	Team	League	GP	G	A	PTS	PIM	GP	G	A	PTS	PIM
96-97	Macon	CeHL	7	1	2	3	14	5	1	1	2	12

6-3, 232.

Louis Charbonneau — Right Wing

			Regular Season					Playoffs				
Season	Team	League	GP	G	A	PTS	PIM	GP	G	A	PTS	PIM
95-96	Cornwall	AHL	1	0	0	0	0	—	—	—	—	—
95-96	Roanoke	ECHL	22	6	1	7	94	—	—	—	—	—
95-96	Erie	ECHL	25	2	3	5	187	—	—	—	—	—
96-97	Syracuse	AHL	2	0	0	0	2	—	—	—	—	—
96-97	Jacksonville	ECHL	27	3	6	9	241	—	—	—	—	—
96-97	Wheeling	ECHL	23	4	3	7	159	1	0	0	0	0
	AHL	Totals	3	0	0	0	2	—	—	—	—	—
	ECHL	Totals	97	15	13	28	681	1	0	0	0	0

Born; 10/27/74, Montreal, Quebec. 6-1, 204.

Patrick Charbonneau — Defenseman

			Regular Season					Playoffs				
Season	Team	League	GP	G	A	PTS	PIM	GP	G	A	PTS	PIM
96-97	Birmingham	ECHL	34	0	2	2	42	1	0	0	0	0

Born; 6/5/75, Napierville, Quebec. 5-10, 183.

Patrick Charbonneau — Goaltender

			Regular Season						Playoffs				
Season	Team	League	GP	W	L	T	MIN	SO	GAVG	GP	W	L	MIN	SO	GAVG
93-94	Prince Edward Island	AHL	3	2	1	0	180	0	3.67	—	—	—	—	—	—
94-95	Prince Edward Island	AHL	2	2	0	0	120	0	2.00	3	0	2	137	0	5.24
95-96	Prince Edward Island	AHL	17	5	8	0	864	0	4.79	—	—	—	—	—	—
95-96	Thunder Bay	CoHL	29	16	7	3	1587	1	3.25	19	10	8	942	0	4.01
96-97	Syracuse	AHL	2	1	0	0	80	1	2.25	—	—	—	—	—	—
96-97	Raleigh	ECHL	40	18	14	4	2105	0	4.13	—	—	—	—	—	—
	AHL	Totals	24	10	9	0	1244	1	4.20	3	0	2	137	0	5.24

Born; 7/22/75, St. Jean, Quebec. 5-11, 217. Drafted by Ottawa Senators (3rd choice, 53rd overall) in 1993 Entry Draft.

Stephane Charbonneau — Right Wing

			Regular Season					Playoffs				
Season	Team	League	GP	G	A	PTS	PIM	GP	G	A	PTS	PIM
91-92	Quebec	NHL	2	0	0	0	0	—	—	—	—	—
91-92	Halifax	AHL	64	22	25	47	183	—	—	—	—	—
92-93	Halifax	AHL	56	18	20	38	125	—	—	—	—	—
93-94	Phoenix	IHL	32	7	6	13	43	—	—	—	—	—
93-94	Erie	ECHL	23	22	8	30	130	—	—	—	—	—
94-95	Portland	AHL	7	3	5	8	0	—	—	—	—	—
94-95	Cornwall	AHL	1	0	1	1	0	—	—	—	—	—
94-95	Fort Wayne	IHL	4	0	0	0	8	—	—	—	—	—
94-95	Erie	ECHL	64	50	41	91	129	—	—	—	—	—
95-96	Portland	AHL	23	5	3	8	23	1	0	0	0	0
95-96	Flint	CoHL	1	1	0	1	0	—	—	—	—	—
96-97	Portland	AHL	9	1	0	1	2	—	—	—	—	—
96-97	Baton Rouge	ECHL	43	19	24	43	63	—	—	—	—	—
96-97	Mississippi	ECHL	13	8	6	14	14	3	2	0	2	18
	AHL	Totals	160	49	53	102	333	1	0	0	0	0
	IHL	Totals	36	7	6	13	51	—	—	—	—	—
	ECHL	Totals	143	99	79	178	336	3	2	0	2	18

Born; 6/27/70, Saint-Adele, Quebec. 6-2, 195. Signed as a free agent by Quebec Nordiques (4/25/91).

Craig Charron — Center

			Regular Season					Playoffs				
Season	Team	League	GP	G	A	PTS	PIM	GP	G	A	PTS	PIM
90-91	Albany	IHL	5	0	2	2	0	—	—	—	—	—
90-91	Winston-Salem	ECHL	30	11	16	27	10	—	—	—	—	—
91-92	Cincinnati	ECHL	64	41	55	96	97	9	5	5	10	10
92-93	Cleveland	IHL	27	6	8	14	8	—	—	—	—	—
92-93	Birmingham	ECHL	23	9	17	26	18	—	—	—	—	—
93-94	N/A											
94-95	Cornwall	AHL	6	5	0	5	0	2	0	0	0	0
94-95	Fort Wayne	IHL	2	1	0	1	4	—	—	—	—	—
94-95	Kalamazoo	IHL	2	0	0	0	0	—	—	—	—	—
94-95	Dayton	ECHL	48	35	47	82	82	9	9	13	22	10
95-96	Rochester	AHL	72	43	52	95	79	19	7	10	17	12
96-97	Rochester	AHL	72	24	41	65	42	10	2	7	9	4
	AHL	Totals	150	72	93	165	121	31	9	17	26	16
	IHL	Totals	36	7	10	17	12	—	—	—	—	—
	ECHL	Totals	165	96	135	231	207	18	14	18	32	20

Born; 11/15/67, North Easton, Massachusetts. 5-10, 183. Member of 1995-96 AHL champion Rochester Americans.

Eric Charron — Defenseman

			Regular Season					Playoffs				
Season	Team	League	GP	G	A	PTS	PIM	GP	G	A	PTS	PIM
88-89	Sherbrooke	AHL	1	0	0	0	0	—	—	—	—	—
89-90	Sherbrooke	AHL	—	—	—	—	—	2	0	0	0	0
90-91	Fredericton	AHL	71	1	11	12	108	2	1	0	1	29
91-92	Fredericton	AHL	59	2	11	13	98	6	1	0	1	4
92-93	Montreal	NHL	3	0	0	0	2	—	—	—	—	—
92-93	Fredericton	AHL	54	3	13	16	93	—	—	—	—	—
92-93	Atlanta	IHL	11	0	2	2	12	3	0	1	1	6
93-94	Tampa Bay	NHL	4	0	0	0	2	—	—	—	—	—
93-94	Atlanta	IHL	66	5	18	23	144	14	1	4	5	28
94-95	Tampa Bay	NHL	45	1	4	5	26	—	—	—	—	—
95-96	Tampa Bay	NHL	14	0	0	0	18	—	—	—	—	—
95-96	Washington	NHL	4	0	1	1	4	6	0	0	0	8

Season	Team	League	GP	G	A	PTS	PIM	GP	G	A	PTS	PIM
95-96	Portland	AHL	45	0	8	8	88	20	1	1	2	33
96-97	Washington	NHL	25	1	1	2	20	—	—	—	—	—
96-97	Portland	AHL	29	6	8	14	55	5	0	3	3	0
	NHL	Totals	101	2	6	8	72	6	0	0	0	8
	AHL	Totals	259	12	51	63	442	35	3	4	7	66
	IHL	Totals	77	5	20	25	156	17	1	5	6	34

Born; 1/14/70, Verdun, Quebec. 6-3, 192. Drafted by Montreal Canadiens (1st choice, 20th overall) in 1988 Entry Draft. Traded to Tampa Bay Lightning by Montreal with Alain Cote and future considerations for Rob Ramage (3/20/93). Traded to Washington Capitals by Tampa Bay for conditional pick in 1997 Entry Draft (11/16/97). Member of 1993-94 IHL champion Atlanta Knights.

Don Chase — Right Wing

Season	Team	League	GP	G	A	PTS	PIM	GP	G	A	PTS	PIM
96-97	Fredericton	AHL	12	0	0	0	2	—	—	—	—	—
96-97	Wheeling	ECHL	53	23	25	48	26	3	2	4	6	0

Born; 3/17/74, Springfield, Massachusetts. 5-11, 190. Drafted by Montreal Canadiens (7th choice, 116th overall) in 1992 Entry Draft.

Tim Chase — Defenseman

Season	Team	League	GP	G	A	PTS	PIM	GP	G	A	PTS	PIM
92-93	Fredericton	AHL	25	4	8	12	16	3	0	0	0	0
93-94	Fredericton	AHL	8	0	4	4	0	—	—	—	—	—
93-94	Atlanta	IHL	1	1	0	1	0	—	—	—	—	—
93-94	Knoxville	ECHL	37	2	15	17	65	—	—	—	—	—
94-95	N/A											
95-96	Jacksonville	ECHL	54	13	18	31	134	16	5	8	13	6
96-97	Jacksonville	ECHL	9	0	2	2	10	—	—	—	—	—
96-97		ECHL	25	6	15	21	20	—	—	—	—	—
96-97	Tallahassee	ECHL	11	1	3	4	18	—	—	—	—	—
	AHL	Totals	33	4	12	16	16	3	0	0	0	0
	ECHL	Totals	136	22	53	76	247	16	5	8	13	6

Born; 3/23/70, Gaithersburg, Maryland. 6-2, 180. Drafted by Montreal Canadiens (8th choice, 146th overall) in 1988 Entry Draft.

Denis Chasse — Right Wing

Season	Team	League	GP	G	A	PTS	PIM	GP	G	A	PTS	PIM
91-92	Halifax	AHL	73	26	35	61	254	—	—	—	—	—
92-93	Halifax	AHL	75	35	41	76	242	—	—	—	—	—
93-94	St. Louis	NHL	3	0	1	1	15	—	—	—	—	—
93-94	Cornwall	AHL	48	27	39	66	194	—	—	—	—	—
94-95	St. Louis	NHL	47	7	9	16	133	7	1	7	8	23
95-96	St. Louis	NHL	42	3	0	3	108	—	—	—	—	—
95-96	Washington	NHL	3	0	0	0	5	—	—	—	—	—
95-96	Winnipeg	NHL	15	0	0	0	12	—	—	—	—	—
95-96	Worcester	AHL	3	0	0	0	6	—	—	—	—	—
96-97	Ottawa	NHL	22	1	4	5	19	—	—	—	—	—
96-97	Detroit	IHL	9	2	1	3	33	—	—	—	—	—
96-97	Indianapolis	IHL	3	0	0	0	10	4	1	1	2	23
	NHL	Totals	132	11	14	25	292	—	—	—	—	—
	AHL	Totals	199	88	115	203	696	7	1	7	8	23
	IHL	Totals	12	2	1	3	43	4	1	1	2	23

Born; 2/7/70, Montreal, Quebec. 6-2, 200. Signed as a free agent by Quebec Nordiques (5/14/91). Traded to St. Louis Blues with Steve Duchesne by Nordiques for Ron Sutter, Bob Bassen and Garth Butcher (1/23/94). Traded to Washington Capitals by Blues for Rob Pearson (1/29/96). Traded to Winnipeg Jets by Washington for Stewart Malgunas (2/15/96).

Steve Chelios — Defenseman

Season	Team	League	GP	G	A	PTS	PIM	GP	G	A	PTS	PIM
89-90	Virginia	ECHL	5	1	2	3	4	—	—	—	—	—
90-91	Roanoke	ECHL	7	1	3	4	28	—	—	—	—	—
90-91	Richmond	ECHL	5	0	2	2	4	—	—	—	—	—
90-91	Johnstown	ECHL	7	0	3	3	8	—	—	—	—	—
90-91	Louisville	ECHL	3	0	1	1	4	—	—	—	—	—
91-92	Roanoke	ECHL	18	2	4	6	44	—	—	—	—	—
91-92	Nashville	ECHL	24	5	11	16	47	—	—	—	—	—
92-93	Dallas	CeHL	30	3	19	22	60	—	—	—	—	—
92-93	Wichita	CeHL	12	4	12	16	32	—	—	—	—	—
93-94	Wichita	CeHL	61	8	51	59	153	9	0	11	11	18
94-95	Daytona	SUN	26	6	31	37	101	—	—	—	—	—
95-96	Birmingham	ECHL	10	1	1	2	4	—	—	—	—	—
95-96	Madison	CoHL	2	1	0	1	0	—	—	—	—	—
95-96	Daytona	SHL	29	5	42	47	152	—	—	—	—	—
96-97	Quad City	CoHL	14	2	8	10	13	14	2	13	15	18
	ECHL	Totals	79	10	27	37	143	—	—	—	—	—
	CeHL	Totals	103	15	82	97	245	9	0	11	11	18
	SHL	Totals	55	11	73	84	253	—	—	—	—	—
	CoHL	Totals	16	3	8	11	13	14	2	13	15	18

Born; 8/24/68, San Diego, California. 5-9, 180. Member of 1993-94 CeHL champion Wichita Thunder. Member of 1996-97 CoHL champion Quad City Mallards.

Vladimir Cherbaturkin — Defenseman

Season	Team	League	GP	G	A	PTS	PIM	GP	G	A	PTS	PIM
96-97	Utah	IHL	68	0	4	4	34	—	—	—	—	—

Born; 4/23/75, Tyumen, Russia. 6-2, 189. Drafted by New Yorl Islanders (3rd choice, 66th overall) in 1993 Entry Draft.

Steve Cheredaryk — Defenseman

Season	Team	League	GP	G	A	PTS	PIM	GP	G	A	PTS	PIM
94-95	Springfield	AHL	3	0	1	1	0	—	—	—	—	—
95-96	Springfield	AHL	32	0	1	1	36	—	—	—	—	—
95-96	Knoxville	ECHL	13	0	10	10	72	6	2	4	6	12
96-97	Springfield	AHL	46	1	2	3	69	—	—	—	—	—
96-97	Fredericton	AHL	14	0	1	1	24	—	—	—	—	—
96-97	Mississippi	ECHL	9	0	1	1	33	—	—	—	—	—
	AHL	Totals	95	1	5	6	129	—	—	—	—	—
	ECHL	Totals	22	0	11	11	105	6	2	4	6	12

Born; 11/20/75, Calgary, Alberta. 6-2, 197. Drafted by Winnipeg Jets (4th choice, 82nd overall) in 1994 Entry Draft. Traded to Montreal Canadiens by Phoenix Coyotes for Pat Jablonski.

Denis Chervyakov — Defenseman

Season	Team	League	GP	G	A	PTS	PIM	GP	G	A	PTS	PIM
92-93	Boston	NHL	2	0	0	0	2	—	—	—	—	—
92-93	Providence	AHL	48	4	12	16	99	—	—	—	—	—
92-93	Atlanta	IHL	1	0	0	0	0	—	—	—	—	—
93-94	Providence	AHL	58	2	16	18	128	—	—	—	—	—
94-95	Providence	AHL	65	1	18	19	130	10	0	2	2	14
95-96	Providence	AHL	64	3	7	10	58	4	1	0	1	21
96-97	Kentucky	AHL	52	2	11	13	78	—	—	—	—	—
	AHL	Totals	235	10	53	63	415	14	1	2	3	35

Born; 4/20/70, St. Petersburg, Russia. 6-0, 190. Drafted by Boston Bruins (9th choice, 256th overall) in 1992 Entry Draft.

Tim Cheveldae — Goaltender

			Regular Season							Playoffs					
Season	Team	League	GP	W	L	T	MIN	SO	GAVG	GP	W	L	MIN	SO	AVG
88-89	Detroit	NHL	2	0	2	0	122	0	4.43	—	—	—	—	—	—
88-89	Adirondack	AHL	30	20	8	0	1694	1	3.47	2	1	0	99	0	5.45
89-90	Detroit	NHL	28	10	9	8	1600	0	3.79	—	—	—	—	—	—
89-90	Adirondack	AHL	31	17	8	6	1848	0	3.77	—	—	—	—	—	—
90-91	Detroit	NHL	65	30	26	5	3615	2	3.55	7	3	4	398	0	3.32
91-92	Detroit	NHL	*72	*38	23	9	*4236	2	3.20	11	3	7	597	*2	2.51
92-93	Detroit	NHL	67	34	24	7	3880	4	3.25	7	3	4	423	0	3.40
93-94	Detroit	NHL	30	16	9	1	1572	1	3.47	—	—	—	—	—	—
93-94	Winnipeg	NHL	14	5	8	1	788	1	3.96	—	—	—	—	—	—
93-94	Adirondack	AHL	2	1	0	1	125	0	3.36	—	—	—	—	—	—
94-95	Winnipeg	NHL	30	8	16	3	1571	0	3.70	—	—	—	—	—	—
95-96	Winnipeg	NHL	30	8	18	3	1695	0	3.93	—	—	—	—	—	—
95-96	Hershey	AHL	8	4	3	0	457	0	4.07	4	2	2	250	0	3.36
96-97	Boston	NHL	2	0	1	0	93	0	3.23	—	—	—	—	—	—
96-97	Fort Wayne	IHL	21	6	9	4	1138	0	3.96	—	—	—	—	—	—
	NHL	Totals	40	149	136	37	19162	10	3.49	25	9	15	1418	2	3.00
	AHL	Totals	71	42	19	7	4124	1	3.67	6	3	2	349	0	3.95

Born; 2/15/68, Melville, Saskatchewan. 5-10, 175. Drafted by Detroit Red Wings (4th choice, 64th overall) in 1986 Entry Draft. Traded to Winnipeg Jets by Detroit with Dallas Drake for Bob Essensa and Sergei Bautin (3/8/94). Traded to Philadelphia Flyers by Winnipeg with Phoenix's third round pick (Chester Gallant) in 1996 Entry draft for Dominic Roussel (2/27/96). Signed as a free agent by Las Vegas (8/97).

Grant Chorney — Right Wing

			Regular Season					Playoffs				
Season	Team	League	GP	G	A	PTS	PIM	GP	G	A	PTS	PIM
92-93	Knoxville	ECHL	52	10	13	23	*443	—	—	—	—	—
93-94	Richmond	ECHL	4	1	1	2	31	—	—	—	—	—
96-97	Central Texas	WPHL	18	1	6	7	90	—	—	—	—	—
96-97	Amarillo	WPHL	21	3	4	7	138	—	—	—	—	—
	ECHL	Totals	56	11	14	25	474	—	—	—	—	—
	WPHL	Totals	39	4	10	14	228	—	—	—	—	—

Born; 1/3/70, Edmonton, Alberta. 6-3, 230.

Troy Christensen — Defenseman

			Regular Season					Playoffs				
Season	Team	League	GP	G	A	PTS	PIM	GP	G	A	PTS	PIM
96-97	Dayton	ECHL	46	3	8	11	30	2	0	0	0	0

Born; Winnipeg, Manitoba. 5-9, 185

Brandon Christian — Left Wing

			Regular Season					Playoffs				
Season	Team	League	GP	G	A	PTS	PIM	GP	G	A	PTS	PIM
94-95	JHN	ECHL	39	7	12	19	226	—	—	—	—	—
95-96	THB	CoHL	26	3	2	5	70	—	—	—	—	—
95-96	JHN	ECHL	37	1	4	5	219	—	—	—	—	—
96-97	Philadelphia	AHL	2	0	0	0	32	—	—	—	—	—
96-97	Johnstown	ECHL	49	1	3	4	140	—	—	—	—	—
	ECHL	Totals	125	9	19	28	585	—	—	—	—	—

Born; 4/21/72, Burlington, Ontario. 6-4, 230.

Gord Christian — Left Wing

			Regular Season					Playoffs				
Season	Team	League	GP	G	A	PTS	PIM	GP	G	A	PTS	PIM
93-94	Johnstown	ECHL	45	29	25	54	95	3	0	0	0	4
94-95	Johnstown	ECHL	4	1	2	3	29	—	—	—	—	—

Season	Team	League	GP	G	A	PTS	PIM	GP	G	A	PTS	PIM
94-95	South Carolina	ECHL	15	1	3	4	17	—	—	—	—	—
94-95	Raleigh	ECHL	8	2	4	6	23	—	—	—	—	—
95-96	San Antonio	CeHL	49	15	24	39	89	—	—	—	—	—
95-96	Wichita	CeHL	7	3	2	5	14	—	—	—	—	—
96-97	New Mexico	WPHL	34	9	12	21	151	—	—	—	—	—
	ECHL	Totals	72	33	34	67	164	3	0	0	0	4
	CeHL	Totals	56	18	26	44	103	—	—	—	—	—

Born; 2/24/69, Mount Hope, Ontario. 6-2, 200.

Jeff Christian — Left Wing

Season	Team	League	GP	G	A	PTS	PIM	GP	G	A	PTS	PIM
90-91	Utica	AHL	80	24	42	66	165	—	—	—	—	—
91-92	New Jersey	NHL	2	0	0	0	2	—	—	—	—	—
91-92	Utica	AHL	76	27	24	51	198	4	0	0	0	16
92-93	Utica	AHL	22	4	6	10	39	—	—	—	—	—
92-93	Hamilton	AHL	11	2	5	7	35	—	—	—	—	—
92-93	Cincinnati	IHL	36	5	12	17	113	—	—	—	—	—
93-94	Albany	AHL	76	34	43	77	227	5	1	2	3	19
94-95	Pittsburgh	NHL	1	0	0	0	0	—	—	—	—	—
94-95	Cleveland	IHL	56	13	24	37	126	2	0	1	1	8
95-96	Pittsburgh	NHL	3	0	0	0	2	—	—	—	—	—
95-96	Cleveland	IHL	66	23	32	55	131	3	0	1	1	8
96-97	Pittsburgh	NHL	11	2	2	4	13	—	—	—	—	—
96-97	Cleveland	IHL	69	40	40	80	262	12	6	8	14	44
	NHL	Totals	17	2	2	4	17	—	—	—	—	—
	AHL	Totals	265	91	120	211	664	9	1	2	3	35
	IHL	Totals	227	81	108	189	632	17	6	10	16	60

Born; 7/30/70, Burlington, Ontario. 6-2, 210. Drafted by New Jersey Devils (2nd choice, 23rd overall) in 1988 Entry Draft. Signed as a free agent by Pittsbugh Penguins (8/2/94). Suspended by IHL for 20 games (1997). Signed as a free agent by Phoenix Coyotes (8/97).

Tim Christian — Right Wing

Season	Team	League	GP	G	A	PTS	PIM	GP	G	A	PTS	PIM
95-96	Roanoke	ECHL	66	24	26	50	33	3	0	1	1	2
96-97	Roanoke	ECHL	68	25	28	53	35	2	1	0	1	0
	ECHL	Totals	134	49	54	103	68	5	1	1	2	2

Born; 5/11/71, 6-0, 180.

Jason Christie — Right Wing

Season	Team	League	GP	G	A	PTS	PIM	GP	G	A	PTS	PIM
91-92	Columbus	ECHL	61	28	56	84	218	—	—	—	—	—
92-93	Hamilton	AHL	11	3	2	5	8	—	—	—	—	—
92-93	Columbus	ECHL	63	20	41	61	190	—	—	—	—	—
93-94	Hamilton	AHL	28	6	9	15	36	—	—	—	—	—
93-94	Charlotte	ECHL	27	10	14	24	55	3	1	1	2	2
94-95	Portland	AHL	71	20	40	60	130	3	1	0	1	0
95-96	Portland	AHL	65	7	21	28	86	23	6	10	16	49
96-97	Manitoba	IHL	34	4	12	16	29	—	—	—	—	—
96-97	Portland	AHL	33	4	14	18	42	5	1	3	4	4
	AHL	Totals	208	40	86	126	302	31	8	13	21	53
	ECHL	Totals	151	58	111	169	463	3	1	1	2	2

Born; 4/25/69, Gibbons, Alberta. 5-8, 180.

Alexsander Chunchukov — Right Wing

			Regular Season					Playoffs				
Season	Team	League	GP	G	A	PTS	PIM	GP	G	A	PTS	PIM
94-95	Raleigh	ECHL	32	7	18	25	30	—	—	—	—	—
94-95	Nashville	ECHL	29	11	25	36	32	11	4	11	15	4
95-96	Nashville	ECHL	55	20	31	51	51	—	—	—	—	—
96-97	Johnstown	ECHL	70	34	58	92	75	—	—	—	—	—
	ECHL	Totals	186	72	132	204	188	11	4	11	15	4

Born; 4/3/71, Riga, Latvia. 6-1, 195.

Brad Church — Left Wing

			Regular Season					Playoffs				
Season	Team	League	GP	G	A	PTS	PIM	GP	G	A	PTS	PIM
96-97	Portland	AHL	50	4	8	12	92	1	0	0	0	0

Born; 11/14/76, Dauphin, Manitoba. 6-1, 210. Drafted by Washington Capitals (1st choice, 17th overall) in 1995 Entry Draft.

Dave Chyzowski — Left Wing

			Regular Season					Playoffs				
Season	Team	League	GP	G	A	PTS	PIM	GP	G	A	PTS	PIM
89-90	Islanders	NHL	34	8	6	14	45	—	—	—	—	—
89-90	Springfield	AHL	4	0	0	0	7	—	—	—	—	—
90-91	Islanders	NHL	56	5	9	14	61	—	—	—	—	—
90-91	Capital District	AHL	7	3	6	9	22	—	—	—	—	—
91-92	Islanders	NHL	12	1	1	2	17	—	—	—	—	—
91-92	Capital District	AHL	55	15	18	33	121	6	1	1	2	23
92-93	Capital District	AHL	66	15	21	36	177	3	2	0	2	0
93-94	Islanders	NHL	3	1	0	1	4	2	0	0	0	0
93-94	Salt Lake City	IHL	66	27	13	40	151	—	—	—	—	—
94-95	Islanders	NHL	13	0	0	0	11	—	—	—	—	—
94-95	Kalamazoo	IHL	4	0	4	4	8	16	9	5	14	27
95-96	Adirondack	AHL	80	44	39	83	160	3	0	0	0	6
96-97	Chicago	NHL	8	0	0	0	6	—	—	—	—	—
96-97	Indianapolis	IHL	76	34	40	74	261	4	0	2	2	38
	NHL	Totals	126	15	16	31	144	2	0	0	0	0
	AHL	Totals	212	77	84	161	487	12	3	1	4	29
	IHL	Totals	146	61	57	118	420	20	9	7	16	65

Born; 7/11/71, Edmonton, Alberta. 6-1, 193. Drafted by New York Islanders (1st choice, 2nd overall) 1989 Entry Draft. Signed as a free agent by Orlando Solar Bears (8/97).

Peter Ciavaglia — Center

			Regular Season					Playoffs				
Season	Team	League	GP	G	A	PTS	PIM	GP	G	A	PTS	PIM
91-92	Buffalo	NHL	2	0	0	0	0	—	—	—	—	—
91-92	Rochester	AHL	77	37	61	98	16	6	2	5	7	6
92-93	Buffalo	NHL	3	0	0	0	0	—	—	—	—	—
92-93	Rochester	AHL	64	35	67	102	32	17	9	16	25	12
93-94	United States	National										
94-95	Detroit	IHL	73	22	59	81	83	5	1	1	2	6
95-96	Detroit	IHL	75	22	56	78	38	12	6	11	17	12
96-97	Detroit	IHL	72	21	51	72	54	21	*14	19	*33	32
	NHL	Totals	5	0	0	0	0	—	—	—	—	—
	IHL	Totals	220	65	166	231	175	17	7	12	19	18
	AHL	Totals	141	72	128	200	48	23	11	21	32	18

Born; 7/15/69, Albany, New York. 5-10, 180. Drafted by Calgary Flames (8th choice, 145th overall) in 1987 Entry Draft. Signed as a free agent by Buffalo Sabres (8/30/91). 1996-97 IHL Playoff MVP. Member of 1996-97 IHL Champion Detroit Vipers.

Chris Cichocki — Right Wing

Regular Season / Playoffs

Season	Team	League	GP	G	A	PTS	PIM	GP	G	A	PTS	PIM
85-86	Detroit	NHL	59	10	11	21	21	—	—	—	—	—
85-86	Adirondack	AHL	9	4	4	8	6	—	—	—	—	—
86-87	Detroit	NHL	2	0	0	0	2	—	—	—	—	—
86-87	Adirondack	AHL	55	31	34	65	27	—	—	—	—	—
86-87	Maine	AHL	7	2	2	4	0	—	—	—	—	—
87-88	New Jersey	NHL	5	1	0	1	2	—	—	—	—	—
87-88	Utica	AHL	69	36	30	66	66	—	—	—	—	—
88-89	New Jersey	NHL	2	0	1	1	2	—	—	—	—	—
88-89	Utica	AHL	59	32	31	63	50	5	0	1	1	2
89-90	Utica	AHL	11	3	1	4	10	—	—	—	—	—
89-90	Binghamton	AHL	60	21	26	47	22	—	—	—	—	—
90-91	Binghamton	AHL	80	35	30	65	70	9	0	4	4	2
91-92	Binghamton	AHL	75	28	29	57	132	6	5	4	9	4
92-93	Binghamton	AHL	65	23	29	52	78	9	3	2	5	25
93-94	Cincinnati	IHL	69	22	20	42	101	11	2	2	4	12
94-95	Cincinnati	IHL	75	22	30	52	50	8	0	3	3	6
95-96	Cincinnati	IHL	57	4	7	11	30	14	0	1	1	10
96-97	Cincinnati	IHL	35	6	9	15	30	1	0	0	0	0
	NHL	Totals	68	11	12	23	27	—	—	—	—	—
	AHL	Totals	490	215	216	431	461	29	8	11	19	33
	IHL	Totals	236	54	66	120	231	34	2	6	8	28

Born; 9/17/63, Detroit, Michigan. 5-11, 185. Signed as a free agent by Detroit Red Wings (6/28/85). Traded to New Jersey Devils by Detroit with Detroit's third round choice (later traded to Buffalo Sabres-Buffalo selected Andrew MacVicar) in 1987 Entry Draft for Mel Bridgman (3/9/87). Traded to Hartford Whalers by New Jersey for Jim Thomson (10/31/89). Signed as a free agent by New York Rangers (9/6/90). Re-signed by Cincinnati Cyclones (8/96).

Jozef Cierny — Left Wing

Regular Season / Playoffs

Season	Team	League	GP	G	A	PTS	PIM	GP	G	A	PTS	PIM
92-93	Rochester	AHL	54	27	27	54	36	—	—	—	—	—
93-94	Edmonton	NHL	1	0	0	0	0	—	—	—	—	—
93-94	Cape Breton	AHL	73	30	27	57	88	4	1	1	2	4
94-95	Cape Breton	AHL	73	28	24	52	58	—	—	—	—	—
95-96	Detroit	IHL	20	2	5	7	16	—	—	—	—	—
95-96	Los Angeles	IHL	43	23	16	39	36	—	—	—	—	—
96-97	Long Beach	IHL	68	27	27	54	106	16	8	5	13	7
	AHL	Totals	200	85	78	163	182	4	1	1	2	4
	IHL	Totals	131	52	48	100	158	16	8	5	13	7

Born; 5/13/74, Zvolen, Slovakia. 6-2, 190. Drafted by Buffalo Sabres (2nd choice, 35th overall) in 1992 Entry Draft. Traded to Edmonton Oilers by Buffalo with Buffalo's fourth round choice (Jussi Tarvainen) in 1994 Entry Draft for Craig Simpson (9/1/93).

Jason Cipolla — Center

Regular Season / Playoffs

Season	Team	League	GP	G	A	PTS	PIM	GP	G	A	PTS	PIM
94-95	St. John's	AHL	4	0	0	0	0	—	—	—	—	—
95-96	St. John's	AHL	38	8	9	17	42	4	0	1	1	2
95-96	South Carolina	ECHL	39	21	32	53	73	—	—	—	—	—
96-97	St. John's	AHL	45	7	13	20	74	—	—	—	—	—
96-97	South Carolina	ECHL	9	7	4	11	20	18	11	13	24	20
	AHL	Totals	87	15	22	37	116	4	0	1	1	2
	ECHL	Totals	48	28	36	64	93	18	11	13	24	20

Born; 12/30/72, Toronto, Ontario. 5-9, 170. Member of 1996-97 ECHL Champion South Carolina Stingrays.

Mark Cipriano — Defenseman

			Regular Season					Playoffs				
Season	Team	League	GP	G	A	PTS	PIM	GP	G	A	PTS	PIM
91-92	Columbus	ECHL	48	17	14	31	333	—	—	—	—	—
92-93	Columbus	ECHL	18	4	4	8	64	—	—	—	—	—
92-93	Hamilton	AHL	24	6	3	9	49	—	—	—	—	—
93-94	Columbus	ECHL	22	2	11	13	136	—	—	—	—	—
95-96	Houston	IHL	4	1	0	1	2	—	—	—	—	—
95-96	Bakersfield	WCHL	7	5	1	6	2	—	—	—	—	—
96-97	Bakersfield	WCHL	33	7	14	21	151	4	3	0	3	19
	ECHL	Totals	88	23	29	52	533	—	—	—	—	—
	WCHL	Totals	40	12	15	27	153	4	3	0	3	19

Born; 6/1/71, Delta, British Columbia. 5-11, 195. Drafted by Vancouver Canucks (8th choice, 170th overall) in 1990 Entry Draft.

Aigars Cipruss — Center

			Regular Season					Playoffs				
Season	Team	League	GP	G	A	PTS	PIM	GP	G	A	PTS	PIM
94-95	Atlanta	IHL	11	3	7	10	2	—	—	—	—	—
94-95	Nashville	ECHL	57	25	32	57	96	12	5	10	15	20
95-96	Atlanta	IHL	2	0	2	2	0	—	—	—	—	—
95-96	Providence	AHL	15	3	3	6	6	—	—	—	—	—
95-96	Nashville	ECHL	49	26	50	76	57	—	—	—	—	—
96-97	Grand Rapids	IHL	1	0	1	1	0	—	—	—	—	—
96-97	Quebec	IHL	41	7	24	31	2	—	—	—	—	—
	Muskegon	CoHL	23	13	19	32	13	—	—	—	—	—
	IHL	Totals	55	10	34	44	4	—	—	—	—	—
	ECHL	Totals	106	51	82	133	153	12	5	10	15	20

Born; 1/12/72, Riga, Latvia. 5-10, 175.

Jason Cirone — Center

			Regular Season					Playoffs				
Season	Team	League	GP	G	A	PTS	PIM	GP	G	A	PTS	PIM
91-92	Winnipeg	NHL	3	0	0	0	2	—	—	—	—	—
91-92	Moncton	AHL	64	32	27	59	124	10	1	1	2	8
92-93	Italy											
93-94	Cincinnati	IHL	26	4	2	6	61	—	—	—	—	—
93-94	Birmingham	ECHL	11	3	3	6	45	10	8	8	16	*67
94-95	Cincinnati	IHL	74	22	15	37	170	9	1	1	2	14
95-96	Rochester	AHL	24	4	5	9	34	—	—	—	—	—
95-96	Los Angeles	IHL	26	8	10	18	47	—	—	—	—	—
95-96	San Diego	WCHL	3	2	1	3	20	—	—	—	—	—
96-97	Long Beach	IHL	11	4	3	7	14	—	—	—	—	—
96-97	Kansas City	IHL	70	18	38	56	88	3	0	3	3	2
	IHL	Totals	207	56	68	124	380	12	1	4	5	16
	AHL	Totals	88	36	32	68	158	10	1	1	2	8

Drafted by Winnipeg Jets (3rd choice, 46th overall) in 1989 Entry Draft. Traded to Florida Panthers by Winnipeg for Dave Tomlinson (8/3/93).

Derek Clancey — Center

			Regular Season					Playoffs				
Season	Team	League	GP	G	A	PTS	PIM	GP	G	A	PTS	PIM
91-92	Erie	ECHL	16	7	6	13	24	—	—	—	—	—
91-92	Toledo	ECHL	5	2	5	7	0	—	—	—	—	—
91-92	Winston-Salem	ECHL	9	4	3	7	2	—	—	—	—	—
92-93	Detroit	CoHL	11	4	13	17	6	1	0	0	0	2
93-94	Columbus	ECHL	45	16	42	58	34	6	1	5	6	4
94-95	Columbus	ECHL	63	21	66	87	20	3	3	2	5	6
95-96	Columbus	ECHL	67	32	77	109	40	3	0	2	2	0

Season	Team	League	GP	G	A	PTS	PIM	GP	G	A	PTS	PIM
96-97	Waco	WPHL	9	3	10	13	2	—	—	—	—	—
96-97	Columbus	ECHL	46	26	33	59	32	8	1	2	3	8
	ECHL	Totals	251	108	232	340	152	21	5	11	16	20

Born; 4/16/69, St. John's, Newfoundland. 5-10, 180.

Chris Clancy — Left Wing

Season	Team	League	GP	G	A	PTS	PIM	GP	G	A	PTS	PIM
96-97	Syracuse	AHL	3	0	1	1	0	2	0	0	0	0

Born; 11/28/72, Kitchener, Ontario. 6-3, 195. Drafted by Buffalo Sabres (12th choice, 251st overall) in 1992 Entry Draft.

Jason Clark — Center

Season	Team	League	GP	G	A	PTS	PIM	GP	G	A	PTS	PIM
96-97	Syracuse	AHL	11	3	3	6	2	—	—	—	—	—
96-97	Wheeling	ECHL	38	10	14	24	14	—	—	—	—	—
96-97	Jacksonville	ECHL	28	10	24	34	8	—	—	—	—	—
	ECHL	Totals	66	20	38	58	22	—	—	—	—	—

Born; 5/6/72, Belmont, Ontario. 6-1, 185. Drafted by Vancouver Canucks (8th choice, 141st overall) in 1992 Entry Draft.

Kerry Clark — Right Wing

Season	Team	League	GP	G	A	PTS	PIM	GP	G	A	PTS	PIM
88-89	Springfield	AHL	63	7	7	14	264	—	—	—	—	—
88-89	Indianapolis	IHL	3	0	1	1	12	—	—	—	—	—
89-90	Springfield	AHL	21	0	1	1	73	—	—	—	—	—
89-90	Phoenix	IHL	38	4	8	12	262	—	—	—	—	—
90-91	Salt Lake City	IHL	62	14	14	28	372	4	1	1	2	12
91-92	Salt Lake City	IHL	74	12	14	26	266	5	1	0	1	34
92-93	Salt Lake City	IHL	64	14	15	29	255	—	—	—	—	—
93-94	Portland	AHL	55	9	5	14	309	5	0	0	0	26
94-95	Portland	AHL	57	9	12	21	282	1	0	0	0	0
95-96	Orlando	IHL	64	3	6	9	228	8	1	0	1	17
96-97	Orlando	IHL	48	6	1	7	204	7	0	1	1	15
	IHL	Totals	353	53	59	112	1599	24	3	2	5	78
	AHL	Totals	196	25	25	50	928	6	0	0	0	26

Born; 8/21/68, Kelvington, Saskatchewan. 6-1, 205. Drafted by New York Islanders (12th choice, 206th overall) in 1986 Entry Draft. Signed as a free agent by Calgary Flames (7/23/90). Signed as a free agent by Washington Capitals (9/23/94). Member of 1993-94 AHL champion Portland Pirates.

Cosmo Clarke — Left Wing

Season	Team	League	GP	G	A	PTS	PIM	GP	G	A	PTS	PIM
94-95	Brantford	CoHL	5	0	0	0	2	—	—	—	—	—
95-96	Flint	CoHL	4	0	0	0	2	—	—	—	—	—
95-96	Huntsville	SHL	52	21	27	48	83	9	0	0	0	9
96-97	Dayton	CoHL	69	27	21	48	77	—	—	—	—	—
	CoHL	Totals	78	27	21	48	81	—	—	—	—	—

Born; 5/1/70, Kanata, Ontario. 6-3, 238. Member of 1995-96 SHL champion Huntsville Channel Cats.

Jason Clarke — Right Wing

Season	Team	League	GP	G	A	PTS	PIM	GP	G	A	PTS	PIM
93-94	Erie	ECHL	3	1	0	1	57	—	—	—	—	—
93-94	Charlotte	ECHL	11	2	2	4	100	—	—	—	—	—
93-94	Brantford	CoHL	24	8	13	21	264	1	0	0	0	0
94-95	Roanoke	ECHL	63	11	18	29	*467	8	1	4	5	64
95-96	Roanoke	ECHL	59	20	18	38	491	3	0	1	1	20

Season	Team	League	GP	G	A	PTS	PIM	GP	G	A	PTS	PIM
96-97	Brimingham	ECHL	8	1	2	3	90	—	—	—	—	—
96-97	Central Texas	WPHL	31	7	13	20	226	9	1	4	5	63
	ECHL	Totals	144	35	40	75	1205	11	1	5	6	84

Born; 2/28/73, Cobourg, Ontario. 6-1, 232.

Joe Clarke — Left Wing
Regular Season / **Playoffs**

Season	Team	League	GP	G	A	PTS	PIM	GP	G	A	PTS	PIM
96-97	Muskegon	CoHL	71	6	8	14	64	3	0	0	0	4

Born; 5/6/72, London, Ontario. 6-0, 200.

Taylor Clarke — Left Wing
Regular Season / **Playoffs**

Season	Team	League	GP	G	A	PTS	PIM	GP	G	A	PTS	PIM
96-97	Richmond	ECHL	22	6	11	17	13	—	—	—	—	—

Born; 2/7/73, Atlanta, Georgia. 6-2, 200.

Will Clarke — Goaltender
Regular Season / **Playoffs**

Season	Team	League	GP	W	L	T	MIN	SO	GAVG	GP	W	L	MIN	SO	AVG
95-96	Tallahassee	ECHL	1	0	1	0	59	0	4.04	—	—	—	—	—	—
95-96	Columbus	ECHL	16	7	5	1	810	0	3.48	1	0	1	27	0	6.65
96-97	Columbus	ECHL	3	0	2	0	108	0	3.89	—	—	—	—	—	—
96-97	Dayton	ECHL	21	7	13	1	1192	1	3.83	—	—	—	—	—	—
	ECHL	Totals	41	14	21	2	2169	1	3.71	1	0	1	27	0	6.65

Born; 2/9/72, Royal Oak, Michigan. 6-2, 188. Last amateur club; Bowling Green University (CCHA).

Patrick Clement — Defenseman
Regular Season / **Playoffs**

Season	Team	League	GP	G	A	PTS	PIM	GP	G	A	PTS	PIM
96-97	Jacksonville	ECHL	17	1	1	2	62	—	—	—	—	—
96-97	Memphis	CeHL	15	2	7	9	78	18	3	6	9	29

Born; 3/18/73, Lachine, Quebec. 6-2, 220.

Brian Clifford — Right Wing
Regular Season / **Playoffs**

Season	Team	League	GP	G	A	PTS	PIM	GP	G	A	PTS	PIM
96-97	Toledo	ECHL	21	6	9	15	10	—	—	—	—	—

Born; 6/18/73, Buffalo, New York. 6-0, 185. Drafted by Pittsburgh Penguins (6th choice, 126th overall) in 1991 Entry Draft.

Bob Clouston — Center
Regular Season / **Playoffs**

Season	Team	League	GP	G	A	PTS	PIM	GP	G	A	PTS	PIM
93-94	Huntington	ECHL	7	1	1	2	6	—	—	—	—	—
94-95	Flint	CoHL	33	3	9	12	29	—	—	—	—	—
94-95	Utica	CoHL	27	5	5	10	22	—	—	—	—	—
95-96	Quad City	CoHL	2	0	0	0	0	—	—	—	—	—
95-96	Huntsville	SHL	46	19	45	64	124	10	3	14	17	22
96-97	Dayton	CoHL	60	9	50	59	64	—	—	—	—	—
	CoHL	Totals	62	8	14	22	51	—	—	—	—	—

Born; 8/14/73, Detroit, Michigan. 5-8, 175. Member of 1995-96 SHL champion Huntsville Channel Cats.

Colin Cloutier — Center
Regular Season / **Playoffs**

Season	Team	League	GP	G	A	PTS	PIM	GP	G	A	PTS	PIM
96-97	Adirondack	AHL	52	5	15	20	127	2	0	0	0	0

Born; 1/27/76, Winnipeg, Manitoba. Drafted by Tampa Bay Lightning (2nd choice, 34th overall) in 1994 Entry Draft.

Dan Cloutier — Goaltender

			Regular Season							Playoffs					
Season	Team	League	GP	W	L	T	MIN	SO	GAVG	GP	W	L	MIN	SO	GAVG
96-97	Binghamton	AHL	60	23	*28	8	3367	3	3.55	4	1	3	236	0	3.31

Born; 4/22/76, Mont-Laurier, Quebec. 6-1, 182. Drafted by New York Rangers (1st choice, 26th overall) in 1994 Entry Draft. Member of 1996-97 AHL All-Rookie Team.

Eric Cloutier — Left Wing

			Regular Season					Playoffs				
Season	Team	League	GP	G	A	PTS	PIM	GP	G	A	PTS	PIM
95-96	Providence	AHL	6	0	0	0	31	—	—	—	—	—
95-96	Charlotte	ECHL	14	2	5	7	133	—	—	—	—	—
95-96	Louisiana	ECHL	15	5	3	8	104	4	0	2	2	8
96-97	Houston	IHL	3	0	0	0	6	—	—	—	—	—
96-97	Jacksonville	ECHL	47	13	11	24	334	—	—	—	—	—
	ECHL	Totals	76	20	19	39	571	4	0	2	2	8

Born; 3/7/75, Mont-Laurier, Quebec. 6-0, 185.

Sylvain Cloutier — Center

			Regular Season					Playoffs				
Season	Team	League	GP	G	A	PTS	PIM	GP	G	A	PTS	PIM
93-94	Adirondack	AHL	2	0	2	2	2	—	—	—	—	—
94-95	Adirondack	AHL	71	7	26	33	144	—	—	—	—	—
95-96	Adirondack	AHL	65	11	17	28	118	3	0	0	0	4
95-96	Toledo	ECHL	6	4	2	6	4	—	—	—	—	—
96-97	Adirondack	AHL	77	13	36	49	190	4	0	2	2	4
	AHL	Totals	215	31	81	112	454	7	0	2	2	8

Born; 2/13/74, Mont-Laurier, Quebec. 6-0, 195. Drafted by Detroit Red Wings (3rd choice, 70th overall) 1992 Entry Draft.

Barry Clukey — Center

			Regular Season					Playoffs				
Season	Team	League	GP	G	A	PTS	PIM	GP	G	A	PTS	PIM
95-96	Utica	CoHL	6	0	0	0	4	—	—	—	—	—
96-97	Jacksonville	ECHL	45	12	8	20	112	—	—	—	—	—

Born; 7/27/73, Waterville, Maine. 5-10, 190.

Brodie Coffin — Forward

			Regular Season					Playoffs				
Season	Team	League	GP	G	A	PTS	PIM	GP	G	A	PTS	PIM
96-97	Huntington	ECHL	63	12	13	25	147	—	—	—	—	—

Born; 4/9/74, Charlottetown, Prince Edward Island. 6-1, 195.

Tom Colasanto — Center

			Regular Season					Playoffs				
Season	Team	League	GP	G	A	PTS	PIM	GP	G	A	PTS	PIM
96-97	Utica	CoHL	23	4	3	7	35	—	—	—	—	—
96-97	Dayton	CoHL	29	3	6	9	31	—	—	—	—	—
	CoHL	Totals	52	7	9	16	66	—	—	—	—	—

Born; 4/9/73, Commack, New York. 5-7, 175.

Darren Colbourne — Right Wing

			Regular Season					Playoffs				
Season	Team	League	GP	G	A	PTS	PIM	GP	G	A	PTS	PIM
91-92	Kalamazoo	IHL	1	0	1	1	0	—	—	—	—	—
91-92	Dayton	ECHL	64	*69	50	119	70	3	1	0	1	14
92-93	Peoria	IHL	6	1	1	2	2	—	—	—	—	—
92-93	Dayton	ECHL	32	19	11	30	41	—	—	—	—	—

Season	Team	League	GP	G	A	PTS	PIM	GP	G	A	PTS	PIM
92-93	Richmond	ECHL	29	26	23	49	12	1	0	1	1	0
93-94	St. John's	AHL	1	0	0	0	0	—	—	—	—	—
93-94	Richmond	ECHL	68	69	35	104	100	—	—	—	—	—
95-96	Raleigh	ECHL	36	27	14	41	16	4	0	0	0	0
96-97	Raleigh	ECHL	69	53	48	101	32	—	—	—	—	—
	IHL	Totals	7	1	2	3	2	—	—	—	—	—
	ECHL	Totals	298	263	181	444	271	4	1	1	2	2

Born; 1/5/68, Corner Brook, Newfoundland. 6-0, 195. Drafted by Detroit Red Wings (10th choice, 227th overall) in 1988 Entry Draft. 1991-92 ECHL Rookie of the Year. 1991-92 ECHL First Team All-Star. 1993-94 ECHL Second Team All-Star.

Danton Cole — Right Wing

Season	Team	League	GP	G	A	PTS	PIM	GP	G	A	PTS	PIM
89-90	Winnipeg	NHL	2	1	1	2	0	—	—	—	—	—
89-90	Moncton	AHL	80	31	42	73	18	—	—	—	—	—
90-91	Winnipeg	NHL	66	13	11	24	24	—	—	—	—	—
90-91	Moncton	AHL	3	1	1	2	0	—	—	—	—	—
91-92	Winnipeg	NHL	52	7	5	12	32	—	—	—	—	—
92-93	Tampa Bay	NHL	67	12	15	27	23	—	—	—	—	—
92-93	Atlanta	IHL	1	1	0	1	2	—	—	—	—	—
93-94	Tampa Bay	NHL	81	20	23	43	32	—	—	—	—	—
94-95	Tampa Bay	NHL	26	3	3	6	6	—	—	—	—	—
94-95	New Jersey	NHL	12	1	2	3	8	1	0	0	0	0
95-96	Islanders	NHL	10	1	0	1	0	—	—	—	—	—
95-96	Chicago	NHL	2	0	0	0	0	—	—	—	—	—
95-96	Utah	IHL	34	28	15	43	22	—	—	—	—	—
95-96	Indianapolis	IHL	32	9	12	21	20	5	1	5	6	8
96-97	Grand Rapids	IHL	35	8	18	26	24	5	3	1	4	2
	NHL	Totals	318	58	60	118	125	1	0	0	0	0
	IHL	Totals	102	46	45	91	68	10	4	6	10	10
	AHL	Totals	83	32	43	75	18	—	—	—	—	—

Born; 1/10/67, Pontiac, Michigan. 5-11, 185. Drafted by Winnipeg Jets (6th choice, 123rd overall) in 1985 Entry Draft. Traded to Tampa Bay Lightning by Winnipeg for future considerations (6/19/92). Traded to New Jersey Devils by Tampa Bay with Shawn Chambers for Alexander Semak and Ben Hankinson (3/14/95).

Lee Cole — Defenseman

Season	Team	League	GP	G	A	PTS	PIM	GP	G	A	PTS	PIM
96-97	Toledo	ECHL	8	0	1	1	18	1	0	0	0	2

Born; 7/13/76, Timmons, Ontario. 6-2, 220.

Tom Cole — Goaltender

Season	Team	League	GP	W	L	T	MIN	SO	GAVG	GP	W	L	MIN	SO	GAVG
92-93	Nashville	ECHL	27	15	9	2	1401	0	4.41	1	0	0	20	0	0.00
93-94	Nashville	ECHL	29	11	14	0	1612	0	3.87	—	—	—	—	—	—
94-95	Worcester	AHL	1	0	0	0	28	0	4.23	—	—	—	—	—	—
94-95	Utica	CoHL	36	13	20	2	1993	0	4.34	6	2	4	362	1	2.66
95-96	Utica	CoHL	16	3	10	1	783	0	5.52	—	—	—	—	—	—
96-97	Utica	CoHL	16	4	7	2	757	0	4.83	1	0	0	0:06	0	0
	CoHL	Totals	68	20	47	5	3533	0	4.70	7	2	4	362	1	2.66
	ECHL	Totals	56	26	23	2	3013	0	4.12	1	0	0	20	0	0.00

Born; 2/8/69, Woburn, Massachusetts. 6-0, 183. Drafted by Edmonton Oilers (10th choice, 187th overall) in 1988 Entry Draft.

Bruce Coles — Right Wing

Season	Team	League	GP	G	A	PTS	PIM	GP	G	A	PTS	PIM
91-92	Winston-Salem	ECHL	16	2	6	8	37	—	—	—	—	—

Season	Team	League	GP	G	A	PTS	PIM	GP	G	A	PTS	PIM
91-92	Johnstown	ECHL	43	32	45	77	113	6	3	1	4	12
92-93	Canadian	National										
92-93	Johnstown	ECHL	28	28	26	54	61	5	1	3	4	29
93-94	Johnstown	ECHL	24	23	20	43	56	3	0	1	1	10
94-95	Hershey	AHL	51	16	25	41	73	6	1	5	6	14
94-95	Johnstown	ECHL	29	20	25	45	56	—	—	—	—	—
95-96	Hershey	AHL	68	23	29	52	75	5	2	2	4	6
96-97	Philadelphia	AHL	79	31	49	80	152	10	2	5	7	28
	AHL	Totals	198	70	103	173	300	21	5	12	17	48
	ECHL	Totals	140	105	122	227	323	14	4.	5	9	51

Born; 12/6/68, Montreal, Quebec. 5-9, 185. Drafted by Montreal Canadiens (1st choice, 23rd overall) in 1990 Supplemental Draft. Signed as a free agent by Philadelphia Flyers (5/31/95).

Clint Collins — Right Wing

Season	Team	League	GP	G	A	PTS	PIM	GP	G	A	PTS	PIM
95-96	Fort Worth	CeHL	2	1	0	1	39	—	—	—	—	—
95-96	Tulsa	CeHL	2	1	0	1	4	—	—	—	—	—
96-97	New Mexico	WPHL	7	1	1	2	82	—	—	—	—	—
96-97	Wichita	CeHL	4	0	0	0	57	—	—	—	—	—
96-97	Columbus	CeHL	5	1	2	3	63	3	1	0	1	14
	CeHL	Totals	13	3	2	5	163	3	1	0	1	14

Born; 8/5/74, Vancouver, British Columbia. 6-0, 192.

Jason Collins — Center

Season	Team	League	GP	G	A	PTS	PIM	GP	G	A	PTS	PIM
96-97	Central Texas	WPHL	55	14	23	37	36	10	3	3	6	2

Born; 6/7/74, Devon, Alberta. 5-11, 175.

Brendan Concannon — Forward

Season	Team	League	GP	G	A	PTS	PIM	GP	G	A	PTS	PIM
96-97	Pensacola	ECHL	68	15	31	46	41	12	3	4	7	9

Born; 9/8/72, Boston, Massachusetts. 5-10, 185. Last amateur team; Lowell (Hockey East).

Rob Concannon — Left Wing

Season	Team	League	GP	G	A	PTS	PIM	GP	G	A	PTS	PIM
95-96	St. John's	AHL	20	1	2	3	4	—	—	—	—	—
95-96	South Carolina	ECHL	45	18	28	46	28	4	0	3	3	10
96-97	South Carolina	ECHL	69	24	46	70	163	18	3	5	8	39
	ECHL	Totals	114	42	74	116	191	22	3	8	11	49

Born; 12/2/70, Dorchester, Massachusetts. 6-0, 175. Member of 1996-97 ECHL Champion South Carolina Stingrays.

Craig Conley — Right Wing

Season	Team	League	GP	G	A	PTS	PIM	GP	G	A	PTS	PIM
95-96	Detroit	CoHL	20	7	13	20	12	—	—	—	—	—
95-96	Lakeland	SHL	7	4	7	11	2	—	—	—	—	—
95-96	Winston-Salem	SHL	15	3	7	10	2	9	2	5	7	8
96-97	Saginaw	CoHL	16	4	13	17	14	—	—	—	—	—
96-97	Dayton	CoHL	28	6	12	18	18	—	—	—	—	—
96-97	Flint	CoHL	15	0	4	4	8	—	—	—	—	—
	CoHL	Totals	79	17	42	59	52	—	—	—	—	—
	SHL	Totals	22	7	14	21	4	9	2	5	7	8

Born; 10/25/70, St. Clair Shores, Michigan. 5-11, 170.

Rob Conn — Right Wing

			Regular Season					Playoffs				
Season	Team	League	GP	G	A	PTS	PIM	GP	G	A	PTS	PIM
91-92	Chicago	NHL	2	0	0	0	2	—	—	—	—	—
91-92	Indianapolis	IHL	72	19	16	35	100	—	—	—	—	—
92-93	Indianapolis	IHL	75	13	14	27	81	5	0	1	1	6
93-94	Indianapolis	IHL	51	16	11	27	46	—	—	—	—	—
94-95	Indianapolis	IHL	10	4	4	8	11	—	—	—	—	—
94-95	Albany	AHL	68	35	32	67	76	14	4	6	10	16
95-96	Buffalo	NHL	28	2	5	7	18	—	—	—	—	—
95-96	Rochester	AHL	36	22	15	37	40	19	7	6	13	10
96-97	Indianapolis	IHL	72	25	32	57	81	4	0	0	0	8
	NHL	Totals	30	2	5	7	20	—	—	—	—	—
	IHL	Totals	280	77	77	154	319	9	0	1	1	14
	AHL	Totals	104	57	47	104	116	33	11	12	23	26

Born; 9/3/68, Calgary, Alberta. 6-2, 200. Signed as a free agent by Chicago Blackhawks (7/31/91). Traded to New Jersey Devils by Chicago for Dean Malkoc (1/30/95). Member of 1994-95 AHL champion Albany RiverRats. Member of 1995-96 AHL champion Rochester Americans.

Al Conroy — Center

			Regular Season					Playoffs				
Season	Team	League	GP	G	A	PTS	PIM	GP	G	A	PTS	PIM
86-87	Switzerland											
86-87	Rochester	AHL	13	4	4	8	40	13	1	3	4	50
87-88	Italy											
87-88	Adirondack	AHL	13	5	8	13	20	11	1	3	4	41
88-89	West Germany											
89-90	Adirondack	AHL	77	23	33	56	147	5	0	0	0	20
90-91	Adirondack	AHL	80	26	39	65	172	2	1	1	2	0
91-92	Philadelphia	NHL	31	2	9	11	74	—	—	—	—	—
91-92	Hershey	AHL	47	17	28	45	90	6	4	2	6	12
92-93	Philadelphia	NHL	21	3	2	5	17	—	—	—	—	—
92-93	Hershey	AHL	60	28	32	60	130	—	—	—	—	—
93-94	Philadelphia	NHL	62	4	3	7	65	—	—	—	—	—
94-95	Detroit	IHL	71	18	40	58	151	—	—	—	—	—
94-95	Houston	IHL	9	3	4	7	17	4	1	2	3	8
95-96	Houston	IHL	82	24	38	62	134	—	—	—	—	—
96-97	Houston	IHL	70	15	32	47	171	13	4	10	14	26
	NHL	Totals	114	9	14	23	156	—	—	—	—	—
	AHL	Totals	290	103	144	247	599	37	7	9	16	123
	IHL	Totals	232	60	114	174	473	17	5	12	17	34

Born; 1/17/66, Calgary, Alberta. 5-8, 170. Signed as a free agent by Detroit Red Wings (8/16/89). Signed as a free agent by Philadelphia Flyers (8/21/91). Member of 1986-87 AHL champion Rochester Americans.

Trevor Converse — Right Wing

			Regular Season					Playoffs				
Season	Team	League	GP	G	A	PTS	PIM	GP	G	A	PTS	PIM
91-92	Thunder Bay	CoHL	22	8	12	20	84	13	4	7	11	18
91-92	Richmond	ECHL	13	4	7	11	75	—	—	—	—	—
92-93	Thunder Bay	CoHL	7	0	5	5	23	—	—	—	—	—
92-93	Richmond	ECHL	2	0	0	0	4	—	—	—	—	—
95-96	Fort Worth	CeHL	62	14	21	35	195	—	—	—	—	—
96-97	Baltimore	AHL	2	0	1	1	12	—	—	—	—	—
96-97	Hershey	AHL	2	0	0	0	5	—	—	—	—	—
96-97	Johnstown	ECHL	42	6	8	14	160	—	—	—	—	—
96-97	Mobile	ECHL	10	2	2	4	53	3	2	1	3	2
	ECHL	Totals	67	12	17	29	292	3	2	1	3	2
	CoHL	Totals	29	8	17	25	107	13	4	7	11	18

Born; 2/4/70, North Battleford, Saskatchewan. 6-1, 210. Member of 1991-92 CoHL champion Thunder Bay Senators. Did not play professional hockey in North America between the 1993-94 and 1994-95 seasons.

Brandon Convery — Center

Season	Team	League	GP	G	A	PTS	PIM	GP	G	A	PTS	PIM
92-93	St. John's	AHL	3	0	0	0	0	5	0	1	1	0
93-94	St. John's	AHL	—	—	—	—	—	1	0	0	0	0
94-95	St. John's	AHL	76	34	37	71	43	5	2	2	4	4
95-96	Toronto	NHL	11	5	2	7	4	5	0	0	0	2
95-96	St. John's	AHL	57	22	23	45	28	—	—	—	—	—
96-97	Toronto	NHL	39	2	8	10	20	—	—	—	—	—
96-97	St. John's	AHL	25	14	14	28	15	—	—	—	—	—
	NHL	Totals	50	7	10	17	24	5	0	0	0	2
	AHL	Totals	161	70	74	144	86	11	2	3	5	4

Born; 2/4/74, Kingston, Ontario. 6-0, 180. Drafted by Toronto Maple Leafs (1st choice, 8th overall) in 1992 Entry Draft.

Brad Cook — Defenseman

Season	Team	League	GP	G	A	PTS	PIM	GP	G	A	PTS	PIM
96-97	Dayton	CoHL	61	4	19	23	53	—	—	—	—	—

2/26/75, Southgate, Michigan. 5-10, 195.

Jamie Cooke — Right Wing

Season	Team	League	GP	G	A	PTS	PIM	GP	G	A	PTS	PIM
91-92	Hershey	AHL	66	15	26	41	49	—	—	—	—	—
92-93	Hershey	AHL	36	11	7	18	12	—	—	—	—	—
93-94	Birmingham	ECHL	52	24	23	47	55	10	1	4	5	8
94-95	Memphis	CeHL	35	23	22	45	11	—	—	—	—	—
95-96	Memphis	CeHL	63	28	43	71	37	6	3	2	5	11
96-97	Memphis	CeHL	59	25	31	56	57	18	8	13	21	22
	AHL	Totals	102	26	33	59	61	—	—	—	—	—
	CeHL	Totals	157	76	96	172	155	24	11	15	26	33

Born; 5/11/68, Toronto, Ontario. 6-1, 200. Drafted by Philadelphia Flyers (8th choice, 140th overall) in 1988 Entry Draft. Signed as a player/assistant coach with the Idaho Steelheads for 1997-98 season.

Joe Coombs — Forward

Season	Team	League	GP	G	A	PTS	PIM	GP	G	A	PTS	PIM
96-97	Columbus	ECHL	66	28	31	59	127	8	3	4	7	10

Last amateur club; Belleville (OHL).

David Cooper — Defenseman

Season	Team	League	GP	G	A	PTS	PIM	GP	G	A	PTS	PIM
92-93	Rochester	AHL	—	—	—	—	—	2	0	0	0	2
93-94	Rochester	AHL	68	10	25	35	82	4	1	1	2	2
94-95	Rochester	AHL	21	2	4	6	48	—	—	—	—	—
94-95	South Carolina	ECHL	39	9	19	28	90	9	3	8	11	24
95-96	Rochester	AHL	67	9	18	27	79	8	0	1	1	12
96-97	Toronto	NHL	19	3	3	6	16	—	—	—	—	—
96-97	St. John's	AHL	44	16	19	35	65	—	—	—	—	—
	AHL	Totals	200	37	66	103	274	14	1	2	3	16

Born; 11/2/73, Williamsville, New York. 6-2, 204. Drafted by Buffalo Sabres (1st choice, 11th overall) in 1992 Entry Draft. Member of 1995-96 AHL champion Rochester Americans.

Brian Corcoran — Defenseman

Season	Team	League	GP	G	A	PTS	PIM	GP	G	A	PTS	PIM
95-96	Baltimore	AHL	18	0	2	2	24	6	0	0	0	4
95-96	Raleigh	ECHL	56	3	13	16	165	—	—	—	—	—
96-97	Baltimore	AHL	41	2	5	7	114	3	0	1	1	4
	AHL	Totals	59	2	7	9	138	9	0	1	1	8

Born; 4/23/72, Baldwinsville, New York. 6-2, 215. Signed as a free agent by Anaheim Mighty Ducks (3/29/95).

Mario Cormier — Defenseman

Season	Team	League	GP	G	A	PTS	PIM	GP	G	A	PTS	PIM
96-97	South Carolina	ECHL	4	0	0	0	4	2	0	1	1	2

Member of 1996-97 ECHL Champion South Carolina Stingrays.

Mark Cornforth — Defenseman

Season	Team	League	GP	G	A	PTS	PIM	GP	G	A	PTS	PIM
94-95	Syracuse	AHL	2	0	1	1	2	—	—	—	—	—
95-96	Boston	NHL	6	0	0	0	4	—	—	—	—	—
95-96	Providence	AHL	65	5	10	15	117	4	0	0	0	4
96-97	Providence	AHL	61	8	12	20	47	—	—	—	—	—
96-97	Cleveland	IHL	13	1	4	5	25	14	1	3	4	29
	AHL	Totals	128	13	23	36	166	4	0	0	0	4

Born; 11/13/72, Montreal, Quebec. 6-1, 193. Signed as a free agent by Boston Bruins (10/6/95).

Keli Corpse — Center

Season	Team	League	GP	G	A	PTS	PIM	GP	G	A	PTS	PIM
95-96	Fredericton	AHL	5	0	1	1	0	—	—	—	—	—
95-96	Wheeling	ECHL	63	32	62	94	40	6	0	4	4	4
96-97	Baltimore	AHL	2	0	1	1	2	—	—	—	—	—
96-97	Grand Rapids	IHL	19	3	4	7	2	—	—	—	—	—
96-97	Fort Wayne	IHL	33	4	15	19	26	—	—	—	—	—
96-97	Wheeling	ECHL	24	12	17	29	10	—	—	—	—	—
	IHL	Totals	52	7	19	26	28	—	—	—	—	—
	AHL	Totals	7	0	2	2	2	—	—	—	—	—
	ECHL	Totals	87	44	79	123	50	6	0	4	4	4

Born; 5/14/74, London, Ontario. 5-11, 175. Drafted by Montreal Canadiens (3rd choice, 44th overall) in 1992 Entry Draft. 1995-96 ECHL Rookie of the Year. 1995-96 ECHL Second Team All-Star.

Yvon Corriveau — Left Wing

Season	Team	League	GP	G	A	PTS	PIM	GP	G	A	PTS	PIM
85-86	Washington	NHL	2	0	0	0	0	4	0	3	3	2
86-87	Washington	NHL	17	1	1	2	24	—	—	—	—	—
86-87	Binghamton	AHL	7	0	0	0	2	8	0	1	1	0
87-88	Washington	NHL	44	10	9	19	84	13	1	2	3	30
87-88	Binghamton	AHL	35	15	14	29	64	—	—	—	—	—
88-89	Washington	NHL	33	3	2	5	62	1	0	0	0	0
88-89	Baltimore	AHL	33	16	23	39	65	—	—	—	—	—
89-90	Washington	NHL	50	9	6	15	50	—	—	—	—	—
89-90	Hartford	NHL	13	4	1	5	22	4	1	0	1	0
90-91	Hartford	NHL	23	1	1	2	18	—	—	—	—	—
90-91	Springfield	AHL	44	17	25	42	10	18	*10	6	16	31
91-92	Hartford	NHL	38	12	8	20	36	7	3	2	5	18
91-92	Springfield	AHL	39	26	15	41	40	—	—	—	—	—

Season	Team	League	GP	G	A	PTS	PIM	GP	G	A	PTS	PIM
92-93	San Jose	NHL	20	3	7	10	0	—	—	—	—	—
92-93	Hartford	NHL	37	5	5	10	14	—	—	—	—	—
93-94	Hartford	NHL	3	0	0	0	0	—	—	—	—	—
93-94	Springfield	AHL	71	42	39	81	53	6	7	3	10	20
94-95	Minnesota	IHL	62	18	24	42	26	3	1	1	2	0
95-96	Minnesota	IHL	60	21	22	43	40	—	—	—	—	—
95-96	Detroit	IHL	14	5	6	11	12	4	0	1	1	6
96-97	Detroit	IHL	52	9	9	18	85	21	2	1	3	34
	NHL	Totals	280	48	40	88	310	29	5	7	12	50
	AHL	Totals	229	116	116	232	234	32	17	10	27	51
	IHL	Totals	188	53	61	114	163	28	3	3	6	40

Born; 2/8/67, Welland, Ontario. 6-1, 195. Drafted by Washington Capitals (1st choice, 19th overall) in 1985 Entry Draft. Traded to Hartford Whalers by Washington for Mike Liut (3/6/90). Traded to Washington by Hartford to complete (6/15/92) deal in which Mark Hunter and future considerations were traded to Washington for Nick Kypreos (8/20/92). Claimed by San Jose Sharks from Washington in NHL Waiver Draft (10/4/92). Traded to Hartford by San Jose to complete (10/9/92) trade in which Michel Picard was traded to San Jose for future considerations (1/21/93). Member of 1990-91 AHL champion Springfield Indians. Member of 1996-97 IHL Champion Detroit Vipers.

Bryan Cossette — Defenseman

Season	Team	League	GP	G	A	PTS	PIM	GP	G	A	PTS	PIM
96-97	Roanoke	ECHL	3	0	1	1	2	2	0	0	0	0

Born; Estevan, Saskatchewan. 6-0, 200.

Mark Costea — Defenseman

Season	Team	League	GP	G	A	PTS	PIM	GP	G	A	PTS	PIM
96-97	Fresno	WCHL	1	0	0	0	0	—	—	—	—	—
96-97	Alaska	WCHL	30	3	16	19	34	—	—	—	—	—
	WCHL	Totals	31	3	16	19	34	—	—	—	—	—

Born;

Alain Cote — Defenseman

Season	Team	League	GP	G	A	PTS	PIM	GP	G	A	PTS	PIM
85-86	Moncton	AHL	3	0	0	0	0	—	—	—	—	—
85-86	Boston	NHL	32	0	6	6	14	—	—	—	—	—
86-87	Boston	NHL	3	0	0	0	0	—	—	—	—	—
87-88	Boston	NHL	2	0	0	0	0	—	—	—	—	—
87-88	Maine	AHL	69	9	34	43	108	9	2	4	6	19
88-89	Boston	NHL	31	2	3	5	51	—	—	—	—	—
88-89	Maine	AHL	37	5	16	21	111	—	—	—	—	—
89-90	Washington	NHL	2	0	0	0	7	—	—	—	—	—
89-90	Baltimore	AHL	57	5	19	24	161	3	0	0	0	9
90-91	Montreal	NHL	28	0	6	6	26	11	0	2	2	26
90-91	Fredericton	AHL	49	8	19	27	110	—	—	—	—	—
91-92	Montreal	NHL	13	0	3	3	22	—	—	—	—	—
91-92	Fredericton	AHL	20	1	10	11	24	7	0	1	1	4
92-93	Tampa Bay	NHL	2	0	0	0	0	—	—	—	—	—
92-93	Fredericton	AHL	61	10	17	27	83	—	—	—	—	—
92-93	Atlanta	IHL	8	1	0	1	0	1	0	0	0	0
93-94	Quebec	NHL	6	0	0	0	4	—	—	—	—	—
93-94	Cornwall	AHL	67	10	34	44	80	11	0	2	2	11
94-95	N/A											
95-96	San Francisco	IHL	80	5	26	31	133	4	0	0	0	10
96-97	Quebec	IHL	76	8	17	25	102	9	0	2	2	30
	NHL	Totals	119	2	18	20	124	11	0	2	2	26
	AHL	Totals	363	48	149	197	677	30	2	7	9	60
	IHL	Totals	164	14	43	57	235	14	0	2	2	40

Born; 4/14/67. Montmagny, Quebec. 6-0, 200. Drafted by Boston Bruins (1st choice, 31st overall) in 1985 Entry Draft. Traded to Washington Capitals by Boston for Bobby Gould (9/27/89). Traded to Montreal Canadiens by Washington for Marc Deschamps (6/23/90). Traded to Tampa Bay Lightning by Montreal with Eric Charron and future considerations for Rob Ramage (3/20/93) Canadiens sent Donald Dufresene to Tampa Bay to complete deal (6/18/93). Signed as a freee agent by Quebec Nordiques (7/3/93).

Alain Cote — Left Wing

Season	Team	League	GP	G	A	PTS	PIM	GP	G	A	PTS	PIM
			Regular Season					Playoffs				
94-95	Thunder Bay	CoHL	74	13	11	24	20	11	1	4	5	4
95-96	Winston-Salem	SHL	60	19	25	44	35	9	0	2	2	0
96-97	Macon	CeHL	65	23	33	56	76	5	2	1	3	2

Born; 8/13/73, Beauport, Quebec. 5-11, 200. Member of 1994-95 Colonial League champion Thunder Bay Senators.

Patrick Cote — Left Wing

Season	Team	League	GP	G	A	PTS	PIM	GP	G	A	PTS	PIM
			Regular Season					Playoffs				
95-96	Dallas	NHL	2	0	0	0	5	—	—	—	—	—
95-96	Michigan	IHL	57	4	6	10	239	3	0	0	0	2
96-97	Dallas	NHL	3	0	0	0	27	—	—	—	—	—
96-97	Michigan	IHL	58	14	10	24	237	4	2	0	2	6
	NHL	Totals	5	0	0	0	32	—	—	—	—	—
	IHL	Totals	115	18	16	34	476	7	2	0	2	8

Born; 1/24/75, Lasalle, Quebec. 6-3, 199. Drafted by Dallas Stars (2nd choice, 37th overall) in 1995 Entry Draft.

Ed Courtenay — Right Wing

Season	Team	League	GP	G	A	PTS	PIM	GP	G	A	PTS	PIM
			Regular Season					Playoffs				
88-89	Kalamazoo	IHL	1	0	0	0	0	1	0	0	0	2
89-90	Kalamazoo	IHL	57	25	28	53	16	3	0	0	0	0
90-91	Kalamazoo	IHL	76	35	36	71	37	8	2	3	5	12
91-92	San Jose	NHL	5	0	0	0	0	—	—	—	—	—
91-92	Kansas City	IHL	36	14	12	26	46	15	8	9	17	15
92-93	San Jose	NHL	39	7	13	20	10	—	—	—	—	—
92-93	Kansas City	IHL	32	15	11	26	25	—	—	—	—	—
93-94	Kansas City	IHL	62	27	21	48	60	—	—	—	—	—
94-95	Chicago	IHL	47	14	16	30	20	—	—	—	—	—
94-95	Peoria	IHL	9	5	0	5	4	9	5	3	8	2
95-96	San Fransisco	IHL	20	6	3	9	8	—	—	—	—	—
95-96	Jacksonville	ECHL	3	0	2	2	4	18	5	12	17	23
95-96	Reno	WCHL	7	3	7	10	8	—	—	—	—	—
96-97	South Carolina	ECHL	68	54	56	*110	70	—	—	—	—	—
	NHL	Totals	44	7	13	20	10	—	—	—	—	—
	IHL	Totals	340	141	127	268	216	36	15	15	30	31
	ECHL	Totals	71	54	58	112	74	18	5	12	17	23

Born; 2/2/68, Verdun, Quebec. 6-4, 200. Signed as a free agent by Minnesota North Stars (10/1/89). Selected by San Jose Sharks in NHL dispersal draft (5/30/91). 1996-97 ECHL First Team All-Star. Missed playoffs (1997) after being suspended by ECHL for 25 games due to a high-sticking incident.

Jason Courtemanche — Defenseman

Season	Team	League	GP	G	A	PTS	PIM	GP	G	A	PTS	PIM
			Regular Season					Playoffs				
93-94	Nashville	ECHL	46	6	6	12	140	2	0	0	0	10
94-95	Nashville	ECHL	45	1	8	9	223	—	—	—	—	—
95-96	Johnstown	ECHL	60	5	15	20	363	—	—	—	—	—
95-96	San Diego	WCHL	5	0	1	1	2	9	0	1	1	13
96-97	Houston	IHL	1	0	0	0	5	—	—	—	—	—
96-97	Utah	IHL	2	0	0	0	0	—	—	—	—	—

Season	Team	League	GP	G	A	PTS	PIM	GP	G	A	PTS	PIM
96-97	Long Beach	IHL	12	0	0	0	25	2	0	0	0	5
96-97	San Diego	WCHL	45	13	16	29	285	6	1	2	3	50
	IHL	Totals	15	0	0	0	30	2	0	0	0	5
	ECHL	Totals	151	12	29	41	726	2	0	0	0	10
	WCHL	Totals	50	13	17	30	287	15	1	3	4	63

Born; 7/31/70, Hartford, Connecticut. 6-1, 215. Member of 1995-96 WCHL champion San Diego Gulls. Member of 1996-97 WCHL Champion San Diego Gulls.

Larry Courville — Left Wing

			Regular Season					Playoffs				
Season	Team	League	GP	G	A	PTS	PIM	GP	G	A	PTS	PIM
93-94	Moncton	AHL	8	2	0	2	37	—	—	—	—	—
95-96	Vancouver	NHL	3	1	0	1	0	—	—	—	—	—
95-96	Syracuse	AHL	71	17	32	49	127	14	5	3	8	10
96-97	Vancouver	NHL	19	0	2	2	11	—	—	—	—	—
96-97	Syracuse	AHL	54	20	24	44	103	3	0	1	1	20
	NHL	Totals	22	1	2	3	11	—	—	—	—	—
	AHL	Totals	133	39	56	95	267	17	5	4	9	30

Born; 4/2/74, Timmins, Ontario. 6-1, 180. Drafted by Winnipeg Jets (6th choice, 119th overall) in 1993 Entry Draft. Re-entered Entry Draft, selected by Vancouver Canucks (2nd choice, 61st overall) in 1995 Entry Draft.

Marcel Cousineau — Goaltender

			Regular Season							Playoffs					
Season	Team	League	GP	W	L	T	MIN	SO	GAVG	GP	W	L	MIN	SO	GAVG
93-94	St. John's	AHL	37	13	11	9	2015	0	3.51	—	—	—	—	—	—
94-95	St. John's	AHL	58	22	27	6	3342	4	3.07	3	0	3	179	0	3.01
95-96	St. John's	AHL	62	21	26	13	3629	1	3.17	4	1	3	257	0	2.56
96-97	Toronto	NHL	13	3	5	1	566	1	3.29	—	—	—	—	—	—
96-97	St. John's	AHL	19	7	8	3	1053	0	3.30	11	6	5	658	0	2.55
	AHL	Totals	176	63	72	31	10039	5	3.22	18	7	11	1094	0	2.63

Born; 4/30/73, Delson, Quebec. 5-9, 180. Drafted by Boston Bruins (3rd choice, 62nd overall) in 1991 Entry Draft. Signed as a free agent by Toronto Maple Leafs (11/13/93). Shared a shutout with Felix Potvin (12/3/96) versus St. Louis.

Sylvain Couturier — Center

			Regular Season					Playoffs				
Season	Team	League	GP	G	A	PTS	PIM	GP	G	A	PTS	PIM
88-89	Los Angeles	NHL	16	1	3	4	2	—	—	—	—	—
88-89	New Haven	AHL	44	18	20	38	33	10	2	2	4	11
89-90	New Haven	AHL	50	9	8	17	47	—	—	—	—	—
90-91	Los Angeles	NHL	3	0	1	1	0	—	—	—	—	—
90-91	Phoenix	IHL	66	50	37	87	49	10	8	2	10	10
91-92	Los Angeles	NHL	14	3	1	4	2	—	—	—	—	—
91-92	Phoenix	IHL	39	19	20	39	68	—	—	—	—	—
92-93	Phoenix	IHL	38	23	16	39	63	—	—	—	—	—
92-93	Fort Wayne	IHL	—	—	—	—	—	4	2	3	5	2
92-93	Adirondack	AHL	29	17	17	34	12	11	3	5	8	10
93-94	Milwaukee	IHL	80	41	51	92	123	4	1	2	3	2
94-95	Milwaukee	IHL	77	31	41	72	77	15	1	4	5	10
95-96	Milwaukee	IHL	82	33	52	85	60	5	1	0	1	2
96-97	Milwaukee	IHL	79	26	24	50	42	3	0	1	1	2
	NHL	Totals	33	4	5	9	4	—	—	—	—	—
	IHL	Totals	461	223	241	464	482	36	12	12	24	26
	AHL	Totals	123	44	45	89	92	21	5	7	12	21

Born; 4/23/68, Greenfield Park, Quebec. 6-2, 205. Drafted by Los Angeles Kings (3rd choice, 65th overall) in 1986 Entry Draft. Traded to Detroit Red Wings by Los Angeles with Paul Coffey and Jim Hiller for Jimmy Carson, Marc Potvin and Gary Shuchuk. Member of 1992-93 IHL champion Fort Wayne Komets.

Mike Couvrette — Center

			Regular Season					Playoffs				
Season	Team	League	GP	G	A	PTS	PIM	GP	G	A	PTS	PIM
89-90	Virginia	ECHL	11	12	11	23	10	—	—	—	—	—
93-94	Detroit	CoHL	6	1	1	2	0	—	—	—	—	—
93-94	Utica	CoHL	1	0	0	0	0	—	—	—	—	—
93-94	Jacksonville	SUN	11	5	6	11	4	—	—	—	—	—
94-95	Tulsa	CeHL	40	22	19	41	27	—	—	—	—	—
94-95	Memphis	CeHL	3	0	1	1	0	—	—	—	—	—
94-95	Oklahoma City	CeHL	10	1	3	4	4	5	3	1	4	14
95-96	San Diego	WCHL	52	22	36	58	73	9	1	1	2	8
96-97	San Antonio	CeHL	7	4	1	5	6	—	—	—	—	—
96-97	San Diego	WCHL	7	2	4	6	6	—	—	—	—	—
96-97	Bakersfield	WCHL	11	8	8	16	10	—	—	—	—	—
	WCHL	Totals	70	32	48	80	89	9	1	1	2	8
	CeHL	Totals	60	27	24	51	37	5	3	1	4	14
	CoHL	Totals	7	1	1	2	0	—	—	—	—	—

Born; 11/11/65, Verdun, France. 5-10, 193. Did not play professional hockey in North America between the 1989-90 season and the 1993-94 season. Member of 1995-96 WCHL champion San Diego Gulls.

Jeff Cowan — Left Wing

			Regular Season					Playoffs				
Season	Team	League	GP	G	A	PTS	PIM	GP	G	A	PTS	PIM
96-97	Saint John	AHL	22	5	5	10	8	—	—	—	—	—
96-97	Roanoke	ECHL	47	21	13	34	42	—	—	—	—	—

Born; 9/27/76, Scarborough, Ontario. 6-2, 185. Last amateur club; Barrie (OHL).

Craig Coxe — Right Wing

			Regular Season					Playoffs				
Season	Team	League	GP	G	A	PTS	PIM	GP	G	A	PTS	PIM
84-85	Vancouver	NHL	9	0	0	0	49	—	—	—	—	—
84-85	Fredericton	AHL	62	8	7	15	242	4	2	1	3	16
85-86	Vancouver	NHL	57	3	5	8	176	3	0	0	0	2
86-87	Vancouver	NHL	15	1	0	1	31	—	—	—	—	—
86-87	Fredericton	AHL	46	1	12	13	168	—	—	—	—	—
87-88	Vancouver	NHL	64	5	12	17	186	—	—	—	—	—
87-88	Calgary	NHL	7	2	3	5	32	2	1	0	1	16
88-89	St. Louis	NHL	41	0	7	7	127	—	—	—	—	—
88-89	Peoria	IHL	8	2	7	9	38	—	—	—	—	—
89-90	Vancouver	NHL	25	1	4	5	66	—	—	—	—	—
89-90	Milwaukee	IHL	5	0	5	5	4	—	—	—	—	—
90-91	Vancouver	NHL	7	0	0	0	27	—	—	—	—	—
90-91	Milwaukee	IHL	36	9	21	30	116	6	3	2	5	22
91-92	San Jose	NHL	10	2	0	2	19	—	—	—	—	—
91-92	Kansas City	IHL	51	17	21	38	106	—	—	—	—	—
91-92	Kalamazoo	IHL	6	4	5	9	13	10	2	4	6	37
92-93	Kalamazoo	IHL	12	1	1	2	8	—	—	—	—	—
92-93	Cincinnati	IHL	20	5	3	8	34	—	—	—	—	—
93-94	Tulsa	CeHL	64	26	57	83	236	11	4	9	13	38
94-95	Tulsa	CeHL	12	7	7	14	28	7	0	1	1	30
95-96	Huntsville	SHL	20	7	13	20	56	10	8	13	21	33
96-97	Tulsa	CeHL	64	29	59	88	95	5	2	2	4	8
	NHL	Totals	235	14	31	45	713	5	1	0	1	18
	IHL	Totals	138	38	63	101	319	16	5	6	11	59
	AHL	Totals	108	9	19	28	410	4	2	1	3	16
	CeHL	Totals	140	62	123	185	359	23	6	12	16	76

Born; 1/21/64, Chula Vista, California. 6-4, 220. Drafted by Detroit Red Wings (4th choice, 66th overall) in 1982 Entry Draft. Traded by Vancouver Canucks to Calgary Flames for Brian Bradley, Peter Bakovic and future considerations (Kevan Guy) (3/88). Traded to St. Louis Blues by calgary with Mike Bullard and Tim Corkey for Doug Gilmour, Mark Hunter, Steve Bozek and Michael Dark (9/5/88). Sold to Chicago Blackhawks by St. Louis to complete future considerations of Rik Wilson trade made on September 27 (9/28/89). Claimed by Canucks in NHL waiver draft (10/2/89). Selected by San Jose Sharks in 1991 NHL expansion draft (5/30/91). Member of 1995-96 SHL champion Huntsville Channel Cats.

David Craievich — Defenseman

Season	Team	League	GP	G	A	PTS	PIM	GP	G	A	PTS	PIM
91-92	Utica	AHL	9	0	0	0	4	1	0	0	0	4
91-92	Cincinnati	ECHL	50	11	29	40	166	8	1	8	9	15
92-93	Cincinnati	IHL	21	0	3	3	33	—	—	—	—	—
92-93	Birmingham	ECHL	56	10	35	45	139	—	—	—	—	—
93-94	Cincinnati	IHL	3	0	0	0	0	—	—	—	—	—
93-94	Birmingham	ECHL	61	18	58	76	218	10	5	10	15	14
94-95	Minnesota	IHL	2	0	0	0	0	—	—	—	—	—
94-95	Birmingham	ECHL	59	20	46	66	140	7	4	4	8	10
95-96	Mobile	ECHL	65	23	51	74	157	—	—	—	—	—
96-97	Hershey	AHL	2	0	0	0	2	—	—	—	—	—
96-97	Mobile	ECHL	65	13	25	38	125	3	0	1	1	0
	IHL	Totals	26	0	3	3	33	—	—	—	—	—
	AHL	Totals	11	0	0	0	6	1	0	0	0	4
	ECHL	Totals	356	95	244	339	945	28	10	23	33	39

Born; 5/3/71, Chatham, Ontario. 6-2, 208. Drafted by New Jersey Devils (7th choice, 143rd overall) in 1991 Entry Draft. 1993-94 ECHL Second Team All-Star. 1995-96 ECHL Second Team All-Star.

John Craighead — Left Wing

Season	Team	League	GP	G	A	PTS	PIM	GP	G	A	PTS	PIM
92-93	Louisville	ECHL	5	1	0	1	33	—	—	—	—	—
93-94	Huntington	ECHL	9	4	2	6	44	—	—	—	—	—
93-94	Richmond	ECHL	28	18	12	30	89	—	—	—	—	—
94-95	Detroit	IHL	44	5	7	12	285	3	0	1	1	4
95-96	Detroit	IHL	63	7	9	16	368	10	2	3	5	28
96-97	Toronto	NHL	5	0	0	0	10	—	—	—	—	—
96-97	St. John's	AHL	53	9	10	19	318	7	1	1	2	22
	IHL	Totals	107	12	16	28	653	13	2	4	6	32
	ECHL	Totals	42	23	14	37	166	—	—	—	—	—

Born; 11/23/71, Richmond, Virginia. 6-1, 200. Signed as a free agent by Toronto Maple Leafs (7/96).

Dale Craigwell — Center

Season	Team	League	GP	G	A	PTS	PIM	GP	G	A	PTS	PIM
91-92	San Jose	NHL	32	5	11	16	8	—	—	—	—	—
91-92	Kansas City	IHL	48	6	19	25	29	12	4	7	11	4
92-93	San Jose	NHL	8	3	1	4	4	—	—	—	—	—
92-93	Kansas City	IHL	60	15	38	53	24	12	*7	5	12	2
93-94	San Jose	NHL	58	3	6	9	16	—	—	—	—	—
93-94	Kansas City	IHL	5	3	1	4	0	—	—	—	—	—
94-95	Injured	DNP										
95-96	San Fransico	IHL	75	11	49	60	38	4	2	0	2	2
96-97	Kansas City	IHL	82	17	51	68	34	3	1	0	1	0
	NHL	Totals	98	11	18	29	28	—	—	—	—	—
	IHL	Totals	270	52	158	200	125	31	14	12	26	8

Born; 4/24/71, Toronto, Ontario. 5-10, 178. Drafted by San Jose Sharks (11th choice, 199th overall) in 1991 Entry Draft. Member of 1991-92 IHL champion Kansas City Blades.

Jason Crane — Right Wing

			Regular Season					Playoffs				
Season	Team	League	GP	G	A	PTS	PIM	GP	G	A	PTS	PIM
95-96	Lakeland	SHL	48	12	22	34	24	4	0	2	2	2
96-97	Columbus	CeHL	43	11	14	25	16	2	1	0	1	2

Born; 1/13/72, Toronto, Ontario. 5-9, 180.

Derek Crawford — Left Wing

			Regular Season					Playoffs				
Season	Team	League	GP	G	A	PTS	PIM	GP	G	A	PTS	PIM
90-91	Greensboro	ECHL	8	2	5	7	73	—	—	—	—	—
91-92	Dayton	ECHL	61	37	37	74	231	3	0	0	0	14
92-93	Dayton	ECHL	21	4	9	13	91	—	—	—	—	—
92-93	Dallas	CeHL	22	19	11	30	37	7	5	2	7	27
93-94	Dallas	CeHL	61	26	50	76	171	7	1	4	5	27
94-95	Dallas	CeHL	27	6	4	10	111	—	—	—	—	—
95-96	Reno	WCHL	57	19	21	40	139	2	0	1	1	2
96-97	New Mexico	WPHL	53	15	25	40	206	6	1	3	4	18
	CeHL	Totals	110	51	65	116	319	14	6	6	12	54
	ECHL	Totals	90	43	51	94	395	3	0	0	0	14

Born; 4/14/69, Hamilton, Ontario. 6-3, 220.

Brendan Creagh — Defenseman

			Regular Season					Playoffs				
Season	Team	League	GP	G	A	PTS	PIM	GP	G	A	PTS	PIM
93-94	Cornwall	AHL	1	0	0	0	0	—	—	—	—	—
93-94	Greensboro	ECHL	61	20	16	36	112	6	0	0	0	10
94-95	Greensboro	ECHL	21	4	7	11	39	—	—	—	—	—
94-95	Birmingham	ECHL	30	3	8	11	42	7	1	1	2	12
95-96	Birmingham	ECHL	66	6	25	31	100	—	—	—	—	—
96-97	Birmingham	ECHL	49	7	16	23	52	—	—	—	—	—
96-97	Peoria	ECHL	17	3	10	13	31	10	2	3	5	8
	ECHL	Totals	244	43	82	125	376	23	3	4	7	30

Born; 2/1/70, Hartford, Connecticut. 6-0, 200.

Derek Crimin — Center

			Regular Season					Playoffs				
Season	Team	League	GP	G	A	PTS	PIM	GP	G	A	PTS	PIM
95-96	Nashville	ECHL	4	1	5	6	0	2	1	0	1	0
96-97	Pensacola	ECHL	16	5	10	15	4	—	—	—	—	—
96-97	Wheeling	ECHL	29	8	8	16	8	—	—	—	—	—
96-97	Charlotte	ECHL	16	2	8	10	8	3	2	1	3	8
	ECHL	Totals	65	16	31	47	20	5	3	1	4	8

Born; 4/3/73, Sault Ste. Marie, Michigan. 6-0, 185. Last amateur club; Ferris State (CCHA).

Earl Cronan — Left Wing

			Regular Season					Playoffs				
Season	Team	League	GP	G	A	PTS	PIM	GP	G	A	PTS	PIM
96-97	Fredericton	AHL	50	5	3	8	33	—	—	—	—	—

Born; 1/2/73, Warwick, Rhode Island. 6-1, 195. Drafted by Montreal Canadiens (11th choice, 212th overall) in 1992 Entry Draft.

Paul Croteau — Defenseman

			Regular Season					Playoffs				
Season	Team	League	GP	G	A	PTS	PIM	GP	G	A	PTS	PIM
95-96	Roanoke	ECHL	23	2	2	4	2	—	—	—	—	—
95-96	Raleigh	ECHL	4	0	0	0	0	—	—	—	—	—
95-96	Erie	ECHL	28	1	9	10	4	—	—	—	—	—
96-97	Baton Rouge	ECHL	61	5	29	34	24	—	—	—	—	—

| | ECHL | Totals | 116 | 8 | 40 | 48 | 30 | — | — | — | — | — |

Born; 5/21/72, Lewiston, Maine. 6-0, 200.

Phil Crowe — Right Wing

Season	Team	League	GP	G	A	PTS	PIM	GP	G	A	PTS	PIM
91-92	Adirondack	AHL	6	1	0	1	29	—	—	—	—	—
91-92	Columbus	ECHL	32	4	7	11	145	—	—	—	—	—
91-92	Toledo	ECHL	2	0	0	0	0	5	0	0	0	58
92-93	Phoenix	IHL	53	3	3	6	190	—	—	—	—	—
93-94	Fort Wayne	IHL	5	0	1	1	26	—	—	—	—	—
93-94	Phoenix	IHL	2	0	0	0	0	—	—	—	—	—
93-94	Los Angeles	NHL	31	0	2	2	77	—	—	—	—	—
94-95	Hershey	AHL	46	11	6	17	132	6	0	1	1	19
95-96	Philadelphia	NHL	16	1	1	2	28	—	—	—	—	—
95-96	Hershey	AHL	39	6	8	14	105	5	1	2	3	19
96-97	Ottawa	NHL	26	0	1	1	30	3	0	0	0	16
96-97	Detroit	IHL	41	7	7	14	83	—	—	—	—	—
	NHL	Totals	73	1	4	5	135	3	0	0	0	16
	IHL	Totals	101	10	11	21	299	—	—	—	—	—
	AHL	Totals	91	18	14	32	266	11	1	3	4	37
	ECHL	Totals	34	4	7	11	145	5	0	0	0	58

Born; 4/14/70, Nanton, Alberta. 6-2, 220. Signed as a free agent by Los Angeles Kings (11/8/93). Signed as a free agent by Philadelphia Flyers (7/19/94). Signed as a free agent by Ottawa Senators (7/96).

Ted Crowley — Defenseman

Season	Team	League	GP	G	A	PTS	PIM	GP	G	A	PTS	PIM
91-92	United States	National										
91-92	St. John's	AHL	29	5	4	9	33	10	3	1	4	11
92-93	St. John's	AHL	79	19	38	57	41	9	2	2	4	4
93-94	United States	National										
93-94	Hartford	NHL	21	1	2	3	10	—	—	—	—	—
94-95	Chicago	IHL	53	8	23	31	68	—	—	—	—	—
94-95	Houston	IHL	23	4	9	13	35	3	0	1	1	0
95-96	Providence	AHL	72	12	30	42	47	4	1	2	3	2
96-97	Cincinnati	IHL	39	9	9	18	24	—	—	—	—	—
96-97	Phoenix	IHL	30	5	8	13	21	—	—	—	—	—
	AHL	Totals	180	36	72	108	121	23	6	5	11	17
	IHL	Totals	145	26	49	75	148	3	0	1	1	0

Born; 5/3/70, Boxborough, Massachusetts. 6-2, 188. Drafted by Toronto Maple Leafs (4th choice, 69th overall) in 1988 Entry Draft. Traded to Hartford Whalers by Toronto for Mark Greig and Hartford's sixth round choice (later traded to New York Rangers, Rangers selected Yuri Litvinov) in 1994 Entry Draft (1/25/94). Signed as a free agent by Boston Bruins (8/9/95). Signed as a free agent by Phoenix Coyotes (1997).

Trent Cull — Defenseman

Season	Team	League	GP	G	A	PTS	PIM	GP	G	A	PTS	PIM
94-95	St. John's	AHL	43	0	1	1	53	—	—	—	—	—
95-96	St. John's	AHL	46	2	1	3	118	4	0	0	0	6
96-97	St. John's	AHL	75	4	5	9	219	8	0	1	1	18
	AHL	Totals	164	6	7	13	390	12	0	1	1	24

Born; 9/27/73, Georgetown, Ontario. 6-3, 210. Signed as a free agent by Toronto Maple Leafs (6/4/94).

Brent Cullaton

Season	Team	League	GP	G	A	PTS	PIM	GP	G	A	PTS	PIM
96-97	Kansas City	IHL	67	19	14	33	32	3	0	1	1	0
96-97	Mobile	ECHL	4	1	4	5	16	—	—	—	—	—

Born; 11/12/74, Cambridge, Ontario. 6-0, 210.

Matt Cullen — Center

			Regular Season					Playoffs				
Season	Team	League	GP	G	A	PTS	PIM	GP	G	A	PTS	PIM
96-97	Baltimore	AHL	6	3	3	6	7	3	0	2	2	0

Born; 11/2/76, Virginia, Minnesota. 6-1, 182. Drafted by Anaheim Mighty Ducks (2nd choice, 35th overall) in 1996 Entry Draft.

David Cunniff — Center

			Regular Season					Playoffs				
Season	Team	League	GP	G	A	PTS	PIM	GP	G	A	PTS	PIM
96-97	Jacksonville	ECHL	16	4	5	9	75	—	—	—	—	—
96-97	Raleigh	ECHL	46	14	6	20	67	—	—	—	—	—
	ECHL	Totals	62	18	11	29	142	—	—	—	—	—

Born; 10/9/73, South Boston, Massachusetts. 5-10, 185.

Bob Cunningham — Center

			Regular Season					Playoffs				
Season	Team	League	GP	G	A	PTS	PIM	GP	G	A	PTS	PIM
95-96	Mobile	ECHL	25	5	9	14	16	—	—	—	—	—
96-97	Fort Worth	CeHL	10	4	7	11	15	—	—	—	—	—
96-97	Memphis	CeHL	56	33	38	71	79	17	4	7	11	22
	CeHL	Totals	66	37	45	82	94	17	4	7	11	22

Born; 8/13/75, Delson, Quebec. 6-3, 205.

Dan Currie — Left Wing

			Regular Season					Playoffs				
Season	Team	League	GP	G	A	PTS	PIM	GP	G	A	PTS	PIM
87-88	Nova Scotia	AHL	3	4	2	6	0	5	4	3	7	0
88-89	Cape Breton	AHL	77	29	36	65	29	—	—	—	—	—
89-90	Cape Breton	AHL	77	36	40	76	28	6	4	4	8	0
90-91	Edmonton	NHL	5	0	0	0	0	—	—	—	—	—
90-91	Cape Breton	AHL	71	47	45	92	51	4	3	1	4	8
91-92	Edmonton	NHL	7	1	0	1	0	—	—	—	—	—
91-92	Cape Breton	AHL	66	*50	42	92	39	5	4	5	9	4
92-93	Edmonton	NHL	5	0	0	0	4	—	—	—	—	—
92-93	Cape Breton	AHL	75	57	41	98	73	16	7	4	11	29
93-94	Los Angeles	NHL	5	1	1	2	0	—	—	—	—	—
93-94	Phoenix	IHL	74	37	49	86	96	—	—	—	—	—
94-95	Phoenix	IHL	16	2	6	8	8	—	—	—	—	—
94-95	Minnesota	IHL	54	18	35	53	34	3	0	0	0	2
95-96	Chicago	IHL	79	39	34	73	53	9	5	4	9	12
96-97	Chicago	IHL	55	18	10	28	18	—	—	—	—	—
96-97	Fort Wayne	IHL	24	10	12	22	6	—	—	—	—	—
	NHL	Totals	22	2	1	3	4	—	—	—	—	—
	AHL	Totals	369	223	206	429	220	36	22	17	39	41
	IHL	Totals	302	124	146	270	219	12	5	4	9	12

Born; 3/15/68, Burlington, Ontario. 6-2, 195. Drafted by Edmonton Oilers (4th choice, 84th overall) in 1986 Entry Draft. Signed as a free agent by Los Angeles Kings (7/16/93). 1991-92 AHL Second Team All-Star. 1992-93 AHL First Team All-Star. Member of 1992-93 AHL champion Cape Breton Oilers.

Jamie Dabonovich — Defenseman

Season	Team	League	GP	G	A	PTS	PIM	GP	G	A	PTS	PIM
91-92	Flint	CoHL	3	1	0	1	14	—	—	—	—	—
91-92	Knoxville	ECHL	36	4	9	13	23	—	—	—	—	—
92-93	Knoxville	ECHL	12	1	1	2	37	—	—	—	—	—
92-93	Chatham	CoHL	35	7	15	22	9	15	1	3	4	4
94-95	Detroit	CoHL	43	7	11	18	18	5	0	0	0	2
96-97	Port Huron	CoHL	60	9	18	27	60	5	0	2	2	0
	CoHL	Totals	141	24	44	68	101	25	1	5	6	6
	ECHL	Totals	48	5	10	15	60	—	—	—	—	—

Born; 8/8/68, Sarnia, Ontario. 6-0, 210.

Jeff Dacosta — Defenseman

Season	Team	League	GP	G	A	PTS	PIM	GP	G	A	PTS	PIM
96-97	New Mexico	WPHL	55	7	39	46	63	—	—	—	—	—
96-97	El Paso	WPHL	2	1	0	1	2	10	1	5	6	10
	WPHL	Totals	57	8	39	47	65	10	1	5	6	10

Born; 5/16/76, Toronto, Ontario. 5-10, 201. Member of 1996-97 WPHL Champion El Paso Buzzards.

Kevin Dahl — Defenseman

Season	Team	League	GP	G	A	PTS	PIM	GP	G	A	PTS	PIM
90-91	Fredericton	AHL	32	1	15	16	45	9	0	1	1	11
90-91	Winston-Salem	ECHL	36	7	17	24	58	—	—	—	—	—
91-92	Salt Lake City	IHL	13	0	2	2	12	5	0	0	0	13
92-93	Calgary	NHL	61	2	9	11	56	6	0	2	2	8
93-94	Calgary	NHL	33	0	3	3	23	6	0	0	0	4
93-94	Saint John	AHL	2	0	0	0	0	—	—	—	—	—
94-95	Calgary	NHL	34	4	8	12	38	3	0	0	0	0
95-96	Calgary	NHL	32	1	1	2	26	1	0	0	0	0
95-96	Saint John	AHL	23	4	11	15	37	—	—	—	—	—
96-97	Phoenix	NHL	2	0	0	0	0	—	—	—	—	—
96-97	Las Vegas	IHL	73	10	21	31	101	3	0	0	0	2
	NHL	Totals	162	7	21	28	143	16	0	2	2	12
	IHL	Totals	86	10	23	33	113	8	0	0	0	15
	AHL	Totals	57	5	26	31	82	9	0	1	1	11

Born; 12/30/68, Regina, Saskatchewan. 5-11, 190. Drafted by Montreal Canadiens (12th choice, 230th overall) in 1987 Entry Draft. Signed as a free agent by Calgary Flames (7/27/91).

Chris Dahlquist — Defenseman

Season	Team	League	GP	G	A	PTS	PIM	GP	G	A	PTS	PIM
85-86	Pittsburgh	NHL	5	1	2	3	2	—	—	—	—	—
85-86	Baltimore	AHL	65	4	21	25	64	—	—	—	—	—
86-87	Pittsburgh	NHL	19	0	1	1	20	—	—	—	—	—
86-87	Baltimore	AHL	51	1	16	17	50	—	—	—	—	—
87-88	Pittsburgh	NHL	44	3	6	9	69	—	—	—	—	—
88-89	Pittsburgh	NHL	43	1	5	6	42	2	0	0	0	0
88-89	Muskegon	IHL	10	3	6	9	14	—	—	—	—	—
89-90	Pittsburgh	NHL	62	4	10	14	56	—	—	—	—	—
89-90	Muskegon	IHL	6	1	1	2	8	—	—	—	—	—
90-91	Pittsburgh	NHL	22	1	2	3	30	—	—	—	—	—
90-91	Minnesota	NHL	42	2	6	8	33	23	1	6	7	20
91-92	Minnesota	NHL	74	1	13	14	68	7	0	0	0	6
92-93	Calgary	NHL	74	3	7	10	66	6	3	1	4	4

Season	Team	League	GP	G	A	PTS	PIM	GP	G	A	PTS	PIM
93-94	Calgary	NHL	77	1	11	12	52	1	0	0	0	0
94-95	Ottawa	NHL	46	1	7	8	36	—	—	—	—	—
95-96	Ottawa	NHL	24	1	1	2	14	—	—	—	—	—
95-96	Cincinnati	IHL	38	4	8	12	50	2	1	3	4	0
96-97	Las Vegas	IHL	18	1	4	5	26	—	—	—	—	—
	NHL	Totals	532	19	71	90	488	39	4	7	11	30
	AHL	Totals	116	5	37	42	114	—	—	—	—	—
	IHL	Totals	72	9	19	28	98	2	1	3	4	0

Born; 12/14/62, Fridley, Minnesota. 6-1, 195. Signed as a free agent by Pittsburgh Penguins (5/7/85). Traded to Minnesota North Stars by Pittsburgh with Jim Johnosn for Larry Murphy and Peter Taglianetti (12/11/90). Claimed by Calgary Flames from Minnesota in NHL Waiver Draft (10/4/92). Signed as a free agent by Ottawa Senators (7/4/94). Missed most of 96-97 with injury.

Phil Daigle — Center

			Regular Season					Playoffs				
Season	Team	League	GP	G	A	PTS	PIM	GP	G	A	PTS	PIM
95-96	Huntington	ECHL	2	0	0	0	0	—	—	—	—	—
95-96	Utica	CoHL	8	2	1	3	10	—	—	—	—	—
95-96	Jacksonville	SUN	9	3	4	7	57	—	—	—	—	—
95-96	Huntsville	SHL	8	4	3	7	36	10	1	5	6	45
96-97	Huntsville	CeHL	55	18	23	41	217	9	6	4	10	16
	SHL	Totals	17	7	7	14	93	10	1	5	6	45

Born; 12/21/69, Fredericton, Manitoba. 5-7, 180. Member of 1995-96 SHL champion Huntsville Channel Cats.

Sylvain Daigle — Goaltender

			Regular Season							Playoffs					
Season	Team	League	GP	W	L	T	MIN	SO	GAVG	GP	W	L	MIN	SO	GAVG
96-97	Springfield	AHL	13	8	3	0	691	1	2.00	6	1	4	312	0	3.47
96-97	Las Vegas	IHL	1	0	0	0	42	0	7.17	—	—	—	—	—	—
96-97	Mississippi	ECHL	34	20	8	5	1951	2	3.08	—	—	—	—	—	—

Born; 10/20/76, St. Hyacinthe, Quebec. 5-8, 185. Drafted by Winnipeg Jets (7th choice, 136th overall) in 1995 Entry Draft.

Andrew Dale — Center

			Regular Season					Playoffs				
Season	Team	League	GP	G	A	PTS	PIM	GP	G	A	PTS	PIM
96-97	Phoenix	IHL	32	7	6	13	19	—	—	—	—	—
96-97	Mississippi	ECHL	19	6	9	15	16	2	0	1	1	0

Born; 2/16/76, Sudbury, Ontario. 6-1, 196. Drafted by Los Angeles Kings (6th choice, 189th overall) in 1994 Entry Draft.

Chad Dameworth — Defenseman

			Regular Season					Playoffs				
Season	Team	League	GP	G	A	PTS	PIM	GP	G	A	PTS	PIM
94-95	Cape Breton	AHL	1	0	0	0	0	—	—	—	—	—
95-96	Cape Breton	AHL	24	2	2	4	31	—	—	—	—	—
95-96	Wheeling	ECHL	35	2	9	11	10	—	—	—	—	—
96-97	Worcester	AHL	36	1	6	7	101	4	0	0	0	4
96-97	Wheeling	ECHL	20	1	3	4	25	—	—	—	—	—
96-97	Johnstown	ECHL	4	2	0	2	4	—	—	—	—	—
	AHL	Totals	61	3	8	11	132	4	0	0	0	4
	ECHL	Totals	59	5	12	17	39	—	—	—	—	—

Born; 7/6/72, Marquette, Michigan. 6-2, 215. Drafted by Edmonton Oilers (1st choice, 6th overall) in 1994 Supplemental Draft.

Eric Dandenault — Defenseman

			Regular Season					Playoffs				
Season	Team	League	GP	G	A	PTS	PIM	GP	G	A	PTS	PIM
93-94	Johnstown	ECHL	2	1	1	2	6	—	—	—	—	—
93-94	Hershey	AHL	14	2	1	3	49	—	—	—	—	—
95-96	Cincinnati	IHL	16	1	2	3	45	17	1	6	7	30

	95-96	Saginaw	CoHL	61	5	30	35	160	—	—	—	—	—
	96-97	Cincinnati	IHL	77	5	14	19	240	3	0	0	0	7
		IHL	Totals	93	6	16	22	285	20	1	6	7	37

Born; 3/10/70, Sherbrooke, Quebec. 6-0, 193.

Jeff Daniels — Left Wing

	Regular Season							Playoffs				
Season	Team	League	GP	G	A	PTS	PIM	GP	G	A	PTS	PIM
88-89	Muskegon	IHL	58	21	21	42	58	11	3	5	8	11
89-90	Muskegon	IHL	80	30	47	77	39	6	1	1	2	7
90-91	Pittsburgh	NHL	11	0	2	2	2	—	—	—	—	—
90-91	Muskegon	IHL	62	23	29	52	18	5	1	3	4	2
91-92	Pittsburgh	NHL	2	0	0	0	0	—	—	—	—	—
91-92	Muskegon	IHL	44	19	16	35	38	10	5	4	9	9
92-93	Pittsburgh	NHL	58	5	4	9	14	12	3	2	5	0
92-93	Cleveland	IHL	3	2	1	3	0	—	—	—	—	—
93-94	Pittsburgh	NHL	63	3	5	8	20	—	—	—	—	—
93-94	Florida	NHL	7	0	0	0	0	—	—	—	—	—
94-95	Florida	NHL	3	0	0	0	0	—	—	—	—	—
94-95	Detroit	IHL	25	8	12	20	6	5	1	0	1	0
95-96	Springfield	AHL	72	22	20	42	32	10	3	0	3	2
96-97	Hartford	NHL	10	0	2	2	0	—	—	—	—	—
96-97	Springfield	AHL	38	18	14	32	19	16	7	3	10	4
	NHL	Totals	154	8	13	21	36	12	3	2	5	0
	IHL	Totals	272	103	126	229	159	37	11	13	24	29
	AHL	Totals	110	40	34	74	51	26	10	3	13	6

Born; 6/24/68, Oshawa, Ontario. 6-1, 200. Drafted by Pittsburgh Penguins (6th choice, 109th overall) in 1986 Entry Draft. Traded to Florida Panthers by Pittsburgh for Greg Hawgood (3/19/94). Signed as a free agent by Hartford Whalers (7/18/95).

Kimbi Daniels — Center

	Regular Season							Playoffs				
Season	Team	League	GP	G	A	PTS	PIM	GP	G	A	PTS	PIM
91-92	Philadelphia	NHL	25	1	1	2	4	—	—	—	—	—
93-94	Salt Lake City	IHL	25	6	9	15	8	—	—	—	—	—
93-94	Detroit	CoHL	23	11	28	39	42	—	—	—	—	—
94-95	Minnesota	IHL	10	1	4	5	2	—	—	—	—	—
95-96	Baltimore	AHL	7	2	1	3	2	—	—	—	—	—
95-96	Jacksonville	ECHL	26	12	22	34	129	—	—	—	—	—
95-96	Charlotte	ECHL	18	16	14	30	6	16	8	6	14	24
96-97	Rochester	AHL	6	1	3	4	2	—	—	—	—	—
96-97	Hamilton	AHL	3	0	0	0	0	16	5	8	13	4
96-97	Charlotte	ECHL	32	12	24	36	116	—	—	—	—	—
96-97	Wheeling	ECHL	17	5	24	29	10	3	1	4	5	6
	IHL	Totals	35	7	13	20	10	—	—	—	—	—
	AHL	Totals	16	3	4	7	4	16	5	8	13	4
	ECHL	Totals	93	45	84	129	261	19	9	10	19	30

Born; 1/19/72, Brandon, Manitoba. 5-10, 175. Drafted by Philadelphia Flyers (5th choice, 44th overall) in 1990 Entry Draft. Member of 1995-96 ECHL champion Charlotte Checkers.

Craig Darby — Center

	Regular Season							Playoffs				
Season	Team	League	GP	G	A	PTS	PIM	GP	G	A	PTS	PIM
93-94	Fredericton	AHL	66	23	33	56	51	—	—	—	—	—
94-95	Montreal	NHL	10	0	2	2	0	—	—	—	—	—
94-95	Islanders	NHL	3	0	0	0	0	—	—	—	—	—
94-95	Fredericton	AHL	64	21	47	68	82	—	—	—	—	—
95-96	Islanders	NHL	10	0	2	2	0	—	—	—	—	—

Season	Team	League	GP	G	A	PTS	PIM	GP	G	A	PTS	PIM
95-96	Worcester	AHL	68	22	28	50	47	4	1	1	2	2
96-97	Philadelphia	NHL	9	1	4	5	2	—	—	—	—	—
96-97	Philadelphia	AHL	59	26	33	59	24	10	3	6	9	0
	NHL	Totals	32	1	8	9	2	—	—	—	—	—
	AHL	Totals	257	92	141	233	204	14	4	7	11	2

Born; 9/25/67, Oneida, New York. 6-1, 195. Drafted by Montreal Canadiens (3rd choice, 43rd overall) in 1991 Entry Draft. Traded to New York Islanders by Montreal with Kirk Muller and Mathieu Schneider for Pierre Turgeon and Vladimir Malakhov (4/5/95).

Michael Dark — Defenseman

Season	Team	League	GP	G	A	PTS	PIM	GP	G	A	PTS	PIM
86-87	St. Louis	NHL	13	2	0	2	2	—	—	—	—	—
86-87	Peoria	IHL	42	4	11	15	93	—	—	—	—	—
87-88	St. Louis	NHL	30	3	6	9	12	—	—	—	—	—
87-88	Peoria	IHL	37	21	12	33	97	2	0	0	0	4
88-89	Salt Lake City	IHL	36	3	12	15	57	—	—	—	—	—
88-89	New Haven	AHL	7	0	4	4	4	—	—	—	—	—
91-92	Flint	CoHL	1	0	0	0	15	—	—	—	—	—
91-92	St. Thomas	CoHL	2	0	0	0	0	—	—	—	—	—
95-96	Brantford	CoHL	11	3	12	15	33	3	1	0	1	2
96-97	Port Huron	CoHL	17	0	2	2	10	5	1	3	4	0
	NHL	Totals	43	5	6	11	14	—	—	—	—	—
	IHL	Totals	115	28	35	63	247	2	0	0	0	4
	CoHL	Totals	31	3	14	17	58	8	2	3	5	2

9/17/63, Sarnia, Ontario. 6-3, 210. Drafted by Montreal Canadiens (10th choice, 124th overall) in 1982 Entry Draft. NHL Rights traded to St. Louis Blues with Mark Hunter and future considerations for St. Louis' first round choice (Jose Charbonneau) and a switch of other choices (6/85).

Dion Darling — Defenseman

Season	Team	League	GP	G	A	PTS	PIM	GP	G	A	PTS	PIM
93-94	WHL	ECHL	3	0	1	1	7	9	0	1	1	14
94-95	FRE	AHL	51	0	2	2	153	—	—	—	—	—
94-95	WHL	ECHL	4	0	0	0	24	—	—	—	—	—
95-96	FRE	AHL	74	3	2	5	215	6	0	0	0	5
96-97	Fredericton	AHL	58	2	6	8	150	—	—	—	—	—
	AHL	Totals	183	5	10	15	518	6	0	0	0	5
	ECHL	Totals	7	0	1	1	31	9	0	1	1	14

Born; 10/22/74, Edmonton, Alberta. 6-3, 210. Drafted by Montreal Canadiens (7th choice, 125th overall) in 1993 Entry Draft.

David Dartsch — Forward

Season	Team	League	GP	G	A	PTS	PIM	GP	G	A	PTS	PIM
96-97	Richmond	ECHL	65	4	20	24	214	8	1	1	2	51

Born; 2/17/74, Pointe-Claire, Quebec. 5-10, 187.

Chris Dashney — Defenseman

Season	Team	League	GP	G	A	PTS	PIM	GP	G	A	PTS	PIM
96-97	Tulsa	CeHL	66	1	15	16	56	5	0	0	0	14

Born; 10/16/72, Ottawa, Ontario. 6-1, 195.

Brent Daugherty — Right Wing

Season	Team	League	GP	G	A	PTS	PIM	GP	G	A	PTS	PIM
96-97	Port Huron	CoHL	2	0	1	1	0	—	—	—	—	—
96-97	Muskegon	CoHL	66	8	8	16	69	—	—	—	—	—
	CoHL	Totals	68	8	9	17	69	—	—	—	—	—

Born; 7/3/67, Chatham, Ontario. 6-0, 205.

Bill Davidson — Defenseman

Season	Team	League	GP	G	A	PTS	PIM	GP	G	A	PTS	PIM
90-91	Louisville	ECHL	5	0	2	2	19	—	—	—	—	—
90-91	Knoxville	ECHL	14	1	5	6	45	—	—	—	—	—
93-94	West Palm Beach	SUN	44	3	12	15	62	5	0	4	4	6
94-95	Fresno	SUN	2	0	0	0	0	—	—	—	—	—
94-95	Memphis	CeHL	11	1	1	2	17	—	—	—	—	—
96-97	New Mexico	WPHL	28	1	3	4	120	—	—	—	—	—
	SUN	Totals	46	3	12	15	62	5	0	4	4	6
	ECHL	Totals	19	1	7	8	64	—	—	—	—	—

Born; 4/16/67, Edmonton, Alberta. 6-0, 195. Member of 1993-94 Sunshine League Champion West Palm Beach Blaze.

Bryce Davidson — Right Wing

Season	Team	League	GP	G	A	PTS	PIM	GP	G	A	PTS	PIM
95-96	Daytona Beach	SHL	51	4	5	9	*413	2	0	2	2	17
96-97	Saginaw	CoHL	48	5	9	14	*440	—	—	—	—	—

Born; 11/11/74, Mississauga, Ontario. 5-9, 195.

Lee Davidson — Center

Season	Team	League	GP	G	A	PTS	PIM	GP	G	A	PTS	PIM
90-91	Moncton	AHL	69	15	17	32	24	—	—	—	—	—
91-92	Moncton	AHL	43	3	12	15	32	—	—	—	—	—
91-92	Fort Wayne	IHL	22	4	10	14	30	7	2	5	7	8
92-93	Fort Wayne	IHL	60	22	20	42	58	12	2	0	2	21
93-94	Fort Wayne	IHL	74	25	42	67	32	17	4	12	16	10
94-95	Chicago	IHL	76	28	37	65	36	3	2	0	2	2
95-96	Chicago	IHL	18	6	14	20	18	—	—	—	—	—
95-96	Atlanta	IHL	55	25	36	61	34	3	3	1	4	0
96-97	Fort Wayne	IHL	73	24	51	75	60	—	—	—	—	—
	IHL	Totals	378	134	210	344	268	42	13	18	31	41
	AHL	Totals	112	18	29	47	56	—	—	—	—	—

Born; 6/30/68, Winnipeg, Manitoba. 5-11, 180. Drafted by Washington Capitals (9th choice, 166th overall) in 1986 Entry Draft. Signed as a free agent by Winnipeg Jets (9/4/90). Member of 1992-93 IHL champion Fort Wayne Komets.

Scott Davis — Defenseman

Season	Team	League	GP	G	A	PTS	PIM	GP	G	A	PTS	PIM
96-97	New Mexico	WPHL	10	0	5	5	18	5	0	0	0	9

6-0, 188. Drafted by Quebec Nordiques (8th choice, 190th overall) in 1990 Entry Draft.

Jeff Daw — Center

Season	Team	League	GP	G	A	PTS	PIM	GP	G	A	PTS	PIM
96-97	Hamilton	AHL	56	11	8	19	39	19	4	5	9	0
96-97	Wheeling	ECHL	13	3	8	11	26	—	—	—	—	—

Born; 2/28/72, Carlisle, Ontario. 6-3, 200. Last amateur club; Lowell University (Hockey East).

Joe Day — Center

Season	Team	League	GP	G	A	PTS	PIM	GP	G	A	PTS	PIM
90-91	Springfield	AHL	75	24	29	53	82	18	5	5	10	27
91-92	Hartford	NHL	24	0	3	3	10	—	—	—	—	—
91-92	Springfield	AHL	50	33	25	58	92	—	—	—	—	—

Season	Team	League	GP	G	A	PTS	PIM	GP	G	A	PTS	PIM
92-93	Hartford	NHL	24	1	7	8	47	—	—	—	—	—
92-93	Springfield	AHL	33	15	20	35	118	15	0	8	8	40
93-94	Islanders	NHL	24	0	0	0	30	—	—	—	—	—
93-94	Salt Lake City	IHL	33	16	10	26	153	—	—	—	—	—
94-95	Detroit	IHL	32	16	10	26	126	5	0	2	2	21
95-96	Detroit	IHL	53	19	19	38	105	—	—	—	—	—
95-96	Las Vegas	IHL	29	11	17	28	70	15	7	3	10	46
96-97	Baltimore	AHL	11	3	0	3	22	—	—	—	—	—
96-97	Las Vegas	IHL	30	9	14	23	41	3	0	0	0	6
	NHL	Totals	72	1	10	11	87	—	—	—	—	—
	IHL	Totals	196	71	70	141	495	23	7	5	12	73
	AHL	Totals	169	75	74	149	314	33	5	13	18	67

Born; 5/11/68, Chicago, Illinois. 5-11, 180. Drafted by Hartford Whalers (8th choice, 186th overall) in 1987 Entry Draft. Signed as a free agent by New York Islanders (8/24/93). Signed as a free agent by Anaheim Mighty Ducks (8/19/96). Member of 1990-91 AHL champion Springfield Indians.

Jake Deadmarsh — Defenseman

Season	Team	League	GP	G	A	PTS	PIM	GP	G	A	PTS	PIM
96-97	Charlotte	ECHL	9	0	0	0	15	—	—	—	—	—
96-97	Huntington	ECHL	16	0	3	3	6	—	—	—	—	—
	ECHL	Totals	25	0	3	3	21	—	—	—	—	—

Born; 1/30/77, Fruitvale, British Columbia. 6-0, 195. Drafted by San Jose Sharks (6th choice, 164th overall) in 1996 Entry Draft.

Mark Deazeley — Left Wing

Season	Team	League	GP	G	A	PTS	PIM	GP	G	A	PTS	PIM
92-93	Toledo	ECHL	63	27	18	45	263	15	8	6	14	66
93-94	Toledo	ECHL	57	41	36	77	231	14	*16	10	*26	37
93-94	Fort Wayne	IHL	1	0	0	0	2	—	—	—	—	—
94-95	Springfield	AHL	26	2	0	2	141	—	—	—	—	—
94-95	Toledo	ECHL	14	5	1	6	136	—	—	—	—	—
95-96	Tallahassee	ECHL	67	29	36	65	141	12	7	6	13	17
96-97	Austin	WPHL	20	5	8	13	28	—	—	—	—	—
96-97	Tallahassee	ECHL	43	17	10	27	89	3	0	0	0	14
	ECHL	Totals	244	119	101	220	860	44	31	22	53	134

Born; 4/8/72, Toronto, Ontario. 6-4, 237. Signed as a free agent by Winnipeg Jets (6/17/94). 1993-94 ECHL Playoff MVP. Member of 1992-93 ECHL champion Toledo Storm. Member of 1993-94 ECHL champion Toledo Storm.

Alain Deeks — Defenseman

Season	Team	League	GP	G	A	PTS	PIM	GP	G	A	PTS	PIM
91-92	Columbus	ECHL	46	15	24	39	73	—	—	—	—	—
92-93	Hamilton	AHL	18	0	6	6	6	—	—	—	—	—
92-93	New Haven	AHL	1	0	0	0	0	—	—	—	—	—
92-93	Columbus	ECHL	23	5	11	16	34	—	—	—	—	—
93-94	Prince Edward Island	AHL	35	1	3	4	36	—	—	—	—	—
93-94	Thunder Bay	CoHL	22	1	5	6	16	9	3	6	9	13
94-95	Las Vegas	IHL	13	1	2	3	27	5	1	1	2	6
94-95	Knoxville	ECHL	58	15	13	28	150	1	0	0	0	0
95-96	Baltimore	AHL	35	1	1	2	21	—	—	—	—	—
96-97	Baltimore	AHL	16	0	2	2	17	—	—	—	—	—
	AHL	Totals	105	2	12	14	80	—	—	—	—	—
	ECHL	Totals	127	35	48	83	257	1	0	0	0	0

Born; 4/15/69, Hawkesbury, Ontario. 6-5, 225. Signed as a free agent by Ottawa Senators (7/2/93). Signed as a free agent by Anaheim Mighty Ducks (7/10/95). Member of 1993-94 CoHL champion Thunder Bay Senators.

Alexei Deev — Center

			Regular Season					Playoffs				
Season	Team	League	GP	G	A	PTS	PIM	GP	G	A	PTS	PIM
93-94	Charlotte	ECHL	10	3	3	6	0	—	—	—	—	—
93-94	Huntington	ECHL	12	3	6	9	2	—	—	—	—	—
94-95	Charlotte	ECHL	6	0	0	0	0	—	—	—	—	—
95-96	Winston-Salem	SHL	59	37	51	88	78	9	5	8	13	8
96-97	Macon	CeHL	66	38	54	92	28	4	2	2	4	6
	ECHL	Totals	28	6	9	15	2	—	—	—	—	—

Born; 12/29/73, Siberia, Russia. 5-11, 172.

Dale DeGray — Defenseman

			Regular Season					Playoffs				
Season	Team	League	GP	G	A	PTS	PIM	GP	G	A	PTS	PIM
83-84	Colorado	CHL	67	16	14	30	67	6	1	1	2	2
84-85	Moncton	AHL	77	24	37	61	63	—	—	—	—	—
85-86	Calgary	NHL	1	0	0	0	0	—	—	—	—	—
85-86	Moncton	AHL	76	10	31	41	128	6	0	1	1	0
86-87	Calgary	NHL	27	6	7	13	29	—	—	—	—	—
86-87	Moncton	AHL	45	10	22	32	57	5	2	1	3	19
87-88	Toronto	NHL	56	6	18	24	63	5	0	1	1	16
87-88	New Haven	AHL	8	2	10	12	38	—	—	—	—	—
88-89	Los Angeles	NHL	63	6	22	28	97	8	1	2	3	12
89-90	Buffalo	NHL	6	0	0	0	6	—	—	—	—	—
89-90	New Haven	AHL	16	2	10	12	38	—	—	—	—	—
89-90	Rochester	AHL	50	6	25	31	118	17	5	6	11	59
90-91	Rochester	AHL	64	9	25	34	121	15	3	4	7	*76
91-92	Italy											
92-93	San Diego	IHL	79	18	64	82	181	14	3	11	14	77
93-94	San Diego	IHL	80	20	50	70	163	9	2	1	3	8
94-95	Detroit	IHL	14	1	8	9	18	—	—	—	—	—
94-95	Cleveland	IHL	64	19	49	68	134	4	0	4	4	10
95-96	Cincinnati	IHL	79	13	46	59	96	16	1	6	7	35
96-97	Cincinnati	IHL	30	5	16	21	55	—	—	—	—	—
96-97	Manitoba	IHL	44	9	15	24	42	—	—	—	—	—
	NHL	Totals	153	18	47	65	195	13	1	3	4	28
	IHL	Totals	390	85	295	380	689	43	6	22	28	130
	AHL	Totals	336	63	160	223	533	43	10	12	22	154

Born; 9/3/63, Oshawa, Ontario. 6-0, 206. Drafted by Calgary Flames (7th choice, 162nd overall) in 1981 Entry Draft. Traded to Toronto Maple Leafs by Calgary for future considerations (9/87). Selected by Los Angeles Kings in 1988 Waiver Draft (10/3/88). Traded to Buffalo Sabres by Los Angeles for Bob Halkidis (11/24/89). Signed as a free agent by San Diego Gulls (8/27/92). Signed as a free agent by Detroit Vipers (1994). Traded by Detroit to Cleveland Lumberjacks to complete earlier trade (11/16/94). 1984-85 AHL Second All-Star Team. 1992-93 IHL Second Team All-Star. 1994-95 IHL Second Team All-Star.

Mike Degurse — Forward

			Regular Season					Playoffs				
Season	Team	League	GP	G	A	PTS	PIM	GP	G	A	PTS	PIM
95-96	Winston-Salem	SHL	56	18	20	38	302	9	1	0	1	40
96-97	Huntsville	CeHL	62	31	15	46	282	8	3	6	9	46

Born; 10/4/74, Sarnia Reserve, Ontario. 6-2, 220.

Ray Delarosibil — Defenseman

			Regular Season					Playoffs				
Season	Team	League	GP	G	A	PTS	PIM	GP	G	A	PTS	PIM
96-97	Macon	CeHL	4	0	2	2	5	5	0	2	2	2

Born;

Matt DelGuidice — Goaltender

Regular Season / Playoffs

Season	Team	League	GP	W	L	T	MIN	SO	GAVG	GP	W	L	MIN	SO	GAVG
90-91	Boston	NHL	1	0	0	0	10	0	0.00	—	—	—	—	—	—
90-91	Maine	AHL	52	23	18	9	2893	2	3.32	2	1	1	82	0	3.66
91-92	Boston	NHL	10	2	5	1	424	0	3.96	—	—	—	—	—	—
91-92	Maine	AHL	25	5	15	0	1369	0	4.43	—	—	—	—	—	—
92-93	Providence	AHL	9	0	7	1	478	0	7.28	—	—	—	—	—	—
92-93	San Diego	IHL	1	0	0	0	20	0	6.00	—	—	—	—	—	—
93-94	Albany	AHL	5	1	2	2	310	0	3.68	—	—	—	—	—	—
93-94	Springfield	AHL	1	0	0	1	65	0	2.77	—	—	—	—	—	—
93-94	Raleigh	ECHL	31	18	9	4	1878	1	2.94	12	6	4	707	0	3.14
94-95	Atlanta	IHL	1	0	0	0	53	0	5.70	—	—	—	—	—	—
94-95	Charlotte	ECHL	5	2	2	1	303	0	2.97	—	—	—	—	—	—
94-95	Nashville	ECHL	18	7	8	2	1009	0	4.82	2	0	1	74	0	4.84
95-96	Albany	AHL	1	0	0	0	0	0	0.00	—	—	—	—	—	—
95-96	Raleigh	ECHL	35	13	10	3	1738	0	3.56	2	0	1	60	0	2.98
96-97	Amarillo	WPHL	49	13	*26	7	2620	0	4.42	—	—	—	—	—	—
	NHL	Totals	11	2	5	1	434	0	3.87	—	—	—	—	—	—
	AHL	Totals	93	29	42	13	5115	2	4.00	2	1	1	82	0	3.66
	IHL	Totals	2	0	0	0	73	0	5.74	—	—	—	—	—	—
	ECHL	Totals	84	40	29	10	4928	1	3.54	16	6	6	841	0	3.28

Born; 3/15/67, West Haven, Connecticut. 5-10, 170. Drafted by Boston Bruins (4th choice, 77th overall) in 1987 Entry Draft.

Marc Delorme — Goaltender

Regular Season / Playoffs

Season	Team	League	GP	W	L	T	MIN	SO	GAVG	GP	W	L	MIN	SO	GAVG
94-95	Brantford	CoHL	25	12	8	2	1339	1	3.85	—	—	—	—	—	—
95-96	Brantford	CoHL	*55	*35	13	3	*3020	1	3.40	12	7	4	688	1	3.31
96-97	Detroit	IHL	1	0	0	1	38	0	0.00	—	—	—	—	—	—
96-97	Louisiana	ECHL	56	*36	14	3	3115	2	3.06	14	7	*6	753	0	4.54
	CoHL	Totals	80	47	21	5	4359	2	3.54	12	7	4	688	1	3.31

Born; 6/19/70, Montreal, Quebec. 5-11, 170. 1995-96 CoHL Second Team All-Star. 1996-97 ECHL Goaltender of the Year. 1996-97 ECHL First Team All-Star.

Bob DeLorimiere — Goaltender

Regular Season / Playoffs

Season	Team	League	GP	W	L	T	MIN	SO	GAVG	GP	W	L	MIN	SO	GAVG
94-95	Brantford	CoHL	14	2	6	3	702	0	4.61	—	—	—	—	—	—
94-95	Utica	CoHL	3	0	2	0	123	0	10.17	—	—	—	—	—	—
95-96	Utica	CoHL	28	9	10	2	1224	1	4.02	—	—	—	—	—	—
96-97	Fort Worth	CeHL	17	7	7	0	970	0	3.84	1	0	0	10	0	5.89
	CoHL	Totals	45	11	18	5	2049	1	4.60	—	—	—	—	—	—

Born; 6/17/70, North Tonawanda, New York. 5-8, 180. Member of 1996-97 CeHL Champion Fort Worth Fire.

Pavol Demitra — Left Wing

Regular Season / Playoffs

Season	Team	League	GP	G	A	PTS	PIM	GP	G	A	PTS	PIM
93-94	Ottawa	NHL	12	1	1	2	4	—	—	—	—	—
93-94	Prince Edward Island	AHL	41	18	23	41	8	—	—	—	—	—
94-95	Ottawa	NHL	16	4	3	7	0	—	—	—	—	—
94-95	Prince Edward Island	AHL	61	26	48	74	23	5	0	7	7	0
95-96	Ottawa	NHL	31	7	10	17	6	—	—	—	—	—
95-96	Prince Edward Island	AHL	48	28	53	81	44	—	—	—	—	—
96-97	St. Louis	NHL	8	3	0	3	2	6	1	3	4	6
96-97	Las Vegas	IHL	22	8	13	21	10	—	—	—	—	—
96-97	Grand Rapids	IHL	42	20	30	50	24	—	—	—	—	—

		NHL	Totals	67	15	14	29	12	6	1	3	4	6
		AHL	Totals	150	72	124	196	75	5	0	7	7	0
		IHL	Totals	64	28	43	71	34	—	—	—	—	—

Born; 11/29/74, Dubnica, Czechoslovakia. 5-11, 178. Drafted by Ottawa Senators (9th choice, 227th overall) in 1993 Entry Draft.

Nathan Dempsey — Defenseman

			Regular Season					Playoffs				
Season	Team	League	GP	G	A	PTS	PIM	GP	G	A	PTS	PIM
92-93	St. John's	AHL	—	—	—	—	—	2	0	0	0	0
94-95	St. John's	AHL	74	7	30	37	91	5	1	0	1	11
95-96	St. John's	AHL	73	5	15	20	103	4	1	0	1	9
96-97	Toronto	NHL	14	1	1	2	2	—	—	—	—	—
96-97	St. John's	AHL	52	8	18	26	108	6	1	0	1	4
	AHL	Totals	199	20	63	83	302	17	3	0	3	24

Born; 7/14/74, Spruce Grove, Alberta. 6-0, 170. Drafted by Toronto Maple Leafs (11th choice, 148th overall) in 1992 Entry Draft.

Marc Denis — Goaltender

			Regular Season							Playoffs					
Season	Team	League	GP	W	L	T	MIN	SO	GAVG	GP	W	L	MIN	SO	GAVG
96-97	Colorado	NHL	1	0	1	0	60	0	3.00	—	—	—	—	—	—
96-97	Hershey	AHL	—	—	—	—	—	—	—	4	1	0	56	0	*1.08

Born; 8/1/77, Montreal, Quebec. 6-0, 188. Drafted by Colorado Avalanche (1st choice, 25th overall) in 1995 Entry Draft. Member of 1996-97 AHL Champion Hershey Bears.

Mike Dennis — Defenseman

			Regular Season					Playoffs				
Season	Team	League	GP	G	A	PTS	PIM	GP	G	A	PTS	PIM
94-95	Dayton	ECHL	3	0	1	1	15	—	—	—	—	—
94-95	Johnstown	ECHL	59	5	18	23	86	5	0	1	1	28
95-96	Raleigh	ECHL	19	2	2	4	35	—	—	—	—	—
95-96	Mobile	ECHL	45	5	18	23	104	—	—	—	—	—
96-97	Mobile	ECHL	59	6	21	27	155	3	0	0	0	6
	ECHL	Totals	181	18	60	78	395	8	0	1	1	34

Born; 5/18/71, Kansas City, Kansas. 5-10, 185.

Larry DePalma — Left Wing

			Regular Season					Playoffs				
Season	Team	League	GP	G	A	PTS	PIM	GP	G	A	PTS	PIM
85-86	Minnesota	NHL	1	0	0	0	0	—	—	—	—	—
86-87	Minnesota	NHL	56	9	6	15	219	—	—	—	—	—
86-87	Springfield	AHL	9	2	2	4	82	—	—	—	—	—
87-88	Minnesota	NHL	7	1	1	2	15	—	—	—	—	—
87-88	Baltimore	AHL	16	8	10	18	121	—	—	—	—	—
87-88	Kalamazoo	IHL	22	6	11	17	215	—	—	—	—	—
88-89	Minnesota	NHL	43	5	7	12	102	2	0	0	0	6
89-90	Kalamazoo	IHL	36	7	14	21	218	4	1	1	2	32
90-91	Minnesota	NHL	14	3	0	3	26	—	—	—	—	—
90-91	Kalamazoo	IHL	55	27	32	59	160	11	5	4	9	25
91-92	Kansas City	IHL	62	28	29	57	188	15	7	*13	20	34
92-93	San Jose	NHL	20	2	6	8	41	—	—	—	—	—
92-93	Kansas City	IHL	30	11	11	22	83	10	1	4	5	20
93-94	Pittsburgh	NHL	7	1	0	1	5	1	0	0	0	0
93-94	Atlanta	IHL	30	10	10	20	109	—	—	—	—	—
93-94	Salt Lake City	IHL	34	4	12	16	125	—	—	—	—	—
93-94	Las Vegas	IHL	1	0	0	0	17	—	—	—	—	—
93-94	Cleveland	IHL	9	4	1	5	49	—	—	—	—	—
94-95	Cleveland	IHL	25	6	6	12	113	—	—	—	—	—
94-95	San Diego	IHL	38	14	8	22	86	2	0	0	0	20

95-96	Minnesota	IHL	55	9	17	26	173	—	—	—	—	—
96-97	Milwaukee	IHL	68	13	13	26	131	3	0	1	1	4
	NHL	Totals	148	21	20	41	408	3	0	0	0	6
	IHL	Totals	456	139	164	303	1667	45	14	22	36	135
	AHL	Totals	25	10	12	22	203	—	—	—	—	—

Born; 10/27/65, Trenton, Michigan. 5-11, 200. Signed as a free agent by Minnesota North Stars (5/12/86). Signed as a free agent by San Jose (8/30/91). Signed as a free agent by New York Islanders (11/29/93). Claimed on waivers by Pittsburgh Penguins from Islanders. Member of 1991-92 IHL champion Kansas City Blades.

John DePourcq — Center

			Regular Season					Playoffs				
Season	Team	League	GP	G	A	PTS	PIM	GP	G	A	PTS	PIM
93-94	Erie	ECHL	28	14	29	43	4	—	—	—	—	—
94-95	Wichita	CeHL	59	28	53	81	10	6	2	6	8	2
95-96	Louisiana	ECHL	55	22	53	75	20	3	2	1	3	0
96-97	Louisiana	ECHL	68	28	63	91	14	13	2	8	10	6
	ECHL	Totals	151	64	145	209	38	16	4	9	13	6

Born; 2/6/68, Summerland, British Columbia. 5-8, 171. Member of 1994-95 CeHL Champion Wichita Thunder.

Chris Deprofio — Center

			Regular Season					Playoffs				
Season	Team	League	GP	G	A	PTS	PIM	GP	G	A	PTS	PIM
96-97	Roanoke	ECHL	7	1	1	2	4	—	—	—	—	—
96-97	Louisville	ECHL	44	23	26	49	37	—	—	—	—	—
	ECHL	Totals	51	24	27	51	41	—	—	—	—	—

Born; 5/22/73, Mississauga, Ontario. 6-1, 185.

Duane Derksen — Goaltender

			Regular Season							Playoffs					
Season	Team	League	GP	MIN	GAVG	W	L	T	SO	GP	MIN	GAVG	W	L	SO
92-93	Baltimore	AHL	26	1247	4.14	6	13	3	0	4	188	2.23	1	1	0
92-93	Hampton Roads	ECHL	13	747	3.86	7	5	0	0	—	—	—	—	—	—
93-94	Adirondack	AHL	11	600	3.70	4	6	0	0	—	—	—	—	—	—
93-94	Milwaukee	IHL	9	490	3.42	4	2	2	0	—	—	—	—	—	—
94-95	Minnesota	IHL	7	251	5.02	1	3	3	0	—	—	—	—	—	—
94-95	Richmond	ECHL	27	1558	3.20	15	8	2	0	4	99	3.62	1	0	0
95-96	Fort Wayne	IHL	1	22	8.01	0	0	0	0	—	—	—	—	—	—
95-96	Milwaukee	IHL	1	34	1.79	0	0	0	0	—	—	—	—	—	—
95-96	Madison	CoHL	40	2209	3.48	19	15	3	1	6	362	4.47	2	4	0
96-97	Milwaukee	IHL	1	60	2.00	0	0	1	0	—	—	—	—	—	—
96-97	Madison	CoHL	59	3365	3.39	36	17	5	0	5	279	3.66	2	3	0
	AHL	Totals	37	1847	4.00	10	19	3	0	4	188	2.23	1	1	0
	IHL	Totals	19	857	3.85	5	5	6	0	—	—	—	—	—	—
	CoHL	Totals	99	5574	3.42	55	32	8	1	11	641	4.12	4	7	0
	ECHL	Totals	40	2305	3.41	22	13	2	0	4	99	3.62	1	0	0

Born; 7/7/68, St. Boniface, Manitoba. 6-1, 188. Selected by Washington Capitals (fourth round, 57th overall) 6/11/88. Member of 1994-95 Riley Cup Champion Richmond Renegades. 1996-97 CoHL Second Team All-Star.

Phillipe DeRouville — Goaltender

			Regular Season							Playoffs					
Season	Team	League	GP	W	L	T	MIN	SO	GAVG	GP	W	L	MIN	SO	GAVG
94-95	PIT	NHL	1	1	0	0	60	0	3.00	—	—	—	—	—	—
94-95	CLV	IHL	41	24	10	5	2369	1	3.32	4	1	3	263	0	4.09
95-96	CLV	IHL	38	19	11	3	2007	1	3.86	—	—	—	—	—	—
96-97	Pittsburgh	NHL	2	0	2	0	111	0	3.24	—	—	—	—	—	—
96-97	Kansas City	IHL	26	11	11	4	1470	2	2.82	2	0	1	33	0	7.35
	NHL	Totals	3	1	2	0	171	0	3.16	—	—	—	—	—	—
	IHL	Totals	105	54	32	12	5846	4	3.38	6	1	4	296	0	4.46

Born; 8/7/74, Victoriaville, Quebec. 6-1, 183. Drafted by Pittsburgh Penguins (5th choice, 115th overall) in 1992 Entry Draft.

Mark DeSantis — Defenseman

			Regular Season					Playoffs				
Season	Team	League	GP	G	A	PTS	PIM	GP	G	A	PTS	PIM
93-94	San Diego	IHL	54	5	10	15	95	—	—	—	—	—
94-95	San Diego	IHL	8	0	0	0	23	—	—	—	—	—
94-95	Greensboro	ECHL	57	10	34	44	196	15	0	4	4	71
95-96	Baltimore	AHL	8	0	0	0	21	—	—	—	—	—
95-96	Jacksonville	ECHL	51	12	32	44	243	18	6	15	21	56
96-97	San Antonio	IHL	61	7	15	22	184	2	0	1	1	2
	IHL	Totals	123	12	25	37	302	2	0	1	1	2
	ECHL	Totals	108	22	66	88	439	33	6	19	25	127

Born; 1/12/72, Brampton, Ontario. 6-0, 205. Signed as a free agent by Anaheim Mighty Ducks (8/2/93).

Kevin Deschambeault — Goaltender

			Regular Season						Playoffs					
Season	Team	League	GP	W	L	T	MIN	SO	GAVG	GP	W	L	MIN	SO	GAVG
96-97	Columbus	CeHL	35	16	13	2	1911	0	3.96	—	—	—	—	—	—
96-97	Memphis	CeHL	5	2	2	1	294	0	4.29	4	1	2	192	0	*2.50
	CeHL	Totals	40	18	15	3	2205	0	4.00	4	1	2	192	0	2.50

Born; 5/29/72, Leeds, Maine. 5-10, 175. Last amateur club; Miami of Ohio (CCHA).

Frederic Deschenes — Goaltender

			Regular Season						Playoffs					
Season	Team	League	GP	W	L	T	MIN	SO	GAVG	GP	W	L	MIN	SO	GAVG
96-97	Rochester	AHL	38	15	13	3	1898	2	2.85	10	6	4	628	0	2.68
96-97	Flint	CoHL	3	3	0	0	180	0	1.67	—	—	—	—	—	—

Born; 1/12/76, Quebec, Quebec. 5-9, 164. Drafted by Detroit Red Wings (4th choice, 114th overall) in 1994 Entry Draft.

Stephane Desjardins — Defenseman

			Regular Season					Playoffs				
Season	Team	League	GP	G	A	PTS	PIM	GP	G	A	PTS	PIM
93-94	Fort Worth	CeHL	37	7	16	23	58	—	—	—	—	—
94-95	Roanoke	ECHL	58	2	5	7	64	7	0	0	0	9
95-96	Nashville	ECHL	39	3	13	16	55	—	—	—	—	—
95-96	Columbus	ECHL	20	1	3	4	6	3	0	0	0	0
96-97	Austin	WPHL	37	2	8	10	84	—	—	—	—	—
96-97	Central Texas	WPHL	8	2	3	5	24	—	—	—	—	—
96-97	Waco	WPHL	16	4	3	7	18	—	—	—	—	—
	ECHL	Totals	117	6	21	27	125	10	0	0	0	9
	WPHL	Totals	61	8	14	22	126					

Born; 6/23/72, Anjou, Quebec. 5-11, 195.

Jarrett Deuling — Left Wing

			Regular Season					Playoffs				
Season	Team	League	GP	G	A	PTS	PIM	GP	G	A	PTS	PIM
94-95	Worcester	AHL	63	11	8	19	37	—	—	—	—	—
95-96	Islanders	NHL	14	0	1	1	11	—	—	—	—	—
95-96	Worcester	AHL	57	16	7	23	57	4	1	2	3	2
96-97	Islanders	NHL	1	0	0	0	0	—	—	—	—	—
96-97	Kentucky	AHL	58	15	31	46	57	4	3	0	3	8
	NHL	Totals	15	0	1	1	11	—	—	—	—	—
	AHL	Totals	178	42	46	88	151	8	4	2	6	10

Born; 3/4/74, Vernon, British Columbia. 5-11, 195. Drafted by New York Islanders (2nd choice, 56th overall) in 1992 Entry Draft.

Boyd Devereaux — Center

			Regular Season					Playoffs				
Season	Team	League	GP	G	A	PTS	PIM	GP	G	A	PTS	PIM
96-97	Hamilton	AHL	—	—	—	—	—	1	0	1	1	0

Born; 45/16/78, Seaforth, Ontario. Drafted by Edmonton Oilers (1st choice, 6th overall) in 1996 Entry Draft.

John Devereaux — Center

			Regular Season					Playoffs				
Season	Team	League	GP	G	A	PTS	PIM	GP	G	A	PTS	PIM
88-89	Flint	IHL	11	3	1	4	11	—	—	—	—	—
88-89	Carolina	ECHL	28	18	31	49	32	11	7	7	14	10
89-90	Winston-Salem	ECHL	58	22	48	70	110	8	1	2	3	11
90-91	Winston-Salem	ECHL	57	20	37	57	47	—	—	—	—	—
91-92	Winston-Salem	ECHL	2	1	1	2	2	—	—	—	—	—
91-92	Greensboro	ECHL	32	5	16	21	77	11	3	4	7	10
93-94	Greensboro	ECHL	1	0	0	0	0	—	—	—	—	—
95-96	Winston-Salem	SHL	43	19	32	51	50	9	2	10	12	4
96-97	Reno	WCHL	32	12	23	35	62	—	—	—	—	—
96-97	Bakersfield	WCHL	20	10	19	29	10	4	0	1	1	29
	ECHL	Totals	178	66	133	199	268	30	11	13	24	31
	WCHL	Totals	52	22	42	64	72	4	0	1	1	29

Born; 6/6/65, Cincinnati, Ohio. 6-0, 205. Drafted by Hartford Whalers (4th choice, 173rd overall) in 1984 Entry Draft.

Greg deVries — Defenseman

			Regular Season					Playoffs				
Season	Team	League	GP	G	A	PTS	PIM	GP	G	A	PTS	PIM
93-94	Cape Breton	AHL	9	0	0	0	11	1	0	0	0	0
94-95	Cape Breton	AHL	77	5	19	24	68	—	—	—	—	—
95-96	Edmonton	NHL	13	1	1	2	12	—	—	—	—	—
95-96	Cape Breton	AHL	58	9	30	39	174	—	—	—	—	—
96-97	Edmonton	NHL	37	0	4	4	52	12	0	1	1	8
96-97	Hamilton	AHL	34	4	14	18	26	—	—	—	—	—
	NHL	Totals	50	1	5	6	64	12	0	1	1	8
	AHL	Totals	187	18	45	63	279	1	0	0	0	0

Born; 1/4/73, Sundridge, Ontario. 6-3, 218. Signed as a free agent by Edmonton Oilers (3/20/94).

Len Devuono — Defenseman

			Regular Season					Playoffs				
Season	Team	League	GP	G	A	PTS	PIM	GP	G	A	PTS	PIM
91-92	Moncton	AHL	1	0	0	0	0	—	—	—	—	—
91-92	Brantford	CoHL	6	0	0	0	19	—	—	—	—	—
93-94	West Palm Beach	SUN	5	0	5	5	22	—	—	—	—	—
95-96	Wichita	CeHL	47	2	9	11	171	—	—	—	—	—
96-97	Reno	WCHL	40	5	11	16	109	—	—	—	—	—
96-97	Wichita	CeHL	9	0	1	1	67	—	—	—	—	—
96-97	Utica	CoHL	9	3	3	6	2	—	—	—	—	—
	CeHL	Totals	56	2	10	12	238	—	—	—	—	—
	CoHL	Totals	15	3	3	6	21	—	—	—	—	—

Born; 2/7/71, Sault Ste. Marie, Ontario. 6-0, 193.

Brad Dexter — Defenseman

			Regular Season					Playoffs				
Season	Team	League	GP	G	A	PTS	PIM	GP	G	A	PTS	PIM
96-97	Raleigh	ECHL	52	8	32	40	20	—	—	—	—	—
96-97	South Carolina	ECHL	16	0	17	17	12	18	3	*23	26	8
	ECHL	Totals	68	8	49	57	32	18	3	23	26	8

Born; 3/29/72, Kingston, Ontario. 6-3, 180. Member of 1996-97 ECHL Champion South Carolina Stingrays.

Jason Dexter — Center

			Regular Season					Playoffs				
Season	Team	League	GP	G	A	PTS	PIM	GP	G	A	PTS	PIM
94-95	Birmingham	ECHL	19	5	10	15	0	7	3	4	7	2
95-96	Birmingham	ECHL	63	18	18	36	20	—	—	—	—	—
96-97	Columbus	CeHL	66	29	44	73	27	3	1	1	2	0
	ECHL	Totals	82	23	28	51	20	7	3	4	7	2

Born; 3/12/71, Kingston, Ontario. 6-1, 210.

Mark Deyell — Center

			Regular Season					Playoffs				
Season	Team	League	GP	G	A	PTS	PIM	GP	G	A	PTS	PIM
96-97	St. John's	AHL	58	15	27	42	30	10	1	5	6	6

Born; 3/26/76, Regina, Saskatchewan. 5-11, 170. Drafted by Toronto Maple Leafs (4th choice, 126th overall) in 1994 Entry Draft.

Norm Dezainde — Left Wing

			Regular Season					Playoffs				
Season	Team	League	GP	G	A	PTS	PIM	GP	G	A	PTS	PIM
93-94	Toledo	ECHL	—	—	—	—	—	6	0	1	1	6
94-95	Syracuse	AHL	6	0	1	1	17	—	—	—	—	—
94-95	Toledo	ECHL	20	6	15	21	47	—	—	—	—	—
94-95	South Carolina	ECHL	9	0	0	0	6	—	—	—	—	—
95-96	Toledo	ECHL	66	21	19	40	238	5	0	1	1	8
96-97	Adirondack	AHL	2	1	0	1	4	—	—	—	—	—
96-97	Toledo	ECHL	49	7	16	23	197	—	—	—	—	—
96-97	Dayton	ECHL	15	3	4	7	78	4	3	0	3	10
	AHL	Totals	8	1	1	2	21	—	—	—	—	—
	ECHL	Totals	159	37	54	91	566	15	3	2	5	24

Born; 1/29/73, Jarvis, Ontario. 5-10, 180. Member of 1993-94 ECHL champion Toledo Storm.

Gord Dineen — Defenseman

			Regular Season					Playoffs				
Season	Team	League	GP	G	A	PTS	PIM	GP	G	A	PTS	PIM
82-83	Islanders	NHL	2	0	0	0	4	—	—	—	—	—
82-83	Indianapolis	CHL	73	10	47	57	78	13	2	10	12	29
83-84	Islanders	NHL	43	1	11	12	32	9	1	1	2	28
83-84	Indianapolis	CHL	26	4	13	17	63	—	—	—	—	—
84-85	Islanders	NHL	48	1	12	13	89	10	0	0	0	26
84-85	Springfield	AHL	25	1	8	9	46	—	—	—	—	—
85-86	Islanders	NHL	57	1	8	9	81	3	0	0	0	2
85-86	Springfield	AHL	11	2	3	5	20	—	—	—	—	—
86-87	Islanders	NHL	71	4	10	14	110	7	0	4	4	4
87-88	Islanders	NHL	57	4	12	16	62	—	—	—	—	—
87-88	Minnesota	NHL	13	1	1	2	21	—	—	—	—	—
88-89	Minnesota	NHL	2	0	1	1	2	—	—	—	—	—
88-89	Pittsburgh	NHL	38	1	2	3	42	11	0	2	2	8
88-89	Kalamazoo	IHL	25	2	6	8	49	—	—	—	—	—
89-90	Pittsburgh	NHL	69	1	8	9	125	—	—	—	—	—
90-91	Pittsburgh	NHL	9	0	0	0	4	—	—	—	—	—
90-91	Muskegon	IHL	40	1	14	15	57	5	0	2	2	0
91-92	Pittsburgh	NHL	1	0	0	0	0	—	—	—	—	—
91-92	Muskegon	IHL	79	8	37	45	83	14	2	4	6	33
92-93	Ottawa	NHL	32	2	4	6	30	—	—	—	—	—
92-93	San Diego	IHL	41	6	23	29	36	—	—	—	—	—
93-94	Ottawa	NHL	77	0	21	21	89	—	—	—	—	—
93-94	San Diego	IHL	3	0	0	0	2	—	—	—	—	—
94-95	Islanders	NHL	9	0	0	0	2	—	—	—	—	—
94-95	Denver	IHL	68	5	27	32	75	17	1	6	7	8

Season	Team	League	GP	G	A	PTS	PIM	GP	G	A	PTS	PIM
95-96	Utah	IHL	82	1	17	18	89	22	0	3	3	14
96-97	Utah	IHL	81	5	29	34	62	7	0	3	3	4
	NHL	Totals	528	16	90	106	693	40	1	7	8	68
	IHL	Totals	419	28	153	181	453	65	3	18	21	59
	CHL	Totals	99	14	60	74	141	13	2	10	12	29
	AHL	Totals	36	3	11	14	66	—	—	—	—	—

Born; 9/21/62, Quebec City, Quebec. 6-0, 195. Drafted by New York Islanders (2nd choice, 42nd overall) in 1981 Entry Draft. Traded to Monnesota North Stars by Islanders for Chris Pryor and future considerations (3/8/88). Traded to Pittsburgh Penguins by Minnesota with Scott Bjustad for Ville Siren and Steve Gotaas (12/17/88). Signed as a free agent by Ottawa Senators (8/31/92). Signed as a free agent by Islanders (7/26/94). 1982-83 CHL First All-Star Team. 1982-83 Won Bob Gassoff Trophy (CHL's Most Improved Defenseman). 1982-83 Won Bobby Orr Trophy (CHL's Top Defenseman). 1991-92 IHL First Team All-Star. Member of 1982-83 CHL champion Indianapolis Checkers. Member of 1994-95 IHL champion Denver Grizzlies. Member of 1995-96 IHL champion Utah Grizzlies.

Chris Dingman — Left Wing

			Regular Season					Playoffs				
Season	Team	League	GP	G	A	PTS	PIM	GP	G	A	PTS	PIM
95-96	Saint John	AHL	—	—	—	—	—	1	0	0	0	0
96-97	Saint John	AHL	71	5	6	11	195	—	—	—	—	—
	AHL	Totals	71	5	6	11	195	1	0	0	0	0

Born; 7/6/76, Edmonton, Alberta. 6-4, 225. Drafted by Calgary Flames (1st choice, 19th overall) in 1994 Entry Draft.

Gilbert Dionne — Left Wing

			Regular Season					Playoffs				
Season	Team	League	GP	G	A	PTS	PIM	GP	G	A	PTS	PIM
90-91	Montreal	NHL	2	0	0	0	0	—	—	—	—	—
90-91	Fredericton	AHL	77	40	47	87	62	9	6	5	11	8
91-92	Montreal	NHL	39	21	13	34	10	11	3	4	7	10
91-92	Fredericton	AHL	29	19	27	46	20	—	—	—	—	—
92-93	Montreal	NHL	75	20	28	48	63	20	6	6	12	20
92-93	Fredericton	AHL	3	4	3	7	0	—	—	—	—	—
93-94	Montreal	NHL	74	19	26	45	31	5	1	2	3	0
94-95	Montreal	NHL	6	0	3	3	2	—	—	—	—	—
94-95	Philadelphia	NHL	20	0	6	6	2	3	0	0	0	4
95-96	Philadelphia	NHL	2	0	1	1	0	—	—	—	—	—
95-96	Florida	NHL	5	1	2	3	0	—	—	—	—	—
95-96	Carolina	AHL	55	43	58	101	29	—	—	—	—	—
96-97	Carolina	AHL	72	41	47	88	69	—	—	—	—	—
	NHL	Totals	223	61	79	140	108	39	10	12	22	34
	AHL	Totals	164	106	135	241	111	9	6	5	11	8

Born; 9/19/70, Drummondville, Quebec. 6-0, 194. Drafted by Montreal Canadiens (5th choice, 81st overall) in 1990 Entry Draft. Traded to Philadelphia Flyers by Montreal with Eric Desjardins and John LeClair for Mark Recchi and Philadelphia's third round choice (Martin Hohenberger) in 1995 Entry Draft (2/9/95). Member of 1992-93 Stanley Cup champion Montreal Canadiens. 1995-96 AHL Second Team All-Star.

Paul DiPietro — Center

			Regular Season					Playoffs				
Season	Team	League	GP	G	A	PTS	PIM	GP	G	A	PTS	PIM
90-91	Fredericton	AHL	78	39	31	70	38	9	5	6	11	2
91-92	Montreal	NHL	33	4	6	10	25	—	—	—	—	—
91-92	Fredericton	AHL	43	26	31	57	52	7	3	4	7	8
92-93	Montreal	NHL	29	4	13	17	14	17	8	5	13	8
92-93	Fredericton	AHL	26	8	16	24	16	—	—	—	—	—
93-94	Montreal	NHL	70	13	20	33	37	7	2	4	6	2
94-95	Montreal	NHL	22	4	5	9	4	—	—	—	—	—
94-95	Toronto	NHL	12	1	1	2	6	7	1	1	2	0
95-96	Toronto	NHL	20	4	4	8	4	—	—	—	—	—
95-96	St. John's	AHL	2	2	2	4	0	—	—	—	—	—
95-96	Houston	IHL	36	18	23	41	44	—	—	—	—	—
95-96	Las Vegas	IHL	13	5	6	11	10	13	4	8	12	16

Season	Team	League	GP	G	A	PTS	PIM	GP	G	A	PTS	PIM
96-97	Los Angeles	NHL	6	1	0	1	6	—	—	—	—	—
96-97	Phoenix	IHL	33	9	20	29	32	—	—	—	—	—
96-97	Cincinnati	IHL	32	15	14	29	28	3	1	1	2	2
	NHL	Totals	192	31	49	80	96	31	11	10	21	10
	AHL	Totals	149	75	80	155	110	16	8	10	18	10
	IHL	Totals	114	47	63	110	114	16	5	9	14	18

Born; 9/8/70, Sault Ste. Marie, Ontario. 5-9, 181. Drafted by Montreal Canadiens (6th choice, 102nd overall) in 1990 Entry Draft. Traded to Toronto Maple Leafs by Montreal for a conditional fourth round draft choice (4/6/95). Signed as a free agent by Los Angeles Kings (1996). Member of 1992-93 Stanley Cup champion Montreal Canadiens.

Robert Dirk — Defenseman

			Regular Season					Playoffs				
Season	Team	League	GP	G	A	PTS	PIM	GP	G	A	PTS	PIM
86-87	Peoria	IHL	76	5	17	22	155	—	—	—	—	—
87-88	St. Louis	NHL	7	0	1	1	16	6	0	1	1	2
87-88	Peoria	IHL	54	4	21	25	126	—	—	—	—	—
88-89	St. Louis	NHL	9	0	1	1	11	—	—	—	—	—
88-89	Peoria	IHL	22	0	2	2	54	—	—	—	—	—
89-90	St. Louis	NHL	37	1	1	2	128	3	0	0	0	0
89-90	Peoria	IHL	24	1	2	3	79	—	—	—	—	—
90-91	St. Louis	NHL	41	1	3	4	100	—	—	—	—	—
90-91	Vancouver	NHL	11	1	0	1	20	6	0	0	0	13
90-91	Peoria	IHL	3	0	0	0	2	—	—	—	—	—
91-92	Vancouver	NHL	72	2	7	9	126	13	0	0	0	20
92-93	Vancouver	NHL	69	4	8	12	150	9	0	0	0	6
93-94	Vancouver	NHL	65	2	3	5	105	—	—	—	—	—
93-94	Chicago	NHL	6	0	0	0	26	2	0	0	0	15
94-95	Anaheim	NHL	38	1	3	4	56	—	—	—	—	—
95-96	Anaheim	NHL	44	1	2	3	42	—	—	—	—	—
95-96	Montreal	NHL	3	0	0	0	6	—	—	—	—	—
96-97	Detroit	IHL	48	2	8	10	36	—	—	—	—	—
96-97	Chicago	IHL	31	1	5	6	26	3	0	0	0	0
	NHL	Totals	402	13	29	42	786	39	0	1	1	56
	IHL	Totals	258	13	55	68	478	3	0	0	0	0

Born; 8/20/66, Regina, Saskatchewan. 6-4, 210. Drafted by St. Louis Blues (4th choice, 53rd overall) in 1984 Entry Draft. Traded to Vancouver Canucks by St.Louis with Geoff Courtnall, Sergio Momesso, Cliff Ronning and St. Louis' fifth round choice (Brian Loney) in 1992 Entry Draft for Dan Quinn and Garth Butcher, 3/5/91. Traded to Chicago Blackhawks by Vancouver for Chicago's forth round choice (Mike Dubinsky) in 1994 Entry Draft, 3/21/94. Traded to Anaheim Mighty Ducks by Chicago for Tampa Bay's fourth round choice (previously acquired by Anaheim-Chicago selected Chris Van Dyk) in 1995 Entry Draft, 7/21/94. Traded to Montreal Canadiens by Anaheim for Jim Campbell, 1/21/96). Named coach of the Winston-Salem IceHawks beginning with 1997 season.

Jason Disher — Defenseman

			Regular Season					Playoffs				
Season	Team	League	GP	G	A	PTS	PIM	GP	G	A	PTS	PIM
95-96	Prince Edward Island	AHL	10	0	1	1	13	—	—	—	—	—
95-96	Thunder Bay	CoHL	40	0	15	15	167	18	1	4	5	73
96-97	Thunder Bay	CoHL	60	9	13	22	240	11	6	3	9	56
	CoHL	Totals	100	9	28	37	407	29	7	7	14	129

Born; 5/28/75, Windsor, Ontario. 6-2, 208. Drafted by Ottawa Senators (7th choice, 183rd overall) in 1993 Entry Draft.

Brian Dobbin — Right Wing

			Regular Season					Playoffs				
Season	Team	League	GP	G	A	PTS	PIM	GP	G	A	PTS	PIM
85-86	Hershey	AHL	2	1	0	1	0	18	5	5	10	21
86-87	Philadelphia	NHL	12	2	1	3	14	—	—	—	—	—
86-87	Hershey	AHL	52	26	35	61	66	5	4	2	6	15
87-88	Philadelphia	NHL	21	3	5	8	6	—	—	—	—	—
87-88	Hershey	AHL	54	36	47	83	58	12	7	8	15	15
88-89	Philadelphia	NHL	14	0	1	1	8	2	0	0	0	17

Season	Team	League	GP	G	A	PTS	PIM	GP	G	A	PTS	PIM
88-89	Hershey	AHL	59	43	48	91	61	11	7	6	13	12
89-90	Philadelphia	NHL	9	1	1	2	11	—	—	—	—	—
89-90	Hershey	AHL	68	38	47	85	58	—	—	—	—	—
90-91	Hershey	AHL	80	33	43	76	82	7	1	2	3	7
91-92	Boston	NHL	7	1	0	12	22	—	—	—	—	—
91-92	New Haven	AHL	33	16	21	37	20	—	—	—	—	—
91-92	Maine	AHL	33	21	15	36	14	—	—	—	—	—
92-93	Milwaukee	IHL	80	39	45	84	50	6	4	3	7	6
93-94	Milwaukee	IHL	81	48	53	101	73	4	1	0	1	4
94-95	Milwaukee	IHL	76	21	40	61	62	9	0	4	4	2
95-96	Cincinnati	IHL	82	28	37	65	97	17	2	2	4	14
96-97	Grand Rapids	IHL	29	4	5	9	39	—	—	—	—	—
96-97	Muskegon	CoHL	2	0	0	0	2	—	—	—	—	—
96-97	Austin	WPHL	23	14	18	32	25	6	2	5	7	11
	NHL	Totals	63	7	8	15	61	2	0	0	0	17
	IHL	Totals	348	140	180	320	321	36	7	9	16	26
	AHL	Totals	331	214	256	470	240	53	24	23	47	70

Born; 8/18/66, Petrolia, Ontario. 6-1, 205. Drafted by Philadelphia Flyers (6th choice, 100th overall) in 1984 Entry Draft (6/9/84). Traded to Boston Bruins by Philadelphia with Gord Murphy and third round pick in 1992 Draft (Sergei Zholtok) for Garry Galley, Wes Walz and future considerations (1/2/92). 1988-89 AHL First Team All-Star. 1989-90 AHL Second Team All-Star. 1993-94 IHL Second Team All-Star.

Jason Doig — Defenseman

Season	Team	League	GP	G	A	PTS	PIM	GP	G	A	PTS	PIM
95-96	Winnipeg	NHL	15	1	1	2	28	—	—	—	—	—
95-96	Springfield	AHL	5	0	0	0	28	—	—	—	—	—
96-97	Las Vegas	IHL	6	0	1	1	19	—	—	—	—	—
96-97	Springfield	AHL	5	0	3	3	2	17	1	4	5	37
	AHL	Totals	10	0	3	3	30	17	1	4	5	37

Born; 1/29/77, Montreal, Quebec. 6-3, 216. Drafted by Winnipeg Jets (3rd choice, 34th overall) in 1995 Entry Draft.

Robert Dome — Right Wing

Season	Team	League	GP	G	A	PTS	PIM	GP	G	A	PTS	PIM
95-96	Utah	IHL	56	10	9	19	28	—	—	—	—	—
96-97	Long Beach	IHL	13	4	6	10	14	—	—	—	—	—
96-97	Las Vegas	IHL	43	10	7	17	22	—	—	—	—	—
	IHL	Totals	112	24	22	46	64	—	—	—	—	—

Born; 1/29/79, Skalica, Czechoslovakia. 6-2, 205. Drafted by Pittsburgh Penguins (1st choice, 17th overall) in 1997 Entry Draft.

Hnat Domenichelli — Center

Season	Team	League	GP	G	A	PTS	PIM	GP	G	A	PTS	PIM
96-97	Hartford	NHL	13	2	1	3	7	—	—	—	—	—
96-97	Calgary	NHL	10	1	2	3	2	—	—	—	—	—
96-97	Springfield	AHL	39	24	24	48	12	—	—	—	—	—
96-97	Saint John	AHL	1	1	1	2	0	5	5	0	5	2
	NHL	Totals	23	3	3	6	9	—	—	—	—	—
	AHL	Totals	40	25	25	50	12	5	5	0	5	2

Born; 2/17/76, Edmonton, Alberta. 6-0, 175. Drafted by Hartford Whalers (2nd choice, 83rd overall) in 1994 Entry Draft. Traded to Calgary Flames by Hartford with Glen Featherstone, Second round pick (originally acquired from New Jersey—Dimitri Kokorev), and third round pick in 1998 Entry Draft for Steve Chiasson and third round pick (originally acquired from Colorado and New York Islanders—Francis Lessard), March 5, 1997.

Mark Donahue — Right Wing

Season	Team	League	GP	G	A	PTS	PIM	GP	G	A	PTS	PIM
94-95	Saginaw	CoHL	18	4	6	10	52	9	3	3	6	15

95-96	Saginaw	CoHL	58	25	24	49	121	3	3	1	4	4
96-97	Birmingham	ECHL	61	15	14	29	120	8	2	1	3	12
	CoHL	Totals	76	29	30	59	173	12	6	4	10	19

Born; 2/18/73, Farmington Hills, Michigan. 6-0, 199.

Derek Donald — Right Wing

			Regular Season					Playoffs				
Season	Team	League	GP	G	A	PTS	PIM	GP	G	A	PTS	PIM
92-93	Dayton	ECHL	63	22	44	66	56	3	1	2	3	0
93-94	Moncton	AHL	7	4	1	5	0	—	—	—	—	—
93-94	Peoria	IHL	3	0	0	0	2	—	—	—	—	—
93-94	Dayton	ECHL	62	51	51	102	98	3	0	2	2	8
95-96	Anchorage	WCHL	56	38	45	83	109	—	—	—	—	—
96-97	Anchorage	WCHL	57	51	47	98	52	9	2	6	8	36
	ECHL	Totals	125	73	95	168	154	6	1	4	5	8
	WCHL	Totals	113	89	92	181	161	9	2	6	8	36

Born; 5/1/70, Calgary, Alberta. 5-8, 180.

Gord Donnelly — Defenseman

			Regular Season					Playoffs				
Season	Team	League	GP	G	A	PTS	PIM	GP	G	A	PTS	PIM
82-83	Salt Lake City	CHL	67	3	12	15	222	6	1	1	2	8
83-84	Quebec	NHL	38	0	5	5	60	—	—	—	—	—
83-84	Fredericton	AHL	30	2	3	5	146	7	1	1	2	43
84-85	Quebec	NHL	22	0	0	0	33	—	—	—	—	—
84-85	Fredericton	AHL	42	1	5	6	134	6	0	1	1	25
85-86	Quebec	NHL	36	2	2	4	85	1	0	0	0	0
85-86	Fredericton	AHL	38	3	5	8	103	5	0	0	0	33
86-87	Quebec	NHL	38	0	2	2	143	13	0	0	0	53
87-88	Quebec	NHL	63	4	3	7	301	—	—	—	—	—
88-89	Quebec	NHL	16	4	0	4	46	—	—	—	—	—
88-89	Winnipeg	NHL	57	6	10	16	228	—	—	—	—	—
89-90	Winnipeg	NHL	55	3	3	6	222	6	0	1	1	8
90-91	Winnipeg	NHL	57	3	4	7	265	—	—	—	—	—
91-92	Winnipeg	NHL	4	0	0	0	11	—	—	—	—	—
91-92	Buffalo	NHL	67	2	3	5	305	6	0	1	1	0
92-93	Buffalo	NHL	60	3	8	11	221	—	—	—	—	—
93-94	Buffalo	NHL	7	0	0	0	31	—	—	—	—	—
93-94	Dallas	NHL	18	0	1	1	66	—	—	—	—	—
94-95	Dallas	NHL	16	1	0	1	52	—	—	—	—	—
94-95	Kalamazoo	IHL	7	2	2	4	18	—	—	—	—	—
95-96	Houston	IHL	73	3	4	7	333	—	—	—	—	—
96-97	Houston	IHL	5	0	0	0	25	—	—	—	—	—
96-97	Chicago	IHL	59	3	5	8	144	4	0	2	2	28
	NHL	Totals	554	28	41	69	2069	26	0	2	2	61
	IHL	Totals	144	8	11	19	520	4	0	2	2	28
	AHL	Totals	110	6	13	19	383	18	1	2	3	101

Born; 4/5/62, Montreal, Quebec. 6-1, 202. Drafted by St. Louis Blues (3rd choice, 62nd overall) in 1981 Entry Draft. Rights transferred to Quebec Nordiques by St. Louis with rights to Claude Julien when St. Louis signed Jacques Demers as coach (8/19/83). Traded to Winnipeg Jets by Quebec for Mario Marois (12/6/88). Traded to Buffalo Sabres by Winnipeg with Dave McLlwain, Winnipeg's fifth round choice (Yuri Khymlev) in 1992 Entry Draft and future considerations for Darrin Shannon, Mike Hartman and Dean Kennedy (10/11/91). Traded to Dallas Stars by Buffalo for James Black and Dallas' seventh round choice (Steve Webb) in 1994 Entry Draft (12/15/93).

Mike Donnelly — Left Wing

			Regular Season					Playoffs				
Season	Team	League	GP	G	A	PTS	PIM	GP	G	A	PTS	PIM
86-87	Rangers	NHL	5	1	1	2	0	—	—	—	—	—
86-87	New Haven	AHL	58	27	34	61	52	7	2	0	2	9
87-88	Rangers	NHL	17	2	2	4	8	—	—	—	—	—

Season	Team	League	GP	G	A	PTS	PIM	GP	G	A	PTS	PIM
87-88	Buffalo	NHL	40	6	8	14	44	—	—	—	—	—
87-88	Colorado	IHL	8	7	11	18	15	—	—	—	—	—
88-89	Buffalo	NHL	22	4	6	10	10	—	—	—	—	—
88-89	Rochester	AHL	53	32	37	69	53	—	—	—	—	—
89-90	Buffalo	NHL	12	1	2	3	8	—	—	—	—	—
89-90	Rochester	AHL	68	43	55	98	71	16	*12	7	19	9
90-91	Los Angeles	NHL	53	7	5	12	41	12	5	4	9	6
90-91	New Haven	AHL	18	10	6	16	2	—	—	—	—	—
91-92	Los Angeles	NHL	80	29	16	45	20	6	1	0	1	4
92-93	Los Angeles	NHL	84	29	40	69	45	24	6	7	13	14
93-94	Los Angeles	NHL	81	21	21	42	34	—	—	—	—	—
94-95	Los Angeles	NHL	9	1	1	2	4	—	—	—	—	—
94-95	Dallas	NHL	35	11	14	25	29	5	0	1	1	6
95-96	Dallas	NHL	24	2	5	7	10	—	—	—	—	—
95-96	Michigan	IHL	21	8	15	23	20	8	3	0	3	10
96-97	Islanders	NHL	3	0	0	0	2	—	—	—	—	—
96-97	Utah	IHL	14	7	2	9	33	—	—	—	—	—
96-97	Detroit	IHL	19	4	4	8	12	—	—	—	—	—
	NHL	Totals	465	114	121	235	255	47	12	12	24	30
	AHL	Totals	197	112	132	244	178	23	14	7	21	18
	IHL	Totals	62	26	32	58	80	8	3	0	3	10

Born; 10/10/63, Detroit, Michigan. 5-11, 185. Signed as a free agent by New York Rangers (8/15/86). Traded to Buffalo Sabres by Rangers with Rangers' fifth round pick (Alexander Mogilny) in 1988 Entry Draft for Paul Cyr and Buffalo's tenth round choice (Eric Fenton) in 1988 Entry Draft (12/31/87). Traded to Los Angeles Kings by Buffalo for Mikko Makela (9/30/90). Traded to Dallas Stars by Los Angeles with Los Angeles' seventh round choice (Eoin Mcinerney) in 1996 Entry Draft for Dallas' fourth round choice (later traded to Washington-Washington selected Justin Davis) in 1996 Entry draft (2/17/95) Signed as a free agent by New York Islanders (8/19/96).

Rob Dobson — Goaltender

			Regular Season							Playoffs				
Season	Team	League	GP	W	L	T	MIN	SO	GAVG	GP	W	L	MIN	SO	GAVG
90-91	Muskegon	IHL	24	10	10	0	1243	0	4.34	—	—	—	—	—	—
90-91	Louisville	ECHL	3	3	0	0	180	0	4.00	5	3	1	270	0	3.55
91-92	Muskegon	IHL	28	13	12	2	1655	4	3.26	12	8	4	697	0	3.44
92-93	Cleveland	IHL	50	26	15	3	2825	1	3.55	4	0	4	203	0	5.91
93-94	Pittsburgh	NHL	2	0	0	0	45	0	4.00	—	—	—	—	—	—
93-94	Cleveland	IHL	32	9	10	8	1681	0	3.89	—	—	—	—	—	—
94-95	Houston	IHL	41	17	16	2	2102	0	3.40	1	0	0	40	0	9.00
95-96	Louisiana	ECHL	2	1	0	1	120	0	2.00	—	—	—	—	—	—
95-96	Houston	IHL	38	10	13	3	1700	0	3.74	—	—	—	—	—	—
96-97	Houston	IHL	12	5	4	1	637	0	3.39	—	—	—	—	—	—
	IHL	Totals	225	90	80	19	11843	5	3.58	17	8	8	940	0	4.21

Born; 8/21/67, Smith Falls, Ontario. 6-0, 205. Signed as a free agent by Houston (7/6/91).

David Dorosh — Goaltender

			Regular Season							Playoffs					
Season	Team	League	GP	W	L	T	MIN	SO	GAVG	GP	W	L	MIN	SO	GAVG
94-95	Daytona Beach	SUN	12	3	7	0	598	0	4.72	—	—	—	—	—	—
95-96	N/A														
96-97	Brantford	CoHL	12	5	3	2	544	0	4.85	1	0	0	23	0	5.19

Born; Mississauga, Ontario. 6-0, 175.

Cory Dosdall — Center

			Regular Season					Playoffs				
Season	Team	League	GP	G	A	PTS	PIM	GP	G	A	PTS	PIM
96-97	Wichita	CeHL	62	36	36	72	272	9	2	3	5	23

Born; 2/1/73, Regina, Saskatchewan. 5-10, 185. 1996-97 CeHL Rookie of the Year.

Dave D. Doucet — Defenseman

			Regular Season					Playoffs				
Season	Team	League	GP	G	A	PTS	PIM	GP	G	A	PTS	PIM
94-95	Daytona Beach	SUN	33	8	9	17	108	—	—	—	—	—
95-96	Daytona Beach	SHL	58	12	35	47	197	4	0	0	0	6
96-97	Anchorage	WCHL	53	3	13	16	204	9	0	4	4	59
	SHL	Totals	91	20	44	64	305	4	0	0	0	6

Born; 5/29/73, Quebec City, Quebec. 5-10, 200.

Dave Doucette — Defenseman

			Regular Season					Playoffs				
Season	Team	League	GP	G	A	PTS	PIM	GP	G	A	PTS	PIM
89-90	Erie	ECHL	37	6	31	37	17	—	—	—	—	—
89-90	Winston-Salem	ECHL	21	3	23	26	22	10	0	8	8	4
90-91	Erie	ECHL	40	0	24	24	25	5	0	0	0	2
91-92	Raleigh	ECHL	46	3	14	17	12	2	0	1	1	2
92-93	Dallas	CeHL	50	10	46	56	66	7	0	10	10	10
93-94	Dallas	CeHL	52	9	53	62	93	—	—	—	—	—
93-94	Tulsa	CeHL	10	1	10	11	8	11	2	11	13	6
94-95	Wichita	CeHL	64	20	70	90	81	11	2	12	14	6
95-96	Wichita	CeHL	39	9	28	37	132	—	—	—	—	—
96-97	New Mexico	WPHL	51	5	35	40	45	6	2	5	7	2
	CeHL	Totals	215	49	207	256	380	29	4	33	37	22
	ECHL	Totals	144	12	92	104	76	17	0	9	9	8

Born; 9/22/65, Toronto, Ontario. 5-11, 190. 1989-90 ECHL First Team All-Star. 1992-93 CeHL Defenseman of the Year. 1992-93 CeHL First Team All-Star. 1993-94 CeHL First Team All-Star. 1994-95 CeHL First Team All-Star. Member of 1994-95 CeHL champion Wichita Thunder.

Todd Dougherty — Defenseman

			Regular Season					Playoffs				
Season	Team	League	GP	G	A	PTS	PIM	GP	G	A	PTS	PIM
94-95	Richmond	ECHL	3	0	0	0	15	—	—	—	—	—
94-95	Utica	CoHL	21	0	7	7	92	—	—	—	—	—
94-95	Lakeland	SUN	5	2	1	3	19	—	—	—	—	—
95-96	Huntsville	SHL	37	3	15	18	164	6	0	1	1	29
96-97	Huntsville	CeHL	44	3	12	15	201	6	0	0	0	28
	SHL	Totals	42	5	16	21	183	6	0	1	1	29

Born; 2/17/71, Alburg, Vermont. 6-0, 215. Member of 1995-96 SHL champion Huntsville Channel Cats.

Peter Douris — Right Wing

			Regular Season					Playoffs				
Season	Team	League	GP	G	A	PTS	PIM	GP	G	A	PTS	PIM
85-86	Winnipeg	NHL	11	0	0	0	0	—	—	—	—	—
85-86	Canadian	Olympic	33	16	7	23	18	—	—	—	—	—
86-87	Winnipeg	NHL	6	0	0	0	0	—	—	—	—	—
86-87	Sherbrooke	AHL	62	14	28	42	24	17	7	*15	*22	16
87-88	Winnipeg	NHL	4	0	2	2	0	1	0	0	0	0
87-88	Moncton	AHL	73	42	37	79	53	—	—	—	—	—
88-89	Peoria	IHL	81	28	41	69	32	4	1	2	3	0
89-90	Boston	NHL	36	5	6	11	15	8	0	1	1	8
89-90	Maine	AHL	38	17	20	37	14	—	—	—	—	—
90-91	Boston	NHL	39	2	5	7	9	7	0	1	1	6
90-91	Maine	AHL	35	16	15	31	9	2	3	0	3	2
91-92	Boston	NHL	54	10	13	23	10	7	2	3	5	0
91-92	Maine	AHL	12	4	3	7	2	—	—	—	—	—
92-93	Boston	NHL	19	4	4	8	4	4	1	0	1	0
92-93	Providence	AHL	50	29	26	55	12	—	—	—	—	—

Season	Team	League	GP	G	A	PTS	PIM	GP	G	A	PTS	PIM
93-94	Anaheim	NHL	74	12	22	34	21	—	—	—	—	—
94-95	Anaheim	NHL	46	10	11	21	12	—	—	—	—	—
95-96	Anaheim	NHL	31	8	7	15	9	—	—	—	—	—
96-97	Milwaukee	IHL	80	36	36	72	14	3	2	2	4	2
	NHL	Totals	320	54	67	121	80	27	3	5	8	14
	AHL	Totals	270	122	129	251	114	19	10	15	25	18
	IHL	Totals	161	64	77	141	46	7	3	4	7	2

Born; 2/19/66, Toronto, Ontario. 6-1, 195. Drafted by Winnipeg Jets (1st choice, 30th overall) in 1984 Entry Draft. Traded to St. Louis Blues for Kent Carlson and St. Louis' twelfth round selection (Sergei Kharin) in 1989 Entry Draft and St. Louis' fourth round choice (Scott Levins) in 1990 Entry Draft, 9/29/88. Signed as a free agent by Boston Bruins (6/27/89). Signed as a free agent by Anaheim Mighty Ducks (7/22/93).

Jim Dowd — Center

			Regular Season					Playoffs				
Season	Team	League	GP	G	A	PTS	PIM	GP	G	A	PTS	PIM
91-92	New Jersey	NHL	1	0	0	0	0	—	—	—	—	—
91-92	Utica	AHL	78	17	42	59	47	4	2	2	4	4
92-93	New Jersey	NHL	1	0	0	0	0	—	—	—	—	—
92-93	Utica	AHL	78	27	45	72	62	5	1	7	8	10
93-94	New Jersey	NHL	15	5	10	15	0	19	2	6	8	8
93-94	Albany	AHL	58	26	37	63	76	—	—	—	—	—
94-95	New Jersey	NHL	10	1	4	5	0	11	2	1	3	8
95-96	New Jersey	NHL	28	4	9	13	17	—	—	—	—	—
95-96	Vancouver	NHL	38	1	6	7	6	1	0	0	0	0
96-97	Islanders	NHL	3	0	0	0	0	—	—	—	—	—
96-97	Utah	IHL	48	10	21	31	27	—	—	—	—	—
96-97	Saint John	AHL	24	5	11	16	18	5	1	2	3	0
	NHL	Totals	96	11	29	40	23	31	4	7	11	16
	AHL	Totals	238	75	135	210	203	14	4	11	15	14

Born; 12/25/68, Brick, New Jersey. 6-1, 190. Drafted by New Jersey Devils (7th choice, 149th overall) in 1987 Entry Draft. Traded to Hartford Whalers by New Jersey with New Jersey second round choice in 1997 Entry Draft (Dmitri Kokorev) for Jocelyn Lemieux and Hartford's second round choice in 1998 Entry Draft, (12/19/95). Traded to Vancouver Canucks by Hartford with Frantisek Kucera and Hartford's second round choice (Dmitri Kokorev) in 1997 Entry Draft for Jeff Brown and Vancouver's third round choice in 1998 Entry Draft, (12/19/95). Member of 1994-95 Stanley Cup champion New Jersey Devils.

Steve Dowhy — Center

			Regular Season					Playoffs				
Season	Team	League	GP	G	A	PTS	PIM	GP	G	A	PTS	PIM
95-96	Bakersfield	WCHL	58	36	53	89	58	—	—	—	—	—
96-97	Bakersfield	WCHL	63	51	73	124	84	4	2	3	5	12
	WCHL	Totals	121	87	126	213	142	4	2	3	5	12

Born; 7/18/74, Winnipeg, Manitoba. 6-0, 190. 1996-97 WCHL First Team All-Star.

Aaron Downey — Right Wing

			Regular Season					Playoffs				
Season	Team	League	GP	G	A	PTS	PIM	GP	G	A	PTS	PIM
95-96	Hampton Roads	ECHL	65	12	11	23	354	—	—	—	—	—
96-97	Manitoba	IHL	2	0	0	0	17	—	—	—	—	—
96-97	Portland	AHL	3	0	0	0	19	—	—	—	—	—
96-97	Hamton Roads	ECHL	64	8	8	16	338	9	0	3	3	26
	ECHL	Totals	129	20	19	39	692	9	0	3	3	26

Born; 8/27/74, Orangeville, Ontario. 6-0, 205.

Brian Downey — Left Wing

			Regular Season					Playoffs				
Season	Team	League	GP	G	A	PTS	PIM	GP	G	A	PTS	PIM
92-93	New Haven	AHL	6	0	2	2	0	—	—	—	—	—
92-93	Thunder Bay	CoHL	43	17	31	48	14	11	4	5	9	14
93-94	Thunder Bay	CoHL	61	30	51	81	17	9	3	11	14	2

Season	Team	League	GP	G	A	PTS	PIM	GP	G	A	PTS	PIM
94-95	Thunder Bay	CoHL	25	13	18	31	23	11	5	7	12	2
95-96	Madison	CoHL	74	30	50	80	62	6	1	6	7	2
96-97	Milwaukee	IHL	1	0	0	0	0	—	—	—	—	—
96-97	Madison	CoHL	63	25	49	74	26	5	0	3	3	2
	CoHL	Totals	266	115	199	314	142	42	13	32	45	22

Born; 6/30/68, Ottawa, Ontario. 6-1, 190. 1995-96 CoHL Best Defensive Forward. Member of 1993-94 and 1994-95 Colonial Cup Champion Thunder Bay Senators. 1996-97 CoHL Best Defensive Forward.

Jason Downey — Defenseman

Season	Team	League	GP	G	A	PTS	PIM	GP	G	A	PTS	PIM
93-94	Fredericton	AHL	15	0	1	1	35	—	—	—	—	—
93-94	Dayton	ECHL	35	2	22	24	176	3	0	0	0	12
94-95	Cornwall	AHL	—	—	—	—	—	7	0	0	0	28
94-95	Kalamazoo	IHL	3	0	0	0	2	—	—	—	—	—
94-95	Peoria	IHL	4	0	0	0	14	—	—	—	—	—
94-95	Dayton	ECHL	62	7	23	30	282	9	2	15	17	57
95-96	Dayton	ECHL	58	8	22	30	354	3	0	0	0	32
96-97	Dayton	ECHL	50	3	7	10	166	4	1	2	3	16
	AHL	Totals	15	0	1	1	35	7	0	0	0	28
	IHL	Totals	7	0	0	0	16	—	—	—	—	—
	ECHL	Totals	205	20	74	94	978	19	3	17	20	117

Born; 7/22/72, Sault Ste. Marie, Ontario. 5-8, 198.

Shane Doyle — Defenseman

Season	Team	League	GP	G	A	PTS	PIM	GP	G	A	PTS	PIM
87-88	Utica	AHL	14	0	1	1	38	—	—	—	—	—
87-88	Flint	IHL	13	1	1	2	81	—	—	—	—	—
88-89	Indianapolis	IHL	62	4	36	40	224	—	—	—	—	—
89-90	Winston-Salem	ECHL	7	1	4	5	44	—	—	—	—	—
95-96	Detroit	CoHL	13	0	2	2	62	—	—	—	—	—
95-96	Saginaw	CoHL	15	1	3	4	68	—	—	—	—	—
95-96	Toledo	ECHL	2	0	0	0	23	—	—	—	—	—
95-96	Daytona Beach	SHL	8	4	7	11	48	4	0	0	0	50
96-97	Alaska	WCHL	22	3	13	16	106	—	—	—	—	—
96-97	Jacksonville	ECHL	14	0	4	4	83	—	—	—	—	—
	IHL	Totals	75	5	37	42	305	—	—	—	—	—
	CoHL	Totals	28	1	5	6	130	—	—	—	—	—
	ECHL	Totals	23	1	8	9	150	—	—	—	—	—

Born; 4/26/67, Lindsay, Ontario. 6-3, 222. Drafted by Vancouver Canucks (3rd choice, 85th overall) in 1985 Entry Draft. Did not play professional hockey in North America from the 1990-91 season until the 1995-96 season.

Trevor Doyle — Defenseman

Season	Team	League	GP	G	A	PTS	PIM	GP	G	A	PTS	PIM
94-95	Cincinnati	IHL	52	0	3	3	139	6	0	0	0	13
95-96	Carolina	AHL	48	1	2	3	117	—	—	—	—	—
96-97	Carolina	AHL	47	3	10	13	288	—	—	—	—	—
	AHL	Totals	95	4	12	16	405	—	—	—	—	—

Born; 1/1/74, Ottawa, Ontario. 6-3, 212.

Tom Draper — Goaltender

Season	Team	League	GP	W	L	T	MIN	SO	GAVG	GP	W	L	MIN	SO	GAVG
88-89	Winnipeg	NHL	2	1	1	0	120	0	6.00	—	—	—	—	—	—
88-89	Moncton	AHL	*54	27	17	5	*2962	2	3.46	7	5	2	419	0	3.44
89-90	Winnipeg	NHL	6	2	4	0	359	0	4.35	—	—	—	—	—	—
89-90	Moncton	AHL	51	20	24	3	2844	1	3.52	—	—	—	—	—	—
90-91	Moncton	AHL	30	15	13	2	1779	1	3.20	—	—	—	—	—	—
90-91	Fort Wayne	IHL	10	5	3	1	564	0	3.40	—	—	—	—	—	—
90-91	Peoria	IHL	10	6	3	1	584	0	3.70	4	2	1	214	0	2.80
91-92	Buffalo	NHL	26	10	9	5	1403	1	3.21	7	3	4	433	1	2.63
91-92	Rochester	AHL	9	4	3	2	531	0	3.16	—	—	—	—	—	—
92-93	Buffalo	NHL	11	5	6	0	664	0	3.70	—	—	—	—	—	—
92-93	Rochester	AHL	5	3	2	0	303	0	4.36	—	—	—	—	—	—
93-94	Islanders	NHL	7	1	3	0	227	0	4.23	—	—	—	—	—	—
93-94	Salt Lake City	IHL	35	7	23	3	1933	0	4.34	—	—	—	—	—	—
94-95	Minnesota	IHL	59	25	20	6	3063	1	3.66	2	0	2	118	0	5.07
95-96	Winnipeg	NHL	1	0	0	0	34	0	5.29	—	—	—	—	—	—
95-96	Milwaukee	IHL	31	14	12	3	1793	1	3.38	—	—	—	—	—	—
96-97	Long Beach	IHL	39	28	7	3	2267	2	2.39	*18	*13	5	*1097	*2	2.24
	NHL	Totals	53	19	23	5	2807	1	3.70	7	3	4	433	1	2.63
	IHL	Totals	184	85	68	17	10204	2	3.43	24	15	8	1429	2	2.56
	AHL	Totals	149	69	59	12	8419	4	3.44	7	5	2	419	0	3.44

Born; 11/20/66, Outremont, Quebec. 5-11, 180. Drafted by Winnipeg Jets (8th choice, 165th overall) in 1985 Entry Draft. Traded to St. Louis Blues by Winnipeg for future considerations (Jim Vesey, 5/24/91) (2/28/91). Traded to Winnipeg by St. Louis for future considerations (5/24/91). Traded to Buffalo Sabres by Winnipeg for Buffalo's seventh round choice (Artur Oktyabrev) in 1992 Entry Draft (6/22/91). Traded to New York Islanders by Buffalo for Islanders' seventh round choice (Steve Plouffe) in 1994 Entry Draft (9/30/93). 1988-89 AHL Second Team All-Star. Member of 1990-91 IHL champion Peoria Rivermen.

Barry Dreger — Defenseman

Season	Team	League	GP	G	A	PTS	PIM	GP	G	A	PTS	PIM
91-92	Columbus	ECHL	57	4	24	28	362	—	—	—	—	—
92-93	Columbus	ECHL	37	4	12	16	301	—	—	—	—	—
92-93	Hamilton	AHL	13	0	3	3	50	—	—	—	—	—
93-94	San Diego	IHL	57	2	6	8	166	1	0	0	0	2
94-95	San Diego	IHL	60	5	6	11	217	—	—	—	—	—
95-96	Orlando	IHL	70	4	5	9	314	23	2	1	3	51
96-97	Orlando	IHL	81	10	14	24	387	10	0	0	0	57
	IHL	Totals	268	21	31	52	1084	34	2	1	3	110
	ECHL	Totals	94	8	36	44	663	—	—	—	—	—

Born; 11/28/69, Winnipeg, Manitoba. 6-0, 190.

Greg Dreveny — Goaltender

Season	Team	League	GP	W	L	T	MIN	SO	GAVG	GP	W	L	MIN	SO	GAVG
96-97	Birmingham	ECHL	35	21	10	1	1816	0	3.77	8	5	3	511	0	3.87

Born;

Jimmy Drolet — Defenseman

Season	Team	League	GP	G	A	PTS	PIM	GP	G	A	PTS	PIM
96-97	Fredericton	AHL	57	3	2	5	43	—	—	—	—	—

Born; 2/19/76, Vanier, Quebec. 6-1, 180. Drafted by Montreal Canadiens (7th choice, 122nd overall) in 1994 Entry Draft.

Ivan Droppa — Defenseman

Season	Team	League	GP	G	A	PTS	PIM	GP	G	A	PTS	PIM
92-93	Indianapolis	IHL	77	14	29	43	92	5	0	1	1	2
93-94	Chicago	NHL	12	0	1	1	12	—	—	—	—	—
93-94	Indianapolis	IHL	55	9	10	19	71	—	—	—	—	—
94-95	Indianapolis	IHL	67	5	28	33	91	—	—	—	—	—
95-96	Chicago	NHL	7	0	0	0	2	—	—	—	—	—
95-96	Indianapolis	IHL	72	6	30	36	71	3	0	1	1	2
96-97	Indianapolis	IHL	26	1	13	14	44	—	—	—	—	—
96-97	Carolina	AHL	47	4	22	26	48	—	—	—	—	—
	NHL	Totals	19	0	1	1	14	—	—	—	—	—
	IHL	Totals	297	35	100	135	369	8	0	2	2	4

Born; 2/1/72, Liptousky Mikulas, Czechoslovakia. 6-2, 209. Drafted by Chicago Blackhawks (2nd choice, 37th overall) in 1990 Entry Draft.

P.C. Drouin — Left Wing

Season	Team	League	GP	G	A	PTS	PIM	GP	G	A	PTS	PIM
96-97	Boston	NHL	3	0	0	0	0	—	—	—	—	—
96-97	Providence	AHL	42	12	11	23	10	—	—	—	—	—

Born; 4/22/76, St. Lambert, Quebec. 6-2, 205. Last amateur club; Cornell (ECAC).

Stan Drulia — Center

Season	Team	League	GP	G	A	PTS	PIM	GP	G	A	PTS	PIM
88-89	Maine	AHL	3	1	1	2	0	—	—	—	—	—
89-90	Cape Breton	AHL	31	5	7	12	2	—	—	—	—	—
89-90	Phoenix	IHL	16	6	3	9	2	—	—	—	—	—
90-91	Knoxville	ECHL	64	*63	77	*140	39	3	3	2	5	4
91-92	New Haven	AHL	77	49	53	102	46	5	2	4	6	4
92-93	Tampa Bay	NHL	24	2	1	3	10	—	—	—	—	—
92-93	Atlanta	IHL	47	28	26	54	38	3	2	3	5	4
93-94	Atlanta	IHL	79	54	60	114	70	14	13	12	25	8
94-95	Atlanta	IHL	66	41	49	90	60	5	1	5	6	2
95-96	Atlanta	IHL	75	38	56	94	80	3	0	2	2	18
96-97	Detroit	IHL	73	33	38	71	42	21	5	*21	26	14
	IHL	Totals	356	200	232	432	292	46	21	43	64	46
	AHL	Totals	111	55	61	116	48	5	2	4	6	4

Born; 1/5/68, Elmira, New York. 5-10, 180. Drafted by Pittsburgh Penguins (11th choice, 214th overall) in 1986 Entry Draft. Signed as a free agent by Edmonton Oilers (5/89). Signed as a free agent by Tampa Bay Lightning (9/1/92). 1990-91 First Team ECHL All-Star. 1990-91 ECHL MVP. 1991-92 AHL Second Team All-Star. 1993-94 IHL First Team All-Star. 1994-95 IHL First Team All-Star. Member of 1993-94 IHL champion Atlanta Knights. Member of 1996-97 IHL Champion Detroit Vipers.

Steve Dubinsky — Center

Season	Team	League	GP	G	A	PTS	PIM	GP	G	A	PTS	PIM
93-94	Chicago	NHL	27	2	6	8	16	6	0	0	0	10
93-94	Indianapolis	IHL	54	15	25	40	63	—	—	—	—	—
94-95	Chicago	NHL	16	0	0	0	8	—	—	—	—	—
94-95	Indianapolis	IHL	62	16	11	27	29	—	—	—	—	—
95-96	Chicago	NHL	43	2	3	5	14	—	—	—	—	—
95-96	Indianapolis	IHL	16	8	8	16	10	—	—	—	—	—
96-97	Chicago	NHL	5	0	0	0	0	4	1	0	1	4
96-97	Indianapolis	IHL	77	32	40	72	53	1	3	1	4	0
	NHL	Totals	91	4	9	13	38	10	1	0	1	14
	IHL	Totals	2090	71	84	155	155	1	3	1	4	0

Born; 7/9/70, Montreal, Quebec. 6-0, 190. Drafted by Chicago Blackhawks (9th choice, 226th overall) in 1990 Entry Draft.

Ilya Dubkov — Center

			Regular Season					Playoffs				
Season	Team	League	GP	G	A	PTS	PIM	GP	G	A	PTS	PIM
93-94	Roanoke	ECHL	68	25	39	64	88	2	0	0	0	15
94-95	Roanoke	ECHL	68	28	47	75	78	8	5	3	8	4
95-96	Roanoke	ECHL	69	20	52	72	99	3	1	0	1	2
96-97	Hamilton	AHL	3	0	1	1	2	—	—	—	—	—
96-97	Roanoke	ECHL	53	25	50	75	44	4	0	3	3	6
	ECHL	Totals	258	98	188	286	309	17	6	6	12	27

Born; 2/17/72, Moscow, Russia. 6-3, 180.

Eric Dubois — Defenseman

			Regular Season					Playoffs				
Season	Team	League	GP	G	A	PTS	PIM	GP	G	A	PTS	PIM
91-92	Halifax	AHL	14	0	0	0	8	—	—	—	—	—
91-92	New Haven	AHL	1	0	0	0	2	—	—	—	—	—
91-92	Greensboro	ECHL	36	7	17	24	62	11	4	4	8	40
92-93	Oklahoma City	CeHL	25	5	20	25	70	—	—	—	—	—
92-93	Atlanta	IHL	43	3	9	12	44	9	0	0	0	10
93-94	Atlanta	IHL	80	13	26	39	174	14	0	7	7	48
94-95	Atlanta	IHL	56	3	25	28	56	5	0	3	3	24
95-96	Atlanta	IHL	20	1	5	6	40	—	—	—	—	—
95-96	Chicago	IHL	45	2	8	10	39	—	—	—	—	—
96-97	Manitoba	IHL	80	8	17	25	60	—	—	—	—	—
	IHL	Totals	324	30	90	120	413	28	0	10	10	82
	AHL	Totals	15	0	0	0	10	—	—	—	—	—

Born; 5/9/70, Montreal, Quebec. 6-0, 195. Drafted by Quebec Nordiques (6th choice, 76th overall) in 1989 Entry Draft. Signed as a free agent by Tampa Bay Lightning (6/2/93). Member of 1993-94 IHL champion Atlanta Knights.

Jonathan DuBois — Center

			Regular Season					Playoffs				
Season	Team	League	GP	G	A	PTS	PIM	GP	G	A	PTS	PIM
95-96	Huntsville	SHL	59	28	55	83	230	10	5	6	11	37
95-96	Flint	CoHL	1	0	0	0	0	8	1	1	2	14
96-97	Hunstsville	CeHL	62	15	49	64	307	9	2	13	15	17

Born; 3/8/74, Drummondville, Quebec. 5-9, 180. Member of 1995-96 SHL Champion Huntsville Channel Cats. Member of 1995-96 CoHL Champion Flint Generals.

Robert Dubois — Right Wing

			Regular Season					Playoffs				
Season	Team	League	GP	G	A	PTS	PIM	GP	G	A	PTS	PIM
96-97	Dayton	CoHL	12	3	4	7	8	—	—	—	—	—
96-97	Thunder Bay	CoHL	21	6	7	13	6	—	—	—	—	—
96-97	Brantford	CoHL	18	7	5	12	22	—	—	—	—	—
96-97	Madison	CoHL	6	2	4	6	4	3	0	0	0	0
	CoHL	Totals	57	18	20	38	40	3	0	0	0	0

Born; 3/19/76, Sudbury, Ontario. 6-0, 200.

Gaeten Duchesne — Left Wing

			Regular Season					Playoffs				
Season	Team	League	GP	G	A	PTS	PIM	GP	G	A	PTS	PIM
81-82	Washington	NHL	74	9	14	23	46	—	—	—	—	—
82-83	Hershey	AHL	1	1	0	1	0	—	—	—	—	—
82-83	Washington	NHL	77	18	19	37	52	4	1	1	2	4
83-84	Washington	NHL	79	17	19	36	29	8	2	1	3	2
84-85	Washington	NHL	67	15	23	38	32	5	0	1	1	7
85-86	Washington	NHL	80	11	28	39	39	9	4	3	7	12

Season	Team	League	GP	G	A	PTS	PIM	GP	G	A	PTS	PIM
86-87	Washington	NHL	74	17	35	52	53	7	3	0	3	14
87-88	Quebec	NHL	80	24	23	47	83	—	—	—	—	—
88-89	Quebec	NHL	70	8	21	29	56	—	—	—	—	—
89-90	Minnesota	NHL	72	12	8	20	33	7	0	0	0	6
90-91	Minnesota	NHL	68	9	9	18	18	23	2	3	5	34
91-92	Minnesota	NHL	73	8	15	23	102	7	1	0	1	6
92-93	Minnesota	NHL	84	16	13	29	30	—	—	—	—	—
93-94	San Jose	NHL	84	12	18	30	28	14	1	4	5	12
94-95	San Jose	NHL	33	2	7	9	16	—	—	—	—	—
94-95	Florida	NHL	13	1	2	3	0	—	—	—	—	—
95-96	N/A											
96-97	Quebec	IHL	66	10	18	28	54	9	5	0	5	4
	NHL	Totals	1028	179	254	433	617	84	14	13	27	97

Born; 7/11/62, Quebec City, Quebec. 5-11, 200. Drafted by Washington Capitals (eighth pick, 152nd overall) in 1981 Entry Draft. Traded to Quebec Nordiques with Alan Haworth and first round pick in 1987 (Joe Sakic) by Washington for Dale Hunter and Clint Malarchuk, June 1987. Traded to Minnesota North Stars by Quebec for Kevin Kaminski (6/18/89). Traded to San Jose Sharks by Minnesota for sixth round pick in 1993 Entry Draft, 6/20/93. Traded by Florida Panthers by San Jose for sixth round pick (Timo Hakanen) in 1995 Entry Draft, 4/7/95.

Jason Duda — Left Wing

			Regular Season					Playoffs				
Season	Team	League	GP	G	A	PTS	PIM	GP	G	A	PTS	PIM
96-97	Oklahoma City	CeHL	15	2	6	8	11	—	—	—	—	—
96-97	Wichita	CeHL	39	15	15	30	34	9	2	7	9	19
	CeHL	Totals	54	17	21	38	45	9	2	7	9	19

Born; 5/5/75, Sexsmith, Alberta. 5-10, 185. Traded to Wichita Thunder by Oklahoma City Blazers for David Shute (1997).

Rhett Dudley — Defenseman

			Regular Season					Playoffs				
Season	Team	League	GP	G	A	PTS	PIM	GP	G	A	PTS	PIM
95-96	Wheeling	ECHL	1	0	0	0	0	—	—	—	—	—
95-96	Knoxville	ECHL	3	0	0	0	14	—	—	—	—	—
96-97	Tulsa	CeHL	65	8	12	20	114	5	0	2	2	10
	ECHL	Totals	4	0	0	0	14	—	—	—	—	—

Born; 11/9/74, Wetaskiwia, Alberta. 6-1, 185.

Parris Duffus — Goaltender

			Regular Season							Playoffs						
Season	Team	League	GP	W	L	T	MIN	SO	GAVG	GP	W	L	MIN	SO	GAVG
92-93	Hampton Roads	ECHL	4	3	1	0	245	0	3.18	—	—	—	—	—	—
92-93	Peoria	IHL	37	16	15	4	2149	0	3.96	1	0	1	59	0	5.08
93-94	Peoria	IHL	36	19	10	3	1845	0	4.58	2	0	1	92	0	3.88
94-95	Peoria	IHL	29	17	7	3	1581	*3	2.69	7	4	2	409	0	2.49
95-96	Minnesota	IHL	35	10	17	2	1812	1	3.31	—	—	—	—	—	—
96-97	Phoenix	NHL	1	0	0	0	29	0	2.07	—	—	—	—	—	—
96-97	Las Vegas	IHL	58	28	19	6	3267	3	3.23	3	0	3	176	0	2.73
	IHL	Totals	195	90	68	18	10654	7	3.55	13	4	7	560	0	2.93

Born; 1/27/70, Denver, Colorado. 6-2, 192. Drafted by St. Louis Blues (6th choice, 180th overall) in 1990 Entry Draft. Signed as a free agent by Winnipeg Jets (8/4/95).

Jim Duhart — Right Wing

			Regular Season					Playoffs				
Season	Team	League	GP	G	A	PTS	PIM	GP	G	A	PTS	PIM
93-94	Flint	CoHL	62	18	24	42	211	9	1	4	5	70
94-95	Raleigh	ECHL	20	8	8	16	112	—	—	—	—	—
94-95	Flint	CoHL	30	10	7	17	110	—	—	—	—	—
95-96	Flint	CoHL	57	8	25	33	285	5	0	0	0	20
96-97	Saginaw	CoHL	27	11	10	21	79	—	—	—	—	—
96-97	Madison	CoHL	41	26	16	42	108	5	3	4	7	8

| | | CoHL | Totals | 213 | 71 | 83 | 154 | 793 | 19 | 4 | 8 | 12 | 98 |

Born; 7/24/71, Ottawa, Ontario. 5-10, 202. Member of 1995-96 Colonial Cup Champion Flint Generals.

Rob Dumas — Defenseman

			Regular Season					Playoffs				
Season	Team	League	GP	G	A	PTS	PIM	GP	G	A	PTS	PIM
88-89	Peoria	IHL	10	0	0	0	51	4	0	0	0	23
89-90	N/A											
90-91	Greensboro	ECHL	64	4	29	33	201	13	2	0	2	32
91-92	Nashville	ECHL	63	9	37	46	215	—	—	—	—	—
92-93	Milwaukee	IHL	1	0	0	0	0	—	—	—	—	—
92-93	Nashville	ECHL	63	13	45	58	191	9	2	0	2	37
93-94	Milwaukee	IHL	8	0	0	0	16	—	—	—	—	—
93-94	Nashville	ECHL	52	11	36	47	203	2	1	0	1	2
94-95	Nashville	ECHL	22	3	8	11	47	—	—	—	—	—
94-95	Tallahassee	ECHL	35	8	27	35	68	13	4	3	7	40
95-96	N/A											
96-97	Tallahassee	ECHL	63	17	33	50	118	3	0	1	1	5
	IHL	Totals	19	0	0	0	67	4	0	0	0	23
	ECHL	Totals	362	65	215	280	1043	40	9	4	13	116

Born; 5/19/69, Spirit River, Alberta. 6-0, 200. Drafted by St. Louis Blues (9th choice, 180th overall) in 1987 Entry Draft.

Louis Dumont — Center

			Regular Season					Playoffs				
Season	Team	League	GP	G	A	PTS	PIM	GP	G	A	PTS	PIM
94-95	Tallahassee	ECHL	5	1	0	1	4	—	—	—	—	—
94-95	Wheeling	ECHL	62	25	33	58	81	3	1	1	2	4
95-96	Wheeling	ECHL	66	24	39	63	57	6	0	3	3	6
96-97	Louisiana	ECHL	64	42	45	87	106	17	6	11	17	8
	ECHL	Totals	187	92	117	209	248	26	7	15	22	18

Born; 1/30/73, Calgary, Alberta. 5-10, 180.

Mario Dumoulin — Defenseman

			Regular Season					Playoffs				
Season	Team	League	GP	G	A	PTS	PIM	GP	G	A	PTS	PIM
94-95	Greensboro	ECHL	—	—	—	—	—	3	0	0	0	4
95-96	Brantford	CoHL	63	3	15	18	102	—	—	—	—	—
95-96	Detroit	CoHL	7	2	1	3	20	7	0	1	1	6
96-97	Birmingham	ECHL	61	3	12	15	328	8	1	6	7	28
	CoHL	Totals	70	5	16	21	122	7	0	1	1	6
	ECHL	Totals	61	3	12	15	328	11	1	6	7	32

Born; 1/11/74, Drummondville, Quebec. 6-1, 193.

Brett Duncan — Defenseman

			Regular Season					Playoffs				
Season	Team	League	GP	G	A	PTS	PIM	GP	G	A	PTS	PIM
95-96	Saint John	AHL	19	0	0	0	109	—	—	—	—	—
95-96	Los Angeles	IHL	7	0	0	0	32	—	—	—	—	—
96-97	Birmingham	ECHL	27	2	1	3	99	8	0	1	1	8

Born; 2/15/73, Kitchener, Ontario. 6-0, 220. Drafted by Tampa Bay Lightning (10th choice, 237th overall) in 1993 Entry Draft.

Craig Duncanson — Left Wing

			Regular Season					Playoffs				
Season	Team	League	GP	G	A	PTS	PIM	GP	G	A	PTS	PIM
85-86	Los Angeles	NHL	2	0	1	1	0	—	—	—	—	—
85-86	New Haven	AHL	—	—	—	—	—	6	4	7	11	2
86-87	Los Angeles	NHL	2	0	0	0	24	—	—	—	—	—
87-88	Los Angeles	NHL	9	0	0	0	12	—	—	—	—	—

Season	Team	League	GP	G	A	PTS	PIM	GP	G	A	PTS	PIM
87-88	New Haven	AHL	57	15	25	40	170	—	—	—	—	—
88-89	Los Angeles	NHL	5	0	0	0	0	—	—	—	—	—
88-89	New Haven	AHL	69	25	39	64	200	17	4	8	12	60
89-90	Los Angeles	NHL	10	3	2	5	9	—	—	—	—	—
89-90	New Haven	AHL	51	17	30	47	152	—	—	—	—	—
90-91	Winnipeg	NHL	7	2	0	2	16	—	—	—	—	—
90-91	Moncton	AHL	58	16	34	50	107	9	3	11	14	31
91-92	Baltimore	AHL	46	20	26	46	98	—	—	—	—	—
91-92	Moncton	AHL	19	12	9	21	6	11	6	4	10	10
92-93	Rangers	NHL	3	0	1	1	0	—	—	—	—	—
92-93	Binghamton	AHL	69	35	59	94	126	14	7	5	12	9
93-94	Binghamton	AHL	70	25	44	69	83	—	—	—	—	—
94-95	Binghamton	AHL	62	21	43	64	105	11	4	4	8	16
95-96	Orlando	IHL	79	19	24	43	123	22	3	10	13	16
96-97	Fort Wayne	IHL	61	14	24	38	64	—	—	—	—	—
96-97	Cincinnati	IHL	21	3	11	14	19	3	1	1	2	0
	NHL	Totals	38	5	4	9	61	—	—	—	—	—
	AHL	Totals	501	186	309	495	1047	68	28	39	67	128
	IHL	Totals	161	36	59	95	206	25	4	11	15	16

Born; 3/17/67, Sudbury, Ontario. 6-0, 200. Drafted by Los Angeles Kings (1st choice, 9th overall) in 1985 Entry Draft. traded to Minnesota North Stars by Los Angeles for Daniel Berthiaume (9/6/90). Traded to Winnipeg Jets by Minnesota for Brian Hunt (9/6/90). Traded to Washington Capitals by Winnipeg with Brent Hughes and Simon Wheeldon for Bob Joyce, Tyler Larter and Kent Paynter (5/21/91). Signed as a free agent by New York Rangers (9/4/92).

Shane Dungey — Defenseman

			Regular Season					Playoffs				
Season	Team	League	GP	G	A	PTS	PIM	GP	G	A	PTS	PIM
96-97	Brantford	CoHL	6	0	1	1	10	10	0	1	1	10

Born; 9/23/71, Richmond Hill, Ontario. 6-4, 220.

Brett Dunleavy — Forward

			Regular Season					Playoffs				
Season	Team	League	GP	G	A	PTS	PIM	GP	G	A	PTS	PIM
93-94	Jacksonville	SUN	28	6	5	11	32	—	—	—	—	—
94-95	Lakeland	SUN	55	11	18	29	24	1	0	0	0	0
95-96	N/A											
96-97	Charlotte	ECHL	1	1	0	1	0	—	—	—	—	—
96-97	Bakersfield	WCHL	19	3	4	7	6	—	—	—	—	—
	SUN	Totals	83	17	23	40	56	1	0	0	0	0

Born; 4/27/71, Charlotte, North Carolina. 6-0, 175.

Jamie Dunn — Right Wing

			Regular Season					Playoffs				
Season	Team	League	GP	G	A	PTS	PIM	GP	G	A	PTS	PIM
96-97	Waco	WPHL	55	27	24	51	85	—	—	—	—	—

Born;

Pat Dunn — Right Wing

			Regular Season					Playoffs				
Season	Team	League	GP	G	A	PTS	PIM	GP	G	A	PTS	PIM
96-97	Utah	IHL	2	0	0	0	0	—	—	—	—	—
96-97	New Mexico	WPHL	51	23	35	58	62	2	0	2	2	0

Born; 3/15/63, Trois-Rivieres, Quebec. 5-11, 190.

Stu Dunn — Goaltender

			Regular Season							Playoffs					
Season	Team	League	GP	W	L	T	MIN	SO	GAVG	GP	W	L	MIN	SO	GAVG
96-97	Tallahassee	ECHL	3	0	0	0	76	0	2.36	—	—	—	—	—	—
96-97	Mobile	ECHL	7	0	4	1	366	0	4.59	—	—	—	—	—	—
96-97	Knoxville	ECHL	2	0	1	0	77	0	3.89	—	—	—	—	—	—
	ECHL	Totals	12	0	5	1	519	0	3.99	—	—	—	—	—	—

Born; 5/18/74, Charlottetown, Prince Edward Island. 5-11, 180.

George Dupont — Center

			Regular Season					Playoffs				
Season	Team	League	GP	G	A	PTS	PIM	GP	G	A	PTS	PIM
93-94	Oklahoma City	CeHL	4	4	0	4	27	7	4	4	8	48
94-95	Oklahoma City	CeHL	65	27	78	105	250	5	2	4	6	31
95-96	Oklahoma City	CeHL	61	28	83	111	274	13	2	12	14	64
96-97	Oklahoma City	CeHL	63	31	60	91	328	4	0	6	6	13
	CeHL	Totals	193	90	221	311	879	29	8	26	34	156

Born; 3/12/67, Nepean, Ontario. 5-10, 200. 1994-95 CeHL Second Team All-Star. Member of 1995-96 CeHL champion Oklahoma City Blazers.

Guy Dupuis — Defenseman

			Regular Season					Playoffs				
Season	Team	League	GP	G	A	PTS	PIM	GP	G	A	PTS	PIM
90-91	Adirondack	AHL	57	4	10	14	73	—	—	—	—	—
91-92	Adirondack	AHL	49	3	6	9	59	3	0	0	0	4
91-92	Fort Wayne	IHL	10	2	7	9	0	—	—	—	—	—
92-93	Fort Wayne	IHL	53	4	11	15	57	4	0	1	1	6
92-93	Adirondack	AHL	1	0	0	0	0	—	—	—	—	—
93-94	Fort Wayne	IHL	73	9	26	35	70	17	1	7	8	28
94-95	Fort Wayne	IHL	77	9	26	35	125	4	0	0	0	6
95-96	Fort Wayne	IHL	81	5	29	34	118	5	0	0	0	2
96-97	Fort Wayne	IHL	80	6	23	29	84	—	—	—	—	—
	IHL	Totals	374	35	122	157	454	30	1	8	9	42
	AHL	Totals	107	7	16	23	132	3	0	0	0	4

Born; 5/10/70, Moncton, New Brunswick. 6-2, 200. Drafted by Detroit Red Wings (3rd choice, 47th overall) in 1988 Entry Draft. Member of 1992-93 IHL champion Fort Wayne Komets.

Marc Dupuis — Defenseman

			Regular Season					Playoffs				
Season	Team	League	GP	G	A	PTS	PIM	GP	G	A	PTS	PIM
96-97	Indianapolis	IHL	32	0	3	3	14	1	0	0	0	0
96-97	Columbus	ECHL	23	2	13	15	8	8	0	3	3	4

Born; 4/22/76, Cornwall, Ontario. 6-0, 200.

Martin Duris — Defenseman

			Regular Season					Playoffs				
Season	Team	League	GP	G	A	PTS	PIM	GP	G	A	PTS	PIM
96-97	Louisville	ECHL	7	0	2	2	2	—	—	—	—	—
96-97	Raleigh	ECHL	2	0	0	0	0	—	—	—	—	—
96-97	Toledo	ECHL	14	0	1	1	14	—	—	—	—	—
	ECHL	Totals	23	0	3	3	16	—	—	—	—	—

Born;

Martin Duval — Right Wing

			Regular Season					Playoffs				
Season	Team	League	GP	G	A	PTS	PIM	GP	G	A	PTS	PIM
95-96	Tulsa	CeHL	9	4	2	6	6	6	2	2	4	9
96-97	Tulsa	CeHL	31	10	5	15	42	—	—	—	—	—
96-97	Austin	WPHL	28	5	7	12	41	1	0	0	0	0
	CeHL	Totals	40	14	7	21	48	6	2	2	4	9

Born; 3/8/71, St. Leonard, Quebec. 5-11, 190.

Larry Dyck — Goaltender

			Regular Season							Playoffs					
Season	Team	League	GP	W	L	T	MIN	SO	GAVG	GP	W	L	MIN	SO	GAVG
88-89	Kalamazoo	IHL	42	17	20	2	2308	0	4.37	—	—	—	—	—	—
89-90	Kalamazoo	IHL	36	20	12	2	1959	0	3.55	7	2	3	353	0	3.74
89-90	Knoxville	ECHL	3	1	1	1	184	0	3.91	—	—	—	—	—	—
90-91	Kalamazoo	IHL	38	21	15	0	2182	1	3.66	1	0	1	60	0	6.00
91-92	Kalamazoo	IHL	57	25	23	6	*3305	0	3.54	12	5	7	690	0	3.74
92-93	Milwaukee	IHL	40	23	9	0	2328	0	3.38	3	1	2	180	0	3.33
93-94	Milwaukee	IHL	41	15	13	7	2145	0	3.38	3	0	3	120	0	5.47
94-95	Kansas City	IHL	21	13	6	2	1258	1	2.48	19	11	8	1291	1	2.60
95-96	Kansas City	IHL	39	18	17	2	2174	2	3.84	4	2	2	207	0	2.61
95-96	Mobile	ECHL	3	1	1	1	180	0	4.67	—	—	—	—	—	—
96-97	Kansas City	IHL	58	26	14	11	3146	2	3.03	3	0	2	159	0	3.02
	IHL	Totals	372	178	129	32	20805	6	3.50	52	21	28	3060	1	3.24
	ECHL	Totals	6	2	2	2	364	0	4.28	—	—	—	—	—	—

Born; 12/15/65, Winkler, Manitoba. 5-11, 180. Signed as a free agent by Minnesota North Stars (8/88).

Paul Dyck — Defenseman

			Regular Season					Playoffs				
Season	Team	League	GP	G	A	PTS	PIM	GP	G	A	PTS	PIM
91-92	Muskegon	IHL	73	6	21	27	40	14	1	3	4	4
92-93	Cleveland	IHL	69	6	21	27	69	1	0	0	0	0
93-94	Cleveland	IHL	60	1	10	11	57	—	—	—	—	—
94-95	Cleveland	IHL	79	5	12	17	59	4	1	3	4	4
95-96	Kansas City	IHL	51	2	5	7	76	—	—	—	—	—
95-96	Detroit	IHL	5	1	1	2	8	7	0	0	0	12
96-97	Kansas City	IHL	49	2	8	10	39	—	—	—	—	—
96-97	Houston	IHL	30	1	4	5	32	13	0	1	1	12
	IHL	Totals	416	24	82	106	380	39	2	7	9	32

Born; 4/15/71, Winnipeg, Manitoba. 6-1, 200. Drafted by Pittsburgh Penguins (11th pick, 236th overall) in 1991 Entry Draft.

Joe Eagan — Defenseman

			Regular Season					Playoffs				
Season	Team	League	GP	G	A	PTS	PIM	GP	G	A	PTS	PIM
92-93	Dallas	CeHL	16	1	2	3	12	4	0	1	1	2
93-94	Louisville	ECHL	21	0	2	2	49	—	—	—	—	—
94-95	Birmingham	ECHL	12	1	0	1	18	—	—	—	—	—
94-95	Johnstown	ECHL	3	0	0	0	2	—	—	—	—	—
95-96	Bakersfield	WCHL	22	0	9	9	73	—	—	—	—	—
96-97	Nashville	CeHL	31	5	14	19	112	—	—	—	—	—
96-97	Tulsa	CeHL	25	1	2	3	24	5	0	1	1	4
	CeHL	Totals	72	7	18	25	148	9	0	2	2	6
	ECHL	Totals	36	1	2	3	69	—	—	—	—	—

Born; 4/30/70, Darien, Connecticut. 5-11, 190.

Dallas Eakins — Defenseman

			Regular Season					Playoffs				
Season	Team	League	GP	G	A	PTS	PIM	GP	G	A	PTS	PIM
88-89	Baltimore	AHL	62	0	10	10	139	—	—	—	—	—
89-90	Moncton	AHL	75	2	11	13	189	—	—	—	—	—
90-91	Moncton	AHL	75	1	12	13	132	9	0	1	1	44
91-92	Moncton	AHL	67	3	13	16	136	11	2	1	3	16
92-93	Winnipeg	NHL	14	0	2	2	38	—	—	—	—	—
92-93	Moncton	AHL	55	4	6	10	132	—	—	—	—	—
93-94	Florida	NHL	1	0	0	0	0	—	—	—	—	—
93-94	Cincinnati	IHL	80	1	18	19	143	8	0	1	1	41
94-95	Florida	NHL	17	0	1	1	35	—	—	—	—	—
94-95	Cincinnati	IHL	59	6	12	18	69	—	—	—	—	—
95-96	St. Louis	NHL	16	0	1	1	34	—	—	—	—	—
95-96	Winnipeg	NHL	2	0	0	0	0	—	—	—	—	—
95-96	Worcester	AHL	4	0	0	0	12	—	—	—	—	—
96-97	Phoenix	NHL	4	0	0	0	6	—	—	—	—	—
96-97	Rangers	NHL	3	0	0	0	6	4	0	0	0	4
96-97	Springfield	AHL	38	6	7	13	63	—	—	—	—	—
96-97	Binghamton	AHL	19	1	7	8	15	—	—	—	—	—
	NHL	Totals	57	0	4	4	123	4	0	0	0	4
	AHL	Totals	395	17	66	83	818	20	2	2	4	60
	IHL	Totals	139	7	30	37	212	8	0	1	1	41

Born; 2/27/67, Dade City, Florida. 6-2, 195. Drafted by Washington Capitals (11th choice, 208th overall) in 1985 Entry Draft. Signed as a free agent by Winnipeg Jets (10/17/89). Signed as a free agent by Florida Panthers (7/8/93). Traded to St. Louis Blues by Florida for St. Louis' fourth round choice in 1997 Entry Draft (Ivan Novoseltsev), 9/28/95. Claimed on waivers by Winnipeg from St. Louis (3/20/96). Traded to New York Rangers with Mike Eastwood by Phoenix Coyotes for Jayson More (2/6/97). Played forward for Rangers in 1997 playoffs.

J.D. Eaton — Right Wing

			Regular Season					Playoffs				
Season	Team	League	GP	G	A	PTS	PIM	GP	G	A	PTS	PIM
95-96	Utica	CoHL	58	5	9	14	184	—	—	—	—	—
96-97	Saginaw	CoHL	64	22	34	56	301	—	—	—	—	—
	CoHL	Totals	122	27	43	70	485	—	—	—	—	—

Born; 5/28/73, Sudbury, Ontario. 5-11, 205.

Derek Eberle — Defenseman

			Regular Season					Playoffs				
Season	Team	League	GP	G	A	PTS	PIM	GP	G	A	PTS	PIM
93-94	Providence	AHL	17	0	3	3	20	—	—	—	—	—
93-94	Charlotte	ECHL	46	8	21	29	97	3	0	3	3	4
94-95	Atlanta	IHL	13	2	1	3	4	2	0	0	0	0
94-95	Nashville	ECHL	57	25	32	57	96	12	5	10	15	20

95-96	Nashville	IHL	2	0	0	0	0	—	—	—	—	—
95-96	Nashville	ECHL	50	15	43	58	20	5	2	6	8	10
96-97	Carolina	AHL	7	0	3	3	0	—	—	—	—	—
96-97	Manitoba	IHL	3	0	0	0	0	—	—	—	—	—
96-97	Port Huron	CoHL	63	11	40	51	62	—	—	—	—	—
	AHL	Totals	24	0	6	6	20	—	—	—	—	—
	IHL	Totals	18	2	1	3	4	2	0	0	0	0
	ECHL	Totals	153	48	96	144	213	20	7	19	26	34

7/18/72, Regina, Saskatchewan. 5-10, 205.

Robert Edholm — Defenseman

Season	Team	League	GP	G	A	PTS	PIM	GP	G	A	PTS	PIM
96-97	Fresno	WCHL	30	7	13	20	75	4	1	3	4	14

Born; 2/19/71, Stockholm, Sweden. 5-11, 195.

Ray Edwards — Right Wing

Season	Team	League	GP	G	A	PTS	PIM	GP	G	A	PTS	PIM
91-92	Dayton	ECHL	23	5	10	15	120	3	0	0	0	18
92-93	Dayton	ECHL	29	7	7	14	107	—	—	—	—	—
92-93	Birmingham	ECHL	16	0	7	7	60	—	—	—	—	—
93-94	Dayton	ECHL	51	14	10	24	167	—	—	—	—	—
94-95	Huntington	ECHL	32	3	5	8	129	4	0	1	1	6
95-96	Huntington	ECHL	65	20	10	30	330	—	—	—	—	—
96-97	Huntington	ECHL	45	13	15	28	166	—	—	—	—	—
	ECHL	Totals	261	62	64	126	1079	7	0	1	1	24

Born; 6/11/70, Hanover, Ontario. 5-11, 200.

Allan Egeland — Center

Season	Team	League	GP	G	A	PTS	PIM	GP	G	A	PTS	PIM
94-95	Atlanta	IHL	60	8	16	24	112	5	0	1	1	16
95-96	Tampa Bay	NHL	5	0	0	0	2	—	—	—	—	—
95-96	Atlanta	IHL	68	22	22	44	182	3	0	1	1	0
96-97	Tampa Bay	NHL	4	0	0	0	5	—	—	—	—	—
96-97	Adirondack	AHL	52	18	32	50	184	2	0	1	1	4
	NHL	Totals	9	0	0	0	7	—	—	—	—	—
	IHL	Totals	128	30	38	68	294	8	0	1	1	16

Born; 1/31/73, Lethbridge, Alberta. 6-0, 184. Drafted by Tampa Bay Lightning (3rd choice, 55th overall) in 1993 Entry Draft.

Tracy Egeland — Right Wing

Season	Team	League	GP	G	A	PTS	PIM	GP	G	A	PTS	PIM
90-91	Indianapolis	IHL	79	17	22	39	205	7	2	1	3	21
91-92	Indianapolis	IHL	66	20	11	31	214	—	—	—	—	—
92-93	Indianapolis	IHL	43	11	14	25	122	—	—	—	—	—
93-94	Hershey	AHL	57	7	11	18	266	4	0	0	0	2
94-95	Hershey	AHL	37	5	5	10	83	—	—	—	—	—
95-96	Los Angeles	IHL	54	5	1	6	182	—	—	—	—	—
96-97	Huntington	ECHL	43	36	27	63	156	—	—	—	—	—
	IHL	Totals	242	53	48	101	723	7	2	1	3	21
	AHL	Totals	94	12	16	28	349	4	0	0	0	2

Born; 8/20/70, Lethbridge, Alberta. 6-2, 180. Drafted by Chicago Blackhawks (5th choice, 132nd overall) in 1989 Entry Draft. Signed as a free agent by Philadelphia Flyers (8/4/93).

Trent Eigner — Defenseman

Season	Team	League	GP	G	A	PTS	PIM	GP	G	A	PTS	PIM
94-95	Raleigh	ECHL	7	1	2	3	10	—	—	—	—	—
94-95	Huntington	ECHL	59	8	25	33	164	4	0	1	1	12
95-96	Huntington	ECHL	70	6	34	40	209	—	—	—	—	—
96-97	Huntington	ECHL	8	0	1	1	8	—	—	—	—	—
96-97	El Paso	WPHL	50	14	43	57	89	11	1	8	9	29
	ECHL	Totals	144	15	62	77	391	4	0	1	1	12

Born; 7/6/70, Oshkosh, Wisconsin. 6-0, 195. Member of 1996-97 WPHL Champion El Paso Buzzards.

Neil Eisenhut — Center

Season	Team	League	GP	G	A	PTS	PIM	GP	G	A	PTS	PIM
91-92	Milwaukee	IHL	76	13	23	36	26	2	1	2	3	0
92-93	Hamilton	AHL	72	22	40	62	41	—	—	—	—	—
93-94	Vancouver	NHL	13	1	3	4	21	—	—	—	—	—
93-94	Hamilton	AHL	60	17	36	53	30	4	1	4	5	0
94-95	Calgary	NHL	3	0	0	0	0	—	—	—	—	—
94-95	Saint John	AHL	75	16	39	55	30	5	1	1	2	6
95-96	Orlando	IHL	59	10	18	28	30	—	—	—	—	—
95-96	Binghamton	AHL	10	3	3	6	2	4	3	2	5	0
96-97	Binghamton	AHL	55	25	26	51	16	4	1	2	3	0
96-97	Flint	CoHL	21	10	33	43	20	5	1	4	5	8
	NHL	Totals	16	1	3	4	21	—	—	—	—	—
	AHL	Totals	272	83	144	227	119	17	6	9	15	6
	IHL	Totals	135	23	41	64	56	2	1	2	3	0

Born; 6/9/67, Osoyoos, British Columbia. 6-1, 195. Drafted by Vancouver Canucks (11th choice, 238th overall) in 1987 Entry Draft. Signed as a free agent by Calgary Flames (6/16/94).

Jason Elders — Left Wing

Season	Team	League	GP	G	A	PTS	PIM	GP	G	A	PTS	PIM
95-96	Mobile	ECHL	70	38	31	69	28	—	—	—	—	—
96-97	Kansas City	IHL	2	1	0	1	0	—	—	—	—	—
96-97	Mobile	ECHL	68	42	43	85	22	3	1	1	2	0
	ECHL	Totals	138	80	74	154	50	3	1	1	2	0

Born; 12/28/70, Winnipeg, Manitoba. 5-10, 195. 1996-97 ECHL Second Team All-Star.

Patrick Elias — Left Wing

Season	Team	League	GP	G	A	PTS	PIM	GP	G	A	PTS	PIM
95-96	New Jersey	NHL	1	0	0	0	0	—	—	—	—	—
95-96	Albany	AHL	74	27	36	63	83	4	1	1	2	2
96-97	New Jersey	NHL	17	2	3	5	2	—	—	—	—	—
96-97	Albany	AHL	57	24	43	67	76	5	1	2	3	6
	NHL	Totals	18	2	3	5	2	—	—	—	—	—
	AHL	Totals	131	51	79	130	159	9	2	3	5	8

Born; 4/13/76, Trebic, Czechoslovakia. 6-0, 175. Drafted by New Jersey Devils (2nd choice, 51st overall) in 1994 Entry Draft.

Mickey Elick — Defenseman

Season	Team	League	GP	G	A	PTS	PIM	GP	G	A	PTS	PIM
96-97	Binghamton	AHL	1	0	1	1	2	—	—	—	—	—
96-97	Charlotte	ECHL	70	25	36	61	79	3	1	0	1	14

Born; 3/17/74, Calgary, Alberta. 6-1, 180. Drafted by New York Rangers (8th choice, 192nd overall) in 1992 Entry Draft.

Todd Elik — Center

			Regular Season					Playoffs				
Season	Team	League	GP	G	A	PTS	PIM	GP	G	A	PTS	PIM
87-88	Colorado	IHL	81	44	56	100	83	12	8	12	20	9
88-89	Denver	IHL	28	20	15	35	22	—	—	—	—	—
88-89	New Haven	AHL	43	11	25	36	31	17	10	12	22	44
89-90	Los Angeles	NHL	48	10	23	33	41	10	3	9	12	10
89-90	New Haven	AHL	32	20	23	43	42	—	—	—	—	—
90-91	Los Angeles	NHL	74	21	37	58	58	12	2	7	9	6
91-92	Minnesota	NHL	62	14	32	46	125	5	1	1	2	2
92-93	Minnesota	NHL	46	13	18	31	48	—	—	—	—	—
92-93	Edmonton	NHL	14	1	9	10	8	—	—	—	—	—
93-94	Edmonton	NHL	4	0	0	0	6	—	—	—	—	—
93-94	San Jose	NHL	75	25	41	66	89	14	5	5	10	12
94-95	San Jose	NHL	22	7	10	17	18	—	—	—	—	—
94-95	St. Louis	NHL	13	2	4	6	4	7	4	3	7	2
95-96	Boston	NHL	59	13	33	46	40	4	0	2	2	16
95-96	Providence	AHL	7	2	7	9	10	—	—	—	—	—
96-97	Boston	NHL	31	4	12	16	16	—	—	—	—	—
96-97	Providence	AHL	37	16	29	45	63	10	1	6	7	33
	NHL	Totals	448	110	219	329	453	52	15	27	42	48
	AHL	Totals	113	49	84	133	146	27	11	18	29	77
	IHL	Totals	109	64	71	135	105	12	8	12	20	9

Born; 4/15/66, Brampton, Ontario. 6-2, 195. Signed as a free agent by New York Rangers (2/26/88). Traded to Los Angeles Kings by Rangers with Igor Liba, Michael Boyce and future considerations for Dean Kennedy and Denis Larocque (12/12/88). Traded to Minnesota North Stars by Los Angeles for Randy Gilhen, Charlie Huddy, Jim Thomson and Rangers fourth round choice (previously acquired by Minnesota—Los Angeles selected Alexei Zhitnik) in 1991 Entry Draft, 6/22/91. Traded to Edmonton Oilers by Minnesota for Brent Gilchrist (3/5/93). Claimed on waivers by San Jose Sharks from Edmonton (10/26/93). Traded to St. Louis Blues by San Jose for Kevin Miller (3/23/95). Signed as a free agent by Boston Bruins (8/8/95).

Aaron Ellis — Goaltender

			Regular Season							Playoffs					
Season	Team	League	GP	W	L	T	MIN	SO	GAVG	GP	W	L	MIN	SO	GAVG
94-95	Memphis	CeHL	11	4	6	1	629	1	5.34	—	—	—	—	—	—
95-96	Cornwall	AHL	1	0	0	0	31	0	3.86	—	—	—	—	—	—
95-96	Brantford	CoHL	30	10	11	2	1411	0	4.29	1	0	1	42	0	2.85
96-97	Binghamton	AHL	1	0	0	0	20	0	0.00	—	—	—	—	—	—
96-97	Utica	CoHL	27	8	6	4	1302	0	4.61	—	—	—	—	—	—
	AHL	Totals	2	0	0	0	51	0	2.35	—	—	—	—	—	—
	CoHL	Totals	57	18	17	6	2713	0	4.44	1	0	1	42	0	2.85

Born; 5/13/74, Indianapolis, Indiana. 6-1, 187. Drafted by Quebec Nordiques (11th choice, 244th overall) in 1992 Entry Draft.

Mikko Elomo — Left Wing

			Regular Season					Playoffs				
Season	Team	League	GP	G	A	PTS	PIM	GP	G	A	PTS	PIM
96-97	Portland	AHL	52	8	9	17	37	—	—	—	—	—

Born; 4/21/77, Turku, Finland. 6-0, 180. Drafted by Washington Capitals (2nd choice, 23rd overall) in 1995 Entry Draft.

Dan Elsener — Defenseman

			Regular Season					Playoffs				
Season	Team	League	GP	G	A	PTS	PIM	GP	G	A	PTS	PIM
91-92	Cincinnati	ECHL	11	0	6	6	17	—	—	—	—	—
92-93	Memphis	CeHL	26	2	8	10	54	—	—	—	—	—
92-93	Wichita	CeHL	8	0	4	4	15	—	—	—	—	—
92-93	Muskegon	CoHL	4	0	3	3	0	—	—	—	—	—
93-94	Flint	CoHL	47	6	9	15	49	—	—	—	—	—
93-94	St. Thomas	CoHL	3	1	2	3	2	3	1	1	2	0

Season	Team	League	GP	G	A	PTS	PIM	GP	G	A	PTS	PIM
94-95	N/A											
95-96	N/A											
96-97	San Diego	WCHL	8	0	8	8	4	3	0	2	2	4
	CoHL	Totals	54	7	14	21	51	3	0	2	2	4
	CeHL	Totals	34	2	12	14	69	—	—	—	—	—

Born; 7/6/66, Kloton, Switzerland. 5-11, 195. Member of 1996-97 WCHL Champion San Diego Gulls.

Pat Elynuik — Right Wing

			Regular Season					Playoffs				
Season	Team	League	GP	G	A	PTS	PIM	GP	G	A	PTS	PIM
87-88	Winnipeg	NHL	13	1	3	4	12	—	—	—	—	—
87-88	Moncton	AHL	30	11	18	29	35	—	—	—	—	—
88-89	Winnipeg	NHL	59	26	25	51	29	—	—	—	—	—
88-89	Moncton	AHL	7	8	2	10	2	—	—	—	—	—
89-90	Winnipeg	NHL	80	32	42	74	83	7	2	4	6	2
90-91	Winnipeg	NHL	80	31	34	65	73	—	—	—	—	—
91-92	Winnipeg	NHL	60	25	25	50	65	7	2	2	4	4
92-93	Washington	NHL	80	22	35	57	66	6	2	3	5	19
93-94	Washington	NHL	4	1	1	2	0	—	—	—	—	—
93-94	Tampa Bay	NHL	63	12	14	26	64	—	—	—	—	—
94-95	Ottawa	NHL	41	3	7	10	51	—	—	—	—	—
95-96	Ottawa	NHL	29	1	2	3	16	—	—	—	—	—
95-96	Fort Wayne	IHL	42	22	28	50	43	—	—	—	—	—
96-97	Michigan	IHL	81	24	34	58	62	4	1	0	1	0
	NHL	Totals	506	154	188	342	459	20	6	9	15	25
	IHL	Totals	123	46	62	108	105	4	1	0	1	0
	AHL	Totals	37	19	20	39	37	—	—	—	—	—

Born; 10/30/67, Foam Lake, Saskatchewan. 6-0, 185. Drafted by Winnipeg Jets (1st choice, 8th overall) in 1986 Entry Draft. Traded to Washington Capitals by Winnipeg for John Druce and Toronto's fourth round choice (previously acquired by Washington-later traded to Detroit-Detroit selected John Jakopin) in 1993 Entry Draft (10/1/92). Traded to Tampa Bay Lightning by Washington for future draft choices (10/22/93). Signed as a free agent by Otaawa Senators (6/21/94).

David Emma — Center

			Regular Season					Playoffs				
Season	Team	League	GP	G	A	PTS	PIM	GP	G	A	PTS	PIM
91-92	United States	National										
91-92	Utica	AHL	15	4	7	11	12	4	1	1	2	2
92-93	New Jersey	NHL	2	0	0	0	0	—	—	—	—	—
92-93	Utica	AHL	61	21	40	61	47	5	2	1	3	6
93-94	New Jersey	NHL	15	5	5	10	2	—	—	—	—	—
93-94	Albany	AHL	56	26	29	55	53	5	1	2	3	8
94-95	New Jersey	NHL	6	0	1	1	0	—	—	—	—	—
94-95	Albany	AHL	1	0	0	0	0	—	—	—	—	—
95-96	Detroit	IHL	79	30	32	62	75	11	5	2	7	2
96-97	Boston	NHL	5	0	0	0	0	—	—	—	—	—
96-97	Providence	AHL	53	10	18	28	24	—	—	—	—	—
96-97	Phoenix	IHL	8	0	4	4	4	—	—	—	—	—
	NHL	Totals	28	5	6	11	2	—	—	—	—	—
	AHL	Totals	133	51	76	127	112	14	4	4	8	16
	IHL	Totals	87	30	36	66	79	11	5	2	7	2

Born; 1/14/69, Cranston, Rhode Island. 5-11, 180. Drafted by New Jersey Devils (6th choice, 110th overall) in 1989 Entry Draft.

Rick Emmett — Defenseman

			Regular Season					Playoffs				
Season	Team	League	GP	G	A	PTS	PIM	GP	G	A	PTS	PIM
95-96	Brantford	CoHL	1	1	0	1	0	—	—	—	—	—
95-96	South Carolina	ECHL	7	0	2	2	4	—	—	—	—	—

Season	Team	League	GP	G	A	PTS	PIM	GP	G	A	PTS	PIM
95-96	Columbus	ECHL	7	1	4	5	0	—	—	—	—	—
95-96	Johnstown	ECHL	24	2	15	17	12	—	—	—	—	—
96-97	Quad City	CoHL	46	11	26	37	32	15	5	8	13	24
	CoHL	Totals	47	12	26	38	32	15	5	8	13	24
	ECHL	Totals	38	3	21	24	16	—	—	—	—	—

Born; 2/12/75, Etobicoke, Ontario. 5-10, 195. Member of 1996-97 CoHL Champion Quad City Mallards.

Gary Emmons — Center

			Regular Season					Playoffs				
Season	Team	League	GP	G	A	PTS	PIM	GP	G	A	PTS	PIM
87-88	Milwaukee	IHL	13	3	4	7	4	—	—	—	—	—
87-88	Nova Scotia	AHL	59	18	27	45	22	—	—	—	—	—
88-89	Canada	National										
89-90	Kalamazoo	IHL	81	41	59	100	38	8	2	7	9	2
90-91	Kalamazoo	IHL	62	25	33	58	26	11	5	8	13	6
91-92	Kansas City	IHL	80	29	54	83	60	15	6	13	19	8
92-93	Kansas City	IHL	80	37	44	81	80	12	*7	6	13	8
93-94	San Jose	NHL	3	1	0	1	0	—	—	—	—	—
93-94	Kansas City	IHL	63	20	49	69	28	—	—	—	—	—
94-95	Kansas City	IHL	81	22	38	60	42	21	9	19	28	24
95-96	Kansas City	IHL	73	24	39	63	72	1	0	0	0	4
96-97	Kansas City	IHL	67	15	30	45	36	3	0	1	1	4
	IHL	Totals	600	216	350	566	386	71	29	54	83	56

Born; 12/30/63, Winnipeg, Manitoba. 5-9, 180. Drafted by New York Rangers (1st choice, 14th overall) in 1986 Supplemental Draft. Signed as a free agent by Edmonton Oilers (7/27/87). Signed as a free agent by Minnesota North Stars (7/11/89). Signed as a free agent by San Jose Sharks (10/19/93).

John Emmons — Center

			Regular Season					Playoffs				
Season	Team	League	GP	G	A	PTS	PIM	GP	G	A	PTS	PIM
96-97	Fort Wayne	IHL	1	0	0	0	0	—	—	—	—	—
96-97	Dayton	ECHL	69	20	37	57	62	4	0	1	1	2

Born; 8/17/74, San Jose, California. Drafted by Calgary Flames (7th choice, 122nd overall) in 1993 Entry Draft.

Larry Empey — Defenseman

			Regular Season					Playoffs				
Season	Team	League	GP	G	A	PTS	PIM	GP	G	A	PTS	PIM
94-95	Syracuse	AHL	1	0	0	0	0	—	—	—	—	—
94-95	Erie	ECHL	23	0	1	1	52	—	—	—	—	—
94-95	Utica	CoHL	27	0	5	5	29	6	0	1	1	6
95-96	Utica	CoHL	72	4	8	12	106	—	—	—	—	—
96-97	Utica	CoHL	73	1	10	11	83	3	0	1	1	6
	CoHL	Totals	172	5	23	28	218	9	0	2	2	12

Born; 7/25/73, Swift Current, Saskatchewan. 6-3, 220.

Ryan Equale — Forward

			Regular Season					Playoffs				
Season	Team	League	GP	G	A	PTS	PIM	GP	G	A	PTS	PIM
96-97	Roanoke	ECHL	39	4	10	14	47	4	0	0	0	2

Born; 2/22/73, Wilton, Connecticut. 6-0, 195.

Chad Erickson — Goaltender

			Regular Season						Playoffs					
Season	Team	League	GP	W	L	T	MIN	SO	AVG	GP	W	L	MIN	SO	GAVG
91-92	New Jersey	NHL	2	1	1	0	120	0	4.50	—	—	—	—	—	—
91-92	Utica	AHL	44	18	19	3	2341	2	3.77	2	0	2	127	0	5.20
92-93	Cincinnati	IHL	10	2	6	1	516	0	4.88	—	—	—	—	—	—
92-93	Birmingham	ECHL	14	6	6	2	856	0	3.79	—	—	—	—	—	—

Season	Team	League	GP	G	A	PTS	PIM	GAA	GP	G	A	PTS	PIM	GAA
92-93	Albany	AHL	9	1	7	1	505	0	5.58	—	—	—	—	—
93-94	Albany	AHL	4	2	1	0	184	0	4.25	—	—	—	—	—
93-94	Raleigh	ECHL	32	19	9	3	1884	0	3.22	6	3	1	287	0	4.40
94-95	Albany	AHL	1	1	0	0	60	0	2.00	—	—	—	—	—
94-95	Providence	AHL	7	1	6	0	351	0	5.63	—	—	—	—	—
94-95	Springfield	AHL	1	0	0	0	23	0	7.78	—	—	—	—	—
94-95	Raleigh	ECHL	11	1	8	1	587	0	4.60	—	—	—	—	—
95-96	Birmingham	ECHL	44	16	20	4	2410	0	5.00	—	—	—	—	—
96-97	Austin	WPHL	32	18	11	2	1875	0	3.90	5	2	2	281	0	4.06
	AHL	Totals	66	23	33	4	3464	2	4.24	2	0	2	127	0	5.20
	ECHL	Totals	101	42	43	10	5737	0	3.63	6	3	1	287	0	4.40

Born; 8/21/70, Minneapolis, Minnesota. 5-9, 175. Drafted by New Jersey Devils (8th choice, 138th overall) in 1988 Entry Draft.

Anders Eriksson — Defense

			Regular Season					Playoffs				
Season	Team	League	GP	G	A	PTS	PIM	GP	G	A	PTS	PIM
95-96	Detroit	NHL	1	0	0	0	2	3	0	0	0	0
95-96	Adirondack	AHL	75	6	36	42	64	3	0	0	0	0
96-97	Detroit	NHL	23	0	6	6	10	—	—	—	—	—
96-97	Adirondack	AHL	44	3	25	28	36	4	0	1	1	4
	NHL	Totals	24	0	6	6	12	3	0	0	0	0
	AHL	Totals	119	9	61	70	100	7	0	1	1	4

Born; 1/9/75, Bolinas, Sweden. 6-3, 218. Drafted by Detroit Red Wings (1st choice, 22nd overall) 1993 Entry Draft.

Valeri Ermolov — Center

			Regular Season					Playoffs				
Season	Team	League	GP	G	A	PTS	PIM	GP	G	A	PTS	PIM
96-97	Huntington	ECHL	40	5	29	34	18	—	—	—	—	—

Born; 8/22/75, Minsk, Belarus. 6-2, 200.

Len Esau — Defenseman

			Regular Season					Playoffs				
Season	Team	League	GP	G	A	PTS	PIM	GP	G	A	PTS	PIM
90-91	Newmarket	AHL	76	4	14	18	28	—	—	—	—	—
91-92	Toronto	NHL	2	0	0	0	0	—	—	—	—	—
91-92	St. John's	AHL	78	9	29	38	68	13	0	2	2	14
92-93	Quebec	NHL	4	0	1	1	2	—	—	—	—	—
92-93	Halifax	AHL	75	11	31	42	79	—	—	—	—	—
93-94	Calgary	NHL	6	0	3	3	7	—	—	—	—	—
93-94	Saint John	AHL	75	12	36	48	129	7	2	2	4	6
94-95	Edmonton	NHL	14	0	6	6	15	—	—	—	—	—
94-95	Calgary	NHL	1	0	0	0	0	—	—	—	—	—
94-95	Saint John	AHL	54	13	27	40	73	5	0	2	2	0
95-96	Cincinnati	IHL	82	15	21	36	150	17	5	6	11	26
96-97	Milwaukee	IHL	49	6	16	22	70	—	—	—	—	—
96-97	Detroit	IHL	30	6	8	14	36	13	1	4	5	38
	NHL	Totals	27	0	10	10	24	—	—	—	—	—
	AHL	Totals	358	49	137	186	377	25	2	6	8	20
	IHL	Totals	161	27	45	72	256	30	6	10	16	64

Born; 3/16/68, Meadow Lake, Saskatchewan. 6-3, 195. Drafted by Toronto Maple Leafs (5th choice, 86th overall) in 1988 Entry Draft. Traded to Quebec Nordiques by Toronto for Ken McRae (7/21/92). Signed as a free agent by Calgary Flames (9/6/93). Claimed by Edmonton Oilers from Calgary in NHL Waiver Draft (1/18/95). Claimed on waivers by Calgary from Edmonton (3/7/95). Signed as a free agent by Florida Panthers (7/27/95). Member of 1996-97 IHL Champions Detroit Vipers.

Brad Essex — Center

Season	Team	League	GP	G	A	PTS	PIM	GP	G	A	PTS	PIM
96-97	Peoria	ECHL	53	6	9	15	181	10	0	4	4	34

Born;

Doug Evans — Defenseman

Season	Team	League	GP	G	A	PTS	PIM	GP	G	A	PTS	PIM
92-93	Dayton	ECHL	58	5	18	23	71	3	0	0	0	0
93-94	Charlotte	EHL	45	4	9	13	58	3	0	0	0	6
94-95	Rochester	AHL	2	0	0	0	0	—	—	—	—	—
94-95	Greensboro	ECHL	59	10	15	25	151	18	1	2	3	34
95-96	Jacksonville	ECHL	55	5	11	16	262	—	—	—	—	—
96-97	Jacksonville	ECHL	55	2	10	12	251	—	—	—	—	—
	ECHL	Totals	272	26	63	89	795	24	1	2	3	40

Born; 7/12/71, San Jose, California. 6-0, 205.

Doug Evans — Left Wing

Season	Team	League	GP	G	A	PTS	PIM	GP	G	A	PTS	PIM
84-85	Peoria	IHL	81	36	61	97	189	20	18	14	32	*88
85-86	St. Louis	NHL	13	1	0	1	2	—	—	—	—	—
85-86	Peoria	IHL	69	46	51	97	179	10	4	6	10	32
86-87	St. Louis	NHL	53	3	13	16	91	5	0	0	0	10
86-87	Peoria	IHL	18	10	15	25	39	—	—	—	—	—
87-88	St. Louis	NHL	41	5	7	12	49	2	0	0	0	0
87-88	Peoria	IHL	11	4	16	20	64	—	—	—	—	—
88-89	St. Louis	NHL	53	7	12	19	81	7	1	2	3	16
89-90	St. Louis	NHL	3	0	0	0	0	—	—	—	—	—
89-90	Winnipeg	NHL	27	10	8	18	33	7	2	2	4	10
89-90	Peoria	IHL	42	19	28	47	128	—	—	—	—	—
90-91	Winnipeg	NHL	70	7	27	34	108	—	—	—	—	—
91-92	Winnipeg	NHL	30	7	7	14	68	1	0	0	0	2
91-92	Peoria	IHL	16	5	14	19	38	—	—	—	—	—
91-92	Moncton	AHL	10	7	8	15	10	—	—	—	—	—
92-93	Philadelphia	NHL	65	8	13	21	70	—	—	—	—	—
93-94	Peoria	IHL	76	27	63	90	108	6	2	6	8	10
94-95	Peoria	IHL	74	13	39	52	103	9	2	9	11	10
95-96	Peoria	IHL	74	19	48	67	81	1	0	0	0	0
96-97	Peoria	ECHL	67	23	59	82	128	10	10	12	22	20
	NHL	Totals	355	48	87	135	502	22	3	4	7	38
	IHL	Totals	461	179	335	514	929	46	26	35	61	140

Born; 6/2/63, Peterborough, Ontario. 5-9, 185. Signed as a free agent by St. louis Blues (6/10/85). Traded to Winnipeg Jets by St. Louis for Ron Wilson (1/22/90). Loaned to Peoria Rivermen (11/9/91, returned 12/15/91). Traded to Boston Bruins by Winnipeg for Daniel Berthiaume (6/10/92). Selected by Philadelphia Flyers in NHL waiver draft (10/4/92). Signed as a free agent by Peoria (8/2/93). 1985-86 IHL First Team All-Star. Member of 1984-85 IHL champion Peoria Rivermen.

Kevin Evans — Left Wing

Season	Team	League	GP	G	A	PTS	PIM	GP	G	A	PTS	PIM
85-86	Kalamazoo	IHL	11	3	5	8	97	6	3	0	3	56
86-87	Kalamazoo	IHL	73	19	31	50	*648	—	—	—	—	—
87-88	Kalamazoo	IHL	54	9	28	37	404	5	1	1	2	46
88-89	Kalmazoo	IHL	54	22	32	54	328	—	—	—	—	—
89-90	Kalmazoo	IHL	76	30	54	84	346	—	—	—	—	—
90-91	Minnesota	NHL	4	0	0	0	19	—	—	—	—	—

Season	Team	League	GP	G	A	PTS	PIM	GP	G	A	PTS	PIM
90-91	Kalamazoo	IHL	16	10	12	22	70	—	—	—	—	—
91-92	San Jose	NHL	5	0	1	1	25	—	—	—	—	—
91-92	Kansas City	IHL	66	10	39	49	342	14	2	13	15	70
92-93	Kalamazoo	IHL	49	7	24	31	283	—	—	—	—	—
93-94	Peoria	IHL	67	10	29	39	254	4	0	0	0	6
94-95	Peoria	IHL	29	5	9	14	121	—	—	—	—	—
94-95	Kansas City	IHL	26	3	6	9	192	19	2	4	6	11
95-96	Memphis	CeHL	38	11	32	43	356	6	2	9	11	48
96-97	Mississippi	ECHL	63	19	27	46	*505	3	1	1	2	21
	NHL	Totals	9	0	1	1	44	—	—	—	—	—
	IHL	Totals	521	128	269	397	3085	48	8	18	26	189

Born; 7/18/65, Peterborough, Ontario. 5-10, 182. Signed as a free agent by Minnesota North Stars (8/8/88). Selected by San Jose Sharks in NHL dispersal draft (5/30/91). Signed as a free agent by Minnesota (7/17/92). Signed as player/assistant coach by Mississippi Sea Wolves.

Michael Evans — Center

			Regular Season					Playoffs				
Season	Team	League	GP	G	A	PTS	PIM	GP	G	A	PTS	PIM
96-97	Waco	WPHL	60	14	15	29	66	—	—	—	—	—

Born; Brooks, Alberta. 5-10, 185.

Shawn Evans — Defenseman

			Regular Season					Playoffs				
Season	Team	League	GP	G	A	PTS	PIM	GP	G	A	PTS	PIM
85-86	Peria	IHL	55	8	26	34	36	—	—	—	—	—
85-86	St. Louis	NHL	7	0	0	0	2	—	—	—	—	—
86-87	Nova Scotia	AHL	55	7	28	35	29	5	0	4	4	6
87-88	Nova Scotia	AHL	79	8	62	70	109	5	1	1	2	40
88-89	Springfield	AHL	68	9	50	59	125	—	—	—	—	—
89-90	Islanders	NHL	2	1	0	1	0	—	—	—	—	—
89-90	Springfield	AHL	63	6	35	41	102	18	6	11	17	35
90-91	Switzerland											
90-91	Maine	AHL	51	9	37	46	44	2	0	1	1	0
91-92	Springfield	AHL	80	11	67	78	81	11	0	8	8	16
92-93	Milwaukee	IHL	79	13	65	78	83	6	0	3	3	6
93-94	N/A											
94-95	Milwaukee	IHL	58	6	34	40	20	—	—	—	—	—
94-95	Fort Wayne	IHL	11	2	8	10	6	4	1	3	4	2
95-96	Fort Wayne	IHL	81	5	61	66	78	5	3	3	6	2
96-97	Fort Wayne	IHL	41	7	13	20	34	—	—	—	—	—
96-97	Manitoba	IHL	17	2	3	5	4	—	—	—	—	—
96-97	Cincinnati	IHL	21	3	9	12	24	3	0	0	0	19
	NHL	Totals	9	1	0	1	2	—	—	—	—	—
	AHL	Totals	396	50	279	329	490	41	7	25	32	97
	IHL	Totals	363	46	219	265	285	18	4	9	13	29

Born; 9/7/65, Kingston, Ontario. 6-3, 190. Drafted by New Jersey Devils (2nd choice, 24th overall) in 1983 Entry Draft. Traded to St. Louis Blues by New Jersey with fifth round pick (Mike Wolak) in 1986 for Mark Johnson (9/19/85). Traded to Edmonton Oilers by St. Louis for Todd Ewen (10/15/86). Signed as a free agent by New York Islanders (6/20/88). Signed as a free agent by Hartford Whalers (8/14/91). 1991-92 AHL First Team All-Star. 1992-93 AHL First Team All-Star. Member of 1989-90 AHL champion Springfield Indians.

Chris Everett — Center

			Regular Season					Playoffs				
Season	Team	League	GP	G	A	PTS	PIM	GP	G	A	PTS	PIM
96-97	Tulsa	CeHL	58	10	17	27	8	—	—	—	—	—
96-97	Oklahoma City	CeHL	5	1	0	1	2	4	0	1	1	2
	CeHL	Totals	63	11	17	28	10	4	0	1	1	2

Born; 4/3/73, Calgary, Alberta. 6-0, 185.

Dean Ewen — Left Wing

Season	Team	League	Regular Season					Playoffs				
			GP	G	A	PTS	PIM	GP	G	A	PTS	PIM
89-90	Springfield	AHL	34	0	7	7	194	—	—	—	—	—
91-92	Capital District	AHL	41	5	8	13	106	—	—	—	—	—
93-94	San Diego	IHL	19	0	3	3	45	3	1	0	1	8
94-95	San Diego	IHL	36	4	3	7	187	4	0	0	0	10
95-96	Kansas City	IHL	50	1	6	7	203	5	0	1	1	11
96-97	Kansas City	IHL	36	7	2	9	132	2	0	0	0	0
	IHL	Totals	141	12	14	31	567	14	1	1	2	29
	AHL	Totals	75	5	15	20	300	—	—	—	—	—

Born; 2/28/69, St. Albert, Alberta. 6-1, 225. Drafted by New York Islanders (3rd choice, 55th overall) in 1987 Entry Draft. Signed as a free agent by Anaheim Mighty Ducks (1/21/94). Signed as a free agent by Kansas City Blades (7/19/95).

Dominic Fafard — Defenseman

			Regular Season					Playoffs				
Season	Team	League	GP	G	A	PTS	PIM	GP	G	A	PTS	PIM
94-95	Wheeling	ECHL	39	2	8	10	44	—	—	—	—	—
94-95	South Carolina	ECHL	7	0	1	1	4	8	1	0	1	6
95-96	Wheeling	ECHL	2	0	0	0	0	—	—	—	—	—
95-96	Raleigh	ECHL	4	0	1	1	2	—	—	—	—	—
95-96	Oklahoma City	CeHL	56	6	26	32	77	13	0	3	3	10
96-97	Oklahoma City	CeHL	66	2	20	22	111	4	1	0	1	4
	CeHL	Totals	122	8	46	54	188	17	1	3	4	14
	ECHL	Totals	52	2	10	12	50	8	1	0	1	6

Born; 7/13/74, Longeuil, Quebec. 6-5, 230. Signed as a free agent by Edmonton Oilers (9/30/94). Member of 1995-96 CeHL champion Oklahoma City Blazers.

Quinn Fair — Defenseman

			Regular Season					Playoffs				
Season	Team	League	GP	G	A	PTS	PIM	GP	G	A	PTS	PIM
96-97	Grand Rapids	IHL	2	0	0	0	0	—	—	—	—	—
96-97	Baltimore	AHL	9	0	0	0	2	—	—	—	—	—
96-97	Mississippi	ECHL	58	12	22	34	54	3	0	1	1	0

Born; 5/23/73, Campbell River, British Columbia. 6-1, 210. Drafted by Los Angeles Kings (1st choice, 7th overall) in 1994 Supplemental Draft. Last amateur club; Bowling Green University (CCHA).

Kelly Fairchild — Center

			Regular Season					Playoffs				
Season	Team	League	GP	G	A	PTS	PIM	GP	G	A	PTS	PIM
94-95	St. John's	AHL	53	27	23	50	51	4	0	2	2	4
95-96	Toronto	NHL	1	0	1	1	2	—	—	—	—	—
95-96	St. John's	AHL	78	29	47	78	85	2	0	1	1	4
96-97	Toronto	NHL	22	0	2	2	2	—	—	—	—	—
96-97	St. John's	AHL	29	9	22	31	36	—	—	—	—	—
96-97	Orlando	IHL	25	9	6	15	20	9	6	5	11	16
	NHL	Totals	23	0	3	3	4	—	—	—	—	—
	AHL	Totals	160	65	92	157	172	6	0	3	3	8

Born; 4/9/73, Hibbing, Minnesota. 5-11, 180. Drafted by Los Angeles Kings (7th choice, 152nd overall) in 1991 Entry Draft. Traded to Toronto Maple Leafs by Los Angeles with Dixon Ward, Guy Leveque and Shayne Toporowski for Eric Lacroix, Chris Snell and Toronto's fourth round choice (Eric Belanger) in 1996 Entry Draft.

Chris Fargher — Defenseman

			Regular Season					Playoffs				
Season	Team	League	GP	G	A	PTS	PIM	GP	G	A	PTS	PIM
96-97	Jacksonville	ECHL	33	4	4	8	35	—	—	—	—	—

Born; 6/9/70, Annapolis, Maryland. 6-0, 189.

Brian Farrell — Left Wing

			Regular Season					Playoffs				
Season	Team	League	GP	G	A	PTS	PIM	GP	G	A	PTS	PIM
94-95	Cleveland	IHL	46	7	11	18	28	—	—	—	—	—
95-96	Utah	IHL	1	0	0	0	6	—	—	—	—	—
95-96	Jacksonville	ECHL	41	14	22	36	128	—	—	—	—	—
95-96	Toledo	ECHL	20	6	7	13	41	11	3	4	7	10
96-97	Fort Wayne	IHL	45	8	7	15	36	—	—	—	—	—
96-97	Chicago	IHL	22	5	5	10	16	4	2	0	2	4
	IHL	Totals	47	7	11	18	34	—	—	—	—	—
	ECHL	Totals	61	20	29	49	169	11	3	4	7	10

Born; 4/16/72, Hartford, Connecticut. 5-11, 170. Drafted by Pittsburgh Penguins (4th choice, 89th overall) in 1990 Entry Draft.

Rich Fatrola — Left Wing

			Regular Season					Playoffs				
Season	Team	League	GP	G	A	PTS	PIM	GP	G	A	PTS	PIM
95-96	Muskegon	CoHL	31	9	4	13	56	—	—	—	—	—
95-96	Utica	CoHL	20	12	6	18	39	—	—	—	—	—
96-97	Utica	CoHL	30	6	11	17	27	—	—	—	—	—
96-97	Dayton	CoHL	29	17	23	40	28	—	—	—	—	—
	CoHL	Totals	110	44	44	88	150	—	—	—	—	—

Born; 10/29/70, Toronto, Ontario. 6-0, 200.

Andy Faulkner — Center

			Regular Season					Playoffs				
Season	Team	League	GP	G	A	PTS	PIM	GP	G	A	PTS	PIM
96-97	Quad City	CoHL	69	20	25	45	18	14	1	4	5	6

Born; 1/8/71, Enderby, British Columbia. 5-11, 195. Member of 1996-97 Colonial League Champion Quad City Mallards.

Kent Fearns — Defenseman

			Regular Season					Playoffs				
Season	Team	League	GP	G	A	PTS	PIM	GP	G	A	PTS	PIM
95-96	Cape Breton	AHL	6	0	0	0	4	—	—	—	—	—
95-96	Flint	CoHL	24	5	6	11	23	—	—	—	—	—
95-96	Knoxville	ECHL	21	1	8	9	24	8	1	5	6	6
96-97	Las Vegas	IHL	21	3	8	11	6	—	—	—	—	—
96-97	Manitoba	IHL	10	1	4	5	6	—	—	—	—	—
96-97	Knoxville	ECHL	37	11	21	32	37	—	—	—	—	—
	IHL	Totals	31	4	12	16	12	—	—	—	—	—
	ECHL	Totals	58	12	29	41	61	8	1	5	6	6

Born; 9/13/72, Langley, British Columbia. 6-0, 190.

Mike Feasby — Right Wing

			Regular Season					Playoffs				
Season	Team	League	GP	G	A	PTS	PIM	GP	G	A	PTS	PIM
96-97	Muskegon	CoHL	5	1	0	1	5	3	0	0	0	12

Born; 4/19/73, Port Perry, Ontario. 6-2, 205.

Scott Feasby — Defenseman

			Regular Season					Playoffs				
Season	Team	League	GP	G	A	PTS	PIM	GP	G	A	PTS	PIM
90-91	Roanoke	ECHL	24	3	5	8	57	—	—	—	—	—
91-92	Raleigh	ECHL	20	0	5	5	47	—	—	—	—	—
91-92	Brantford	CoHL	36	2	11	13	40	6	2	1	3	4
92-93	N/A											
93-94	Muskegon	CoHL	62	7	17	24	156	3	0	1	1	5
94-95	Detroit	IHL	1	0	0	0	2	—	—	—	—	—
94-95	Kalamazoo	IHL	2	0	1	1	0	—	—	—	—	—
94-95	Phoenix	IHL	6	0	0	0	4	—	—	—	—	—
94-95	Muskegon	CoHL	63	4	15	19	75	17	0	4	4	10
95-96	Detroit	IHL	4	0	2	2	0	—	—	—	—	—
95-96	Los Angeles	IHL	22	0	1	1	34	—	—	—	—	—
95-96	Rochester	AHL	12	0	2	2	6	1	0	0	0	0
95-96	Muskegon	CoHL	44	4	8	12	107	—	—	—	—	—
96-97	Detroit	IHL	5	0	1	1	2	—	—	—	—	—
96-97	Rochester	AHL	1	0	0	0	2	—	—	—	—	—
96-97	Muskegon	CoHL	69	5	31	36	122	3	0	0	0	4
	IHL	Totals	40	0	5	5	42	—	—	—	—	—
	AHL	Totals	13	0	2	2	8	1	0	0	0	0
	CoHL	Totals	274	22	82	104	500	29	2	6	8	23
	ECHL	Totals	44	3	10	13	104	—	—	—	—	—

Born; 11/20/70, Oxbridge, Ontario. 6-2, 200. Member of 1995-96 AHL champion Rochester Americans.

Anton Fedorov — Center

Season	Team	League	GP	G	A	PTS	PIM	GP	G	A	PTS	PIM
94-95	Detroit	CoHL	4	0	0	0	0	—	—	—	—	—
94-95	Raleigh	ECHL	21	2	6	8	6	—	—	—	—	—
94-95	Johnstown	ECHL	13	5	6	11	2	5	1	1	2	0
95-96	Wichita	CeHL	64	26	38	64	62	—	—	—	—	—
96-97	Kansas City	IHL	2	0	0	0	0	—	—	—	—	—
96-97	Wichita	CeHL	66	24	41	65	79	9	0	3	3	5
	CeHL	Totals	130	50	79	129	141	9	0	3	3	5
	ECHL	Totals	34	7	12	19	8	5	1	1	2	0

Born; 6/29/72, St. Petersbug, Russia. 5-11, 198.

Brian Felsner — Center

Season	Team	League	GP	G	A	PTS	PIM	GP	G	A	PTS	PIM
96-97	Orlando	IHL	75	29	41	70	38	7	2	3	5	6

Born; 11/7/72, Mt. Clemens, Michigan. 6-0, 190. Last amateur club; Lake Superior State (CCHA). 1996-97 IHL American Born Rookie of the Year.

Denny Felsner — Left Wing

Season	Team	League	GP	G	A	PTS	PIM	GP	G	A	PTS	PIM
91-92	St. Louis	NHL	3	0	1	1	0	1	0	0	0	0
92-93	St. Louis	NHL	6	0	3	3	2	9	2	3	5	2
92-93	Peoria	IHL	29	14	21	35	8	—	—	—	—	—
93-94	St. Louis	NHL	6	1	0	1	2	—	—	—	—	—
93-94	Peoria	IHL	6	8	3	11	14	—	—	—	—	—
94-95	St. Louis	NHL	3	0	0	0	2	—	—	—	—	—
94-95	Peoria	IHL	25	10	12	22	14	8	2	3	5	0
95-96	Syracuse	AHL	66	23	34	57	22	14	5	12	17	0
96-97	Chicago	IHL	39	10	12	22	4	—	—	—	—	—
96-97	Milwaukee	IHL	14	1	3	4	2	—	—	—	—	—
	NHL	Totals	18	1	4	5	6	10	2	3	5	2
	IHL	Totals	113	43	51	94	42	8	2	3	5	0

Born; 4/29/70, Warren, Michigan. 6-0, 195. Drafted by St. Louis Blues (3rd choice, 55th overall) in 1989 Entry Draft.

Eric Fenton — Right Wing

Season	Team	League	GP	G	A	PTS	PIM	GP	G	A	PTS	PIM
93-94	Hampton Roads	ECHL	24	12	16	28	39	—	—	—	—	—
93-94	Portland	AHL	25	2	5	7	104	—	—	—	—	—
94-95	Charlotte	ECHL	58	11	26	37	269	2	0	0	0	4
94-95	Peoria	IHL	8	1	1	2	20	2	0	0	0	8
95-96	Peoria	IHL	33	2	7	9	102	12	3	1	4	38
95-96	Charlotte	ECHL	4	2	1	3	36	4	1	0	1	33
96-97	Milwaukee	IHL	43	3	5	8	169	3	1	0	1	6
96-97	Charlotte	ECHL	29	15	9	24	163	—	—	—	—	—
	IHL	Totals	84	6	13	19	291	17	4	1	5	52
	ECHL	Totals	115	40	52	92	507	6	1	0	1	37

Born; 7/17/69, Troy, New York. 6-2, 190. Member of 1995-96 ECHL Champion Charlotte Checkers.

Craig Ferguson — Right Wing

Season	Team	League	GP	G	A	PTS	PIM	GP	G	A	PTS	PIM
92-93	FRE	AHL	55	15	13	28	20	5	0	1	1	2
92-93	WHL	ECHL	9	6	5	11	24	—	—	—	—	—
93-94	MTL	NHL	2	0	1	1	0	—	—	—	—	—
93-94	FRE	AHL	57	29	32	61	60	—	—	—	—	—
94-95	MTL	NHL	1	0	0	0	0	—	—	—	—	—
94-95	FRE	AHL	80	27	35	62	62	17	6	2	8	6
95-96	MTL	NHL	10	1	0	1	2	—	—	—	—	—
95-96	CAL	NHL	8	0	0	0	4	—	—	—	—	—
95-96	SJN	AHL	18	5	13	18	8	—	—	—	—	—
95-96	PHX	IHL	31	6	9	15	25	4	0	2	2	6
96-97	Florida	NHL	3	0	0	0	0	—	—	—	—	—
96-97	Carolina	AHL	74	29	41	70	57	—	—	—	—	—
	NHL	Totals	24	1	1	2	6	—	—	—	—	—
	AHL	Totals	284	105	134	239	207	22	6	3	9	8

Born; 8/4/70, Castro Valley, California. 6-0, 185. Drafted by Montreal Canadiens (7th choice, 146th overall) in 1989 Entry Draft. Traded to Calgary Flames by Montreal with Yves Sarault for a conditional draft pick (11/26/95). Traded to Los Angeles Kings by Calgary for Pat Conacher (2/10/96). Signed as a free agent by Florida Panthers (8/96).

Dallas Ferguson — Defenseman

Season	Team	League	GP	G	A	PTS	PIM	GP	G	A	PTS	PIM
96-97	Alaska	WCHL	15	1	13	14	12	—	—	—	—	—
96-97	Richmond	ECHL	18	1	2	3	6	—	—	—	—	—

Born; 11/24/72, Wainwright, Alberta. 5-10, 200. Last amateur club; Alaska-Fairbanks (WCHA).

Dan Ferguson — Left Wing

Season	Team	League	GP	G	A	PTS	PIM	GP	G	A	PTS	PIM
96-97	El Paso	WPHL	22	0	5	5	110	—	—	—	—	—

Born; 5/3/71, Fredericton, New Brunswick. 6-1, 215.

Jeff Ferguson — Goaltender

Season	Team	League	GP	W	L	T	MIN	SO	GAVG	GP	W	L	MIN	SO	GAVG
94-95	Fresno	SUN	8	3	4	0	367	0	5.06	—	—	—	—	—	—
95-96	Fresno	WCHL	47	22	17	7	2719	1	3.75	1	1	0	60	0	4.00
96-97	Fresno	WCHL	51	26	18	6	2895	0	3.92	5	3	2	286	0	4.62
	WCHL	Totals	98	48	45	13	5614	1	3.84	6	4	2	346	0	4.51

Born; 7/23/69, Calgary, Alberta. 5-8, 175. 1996-97 WCHL Second Team All-Star.

Kyle Ferguson — Right Wing

Season	Team	League	GP	G	A	PTS	PIM	GP	G	A	PTS	PIM
96-97	South Carolina	ECHL	42	6	9	15	172	—	—	—	—	—
96-97	Louisville	ECHL	18	6	6	12	30	—	—	—	—	—
	ECHL	Totals	60	12	15	27	202	—	—	—	—	—

Born; 8/12/73, Toronto, Ontario. 6-3, 230. Drafted by Toronto Maple Leafs (7th choice, 253rd overall) in 1993 Entry Draft.

Scott Ferguson — Defenseman

Season	Team	League	GP	G	A	PTS	PIM	GP	G	A	PTS	PIM
94-95	Cape Breton	AHL	58	4	6	10	103	—	—	—	—	—
94-95	Wheeling	ECHL	5	1	5	6	16	—	—	—	—	—
95-96	Cape Breton	AHL	80	5	16	21	196	—	—	—	—	—

Season	Team	League	GP	G	A	PTS	PIM	GP	G	A	PTS	PIM
96-97	Hamilton	AHL	74	6	14	20	115	21	5	7	12	59
	AHL	Totals	212	15	36	51	414	21	5	7	12	59

Born; 1/6/73, Camrose, Alberta. 6-1, 191. Signed as a free agent by Edmonton Oilers (6/2/94).

Emmanual Fernandez — Goaltender

			Regular Season							Playoffs				
Season	Team	League	GP	W	L	T	MIN	SO	GAVG	GP	W	L	MIN	SO	GAVG
94-95	Dallas	NHL	1	0	1	0	59	0	3.05	—	—	—	—	—	—
94-95	Kalamazoo	IHL	46	21	10	9	2470	2	2.79	14	10	2	753	1	2.71
95-96	Dallas	NHL	5	0	1	1	249	0	4.58	—	—	—	—	—	—
95-96	Michigan	IHL	47	22	15	9	2663	4	3.00	6	5	1	372	0	2.26
96-97	Michigan	IHL	48	20	24	2	2721	2	3.13	4	1	3	277	0	3.25
	NHL	Totals	6	0	2	1	308	0	4.29	—	—	—	—	—	—
	IHL	Totals	141	63	49	20	7843	8	2.98	24	16	6	1402	1	2.70

Born; 8/27/74, Etobicoke, Ontario. 6-0, 185. Drafted by Quebec Nordiques (4th choice, 52nd overall) in 1992 Entry Draft. Rights traded to Dallas Stars by Quebec for Tommy Sjodin and Dallas' third round choice (Chris Drury) in 1994 Entry Draft (2/13/94).

Mark Ferner — Defenseman

			Regular Season					Playoffs				
Season	Team	League	GP	G	A	PTS	PIM	GP	G	A	PTS	PIM
85-86	Rochester	AHL	63	3	14	17	87	—	—	—	—	—
86-87	Buffalo	NHL	13	0	3	3	9	—	—	—	—	—
86-87	Rochester	AHL	54	0	12	12	157	—	—	—	—	—
87-88	Rochester	AHL	69	1	25	26	165	7	1	4	5	31
88-89	Buffalo	NHL	2	0	0	0	2	—	—	—	—	—
88-89	Rochester	AHL	55	0	18	18	97	—	—	—	—	—
89-90	Washington	NHL	2	0	0	0	0	—	—	—	—	—
89-90	Baltimore	AHL	74	7	28	35	76	11	1	2	3	21
90-91	Washington	NHL	7	0	1	1	4	—	—	—	—	—
90-91	Baltimore	AHL	61	14	40	54	38	6	1	4	5	24
91-92	Baltimore	AHL	57	7	38	45	67	—	—	—	—	—
91-92	St. John's	AHL	15	1	8	9	6	14	2	14	16	38
92-93	New Haven	AHL	34	5	7	12	69	—	—	—	—	—
92-93	San Diego	IHL	26	0	15	15	34	11	1	2	3	8
93-94	Anaheim	NHL	50	3	5	8	30	—	—	—	—	—
94-95	Anaheim	NHL	14	0	1	1	6	—	—	—	—	—
94-95	Detroit	NHL	3	0	0	0	0	—	—	—	—	—
94-95	San Diego	IHL	46	3	12	15	51	—	—	—	—	—
94-95	Adirondack	AHL	3	0	0	0	2	1	0	0	0	0
95-96	Orlando	IHL	43	4	18	22	37	23	4	10	14	8
96-97	Orlando	IHL	61	12	18	30	55	—	—	—	—	—
96-97	Long Beach	IHL	17	2	6	8	31	18	3	4	7	6
	NHL	Totals	91	3	10	13	51	—	—	—	—	—
	AHL	Totals	485	38	198	236	764	39	5	24	29	114
	IHL	Totals	193	21	69	90	198	52	8	16	24	22

Born; 9/5/65, Regina, Saskatchewan. 6-0, 195. Drafted by Buffalo Sabres (12th choice, 194th overall) in 1983 Entry Draft. Traded to Washington Capitals by Buffalo for Scott McCrory (6/1/89). Traded to Toronto Maple Leafs by Washington for future considerations (2/27/92). Signed as a free agent by Ottawa Senators (8/6/92). Claimed by Anaheim Might Ducks from Ottawa in Expansion Draft (6/24/93). Traded to Detroit Red Wings by Anaheim with Stu Grimson and Anaheim's sixth pick (Magnus Nilsson) for Mike Sillinger and Jason York (4/4/95). 1990-91 AHL Second Team All-Star.

Chris Ferraro — Right Wing

			Regular Season					Playoffs				
Season	Team	League	GP	G	A	PTS	PIM	GP	G	A	PTS	PIM
94-95	Atlanta	IHL	54	13	14	27	72	—	—	—	—	—
94-95	Binghamton	AHL	13	6	4	10	38	10	2	3	5	16
95-96	Rangers	NHL	2	1	0	1	0	—	—	—	—	—
95-96	Binghamton	AHL	77	32	67	99	208	4	4	2	6	13

Season	Team	League	GP	G	A	PTS	PIM	GP	G	A	PTS	PIM
96-97	Rangers	NHL	12	1	1	2	6	—	—	—	—	—
96-97	Binghamton	AHL	53	29	34	63	94	—	—	—	—	—
	NHL	Totals	14	2	1	3	0	—	—	—	—	—
	AHL	Totals	143	67	105	172	340	14	6	5	11	29

Born; 1/24/73, Long Island, New York. 5-10, 188. Drafted by New York Rangers (4th choice, 85th overall) in 1992 Entry Draft.

Peter Ferraro — Center

Season	Team	League	GP	G	A	PTS	PIM	GP	G	A	PTS	PIM
94-95	Atlanta	IHL	61	15	24	39	118	—	—	—	—	—
94-95	Binghamton	AHL	12	2	6	8	67	11	4	3	7	51
95-96	Rangers	NHL	5	0	1	1	0	—	—	—	—	—
95-96	Binghamton	AHL	68	48	53	101	157	4	1	6	7	22
96-97	Rangers	NHL	2	0	0	0	0	2	0	0	0	0
96-97	Binghamton	AHL	75	38	39	77	171	4	3	1	4	18
	NHL	Totals	7	0	1	1	0	2	0	0	0	0
	AHL	Totals	155	88	98	186	395	19	8	10	18	91

Born; 1/24/73, Long Island, New York. 5-10, 190. Drafted by New York Rangers (1st choice, 24th overall) in 1992 Entry Draft. 1995-96 AHL First Team All-Star.

Pat Ferschweiler — Center

Season	Team	League	GP	G	A	PTS	PIM	GP	G	A	PTS	PIM
93-94	Roanoke	ECHL	68	27	58	85	79	2	0	1	1	2
94-95	Roanoke	ECHL	22	8	22	30	44	—	—	—	—	—
94-95	Minnesota	IHL	1	0	0	0	0	—	—	—	—	—
94-95	Kansas City	IHL	49	11	18	29	28	20	2	4	6	22
95-96	Kansas City	IHL	16	0	3	3	8	—	—	—	—	—
95-96	San Francisco	IHL	42	3	7	10	42	4	0	0	0	0
96-97	Kansas City	IHL	49	4	6	10	42	2	0	1	1	2
	IHL	Totals	147	18	34	52	120	26	2	5	7	24
	ECHL	Totals	90	35	80	115	113	2	0	1	1	2

Born; 2/20/70, Rochester, Minnesota. 6-1, 205.

Chris Fess — Right Wing

Season	Team	League	GP	G	A	PTS	PIM	GP	G	A	PTS	PIM
94-95	Knoxville	ECHL	48	7	11	18	77	4	0	0	0	4
95-96	Knoxville	ECHL	63	16	14	30	121	8	0	2	2	14
96-97	Knoxville	ECHL	70	25	33	58	107	—	—	—	—	—
	ECHL	Totals	181	48	58	106	295	12	0	2	2	18

Born; 8/11/71, Rochester, New York. 6-2, 200.

Jed Fiebelkorn — Right Wing

Season	Team	League	GP	G	A	PTS	PIM	GP	G	A	PTS	PIM
95-96	Worcester	AHL	13	0	1	1	5	—	—	—	—	—
95-96	Jacksonville	ECHL	29	3	8	11	57	—	—	—	—	—
95-96	Tallahassee	ECHL	21	6	6	12	18	12	1	2	3	10
96-97	Tallahassee	ECHL	66	21	18	39	101	3	0	0	0	4
	ECHL	Totals	116	30	32	62	176	15	1	2	3	14

Born; 9/1/72, Minneapolis, Minnesota. 6-3, 220. Drafted by St. Louis Blues (9th choice, 197th overall) in 1991 Entry Draft.

Sam Fields — Defenseman

Season	Team	League	GP	G	A	PTS	PIM	GP	G	A	PTS	PIM
96-97	Nashville	CeHL	23	2	6	8	88	—	—	—	—	—
96-97	Wichita	CeHL	2	0	0	0	16	—	—	—	—	—

Season	Team	League	GP	G	A	PTS	PIM	GP	G	A	PTS	PIM
96-97	Huntsville	CeHL	6	0	0	0	25	—	—	—	—	—
	CeHL	Totals	31	2	6	8	129	—	—	—	—	—

Born; 8/31/76, Chicago, Illinois. 6-3, 200.

Mike Figliomeni — Left Wing
Regular Season / Playoffs

Season	Team	League	GP	G	A	PTS	PIM	GP	G	A	PTS	PIM
95-96	South Carolina	ECHL	5	2	2	4	2	—	—	—	—	—
96-97	Waco	WPHL	14	4	4	8	6	—	—	—	—	—
96-97	Thunder Bay	CoHL	53	22	35	57	21	11	2	5	7	4

Born; 5/3/72, Thunder Bay, Ontario. 5-5, 155.

Jean-ian Filiatreault — Goaltender
Regular Season / Playoffs

Season	Team	League	GP	W	L	T	MIN	SO	GAVG	GP	W	L	MIN	SO	GAVG
95-96	Oklahoma City	CeHL	42	*30	7	2	2350	1	3.57	12	8	4	722	0	2.74
96-97	Oklahoma City	CeHL	41	26	9	4	2186	1	*2.80	—	—	—	—	—	—
	CeHL	Totals	83	56	16	6	4536	2	3.20	12	8	4	722	0	2.74

Born; 3/5/74, Laval West, Quebec. 5-11, 165. 1995-96 CeHL Goaltender of the Year. 1995-96 CeHL Second Team All-Star. 1995-96 President Trophy (CeHL Playoff MVP) winner. Member of 1995-96 CeHL Champion Oklahoma City Blazers. 1996-97 CeHL Second Team All-Star.

Claude Fillion — Defenseman
Regular Season / Playoffs

Season	Team	League	GP	G	A	PTS	PIM	GP	G	A	PTS	PIM
94-95	Providence	AHL	1	0	0	0	0	—	—	—	—	—
95-96	Hampton Roads	ECHL	39	2	14	16	144	3	0	2	2	8
96-97	Macon	CeHL	62	15	30	45	246	5	1	2	3	36

Born; 7/9/74, Baie-St. Paul, Quebec. 6-3, 207.

Tim Fingerhut — Left Wing
Regular Season / Playoffs

Season	Team	League	GP	G	A	PTS	PIM	GP	G	A	PTS	PIM
92-93	Chatham	CoHL	5	1	2	3	0	—	—	—	—	—
92-93	Muskegon	CoHL	44	13	7	20	9	—	—	—	—	—
93-94	Utica	CoHL	58	24	34	58	53	—	—	—	—	—
94-95	Utica	CoHL	56	28	30	58	79	6	1	4	5	4
95-96	Utica	CoHL	58	25	23	58	95	—	—	—	—	—
95-96	Detroit	CoHL	13	3	7	10	25	10	4	2	6	12
96-97	Port Huron	CoHL	35	7	11	18	45	—	—	—	—	—
96-97	Utica	CoHL	39	9	23	32	42	3	1	0	1	9
	CoHL	Totals	308	110	137	247	348	19	6	6	12	25

Born; 5/20/71, Pennsauken, New Jersey. 6-0, 195. Drafted by Pittsburgh Penguins (12th choice, 194th overall) in 1990 Entry Draft.

Shannon Finn — Defenseman
Regular Season / Playoffs

Season	Team	League	GP	G	A	PTS	PIM	GP	G	A	PTS	PIM
94-95	Canadian	National										
94-95	Minnesota	IHL	3	0	2	2	6	—	—	—	—	—
95-96	Peoria	IHL	67	4	22	26	75	12	1	1	2	10
96-97	Fort Wayne	IHL	1	0	1	1	0	—	—	—	—	—
96-97	Utah	IHL	2	0	2	2	0	—	—	—	—	—
96-97	Milwaukee	IHL	70	7	8	15	83	3	1	1	2	2
	IHL	Totals	143	11	35	46	164	15	2	2	4	12

Born; 1/25/72, Toronto, Ontario. 6-2, 195. Drafted by Philadelphia Flyers (1st choice, 10th overall) in 1993 Supplemental Draft.

John Finstrom — Center

			Regular Season					Playoffs				
Season	Team	League	GP	G	A	PTS	PIM	GP	G	A	PTS	PIM
93-94	Huntsville	ECHL	5	0	1	1	0	—	—	—	—	—
93-94	Daytona Beach	SUN	54	8	18	26	107	2	0	1	1	2
94-95	Daytona Beach	SUN	4	0	1	1	17	—	—	—	—	—
95-96	Detroit	CoHL	68	15	23	38	211	10	0	1	1	33
96-97	Port Huron	CoHL	49	4	12	16	64	5	2	5	7	8
	CoHL	Totals	117	19	35	54	275	15	2	6	8	41
	SUN	Totals	58	8	19	27	124	2	0	1	1	2

Born; 9/2/71, Los Angeles, California. 5-10, 180.

Peter Fiorentino — Defenseman

			Regular Season					Playoffs				
Season	Team	League	GP	G	A	PTS	PIM	GP	G	A	PTS	PIM
88-89	Denver	IHL	10	0	0	0	39	4	0	0	0	24
89-90	Flint	IHL	64	2	7	9	302	—	—	—	—	—
90-91	Binghamton	AHL	55	2	11	13	361	1	0	0	0	0
91-92	Rangers	NHL	1	0	0	0	0	—	—	—	—	—
91-92	Binghamton	AHL	70	2	11	13	340	5	0	1	1	24
92-93	Binghamton	AHL	64	9	5	14	286	13	0	3	3	22
93-94	Binghamton	AHL	68	7	15	22	220	—	—	—	—	—
94-95	Binghamton	AHL	66	9	16	25	183	2	0	1	1	11
95-96	Las Vegas	IHL	54	5	7	12	192	—	—	—	—	—
95-96	Indianapolis	IHL	10	0	0	0	27	5	0	0	0	2
96-97	Binghamton	AHL	63	1	10	11	191	4	0	2	2	0
	AHL	Totals	386	30	68	98	1581	25	0	7	7	57
	IHL	Totals	138	7	14	21	560	9	0	0	0	26

Born; 12/22/68, Niagra Falls, Ontario. 6-1, 205. Drafted by New York Rangers (11th choice, 215th overall) in 1988 Entry Draft.

Jason Firth — Center

			Regular Season					Playoffs				
Season	Team	League	GP	G	A	PTS	PIM	GP	G	A	PTS	PIM
92-93	New Haven	AHL	4	0	1	1	4	—	—	—	—	—
92-93	Thunder Bay	CoHL	49	36	64	100	10	11	8	9	17	2
93-94	Prince Edward Island	AHL	61	15	46	61	66	—	—	—	—	—
93-94	Thunder Bay	CoHL	13	10	16	26	2	—	—	—	—	—
94-95	Prince Edward Island	AHL	4	1	0	1	2	—	—	—	—	—
94-95	Syracuse	AHL	20	4	13	17	4	—	—	—	—	—
94-95	Thunder Bay	CoHL	59	29	65	94	37	11	6	*22	28	8
95-96	Thunder Bay	CoHL	74	39	94	133	50	19	10	*23	*33	24
96-97	Thunder Bay	CoHL	56	37	83	120	22	11	7	14	21	8
	AHL	Totals	89	20	60	80	76	—	—	—	—	—
	CoHL	Totals	251	151	322	473	121	52	31	68	99	42

Born; 3/29/71, Dartmouth, Nova Scotia. 5-11, 186. Drafted by Detroit Red Wings (8th choice, 208th overall) in 1991 Entry Draft. 1992-93 CoHL Rookie of the Year. 1992-93 CoHL MVP. 1992-93 CoHL Second Team All-Star. 1995-96 CoHL Second Team All-Star. Member of 1994-95 CoHL champion Thunder Bay Senators. 1996-97 Second Team CoHL All-Star.

Craig Fisher — Left Wing

			Regular Season					Playoffs				
Season	Team	League	GP	G	A	PTS	PIM	GP	G	A	PTS	PIM
89-90	Philadelphia	NHL	2	0	0	0	0	—	—	—	—	—
90-91	Philadelphia	NHL	2	0	0	0	0	—	—	—	—	—
90-91	Hershey	AHL	77	43	36	79	46	7	5	3	8	2
91-92	Cape Breton	AHL	60	20	25	45	28	1	0	0	0	0
92-93	Cape Breton	AHL	75	32	29	61	74	1	0	0	0	0
93-94	Winnipeg	NHL	4	0	0	0	2	—	—	—	—	—

Season	Team	League	GP	G	A	PTS	PIM	GP	G	A	PTS	PIM
93-94	Cape Breton	AHL	16	5	5	10	11	—	—	—	—	—
93-94	Moncton	AHL	46	26	35	61	36	21	11	11	22	28
94-95	Indianapolis	IHL	77	53	40	93	65	—	—	—	—	—
95-96	Orlando	IHL	82	*74	56	130	81	14	10	7	17	6
96-97	Florida	NHL	4	0	0	0	0	—	—	—	—	—
96-97	Utah	IHL	15	6	7	13	4	—	—	—	—	—
96-97	Carolina	AHL	42	33	29	62	16	—	—	—	—	—
	NHL	Totals	12	0	0	0	2	—	—	—	—	—
	AHL	Totals	316	159	159	318	211	30	16	14	30	30
	IHL	Totals	174	133	103	236	150	14	10	7	17	6

Born; 6/30/70, Oshawa, Ontario. 6-3, 180. Drafted by Philadelphia Flyers (3rd choice, 56th overall) in 1988 Entry Draft. Traded to Edmonton Oilers by Philadelphia with Scott Mellanby and Craig Berube for Dave Brown, Corey Foster and Jari Kurri (5/30/91). Traded to Winnipeg Jets by Edmonton for cash (12/9/93). Signed as a free agent by Chicago (6/9/94). Signed as a free agent by New York Islanders (8/96). Traded to Florida Panthers by Islanders for cash (12/7/96). 1995-96 IHL First Team All-Star. Member of 1992-93 AHL champion Cape Breton Oilers.

Shane Fisher — Defenseman

Season	Team	League	GP	G	A	PTS	PIM	GP	G	A	PTS	PIM
96-97	Tulsa	CeHL	1	0	0	0	2	—	—	—	—	—
96-97	Alaska	WCHL	55	3	10	13	73	—	—	—	—	—

Born; 2/17/75, Bellevue, Alberta. 5-10, 190.

Jay Fitzpatrick — Defenseman

Season	Team	League	GP	G	A	PTS	PIM	GP	G	A	PTS	PIM
96-97	Wichita	CeHL	46	3	7	10	173	—	—	—	—	—

Born; 9/3/75, Wood Mountain, Saskatchewan. 5-11, 190.

Rory Fitzpatrick — Defenseman

Season	Team	League	GP	G	A	PTS	PIM	GP	G	A	PTS	PIM
94-95	Fredericton	AHL	—	—	—	—	—	10	1	2	3	5
95-96	Montreal	NHL	42	0	2	2	18	6	1	1	2	0
95-96	Fredericton	AHL	18	4	6	10	36	—	—	—	—	—
96-97	Montreal	NHL	6	0	1	1	6	—	—	—	—	—
96-97	St. Louis	NHL	2	0	0	0	2	—	—	—	—	—
96-97	Worcester	AHL	49	4	13	17	78	5	1	2	3	0
	NHL	Totals	50	0	3	3	26	6	1	1	2	0
	AHL	Totals	67	8	19	27	114	15	2	4	6	5

Born; 1/11/75, Rochester, New York. 6-1, 195. Drafted by Montreal Canadiens (2nd choice, 47th overall) in 1993 Entry Draft. Traded to St. Louis Blues with Pierre Turgeon and Craig Conroy by Montreal for Murray Baron, Shayne Corson and fifth round pick in 1997 Entry Draft (Gennady Razin) 10/29/96.

Jason Fitzsimmons — Goaltender

Season	Team	League	GP	W	L	T	MIN	SO	GAVG	GP	W	L	MIN	SO	GAVG
92-93	Hamilton	AHL	14	5	8	1	788	0	4.04	—	—	—	—	—	—
92-93	Columbus	ECHL	23	10	9	3	1340	0	4.07	—	—	—	—	—	—
93-94	Hamilton	AHL	17	2	8	0	709	0	4.15	2	0	2	98	0	3.67
94-95	South Carolina	ECHL	37	24	7	4	2125	1	2.97	7	4	3	418	0	3.59
95-96	Cape Breton	AHL	36	12	17	3	1866	3	3.99	—	—	—	—	—	—
96-97	Syracuse	AHL	6	0	2	0	230	0	3.64	—	—	—	—	—	—
96-97	South Carolina	ECHL	11	8	1	1	585	1	3.38	*17	*13	4	*1011	0	3.38
	AHL	Totals	73	19	35	4	3593	3	4.01	2	0	2	98	0	3.67
	ECHL	Totals	71	42	17	8	4050	2	3.39	24	17	7	1429	0	3.44

Born; 6/3/71, Regina, Saskatchewan. 5-11, 185. Drafted by Vancouver Canucks (10th choice, 227th overall) in 1991 Entry Draft. Member of 1996-97 ECHL Champion South Carolina Stingrays. 1996-97 ECHL Playoff MVP.

Brett Fizzell — Defenseman

			Regular Season					Playoffs				
Season	Team	League	GP	G	A	PTS	PIM	GP	G	A	PTS	PIM
96-97	Reno	WCHL	19	1	3	4	61	—	—	—	—	—
96-97	El Paso	WPHL	2	0	0	0	19	—	—	—	—	—
96-97	Austin	WPHL	27	0	1	1	88	—	—	—	—	—
	WPHL	Totals	29	0	1	1	107	—	—	—	—	—

Born; 3/5/75, Calgary, Alberta. 6-5, 220.

Wade Flaherty — Goaltender

			Regular Season							Playoffs					
Season	Team	League	GP	W	L	T	MIN	SO	GAVG	GP	W	L	MIN	SO	GAVG
89-90	Greensboro	ECHL	27	12	10	0	1308	0	4.40	—	—	—	—	—	—
90-91	Kansas City	IHL	*56	16	31	4	2990	0	4.49	—	—	—	—	—	—
91-92	San Jose	NHL	3	0	3	0	178	0	4.38	—	—	—	—	—	—
91-92	Kansas City	IHL	43	26	14	3	2603	1	3.23	1	0	0	1	0	0.00
92-93	San Jose	NHL	1	0	1	0	60	0	5.00	—	—	—	—	—	—
92-93	Kansas City	IHL	*61	*34	19	7	*3642	2	3.21	*12	6	6	733	*1	2.78
93-94	Kansas City	IHL	*60	32	19	9	*3564	0	3.40	—	—	—	—	—	—
94-95	San Jose	NHL	18	5	6	1	852	1	3.10	7	2	3	377	0	4.93
95-96	San Jose	NHL	24	3	12	1	1137	0	4.85	—	—	—	—	—	—
96-97	San Jose	NHL	7	2	4	0	359	0	5.18	—	—	—	—	—	—
96-97	Kentucky	AHL	19	8	6	2	1032	1	3.14	3	1	2	200	0	3.30
	NHL	Totals	53	10	26	2	2586	1	4.29	7	2	3	377	0	4.93
	IHL	Totals	220	108	83	23	12799	3	3.57	13	6	6	734	1	2.78

Born; 1/11/68, Terrace, British Columbia. 6-0, 170. Drafted by Buffalo Sabres (10th choice, 181st overall) 1988 Entry Draft. Signed as a free agent by San Jose (9/3/91). Won James Norris Trophy (fewest goals against-IHL) with Arturs Irbe (1991-92). 1992-93 IHL Second All-Star Team. 1993-94 IHL Second All-Star Team. Member of 1991-92 IHL Champion Kansas City Blades.

Brent Fleetwood — Left Wing

			Regular Season					Playoffs				
Season	Team	League	GP	G	A	PTS	PIM	GP	G	A	PTS	PIM
90-91	Fredericton	AHL	5	0	1	1	2	—	—	—	—	—
90-91	Winston-Salem	ECHL	61	28	32	60	75	—	—	—	—	—
91-92	Fredericton	AHL	3	0	0	0	0	—	—	—	—	—
91-92	Winston-Salem	ECHL	56	27	32	59	73	4	0	0	0	7
92-93	Greensboro	ECHL	36	9	18	27	57	—	—	—	—	—
92-93	Hampton Roads	ECHL	13	5	2	7	4	4	1	0	1	0
93-94	West Palm Beach	SUN	52	34	48	82	81	5	6	3	9	*34
94-95	Memphis	CeHL	66	28	32	60	94	—	—	—	—	—
95-96	Memphis	CeHL	64	35	42	77	132	6	2	0	2	10
96-97	Memphis	CeHL	52	17	27	44	52	—	—	—	—	—
96-97	San Antonio	CeHL	5	3	4	7	0	—	—	—	—	—
	AHL	Totals	8	0	1	1	2					
	CeHL	Totals	193	83	105	188	278	6	2	0	2	10
	ECHL	Totals	166	69	84	153	209	8	1	0	1	7

Born; 6/4/70, Edmonton, Alberta. 6-2, 202. Drafted by Montreal Canadiens (9th choice, 165th overall) in 1990 Entry Draft. Member of 1993-94 Sunshine champion West Palm Beach. Selected by Macon Whoopee in CeHL Dispersal (6/10/97).

Gerry Fleming — Left Wing

			Regular Season					Playoffs				
Season	Team	League	GP	G	A	PTS	PIM	GP	G	A	PTS	PIM
91-92	Fredericton	AHL	37	4	6	10	133	1	0	0	0	7
92-93	Fredericton	AHL	64	9	17	26	262	5	1	2	3	14
93-94	Montreal	AHL	5	0	0	0	25	—	—	—	—	—
93-94	Fredericton	AHL	46	6	16	22	188	—	—	—	—	—
94-95	Montreal	NHL	6	0	0	0	17	—	—	—	—	—

Season	Team	League	GP	G	A	PTS	PIM	GP	G	A	PTS	PIM
94-95	Fredericton	AHL	16	3	3	6	60	10	2	0	2	67
95-96	Fredericton	AHL	40	8	9	17	127	10	3	1	4	19
96-97	Fredericton	AHL	40	5	11	16	164	—	—	—	—	—
	NHL	Totals	11	0	0	0	42	—	—	—	—	—
	AHL	Totals	248	35	62	97	934	26	6	3	9	107

Born; 10/16/67, Montreal, Quebec. 6-5, 240. Signed as a free agent by Montreal Canadiens (2/17/92).

David Fletcher — Goaltender

			Regular Season						Playoffs				
Season	Team	League	GP	W	L	T	MIN	SO	GAVG	GP	W	L	MIN	SO	GAVG
96-97	Quad City	CoHL	19	9	5	1	941	0	4.02	1	0	0	33	0	0.00

Born; 5/27/71, Livonia, Michigan. 5-9, 171. Member of 1996-97 Colonial League Champion Quad City Mallards.

Carl Fleury — Center

			Regular Season					Playoffs				
Season	Team	League	GP	G	A	PTS	PIM	GP	G	A	PTS	PIM
94-95	Roanoke	ECHL	16	1	1	2	35	—	—	—	—	—
94-95	Erie	ECHL	43	13	15	28	79	—	—	—	—	—
95-96	Erie	ECHL	63	8	32	40	139	—	—	—	—	—
96-97	Johnstown	ECHL	68	30	37	67	102	—	—	—	—	—
	ECHL	Totals	190	52	85	137	355	—	—	—	—	—

Born; 10/22/73, St. Claire, Quebec. 6-1, 198.

Marty Flichel — Right Wing

			Regular Season					Playoffs				
Season	Team	League	GP	G	A	PTS	PIM	GP	G	A	PTS	PIM
96-97	Michigan	IHL	19	2	3	5	10	—	—	—	—	—
96-97	Dayton	ECHL	28	17	16	33	24	2	0	1	1	4

Born; 3/6/76, Hodgeville, Saskatchewan. 5-11, 175. Drafted by Dallas Stars (6th choice, 228th overall) in 1994 Entry Draft.

Eric Flinton — Left Wing

			Regular Season					Playoffs				
Season	Team	League	GP	G	A	PTS	PIM	GP	G	A	PTS	PIM
95-96	Charlotte	ECHL	69	20	26	46	29	16	5	8	13	4
96-97	Binghamton	AHL	68	6	18	24	22	4	0	0	0	2

Born; 2/2/72, William Lake, British Columbia. 6-2, 200. Drafted by Ottawa Senators in 1993 Supplemental Draft. Signed as a free agent by New York Rangers (9/12/95). Member of 1995-96 ECHL champion Charlotte Checkers.

Bryan Fogarty — Defenseman

			Regular Season					Playoffs				
Season	Team	League	GP	G	A	PTS	PIM	GP	G	A	PTS	PIM
89-90	Quebec	NHL	45	4	10	14	31	—	—	—	—	—
89-90	Halifax	AHL	22	5	14	19	6	6	2	4	6	0
90-91	Quebec	NHL	45	9	22	31	24	—	—	—	—	—
90-91	Halifax	AHL	5	0	2	2	0	—	—	—	—	—
91-92	Quebec	NHL	20	3	12	15	16	—	—	—	—	—
91-92	Halifax	AHL	2	0	0	0	2	—	—	—	—	—
91-92	New Haven	AHL	4	0	1	1	6	—	—	—	—	—
91-92	Muskegon	IHL	8	2	4	6	30	—	—	—	—	—
92-93	Pittsburgh	NHL	12	0	4	4	4	—	—	—	—	—
92-93	Cleveland	IHL	15	2	5	7	8	3	0	1	1	17
93-94	Montreal	NHL	13	1	2	3	10	—	—	—	—	—
93-94	Atlanta	IHL	8	1	5	6	4	—	—	—	—	—
93-94	Las Vegas	IHL	33	3	16	19	38	—	—	—	—	—
93-94	Kansas City	IHL	3	2	1	3	2	—	—	—	—	—
94-95	Montreal	NHL	21	5	2	7	34	—	—	—	—	—
95-96	Minnesota	IHL	17	3	12	15	24	—	—	—	—	—
95-96	Detroit	IHL	18	1	5	6	11	—	—	—	—	—

Season	Team	League	GP	G	A	PTS	PIM	GP	G	A	PTS	PIM
96-97	Kansas City	IHL	22	3	9	12	10	—	—	—	—	—
	NHL	Totals	156	22	52	74	119	—	—	—	—	—
	IHL	Totals	124	17	57	74	127	3	0	1	1	17
	AHL	Totals	33	5	17	22	14	6	2	4	6	0

Born; 6/11/69, Brantford, Ontario. 6-2, 198. Drafted by Quebec Nordiques (1st choice, 9th overall) in 1987 Entry Draft. Traded to Pittsburgh Penguins by Quebec for Scott Young (3/10/92). Signed as a free agent by Tampa Bay Lightning (9/28/93). Signed as a free agent by Montreal Canadiens (2/25/94).

Colin Foley — Center

			Regular Season					Playoffs				
Season	Team	League	GP	G	A	PTS	PIM	GP	G	A	PTS	PIM
94-95	Greensboro	ECHL	28	12	6	18	58	—	—	—	—	—
95-96	Erie	ECHL	50	22	28	50	65	—	—	—	—	—
96-97	Alaska	WCHL	60	23	48	71	45	—	—	—	—	—
	ECHL	Totals	78	34	34	68	123	—	—	—	—	—

Born; 4/1/74, Victoria, British Columbia. 5-11, 185.

Colin Forbes — Left Wing

			Regular Season					Playoffs				
Season	Team	League	GP	G	A	PTS	PIM	GP	G	A	PTS	PIM
95-96	Hershey	AHL	2	1	0	1	2	4	0	2	2	2
96-97	Philadelphia	NHL	3	1	0	1	0	3	0	0	0	0
96-97	Philadlephia	AHL	74	21	28	49	108	10	5	5	10	33
	AHL	Totals	76	22	28	50	110	14	5	7	12	35

Born; 2/16/76, New Westminster, Alberta. 6-3, 205. Drafted by Philadelphia Flyers (5th choice, 166th overall) in 1994 Entry Draft.

Nick Forbes — Left Wing

			Regular Season					Playoffs				
Season	Team	League	GP	G	A	PTS	PIM	GP	G	A	PTS	PIM
95-96	Utica	CoHL	53	10	12	22	154	—	—	—	—	—
95-96	Flint	CoHL	7	1	3	4	32	13	2	0	2	14
96-97	Detroit	IHL	1	0	0	0	0	—	—	—	—	—
96-97	Michigan	IHL	1	0	0	0	0	—	—	—	—	—
96-97	Flint	CoHL	68	23	24	47	222	14	2	4	6	18
	IHL	Totals	2	0	0	0	0	—	—	—	—	—
	CoHL	Totals	128	34	39	73	408	27	4	4	8	32

Born; 4/27/72, Montreal, Quebec. 6-1, 205. Member of 1995-96 Colonial Cup Champion Flint Generals

Bryan Forslund — Left Wing

			Regular Season					Playoffs				
Season	Team	League	GP	G	A	PTS	PIM	GP	G	A	PTS	PIM
95-96	Tulsa	CeHL	59	18	15	33	78	6	0	0	0	25
96-97	Tulsa	CeHL	55	19	20	39	64	5	0	1	1	0
	CeHL	Totals	114	37	35	72	142	11	0	1	1	25

Born; 6/8/74, Sherwood Park, Alberta 6-0, 190.

Sebastien Fortier — Left Wing

			Regular Season					Playoffs				
Season	Team	League	GP	G	A	PTS	PIM	GP	G	A	PTS	PIM
93-94	Fredericton	AHL	4	0	3	3	11	—	—	—	—	—
93-94	Wheeling	ECHL	62	6	22	28	36	—	—	—	—	—
94-95	Brantford	CoHL	25	5	10	15	21	—	—	—	—	—
94-95	Utica	CoHL	33	5	14	19	86	—	—	—	—	—
95-96	Utica	CoHL	19	1	7	8	15	—	—	—	—	—
95-96	Thunder Bay	CoHL	43	3	10	13	105	17	1	2	3	96
96-97	Birmingham	ECHL	48	7	8	15	150	—	—	—	—	—
96-97	Richmond	ECHL	15	7	10	17	28	7	3	4	7	10

	ECHL	Totals	125	20	40	60	214	7	3	4	7	10
	CoHL	Totals	120	14	41	55	227	17	1	2	3	96

Born; 10/12/73, Greenfield Park, Quebec. 6-0, 198.

Corey Foster — Defenseman

Season	Team	League	GP	G	A	PTS	PIM	GP	G	A	PTS	PIM
88-89	New Jersey	NHL	2	0	0	0	0	—	—	—	—	—
89-90	Cape Breton	AHL	54	7	17	24	32	1	0	0	0	0
90-91	Cape Breton	AHL	67	14	11	25	51	4	2	4	6	4
91-92	Philadelphia	NHL	25	3	4	7	20	—	—	—	—	—
91-92	Hershey	AHL	19	5	9	14	26	6	1	1	2	5
92-93	Hershey	AHL	80	9	25	34	102	—	—	—	—	—
93-94	Hershey	AHL	66	21	37	58	96	9	2	5	7	10
94-95	Prince Edward Island	AHL	78	13	34	47	61	11	2	5	7	12
95-96	Pittsburgh	NHL	11	2	2	4	2	3	0	0	0	4
95-96	Cleveland	IHL	61	10	36	46	93	—	—	—	—	—
96-97	Cleveland	IHL	51	5	29	34	71	14	0	9	9	22
	NHL	Totals	38	5	6	11	22	3	0	0	0	4
	AHL	Totals	364	69	133	202	368	31	7	17	24	31
	IHL	Totals	112	15	65	80	164	14	0	9	9	22

Born; 10/27/69, Ottawa, Ontario. 6-3, 204. Drafted by New Jersey (1st choice, 12th overall) in 1988 Entry Draft. Traded to Edmonton Oilers by New Jersey for Edmonton's first round choice (Jason Miller) in 1989 Entry Draft (6/17/89). Traded to Philadelphia Flyers by Edmonton with Dave Brown and Jari Kurri for Craig Fisher, Scott Mellanby and Craig Berube (5/30/91). Signed as a free agent by Ottawa Senators (6/20/94). Signed as a free agent by Pittsburgh Penguins (8/7/95).

Mike Fountain — Goaltender

Season	Team	League	GP	W	L	T	MIN	SO	GAVG	GP	W	L	MIN	SO	GAVG
92-93	Hamilton	AHL	12	2	8	0	618	0	4.47	—	—	—	—	—	—
93-94	Hamilton	AHL	*70	*34	28	6	*4005	*4	3.61	3	0	2	146	0	4.92
94-95	Syracuse	AHL	61	25	29	7	3618	2	3.73	—	—	—	—	—	—
95-96	Syracuse	AHL	54	21	27	3	3060	1	3.61	15	8	7	915	2	3.74
96-97	Vancouver	NHL	6	2	2	0	245	1	3.43	—	—	—	—	—	—
96-97	Syracuse	AHL	25	8	14	2	1462	1	3.20	2	0	2	120	0	6.02
	AHL	Totals	222	90	106	18	12763	8	3.64	20	8	11	1181	2	4.12

Born; 1/26/72, North York, Ontario. 6-1, 176. Drafted by Vancouver Canucks (4th choice, 69th overall) in 1992 Entry Draft. 1993-94 AHL Second Team All-Star. Signed as a free agent by Carolina Hurricanes (8/97).

Petr Franek — Goaltender

Season	Team	League	GP	W	L	T	MIN	SO	GAVG	GP	W	L	MIN	SO	GAVG
96-97	Quebec	IHL	6	3	3	0	358	0	3.02	1	0	1	40	0	6.00
96-97	Hershey	AHL	15	4	1	0	457	3	3.02	—	—	—	—	—	—
96-97	Brantford	CoHL	6	4	1	0	322	0	2.61	—	—	—	—	—	—

Born; 4/6/75, Most, Czechoslovakia. 5-11, 187. Drafted by Quebec Nordiques (10th choice, 205th overall) in 1993 Entry Draft.

Jeff Frankel — Forward

Season	Team	League	GP	G	A	PTS	PIM	GP	G	A	PTS	PIM
96-97	Knoxville	ECHL	3	0	0	0	0	—	—	—	—	—
96-97	Huntsville	CeHL	17	4	5	9	38	—	—	—	—	—
96-97	Nashville	CeHL	12	1	0	1	21	—	—	—	—	—
	CeHL	Totals	29	5	5	10	59	—	—	—	—	—

Born; 5/9/74, Philadelphia, Pennsylvania. 6-2, 205.

Shawn Frappier — Defenseman

Season	Team	League	GP	G	A	PTS	PIM	GP	G	A	PTS	PIM
96-97	Grand Rapids	IHL	3	0	0	0	0	—	—	—	—	—
96-97	Mississippi	ECHL	48	4	15	19	70	—	—	—	—	—

Born; 7/2/75, Sudbury, Ontario. 6-0, 195. Last amateur club; Barrie (OHL).

Iain Fraser — Center

Season	Team	League	GP	G	A	PTS	PIM	GP	G	A	PTS	PIM
90-91	Capital District	AHL	32	5	13	18	16	—	—	—	—	—
90-91	Richmond	ECHL	3	1	1	2	0	—	—	—	—	—
91-92	Capital District	AHL	45	9	11	20	24	—	—	—	—	—
92-93	Islanders	NHL	7	2	2	4	2	—	—	—	—	—
92-93	Capital District	AHL	74	41	69	110	16	4	0	1	1	0
93-94	Quebec	NHL	60	17	20	37	23	—	—	—	—	—
94-95	Dallas	NHL	4	0	0	0	0	—	—	—	—	—
94-95	Edmonton	NHL	9	3	0	3	0	—	—	—	—	—
94-95	Denver	IHL	1	0	0	0	0	—	—	—	—	—
95-96	Winnipeg	NHL	12	1	1	2	4	4	0	0	0	0
95-96	Springfield	AHL	53	24	47	71	27	6	0	6	6	2
96-97	San Jose	NHL	2	0	0	0	2	—	—	—	—	—
96-97	Kentucky	AHL	57	27	33	60	24	—	—	—	—	—
	NHL	Totals	94	23	23	46	31	4	0	0	0	0
	AHL	Totals	261	106	173	279	107	10	0	7	7	2

Born; 8/10/69, Scarborough, Ontario. 5-10, 175. Drafted by New York Islanders (12th choice, 233rd overall) in 1989 Entry Draft. Signed as a free agent by Quebec (8/3/93). Traded to Dallas Stars by Quebec for a conditional choice in 1996 Entry Draft (1/31/95). Claimed on waivers by Edmonton Oilers from Dallas (3/3/95). 1992-93 AHL Second Team All-Star.

Scott Fraser — Center

Season	Team	League	GP	G	A	PTS	PIM	GP	G	A	PTS	PIM
94-95	FRE	AHL	65	23	25	48	36	16	3	5	8	14
94-95	WHL	ECHL	8	4	2	6	8	—	—	—	—	—
95-96	MTL	NHL	14	2	0	2	4	—	—	—	—	—
95-96	FRE	AHL	58	37	37	74	43	10	9	7	16	2
96-97	Fredericton	AHL	7	3	8	11	0	—	—	—	—	—
96-97	Saint John	AHL	37	22	10	32	24	—	—	—	—	—
96-97	Carolina	AHL	18	9	19	28	12	—	—	—	—	—
96-97	San Antonio	IHL	8	0	1	1	2	—	—	—	—	—
	AHL	Totals	185	94	99	193	115	26	12	12	24	16

Born; 5/3/72, Moncton, New Brunswick. 6-1, 200. Drafted by Montreal Canadiens (12th choice, 193rd overall) in 1991 Entry Draft. Traded to Calgary Flames by Montreal for David Ling and Calgary's 6th round pick in the 1998 Entry Draft (/1024/96).

Dan Frawley — Right Wing

Season	Team	League	GP	G	A	PTS	PIM	GP	G	A	PTS	PIM
82-83	Springfield	AHL	80	30	27	57	107	—	—	—	—	—
83-84	Chicago	NHL	3	0	0	0	0	—	—	—	—	—
83-84	Springfield	AHL	69	22	34	56	137	4	0	1	1	2
84-85	Chicago	NHL	30	4	3	7	64	1	0	0	0	0
84-85	Milwaukee	IHL	26	11	12	23	125	—	—	—	—	—
85-86	Pittsburgh	NHL	69	10	11	21	174	—	—	—	—	—
86-87	Pittsburgh	NHL	78	14	14	28	218	—	—	—	—	—
87-88	Pittsburgh	NHL	47	6	8	14	152	—	—	—	—	—
88-89	Pittsburgh	NHL	46	3	4	7	66	—	—	—	—	—

Season	Team	League	GP	G	A	PTS	PIM	GP	G	A	PTS	PIM
88-89	Muskegon	IHL	24	12	16	28	35	14	6	4	10	31
89-90	Muskegon	IHL	82	31	47	78	165	15	9	12	21	51
90-91	Rochester	AHL	74	15	31	46	152	14	4	7	11	34
91-92	Rochester	AHL	78	28	23	51	208	16	7	5	12	35
92-93	Rochester	AHL	75	17	27	44	216	17	1	7	8	70
93-94	N/A											
94-95	N/A											
95-96	Rochester	AHL	77	12	15	27	194	19	5	6	11	8
96-97	Rochester	AHL	77	11	22	33	115	10	2	2	4	8
	NHL	Totals	273	37	40	77	674	1	0	0	0	0
	AHL	Totals	530	135	179	314	1129	80	19	28	47	157
	IHL	Totals	132	54	75	129	325	29	15	16	31	82

Born; 6/2/62, Sturgeon Falls, Ontario. 6-0, 198. Drafted by Chicago Blackhawks (15th choice, 204th overall) in 1980 Entry Draft. Selected by Pittsburgh Penguins in NHL waiver draft (10/7/85). Signed as a free agent by Buffalo Sabres (9/90). Member of 1988-89 IHL champion Muskegon Lumberjacks. Member of 1995-96 AHL champion Rochester Americans.

Joe Frederick — Right Wing

			Regular Season					Playoffs				
Season	Team	League	GP	G	A	PTS	PIM	GP	G	A	PTS	PIM
92-93	Adirondack	AHL	5	0	1	1	2	8	0	0	0	6
93-94	Adirondack	AHL	68	28	30	58	130	12	11	4	15	22
94-95	Adirondack	AHL	71	27	28	55	124	4	0	0	0	10
95-96	Orlando	IHL	63	22	14	36	194	23	6	2	8	36
96-97	Orlando	IHL	48	16	9	25	82	—	—	—	—	—
96-97	Phoenix	IHL	9	2	3	5	10	—	—	—	—	—
96-97	Chicago	IHL	8	1	1	2	14	1	1	0	1	0
	AHL	Totals	144	55	59	114	256	24	11	4	15	38
	IHL	Totals	128	41	27	68	300	24	7	2	1	

Born; 6/18/69, Madison, Wisconsin. 6-1, 190. Drafted by Detroit Red Wings (13th choice, 242nd overall) in 1989 Entry Draft.

Troy Frederick — Left Wing

			Regular Season					Playoffs				
Season	Team	League	GP	G	A	PTS	PIM	GP	G	A	PTS	PIM
90-91	Knoxville	ECHL	4	0	3	3	41	—	—	—	—	—
90-91	Kansas City	IHL	39	2	3	5	79	—	—	—	—	—
91-92	Kansas City	IHL	13	0	3	3	29	—	—	—	—	—
92-93	Kansas City	IHL	16	0	1	1	27	—	—	—	—	—
92-93	Johnstown	ECHL	8	0	1	1	0	—	—	—	—	—
93-94	Kansas City	IHL	21	0	3	3	55	—	—	—	—	—
93-94	Fort Worth	CeHL	10	3	7	10	2	—	—	—	—	—
94-95	Fort Worth	CeHL	66	38	37	75	99	—	—	—	—	—
95-96	Foth Worth	CeHL	64	28	38	66	87	—	—	—	—	—
96-97	Central Texas	WPHL	64	35	25	60	92	11	4	5	9	10
	IHL	Totals	89	2	10	12	190	—	—	—	—	—
	CeHL	Totals	140	69	82	151	188	—	—	—	—	—
	ECHL	Totals	12	0	4	4	41	—	—	—	—	—

Born; 4/4/69, Virden, Manitoba. 6-5, 235.

Mark Freer — Center

			Regular Season					Playoffs				
Season	Team	League	GP	G	A	PTS	PIM	GP	G	A	PTS	PIM
86-87	Philadelphia	NHL	1	0	1	1	0	—	—	—	—	—
87-88	Philadelphia	NHL	1	0	0	0	0	—	—	—	—	—
88-89	Philadelphia	NHL	5	0	1	1	0	—	—	—	—	—
88-89	Hershey	AHL	75	30	49	79	77	12	4	6	10	2
89-90	Philadelphia	NHL	2	0	0	0	0	—	—	—	—	—
89-90	Hershey	AHL	65	28	36	64	31	—	—	—	—	—
90-91	Hershey	AHL	77	18	44	62	45	7	1	3	4	17

Season	Team	League	GP	G	A	PTS	PIM	GP	G	A	PTS	PIM
91-92	Philadelphia	NHL	50	6	7	13	18	—	—	—	—	—
91-92	Hershey	AHL	31	13	11	24	38	6	0	3	3	2
92-93	Ottawa	NHL	63	10	14	24	39	—	—	—	—	—
93-94	Calgary	NHL	2	0	0	0	4	—	—	—	—	—
93-94	Saint John	AHL	77	33	53	86	45	7	2	4	6	16
94-95	Houston	IHL	80	38	42	80	54	4	0	1	1	4
95-96	Houston	IHL	80	22	31	53	67	—	—	—	—	—
96-97	Houston	IHL	81	21	36	57	43	12	2	3	5	4
	NHL	Totals	124	16	23	39	61	—	—	—	—	—
	AHL	Totals	325	122	193	315	236	32	7	16	23	37
	IHL	Totals	241	81	109	190	164	16	2	4	6	8

Born; 7/14/68, Toronto, Ontario. 5-10, 180. Signed as a free agent by Philadelphia Flyers (10/7/86). Claimed by Ottawa Senators from Philadelphia in Expansion Draft (6/18/92). Signed as a free agent by Calgary Flames (8/10/93).

Adam French — Defenseman

			Regular Season					Playoffs				
Season	Team	League	GP	G	A	PTS	PIM	GP	G	A	PTS	PIM
95-96	Richmond	ECHL	3	0	2	2	0	4	0	0	0	2
96-97	Nashville	CeHL	43	13	15	28	98	—	—	—	—	—
96-97	Macon	CeHL	22	4	15	19	46	5	0	3	3	10
	CeHL	Totals	65	17	30	47	144	5	0	3	3	10

Born; 1/9/72, Ancaster, Ontario. 5-10, 186.

Chris French — Goaltender

			Regular Season							Playoffs					
Season	Team	League	GP	W	L	T	MIN	SO	GAVG	GP	W	L	MIN	SO	GAVG
93-94	Huntington	ECHL	23	4	11	3	1200	0	5.75	—	—	—	—	—	—
93-94	Lakeland	SUN	3	0	2	0	145	0	6.18	—	—	—	—	—	—
93-94	Muskegon	CoHL	5	1	3	0	213	0	5.89	—	—	—	—	—	—
94-95	N/A														
95-96	N/A														
96-97	Alaska	WCHL	35	5	21	2	1770	0	6.27	—	—	—	—	—	—

Born; Barrie, Ontario. 6-3, 205.

Tony Frenette — Right Wing

			Regular Season					Playoffs				
Season	Team	League	GP	G	A	PTS	PIM	GP	G	A	PTS	PIM
96-97	Pensacola	ECHL	9	3	3	6	8	—	—	—	—	—
96-97	Huntsville	CeHL	47	41	31	72	50	9	1	2	3	10

Born; 1/20/73, Edmonton, Alberta. 5-10, 180. Last amateur club; Maine (Hockey East).

Doug Friedman — Left Wing

			Regular Season					Playoffs				
Season	Team	League	GP	G	A	PTS	PIM	GP	G	A	PTS	PIM
94-95	Cornwall	AHL	55	6	9	15	56	3	0	0	0	0
95-96	Cornwall	AHL	80	12	22	34	178	8	1	1	2	17
96-97	Hershey	AHL	61	12	21	33	245	23	6	9	15	49
	AHL	Totals	196	30	52	82	479	34	7	10	17	66

Born; 9/1/71, Cape Elizabeth, Maine. 6-1, 189. Drafted by Quebec Nordiques (11th choice, 222nd overall) in 1991 Entry Draft. Member of 1996-97 AHL Champion Herrshey Bears.

Clarke Funk — Left Wing

			Regular Season					Playoffs				
Season	Team	League	GP	G	A	PTS	PIM	GP	G	A	PTS	PIM
96-97	Wichita	CeHL	26	2	8	10	30	—	—	—	—	—

Born; 6/24/74, Flin Flon, Manitoba. 5-8, 183.

Jeff Gabriel — Right Wing

			Regular Season					Playoffs				
Season	Team	League	GP	G	A	PTS	PIM	GP	G	A	PTS	PIM
94-95	Greensboro	ECHL	66	24	27	51	92	18	7	5	12	10
94-95	Peoria	IHL	2	0	0	0	2	—	—	—	—	—
95-96	Raleigh	ECHL	28	11	8	19	28	—	—	—	—	—
95-96	Jacksonville	ECHL	30	5	15	20	4	18	4	7	11	6
96-97	Austin	WPHL	33	11	17	28	28	—	—	—	—	—
	ECHL	Totals	124	40	50	90	124	36	11	12	23	16

Born; 1/30/72, North York, Ontario. 6-0, 190.

Link Gaetz — Defenseman

			Regular Season					Playoffs				
Season	Team	League	GP	G	A	PTS	PIM	GP	G	A	PTS	PIM
88-89	Minnesota	NHL	12	0	2	2	53	—	—	—	—	—
88-89	Kalamazoo	IHL	37	3	4	7	192	5	0	0	0	56
89-90	Minnesota	NHL	5	0	0	0	33	—	—	—	—	—
89-90	Kalamazoo	IHL	61	5	16	21	318	9	2	2	4	59
90-91	Kalamazoo	IHL	9	0	1	1	44	—	—	—	—	—
90-91	Kansas City	IHL	18	1	10	11	178	—	—	—	—	—
91-92	San Jose	NHL	48	6	6	12	326	—	—	—	—	—
92-93	Nashville	ECHL	3	1	0	1	10	—	—	—	—	—
92-93	Kansas City	IHL	2	0	0	0	14	—	—	—	—	—
93-94	Nashville	ECHL	24	1	1	2	261	—	—	—	—	—
93-94	Cape Breton	AHL	21	0	1	1	140	—	—	—	—	—
93-94	West Palm Beach	SUN	6	0	3	3	15	3	0	1	1	8
94-95	San Antonio	CeHL	13	0	3	3	156	—	—	—	—	—
95-96	San Francisco	IHL	3	0	0	0	37	—	—	—	—	—
96-97	Madison	CoHL	26	2	4	6	178	—	—	—	—	—
	NHL	Totals	65	6	8	14	412	—	—	—	—	—
	IHL	Totals	130	9	31	40	783	14	2	2	4	115
	ECHL	Totals	27	2	1	3	271	—	—	—	—	—

Born; 10/2/68, Vancouver, British Columbia. 6-4, 230. Drafted by Minnesota North Stars (2nd choice, 40th overall) in 19988 Entry Draft. Selected by San Jose Sharks in NHL dispersal draft (5/30/91). Traded to Edmonton Oilers by San Jose for conditional 10th round pick in 1994 Entry Draft, (9/10/93). Member of 1993-94 Sunshine League champion West Palm Beach Blaze.

Joe Gaffney — Forward

			Regular Season					Playoffs				
Season	Team	League	GP	G	A	PTS	PIM	GP	G	A	PTS	PIM
95-96	Nashville	ECHL	29	3	4	7	12	—	—	—	—	—
96-97	Nashville	CeHL	49	11	11	22	29	—	—	—	—	—

Born; 12/4/72, Warwcik, Rhode Island. 5-9, 170.

Joaquin Gage — Goaltender

			Regular Season							Playoffs				
Season	Team	League	GP	W	L	T	MIN	SO	GAVG	GP	W	L	MIN	SO	GAVG
94-95	Edmonton	NHL	2	0	2	0	99	0	4.24	—	—	—	—	—	—
94-95	Cape Breton	AHL	54	17	28	5	3010	0	4.13	—	—	—	—	—	—
95-96	Edmonton	NHL	16	2	8	1	717	0	3.77	—	—	—	—	—	—
95-96	Cape Breton	AHL	21	8	11	0	1162	0	4.13	—	—	—	—	—	—
96-97	Hamilton	AHL	29	7	14	4	1558	0	3.50	—	—	—	—	—	—
96-97	Wheeling	ECHL	3	1	0	0	120	0	4.00	—	—	—	—	—	—
	NHL	Totals	18	2	10	1	816	0	3.82	—	—	—	—	—	—
	AHL	Totals	104	32	53	9	5730	0	3.96	—	—	—	—	—	—

Born; 10/19/73, Vancouver, British Columbia. 6-0, 206. Drafted by Edmonton Ollers (6th choice, 109th overall) in 1992 Entry Draft.

Dave Gagnon — Goaltender

			Regular Season							Playoffs					
Season	Team	League	GP	W	L	T	MIN	SO	GAVG	GP	W	L	MIN	SO	GAVG
90-91	Detroit	NHL	2	0	1	0	35	0	10.29	—	—	—	—	—	—
90-91	Adirondack	AHL	24	7	8	5	1356	0	4.16	—	—	—	—	—	—
90-91	Hampton Roads	ECHL	10	7	1	2	606	2	2.57	11	*10	1	*696	0	*2.33
91-92	Toledo	ECHL	7	4	2	0	354	0	3.05	—	—	—	—	—	—
91-92	Fort Wayne	IHL	2	2	0	0	125	0	3.36	—	—	—	—	—	—
92-93	Fort Wayne	IHL	31	15	11	0	1771	0	3.93	1	0	0	6	0	0.00
92-93	Adirondack	AHL	1	0	1	0	60	0	5.00	—	—	—	—	—	—
93-94	Toledo	ECHL	20	13	5	0	1122	1	3.48	*14	*12	2	*910	0	*2.70
93-94	Fort Wayne	IHL	19	7	6	3	1026	0	3.39	—	—	—	—	—	—
94-95	Minnesota	IHL	16	5	4	2	767	0	4.30	1	0	1	60	0	9.00
94-95	Roanoke	ECHL	29	17	7	5	1738	1	2.83	—	—	—	—	—	—
95-96	Minnesota	IHL	52	18	25	4	2721	0	4.14	—	—	—	—	—	—
96-97	Roanoke	ECHL	60	34	18	6	3387	3	3.21	3	1	2	220	0	2.73
	IHL	Totals	120	37	46	9	6410	0	3.97	2	0	1	66	0	8.18
	AHL	Totals	25	7	9	5	1416	0	4.19	—	—	—	—	—	—
	ECHL	Totals	126	75	33	11	7207	7	3.10	28	23	5	1826	0	2.56

Born; 10/31/67, Windsor, Ontario. 6-0, 195. Signed as a free agent by Detroit Red Wings (6/11/90). 1990-91 ECHL Playoff MVP. 1994-95 ECHL Second Team All-Star. Member of 1990-91 ECHL champion Hampton Roads Admirals. Member of 1992-93 IHL champion Fort Wayne Komets. Member of 1993-94 ECHL champion Toledo Storm.

Pierre Gagnon — Goaltender

			Regular Season							Playoffs					
Season	Team	League	GP	W	L	T	MIN	SO	GAVG	GP	W	L	MIN	SO	GAVG
92-93	Thunder Bay	CoHL	2	1	1	0	124	0	4.35	—	—	—	—	—	—
96-97	Macon	CeHL	*57	33	18	2	*3155	1	3.27	5	2	3	308	0	2.73

Born; LaFontaine, Quebec. Did not play professional hockey in North America between the 92-93 and 96-97 seasons.

Sean Gagnon — Defenseman

			Regular Season					Playoffs				
Season	Team	League	GP	G	A	PTS	PIM	GP	G	A	PTS	PIM
94-95	Dayton	ECHL	68	9	23	32	339	8	0	3	3	69
95-96	Dayton	ECHL	68	7	22	29	326	3	0	1	1	33
96-97	Fort Wayne	IHL	72	7	7	14	*457	—	—	—	—	—
	ECHL	Totals	136	16	45	61	665	11	0	4	4	102

Born; 9/11/73, Sault Ste. Marie, Ontario. 6-2, 210. Signed as a free agent by Phoenix Coyotes (6/97).

Maxim Galanov — Defenseman

			Regular Season					Playoffs				
Season	Team	League	GP	G	A	PTS	PIM	GP	G	A	PTS	PIM
95-96	Binghamton	AHL	72	17	36	53	24	4	1	1	2	0
96-97	Binghamton	AHL	73	13	30	43	30	3	0	0	0	2
	AHL	Totals	145	30	66	96	54	7	1	1	2	2

Born; 3/13/74, Krasnoyarsk, Russia. 6-1, 175. Drafted by New York Rangers (3rd choice, 61st overall) in 1993 Entry Draft.

Murray Galbraith — Defenseman

			Regular Season					Playoffs				
Season	Team	League	GP	G	A	PTS	PIM	GP	G	A	PTS	PIM
96-97	Louisiana	ECHL	5	0	0	0	18	—	—	—	—	—
96-97	Tulsa	CeHL	4	0	1	1	16	—	—	—	—	—
96-97	Alaska	WCHL	10	2	0	2	42	—	—	—	—	—
96-97	San Diego	WCHL	2	0	0	0	0	—	—	—	—	—
	WCHL	Totals	12	2	0	2	42	—	—	—	—	—

Born; 8/3/75, Victory, British Columbia. 6-4, 220.

Igor Galkin — Goaltender

			Regular Season							Playoffs					
Season	Team	League	GP	W	L	T	MIN	SO	GAVG	GP	W	L	MIN	SO	GAVG
96-97	Detroit	IHL	2	1	0	0	73	0	2.47	—	—	—	—	—	—
96-97	Las Vegas	IHL	3	1	2	0	84	0	5.68	—	—	—	—	—	—
96-97	Binghamton	AHL	4	1	1	0	168	0	3.22	—	—	—	—	—	—
96-97	Flint	CoHL	42	31	10	0	2351	1	3.42	12	9	3	707	*1	3.31
	IHL	Totals	5	2	2	0	157	0	4.20	—	—	—	—	—	—

Born; 12/14/74, Moscow, Russia. 5-10, 174. Member of 1996-97 CoHL Rookie Team.

Scott Galt — Goaltender

			Regular Season							Playoffs					
Season	Team	League	GP	W	L	T	MIN	SO	GAVG	GP	W	L	MIN	SO	GAVG
95-96	Jacksonville	ECHL	11	4	5	1	619	0	4.26	—	—	—	—	—	—
96-97	Central Texas	WPHL	11	4	5	0	496	0	4.11	—	—	—	—	—	—

Born; 1/18/74, Penetanguistene, Ontario. 5-10, 175.

Alex Galtcheniouk — Center

			Regular Season					Playoffs				
Season	Team	League	GP	G	A	PTS	PIM	GP	G	A	PTS	PIM
92-93	Milwaukee	IHL	44	13	33	46	22	1	0	0	0	0
93-94	Milwaukee	IHL	33	12	24	36	20	3	1	1	2	0
95-96	Madison	CoHL	12	2	7	9	4	—	—	—	—	—
96-97	Michigan	IHL	52	11	17	28	24	4	2	1	3	0
96-97	Madison	CoHL	22	11	21	32	18	—	—	—	—	—
	IHL	Totals	129	36	74	110	66	8	3	2	5	0
	CoHL	Totals	34	13	28	41	22	—	—	—	—	—

Born; 7/28/67, Minsk, Belarus. 6-1, 195. Did not play professionally in North America during 1994-95 season.

Mike Gamble — Center

			Regular Season					Playoffs				
Season	Team	League	GP	G	A	PTS	PIM	GP	G	A	PTS	PIM
95-96	Huntsville	SHL	54	31	33	64	93	—	—	—	—	—
96-97	Brantford	CoHL	36	12	13	25	55	—	—	—	—	—
96-97	Dayton	CoHL	7	2	1	3	6	—	—	—	—	—
96-97	Huntsville	CeHL	11	10	11	21	18	4	2	1	3	30
	CoHL	Totals	43	14	14	28	61	—	—	—	—	—

Born; 8/17/75, Brantford, Ontario. 5-9, 175. Broke leg in 96-97 playoffs.

Liam Garvey — Defenseman

			Regular Season					Playoffs				
Season	Team	League	GP	G	A	PTS	PIM	GP	G	A	PTS	PIM
95-96	San Antonio	CeHL	50	11	39	50	118	4	0	1	1	12
96-97	Fort Wayne	IHL	55	5	10	15	92	—	—	—	—	—
96-97	Peoria	ECHL	19	4	15	19	61	—	—	—	—	—

Born; 1/2/73, Chicago Heights, Illinois. 5-11, 190. 1995-96 CeHL First Team All-Star.

Matt Garzone — Defenseman

			Regular Season					Playoffs				
Season	Team	League	GP	G	A	PTS	PIM	GP	G	A	PTS	PIM
96-97	Richmond	ECHL	39	4	13	17	38	—	—	—	—	—
96-97	Knoxville	ECHL	23	1	7	8	16	—	—	—	—	—
	ECHL	Totals	62	5	20	25	54	—	—	—	—	—

Born; 10/6/72, Sherborn, Massachusetts. 6-0, 205. Last amateur club; Colgate (ECAC).

Sandy Gasseau — Right Wing

			Regular Season					Playoffs				
Season	Team	League	GP	G	A	PTS	PIM	GP	G	A	PTS	PIM
95-96	San Diego	WCHL	14	9	11	20	20	—	—	—	—	—
96-97	San Diego	WCHL	42	26	22	48	35	6	3	3	6	14
	WCHL	Totals	56	35	33	68	55	6	3	3	6	14

Born; 9/15/70, Ste. Foy, Quebec. 6-2, 195. Member of 1996-97 WCHL Champion San Diego Gulls.

Jim Gattolliat — Defenseman

			Regular Season					Playoffs				
Season	Team	League	GP	G	A	PTS	PIM	GP	G	A	PTS	PIM
96-97	Dayton	ECHL	3	0	1	1	7	4	1	2	3	7

Born; 12/18/76, Edmonton, Alberta. 5-11, 192.

Denis Gauthier — Defenseman

			Regular Season					Playoffs				
Season	Team	League	GP	G	A	PTS	PIM	GP	G	A	PTS	PIM
95-96	Saint John	AHL	5	2	0	2	8	16	1	6	7	20
96-97	Saint John	AHL	73	3	28	31	74	5	0	0	0	6
	AHL	Totals	78	5	28	33	82	21	1	6	7	26

Born; 10/1/76, Montreal, Quebec. 6-2, 195. Drafted by Calgary Flames (1st choice, 20th overall) in 1995 Entry Draft.

Derek Gauthier — Right Wing

			Regular Season					Playoffs				
Season	Team	League	GP	G	A	PTS	PIM	GP	G	A	PTS	PIM
93-94	Charlotte	ECHL	52	12	15	27	118	—	—	—	—	—
94-95	Brantford	CoHL	60	16	26	42	101	—	—	—	—	—
95-96	Louisville	ECHL	65	25	32	57	177	3	1	0	1	4
96-97	Columbus	ECHL	60	33	40	73	164	8	3	4	7	18
	ECHL	Totals	177	70	87	157	459	11	4	4	8	22

Born; 4/3/73, Sudbury, Ontario. 6-0, 195.

Sean Gauthier — Goaltender

			Regular Season							Playoffs					
Season	Team	League	GP	W	L	T	MIN	SO	GAVG	GP	W	L	MIN	SO	GAVG
91-92	Fort Wayne	IHL	18	10	4	2	978	1	3.62	2	0	0	48	0	8.75
91-92	Moncton	AHL	25	8	10	5	1415	1	3.73	2	0	0	26	0	4.62
92-93	Moncton	AHL	38	10	16	9	2196	0	3.96	2	0	1	75	0	4.80
93-94	Moncton	AHL	13	3	5	1	617	0	3.99	—	—	—	—	—	—
93-94	Fort Wayne	IHL	22	9	9	3	1139	0	3.48	—	—	—	—	—	—
94-95	Fort Worth	IHL	5	0	2	1	218	0	4.13	—	—	—	—	—	—
94-95	Canada	National													
95-96	St. John's	AHL	5	1	1	0	173	0	3.12	—	—	—	—	—	—
95-96	South Carolina	ECHL	49	31	11	7	2891	0	3.09	8	5	3	478	0	3.01
96-97	Pensacola	ECHL	46	23	21	1	2693	1	3.74	12	8	4	750	*1	3.52
	AHL	Totals	81	22	32	15	4401	1	3.86	4	0	1	101	0	4.76
	IHL	Totals	45	19	15	6	2335	1	3.60	2	0	0	48	0	8.75
	ECHL	Totals	95	54	32	8	5584	1	3.41	20	13	7	1228	1	3.32

Born; 3/28/71, Sudbury, Ontario. 5-11, 202. Drafted by Winnipeg Jets (7th choice, 181st overall) in 1991 Entry Draft. 1995-96 ECHL Second Team All-Star.

Greg Geldart — Center

			Regular Season					Playoffs				
Season	Team	League	GP	G	A	PTS	PIM	GP	G	A	PTS	PIM
92-93	Detroit	CoHL	44	6	20	26	23	5	0	0	0	4
93-94	Huntsville	ECHL	58	12	28	40	33	—	—	—	—	—
94-95	Tallahassee	ECHL	65	26	47	73	24	13	5	14	19	6
95-96	Tallahassee	ECHL	61	14	42	56	32	12	3	4	7	6

Season	Team	League	GP	G	A	PTS	PIM	GP	G	A	PTS	PIM
96-97	Tallahassee	ECHL	67	17	40	57	28	3	0	1	1	0
	ECHL	Totals	251	69	157	226	117	28	8	19	27	12

Born; 5/12/68, Edmonton, Alberta. 6-0, 195. Drafted by Vancouver Canucks (7th choice, 149th overall) in 1988 Entry Draft.

Martin Gendron — Right Wing

			Regular Season					Playoffs				
Season	Team	League	GP	G	A	PTS	PIM	GP	G	A	PTS	PIM
92-93	Baltimnore	AHL	10	1	2	3	2	3	0	0	0	0
93-94	Canada	National										
94-95	Washington	NHL	8	2	1	3	2	—	—	—	—	—
94-95	Portland	AHL	72	36	32	68	54	4	5	1	6	2
95-96	Washington	NHL	20	2	1	3	8	—	—	—	—	—
95-96	Portland	AHL	48	38	29	67	39	22	*15	18	33	8
96-97	Las Vegas	IHL	81	51	39	90	20	3	2	1	3	0
	NHL	Totals	28	4	2	6	10	—	—	—	—	—
	AHL	Totals	130	75	63	138	95	29	20	19	39	10

Born; 2/15/74, Valleyfield, Quebec. 5-8, 180. Drafted by Washington Capitals (4th choice, 71st overall) in 1992 Entry Draft.

Marc Genest — Center

			Regular Season					Playoffs				
Season	Team	League	GP	G	A	PTS	PIM	GP	G	A	PTS	PIM
96-97	South Carolina	ECHL	35	3	13	16	41	—	—	—	—	—
96-97	Raleigh	ECHL	11	1	2	3	4	—	—	—	—	—
	ECHL	Totals	46	4	15	19	45	—	—	—	—	—

Born; 2/19/73, Orleans, Ontario. 5-11, 188.

Chris George — Right Wing

			Regular Season					Playoffs				
Season	Team	League	GP	G	A	PTS	PIM	GP	G	A	PTS	PIM
94-95	Tallahassee	ECHL	8	1	1	2	4	—	—	—	—	—
95-96	Tallahassee	ECHL	1	0	0	0	0	—	—	—	—	—
95-96	Daytona Beach	SHL	60	45	38	83	28	4	1	3	4	4
96-97	Columbus	CeHL	3	0	1	1	6	—	—	—	—	—
96-97	Huntsville	CeHL	54	27	15	42	21	9	2	2	4	6
	CeHL	Totals	57	27	16	43	27	9	2	2	4	6
	ECHL	Totals	9	1	1	2	4	—	—	—	—	—

Born; 12/3/71, Kitchener, Ontario. 5-10, 192.

Dave Geris — Defense

			Regular Season					Playoffs				
Season	Team	League	GP	G	A	PTS	PIM	GP	G	A	PTS	PIM
96-97	Carolina	AHL	28	1	1	2	59	—	—	—	—	—
96-97	Port Huron	CoHL	42	1	7	8	117	5	0	1	1	0

Born; 6/7/76, North Bay, Ontario. 6-5, 240. Drafted by Florida Panthers (6th choice, 105th overall) in 1994 Entry Draft.

Eric Germain — Defenseman

			Regular Season					Playoffs				
Season	Team	League	GP	G	A	PTS	PIM	GP	G	A	PTS	PIM
86-87	Flint	IHL	21	0	2	2	23	—	—	—	—	—
86-87	Fredericton	AHL	44	2	8	10	28	—	—	—	—	—
87-88	Los Angeles	NHL	4	0	1	1	13	1	0	0	0	4
87-88	New Haven	AHL	69	0	10	10	82	—	—	—	—	—
88-89	New Haven	AHL	55	0	9	9	93	17	0	3	3	23
89-90	New Haven	AHL	59	3	12	15	112	—	—	—	—	—
90-91	Binghamton	AHL	60	4	10	14	144	10	0	1	1	14
91-92	Moncton	AHL	3	0	2	2	4	—	—	—	—	—
91-92	Binghamton	AHL	47	3	6	9	86	3	0	0	0	0
93-94	Richmond	ECHL	56	3	16	19	192	—	—	—	—	—
93-94	Binghamton	AHL	3	0	0	0	6	—	—	—	—	—

Season	Team	League	GP	G	A	PTS	PIM	GP	G	A	PTS	PIM
94-95	Rochester	AHL	18	1	7	8	13	5	0	2	2	18
94-95	Richmond	ECHL	10	0	2	2	55	—	—	—	—	—
95-96	Erie	ECHL	67	4	13	17	245	—	—	—	—	—
96-97	Columbus	CeHL	66	7	15	22	176	3	0	0	0	2
	AHL	Totals	358	13	58	71	568	35	0	6	6	55
	ECHL	Totals	133	7	31	38	492	—	—	—	—	—

Born; 6/26/66, Quebec City, Quebec. 6-1, 195. Signed as a free agent by Los Angeles Kings (6/86).

Ken Gernander — Center
Regular Season / Playoffs

Season	Team	League	GP	G	A	PTS	PIM	GP	G	A	PTS	PIM
91-92	Fort Wayne	IHL	13	7	6	13	2	—	—	—	—	—
91-92	Moncton	AHL	43	8	18	26	9	8	1	1	2	2
92-93	Moncton	AHL	71	18	29	47	20	5	1	4	5	0
93-94	Moncton	AHL	71	22	25	47	12	19	6	1	7	0
94-95	Binghamton	AHL	80	28	25	53	24	11	2	2	4	6
95-96	Rangers	NHL	10	2	3	5	4	6	0	0	0	0
95-96	Binghamton	AHL	63	44	29	73	38	—	—	—	—	—
96-97	Rangers	NHL	—	—	—	—	—	9	0	0	0	0
96-97	Binghamton	AHL	46	13	18	31	30	2	0	1	1	0
	NHL	Totals	10	2	3	5	4	15	0	0	0	0
	AHL	Totals	374	133	144	277	137	51	10	9	19	8

Born; 6/30/69, Coleraine, Minnesota. 5-10, 175. Drafted by Winnipeg Jets (4th choice, 96th overall) in 1987 Entry Draft. Signed as a free agent by New York Rangers (7/4/94).

Hugues Gervais — Right Wing
Regular Season / Playoffs

Season	Team	League	GP	G	A	PTS	PIM	GP	G	A	PTS	PIM
96-97	Hershey	AHL	3	0	0	0	14	9	1	1	2	19
96-97	Mobile	ECHL	57	12	5	17	198	3	1	1	2	10

Born; 1/10/75, Fortierville, Quebec. 6-1, 206. Member of 1996-97 AHL Champion Hershey Bears.

Victor Gervais — Center
Regular Season / Playoffs

Season	Team	League	GP	G	A	PTS	PIM	GP	G	A	PTS	PIM
90-91	Baltimore	AHL	28	2	13	15	28	—	—	—	—	—
90-91	Hampton Roads	ECHL	8	5	14	19	15	—	—	—	—	—
91-92	Baltimore	AHL	21	1	5	6	37	—	—	—	—	—
91-92	Hampton Roads	ECHL	44	30	43	73	79	14	6	8	14	20
92-93	Baltimore	AHL	10	2	4	6	2	—	—	—	—	—
92-93	Hampton Roads	ECHL	59	38	*80	118	137	4	0	3	3	10
93-94	Portland	AHL	3	0	1	1	0	—	—	—	—	—
93-94	Cleveland	IHL	37	16	16	32	18	—	—	—	—	—
93-94	Hampton Roads	ECHL	31	22	53	75	82	—	—	—	—	—
94-95	Cleveland	IHL	52	20	32	52	55	4	1	3	4	4
95-96	Cleveland	IHL	56	10	28	38	58	3	0	1	1	2
95-96	Hampton Roads	ECHL	3	3	0	3	16	—	—	—	—	—
96-97	Grand Rapids	IHL	14	2	4	6	16	—	—	—	—	—
96-97	Hampton Roads	ECHL	52	28	60	88	170	7	2	12	14	12
	IHL	Totals	159	48	80	128	147	7	1	4	5	6
	AHL	Totals	62	5	23	28	67	—	—	—	—	—
	ECHL	Totals	197	126	250	376	499	25	8	23	31	42

Born; 3/13/69, Prince George, British Columbia. 5-9, 170. Drafted by Washington Capitals (8th choice, 187th overall) in 1989 Entry Draft.

John Gibson — Defenseman
Regular Season / Playoffs

Season	Team	League	GP	G	A	PTS	PIM	GP	G	A	PTS	PIM
95-96	Huntsville	SHL	60	11	16	27	108	10	4	2	6	10
96-97	Huntsville	CeHL	66	15	50	65	111	9	5	9	14	0

Born; 9/30/70, Kingston, Ontario. 6-2, 205. Member of 1995-96 SHL champion Huntsville Channel Cats.

Steve Gibson — Left Wing

Season	Team	League	GP	G	A	PTS	PIM	GP	G	A	PTS	PIM
92-93	Johnstown	ECHL	—	—	—	—	—	3	0	1	1	2
93-94	Cape Breton	AHL	3	0	0	0	2	—	—	—	—	—
93-94	Wheeling	ECHL	55	29	30	59	47	9	1	3	4	23
94-95	Portland	AHL	12	1	3	4	2	—	—	—	—	—
94-95	Cornwall	AHL	2	0	0	0	0	—	—	—	—	—
94-95	Wheeling	ECHL	50	37	29	56	61	3	0	3	3	6
95-96	Wheeling	ECHL	70	42	53	95	54	7	5	5	10	6
96-97	Hamilton	AHL	2	0	2	2	0	2	1	0	1	2
96-97	Wheeling	ECHL	16	18	14	32	7	3	5	0	5	6
	AHL	Totals	17	1	3	4	4	—	—	—	—	—
	ECHL	Totals	191	126	126	252	169	25	11	12	23	43

Born; 10/10/72, Listowal, Ontario. 6-0, 200. Drafted by Edmonton Oilers (7th choice, 157th overall) in 1992 Entry Draft.

Wade Gibson — Defenseman

Season	Team	League	GP	G	A	PTS	PIM	GP	G	A	PTS	PIM
94-95	Tallahassee	ECHL	41	3	7	10	129	—	—	—	—	—
94-95	Erie	ECHL	2	0	0	0	0	—	—	—	—	—
95-96	Erie	ECHL	34	4	7	11	40	—	—	—	—	—
95-96	Roanoke	ECHL	27	2	4	6	28	2	0	0	0	20
96-97	New Mexico	WPHL	58	7	15	22	141	5	0	1	1	6
	ECHL	Totals	104	9	18	27	197	2	0	0	0	20

Born; 9/13/73, Kingston, Ontario. 6-2, 205. Selected by Lake Charles in WPHL Expansion Draft (6/2/97).

Lee Giffin — Right Wing

Season	Team	League	GP	G	A	PTS	PIM	GP	G	A	PTS	PIM
86-87	Pittsburgh	NHL	8	1	1	2	0	—	—	—	—	—
87-88	Pittsburgh	NHL	19	0	2	2	9	—	—	—	—	—
87-88	Muskegon	IHL	48	26	37	63	61	6	1	3	4	2
88-89	Muskegon	IHL	63	30	44	74	93	12	5	7	12	8
89-90	Flint	IHL	73	30	44	74	68	4	1	2	3	0
90-91	Kansas City	IHL	60	25	43	68	48	—	—	—	—	—
91-92	Capital District	AHL	77	19	26	45	58	7	3	3	6	18
92-93	Chatham	CoHL	29	14	26	40	65	5	6	3	9	0
93-94	N/A											
94-95	Saginaw	CoHL	13	5	7	12	13	10	2	13	15	24
95-96	Saginaw	CoHL	58	20	47	67	94	5	1	2	3	8
96-97	Kansas City	IHL	2	0	0	0	0	—	—	—	—	—
96-97	Mobile	ECHL	20	7	9	16	4	3	1	0	1	0
	NHL	Totals	27	1	3	4	9	—	—	—	—	—
	IHL	Totals	246	111	168	279	270	22	7	12	19	10
	CoHL	Totals	100	39	80	119	172	20	9	18	27	32

Born; 4/1/67, Chatham, Ontario. 5-11, 200. Drafted by Pittsburgh Penguins (2nd choice, 23rd overall) in 1985 Entry Draft. Signed as a free agent by New York Rangers (9/89). Member of 1989-90 IHL champion Muskegon Lumberjacks.

Randy Gilhen — Center

Season	Team	League	GP	G	A	PTS	PIM	GP	G	A	PTS	PIM
82-83	Hartford	NHL	2	00	1	1	0	—	—	—	—	—
83-84	Binghamton	AHL	73	8	12	20	72	—	—	—	—	—
84-85	Salt Lake City	IHL	57	20	20	40	28	—	—	—	—	—
84-85	Binghamton	AHL	18	3	3	6	9	8	4	1	5	16
85-86	Fort Wayne	IHL	82	44	40	84	48	15	10	8	18	6
86-87	Winnipeg	NHL	2	0	0	0	0	—	—	—	—	—
86-87	Sherbrooke	AHL	75	36	29	65	44	17	7	13	20	10
87-88	Winnipeg	NHL	13	3	2	5	15	4	1	0	1	10
87-88	Moncton	AHL	68	40	47	87	51	—	—	—	—	—
88-89	Winnipeg	NHL	64	5	3	8	38	—	—	—	—	—
89-90	Pittsburgh	NHL	61	5	11	16	54	—	—	—	—	—
90-91	Pittsburgh	NHL	72	15	10	25	51	16	1	0	1	14
91-92	Los Angeles	NHL	33	3	6	9	14	—	—	—	—	—
91-92	Rangers	NHL	40	7	7	14	14	13	1	2	3	2
92-93	Rangers	NHL	33	3	2	5	8	—	—	—	—	—
92-93	Tampa Bay	NHL	11	0	2	2	6	—	—	—	—	—
93-94	Florida	NHL	20	4	4	8	16	—	—	—	—	—
93-94	Winnipeg	NHL	40	3	3	6	34	—	—	—	—	—
94-95	Winnipeg	NHL	44	5	6	11	52	—	—	—	—	—
95-96	Winnipeg	NHL	22	2	3	5	12	—	—	—	—	—
96-97	Manitoba	IHL	79	21	24	45	101	—	—	—	—	—
	NHL	Totals	457	55	60	115	314	33	3	2	5	26
	AHL	Totals	234	87	91	178	176	25	11	14	35	26
	IHL	Totals	218	85	84	169	177	15	10	8	18	6

Born; 6/13/63, Zweibrucken, West Germany. 6-0, 190. Drafted by Hartford Whalers (6th choice, 109th overall) in 1982 NHL Entry Draft. Signed as a free agent by Winnipeg Jets (11/8/85). Traded to Pittsburgh Penguins by Winnipeg with Jim Kyte and Andrew McBain for Randy Cunneyworth, Rick Tabaracci and Dave McLlwain (6/17/89). Claimed by Minnesota North Stars from Pittsburgh in Expansion Draft (5/30/91). Traded to Los Angeles Kings by Minnesota with Charlie Huddy, Jim Thomson and New York Rangers fourth round pick (previously acquired by Minnesota—Los Angeles selected Alexei Zhitnik) in 1991 Entry Draft for Todd Elik (6/22/91). Traded to New York Rangers by Los Angles for Corey Millen (12/23/91). Traded to Tampa Bay Lightning by Rangers for Mike Hartman (3/22/93). Claimed by Florida Panthers from Tampa Bay in Expansion Draft (6/24/93). Traded to Winnipeg Jets by Florida for Stu Barnes and St. Louis' sixth round pick (previously acquired by Winnipeg—later traded to Edmonton—later traded to Winnipeg—Winnipeg selected Chris Kibermanis) 11/25/93. Member of 1990-91 Stanley Cup champion Pittsburgh Penguins. Member of 1985-86 IHL Champion Fort Wayne Komets.

Sean Gillam — Defenseman

Season	Team	League	GP	G	A	PTS	PIM	GP	G	A	PTS	PIM
96-97	Adirondack	AHL	64	1	7	8	50	—	—	—	—	—

Born; 5/7/76, Lethbridge, Alberta. 6-2, 187. Drafted by Detroit Red Wings (3rd choice, 75th overall) in 1994 Entry Draft.

Todd Gillingham — Left Wing

Season	Team	League	GP	G	A	PTS	PIM	GP	G	A	PTS	PIM
91-92	St. John's	AHL	66	12	35	47	306	16	4	7	11	80
91-92	Salt Lake City	IHL	1	0	0	0	2	—	—	—	—	—
92-93	Salt Lake City	IHL	75	12	21	33	267	—	—	—	—	—
93-94	St. John's	AHL	59	20	25	45	260	10	0	2	2	12
94-95	Chicago	IHL	54	8	11	19	208	—	—	—	—	—
94-95	San Diego	IHL	16	1	1	2	60	5	2	3	5	10
95-96	Los Angeles	IHL	69	26	24	50	376	—	—	—	—	—
96-97	Long Beach	IHL	37	9	15	24	129	—	—	—	—	—
96-97	Phoenix	IHL	34	9	10	19	106	—	—	—	—	—
	IHL	Totals	286	65	82	147	1148	5	2	3	5	10
	AHL	Totals	125	32	56	88	566	26	4	9	13	92

Born; 1/31/70. Labrador City, Labrador. 6-2, 205. Loaned to Phoenix Roadrunners for completion of 1996-97 season by Long Beach.

Ryan Gillis — Defenseman

			Regular Season					Playoffs				
Season	Team	League	GP	G	A	PTS	PIM	GP	G	A	PTS	PIM
96-97	Michigan	IHL	11	0	2	2	12	4	0	0	0	12
96-97	Saint John	AHL	4	0	0	0	0	—	—	—	—	—
96-97	Baltimore	AHL	9	1	1	2	15	—	—	—	—	—
96-97	Dayton	ECHL	35	11	12	23	44	—	—	—	—	—
	AHL	Totals	13	1	1	2	15	—	—	—	—	—

Born; 12/31/76, Salisbury, New Brunswick. 6-1, 195. Drafted by Calgary Flames (6th choice, 176th overall) in 1995 Entry Draft.

Rick Girard — Center

			Regular Season					Playoffs				
Season	Team	League	GP	G	A	PTS	PIM	GP	G	A	PTS	PIM
93-94	Hamilton	AHL	1	1	1	2	0	—	—	—	—	—
94-95	Syracuse	AHL	26	10	13	23	22	—	—	—	—	—
95-96	Syracuse	AHL	67	15	21	36	32	16	9	8	17	16
96-97	Syracuse	AHL	66	19	28	47	20	1	1	1	2	2
	AHL	Totals	160	45	63	108	74	17	10	9	19	18

Born; 5/1/74, Edmonton, Alberta. 5-11, 180. Drafted by Vancouver Canucks (2nd choice, 46th overall) in 1993 Entry Draft.

Rick Girhiny — Center

			Regular Season					Playoffs				
Season	Team	League	GP	G	A	PTS	PIM	GP	G	A	PTS	PIM
93-94	Birmingham	ECHL	15	2	1	3	10	—	—	—	—	—
93-94	Dayton	ECHL	5	2	0	2	0	—	—	—	—	—
95-96	Muskegon	CoHL	72	2	8	10	57	5	0	0	0	0
96-97	Austin	WPHL	64	10	9	19	55	6	0	1	1	16
	ECHL	Totals	20	4	1	5	10	—	—	—	—	—

Born; 7/11/73, Niagra Falls, Ontario. 5-9, 175.

Trent Gleason — Defenseman

			Regular Season					Playoffs				
Season	Team	League	GP	G	A	PTS	PIM	GP	G	A	PTS	PIM
95-96	South Carolina	ECHL	2	0	1	1	6	—	—	—	—	—
95-96	Memphis	CeHL	61	5	15	20	111	4	1	1	2	2
96-97	Memphis	CeHL	24	1	6	7	41	—	—	—	—	—
96-97	San Antonio	CeHL	25	3	9	12	25	—	—	—	—	—
	CeHL	Totals	110	9	30	39	177	4	1	1	2	2

Born; 4/29/71, Montreal, Quebec. 6-1, 190.

Jason Glover — Right Wing

			Regular Season					Playoffs				
Season	Team	League	GP	G	A	PTS	PIM	GP	G	A	PTS	PIM
95-96	Brantford	CoHL	3	0	1	1	0	—	—	—	—	—
96-97	Flint	CoHL	59	13	24	37	45	13	5	1	6	20
	CoHL	Totals	62	13	25	38	45	13	5	1	6	20

Born; 3/29/72, London, Ontario. 6-0, 185.

Brian Glynn — Defenseman

			Regular Season					Playoffs				
Season	Team	League	GP	G	A	PTS	PIM	GP	G	A	PTS	PIM
87-88	Calgary	NHL	67	5	14	19	87	1	0	0	0	0
88-89	Calgary	NHL	9	0	1	1	19	—	—	—	—	—
88-89	Salt Lake City	IHL	31	3	10	13	105	14	3	7	10	31
89-90	Calgary	NHL	1	0	0	0	0	—	—	—	—	—
89-90	Salt Lake City	IHL	80	17	44	61	164	—	—	—	—	—
90-91	Minnesota	NHL	66	8	11	19	83	23	2	6	8	18

Season	Team	League	GP	G	A	PTS	PIM	GP	G	A	PTS	PIM
90-91	Salt Lake City	IHL	8	1	3	4	18	—	—	—	—	—
91-92	Minnesota	NHL	37	2	12	14	24	—	—	—	—	—
91-92	Edmonton	NHL	25	2	6	8	6	16	4	1	5	12
92-93	Edmonton	NHL	64	4	12	16	60	—	—	—	—	—
93-94	Ottawa	NHL	48	2	13	15	41	—	—	—	—	—
93-94	Vancouver	NHL	16	0	0	0	12	17	0	3	3	10
94-95	Hartford	NHL	43	1	6	7	32	—	—	—	—	—
95-96	Hartford	NHL	54	0	4	4	44	—	—	—	—	—
96-97	Hartford	NHL	1	1	0	1	2	—	—	—	—	—
96-97	San Antonio	IHL	62	13	11	24	46	9	2	6	8	4
	NHL	Totals	431	25	79	104	410	57	6	10	16	40
	IHL	Totals	181	34	68	102	333	23	5	13	18	35

Born; 11/23/67, Iserlohn, West Germany. 6-4, 218. Drafted by Calgary Flames (2nd choice, 37th overall) in 1986 Entry Draft. Traded to Minnesota North Stars by Calgary for Frantisek Musil (10/26/90). traded to Edmonton Oilers by Minnesota for David Shaw (1/21/92). Traded to Ottawa Seantors by Edmonton for Ottawa's eight round draft choice (Rob Quinn) in 1994 Entry Draft (9/15/93). Claimed on waivers by vancouver Canucks from Ottawa (2/5/94). Claimed by Hartford Whalers from Vancouver in NHL Waiver Draft (1/18/95). Traded to Detroit Red Wings by Hartford with Brendan Shanahan for Keith Primeau, Paul Coffey and Detroit's first round choice (Nick Tselios) in 1997 Entry Draft. 1989-90 IHL First Team All-Star. 1989-90 Won IHL's Governor's Trophy (Top Defenseman).

Bob Gohde — Defenseman

Season	Team	League	GP	G	A	PTS	PIM	GP	G	A	PTS	PIM
94-95	Nashville	ECHL	2	0	0	0	0	—	—	—	—	—
95-96	Jacksonville	ECHL	3	0	0	0	4	—	—	—	—	—
95-96	Huntington	ECHL	53	2	5	7	64	—	—	—	—	—
96-97	Dayton	CoHL	29	0	4	4	35	—	—	—	—	—
96-97	Brantford	CoHL	37	2	7	9	25	10	0	1	1	6
	CoHL	Totals	66	2	11	13	60	10	0	1	1	6
	ECHL	Totals	58	2	5	7	68	—	—	—	—	—

Born; 6/9/71, Rolling Meadows, Illinois. 6-1, 205.

Fred Goltz — Left Wing

Season	Team	League	GP	G	A	PTS	PIM	GP	G	A	PTS	PIM
94-95	San Antonio	CeHL	61	25	19	44	150	13	2	1	3	45
95-96	Louisiana	ECHL	38	16	14	30	104	—	—	—	—	—
96-97	San Antonio	CeHL	26	13	10	23	15	—	—	—	—	—
96-97	Columbus	CeHL	14	4	9	13	16	3	0	0	0	24
	CeHL	Totals	101	42	38	80	181	16	2	1	3	69

Born; 6/4/71, Kingston, Ontario. 6-0, 200.

Yan Golubovsky — Defense

Season	Team	League	GP	G	A	PTS	PIM	GP	G	A	PTS	PIM
94-95	Adirondack	AHL	57	4	2	6	39	—	—	—	—	—
95-96	Adirondack	AHL	71	5	16	21	97	3	0	0	0	2
96-97	Adirondack	AHL	62	2	11	13	67	4	0	0	0	0
	AHL	Totals	190	11	29	40	203	7	0	0	0	2

Born; 3/9/76, Novosibirisk, Russia. 6-3, 183. Drafted by Detroit Red Wings (1st choice, 23rd overall) 1994 Entry Draft.

Tom Gomes — Right Wing

Season	Team	League	GP	G	A	PTS	PIM	GP	G	A	PTS	PIM
94-95	Oklahoma City	CeHL	57	20	22	42	52	5	4	0	4	0
95-96	Nashville	ECHL	1	0	0	0	2	—	—	—	—	—
95-96	Oklahoma City	CeHL	64	28	30	58	90	13	4	5	9	15
96-97	Oklahoma City	CeHL	66	25	25	50	155	4	1	0	1	18
	CeHL	Totals	187	73	77	150	297	22	9	5	14	33

Born; 4/29/72, Harrow, Ontario. 5-10, 200. Member of 1995-96 CeHL champion Oklahoma City Blazers.

Daniel Goneau — Left Wing

			Regular Season					Playoffs				
Season	Team	League	GP	G	A	PTS	PIM	GP	G	A	PTS	PIM
96-97	Rangers	NHL	41	10	3	13	10	—	—	—	—	—
96-97	Binghamton	AHL	39	15	15	30	10	—	—	—	—	—

Born; 1/16/76, Montreal, Quebec. 6-1, 196. Drafted by Boston Bruins (2nd choice, 47th overall) in 1994 Entry Draft. Re-entered NHL Entry Draft sleceted by New York Rangers (2nd choice, 48th overall) in 1996 Entry Draft.

Chris Gordon — Goaltender

			Regular Season							Playoffs					
Season	Team	League	GP	MIN	GAVG	W	L	OTL	SO	GP	MIN	GAVG	W	L	SO
94-95	Worcester	AHL	17	993	4.05	7	10	0	0	—	—	—	—	—	—
94-95	Huntington	ECHL	30	1484	2.55	17	6	2	2	—	—	—	—	—	—
95-96	Detroit	IHL	1	42	7.11	0	1	0	0	—	—	—	—	—	—
95-96	Flint	CoHL	36	2042	2.85	22	9	3	2	9	503	3.22	7	2	0
96-97	El Paso	WPHL	50	2762	4.06	26	18	5	0	*11	652	3.68	*8	3	0

Born; 2/16/70, Grand Rapids, Michigan. 5-11, 155. 1994-95 ECHL Goaltender of the Year. 1994-95 First Team ECHL All-Star. Member of 1995-96 Colonial Cup Champion Flint Generals. Member of 1996-97 WPHL Champion El Paso Buzzards.

Ian Gordon — Goaltender

			Regular Season							Playoffs					
Season	Team	League	GP	W	L	T	MIN	SO	GAVG	GP	W	L	MIN	SO	GAVG
95-96	Saint John	AHL	19	2	12	0	768	0	4.37	—	—	—	—	—	—
96-97	Saint John	AHL	21	5	9	1	989	0	3.03	—	—	—	—	—	—
96-97	Grand Rapids	IHL	5	2	2	0	257	0	3.50	1	0	0	1	0	0.00
	AHL	Totals	40	7	21	1	1757	0	3.62	—	—	—	—	—	—

Born; 5/15/75, North Battleford, Saskatchewan. 5-10, 170.

Rhett Gordon — Right Wing

			Regular Season					Playoffs				
Season	Team	League	GP	G	A	PTS	PIM	GP	G	A	PTS	PIM
95-96	Springfield	AHL	2	0	0	0	2	1	0	0	0	0
96-97	Springfield	AHL	54	11	11	22	54	8	1	2	3	6
	AHL	Totals	56	11	11	22	56	9	1	2	3	6

Born; 8/26/76, Regina, Saskatchewan. 5-11, 175. Signed as a free agent by Winnipeg Jets (9/29/94).

Robb Gordon — Center

			Regular Season					Playoffs				
Season	Team	League	GP	G	A	PTS	PIM	GP	G	A	PTS	PIM
96-97	Syracuse	AHL	63	11	14	25	18	3	0	0	0	7

Born; 1/13/76, Murrayville, British Columbia. 5-11, 170. Drafted by Vancouver Canucks (2nd choice, 39th overall) in 1994 Entry Draft.

Jeff Gorman — Forward

			Regular Season					Playoffs				
Season	Team	League	GP	G	A	PTS	PIM	GP	G	A	PTS	PIM
96-97	Bakersfield	WCHL	14	12	9	21	4	4	3	2	5	4

Born; 1/6/73, Winnipeg, Manitoba. 5-11, 190.

Sheldon Gorski — Right Wing

			Regular Season					Playoffs				
Season	Team	League	GP	G	A	PTS	PIM	GP	G	A	PTS	PIM
90-91	Indianapolis	IHL	3	1	0	1	0	—	—	—	—	—
90-91	Louisville	ECHL	62	51	53	104	106	7	5	4	9	20
91-92	Louisville	ECHL	55	56	54	100	94	13	14	8	22	15
92-93	Louisville	ECHL	63	51	47	98	103	—	—	—	—	—
93-94	Louisville	ECHL	41	22	28	50	85	6	1	7	8	4

Season	Team	League	GP	G	A	PTS	PIM	GP	G	A	PTS	PIM
94-95	San Antonio	CeHL	57	45	26	71	96	13	*15	12	27	12
95-96	Louisville	ECHL	48	21	18	39	47	3	1	1	2	8
96-97	Louisville	ECHL	66	38	35	73	96	—	—	—	—	—
	ECHL	Totals	335	239	235	474	531	29	21	20	41	47

Born; 10/16/65, Greenfell, Saskatchewan. 5-10, 185. 1990-91 ECHL Second Team All-Star. 1992-93 ECHL First Team All-Star.

Christian Gosselin — Defenseman

			Regular Season					Playoffs				
Season	Team	League	GP	G	A	PTS	PIM	GP	G	A	PTS	PIM
96-97	Macon	CeHL	63	8	10	18	229	5	0	0	0	29

Born; 8/21/76, Montreal, Quebec. 6-5, 225.

Steve Gosselin — Defenseman

			Regular Season					Playoffs				
Season	Team	League	GP	G	A	PTS	PIM	GP	G	A	PTS	PIM
94-95	Houston	IHL	28	5	5	10	36	—	—	—	—	—
94-95	Chicago	IHL	19	2	2	4	43	1	0	0	0	2
95-96	Chicago	IHL	72	5	17	22	156	3	0	1	1	6
96-97	Chicago	IHL	48	3	16	19	56	—	—	—	—	—
96-97	Detroit	IHL	17	1	6	7	34	11	0	1	1	20
	IHL	Totals	184	16	46	62	325	15	0	2	2	28

Born; 3/27/73, St. Octave, Quebec. 5-9, 195. Member of 1996-97 IHL Champion Detroit Vipers.

Chris Gotziamin — Right Wing

			Regular Season					Playoffs				
Season	Team	League	GP	G	A	PTS	PIM	GP	G	A	PTS	PIM
93-94	Albany	AHL	3	1	1	2	0	—	—	—	—	—
94-95	Saint John	AHL	12	2	2	4	4	—	—	—	—	—
94-95	Columbus	ECHL	56	35	19	54	57	3	4	1	5	15
95-96	Detroit	IHL	12	1	1	2	6	—	—	—	—	—
95-96	Flint	CoHL	63	24	39	63	27	15	3	6	9	28
96-97	Baltimore	AHL	3	0	0	0	0	—	—	—	—	—
96-97	Raleigh	ECHL	48	22	14	36	18	—	—	—	—	—
96-97	Waco	WPHL	9	7	2	9	11	—	—	—	—	—
	AHL	Totals	18	3	3	6	4	—	—	—	—	—
	ECHL	Totals	104	57	33	90	75	3	4	1	5	15

Born; 11/29/71, Roseau, Minnesota. 6-3, 200. Drafted by New Jersey Devils (3rd choice, 29th overall) in 1990 Entry Draft. Member of 1995-96 Colonial Cup Champion Flint Generals.

Brian Goudie — Defenseman

			Regular Season					Playoffs				
Season	Team	League	GP	G	A	PTS	PIM	GP	G	A	PTS	PIM
92-93	Hampton Roads	ECHL	26	0	7	7	138	4	0	0	0	6
93-94	Moncton	AHL	3	0	1	1	30	—	—	—	—	—
93-94	Hamilton	AHL	5	1	0	1	20	—	—	—	—	—
93-94	Hampton Roads	ECHL	55	8	11	19	306	7	2	2	4	57
94-95	Hampton Roads	ECHL	51	5	16	21	278	4	0	5	5	45
95-96	Baltimore	AHL	5	0	1	1	23	12	0	2	2	26
95-96	Springfield	AHL	1	0	0	0	2	—	—	—	—	—
95-96	Richmond	ECHL	53	3	9	12	349	—	—	—	—	—
96-97	Baltimore	AHL	15	0	1	1	31	—	—	—	—	—
96-97	Richmond	ECHL	35	2	4	6	144	8	0	4	4	40
	AHL	Totals	29	1	3	4	106	12	0	2	2	26
	ECHL	Totals	220	18	47	65	1215	23	2	11	13	148

Born; 11/9/72, The Pas, Manitoba. 5-11, 190.

Justin Gould — Defenseman

			Regular Season					Playoffs				
Season	Team	League	GP	G	A	PTS	PIM	GP	G	A	PTS	PIM
96-97	Providence	AHL	9	0	2	2	11	—	—	—	—	—
96-97	Charlotte	ECHL	54	12	15	27	55	3	1	1	2	0

Born; 6/5/74, Dedham, Massachusetts. 6-0, 190. Last amateur club; Providence (Hockey East).

David Goverde — Goaltender

			Regular Season							Playoffs					
Season	Team	League	GP	W	L	T	MIN	SO	GAVG	GP	W	L	MIN	SO	GAVG
90-91	Phoenix	IHL	40	11	19	5	2007	0	4.10	—	—	—	—	—	—
91-92	Los Angeles	NHL	2	1	1	0	120	0	4.50	—	—	—	—	—	—
91-92	Phoenix	IHL	35	11	19	3	1951	1	3.97	—	—	—	—	—	—
91-92	New Haven	AHL	5	1	3	0	248	0	4.11	—	—	—	—	—	—
92-93	Los Angeles	NHL	2	0	2	0	98	0	7.96	—	—	—	—	—	—
92-93	Phoenix	IHL	45	18	21	3	2569	1	4.04	—	—	—	—	—	—
93-94	Los Angeles	NHL	1	0	1	0	60	0	7.00	—	—	—	—	—	—
93-94	Phoenix	IHL	30	15	13	1	1716	0	3.25	—	—	—	—	—	—
93-94	Peoria	IHL	5	4	1	0	299	0	2.61	1	0	1	59	0	7.05
93-94	Portland	AHL	1	0	1	0	59	0	4.01	—	—	—	—	—	—
94-95	Phoenix	IHL	2	0	2	0	76	0	3.95	—	—	—	—	—	—
94-95	Detroit	IHL	15	8	5	0	814	0	3.61	—	—	—	—	—	—
94-95	Detroit	CoHL	4	4	0	0	240	0	2.50	—	—	—	—	—	—
95-96	Saint John	AHL	1	0	0	0	47	0	11.43	—	—	—	—	—	—
95-96	Louisville	ECHL	12	5	5	1	697	*1	3.96	—	—	—	—	—	—
95-96	Toledo	ECHL	31	23	3	4	1817	*1	2.61	11	8	3	666	0	2.88
96-97	Fort Wayne	IHL	1	0	1	0	60	0	7.00	—	—	—	—	—	—
96-97	Toledo	ECHL	44	23	14	5	2554	*5	2.96	5	2	3	347	0	*2.59
	NHL	Totals	5	1	4	0	278	0	6.26	—	—	—	—	—	—
	IHL	Totals	173	67	81	12	9492	2	3.83	1	0	1	59	0	7.05
	AHL	Totals	7	1	4	0	354	0	5.08	—	—	—	—	—	—
	ECHL	Totals	87	51	22	10	5068	7	2.97	16	10	6	1013	0	2.78

Born; 4/9/70, Toronto, Ontario. 6-1, 200. Drafted by Los Angeles Kings (4th choice, 91st overall) in 1990 Entry Draft. 1996-97 ECHL Second Team All-Star. Signed as a free agent by the Phoenix Mustangs (WCHL), (8/97).

Derek Grant — Right Wing

			Regular Season					Playoffs				
Season	Team	League	GP	G	A	PTS	PIM	GP	G	A	PTS	PIM
94-95	Adirondack	AHL	4	0	0	0	15	—	—	—	—	—
94-95	South Carolina	ECHL	—	—	—	—	—	3	1	2	3	4
95-96	South Carolina	ECHL	2	0	0	0	2	—	—	—	—	—
95-96	Memphis	CeHL	52	39	53	92	25	6	5	4	9	8
96-97	Memphis	CeHL	59	35	42	77	59	18	7	10	17	6
	CeHL	Totals	111	74	95	169	84	24	12	14	26	14
	ECHL	Totals	2	0	0	0	2	3	1	2	3	4

Born; 3/18/74, Cornwall, Ontario. 6-0, 175. 1995-96 CeHL Rookie of the Year.

Kevin Grant — Defenseman

			Regular Season					Playoffs				
Season	Team	League	GP	G	A	PTS	PIM	GP	G	A	PTS	PIM
88-89	Salt Lake City	IHL	3	0	1	1	5	3	0	0	0	12
89-90	Salt Lake City	IHL	78	7	17	24	117	11	0	2	2	22
90-91	Salt Lake City	IHL	63	6	19	25	200	3	0	0	0	8
91-92	Salt Lake City	IHL	73	7	16	23	181	—	—	—	—	—
92-93	Salt Lake City	IHL	1	0	0	0	2	—	—	—	—	—
92-93	Phoenix	IHL	49	4	17	21	119	—	—	—	—	—
92-93	Cincinnati	IHL	2	0	0	0	2	—	—	—	—	—

Season	Team	League	GP	G	A	PTS	PIM	GP	G	A	PTS	PIM
93-94	Phoenix	IHL	33	0	3	3	110	—	—	—	—	—
93-94	San Diego	IHL	5	0	0	0	18	—	—	—	—	—
93-94	Milwaukee	IHL	16	3	6	9	64	4	0	4	4	20
94-95	Milwaukee	IHL	3	0	1	1	6	—	—	—	—	—
94-95	Houston	IHL	57	4	9	13	182	4	1	1	2	19
95-96	Houston	IHL	24	1	3	4	43	—	—	—	—	—
95-96	Cincinnati	IHL	22	2	4	6	51	17	1	2	3	28
96-97	Adirondack	AHL	53	1	6	7	54	4	1	2	3	6
	IHL	Totals	429	34	96	130	1100	42	2	9	11	109

Born; 1/9/69, Toronto, Ontario. 6-3, 210. Drafted by Calgary Flames (3rd choice, 40th overall) in 1987 Entry Draft. Traded by Salt Lake City Golden Eagles to Phoenix Roadrunners for Paul Holden (10/16/92).

Benoit Gratton — Left Wing

			Regular Season					Playoffs				
Season	Team	League	GP	G	A	PTS	PIM	GP	G	A	PTS	PIM
96-97	Portland	AHL	76	6	40	46	140	5	2	1	3	14

Born; 12/28/76, Montreal, Quebec. 5-10, 163. Drafted by Washington Capitals (6th choice, 105th overall) in 1995 Entry Draft.

Danny Gratton — Center

			Regular Season					Playoffs				
Season	Team	League	GP	G	A	PTS	PIM	GP	G	A	PTS	PIM
86-87	New Haven	AHL	49	6	10	16	45	2	0	0	0	0
87-88	New Haven	AHL	57	18	28	46	77	—	—	—	—	—
87-88	Los Angeles	NHL	7	1	0	1	5	—	—	—	—	—
88-89	Flint	IHL	20	5	9	14	8	—	—	—	—	—
88-89	New Haven	AHL	29	5	13	18	41	—	—	—	—	—
89-90	Canada	National	68	29	37	66	40	—	—	—	—	—
90-91	Kalamazoo	IHL	44	9	11	20	32	6	1	0	1	14
90-91	Canada	National	N/A									
91-92	Brantford	CoHL	17	8	12	20	6	6	3	9	12	12
92-93	Brantford	CoHL	13	9	8	17	0	10	2	11	13	4
93-94	Hamilton	AHL	2	0	0	0	12	—	—	—	—	—
93-94	Brantford	CoHL	12	9	10	19	16	—	—	—	—	—
96-97	Muskegon	CoHL	60	14	35	49	36	2	1	0	1	19
	AHL	Totals	137	29	41	70	175	2	0	0	0	0
	IHL	Totals	64	14	20	34	40	6	1	0	1	14
	CoHL	Totals	102	40	65	105	58	18	6	20	26	35

Born; 12/7/66, Brantford, Ontario. 6-1, 185. Drafted by Los Angeles Kings (2nd choice, 10th overall) in 1985 Entry Draft. Member of 1992-93 CoHL Champion Brantford Smoke. Did not play professionally in North America between 1993-94 and 1996-97 seasons.

Dan Gravelle — Center

			Regular Season					Playoffs				
Season	Team	League	GP	G	A	PTS	PIM	GP	G	A	PTS	PIM
93-94	Indianapolis	IHL	9	1	1	2	0	—	—	—	—	—
93-94	Greensboro	ECHL	58	38	66	104	73	8	3	3	6	14
94-95	Fort Wayne	IHL	3	0	2	2	0	—	—	—	—	—
94-95	Detroit	CoHL	51	23	33	56	54	12	6	9	15	16
95-96	Carolina	AHL	2	0	0	0	4	—	—	—	—	—
95-96	Detroit	CoHL	18	10	17	27	16	10	6	3	9	15
96-97	San Diego	WCHL	—	—	—	—	—	4	3	3	6	4
	CoHL	Totals	69	33	50	83	70	22	12	12	24	31
	IHL	Totals	12	1	3	4	0	—	—	—	—	—

Born; 3/10/70, Montreal, Quebec. 5-11, 190. 1993-94 ECHL Rookie-of-the-year. 1993-94 2nd Team ECHL all-star. Member of 1996-97 WCHL champion San Diego Gulls.

Brandon Gray — Defenseman

Season	Team	League	GP	G	A	PTS	PIM	GP	G	A	PTS	PIM
96-97	Mississippi	ECHL	20	1	2	3	14	2	0	0	0	0

Born; 4/16/76, Montreal, Quebec. 6-1, 190. Last amateur club; Drummondville (QMJHL).

Roy Gray — Defenseman

Season	Team	League	GP	G	A	PTS	PIM	GP	G	A	PTS	PIM
96-97	Utica	CoHL	39	3	6	9	67	—	—	—	—	—
96-97	Brantford	CoHL	5	0	1	1	12	8	0	1	1	10
	CoHL	Totals	44	3	7	10	79	8	0	1	1	10

Born; 4/22/76, Toronto, Ontario. 5-8, 184. Last amateur club; Ottawa (OHL).

Mark Green — Center

Season	Team	League	GP	G	A	PTS	PIM	GP	G	A	PTS	PIM
91-92	Johnstown	ECHL	64	68	49	117	44	6	2	3	5	4
92-93	Atlanta	IHL	5	0	1	1	0	—	—	—	—	—
92-93	Louisville	ECHL	61	48	29	77	57	—	—	—	—	—
93-94	South Carolina	ECHL	65	25	29	54	54	3	1	1	2	0
94-95	Adirondack	AHL	4	0	3	3	2	—	—	—	—	—
94-95	Utica	CoHL	71	*71	56	127	76	6	5	2	7	8
95-96	Utica	CoHL	60	51	35	86	42	—	—	—	—	—
95-96	Daytona Beach	SHL	10	11	14	25	10	4	1	2	3	4
96-97	Saginaw	CoHL	72	*80	65	145	85	—	—	—	—	—
	CoHL	Totals	203	202	156	358	203	6	5	2	7	8
	ECHL	Totals	190	141	107	248	155	9	3	4	7	4

Born; 12/26/67, Watertown, New York. 6-4, 200. Drafted by Winnipeg Jets (8th choice, 176th overall) in 1986 Entry Draft. 1991-92 ECHL First Team All-Star. 1994-95 shared CoHL MVP Award with Paul Polillo.

Scott Green — Center

Season	Team	League	GP	G	A	PTS	PIM	GP	G	A	PTS	PIM
96-97	Tulsa	CeHL	49	10	15	25	35	5	1	1	2	2

Born;

Shayne Green — Right Wing

Season	Team	League	GP	G	A	PTS	PIM	GP	G	A	PTS	PIM
92-93	Dayton	ECHL	55	17	24	41	117	3	0	1	1	0
92-93	Kalamazoo	IHL	1	0	0	0	0	—	—	—	—	—
93-94	Erie	ECHL	5	1	5	6	0	—	—	—	—	—
96-97	Fresno	WCHL	29	15	22	37	32	5	4	1	5	2
	ECHL	Totals	60	18	29	47	117	3	0	1	1	0

Born; 8/13/71, Quesnel, British Columbia. 6-0, 200. Drafted by Minnesota North Stars (9th choice, 228th overall) in 1991 Entry Draft.

Tim Green — Defenseman

Season	Team	League	GP	G	A	PTS	PIM	GP	G	A	PTS	PIM
95-96	Columbus	ECHL	47	2	11	13	62	—	—	—	—	—
95-96	San Antonio	CeHL	11	1	1	2	10	13	1	1	2	27
96-97	Waco	WPHL	64	9	26	35	75	—	—	—	—	—

Born; 6/25/69, Calgary, Alberta. 5-10, 180.

Jeff Greenlaw — Left Wing

			Regular Season					Playoffs				
Season	Team	League	GP	G	A	PTS	PIM	GP	G	A	PTS	PIM
86-87	Washington	NHL	22	0	3	3	44	—	—	—	—	—
86-87	Binghamton	AHL	4	0	2	2	0	—	—	—	—	—
87-88	Washington	NHL	—	—	—	—	—	1	0	0	0	19
87-88	Binghamton	AHL	56	8	7	15	142	1	0	0	0	2
88-89	Baltimore	AHL	55	12	15	27	115	—	—	—	—	—
89-90	Baltimore	AHL	10	3	2	5	26	7	1	0	1	13
90-91	Washington	NHL	10	2	0	2	10	1	0	0	0	2
90-91	Baltimore	AHL	50	17	17	34	93	3	1	1	2	2
91-92	Washington	NHL	5	0	1	1	34	—	—	—	—	—
91-92	Baltimore	AHL	37	6	8	14	57	—	—	—	—	—
92-93	Washington	NHL	16	1	1	2	18	—	—	—	—	—
92-93	Baltimore	AHL	49	12	14	26	66	7	3	1	4	0
93-94	Florida	NHL	4	0	1	1	2	—	—	—	—	—
93-94	Cincinnati	IHL	55	14	15	29	85	11	2	2	4	28
94-95	Cincinnati	IHL	67	10	21	31	117	10	2	0	2	22
95-96	Cincinnati	IHL	64	17	15	32	112	17	2	4	6	36
96-97	Cincinnati	IHL	27	6	6	12	70	1	0	1	1	2
	NHL	Totals	57	3	6	9	108	2	0	0	0	21
	AHL	Totals	261	58	65	123	499	18	5	2	7	17
	IHL	Totals	213	47	57	104	384	39	6	7	13	88

Born; 2/28/68, Toronto, Ontario. 6-0, 230. Drafted by Washington Capitals (1st choice, 19th overall) in 1986 Entry Draft. Signed as a free agent by Florida Panthers (7/14/93).

Davie Greenway — Defenseman

			Regular Season					Playoffs				
Season	Team	League	GP	G	A	PTS	PIM	GP	G	A	PTS	PIM
96-97	Nashville	CeHL	42	1	9	10	22	—	—	—	—	—

Born; 6/27/76, Edmonton, Alberta. 6-3, 195.

Dale Greenwood — Center

			Regular Season					Playoffs				
Season	Team	League	GP	G	A	PTS	PIM	GP	G	A	PTS	PIM
96-97	Saginaw	CoHL	50	10	26	36	30	—	—	—	—	—

Born; 2/13/75, Mississauga, Ontario. 5-11, 185.

Brian Greer — Goaltender

			Regular Season							Playoffs					
Season	Team	League	GP	MIN	GAVG	W	L	OTL	SO	GP	MIN	GAVG	W	L	SO
95-96	Muskegon	CoHL	27	1167	3.75	8	10	2	0	2	77	3.91	0	2	0
96-97	Muskegon	CoHL	30	1595	3.54	15	10	2	0	1	59	4.04	0	1	0
	CoHL	Totals	57	2762	3.63	23	20	4	0	3	136	3.96	0	3	0

Born; 7/5/74, Orillia, Ontario. 5-10, 165.

Shamus Gregga — Goaltender

			Regular Season							Playoffs					
Season	Team	League	GP	W	L	T	MIN	SO	GAVG	GP	W	L	MIN	SO	GAVG
93-94	Hampton Roads	ECHL	10	3	2	0	394	0	3.65	—	—	—	—	—	—
94-95	Hampton Roads	ECHL	18	6	5	2	853	0	3.66	—	—	—	—	—	—
95-96	Cleveland	IHL	3	1	0	1	108	0	3.35	—	—	—	—	—	—
95-96	Huntington	ECHL	21	3	13	3	1053	0	4.62	—	—	—	—	—	—
95-96	Wheeling	ECHL	3	0	0	0	31	0	3.86	—	—	—	—	—	—
96-97	Hampton Roads	ECHL	2	0	1	0	80	0	5.25	—	—	—	—	—	—

96-97	Macon	CeHL	15	4	5	2	672	0	3.93	—	—	— — —
96-97	Wichita	CeHL	1	0	0	0	41	0	2.90	—	—	— — —
	ECHL	Totals	54	12	21	5	2411	0	4.13	—	—	— — —
	CeHL	Totals	16	4	5	2	714	0	3.87	—	—	— — —

Born; 6/21/74, Montreal, Quebec. 5-11, 186.

Dave Gregory — Defenseman

			Regular Season					Playoffs				
Season	Team	League	GP	G	A	PTS	PIM	GP	G	A	PTS	PIM
94-95	London	CoHL	20	0	2	2	17	—	—	—	—	—
96-97	Central Texas	WPHL	16	0	4	4	22	—	—	—	—	—
96-97	Bakersfield	WCHL	6	0	1	1	0	2	0	0	0	4

Born; 5/1/67, Woodstock, Ontario. 6-1, 195.

Jack Greig — Left Wing

			Regular Season					Playoffs				
Season	Team	League	GP	G	A	PTS	PIM	GP	G	A	PTS	PIM
95-96	Huntsville	SHL	47	9	15	24	205	1	0	0	0	0
96-97	Dayton	CoHL	69	0	10	10	213	—	—	—	—	—

Born; 1/11/73, Long Island, New York. 6-0, 200. Member of 1995-96 SHL champion Huntsville Channel Cats.

Mark Greig — Right Wing

			Regular Season					Playoffs				
Season	Team	League	GP	G	A	PTS	PIM	GP	G	A	PTS	PIM
90-91	Hartford	NHL	4	0	0	0	0	—	—	—	—	—
90-91	Springfield	AHL	73	32	55	87	73	17	2	6	8	22
91-92	Hartford	NHL	17	0	5	5	6	—	—	—	—	—
91-92	Springfield	AHL	50	20	27	47	38	9	1	1	2	20
92-93	Hartford	NHL	22	1	7	8	27	—	—	—	—	—
92-93	Springfield	AHL	55	20	38	58	86	—	—	—	—	—
93-94	Hartford	NHL	31	4	5	9	31	—	—	—	—	—
93-94	Toronto	NHL	13	2	2	4	10	—	—	—	—	—
93-94	Springfield	AHL	4	0	4	4	21	—	—	—	—	—
93-94	St. John's	AHL	9	4	6	10	0	11	4	2	6	26
94-95	Calgary	NHL	8	1	1	2	2	—	—	—	—	—
94-95	Saint John	AHL	67	31	50	81	82	2	0	1	1	0
95-96	Atlanta	IHL	71	25	48	73	104	3	2	1	3	4
96-97	Quebec	IHL	5	1	2	3	0	—	—	—	—	—
96-97	Houston	IHL	59	12	30	42	59	13	5	8	13	2
	NHL	Totals	95	8	20	28	76	—	—	—	—	—
	AHL	Totals	258	107	180	287	300	39	7	10	17	68
	IHL	Totals	135	38	80	118	163	16	7	9	16	6

Born; 1/25/70, High River, Alberta. 5-11, 190. Drafted by Hartford Whalers (1st choice, 15th overall) in 1990 Entry Draft. Traded to Toronto Maple Leafs by Hartford with 6th round choice (later traded to New York Rangers-Rangers selected Yuri Litvinov) in 1994 Entry Draft for Ted Crowley (1/25/94). Signed as a free agent by Calgary (8/9/94). Member of 1990-91 AHL champion Springfield Indians.

Chris Grenville — Right Wing

			Regular Season					Playoffs				
Season	Team	League	GP	G	A	PTS	PIM	GP	G	A	PTS	PIM
95-96	Birmingham	ECHL	40	9	7	16	40	—	—	—	—	—
96-97	Columbus	CeHL	36	13	7	20	34	—	—	—	—	—
96-97	Saginaw	CoHL	27	10	12	22	12	—	—	—	—	—

Born; 2/24/74, St. Catharines, Ontario. 6-1, 205.

Brent Gretzky — Center

			Regular Season					Playoffs				
Season	Team	League	GP	G	A	PTS	PIM	GP	G	A	PTS	PIM
92-93	Atlanta	IHL	77	20	34	54	84	9	3	2	5	8

Season	Team	League	GP	G	A	PTS	PIM	GP	G	A	PTS	PIM
93-94	Tampa Bay	NHL	10	1	2	3	2	—	—	—	—	—
93-94	Atlanta	IHL	54	17	23	40	30	14	1	1	2	2
94-95	Tampa Bay	IHL	3	0	1	1	0	—	—	—	—	—
94-95	Atlanta	IHL	67	19	32	51	42	5	4	1	5	4
95-96	St. John's	AHL	68	13	28	41	40	4	0	6	6	0
96-97	Las Vegas	IHL	40	5	12	17	8	—	—	—	—	—
96-97	Quebec	IHL	1	0	0	0	0	—	—	—	—	—
96-97	Pensacola	ECHL	22	9	15	24	4	12	5	8	13	4
	NHL	Totals	13	1	3	4	2	—	—	—	—	—
	IHL	Totals	239	61	101	162	164	28	8	4	12	14

Born; 6/24/69, Sudbury, Ontario. 5-11, 182. Drafted by Tampa Bay Lightning (3rd choice, 49th overall) in 1992 Entry Draft. Signed as a free agent by Toronto Maple Leafs (9/8/95). Member of 1993-94 IHL champion Atlanta Knights.

Brent Grieve — Left Wing

Season	Team	League	GP	G	A	PTS	PIM	GP	G	A	PTS	PIM
90-91	Capital District	AHL	61	14	13	27	80	—	—	—	—	—
90-91	Kansas City	IHL	5	2	2	4	2	—	—	—	—	—
91-92	Capital District	AHL	74	34	32	66	84	7	3	1	4	16
92-93	Capital District	AHL	79	34	28	62	122	4	1	1	2	10
93-94	Islanders	NHL	3	0	0	0	7	—	—	—	—	—
93-94	Edmonton	NHL	24	13	5	18	14	—	—	—	—	—
93-94	Salt Lake City	IHL	22	9	5	14	30	—	—	—	—	—
93-94	Capital District	AHL	20	10	11	21	14	4	2	4	6	16
94-95	Chicago	NHL	24	1	5	6	23	—	—	—	—	—
95-96	Chicago	NHL	28	2	4	6	28	—	—	—	—	—
95-96	Indianapolis	IHL	24	9	10	19	16	—	—	—	—	—
95-96	Phoenix	IHL	13	8	11	19	14	4	2	1	3	18
96-97	Los Angeles	NHL	18	4	2	6	15	—	—	—	—	—
96-97	Phoenix	IHL	31	10	14	24	51	—	—	—	—	—
	NHL	Totals	97	20	16	36	87	—	—	—	—	—
	AHL	Totals	234	92	84	176	300	15	6	6	12	42
	IHL	Totals	95	38	42	80	113	4	2	1	3	18

Born; 5/9/69, Oshawa, Ontario. 6-1, 204. Drafted by New York islanders (4th choice, 65th overall) in 1989 Entry Draft. Traded to Edmonton Oilers by Islanders for Marc Laforge (12/15/93). Signed as a free agent by Chicago (7/7/94). Signed as a free agent by Los Angeles Kings (7/96).

Dean Grillo — Center

Season	Team	League	GP	G	A	PTS	PIM	GP	G	A	PTS	PIM
94-95	Kansas City	IHL	72	15	21	36	24	18	3	5	8	18
95-96	Kansas City	IHL	65	9	10	19	26	5	0	0	0	2
96-97	Kentucky	AHL	67	12	22	34	27	4	0	1	1	2
	IHL	Totals	137	24	31	55	50	23	3	5	8	20

Born; 12/8/72, Bemidji, Minnesota. 6-2, 210. Drafted by San Jose Sharks (9th choice, 155th overall) in 1991 Entry Draft.

Chad Grills — Center

Season	Team	League	GP	G	A	PTS	PIM	GP	G	A	PTS	PIM
94-95	Flint	CoHL	3	0	1	1	8	—	—	—	—	—
95-96	Brantford	CoHL	1	0	0	0	0	—	—	—	—	—
95-96	Flint	CoHL	58	8	18	26	170	15	2	5	7	73
96-97	Detroit	IHL	1	0	0	0	0	—	—	—	—	—
96-97	Flint	CoHL	51	15	29	44	168	14	2	7	9	34
	CoHL	Totals	113	23	48	71	346	29	4	12	16	107

Member of 1995-96 Colonial Cup Champion Flint Generals

Devin Grimeau — Defenseman

Season	Team	League	GP	G	A	PTS	PIM	GP	G	A	PTS	PIM
96-97	El Paso	WPHL	28	1	6	7	36	—	—	—	—	—

Born;

Francois Groleau — Defenseman

Season	Team	League	GP	G	A	PTS	PIM	GP	G	A	PTS	PIM
93-94	Saint John	AHL	73	8	14	22	49	7	0	1	1	2
94-95	Saint John	AHL	65	6	34	40	28	—	—	—	—	—
94-95	Cornwall	AHL	8	1	2	3	7	14	2	7	9	16
95-96	Montreal	NHL	2	0	1	1	2	—	—	—	—	—
95-96	Fredericton	AHL	12	3	5	8	10	10	1	6	7	14
95-96	San Francisco	IHL	63	6	26	32	60	—	—	—	—	—
96-97	Montreal	NHL	5	0	0	0	4	—	—	—	—	—
96-97	Fredericton	AHL	47	8	24	32	43	—	—	—	—	—
	NHL	Totals	7	0	1	1	6	—	—	—	—	—
	AHL	Totals	205	26	79	105	137	31	3	14	17	32

Born; 1/23/73. Longueuil, Quebec. 6-0, 200. Drafted by Calgary Flames (2nd choice, 41st overall) in 1991 Entry Draft. Traded to Quebec Nordiques by Calgary for Ed Ward (3/23/95). Signed as a free agent by Montreal Canadiens (6/17/95).

Tuomas Gronman — Defenseman

Season	Team	League	GP	G	A	PTS	PIM	GP	G	A	PTS	PIM
96-97	Chicago	NHL	16	0	1	1	13	—	—	—	—	—
96-97	Indianapolis	IHL	51	5	16	21	89	4	1	1	2	6

Born; 3/22/74. Viitasaari, Finland. 6-3, 198. Drafted by Quebec Nordiques (3rd choice, 29th overall) in 1992 Entry Draft. Rights traded to Chicago Blackhawks by Colorado for Chicago's second round choice in 1998 Entry Draft (7/10/96).

Garry Gruber — Defenseman

Season	Team	League	GP	G	A	PTS	PIM	GP	G	A	PTS	PIM
96-97	Tallahassee	ECHL	37	2	10	12	26	—	—	—	—	—
96-97	Louisville	ECHL	22	0	7	7	4	—	—	—	—	—
	ECHL	Totals	59	2	17	19	30	—	—	—	—	—

Born; Madison, Wisconsin. 6-0, 190. Last amateur club; Notre Dame (CCHA).

John Gruden — Defenseman

Season	Team	League	GP	G	A	PTS	PIM	GP	G	A	PTS	PIM
93-94	Boston	NHL	7	0	1	1	2	—	—	—	—	—
94-95	Boston	NHL	38	0	6	6	22	—	—	—	—	—
94-95	Providence	AHL	1	0	1	1	0	—	—	—	—	—
95-96	Boston	NHL	14	0	0	0	4	3	0	1	1	0
95-96	Providence	AHL	39	5	19	24	29	—	—	—	—	—
96-97	Providence	AHL	78	18	27	45	52	10	3	6	9	4
	NHL	Totals	59	0	7	7	28	3	0	1	1	0
	AHL	Totals	118	23	47	70	81	10	3	6	9	4

Born; 4/6/70, Hastings, Minnesota. 6-0, 180. Drafted by Boston Bruins (7th choice, 168th overall) in 1990 Entry Draft.

Mike Gruttadauria — Right Wing

Season	Team	League	GP	G	A	PTS	PIM	GP	G	A	PTS	PIM
93-94	Chatham	CoHL	42	3	0	3	77	8	0	0	0	44
94-95	Saginaw	CoHL	41	0	3	3	110	—	—	—	—	—
95-96	Fort Worth	CeHL	3	0	1	1	9	—	—	—	—	—

Season	Team	League	GP	G	A	PTS	PIM	GP	G	A	PTS	PIM
96-97	Utica	CoHL	32	1	0	1	136	—	—	—	—	—
	CoHL	Totals	115	4	3	7	323	8	0	0	0	44

Born; 10/10/70, Rochester, New York. 6-1, 195.

Jeff Guay — Defenseman

Regular Season / Playoffs

Season	Team	League	GP	G	A	PTS	PIM	GP	G	A	PTS	PIM
95-96	Quad City	CoHL	43	2	9	11	30	—	—	—	—	—
95-96	Utica	CoHL	12	0	0	0	2	—	—	—	—	—
96-97	Utica	CoHL	14	0	1	1	6	—	—	—	—	—
96-97	Waco	WPHL	8	0	2	2	15	—	—	—	—	—
96-97	Central Texas	WPHL	12	0	2	2	2	—	—	—	—	—
	CoHL	Totals	69	2	10	12	38	—	—	—	—	—
	WPHL	Totals	20	0	4	4	17	—	—	—	—	—

Born; 2/9/72, Lewiston, Maine. 5-9, 188.

Daniel Guerard — Right Wing

Regular Season / Playoffs

Season	Team	League	GP	G	A	PTS	PIM	GP	G	A	PTS	PIM
92-93	New Haven	AHL	2	2	1	3	0	—	—	—	—	—
93-94	Prince Edward Island	AHL	3	0	0	0	17	—	—	—	—	—
94-95	Ottawa	NHL	2	0	0	0	0	—	—	—	—	—
94-95	Prince Edward Island	AHL	68	20	22	42	95	6	0	1	1	16
95-96	Prince Edward Island	AHL	42	3	7	10	56	—	—	—	—	—
96-97	Worcester	AHL	49	8	8	16	50	—	—	—	—	—
	AHL	Totals	164	33	38	71	218	6	0	1	1	16

Born; 4/9/74, LaSalle, Quebec. 6-4, 215. Drafted by Ottawa Senators (5th choice, 98th overall) in 1992 Entry Draft.

Garry Gulash — Defenseman

Regular Season / Playoffs

Season	Team	League	GP	G	A	PTS	PIM	GP	G	A	PTS	PIM
93-94	West Palm Beach	SUN	8	5	4	9	71	—	—	—	—	—
93-94	Detroit	CoHL	31	7	15	22	146	1	0	2	2	0
93-94	Johnstown	ECHL	3	0	0	0	60	—	—	—	—	—
94-95	Detroit	IHL	3	0	0	0	0	—	—	—	—	—
94-95	Detroit	CoHL	53	10	29	39	239	7	1	3	4	56
95-96	Milwaukee	IHL	4	0	0	0	11	1	0	0	0	0
95-96	Detroit	CoHL	6	1	2	3	44	—	—	—	—	—
95-96	Richmond	ECHL	37	3	9	12	260	7	0	4	4	10
96-97	Richmond	ECHL	29	1	4	5	225	—	—	—	—	—
96-97	Birmingham	ECHL	17	0	3	3	138	8	0	6	6	39
	IHL	Totals	7	0	0	0	11	1	0	0	0	0
	CoHL	Totals	90	18	46	64	429	8	1	5	6	56
	ECHL	Totals	86	4	16	20	683	15	0	10	10	49

Born; 9/22/72, Calgary, Alberta. 5-10, 225.

Glen Gulutzan — Center

Regular Season / Playoffs

Season	Team	League	GP	G	A	PTS	PIM	GP	G	A	PTS	PIM
96-97	Utah	IHL	3	0	0	0	2	—	—	—	—	—
96-97	Las Vegas	IHL	1	0	0	0	0	—	—	—	—	—
96-97	Fresno	WCHL	60	30	*80	110	52	5	0	9	9	8
	IHL	Totals	4	0	0	0	2	—	—	—	—	—

Born; 8/12/71, The Pas, Manitoba. 5-10, 175.

Steve Guolla — Left Wing

			Regular Season					Playoffs				
Season	Team	League	GP	G	A	PTS	PIM	GP	G	A	PTS	PIM
95-96	Prince Edward Island	AHL	72	32	48	80	28	3	0	0	0	0
96-97	San Jose	NHL	43	13	8	21	14	—	—	—	—	—
96-97	Kentucky	AHL	34	22	22	44	10	4	2	1	3	0
	AHL	Totals	106	54	70	124	38	7	2	1	3	0

Born; 3/15/73, Scarborough, Ontario. 6-0, 180. Drafted by Ottawa Senators (1st choice, 3rd overall) in 1994 Supplemental Draft. Signed as a free agent by San Jose Sharks (8/22/96).

Miroslav Guren — Defenseman

			Regular Season					Playoffs				
Season	Team	League	GP	G	A	PTS	PIM	GP	G	A	PTS	PIM
96-97	Fredericton	AHL	79	6	26	32	26	—	—	—	—	—

Born; 9/24/76, Hradiste, Czechoslovakia. 6-2, 215. Drafted by Montreal Canadiens (2nd choice, 60th overall) in 1995 Entry Draft.

Sergei Gusev — Defenseman

			Regular Season					Playoffs				
Season	Team	League	GP	G	A	PTS	PIM	GP	G	A	PTS	PIM
95-96	Michigan	IHL	73	11	17	28	76	—	—	—	—	—
96-97	Michigan	IHL	51	7	8	15	44	4	0	4	4	6
	IHL	Totals	124	18	25	43	120	4	0	4	4	6

Born; 7/31/75, Nizhny Tagil, Russia. 6-1, 195. Drafted by Dallas Stars (4th choice, 69th overall) in 1995 Entry Draft.

Ravil Gusmanov — Left Wing

			Regular Season					Playoffs				
Season	Team	League	GP	G	A	PTS	PIM	GP	G	A	PTS	PIM
94-95	Springfield	AHL	72	18	15	33	14	—	—	—	—	—
95-96	Winnipeg	NHL	4	0	0	0	0	—	—	—	—	—
95-96	Springfield	AHL	60	36	32	68	20	—	—	—	—	—
95-96	Indianapolis	IHL	11	6	10	16	4	5	2	3	5	4
96-97	Indianapolis	IHL	60	21	27	48	14	—	—	—	—	—
96-97	Saint John	AHL	12	4	4	8	2	3	0	1	1	2
	AHL	Totals	144	58	51	109	36	3	0	1	1	2
	IHL	Totals	71	27	37	64	18	5	2	3	5	4

Born; 7/25/72, Naberehnye Chelny, Russia. 6-3, 185. Drafted by Winnipeg Jets (5th choice, 93rd overall) in 1993 Entry Draft. Traded to Chicago Blackhawks by Winnipeg for Chicago's fourth round choice (later traded to Toronto—Toronto selected Vladimir Antipov) in 1996 Entry Draft. Traded to Calgary Flames by Chicago for Marc Hussey (3/18/97).

Brad Guzda — Goaltender

			Regular Season							Playoffs					
Season	Team	League	GP	W	L	T	MIN	SO	GAVG	GP	W	L	MIN	SO	GAVG
94-95	Muskegon	CoHL	—	—	—	—	—	—	—	1	0	1	46	0	6.51
95-96	Muskegon	CoHL	2	0	0	0	12	0	24.46	—	—	—	—	—	—
95-96	Knoxville	ECHL	19	16	1	0	1083	0	3.82	7	3	4	433	0	3.33
96-97	Knoxville	ECHL	35	12	18	2	1853	1	5.38	—	—	—	—	—	—
96-97	Phoenix	IHL	5	0	1	2	165	0	4.37	—	—	—	—	—	—
	ECHL	Totals	54	28	19	2	2936	1	4.80	7	3	4	433	0	3.33

Born; 4/28/73, Banff, Alberta. 6-2, 175. Signed as a free agent by Los Angeles Kings (7/96).

Dwayne Gylywoychuk — Defenseman

Season	Team	League	Regular Season					Playoffs				
			GP	G	A	PTS	PIM	GP	G	A	PTS	PIM
94-95	Greensboro	ECHL	27	1	9	10	42	—	—	—	—	—
95-96	Jacksonville	ECHL	48	1	5	6	105	—	—	—	—	—
95-96	Dayton	ECHL	5	0	0	0	20	—	—	—	—	—
96-97	Central Texas	WPHL	40	1	5	6	45	8	0	1	1	10
	ECHL	Totals	80	2	14	16	167	—	—	—	—	—

Born; 7/27/73, Brandon, Alberta. 6-3, 200. Drafted by Lake Charles Ice Pirates in WPHL Expansion draft. Returned to Central Texas Stampede for rights to Daniel Berthiaume. (6/2/97).

Muskegon's Scott Feasby attempts to corral Border Cat threat Bob McKillop.   Photo courtesy of Border Cats.

174

Robert Haddock — Defenseman

Season	Team	League	GP	G	A	PTS	PIM	GP	G	A	PTS	PIM
93-94	Erie	ECHL	8	0	2	2	16	—	—	—	—	—
93-94	Huntington	ECHL	2	0	0	0	17	—	—	—	—	—
94-95	Tallahassee	ECHL	43	5	14	19	55	13	1	6	7	24
95-96	Bakersfield	WCHL	39	2	17	19	81	—	—	—	—	—
96-97	El Paso	WPHL	55	8	22	30	97	6	0	2	2	14
	ECHL	Totals	53	5	16	21	88	13	1	6	7	24

Born; 4/7/70, Montreal, Quebec. 5-11, 195. Member of 1996-97 WPHL Champion El Paso Buzzards.

Brad Haelzle — Right Wing

Season	Team	League	GP	G	A	PTS	PIM	GP	G	A	PTS	PIM
94-95	Toledo	ECHL	—	—	—	—	—	3	0	1	1	4
95-96	Fresno	WCHL	53	22	20	42	45	7	2	4	6	0
96-97	Fresno	WCHL	49	16	25	41	120	3	0	0	0	24
	WCHL	Totals	102	38	45	83	165	10	2	4	6	24

Born; 1/5/70, Waterloo, Ontario. 6-0, 180.

Ryan Haggerty — Left Wing

Season	Team	League	GP	G	A	PTS	PIM	GP	G	A	PTS	PIM
95-96	Cape Breton	AHL	29	5	6	11	12	—	—	—	—	—
95-96	Wheeling	ECHL	4	0	2	2	0	—	—	—	—	—
96-97	Wheeling	ECHL	67	17	31	48	22	3	1	2	3	0
	ECHL	Totals	71	17	33	50	22	3	1	2	3	0

Born; 5/2/73, Rye, New York. 6-1, 185. Drafted by Edmonton Oilers (6th choice, 93rd overall) in 1991 Entry Draft.

Sean Haggerty — Left Wing

Season	Team	League	GP	G	A	PTS	PIM	GP	G	A	PTS	PIM
95-96	Toronto	NHL	1	0	0	0	0	—	—	—	—	—
95-96	Worcester	AHL	—	—	—	—	—	1	0	0	0	2
96-97	Kentucky	AHL	77	13	22	35	60	4	1	0	1	4
	AHL	Totals	77	13	22	35	60	5	1	0	1	6

Born; 2/11/76, Rye, New York. 6-1, 186. Drafted by Toronto Maple Leafs (2nd choice, 48th overall) in 1994 Entry Draft. Traded to New York Islanders by Toronto with Darby Hendrickson, Kenny Jonsson and Toronto's first round choice (Roberto Luongo) in 1997 Entry Draft for Wendel Clark, Mathieu Schneider and D. J. Smith (3/13/96).

Sean Halifax — Defenseman

Season	Team	League	GP	G	A	PTS	PIM	GP	G	A	PTS	PIM
96-97	Knoxville	ECHL	63	2	15	17	107	—	—	—	—	—

Born; Fruitvale, British Columbia. 6-3, 210.

Bob Halkidis — Defenseman

Season	Team	League	GP	G	A	PTS	PIM	GP	G	A	PTS	PIM
84-85	Buffalo	AHL	—	—	—	—	—	4	0	0	0	19
85-86	Buffalo	NHL	37	1	9	10	115	—	—	—	—	—
86-87	Buffalo	NHL	6	1	1	2	19	—	—	—	—	—
86-87	Rochester	AHL	59	1	8	9	144	8	0	0	0	43
87-88	Buffalo	NHL	30	0	3	3	115	4	0	0	0	22
87-88	Rochester	AHL	15	2	5	7	50	—	—	—	—	—
88-89	Buffalo	NHL	16	0	1	1	66	—	—	—	—	—
88-89	Rochester	AHL	16	0	6	6	64	—	—	—	—	—

Season	Team	League	GP	G	A	PTS	PIM	GP	G	A	PTS	PIM
89-90	Los Angeles	NHL	20	0	4	4	56	8	0	1	1	8
89-90	Rochester	AHL	18	1	13	14	70	—	—	—	—	—
89-90	New Haven	AHL	30	3	17	20	67	—	—	—	—	—
90-91	Los Angeles	NHL	34	1	3	4	133	3	0	0	0	0
90-91	New Haven	AHL	7	1	3	4	10	—	—	—	—	—
90-91	Phoenix	IHL	4	1	5	6	6	—	—	—	—	—
91-92	Toronto	NHL	46	3	3	6	145	—	—	—	—	—
92-93	St. John's	AHL	29	2	13	15	61	—	—	—	—	—
92-93	Milwaukee	IHL	26	0	9	9	79	5	0	1	1	27
93-94	Detroit	NHL	28	1	4	5	93	1	0	0	0	2
93-94	Adirondack	AHL	15	0	6	6	46	—	—	—	—	—
94-95	Detroit	NHL	4	0	1	1	6	—	—	—	—	—
94-95	Tampa Bay	NHL	27	1	3	4	40	—	—	—	—	—
95-96	Tampa Bay	NHL	3	0	0	0	7	—	—	—	—	—
95-96	Islanders	NHL	5	0	0	0	30	—	—	—	—	—
95-96	Atlanta	IHL	21	1	7	8	62	—	—	—	—	—
95-96	Indianapolis	IHL	3	0	2	2	8	—	—	—	—	—
95-96	Utah	IHL	27	0	7	7	72	12	1	1	2	36
96-97	Carolina	AHL	41	5	13	18	47	—	—	—	—	—
	NHL	Totals	256	8	32	40	825	20	0	1	1	51
	AHL	Totals	230	15	84	99	559	8	0	0	0	43
	IHL	Totals	81	2	30	32	227	17	1	2	3	63

Born; 3/5/66, Toronto, Ontario. 5-11, 205. Drafted by Buffalo Sabres (4th choice, 81st overall) in 1984 Entry Draft. Traded to Los Angeles Kings by Buffalo with future considerations for Dale DeGray and future considerations (11/24/89). Signed as a free agent by Toronto Maple Leafs (7/24/91). Signed as a free agent by Detroit Red Wings (9/2/93). Claimed on waivers by Tampa Bay Lightning from Detroit (2/10/95). Traded to New York Islanders by Chicago Balckhawks for Danton Cole (2/2/96). Signed as a free agent by Florida Panthers (7/25/96). Member of 1986-87 AHL champion Rochester Americans. Member of 1995-96 IHL champion Utah Grizzlies.

Steven Halko — Defenseman

			Regular Season					Playoffs				
Season	Team	League	GP	G	A	PTS	PIM	GP	G	A	PTS	PIM
96-97	Springfield	AHL	70	1	5	6	37	11	0	2	2	8

Born; 3/8/74, Etobicoke, Ontario. 6-1, 183. Drafted by Hartford Whalers (10th choice, 225th overall) in 1992 Entry Draft.

Mike Hall — Center

			Regular Season					Playoffs				
Season	Team	League	GP	G	A	PTS	PIM	GP	G	A	PTS	PIM
96-97	Baltimore	AHL	2	0	1	1	2	—	—	—	—	—
96-97	Baton Rouge	ECHL	16	4	5	9	8	—	—	—	—	—
96-97	Raleigh	ECHL	22	3	8	11	26	—	—	—	—	—
96-97	Jacksonville	ECHL	19	8	8	16	8	—	—	—	—	—
	ECHL	Totals	57	15	21	36	42	—	—	—	—	—

Born; 2/13/73, Ottawa, Ontario. 6-2, 180. Last amateur club; Bowling Green State (CCHA).

Todd Hall — Defenseman

			Regular Season					Playoffs				
Season	Team	League	GP	G	A	PTS	PIM	GP	G	A	PTS	PIM
96-97	Binghamton	AHL	40	3	7	10	12	4	0	1	1	0
96-97	Charlotte	ECHL	13	0	2	2	8	—	—	—	—	—

Born; 1/22/73, Hamden, Connecticut. 6-1, 212. Drafted by Hartford Whalers (3rd choice, 53rd overall) in 1991 Entry Draft.

Trevor Halverson — Left Wing

			Regular Season					Playoffs				
Season	Team	League	GP	G	A	PTS	PIM	GP	G	A	PTS	PIM
91-92	Baltimore	AHL	74	10	11	21	181	—	—	—	—	—
92-93	Baltimore	AHL	67	19	21	40	170	2	1	0	1	0
92-93	Hampton Roads	ECHL	9	7	5	12	6	—	—	—	—	—
93-94	San Diego	IHL	58	4	9	13	115	—	—	—	—	—

Season	Team	League	GP	G	A	PTS	PIM	GP	G	A	PTS	PIM
93-94	Milwaukee	IHL	4	1	0	1	8	2	0	0	0	17
94-95	Portland	AHL	5	0	1	1	9	—	—	—	—	—
94-95	Hampton Roads	ECHL	42	14	26	40	194	4	1	1	2	2
95-96	Portland	AHL	3	0	1	1	0	—	—	—	—	—
95-96	Las Vegas	IHL	22	6	9	15	86	—	—	—	—	—
95-96	Utah	IHL	1	0	1	1	0	—	—	—	—	—
95-96	Indianapolis	IHL	12	0	1	1	18	5	0	0	0	4
95-96	Hampton Roads	ECHL	38	34	27	61	152	—	—	—	—	—
96-97	Portland	AHL	50	9	8	17	157	3	1	1	2	4
	AHL	Totals	199	38	42	80	517	5	2	1	3	4
	IHL	Totals	97	11	20	31	227	7	0	0	0	21
	ECHL	Totals	89	55	58	113	352	4	1	1	2	2

Born; 4/6/71, White River, Ontario. 6-1, 200. Drafted by Washington Capitals (2nd choice, 21st overall) in 1991 Entry Draft. Claimed by Anaheim Mighty Ducks in Expansion Draft (6/24/93).

Craig Hamelin — Center

			Regular Season					Playoffs				
Season	Team	League	GP	G	A	PTS	PIM	GP	G	A	PTS	PIM
95-96	Louisville	ECHL	2	0	2	2	4	—	—	—	—	—
95-96	Jacksonville	ECHL	2	0	1	1	2	—	—	—	—	—
95-96	Tulsa	CeHL	49	22	36	58	38	6	1	4	5	14
96-97	New Mexico	WPHL	3	3	1	4	0	4	1	0	1	0
	ECHL	Totals	4	0	3	3	6	—	—	—	—	—

Born; Renfrew, Ontario. 5-9, 175.

Hugo Hamelin — Goaltender

			Regular Season							Playoffs					
Season	Team	League	GP	W	L	T	MIN	SO	GAVG	GP	W	L	MIN	SO	GAVG
95-96	Memphis	CeHL	16	7	7	2	904	1	4.25	—	—	—	—	—	—
95-96	Huntsville	SHL	26	11	13	2	1522	0	4.93	—	—	—	—	—	—
96-97	Kansas City	IHL	1	0	0	0	2	0	0.00	—	—	—	—	—	—
96-97	Memphis	CeHL	35	16	14	2	1918	0	3.75	—	—	—	—	—	—
96-97	Wichita	CeHL	5	2	2	1	298	0	3.83	9	4	5	537	0	3.80
	CeHL	Totals	56	25	23	5	3120	1	3.90	9	4	5	537	0	3.80

Born; 5/5/74, Granby, Quebec. 6-0, 175.

Martin Hamrlik — Defenseman

			Regular Season					Playoffs				
Season	Team	League	GP	G	A	PTS	PIM	GP	G	A	PTS	PIM
92-93	Springfield	AHL	8	1	3	4	16	—	—	—	—	—
93-94	Springfield	AHL	1	0	0	0	0	—	—	—	—	—
93-94	Peoria	IHL	47	1	11	12	61	6	0	1	1	2
94-95	Peoria	IHL	77	5	13	18	120	3	0	0	0	2
95-96	Peoria	IHL	65	6	25	31	91	—	—	—	—	—
96-97	Long Beach	IHL	64	3	14	17	110	—	—	—	—	—
96-97	Orlando	IHL	16	3	3	6	21	10	1	6	7	10
	IHL	Totals	269	18	66	84	403	19	1	7	8	14
	AHL	Totals	9	1	3	4	16	—	—	—	—	—

Born; 5/6/73, Zlin, Czechoslovakia. 5-11, 176. Drafted by Hartford Whalers (2nd choice, 31st overall) in 1991 Entry Draft. Traded to St. Louis Blues by Hartford for cash (11/12/93).

Trevor Hanas — Right Wing

			Regular Season					Playoffs				
Season	Team	League	GP	G	A	PTS	PIM	GP	G	A	PTS	PIM
96-97	Peoria	ECHL	62	20	32	52	167	8	5	9	14	34

Last amateur club; Lethbridge (WHL).

Jason Hanchuk — Defenseman

			Regular Season					Playoffs				
Season	Team	League	GP	G	A	PTS	PIM	GP	G	A	PTS	PIM
95-96	Louisville	ECHL	65	9	34	43	46	3	0	1	1	4
96-97	Louisville	ECHL	62	10	16	26	58	—	—	—	—	—
	ECHL	Totals	127	19	50	69	104	3	0	1	1	4

Born; 1/16/71, Ottawa, Ontario. 6-0, 205.

Darrin Hands — Right Wing

			Regular Season					Playoffs				
Season	Team	League	GP	G	A	PTS	PIM	GP	G	A	PTS	PIM
96-97	Amarillo	WPHL	26	1	5	6	34	—	—	—	—	—

Born; 1/16/72, Jackson, Michigan. 6-0, 210.

Ron Handy — Center

			Regular Season					Playoffs				
Season	Team	League	GP	G	A	PTS	PIM	GP	G	A	PTS	PIM
82-83	Indianapolis	CHL	9	2	7	9	0	10	3	8	11	18
83-84	Indianapolis	CHL	66	29	46	75	40	10	2	5	7	0
84-85	Islanders	NHL	10	0	2	2	0	—	—	—	—	—
84-85	Springfield	AHL	69	29	35	64	38	3	2	2	4	0
85-86	Springfield	AHL	79	13	30	61	66	—	—	—	—	—
86-87	Indianapolis	IHL	82	*55	80	135	57	6	4	3	7	2
87-88	St. Louis	NHL	4	0	1	1	0	—	—	—	—	—
87-88	Peoria	IHL	78	53	63	116	61	7	2	3	5	4
88-89	Indianapolis	IHL	81	43	57	100	52	—	—	—	—	—
89-90	Fort Wayne	IHL	82	36	39	75	52	5	3	1	4	0
90-91	Kansas City	IHL	64	42	39	81	41	—	—	—	—	—
91-92	Kansas City	IHL	38	16	19	35	30	15	13	8	21	8
92-93	Kansas City	IHL	6	1	1	2	2	—	—	—	—	—
92-93	Peoria	IHL	18	0	7	7	16	—	—	—	—	—
92-93	Wichita	CeHL	11	6	12	18	20	—	—	—	—	—
93-94	Wichita	CeHL	57	29	80	109	98	11	12	10	22	12
94-95	Denver	IHL	1	0	0	0	0	—	—	—	—	—
94-95	Wichita	CeHL	46	24	45	69	72	11	15	16	31	4
95-96	Huntsville	SHL	3	3	1	4	0	—	—	—	—	—
95-96	Louisiana	ECHL	58	20	65	85	34	5	2	4	6	2
96-97	Louisiana	ECHL	66	33	*67	100	58	17	5	17	22	0
	NHL	Totals	14	0	3	3	0	—	—	—	—	—
	IHL	Totals	450	246	266	512	311	33	22	15	37	14
	AHL	Totals	148	42	65	107	104	3	2	2	4	0
	CHL	Totals	75	31	53	84	40	20	5	13	18	18
	ECHL	Totals	124	53	132	185	92	22	7	21	28	2
	CeHL	Totals	114	59	137	196	190	22	27	26	53	16

Born; 1/5/63, Toronto, Ontario. 5-11, 175. Drafted by New York Islanders (3rd choice, 57th overall) in 1981 Entry Draft. Signed as a free agent by St. Louis Blues (9/87). Named player/coach of Indianapolis Ice (2/89). Released by St. Louis Blues (5/89). Signed as a free agent by Ft. Wayne Komets (9/89). Signed as a free agent by Kansas City Blades (8/90). Member of 1982-83 Central League champion Indianapolis Checkers. 1983-84 Central League Second Team All-Star. 1986-87 IHL Second Team All-Star. 1987-88 IHL First Team All-Star. 1991-92 IHL Playoff MVP. Member of 1991-92 IHL champion Kansas City Blades. 1993-94 CeHL Second Team All-Star. 1993-94 CeHL Playoff MVP. Member of 1993-94 CeHL champion Wichita Thunder. 1994-95 CeHL Playoff MVP. Member of 1994-95 CeHL champion Wichita Thunder.

Ben Hankinson — Right Wing

			Regular Season					Playoffs				
Season	Team	League	GP	G	A	PTS	PIM	GP	G	A	PTS	PIM
91-92	Utica	AHL	77	17	16	33	186	4	3	1	4	2
92-93	New Jersey	NHL	4	2	1	3	9	—	—	—	—	—

Season	Team	League	GP	G	A	PTS	PIM	GP	G	A	PTS	PIM
92-93	Utica	AHL	75	35	27	62	145	5	2	2	4	6
93-94	New Jersey	NHL	13	1	0	1	23	2	1	0	1	4
93-94	Albany	AHL	29	9	14	23	80	5	3	1	4	6
94-95	New Jersey	NHL	8	0	0	0	7	—	—	—	—	—
94-95	Tampa Bay	NHL	18	0	2	2	6	—	—	—	—	—
94-95	Albany	AHL	1	1	0	1	6	—	—	—	—	—
95-96	Adirondack	AHL	75	25	21	46	210	3	0	0	0	8
96-97	Grand Rapids	IHL	68	16	13	29	219	5	2	2	4	4
	NHL	Totals	43	3	3	6	45	2	1	0	1	4
	AHL	Totals	257	87	78	165	627	17	8	4	12	22

Born; 5/1/69, Edina, Minnesota. 6-2, 210. Drafted by New Jersey Devils (5th choice, 107th overall) in 1987 Entry Draft. Traded to Tampa Bay Lightning with Alexander Semak for Shawn Chambers and Danton Cole (3/14/95). Traded to Detroit Red Wings by Tampa Bay with Marc Bergevin for Shawn Burr and Detroit's third round choice (later traded to the Boston Bruins) in 1996 Entry Draft (8-17-95).

Pat Hanley — Defenseman

			Regular Season					Playoffs				
Season	Team	League	GP	G	A	PTS	PIM	GP	G	A	PTS	PIM
96-97	Thunder Bay	CoHL	54	3	8	11	52	—	—	—	—	—

Born; 11/14/71, Terrance Bay, Ontario. 6-1, 196. Last amateur club; Miami of Ohio (CCHA).

Tavis Hansen — Center

			Regular Season					Playoffs				
Season	Team	League	GP	G	A	PTS	PIM	GP	G	A	PTS	PIM
94-95	Winnipeg	NHL	1	0	0	0	0	—	—	—	—	—
95-96	Springfield	AHL	67	6	16	22	85	5	1	2	3	2
96-97	Springfield	AHL	12	3	1	4	23	—	—	—	—	—
	AHL	Totals	79	9	17	26	108	5	1	2	3	2

Born; 6/17/75, Prince Albert, Saskatchewan. 6-1, 180. Drafted by Winnipeg Jets (3rd choice, 58th overall) in 1984 Entry Draft.

Michael Harder — Right Wing

			Regular Season					Playoffs				
Season	Team	League	GP	G	A	PTS	PIM	GP	G	A	PTS	PIM
96-97	Hamilton	AHL	2	0	1	1	0	—	—	—	—	—
96-97	Milwaukee	IHL	7	1	3	4	6	2	0	1	1	0

Born; 2/8/73, Winnipeg, Manitoba. 6-0, 180. Last amateur club; Colgate (ECAC).

Mike Harding — Right Wing

			Regular Season					Playoffs				
Season	Team	League	GP	G	A	PTS	PIM	GP	G	A	PTS	PIM
95-96	Springfield	AHL	42	5	3	8	50	—	—	—	—	—
95-96	Richmond	ECHL	19	4	4	8	40	—	—	—	—	—
96-97	Springfield	AHL	5	0	2	2	2	—	—	—	—	—
96-97	Richmond	ECHL	67	29	29	58	141	7	1	2	3	18
	AHL	Totals	47	5	5	10	52	—	—	—	—	—
	ECHL	Totals	86	33	33	66	181	7	1	2	3	18

Born; 2/24/71, Edsow, Alberta. 6-4, 225. Drafted by Hartford Whalers (6th choice, 119th overall) in 1991 Entry Draft.

Brett Harkins — Left Wing

			Regular Season					Playoffs				
Season	Team	League	GP	G	A	PTS	PIM	GP	G	A	PTS	PIM
93-94	Adirondack	AHL	80	22	47	69	23	10	1	5	6	4
94-95	Boston	NHL	1	0	1	1	0	—	—	—	—	—
94-95	Providemce	AHL	80	23	*69	92	32	13	8	14	22	4
95-96	Florida	NHL	8	0	3	3	6	—	—	—	—	—
95-96	Carolina	AHL	55	23	*71	94	172	—	—	—	—	—
96-97	Boston	NHL	44	4	14	18	8	—	—	—	—	—
96-97	Providence	AHL	28	9	31	40	32	10	2	10	12	0
	NHL	Totals	53	4	18	22	14	—	—	—	—	—
	AHL	Totals	243	77	218	295	259	33	11	29	40	8

Born; 7/2/70, North Ridgeville, Ohio. 6-1, 185. Drafted by New York Islanders (9th choice, 133rd overall) in 1989 Entry Draft. Signed as a free agent by Boston Bruins (7/1/94). Signed as a free agent by Florida Panthers (7/24/95). Signed as a free agent by Boston (1996).

Todd Harkins — Center

Season	Team	League	GP	G	A	PTS	PIM	GP	G	A	PTS	PIM
90-91	Salt Lake City	IHL	79	15	27	42	113	3	0	0	0	0
91-92	Calgary	NHL	5	0	0	0	7	—	—	—	—	—
91-92	Salt Lake City	IHL	72	32	30	62	67	5	1	1	2	0
92-93	Calgary	NHL	15	2	3	5	22	—	—	—	—	—
92-93	Salt Lake City	IHL	53	13	21	34	90	—	—	—	—	—
93-94	Hartford	NHL	28	1	0	1	49	—	—	—	—	—
93-94	Saint John	AHL	38	13	9	22	64	—	—	—	—	—
93-94	Springfield	AHL	1	0	3	3	2	9	0	0	0	6
94-95	Chicago	IHL	52	18	25	43	136	—	—	—	—	—
94-95	Houston	IHL	25	9	10	19	77	4	1	1	2	28
95-96	Carolina	AHL	69	27	28	55	172	—	—	—	—	—
96-97	Fort Worth	IHL	60	12	13	25	131	—	—	—	—	—
96-97	Phoenix	IHL	16	4	3	7	24	—	—	—	—	—
	NHL	Totals	48	3	3	6	78	—	—	—	—	—
	IHL	Totals	357	103	129	232	638	12	2	2	4	28
	AHL	Totals	108	40	40	80	238	9	0	0	0	6

Born; 10/8/68, Cleveland, Ohio. 6-3, 210. Drafted by Calgary Flames (2nd choice, 42nd overall) in 1988 Entry Draft. Traded to Hartford Whalers by Calgary for Scott Morrow (1/24/94).

David Harlock — Defenseman

Season	Team	League	GP	G	A	PTS	PIM	GP	G	A	PTS	PIM
93-94	Toronto	NHL	6	0	0	0	0	—	—	—	—	—
93-94	St. John's	AHL	10	0	3	3	2	9	0	0	0	6
93-94	Canadian	National										
94-95	Toronto	NHL	1	0	0	0	0	—	—	—	—	—
94-95	St. John's	AHL	58	0	6	6	44	5	0	0	0	0
95-96	Toronto	NHL	1	0	0	0	0	—	—	—	—	—
95-96	St. John's	AHL	77	0	12	12	92	4	0	1	1	2
96-97	San Antonio	IHL	69	3	10	13	82	9	0	0	0	10
	NHL	Totals	8	0	0	0	0	—	—	—	—	—
	AHL	Totals	145	0	21	21	138	18	0	1	1	8

Born; 3/16/71, Toronto, Ontario. 6-2, 195. Drafted by New Jersey Devils (2nd choice, 24th overall) in 1990 Entry Draft. Signed as a free agent by Toronto Maple Leafs (8/20/93).

Duane Harmer — Defenseman

Season	Team	League	GP	G	A	PTS	PIM	GP	G	A	PTS	PIM
95-96	Roanoke	ECHL	69	5	13	18	120	3	0	0	0	4
96-97	Roanoke	ECHL	70	4	28	32	122	4	0	4	4	2
	ECHL	Totals	139	9	41	50	242	7	0	4	4	6

Born; 6/3/74, Fullarton, Ontario. 6-0, 190.

Ryan Harnett — Right Wing

Season	Team	League	GP	G	A	PTS	PIM	GP	G	A	PTS	PIM
96-97	Alaska	WCHL	2	0	0	0	0	—	—	—	—	—
96-97	Brantford	CoHL	37	3	8	11	10	—	—	—	—	—

Born; 2/19/75, Uxbridge, Ontario. 6-1, 195.

Derek Harper — Defenseman

Season	Team	League	GP	G	A	PTS	PIM	GP	G	A	PTS	PIM
95-96	Tulsa	CeHL	4	0	0	0	12	—	—	—	—	—
95-96	Memphis	CeHL	3	0	0	0	0	—	—	—	—	—
95-96	Jacksonville	SHL	46	4	18	22	53	—	—	—	—	—
96-97	Memphis	CeHL	45	1	7	8	169	18	1	0	1	26
	CeHL	Totals	52	1	7	8	181	18	1	0	1	26

Born; 1/5/73, Princeton, British Columbia. 6-3, 210.

Kelly Harper — Right Wing

Season	Team	League	GP	G	A	PTS	PIM	GP	G	A	PTS	PIM
94-95	Huntington	ECHL	60	12	14	26	100	4	2	1	3	2
95-96	Detroit	CoHL	7	1	1	2	7	—	—	—	—	—
95-96	Huntington	ECHL	57	13	32	45	95	—	—	—	—	—
96-97	Huntington	ECHL	58	14	49	63	52	—	—	—	—	—
	ECHL	Totals	175	39	95	134	247	4	2	1	3	2

Born; 5/9/72, Sudbury, Ontario. 6-3, 190. Drafted by Calgary Flames (8th choice, 151st overall) in 1991 Entry Draft.

Regan Harper — Defenseman

Season	Team	League	GP	G	A	PTS	PIM	GP	G	A	PTS	PIM
96-97	Oklahoma City	CeHL	58	4	17	21	59	4	1	0	1	14

Born; 11/23/71, Birch Hills, Saskatchewan. 6-2, 190.

Ross Harris — Left Wing

Season	Team	League	GP	G	A	PTS	PIM	GP	G	A	PTS	PIM
94-95	Dallas	CeHL	40	14	21	35	15	—	—	—	—	—
94-95	San Antonio	CeHL	13	2	2	4	16	—	—	—	—	—
95-96	Bakersfield	WCHL	58	35	48	83	77	—	—	—	—	—
96-97	Oklahoma City	CeHL	15	3	4	7	4	—	—	—	—	—
96-97	Bakersfield	WCHL	22	8	7	15	42	—	—	—	—	—
96-97	Reno	WCHL	35	20	23	43	24	—	—	—	—	—
	WCHL	Totals	115	63	78	141	143	—	—	—	—	—
	CeHL	Totals	68	19	27	46	31	—	—	—	—	—

Born; 12/14/73, Victoria, British Columbia. 6-0, 185. 1995-96 WCHL Second Team All-Star.

Sean Harris — Right Wing

Season	Team	League	GP	G	A	PTS	PIM	GP	G	A	PTS	PIM
96-97	Port Huron	CoHL	3	1	0	1	17	—	—	—	—	—
96-97	Madison	CoHL	25	4	4	8	63	3	0	0	0	0
	CoHL	Totals	28	5	4	9	80	3	0	0	0	0

Born; 8/4/75, Sarnia, Ontario. 5-10, 190.

Tim Harris — Right Wing

Season	Team	League	GP	G	A	PTS	PIM	GP	G	A	PTS	PIM
93-94	South Carolina	ECHL	60	13	35	48	137	2	0	1	1	2
94-95	Utica	CoHL	60	15	28	43	92	6	2	2	4	16
95-96	Detroit	CoHL	59	22	23	45	148	10	1	3	4	14
96-97	Port Huron	CoHL	47	6	14	20	65	—	—	—	—	—
96-97	Utica	CoHL	20	10	10	20	23	3	1	1	2	0
	CoHL	Totals	186	53	75	128	328	19	4	6	10	30

Born; 10/16/67, Uxbridge, Ontario. 6-2, 190. Drafted by Calgary Flames (5th choice, 70th overall) in 1987 Entry Draft.

Todd Harris — Defenseman

Season	Team	League	GP	G	A	PTS	PIM	GP	G	A	PTS	PIM
93-94	Birmingham	ECHL	57	2	15	17	93	—	—	—	—	—
94-95	Birmingham	ECHL	37	3	17	20	50	—	—	—	—	—
94-95	Erie	ECHL	27	6	7	13	49	—	—	—	—	—
95-96	Erie	ECHL	3	1	0	1	0	—	—	—	—	—
95-96	Oklahoma City	CeHL	63	13	52	65	139	13	4	2	6	18
96-97	Oklahoma City	CeHL	16	2	4	6	47	—	—	—	—	—
96-97	New Mexico	WPHL	11	1	3	4	21	—	—	—	—	—
	ECHL	Totals	124	12	39	51	192	—	—	—	—	—
	CeHL	Totals	79	15	56	71	186	13	4	2	6	18

Born; 5/11/72, Calgary, Alberta. 6-4, 210. Drafted by St. Louis Blues (10th choice, 206th overall) in 1992 Entry Draft. Member of 1995-96 CeHL champion Oklahoma City Blazers.

Brad Harrison — Right Wing

Season	Team	League	GP	G	A	PTS	PIM	GP	G	A	PTS	PIM
94-95	Erie	ECHL	34	14	7	21	129	—	—	—	—	—
95-96	Erie	ECHL	66	13	25	38	321	—	—	—	—	—
96-97	Amarillo	WPHL	15	5	7	12	20	—	—	—	—	—
96-97	New Mexico	WPHL	18	3	2	5	101	—	—	—	—	—
	ECHL	Totals	100	27	32	59	450	—	—	—	—	—
	WPHL	Totals	33	8	9	17	121	—	—	—	—	—

Born;

Dan Harrison — Defenseman

Season	Team	League	GP	G	A	PTS	PIM	GP	G	A	PTS	PIM
96-97	Hampton Roads	ECHL	5	1	3	4	0	—	—	—	—	—
96-97	Johnstown	ECHL	26	3	20	23	91	—	—	—	—	—
	ECHL	Totals	31	4	23	27	91	—	—	—	—	—

Born; 4/22/75, Newmarket, Ontario. 5-11, 180. Last amateur club; Ohio State (CCHA).

Ryan Harrison — Center

Season	Team	League	GP	G	A	PTS	PIM	GP	G	A	PTS	PIM
94-95	Tulsa	CeHL	33	13	14	27	39	—	—	—	—	—
95-96	Tulsa	CeHL	54	23	24	47	48	6	3	1	4	4
96-97	Tulsa	CeHL	46	15	10	25	23	5	0	1	1	4
	CeHL	Totals	133	51	48	99	110	11	3	2	5	8

Born; 12/12/71, Kamloops, British Columbia. 5-10, 183.

Mike Hartman — Left Wing

Season	Team	League	GP	G	A	PTS	PIM	GP	G	A	PTS	PIM
86-87	Buffalo	NHL	17	3	3	6	69	—	—	—	—	—
87-88	Buffalo	NHL	18	3	1	4	90	6	0	0	0	35
87-88	Rochester	AHL	57	13	14	27	283	4	1	0	1	22
88-89	Buffalo	NHL	70	8	9	17	316	5	0	0	0	34
89-90	Buffalo	NHL	60	11	10	21	211	6	0	0	0	18
90-91	Buffalo	NHL	60	9	3	12	204	2	0	0	0	17
91-92	Winnipeg	NHL	75	4	4	8	264	2	0	0	0	2
92-93	Tampa Bay	NHL	58	4	4	8	154	—	—	—	—	—
92-93	Rangers	NHL	3	0	0	0	6	—	—	—	—	—
93-94	Rangers	NYR	35	1	1	2	70	—	—	—	—	—
94-95	Rangers	NHL	1	0	0	0	4	—	—	—	—	—
94-95	Detroit	IHL	6	1	0	1	52	1	0	0	0	0

			GP	G	A	PTS	PIM	GP	G	A	PTS	PIM
95-96	Orlando	IHL	77	14	10	24	243	21	2	2	4	31
96-97	Hershey	AHL	42	5	8	13	116	1	0	0	0	0
	NHL	Totals	397	43	35	78	1388	21	0	0	0	106
	AHL	Totals	99	18	22	40	399	5	1	0	1	22
	IHL	Totals	83	15	10	23	295	22	2	2	4	31

Born; 2/7/67, Detroit, Michigan. 6-0, 190. Drafted by Buffalo Sabres (8th choice, 131st overall) in 1986 Entry Draft. Traded to Winnipeg Jets by Buffalo with Darrin Shannon and Dean Kennedy for Dave McLlwain, Gord Donnelly, Winnipeg's fifth round choice (Yuri Khmylev) in 1992 Entry Draft and future considerations (10/11/91). Claimed by Tampa Bay Lightning from Winnipeg in Expansion Draft (6/18/92). Traded to New York Rangers by Tampa Bay for Randy Gilhen (3/22/93). Member of 1996-97 AHL Champion Hershey Bears.

Rob Hartnell — Center

			Regular Season					Playoffs				
Season	Team	League	GP	G	A	PTS	PIM	GP	G	A	PTS	PIM
93-94	Richmond	ECHL	29	4	11	15	87	—	—	—	—	—
93-94	Dayton	ECHL	37	9	15	24	133	3	0	0	0	20
94-95	Dayton	ECHL	62	21	26	47	211	7	1	1	2	15
95-96	Huntington	ECHL	35	8	16	24	132	—	—	—	—	—
96-97	El Paso	WPHL	47	23	37	60	76	—	—	—	—	—
96-97	Waco	WPHL	20	8	18	26	18	—	—	—	—	—
	ECHL	Totals	163	42	68	110	563	10	1	1	2	15
	WPHL	Totals	67	31	55	86	94	—	—	—	—	—

Born; 11/18/72, Rocky Mountain House, Alberta. 5-9, 170.

Brett Hauer — Defenseman

			Regular Season					Playoffs				
Season	Team	League	GP	G	A	PTS	PIM	GP	G	A	PTS	PIM
93-94	United States	National	N/A					—	—	—	—	—
93-94	Las Vegas	IHL	21	0	7	7	8	1	0	0	0	0
94-95	Sweden		N/A									
95-96	Edmonton	NHL	29	4	2	6	30	—	—	—	—	—
95-96	Cape Breton	AHL	17	3	5	8	29	—	—	—	—	—
96-97	Chicago	IHL	81	10	30	40	50	4	2	0	2	4
	IHL	Totals	102	10	37	47	58	5	2	0	2	4

Born; 7/11/71, Edina, Minnesota. 6-2, 205. Drafted by Vancouver Canucks (3rd choice, 71st overall) in 1989 Entry Draft. Traded to Edmonton Oilers by Vancouver for a conditional draft pick.

Kyle Haviland — Defenseman

			Regular Season					Playoffs				
Season	Team	League	GP	G	A	PTS	PIM	GP	G	A	PTS	PIM
92-93	Roanoke	ECHL	3	0	0	0	32	—	—	—	—	—
93-94	Memphis	CeHL	59	2	11	13	151	—	—	—	—	—
94-95	Memphis	CeHL	61	7	19	26	215	—	—	—	—	—
95-96	Muskegon	CoHL	68	2	10	12	180	5	0	1	1	21
96-97	Austin	WPHL	40	1	4	5	130	6	0	1	1	40
	CeHL	Totals	120	9	30	39	366	—	—	—	—	—

Born; 8/10/71, Windsor, Ontario. 6-0, 215.

Todd Hawkins — Right Wing

			Regular Season					Playoffs				
Season	Team	League	GP	G	A	PTS	PIM	GP	G	A	PTS	PIM
87-88	Flint	IHL	50	13	13	26	337	16	3	5	8	*174
87-88	Fredericton	AHL	2	0	4	4	11	—	—	—	—	—
88-89	Vancouver	NHL	4	0	0	0	9	—	—	—	—	—
88-89	Milwaukee	IHL	63	12	14	26	307	9	1	0	1	33
89-90	Vancouver	NHL	4	0	0	0	6	—	—	—	—	—
89-90	Milwaukee	IHL	61	23	17	40	273	5	4	1	5	19
90-91	New Haven	AHL	22	2	5	7	66	—	—	—	—	—

Season	Team	League	GP	G	A	PTS	PIM	GP	G	A	PTS	PIM
90-91	Milwaukee	IHL	39	9	11	20	134	—	—	—	—	—
91-92	Toronto	NHL	2	0	0	0	0	—	—	—	—	—
91-92	St. John's	AHL	66	30	27	57	139	7	1	0	1	10
92-93	St. John's	AHL	72	21	41	62	103	9	1	3	4	10
93-94	Cleveland	IHL	76	19	14	33	115	—	—	—	—	—
94-95	Cleveland	IHL	4	2	0	2	29	—	—	—	—	—
94-95	Minnesota	IHL	47	10	8	18	95	3	0	1	1	12
95-96	Cincinnati	IHL	73	16	12	28	65	17	7	4	11	32
96-97	Cincinnati	IHL	81	13	13	26	162	3	0	1	1	2
	NHL	Totals	10	0	0	0	15	—	—	—	—	—
	IHL	Totals	494	117	102	219	1517	53	15	12	27	272
	AHL	Totals	162	53	77	130	319	16	2	3	5	20

Born; 8/2/66, Kingston, Ontario. 6-1, 195. Drafted by Vancouver Canucks (10th choice, 217th overall) in 1986 Entry Draft. Traded to Toronto Maple Leafs by Vancouver for Brian Blad (1/22/91). Signed as a free agent by Pittsburgh Penguins (8/20/93).

Joe Hawley — Center

Season	Team	League	GP	G	A	PTS	PIM	GP	G	A	PTS	PIM
90-91	Peoria	IHL	5	0	0	0	0	10	1	1	2	8
91-92	Dayton	ECHL	7	3	6	9	12	—	—	—	—	—
91-92	Peoria	IHL	40	6	7	13	42	—	—	—	—	—
92-93	Peoria	IHL	50	12	11	23	52	—	—	—	—	—
93-94	Muskegon	CoHL	45	19	33	52	88	1	0	0	0	0
94-95	Charlotte	ECHL	33	19	22	41	57	—	—	—	—	—
94-95	Roanoke	ECHL	20	4	2	6	15	8	2	3	5	40
95-96	Brantford	CoHL	64	32	65	97	114	12	4	13	17	10
96-97	Brantford	CoHL	11	2	11	13	30	3	2	1	3	8
	IHL	Totals	95	18	18	36	94	—	—	—	—	—
	CoHL	Totals	120	53	109	162	232	16	6	14	20	18
	ECHL	Totals	60	26	30	56	84	8	2	3	5	40

Born; 3/13/71, Peterborough, Ontario. 5-10, 185. Drafted by St. Louis Blues (8th choice, 222nd overall) in 1990 Entry Draft. Member of 1990-91 IHL champion Peoria Rivermen.

Kent Hawley — Center

Season	Team	League	GP	G	A	PTS	PIM	GP	G	A	PTS	PIM
88-89	Hershey	AHL	54	9	17	26	47	—	—	—	—	—
89-90	Hampton Roads	ECHL	13	5	6	11	12	5	2	3	5	17
89-90	Hershey	AHL	24	6	4	10	28	—	—	—	—	—
90-91	Hershey	AHL	6	1	1	2	4	—	—	—	—	—
90-91	Hampton Roads	ECHL	43	17	28	45	95	14	5	9	14	32
91-92	San Diego	IHL	1	0	2	2	0	3	1	0	1	4
91-92	St. Thomas	CoHL	60	30	55	85	85	12	6	14	20	18
92-93	New Haven	AHL	6	1	1	2	2	—	—	—	—	—
92-93	Thunder Bay	CoHL	5	2	8	10	8	—	—	—	—	—
92-93	St. Thomas	CoHL	40	22	38	60	47	15	4	18	22	33
93-94	St. Thomas	CoHL	25	12	34	46	14	—	—	—	—	—
93-94	Brantford	CoHL	26	10	28	38	38	7	3	4	7	2
94-95	London	CoHL	61	35	59	94	54	—	—	—	—	—
95-96	Madison	CoHL	74	28	47	75	84	6	2	2	4	4
96-97	Madison	CoHL	72	28	77	105	48	5	1	5	6	2
	AHL	Totals	90	17	23	40	81	—	—	—	—	—
	CoHL	Totals	363	167	346	513	378	45	16	43	59	59
	ECHL	Totals	56	22	34	56	107	19	7	12	19	49

Born; 2/20/68, Kingston, Ontario. 6-4, 215. Drafted by Philadelphia Flyers (3rd choice, 28th overall) 6/21/86. Member of 1990-91 Riley Cup Champion Hampton Roads Admirals. Named coach of the Madison Monsters at the beginning of the 1997-98 season. 1996-97 CoHL Most Sportsmanlike Player.

Craig Hayden — Defenseman

			Regular Season					Playoffs				
Season	Team	League	GP	G	A	PTS	PIM	GP	G	A	PTS	PIM
96-97	Amarillo	WPHL	31	0	3	3	22	—	—	—	—	—

Born;

Jamie Hayden — Defenseman

			Regular Season					Playoffs				
Season	Team	League	GP	G	A	PTS	PIM	GP	G	A	PTS	PIM
92-93	Thunder Bay	CoHL	59	0	11	11	24	11	4	5	9	2
93-94	Thunder Bay	CoHL	43	2	13	15	22	—	—	—	—	—
93-94	Utica	CoHL	7	0	0	0	0	—	—	—	—	—
94-95	Thunder Bay	CoHL	32	1	5	6	21	—	—	—	—	—
94-95	Utica	CoHL	25	1	6	7	12	6	0	1	1	6
95-96	Thunder Bay	CoHL	42	2	6	8	26	—	—	—	—	—
95-96	Utica	CoHL	12	0	3	3	10	—	—	—	—	—
95-96	Brantford	CoHL	12	2	5	7	10	11	0	0	0	10
96-97	Brantford	CoHL	31	3	9	12	37	—	—	—	—	—
96-97	Utica	CoHL	35	1	9	10	24	3	0	0	0	2
	CoHL	Totals	298	12	67	79	186	31	4	6	10	20

Born; 4/19/72, Saskatoon, Saskatchewan. 6-0, 195.

Rick Hayward — Defenseman

			Regular Season					Playoffs				
Season	Team	League	GP	G	A	PTS	PIM	GP	G	A	PTS	PIM
86-87	Sherbrook	AHL	43	2	3	5	153	3	0	1	1	15
87-88	Sherbrook	AHL	22	1	5	6	91	—	—	—	—	—
87-88	Saginaw	IHL	24	3	4	7	129	—	—	—	—	—
87-88	Salt Lake City	IHL	17	1	3	4	124	13	0	1	1	120
88-89	Salt Lake City	IHL	72	4	20	24	313	10	4	3	7	42
89-90	Salt Lake City	IHL	58	5	13	18	*419	—	—	—	—	—
90-91	Los Angeles	NHL	4	0	0	0	5	—	—	—	—	—
90-91	Phoenix	IHL	60	9	13	22	369	7	1	2	3	44
91-92	Capital District	AHL	27	3	8	11	139	7	0	0	0	58
92-93	Moncton	AHL	47	1	3	4	231	4	1	1	2	27
92-93	Capital District	AHL	19	0	1	1	80	—	—	—	—	—
93-94	Cincinnati	IHL	61	2	6	8	302	8	0	1	1	*99
94-95	Cleveland	IHL	56	1	3	4	269	3	0	0	0	13
95-96	Cleveland	IHL	53	0	6	6	244	3	0	0	0	6
96-97	Cleveland	IHL	73	2	10	12	244	13	0	0	0	36
	IHL	Totals	474	27	78	105	2413	57	5	7	12	360
	AHL	Totals	158	7	20	27	694	14	1	2	3	100

Born; 2/25/66, Toledo, Ohio. 6-2, 200. Drafted by Montreal Canadiens (9th choice, 162nd overall) in 1986 Entry Draft. Traded to Calgary Flames by Montreal for Martin Nicoletti (2/20/88). Signed as a free agent by Los Angeles Kings (8/90). Signed as a free agent by New York Islanders (7/25/91). Signed as a free agent by Winnipeg Jets (7/30/92). Traded to Islanders by Winnipeg for future considerations (2/22/93). Signed as a free agent by Florida Panthers (9/7/93). Signed as a free agent by Cleveland Lumberjacks (6/24/94). Member of 1987-88 IHL champion Salt Lake City Golden Eagles.

Paul Healey — Right Wing

			Regular Season					Playoffs				
Season	Team	League	GP	G	A	PTS	PIM	GP	G	A	PTS	PIM
95-96	Hershey	AHL	60	7	15	22	35	—	—	—	—	—
96-97	Philadelphia	NHL	2	0	0	0	0	—	—	—	—	—
96-97	Philadelphia	AHL	64	21	19	40	56	10	1	4	5	10
	AHL	Totals	124	28	34	62	91	10	1	4	5	10

Born; 3/20/75, Edmonton, Alberta. 6-2, 185. Drafted by Philadelphia Flyers (7th choice, 192nd overall) in 1993 Entry Draft.

Mike Heaney — Defenseman

Season	Team	League	GP	G	A	PTS	PIM	GP	G	A	PTS	PIM
92-93	Richmond	ECHL	10	0	5	5	4	1	0	0	0	2
93-94	Richmond	ECHL	5	0	5	5	8	—	—	—	—	—
93-94	Dayton	ECHL	11	0	7	7	36	—	—	—	—	—
94-95	West Palm Beach	SUN	5	2	1	3	2	—	—	—	—	—
94-95	Daytona Beach	SUN	31	14	27	41	68	—	—	—	—	—
94-95	Wichita	CeHL	4	0	0	0	0	9	0	4	4	12
95-96	Louisiana	ECHL	59	0	6	6	137	1	0	0	0	0
96-97	Reno	WCHL	34	4	29	33	64	—	—	—	—	—
96-97	Wichita	CeHL	8	0	0	0	6	9	1	5	6	32
	ECHL	Totals	85	0	23	23	185	2	0	0	0	2
	SUN	Totals	36	16	28	44	70	—	—	—	—	—
	CeHL	Totals	12	0	0	0	6	18	1	9	10	44

Born; 5/18/69, Toronto, Ontario. 5-10, 185. Member of 1994-95 CeHL champion Wichita Thunder.

Jamie Hearn — Defenseman

Season	Team	League	GP	G	A	PTS	PIM	GP	G	A	PTS	PIM
92-93	Oklahoma City	CeHL	59	10	28	38	161	11	2	5	7	40
93-94	Wichita	CeHL	54	4	16	20	120	—	—	—	—	—
93-94	Memphis	CeHL	10	4	5	9	8	—	—	—	—	—
94-95	Memphis	CeHL	57	6	28	34	154	—	—	—	—	—
95-96	Muskegon	CoHL	48	5	22	27	139	—	—	—	—	—
95-96	Flint	CoHL	13	0	4	4	20	15	4	3	7	50
96-97	Phoenix	IHL	2	0	1	1	0	—	—	—	—	—
96-97	Waco	WPHL	62	14	39	53	166	—	—	—	—	—
	CeHL	Totals	180	24	77	101	443	11	2	5	7	40

Born; 2/23/71, Quesnel, British Columbia. 6-1, 210. Member of 1995-96 Colonial Cup Champion Flint Generals

John Heasty — Defenseman

Season	Team	League	GP	G	A	PTS	PIM	GP	G	A	PTS	PIM
91-92	Flint	CoHL	15	1	5	6	31	—	—	—	—	—
92-93	Flint	CoHL	38	5	11	16	42	5	0	2	2	2
93-94	Flint	CoHL	51	16	4	20	34	8	1	0	1	2
94-95	N/A											
95-96	Flint	CoHL	9	0	0	0	2	—	—	—	—	—
96-97	Saginaw	CoHL	1	0	0	0	0	—	—	—	—	—
96-97	Flint	CoHL	28	2	3	5	4	—	—	—	—	—
	CoHL	Totals	142	24	23	47	113	13	1	2	3	4

Born; 2/28/67, North York, Ontario. 6-0, 195.

Jason Hehr — Defenseman

Season	Team	League	GP	G	A	PTS	PIM	GP	G	A	PTS	PIM
95-96	Kansas City	IHL	7	0	1	1	11	—	—	—	—	—
95-96	Raleigh	ECHL	43	5	11	16	36	4	0	1	1	0
96-97	South Carolina	ECHL	22	6	5	11	38	17	2	7	9	27
	ECHL	Totals	65	11	16	27	74	21	2	8	10	27

Born; 2/8/71, Medicine Hat, Alberta. 6-1, 193. Drafted by New Jersey Devils (11th choice, 253rd overall) in 1991 Entry Draft. Member of 1996-97 ECHL Champion South Carolina Stingrays.

Shawn Heins — Defenseman

Season	Team	League	GP	G	A	PTS	PIM	GP	G	A	PTS	PIM
95-96	Cape Breton	AHL	1	0	0	0	0	—	—	—	—	—
95-96	Mobile	ECHL	62	7	20	27	152	—	—	—	—	—
96-97	Kansas City	IHL	6	0	0	0	9	—	—	—	—	—
96-97	Mobile	ECHL	56	6	17	23	253	3	0	2	2	2
	ECHL	Totals	118	13	37	50	405	3	0	2	2	2

Born; 12/24/73, Eganville, Ontario. 6-3, 215.

Jason Helbing — Center

Season	Team	League	GP	G	A	PTS	PIM	GP	G	A	PTS	PIM
96-97	San Antonio	CeHL	6	0	1	1	0	—	—	—	—	—
96-97	Waco	WPHL	20	1	5	6	4	—	—	—	—	—

Born; 3/29/74, Beaverdam, Wisconsin. 5-8, 172.

Sami Helenius — Defenseman

Season	Team	League	GP	G	A	PTS	PIM	GP	G	A	PTS	PIM
94-95	Saint John	AHL	69	2	5	7	217	—	—	—	—	—
95-96	Saint John	AHL	68	0	3	3	231	10	0	0	0	9
96-97	Calgary	NHL	3	0	1	1	0	—	—	—	—	—
96-97	Saint John	AHL	72	5	10	15	218	2	0	0	0	0
	AHL	Totals	209	7	18	25	666	12	0	0	0	9

Born; 1/22/74, Helsinki, Finland. 6-5, 225. Drafted by Calgary Flames (5th choice, 102nd overall) in 1992 Entry Draft.

Bryan Helmer — Defenseman

Season	Team	League	GP	G	A	PTS	PIM	GP	G	A	PTS	PIM
93-94	Albany	AHL	65	4	19	23	79	5	0	0	0	9
94-95	Albany	AHL	77	7	36	43	101	7	1	0	1	0
95-96	Albany	AHL	80	14	30	44	107	4	2	0	2	6
96-97	Albany	AHL	77	12	27	39	113	16	1	7	8	10
	AHL	Totals	299	37	112	149	400	32	4	7	11	25

Born; 7/15/72, Sault Ste. Marie, Ontario. 6-1, 190. Signed as a free agent by New Jersey Devils (7/10/94). Member of 1994-95 Calder Cup Champion Albany RiverRats.

Mike Henderson — Left Wing

Season	Team	League	GP	G	A	PTS	PIM	GP	G	A	PTS	PIM
96-97	Fresno	WCHL	14	7	3	10	95	—	—	—	—	—
96-97	Amarillo	WPHL	34	7	12	19	215	—	—	—	—	—

Born; 3/24/74, Brampton, Ontario. 6-1, 210.

Todd Henderson — Goaltender

Season	Team	League	GP	W	L	T	MIN	SO	GAVG	GP	W	L	MIN	SO	GAVG
95-96	Alaska	WCHL	33	14	13	5	1782	0	4.95	4	2	2	239	0	4.26
96-97	Alaska	WCHL	33	6	21	1	1596	0	6.84	—	—	—	—	—	—
	WCHL	Totals	66	20	34	6	3378	0	5.84	4	2	2	239	0	4.26

Born; 3/8/69, Thunder Bay, Ontario. 6-1, 168.

Dale Henry — Left Wing

Season	Team	League	GP	G	A	PTS	PIM	GP	G	A	PTS	PIM
84-85	Islanders	NHL	16	2	1	3	19	—	—	—	—	—
84-85	Springfield	AHL	67	11	20	31	133	4	0	0	0	13
85-86	Islanders	NHL	7	1	3	4	15	—	—	—	—	—
85-86	Springfield	AHL	64	14	26	40	162	—	—	—	—	—
86-87	Islanders	NHL	19	3	3	6	46	8	0	0	0	2
86-87	Springfield	AHL	23	9	14	23	49	—	—	—	—	—
87-88	Islanders	NHL	48	5	15	20	115	6	1	0	1	17
87-88	Springfield	AHL	24	9	12	21	103	—	—	—	—	—
88-89	Islanders	NHL	22	2	2	4	66	—	—	—	—	—
88-89	Springfield	AHL	50	13	21	34	83	—	—	—	—	—
90-91	Albany	IHL	55	16	22	38	87	—	—	—	—	—
90-91	Springfield	AHL	20	5	9	14	31	18	2	7	9	24
91-92	Muskegon	IHL	39	5	17	22	28	14	1	4	5	36
92-93	N/A											
93-94	Milwaukee	IHL	49	5	11	16	104	—	—	—	—	—
94-95	San Antonio	CeHL	55	28	36	64	120	13	6	8	14	25
95-96	San Antonio	CeHL	62	27	40	67	177	11	3	8	11	14
96-97	San Antonio	CeHL	23	12	19	31	48	—	—	—	—	—
	NHL	Totals	132	13	26	39	263	14	1	0	1	19
	AHL	Totals	248	61	102	163	561	22	2	7	9	37
	IHL	Totals	143	26	50	76	219	14	1	4	5	36
	CeHL	Totals	140	67	95	162	345	24	9	16	25	39

Born; 9/25/64, Prince Albert, Saskatchewan. 6-0, 200. Drafted by New York Islanders (10th choice, 157th overall) in 1983 Entry Draft. Signed as a free agent by Albany Choppers (9/90). Signed as a free agent by Springfield Indians (2/16/91). Named head coach of the San Antonio Iguanas (7/9/96). Removed as head coach of the Iguanas midway through 96-97 season. 1995-96 CeHL Second Team All-Star. Member of 1990-91 AHL champion Springfield Indians.

Ian Herbers — Defenseman

Season	Team	League	GP	G	A	PTS	PIM	GP	G	A	PTS	PIM
92-93	Cape Breton	AHL	77	7	15	22	129	10	0	1	1	16
93-94	Edmonton	NHL	22	0	2	2	32	—	—	—	—	—
93-94	Cape Breton	AHL	53	7	16	23	122	5	0	3	3	12
94-95	Cape Breton	AHL	36	1	11	12	104	—	—	—	—	—
94-95	Detroit	IHL	37	1	5	6	46	5	1	1	2	6
95-96	Detroit	IHL	73	3	11	14	140	12	3	5	8	29
96-97	Detroit	IHL	67	3	16	19	129	21	0	4	4	34
	IHL	Totals	177	7	32	39	315	38	4	10	14	69
	AHL	Totals	166	15	42	57	355	15	0	4	4	28

Born; 7/18/67, Jasper, Alberta. 6-4, 225. Drafted by Buffalo Sabres (11th choice, 190th overall) in 1987 Entry Draft. Signed as a free agent by Edmonton Oilers (9/9/92). Member of 1992-93 AHL champion Cape Breton Oilers. Member of 1996-97 IHL Champion Detroit Vipers.

Derek Herlofsky — Goaltender

Season	Team	League	GP	W	L	T	MIN	SO	GAVG	GP	W	L	MIN	SO	GAVG
95-96	Dayton	ECHL	42	19	15	4	2166	2	3.02	1	0	1	36	0	5.06
96-97	Providence	AHL	7	6	1	0	423	2	1.56	3	1	2	178	0	2.69
96-97	Michigan	IHL	9	2	4	1	442	0	3.12	—	—	—	—	—	—
96-97	Dayton	ECHL	26	17	4	4	1549	1	2.87	—	—	—	—	—	—
	ECHL	Totals	68	36	19	8	3715	3	2.96	1	0	1	36	0	5.06

Born; 10/1/71, Minneapolis, Minnesota. 5-10, 175. Drafted by Minnesota North Stars (7th choice, 184th overall) in 1991 Entry Draft.

Steve Herniman — Defenseman

Season	Team	League	GP	G	A	PTS	PIM	GP	G	A	PTS	PIM
89-90	Virginia	ECHL	31	2	4	6	238	3	0	0	0	29
89-90	Milwaukee	IHL	15	0	0	0	102	—	—	—	—	—
90-91	Richmond	ECHL	2	0	1	1	0	4	1	1	2	9
90-91	Milwaukee	IHL	38	0	0	0	86	—	—	—	—	—
90-91	Albany	IHL	7	0	1	1	36	—	—	—	—	—
91-92	Kalamazoo	IHL	64	4	6	10	271	1	0	0	0	0
92-93	Fort Wayne	IHL	8	0	1	1	23	—	—	—	—	—
92-93	Muskegon	CoHL	49	9	22	31	173	7	1	1	2	39
93-94	Muskegon	CoHL	4	0	0	0	24	—	—	—	—	—
94-95	Muskegon	CoHL	16	0	2	2	28	—	—	—	—	—
95-96	Muskegon	CoHL	71	1	3	4	158	5	0	0	0	18
96-97	Utica	CoHL	55	0	3	3	72	3	0	0	0	2
	IHL	Totals	132	4	8	12	518	1	0	0	0	0
	CoHL	Totals	195	10	30	40	455	15	1	1	2	59
	ECHL	Totals	33	2	5	7	238	7	1	1	2	38

Born; 6/9/68, Windsor, Ontario. 6-4, 215. Drafted by Vancouver Canucks (5th choice, 112th overall) in 1986 Entry Draft.

Chris Herperger — Left Wing

Season	Team	League	GP	G	A	PTS	PIM	GP	G	A	PTS	PIM
94-95	Hershey	AHL	4	0	0	0	0	—	—	—	—	—
95-96	Hershey	AHL	46	8	12	20	36	—	—	—	—	—
95-96	Baltimore	AHL	21	2	3	5	17	9	2	3	5	6
96-97	Baltimore	AHL	67	19	22	41	88	3	0	0	0	0
	AHL	Totals	138	29	37	66	141	12	2	3	5	6

Born; 2/24/74, Esterhazy, Saskatchewan. 6-0, 190. Drafted by Philadelphia Flyers (10th choice, 223rd overall) in 1992 Entry Draft. Traded by Philadelphia with Phoenix's 7th round pick in 1997 Entry Draft to Anaheim Mighty Ducks for Bob Corkum (2/6/96).

Harold Hersh — Center

Season	Team	League	GP	G	A	PTS	PIM	GP	G	A	PTS	PIM
95-96	Fredericton	AHL	63	5	17	22	30	—	—	—	—	—
96-97	Fredericton	AHL	67	11	11	22	32	—	—	—	—	—
	AHL	Totals	130	16	28	44	62	—	—	—	—	—

Born; 4/18/74, Montreal, Quebec. 6-1, 188.

Jason Herter — Defenseman

Season	Team	League	GP	G	A	PTS	PIM	GP	G	A	PTS	PIM
91-92	Milwaukee	IHL	56	7	18	25	34	1	0	0	0	2
92-93	Hamilton	AHL	70	7	16	23	68	—	—	—	—	—
93-94	Kalamazoo	IHL	68	14	28	42	92	5	3	0	3	14
94-95	Kalamazoo	IHL	60	12	20	32	70	16	2	8	10	10
95-96	Islanders	NHL	1	0	1	1	0	—	—	—	—	—
95-96	Utah	IHL	74	14	31	45	58	20	4	10	14	8
96-97	Kansas City	IHL	71	9	26	35	62	3	0	1	1	0
	IHL	Totals	329	56	123	179	316	45	9	19	28	34

Born; 10/2/70, Hafford, Saskatchewan. 6-1, 202. Drafted by Vancouver Canucks (1st choice, 8th overall) in 1989 Entry Draft. Signed as a free agent by Dallas Stars (8/6/93). Signed as a free agent by New York Islanders (8/10/95). Member of 1995-96 IHL champion Utah Grizzlies.

Jamie Heward — Defenseman

Season	Team	League	GP	G	A	PTS	PIM	GP	G	A	PTS	PIM
91-92	Muskegon	IHL	54	6	21	27	37	14	1	4	5	4
92-93	Cleveland	IHL	58	9	18	27	64	—	—	—	—	—
93-94	Cleveland	IHL	73	8	16	24	72	—	—	—	—	—
94-95	Canadian	National										
95-96	Toronto	NHL	5	0	0	0	0	—	—	—	—	—
95-96	St. John's	AHL	73	22	34	56	33	3	1	1	2	6
96-97	Toronto	NHL	20	1	4	5	6	—	—	—	—	—
96-97	St. John's	AHL	27	8	19	27	26	9	1	3	4	6
	NHL	Totals	25	1	4	5	6	—	—	—	—	—
	IHL	Totals	185	23	55	78	173	14	1	4	5	4
	AHL	Totals	100	30	53	83	59	12	2	4	6	12

Born; 3/30/71, Regina, Saskatchewan. 6-2, 198. Drafted by Pittsburgh Penguins (1st choice, 16th overall) in 1989 Entry Draft. Signed as a free agent by Toronto Maple Leafs (5/4/95). 1995-96 AHL First Team All-Star.

Mike Hiebert — Left Wing

Season	Team	League	GP	G	A	PTS	PIM	GP	G	A	PTS	PIM
96-97	Reno	WCHL	3	0	0	0	15	—	—	—	—	—
96-97	Tulsa	CeHL	15	2	3	5	66	—	—	—	—	—
96-97	San Antonio	CeHL	20	2	6	8	62	—	—	—	—	—
	CeHL	Totals	35	4	9	13	128	—	—	—	—	—

Born; 4/16/75, Winnipeg, Manitoba. 6-0, 188.

Jon Hillebrandt — Goaltender

Season	Team	League	GP	W	L	T	MIN	SO	GAVG	GP	W	L	MIN	SO	GAVG
93-94	United States	National	N/A												
93-94	Binghamton	AHL	7	1	3	0	294	0	3.67	—	—	—	—	—	—
93-94	Erie	ECHL	3	2	0	1	189	1	2.53	—	—	—	—	—	—
94-95	San Diego	IHL	1	0	1	0	40	0	9.00	—	—	—	—	—	—
94-95	Binghamton	AHL	—	—	—	—	—	—	—	1	0	0	5	0	12.00
94-95	Charlotte	ECHL	32	14	11	5	1790	0	4.05	3	0	2	179	0	4.01
95-96	Binghamton	AHL	36	15	14	2	1845	0	4.42	2	1	1	47	0	10.13
96-97	San Antonio	IHL	1	0	0	0	33	0	3.60	—	—	—	—	—	—
96-97	Chicago	IHL	2	0	1	0	54	0	4.46	—	—	—	—	—	—
96-97	Peoria	ECHL	26	18	4	3	1487	2	*2.82	2	1	0	80	0	3.00
	AHL	Totals	43	16	17	2	2139	0	4.32	3	1	1	52	0	10.38
	IHL	Totals	4	0	2	0	127	0	5.53	—	—	—	—	—	—
	ECHL	Totals	61	34	15	9	3466	1	3.44	5	1	2	259	0	3.70

Born; 12/18/71, Cottage Grove, Wisconsin. 5-10, 160. Drafted by New York Rangers (12th choice, 202nd overall) in 1990 Entry Draft.

Kevin Hilton — Center

Season	Team	League	GP	G	A	PTS	PIM	GP	G	A	PTS	PIM
96-97	Worcester	AHL	27	3	7	10	23	4	0	2	2	0
96-97	Quebec	IHL	11	1	0	1	2	—	—	—	—	—
96-97	Mississippi	ECHL	28	8	13	21	9	—	—	—	—	—

Born; 1/5/75, Trenton, Michigan. 5-11, 170. Drafted by Detroit Red Wings (3rd choice, 74th overall) in 1993 Entry Draft.

Mark Hilton — Defenseman

Season	Team	League	GP	G	A	PTS	PIM	GP	G	A	PTS	PIM
91-92	Nashville	ECHL	44	6	17	23	46	—	—	—	—	—
92-93	Louisville	ECHL	2	0	0	0	0	—	—	—	—	—

Season	Team	League	GP	G	A	PTS	PIM	GP	G	A	PTS	PIM
92-93	Dayton	ECHL	2	0	0	0	0	—	—	—	—	—
93-94	Jacksonville	SUN	49	7	41	48	125	5	0	5	5	6
94-95	Wichita	CeHL	50	7	17	24	94	—	—	—	—	—
94-95	Fort Worth	CeHL	15	7	10	17	18	—	—	—	—	—
95-96	Fort Worth	CeHL	28	7	16	23	60	—	—	—	—	—
95-96	San Antonio	CeHL	38	8	26	34	56	13	6	2	8	20
96-97	Waco	WPHL	36	10	19	29	52	—	—	—	—	—
96-97	El Paso	WPHL	15	5	7	12	12	11	5	8	13	6
	CeHL	Totals	131	29	69	98	228	13	6	2	8	20
	WPHL	Totals	51	15	26	41	64	11	5	8	13	6
	ECHL	Totals	48	6	17	23	46	—	—	—	—	—

Born; 2/9/69, Toronto, Ontario. 6-1, 200.

Rod Hinks — Center

			Regular Season					Playoffs				
Season	Team	League	GP	G	A	PTS	PIM	GP	G	A	PTS	PIM
94-95	Johnstown	ECHL	66	30	46	76	90	5	4	1	5	4
94-95	Hershey	AHL	3	0	1	1	0	1	0	0	0	2
95-96	N/A											
96-97	Hershey	AHL	12	2	1	3	4	—	—	—	—	—
96-97	Muskegon	CoHL	55	39	40	79	49	3	1	0	1	6
	AHL	Totals	15	2	2	4	4	1	0	0	0	2

Born; 4/11/73, Toronto, Ontario. 5-11, 185. Drafted by New York Islanders (8th choice, 196th overall) in 1993 Entry Draft.

Shane Hnidy — Defenseman

			Regualr Season					Playoffs				
Season	Team	League	GP	G	A	PTS	PIM	GP	G	A	PTS	PIM
96-97	Saint John	AHL	44	2	12	14	112	—	—	—	—	—
96-97	Baton Rouge	ECHL	21	3	10	13	50	—	—	—	—	—

Born; 8/11/75, Neepawa, Manitoba. 6-1, 200. Drafted by Buffalo Sabres (7th choice, 173rd overall) in 1994 Entry Draft.

Daniel Hodge — Defenseman

			Regular Season					Playoffs				
Season	Team	League	GP	G	A	PTS	PIM	GP	G	A	PTS	PIM
95-96	Providence	AHL	23	1	7	8	12	—	—	—	—	—
96-97	Peoria	ECHL	68	12	34	46	63	10	4	6	10	7

Born; 9/18/71, Melrose, Massachusetts. 6-3, 205. Drafted by Boston Bruins (8th choice, 194th overall) in 1991 Entry Draft.

Kevin Hoffman — Defenseman

			Regular Season					Playoffs				
Season	Team	League	GP	G	A	PTS	PIM	GP	G	A	PTS	PIM
96-97	Raleigh	ECHL	60	5	18	23	50	—	—	—	—	—

Born; 5/2/68, Vancouver, British Columbia. 6-0, 205.

Tim Hogan — Defenseman

			Regular Season					Playoffs				
Season	Team	League	GP	G	A	PTS	PIM	GP	G	A	PTS	PIM
95-96	Indianapolis	IHL	1	0	0	0	0	—	—	—	—	—
95-96	Columbus	ECHL	66	7	10	17	52	3	0	0	0	0
96-97	Columbus	ECHL	70	6	30	36	72	8	1	2	3	0
	ECHL	Totaks	136	13	40	53	124	11	1	2	3	0

Born; 1/7/74, Oshawa, Ontario. 6-2, 185. Drafted by Chicago Blackhawks (5th choice, 113rd overall) in 1992 Entry Draft.

Murray Hogg — Defenseman

			Regular Season					Playoffs				
Season	Team	League	GP	G	A	PTS	PIM	GP	G	A	PTS	PIM
96-97	Fort Worth	CeHL	66	4	13	17	197	12	1	2	3	40

Born; 3/15/76, Millbrook, Ontario. 6-0, 210. Member of 1996-97 CeHL Champion Fort Worth Fire.

Jason Holland — Defenseman

Season	Team	League	GP	G	A	PTS	PIM	GP	G	A	PTS	PIM
96-97	Islanders	NHL	4	1	0	1	0	—	—	—	—	—
96-97	Kentucky	AHL	72	14	25	39	46	4	0	2	2	0

Born; 4/30/76, Morinville, Alberta. 6-2, 193. Drafted by New York Islanders (2nd choice, 38th overall) in 1994 Entry Draft. Member of 1996-97 AHL All-Rookie Team.

Kevin Holliday — Defenseman

Season	Team	League	GP	G	A	PTS	PIM	GP	G	A	PTS	PIM
96-97	Thunder Bay	CoHL	69	1	5	6	403	3	1	1	2	28

Born; 5/6/75, Red Lake, Ontario. 6-2, 225.

Terry Hollinger — Defenseman

Season	Team	League	GP	G	A	PTS	PIM	GP	G	A	PTS	PIM
91-92	Peoria	IHL	1	0	2	2	0	5	0	1	1	0
92-93	Peoria	IHL	72	2	28	30	67	4	1	1	2	0
93-94	St. Louis	NHL	2	0	0	0	0	—	—	—	—	—
93-94	Peoria	IHL	78	12	31	43	96	6	0	3	3	31
94-95	St. Louis	NHL	5	0	0	0	2	—	—	—	—	—
94-95	Peoria	IHL	69	7	25	32	137	4	2	4	6	8
95-96	Rochester	AHL	62	5	50	55	71	19	3	11	14	12
96-97	Rochester	AHL	73	12	51	63	54	10	2	7	9	27
	NHL	Totals	7	0	0	0	2	—	—	—	—	—
	IHL	Totals	220	21	86	107	300	19	3	9	12	39
	AHL	Totals	135	17	101	118	125	29	5	18	23	39

Born; 2/24/71, Regina, Saskatchewan. 6-2, 215. Drafted by St. Louis Blues (7th choice, 153rd overall) in 1991 Entry Draft. Signed as a free agent by Buffalo Sabres (8/19/95). Member of 1995-96 AHL champion Rochester Americans. 1995-96 AHL Second Team All-Star. 1996-97 AHL First Team All-Star.

Scott Hollis — Right Wing

Season	Team	League	GP	G	A	PTS	PIM	GP	G	A	PTS	PIM
93-94	Las Vegas	IHL	23	3	1	4	65	—	—	—	—	—
93-94	Knoxville	ECHL	28	20	16	36	99	3	3	1	4	8
94-95	Adirondack	AHL	48	12	15	27	118	—	—	—	—	—
95-96	Adirondack	AHL	55	18	19	37	111	3	0	1	1	4
95-96	Toledo	ECHL	7	7	11	18	5	—	—	—	—	—
96-97	San Antonio	IHL	73	17	17	34	187	9	1	1	2	6
	AHL	Totals	103	30	34	64	229	3	0	1	1	4
	IHL	Totals	96	20	18	38	252	9	1	1	2	6
	ECHL	Totals	35	27	27	54	104	3	3	1	4	8

Born; 9/18/72, Kingston, Ontario. 5-11, 183. Drafted by Vancouver Canucks (9th choice, 165th overall) 1992 Entry Draft.

Chad Holloway — Defenseman

Season	Team	League	GP	G	A	PTS	PIM	GP	G	A	PTS	PIM
94-95	Saginaw	CoHL	60	1	2	3	97	11	0	0	0	43
95-96	Saginaw	CoHL	68	5	6	11	162	5	1	0	1	5
96-97	Brantford	CoHL	34	2	9	11	37	—	—	—	—	—
96-97	Dayton	CoHL	31	0	8	8	70	—	—	—	—	—
96-97	Utica	CoHL	6	0	1	1	7	3	0	2	2	0
	CoHL	Totals	199	8	26	34	373	169	1	2	3	48

Born; 2/29/72, Burlington, Ontario. 6-1, 195.

Randy Holmes
Center

Season	Team	League	GP	G	A	PTS	PIM	GP	G	A	PTS	PIM
96-97	Madison	CoHL	74	26	45	71	47	5	1	2	3	2

Regular Season / Playoffs

Born; 8/30/72, Kingston, Ontario. 5-9, 180. Last amateur club; Ohio State (CCHA). 1996-97 Member of CoHL All-Rookie Team.

Tom Holmes
Forward

Season	Team	League	GP	G	A	PTS	PIM	GP	G	A	PTS	PIM
96-97	Richmond	ECHL	69	16	33	49	141	8	3	0	3	8

Born; 3/10/73, Rye, New York. 5-11, 190. Last amateur club; Harvard (ECAC).

Dale Hooper
Defenseman

Season	Team	League	GP	G	A	PTS	PIM	GP	G	A	PTS	PIM
96-97	Dayton	ECHL	31	2	8	10	27	—	—	—	—	—
96-97	Huntington	ECHL	16	1	6	7	8	—	—	—	—	—
	ECHL	Totals	47	3	14	17	35	—	—	—	—	—

Born; 11/28/72, North Conway, New Hampshire. 6-1, 195. Last amateur club; Massachusetts (Hockey East).

Ron Hoover
Left Wing

Season	Team	League	GP	G	A	PTS	PIM	GP	G	A	PTS	PIM
89-90	Boston	NHL	2	0	0	0	0	—	—	—	—	—
89-90	Maine	AHL	75	28	26	54	57	—	—	—	—	—
90-91	Boston	NHL	15	4	0	4	31	8	0	0	0	18
90-91	Maine	AHL	62	28	16	44	40	—	—	—	—	—
91-92	St. Louis	NHL	1	0	0	0	0	—	—	—	—	—
91-92	Peoria	IHL	71	27	34	61	30	10	4	4	8	4
92-93	Peoria	IHL	58	17	13	30	28	4	1	1	2	2
93-94	Peoria	IHL	80	26	24	50	89	6	0	1	1	10
94-95	Peoria	IHL	76	22	20	42	70	9	2	1	3	12
95-96	Peoria	IHL	74	22	15	37	94	12	0	3	3	8
96-97	Cincinnati	IHL	4	1	1	2	0	—	—	—	—	—
96-97	San Antonio	IHL	21	2	3	5	18	8	1	1	2	0
	NHL	Totals	18	4	0	4	31	8	0	0	0	18
	IHL	Totals	384	117	110	227	329	49	8	11	19	54
	AHL	Totals	137	56	42	98	97	—	—	—	—	—

Born; 10/28/66, Oakville, Ontario. 5-11, 185. Drafted by Hartford Whalers (7th choice, 158th overall) in 1986 Entry Draft. Signed as a free agent by Boston Bruins (9/1/89). Signed as a free agent by St. Louis Blues (7/23/91).

Tony Horacek
Left Wing

Season	Team	League	GP	G	A	PTS	PIM	GP	G	A	PTS	PIM
86-87	Hershey	AHL	—	—	—	—	—	1	0	0	0	0
87-88	Hershey	AHL	1	0	0	0	0	—	—	—	—	—
88-89	Hershey	AHL	10	0	0	0	38	—	—	—	—	—
88-89	Indianapolis	IHL	43	11	13	24	138	—	—	—	—	—
89-90	Philadelphia	NHL	48	5	5	10	117	—	—	—	—	—
89-90	Hershey	AHL	12	0	5	5	25	—	—	—	—	—
90-91	Philadelphia	NHL	34	3	6	9	49	—	—	—	—	—
90-91	Hershey	AHL	19	5	3	8	35	4	2	0	2	14
91-92	Philadelphia	NHL	34	1	3	4	51	—	—	—	—	—
91-92	Chicago	NHL	12	1	4	5	21	2	1	0	1	2
92-93	Indianapolis	IHL	6	1	1	2	28	5	3	2	5	18
93-94	Chicago	NHL	7	0	0	0	53	—	—	—	—	—
93-94	Indianapolis	IHL	29	6	7	13	63	—	—	—	—	—
94-95	Chicago	NHL	19	0	1	1	25	—	—	—	—	—

Season	Team	League	GP	G	A	PTS	PIM	GP	G	A	PTS	PIM
94-95	Indianapolis	IHL	51	7	19	26	201	—	—	—	—	—
95-96	Hershey	AHL	34	4	9	13	75	5	1	1	2	4
96-97	Cincinnati	IHL	60	4	5	9	158	2	0	1	1	2
	NHL	Totals	154	10	19	29	316	2	1	0	1	2
	IHL	Totals	189	29	45	74	588	7	3	3	6	20
	AHL	Totals	76	9	17	26	173	10	3	1	4	18

Born; 2/3/67, Vancouver, British Columbia. 6-4, 215. Drafted by Philadelphia Flyers (8th choice, 147th overall) in 1985 Entry Draft. Traded to Chicago Blackhawks by Philadelphia for Ryan McGill (2/7/92).

Bill Horn — Goaltender

Regular Season / Playoffs

Season	Team	League	GP	W	L	T	MIN	SO	GAVG	GP	W	L	MIN	SO	GAVG
90-91	Roanoke Valley	ECHL	*51	18	21	6	*2719	1	4.28	—	—	—	—	—	—
90-91	New Haven	AHL	1				60	0	5.00	—	—	—	—	—	—
92-93	Greensboro	ECHL	27	16	9	0	1465	3	3.32	—	—	—	—	—	—
92-93	Rochester	AHL	6				304	0	4.34	1			13	0	0.00
92-93	San Diego	IHL	2				120	0	2.50	—	—	—	—	—	—
93-94	Wheeling	ECHL	4	2	0	0	107	0	2.80	—	—	—	—	—	—
93-94	Rochester	AHL	25	9	9	5	1395	0	3.49	1	0	1	42	0	7.13
94-95	Greensboro	ECHL	20	13	5	1	1135	0	3.07	13	8	5	755	1	3.82
94-95	San Diego	IHL	8	2	1	1	289	0	3.12	—	—	—	—	—	—
96-97	Raleigh	ECHL	29	7	16	2	1512	0	4.01	—	—	—	—	—	—
96-97	Columbus	CeHL	3	2	1	0	159	0	6.43	2	0	2	102	0	6.49
	AHL	Totals	32				1759	0	3.68	2			55	0	5.43
	IHL	Totals	10				409	0	2.93	—	—	—	—	—	—
	ECHL	Totals	131	56	51	9	6938	4	3.80	13	8	5	755	1	3.82

Born; 4/16/67, Whitewood, Saskatchewan. 5-8, 165. Drafted by Hartford Whalers (4th choice, 95th overall) in 1986 Entry Draft.

Eric Houde — Center

Regular Season / Playoffs

Season	Team	League	GP	G	A	PTS	PIM	GP	G	A	PTS	PIM
96-97	Montreal	NHL	13	0	2	2	2	—	—	—	—	—
96-97	Fredericton	AHL	66	30	36	66	20	—	—	—	—	—

Born; 12/19/76, Montreal, Quebec. Drafted by Montreal Canadiens (9th choice, 216th overall) in 1995 Entry Draft. 1996-97 Member of 1996-97 AHL All-Rookie Team.

Bobby House — Right Wing

Regular Season / Playoffs

Season	Team	League	GP	G	A	PTS	PIM	GP	G	A	PTS	PIM
93-94	Indianapolis	IHL	42	10	8	18	51	—	—	—	—	—
93-94	Flint	CoHL	4	3	3	6	0	—	—	—	—	—
94-95	Indianapolis	IHL	26	2	3	5	26	—	—	—	—	—
94-95	Albany	AHL	26	4	7	11	12	8	1	1	2	0
94-95	Columbus	ECHL	9	11	6	17	2	—	—	—	—	—
95-96	Albany	AHL	77	37	49	86	57	4	0	0	0	4
96-97	Albany	AHL	68	18	16	34	65	16	3	2	5	23
	AHL	Totals	171	59	72	131	134	28	4	3	7	27
	IHL	Totals	68	12	11	23	77	—	—	—	—	—

Born; 1/7/73, Whitehorse, Yukon Territories. 6-1, 200. Drafted by Chicago Blackhawks (4th choice, 66th overall) in 1991 Entry Draft. Traded to New Jersey Devils by Chicago for cash (5/21/96). Member of 1994-95 Calder Cup champion Albany RiverRats.

Todd Howarth — Center

Regular Season / Playoffs

Season	Team	League	GP	G	A	PTS	PIM	GP	G	A	PTS	PIM
91-92	Thunder Bay	CoHL	16	5	10	15	20	13	3	7	10	18
92-93	Thunder Bay	CoHL	60	37	42	79	96	11	2	13	15	12
93-94	Thunder Bay	CoHL	49	23	41	64	80	9	7	8	15	19
94-95	Thunder Bay	CoHL	67	27	47	74	168	11	8	8	16	45

Season	Team	League	GP	G	A	PTS	PIM	GP	G	A	PTS	PIM
95-96	Thunder Bay	CoHL	55	33	45	78	185	19	9	20	29	51
96-97	Fort Worth	CeHL	27	15	19	34	100	17	5	9	14	49
	CoHL	Totals	247	125	185	310	549	63	29	56	85	145

Born; 6/16/70, Dryden, Ontario. 5-9, 170. 1992-93 CoHL Best Defensive Forward. Member of 1991-92 CoHL champion Thunder Bay Thunder Hawks. Member of 1993-94 CoHL champion Thunder Bay Senators. Member of 1994-95 CoHL champion Thunder Bay Senators. Member of 1996-97 CeHL Champion Fort Worth Fire.

Jan Hrdina — Right Wing

			Regular Season					Playoffs				
Season	Team	League	GP	G	A	PTS	PIM	GP	G	A	PTS	PIM
96-97	Cleveland	IHL	68	23	31	54	82	13	1	2	3	8

Born; 2/5/76, Hradec Kralove, Czechoslovakia. 6-0, 190. Drafted by Pittsburgh Penguins (4th choice, 128th overall) in 1995 Entry Draft.

Nick Hriczov — Defenseman

			Regular Season					Playoffs				
Season	Team	League	GP	G	A	PTS	PIM	GP	G	A	PTS	PIM
96-97	Amarillo	WPHL	58	1	13	14	161	—	—	—	—	—

Born; 9/24/72, Clifton, New Jersey. 6-4, 235.

Tony Hrkac — Center

			Regular Season					Playoffs				
Season	Team	League	GP	G	A	PTS	PIM	GP	G	A	PTS	PIM
86-87	St. Louis	NHL	—	—	—	—	—	3	0	0	0	0
87-88	St. Louis	NHL	67	11	37	48	22	10	6	1	7	4
88-89	St. Louis	NHL	70	17	28	45	8	4	1	1	2	0
89-90	St. Louis	NHL	28	5	12	17	8	—	—	—	—	—
89-90	Quebec	NHL	22	4	8	12	2	—	—	—	—	—
89-90	Halifax	AHL	20	12	21	33	4	6	5	9	14	4
90-91	Quebec	NHL	70	16	32	48	16	—	—	—	—	—
90-91	Halifax	AHL	3	4	1	5	2	—	—	—	—	—
91-92	San Jose	NHL	22	2	10	12	4	—	—	—	—	—
91-92	Chicago	NHL	18	1	2	3	6	3	0	0	0	2
92-93	Indianapolis	IHL	80	45	*87	*132	70	5	0	2	2	2
93-94	St. Louis	NHL	36	6	5	11	8	4	0	0	0	0
93-94	Peoria	IHL	45	30	51	81	25	1	1	2	3	0
94-95	Milwaukee	IHL	71	24	67	91	26	15	4	9	13	16
95-96	Milwaukee	IHL	43	14	28	42	18	5	1	3	4	4
96-97	Milwaukee	IHL	81	27	61	88	20	3	1	1	2	2
	NHL	Totals	333	62	134	196	74	24	7	2	9	6
	IHL	Totals	320	140	294	434	159	29	7	17	24	24
	AHL	Totals	23	16	22	38	6	6	5	9	14	4

Born; 7/7/66, Thunder Bay, Ontario. 5-11, 170. Drafted by St. Louis Blues (2nd choice, 32nd overall) in 1984 Entry Draft. Traded to Quebec Nordiques by St. louis with Greg Millen for Jeff Brown (12/13/89). Traded to San Jose Sharks by Quebec for Greg Paslawski (5/31/91). Traded to Chicago Blackhawks by San Jose for future considerations (2/7/92). Signed as a free agent by St. Louis Blues (7/30/92). 1992-93 IHL MVP. 1992-93 IHL First Team All-Star.

Kelly Hrycun — Right Wing

			Regular Season					Playoffs				
Season	Team	League	GP	G	A	PTS	PIM	GP	G	A	PTS	PIM
94-95	Fresno	SUN	2	0	0	0	2	—	—	—	—	—
95-96	Alaska	WCHL	34	10	20	30	6	5	4	3	7	0
96-97	Alaska	WCHL	63	38	34	72	44	—	—	—	—	—
	WCHL	Totals	97	48	54	102	50	5	4	3	7	0

Born; 4/21/73, Edmonton, Alberta. 5-10, 180. Selected by Tucson Sabrecats in WCHL Dispersal Draft.

Rob Hrystak — Center

			Regular Season					Playoffs				
Season	Team	League	GP	G	A	PTS	PIM	GP	G	A	PTS	PIM
88-89	Johnstown	ECHL	56	40	49	89	86	11	*8	10	18	18
89-90	Johnstown	ECHL	10	1	7	8	33	—	—	—	—	—
89-90	Knoxville	ECHL	38	17	37	54	51	—	—	—	—	—
90-91	Johnstown	ECHL	40	22	28	50	58	10	4	5	9	10
91-92	Johnstown	ECHL	47	19	27	46	68	—	—	—	—	—
96-97	Austin	WPHL	2	1	1	2	2	—	—	—	—	—
96-97	Central Texas	WPHL	14	6	14	20	21	—	—	—	—	—
96-97	Waco	WPHL	8	3	2	5	12	—	—	—	—	—
96-97	Nashville	CeHL	9	5	3	8	6	—	—	—	—	—
	ECHL	Totals	191	99	148	247	296	21	12	15	27	28
	WPHL	Totals	24	10	17	27	35	—	—	—	—	—

Born; 8/11/65, Saskatoon, Saskatchewan. 5-11, 180. 1988-89 ECHL First Team All-Star.

Roman Hubalek — Left Wing

			Regular Season					Playoffs				
Season	Team	League	GP	G	A	PTS	PIM	GP	G	A	PTS	PIM
91-92	Knoxville	ECHL	50	14	27	41	24	—	—	—	—	—
92-93	Muskegon	CoHL	52	17	25	42	32	—	—	—	—	—
93-94	Muskegon	CoHL	8	1	1	2	0	—	—	—	—	—
93-94	West Palm Beach	SUN	45	25	20	45	55	5	1	4	5	2
94-95	West Palm Beach	SUN	54	38	57	*95	104	5	2	7	9	16
95-96	West Palm Beach	SHL	44	21	25	46	105	—	—	—	—	—
96-97	Reno	WCHL	21	5	22	27	17	—	—	—	—	—
	CoHL	Totals	60	18	26	44	32	—	—	—	—	—
	SHL	Totals	143	84	99	183	264	10	3	11	14	18

Born; 8/30/68, Brno, Czechoslovakia. 5-7, 160. Member of 1993-94 Sunshine League champion West Palm Beach Blaze. Member of 1994-95 Sunshine League champion West Palm Beach Blaze.

Charlie Huddy — Defenseman

			Regular Season					Playoffs				
Season	Team	League	GP	G	A	PTS	PIM	GP	G	A	PTS	PIM
79-80	Houston	CHL	79	14	34	48	46	6	1	0	1	2
80-81	Edmonton	NHL	12	2	5	7	6	—	—	—	—	—
80-81	Wichita	CHL	47	8	36	44	71	17	3	11	14	10
81-82	Edmonton	NHL	41	4	11	15	46	5	1	2	3	14
81-82	Wichita	CHL	32	7	19	26	51	—	—	—	—	—
82-83	Edmonton	NHL	76	20	37	57	58	15	1	6	7	10
83-84	Edmonton	NHL	75	8	34	42	43	12	1	9	10	8
84-85	Edmonton	NHL	80	7	44	51	46	18	3	17	20	17
85-86	Edmonton	NHL	76	6	35	41	55	7	0	2	2	0
86-87	Edmonton	NHL	58	4	15	19	35	21	1	7	8	21
87-88	Edmonton	NHL	77	13	28	41	71	13	4	5	9	10
88-89	Edmonton	NHL	76	11	33	44	52	7	2	0	2	4
89-90	Edmonton	NHL	70	1	23	24	56	22	0	6	6	11
90-91	Edmonton	NHL	53	5	22	27	32	18	3	7	10	10
91-92	Los Angeles	NHL	56	4	19	23	43	6	1	1	2	10
92-93	Los Angeles	NHL	82	2	25	27	64	23	1	4	5	12
93-94	Los Angeles	NHL	79	5	13	18	71	—	—	—	—	—
94-95	Los Angeles	NHL	9	0	1	1	6	—	—	—	—	—
94-95	Buffalo	NHL	32	2	4	6	36	3	0	0	0	0
95-96	Buffalo	NHL	52	5	5	10	59	—	—	—	—	—
95-96	St. Louis	NHL	12	0	0	0	6	13	1	0	1	8
96-97	Buffalo	NHL	1	0	0	0	0	—	—	—	—	—
96-97	Rochester	AHL	63	6	8	14	36	4	0	0	0	0

			GP	G	A	PTS	PIM	GP	G	A	PTS	PIM
	NHL	Totals	1017	99	354	453	785	183	19	66	85	135
	CHL	Totals	158	29	89	118	168	23	4	11	15	12

Born; 6/2/59, Oshawa, Ontario. 6-0, 210. Signed as a free agent by Edmonton Oilers (9/14/79). Claimed by Minnesota North Stars from Edmonton in Expansion draft (5/30/91). Traded to Los Angeles Kings by Minnesota with Randy Gilhen, Jim Thomson and New York Rangers fourth round choice (previously acquired by Minnesota—Los Angeles selected Alexei Zhitnik) in 1991 Entry Draft for Todd Elik (6/22/91). Traded to Buffalo Sabres by Los Angeles with Alexei Zhitnik, Robb Stauber and Los Angeles' fifth round choice (Marian Menhart) in 1995 Entry Draft for Phillippe Boucher, Denis Tsygurov and Grant Fuhr (2/14/95). Traded to St. Louis Blues by Buffalo with Buffalo's seventh round choice (Daniel Corso) in 1996 Entry Draft for Denis Hamel (3/19/96). Member of 1983-84 Stanley Cup Champion Edmonotn Oilers. Member of 1984-85 Stanley Cup Champion Edmonton Oilers. Member of 1986-87 Stanley Cup Champion Edmonton Oilers. Member of 1987-88 Stanley Cup Champion Edmonton Oilers. Member of 1989-90 Stanley Cup Champion Edmonton Oilers.

Mike Hudson — Center

			Regular Season					Playoffs				
Season	Team	League	GP	G	A	PTS	PIM	GP	G	A	PTS	PIM
87-88	Saginaw	IHL	75	18	30	48	44	10	2	3	5	20
88-89	Chicago	NHL	41	7	16	23	20	10	1	2	3	18
88-89	Saginaw	IHL	30	15	17	32	10	—	—	—	—	—
89-90	Chicago	NHL	49	9	12	21	56	4	0	0	0	2
90-91	Chicago	NHL	55	7	9	16	62	6	0	2	2	8
90-91	Indianapolis	IHL	3	1	2	3	0	—	—	—	—	—
91-92	Chicago	NHL	76	14	15	29	92	16	3	5	8	26
92-93	Chicago	NHL	36	1	6	7	44	—	—	—	—	—
92-93	Edmonton	NHL	5	0	1	1	2	—	—	—	—	—
93-94	Rangers	NHL	48	4	7	11	47	—	—	—	—	—
94-95	Pittsburgh	NHL	40	2	9	11	34	11	0	0	0	6
95-96	Toronto	NHL	27	2	0	2	29	—	—	—	—	—
95-96	St. Louis	NHL	32	3	12	15	26	2	0	1	1	4
96-97	Phoenix	NHL	7	0	0	0	2	—	—	—	—	—
96-97	Phoenix	IHL	33	6	9	15	10	—	—	—	—	—
	NHL	Totals	416	49	87	136	414	49	4	10	14	64
	IHL	Totals	141	40	58	98	64	10	2	3	5	20

Born; 2/6/67, Guelph, Ontario. 6-1, 205. Drafted by Chicago Blackhawks (6th choice, 140th overall) in 1986 Entry Draft. Traded to Edmonotn Oilers for Craig Muni (3/22/93). Claimed by New York Rangers from Edmonton in NHL Waiver Draft (10/3/93). Claimed by PIttsburgh Penguins from Rangers in NHL Waiver Draft (1/18/95). Signed as a free agent by Toronto Maple Leafs (9/22/95). Claimed on waivers by St. Louis Blues (1/4/96).

Kerry Huffman — Defenseman

			Regular Season					Playoffs				
Season	Team	League	GP	G	A	PTS	PIM	GP	G	A	PTS	PIM
86-87	Philadelphia	NHL	9	0	0	0	2	—	—	—	—	—
86-87	Hershey	AHL	3	0	1	1	0	4	0	0	0	0
87-88	Philadelphia	NHL	52	6	17	23	34	2	0	0	0	0
88-89	Philadelphia	NHL	29	0	11	11	31	—	—	—	—	—
88-89	Hershey	AHL	29	2	13	15	16	—	—	—	—	—
89-90	Philadelphia	NHL	43	1	12	13	34	—	—	—	—	—
90-91	Philadelphia	NHL	10	1	2	3	10	—	—	—	—	—
90-91	Hershey	AHL	45	5	29	34	20	7	1	2	3	0
91-92	Philadelphia	NHL	60	14	18	32	41	—	—	—	—	—
92-93	Quebec	NHL	52	4	18	22	54	3	0	0	0	0
93-94	Quebec	NHL	28	0	6	6	28	—	—	—	—	—
93-94	Ottawa	NHL	34	4	8	12	12	—	—	—	—	—
94-95	Ottawa	NHL	37	2	4	6	46	—	—	—	—	—
95-96	Ottawa	NHL	43	4	11	15	63	—	—	—	—	—
95-96	Philadelphia	NHL	4	1	1	3	6	6	0	0	0	0
96-97	Las Vegas	IHL	44	5	19	24	38	3	0	0	0	2
	NHL	Totals	401	37	108	145	361	11	0	0	0	2
	AHL	Totals	77	7	43	50	36	11	1	2	3	0

Born; 1/3/68, Peterborough, Ontario. 6-2, 200. Drafted by Philadelphia Flyers (1st choice, 20th overall) in 1986 Entry Draft. Traded to Quebec Nordiques by Philadelphia with Peter Forsberg, Steve Duchesne, Mikke Ricci, Ron Hextall, Chris Simon, Philadelphia's first round choice in the 1993 (Jocelyn Thibault) and 1994 (later traded to Toronto-later traded to Washington-Washington selected Nolan Baumgartner)-Entry Drafts and cash for Eric Lindros (6/30/92). Claimed on waivers by Ottawa Senators from Quebec, (1/15/94). Traded to Flyers by Senators for future considerations (3/19/96).

Ryan Hughes — Center

			Regular Season					Playoffs				
Season	Team	League	GP	G	A	PTS	PIM	GP	G	A	PTS	PIM
93-94	Cornwall	AHL	54	17	12	29	24	13	2	4	6	6
94-95	Cornwall	AHL	72	15	24	39	48	14	0	7	7	10
95-96	Boston	NHL	3	0	0	0	0	—	—	—	—	—
95-96	Providence	AHL	78	22	52	74	89	4	1	2	3	20
96-97	Chicago	IHL	14	2	6	8	12	—	—	—	—	—
96-97	Quebec	IHL	30	2	3	5	24	8	1	1	2	4
	AHL	Totals	204	54	88	132	161	31	3	13	16	36
	IHL	Totals	44	4	9	13	36	8	1	1	2	4

Born; 1/17/72, Montreal, Quebec. 6-2, 196. Drafted by Quebec Nordiques (2nd choice, 22nd overall) in 1990 Entry Draft. Signed as a free agent by Boston Bruins (10/6/95).

Joe Hulbig — Left Wing

			Regular Season					Playoffs				
Season	Team	League	GP	G	A	PTS	PIM	GP	G	A	PTS	PIM
96-97	Edmonton	NHL	6	0	0	0	0	6	0	1	1	2
96-97	Hamilton	AHL	73	18	28	46	59	16	6	10	16	6

Born; 9/29/73, Norwood, Massachusetts. 6-3, 215. Drafted by Edmonton Oilers (1st choice, 13th overall) in 1992 Entry Draft.

Dean Hulett — Left Wing

			Regular Season					Playoffs				
Season	Team	League	GP	G	A	PTS	PIM	GP	G	A	PTS	PIM
93-94	Phoenix	IHL	43	8	7	15	76	—	—	—	—	—
94-95	Greensboro	ECHL	4	1	3	4	15	—	—	—	—	—
94-95	Tallahassee	ECHL	42	10	18	28	160	—	—	—	—	—
94-95	South Carolina	ECHL	15	8	3	11	34	9	3	8	11	30
95-96	South Carolina	ECHL	5	2	2	4	20	—	—	—	—	—
95-96	Louisiana	ECHL	24	9	10	19	131	5	3	5	8	21
96-97	San Antonio	CeHL	41	20	34	54	154	—	—	—	—	—
	ECHL	Totals	90	30	36	66	360	14	6	13	19	51

Born; 7/25/71, San Juan, Puerto Rico. 6-6, 210. Drafted by Los Angeles Kings (7th choice, 154th overall) in 1990 Entry Draft.

Travis Hulse — Defenseman

			Regular Season					Playoffs				
Season	Team	League	GP	G	A	PTS	PIM	GP	G	A	PTS	PIM
95-96	Winston-Salem	SHL	58	3	31	34	44	2	0	0	0	6
96-97	Central Texas	WPHL	15	1	4	5	21	—	—	—	—	—
96-97	Waco	WPHL	17	0	2	2	11	—	—	—	—	—
	WPHL	Totals	32	1	6	7	32	—	—	—	—	—

Born; 12/15/70, Calgary, Alberta. 6-2, 200.

Kent Hulst — Center

			Regular Season					Playoffs				
Season	Team	League	GP	G	A	PTS	PIM	GP	G	A	PTS	PIM
88-89	Flint	IHL	7	0	1	1	4	—	—	—	—	—
88-89	Newmarket	AHL	—	—	—	—	—	2	1	1	2	2
89-90	Newmarket	AHL	80	26	34	60	29	—	—	—	—	—
90-91	Newmarket	AHL	79	28	37	65	57	—	—	—	—	—
91-92	New Haven	AHL	80	21	39	60	59	5	2	2	4	0
93-94	Portland	AHL	72	34	33	67	68	17	4	6	10	14
94-95	Portland	AHL	29	10	17	27	80	7	3	1	4	2

Season	Team	League	GP	G	A	PTS	PIM	GP	G	A	PTS	PIM
95-96	Portland	AHL	75	25	47	72	122	24	11	16	27	30
96-97	Portland	AHL	48	19	31	50	60	5	1	2	3	4
	AHL	Totals	463	163	238	401	475	60	22	28	50	52

Born; 4/8/68, St. Thomas, Ontario. 6-1, 195. Drafted by Toronto Maple Leafs (4th choice, 69th overall) in 1986 Entry Draft. Signed as a free agent by Quebec Nordiques (9/20/91). Signed as a free agent by Portland Pirates (1993). Member of 1993-94 AHL champion Portland Pirates.

Kelly Hultgren — Defenseman

			Regular Season					Playoffs				
Season	Team	League	GP	G	A	PTS	PIM	GP	G	A	PTS	PIM
95-96	Los Angeles	IHL	40	1	7	8	54	—	—	—	—	—
95-96	Louisiana	ECHL	18	1	12	13	31	—	—	—	—	—
95-96	San Diego	WCHL	4	2	3	5	8	—	—	—	—	—
96-97	Long Beach	IHL	2	0	0	0	0	—	—	—	—	—
96-97	Pensacola	ECHL	15	6	4	10	0	10	4	5	9	6
96-97	Fresno	WCHL	44	9	28	37	45	—	—	—	—	—
	IHL	Totals	42	1	7	8	54	—	—	—	—	—
	WCHL	Totals	48	11	31	42	53	—	—	—	—	—
	ECHL	Totals	33	7	16	23	31	10	4	5	9	6

Born; 4/11/71, St. Paul, Minnesota. 6-0, 190.

Casey Hungle — Right Wing

			Regular Season					Playoffs				
Season	Team	League	GP	G	A	PTS	PIM	GP	G	A	PTS	PIM
93-94	Erie	ECHL	64	28	17	45	51	—	—	—	—	—
94-95	Erie	ECHL	45	9	8	17	49	—	—	—	—	—
95-96	Tallahassee	ECHL	28	6	3	9	18	—	—	—	—	—
96-97	Columbus	CeHL	60	26	31	57	71	—	—	—	—	—
96-97	Wichita	CeHL	8	3	3	6	10	9	1	2	3	19
	ECHL	Totals	137	43	28	71	118	—	—	—	—	—
	CeHL	Totals	68	29	34	63	81	9	1	2	3	19

Born; 5/27/72, Shawnigan Lake, British Columbia. 5-11, 180.

Kelly Hurd — Right Wing

			Regular Season					Playoffs				
Season	Team	League	GP	G	A	PTS	PIM	GP	G	A	PTS	PIM
91-92	Adirondack	AHL	35	9	7	16	16	8	1	4	5	2
91-92	Fort Wayne	IHL	30	13	9	22	12	3	3	0	3	9
92-93	Fort Wayne	IHL	71	23	31	54	81	10	4	5	9	12
93-94	Fort Wayne	IHL	75	35	49	84	52	17	6	4	10	10
94-95	Fort Wayne	IHL	59	16	33	49	36	4	3	0	3	4
95-96	San Francisco	IHL	26	5	3	8	20	—	—	—	—	—
95-96	Houston	IHL	44	14	16	30	23	—	—	—	—	—
96-97	Grand Rapids	IHL	4	0	1	1	4	—	—	—	—	—
96-97	Utah	IHL	2	0	0	0	0	—	—	—	—	—
96-97	Mississippi	ECHL	57	25	33	58	72	3	1	3	4	2
	IHL	Totals	311	106	142	248	228	34	16	9	25	35

Born; 5/13/68, Castlegar, British Columbia. Drafted by Detroit Red Wings (6th choice, 143rd overall) in 1988 Entry Draft. Member of 1991-92 AHL champion Adirondack Red Wings. Member of 1992-93 IHL champion Fort Wayne Komets.

Mike Hurlbut — Defenseman

			Regular Season					Playoffs				
Season	Team	League	GP	G	A	PTS	PIM	GP	G	A	PTS	PIM
88-89	Denver	IHL	8	0	2	2	13	4	1	2	3	2
89-90	Flint	IHL	74	3	34	37	38	3	0	1	1	2
90-91	San Diego	IHL	2	1	0	1	0	—	—	—	—	—
90-91	Binghamton	AHL	33	2	11	13	27	3	0	1	1	0
91-92	Binghamton	AHL	79	16	39	55	64	11	2	7	9	8
92-93	Rangers	NHL	23	1	8	9	16	—	—	—	—	—

Season	Team	League	GP	G	A	PTS	PIM	GP	G	A	PTS	PIM
92-93	Binghamton	AHL	45	11	25	36	46	14	2	5	7	12
93-94	Quebec	NHL	1	0	0	0	0	—	—	—	—	—
93-94	Cornwall	AHL	77	13	33	46	100	13	3	7	10	12
94-95	Cornwall	AHL	74	11	49	60	69	3	1	0	1	15
95-96	Minnesota	IHL	22	1	4	5	22	—	—	—	—	—
95-96	Houston	IHL	38	3	12	15	33	—	—	—	—	—
96-97	Houston	IHL	70	11	24	35	62	13	5	8	13	12
	NHL	Totals	24	1	8	9	16	—	—	—	—	—
	AHL	Totals	308	53	157	210	306	44	8	20	28	47
	IHL	Totals	214	19	76	95	168	20	6	11	17	16

Born; 10/7/66, Massensa, New York. 6-2, 200. Drafted by New York Rangers (1st choice, 5th overall) in 1988 Supplemental Draft. Traded to Quebec Nordiques by Rangers for Alexander Karpovtsev (9/7/93). 1994-95 AHL Second Team All-Star.

Ryan Huska — Left Wing

Season	Team	League	GP	G	A	PTS	PIM	GP	G	A	PTS	PIM
95-96	Indianapolis	IHL	28	2	3	5	15	5	1	1	2	27
96-97	Indianapolis	IHL	80	18	12	30	100	4	0	0	0	4
	IHL	Totals	108	20	15	35	115	9	1	1	2	31

Born; 7/2/75, Cranbrook, British Columbia. 6-2, 194. Drafted by Chicago Blackhawks (4th choice, 76th overall) in 1993 Entry Draft.

Marc Hussey — Defenseman

Season	Team	League	GP	G	A	PTS	PIM	GP	G	A	PTS	PIM
94-95	St. John's	AHL	11	0	1	1	20	—	—	—	—	—
95-96	Saint John	AHL	68	10	21	31	120	5	0	0	0	8
96-97	Saint John	AHL	46	6	18	24	62	—	—	—	—	—
96-97	Utah	IHL	8	0	1	1	6	—	—	—	—	—
96-97	Indianapolis	IHL	14	0	2	2	17	4	0	1	1	10
	AHL	Totals	125	16	40	56	202	5	0	0	0	8
	IHL	Totals	22	0	3	3	23	4	0	1	1	10

Born; 1/22/74, Chatham, New Brunswick. 6-4, 182. Drafted by Pittsburgh Penguins (2nd choice, 43rd overall) in 1992 Entry Draft. Traded to Chicago Blackhawks by Calgary Flames for Ravil Gusmanov (3/18/97).

Rob Hutson — Right Wing

Season	Team	League	GP	G	A	PTS	PIM	GP	G	A	PTS	PIM
95-96	Toledo	ECHL	2	0	2	2	0	—	—	—	—	—
96-97	Saginaw	CoHL	5	2	2	4	4	—	—	—	—	—
96-97	Amarillo	WPHL	45	21	25	46	117	—	—	—	—	—

Born; 4/9/72, Bowsman, Manitoba. 5-11, 190. Last amateur club; Illinois-Chicago (CCHA).

Dave Hymovitz — Left Wing

Season	Team	League	GP	G	A	PTS	PIM	GP	G	A	PTS	PIM
96-97	Indianapolis	IHL	6	0	1	1	0	1	0	0	0	0
96-97	Columbus	ECHL	58	39	32	71	29	5	4	1	5	2

Born; 5/30/74, Boston, Massachusetts. 5-11, 170. Drafted by Chicago Blackhawks (9th choice, 209th overall) in 1992 Entry Draft.

Chris Hynnes — Defenseman

Season	Team	League	GP	G	A	PTS	PIM	GP	G	A	PTS	PIM
93-94	Thunder Bay	CoHL	59	13	40	53	45	9	2	6	8	6
94-95	Minnesota	IHL	25	3	4	7	22	—	—	—	—	—
94-95	Prince Edward Island	AHL	14	0	1	1	4	—	—	—	—	—
94-95	Thunder Bay	CoHL	16	6	9	15	10	8	1	5	6	10
95-96	Thunder Bay	CoHL	73	26	47	73	96	19	4	17	21	32
96-97	South Carolina	ECHL	68	22	33	55	86	18	11	16	*27	44

| | CoHL | Totals | 148 | 45 | 96 | 141 | 151 | 36 | 7 | 28 | 35 | 48 |

Born; 8/12/70, Thunder Bay, Ontario. 6-0, 205. 1995-96 CoHL Best Defender. 1995-96 CoHL First Team All-Star. 1996-97 Second Team ECHL All-Star. Member of 1993-94 CoHL champion Thunder Bay Senators. Member of 1994-95 CoHL champion Thunder Bay Senators. Member of 1996-97 ECHL Champion South Carolina Stingrays.

Brian Idalski — Defenseman

			Regular Season					Playoffs				
Season	Team	League	GP	G	A	PTS	PIM	GP	G	A	PTS	PIM
95-96	Madison	CoHL	65	1	8	9	78	6	1	0	1	4
96-97	Madison	CoHL	58	2	15	17	83	—	—	—	—	—
	CoHL	Totals	123	3	23	26	161	6	1	0	1	4

Born; 1/23/71, Warren, Michigan. 6-2, 195.

Viktor Ignatjev — Defenseman

			Regular Season					Playoffs				
Season	Team	League	GP	G	A	PTS	PIM	GP	G	A	PTS	PIM
92-93	Kansas City	IHL	64	5	16	21	68	4	1	2	3	24
93-94	Kansas City	IHL	67	1	24	25	123	—	—	—	—	—
94-95	Oklahoma City	CeHL	47	11	35	46	66	—	—	—	—	—
94-95	Denver	IHL	23	2	11	13	4	17	3	8	11	8
95-96	Utah	IHL	73	9	29	38	67	21	3	8	11	22
96-97	Long Beach	IHL	82	16	53	69	112	16	3	4	7	26
	IHL	Totals	309	33	133	166	374	58	10	22	32	80

Born; 4/26/70, Riga, Latvia. 6-4, 215. Drafted by San Jose Sharks (11th choice, 243rd overall) in 1992 Entry Draft. 1994-95 CeHL Second Team All-Star. 1996-97 IHL Second Team All-Star. Member of 1994-95 IHL champion Denver Grizzlies. Member of 1995-96 IHL champion Utah Grizzlies.

Chris Imes — Defenseman

			Regular Season					Playoffs				
Season	Team	League	GP	G	A	PTS	PIM	GP	G	A	PTS	PIM
94-95	Minnesota	IHL	2	0	0	0	4	3	0	0	0	0
95-96	Minnesota	IHL	80	4	14	18	56	—	—	—	—	—
96-97	Anchorage	WCHL	7	3	3	6	4	9	1	3	4	24
	IHL	Totals	82	4	14	18	60	3	0	0	0	0

Born; 8/27/72, Birchdale, Minnesota. 5-11, 195.

Cal Ingraham — Right Wing

			Regular Season					Playoffs				
Season	Team	League	GP	G	A	PTS	PIM	GP	G	A	PTS	PIM
95-96	Tallahassee	ECHL	69	32	39	71	57	12	8	8	16	10
96-97	Tallahassee	ECHL	70	34	58	92	54	3	1	0	1	2
	ECHL	Totals	139	66	97	163	111	15	9	8	17	12

Born; 6/4/70, Haverhill, Massachusetts. 5-5, 160.

Derek Innanen — Center

			Regular Season					Playoffs				
Season	Team	League	GP	G	A	PTS	PIM	GP	G	A	PTS	PIM
96-97	Mississippi	ECHL	58	9	6	15	131	3	0	0	0	2

5-11, 185. Last amateur club; Western Michigan (CCHA).

Ralph Intranuovo — Center

			Regular Season					Playoffs				
Season	Team	League	GP	G	A	PTS	PIM	GP	G	A	PTS	PIM
93-94	Cape Breton	AHL	66	21	31	52	39	4	1	2	3	2
94-95	Edmonton	NHL	1	0	1	1	0	—	—	—	—	—

Season	Team	League	GP	G	A	PTS	PIM	GP	G	A	PTS	PIM
94-95	Cape Breton	AHL	70	46	47	93	62	—	—	—	—	—
95-96	Edmonton	NHL	13	1	2	3	4	—	—	—	—	—
95-96	Cape Breton	AHL	52	34	29	73	84	—	—	—	—	—
96-97	Edmonton	NHL	8	1	1	2	0	—	—	—	—	—
96-97	Hamilton	AHL	68	36	40	76	88	22	8	4	12	30
	NHL	Totals	22	2	4	6	4	—	—	—	—	—
	AHL	Totals	256	137	147	284	185	26	9	6	15	32

Born; 12/11/73, East York, Ontario. 5-8, 180. Drafted by Edmonton Oilers (5th choice, 96th overall) in 1992 Entry Draft. 1995 AHL Second Team All-Star. 1996-97 AHL Second Team All-Star.

Brad Isbister — Right Wing

Season	Team	League	GP	G	A	PTS	PIM	GP	G	A	PTS	PIM
96-97	Springfield	AHL	7	3	1	4	14	9	1	2	3	10

Born; 5/7/77, Edmonton, Alberta. 6-2, 198. Drafted by Winnipeg Jets (4th choice, 67th overall) in 1995 Entry Draft.

Corey Isen — Right Wing

Season	Team	League	GP	G	A	PTS	PIM	GP	G	A	PTS	PIM
96-97	Utica	CoHL	22	2	7	9	60	—	—	—	—	—
96-97	Brantford	CoHL	27	10	5	15	52	10	2	1	3	10
	CoHL	Totals	49	12	12	24	112	10	2	1	3	10

Born; 5/26/75, London, Ontario. 5-9, 190.

Jason Issel — Left Wing

Season	Team	League	GP	G	A	PTS	PIM	GP	G	A	PTS	PIM
96-97	Dayton	ECHL	3	2	4	6	4	4	0	1	1	4

Born; 3/1/76, Neudorf, Saskatchewan. 6-2, 205. Last amateur club; Prince Albert (WHL).

Dave Ivaska — Defenseman

Season	Team	League	GP	G	A	PTS	PIM	GP	G	A	PTS	PIM
95-96	Detroit	CoHL	59	4	11	15	94	4	1	0	1	4
96-97	Port Huron	CoHL	61	10	9	19	102	5	1	1	2	12
	CoHL	Totals	120	14	20	34	196	9	2	1	3	16

Born; 4/11/73, Boston, Massachusetts. 5-10, 185.

Jeff Jablonski — Left Wing

			Regular Season					Playoffs				
Season	Team	League	GP	G	A	PTS	PIM	GP	G	A	PTS	PIM
90-91	Capital District	AHL	44	6	6	12	4	—	—	—	—	—
90-91	Kansas City	IHL	10	3	4	7	4	—	—	—	—	—
91-92	New Haven	AHL	1	0	0	0	0	—	—	—	—	—
91-92	Capital District	AHL	4	1	1	2	0	—	—	—	—	—
91-92	Nashville	ECHL	63	36	39	75	74	—	—	—	—	—
92-93	Capital District	AHL	6	0	0	0	2	—	—	—	—	—
92-93	Toledo	ECHL	61	26	46	72	93	16	3	11	14	20
93-94	Raleigh	ECHL	20	11	20	31	13	16	6	5	11	20
94-95	N/A											
95-96	Roanoke	ECHL	69	39	22	61	44	3	0	1	1	2
96-97	Roanoke	ECHL	68	52	44	96	30	4	4	0	4	2
	AHL	Totals	55	7	7	14	6	—	—	—	—	—
	ECHL	Totals	281	164	171	335	254	39	13	16	29	44

Born; 6/20/67, Toledo, Ohio. 6-1, 195. Drafted by New York Islanders (11th choice, 185th overall) in 1986 Entry Draft. Member of 1992-93 ECHL champion Toledo Storm. 1996-97 ECHL First Team All-Star.

Dane Jackson — Right Wing

			Regular Season					Playoffs				
Season	Team	League	GP	G	A	PTS	PIM	GP	G	A	PTS	PIM
92-93	Hamilton	AHL	68	23	20	43	59	—	—	—	—	—
93-94	Vancouver	NHL	12	5	1	6	9	—	—	—	—	—
93-94	Hamilton	AHL	60	25	35	60	73	4	2	2	4	16
94-95	Vancouver	NHL	3	1	0	1	4	6	0	0	0	10
94-95	Syracuse	AHL	78	30	28	58	162	—	—	—	—	—
95-96	Buffalo	NHL	22	5	4	9	41	—	—	—	—	—
95-96	Rochester	AHL	50	27	19	46	132	19	3	6	10	53
96-97	Rochester	AHL	78	24	34	58	111	10	7	4	11	14
	NHL	Totals	37	11	5	16	54	6	0	0	0	10
	AHL	Totals	334	129	136	265	537	33	12	12	24	83

Born; 5/17/70, Castlegar, British Columbia. 6-1, 196. Drafted by Vancouver Canucks (3rd choice, 44th overall) in 1988 Entry Draft. Signed as a free agent by Buffalo Sabres (8/16/95). Member of 1995-96 AHL champion Rochester Americans.

Mike Jackson — Right Wing

			Regular Season					Playoffs				
Season	Team	League	GP	G	A	PTS	PIM	GP	G	A	PTS	PIM
90-91	Newmarket	AHL	48	5	9	14	126	—	—	—	—	—
91-92	St. John's	AHL	1	0	0	0	0	—	—	—	—	—
91-92	Brantford	CoHL	49	7	27	34	115	6	2	5	7	8
92-93	Memphis	CeHL	57	24	28	52	182	6	1	4	5	15
93-94	Memphis	CeHL	64	26	37	63	90	—	—	—	—	—
94-95	Memphis	CeHL	52	13	22	35	67	—	—	—	—	—
95-96	Memphis	CeHL	51	12	29	41	155	3	0	0	0	7
96-97	Austin	WPHL	52	11	11	22	192	6	1	2	3	48
	AHL	Totals	49	5	9	14	126	—	—	—	—	—
	CeHL	Totals	224	75	116	191	494	9	1	4	5	22

Born; 2/4/69, Mississauga, Ontario. 6-0, 200. Drafted by Toronto Maple Leafs (12th choice, 213rd overall) in 1989 Entry Draft.

Paul Jackson — Center

			Regular Season					Playoffs				
Season	Team	League	GP	G	A	PTS	PIM	GP	G	A	PTS	PIM
93-94	Wichita	CeHL	59	*71	64	*135	215	11	11	*12	23	20
94-95	San Antonio	CeHL	53	51	49	100	251	11	7	6	13	52
95-96	Utah	IHL	1	0	0	0	0	—	—	—	—	—
95-96	San Antonio	CeHL	62	50	65	115	184	13	9	8	17	65

Season	Team	League	GP	G	A	PTS	PIM	GP	G	A	PTS	PIM
96-97	Las Vegas	IHL	1	0	0	0	0	—	—	—	—	—
96-97	San Antonio	CeHL	61	44	46	90	391	—	—	—	—	—
	IHL	Totals	2	0	0	0	0	—	—	—	—	—
	CeHL	Totals	235	216	224	440	1041	35	27	26	53	137

Born; 2/7/66, Toronto, Ontario. 5-10, 175. 1993-94 CeHL First Team All-Star. 1994-95 CeHL MVP. 1994-95 CeHL First Team All-Star. 1995-96 CeHL Second Team All-Star. Member of 1993-94 CeHL champion Wichita Thunder.

Steve Jaques — Defenseman

Season	Team	League	GP	G	A	PTS	PIM	GP	G	A	PTS	PIM
91-92	Phoenix	IHL	13	2	4	6	69	—	—	—	—	—
92-93	Providence	AHL	51	3	21	24	187	6	1	7	8	13
93-94	Salt Lake City	IHL	3	0	1	1	4	—	—	—	—	—
93-94	Las Vegas	IHL	49	3	5	8	192	5	0	0	0	28
94-95	Houston	IHL	75	2	14	16	233	4	1	1	2	11
95-96	Houston	IHL	70	3	16	19	285	—	—	—	—	—
96-97	Houston	IHL	50	0	8	8	116	—	—	—	—	—
96-97	Kansas City	IHL	28	2	8	10	35	3	0	0	0	8
	IHL	Totals	288	12	56	68	934	12	1	1	2	47

Born; 2/21/69, Burnaby, British Columbia. 5-11, 180. Drafted by Los Angeles Kings (11th choice, 228th overall) in 1989 Entry Draft.

Marko Jantunen — Left Wing

Season	Team	League	GP	G	A	PTS	PIM	GP	G	A	PTS	PIM
96-97	Calgary	NHL	3	0	0	0	0	—	—	—	—	—
96-97	Saint John	AHL	23	8	16	24	18	—	—	—	—	—

Born; 2/14/71, Lalti, Findland. 5-10, 185. Drafted by Calgary Flames (13th choice, 239th overall) in Entry Draft.

Stanislav Jasecko — Defenseman

Season	Team	League	GP	G	A	PTS	PIM	GP	G	A	PTS	PIM
96-97	Grand Rapids	IHL	62	3	15	18	48	—	—	—	—	—

Born; 12/15/72, Koske, Slovakia. 6-3, 205.

Bobby Jay — Defenseman

Season	Team	League	GP	G	A	PTS	PIM	GP	G	A	PTS	PIM
90-91	Fort Wayne	IHL	40	1	8	9	24	14	0	3	3	16
91-92	Fort Wayne	IHL	76	1	19	20	119	7	0	2	2	4
92-93	Fort Wayne	IHL	78	5	21	26	100	8	0	2	2	14
93-94	Los Angeles	NHL	3	0	1	1	0	—	—	—	—	—
93-94	Phoenix	IHL	65	7	15	22	54	—	—	—	—	—
94-95	Detroit	IHL	57	3	8	11	51	5	0	0	0	10
95-96	Detroit	IHL	17	2	2	4	22	6	0	1	1	16
96-97	Detroit	IHL	71	3	11	14	44	21	1	1	2	21
	IHL	Totals	404	22	84	106	414	61	1	9	10	81

Born; 11/18/65, Burlington, Massachusetts. 5-11,185. Signed as a free agent by Los Angeles Kings (7/16/93). Member of 1992-93 IHL champion Fort Wayne Komets. Member of IHL Champion Detroit Vipers 1996-97.

Yanick Jean — Defenseman

Season	Team	League	GP	G	A	PTS	PIM	GP	G	A	PTS	PIM
96-97	Mississippi	ECHL	52	2	9	11	65	3	0	3	3	8

Born; 11/26/75, Alma, Quebec. 6-1, 205. Drafted by Washington Capitals (5th choice, 119th overall) in 1994 Entry Draft.

Grant Jennings — Defenseman

Season	Team	League	GP	G	A	PTS	PIM	GP	G	A	PTS	PIM
85-86	Binghamton	AHL	51	0	4	4	109	—	—	—	—	—
86-87	Fort Wayne	IHL	3	0	0	0	0	—	—	—	—	—
86-87	Binghamton	AHL	47	1	5	6	125	13	0	2	2	17
87-88	Washington	NHL	—	—	—	—	—	1	0	0	0	0
87-88	Binghamton	AHL	56	2	12	14	195	3	1	0	1	15
88-89	Hartford	NHL	55	3	10	13	159	4	1	0	1	17
88-89	Binghamton	AHL	2	0	0	0	2	—	—	—	—	—
89-90	Hartford	NHL	64	3	6	9	171	7	0	0	0	13
90-91	Hartford	NHL	44	1	4	5	82	—	—	—	—	—
90-91	Pittsburgh	NHL	13	1	3	4	26	13	1	1	2	16
91-92	Pittsburgh	NHL	53	4	5	9	104	10	0	0	0	12
92-93	Pittsburgh	NHL	58	0	5	5	65	12	0	0	0	8
93-94	Pittsburgh	NHL	61	2	4	6	126	3	0	0	0	2
94-95	Pittsburgh	NHL	25	0	4	4	36	—	—	—	—	—
94-95	Toronto	NHL	10	0	2	2	7	4	0	0	0	0
95-96	Buffalo	NHL	6	0	0	0	28	—	—	—	—	—
95-96	Rochester	AHL	9	0	1	1	28	—	—	—	—	—
95-96	Atlanta	IHL	3	0	0	0	19	3	0	0	0	20
96-97	Quebec	IHL	42	2	10	12	79	—	—	—	—	—
	NHL	Totals	389	14	43	57	804	54	2	1	3	68
	AHL	Totals	165	3	22	25	459	16	1	2	3	32
	IHL	Totals	48	2	10	12	98	3	0	0	0	20

Born; 5/5/65, Hudson Bay, saskatchewan. 6-3, 210. Signed as a free agent by Washington Capitals (6/25/85). Traded to Hartford Whalers by Washington with Ed Kastelic for Mike Millar and Neil Sheehy (7/6/88). Traded to Pittsburgh Penguins by Hartford with Ron Francis and Ulf Samuelsson for John Cullen, Jeff Parker and Zarley Zalapski (3/4/71). Traded to Toronto Maple Leafs by Pittsburgh for Drake Berehowsky (4/7/95). Member of 1990-91 Stanley Cup champion Pittsburgh Penguins. Member of 1991-92 Stanley Cup champion Pittsburgh Penguins.

Chris Jensen — Right Wing

Season	Team	League	GP	G	A	PTS	PIM	GP	G	A	PTS	PIM
85-86	Rangers	NHL	9	1	3	4	0	—	—	—	—	—
86-87	Rangers	NHL	37	6	7	13	21	—	—	—	—	—
86-87	New Haven	AHL	14	4	9	13	41	—	—	—	—	—
87-88	Rangers	NHL	7	0	1	1	2	—	—	—	—	—
87-88	Colorado	IHL	43	10	23	33	68	10	3	7	10	8
88-89	Hershey	AHL	45	27	31	58	66	10	4	5	9	29
89-90	Philadelphia	NHL	1	0	0	0	2	—	—	—	—	—
89-90	Hershey	AHL	43	16	26	42	101	—	—	—	—	—
90-91	Philadelphia	NHL	18	2	1	3	2	—	—	—	—	—
90-91	Hershey	AHL	50	26	20	46	83	6	2	2	4	10
91-92	Philadelphia	NHL	2	0	0	0	0	—	—	—	—	—
91-92	Hershey	AHL	71	38	33	71	134	6	0	1	1	2
92-93	Hershey	AHL	74	33	47	80	95	—	—	—	—	—
93-94	Portland	AHL	56	33	28	61	52	16	6	10	16	22
94-95	Portland	AHL	67	35	42	77	89	7	4	3	7	0
95-96	Minnesota	IHL	52	25	19	44	109	—	—	—	—	—
95-96	Michigan	IHL	13	5	5	10	7	6	0	2	2	6
96-97	Manitoba	IHL	16	6	4	10	23	—	—	—	—	—
96-97	Long Beach	IHL	18	3	5	8	10	18	2	2	4	28
	NHL	Totals	74	9	12	21	27	—	—	—	—	—
	AHL	Totals	420	212	236	448	661	45	15	23	38	42
	IHL	Totals	142	49	56	105	217	34	5	11	16	42

Born; 10/28/63, Fort St. John, British Columbia. 5-10, 170. Drafted by New York Rangers (4th pick, 78th overall) in 1982 Entry Draft. Traded to Philadelphia Flyers by Rangers for Michael Boyce (9/28/88). Signed as a free agent by Portland Pirates (7/93). Signed as a free agent by Minnesota Moose (6/20/95). Member of 1993-94 AHL champion Portland Pirates.

Jim Jensen — Left Wing

Season	Team	League	GP	G	A	PTS	PIM	GP	G	A	PTS	PIM
95-96	Mobile	ECHL	66	11	13	24	101	—	—	—	—	—
96-97	Mobile	ECHL	54	9	12	21	64	3	0	1	1	4
	ECHL	Totals	120	20	25	45	165	3	0	1	1	4

Born; 5/16/73, Grand Rapids, Michigan. 5-8, 185.

Paul Jerrard — Defenseman

Season	Team	League	GP	G	A	PTS	PIM	GP	G	A	PTS	PIM
87-88	Colorado	IHL	77	20	28	48	182	11	2	4	6	40
88-89	Minnesota	NHL	5	0	0	0	4	—	—	—	—	—
88-89	Denver	IHL	2	1	1	2	21	—	—	—	—	—
88-89	Kalamazoo	IHL	68	15	25	40	195	6	2	1	3	37
89-90	Kalamazoo	IHL	60	9	18	27	134	7	1	1	2	11
90-91	Albany	IHL	7	0	3	3	30	—	—	—	—	—
90-91	Kalamazoo	IHL	62	10	23	33	111	7	0	0	0	13
91-92	Kalamazoo	IHL	76	4	24	28	123	12	1	7	8	31
92-93	Kalamazoo	IHL	80	8	11	19	187	—	—	—	—	—
93-94	Kalamazoo	IHL	24	0	2	2	60	—	—	—	—	—
93-94	Milwaukee	IHL	28	6	3	9	58	2	0	0	0	8
94-95	Hershey	AHL	66	17	11	28	118	6	0	1	1	19
95-96	Hershey	AHL	25	1	7	8	63	—	—	—	—	—
95-96	Fort Wayne	IHL	19	0	1	1	43	4	0	0	0	2
96-97	Hershey	AHL	62	3	13	16	144	22	1	5	6	24
	IHL	Totals	503	73	139	212	1144	49	6	13	19	142
	AHL	Totals	153	21	31	52	325	10	0	1	1	21

Born; 4/20/65, Winnipeg, Manitoba. 6-1, 190. Drafted by New York Rangers (10th choice, 173rd overall) in 1983 Entry Draft. Traded to Minnesota North Stars by Rangers with Mark Tinordi, Mike Sullivan, Brett Barnett and third round pick (Murray Garbutt, pick previosuly acquired from Los Angeles) for Igor Liba, Brian Lawton and rights to Eric Bennett (10/11/88). Member of 1996-97 AHL Champion Hershey Bearrs.

Dave Jesiolowski — Forward

Season	Team	League	GP	G	A	PTS	PIM	GP	G	A	PTS	PIM
96-97	Baton Rouge	ECHL	15	2	4	6	70	—	—	—	—	—
96-97	Knoxville	ECHL	8	1	1	2	27	—	—	—	—	—
	ECHL	Totals	23	3	5	8	97	—	—	—	—	—

Born; 1/1/74, Edmonton, Alberta. 6-0, 185.

Lee Jinman — Center

Season	Team	League	GP	G	A	PTS	PIM	GP	G	A	PTS	PIM
96-97	Michigan	IHL	81	17	40	57	65	4	1	1	2	2

Born; 1/10/76, Toronto, Ontario. 5-10, 160. Drafted by Dallas Stars (2nd choice, 46th overall) in 1994 Entry Draft.

Trevor Jobe — Center

Season	Team	League	GP	G	A	PTS	PIM	GP	G	A	PTS	PIM
88-89	Newmarket	AHL	75	23	24	47	90	5	0	1	1	12
89-90	Newmarket	AHL	1	0	1	1	2	—	—	—	—	—
89-90	Hampton Roads	ECHL	51	48	23	71	143	5	5	5	10	30
90-91	Newmarket	AHL	2	0	1	1	0	—	—	—	—	—
90-91	Nashville	ECHL	59	49	60	109	229	—	—	—	—	—
91-92	Richmond	ECHL	34	36	30	66	74	—	—	—	—	—
91-92	Nashville	ECHL	28	18	19	37	81	—	—	—	—	—
92-93	Prince Edward Island	AHL	3	1	2	3	0	—	—	—	—	—

Season	Team	League	GP	G	A	PTS	PIM	GP	G	A	PTS	PIM
92-93	Nashville	ECHL	61	*85	76	*161	222	9	7	7	14	38
93-94	N/A											
94-95	Nashville	ECHL	18	16	13	29	40	—	—	—	—	—
94-95	Raleigh	ECHL	23	18	22	40	42	—	—	—	—	—
95-96	Johnstown	ECHL	36	33	37	70	72	—	—	—	—	—
95-96	Tallahassee	ECHL	20	10	18	28	26	12	7	1	8	10
96-97	Wichita	CeHL	57	*56	69	*125	139	—	—	—	—	—
96-97	Columbus	CeHL	4	*5	4	*9	8	3	1	2	3	14
	AHL	Totals	81	24	28	52	92	5	0	1	1	12
	ECHL	Totals	330	313	298	611	929	26	19	13	32	78
	CeHL	Totals	61	61	73	134	147	3	1	2	3	14

Born; 5/14/67, Brandon, Manitoba. 6-1, 210. Drafted by Toronto Maple Leafs (7th choice, 133rd overall) in 1987 Entry Draft. 1992-93 ECHL MVP. 1992-93 ECHL First All-Star Team. 1996-97 CeHL Second Team All-Star. 1996-97 CeHL MVP.

Andreas Johansson — Right Wing

			Regular Season					Playoffs				
Season	Team	League	GP	G	A	PTS	PIM	GP	G	A	PTS	PIM
95-96	Islanders	NHL	3	1	1	2	0	—	—	—	—	—
95-96	Worcester	AHL	29	5	5	10	32	—	—	—	—	—
95-96	Utah	IHL	22	4	13	17	28	12	0	5	5	6
96-97	Islanders	NHL	15	2	2	4	0	—	—	—	—	—
96-97	Pittsburgh	NHL	27	2	7	9	20	—	—	—	—	—
96-97	Cleveland	IHL	10	2	4	6	42	11	1	5	6	8
	NHL	Totals	45	5	10	15	20	—	—	—	—	—
	IHL	Totals	32	6	17	23	70	23	1	10	11	14

Born; 5/19/73, Hofors, Sweden. 5-10, 198. Drafted by New York Islanders (7th choice, 136th overall) in 1991 Entry Draft. Traded to Pittsburgh Penguins by Islanders with Darius Kasparaitis for Bryan Smolinski (11/17/96). Member of 1995-96 IHL champion Utah Grizzlies.

Bernie John — Defenseman

			Regular Season					Playoffs				
Season	Team	League	GP	G	A	PTS	PIM	GP	G	A	PTS	PIM
93-94	St. Thomas	CoHL	60	7	33	40	6	3	0	1	1	0
94-95	London	CoHL	46	10	22	32	10	5	1	1	2	2
95-96	Brantford	CoHL	59	6	30	36	32	12	0	18	18	23
96-97	Utah	IHL	1	0	1	1	0	—	—	—	—	—
96-97	Brantford	CoHL	69	16	54	70	25	8	4	5	9	0
	CoHL	Totals	234	39	139	178	73	28	5	25	30	25

Born; 6/4/72, Sudbury, Ontario. 5-11, 208. 1996-97 CoHL Second Team All-Star.

Cory Johnson — Left Wing

			Regular Season					Playoffs				
Season	Team	League	GP	G	A	PTS	PIM	GP	G	A	PTS	PIM
94-95	Saginaw	CoHL	57	13	29	42	22	—	—	—	—	—
94-95	Muskegon	CoHL	7	1	2	3	2	17	4	1	5	19
95-96	Muskegon	CoHL	73	17	32	49	51	5	1	1	2	7
96-97	Grand Rapids	IHL	12	1	2	3	4	—	—	—	—	—
96-97	Muskegon	CoHL	65	20	25	45	26	1	1	0	1	2
	CoHL	Totals	202	51	88	139	75	23	6	2	8	28

Born; 9/15/73, Antigonish, Nova Scotia. 6-2, 203.

Craig Johnson — Right Wing

			Regular Season					Playoffs				
Season	Team	League	GP	G	A	PTS	PIM	GP	G	A	PTS	PIM
92-93	Oklahoma City	CeHL	50	8	11	19	219	11	0	2	2	67
93-94	Oklahoma City	CeHL	48	5	5	10	230	4	0	0	0	2
94-95	Birmingham	ECHL	37	3	0	3	150	—	—	—	—	—
94-95	Wichita	CeHL	14	1	0	1	99	7	2	5	7	14

Season	Team	League	GP	G	A	PTS	PIM	GP	G	A	PTS	PIM
95-96	Saginaw	CoHL	31	3	1	4	139	2	0	0	0	0
96-97	Michigan	IHL	2	0	0	0	2	—	—	—	—	—
96-97	Manitoba	IHL	16	2	2	4	38	—	—	—	—	—
96-97	Mobile	ECHL	4	0	0	0	74	—	—	—	—	—
96-97	Oklahoma City	CeHL	36	6	11	17	134	—	—	—	—	—
	IHL	Totals	18	2	2	4	40	—	—	—	—	—
	CeHL	Totals	148	20	27	47	682	22	2	7	9	83
	ECHL	Totals	41	3	0	3	224	—	—	—	—	—

Born; 11/16/71, Montreal, Quebec. 6-5, 230. Member of 1994-95 CeHL champion Wichita Thunder.

Darren Johnson — Right Wing

Season	Team	League	GP	G	A	PTS	PIM	GP	G	A	PTS	PIM
96-97	Knoxville	ECHL	28	3	2	5	30	—	—	—	—	—

Born; 8/17/74, Flin Flon, Manitoba. 5-10, 195.

Matt Johnson — Center

Season	Team	League	GP	G	A	PTS	PIM	GP	G	A	PTS	PIM
96-97	Tallahassee	ECHL	69	25	39	64	14	3	0	1	1	0

Born; 10/3/72, Norwood, Massachusetts. 5-10, 185. Last amateur club; Vermont (ECAC).

Ryan Johnson — Center

Season	Team	League	GP	G	A	PTS	PIM	GP	G	A	PTS	PIM
96-97	Carolina	AHL	79	18	24	42	28	—	—	—	—	—

Born; 6/14/76, Thunder Bay, Ontario. 6-2, 185. Drafted by Florida Panthers (4th choice, 36th overall) in 1994 Entry Draft.

B.J. Johnston — Right Wing

Season	Team	League	GP	G	A	PTS	PIM	GP	G	A	PTS	PIM
96-97	Baton Rouge	ECHL	61	17	32	49	52	—	—	—	—	—

Born; 10/13/75, Blenheim, Ontario. 6-2, 200.

Chris Johnston — Left Wing

Season	Team	League	GP	G	A	PTS	PIM	GP	G	A	PTS	PIM
95-96	Erie	ECHL	49	12	14	26	59	—	—	—	—	—
95-96	Dayton	ECHL	15	1	9	10	21	3	2	1	3	0
96-97	Dayton	ECHL	24	6	6	12	27	—	—	—	—	—
96-97	Oklahoma City	CeHL	18	8	4	12	24	4	1	0	1	35
	ECHL	Totals	88	19	29	48	80	3	2	1	3	0

Born; 12/25/74, Brandon, Manitoba. 5-10, 180.

Neil Johnston — Center

Season	Team	League	GP	G	A	PTS	PIM	GP	G	A	PTS	PIM
96-97	Wichita	CeHL	65	15	26	41	126	9	1	3	4	22

Born; 7/8/74, Eston, Saskatchewan. 6-1, 190.

Jacques Joubert — Center

Season	Team	League	GP	G	A	PTS	PIM	GP	G	A	PTS	PIM
95-96	Peoria	IHL	73	17	25	42	45	12	2	5	7	2
96-97	Milwaukee	IHL	42	7	9	16	22	—	—	—	—	—
96-97	Rochester	AHL	20	5	3	8	10	—	—	—	—	—
	IHL	Totals	115	24	34	58	67	12	2	5	7	2

Born; 3/23/71, South Bend, Indiana. 6-2, 201. Drafted by Dallas Stars in NHL supplemental draft (6/25/93).

Bob Joyce — Left Wing

			Regular Season					Playoffs				
Season	Team	League	GP	G	A	PTS	PIM	GP	G	A	PTS	PIM
87-88	Canadian	National										
87-88	Boston	NHL	15	7	5	12	10	23	8	6	14	18
88-89	Boston	NHL	77	18	31	49	46	9	5	2	7	2
89-90	Boston	NHL	23	1	2	3	22	—	—	—	—	—
89-90	Washington	NHL	24	5	8	13	4	14	2	1	3	9
90-91	Washington	NHL	17	3	3	6	8	—	—	—	—	—
90-91	Baltimore	AHL	36	10	8	18	14	6	1	0	1	4
91-92	Winnipeg	NHL	1	0	0	0	0	—	—	—	—	—
91-92	Moncton	AHL	66	19	29	48	51	10	0	5	5	9
92-93	Winnipeg	NHL	1	0	0	0	0	—	—	—	—	—
92-93	Moncton	AHL	75	25	32	57	52	5	0	0	0	2
93-94	Las Vegas	IHL	63	15	18	33	45	5	2	1	3	8
94-95	Las Vegas	IHL	60	15	12	27	52	10	4	3	7	26
95-96	Orlando	IHL	55	7	11	18	81	18	2	1	3	12
96-97	Orlando	IHL	76	15	33	48	98	5	0	0	0	2
	NHL	Totals	158	34	49	83	90	46	15	9	24	29
	IHL	Totals	254	52	74	126	276	38	8	5	13	48
	AHL	Totals	177	54	69	123	117	21	1	5	6	15

Born; 7/11/76, St. John's New Brunswick. 6-0, 195. Selected by Boston Bruins (4th choice, 82nd overall) in 1984 Entry Draft. Traded to Washington Capitals by Boston for Dave Christian (12/13/89). Traded to Winnipeg Jets by Washington with Kent Paynter and Tyler Larter for Brent Hughes, Craig Duncanson and Simon Wheeldon (5/21/91). Signed as a free agent by Las Vegas Thunder (7/8/93).

Duane Joyce — Defenseman

			Regular Season					Playoffs				
Season	Team	League	GP	G	A	PTS	PIM	GP	G	A	PTS	PIM
89-90	Kalamazoo	IHL	2	0	0	0	2	—	—	—	—	—
89-90	Fort Wayne	IHL	66	10	26	36	53	—	—	—	—	—
89-90	Muskegon	IHL	13	3	10	13	8	12	3	7	10	13
90-91	Kalamazoo	IHL	80	12	32	44	53	11	0	3	3	6
91-92	Kansas City	IHL	80	12	32	44	62	15	6	11	17	8
92-93	Kansas City	IHL	75	15	25	40	30	12	1	2	3	6
93-94	Dallas	NHL	3	0	0	0	0	—	—	—	—	—
93-94	Kansas City	IHL	43	9	23	32	40	—	—	—	—	—
94-95	Kansas City	IHL	71	9	21	30	31	21	2	5	7	4
95-96	Cincinnati	IHL	49	11	25	36	36	—	—	—	—	—
95-96	Orlando	IHL	34	3	17	20	18	21	4	6	10	2
96-97	Cincinnati	IHL	38	3	16	19	12	3	1	2	3	0
96-97	Carolina	AHL	34	6	18	24	27	—	—	—	—	—
	IHL	Totals	551	87	227	314	345	95	17	36	53	39

Born; 5/5/65, Pembroke, Massachusetts. 6-2, 205. Signed as a free agent by San Jose Sharks (8/13/91). Signed as a free agent by Dallas Stars (12/3/93). Member of 1991-92 IHL champion Kansas City Blades.

Jeff Jubenville — Right Wing

			Regular Season					Playoffs				
Season	Team	League	GP	G	A	PTS	PIM	GP	G	A	PTS	PIM
95-96	Bakersfield	WCHL	52	31	27	58	51	—	—	—	—	—
96-97	Bakersfield	WCHL	50	30	34	64	47	4	1	2	3	4
	WCHL	Totals	102	61	61	121	98	4	1	2	3	4

Born; 2/5/74, Duncan, British Columbia. 6-2, 210.

Rick Judson — Left Wing

Season	Team	League	GP	G	A	PTS	PIM	GP	G	A	PTS	PIM
91-92	Toledo	ECHL	2	1	0	1	2	—	—	—	—	—
92-93	Adirondack	AHL	7	3	0	3	0	—	—	—	—	—
92-93	Toledo	ECHL	56	23	28	51	39	16	7	16	23	10
93-94	Adirondack	AHL	2	1	0	1	0	—	—	—	—	—
93-94	Toledo	ECHL	61	39	49	88	16	14	5	13	18	6
94-95	Las Vegas	IHL	2	0	1	1	0	—	—	—	—	—
94-95	Toledo	ECHL	54	27	41	68	29	4	2	4	6	0
95-96	Utah	IHL	1	0	0	0	0	—	—	—	—	—
95-96	Michigan	IHL	2	0	1	1	0	—	—	—	—	—
95-96	Minnesota	IHL	5	0	1	1	0	—	—	—	—	—
95-96	Toledo	ECHL	59	43	38	81	38	11	9	9	18	2
96-97	Las Vegas	IHL	17	5	2	7	0	2	0	0	0	0
96-97	Toledo	ECHL	54	30	43	73	22	5	3	2	5	0
	IHL	Totals	27	5	5	10	0	2	0	0	0	0
	AHL	Totals	9	4	0	4	0	—	—	—	—	—
	ECHL	Totals	286	163	199	362	146	50	26	44	70	18

Born; 8/13/69, Toledo, Ohio. 5-10, 200. Drafted by Detroit Red Wings (11th choice, 204th overall) in 1989 Entry Draft. 1992-93 ECHL Playoff MVP. 1993-94 ECHL Second Team All-Star. Member of 1992-93 ECHL champion Toledo Storm. Member of 1993-94 ECHL champion Toledo Storm.

Patrick Juhlin — Left Wing

Season	Team	League	GP	G	A	PTS	PIM	GP	G	A	PTS	PIM
94-95	Philadelphia	NHL	42	4	3	7	6	13	1	0	1	2
95-96	Philadelphia	NHL	14	3	3	6	17	—	—	—	—	—
95-96	Hershey	AHL	14	5	2	7	8	1	0	0	0	0
96-97	Philadelphia	AHL	78	31	60	91	24	9	7	6	13	4
	NHL	Totals	56	7	6	13	23	13	1	0	1	2
	AHL	Totals	92	36	62	98	32	10	7	6	13	4

Born; 4/24/70, Huddinge, Sweden. 6-0, 194. Drafted by Philadelphia Flyers (2nd choice, 34th overall) in 1989 Entry Draft. 1996-97 AHL First Team All-Star.

Stephane Julien — Defenseman

Season	Team	League	GP	G	A	PTS	PIM	GP	G	A	PTS	PIM
96-97	Pensacola	ECHL	69	13	25	38	91	12	2	2	4	20

Born; 4/7/74, Shawnigan, Ontario. 5-11, 190.

Claude Jutras — Right Wing

Season	Team	League	GP	G	A	PTS	PIM	GP	G	A	PTS	PIM
94-95	Cape Breton	AHL	25	6	5	11	95	—	—	—	—	—
94-95	Wheeling	ECHL	19	7	7	14	172	3	2	1	3	20
95-96	Cape Breton	AHL	4	0	0	0	11	—	—	—	—	—
95-96	Cornwall	AHL	40	4	4	8	148	5	0	0	0	7
95-96	Brantford	CoHL	1	0	0	0	2	—	—	—	—	—
96-97	Pensacola	ECHL	13	6	5	11	132	—	—	—	—	—
96-97	Tallahassee	ECHL	20	4	8	12	126	—	—	—	—	—
96-97	Knoxville	ECHL	19	1	10	11	141	—	—	—	—	—
	AHL	Totals	69	10	9	19	254	5	0	0	0	7
	ECHL	Totals	71	18	30	48	471	3	2	1	3	20

Born; 9/18/73, Hampstead, Quebec. 6-1, 200. Drafted by Philadelphia Flyers (7th choice, 175th overall) in 1992 Entry Draft. Signed as a free agent by the Cape Breton Oilers (9/30/94).

Marian Kacir — Right Wing

			Regular Season					Playoffs				
Season	Team	League	GP	G	A	PTS	PIM	GP	G	A	PTS	PIM
94-95	Chicago	IHL	29	4	6	10	6	—	—	—	—	—
94-95	Charlotte	ECHL	5	2	3	5	2	—	—	—	—	—
94-95	Nashville	ECHL	9	1	7	8	2	4	1	2	3	6
95-96	Atlanta	IHL	2	0	0	0	0	—	—	—	—	—
95-96	Nashville	ECHL	36	22	33	55	6	—	—	—	—	—
96-97	Adirondack	AHL	3	0	0	0	2	—	—	—	—	—
96-97	Wheeling	ECHL	20	6	13	19	0	—	—	—	—	—
	IHL	Totals	31	4	6	10	6	—	—	—	—	—
	ECHL	Totals	70	31	56	87	10	4	1	2	3	6

Born; 9/29/74, Hodonin, Czechoslovakia. 6-1, 183. Drafted by Tampa Bay Lightning (4th choice, 81st overall) in 1993 Entry Draft.

Butch Kaebel — Left Wing

			Regular Season					Playoffs				
Season	Team	League	GP	G	A	PTS	PIM	GP	G	A	PTS	PIM
90-91	Knoxville	ECHL	54	17	26	43	49	1	0	0	0	0
91-92	Peoria	IHL	30	3	11	14	6	3	0	0	0	0
91-92	Dayton	ECHL	30	4	18	22	13	—	—	—	—	—
91-92	Michigan	CoHL	18	5	7	12	4	—	—	—	—	—
92-93	Birmingham	ECHL	56	17	25	42	61	—	—	—	—	—
93-94	Peoria	IHL	59	16	9	25	31	6	1	0	1	0
93-94	Dayton	ECHL	14	7	7	14	23	—	—	—	—	—
94-95	Peoria	IHL	43	7	2	9	61	3	0	0	0	2
95-96	Peoria	IHL	1	0	1	1	0	—	—	—	—	—
95-96	Quad City	CoHL	51	13	34	47	72	4	2	2	4	8
96-97	Peoria	ECHL	57	27	37	64	41	10	4	2	6	2
	IHL	Totals	133	26	23	49	98	12	1	0	1	2
	ECHL	Totals	211	72	113	185	187	11	4	2	6	2
	CoHL	Totals	69	18	41	59	76	4	2	2	4	8

Born; 11/15/66, Pekin, Illinois. 5-11, 195.

Karson Kaebel — Center

			Regular Season					Playoffs				
Season	Team	League	GP	G	A	PTS	PIM	GP	G	A	PTS	PIM
94-95	Cornwall	AHL	25	3	7	10	17	—	—	—	—	—
94-95	Dayton	ECHL	33	14	33	47	68	9	0	4	4	28
95-96	Jacksonville	ECHL	1	0	0	0	0	—	—	—	—	—
95-96	Quad City	CoHL	57	14	52	66	88	4	1	2	3	0
96-97	Peoria	ECHL	69	23	45	68	68	10	3	4	7	16
	ECHL	Totals	103	37	78	115	136	19	3	8	11	44

Born; 12/5/72, Pekin, Illinois. 5-10, 204.

Darcy Kaminski — Defenseman

			Regular Season					Playoffs				
Season	Team	League	GP	G	A	PTS	PIM	GP	G	A	PTS	PIM
90-91	Hampton Roads	ECHL	42	5	14	19	132	11	0	2	2	58
91-92	Hampton Roads	ECHL	24	2	5	7	110	—	—	—	—	—
92-93	Nashville	ECHL	42	3	6	9	133	3	0	0	0	6
93-94	Wichita	CeHL	10	0	1	1	6	4	0	0	0	21
94-95	Wichita	CeHL	24	1	3	4	38	—	—	—	—	—
96-97	Wichita	CeHL	45	1	7	8	91	—	—	—	—	—
	ECHL	Totals	108	10	25	35	375	14	0	2	2	64
	CeHL	Totals	79	2	11	13	135	4	0	0	0	21

Born; 3/10/64, Lethbridge, Alberta. 6-1, 180. Drafted by Hartford Whalers (14th choice, 224th overall) in 1983 Entry Draft. Member of 1990-91 ECHL Champion Hampton Roads Admirals. Member of 1993-94 CeHL Champion Wichita Thunder. DNP in 1995-96 season.

Yan Kaminsky — Left Wing

Season	Team	League	GP	G	A	PTS	PIM	GP	G	A	PTS	PIM
93-94	Winnipeg	NHL	1	0	0	0	0	—	—	—	—	—
93-94	Moncton	AHL	33	9	13	22	6	—	—	—	—	—
94-95	Islanders	NHL	2	1	1	2	0	—	—	—	—	—
94-95	Denver	IHL	38	17	16	33	14	15	6	6	12	0
95-96	Utah	IHL	16	3	3	6	8	21	3	5	8	4
96-97	Utah	IHL	77	28	27	55	18	7	1	4	5	0
	NHL	Totals	3	1	1	2	0	—	—	—	—	—
	IHL	Totals	131	48	46	94	40	43	10	15	25	4

Born; 7/28/71, Penza, Russia. 6-1, 176. Drafted by Winnipeg Jets (4th choice, 99th overall) in 1991 Entry Draft. Traded to New York Islanders by Winnipeg for Wayne McBean (2/1/94). Member of 1994-95 IHL champion Denver Grizzlies. Member of 1995-96 IHL champion Utah Grizzlies.

Kory Karlander — Left Wing

Season	Team	League	GP	G	A	PTS	PIM	GP	G	A	PTS	PIM
95-96	Columbus	ECHL	17	1	6	7	28	2	0	0	0	4
96-97	Louisville	ECHL	19	3	8	11	6	—	—	—	—	—
96-97	Raleigh	ECHL	36	8	20	28	36	—	—	—	—	—
	ECHL	Totals	72	12	34	46	70	2	0	0	0	4

Born; 3/21/72, Melita, Manitoba. 6-1, 190.

Frederic Karlstrom — Defenseman

Season	Team	League	GP	G	A	PTS	PIM	GP	G	A	PTS	PIM
96-97	Macon	CeHL	28	1	3	4	27	—	—	—	—	—
96-97	Nashville	CeHL	19	4	5	9	18	—	—	—	—	—
	CeHL	Totals	47	5	8	13	45	—	—	—	—	—

Born; 4/25/73, Harno Sand, Sweden. 6-1, 190.

Sergei Karnaoukh — Left Wing

Season	Team	League	GP	G	A	PTS	PIM	GP	G	A	PTS	PIM
96-97	Muskegon	CoHL	20	2	6	8	30	2	0	0	0	2

Born; 8/25/75, Kiev, Ukraine. 6-0, 165.

Mark Karpen — Center

Season	Team	League	GP	G	A	PTS	PIM	GP	G	A	PTS	PIM
92-93	St. Thomas	CoHL	29	9	21	30	16	—	—	—	—	—
92-93	Johnstown	ECHL	38	17	25	42	22	5	1	4	5	4
93-94	Cleveland	IHL	17	6	5	11	0	—	—	—	—	—
93-94	Muskegon	CoHL	45	29	46	75	20	3	1	1	2	0
94-95	Wichita	CeHL	49	32	40	72	45	—	—	—	—	—
95-96	Muskegon	CoHL	9	2	4	6	8	—	—	—	—	—
95-96	Reno	WCHL	55	28	37	65	49	3	0	2	2	0
96-97	Amarillo	WPHL	57	32	36	68	38	—	—	—	—	—
	CoHL	Totals	83	40	71	111	44	3	1	1	2	0

Born; 5/13/69, Eveleth, Minnesota. 5-11, 170. 1995-96 WCHL Second Team All-Star.

Igor Karpenko — Goaltender

Regular Season | | | | | | | | | **Playoffs**

Season	Team	League	GP	W	L	T	MIN	SO	AVG	GP	W	L	MIN	SO	AVG
96-97	Port Huron	CoHL	23	9	9	1	1149	0	3.50	3	1	2	179	0	5.36
96-97	Las Vegas	IHL	3	0	2	0	134	0	5.38	—	—	—	—	—	—

Born; 7/23/76, Liev, Russia. Drafted by Anaheim Mighty Ducks (7th choice, 185th overall) in 1995 Entry Draft.

Valeri Karpov — Right Wing

Regular Season | | | | | | | **Playoffs**

Season	Team	League	GP	G	A	PTS	PIM	GP	G	A	PTS	PIM
94-95	Anaheim	NHL	30	4	7	11	6	—	—	—	—	—
94-95	San Diego	IHL	5	3	3	6	0	—	—	—	—	—
95-96	Anaheim	NHL	37	9	8	17	10	—	—	—	—	—
96-97	Anaheim	NHL	9	1	0	1	16	—	—	—	—	—
96-97	Baltimore	AHL	10	4	8	12	8	—	—	—	—	—
96-97	Long Beach	IHL	30	18	17	35	19	18	8	7	15	18
	NHL	Totals	76	14	15	29	32	—	—	—	—	—
	IHL	Totals	35	21	20	41	19	18	8	7	15	18

Born; 8/5/71, Chelyabinsk, Russia. 5-10, 176. Drafted by Anaheim Mighty Ducks (3rd choice, 56th overall) in 1993 Entry Draft.

Dan Keczmer — Defenseman

Regular Season | | | | | | | **Playoffs**

Season	Team	League	GP	G	A	PTS	PIM	GP	G	A	PTS	PIM
90-91	Minnesota	NHL	9	0	1	1	6	—	—	—	—	—
90-91	Kalamazoo	IHL	60	4	20	24	60	9	1	2	3	10
91-92	United States	National										
91-92	Hartford	NHL	1	0	0	0	0	—	—	—	—	—
91-92	Springfield	AHL	18	3	4	7	10	4	0	0	0	6
92-93	Hartford	NHL	23	4	4	8	28	—	—	—	—	—
92-93	Springfield	AHL	37	1	13	14	38	12	0	4	4	14
93-94	Hartford	NHL	12	0	1	1	12	—	—	—	—	—
93-94	Calgary	NHL	57	1	20	21	48	3	0	0	0	4
93-94	Springfield	AHL	7	0	1	1	4	—	—	—	—	—
94-95	Calgary	NHL	28	2	3	5	10	7	0	1	1	2
95-96	Calgary	NHL	13	0	0	0	14	—	—	—	—	—
95-96	Saint John	AHL	22	3	11	14	14	—	—	—	—	—
95-96	Albany	AHL	17	0	4	4	4	1	0	0	0	0
96-97	Dallas	NHL	13	0	1	1	6	—	—	—	—	—
96-97	Michigan	IHL	42	3	17	20	24	—	—	—	—	—
	NHL	Totals	156	7	30	37	124	10	0	1	1	6
	IHL	Totals	102	7	37	44	84	9	1	2	3	10
	AHL	Totals	101	7	33	40	70	17	0	4	4	20

Born; 5/25/68, Mt. Clemens, Michigan. 6-1, 190. Drafted by Minnesota North Stars (11th choice, 201st overall) in 1986 Entry Draft. Claimed by San Jose Sharks from Minnesota in Dispersal Draft (5/30/91). Traded to Hartford Whalers by San Jose for Dean Evason (10/2/91). Traded to Calgary Flames by Hartford for Jeff Reese (11/19/93). Traded to New Jersey Devils by Calgary Flames with Phil Housley for Tommy Albelin, Cal Hulse and Jocelyn Lemieux. Signed as a free agent by Dallas Stars (8/19/96).

Jason Keith — Center

Regular Season | | | | | | | **Playoffs**

Season	Team	League	GP	G	A	PTS	PIM	GP	G	A	PTS	PIM
95-96	Reno	WCHL	51	14	22	36	56	—	—	—	—	—
96-97	Reno	WCHL	46	9	10	19	44	—	—	—	—	—
96-97	Alaska	WCHL	6	1	3	4	4	—	—	—	—	—
	WCHL	Totals	103	24	35	59	104	—	—	—	—	—

Born; 7/1/74, 5-10, 170.

Aaron Keller — Defenseman

Season	Team	League	GP	G	A	PTS	PIM	GP	G	A	PTS	PIM
96-97	Baltimore	AHL	11	3	2	5	2	1	0	0	0	0
96-97	Chicago	IHL	23	1	3	4	4	—	—	—	—	—
96-97	Peoria	ECHL	22	0	8	8	24	—	—	—	—	—

Born; 3/1/75, Kamloops, British Columbia. 6-0, 175. Last amateur club; Kamloops (WHL).

Jason Kelly — Right Wing

Season	Team	League	GP	G	A	PTS	PIM	GP	G	A	PTS	PIM
95-96	Charlotte	ECHL	42	2	15	17	95	14	1	3	4	14
96-97	Baton Rouge	ECHL	60	3	14	17	81	—	—	—	—	—
	ECHL	Totals	102	5	29	34	176	14	1	3	4	14

Born; 5/30/72, Thunder Bay, Ontario. 6-2, 208. Member of 1995-96 ECHL champion Charlotte Checkers.

Steve Kelly — Center

Season	Team	League	GP	G	A	PTS	PIM	GP	G	A	PTS	PIM
96-97	Edmonton	NHL	8	1	0	1	6	6	0	0	0	2
96-97	Hamilton	AHL	48	9	29	38	111	11	3	3	6	24

Born; 10/26/76, Vancouver, British Columbia. 6-1, 190. Drafted by Edmonton Oilers (1st choice, 6th overall) in 1995 Entry Draft.

Scott Kelsey — Defenseman

Season	Team	League	GP	G	A	PTS	PIM	GP	G	A	PTS	PIM
93-94	Utica	CoHL	12	1	2	3	2	—	—	—	—	—
93-94	Muskegon	CoHL	10	0	1	1	8	—	—	—	—	—
93-94	Louisville	ECHL	27	0	3	3	10	6	0	0	0	9
94-95	San Antonio	CeHL	32	4	7	11	84	—	—	—	—	—
94-95	Memphis	CeHL	31	1	5	6	40	—	—	—	—	—
95-96	Memphis	CeHL	63	4	12	16	121	6	0	1	1	17
96-97	Memphis	CeHL	66	2	18	20	168	18	3	3	6	30
	CeHL	Totals	192	11	42	53	413	24	3	4	7	47
	CoHL	Totals	22	1	3	4	10	—	—	—	—	—

Born; 1/31/71, New Hartford, New York. 6-1, 195.

Mick Kempffer — Defenseman

Season	Team	League	GP	G	A	PTS	PIM	GP	G	A	PTS	PIM
94-95	Chicago	IHL	35	2	5	7	26	—	—	—	—	—
94-95	Charlotte	ECHL	12	1	6	7	16	—	—	—	—	—
95-96	Charlotte	ECHL	65	1	21	22	82	16	0	3	3	33
96-97	Charlotte	ECHL	43	4	18	22	27	—	—	—	—	—
96-97	Jacksonville	ECHL	23	2	6	8	24	—	—	—	—	—
	ECHL	Totals	143	8	51	59	149	16	0	3	3	33

Born; 4/17/70, Duluth, Minnesota. 6-0, 184. Member of 1995-96 ECHL champion Charlotte Checkers.

Chris Kenady — Right Wing

Season	Team	League	GP	G	A	PTS	PIM	GP	G	A	PTS	PIM
95-96	Worcester	AHL	43	9	10	19	58	2	0	0	0	0
96-97	Worcester	AHL	73	23	26	49	131	5	0	1	1	2
	AHL	Totals	116	32	36	68	189	7	0	1	1	2

Born; 4/10/73, Mound, Minnesota. 6-2, 195. Drafted by St. Louis Blues (8th choice, 175th overall) in 1991 Entry Draft.

Troy Kennedy — Right Wing

			Regular Season					Playoffs				
Season	Team	League	GP	G	A	PTS	PIM	GP	G	A	PTS	PIM
96-97	Central Texas	WPHL	64	16	50	66	47	11	3	9	12	12

Born; 3/12/68, Brandon, Manitoba. Drafted by Calgary Flames (8th choice, 168th overall) in 1988 Entry Draft.

Jay Kenney — Defenseman

			Regular Season					Playoffs				
Season	Team	League	GP	G	A	PTS	PIM	GP	G	A	PTS	PIM
96-97	Charlotte	ECHL	62	2	14	16	61	3	0	1	1	4

Born; 9/21/73, New York, New York. 6-2, 190. Drafted by Ottawa Senators (8th choice, 169th overall) in 1992 Entry Draft.

Rob Kenny — Right Wing

			Regular Season					Playoffs				
Season	Team	League	GP	G	A	PTS	PIM	GP	G	A	PTS	PIM
92-93	Binghamton	AHL	66	12	11	23	56	8	2	4	6	8
93-94	Binghamton	AHL	63	27	14	41	90	—	—	—	—	—
94-95	Binghamton	AHL	17	2	9	11	32	—	—	—	—	—
95-96	Los Angeles	IHL	74	15	19	34	124	—	—	—	—	—
96-97	Long Beach	IHL	76	18	15	33	127	18	4	2	6	44
	IHL	Totals	150	33	34	67	251	18	4	2	6	44
	AHL	Totals	146	41	34	75	178	8	2	4	6	8

Born; 10/19/68, Bronx, New York. 6-1, 205.

Kevin Kerr — Right Wing

			Regular Season					Playoffs				
Season	Team	League	GP	G	A	PTS	PIM	GP	G	A	PTS	PIM
87-88	Rochester	AHL	72	18	11	29	352	5	1	3	4	42
88-89	Rochester	AHL	66	20	18	38	306	—	—	—	—	—
89-90	Rochester	AHL	8	0	1	1	22	—	—	—	—	—
89-90	Fort Wayne	IHL	43	11	16	27	219	5	0	1	1	33
89-90	Phoenix	IHL	6	0	0	0	25	—	—	—	—	—
90-91	Fort Wayne	IHL	13	1	6	7	32	—	—	—	—	—
90-91	Cincinnati	ECHL	36	25	34	59	228	4	0	6	6	23
91-92	Utica	AHL	19	3	3	6	25	—	—	—	—	—
91-92	Cincinnati	ECHL	37	27	18	45	203	9	4	9	13	64
92-93	Cincinnati	IHL	39	18	23	41	93	—	—	—	—	—
92-93	Birmingham	ECHL	39	30	34	64	217	—	—	—	—	—
93-94	Portland	AHL	4	2	0	2	2	8	0	3	3	21
93-94	Phoenix	IHL	12	2	4	6	9	—	—	—	—	—
93-94	Flint	CoHL	45	57	55	112	299	10	6	7	13	79
94-95	Flint	CoHL	62	63	56	119	284	4	6	1	7	2
95-96	Flint	CoHL	66	53	47	100	204	15	11	15	26	24
96-97	Flint	CoHL	68	72	53	125	200	13	10	6	16	35
	AHL	Totals	169	43	33	76	707	13	1	6	7	63
	IHL	Totals	113	32	49	81	378	5	0	1	1	33
	CoHL	Totals	241	245	211	456	987	42	33	29	62	140
	ECHL	Totals	112	82	86	168	648	13	4	15	19	87

Born; 9/18/67, North Bay, Ontario. 5-10, 190. Drafted by Buffalo Sabres (4rth choice, 56th overall) 6/21/86. 1993-94 CoHL First Team All-Star, 1994-95 CoHL Second Team All-Star, 1995-96 CoHL First Team All-Star. 1996-97 CoHL First Team All-Star. Member of 1993-94 Calder Cup Champion Portland Pirates. Member of 1995-96 Colonial Cup Champion Flint Generals.

Dan Kesa — Right Wing

			Regular Season					Playoffs				
Season	Team	League	GP	G	A	PTS	PIM	GP	G	A	PTS	PIM
92-93	Hamilton	AHL	62	16	24	40	76	—	—	—	—	—
93-94	Vancouver	NHL	5	0	0	0	2	—	—	—	—	—

Season	Team	League	GP	G	A	PTS	PIM	GP	G	A	PTS	PIM
93-94	Hamilton	AHL	53	37	33	70	33	4	1	4	5	4
94-95	Syracuse	AHL	70	34	44	78	81	—	—	—	—	—
95-96	Dallas	NHL	3	0	0	0	0	—	—	—	—	—
95-96	Springfield	AHL	22	10	5	15	13	—	—	—	—	—
95-96	Michigan	IHL	15	4	11	15	33	—	—	—	—	—
95-96	Detroit	IHL	27	9	6	15	22	12	6	4	10	4
96-97	Detroit	IHL	60	22	21	43	19	20	7	5	12	20
	NHL	Totals	8	0	0	0	2	—	—	—	—	—
	AHL	Totals	207	97	106	203	203	4	1	4	5	4
	IHL	Totals	102	35	38	73	74	32	13	9	22	24

Born; 11/23/71, Vancouver, British Columbia. 6-0, 208. Drafted by Vancouver Canucks (5th choice, 95th overall) in 1991 Entry Draft. Traded to Dallas Stars by Vancouver with Greg Adams and Vancouver's fifth round choice (later traded to Los Angeles-Los Angeles selected Jason Morgan) in 1995 Entry Draft for Russ Courtnall (4/7/95) and conditional pick in 1997 Entry Draft to Hartford for Robert Petrovicky (11/29/95). Member of 1996-97 IHL Champion Detroit Vipers.

Sergei Kharin — Right Wing

			Regular Season					Playoffs				
Season	Team	League	GP	G	A	PTS	PIM	GP	G	A	PTS	PIM
90-91	Winnipeg	NHL	7	2	3	5	2	—	—	—	—	—
90-91	Moncton	AHL	66	22	18	40	38	5	1	0	1	2
91-92	Halifax	AHL	40	10	12	22	15	—	—	—	—	—
92-93	Cincinnati	IHL	60	13	18	31	25	—	—	—	—	—
92-93	Birmingham	ECHL	2	0	3	3	0	—	—	—	—	—
93-94	Dayton	ECHL	59	30	59	89	56	3	2	0	2	4
94-95	Cincinnati	IHL	56	14	29	43	24	1	0	0	0	0
95-96	Worcester	AHL	28	7	12	19	10	3	1	1	2	2
95-96	Dayton	ECHL	25	7	9	16	25	—	—	—	—	—
96-97	Port Huron	CoHL	49	20	24	44	20	—	—	—	—	—
96-97	Muskegon	CoHL	19	12	16	28	12	3	0	2	2	0
	AHL	Totals	134	39	42	81	63	8	2	1	3	4
	IHL	Totals	116	27	47	74	49	1	0	0	0	0
	ECHL	Totals	86	37	71	108	81	3	2	0	2	4
	CoHL	Totals	68	32	40	72	32	3	0	2	2	0

Born; 2/20/63, Odintsovo, Russia. 6-0, 190. Drafted by Winnipeg Jets (15th choice, 240th overall) in 1989 Entry Draft. Traded to Quebec Nordiques by Jets for Shawn Anderson (10/22/91).

Alexander Kharlomov — Left Wing

			Regular Season					Playoffs				
Season	Team	League	GP	G	A	PTS	PIM	GP	G	A	PTS	PIM
95-96	Portland	AHL	65	14	18	32	35	14	2	3	5	8
96-97	Portland	AHL	56	9	15	24	28	—	—	—	—	—
	AHL	Totals	121	23	33	56	63	14	2	3	5	8

Born; 9/23/75, Moscow, Russia. 5-11, 183. Drafted by Washington Capitals (2nd choice, 15th overall) in 1994 Entry Draft.

Alex Kholomeyev — Right Wing

			Regular Season					Playoffs				
Season	Team	League	GP	G	A	PTS	PIM	GP	G	A	PTS	PIM
92-93	Fort Worth	CeHL	42	23	22	45	124	—	—	—	—	—
93-94	Fort Worth	CeHL	53	21	21	42	76	—	—	—	—	—
94-95	Fort Worth	CeHL	63	31	29	60	91	—	—	—	—	—
95-96	Huntsville	SHL	47	36	35	71	68	10	5	5	10	23
96-97	Waco	WPHL	4	1	3	4	10	—	—	—	—	—
96-97	Huntsville	CeHL	57	37	58	95	90	9	13	1	14	24
	CeHL	Totals	215	112	130	242	381	9	13	1	14	24

Born; 3/29/69, St. Petersburg, Russia. 6-2, 200. Drafted by San Jose Sharks (10th choice, 219th overall) in 1992 Entry Draft. Member of 1995-96 SHL champion Huntsville Channel Cats.

Yuri Khmylev — Left Wing

Season	Team	League	GP	G	A	PTS	PIM	GP	G	A	PTS	PIM
92-93	Buffalo	NHL	68	20	19	39	28	8	4	3	7	4
93-94	Buffalo	NHL	72	27	31	58	49	7	3	1	4	8
94-95	Buffalo	NHL	48	8	17	25	14	5	0	1	1	8
95-96	Buffalo	NHL	66	8	20	28	40	—	—	—	—	—
95-96	St. Louis	NHL	7	0	1	1	0	6	1	1	2	4
96-97	St. Louis	NHL	2	1	0	1	2	—	—	—	—	—
96-97	Quebec	IHL	15	1	7	8	4	—	—	—	—	—
96-97	Hamilton	AHL	52	5	19	24	43	22	6	7	13	12
	NHL	Totals	263	64	88	152	133	26	8	6	14	24

Born; 8/9/64, Moscow, Russia. 6-1, 189. Drafted by Buffalo Sabres (7th choice, 108th overall) in 1992 Entry Draft. Traded to St. Louis Blues by Buffalo with Buffalo's eighth round choice (Andrei Podkonicky) in 1996 Entry Draft for Jean-Luc Grand Pierre, Ottawa's second round chocice (previously acquired by St. Louis—Buffalo selected Cory Sarich) in 1996 Entry Draft and St. Louis' third round selection (Maxim Afinogenov) in 1997 Entry Draft (3/20/96).

Chad Kilger — Center

Season	Team	League	GP	G	A	PTS	PIM	GP	G	A	PTS	PIM
95-96	Anaheim	NHL	45	5	7	12	22	—	—	—	—	—
95-96	Winnipeg	NHL	29	2	3	5	12	4	1	0	1	0
96-97	Phoenix	NHL	24	4	3	7	13	—	—	—	—	—
96-97	Springfield	AHL	52	17	28	45	36	16	5	7	12	56
	NHL	Totals	98	11	13	24	47	4	1	0	1	0

Born; 11/27/76, Cornwall, Ontario. Drafted by Anaheim Mighty Ducks (1st choice, 4th overall) in 1995 Entry Draft. Traded to Winnipeg Jets by Anaheim with Oleg Tverdovsky and Anaheim's third round choice (Per-Anton Lundstrom) in 1996 Entry Draft for Teemu Sellanne, Marc Chouinard and Winnipeg's fourth round choice (later traded to Toronto—later traded to Montreal—Montreal selected Kim Staal) in 1996 Entry Draft, (2/7/96).

Darin Kimble — Right Wing

Season	Team	League	GP	G	A	PTS	PIM	GP	G	A	PTS	PIM
88-89	Quebec	NHL	26	3	1	4	149	—	—	—	—	—
88-89	Halifax	AHL	39	8	6	14	188	—	—	—	—	—
89-90	Quebec	NHL	44	5	5	10	185	—	—	—	—	—
89-90	Halifax	AHL	18	6	6	12	37	6	1	1	2	61
90-91	Quebec	NHL	35	2	5	7	114	—	—	—	—	—
90-91	St. Louis	NHL	26	1	1	2	128	13	0	0	0	38
90-91	Halifax	AHL	7	1	4	5	20	—	—	—	—	—
91-92	St. Louis	NHL	46	1	3	4	166	5	0	0	0	7
92-93	Boston	NHL	55	7	3	10	177	4	0	0	0	2
92-93	Providence	AHL	12	1	4	5	34	—	—	—	—	—
93-94	Chicago	NHL	65	4	2	6	133	1	0	0	0	5
94-95	Chicago	NHL	14	0	0	0	30	—	—	—	—	—
95-96	Indianapolis	IHL	9	1	0	1	15	—	—	—	—	—
95-96	Albany	AHL	60	4	15	19	144	3	0	0	0	2
96-97	Manitoba	IHL	39	3	4	7	115	—	—	—	—	—
96-97	Kansas City	IHL	33	9	9	18	106	2	0	0	0	0
	NHL	Totals	311	23	20	42	1082	23	0	0	0	52
	AHL	Totals	136	20	35	55	423	9	1	1	2	63
	IHL	Totals	81	13	13	26	236	2	0	0	0	0

Born; 11/22/68, Lucky Lake, Saskatchewan. 6-2, 210. Drafted by Quebec Nordiques (5th choice, 66th overall) in 1988 Entry Draft. Traded to St. Louis Blues by Quebec for Herb Raglan, Tony Twist and Andy Rymsha (2/4/91). Traded to Tampa Bay Lightning by St. Louis with Pat Jablonski and Steve Tuttle for future considerations (6/19/92). Traded to Boston Bruins by Tampa Bay with future considerations for Ken Hodge and Matt Hervey (9/4/92). Signed as a free agent by Florida Panthers (7/9/93). Traded to Chicago Blackhawks by Florida for Keith Brown (9/30/93). Traded to New Jersey Devils by Chicago for Michael Vukonich and Bill Armstrong (11/1/96). Signed as a free agent by Phoenix Coyotes (7/97).

Steven King — Right Wing

			Regular Season					Playoffs				
Season	Team	League	GP	G	A	PTS	PIM	GP	G	A	PTS	PIM
91-92	Binghamton	AHL	66	27	15	42	56	10	2	0	2	14
92-93	Rangers	NHL	24	7	5	12	16	—	—	—	—	—
92-93	Binghamton	AHL	53	35	33	68	100	14	7	9	16	26
93-94	Anaheim	NHL	36	8	3	11	44	—	—	—	—	—
94-95	DNP	Injured										
95-96	Anaheim	NHL	7	2	0	2	15	—	—	—	—	—
95-96	Baltimore	AHL	68	40	21	62	95	12	7	5	12	20
96-97	Philadelphia	AHL	39	17	10	27	47	—	—	—	—	—
96-97	Michigan	IHL	39	15	11	26	39	4	1	2	3	12
	NHL	Totals	67	17	8	25	75	—	—	—	—	—
	AHL	Totals	226	119	79	198	298	36	16	14	30	60

Born; 7/22/69, Greenwich, Rhode Island. 6-0, 195. Drafted by New York Rangers (1st choice. 21st overall) in 1991 Supplemental Draft. Claimed by Anaheim Mighty Ducks in Expansion Draft (6/24/93). Signed as a free agent by Philadelphia Flyers (7/31/96).

Geordie Kinnear — Defenseman

			Regular Season					Playoffs				
Season	Team	League	GP	G	A	PTS	PIM	GP	G	A	PTS	PIM
93-94	ALB	AHL	59	3	12	15	197	5	0	0	0	21
94-95	ALB	AHL	68	5	11	16	136	9	1	1	2	7
95-96	ALB	AHL	73	4	7	11	170	4	0	1	1	2
96-97	Albany	AHL	59	2	9	11	175	10	0	1	1	15
	AHL	Totals	259	14	39	53	678	28	1	3	4	45

Born; 7/9/73, Simcoe, Ontario. 6-1, 200. Drafted by New Jersey Devils (7th choice, 162nd overall) in 1992 Entry Draft. Member of 1994-95 Calder Cup champion Albany RiverRats.

Travis Kirby — Goaltender

			Regular Season						Playoffs					
Season	Team	League	GP	W	L	T	MIN	SO	AVG	GP	W	L	MIN	SO	AVG
96-97	Nashville	CeHL	1	0	1	0	60	0	9.00	—	—	—	—	—	—
96-97	San Antonio	CeHL	8	0	5	0	315	0	7.99	—	—	—	—	—	—
96-97	Wichita	CeHL	12	3	7	2	661	0	5.26	1	0	0	1	0	0.00
	CeHL	Totals	21	3	12	2	1037	0	6.31	1	0	0	1	0	0.00

Born; 6/15/74, Parksville, British Columbia. 5-10, 190.

Kyle Kirkpatrick — Defenseman

			Regular Season					Playoffs				
Season	Team	League	GP	G	A	PTS	PIM	GP	G	A	PTS	PIM
94-95	Raleigh	ECHL	8	1	3	4	2	—	—	—	—	—
95-96	Raleigh	ECHL	7	0	0	0	8	—	—	—	—	—
95-96	Huntington	ECHL	52	5	8	13	58	—	—	—	—	—
96-97	Huntington	ECHL	44	1	14	15	70	—	—	—	—	—
	ECHL	Totals	111	7	25	32	138	—	—	—	—	—

Born; 8/14/71, Dearborn, Michigan. 5-10, 190.

Scott Kirton — Right Wing

			Regular Season					Playoffs				
Season	Team	League	GP	G	A	PTS	PIM	GP	G	A	PTS	PIM
95-96	Providence	AHL	2	0	1	1	0	—	—	—	—	—
95-96	Charlotte	ECHL	56	17	19	36	176	16	4	6	10	50
96-97	Charlotte	ECHL	62	16	35	51	170	3	0	1	1	2
	ECHL	Totals	118	33	54	87	346	19	4	7	11	52

Born; 10/4/71, Penetanguishene, Ontario. 6-4, 215. Drafted by Chicago Blackhawks (10th choice, 154th overall) in 1991 Entry Draft. Signed as a free agent by Boston Bruins (8/28/95). Member of 1995-96 ECHL champion Charlotte Checkers.

Olaf Kjenstad — Left Wing

			Regular Season					Playoffs				
Season	Team	League	GP	G	A	PTS	PIM	GP	G	A	PTS	PIM
93-94	St. John's	AHL	7	1	0	1	2	—	—	—	—	—
94-95	Birmingham	ECHL	62	29	30	59	107	7	4	2	6	8
95-96	Cape Breton	AHL	1	0	1	1	0	—	—	—	—	—
95-96	Birmingham	ECHL	67	30	36	66	128	—	—	—	—	—
96-97	Knoxville	ECHL	44	19	31	50	92	—	—	—	—	—
96-97	Tallahassee	ECHL	18	4	11	15	14	2	1	0	1	4
	AHL	Totals	8	1	1	2	2	—	—	—	—	—
	ECHL	Totals	191	82	108	190	341	9	5	2	7	12

Born; 6/15/73, Kamloops, British Columbia. 6-0, 185.

Sergei Klimentiev — Defenseman

			Regular Season					Playoffs				
Season	Team	League	GP	G	A	PTS	PIM	GP	G	A	PTS	PIM
94-95	Rochester	AHL	7	0	0	0	8	1	0	0	0	0
95-96	Rochester	AHL	70	7	29	36	74	19	2	8	10	16
96-97	Rochester	AHL	77	14	28	42	114	10	1	4	5	28
	AHL	Totals	154	21	57	78	196	30	3	12	15	44

Born; 4/5/75, Kiev, Ukraine. 5-11, 200. Drafted by Buffalo Sabres (4th choice, 121st overall) in 1992 Entry Draft. Member of 1995-96 AHL champion Rochester Americans.

Sergei Klimovich — Center

			Regular Season					Playoffs				
Season	Team	League	GP	G	A	PTS	PIM	GP	G	A	PTS	PIM
94-95	Indianapolis	IHL	71	14	30	44	20	—	—	—	—	—
95-96	Indianapolis	IHL	68	17	21	38	28	5	1	1	2	6
96-97	Chicago	NHL	1	0	0	0	2	—	—	—	—	—
96-97	Indianapolis	IHL	75	20	37	57	98	3	1	2	3	0
	IHL	Totals	214	51	88	139	146	8	2	3	5	6

Born; 3/8/74, Novosibrisk, Russia. 6-3, 189. Drafted by Chicago Blackhawks (3rd choice, 41st overall) in 1992 Entry Draft.

Lorne Knauft — Defenseman

			Regular Season					Playoffs				
Season	Team	League	GP	G	A	PTS	PIM	GP	G	A	PTS	PIM
92-93	New Haven	AHL	59	4	6	10	107	—	—	—	—	—
92-93	Thunder Bay	CoHL	3	0	0	0	2	1	0	1	1	2
93-94	Flint	CoHL	51	20	36	56	180	6	0	5	5	47
93-94	Portland	AHL	7	3	1	4	16	7	2	2	4	14
94-95	Muskegon	CoHL	16	2	7	9	48	—	—	—	—	—
94-95	Brantford	CoHL	29	12	19	31	80	—	—	—	—	—
94-95	Rochester	AHL	5	0	2	2	8	—	—	—	—	—
94-95	Adirondack	AHL	2	0	1	1	6	—	—	—	—	—
95-96	Anchorage	WCHL	41	12	27	39	180	—	—	—	—	—
96-97	Houston	IHL	7	1	0	1	2	—	—	—	—	—
96-97	Flint	CoHL	67	19	40	59	144	14	2	7	9	37
	AHL	Totals	73	7	10	17	137	7	2	2	4	14
	CoHL	Totals	166	53	102	155	454	21	2	13	15	86

Born; 7/7/68, Hanna, Alberta. 6-2, 200. Member of 1993-94 AHL champion Portland Pirates.

Rick Knickle — Goaltender

Regular Season / Playoffs

Season	Team	League	GP	W	L	T	MIN	SO	GAVG	GP	W	L	MIN	SO	GAVG
79-80	Muskegon	IHL	16	—	—	—	829	0	3.76	3	—	—	156	0	6.54
80-81	Erie	EHL	43	—	—	—	2347	1	*3.20	8	—	—	446	0	*1.88
81-82	Rochester	AHL	31	10	12	5	1753	1	3.70	3	0	2	125	0	3.37
82-83	Flint	IHL	27	—	—	—	1638	2	3.37	3	—	—	193	0	3.11
82-83	Rochester	AHL	4	0	3	0	143	0	4.64	—	—	—	—	—	—
83-84	Flint	IHL	60	32	21	5	3518	3	3.46	8	8	0	480	0	3.00
84-85	Sherbrooke	AHL	14	7	6	0	780	0	4.08	—	—	—	—	—	—
84-85	Flint	IHL	36	18	11	3	2018	2	3.42	7	3	4	401	0	4.04
85-86	Saginaw	IHL	39	16	15	0	2235	2	3.62	3	2	1	193	0	3.73
86-87	Saginaw	IHL	26	9	13	0	1413	0	4.80	5	1	4	329	0	3.83
87-88	Flint	IHL	1	0	1	0	60	0	4.00	—	—	—	—	—	—
87-88	Peoria	IHL	13	2	8	1	705	0	4.94	6	3	3	294	0	4.08
88-89	Fort Wayne	IHL	47	22	16	0	2716	1	*3.11	4	1	2	173	0	5.20
89-90	Flint	IHL	55	25	24	1	2998	1	4.20	2	0	2	101	0	7.72
90-91	Albany	IHL	14	4	6	2	679	0	4.59	—	—	—	—	—	—
90-91	Springfield	AHL	9	6	0	2	509	0	3.30	—	—	—	—	—	—
91-92	San Diego	IHL	46	*28	13	4	2686	0	3.46	2	0	1	78	0	2.31
92-93	Los Angeles	NHL	10	6	4	0	532	0	3.95	—	—	—	—	—	—
92-93	San Diego	IHL	41	33	4	4	2437	*4	*2.17	—	—	—	—	—	—
93-94	Los Angeles	NHL	4	1	2	0	174	0	3.10	—	—	—	—	—	—
93-94	Phoenix	IHL	25	8	9	3	1292	1	4.13	—	—	—	—	—	—
94-95	Detroit	IHL	49	24	15	5	2725	*3	2.95	—	—	—	—	—	—
95-96	Detroit	IHL	18	9	5	1	872	0	3.44	—	—	—	—	—	—
95-96	Las Vegas	IHL	7	6	1	0	420	0	3.86	4	1	0	126	0	3.33
96-97	Milwaukee	IHL	19	5	9	1	941	0	3.83	—	—	—	—	—	—
	NHL	Totals	14	7	6	0	706	0	3.74	—	—	—	—	—	—
	*IHL	Totals	539	241	171	30	30362	19	3.51	47	19	17	2524	0	4.02
	AHL	Totals	58	23	21	7	3185	1	3.77	3	0	2	125	0	3.37

Born; 2/26/60, Chatham, New Brunswick. 5-11, 170. * Win/Loss totals from 1979-80 and 1982-83 seasons were not available. Drafted by Buffalo Sabres (7th choice, 116th overall) in 1979 Entry Draft. Signed as a free agent by Montreal Canadiens (2/8/85). Signed as a free agent by Los Angeles Kings (2/16/93). 1980-81 EHL First Team All-Star. 1988-89 IHL First Team All-Star. 1992-93 IHL First Team All-Star. 1983-84 IHL Second Team All-Star. 1991-92 IHL First Team All-Star. 1988-89 IHL won James Norris Trophy (fewest goals against). 1992-93 IHL Shared James Norris Trophy with Clint Malarchuk. Member of 1980-81 EHL champion Erie Blades. Member of 1983-84 IHL champion Flint Generals.

Fred Knipscheer — Left Wing

Regular Season / Playoffs

Season	Team	League	GP	G	A	PTS	PIM	GP	G	A	PTS	PIM
93-94	Boston	NHL	11	3	2	5	14	12	2	1	3	6
93-94	Providence	AHL	62	26	13	39	50	—	—	—	—	—
94-95	Boston	NHL	16	3	1	4	2	4	0	0	0	0
94-95	Providence	AHL	71	29	34	63	81	—	—	—	—	—
95-96	St. Louis	NHL	1	0	0	0	0	—	—	—	—	—
95-96	Worcester	AHL	68	36	37	73	93	3	0	0	0	2
96-97	Phoenix	IHL	24	5	11	16	19	—	—	—	—	—
96-97	Indianapolis	IHL	41	10	9	19	46	4	0	2	2	10
	NHL	Totals	28	6	3	9	16	16	2	1	3	6
	AHL	Totals	171	91	84	175	224	3	0	0	0	2
	IHL	Totals	65	15	20	35	65	4	0	2	2	10

Born; 9/3/69, Fort Wayne, Indiana. 5-11, 190. Signed as a free agent by Boston Bruins (4/30/93). Traded to St. Louis by Boston for Rick Zombo (10/2/95).

Kevin Knopp — Defenseman

			Regular Season					Playoffs				
Season	Team	League	GP	G	A	PTS	PIM	GP	G	A	PTS	PIM
95-96	Dayton	ECHL	5	0	1	1	4	—	—	—	—	—
95-96	South Carolina	ECHL	54	11	13	24	81	8	1	5	6	26
96-97	Baltimore	AHL	2	0	0	0	0	—	—	—	—	—
96-97	South Carolina	ECHL	65	10	41	51	108	18	4	2	6	43
	ECHL	Totals	124	21	55	76	193	26	5	7	12	69

Born; 10/24/69, Edmonton, Alberta. 6-2, 200. Member of 1996-97 ECHL Champion South Carolina Stingrays.

Derek Knorr — Center

			Regular Season					Playoffs				
Season	Team	League	GP	G	A	PTS	PIM	GP	G	A	PTS	PIM
95-96	Flint	CoHL	62	5	15	20	82	6	1	1	2	2
96-97	Muskegon	CoHL	72	26	35	61	127	3	0	3	3	8
	CoHL	Totals	134	31	50	81	209	9	1	4	5	10

Born; 11/13/72, Kerrobert, Saskatchewan. 5-9, 190. Member of 1995-96 Colonial Cup Champion Flint Generals

Jason Knox — Defenseman

			Regular Season					Playoffs				
Season	Team	League	GP	G	A	PTS	PIM	GP	G	A	PTS	PIM
96-97	Fresno	WCHL	58	9	14	23	106	5	1	1	2	13

Born; 4/10/71, Williams Lake, British Columbia. 6-2, 205.

Mike Knuble — Right Wing

			Regular Season					Playoffs				
Season	Team	League	GP	G	A	PTS	PIM	GP	G	A	PTS	PIM
94-95	Adirondack	AHL	—	—	—	—	—	3	0	0	0	0
95-96	Adirondack	AHL	80	22	23	45	59	3	1	0	1	0
96-97	Detroit	NHL	9	1	0	1	0	—	—	—	—	—
96-97	Adirondack	AHL	68	28	35	63	54	—	—	—	—	—
	AHL	Totals	148	50	58	108	113	6	1	0	1	0

Born; 7/4/72, Toronto, Ontario. 6-3, 208. Drafted by Detroit Red Wings (4th choice, 76th overall) in 1991 Entry Draft.

Paul Koch — Defenseman

			Regular Season					Playoffs				
Season	Team	League	GP	G	A	PTS	PIM	GP	G	A	PTS	PIM
95-96	Atlanta	IHL	4	0	0	0	2	—	—	—	—	—
95-96	Adirondack	AHL	3	0	1	1	0	—	—	—	—	—
95-96	Toledo	ECHL	67	6	19	25	142	8	1	6	7	10
96-97	Fort Wayne	IHL	2	0	0	0	0	—	—	—	—	—
96-97	Chicago	IHL	39	4	8	12	34	4	0	2	2	10
96-97	Toledo	ECHL	34	6	11	17	68	—	—	—	—	—
	IHL	Totals	45	4	8	12	36	4	0	2	2	10
	ECHL	Totals	101	10	27	37	210	8	1	6	7	10

Born; 6/30/71, St. Paul, Minnesota. 6-3, 220. Drafted by Quebec Nordiques (12th choice, 200th overall) in 1991 Entry Draft.

Ladislav Kohn — Right Wing

			Regular Season					Playoffs				
Season	Team	League	GP	G	A	PTS	PIM	GP	G	A	PTS	PIM
94-95	Saint John	AHL	1	0	0	0	0	—	—	—	—	—
95-96	Calgary	NHL	5	1	0	1	2	—	—	—	—	—
95-96	Saint John	AHL	73	28	45	73	97	16	6	5	11	12
96-97	Saint John	AHL	76	28	29	57	81	5	0	0	0	0
	AHL	Totals	150	56	74	130	178	21	6	5	11	12

Born; 3/4/75, Uherske Hradiste, Czechoslovakia. 5-10, 175. Drafted by Calgary Flames (9th choice, 175th overall) in 1994 Entry Draft.

Michael Koiranen — Left Wing

			Regular Season					Playoffs				
Season	Team	League	GP	G	A	PTS	PIM	GP	G	A	PTS	PIM
96-97	Thunder Bay	CoHL	39	9	11	20	16	7	0	1	1	15

Born; 4/7/74, Thunder Bay, Ontario. 5-10, 185. Last amateur club; Northern Michigan (WCHA).

Mike Kolenda — Defenseman

			Regular Season					Playoffs				
Season	Team	League	GP	G	A	PTS	PIM	GP	G	A	PTS	PIM
95-96	Toledo	ECHL	48	0	10	10	93	7	0	0	0	47
96-97	Fort Wayne	IHL	6	1	0	1	0	—	—	—	—	—
96-97	Toledo	ECHL	52	4	15	19	73	3	0	0	0	0
	ECHL	Totals	100	4	25	29	166	10	0	0	0	47

Born; 3/6/72, Grand Rapids, Michigan. 6-0, 197.

Mark Kolesar — Right Wing

			Regular Season					Playoffs				
Season	Team	League	GP	G	A	PTS	PIM	GP	G	A	PTS	PIM
94-95	St. John's	AHL	65	12	18	30	62	5	1	0	1	2
95-96	Toronto	NHL	21	2	2	4	14	3	1	0	1	2
95-96	St. John's	AHL	52	22	13	35	47	—	—	—	—	—
96-97	Toronto	NHL	7	0	0	0	0	—	—	—	—	—
96-97	St. John's	AHL	62	22	28	50	64	10	1	3	4	6
	NHL	Totals	28	2	2	4	14	3	1	0	1	2
	AHL	Totals	179	56	59	115	173	15	2	3	5	8

Born; 1/23/73, Nepawa, Manitoba. 6-1, 188. Signed as a free agent by Toronto Maple Leafs (5/24/94).

Dean Kolstad — Defenseman

			Regular Season					Playoffs				
Season	Team	League	GP	G	A	PTS	PIM	GP	G	A	PTS	PIM
88-89	Minnesota	NHL	25	1	5	6	42	—	—	—	—	—
88-89	Kalamazoo	IHL	51	10	23	33	91	6	1	0	1	23
89-90	Kalamazoo	IHL	77	10	40	50	172	10	3	4	7	14
90-91	Minnesota	NHL	5	0	0	0	15	—	—	—	—	—
90-91	Kalamazoo	IHL	33	4	8	12	50	9	1	6	7	4
91-92	Kansas City	IHL	74	9	20	29	83	15	3	6	9	8
92-93	San Jose	NHL	10	0	2	2	12	—	—	—	—	—
92-93	Kansas City	IHL	63	9	21	30	79	3	0	0	0	2
93-94	Binghamton	AHL	68	7	26	33	92	—	—	—	—	—
94-95	Minnesota	IHL	73	6	18	24	71	1	0	0	0	2
95-96	Portland	AHL	12	1	1	2	14	—	—	—	—	—
96-97	Central Texas	WPHL	17	2	10	12	44	11	4	7	11	12
	NHL	Totals	40	1	7	8	69	—	—	—	—	—
	IHL	Totals	371	48	130	178	546	44	8	16	24	53
	AHL	Totals	80	8	27	35	106	—	—	—	—	—

Born; 6/16/68, Edmonton, Alberta. 6-6, 228. Drafted by Minnesota North Stars (3rd choice, 33rd overall) in 1986 Entry Draft. Selected by san Jose Sharks in dispersal draft (5/30/91). Signed as a free agent by New York Rangers (9/1/93). 1989-90 IHL Second Team All-Star. Member of 1991-92 IHL Champion Kansas City Blades.

Brad Konick — Center

			Regular Season					Playoffs				
Season	Team	League	GP	G	A	PTS	PIM	GP	G	A	PTS	PIM
96-97	Providence	AHL	32	4	7	11	28	—	—	—	—	—
96-97	Charlotte	ECHL	13	2	4	6	6	—	—	—	—	—

Born; 2/27/68, Bloomington, Minnesota. 5-11, 190. Last amateur club; Harvard (ECAC).

Chris Kontos — Left Wing

			Regular Season					Playoffs				
Season	Team	League	GP	G	A	PTS	PIM	GP	G	A	PTS	PIM
82-83	Rangers	NHL	44	8	7	15	33	—	—	—	—	—
83-84	Rangers	NHL	6	0	1	1	8	—	—	—	—	—
83-84	Tulsa	CHL	21	5	13	18	8	—	—	—	—	—
84-85	Rangers	NHL	28	4	8	12	24	—	—	—	—	—
84-85	New Haven	AHL	48	19	24	43	30	—	—	—	—	—
85-86	New Haven	AHL	21	8	15	23	12	5	4	2	6	4
86-87	Pittsburgh	NHL	31	8	9	17	6	—	—	—	—	—
86-87	New Haven	AHL	36	14	17	31	29	—	—	—	—	—
87-88	Pittsburgh	NHL	36	1	7	8	12	—	—	—	—	—
87-88	Los Angeles	NHL	6	2	10	12	2	4	1	0	1	4
87-88	Muskegon	IHL	10	3	6	9	8	—	—	—	—	—
87-88	New Haven	AHL	16	8	16	24	4	—	—	—	—	—
88-89	Los Angeles	NHL	7	2	1	3	2	11	9	0	9	8
89-90	Los Angeles	NHL	6	2	2	4	4	5	1	0	1	0
89-90	New Haven	AHL	42	10	20	30	25	—	—	—	—	—
90-91	Phoenix	IHL	69	26	36	62	19	11	9	12	21	0
91-92	Canadian	National										
92-93	Tampa Bay	NHL	66	27	24	51	12	—	—	—	—	—
93-94	Canadian	National										
94-95	Canadian	National										
95-96	Cincinnati	IHL	81	26	44	70	13	17	5	8	13	0
96-97	Cincinnati	IHL	11	1	3	4	4	—	—	—	—	—
96-97	Manitoba	IHL	40	17	18	35	12	—	—	—	—	—
	NHL	Totals	230	54	69	123	103	20	11	0	11	12
	IHL	Totals	211	73	107	180	56	28	14	20	34	0
	AHL	Totals	163	59	92	151	100	5	4	2	6	4

Born; 12/10/63, Toronto, Ontario. 6-1, 195. Drafted by New York Rangers (1st choice, 15th overall) in 1982 Entry Draft. Traded to Pittsburgh Penguins by Rangers for Ron Duguay, (1/21/87). Traded to Los Angeles Kings by Pittsburgh with Pittsburgh's sixth round choice (Micah Aivazoff) in 1988 Entry Draft for Bryan Erickson (2/5/88). Signed as a free agent by Tampa Bay Lightning (7/21/92). Signed as a free agent by Florida Panthers (7/7/95).

Dan Kopec — Defenseman

			Regular Season					Playoffs				
Season	Team	League	GP	G	A	PTS	PIM	GP	G	A	PTS	PIM
96-97	Wichita	CeHL	46	6	10	16	365	9	0	2	2	70

Born; 3/3/73, Weyburn, Saskatchewan. 6-4, 225. Traded to Nashville Ice Flyers by Wichita for first pick in Dispersal Draft (6/10/97).

Mervin Kopeck — Defenseman

			Regular Season					Playoffs				
Season	Team	League	GP	G	A	PTS	PIM	GP	G	A	PTS	PIM
95-96	Oklahoma City	CeHL	63	5	24	29	76	13	1	3	4	4
96-97	Oklahoma City	CeHL	62	3	14	17	57	4	0	0	0	2
	CeHL	Totals	125	8	38	46	133	17	1	3	4	6

Born; 4/7/73, Regina, Saskatchewan. 5-10, 185. Member of 1995-96 CeHL Champion Oklahoma City Blazers.

Alexander Korolyuk — Center

			Regular Season					Playoffs				
Season	Team	League	GP	G	A	PTS	PIM	GP	G	A	PTS	PIM
96-97	Manitoba	IHL	42	20	16	36	71	—	—	—	—	—

Born; 1/15/76, Moscow, Russia. 5-9, 170. Drafted by San Jose Sharks (6th chioce, 141st overall) in 1994 Entry Draft.

John Kosobud — Left Wing

Regular Season / Playoffs

Season	Team	League	GP	G	A	PTS	PIM	GP	G	A	PTS	PIM
96-97	Mississippi	ECHL	52	9	12	21	40	2	0	0	0	0

Born; 8/26/72, North Dakota. 6-0, 205.

Chris Kostopoulos — Forward

Regular Season / Playoffs

Season	Team	League	GP	G	A	PTS	PIM	GP	G	A	PTS	PIM
96-97	Waco	WPHL	6	1	1	2	7	—	—	—	—	—
96-97	Columbus	CeHL	9	2	3	5	21	—	—	—	—	—
96-97	Huntsville	CeHL	22	8	12	20	26	9	3	3	6	6
	CeHL	Totals	31	10	15	25	47	9	3	3	6	6

Born; 7/24/73, Mississauga, Ontario. 6-1, 200.

Jeff Kostuch — Center

Regular Season / Playoffs

Season	Team	League	GP	G	A	PTS	PIM	GP	G	A	PTS	PIM
95-96	Hampton Roads	ECHL	67	18	23	41	60	3	0	2	2	4
96-97	Louisville	ECHL	67	19	23	42	87	—	—	—	—	—
	ECHL	Totals	134	37	46	83	147	3	0	2	2	4

Born; 2/18/74, Brockville, Ontario. 6-1, 205.

Jack Kowal — Right Wing

Regular Season / Playoffs

Season	Team	League	GP	G	A	PTS	PIM	GP	G	A	PTS	PIM
95-96	Anchorage	WCHL	5	2	3	5	4	—	—	—	—	—
96-97	Kentucky	AHL	40	5	8	13	37	—	—	—	—	—
96-97	Louisville	ECHL	33	11	16	27	18	—	—	—	—	—

Born; 2/14/73, Anchorage, Alaska. 6-1, 195. Last amateur club; Alaska-Anchorage (WCHA).

Rick Kowalsky — Right Wing

Regular Season / Playoffs

Season	Team	League	GP	G	A	PTS	PIM	GP	G	A	PTS	PIM
93-94	Cornwall	AHL	65	9	8	17	86	—	—	—	—	—
94-95	Cornwall	AHL	9	2	1	3	38	—	—	—	—	—
94-95	Hampton Roads	ECHL	49	29	24	53	114	4	0	4	4	4
95-96	Hampton Roads	ECHL	52	21	29	50	121	—	—	—	—	—
96-97	Portland	AHL	22	7	8	15	10	—	—	—	—	—
96-97	Hampton Roads	ECHL	52	14	26	40	94	9	5	4	9	16
	AHL	Totals	96	18	17	35	134	—	—	—	—	—
	ECHL	Totals	153	64	79	143	329	13	5	8	13	20

Born; 3/20/72, Simcoe, Ontario. 6-1, 195. Drafted by Buffalo Sabres (11th choice, 227th overall) in 1992 Entry Draft.

Brian Kraft — Left Wing

Regular Season / Playoffs

Season	Team	League	GP	G	A	PTS	PIM	GP	G	A	PTS	PIM
95-96	Anchorage	WCHL	50	18	32	50	106	—	—	—	—	—
96-97	Anchorage	WCHL	44	12	20	32	68	8	2	2	4	36
	WCHL	Totals	94	30	52	82	174	8	2	2	4	36

Born; 1/29/67, Melrose Park, Illinois. 5-8, 180.

Paul Krake — Goaltender

Regular Season / Playoffs

Season	Team	League	GP	W	L	T	MIN	SO	GAVG	GP	W	L	MIN	SO	GAVG
92-93	Halifax	AHL	17	8	6	1	916	1	3.73	—	—	—	—	—	—
92-93	Oklahoma City	CeHL	17	13	4	0	1029	0	3.50	—	—	—	—	—	—

Season	Team	League	GP	W	L	T	MIN	SO	GAA	GP	W	L	T	MIN	GAA
93-94	Cornwall	AHL	28	8	13	4	1383	0	4.17	—	—	—	—	—	—
94-95	Cornwall	AHL	7	2	4	0	359	0	4.01	—	—	—	—	—	—
94-95	Erie	ECHL	10	1	8	1	597	0	6.13	—	—	—	—	—	—
94-95	Memphis	CeHL	5	4	1	0	260	0	4.38	—	—	—	—	—	—
95-96	Charlotte	ECHL	10	3	3	0	417	0	3.59	—	—	—	—	—	—
95-96	Wichita	CeHL	22	7	9	0	1010	0	6.00	—	—	—	—	—	—
96-97	Cleveland	IHL	2	0	1	0	76	0	6.28	—	—	—	—	—	—
96-97	Brantford	CoHL	52	29	16	4	2996	*3	3.40	10	4	*6	0	596	4.43
	AHL	Totals	52	18	23	5	2658	1	4.00	—	—	—	—	—	—
	CeHL	Totals	44	24	14	0	2299	0	4.70	—	—	—	—	—	—
	ECHL	Totals	20	4	11	1	1014	0	5.09	—	—	—	—	—	—

Born; 3/25/69, Lloydminster, Alberta. 5-11, 180. Drafted by Quebec Nordiques (10th pick, 148th overall) in 1989 Entry Draft.

Justin Krall — Defenseman

			Regular Season					Playoffs			
Season	Team	League	GP	G	A	PTS	PIM	GP	G	A	PTS	PIM
96-97	Peoria	ECHL	69	10	27	37	57	10	3	5	8	8

Born; 2/20/74, Toledo, Ohio. 6-2, 170. Drafted by Detroit Red Wings (8th choice, 183rd overall) in 1992 Entry Draft.

Mikhail Kravets — Right Wing

			Regular Season					Playoffs			
Season	Team	League	GP	G	A	PTS	PIM	GP	G	A	PTS	PIM
91-92	Kansas City	IHL	74	10	32	42	172	15	6	8	14	12
91-92	San Jose	NHL	1	0	0	0	0	—	—	—	—	—
92-93	San Jose	NHL	1	0	0	0	0	—	—	—	—	—
92-93	Kansas City	IHL	71	19	49	68	153	10	2	5	7	55
93-94	Kansas City	IHL	63	14	44	58	171	—	—	—	—	—
94-95	Detroit	IHL	7	0	0	0	4	—	—	—	—	—
94-95	Minnesota	IHL	37	7	15	22	21	—	—	—	—	—
94-95	Syracuse	AHL	7	2	2	4	8	—	—	—	—	—
95-96	Milwaukee	IHL	7	0	1	1	4	—	—	—	—	—
95-96	Wichita	CeHL	37	14	57	71	89	—	—	—	—	—
96-97	Louisiana	ECHL	57	22	45	67	93	17	4	9	13	18
	NHL	Totals	2	0	0	0	0	—	—	—	—	—
	IHL	Totals	259	50	141	191	525	25	8	13	21	67

Born; 11/12/63, Leningrad, Russia. 5-10, 182. Drafted by San Jose Sharks (13th choice, 243rd overall) in 1991 Entry Draft. Member of 1991-92 Turner Cup champion Kansas City Blades.

Jim Krayer — Center

			Regular Season					Playoffs			
Season	Team	League	GP	G	A	PTS	PIM	GP	G	A	PTS	PIM
95-96	Johnstown	ECHL	36	3	7	10	19	—	—	—	—	—
95-96	Lakeland	SHL	23	9	13	22	8	3	2	1	3	2
96-97	Johnstown	ECHL	56	10	13	23	14	—	—	—	—	—
	ECHL	Totals	92	13	20	33	33	—	—	—	—	—

Born; 12/25/72, Acton, Massachusetts. 5-10, 175.

Aaron Kriss — Defenseman

			Regular Season					Playoffs			
Season	Team	League	GP	G	A	PTS	PIM	GP	G	A	PTS	PIM
95-96	Utah	IHL	4	0	0	0	0	—	—	—	—	—
95-96	Tallahassee	ECHL	60	4	12	16	124	12	0	3	3	4
96-97	Dayton	ECHL	7	0	4	4	4	—	—	—	—	—
	ECHL	Totals	67	4	16	20	128	12	0	3	3	4

Born; 9/17/72, Parma, Ohio. 6-2, 200. Drafted by San Jose Sharks (12th choice, 221st overall) in 1991 Entry Draft.

Alexei Krivchenkov
Defenseman

Season	Team	League	GP	G	A	PTS	PIM	GP	G	A	PTS	PIM
95-96	Cleveland	IHL	37	1	4	5	30	—	—	—	—	—
95-96	Hampton Roads	ECHL	16	3	3	6	28	—	—	—	—	—
96-97	Long Beach	IHL	7	0	3	3	10	—	—	—	—	—
96-97	Johnstown	ECHL	5	1	1	2	24	—	—	—	—	—
96-97	Hampton Roads	ECHL	36	3	32	26	57	6	1	2	3	18
	IHL	Totals	44	1	7	8	40	—	—	—	—	—
	ECHL	Totals	57	7	36	43	109	6	1	2	3	18

Born; 6/11/74, Novosibirsk, Russia. 6-0, 185. Drafted by Pittsburgh Penguins (5th choice, 12th overall) in 1994 Entry Draft.

Yuri Krivokhija
Defenseman

Season	Team	League	GP	G	A	PTS	PIM	GP	G	A	PTS	PIM
92-93	Detroit	CoHL	32	7	9	16	25	5	1	4	5	6
92-93	Springfield	AHL	9	0	2	2	8	—	—	—	—	—
93-94	Detroit	CoHL	13	3	6	9	41	—	—	—	—	—
93-94	Milwaukee	IHL	50	10	28	38	59	2	0	1	1	6
94-95	Cincinnati	IHL	57	9	9	18	67	5	0	0	0	2
95-96	Detroit	IHL	18	2	5	7	18	—	—	—	—	—
95-96	Indianapolis	IHL	55	5	17	22	68	5	0	0	0	20
96-97	Fort Wayne	IHL	18	2	4	6	12	—	—	—	—	—
96-97	Michigan	IHL	6	2	1	3	0	—	—	—	—	—
	IHL	Totals	204	30	64	94	224	12	0	1	1	28
	CoHL	Totals	45	10	15	25	66	5	1	4	5	6

Born; 5/30/68, Minsk, Russia. 6-2, 210.

Gord Kruppke
Defenseman

Season	Team	League	GP	G	A	PTS	PIM	GP	G	A	PTS	PIM
89-90	Adirondack	AHL	59	2	12	14	103	—	—	—	—	—
90-91	Detroit	NHL	4	0	0	0	0	—	—	—	—	—
90-91	Adirondack	AHL	45	1	8	9	153	—	—	—	—	—
91-92	Adirondack	AHL	65	3	9	12	208	16	0	1	1	52
92-93	Detroit	NHL	10	0	0	0	20	—	—	—	—	—
92-93	Adirondack	AHL	41	2	12	14	197	9	1	2	3	20
93-94	Detroit	NHL	9	0	0	0	12	—	—	—	—	—
93-94	Adirondack	AHL	54	2	9	11	210	12	1	3	4	32
94-95	Adirondack	AHL	48	2	9	11	157	—	—	—	—	—
94-95	St. John's	AHL	3	0	1	1	6	—	—	—	—	—
95-96	Houston	IHL	50	0	4	4	119	—	—	—	—	—
96-97	Houston	IHL	43	0	5	5	91	9	0	1	1	14
	NHL	Totals	23	0	0	0	32	—	—	—	—	—
	AHL	Totals	315	12	60	72	1034	37	2	6	8	104
	IHL	Totals	93	0	9	9	210	9	0	1	1	14

Born; 4/2/69, Slave Lake, Alberta. 6-1, 200. Drafted by Detroit Red Wings (2nd choice, 32nd overall) in 1987 Entry Draft. Traded to Toronto Maple Leafs by Detroit for other considerations (4/7/95). Member of 1991-92 AHL champion Adirondack Red Wings.

Mark Krys
Defenseman

Season	Team	League	GP	G	A	PTS	PIM	GP	G	A	PTS	PIM
91-92	Maine	AHL	28	1	2	3	18	—	—	—	—	—
91-92	Johnstown	ECHL	43	8	12	20	73	—	—	—	—	—
92-93	Providence	AHL	34	1	10	11	36	6	0	0	0	2
92-93	Johnstown	ECHL	25	4	14	18	18	—	—	—	—	—
92-93	Cincinnati	IHL	3	0	1	1	2	—	—	—	—	—

Season	Team	League	GP	G	A	PTS	PIM	GP	G	A	PTS	PIM
93-94	Providence	AHL	23	1	2	3	32	—	—	—	—	—
93-94	Rochester	AHL	58	2	13	15	77	4	0	1	1	6
94-95	Rochester	AHL	70	3	16	19	113	3	0	0	0	0
95-96	Los Angeles	IHL	78	6	11	17	96	—	—	—	—	—
96-97	Syracuse	AHL	69	10	15	25	61	—	—	—	—	—
	AHL	Totals	282	18	58	76	337	13	0	1	1	8
	ECHL	Totals	68	12	26	38	91	—	—	—	—	—

Born; 5/29/69, Timmins, Ontario. 6-0, 193. Drafted by Boston Bruins (6th choice, 165th overall) in 1988 Entry Draft.

Filip Kuba — Defenseman

Season	Team	League	GP	G	A	PTS	PIM	GP	G	A	PTS	PIM
96-97	Carolina	AHL	51	0	12	12	38	—	—	—	—	—

Born; 12/29/76, Ostrava, Czechoslovakia. 6-3, 202. Drafted by Florida Panthers (8th choice, 192nd overall) in 1995 Entry Draft.

Frantisek Kucera — Defenseman

Season	Team	League	GP	G	A	PTS	PIM	GP	G	A	PTS	PIM
90-91	Chicago	NHL	40	2	12	14	32	—	—	—	—	—
90-91	Indianapolis	IHL	35	8	19	27	23	7	0	1	1	15
91-92	Chicago	NHL	61	3	10	13	36	6	0	0	0	0
91-92	Indianapolis	IHL	7	1	2	3	4	—	—	—	—	—
92-93	Chicago	NHL	71	5	14	19	59	—	—	—	—	—
93-94	Chicago	NHL	60	4	13	17	34	—	—	—	—	—
93-94	Hartford	NHL	16	1	3	4	14	—	—	—	—	—
94-95	Hartford	NHL	48	3	17	20	30	—	—	—	—	—
95-96	Hartford	NHL	30	2	6	8	10	—	—	—	—	—
95-96	Vancouver	NHL	24	1	0	1	10	6	0	1	1	0
96-97	Vancouver	NHL	2	0	0	0	0	—	—	—	—	—
96-97	Philadelphia	NHL	2	0	0	0	2	—	—	—	—	—
96-97	Houston	IHL	12	0	3	3	20	—	—	—	—	—
96-97	Syracuse	AHL	42	6	29	35	36	—	—	—	—	—
96-97	Philadelphia	AHL	9	1	5	6	2	10	1	6	7	20
	NHL	Totals	354	21	75	96	227	12	0	1	1	0
	IHL	Totals	54	9	24	33	47	7	0	1	1	15
	AHL	Totals	51	7	34	41	38	10	1	6	7	20

Born; 2/3/68, Prague, Czechoslovakia. 6-2, 205. Drafted by Chicago Blackhawks (3rd choice, 77th overall) in 1986 Entry Draft. Traded to Hartford Whalers by Chicago with Jocelyn Lemieux for gary Suter, Randy Cunneyworth and Hartford's third round draft choice (later traded to Vancouver—Vancouver selected Larry Courville) in 1995 Entry Draft, (3/11/94). Traded to Vancouver Canucks by Hartford with Jim Dowd and Hartford's second choice (Ryan Bonni) in 1997 Entry Draft for Jeff Brown and Vancouver's third round choice in 1998 Entry Draft, (12/19/95). Traded to Philadelphia Flyers by Vancouver for future considerations (3/18/97).

Stu Kulak — Right Wing

Season	Team	League	GP	G	A	PTS	PIM	GP	G	A	PTS	PIM
82-83	Vancouver	NHL	4	1	1	2	0	—	—	—	—	—
83-84	Fredericton	AHL	52	12	16	28	55	5	0	0	0	59
84-85	DNP	Injured										
85-86	Fredericton	AHL	3	1	0	1	0	6	2	1	3	0
85-86	Kalamazoo	IHL	30	14	8	22	38	2	2	0	2	0
86-87	Vancouver	NHL	28	1	1	2	37	—	—	—	—	—
86-97	Edmonton	NHL	23	3	1	4	41	—	—	—	—	—
86-87	Rangers	NHL	3	0	0	0	0	—	—	—	—	—
87-88	Quebec	NHL	14	1	1	2	28	—	—	—	—	—
87-88	Moncton	AHL	37	9	12	21	58	—	—	—	—	—
88-89	Winnipeg	NHL	18	2	0	2	24	—	—	—	—	—
88-89	Moncton	AHL	51	30	29	59	98	10	5	6	11	16
89-90	Moncton	AHL	56	14	23	37	72	—	—	—	—	—

Season	Team	League	GP	G	A	PTS	PIM	GP	G	A	PTS	PIM
90-91	Kansas City	IHL	47	13	28	41	20	—	—	—	—	—
91-92	N/A											
92-93	Erie	ECHL	21	13	8	21	23	—	—	—	—	—
93-94	Tulsa	CeHL	59	17	29	46	101	8	0	0	0	28
94-95	San Antonio	CeHL	65	30	38	68	97	13	3	3	6	26
95-96	Reno	WCHL	43	16	25	41	60	3	1	1	2	0
96-97	Reno	WCHL	36	12	18	30	60	—	—	—	—	—
96-97	New Mexico	WPHL	5	0	0	0	0	6	1	1	2	8
	NHL	Totals	90	8	4	12	130	—	—	—	—	—
	AHL	Totals	199	66	80	146	283	21	7	7	14	75
	IHL	Totals	77	27	36	63	58	2	2	0	2	0
	CeHL	Totals	124	47	67	114	198	21	3	3	6	54
	WCHL	Totals	79	28	43	71	120	3	1	1	2	0

Born; 3/10/63, Stony Plain, Alberta. 5-10, 185. Drafted by Vancouver Canucks (5th choice, 115th overall) in 1981 Entry Draft. Acquired by Edmonton Oilers on waivers from Vancouver Canucks (12/86). Sent to New York Rangers by Edmonton as compensation for Reijo Ruotsalainen signing with Edmonton. The Rangers also sent a 12th round pick (Jesper Duus) in 1987 to the Oilers as part of the deal. Traded to Winnipeg Jets by Quebec Nordiques for Bobby Dollas. (12/87). Signed by Kansas City Blades as a free agent (9/6/90).

Jeff Kungle — Defenseman

Season	Team	League	GP	G	A	PTS	PIM	GP	G	A	PTS	PIM
95-96	Milwaukee	IHL	1	0	0	0	0	—	—	—	—	—
96-97	Milwaukee	IHL	3	0	0	0	0	—	—	—	—	—
96-97	Peoria	ECHL	65	6	23	29	68	10	2	4	6	11
	IHL	Totals	4	0	0	0	0	—	—	—	—	—

Born; 10/26/72, Waka, Saskatchewan. 6-0, 205. Last amateur club; St. Lawrence (ECAC).

Les Kuntar — Goaltender

Season	Team	League	GP	W	L	T	MIN	SO	GAVG	GP	W	L	MIN	SO	GAVG
91-92	Fredericton	AHL	11	7	3	0	638	0	2.45	—	—	—	—	—	—
91-92	United States	National													
92-93	Fredericton	AHL	42	16	14	7	2315	0	3.37	1	0	1	64	0	5.63
93-94	Montreal	NHL	6	2	2	0	302	0	3.18	—	—	—	—	—	—
93-94	Fredericton	AHL	34	10	17	3	1804	1	3.62	—	—	—	—	—	—
94-95	Worcester	AHL	24	6	10	5	1241	2	3.72	—	—	—	—	—	—
94-95	Hershey	AHL	32	15	13	2	1802	0	2.96	2	0	1	70	0	4.28
95-96	Hershey	AHL	20	7	8	2	1020	0	4.18	—	—	—	—	—	—
95-96	Fort Wayne	IHL	8	2	3	1	387	1	4.03	—	—	—	—	—	—
96-97	Cleveland	IHL	1	1	0	0	60	0	4.00	—	—	—	—	—	—
96-97	Utah	IHL	3	1	0	0	87	0	0.69	—	—	—	—	—	—
96-97	Rochester	AHL	21	6	9	3	1052	0	3.42	—	—	—	—	—	—
96-97	Pensacola	ECHL	4	2	2	0	220	0	3.55	—	—	—	—	—	—
	AHL	Totals	184	67	74	22	9872	3	3.42	3	0	2	134	0	4.93
	IHL	Totals	12	4	3	1	534	1	3.48	—	—	—	—	—	—

Born; 7/28/69, Elma, New York. 6-2, 195. Drafted by Montreal Canadiens (8th choice, 122nd overall) in 1987 Entry Draft. Signed as a free agent by Philadelphia Flyers (6/30/95).

Mark Kuntz — Defenseman

Season	Team	League	GP	G	A	PTS	PIM	GP	G	A	PTS	PIM
91-92	Richmond	ECHL	46	6	13	19	187	7	1	2	3	52
92-93	Richmond	ECHL	60	12	15	27	215	1	0	0	0	0
93-94	Richmond	ECHL	4	2	0	2	32	—	—	—	—	—
93-94	Dayton	ECHL	57	3	15	18	255	1	0	0	0	0
94-95	Columbus	ECHL	25	6	4	10	91	—	—	—	—	—
95-96	Fresno	WCHL	54	4	10	14	215	7	3	0	3	8

Season	Team	League	GP	G	A	PTS	PIM	GP	G	A	PTS	PIM
96-97	Fresno	WCHL	59	4	15	19	239	3	1	0	1	57
	ECHL	Totals	192	29	47	76	995	9	1	2	3	52
	WCHL	Totals	113	8	25	33	454	10	4	0	4	65

Born; 2/24/68, Medicine Hat, Alberta. 6-0, 200.

Arturs Kupacs — Defenseman

			Regular Season					Playoffs				
Season	Team	League	GP	G	A	PTS	PIM	GP	G	A	PTS	PIM
94-95	Greensboro	ECHL	63	14	30	44	89	18	5	10	15	24
95-96	Las Vegas	IHL	3	0	0	0	2	—	—	—	—	—
95-96	Detroit	CoHL	67	18	39	57	94	8	0	5	5	20
96-97	Las Vegas	IHL	6	0	0	0	10	—	—	—	—	—
96-97	Toledo	ECHL	52	13	30	43	112	—	—	—	—	—
	IHL	Totals	9	0	0	0	12	—	—	—	—	—
	ECHL	Totals	115	27	60	87	201	18	5	10	15	24

Born; 7/14/73, Riga, Latvia. 6-0, 190.

Maxim Kuznetsov — Defense

			Regular Season					Playoffs				
Season	Team	League	GP	G	A	PTS	PIM	GP	G	A	PTS	PIM
96-97	Adirondack	AHL	2	0	1	1	6	2	0	0	0	0

Born; 3/24/77, Pavlodar, Russia. 6-5, 198. Drafted by Detroit Red Wings (1st choice, 26th overall) in 1995 Entry Draft.

Jim Kyte — Defenseman

			Regular Season					Playoffs				
Season	Team	League	GP	G	A	PTS	PIM	GP	G	A	PTS	PIM
82-83	Winnipeg	NHL	2	0	0	0	0	—	—	—	—	—
83-84	Winnipeg	NHL	58	1	2	3	55	3	0	0	0	11
84-85	Winnipeg	NHL	71	0	3	3	111	8	0	0	0	14
85-86	Winnipeg	NHL	71	1	3	4	126	3	0	0	0	23
86-87	Winnipeg	NHL	72	5	5	10	162	10	0	4	4	36
87-88	Winnipeg	NHL	51	1	3	4	128	—	—	—	—	—
88-89	Winnipeg	NHL	74	3	9	12	190	—	—	—	—	—
89-90	Pittsburgh	NHL	56	3	1	4	125	—	—	—	—	—
90-91	Pittsburgh	NHL	1	0	0	0	2	—	—	—	—	—
90-91	Muskegon	IHL	25	2	5	7	157	—	—	—	—	—
90-91	Calgary	NHL	42	0	9	9	153	7	0	0	0	7
91-92	Calgary	NHL	21	0	1	1	107	—	—	—	—	—
91-92	Salt Lake City	IHL	6	0	1	1	9	—	—	—	—	—
92-93	Ottawa	NHL	4	0	1	1	4	—	—	—	—	—
92-93	New Haven	AHL	63	6	18	24	163	—	—	—	—	—
93-94	Las Vegas	IHL	75	2	16	18	246	4	0	1	1	51
94-95	San Jose	NHL	18	2	5	7	33	11	0	2	2	14
94-95	Las Vegas	IHL	76	3	17	20	195	—	—	—	—	—
95-96	San Jose	NHL	57	1	7	8	146	—	—	—	—	—
96-97	Kansas City	IHL	76	3	8	11	259	3	0	0	0	2
	NHL	Totals	598	17	49	66	1342	42	0	6	6	94
	IHL	Totals	258	10	47	57	866	7	0	1	1	53

Born; 3/21/64, Ottawa, Ontario. 6-5, 210. Drafted by Winnipeg Jets (1st choice, 12th overall) in 1982 Entry Draft. Traded to Pittsburgh Penguins by Winnipeg with Andrew McBain and Randy Gilhen for Randy Cunneyworth, Rick Tabaracci and Dave McLlwain, (6/17/89). Traded to Calgary Flames by Pittsburgh for Jiri Hrdina, (12/13/90). Signed as a free agent by Ottawa Senators (9/10/92). Signed as a free agent by San Jose, (3/31/95).

Jean-Francois Labbe — Goaltender

			Regular Season							Playoffs					
Season	Team	League	GP	W	L	T	MIN	SO	GAVG	GP	W	L	MIN	SO	GAVG
93-94	Thunder Bay	CoHL	52	*35	11	4	*2900	*2	*3.10	8	7	1	493	*2	*2.19
93-94	Prince Edward Island	AHL	7	4	3	0	389	0	3.39	—	—	—	—	—	—
94-95	Prince Edward Island	AHL	32	13	14	3	1817	2	3.10	—	—	—	—	—	—
95-96	Cornwall	AHL	55	25	21	5	2971	3	2.91	8	3	5	470	1	2.68
96-97	Hershey	AHL	66	*34	22	9	3811	*6	*2.52	*23	*14	8	*1364	1	2.60
	AHL	Totals	160	76	60	17	8988	11	2.80	31	17	13	1834	2	2.62

Born; 6/15/72, Sherbrooke, Quebec. 5-9, 165. Signed as a free agent by Ottawa Senators (5/12/94). Traded to Colorado Avalanche by Ottawa for a conditional draft pick (9/20/95). Signed as a free agent by Edmonton Oilers (8/97). 1994 CoHL First Team All-Star. 1994 CoHL Rookie of the Year. 1994 CoHL Outstanding Goaltender. 1996-97 AHL Outstanding Netminder. 1996-97 AHL MVP. 1996-97 AHL First Team All-Star. Member of 1996-97 AHL Champion Hershey Bears.

Marc LaBelle — Left Wing

			Regular Season					Playoffs				
Season	Team	League	GP	G	A	PTS	PIM	GP	G	A	PTS	PIM
90-91	Fredericton	AHL	24	1	4	5	95	4	0	2	2	25
90-91	Richmond	ECHL	5	1	1	2	37	—	—	—	—	—
91-92	Fredericton	AHL	62	7	10	17	238	3	0	0	0	6
92-93	New Haven	AHL	31	5	4	9	124	—	—	—	—	—
92-93	San Diego	IHL	5	0	2	2	5	—	—	—	—	—
92-93	Thunder Bay	CoHL	9	0	5	5	17	7	0	1	1	11
93-94	Ciccinnati	IHL	37	2	1	3	133	4	0	1	1	6
94-95	Cincinnati	IHL	54	3	4	7	173	8	0	0	0	7
95-96	Cincinnati	IHL	57	6	11	17	218	—	—	—	—	—
95-96	Milwaukee	IHL	20	5	3	8	50	5	1	1	2	4
96-97	Milwaukee	IHL	14	1	1	2	33	—	—	—	—	—
96-97	Michigan	IHL	46	4	7	11	148	3	0	0	0	6
	IHL	Totals	233	21	29	50	760	20	1	2	3	23
	AHL	Totals	117	13	18	31	457	7	0	2	2	31

Born; 12/20/69, Maniwaki, Quebec. 6-2, 205. Signed as a free agent by Montreal Canadiens (1/21/91). Signed as a free agent by Ottawa Senators (8/6/92). Selected by Florida Panthers in Expansion Draft (6/24/93). Signed as a free agent by Ottawa Senators (6/97).

Patrick Labreque — Goaltender

			Regular Season							Playoffs					
Season	Team	League	GP	W	L	T	MIN	SO	GAVG	GP	W	L	MIN	SO	GAVG
91-92	Halifax	AHL	29	5	12	8	1570	0	4.36	—	—	—	—	—	—
92-93	Halifax	AHL	20	3	12	2	914	0	4.99	—	—	—	—	—	—
92-93	Greensboro	ECHL	11	6	3	2	650	0	2.86	1	0	1	59	0	5.08
93-94	Cornwall	AHL	4	1	2	0	198	1	2.42	—	—	—	—	—	—
93-94	Greensboro	ECHL	29	17	8	2	1609	0	3.32	1	0	0	22	0	10.80
94-95	Fredericton	AHL	35	15	17	1	1913	1	3.26	*16	*10	6	*967	1	2.48
94-95	Wheeling	ECHL	5	2	3	0	281	0	4.69	—	—	—	—	—	—
95-96	Montreal	NHL	2	0	1	0	98	0	4.29	—	—	—	—	—	—
95-96	Fredericton	AHL	48	23	18	6	2685	3	3.42	7	3	3	404	0	4.59
96-97	Fredericton	AHL	12	1	7	1	602	0	3.09	—	—	—	—	—	—
96-97	Quebec	IHL	9	2	6	0	482	0	3.61	—	—	—	—	—	—
	AHL	Totals	148	48	68	18	7882	5	3.70	23	13	9	1371	0	3.11
	ECHL	Totals	45	25	14	4	2540	0	3.35	2	0	1	81	0	6.67

Born; 3/6/71, Laval, Quebec. 6-0, 190. Drafted by Quebec Nordiques (5th choice, 90th overall) in 1991 Entry Draft. Signed as a free agent by Montreal Canadiens (6/21/94).

Martin Lachaine — Center

			Regular Season					Playoffs				
Season	Team	League	GP	G	A	PTS	PIM	GP	G	A	PTS	PIM
96-97	Huntington	ECHL	9	0	0	0	7	—	—	—	—	—
96-97	Pensacola	ECHL	33	0	9	9	63	—	—	—	—	—

Born; 1/30/73, St. Eustache, Quebec. 5-11, 201.

Bob Lachance — Right Wing

Season	Team	League	GP	G	A	PTS	PIM	GP	G	A	PTS	PIM
			Regular Season					Playoffs				
95-96	Worcester	AHL	7	1	0	1	6	—	—	—	—	—
96-97	Worcester	AHL	74	21	35	56	66	5	0	2	2	4
	AHL	Totals	81	22	35	57	72	5	0	2	2	4

Born; 2/1/74, Northhampton, Massachusetts. 5-11, 180. Drafted by St. Louis Blues (5th choice, 134th overall) in 1991 Entry Draft.

Patrick Lacombe — Defenseman

Season	Team	League	GP	G	A	PTS	PIM	GP	G	A	PTS	PIM
			Regular Season					Playoffs				
95-96	Brantford	CoHL	63	2	5	7	180	11	0	1	1	49
96-97	Brantford	CoHL	67	5	27	32	272	6	0	5	5	18
	CoHL	Totals	130	7	32	39	452	17	0	6	6	67

Born; 2/4/74, Montreal, Quebec. 5-11, 200.

Nathan Lafayette — Center

Season	Team	League	GP	G	A	PTS	PIM	GP	G	A	PTS	PIM
			Regular Season					Playoffs				
93-94	St. Louis	NHL	38	2	3	5	14	—	—	—	—	—
93-94	Vancouver	NHL	11	1	1	2	4	20	2	7	9	4
93-94	Peoria	IHL	27	13	11	24	20	—	—	—	—	—
94-95	Vancouver	NHL	27	4	4	8	2	—	—	—	—	—
94-95	Rangers	NHL	12	0	0	0	0	8	0	0	0	2
94-95	Syracuse	AHL	27	9	9	18	10	—	—	—	—	—
95-96	Binghamton	AHL	57	21	27	48	32	—	—	—	—	—
95-96	Rangers	NHL	5	0	0	0	2	—	—	—	—	—
95-96	Los Angeles	NHL	12	2	4	6	6	—	—	—	—	—
96-97	Los Angeles	NHL	15	1	3	4	8	—	—	—	—	—
96-97	Phoenix	IHL	31	2	5	7	16	—	—	—	—	—
96-97	Syracuse	AHL	26	14	11	25	18	3	1	0	1	2
	NHL	Totals	120	10	15	25	36	28	2	7	9	6
	AHL	Totals	110	44	47	91	60	3	1	0	1	2
	IHL	Totals	58	15	16	31	36	—	—	—	—	—

Born; 2/17/73, New Westminster, British Columbia. 6-1, 195. Drafted by St. Louis Blues (3rd choice, 65th overall) in 1991 Entry Draft. Traded to Vancouver Canucks by St. Louis Blues with Jeff Brown and Bret Hedican for Craig Janney (3/21/94). Traded to New York Rangers by Vancouver for Corey Hirsch (4/7/95). Traded to Los Angeles Kings by Rangers with Ray Ferraro, Mattias Norstrom, Ian Laperriere, and Rangers fourth round choice (Sean Blanchard) in 1997 Entry Draft for Marty McSorley, Jari Kurri and Shane Churla, (3/14/96).

Christian LaFlamme — Defenseman

Season	Team	League	GP	G	A	PTS	PIM	GP	G	A	PTS	PIM
			Regular Season					Playoffs				
96-97	Chicago	NHL	4	0	1	1	2	—	—	—	—	—
96-97	Indianapolis	IHL	62	5	15	20	60	4	1	1	2	16

Born; 11/24/76, St. Charles, Quebec. 6-1, 195. Drafted by Chicago Blackhawks (2nd choice, 45th overall) in 1995 Entry Draft.

Mark Laforest — Goaltender

Season	Team	League	GP	W	L	T	MIN	SO	GAVG	GP	W	L	MIN	SO	GAVG
			Regular Season							Playoffs					
83-84	Adirondack	AHL	7	3	3	1	351	0	4.96	—	—	—	—	—	—
83-84	Kalamazoo	IHL	13	4	5	2	718	1	4.01	—	—	—	—	—	—
84-85	Adirondack	AHL	11	2	3	1	430	0	4.88	—	—	—	—	—	—
85-86	Detroit	NHL	28	4	21	0	1383	1	4.95	—	—	—	—	—	—
85-86	Adirondack	AHL	19	13	5	1	1142	0	2.99	*17	*12	5	*1075	0	3.24
86-87	Detroit	NHL	5	2	1	0	219	0	3.29	—	—	—	—	—	—

Season	Team	League	GP	W	L	T	Mins	SO	GAA	GP	W	L	Mins	SO	GAA
86-87	Adirondack	AHL	37	23	8	0	2229	*3	2.83	—	—	—	—	—	—
87-88	Philadelphia	NHL	21	5	9	2	972	1	3.70	2	1	0	48	0	1.25
87-88	Hershey	AHL	5	2	1	2	309	0	2.52	—	—	—	—	—	—
88-89	Philadelphia	NHL	17	5	7	2	933	0	4.12	—	—	—	—	—	—
88-89	Hershey	AHL	3	2	0	0	185	0	2.92	12	7	5	744	1	2.18
89-90	Toronto	NHL	27	9	14	0	1343	0	3.89	—	—	—	—	—	—
89-90	Newmarket	AHL	10	6	4	0	604	1	3.28	—	—	—	—	—	—
90-91	Binghamton	AHL	45	25	14	2	2452	0	3.16	9	3	4	442	1	3.80
91-92	Binghamton	AHL	43	25	15	3	2559	1	3.42	11	7	4	662	0	3.08
92-93	New Haven	AHL	30	10	18	1	1688	1	4.30	—	—	—	—	—	—
92-93	Brantford	CoHL	10	5	3	1	563	1	3.72	—	—	—	—	—	—
93-94	Ottawa	NHL	5	0	2	0	182	0	5.60	—	—	—	—	—	—
93-94	Prince Edward Island	AHL	43	9	25	5	2359	0	4.09	—	—	—	—	—	—
94-95	Milwaukee	IHL	42	19	13	7	2325	2	3.17	15	8	7	937	*2	2.56
95-96	Milwaukee	IHL	53	26	20	7	3078	0	3.72	5	2	3	315	0	3.42
96-97	Binghamton	AHL	9	0	4	1	393	0	3.97	—	—	—	—	—	—
96-97	Utica	CoHL	6	1	2	2	313	0	5.95	—	—	—	—	—	—
	NHL	Totals	103	25	54	4	5032	2	4.22	2	1	0	48	0	1.25
	AHL	Totals	262	120	100	12	14701	6	3.53	49	29	18	2923	2	3.02
	IHL	Totals	108	49	38	16	6121	2	3.55	20	10	10	1252	2	2.78
	CoHL	Totals	16	6	5	3	876	1	4.52	—	—	—	—	—	—

Born; 7/10/62, Welland, Ontario. 5-11, 190. Signed as a free agent by Detroit Red Wings (4/29/83). Traded to Philadelphia Flyers by Detroit for Philadelphia's second round choice (Bob Wilkie) in 1987 Entry Draft (6/13/87), Traded to Toronto Maple Leafs by Philadelphia for Toronto's sixth round choice in 1991 Entry Draft and seventh round choice in 1991 Entry Draft (9/8/89). Traded to New York Rangers by Toronto with Tie Domi for Greg Johnston (6/28/90). Claimed by Ottawa Senators from Rangers in Expansion Draft (6/18/93). 1986-87 AHL Top Goaltender (Baz Bastien Trophy). 1990-91 AHL Top Goaltender. 1990-91 AHL Second Team All-Star. Member of 1985-86 AHL champion Adirondack Red Wings.

Marc Laforge — Defenseman

			Regular Season					Playoffs				
Season	Team	League	GP	G	A	PTS	PIM	GP	G	A	PTS	PIM
86-87	Binghamton	AHL	—	—	—	—	—	4	0	0	0	7
88-89	Binghamton	AHL	38	2	2	4	179	—	—	—	—	—
88-89	Indianapolis	IHL	14	0	2	2	138	—	—	—	—	—
89-90	Hartford	NHL	9	0	0	0	43	—	—	—	—	—
89-90	Binghamton	AHL	25	2	6	8	111	—	—	—	—	—
89-90	Cape Breton	AHL	3	0	1	1	24	3	0	0	0	27
90-91	Cape Breton	AHL	49	1	7	8	217	—	—	—	—	—
91-92	Cape Breton	AHL	59	0	14	14	341	4	0	0	0	24
92-93	Cape Breton	AHL	77	1	12	13	208	15	1	2	3	*78
93-94	Edmonton	NHL	5	0	0	0	21	—	—	—	—	—
93-94	Cape Breton	AHL	14	0	0	0	91	—	—	—	—	—
93-94	Salt Lake City	IHL	43	0	2	2	242	—	—	—	—	—
94-95	Cape Breton	AHL	18	0	1	1	80	—	—	—	—	—
94-95	Syracuse	AHL	39	1	5	6	202	—	—	—	—	—
95-96	Minnesota	IHL	20	0	2	2	102	—	—	—	—	—
96-97	San Antonio	IHL	67	1	7	8	311	7	0	0	0	26
	NHL	Totals	14	0	0	0	64	—	—	—	—	—
	AHL	Totals	322	7	48	55	1453	26	1	2	3	136
	IHL	Totals	144	1	13	14	793	7	0	0	0	26

Born; 1/3/68, Sudbury, Ontario. 6-2, 210. Drafted by Hartford Whalers (2nd choice, 32nd overall) in 1986 Entry Draft. Traded to Edmonton Oilers by Hartford for the rights to Cam Brauer (3/16/90). Traded to New York Islanders by Edmonton for Brent Grieve (12/15/93). Member of 1992-93 AHL champion Cape Breton Oilers.

Darryl Lafrance
Right Wing

			Regular Season					Playoffs				
Season	Team	League	GP	G	A	PTS	PIM	GP	G	A	PTS	PIM
95-96	Chicago	IHL	42	5	5	10	20	5	0	0	0	2
95-96	Flint	CoHL	6	5	3	8	2	—	—	—	—	—
96-97	Chicago	IHL	47	12	14	26	18	3	1	1	2	0
96-97	Peoria	ECHL	7	4	4	8	4	—	—	—	—	—
	IHL	Totals	89	17	19	36	38	8	1	1	2	2

3/20/74, Sudbury, Ontario. 6-0, 195. Drafted by Calgary Flames (6th choice, 121st overall) in 1993 Entry Draft.

Chris Laganas
Right Wing

			Regular Season					Playoffs				
Season	Team	League	GP	G	A	PTS	PIM	GP	G	A	PTS	PIM
92-93	Oklahoma City	CeHL	57	18	22	40	193	11	1	2	3	16
93-94	Oklahoma City	CeHL	58	20	22	42	157	7	3	3	6	30
94-95	Oklahoma City	CeHL	59	9	13	22	177	5	1	1	2	14
95-96	Oklahoma City	CeHL	3	1	0	1	4	—	—	—	—	—
95-96	West Palm Beach	SHL	14	4	4	8	12	—	—	—	—	—
95-96	Reno	WCHL	8	2	0	2	12	3	2	1	3	2
96-97	Reno	WCHL	59	25	29	54	122	—	—	—	—	—
	CeHL	Totals	177	48	57	105	531	23	5	6	11	60
	WCHL	Totals	67	27	29	56	134	3	2	1	3	2

Born; 5/31/66, Seabrook Beach, New Hampshire. 5-10, 190.

Scott LaGrand
Goaltender

			Regular Season							Playoffs					
Season	Team	League	GP	W	L	T	MIN	SO	GAVG	GP	W	L	MIN	SO	GAVG
92-93	Hershey	AHL	32	8	17	4	1854	0	4.69	—	—	—	—	—	—
93-94	Hershey	AHL	40	16	13	3	2032	2	3.45	—	—	—	—	—	—
94-95	Hershey	AHL	21	7	9	3	1104	1	3.86	—	—	—	—	—	—
94-95	Atlanta	IHL	21	7	7	3	993	0	4.04	3	0	2	101	0	5.91
95-96	Orlando	IHL	33	17	7	3	1618	1	3.82	3	0	0	51	0	1.17
96-97	Orlando	IHL	35	16	10	2	1747	2	2.92	4	0	2	153	0	1.96
	AHL	Totals	93	31	39	10	4990	3	4.00	—	—	—	—	—	—
	IHL	Totals	89	40	24	8	4358	3	3.51	10	0	4	305	0	3.15

Born; 2/11/70, Potsdam, New York. 6-0, 165. Drafted by Philadelphia Flyers (5th choice, 77th overall) in 1988 Entry Draft. Traded to Tampa Bay Lightning by Philadelphia for Mike Greenlay (2/2/95). Last amateur club; Boston College (Hockey East).

Martin Laitre
Left Wing

			Regular Season					Playoffs				
Season	Team	League	GP	G	A	PTS	PIM	GP	G	A	PTS	PIM
94-95	Denver	IHL	1	0	0	0	18	—	—	—	—	—
94-95	Brantford	CoHL	28	2	5	7	161	—	—	—	—	—
94-95	Hampton Roads	ECHL	5	0	0	0	4	—	—	—	—	—
94-95	West Palm Beach	SUN	17	4	2	6	153	—	—	—	—	—
95-96	Cornwall	AHL	34	0	2	2	231	—	—	—	—	—
95-96	Brantford	CoHL	6	1	2	3	4	1	0	0	0	0
96-97	Hamilton	AHL	42	1	3	4	297	3	0	0	0	0
	AHL	Totals	76	1	5	6	528	3	0	0	0	0
	CoHL	Totals	34	3	7	10	165	1	0	0	0	0

Born; 4/11/73, Cold Lake, Alberta. 6-1, 220.

Greg Lakovic — Left Wing

Regular Season / Playoffs

Season	Team	League	GP	G	A	PTS	PIM	GP	G	A	PTS	PIM
96-97	Las Vegas	IHL	4	0	0	0	20	—	—	—	—	—
96-97	Tallahassee	ECHL	16	1	1	2	70	—	—	—	—	—
96-97	Toledo	ECHL	32	2	7	9	76	4	0	0	0	16
	ECHL	Totals	48	3	8	11	146	4	0	0	0	16

Born; 1/31/75, Vancouver, British Columbia. 6-2, 210.

Sasha Lakovic — Left Wing

Regular Season / Playoffs

Season	Team	League	GP	G	A	PTS	PIM	GP	G	A	PTS	PIM
92-93	Binghamton	AHL	3	0	0	0	0	—	—	—	—	—
92-93	Columbus	ECHL	27	7	9	16	162	—	—	—	—	—
92-93	Chatham	CoHL	28	7	5	12	235	5	2	1	3	62
93-94	Toledo	ECHL	24	5	10	15	198	—	—	—	—	—
93-94	Chatham	CoHL	13	11	7	18	61	—	—	—	—	—
94-95	Tulsa	CeHL	40	20	24	44	214	5	1	3	4	88
95-96	Las Vegas	IHL	49	1	2	3	416	13	1	1	2	57
96-97	Calgary	NHL	19	0	1	1	54	—	—	—	—	—
96-97	Saint John	AHL	18	1	8	9	182	—	—	—	—	—
96-97	Las Vegas	IHL	10	0	0	0	81	2	0	0	0	14
	IHL	Totals	59	1	2	3	497	15	1	1	2	71
	AHL	Totals	21	1	8	9	182	—	—	—	—	—
	ECHL	Totals	51	12	19	31	360	—	—	—	—	—
	CoHL	Totals	41	18	12	30	296	5	2	1	3	62

Born; 9/7/71, East Vancouver, British Columbia. 6-0, 198.

Martin Lamarche — Left Wing

Regular Season / Playoffs

Season	Team	League	GP	G	A	PTS	PIM	GP	G	A	PTS	PIM
95-96	Prince Edward Island	AHL	30	0	1	1	88	—	—	—	—	—
96-97	Saint John	AHL	33	4	5	9	114	4	0	0	0	21
	AHL	Totals	63	4	6	10	202	4	0	0	0	21

Born; 10/2/75, Ste-Justine, Quebec. 6-1, 206. Signed as a free agent by Ottawa (3/3/95).

Mark Lamb — Center

Regular Season / Playoffs

Season	Team	League	GP	G	A	PTS	PIM	GP	G	A	PTS	PIM
82-83	Colorado	CHL	—	—	—	—	—	6	0	2	2	0
84-85	Moncton	AHL	80	23	49	72	53	—	—	—	—	—
85-86	Calgary	NHL	1	0	0	0	0	—	—	—	—	—
85-86	Moncton	AHL	79	26	50	76	51	10	2	6	8	17
86-87	Detroit	NHL	22	2	1	3	8	11	0	0	0	11
86-87	Adirondack	AHL	49	14	36	50	45	—	—	—	—	—
87-88	Edmonton	NHL	2	0	0	0	0	—	—	—	—	—
87-88	Nova Scotia	AHL	69	27	61	88	45	5	0	5	5	6
88-89	Edmonton	NHL	20	2	8	10	14	6	0	2	2	8
88-89	Cape Breton	AHL	54	33	49	82	29	—	—	—	—	—
89-90	Edmonton	NHL	58	12	26	28	42	22	6	11	17	2
90-91	Edmonton	NHL	37	4	8	12	25	15	0	5	5	20
91-92	Edmonton	NHL	59	6	22	28	46	16	1	1	2	10
92-93	Ottawa	NHL	71	7	19	26	64	—	—	—	—	—
93-94	Ottawa	NHL	66	11	18	29	56	—	—	—	—	—
93-94	Philadelphia	NHL	19	1	6	7	16	—	—	—	—	—
94-95	Philadelphia	NHL	8	0	2	2	2	—	—	—	—	—
94-95	Montreal	NHL	39	1	0	1	18	—	—	—	—	—

Season	Team	League	GP	G	A	PTS	PIM	GP	G	A	PTS	PIM
95-96	Houston	IHL	67	17	60	77	65	—	—	—	—	—
96-97	Houston	IHL	81	25	53	78	83	13	3	12	15	10
	NHL	Totals	402	46	100	146	291	70	7	19	26	51
	AHL	Totals	331	123	245	368	223	15	2	11	13	23
	IHL	Totals	148	42	113	155	148	13	3	12	15	10

Born; 8/3/64, Swift Current, Saskatchewan. 5-9, 180. Drafted by Calgary Flames (5th choice, 72nd overall) in 1982 Entry Draft. Signed as a free agent by Detroit Red Wings (7/28/86). Claimed by Edmonton Oilers from Detroit in NHL Waiver Draft (10/5/87). Claimed by Ottawa from Edmonton in Expansion Draft (6/18/92). Traded to Philadelphia Flyers by Ottawa for Claude Boivin and Kirk Daubenspeck (3/5/94). Traded to Montreal Canadiens by Philadelphia for cash (2/10/95). Member of 1989-90 Stanley Cup champion Edmonton Oilers.

Dan Lambert — Defenseman

			Regular Season					Playoffs				
Season	Team	League	GP	G	A	PTS	PIM	GP	G	A	PTS	PIM
90-91	Quebec	NHL	1	0	0	0	0	—	—	—	—	—
90-91	Halifax	AHL	30	7	13	20	20	—	—	—	—	—
90-91	Fort Wayne	IHL	49	10	27	37	65	19	4	10	14	20
91-92	Quebec	NHL	28	6	9	15	22	—	—	—	—	—
91-92	Halifax	AHL	47	3	28	31	33	—	—	—	—	—
92-93	Moncton	AHL	73	11	30	41	100	5	1	2	3	2
93-94	Fort Wayne	IHL	62	10	27	37	138	18	3	12	15	20
94-95	San Diego	IHL	70	6	19	25	95	5	0	5	5	10
95-96	Los Angeles	IHL	81	22	65	87	121	—	—	—	—	—
96-97	Long Beach	IHL	71	15	50	65	70	18	2	8	10	8
	NHL	Totals	29	6	9	15	22	—	—	—	—	—
	IHL	Totals	333	63	188	251	489	60	9	35	44	58
	AHL	Totals	150	21	71	92	153	5	1	2	3	2

Born; 1/12/70, St. Boniface, Manitoba. 5-8, 177. Drafted by Quebec Nordiques (8th choice, 106th overall) in 1989 Entry Draft. Traded to Winnipeg Jets by Quebec for Shawn Cronin (8/25/92).

Lane Lambert — Right Wing

			Regular Season					Playoffs				
Season	Team	League	GP	G	A	PTS	PIM	GP	G	A	PTS	PIM
83-84	Detroit	NHL	73	20	15	35	115	4	0	0	0	10
84-85	Detroit	NHL	69	14	11	25	104	—	—	—	—	—
85-86	Adirondack	AHL	45	16	25	41	69	16	5	5	10	9
85-86	Detroit	NHL	34	2	3	5	130	—	—	—	—	—
86-87	New Haven	AHL	11	3	3	6	19	—	—	—	—	—
86-87	Rangers	NHL	18	2	2	4	33	—	—	—	—	—
86-87	Quebec	NHL	15	5	6	11	18	13	2	4	6	30
87-88	Quebec	NHL	61	13	28	41	98	—	—	—	—	—
88-89	Quebec	NHL	13	2	2	4	23	—	—	—	—	—
88-89	Halifax	AHL	59	25	35	60	162	4	0	2	2	2
89-90	Canada	National										
96-97	Cleveland	IHL	75	24	20	44	94	13	4	5	9	21
	NHL	Totals	283	58	66	124	521	17	2	4	6	40
	AHL	Totals	115	44	63	107	250	20	5	7	12	11

Born; 11/18/64, Melfort, Saskatchewan. 6-0, 185. Drafted by Detroit Red Wings (2nd choice, 25th overall) in 1983 Entry Draft. Traded to New York Rangers with Kelly Kisio, Jim Leavins and a fifth round 1988 draft pick by Detroit for Glen Hanlon and third round 1987 (Dennis Holland) and 1988 draft picks and future considerations, (7/29/86). Traded to Quebec Nordiques by Rangers for Pat Price (3/5/87). Member of 1985-86 AHL Champion Adirondack Red Wings.

Marc Lamothe — Goaltender

			Regular Season							Playoffs					
Season	Team	League	GP	W	L	T	MIN	SO	GAVG	GP	W	L	MIN	SO	GAVG
94-95	Fredericton	AHL	9	2	5	0	428	0	4.48	—	—	—	—	—	—
94-95	Wheeling	ECHL	12	9	2	1	736	0	3.10	—	—	—	—	—	—
95-96	Fredericton	AHL	23	5	9	3	1165	1	3.76	3	1	2	160	0	3.36

Season	Team	League	GP										
96-97	Indianapolis	IHL	38	20	14	4	2271	1	2.64	1	0	0	20	0	3.00
	AHL	Totals	32	7	14	3	1593	1	3.84	3	1	2	160	0	3.36

Born; 2/27/74, New Liskeard, Ontario. 6-1, 204. Drafted by Montreal Canadiens (6th choice, 92nd overall) in 1992 Entry Draft.

Denis Lamoureux — Forward

			Regular Season					Playoffs				
Season	Team	League	GP	G	A	PTS	PIM	GP	G	A	PTS	PIM
96-97	Hampton Roads	ECHL	18	4	6	10	4	—	—	—	—	—
96-97	Johnstown	ECHL	29	8	9	17	4	—	—	—	—	—
	ECHL	Totals	47	12	15	27	8	—	—	—	—	—

Born; 6/28/75, LaSalle, Quebec. 6-1, 195.

Mitch Lamoureux — Center

			Regular Season					Season				
Season	Team	League	GP	G	A	PTS	PIM	GP	G	A	PTS	PIM
82-83	Baltimore	AHL	80	*57	50	107	107	—	—	—	—	—
83-84	Pittsburgh	NHL	8	1	1	2	6	—	—	—	—	—
83-84	Baltimore	AHL	68	30	38	68	136	9	1	3	4	2
84-85	Pittsburgh	NHL	62	11	8	19	53	—	—	—	—	—
84-85	Baltimore	AHL	18	10	14	24	34	—	—	—	—	—
85-86	Baltimore	AHL	75	22	31	53	129	—	—	—	—	—
86-87	Hershey	AHL	78	43	46	89	122	5	1	2	3	8
87-88	Philadelphia	NHL	3	0	0	0	0	—	—	—	—	—
87-88	Hershey	AHL	78	35	52	87	171	12	9	7	16	48
88-89	Hershey	AHL	9	9	7	16	14	9	1	4	5	14
89-90	Maine	AHL	10	4	7	11	10	—	—	—	—	—
90-91	N/A											
91-92	N/A											
92-93	San Diego	IHL	71	28	39	67	130	4	0	0	0	11
93-94	Hershey	AHL	80	45	60	105	92	11	3	4	7	26
94-95	Hershey	AHL	76	39	46	85	112	6	0	2	2	8
95-96	Providence	AHL	63	22	29	51	62	4	2	3	5	2
96-97	Providence	AHL	75	25	29	54	70	3	0	0	0	4
	NHL	Totals	73	12	9	21	59	—	—	—	—	—
	AHL	Totals	710	341	409	750	1059	59	17	25	42	112

Born; 8/22/62, Ottawa, Ontario. 5-6, 191. Drafted by Pittsburgh Penguins (6th choice, 154th overall) in 1981 Entry Draft. 1982-83 AHL Rookie of the Year. 1982-83 AHL Second Team All Star.

Patrick Lampron — Defenseman

			Regular Season					Playoffs				
Season	Team	League	GP	G	A	PTS	PIM	GP	G	A	PTS	PIM
95-96	Brantford	CoHL	16	1	2	3	14	—	—	—	—	—
95-96	Quad City	CoHL	28	2	9	11	46	—	—	—	—	—
96-97	Central Texas	WPHL	33	7	11	18	61	—	—	—	—	—
96-97	Amarillo	WPHL	27	8	15	23	36	—	—	—	—	—
	WPHL	Totals	60	15	26	41	97	—	—	—	—	—
	CoHL	Totals	44	3	11	14	60	—	—	—	—	—

Born; 1/4/74, Cap De La Madeleine, Quebec. 6-1, 188.

Eric Landry — Center

			Regular Season					Playoffs				
Season	Team	League	GP	G	A	PTS	PIM	GP	G	A	PTS	PIM
95-96	Cape Breton	AHL	74	19	33	52	187	—	—	—	—	—
96-97	Hamilton	AHL	74	15	17	32	139	22	6	7	13	42
	AHL	Totals	148	34	50	84	326	22	6	7	13	42

Born; 1/20/75, Hull, Quebec. 5-10, 180.

Eric M. Landry — Right Wing

Regular Season | | | | | | | Playoffs
Season	Team	League	GP	G	A	PTS	PIM	GP	G	A	PTS	PIM
96-97	Saint John	AHL	12	2	0	2	36	—	—	—	—	—
96-97	Roanoke	ECHL	1	0	0	0	0	4	2	2	4	17

Born; 1/29/76, Cornwall, Ontario. 6-0, 200. Drafted by San Jose Sharks (8th choice, 193rd overall) in 1994 Entry Draft.

Chad Lang — Goaltender

Regular Season | | | | | | | | | Playoffs
Season	Team	League	GP	W	L	T	MIN	SO	GAVG	GP	W	L	MIN	SO	GAVG
95-96	Raleigh	ECHL	8	2	6	0	461	0	3.64	—	—	—	—	—	—
95-96	Columbus	ECHL	4	3	1	0	237	1	2.27	3	0	2	147	0	2.85
96-97	Huntington	ECHL	15	5	5	2	738	0	4.55	—	—	—	—	—	—
	ECHL	Totals	27	10	12	2	1436	1	3.89	3	0	2	147	0	2.85

Born; 2/11/75, Newmarket, Ontario. 5-11, 200. Drafted by Dallas Stars (3rd choice, 87th overall) in 1993 Entry draft.

Scott Langkow — Goaltender

Regular Season | | | | | | | | | Playoffs
Season	Team	League	GP	W	L	T	MIN	SO	GAVG	GP	W	L	MIN	SO	GAVG
95-96	Winnipeg	NHL	1	0	0	0	6	0	0.00	—	—	—	—	—	—
95-96	Springfield	AHL	39	18	15	6	2329	3	2.99	7	4	2	392	0	3.51
96-97	Springfield	AHL	33	15	9	7	1929	0	2.64	—	—	—	—	—	—
	AHL	Totals	72	33	24	13	4258	3	2.83	7	4	2	392	0	3.51

Born; 4/21/75, Sherwood Park, Alberta. 5-11, 190. Drafted by Winnipeg Jets (2nd choice, 31st overall) in 1993 Entry Draft.

Jocelyn Langlois — Forward

Regular Season | | | | | | | Playoffs
Season	Team	League	GP	G	A	PTS	PIM	GP	G	A	PTS	PIM
96-97	Jacksonville	ECHL	39	6	13	19	17	—	—	—	—	—
96-97	Macon	CeHL	5	1	5	6	15	5	4	2	6	8

Born; 11/3/73, Montreal, Quebec. 6-0, 190.

Brian Langlot — Goaltender

Regular Season | | | | | | | | | Playoffs
Season	Team	League	GP	W	L	T	MIN	SO	GAVG	GP	W	L	MIN	SO	GAVG
93-94	Columbus	ECHL	3	1	1	0	159	0	3.76	—	—	—	—	—	—
93-94	Raleigh	ECHL	4	1	2	0	168	0	3.57	—	—	—	—	—	—
93-94	Albany	AHL	1	0	0	0	10	0	0.00	—	—	—	—	—	—
94-95	N/A														
95-96	Fresno	WCHL	1	0	0	0	12	0	0.00	—	—	—	—	—	—
96-97	Wichita	CeHL	25	7	5	3	1106	0	4.45	—	—	—	—	—	—
	ECHL	Totals	7	2	3	0	327	0	3.67	—	—	—	—	—	—

Born; 9/1/69, Seattle, Washington. 5-11, 190.

Marc Laniel — Defenseman

Regular Season | | | | | | | Playoffs
Season	Team	League	GP	G	A	PTS	PIM	GP	G	A	PTS	PIM
87-88	Utica	AHL	2	0	0	0	0	—	—	—	—	—
88-89	Utica	AHL	80	6	28	34	43	5	0	1	1	2
89-90	Utica	AHL	20	0	0	0	25	—	—	—	—	—
89-90	Phoenix	IHL	26	3	15	18	10	—	—	—	—	—
90-91	Utica	AHL	57	6	9	15	45	—	—	—	—	—
91-92	Winston-Salem	ECHL	57	15	36	51	90	5	2	5	7	4
91-92	San Diego	IHL	10	0	2	2	16	—	—	—	—	—
92-93	Birmingham	ECHL	21	5	9	14	26	—	—	—	—	—
92-93	Cincinnati	IHL	13	1	9	10	2	—	—	—	—	—
92-93	Fredericton	AHL	7	0	1	1	6	5	0	2	2	23

Season	Team	League	GP	G	A	PTS	PIM	GP	G	A	PTS	PIM
93-94	Fredericton	AHL	79	6	41	47	76	—	—	—	—	—
94-95	Cincinnati	IHL	70	5	29	34	34	—	—	—	—	—
94-95	Houston	IHL	2	0	0	0	0	4	0	2	2	6
95-96	Houston	IHL	65	5	25	30	40	—	—	—	—	—
95-96	Las Vegas	IHL	9	2	2	4	6	14	0	0	0	14
96-97	Cincinnati	IHL	61	4	14	18	30	—	—	—	—	—
96-97	Fort Wayne	IHL	21	2	5	7	19	—	—	—	—	—
	IHL	Totals	277	22	101	123	157	18	0	2	2	20
	AHL	Totals	245	18	79	97	195	10	0	3	3	25
	ECHL	Totals	78	20	45	65	116	5	2	5	7	4

Born; 1/16/68, Oshawa, Ontario. 6-1, 190. Drafted by New Jersey Devils (4th choice, 62nd overall) in 1986 Entry Draft. 1991-92 ECHL Second Team All-Star.

Jeff Lank — Defenseman

Season	Team	League	GP	G	A	PTS	PIM	GP	G	A	PTS	PIM
95-96	Hershey	AHL	72	7	13	20	70	5	0	0	0	8
96-97	Philadelphia	AHL	44	2	12	14	49	7	2	1	3	4
	AHL	Totals	116	9	25	34	119	12	2	1	3	12

Born; 3/1/75, Indian Head, Saskatchewan. 6-3, 185. Drafted by Montreal Canadiens (6th choice, 113th overall) in 1993 Entry Draft. Re-entered NHL Entry Draft. Drafted by Philadelphia Flyers (9th choice, 230th overall) in 1995 Entry Draft.

Daniel Laperriere — Defenseman

Season	Team	League	GP	G	A	PTS	PIM	GP	G	A	PTS	PIM
92-93	St. Louis	NHL	5	0	1	1	0	—	—	—	—	—
92-93	Peoria	IHL	54	4	20	24	28	—	—	—	—	—
93-94	St. Louis	NHL	20	1	3	4	8	—	—	—	—	—
93-94	Peoria	IHL	56	10	37	47	16	6	0	2	2	2
94-95	St. Louis	NHL	4	0	0	0	15	—	—	—	—	—
94-95	Ottawa	NHL	13	1	1	2	0	—	—	—	—	—
94-95	Peoria	IHL	65	19	33	52	42	—	—	—	—	—
95-96	Ottawa	NHL	6	0	0	0	4	—	—	—	—	—
95-96	Prince Edward Island	AHL	15	2	7	9	4	—	—	—	—	—
95-96	Atlanta	IHL	15	4	9	13	4	—	—	—	—	—
95-96	Kansas City	IHL	23	2	6	8	11	5	0	1	1	0
96-97	Portland	AHL	69	14	26	40	33	5	0	2	2	2
	NHL	Totals	48	2	5	7	27	—	—	—	—	—
	IHL	Totals	213	39	105	144	101	11	0	3	3	2
	AHL	Totals	84	16	33	49	37	5	0	2	2	2

Born; 3/28/69, Laval, Quebec. 6-1, 195. Drafted by St. Louis Blues (4th choice, 93rd overall) in 1989 Entry Draft. Traded to Ottawa Senators by St. Louis with St. Louis' ninth round choice (Erik Kasminski) in 1995 Entry Draft for Ottawa ninth round choice (Libor Zabransky) in 1995 Entry Draft (4/7/95).

Sebastian LaPlante — Left Wing

Season	Team	League	GP	G	A	PTS	PIM	GP	G	A	PTS	PIM
93-94	Cornwall	AHL	5	1	0	1	0	—	—	—	—	—
93-94	Greensboro	ECHL	60	35	38	73	206	8	0	1	1	26
94-95	N/A											
95-96	San Antonio	CeHL	54	29	37	66	153	13	4	11	15	29
96-97	Fort Wayne	IHL	10	1	2	3	17	—	—	—	—	—
96-97	Quad City	CoHL	20	2	14	16	32	4	2	0	2	15
96-97	San Antonio	CeHL	23	8	24	32	127	—	—	—	—	—
	CeHL	Totals	77	37	61	98	280	13	4	11	15	29

Born; 4/23/71, Cap-Rouge, Quebec. 5-11, 190. 1995-96 CeHL First Team All-Star. Member of 1996-97 CoHL Champion Quad City Mallards.

Alexandre LaPorte — Defenseman

			Regular Season					Playoffs				
Season	Team	League	GP	G	A	PTS	PIM	GP	G	A	PTS	PIM
95-96	Atlanta	IHL	14	0	1	1	5	—	—	—	—	—
95-96	Nashville	ECHL	38	2	9	11	60	5	0	0	0	8
96-97	Adirondack	AHL	38	0	3	3	39	1	0	0	0	0

Born; 5/1/75, Cowansville, Quebec. 6-3, 210. Drafted by Tampa Bay Lightning (9th choice, 211th overall) in 1993 Entry Draft.

Georges Laraque — Right Wing

			Regular Season					Playoffs				
Season	Team	League	GP	G	A	PTS	PIM	GP	G	A	PTS	PIM
96-97	Hamilton	AHL	73	14	20	34	179	15	1	3	4	12

Born; 12/7/76, Montreal, Quebec. 6-3, 235. Drafted by Edmonton Oilers (2nd choice, 31st overall) in 1996 Entry Draft.

Francis Larivee — Goaltender

			Regular Season							Playoffs					
Season	Team	League	GP	W	L	T	MIN	SO	GAVG	GP	W	L	MIN	SO	GAVG
96-97	St. John's	AHL	4	3	1	0	244	0	2.21	1	0	0	1	0	0.00

Born; 12/8/77, Montreal, Quebec. 6-2, 198. Drafted by Toronto Maple Leafs (2nd choice, 50th overall) in 1996 Entry Draft.

Mike Larkin — Defenseman

			Regular Season					Playoffs				
Season	Team	League	GP	G	A	PTS	PIM	GP	G	A	PTS	PIM
95-96	Hampton Roads	ECHL	9	2	10	12	8	—	—	—	—	—
95-96	Lakeland	SHL	33	5	29	34	47	4	1	0	1	8
96-97	Hampton Roads	ECHL	34	2	10	12	80	8	1	3	4	35
	ECHL	Totals	43	4	20	24	88	8	1	3	4	35

Born; 3/15/73, South Weymouth, Massachusetts. 6-3, 210.

Don Larner — Right Wing

			Regular Season					Playoffs				
Season	Team	League	GP	G	A	PTS	PIM	GP	G	A	PTS	PIM
96-97	Las Vegas	IHL	2	0	0	0	14	—	—	—	—	—
96-97	Port Huron	CoHL	14	3	5	8	16	—	—	—	—	—
96-97	Toledo	ECHL	34	9	15	24	117	—	—	—	—	—

Born; 2/16/75, Langham, Saskatchewan. 6-1, 205.

Stephane Larocque — Right Wing

			Regular Season					Playoffs				
Season	Team	League	GP	G	A	PTS	PIM	GP	G	A	PTS	PIM
95-96	South Carolina	ECHL	9	1	2	3	32	—	—	—	—	—
95-96	Thunder Bay	CoHL	44	22	35	57	110	18	4	7	11	24
96-97	Fort Worth	CeHL	59	41	39	80	354	17	*14	10	*24	66

Born; 7/24/74, Hull, Quebec. 6-2, 205. Member of 1996-97 CeHL Champion Fort Worth Fire.

Guy Larose

			Regular Season					Playoffs				
Season	Team	League	GP	G	A	PTS	PIM	GP	G	A	PTS	PIM
87-88	Moncton	AHL	77	22	31	53	127	—	—	—	—	—
88-89	Winnipeg	NHL	3	0	1	1	6	—	—	—	—	—
88-89	Moncton	AHL	72	32	27	59	176	10	4	4	8	37
89-90	Moncton	AHL	79	44	26	70	232	—	—	—	—	—
90-91	Winnipeg	NHL	7	0	0	0	8	—	—	—	—	—
90-91	Moncton	AHL	35	14	10	24	60	—	—	—	—	—
90-91	Binghamton	AHL	34	21	15	36	48	10	8	5	13	37
91-92	Toronto	NHL	34	9	5	14	27	—	—	—	—	—
91-92	Binghamton	AHL	30	10	11	21	36	—	—	—	—	—

			GP	G	A	PTS	PIM	GP	G	A	PTS	PIM
91-92	St. John's	AHL	15	7	7	14	26	—	—	—	—	—
92-93	Toronto	NHL	9	0	0	0	8	—	—	—	—	—
92-93	St. John's	AHL	5	0	1	1	8	9	5	2	7	6
93-94	Toronto	NHL	10	1	2	3	10	—	—	—	—	—
93-94	Calgary	NHL	7	0	1	1	4	—	—	—	—	—
93-94	St. John's	AHL	23	13	16	29	41	—	—	—	—	—
93-94	Saint John	AHL	15	11	11	22	20	7	3	2	5	22
94-95	Boston	NHL	—	—	—	—	—	4	0	0	0	0
94-95	Providence	AHL	68	25	33	58	93	12	4	6	10	22
95-96	Detroit	IHL	50	28	15	43	53	—	—	—	—	—
95-96	Las Vegas	IHL	25	10	22	32	54	15	3	6	9	14
96-97	Houston	IHL	79	29	25	54	108	13	6	7	13	12
	NHL	Totals	70	10	9	19	63	4	0	0	0	0
	AHL	Totals	453	186	188	374	867	48	24	19	43	124
	IHL	Totals	154	67	62	129	215	28	9	13	22	26

Born; 8/31/67, Hull, Quebec. 5-9, 175. Drafted by Buffalo Sabres (11th choice, 224th overall) in 1985 Entry Draft. Signed as a free agent by Winnipeg Jets 97/16/87). Traded to New York Rangers by Winnipeg for Rudy Poeschek (1/22/91). Traded to Toronto Maple Leafs by Rangers for Mike Stevens (12/26/91). Claimed on waivers by Calgary Flames from Toronto (1/1/94). Signed as a free agent by Boston Bruins (7/11/94).

Steve Larouche — Center

			Regular Season					Playoffs				
Season	Team	League	GP	G	A	PTS	PIM	GP	G	A	PTS	PIM
91-92	Fredericton	AHL	74	21	35	56	41	7	1	0	1	0
92-93	Fredericton	AHL	77	27	65	92	52	5	2	5	7	6
93-94	Atlanta	IHL	80	43	53	96	73	14	*16	10	*26	16
94-95	Ottawa	NHL	18	8	7	15	6	—	—	—	—	—
94-95	Prince Edward Island	AHL	70	*53	48	101	54	2	1	0	1	0
95-96	Rangers	NHL	1	0	0	0	0	—	—	—	—	—
95-96	Los Angeles	NHL	7	1	2	3	4	—	—	—	—	—
95-96	Binghamton	AHL	39	20	46	66	47	—	—	—	—	—
95-96	Phoenix	IHL	33	19	17	36	14	4	0	1	1	8
96-97	Quebec	IHL	79	49	53	102	78	9	3	10	13	18
	NHL	Totals	26	9	9	18	10	—	—	—	—	—
	AHL	Totals	260	121	194	315	194	14	4	5	9	14
	IHL	Totals	192	111	123	234	165	27	19	21	40	42

Born; 4/14/71, Rouyn, Quebec. 6-0, 180. Drafted by Montreal Canadiens (3rd choice, 41st overall) in 1989 Entry Draft. Signed as a free agent by Ottawa Senators (9/11/94). Traded to New York Rangers by Ottawa for Jean Yves-Roy (10/5/95). Traded to Los Angeles Kings by Rangers for Chris Snell (1/14/96). 1994-95 AHL First Team All-Star. 1994-95 AHL Fred Hunt Trophy winner (Sportsmanship). 1994-95 AHL MVP. 1996-97 IHL First Team All-Star. Member of 1993-94 IHL champion Atlanta Knights.

Brett Larson — Defenseman

			Regular Season					Playoffs				
Season	Team	League	GP	G	A	PTS	PIM	GP	G	A	PTS	PIM
95-96	Madison	CoHL	70	12	31	43	37	6	2	1	3	18
96-97	Louisville	ECHL	27	4	13	17	4	—	—	—	—	—

Born; 8/20/72, Duluth, Minnesota. 6-0, 175.

David Larson — Left Wing

			Regular Season					Playoffs				
Season	Team	League	GP	G	A	PTS	PIM	GP	G	A	PTS	PIM
96-97	Quad City	CoHL	71	13	13	26	169	15	2	3	5	10

Born; 7/10/72, Livonia, Michigan. 6-0, 223. Member of 1996-97 CoHL Champion Quad City Mallards.

Dean Larson — Center

Regular Season / **Playoffs**

Season	Team	League	GP	G	A	PTS	PIM	GP	G	A	PTS	PIM
95-96	Anchorage	WCHL	54	31	61	92	71	—	—	—	—	—
96-97	Anchorage	WCHL	58	29	79	108	54	9	4	6	10	4
	WCHL	Totals	112	60	140	200	125	9	4	6	10	4

Born; 6/4/69, 5-8, 160. 1996-97 WCHL Second team All-Star.

Jon Larson — Defenseman

Regular Season / **Playoffs**

Season	Team	League	GP	G	A	PTS	PIM	GP	G	A	PTS	PIM
93-94	Knoxville	ECHL	51	10	19	29	66	—	—	—	—	—
94-95	Knoxville	ECHL	67	11	17	28	132	8	0	1	1	19
95-96	Knoxville	ECHL	36	5	15	20	46	—	—	—	—	—
95-96	Raleigh	ECHL	35	4	9	13	32	4	1	3	4	2
96-97	Syracuse	AHL	5	1	1	2	4	—	—	—	—	—
96-97	Raleigh	ECHL	47	9	15	24	107	—	—	—	—	—
	ECHL	Totals	236	39	675	114	383	12	1	4	5	21

Born; 4/12/71, Roseau, Minnesota. 6-1, 205. Drafted by New York Islanders (8th choice, 128th overall) in 1989 Entry Draft.

Mike Latendresse — Right Wing

Regular Season / **Playoffs**

Season	Team	League	GP	G	A	PTS	PIM	GP	G	A	PTS	PIM
94-95	Adirondack	AHL	2	0	0	0	0	—	—	—	—	—
94-95	Toledo	ECHL	43	36	20	56	23	4	1	3	4	2
95-96	Detroit	IHL	1	0	0	0	0	—	—	—	—	—
95-96	Birmingham	ECHL	28	21	28	49	32	—	—	—	—	—
96-97	Birmingham	ECHL	61	20	28	48	82	2	0	1	1	0
	ECHL	Totals	132	77	76	153	137	6	1	4	5	2

Born; 2/11/71, Montreal, Quebec. 5-10, 160.

Jim Latos — Right Wing

Regular Season / **Playoffs**

Season	Team	League	GP	G	A	PTS	PIM	GP	G	A	PTS	PIM
87-88	Colorado	IHL	38	11	12	23	98	—	—	—	—	—
88-89	Denver	IHL	37	7	5	12	157	4	0	0	0	17
88-89	Rangers	NHL	1	0	0	0	0	—	—	—	—	—
89-90	Flint	IHL	71	12	15	27	244	4	0	0	0	4
90-91	Kansas City	IHL	61	14	14	28	187	—	—	—	—	—
91-92	St. Thomas	CoHL	27	7	13	20	62	—	—	—	—	—
91-92	Muskegon	IHL	27	4	4	8	54	6	0	1	1	10
91-92	Knoxville	ECHL	10	5	2	7	24	—	—	—	—	—
92-93	Muskegon	CoHL	59	10	24	34	163	7	2	0	2	4
92-93	Cleveland	IHL	1	0	0	0	0	—	—	—	—	—
93-94	Wichita	CeHL	63	19	34	53	227	11	4	5	9	27
94-95	Wichita	CeHL	55	13	23	36	167	11	2	5	7	44
95-96	Louisiana	ECHL	8	2	1	3	30	—	—	—	—	—
96-97	Louisiana	ECHL	32	4	7	11	150	—	—	—	—	—
	IHL	Totals	235	48	50	98	740	14	0	1	1	31
	CeHL	Totals	118	32	57	89	394	22	6	10	16	71
	CoHL	Totals	86	17	37	54	225	7	2	0	2	4
	ECHL	Totals	50	11	10	21	204	—	—	—	—	—

Born; 1/4/66, Wakaw, Saskatchewan. 6-1, 200. Signed as a free agent by New York Rangers (6/5/87). Signed as a free agent by Kansas City Blades (9/90). Member of 1993-94 CeHL Champion Wichita Thunder. Member of 1994-95 CeHL Champion Wichita Thunder.

Brad Lauer — Left Wing

Season	Team	League	GP	G	A	PTS	PIM	GP	G	A	PTS	PIM
86-87	Islanders	NHL	61	7	14	21	65	6	2	0	2	4
87-88	Islanders	NHL	69	17	18	35	67	5	3	1	4	4
88-89	Islanders	NHL	14	3	2	5	2	—	—	—	—	—
88-89	Springfield	AHL	8	1	5	6	0	—	—	—	—	—
89-90	Islanders	NHL	63	6	18	24	19	4	0	2	2	10
89-90	Springfield	AHL	7	4	2	6	0	—	—	—	—	—
90-91	Islanders	NHL	44	4	8	12	45	—	—	—	—	—
90-91	Capital District	AHL	11	5	11	16	14	—	—	—	—	—
91-92	Islanders	NHL	8	1	0	1	2	—	—	—	—	—
91-92	Chicago	NHL	6	0	0	0	4	7	1	1	2	2
91-92	Indianapolis	IHL	57	24	30	54	46	—	—	—	—	—
92-93	Chicago	NHL	7	0	1	1	2	—	—	—	—	—
92-93	Indianapolis	IHL	62	*50	41	91	80	5	3	1	4	6
93-94	Ottawa	NHL	30	2	5	7	6	—	—	—	—	—
93-94	Las Vegas	IHL	32	21	21	42	30	4	1	0	1	2
94-95	Cleveland	IHL	51	32	27	59	48	4	4	2	6	6
95-96	Pittsburgh	NHL	21	4	1	5	6	12	1	1	2	4
95-96	Cleveland	IHL	53	25	27	52	44	—	—	—	—	—
96-97	Cleveland	IHL	64	27	21	48	61	14	4	6	10	8
	NHL	Totals	323	44	67	111	218	34	7	5	12	24
	IHL	Totals	319	179	167	346	309	27	12	9	21	22
	AHL	Totals	26	10	18	28	14	—	—	—	—	—

Born; 10/27/66, Humboldt, Saskatchewan. 6-0, 195. Drafted by New York Islanders (3rd choice, 34th overall) in 1985 Entry Draft. Traded to Chicago Blackhawks by Islanders with Brent Sutter for Adam Creighton and Steve Thomas (10/25/91). Signed as a free agent by Ottawa Senators (1/3/94). Signed as a free agent by Pittsburgh Penguins (8/10/95). 1992-93 IHL First Team All-Star.

Rob Laurie — Goaltender

Season	Team	League	GP	W	L	T	MIN	SO	GAVG	GP	W	L	MIN	SO	GAVG
92-93	Roanoke	ECHL	14	5	7	0	716	0	4.61	—	—	—	—	—	—
92-93	Dayton	ECHL	22	11	7	1	1197	0	4.51	1	0	1	68	0	3.53
93-94	Dayton	ECHL	2	1	1	0	120	0	4.50	—	—	—	—	—	—
93-94	Johnstwon	ECHL	34	18	13	1	1942	0	3.96	3	1	2	153	0	4.31
94-95	Johnstwon	ECHL	26	7	16	2	1456	0	4.66	—	—	—	—	—	—
94-95	Greensboro	ECHL	10	4	4	1	514	0	4.55	—	—	—	—	—	—
95-96	Adirondack	AHL	1	0	1	0	23	0	2.64	—	—	—	—	—	—
95-96	Toledo	ECHL	19	13	3	2	1125	0	3.73	—	—	—	—	—	—
95-96	Tallahassee	ECHL	17	8	5	0	774	0	3.49	3	1	2	196	0	2.76
96-97	Huntington	ECHL	56	27	25	2	3198	1	4.00	—	—	—	—	—	—
	ECHL	Totals	200	94	81	9	11042	1	4.14	7	2	5	417	0	3.45

Born; 5/19/70, Esat Lansing, Michigan. 5-10, 175. @ ECHL win/loss totals are not complete.

Todd Laurin — Goaltender

Season	Team	League	GP	W	L	T	MIN	SO	GAVG	GP	W	L	MIN	SO	GAVG
96-97	Amarillo	WPHL	25	4	13	1	1200	0	5.40	—	—	—	—	—	—

Born; 3/10/75, Gloucester, Ontario. 5-6, 145.

Brian LaVack — Defenseman

Season	Team	League	GP	G	A	PTS	PIM	GP	G	A	PTS	PIM
96-97	Madison	CoHL	25	0	4	4	32	—	—	—	—	—
96-97	Saginaw	CoHL	39	1	6	7	61	—	—	—	—	—
	CoHL	Totals	64	1	10	11	93	—	—	—	—	—

Born; 5/12/75, Massena, New York. 6-1, 195.

Eric Lavigne — Defenseman

			Regular Season					Playoffs				
Season	Team	League	GP	G	A	PTS	PIM	GP	G	A	PTS	PIM
93-94	Phoenix	IHL	62	3	11	14	168	—	—	—	—	—
94-95	Los Angeles	NHL	2	0	0	0	0	—	—	—	—	—
94-95	Phoenix	IHL	69	4	10	14	233	—	—	—	—	—
94-95	Detroit	IHL	1	0	0	0	2	5	0	0	0	26
95-96	Prince Edward Island	AHL	72	5	13	18	154	2	0	0	0	6
96-97	Rochester	AHL	46	1	6	7	89	6	0	1	1	21
	IHL	Totals	132	7	21	28	403	5	0	0	0	26
	AHL	Totals	118	6	19	25	243	8	0	1	1	27

Born; 10/14/72, Victoriaville, Quebec. 6-3, 194. Drafted by Washington Capitals (3rd choice, 25th overall) in 1991 Entry Draft. Signed as a free agent by Los Angeles Kings (10/13/93). Signed as a free agent by Ottawa Senators (8/10/95).

Rodrigo Lavinsh — Defenseman

			Regular Season					Playoffs				
Season	Team	League	GP	G	A	PTS	PIM	GP	G	A	PTS	PIM
94-95	Raleigh	ECHL	25	2	7	9	30	—	—	—	—	—
94-95	Tallahassee	ECHL	44	3	9	12	36	11	0	3	3	8
95-96	Tallahassee	ECHL	52	10	14	24	86	2	0	1	1	0
96-97	Tallahassee	ECHL	50	11	27	38	45	1	0	0	0	2
96-97	Muskegon	CoHL	16	4	4	8	16	—	—	—	—	—
	ECHL	Totals	171	26	57	83	197	14	0	4	4	10

Born; 8/3/74, Riga, Latvia. 5-11, 185.

Danny Laviolette — Goaltender

			Regular Season						Playoffs				
Season	Team	League	GP	W	L	T	MIN	SO	GAVG	GP	W	L	MIN	SO	GAVG
96-97	San Diego	WCHL	19	12	4	0	995	0	3.44	1	0	0	15	0	0.00

Born; Last amateur club, Drummondville (QMJHL).

Peter Laviolette — Defenseman

			Regular Season					Playoffs				
Season	Team	League	GP	G	A	PTS	PIM	GP	G	A	PTS	PIM
86-87	Indianapolis	IHL	72	10	20	30	146	5	0	2	2	12
87-88	Colorado	IHL	19	2	5	7	27	9	3	5	8	7
87-88	United States	National										
88-89	Rangers	NHL	12	0	0	0	6	—	—	—	—	—
88-89	Denver	IHL	57	6	19	25	120	3	0	0	0	4
89-90	Flint	IHL	62	6	18	24	82	4	0	0	0	4
90-91	Binghamton	AHL	65	12	24	36	72	10	2	7	9	30
91-92	Binghamton	AHL	50	4	10	14	50	11	2	7	9	9
92-93	Providence	AHL	74	13	42	55	64	6	0	4	4	10
93-94	San Diego	IHL	17	3	4	7	20	9	3	0	3	6
93-94	United States	National										
94-95	Providence	AHL	65	7	23	30	84	13	2	8	10	17
95-96	Providence	AHL	72	9	17	26	53	4	1	1	2	8
96-97	Providence	AHL	41	6	8	14	40	—	—	—	—	—
	AHL	Totals	367	51	124	175	363	44	7	27	34	74
	IHL	Totals	227	27	66	93	395	30	6	7	13	33

Born; 12/7/64, Franklin, Massachusetts. 6-2, 200. Signed as a free agent by New York Rangers (6/87). Signed as a free agent by Boston Bruins (9/8/92). Named as head coach of the Wheeling Nailers (ECHL), 7/97.

Paul Lawless — Left Wing

			Regular Season					Playoffs				
Season	Team	League	GP	G	A	PTS	PIM	GP	G	A	PTS	PIM
82-83	Hartford	NHL	47	6	9	15	4	—	—	—	—	—
83-84	Hartford	NHL	6	0	3	3	0	—	—	—	—	—
84-85	Binghamton	AHL	8	1	1	2	0	—	—	—	—	—
84-85	Salt Lake City	IHL	72	49	48	97	14	7	5	3	8	20
85-86	Hartford	NHL	64	17	21	38	20	1	0	0	0	0
86-87	Hartford	NHL	60	22	32	54	14	2	0	2	2	2
87-88	Hartford	NHL	27	4	5	9	16	—	—	—	—	—
87-88	Philadelphia	NHL	8	0	5	5	0	—	—	—	—	—
87-88	Vancouver	NHL	13	0	1	1	0	—	—	—	—	—
88-89	Toronto	NHL	7	0	0	0	0	—	—	—	—	—
88-89	Milwaukee	IHL	53	30	35	65	58	—	—	—	—	—
89-90	Toronto	NHL	6	0	1	1	0	—	—	—	—	—
89-90	Newmarket	AHL	3	1	0	1	0	—	—	—	—	—
90-91												
91-92												
92-93	New Haven	AHL	20	10	12	22	63	—	—	—	—	—
92-93	Cincinnati	IHL	29	29	25	54	64	—	—	—	—	—
93-94	Cincinnati	IHL	71	30	27	57	112	11	4	4	8	4
94-95	Cincinnati	IHL	64	44	52	96	119	10	9	9	18	8
95-96	Cincinnati	IHL	77	27	58	85	99	17	4	6	10	16
96-97	Cincinnati	IHL	14	2	10	12	14	—	—	—	—	—
96-97	Austin	WPHL	30	11	35	46	54	6	2	4	6	26
	NHL	Totals	238	49	77	126	54	3	0	2	2	2
	IHL	Totals	380	211	255	466	480	45	22	22	44	48
	AHL	Totals	31	12	13	25	63	—	—	—	—	—

Born; 7/2/64, Scarborough, Ontario. 5-11, 185. Drafted by Hartford Whalers (1st choice, 14th overall) in 1982 Entry Draft. Traded to Philadelphia Flyers by Hartford for Lindsay Carson (1/88). Traded to Vancouver Canucks by Philadelphia with Vancouver's fifth round choice (acquired 3/7/89) by Edmonton, who selected Peter White) in 1989 Entry Draft, acquired earlier by Philadelphia for Willie Huber (3/1/88). Traded to Toronto Maple Leafs by Vancouver for the rights to Peter Deboer (2/27/89).

Doug Lawrence — Left Wing

			Regular Season					Playoffs				
Season	Team	League	GP	G	A	PTS	PIM	GP	G	A	PTS	PIM
89-90	Fort Wayne	IHL	3	0	0	0	0	—	—	—	—	—
89-90	Greensboro	ECHL	53	16	42	58	94	11	2	7	9	67
90-91	Greensboro	ECHL	47	17	44	61	89	—	—	—	—	—
90-91	Erie	ECHL	7	1	7	8	27	4	0	1	1	61
91-92	Erie	ECHL	60	19	74	93	120	4	1	1	2	35
92-93	Memphis	CeHL	19	8	*26	34	47	—	—	—	—	—
92-93	Tulsa	CeHL	38	14	*47	61	114	12	3	*15	18	43
93-94	Tulsa	CeHL	63	25	*93	118	199	11	3	11	14	52
94-95	Nashville	ECHL	33	7	37	44	129	—	—	—	—	—
94-95	Tulsa	CeHL	19	8	15	23	87	7	0	3	3	33
95-96	Oklahoma City	CeHL	54	6	53	59	346	10	2	5	7	61
96-97	Tulsa	CeHL	66	27	*100	127	250	3	1	1	2	43
	CeHL	Totals	259	88	334	422	1043	43	9	35	44	232
	ECHL	Totals	200	60	204	264	459	19	3	9	12	163

Born; 4/11/68, Richmond, British Columbia. 5-10, 180. 1992-93 CeHL Second Team All-Star. 1993-94 CeHL First Team All-Star. 1996-97 CeHL First Team All-Star. Member of 1989-90 ECHL champion Greensboro Monarchs. Member of 1992-93 CeHL champion Tulsa Oilers. Member of 1995-96 CeHL champion Oklahoma City Blazers.

Mark Lawrence — Right Wing

			Regular Season					Playoffs				
Season	Team	League	GP	G	A	PTS	PIM	GP	G	A	PTS	PIM
92-93	Dayton	ECHL	20	8	14	22	46	—	—	—	—	—
92-93	Kalamazoo	IHL	57	22	13	35	47	—	—	—	—	—
93-94	Kalamazoo	IHL	64	17	20	37	90	—	—	—	—	—
94-95	Dallas	NHL	2	0	0	0	0	—	—	—	—	—
94-95	Kalamazoo	IHL	77	21	29	50	92	16	3	7	10	28
95-96	Dallas	NHL	13	0	1	1	17	—	—	—	—	—
95-96	Michigan	IHL	55	15	14	29	92	10	3	4	7	30
96-97	Michigan	IHL	68	15	21	36	141	4	0	0	0	18
	NHL	Totals	15	0	1	1	17	—	—	—	—	—
	IHL	Totals	321	90	97	187	462	30	6	11	17	76

Born; 1/27/72, Burlington, Ontario. 6-3, 210. Drafted by Minnesota North Stars (6th choice, 118th overall) in 1991 Entry Draft.

Brad Layzell — Defenseman

			Regular Season					Playoffs				
Season	Team	League	GP	G	A	PTS	PIM	GP	G	A	PTS	PIM
94-95	Fredericton	AHL	24	1	2	3	8	—	—	—	—	—
94-95	Wheeling	ECHL	31	2	16	18	29	3	0	1	1	4
95-96	Portland	AHL	3	0	2	2	0	13	2	1	3	6
96-97	San Antonio	IHL	1	0	0	0	0	—	—	—	—	—
96-97	Detroit	IHL	11	1	2	3	2	—	—	—	—	—
96-97	Fort Wayne	IHL	15	0	2	2	17	—	—	—	—	—
96-97	Milwaukee	IHL	20	1	2	3	12	3	1	1	2	4
	IHL	Totals	47	2	6	8	31	3	1	1	2	4
	AHL	Totals	27	1	4	5	8	13	2	1	3	10

Born; 3/15/72, Beaconsfield, Quebec. 6-3, 200. Drafted by Montreal Canadiens (7th choice, 100th overall) in 1991 Entry Draft.

Carl LeBlanc — Defenseman

			Regular Season					Playoffs				
Season	Team	League	GP	G	A	PTS	PIM	GP	G	A	PTS	PIM
92-93	Knoxville	ECHL	59	6	16	22	110	—	—	—	—	—
93-94	Knoxville	ECHL	68	15	42	57	157	3	0	1	1	12
94-95	Houston	IHL	2	0	0	0	5	—	—	—	—	—
94-95	Knoxville	ECHL	62	6	47	53	192	4	0	2	2	19
95-96	Knoxville	ECHL	61	3	31	34	86	8	0	3	3	32
96-97	Quad City	CoHL	72	2	38	40	101	15	0	8	8	14
	ECHL	Totals	250	30	136	166	545	15	0	6	6	63

Born; 9/6/71, Drummondville, Quebec. 6-0, 205. Drafted by Washington Capitals (11th choice, 212nd overall) in 1991 Entry Draft. Member of 1996-97 CoHL Champion Quad City Mallards.

John LeBlanc — Left Wing

			Regular Season					Playoffs				
Season	Team	League	GP	G	A	PTS	PIM	GP	G	A	PTS	PIM
86-87	Vancouver	NHL	2	1	0	1	0	—	—	—	—	—
86-87	Fredericton	AHL	75	40	30	70	27	—	—	—	—	—
87-88	Vancouver	NHL	41	12	10	22	18	—	—	—	—	—
87-88	Fredericton	AHL	35	26	25	51	54	15	6	7	13	34
88-89	Edmonton	NHL	2	1	0	1	0	1	0	0	0	0
88-89	Milwaukee	IHL	61	39	31	70	42	—	—	—	—	—
88-89	Cape Breton	AHL	3	4	0	4	0	—	—	—	—	—
89-90	Cape Breton	AHL	77	*54	34	88	50	6	4	0	4	4
91-92	Winnipeg	NHL	16	6	1	7	6	—	—	—	—	—
91-92	Moncton	AHL	56	31	22	53	24	10	3	2	5	8
92-93	Winnipeg	NHL	3	0	0	0	2	—	—	—	—	—
92-93	Moncton	AHL	77	48	40	88	29	5	2	1	3	6

93-94	Winnipeg	NHL	17	6	2	8	2	—	—	—	—	—
93-94	Moncton	AHL	41	25	26	51	38	20	3	6	9	6
94-95	Winnipeg	NHL	2	0	0	0	0	—	—	—	—	—
94-95	Springfield	AHL	65	39	34	73	32	—	—	—	—	—
95-96	Orlando	IHL	60	22	24	46	20	—	—	—	—	—
95-96	Fort Wayne	IHL	16	12	11	23	4	5	0	2	2	14
96-97	Fort Wayne	IHL	77	30	31	61	22	—	—	—	—	—
	NHL	Totals	83	26	13	39	28	1	0	0	0	0
	AHL	Totals	429	267	211	478	296	56	18	16	34	58
	IHL	Totals	214	103	97	200	88	5	0	2	2	14

Born; 1/21/64, Campbelltown, New Brunswick. 6-1, 190. Signed as a free agent by Vancouver Canucks (4/12/86). traded to Edmonton Oilers by Vancouver with Vancouver's fifth round choice (Peter White) in 1989 Entry Draft for Doug Smith and Gregory C. Adams (3/7/89). Traded to Winnipeg Jets by Edmonton with Edmonton's tenth round choice (Teemu Numminen) in 1992 Entry Draft for Winnipeg's fifth round choice (Ryan Haggerty) in 1991 Entry Draft (6/12/91).

Ray LeBlanc — Goaltender

Regular Season / Playoffs

Season	Team	League	GP	W	L	T	MIN	SO	GAVG	GP	W	L	MIN	SO	GAVG
84-85	Pinebridge	ECHL	40	-	-	-	2178	0	4.13	—	—	—	—	—	—
85-86	Carolina	ECHL	42	-	-	-	2505	3	3.19	—	—	—	—	—	—
86-87	Flint	IHL	64	33	23	1	3417	0	3.90	4	1	3	233	0	4.38
87-88	Flint	IHL	62	27	19	8	3269	1	4.39	16	10	6	925	1	3.57
88-89	Flint	IHL	15	5	9	0	852	0	4.72	—	—	—	—	—	—
88-89	Saginaw	IHL	29	19	7	2	1655	0	3.59	1	0	1	59	0	3.05
88-89	New Haven	AHL	1	0	0	0	20	0	9.00	—	—	—	—	—	—
89-90	Indianapolis	IHL	23	15	6	2	1334	2	3.19	—	—	—	—	—	—
89-90	Fort Wayne	IHL	15	3	3	3	680	0	3.88	3	0	2	139	0	4.75
90-91	Fort Wayne	IHL	21	10	8	0	1072	0	3.86	—	—	—	—	—	—
90-91	Indianapolis	IHL	3	2	0	0	145	0	2.90	1	0	0	19	0	3.20
91-92	United States	National													
91-92	Chicago	NHL	1	1	0	0	60	0	1.00	—	—	—	—	—	—
91-92	Indianapolis	IHL	25	14	9	2	1468	2	3.43	—	—	—	—	—	—
92-93	Indianapolis	IHL	56	23	22	7	3201	0	3.86	5	1	4	276	0	5.00
93-94	Indianapolis	IHL	2	0	1	0	112	0	4.25	—	—	—	—	—	—
93-94	Cincinnati	IHL	34	17	9	3	1779	1	3.51	5	0	3	159	0	3.39
94-95	Chicago	IHL	44	19	14	6	2375	1	3.26	3	0	3	177	0	4.73
95-96	Chicago	IHL	31	10	14	2	1614	0	3.61	—	—	—	—	—	—
96-97	Chicago	IHL	38	15	14	2	1911	2	3.23	—	—	—	—	—	—
	IHL	Totals	462	212	158	38	24884	9	3.73	38	12	22	1754	1	3.97
	ECHL	Totals	82	-	-	-	4683	3	3.63	—	—	—	—	—	—

Born; 10/24/64, Fitchburg, Massachusetts. 5-10, 170. Signed as a free agent by Chicago Blackhawks (7/5/89).

Peter Leboutillier — Right Wing

Regular Season / Playoffs

Season	Team	League	GP	G	A	PTS	PIM	GP	G	A	PTS	PIM
95-96	BAL	AHL	68	7	9	16	228	11	0	0	0	33
96-97	Anaheim	NHL	23	1	0	1	121	—	—	—	—	—
96-97	Baltimore	AHL	47	6	12	18	175	—	—	—	—	—
	AHL	Totals	115	13	21	34	403	11	0	0	0	33

Born; 1/11/75, Neepawa, manitoba. 6-1, 195. Drafted by New York Islanders (6th choice, 144th overall) in 1993 Entry Draft. Re-entered NHL Entry Draft, Anaheim Mighty Ducks (5th choice, 133rd overall) in 1995 Entry Draft.

Shane LeBreton — Forward

Regular Season / Playoffs

Season	Team	League	GP	G	A	PTS	PIM	GP	G	A	PTS	PIM
95-96	Winston-Salem	SHL	9	2	2	4	48	—	—	—	—	—
95-96	Jacksonville	SHL	2	0	0	0	6	—	—	—	—	—

96-97	Alaska	WCHL	21	2	2	4	57	—	—	—	—	—
	SHL	Totals	11	2	2	4	54	—	—	—	—	—

Born;

Mike Leclerc — Left Wing

			Regular Season					Playoffs				
Season	Team	League	GP	G	A	PTS	PIM	GP	G	A	PTS	PIM
96-97	Anaheim	NHL	5	1	1	2	0	1	0	0	0	0
96-97	Baltimore	AHL	71	29	27	56	134	—	—	—	—	—

Born; 11/10/76, Winnipeg, Manitoba. 6-1, 205. Drafted by Anaheim Mighty Ducks (3rd choice, 55th overall) in 1995 Entry Draft. Member of AHL 1996-97 All Rookie Team

Eric Lecompte — Left Wing

			Regular Season					Playoffs				
Season	Team	League	GP	G	A	PTS	PIM	GP	G	A	PTS	PIM
94-95	Indianapolis	IHL	3	2	0	2	2	—	—	—	—	—
95-96	Indianapolis	IHL	79	24	20	44	131	—	—	—	—	—
96-97	Indianapolis	IHL	35	2	3	5	74	—	—	—	—	—
96-97	Fort Wayne	IHL	14	1	2	3	62	—	—	—	—	—
96-97	Worcester	AHL	8	0	1	1	4	—	—	—	—	—
	IHL	Totals	131	29	25	54	269	—	—	—	—	—

Born; 4/4/75, Montreal, Quebec. 6-4, 190. Drafted by Chicago Blackhawks (1st choice, 24th overall) in 1993 Entry Draft.

Gary Leeman — Right Wing

			Regular Season					Playoffs				
Season	Team	League	GP	G	A	PTS	PIM	GP	G	A	PTS	PIM
82-83	Toronto	NHL	—	—	—	—	—	2	0	0	0	0
83-84	Toronto	NHL	52	4	8	12	31	—	—	—	—	—
84-85	Toronto	NHL	53	5	26	31	72	—	—	—	—	—
84-85	St. Catharines	AHL	7	2	2	4	11	—	—	—	—	—
85-86	Toronto	NHL	53	9	23	32	20	10	2	10	12	2
85-86	St. Catharines	AHL	25	15	13	28	6	—	—	—	—	—
86-87	Toronto	NHL	80	21	31	52	66	5	0	1	1	14
87-88	Toronto	NHL	80	30	31	61	62	2	2	0	2	2
88-89	Toronto	NHL	61	32	43	75	66	—	—	—	—	—
89-90	Toronto	NHL	80	51	44	95	63	5	3	3	6	16
90-91	Toronto	NHL	52	17	12	29	39	—	—	—	—	—
91-92	Toronto	NHL	34	7	13	20	44	—	—	—	—	—
91-92	Calgary	NHL	29	2	7	9	27	—	—	—	—	—
92-93	Calgary	NHL	30	9	5	14	10	—	—	—	—	—
92-93	Montreal	NHL	20	6	12	18	14	11	1	2	3	2
93-94	Montreal	NHL	31	4	11	15	17	1	0	0	0	0
93-94	Fredericton	AHL	23	18	8	26	16	—	—	—	—	—
94-95	Vancouver	NHL	10	2	0	2	0	—	—	—	—	—
95-96	N/A											
96-97	St. Louis	NHL	2	0	1	1	0	—	—	—	—	—
96-97	Worcester	AHL	24	9	7	16	41	—	—	—	—	—
96-97	Utah	IHL	15	6	1	7	20	4	0	3	3	4
	NHL	Totals	667	199	267	466	531	36	8	16	24	36
	AHL	Totals	79	44	30	74	74	—	—	—	—	—

Born; 2/19/64, Toronto, Ontario. 5-11, 175. Drafted by Toronto Maple Leafs (2nd choice, 24th overall) in 1982 Entry Draft. Traded to Calgary Flames by Toronto with Craig Berube, Alexander Godynyuk, Michel Petit and Jeff Reese for Doug Gilmour, Jamie Macoun, Ric Nattress, Rick Wamsley and Kent Manderville, (1/2/92). Traded to Montreal Canadiens by Calgary Flames for Brian Skrudland (1/28/93). Signed as a free agent by Vancouver Canucks (1/18/95). member of 1992-93 Stanley Cup Champion Montreal Canadiens.

Patrice Lefebvre — Right Wing

			Regular Season					Playoffs				
Season	Team	League	GP	G	A	PTS	PIM	GP	G	A	PTS	PIM
90-91	Springfield	AHL	1	0	0	0	2	—	—	—	—	—
90-91	Louisville	ECHL	26	17	26	43	32	—	—	—	—	—
90-91	Milwaukee	IHL	16	6	4	10	13	—	—	—	—	—
91-92	N/A											
92-93	N/A											
93-94	Las Vegas	IHL	76	31	67	98	71	5	3	4	7	4
94-95	Las Vegas	IHL	75	32	62	94	74	10	2	3	5	2
95-96	Las Vegas	IHL	77	36	78	114	85	15	9	11	20	12
96-97	Las Vegas	IHL	82	21	73	94	94	3	0	2	2	2
	IHL	Totals	326	126	284	410	337	33	14	20	34	20

Born; 6/28/67, Montreal, Quebec. 5-6, 160. Signed as a free agent by Las Vegas Thunder (1993) and (1996).

Manny Legace — Goaltender

			Regular Season							Playoffs					
Season	Team	League	GP	W	L	T	MIN	SO	GAVG	GP	W	L	MIN	SO	GAVG
94-95	Springfield	AHL	39	12	17	6	2169	2	3.54	—	—	—	—	—	—
95-96	Springfield	AHL	37	20	12	4	2196	*5	*2.27	4	1	3	220	0	4.91
96-97	Springfield	AHL	36	17	14	5	2119	1	3.03	12	9	3	745	*2	2.01
96-97	Richmond	ECHL	3	2	1	0	158	0	3.05	—	—	—	—	—	—
	AHL	Totals	112	49	43	15	6484	8	2.94	16	10	6	965	2	2.67

Born; 2/4/73, Toronto, Ontario. 5-9, 162. Drafted by Hartford Whalers (5th choice, 188th overall) in 1993 Entry Draft. 1995-96 AHL First Team All-Star. 1995-96 AHL Top Goaltender.

Jeramie Legault — Right Wing

			Regular Season					Playoffs				
Season	Team	League	GP	G	A	PTS	PIM	GP	G	A	PTS	PIM
96-97	Madison	CoHL	33	3	5	8	20	—	—	—	—	—
96-97	Saginaw	CoHL	27	1	3	4	26	—	—	—	—	—
	CoHL	Totals	60	4	8	12	46	—	—	—	—	—

Born; Born; 7/6/75, Ottawa, Ontario. 6-1, 202.

Alan Leggett — Defenseman

			Regular Season					Playoffs				
Season	Team	League	GP	G	A	PTS	PIM	GP	G	A	PTS	PIM
91-92	San Diego	IHL	55	2	16	18	21	2	0	1	1	2
92-93	Raleigh	ECHL	64	16	30	46	79	10	1	4	5	10
93-94	Saint John	AHL	3	0	0	0	5	—	—	—	—	—
93-94	Raleigh	ECHL	61	10	34	44	87	16	5	10	15	8
94-95	Fresno	SUN	1	0	0	0	0	—	—	—	—	—
95-96	San Diego	WCHL	48	17	39	56	72	8	1	6	7	10
96-97	Houston	IHL	2	0	0	0	0	—	—	—	—	—
96-97	San Diego	WCHL	57	18	45	63	98	8	2	6	8	29
	IHL	Totals	57	2	16	18	21	2	0	1	1	2
	ECHL	Totals	125	26	64	90	166	26	6	14	20	18
	WCHL	Totals	105	35	84	129	170	16	3	12	15	39

Born; 6/21/65, Wainwright, Alberta. 6-2, 205. 1992-93 ECHL Second Team All-Star. 1995-96 WCHL Second Team All-Star. 1996-97 WCHL Defenseman of the Year. 1996-97 WCHL First Team All-Star Team. 1996-97 WCHL Playoff MVP. Member of 1995-96 WCHL champion San Diego Gulls. Member of 1996-97 WCHL Champion San Diego Gulls.

Guy Lehoux — Defenseman

			Regular Season					Playoffs				
Season	Team	League	GP	G	A	PTS	PIM	GP	G	A	PTS	PIM
91-92	St. John's	AHL	67	1	7	8	134	—	—	—	—	—
92-93	St. John's	AHL	42	3	2	5	89	—	—	—	—	—

Season	Team	League	GP	G	A	PTS	PIM	GP	G	A	PTS	PIM
92-93	Brantford	CoHL	13	0	5	5	28	4	0	1	1	15
93-94	St. John's	AHL	71	2	8	10	217	9	1	1	2	8
94-95	St. John's	AHL	77	4	9	13	255	5	0	0	0	2
95-96	St. John's	AHL	66	1	5	6	211	4	0	0	0	2
96-97	St. John's	AHL	69	1	6	7	229	11	0	2	2	20
	AHL	Totals	392	12	37	49	1135	29	1	3	4	32

Born; 10/19/71, Diraeli, Quebec. 5-11, 185. Drafted by Toronto Maple Leafs (10th choice, 179th overall) in 1991 Entry Draft.

Dave Lemanowicz — Goaltender

			Regular Season							Playoffs				
Season	Team	League	GP	W	L	T	MIN	SO	GAVG	GP	W	L	MIN	SO	GAVG
96-97	Carolina	AHL	33	11	18	0	1796	2	3.91	—	—	—	—	—	—
96-97	Port Huron	CoHL	3	1	2	0	168	0	3.94	—	—	—	—	—	—

Born; 3/8/76, Edmonton, Alberta. 6-2, 190. Drafted by Florida Panthers (9th choice, 218th overall) in 1996 Entry Draft.

Jocelyn Lemieux — Right Wing

			Regular Season					Playoffs				
Season	Team	League	GP	G	A	PTS	PIM	GP	G	A	PTS	PIM
86-87	St. Louis	NHL	53	10	8	18	94	5	0	1	1	6
87-88	St. Louis	NHL	23	1	0	1	42	5	0	0	0	15
87-88	Peoria	IHL	8	0	5	5	35	—	—	—	—	—
88-89	Montreal	NHL	1	0	1	1	0	—	—	—	—	—
88-89	Sherbrooke	AHL	73	25	28	53	134	4	3	1	4	6
89-90	Montreal	NHL	34	4	2	6	61	—	—	—	—	—
89-90	Chicago	NHL	39	10	11	21	47	18	1	8	9	28
90-91	Chicago	NHL	67	6	7	13	119	4	0	0	0	0
91-92	Chicago	NHL	78	6	10	16	80	18	3	1	4	33
92-93	Chicago	NHL	81	10	21	31	111	4	1	0	1	2
93-94	Chicago	NHL	66	12	8	20	63	—	—	—	—	—
93-94	Hartford	NHL	16	6	1	7	19	—	—	—	—	—
94-95	Hartford	NHL	41	6	5	11	32	—	—	—	—	—
95-96	Hartford	NHL	29	1	2	3	31	—	—	—	—	—
95-96	New Jersey	NHL	18	0	1	1	4	—	—	—	—	—
95-96	Calgary	NHL	20	4	4	8	10	4	0	0	0	0
96-97	Long Beach	IHL	28	4	10	14	54	—	—	—	—	—
96-97	Phoenix	NHL	2	1	0	1	0	2	0	0	0	4
	NHL	Totals	568	76	81	157	713	60	5	10	15	88
	IHL	Totals	36	4	15	19	89	—	—	—	—	—

Born; 11/18/67, Mont-Laurier, Quebec. 5-10, 200. Drafted by St. Louis Blues (1st choice, 10th overall) in 1986 Entry Draft. Traded to Montreal Canadiens by St. Louis with Darrell May and St. Louis' second round choice (Patrice Brisebois) in 1989 Entry Draft for Sergio Momesso and Vincent Riendeau, (8/9/88). Traded to Chicago Blackhawks by Montreal for Chicago's third round choice (Charles Poulin) in 1990 Entry Draft, (1/5/90). Traded to Hartford Whalers by Chicago with Frantisek Kucera for Gary Suter, Randy Cunneyworth and Hartford's third round choice (later traded to Vancouver—Vancouver selected Larry Courville) in 1995 Entry Draft, (3/11/94). Traded to New Jersey Devils by Hartford with Hartford's second round choice in 1998 Entry Draft for Jim Dowd and New Jersey's choice in 1997 Entry Draft (later traded to Calgary—Calgary selected Dmitri Kokorev), (12/19/95). Traded to Calgary Flames by New Jersey with Tommy Albelin and Cal Hulse for Phil Housley and Dan Keczmer, (2/26/96). Signed as a free agent by Phoenix Coyotes (1997).

Mike Lenarduzzi — Goaltender

			Regular Season							Playoffs				
Season	Team	League	GP	W	L	T	MIN	SO	GAVG	GP	W	L	MIN	SO	GAVG
91-92	Springfield	AHL	—	—	—	—	—	—	—	1	0	0	39	0	3.08
92-93	Springfield	AHL	36	10	17	5	1945	0	4.38	2	1	0	100	0	3.00
92-93	Hartford	NHL	3	1	1	1	168	0	3.21	—	—	—	—	—	—
93-94	Hartford	NHL	1	0	0	0	21	0	2.86	—	—	—	—	—	—
93-94	Springfield	AHL	22	5	7	2	984	0	4.45	—	—	—	—	—	—
93-94	Salt Lake City	IHL	4	0	4	0	211	0	6.26	—	—	—	—	—	—
94-95	London	CoHL	43	19	16	0	2198	0	4.69	5	1	3	274	0	4.37
95-96	Saginaw	CoHL	43	14	15	3	2153	0	4.32	5	1	4	299	0	3.82

Season	Team	League	GP	W	L	T	MIN	SO	GAVG	GP	W	L	MIN	SO	GAVG
96-97	Hershey	AHL	2	0	0	0	13	0	0.00	—	—	—	—	—	—
96-97	Mobile	ECHL	37	15	10	8	1932	1	3.66	1	0	1	60	0	4.00
	NHL	Totals	4	1	1	1	189	0	3.17	—	—	—	—	—	—
	AHL	Totals	60	15	24	7	2942	0	4.39	3	1	0	139	0	3.02
	CoHL	Totals	86	33	31	3	4351	0	4.51	10	2	7	573	0	4.08

Born; 9/14/72, London, Ontario. 6-1, 165. Drafted by Hartford Whalers (3rd choice, 57th overall) in 1990 Entry Draft.

Taras Lendzyk — Goaltender

			Regular Season							Playoffs					
Season	Team	League	GP	W	L	T	MIN	SO	GAVG	GP	W	L	MIN	SO	GAVG
96-97	South Carolina	ECHL	47	28	10	7	2590	0	3.20	1	0	0	20	0	0.00

Born; 3/7/72, Wynyard, Saskatchewan. 5-9, 180. Member of 1996-97 ECHL Champion South Carolina Stingrays.

Dmitri Leonov — Left Wing

			Regular Season					Playoffs				
Season	Team	League	GP	G	A	PTS	PIM	GP	G	A	PTS	PIM
96-97	Worcester	AHL	9	0	1	1	6	—	—	—	—	—
96-97	Baton Rouge	ECHL	55	14	24	38	66	—	—	—	—	—

Born; 2/5/75, Chelyabinsk, Russia. 5-10, 185. Last amateur club; Spokane (WHL).

Martin LePage — Defenseman

			Regular Season					Playoffs				
Season	Team	League	GP	G	A	PTS	PIM	GP	G	A	PTS	PIM
94-95	Nashville	ECHL	10	0	2	2	2	—	—	—	—	—
95-96	Wheeling	ECHL	65	5	17	22	235	7	2	1	3	11
96-97	Wheeling	ECHL	63	7	38	45	175	3	0	2	2	16
	ECHL	Totals	138	12	57	69	412	10	2	3	5	27

Born; 2/26/74, McMasterville, Quebec. 6-2, 205. Drafted by Quebec Nordiques (8th choice, 148th overall) in 1992 Entry Draft.

Paul Lepler — Defenseman

			Regular Season					Playoffs				
Season	Team	League	GP	G	A	PTS	PIM	GP	G	A	PTS	PIM
96-97	Louisville	ECHL	15	1	3	4	13	—	—	—	—	—
96-97	Richmond	ECHL	47	3	9	12	48	—	—	—	—	—
	ECHL	Totals	62	4	12	16	61	—	—	—	—	—

Born; 11/26/72, Granite Falls, Minnesota. 6-3, 190. Drafted by Montreal Canadiens (14th choice, 237th overall) in 1991 Entry Draft.

Francois Leroux — Left Wing

			Regular Season					Playoffs				
Season	Team	League	GP	G	A	PTS	PIM	GP	G	A	PTS	PIM
94-95	Greensboro	ECHL	36	16	16	32	79	17	8	9	17	78
94-95	Cornwall	AHL	18	5	0	5	23	—	—	—	—	—
95-96	Saginaw	CoHL	15	3	8	11	21	—	—	—	—	—
95-96	Jacksonville	ECHL	21	6	14	20	57	—	—	—	—	—
96-97	Jacksonville	ECHL	41	5	14	19	60	—	—	—	—	—
96-97	Charlotte	ECHL	17	6	7	13	14	3	1	1	2	2
	ECHL	Totals	115	33	51	84	210	20	9	10	19	80

Born; 3/1/73, La Praire, Quebec. 5-11, 190.

Jean-Yves Leroux — Left Wing

			Regular Season					Playoffs				
Season	Team	League	GP	G	A	PTS	PIM	GP	G	A	PTS	PIM
96-97	Chicago	NHL	1	0	1	1	5	—	—	—	—	—
96-97	Indianapolis	IHL	69	14	17	31	112	4	1	0	1	2

Born; 6/24/76, Montreal, Quebec. 6-2, 193. Drafted by Chicago Blackhawks (2nd choice, 40th overall) in 1994 Entry Draft.

Kelly Leroux — Defenseman

			Regular Season					Playoffs				
Season	Team	League	GP	G	A	PTS	PIM	GP	G	A	PTS	PIM
96-97	Johnstown	ECHL	27	0	1	1	57	—	—	—	—	—

Born; 3/2/72, Abbotsford, Saskatchewan. 6-2, 215.

Lance Leslie — Goaltender

			Regular Season							Playoffs					
Season	Team	League	GP	W	L	T	MIN	SO	GAVG	GP	W	L	MIN	SO	GAVG
94-95	Prince Edward Island	AHL	1	0	0	1	65	0	1.85	—	—	—	—	—	—
94-95	Thunder Bay	CoHL	42	*29	10	3	2420	*2	3.22	10	*7	2	587	*1	3.58
95-96	Prince Edward Island	AHL	28	12	12	3	1444	1	3.86	—	—	—	—	—	—
95-96	Thunder Bay	CoHL	11	5	3	2	588	0	3.57	—	—	—	—	—	—
95-96	Toledo	ECHL	4	3	0	0	212	0	2.83	—	—	—	—	—	—
96-97	Louisville	ECHL	22	10	8	3	1249	0	3.75	—	—	—	—	—	—
96-97	Kentucky	AHL	14	3	8	2	731	0	4.02	—	—	—	—	—	—
	AHL	Totals	43	15	20	6	2240	1	3.86	—	—	—	—	—	—
	CoHL	Totals	53	34	13	5	3008	2	3.29	10	7	2	587	1	3.58
	ECHL	Totals	26	13	8	3	1461	0	3.61	—	—	—	—	—	—

Born; 6/21/74, Dawson Creek, British Columbia. 5-10, 190. Signed as a free agent by Ottawa Senators (10/4/93). 1994-95 CoHL First All-Star Team. 1994-95 CoHL Rookie of the Year. Member of 1994-95 CoHL champion Thunder Bay Senators.

Lee J. Leslie — Left Wing

			Regular Season					Playoffs				
Season	Team	League	GP	G	A	PTS	PIM	GP	G	A	PTS	PIM
92-93	Peoria	IHL	72	22	24	46	46	4	0	3	3	2
93-94	Kansas City	IHL	43	8	7	15	21	—	—	—	—	—
94-95	Canadian	National										
94-95	Kansa City	IHL	10	2	5	7	4	—	—	—	—	—
95-96	Peoria	IHL	72	23	27	50	30	7	0	0	0	0
96-97	Raleigh	ECHL	25	10	14	24	16	—	—	—	—	—
	IHL	Totals	197	55	63	118	101	11	0	3	3	2

Born; 8/14/72, Prince George, British Columbia. 6-4, 203. Drafted by St. Louis Blues (4th choice, 86th overall) in 1992 Entry Draft. Signed as a free agent by San Jose Sharks (6/21/93).

David Lessard — Forward

			Regular Season					Playoffs				
Season	Team	League	GP	G	A	PTS	PIM	GP	G	A	PTS	PIM
96-97	Bakersfield	WCHL	63	34	45	79	95	1	0	0	0	0

Born; 6/18/75, Tring Junction, Quebec. 6-0, 205. Last amateur club; Drummondville (QMJHL).

Jim Lessard — Defenseman

			Regular Season					Playoffs				
Season	Team	League	GP	G	A	PTS	PIM	GP	G	A	PTS	PIM
92-93	Erie	ECHL	48	6	17	23	214	—	—	—	—	—
93-94	Erie	ECHL	17	5	10	15	93	—	—	—	—	—
93-94	Dayton	ECHL	46	17	27	44	205	3	1	0	1	2
94-95	Dayton	ECHL	66	14	30	44	199	8	1	2	3	9
95-96	Fresno	WCHL	49	14	30	44	164	—	—	—	—	—
96-97	Bakersfield	WCHL	19	2	10	12	64	—	—	—	—	—
96-97	Dayton	CoHL	15	3	1	4	119	—	—	—	—	—
	ECHL	Totals	177	42	84	126	711	11	2	2	4	11
	WCHL	Totals	68	16	40	56	228	—	—	—	—	—

Born; 10/19/71, Fort St. James, British Columbia. 5-9, 170.

Owen Lessard — Left Wing

Season	Team	League	GP	G	A	PTS	PIM	GP	G	A	PTS	PIM
90-91	Indianapolis	IHL	73	8	14	22	52	1	0	0	0	0
91-92	Indianapolis	IHL	41	3	2	5	53	—	—	—	—	—
92-93	Brantford	CoHL	5	1	3	4	2	—	—	—	—	—
92-93	Dayton	ECHL	8	2	2	4	4	—	—	—	—	—
92-93	Indianapolis	IHL	1	0	0	0	2	—	—	—	—	—
95-96	Brantford	CoHL	1	0	0	0	0	—	—	—	—	—
96-97	Huntington	ECHL	61	13	31	44	19	—	—	—	—	—
	IHL	Totals	115	11	16	27	107	1	0	0	0	0
	ECHL	Totals	69	15	33	48	23	—	—	—	—	—
	CoHL	Totals	6	1	3	4	2	—	—	—	—	—

Born; 1/11/70, Sudbury, Ontario. 6-1, 196.

Don Lester — Defenseman

Season	Team	League	GP	G	A	PTS	PIM	GP	G	A	PTS	PIM
94-95	Richmond	ECHL	26	1	16	17	32	—	—	—	—	—
95-96	Alaska	WCHL	45	9	34	43	82	5	0	0	0	6
96-97	Alaska	WCHL	30	6	24	30	61	—	—	—	—	—
	WCHL	Totals	75	15	58	73	143	5	0	0	0	6

Born; 4/29/70. Forest, Ontario. 5-11, 180. Selected by Idaho Steelheads in WCHL Dispersal Draft (1997).

Alan Letang — Defenseman

Season	Team	League	GP	G	A	PTS	PIM	GP	G	A	PTS	PIM
95-96	Fredericton	AHL	71	0	26	26	40	10	0	3	3	4
96-97	Fredericton	AHL	60	2	9	11	8	—	—	—	—	—
	AHL	Totals	131	2	35	37	48	10	0	3	3	4

Born; 9/4/75, Renfrew, Ontario. 6-0, 185. Drafted by Montreal Canadiens (10th choice, 203rd overall) in 1993 Entry Draft.

Scott Levins — Left Wing

Season	Team	League	GP	G	A	PTS	PIM	GP	G	A	PTS	PIM
90-91	Moncton	AHL	74	12	26	38	133	4	0	0	0	4
91-92	Moncton	AHL	69	15	18	33	271	11	3	4	7	30
92-93	Winnipeg	NHL	9	0	1	1	18	—	—	—	—	—
92-93	Moncton	AHL	54	22	26	48	158	5	1	3	4	14
93-94	Florida	NHL	29	5	6	11	69	—	—	—	—	—
93-94	Ottawa	NHL	33	3	5	8	93	—	—	—	—	—
94-95	Ottawa	NHL	24	5	6	11	51	—	—	—	—	—
94-95	Prince Edward Island	AHL	6	0	4	4	14	—	—	—	—	—
95-96	Ottawa	NHL	27	0	2	2	80	—	—	—	—	—
95-96	Detroit	IHL	9	0	0	0	9	—	—	—	—	—
96-97	Springfield	AHL	68	24	23	47	267	11	5	4	9	37
	NHL	Totals	122	13	20	33	311	—	—	—	—	—
	AHL	Totals	271	73	97	170	843	31	8	11	19	85

Born; 1/30/70, Apokane, Washington. 6-4, 210. Drafted by Winnipeg Jets (4th choice, 75th overall) in 1990 Entry Draft. Claimed by Florida Panthers in NHL Expansion Draft (6/24/93). Traded to Ottawa Senators by Florida with Evgeny Davydov, Florida's sixth round choice (Mike Gaffney) in 1994 Entry Draft and Dallas' fourth round choice (previously acquired by Florida—Ottawa selected Kevin Bolibruck) in 1995 Entry Draft for Bob Kudelski (1/6/94). Signed as a free agent by Phoenix Coyotes (8/97).

Duane Lewis — Right Wing

Season	Team	League	GP	G	A	PTS	PIM	GP	G	A	PTS	PIM
96-97	New Mexico	WPHL	7	0	6	6	2	—	—	—	—	—

Season	Team	League	GP	G	A	PTS	PIM	GP	G	A	PTS	PIM
96-97	Amarillo	WPHL	43	13	12	25	22	—	—	—	—	—
	WPHL	Totals	50	13	18	31	24	—	—	—	—	—

Born;

Brett Lievers — Center

Season	Team	League	GP	G	A	PTS	PIM	GP	G	A	PTS	PIM
95-96	Utah	IHL	79	36	27	63	42	20	10	3	13	6
96-97	Utah	IHL	74	22	26	48	11	7	2	0	2	0
	IHL	Totals	153	58	53	111	53	27	12	3	15	6

Born; 6/18/71, Syracuse, New York. 6-1, 190. Drafted by New York Rangers (13th choice, 223rd overall) in 1990 Entry Draft. 1995-96 IHL USA-born rookie of the year. Member of 1995-96 IHL champion Utah Grizzlies.

John Lilley — Right Wing

Season	Team	League	GP	G	A	PTS	PIM	GP	G	A	PTS	PIM
93-94	Anaheim	NHL	13	1	6	7	8	—	—	—	—	—
93-94	San Diego	IHL	2	2	1	3	0	—	—	—	—	—
94-95	San Diego	IHL	45	9	15	24	71	2	0	0	0	2
94-95	Anaheim	NHL	9	2	2	4	5	—	—	—	—	—
95-96	Baltimore	AHL	12	2	4	6	7	—	—	—	—	—
95-96	Anaheim	NHL	1	0	0	0	0	—	—	—	—	—
95-96	Los Angeles	IHL	64	12	20	32	112	—	—	—	—	—
96-97	Detroit	IHL	1	0	0	0	2	—	—	—	—	—
96-97	Rochester	AHL	1	0	2	2	15	—	—	—	—	—
96-97	Providence	AHL	63	12	25	37	130	10	3	0	3	24
	NHL	Totals	23	3	8	11	13	—	—	—	—	—
	IHL	Totals	112	23	36	59	185	2	0	0	0	2
	AHL	Totals	76	14	31	45	152	10	3	0	3	24

Born; 8/3/72, Wakefield, Massachusetts. 5-9, 175. Drafted by Winnipeg Jets (8th choice, 140th overall) in 1990 Entry Draft. Signed as a free agent by Anaheim Mighty Ducks (3/9/94).

Jamie Linden — Right Wing

Season	Team	League	GP	G	A	PTS	PIM	GP	G	A	PTS	PIM
93-94	Cincinnati	IHL	47	1	5	6	55	2	0	0	0	2
93-94	Birmingham	ECHL	16	3	7	10	38	—	—	—	—	—
94-95	Florida	NHL	4	0	0	0	17	—	—	—	—	—
94-95	Cincinnati	IHL	51	3	6	9	173	—	—	—	—	—
95-96	Carolina	AHL	50	4	8	12	92	—	—	—	—	—
96-97	Carolina	AHL	3	0	0	0	5	—	—	—	—	—
96-97	Grand Rapids	IHL	48	8	8	16	138	5	1	1	2	4
	IHL	Totals	146	12	19	31	366	7	1	1	2	6
	AHL	Totals	53	4	8	12	97	—	—	—	—	—

Born; 7/19/72, Medicine Hat, Alberta. 6-3, 185. Signed as a free agent by Florida Panthers (10/4/93).

Terry Lindgren — Defenseman

Season	Team	League	GP	G	A	PTS	PIM	GP	G	A	PTS	PIM
96-97	Kentucky	AHL	35	4	3	7	58	1	0	0	0	0
96-97	Louisville	ECHL	29	1	9	10	66	—	—	—	—	—

Born; 10/11/75, Edmonton, Alberta. 6-1, 187. Last amateur club; Red Deer, WHL.

David Ling — Right Wing

Season	Team	League	GP	G	A	PTS	PIM	GP	G	A	PTS	PIM
95-96	Saint John	AHL	75	24	32	56	179	9	0	5	5	12
96-97	Montreal	NHL	2	0	0	0	0	—	—	—	—	—

Season	Team	League	GP	G	A	PTS	PIM	GP	G	A	PTS	PIM
96-97	Saint John	AHL	5	0	2	2	19	—	—	—	—	—
96-97	Fredericton	AHL	48	22	36	58	229	—	—	—	—	—
	AHL	Totals	128	46	70	116	427	9	0	5	5	12

Born; 1/9/75, Halifax, Nova Scotia. 5-9, 185. Drafted by Quebec Nordiques (9th choice, 179th overall) in 1993 Entry Draft. Traded to Calgary Flames by Quebec with Quebec's 9th round choice (Steve Shirreffs) in 1995 Entry Draft for Calgary's 9th round choice (Chris George) in 1995 Entry Draft. Traded to Montreal Canadiens by Calgary with Calgary's 6th choice in 1998 Entry Draft for Scott Fraser (10/24/96).

Jamie Ling — Center

			Regular Season					Playoffs				
Season	Team	League	GP	G	A	PTS	PIM	GP	G	A	PTS	PIM
96-97	Hershey	AHL	2	0	2	2	2	—	—	—	—	—
96-97	Milwaukee	IHL	3	0	0	0	0	—	—	—	—	—
96-97	Mobile	ECHL	66	19	61	80	51	3	0	0	0	2

Born; 2/22/73, Charlottetown, Prince Edward Island. 5-11, 190. Last amateur club; Notre Dame (CCHA).

Steve Lingren — Defenseman

			Regular Season					Playoffs				
Season	Team	League	GP	G	A	PTS	PIM	GP	G	A	PTS	PIM
93-94	Kalamazoo	IHL	2	0	0	0	0	—	—	—	—	—
94-95	Kalamazoo	IHL	4	0	0	0	0	—	—	—	—	—
94-95	Dayton	ECHL	64	11	23	34	128	9	2	8	10	16
95-96	Michigan	IHL	2	0	0	0	2	—	—	—	—	—
95-96	Cornwall	AHL	1	0	0	0	0	—	—	—	—	—
95-96	Dayton	ECHL	51	15	28	43	83	—	—	—	—	—
96-97	Hershey	AHL	40	3	10	13	67	12	1	2	3	8
96-97	Dayton	ECHL	9	2	5	7	15	—	—	—	—	—
	AHL	Totals	41	3	10	13	67	12	1	2	3	8
	IHL	Totals	8	0	0	0	2	—	—	—	—	—
	ECHL	Totals	124	28	56	84	226	9	2	8	10	16

Born; 4/15/73, Lake Cowichan, British Columbia. 6-0, 185. 1995-96 ECHL First Team All-Star. Member of 1996-97 AHL Champion Hershey Bears.

Chris Lipsett — Forward

			Regular Season					Playoffs				
Season	Team	League	GP	G	A	PTS	PIM	GP	G	A	PTS	PIM
96-97	Roanoke	ECHL	70	19	27	46	40	3	1	2	3	0

Born; 9/24/74, Ottawa, Ontario. 6-0, 187. Last amateur club; Clarkson (ECAC).

Pete Liptrott — Defenseman

			Regular Season					Playoffs				
Season	Team	League	GP	G	A	PTS	PIM	GP	G	A	PTS	PIM
91-92	Richmond	ECHL	10	0	2	2	59	—	—	—	—	—
94-95	Brantford	CoHL	64	3	12	15	90	—	—	—	—	—
95-96	Louisville	ECHL	67	3	11	14	91	3	0	1	1	10
96-97	Louisville	ECHL	23	0	3	3	35	—	—	—	—	—
	ECHL	Totals	100	3	16	19	185	3	0	1	1	10

Born; 7/17/69, St. Catharines, Ontario. 6-1, 195.

Chris LiPuma — Defenseman

			Regular Season					Playoffs				
Season	Team	League	GP	G	A	PTS	PIM	GP	G	A	PTS	PIM
92-93	Tampa Bay	NHL	15	0	5	5	34	—	—	—	—	—
92-93	Atlanta	IHL	66	4	14	18	379	9	1	1	2	35
93-94	Tampa Bay	NHL	27	0	4	4	77	—	—	—	—	—
93-94	Atlanta	IHL	42	2	10	12	254	11	1	1	2	28
94-95	Tampa Bay	NHL	1	0	0	0	0	—	—	—	—	—
94-95	Atlanta	IHL	41	5	12	17	191	—	—	—	—	—
94-95	Nashville	ECHL	1	0	0	0	0	—	—	—	—	—

Season	Team	League	GP	W	L	T	MIN	SO	GAVG	GP	W	L	MIN	SO	GAVG
95-96	Tampa Bay	NHL	21	0	0	0	13	—	—	—	—	—	—	—	—
95-96	Atlanta	IHL	48	5	11	16	146	—	—	—	—	—	—	—	—
96-97	San Jose	NHL	8	0	0	0	22	—	—	—	—	—	—	—	—
96-97	Kentucky	AHL	48	6	17	23	93	4	0	3	3	6			
	NHL	Totals	72	0	9	9	146	—	—	—	—	—	—	—	—
	IHL	Totals	197	16	47	63	970	20	2	2	4	63			

Born; 3/23/71, Bridgeview, Illinois. 6-1, 210. Signed as a free agent by Tampa Bay Lightning (29/92). Member of 1993-94 IHL champion Atlanta Knights. Signed as a free agent by San Jose Sharks (8/26/96).

Neil Little — Goaltender

			Regular Season							Playoffs					
Season	Team	League	GP	W	L	T	MIN	SO	GAVG	GP	W	L	MIN	SO	GAVG
93-94	Hershey	AHL	1	0	0	0	18	0	3.23	—	—	—	—	—	—
94-95	Hershey	AHL	19	5	7	3	919	0	3.91	—	—	—	—	—	—
94-95	Johnstown	ECHL	16	7	6	1	897	0	3.68	3	0	2	144	0	4.55
95-96	Hershey	AHL	48	21	18	6	2679	0	3.34	1	0	1	59	0	4.02
96-97	Philadelphia	AHL	54	31	12	7	3007	0	2.89	10	6	4	620	1	1.94
	AHL	Totals	122	57	37	16	6623	0	3.22	11	6	5	679	1	2.12

Born; 12/18/71, Medicine Hat, Alberta. 6-1, 175. Drafted by Philadelphia Flyers (11th choice, 226th overall) in 1991 Entry Draft.

David Littman — Goaltender

			Regular Season							Playoffs					
Season	Team	League	GP	W	L	T	MIN	SO	GAVG	GP	W	L	MIN	SO	GAVG
89-90	Rochester	AHL	14	5	6	1	681	0	3.26	—	—	—	—	—	—
89-90	Phoenix	IHL	18	8	7	2	1047	0	3.67	—	—	—	—	—	—
90-91	Buffalo	NHL	1	0	0	0	36	0	5.00	—	—	—	—	—	—
90-91	Rochester	AHL	*56	*33	13	5	*3155	3	3.04	8	4	2	378	0	2.54
91-92	Buffalo	NHL	1	0	1	0	60	0	4.00	—	—	—	—	—	—
91-92	Rochester	AHL	*61	*29	20	9	*3558	*3	2.93	15	8	7	879	*1	2.94
92-93	Tampa Bay	NHL	1	0	1	0	45	0	9.33	—	—	—	—	—	—
92-93	Atlanta	IHL	44	23	12	4	2390	0	3.36	3	1	2	178	0	2.70
93-94	Fredericton	AHL	16	8	7	0	872	0	4.33	—	—	—	—	—	—
93-94	Providence	AHL	25	10	11	3	1385	0	3.60	—	—	—	—	—	—
94-95	Richmond	ECHL	8	4	2	0	346	1	2.25	*17	*12	4	*952	*3	*2.33
95-96	Los Angeles	IHL	43	17	16	5	2244	1	3.88	—	—	—	—	—	—
96-97	San Antonio	IHL	45	20	16	5	2438	2	3.23	4	1	3	230	0	2.87
	NHL	Totals	3	0	2	0	141	0	5.96	—	—	—	—	—	—
	AHL	Totals	172	85	57	18	9651	6	3.21	23	12	9	1257	1	2.82
	IHL	Totals	150	68	51	16	8119	3	3.55	7	2	5	408	0	2.79

Born; 6/13/67, Cranston, Rhode Island. 6-0, 175. Drafted by Buffalo Sabres (12th choice, 211th overall) in 1987 Entry Draft. Signed as a free agent by Tampa Bay Lightning (8/27/92). Signed as a free agent by Boston Bruins (8/6/93). 1990-91 Shared Harry "Hap" Holmes (fewest goals against-AHL) with Darcy Wakaluk. 1990-91 AHL First Team All-Star. 1991-92 AHL Second Team All-Star. Member of 1994-95 ECHL champion Richmond Renegades.

Lonnie Loach — Left Wing

			Regular Season					Playoffs				
Season	Team	League	GP	G	A	PTS	PIM	GP	G	A	PTS	PIM
88-89	Flint	IHL	41	22	26	48	30	—	—	—	—	—
88-89	Saginaw	IHL	32	7	6	13	27	—	—	—	—	—
89-90	Indianapolis	IHL	3	0	0	0	0	—	—	—	—	—
89-90	Fort Wayne	IHL	54	15	33	48	40	5	4	2	6	15
89-90	Canadian	National										
90-91	Ft. Wayne	IHL	81	55	76	*131	45	19	5	11	16	13
91-92	Adirondack	AHL	67	37	49	86	69	19	*13	4	17	10
92-93	Ottawa	NHL	3	0	0	0	0	—	—	—	—	—
92-93	Los Angeles	NHL	50	10	13	23	27	1	0	0	0	0
92-93	Phoenix	IHL	4	2	3	5	10	—	—	—	—	—
93-94	Anaheim	NHL	3	0	0	0	2	—	—	—	—	—

Season	Team	League	GP	G	A	PTS	PIM	GP	G	A	PTS	PIM
93-94	San Diego	IHL	74	42	49	91	65	9	4	10	14	6
94-95	San Diego	IHL	13	3	10	13	21	—	—	—	—	—
94-95	Detroit	IHL	64	32	43	75	45	3	2	1	3	2
95-96	Detroit	IHL	79	35	51	86	75	11	1	5	6	8
96-97	San Antonio	IHL	70	24	37	61	45	9	1	3	4	10
	NHL	Totals	56	10	13	23	29	1	0	0	0	0
	IHL	Totals	515	237	334	571	403	56	17	32	49	54

Born; 4/14/68, New Likseard, Ontario. 5-10, 185. Drafted by Chicago Blackhawks (4th choice, 98th overall) in 1986 Entry Draft. Signed as a free agent by Detroit Red Wings (6/7/91). Claimed by Ottawa Senators from Detroit in Expansion Draft (6/18/92). Claimed on waivers by Los Angeles Kings from Ottawa (10/21/92). Claimed by Anaheim Mighty Ducks from Los Angeles in Expansion Draft (6/24/93). 1990-91 IHL Second Team All-Star. Member of 1991-92 AHL champion Adirondack Red Wings.

Mike Loach — Right Wing

			Regular Season					Playoffs				
Season	Team	League	GP	G	A	PTS	PIM	GP	G	A	PTS	PIM
96-97	Toledo	ECHL	3	0	1	1	0	4	0	0	0	6

Born; 9/6/76, New Likseard, Ontario. 6-1, 200. Drafted by New York Islanders (8th choice, 194th overall) in 1994 Entry Draft.

Mike Lobinowich — Defenseman

			Regular Season					Playoffs				
Season	Team	League	GP	G	A	PTS	PIM	GP	G	A	PTS	PIM
96-97	Brantford	CoHL	47	2	12	14	59	—	—	—	—	—
96-97	Saginaw	CoHL	28	3	6	9	21	—	—	—	—	—
	CoHL	Totals	75	5	18	23	80	—	—	—	—	—

Born; 4/28/71, Brampton, Ontario. 6-0, 190.

Jeff Loder — Center

			Regular Season					Playoffs				
Season	Team	League	GP	G	A	PTS	PIM	GP	G	A	PTS	PIM
96-97	Manitoba	IHL	7	0	2	2	4	—	—	—	—	—
96-97	Roanoke	ECHL	54	23	22	45	53	4	2	4	6	0

Born; 1/6/76, Cornerbrook, Newfoundland. 5-10, 195. Last amateur club; Beauport (QMJHL).

Matt Loen — Center

			Regular Season					Playoffs				
Season	Team	League	GP	G	A	PTS	PIM	GP	G	A	PTS	PIM
95-96	Madison	CoHL	68	36	39	75	26	6	4	3	7	2
96-97	Madison	CoHL	73	47	56	103	16	5	2	3	5	2
	CoHL	Totals	141	83	95	178	42	11	6	6	12	4

Born; 11/9/92, Coon Rapids, Minnesota. 6-1, 190. 1995-96 CoHL Rookie of the Year

Darcy Loewen — Left Wing

			Regular Season					Playoffs				
Season	Team	League	GP	G	A	PTS	PIM	GP	G	A	PTS	PIM
89-90	Buffalo	NHL	4	0	0	0	4	—	—	—	—	—
89-90	Rochester	AHL	50	7	11	18	193	5	1	0	1	6
90-91	Buffalo	NHL	6	0	0	0	8	—	—	—	—	—
90-91	Rochester	AHL	71	13	15	28	130	15	1	5	6	14
91-92	Buffalo	NHL	2	0	0	0	2	—	—	—	—	—
91-92	Rochester	AHL	73	11	20	31	193	4	0	1	1	8
92-93	Ottawa	NHL	79	4	5	9	145	—	—	—	—	—
93-94	Ottawa	NHL	44	0	3	3	52	—	—	—	—	—
94-95	Las Vegas	IHL	64	9	21	30	183	7	1	1	2	16
95-96	Las Vegas	IHL	72	14	23	37	198	—	—	—	—	—
96-97	Las Vegas	IHL	76	14	19	33	177	3	0	0	0	0
	NHL	Totals	135	4	8	12	211	—	—	—	—	—
	IHL	Totals	212	37	63	100	558	10	1	1	2	16
	AHL	Totals	194	31	46	77	516	24	2	6	8	28

Born; 2/26/69, Calgary, Alberta. 5-10, 185. Drafted by Buffalo Sabres (2nd choice, 55th overall) in 1988 Entry Draft. Claimed by Ottawa Senators from Buffalo in Expansion Draft (6/18/92).

Shawn Lofroth — Defenseman

			Regular Season					Playoffs				
Season	Team	League	GP	G	A	PTS	PIM	GP	G	A	PTS	PIM
96-97	Alaska	WCHL	36	4	11	15	134	—	—	—	—	—

Born;

Alexei Lojkin — Right Wing

			Regular Season					Playoffs				
Season	Team	League	GP	G	A	PTS	PIM	GP	G	A	PTS	PIM
94-95	Tallahassee	ECHL	1	3	1	4	0	—	—	—	—	—
95-96	Fredericton	AHL	74	24	33	57	16	7	1	3	4	0
96-97	Fredericton	AHL	79	33	56	89	41	—	—	—	—	—
	AHL	Totals	153	57	89	146	57	7	1	3	4	0

Born; 2/21/74, Minsk, Russia. 5-9, 170.

Brian Loney — Right Wing

			Regular Season					Playoffs				
Season	Team	League	GP	G	A	PTS	PIM	GP	G	A	PTS	PIM
92-93	Hamilton	AHL	3	0	2	2	0	—	—	—	—	—
92-93	Canadian	National										
93-94	Hamilton	AHL	67	18	16	34	76	4	0	0	0	8
94-95	Syracuse	AHL	67	23	17	40	98	—	—	—	—	—
95-96	Vancouver	NHL	12	2	3	5	6	—	—	—	—	—
95-96	Syracuse	AHL	48	34	17	51	157	14	3	8	11	20
96-97	Syracuse	AHL	76	19	39	58	123	3	0	0	0	0
	AHL	Totals	251	94	91	185	454	21	3	8	11	28

Born; 8/9/72, Winnipeg, Manitoba. 6-1, 195. Drafted by Vancouver Canucks (6th choice, 110th overall) in 1992 Entry Draft.

Eric Long — Defenseman

			Regular Season					Playoffs				
Season	Team	League	GP	G	A	PTS	PIM	GP	G	A	PTS	PIM
94-95	Raleigh	ECHL	53	4	15	19	55	—	—	—	—	—
95-96	Mobile	ECHL	54	6	25	31	87	—	—	—	—	—
96-97	Mobile	ECHL	65	11	15	26	69	3	0	3	3	6
	ECHL	Totals	172	21	55	76	211	3	0	3	3	6

Born; 7/26/72, Westfield, Massachusetts. 6-0, 190.

Chris Longo — Right Wing

			Regular Season					Playoffs				
Season	Team	League	GP	G	A	PTS	PIM	GP	G	A	PTS	PIM
92-93	Baltimore	AHL	74	7	18	25	52	7	0	1	1	0
93-94	Portland	AHL	69	6	19	25	69	17	2	4	6	11
94-95	Portland	AHL	57	8	13	21	33	2	0	0	0	0
95-96	N/A											
96-97	Springfield	AHL	71	9	22	31	24	17	1	4	5	4
	AHL	Totals	271	30	72	102	178	43	3	9	12	15

Born; 1/5/72, Belleville, Ontario. 5-10, 180. Drafted by Washington Capitals (3rd choice, 51st overall) in 1990 Entry Draft.

Danny Lorenz — Goaltender

			Regular Season							Playoffs					
Season	Team	League	GP	W	L	T	MIN	SO	GAVG	GP	W	L	MIN	SO	GAVG
88-89	Springfield	AHL	4	2	1	0	210	0	3.43	—	—	—	—	—	—
90-91	Islanders	NHL	2	0	1	0	80	0	3.75	—	—	—	—	—	—
90-91	Capital District	AHL	17	5	9	2	940	0	4.47	—	—	—	—	—	—
90-91	Richmond	ECHL	20	6	9	2	1020	0	4.41	—	—	—	—	—	—
91-92	Islanders	NHL	2	0	2	0	120	0	5.00	—	—	—	—	—	—

Season	Team	League												
91-92	Capital District	AHL	53	22	22	7	3050	2	3.56	7	3	4	442	0	3.39
92-93	Islanders	NHL	4	1	2	0	157	0	3.82	—	—	—	—	—	—
92-93	Capital District	AHL	44	16	17	5	2412	1	3.63	4	0	3	219	0	3.29
93-94	Salt Lake City	IHL	20	4	12	0	982	0	5.56	—	—	—	—	—	—
93-94	Springfield	AHL	14	5	7	1	801	0	4.42	2	0	0	35	0	0.00
94-95	Cincinnati	IHL	41	24	10	2	2222	0	3.40	5	2	3	308	0	3.12
95-96	Cincinnati	IHL	46	28	12	5	2693	1	3.10	5	1	2	199	0	3.31
96-97	Milwaukee	IHL	67	33	27	6	3903	0	3.40	3	0	3	187	0	3.53
	NHL	Totals	8	1	5	0	357	0	4.20	—	—	—	—	—	—
	IHL	Totals	174	89	61	13	9800	1	3.53	13	3	8	694	0	3.28
	AHL	Totals	128	45	56	15	7413	3	4.33	13	3	7	696	0	3.19

Born; 12/12/69, Murrayville, British Columbia. 5-10, 185. Drafted by New York Islanders (4th choice, 58th overall) in 1988 Entry Draft. Signed as a free agent by Florida Panthers (6/14/94).

John Lovell — Forward

			Regular Season					Playoffs				
Season	Team	League	GP	G	A	PTS	PIM	GP	G	A	PTS	PIM
96-97	Richmond	ECHL	29	7	7	14	10	—	—	—	—	—

Born; 11/20/65, Springfield, Massachusetts. 6-1, 205.

Brad Lukowich — Defenseman

			Regular Season					Playoffs				
Season	Team	League	GP	G	A	PTS	PIM	GP	G	A	PTS	PIM
96-97	Michigan	IHL	69	2	6	8	77	4	0	1	1	2

Born; 8/12/76, Cranbrook, British Columbia. 6-1, 170. Drafted by New York Islanders (4th choice, 90th overall) in 1994 Entry Draft. Traded to Dallas Stars by Islanders for Dallas third round choice (Robert Schnabel) in 1997 Entry Draft (6/1/96).

Justin Lund — Left Wing

			Regular Season					Playoffs				
Season	Team	League	GP	G	A	PTS	PIM	GP	G	A	PTS	PIM
96-97	Toledo	ECHL	1	0	0	0	2	—	—	—	—	—
96-97	Bakersfield	WCHL	3	0	0	0	2	—	—	—	—	—
96-97	Reno	WCHL	5	0	0	0	17	—	—	—	—	—
96-97	Memphis	CeHL	2	0	0	0	2	—	—	—	—	—
96-97	Nashville	CeHL	12	1	2	3	68	—	—	—	—	—
	CeHL	Totals	14	1	2	3	70	—	—	—	—	—
	WCHL	Totals	8	0	0	0	19	—	—	—	—	—

Born; 1/29/72, Toronto, Ontario. 5-11, 190.

Kevin Lune — Forward

			Regular Season					Playoffs				
Season	Team	League	GP	G	A	PTS	PIM	GP	G	A	PTS	PIM
95-96	Wheeling	ECHL	3	0	0	0	16	—	—	—	—	—
95-96	Oklahoma City	CeHL	48	24	20	44	186	9	2	3	5	17
96-97	Peoria	ECHL	43	9	14	23	111	—	—	—	—	—
	ECHL	Totals	46	9	14	23	127	—	—	—	—	—

Born; 6/8/71, Brantford, Ontario. 6-3, 214. Member of 1995-96 CeHL champion Oklahoma City Blazers.

Chris Luongo — Defenseman

			Regular Season					Playoffs				
Season	Team	League	GP	G	A	PTS	PIM	GP	G	A	PTS	PIM
89-90	Adirondack	AHL	53	9	14	23	37	3	0	0	0	0
89-90	Phoenix	IHL	23	5	9	14	41	—	—	—	—	—
90-91	Detroit	NHL	4	0	1	1	4	—	—	—	—	—
90-91	Adirondack	AHL	76	14	25	39	71	2	0	0	0	7
91-92	Adirondack	AHL	80	6	20	26	60	19	3	5	8	10
92-93	Ottawa	NHL	76	3	9	12	68	—	—	—	—	—

Season	Team	League	GP	G	A	PTS	PIM	GP	G	A	PTS	PIM
92-93	New Haven	AHL	7	0	2	2	2	—	—	—	—	—
93-94	Islanders	NHL	17	1	3	4	13	—	—	—	—	—
93-94	Salt Lake City	IHL	51	9	31	40	54	—	—	—	—	—
94-95	Denver	IHL	41	1	14	15	26	—	—	—	—	—
94-95	Islanders	NHL	47	1	3	4	36	—	—	—	—	—
95-96	Islanders	NHL	74	3	7	10	55	—	—	—	—	—
96-97	Milwaukee	IHL	81	10	35	45	69	2	0	0	0	0
	NHL	Totals	218	8	23	31	176	—	—	—	—	—
	AHL	Totals	216	29	61	90	170	24	3	5	8	10
	IHL	Totals	196	25	89	114	190	2	0	0	0	0

Born; 3/17/67, Detroit, Michigan. Drafted by Detroit Red Wings (5th choice, 92nd overall) in 1985 Entry Draft. Signed as a free agent by Ottawa Senators (9/9/92). Traded to New York Islanders by Ottawa for Jeff Finley, (6/30/93). Member of 1991-92 AHL Champion Adirondack Red Wings.

Dan Lupo — Left Wing

			Regular Season					Playoffs				
Season	Team	League	GP	G	A	PTS	PIM	GP	G	A	PTS	PIM
96-97	Utah	IHL	3	0	0	0	0	—	—	—	—	—
96-97	Tallahassee	ECHL	63	28	36	64	60	3	2	0	2	0

Born; 11/1/72, Somerville, Massachusetts. 5-10, 190.

Jeff Lupu — Center

			Regular Season					Playoffs				
Season	Team	League	GP	G	A	PTS	PIM	GP	G	A	PTS	PIM
96-97	Dayton	CoHL	28	5	16	21	12	—	—	—	—	—

Born; 4/5/71, Rochester Hills, Michigan. 5-8, 170.

Craig Lutes — Center

			Regular Season					Playoffs				
Season	Team	League	GP	G	A	PTS	PIM	GP	G	A	PTS	PIM
94-95	Birmingham	ECHL	66	23	26	49	139	7	6	3	9	6
95-96	Birmingham	ECHL	24	9	10	19	50	—	—	—	—	—
95-96	Johnstown	ECHL	20	7	11	18	12	—	—	—	—	—
95-96	Jacksonville	ECHL	21	9	7	16	17	16	6	6	12	42
96-97	Jacksonville	ECHL	4	1	1	2	6	—	—	—	—	—
96-97	Birmingham	ECHL	63	35	29	64	36	8	4	6	10	2
	ECHL	Totals	198	84	84	168	260	31	16	15	31	50

Born; 2/18/73, Orillia, Ontario. 6-0, 195.

Dave Lylyk — Left Wing

			Regular Season					Playoffs				
Season	Team	League	GP	G	A	PTS	PIM	GP	G	A	PTS	PIM
96-97	Charlotte	ECHL	4	0	0	0	0	—	—	—	—	—
96-97	San Antonio	CeHL	63	23	21	44	29	—	—	—	—	—

Born; 12/22/75, Whitby, Ontario. 6-2, 190. Last amateur club; Regina (WHL).

Corey Lyons — Right Wing

			Regular Season					Playoffs				
Season	Team	League	GP	G	A	PTS	PIM	GP	G	A	PTS	PIM
89-90	Salt Lake City	IHL	—	—	—	—	—	1	0	0	0	0
90-91	Salt Lake City	IHL	51	15	12	27	22	3	0	2	2	0
91-92	Salt Lake City	IHL	26	3	3	6	4	—	—	—	—	—
91-92	Roanoke Valley	ECHL	22	10	13	23	13	7	4	3	7	4
92-93	Brantford	CoHL	4	0	1	1	0	—	—	—	—	—
96-97	Fresno	WCHL	64	39	41	80	52	5	6	3	9	12
	IHL	Totals	77	18	15	33	26	4	0	2	2	0

Born; 6/13/70, Calgary, Alberta. 5-11, 205. Drafted by Calgary Flames (4th choice, 63rd overall) in 1989 Entry Draft.

Craig Lyons
Right Wing

			Regular Season					Playoffs				
Season	Team	League	GP	G	A	PTS	PIM	GP	G	A	PTS	PIM
93-94	Springfield	AHL	46	7	14	21	16	2	0	0	0	0
96-97	Long Beach	IHL	1	0	0	0	0	—	—	—	—	—
96-97	Fresno	WCHL	61	51	60	111	108	5	3	2	5	6

Born; 12/25/72, Calgary, Alberta. 6-2, 195. 1996-97 WCHL First Team All-Star.

Anchorage's Dean Larson is one of the top playmakers in the WCHL.   Photo courtesy of Anchorage Aces

Brett MacDonald — Defenseman

			Regular Season					Playoffs				
Season	Team	League	GP	G	A	PTS	PIM	GP	G	A	PTS	PIM
86-87	Fredericton	AHL	49	0	9	9	29	—	—	—	—	—
87-88	Vancouver	NHL	1	0	0	0	0	—	—	—	—	—
87-88	Fredericton	AHL	15	1	5	6	23	—	—	—	—	—
87-88	Flint	IHL	49	2	21	23	43	15	2	2	4	12
88-89	Flint	IHL	57	3	24	27	53	—	—	—	—	—
88-89	New Haven	AHL	15	2	4	6	6	—	—	—	—	—
90-91	Nashville	ECHL	64	19	62	81	56	—	—	—	—	—
90-91	San Diego	IHL	3	0	1	1	0	—	—	—	—	—
90-91	Moncton	AHL	2	0	0	0	0	7	1	3	4	4
91-92	Moncton	AHL	3	0	0	0	2	—	—	—	—	—
91-92	Flint	CoHL	46	12	33	45	23	—	—	—	—	—
92-93	Flint	CoHL	60	12	39	51	60	6	0	5	5	21
93-94	Chatham	CoHL	42	8	31	39	29	14	6	9	15	4
94-95	Saginaw	CoHL	62	17	42	59	42	—	—	—	—	—
94-95	Muskegon	CoHL	11	3	8	11	14	16	2	5	7	12
95-96	Flint	CoHL	62	16	39	55	55	15	1	8	9	2
96-97	Flint	CoHL	74	8	64	72	44	14	1	11	12	12
	IHL	Totals	109	5	46	51	96	15	2	2	4	12
	AHL	Totals	84	3	18	21	60	7	1	3	4	4
	CoHL	Totals	362	76	256	332	269	72	11	41	52	55

Born; 1/5/66, Bothwell, Ontario. 6-1, 205. 1990-91 ECHL Defenseman of the Year. 1990-91 ECHL First Team All-Star. 1991-92 CoHL Second Team All-Star. 1992-93 CoHL First Team All-Star. 1995-96 CoHL First Team All-Star. 1996-97 CoHL First Team All-Star. Member of 1995-96 Colonial Cup Champion Flint Generals.

Chris MacDonald — Left Wing

			Regular Season					Playoffs				
Season	Team	League	GP	G	A	PTS	PIM	GP	G	A	PTS	PIM
94-95	Brantford	CoHL	4	0	1	1	0	—	—	—	—	—
94-95	Peoria	IHL	4	1	0	1	4	—	—	—	—	—
95-96	Detroit	CoHL	23	9	17	26	25	—	—	—	—	—
96-97	Central Texas	WPHL	13	2	2	4	14	—	—	—	—	—
96-97	Waco	WPHL	27	5	4	9	15	—	—	—	—	—
	WPHL	Totals	40	7	6	13	29	—	—	—	—	—
	CoHL	Totals	27	9	18	27	25	—	—	—	—	—

Born; 3/17/71, Charlottetown, Prince Edward Island. 6-4, 210.

Doug Macdonald — Left Wing

			Regular Season					Playoffs				
Season	Team	League	GP	G	A	PTS	PIM	GP	G	A	PTS	PIM
92-93	Buffalo	NHL	5	1	0	1	2	—	—	—	—	—
92-93	Rochester	AHL	64	25	33	58	58	7	0	2	2	4
93-94	Buffalo	NHL	4	0	0	0	0	—	—	—	—	—
93-94	Rochester	AHL	63	25	19	44	46	4	1	1	2	8
94-95	Buffalo	NHL	2	0	0	0	0	—	—	—	—	—
94-95	Rochester	AHL	58	21	25	46	73	5	0	1	1	0
95-96	Cincinnati	IHL	71	19	40	59	66	15	1	3	4	14
96-97	Cincinnati	IHL	65	20	34	54	36	3	0	0	0	0
	NHL	Totals	11	1	0	1	2	—	—	—	—	—
	AHL	Totals	185	71	77	148	177	16	1	4	5	12
	IHL	Totals	136	39	74	113	102	18	1	3	4	14

Born; 2/8/69, Assiniboia, British Columbia, 6-0, 198. Drafted by Buffalo Sabres (3rd choice, 77th overall) in 1989 Entry Draft.

Jason MacDonald — Right Wing

			Regular Season					Playoffs				
Season	Team	League	GP	G	A	PTS	PIM	GP	G	A	PTS	PIM
93-94	Adirondack	AHL	—	—	—	—	—	1	0	0	0	0
94-95	Adirondack	AHL	68	14	21	35	238	4	0	0	0	2
95-96	Adirondack	AHL	43	9	13	22	99	—	—	—	—	—
95-96	Toledo	ECHL	9	5	5	10	26	9	3	1	4	39
96-97	Adirondack	AHL	1	0	0	0	2	—	—	—	—	—
96-97	Fredericton	AHL	63	22	25	47	189	—	—	—	—	—
	AHL	Totals	175	45	59	104	530	5	0	0	0	2

Born; 4/1/74, Charlottetown, Prince Edward Island. 6-0, 195. Drafted by Detroit Red Wings (5th choice, 142nd overall) in 1992 Entry Draft. Traded to Montreal Canadiens by Detroit for cash (11/8/96).

Kevin MacDonald — Defenseman

			Regular Season					Playoffs				
Season	Team	League	GP	G	A	PTS	PIM	GP	G	A	PTS	PIM
88-89	Muskegon	IHL	64	2	13	15	190	11	2	3	5	22
89-90	New Haven	AHL	27	0	1	1	111	—	—	—	—	—
89-90	Phoenix	IHL	30	1	5	6	201	—	—	—	—	—
90-91	Phoenix	IHL	74	1	9	10	327	11	0	1	1	22
91-92	Phoenix	IHL	76	7	14	21	304	—	—	—	—	—
92-93	Phoenix	IHL	6	0	1	1	23	—	—	—	—	—
92-93	Fort Wayne	IHL	66	4	9	13	283	11	0	0	0	21
93-94	Fort Wayne	IHL	29	0	3	3	140	15	0	4	4	76
93-94	Prince Edward Island	AHL	40	2	4	6	245	—	—	—	—	—
93-94	Ottawa	NHL	1	0	0	0	2	—	—	—	—	—
94-95	Chicago	IHL	75	1	12	13	*390	3	0	0	0	17
95-96	Chicago	IHL	75	2	6	8	274	9	0	3	3	23
96-97	Fort Wayne	IHL	53	1	2	3	251	—	—	—	—	—
96-97	Hershey	AHL	16	1	1	2	74	12	1	0	1	13
	IHL	Totals	548	19	74	93	2383	60	2	11	13	181
	AHL	Totals	83	3	6	9	430	12	1	0	1	13

Born; 2/24/66, Brockville, Ontario. 6-0, 200. Signed as a free agent by Los Angeles Kings (7/90). Signed as a free agent by Ottawa Senators (12/22/93). Member of 1988-89 IHL champion Muskegon Lumberjacks. Member of 1992-93 IHL champion Fort Wayne Komets. Member of 1996-97 AHL Champion Hershey Bears.

Todd MacDonald — Goaltender

			Regular Season							Playoffs					
Season	Team	League	GP	W	L	T	MIN	SO	GAVG	GP	W	L	MIN	SO	GAVG
95-96	Detroit	CoHL	2	1	1	0	120	0	4.01	2	1	1	133	0	1.36
95-96	Carolina	AHL	18	3	12	2	979	0	4.78	—	—	—	—	—	—
96-97	Cincinnati	IHL	31	11	9	5	1617	2	2.71	1	0	0	20	0	3.00
96-97	Carolina	AHL	1	0	1	0	58	0	4.14	—	—	—	—	—	—
	AHL	Totals	19	3	13	2	1037	0	4.75	—	—	—	—	—	—

Born; 7/5/75, Charlottetown, Prince Edward Island. 6-0, 167. Drafted by Florida Panthers (7th choice, 109th overall) in 1993 Entry Draft.

Tom MacDonald — Forward

			Regular Season					Playoffs				
Season	Team	League	GP	G	A	PTS	PIM	GP	G	A	PTS	PIM
96-97	Pensacola	ECHL	19	7	7	14	125	—	—	—	—	—
96-97	Louisville	ECHL	20	3	6	9	87	—	—	—	—	—
96-97	Richmond	ECHL	10	5	0	5	51	—	—	—	—	—
	ECHL	Totals	49	15	13	28	263	—	—	—	—	—

Born; 4/14/74, Toronto, Ontario. 6-1, 205.

Greg MacEachern — Defenseman

			Regular Season					Playoffs				
Season	Team	League	GP	G	A	PTS	PIM	GP	G	A	PTS	PIM
91-92	Fredericton	AHL	20	0	5	5	12	—	—	—	—	—
92-93	Tulsa	CeHL	56	4	3	7	107	12	1	1	2	32
93-94	Tulsa	CeHL	12	0	3	3	8	—	—	—	—	—
93-94	Dallas	CeHL	5	0	1	1	4	1	0	1	1	0
94-95	Dallas	CeHL	35	3	7	10	44	—	—	—	—	—
95-96	Reno	WCHL	57	7	17	24	108	3	2	2	4	2
96-97	New Mexico	WPHL	37	3	10	13	94	6	0	0	0	8
	CeHL	Totals	108	7	14	21	163	13	1	2	3	32

Born; 11/16/71, Port Hood, Nova Scotia. 6-3, 215. Drafted by the Montreal Canadiens (13th choice, 215th overall) in 1991 Entry Draft. Member of 1992-93 CeHL champion Tulsa Oilers.

Mark Macera — Defenseman

			Regular Season					Playoffs				
Season	Team	League	GP	G	A	PTS	PIM	GP	G	A	PTS	PIM
96-97	Nashville	CeHL	4	1	0	1	23	—	—	—	—	—
96-97	Wichita	CeHL	31	4	11	15	75	—	—	—	—	—
96-97	San Antonio	CeHL	21	2	7	9	60	—	—	—	—	—
	CeHL	Totals	56	7	18	25	158	—	—	—	—	—

Born; 12/20/71, London, Ontario. 5-11, 195.

Martin Machecek — Forward

			Regular Season					Playoffs				
Season	Team	League	GP	G	A	PTS	PIM	GP	G	A	PTS	PIM
96-97	Amarillo	WPHL	31	4	6	10	13	—	—	—	—	—
96-97	Raleigh	ECHL	1	0	0	0	0	—	—	—	—	—

Born; 6/9/73, Scarborough, Ontario. 6-1, 200.

Rob MacInnis — Defenseman

			Regular Season					Playoffs				
Season	Team	League	GP	G	A	PTS	PIM	GP	G	A	PTS	PIM
85-86	Moncton	AHL	2	0	0	0	0	—	—	—	—	—
86-87	N/A											
87-88	N/A											
88-89	Cape Breton	AHL	62	8	18	26	170	—	—	—	—	—
89-90	Maine	AHL	34	3	12	15	48	—	—	—	—	—
90-91	Albany	IHL	38	9	9	18	74	—	—	—	—	—
90-91	San Diego	IHL	21	2	14	16	44	—	—	—	—	—
91-92	N/A											
92-93	Cape Breton	AHL	2	0	2	2	0	—	—	—	—	—
93-94	Richmond	ECHL	27	9	18	27	75	—	—	—	—	—
94-95	Hampton Roads	ECHL	54	11	44	55	247	4	0	3	3	12
95-96	Utica	CoHL	54	15	48	63	199	—	—	—	—	—
96-97	Hampton Roads	ECHL	3	0	1	1	4	—	—	—	—	—
96-97	Utica	CoHL	60	15	47	62	169	3	1	1	2	14
	AHL	Totals	100	11	32	43	218	—	—	—	—	—
	IHL	Totals	59	11	23	34	118	—	—	—	—	—
	CoHL	Totals	114	30	95	125	368	7	1	4	5	26
	ECHL	Totals	84	20	63	83	326	4	0	3	3	12

Born; 9/12/65, Inverness, Nova Scotia. 6-0, 210. Signed as a free agent by Cape Breton Oilers (10/88).

Andy MacIntyre — Left Wing

			Regular Season					Playoffs				
Season	Team	League	GP	G	A	PTS	PIM	GP	G	A	PTS	PIM
94-95	Indianapolis	IHL	51	9	8	17	17	—	—	—	—	—

Season	Team	League	GP	G	A	PTS	PIM	GP	G	A	PTS	PIM
94-95	Columbus	ECHL	22	7	8	15	5	—	—	—	—	—
95-96	Indianapolis	IHL	21	2	7	9	11	—	—	—	—	—
95-96	Columbus	ECHL	27	5	7	12	31	2	0	1	1	0
96-97	Indianapolis	IHL	22	2	4	6	26	—	—	—	—	—
96-97	Jacksonville	ECHL	37	13	13	26	17	—	—	—	—	—
	IHL	Totals	94	13	19	32	54	—	—	—	—	—
	ECHL	Totals	96	25	28	53	53	2	0	1	1	0

Born; 4/16/74, Thunder Bay, Ontario. 6-1, 190. Drafted by Chicago Blackhawks (4th choice, 89th overall) in 1992 Entry Draft.

Corey MacIntyre — Left Wing

Season	Team	League	GP	G	A	PTS	PIM	GP	G	A	PTS	PIM
95-96	Louisville	ECHL	4	0	0	0	4	—	—	—	—	—
96-97	Oklahoma City	CeHL	64	15	29	44	61	4	1	1	2	4

Born; 8/10/70, Shawville, Quebec. 6-1, 190.

Dave MacIntyre — Defenseman

Season	Team	League	GP	G	A	PTS	PIM	GP	G	A	PTS	PIM
91-92	Johnstown	ECHL	63	21	37	58	84	6	1	2	3	4
91-92	Moncton	AHL	6	0	1	1	0	11	2	2	4	16
92-93	Monton	AHL	50	5	17	22	37	2	0	0	0	0
92-93	Dayton	ECHL	6	2	4	6	10	—	—	—	—	—
93-94	Salt Lake City	IHL	71	9	27	36	69	—	—	—	—	—
94-95	Peoria	IHL	71	10	31	41	52	8	2	3	5	0
95-96	Peoria	IHL	74	11	35	46	60	6	0	0	0	8
96-97	San Antonio	IHL	76	17	36	53	104	8	1	4	5	2
	IHL	Totals	292	47	129	176	285	22	3	7	10	10
	AHL	Totals	56	5	18	23	37	13	2	2	4	16
	ECHL	Totals	69	23	41	64	94	6	1	2	3	4

Born; 10/28/68, New Glasgcow, Nova Scotia. 5-11, 190.

Jason MacIntyre — Defenseman

Season	Team	League	GP	G	A	PTS	PIM	GP	G	A	PTS	PIM
96-97	Hampton Roads	ECHL	15	1	1	2	49	—	—	—	—	—
96-97	Bakersfield	WCHL	41	3	18	21	270	4	0	0	0	32

Born; 7/14/72, Halifax, Nova Scotia. 5-10, 190.

Dave MacIssac — Defenseman

Season	Team	League	GP	G	A	PTS	PIM	GP	G	A	PTS	PIM
94-95	Milwaukee	IHL	2	0	0	0	5	9	0	2	2	2
95-96	Milwaukee	IHL	71	7	16	23	165	—	—	—	—	—
96-97	Philadelphia	AHL	61	3	15	18	187	10	0	1	1	31
	IHL	Totals	73	7	16	23	170	9	0	2	2	2

Born; 4/23/72, Cambridge, Massachusetts. 6-2, 225.

Todd MacIsaac — Center

Season	Team	League	GP	G	A	PTS	PIM	GP	G	A	PTS	PIM
95-96	Columbus	ECHL	38	11	13	24	95	—	—	—	—	—
95-96	Erie	ECHL	14	6	3	9	10	—	—	—	—	—
96-97	Baton Rouge	ECHL	48	8	19	27	44	—	—	—	—	—
96-97	Roanoke	ECHL	16	1	2	3	16	4	0	0	0	6
	ECHL	Totals	116	26	37	63	165	4	0	0	0	6

Born; 5/25/74, Country Harbour, Nova Scotia. 5-10, 180.

Chris MacKenzie — Center

			Regular Season					Playoffs				
Season	Team	League	GP	G	A	PTS	PIM	GP	G	A	PTS	PIM
92-93	Hampton Roads	ECHL	3	0	1	1	0	—	—	—	—	—
92-93	Louisville	ECHL	2	0	0	0	0	—	—	—	—	—
92-93	Roanoke	ECHL	22	8	14	22	4	—	—	—	—	—
93-94	Daytona Beach	SHL	25	27	11	38	12	2	1	0	1	0
93-94	Detroit	CoHL	21	6	17	23	7	3	1	3	4	0
94-95	Detroit	CoHL	50	20	38	58	24	7	2	4	6	6
95-96	N/A											
96-97	El Paso	WPHL	55	29	55	84	50	11	*9	11	*20	10
	CoHL	Totals	71	26	55	81	31	10	3	7	10	6
	ECHL	Totals	27	8	15	23	4	—	—	—	—	—

Born; 9/16/71, Toronto, Ontario. 6-1, 210. Drafted by St. Louis Blues (10th choice, 219th overall) in 1991 Entry Draft. 1996-97 WPHL Playoff MVP. Member of 1996-97 WPHL Champion El Paso Buzzards.

Darrin MacKay — Left Wing

			Regular Season					Playoffs				
Season	Team	League	GP	G	A	PTS	PIM	GP	G	A	PTS	PIM
96-97	Waco	WPHL	61	21	16	37	22	—	—	—	—	—

Born; 2/4/70, Yorktown, Saskatchewan. 5-10, 185.

Dave Mackey — Left Wing

			Regular Season					Playoffs				
Season	Team	League	GP	G	A	PTS	PIM	GP	G	A	PTS	PIM
86-87	Saginaw	IHL	81	26	49	75	173	10	3	7	10	44
87-88	Chicago	NHL	23	1	3	4	71	—	—	—	—	—
87-88	Saginaw	IHL	62	29	22	51	211	10	3	7	10	44
88-89	Chicago	NHL	23	1	2	3	78	—	—	—	—	—
88-89	Saginaw	IHL	57	22	23	45	223	—	—	—	—	—
89-90	Minnesota	NHL	16	2	0	2	28	—	—	—	—	—
90-91	Milwaukee	IHL	82	28	30	58	226	6	7	2	9	6
91-92	St. Louis	NHL	19	1	0	1	49	1	0	0	0	0
91-92	Peoria	IHL	35	20	17	37	90	—	—	—	—	—
92-93	St. Louis	NHL	15	1	4	5	23	—	—	—	—	—
92-93	Peoria	IHL	42	24	22	46	112	4	1	0	1	22
93-94	St. Louis	NHL	30	2	3	5	56	2	0	0	0	2
93-94	Peoria	IHL	49	14	21	35	132	—	—	—	—	—
94-95	Milwaukee	IHL	74	19	18	37	261	15	6	4	10	34
95-96	Milwaukee	IHL	77	15	16	31	235	4	2	1	3	10
96-97	Milwaukee	IHL	79	15	15	30	223	3	0	0	0	19
	NHL	Totals	126	8	12	20	305	3	0	0	0	2
	IHL	Totals	638	212	233	445	1886	52	22	21	43	179

Born; 7/24/66, New Westminster, British Columbia. 6-3, 205. Drafted by Chicago Blackhawks (12th choice, 224th overall) in 1984 Entry Draft. Claimed by Minnesota North Stars from Chicago in Waiver Draft (10/2/89). Traded to Vancouver Canucks by Minnesota for future considerations (9/7/90). Signed as a free agent by St. Louis Blues (8/7/91).

Pat MacLeod — Defenseman

			Regular Season					Playoffs				
Season	Team	League	GP	G	A	PTS	PIM	GP	G	A	PTS	PIM
89-90	Kalamazoo	IHL	82	9	38	47	27	10	1	6	7	2
90-91	Minnesota	NHL	1	0	1	1	0	—	—	—	—	—
90-91	Kalamazoo	IHL	59	10	30	40	16	11	1	2	3	5
91-92	San Jose	NHL	37	5	11	16	4	—	—	—	—	—
91-92	Kansas City	IHL	45	9	21	30	19	11	1	4	5	4
92-93	San Jose	NHL	13	0	1	1	10	—	—	—	—	—
92-93	Kansas City	IHL	18	8	8	16	14	10	2	4	6	7

Season	Team	League	GP	G	A	PTS	PIM	GP	G	A	PTS	PIM
93-94	Milwaukee	IHL	73	21	52	73	18	3	1	2	3	0
94-95	Milwaukee	IHL	69	11	36	47	16	15	3	6	9	8
95-96	Dallas	NHL	2	0	0	0	0	—	—	—	—	—
95-96	Michigan	IHL	50	3	23	26	18	7	0	3	3	0
96-97	Kansas City	IHL	41	5	8	13	8	3	2	0	2	0
	NHL	Totals	53	5	13	18	14	—	—	—	—	—
	IHL	Totals	437	76	216	292	136	70	11	27	38	26

Born; 6/15/69, Melfort, Saskatchewan. 5-11, 190. Drafted by Minnesota North Stars (5th choice, 87th overall) in 1989 Entry Draft. Claimed by San Jose Sharks from Minnesota in Dispersal Draft (5/30/91). 1993-94 IHL First Team All-Star. Member of 1991-92 IHL champion Kansas City Blades.

B.J. MacPherson — Left Wing

Season	Team	League	GP	G	A	PTS	PIM	GP	G	A	PTS	PIM
94-95	Worcester	AHL	2	0	0	0	8	—	—	—	—	—
94-95	Greensboro	ECHL	15	4	7	11	34	—	—	—	—	—
94-95	Toledo	ECHL	54	16	30	46	117	3	1	3	4	18
95-96	Worcester	AHL	11	1	1	2	10	—	—	—	—	—
95-96	Toledo	ECHL	64	22	45	67	251	5	1	3	4	10
96-97	Long Beach	IHL	4	0	0	0	7	—	—	—	—	—
96-97	Las Vegas	IHL	1	0	0	0	0	—	—	—	—	—
96-97	San Diego	WCHL	60	29	47	76	157	8	4	8	12	30
	AHL	Totals	13	1	1	2	18	—	—	—	—	—
	ECHL	Totals	133	42	82	124	402	8	2	6	8	28
	IHL	Totals	5	0	0	0	7	—	—	—	—	—

Born; 9/23/73, Mississauga, Ontario. 6-2, 200. Drafted by Washington Capitals (10th choice, 263rd overall) in 1992 Entry Draft. Member of 1996-97 WCHL Champion San Diego Gulls.

Don MacPherson — Defenseman

Season	Team	League	GP	G	A	PTS	PIM	GP	G	A	PTS	PIM
94-95	Daytona Beach	SUN	49	14	28	42	49	—	—	—	—	—
95-96	Daytona Beach	SHL	58	15	53	68	196	4	2	2	4	14
96-97	Huntville	CeHL	54	14	47	61	64	9	3	5	8	12
	SHL	Totals	107	29	81	110	245	4	2	2	4	14

Born; 3/29/73, Fredericton, New Brunswick. 5-11, 189.

Forbes MacPherson — Center

Season	Team	League	GP	G	A	PTS	PIM	GP	G	A	PTS	PIM
96-97	Fort Wayne	IHL	2	0	1	1	4	—	—	—	—	—
96-97	Thunder Bay	CoHL	72	42	61	103	68	11	1	12	13	13

Born; 6/5/72, Charlottetown, Prince Edward Island. 5-10, 178. 1996-97 CoHL Rookie of the Year. Mmeber of 1996-97 CoHL All-Rookie Team.

Steve MacSwain — Center

Season	Team	League	GP	G	A	PTS	PIM	GP	G	A	PTS	PIM
87-88	Salt Lake City	IHL	61	16	20	36	52	3	0	0	0	2
92-93	Flint	CoHL	7	2	5	7	2	—	—	—	—	—
95-96	Anchorage	WCHL	44	24	27	51	59	—	—	—	—	—
96-97	Anchorage	WCHL	41	13	17	30	33	—	—	—	—	—
	WCHL	Totals	85	37	44	81	92	—	—	—	—	—

Born; 8/8/65, Anchorage, Alaska. 5-8, 180. Selected in 1986 NHL Supplemental Draft by Calgary Flames. Member of 1987-88 IHL Champion Salt Lake City Golden Eagles.

Mike MacWilliam — Left Wing

			Regular Season					Playoffs				
Season	Team	League	GP	G	A	PTS	PIM	GP	G	A	PTS	PIM
88-89	Milwaukee	IHL	6	1	1	2	28	1	0	0	0	0
88-89	Flint	IHL	18	0	0	0	92	—	—	—	—	—
89-90		Did	Not	Play	Injured							
90-91	Adirondack	AHL	8	0	0	0	32	—	—	—	—	—
90-91	Greensboro	ECHL	15	2	7	9	209	9	3	1	4	*118
91-92	St. John's	AHL	44	7	8	15	301	2	0	0	0	8
91-92	Greensboro	ECHL	8	2	5	7	94	—	—	—	—	—
92-93	Greensboro	ECHL	12	5	5	10	137	—	—	—	—	—
93-94	Tulsa	CeHL	39	16	12	28	326	8	4	0	4	88
94-95	Denver	IHL	30	5	6	11	218	12	2	2	4	56
95-96	Islanders	NHL	6	0	0	0	14	—	—	—	—	—
95-96	Utah	IHL	53	8	16	24	317	6	0	2	2	53
96-97	Phoenix	IHL	29	1	3	4	169	—	—	—	—	—
	IHL	Totals	136	15	26	41	791	19	6	4	10	109
	AHL	Totals	52	7	8	15	333	2	0	0	0	8
	ECHL	Totals	35	9	17	26	440	9	3	1	4	118

Signed as a free agent by Philadelphia Flyers (10/7/86). Signed as a free agent by Toronto Maple Leafs (7/30/91). Signed as a free agent by New York Islanders (7/25/95). Signed as a free agent by Phoenix Roadrunners (1996). Member of 1994-95 IHL champion Denver Grizzlies. Member of 1995-96 IHL champion Utah Grizzlies.

Darrin Madeley — Goaltender

			Regular Season							Playoffs					
Season	Team	League	GP	W	L	T	MIN	SO	GAVG	GP	W	L	MIN	SO	GAVG
92-93	Ottawa	NHL	2	0	2	0	90	0	6.67	—	—	—	—	—	—
92-93	New Haven	AHL	41	10	16	9	2295	0	3.32	—	—	—	—	—	—
93-94	Ottawa	NHL	32	3	18	5	1583	0	4.36	—	—	—	—	—	—
93-94	Prince Edward Island	AHL	6	0	4	0	270	0	5.77	—	—	—	—	—	—
94-95	Ottawa	NHL	5	1	3	0	255	0	3.53	—	—	—	—	—	—
94-95	Prince Edward Island	AHL	3	1	1	1	185	0	2.59	—	—	—	—	—	—
94-95	Detroit	IHL	9	7	2	0	498	1	2.41	—	—	—	—	—	—
95-96	Prince Edward Island	AHL	1	1	0	0	60	0	4.00	—	—	—	—	—	—
95-96	Detroit	IHL	40	16	14	4	2047	0	3.17	7	3	3	354	0	3.89
96-97	Detroit	IHL	4	2	0	0	177	0	3.72	—	—	—	—	—	—
96-97	Saint John	AHL	46	11	18	11	2316	0	3.21	2	0	0	58	0	0.00
	NHL	Totals	39	4	23	5	1928	0	4.36	—	—	—	—	—	—
	AHL	Totals	97	23	39	21	5126	0	3.38	2	0	0	58	0	0.00
	IHL	Totals	53	25	16	4	2722	1	3.06	7	3	3	354	0	3.89

Born; 2/25/68, Holland Landing, Ontario. 5-11, 165. Signed as a free agent by Ottawa Senators (6/20/92). 1992-93 AHL Second Team All-Star. Last amateur club; Lake Superior State (CCHA).

Jeff Madill — Right Wing

			Regular Season					Playoffs				
Season	Team	League	GP	G	A	PTS	PIM	GP	G	A	PTS	PIM
87-88	Utica	AHL	58	18	15	33	127	—	—	—	—	—
88-89	Utica	AHL	69	23	25	48	225	4	1	0	1	35
89-90	Utica	AHL	74	43	26	69	233	4	1	2	3	33
90-91	New Jersey	NHL	14	4	0	4	46	7	0	2	2	8
90-91	Utica	AHL	54	42	35	77	151	—	—	—	—	—
91-92	Kansa City	IHL	62	32	20	52	167	6	2	2	4	30
92-93	Cincinnati	IHL	58	36	17	53	175	—	—	—	—	—
92-93	Milwaukee	IHL	23	13	6	19	53	4	3	0	3	9
93-94	Atlanta	IHL	80	42	44	86	186	14	4	2	6	33
94-95	Denver	IHL	73	35	30	65	207	17	8	6	14	53
95-96	San Francisco	IHL	27	16	13	29	73	—	—	—	—	—

Season	Team	League	GP	G	A	PTS	PIM	GP	G	A	PTS	PIM
95-96	Kansas City	IHL	41	17	16	33	169	5	4	2	6	21
96-97	Kansas City	IHL	59	18	18	36	142	—	—	—	—	—
96-97	Phoenix	IHL	9	5	2	7	22	—	—	—	—	—
	IHL	Totals	432	214	166	380	1194	46	21	12	33	146
	AHL	Totals	255	126	101	227	736	8	2	2	4	68

Born; 6/21/65, Oshawa, Ontario. 5-11, 212. Drafted by New Jersey Devils (2nd choice, 7th overall) in 1987 Supplemental Draft. Claimed by San Jose Sharks from New Jersey in NHL Expansion Draft (5/30/91). Signed as a free agent by New York Islanders (8/25/94). 1990-91 AHL Second Team All-Star. 1992-93 IHL Second Team All-Star. Member of 1991-92 IHL champion Kansas City Blades. Member of 1993-94 IHL champion Atlanta Knights. Member of 1994-95 IHL champion Denver Grizzlies.

Stephen Madore — Defenseman

			Regular Season					Playoffs				
Season	Team	League	GP	G	A	PTS	PIM	GP	G	A	PTS	PIM
95-96	Louisville	ECHL	59	1	7	8	179	2	1	0	1	6
96-97	Kentucky	AHL	7	0	1	1	32	—	—	—	—	—
96-97	Louisville	ECHL	56	5	14	19	200	—	—	—	—	—
	ECHL	Totals	115	6	21	27	379	2	1	0	1	6

Born; 3/13/74, Hull, Quebec. 6-2, 188.

Steve Magnusson — Left Wing

			Regular Season					Playoffs				
Season	Team	League	GP	G	A	PTS	PIM	GP	G	A	PTS	PIM
94-95	Memphis	CeHL	65	17	39	56	119	—	—	—	—	—
95-96	Memphis	CeHL	63	24	40	64	142	6	0	1	1	37
96-97	Memphis	CeHL	34	15	19	34	38	—	—	—	—	—
96-97	San Antonio	CeHL	5	0	1	1	10	—	—	—	—	—
	CeHL	Totals	167	56	99	155	309	6	0	1	1	37

Born; 11/15/72, Anoka, Minnesota. 6-0, 185. Drafted by Calgary Flames (5th choice, 85th overall) in 1991 Entry Draft.

John Mahoney — Left Wing

			Regular Season					Playoffs				
Season	Team	League	GP	G	A	PTS	PIM	GP	G	A	PTS	PIM
96-97	Dayton	ECHL	29	5	8	13	42	—	—	—	—	—
96-97	Johnstown	ECHL	15	1	6	7	39	—	—	—	—	—
	ECHL	Totals	44	6	14	20	81	—	—	—	—	—

Born; 1/31/73, Hull, Massachusetts. 5-10, 185.

Jacques Mailhot — Defenseman

			Regular Season					Playoffs				
Season	Team	League	GP	G	A	PTS	PIM	GP	G	A	PTS	PIM
87-88	Fredericton	AHL	28	2	6	8	137	8	0	0	0	18
87-88	Baltimore	AHL	15	2	0	2	167	—	—	—	—	—
88-89	Quebec	NHL	5	0	0	0	33	—	—	—	—	—
88-89	Halifax	AHL	35	4	1	5	259	1	0	0	0	5
89-90	Hampton Roads	ECHL	5	0	2	2	62	—	—	—	—	—
89-90	Phoenix	IHL	15	0	0	0	70	—	—	—	—	—
89-90	Cape Breton	AHL	6	0	1	1	12	—	—	—	—	—
89-90	Moncton	AHL	6	0	0	0	20	—	—	—	—	—
90-91	Moncton	AHL	13	0	0	0	43	—	—	—	—	—
90-91	San Diego	IHL	1	0	0	0	2	—	—	—	—	—
91-92	Flint	CoHL	29	15	12	27	237	—	—	—	—	—
91-92	Detroit	CoHL	5	2	2	4	44	4	0	1	1	27
92-93	Detroit	CoHL	48	14	21	35	273	4	2	4	6	12
93-94	Detroit	CoHL	21	1	9	10	122	3	0	1	1	49
94-95	Rochester	AHL	15	0	1	1	52	—	—	—	—	—
94-95	Utica	CoHL	59	11	17	28	302	—	—	—	—	—
95-96	Utica	CoHL	8	1	0	1	71	—	—	—	—	—
95-96	Quad City	CoHL	50	14	8	22	253	3	0	0	0	52

Season	Team	League	GP	G	A	PTS	PIM	GP	G	A	PTS	PIM
96-97	Utah	IHL	4	0	0	0	32	—	—	—	—	—
96-97	Central Texas	WPHL	34	5	8	13	247	8	0	3	3	24
	AHL	Totals	118	8	9	17	690	9	0	0	0	23
	IHL	Totals	20	0	0	0	104	—	—	—	—	—
	CoHL	Totals	220	58	69	127	1302	14	2	6	8	140

Born; 12/5/61, Shawnigan, Quebec. 6-2, 208.

Mark Major — Left Wing

			Regular Season					Playoffs				
Season	Team	League	GP	G	A	PTS	PIM	GP	G	A	PTS	PIM
90-91	Muskegon	IHL	60	8	10	18	160	5	0	0	0	0
91-92	Muskegon	IHL	80	13	18	31	302	12	1	3	4	29
92-93	Cleveland	IHL	82	13	15	28	155	3	0	0	0	0
93-94	Providence	AHL	61	17	9	26	176	—	—	—	—	—
94-95	Detroit	IHL	78	17	19	36	229	5	0	1	1	23
95-96	Adirondack	AHL	78	10	19	29	234	3	0	0	0	21
96-97	Detroit	NHL	2	0	0	0	5	—	—	—	—	—
96-97	Adirondack	AHL	78	17	18	35	213	4	0	0	0	13
	IHL	Totals	300	51	62	113	846	25	1	4	5	52
	AHL	Totals	217	44	46	90	623	7	0	0	0	34

Born; 3/20/70, Toronto, Ontario. 6-4, 216. Drafted by Pittsburgh Penguins (2nd choice, 25th overall) in 1988 Entry Draft. Signed as a free agent by Boston Bruins (7/22/93).

Kevin Malgunas — Right Wing

			Regular Season					Playoffs				
Season	Team	League	GP	G	A	PTS	PIM	GP	G	A	PTS	PIM
92-93	Richmond	ECHL	29	7	5	12	106	—	—	—	—	—
92-93	Hampton Roads	ECHL	27	14	18	32	94	4	2	1	3	4
93-94	Hampton Roads	ECHL	37	12	28	40	132	—	—	—	—	—
93-94	Raleigh	ECHL	10	6	3	9	26	14	2	4	6	41
94-95	Detroit	CoHL	39	13	21	34	127	—	—	—	—	—
94-95	Detroit	IHL	17	0	1	1	52	—	—	—	—	—
94-95	Houston	IHL	20	2	5	7	58	2	1	0	1	12
95-96	Houston	IHL	31	1	4	5	60	—	—	—	—	—
96-97	Portland	AHL	3	0	0	0	4	—	—	—	—	—
96-97	Orlando	IHL	2	0	1	1	0	—	—	—	—	—
96-97	Tallahassee	ECHL	54	17	18	35	197	3	0	0	0	11
	IHL	Totals	70	3	11	14	170	2	1	0	1	12
	ECHL	Totals	157	56	72	128	555	21	4	5	9	56

Born; 7/12/71, Prince George, British Columbia. 5-11, 190.

Stewart Malgunas — Defenseman

			Regular Season					Playoffs				
Season	Team	League	GP	G	A	PTS	PIM	GP	G	A	PTS	PIM
90-91	Adirondack	AHL	78	5	19	24	70	2	0	0	0	4
91-92	Adirondack	AHL	69	4	28	32	82	18	2	6	8	28
92-93	Adirondack	AHL	45	3	12	15	39	11	3	3	6	8
93-94	Philadelphia	NHL	67	1	3	4	86	—	—	—	—	—
94-95	Philadelphia	NHL	4	0	0	0	4	—	—	—	—	—
94-95	Hershey	AHL	32	3	5	8	28	6	2	1	3	31
95-96	Winnipeg	NHL	29	0	1	1	32	—	—	—	—	—
95-96	Washington	NHL	1	0	0	0	0	—	—	—	—	—
95-96	Portland	AHL	16	2	5	7	18	13	1	3	4	19
96-97	Washington	NHL	6	0	0	0	2	—	—	—	—	—
96-97	Portland	AHL	68	6	12	18	59	5	0	0	0	8
	NHL	Totals	107	1	4	5	124	—	—	—	—	—
	AHL	Totals	308	23	81	104	296	55	8	13	21	98

Born; 4/21/70, Prince George, British Columbia. 5-11, 190. Drafted by Detroit Red Wings (3rd choice, 66th overall) in 1990 Entry Draft. Traded to Philadelphia Flyers by Detroit for Philadelphia's fifth round choice (David Arsenault) in 1995 Draft (9/9/93). Signed as a free agent by Winnipeg Jets (8/9/95). Traded to Washington Capitals by Winnipeg for Denis Chasse (2/15/96). Member of 1991-92 AHL champion Adirondack Red Wings.

Kurt Mallett — Center

Season	Team	League	GP	G	A	PTS	PIM	GP	G	A	PTS	PIM
94-95	Richmond	ECHL	68	24	27	51	24	17	6	10	16	4
95-96	Richmond	ECHL	46	13	21	34	18	—	—	—	—	—
95-96	Jacksonville	ECHL	17	2	14	16	10	18	9	9	18	2
96-97	Jacksonville	ECHL	61	25	48	73	20	—	—	—	—	—
96-97	Phoenix	IHL	12	4	2	6	2	—	—	—	—	—
	ECHL	Totals	192	64	110	174	72	35	15	19	34	6

Born; 3/27/71, Saugus, Massachusetts. 6-0, 185. Member of 1994-95 ECHL champion Richmond Renegades.

Jason Mallon — Right Wing

Season	Team	League	GP	G	A	PTS	PIM	GP	G	A	PTS	PIM
95-96	Richmond	ECHL	66	17	22	39	52	7	5	2	7	10
96-97	Thunder Bay	CoHL	50	17	33	50	52	11	5	5	10	24

Born; 10/1/70, Thunder Bay, Ontario. 5-11, 190.

Scott Malone — Defenseman

Season	Team	League	GP	G	A	PTS	PIM	GP	G	A	PTS	PIM
94-95	Binghamton	AHL	48	3	14	17	85	11	0	2	2	12
94-95	Birmingham	ECHL	8	1	4	5	36	—	—	—	—	—
95-96	Binghamton	AHL	58	3	13	16	94	4	0	0	0	21
96-97	Charlotte	ECHL	26	2	7	9	63	—	—	—	—	—
96-97	Binghamton	AHL	11	0	1	1	21	—	—	—	—	—
96-97	Orlando	IHL	12	0	0	0	26	—	—	—	—	—
96-97	Quebec	IHL	18	0	2	2	12	9	0	0	0	8
	AHL	Totals	117	6	28	34	200	15	0	2	2	33
	IHL	Totals	30	0	2	2	38	9	0	0	0	8
	ECHL	Totals	34	3	11	14	115	—	—	—	—	—

Born; 1/16/71, South Boston, Massachusetts. 6-0, 180. Drafted by Toronto Maple Leafs (10th choice, 220th overall) in 1990 Entry Draft. Rights traded to New York Rangers by Toronto with Glenn Anderson and Toronto's fourth round choice (Alexander Korobolin) in 1994 Entry Draft for Mike Gartner (3/21/94).

Darren Maloney — Defenseman

Season	Team	League	GP	G	A	PTS	PIM	GP	G	A	PTS	PIM
96-97	Chicago	IHL	8	0	0	0	6	—	—	—	—	—
96-97	San Antonio	IHL	3	0	0	0	2	—	—	—	—	—
96-97	Peoria	ECHL	49	5	22	27	56	10	0	3	3	8
	IHL	Totals	11	0	0	0	8	—	—	—	—	—

Born; 3/10/72, Claresholm, Alberta. 6-2, 200. Last amateur club; Western Michigan (CCHA).

Dominic Maltais — Right Wing

Season	Team	League	GP	G	A	PTS	PIM	GP	G	A	PTS	PIM
93-94	Rochester	AHL	1	0	0	0	0	—	—	—	—	—
93-94	Fort Worth	CeHL	64	44	27	71	88	—	—	—	—	—
94-95	Fort Worth	CeHL	66	40	38	78	204	—	—	—	—	—
95-96	Hampton Roads	ECHL	54	31	32	63	163	—	—	—	—	—
96-97	Portland	AHL	3	0	0	0	4	—	—	—	—	—
96-97	Hampton Roads	ECHL	68	42	55	97	211	9	10	7	17	20

	AHL	Totals	4	0	0	0	4	—	—	—	—	—
	CeHL	Totals	130	84	65	149	292	—	—	—	—	—
	ECHL	Totals	122	73	87	160	374	9	10	7	17	20

Born; 5/31/72, Longueil, Quebec. 5-11, 188. 1996-97 ECHL Second Team All-Star.

Steve Maltais — Left Wing

Regular Season / Playoffs

Season	Team	League	GP	G	A	PTS	PIM	GP	G	A	PTS	PIM
88-89	Fort Wayne	IHL	—	—	—	—	—	4	2	1	3	0
89-90	Washington	NHL	8	0	0	0	2	1	0	0	0	0
89-90	Baltimore	AHL	67	29	37	66	54	12	6	10	16	6
90-91	Washington	NHL	7	0	0	0	2	—	—	—	—	—
90-91	Baltimore	AHL	73	36	43	79	97	6	1	4	5	10
91-92	Minnesota	NHL	12	2	1	3	2	—	—	—	—	—
91-92	Kalamazoo	IHL	48	25	31	56	51	—	—	—	—	—
91-92	Halifax	AHL	10	3	3	6	0	—	—	—	—	—
92-93	Tampa Bay	NHL	63	7	13	20	35	—	—	—	—	—
92-93	Atlanta	IHL	16	14	10	24	22	—	—	—	—	—
93-94	Detroit	NHL	4	0	1	1	0	—	—	—	—	—
93-94	Adirondack	AHL	73	35	49	84	79	12	5	11	16	14
94-95	Chicago	IHL	79	*57	40	97	145	3	1	1	2	0
95-96	Chicago	IHL	81	56	66	122	161	9	7	7	14	20
96-97	Chicago	IHL	81	*60	54	114	62	4	2	0	2	4
	NHL	Totals	94	9	15	24	41	1	0	0	0	0
	IHL	Totals	305	212	201	413	441	20	12	9	21	24
	AHL	Totals	223	103	132	235	230	30	12	25	37	30

Born; 1/25/69, Arvida, Quebec. 6-2, 210. Drafted by Washington Capitals (2nd choice, 57th overall) in 1987 Entry Draft. Traded to Minnesota North Stars by Washington with Trent Klatt for Shawn Chambers (6/21/91). Traded to Quebec Nordiques by Minnesota for Kip Miller (3/8/92). Claimed by Tampa Bay Lightning from Quebec in Expansion Draft (6/18/92). Traded to Detroit Red Wings by Tampa Bay for Dennis Vial (6/8/93). 1994-95 IHL First Team All-Star. 1995-96 IHL Second Team All-Star. 1996-97 IHL Second team All-Star.

Kent Manderville — Left Wing

Regular Season / Playoffs

Season	Team	League	GP	G	A	PTS	PIM	GP	G	A	PTS	PIM
91-92	Toronto	NHL	15	0	4	4	0	—	—	—	—	—
91-92	St. John's	AHL	—	—	—	—	—	12	5	9	14	14
92-93	Toronto	NHL	18	1	1	2	17	18	1	0	1	8
92-93	St, John's	AHL	56	19	28	47	86	2	0	2	2	0
93-94	Toronto	NHL	67	7	9	16	63	12	1	0	1	4
94-95	Toronto	NHL	36	0	1	1	22	7	0	0	0	6
95-96	Edmonton	NHL	37	3	5	8	38	—	—	—	—	—
95-96	St. John's	AHL	27	16	12	28	26	—	—	—	—	—
96-97	Springfield	AHL	23	5	20	25	18	—	—	—	—	—
96-97	Hartford	NHL	44	6	5	11	18	—	—	—	—	—
	NHL	Totals	217	17	25	42	158	37	2	0	2	18
	AHL	Totals	106	40	60	100	112	14	5	11	16	14

Born; 4/12/71, Edmonton, Alberta. 6-3, 207. Drafted by Calgary Flames (1st choice, 24th overall) in 1989 Entry Draft. Traded to Toronto Maple Leafs by Calgary with Doug Gilmour, Jamie Macoun, Rick Wamsley and Ric Nattress for Gary Leeman, Alexander Godynyuk, Jeff Reese, Michel Petit and Craig Berube (1/2/92). Traded to Edmonton Oilers by Toronto for Peter White and Edmonton's sixth round pick (Dimitriy Yakushin) in 1996 Entry Draft (12/4/95). Signed as a free agent by Hartford Whalers, (1996).

Mike Maneluk — Left Wing

Regular Season / Playoffs

Season	Team	League	GP	G	A	PTS	PIM	GP	G	A	PTS	PIM
93-94	San Diego	IHL	—	—	—	—	—	1	0	0	0	0
94-95	Canadian	National										
94-95	San Diego	IHL	10	0	1	1	4	—	—	—	—	—
95-96	Baltimore	AHL	74	33	38	71	73	6	4	3	7	14

Season	Team	League	GP	G	A	PTS	PIM	GP	G	A	PTS	PIM
96-97	Worcester	AHL	70	27	27	54	89	5	1	1	2	14
	AHL	Totals	144	60	65	125	162	11	5	4	9	28
	IHL	Totals	10	0	1	1	4	1	0	0	0	0

Born; 10/1/73, Winnipeg, Manitoba. 5-11, 188. Signed as a free agent by Anaheim Mighty Ducks (1/28/94). Traded to Ottawa Senators by Anaheim for Kevin Brown (7/1/96).

Sal Manganaro — Right Wing

			Regular Season					Playoffs				
Season	Team	League	GP	G	A	PTS	PIM	GP	G	A	PTS	PIM
96-97	Fort Wayne	IHL	7	0	0	0	0	—	—	—	—	—
96-97	Dayton	ECHL	62	24	23	47	118	4	1	1	2	0

Born; 12/20/72, Boston, Massachusetts. 5-11, 183.

Eric Manlow — Center

			Regular Season					Playoffs				
Season	Team	League	GP	G	A	PTS	PIM	GP	G	A	PTS	PIM
95-96	Indianapolis	IHL	75	6	11	17	32	4	0	1	1	4
96-97	Baltimore	AHL	36	6	6	12	13	3	0	0	0	0
96-97	Columbus	ECHL	32	18	18	36	20	—	—	—	—	—

Born; 4/7/75, Belleville, Ontario. 6-0, 190. Drafted by Chicago Blackhawks (2nd choice, 50th overall) in 1993 Entry Draft.

Doug Mann — Right Wing

			Regular Season					Playoffs				
Season	Team	League	GP	G	A	PTS	PIM	GP	G	A	PTS	PIM
94-95	Lakeland	SUN	15	2	3	5	109	—	—	—	—	—
95-96	Lakeland	SHL	46	6	6	12	141	5	1	1	2	17
96-97	Raleigh	ECHL	52	4	1	5	203	—	—	—	—	—
	SHL	Totals	61	8	9	17	250	5	1	1	2	17

Born; 7/4/73, Etobicoke, Ontario. 6-0, 195.

Troy Mann — Left Wing

			Regular Season					Playoffs				
Season	Team	League	GP	G	A	PTS	PIM	GP	G	A	PTS	PIM
95-96	Saginaw	CoHL	58	30	29	59	30	—	—	—	—	—
96-97	Mississippi	ECHL	63	33	33	66	38	3	1	0	1	6

Born; 9/3/69, New Richmond, Quebec. 5-10, 185.

Blair Manning — Center

			Regular Season					Playoffs				
Season	Team	League	GP	G	A	PTS	PIM	GP	G	A	PTS	PIM
96-97	Grand Rapids	IHL	8	1	1	2	4	1	0	1	1	0
96-97	Saint John	AHL	2	0	0	0	0	—	—	—	—	—
96-97	Baton Rouge	ECHL	60	13	33	46	77	—	—	—	—	—

Born; 5/27/75, Vancouver, British Columbia. Last amateur club; Medicine Hat (WHL).

Norm Maracle — Goaltender

			Regular Season							Playoffs					
Season	Team	League	GP	W	L	T	MIN	SO	GAVG	GP	W	L	MIN	SO	GAVG
94-95	Adirondack	AHL	39	12	15	2	1997	0	3.57	—	—	—	—	—	—
95-96	Adirondack	AHL	54	24	18	6	2949	2	2.75	1	0	1	29	0	8.11
96-97	Adirondack	AHL	*68	*34	22	9	*3843	5	2.70	4	1	3	192	1	3.13
	AHL	Totals	161	70	55	17	8789	7	2.92	5	1	4	221	1	3.80

Born; 10/2/74, Belleville, Ontario. 5-9, 175. Drafted by Detroit Red Wings (6th choice, 126th overall) in 1993 Entry Draft. 1996-97 AHL Second Team All-Star.

Derek Marchand — Forward

			Regular Season					Playoffs				
Season	Team	League	GP	G	A	PTS	PIM	GP	G	A	PTS	PIM
95-96	Lakeland	SHL	59	27	29	56	36	5	0	3	3	0
96-97	Columbus	CeHL	60	16	16	32	57	3	0	0	0	22

Born; 12/16/71, Mantunuck, Rhode Island. 6-2, 200.

Eddy Marchant — Right Wing

			Regular Season					Playoffs				
Season	Team	League	GP	G	A	PTS	PIM	GP	G	A	PTS	PIM
96-97	Muskegon	CoHL	10	2	4	6	26	—	—	—	—	—
96-97	Wichita	CeHL	50	16	18	34	226	9	4	3	7	33

Born; 1/8/74, Santiago, Chile, 6-1, 185.

Dave Marcinyshyn — Defenseman

			Regular Season					Playoffs				
Season	Team	League	GP	G	A	PTS	PIM	GP	G	A	PTS	PIM
87-88	Utica	AHL	73	2	7	9	179	—	—	—	—	—
87-88	Flint	IHL	3	0	0	0	4	16	0	2	2	31
88-89	Utica	AHL	74	4	14	18	101	5	0	0	0	13
89-90	Utica	AHL	74	6	18	24	164	5	0	2	2	21
90-91	New Jersey	NHL	9	0	1	1	21	—	—	—	—	—
90-91	Utica	AHL	52	4	9	13	81	—	—	—	—	—
91-92	Quebec	NHL	5	0	0	0	26	—	—	—	—	—
91-92	Halifax	AHL	74	10	42	52	138	—	—	—	—	—
92-93	Rangers	NHL	2	0	0	0	2	—	—	—	—	—
92-93	Binghamton	AHL	67	5	25	30	184	6	0	3	3	14
93-94	Milwaukee	IHL	1	0	0	0	0	—	—	—	—	—
94-95	Milwaukee	IHL	63	2	14	16	176	—	—	—	—	—
94-95	Kalamazoo	IHL	3	0	0	0	6	16	0	1	1	16
95-96	Cincinnati	IHL	65	6	13	19	160	17	0	2	2	10
96-97	Cincinnati	IHL	74	1	9	10	141	—	—	—	—	—
	NHL	Totals	16	0	1	1	49	—	—	—	—	—
	AHL	Totals	414	31	115	146	847	16	0	5	5	48
	IHL	Totals	209	9	36	45	487	49	0	5	5	57

Born; 2/4/67, Edmonton, Alberta. 6-3, 210. Signed as a free agent by New Jersey Devils (9/26/86). Traded to Quebec Nordiques by New Jersey for Brent Severyn (6/3/91). Signed as a free agent by New York Rangers (8/26/92).

Peter Marek — Center

			Regular Season					Playoffs				
Season	Team	League	GP	G	A	PTS	PIM	GP	G	A	PTS	PIM
93-94	Cape Breton	AHL	27	7	8	15	12	—	—	—	—	—
93-94	Wheeling	ECHL	14	7	13	20	27	7	1	3	4	12
94-95	Wheeling	ECHL	25	3	17	20	37	—	—	—	—	—
94-95	Birmingham	ECHL	23	8	16	24	26	7	3	5	8	2
95-96	Reno	WCHL	49	27	24	41	24	3	1	2	3	8
96-97	Reno	WCHL	56	28	35	63	80	—	—	—	—	—
	WCHL	Totals	105	55	59	104	104	3	1	2	3	8
	ECHL	Totals	62	18	46	64	90	14	4	8	12	14

Born; 1/13/69, Slany, Czechoslovakia. 6-3, 205.

Don Margettie — Right Wing

			Regular Season					Playoffs				
Season	Team	League	GP	G	A	PTS	PIM	GP	G	A	PTS	PIM
96-97	Nashville	CeHL	24	13	14	27	89	—	—	—	—	—
96-97	San Antonio	CeHL	40	19	27	46	66	—	—	—	—	—
	CeHL	Totals	64	32	41	73	155	—	—	—	—	—

Born; 7/10/75, Niagra Fall, Ontario. 5-10, 186. Selected by Wichita Thunder in San Antonio Dispersal Draft (6/10/97).

Josef Marha — Center

Season	Team	League	GP	G	A	PTS	PIM	GP	G	A	PTS	PIM
95-96	Colorado	NHL	2	0	1	1	0	—	—	—	—	—
95-96	Cornwall	AHL	74	18	30	48	30	8	1	2	3	10
96-97	Colorado	NHL	6	0	1	1	0	—	—	—	—	—
96-97	Hershey	AHL	67	23	49	72	44	19	6	*16	*22	10
	NHL	Totals	8	0	2	2	0	—	—	—	—	—
	AHL	Totals	141	41	79	140	74	27	7	18	25	20

Born; 6/2/76, Chavlickov, Czechoslovakia. 6-0, 170. Drafted by Quebec Nordiques (3rd choice, 35th overall) in 1994 Entry Draft. Member of 1996-97 AHL Champion Hershey Bears.

Brett Marietti — Right Wing

Season	Team	League	GP	G	A	PTS	PIM	GP	G	A	PTS	PIM
94-95	South Carolina	ECHL	67	23	33	56	103	9	2	0	2	16
95-96	South Carolina	ECHL	64	28	34	62	121	8	8	5	13	17
96-97	South Carolina	ECHL	61	25	41	66	103	18	*12	11	23	58
	ECHL	Totals	192	76	108	184	327	35	22	16	38	91

Born; 2/9/73, Haileybury, Ontario. 5-11, 183. Member of 1996-97 ECHL Champion South Carolina Stingrays.

Chris Marinucci — Left Wing

Season	Team	League	GP	G	A	PTS	PIM	GP	G	A	PTS	PIM
94-95	Denver	IHL	74	29	40	69	42	14	3	4	7	12
94-95	Islanders	NHL	12	1	4	5	2	—	—	—	—	—
95-96	Utah	IHL	8	3	5	8	8	—	—	—	—	—
96-97	Los Angeles	NHL	1	0	0	0	0	—	—	—	—	—
96-97	Utah	IHL	21	3	13	16	6	—	—	—	—	—
96-97	Phoenix	IHL	62	23	29	52	26	—	—	—	—	—
	NHL	Totals	13	1	4	5	2	—	—	—	—	—
	IHL	Totals	165	58	87	145	82	14	3	4	7	12

Born; 12/29/71, Grand Rapids, Minnesota. 6-0, 188. Drafted by New York Islanders (4th choice, 90th overall) in 1990 Entry Draft. Traded to Los Angeles Kings by Islanders for Nicholas Vachon (1996).

Wayne Marion — Goaltender

Season	Team	League	GP	W	L	T	MIN	SO	GAVG	GP	W	L	MIN	SO	GAVG
91-92	Raleigh	ECHL	3	—	—	—	159	0	6.04	—	—	—	—	—	—
91-92	St. Thomas	CoHL	23	8	9	4	1228	0	5.13	—	—	—	—	—	—
92-93	St. Thomas	CoHL	28	10	11	3	1433	0	5.44	1	0	1	60	0	6.00
93-94	Utica	CoHL	36	13	17	2	1953	0	4.89	—	—	—	—	—	—
94-95	Utica	CoHL	27	12	8	3	1565	1	4.22	—	—	—	—	—	—
94-95	Brantford	CoHL	13	4	7	1	682	0	4.48	—	—	—	—	—	—
95-96	Winston-Salem	SHL	*49	*25	17	6	*2722	0	4.25	9	4	5	544	0	*3.75
96-97	Nashville	CeHL	2	0	1	0	100	0	6.60	—	—	—	—	—	—
96-97	Reno	WCHL	29	8	17	2	1540	0	6.43	—	—	—	—	—	—
	CoHL	Totals	127	47	52	13	6861	1	4.85	1	0	1	60	0	6.00

Born; 2/18/71, Hull, Quebec. 5-11, 185.

Danil Markov — Defenseman

Season	Team	League	GP	G	A	PTS	PIM	GP	G	A	PTS	PIM
96-97	St. John's	AHL	10	2	4	6	18	11	2	6	8	14

Born; 7/11/76, Moscow, Russia. 5-11, 176. Drafted by Toronto Maple Leafs (7th choice, 223rd overall) in 1995 Entry Draft.

Daniel Marois — Right Wing

			Regular Season					Playoffs				
Season	Team	League	GP	G	A	PTS	PIM	GP	G	A	PTS	PIM
87-88	Newmarket	AHL	8	4	4	8	4	—	—	—	—	—
87-88	Toronto	NHL	—	—	—	—	—	3	1	0	1	0
88-89	Toronto	NHL	76	31	23	54	76	—	—	—	—	—
89-90	Toronto	NHL	68	39	37	76	82	5	2	2	4	12
90-91	Toronto	NHL	78	21	9	30	112	—	—	—	—	—
91-92	Toronto	NHL	63	15	11	26	76	—	—	—	—	—
91-92	Islanders	NHL	12	2	5	7	18	—	—	—	—	—
92-93	Islanders	NHL	28	2	5	7	35	—	—	—	—	—
92-93	Capital Distrct	AHL	4	2	0	2	0	—	—	—	—	—
93-94	Boston	NHL	22	7	3	10	18	11	0	1	1	16
93-94	Providence	AHL	6	1	2	3	6	—	—	—	—	—
94-95			DID	NOT	PLAY							
95-96	Michigan	IHL	61	28	28	56	105	—	—	—	—	—
95-96	Minnesota	IHL	13	4	3	7	20	—	—	—	—	—
96-97	Quebec	IHL	7	1	1	2	12	—	—	—	—	—
96-97	Utah	IHL	29	7	9	16	58	—	—	—	—	—
	NHL	Totals	347	117	93	210	417	19	3	3	6	28
	IHL	Totals	110	40	41	81	195	—	—	—	—	—
	AHL	Totals	18	7	6	13	10	—	—	—	—	—

Born; 10/3/68, Montreal, Quebec. 6-0, 190. Drafted by Toronto Maple Leafs (2nd choice, 28th overall) in 1987 Entry Draft. Traded to New York Islanders by Toronto with Claude Loiselle for Ken Baumgartner and Dave McLlwain (3/10/92). Traded to Boston Bruins by Islanders for Boston's eighth round choice (Peter Hogardh) in 1994 Entry Draft (3/18/93). Signed as a free agent by Toronto (8/20/96).

Bobby Marshall — Defenseman

			Regular Season					Playoffs				
Season	Team	League	GP	G	A	PTS	PIM	GP	G	A	PTS	PIM
94-95	Saint John	AHL	77	7	24	31	62	5	0	0	0	4
95-96	Saint John	AHL	10	0	5	5	8	—	—	—	—	—
95-96	Baltimore	AHL	67	3	28	31	38	12	2	8	10	8
96-97	Baltimore	AHL	79	1	35	36	45	3	0	1	1	4
	AHL	Totals	233	11	92	103	153	20	2	9	11	16

Born; 4/11/72, North York, Ontario. 6-1, 190. Drafted by Calgary Flames (6th choice, 129th overall) in 1991 Entry Draft. Traded by Calgary to Anaheim Mighty Ducks for Jarrod Skalde (10/30/95).

Craig Martin — Right Wing

			Regular Season					Playoffs				
Season	Team	League	GP	G	A	PTS	PIM	GP	G	A	PTS	PIM
91-92	Moncton	AHL	11	1	1	2	70	—	—	—	—	—
91-92	Fort Wayne	IHL	24	0	0	0	115	—	—	—	—	—
92-93	Moncton	AHL	64	5	13	18	198	5	0	1	1	22
93-94	Adirondack	AHL	76	15	24	39	297	12	2	2	4	63
94-95	Winnipeg	NHL	20	0	1	1	19	—	—	—	—	—
94-95	Springfield	AHL	6	0	1	1	21	—	—	—	—	—
95-96	Springfield	AHL	48	6	5	11	245	8	0	1	1	34
96-97	Carolina	AHL	44	1	2	3	239	—	—	—	—	—
96-97	San Antonio	IHL	15	3	3	6	99	6	0	1	1	25
	AHL	Totals	249	28	46	74	1060	25	2	4	6	119
	IHL	Totals	39	3	3	6	214	6	0	1	1	25

Born; 1/21/71, Amherst, Nova Scotia. 6-2, 215. Drafted by Winnipeg Jets (6th choice, 98th overall) in 1990 Entry Draft. Signed as a free agent by Detroit Red Wings (7/28/93).

Mike Martin — Defenseman

Season	Team	League	GP	G	A	PTS	PIM	GP	G	A	PTS	PIM
			Regular Season					Playoffs				
96-97	Binghamton	AHL	62	2	7	9	45	3	0	1	1	2

Born; 10/27/76, Stratford, Ontario. 6-2, 204. Drafted by New York Rangers (2nd choice, 65th overall) in 1995 Entry Draft.

Neil Martin — Defenseman

Season	Team	League	GP	G	A	PTS	PIM	GP	G	A	PTS	PIM
			Regular Season					Playoffs				
96-97	Portland	AHL	1	0	2	2	0	—	—	—	—	—
96-97	San Antonio	IHL	1	0	0	0	0	—	—	—	—	—
96-97	Hampton Roads	ECHL	54	3	19	22	89	9	0	2	2	4

Born; 9/8/75, Sudbury, Ontario. 5-10, 193.

Tony Martino — Goaltender

Season	Team	League	GP	W	L	T	MIN	SO	GAVG	GP	W	L	MIN	SO	GAVG
			Regular Season							Playoffs					
92-93	Tulsa	CeHL	39	23	13	2	2182	*2	*3.66	*11	*7	2	622	0	4.05
93-94	Tulsa	CeHL	48	30	12	4	2721	1	3.82	*11	4	7	*662	0	4.62
94-95	Tulsa	CeHL	42	25	14	3	2482	0	4.06	7	3	4	421	0	4.41
95-96	Tulsa	CeHL	*51	22	*25	4	*2952	0	4.47	6	2	4	386	0	2.64
96-97	New Mexico	WPHL	51	*33	13	1	2846	1	3.50	5	2	3	312	0	*3.65
	CeHL	Totals	180	100	64	13	10337	3	4.03	35	18	17	2091	0	4.05

Born; 8/13/64, Montreal, Quebec. 5-10, 185. 1992-93 CeHL Outstanding Goaltender. 1992-93 CeHL First Team All-Star. Member of 1992-93 CeHL champion Tulsa Oilers.

Steve Martins — Center

Season	Team	League	GP	G	A	PTS	PIM	GP	G	A	PTS	PIM
			Regular Season					Playoffs				
95-96	Hartford	NHL	23	1	3	4	8	—	—	—	—	—
95-96	Springfield	AHL	30	9	20	29	10	—	—	—	—	—
96-97	Hartford	NHL	2	0	1	1	0	—	—	—	—	—
96-97	Springfield	AHL	63	12	31	43	78	17	1	3	4	26
	NHL	Totals	25	1	4	5	8	—	—	—	—	—
	AHL	Totals	93	21	51	72	88	17	1	2	3	26

Born; 4/13/72, Gatineau, Quebec. 5-9, 175. Drafted by Hartford Whalers (1st choice, 5th overall) in 1994 Supplemental Draft.

Martin Masa — Left Wing

Season	Team	League	GP	G	A	PTS	PIM	GP	G	A	PTS	PIM
			Regular Season					Playoffs				
94-95	Kansas City	IHL	3	0	0	0	0	—	—	—	—	—
94-95	Fort Worth	CeHL	61	31	35	66	104	—	—	—	—	—
95-96	Knoxville	ECHL	17	6	3	9	22	—	—	—	—	—
96-97	Johnstown	ECHL	59	36	32	68	114	—	—	—	—	—
	ECHL	Totals	76	42	35	77	136	—	—	—	—	—

Born; 8/10/73, Sokolov, Czechoslovakia. 6-1, 205.

Jeff Massey — Center

Season	Team	League	GP	G	A	PTS	PIM	GP	G	A	PTS	PIM
			Regular Season					Playoffs				
92-93	Kansas City	IHL	3	0	0	0	0	—	—	—	—	—
92-93	Johnstown	ECHL	56	17	12	29	38	—	—	—	—	—
93-94	Oklahoma City	CeHL	63	21	21	42	64	7	3	5	8	2
94-95	Fort Worth	CeHL	57	23	29	52	41	—	—	—	—	—
95-96	Fort Worth	CeHL	28	9	10	19	25	—	—	—	—	—
95-96	San Antonio	CeHL	28	14	8	22	47	13	1	1	2	2

Season	Team	League	GP	G	A	PTS	PIM	GP	G	A	PTS	PIM
96-97	Austin	WPHL	2	0	0	0	0	—	—	—	—	—
96-97	San Antonio	CeHL	26	4	13	17	66	—	—	—	—	—
96-97	Memphis	CeHL	6	2	2	4	0	18	7	3	10	12
	CeHL	Totals	208	73	83	156	243	38	11	9	20	16

Born; 9/17/68, Swampscott, Massachusetts. 6-4, 205.

Milt Mastad — Defenseman

			Regular Season					Playoffs				
Season	Team	League	GP	G	A	PTS	PIM	GP	G	A	PTS	PIM
95-96	Providence	AHL	18	0	2	2	52	—	—	—	—	—
96-97	Providence	AHL	33	0	2	2	106	—	—	—	—	—
96-97	Charlotte	ECHL	9	0	0	0	25	3	0	1	1	4
	AHL	Totals	51	0	4	4	158	—	—	—	—	—

Born; 3/5/75, Regina, Saskatchewan. 6-4, 225. Drafted by Boston Bruins (6th choice, 155th overall) in 1993 Entry Draft.

Mike Mathers — Forward

			Regular Season					Playoffs				
Season	Team	League	GP	G	A	PTS	PIM	GP	G	A	PTS	PIM
96-97	Fresno	WCHL	51	24	37	61	31	5	0	0	0	7

Born; 6/20/72, Edmonton, Alberta. 6-0, 200. Drafted by Washington Capitals (7th choice, 191st overall) in 1992 Entry Draft.

Marquis Mathieu — Center

			Regular Season					Playoffs				
Season	Team	League	GP	G	A	PTS	PIM	GP	G	A	PTS	PIM
93-94	Fredericton	AHL	22	4	6	10	28	—	—	—	—	—
93-94	Wheeling	ECHL	42	12	11	23	75	9	1	3	4	23
94-95	Worcester	AHL	2	0	0	0	0	—	—	—	—	—
94-95	Toledo	ECHL	33	13	22	35	168	—	—	—	—	—
94-95	Raleigh	ECHL	33	15	17	32	181	—	—	—	—	—
95-96	Worcester	AHL	17	3	10	13	26	—	—	—	—	—
95-96	Houston	IHL	2	1	0	1	9	—	—	—	—	—
95-96	Johnstown	ECHL	25	4	17	21	89	—	—	—	—	—
95-96	Birmingham	ECHL	18	5	7	12	87	—	—	—	—	—
96-97	Worcester	AHL	30	8	16	24	88	1	0	0	0	0
	AHL	Totals	71	15	32	47	142	1	0	0	0	0
	ECHL	Totals	151	49	74	123	600	9	1	3	4	23

Born; 5/31/73, Hartford, Connecticut. 5-11, 190.

David Matsos — Left Wing

			Regular Season					Playoffs				
Season	Team	League	GP	G	A	PTS	PIM	GP	G	A	PTS	PIM
96-97	Adirondack	AHL	56	20	12	32	21	4	0	1	1	0

Born; 11/12/73, Burlington, Ontario. 6-1, 201. Signed as a free agent by Tampa Bay Lightning (5/1/96).

Christian Matte — Right Wing

			Regular Season					Playoffs				
Season	Team	League	GP	G	A	PTS	PIM	GP	G	A	PTS	PIM
93-94	COR	AHL	1	0	0	0	0	—	—	—	—	—
94-95	COR	AHL	—	—	—	—	—	3	0	1	1	2
95-96	COR	AHL	64	20	32	52	51	7	1	1	2	6
96-97	Colorado	NHL	5	1	1	2	0	—	—	—	—	—
96-97	Hershey	AHL	49	18	18	36	78	22	8	3	11	25
	AHL	Totals	114	38	50	88	129	32	9	5	14	33

Born; 1/20/75, Hull, Quebec. 5-11, 164. Drafted by Quebec Nordiques (8th choice, 153rd overall) in 1993 Entry Draft. Member of 1996-97 AHL Champion Hershey Bears.

Darcy Mattersdorfer — Center

Regular Season / **Playoffs**

Season	Team	League	GP	G	A	PTS	PIM	GP	G	A	PTS	PIM
96-97	El Paso	WPHL	20	4	12	16	12	—	—	—	—	—

Born; 10/31/75, Fernie, British Columbia. 5-8, 180.

Mike Matteucci — Defenseman

Regular Season / **Playoffs**

Season	Team	League	GP	G	A	PTS	PIM	GP	G	A	PTS	PIM
95-96	Los Angeles	IHL	4	0	0	0	7	—	—	—	—	—
96-97	Long Beach	IHL	81	4	4	8	254	18	0	1	1	42
	IHL	Totals	85	4	4	8	261	18	0	1	1	42

Born; 12/27/71, Trail, British Columbia. 6-2, 210.

Dale Matthew — Defenseman

Regular Season / **Playoffs**

Season	Team	League	GP	G	A	PTS	PIM	GP	G	A	PTS	PIM
96-97	Macon	CeHL	18	0	1	1	15	—	—	—	—	—
96-97	Memphis	CeHL	19	0	2	2	8	—	—	—	—	—
96-97	Fort Worth	CeHL	9	0	0	0	4	5	0	0	0	2
	CeHL	Totals	46	0	3	3	27	5	0	0	0	2

Born; 8/3/72, Nashua, New Hampshire. 6-4, 215. Member of 1996-97 CeHL Champion Fort Worth Fire.

Jesper Mattson — Center

Regular Season / **Playoffs**

Season	Team	League	GP	G	A	PTS	PIM	GP	G	A	PTS	PIM
95-96	Saint John	AHL	73	12	26	38	18	9	1	1	2	2
96-97	Saint John	AHL	72	22	18	40	32	3	1	1	2	0
	AHL	Totals	145	34	44	78	50	12	2	2	4	2

Born; 5/13/75, Malmo, Sweden. 6-0, 185. Drafted by Calgary Flames (1st choice, 18th overall) in 1993 Entry Draft.

Alex Matvichuk — Center

Regular Season / **Playoffs**

Season	Team	League	GP	G	A	PTS	PIM	GP	G	A	PTS	PIM
96-97	Toledo	ECHL	39	11	24	35	39	—	—	—	—	—
96-97	Wheeling	ECHL	26	8	23	31	23	3	0	3	3	2
	ECHL	Totals	65	19	47	66	62	3	0	3	3	2

Born; 5/13/75, Kiev, Ukraine. 5-8, 170. Last amateur club; North Bay (OHL).

Bob Maudie — Center

Regular Season / **Playoffs**

Season	Team	League	GP	G	A	PTS	PIM	GP	G	A	PTS	PIM
96-97	Binghamton	AHL	19	0	3	3	6	2	0	0	0	0
96-97	Charlotte	ECHL	6	1	1	2	4	—	—	—	—	—

Born; 9/17/76, Cranbrook, British Columbia. 5-11, 180. Drafted by New York Rangers (9th choice, 221st overall) in 1995 Entry Draft.

Michael Maurice — Center

Regular Season / **Playoffs**

Season	Team	League	GP	G	A	PTS	PIM	GP	G	A	PTS	PIM
91-92	Toledo	ECHL	62	39	72	111	51	5	1	2	3	6
92-93	Brantford	CoHL	11	11	6	17	14	—	—	—	—	—
92-93	Hamilton	AHL	13	3	7	10	6	—	—	—	—	—
92-93	Adirondack	AHL	25	4	7	11	4	2	0	0	0	2
93-94	Adirondack	AHL	70	25	30	55	53	12	7	6	13	4
94-95	Houston	IHL	71	20	26	46	64	4	1	2	3	6
95-96	Houston	IHL	68	17	19	36	32	—	—	—	—	—

Season	Team	League	GP	G	A	PTS	PIM	GP	G	A	PTS	PIM
96-97	St. John's	AHL	2	1	1	2	2	—	—	—	—	—
96-97	Grand Rapids	IHL	2	0	1	1	0	—	—	—	—	—
96-97	Mississippi	ECHL	6	2	5	7	2	—	—	—	—	—
96-97	Brantford	CoHL	60	48	76	124	48	10	6	14	20	16
	IHL	Totals	141	37	46	83	96	4	1	2	3	6
	AHL	Totals	110	33	45	78	65	14	7	6	13	6
	CoHL	Totals	71	59	82	141	62	10	6	14	20	16
	ECHL	Totals	68	41	77	118	53	5	1	2	3	6

Born; 4/22/66, Hamilton, Ontario. 6-1, 210. 1991-92 ECHL First Team All-Star. 1996-97 CoHL Second Team All-Star.

Dennis Maxwell — Left Wing

			Regular Season					Playoffs				
Season	Team	League	GP	G	A	PTS	PIM	GP	G	A	PTS	PIM
94-95	Muskegon	CoHL	—	—	—	—	—	10	0	1	1	36
95-96	Binghamton	AHL	8	0	1	1	7	—	—	—	—	—
95-96	Charlotte	ECHL	51	25	19	44	291	14	5	5	10	*78
96-97	Tallahassee	ECHL	30	13	22	35	175	—	—	—	—	—
96-97	Carolina	AHL	2	0	0	0	2	—	—	—	—	—
96-97	St. John's	AHL	20	2	2	4	97	—	—	—	—	—
96-97	San Antonio	IHL	14	1	4	5	32	4	1	0	1	41
	AHL	Totals	30	2	3	5	106	—	—	—	—	—
	ECHL	Totals	81	38	41	79	466	14	5	5	10	78

Born; 6/4/74, Dauphin, Manitoba. 6-2, 210. Member of 1995-96 ECHL champion Charlotte Checkers.

Roger Maxwell — Right Wing

			Regular Season					Playoffs				
Season	Team	League	GP	G	A	PTS	PIM	GP	G	A	PTS	PIM
96-97	Utah	IHL	1	0	0	0	5	—	—	—	—	—
96-97	Phoenix	IHL	2	0	0	0	12	—	—	—	—	—
96-97	Hershey	AHL	18	1	0	1	137	—	—	—	—	—
96-97	Mississippi	ECHL	38	2	4	6	276	—	—	—	—	—
	IHL	Totals	3	0	0	0	17	—	—	—	—	—

Born; 11/21/75, Toronto, Ontario. 6-3, 237.

Alan May — Left Wing

			Regular Season					Playoffs				
Season	Team	League	GP	G	A	PTS	PIM	GP	G	A	PTS	PIM
86-87	Springfield	AHL	4	0	2	2	11	—	—	—	—	—
86-87	Carolina	ACHL	42	23	14	37	310	5	2	2	4	57
87-88	Boston	NHL	3	0	0	0	15	—	—	—	—	—
87-88	Maine	AHL	61	14	11	25	257	—	—	—	—	—
87-88	Nova Scotia	AHL	13	4	1	5	54	4	0	0	0	51
88-89	Edmonton	NHL	3	1	0	1	7	—	—	—	—	—
88-89	Cape Breton	AHL	50	12	13	25	214	—	—	—	—	—
88-89	New Haven	AHL	12	2	8	10	99	16	6	3	9	*105
89-90	Washington	NHL	77	7	10	17	339	15	0	0	0	37
90-91	Washington	NHL	67	4	6	10	264	11	1	1	2	37
91-92	Washington	NHL	75	6	9	15	221	7	0	0	0	0
92-93	Washington	NHL	83	6	10	16	268	6	0	1	1	6
93-94	Washington	NHL	43	4	7	11	97	—	—	—	—	—
93-94	Dallas	NHL	8	1	0	1	18	1	0	0	0	0
94-95	Dallas	NHL	27	1	1	2	106	—	—	—	—	—
94-95	Calgary	NHL	7	1	2	3	13	—	—	—	—	—
95-96	Orlando	IHL	4	0	0	0	11	—	—	—	—	—
95-96	Detroit	IHL	17	2	5	7	49	—	—	—	—	—
95-96	Utah	IHL	53	13	12	25	108	14	1	2	3	14
96-97	Houston	IHL	82	7	11	18	270	13	1	2	3	28

	NHL	Totals	393	31	45	76	1348	40	1	2	3	80
	IHL	Totals	155	22	28	50	438	27	2	4	6	42
	AHL	Totals	140	32	35	67	635	20	6	3	9	156

Born; 1/14/65, Barrhead, Alberta. 6-1, 200. Signed as a free agent by Boston Bruins (10/30/87). Traded to Edmonton Oilers by Boston for Moe Lemay (3/8/88). Traded to Los Angeles Kings by Edmonton with Jim Wiemer for Brian Wilks and John English (3/7/89). Traded to Washington Capitals by Los Angeles for Washington's fifth round choice (Thomas Newman) in 1989 Entry Draft (6/17/89). Traded to Dallas Stars by Washington with Washington's seventh round choice (Jeff Dewar) in 1995 Entry Draft for Jim Johnson (3/21/94). Traded to Calgary Flames by Dallas for Calgary's eighth round choice (Sergei Luchinkin) in 1995 Entry Draft (4/7/95). Member of 1995-96 IHL Champion Utah Grizzlies.

Jamal Mayers — Centers

Season	Team	League	GP	G	A	PTS	PIM	GP	G	A	PTS	PIM
96-97	St. Louis	NHL	6	0	1	1	2	—	—	—	—	—
96-97	Worcester	AHL	62	12	14	26	104	5	4	5	9	4

Born; 10/24/74, Toronto, Ontario. 6-0, 190. Drafted by St. Louis Blues (3rd choice, 89th overall) in 1993 Entry Draft.

David Mayes — Defenseman

Season	Team	League	GP	G	A	PTS	PIM	GP	G	A	PTS	PIM
96-97	St. John's	AHL	2	0	0	0	0	—	—	—	—	—
96-97	South Carolina	ECHL	66	10	22	32	61	11	3	3	6	28

Born; 7/26/74, Thunder Bay, Ontario. 6-0, 188. Member of 1996-97 ECHL Champion South Carolina Stingrays.

Martin Mayhew — Right Wing

Season	Team	League	GP	G	A	PTS	PIM	GP	G	A	PTS	PIM
96-97	Mobile	ECHL	55	16	22	38	215	1	0	0	0	0
96-97	Kansas City	IHL	1	0	0	0	0	—	—	—	—	—

Born; 3/10/74, Windsor, Ontario. 6-3, 220.

Pat Mazzoli — Goaltender

Season	Team	League	GP	W	L	T	MIN	SO	GAVG	GP	W	L	MIN	SO	GAVG
96-97	Grand Rapids	IHL	5	2	0	0	169	0	3.56	—	—	—	—	—	—
96-97	Fort Wayne	IHL	15	1	6	0	673	0	3.75	—	—	—	—	—	—
96-97	Muskegon	CoHL	25	13	10	2	1429	1	3.02	—	—	—	—	—	—
	IHL	Totals	20	3	6	0	841	0	3.71	—	—	—	—	—	—

Born; 3/16/70, Markham, Ontario. 5-10, 185. Drafted by Quebec Nordiques (8th choice, 169th overall) in 1990 Entry Draft.

Chris McAllister — Defenseman

Season	Team	League	GP	G	A	PTS	PIM	GP	G	A	PTS	PIM
95-96	Syracuse	AHL	68	0	2	2	142	16	0	0	0	34
96-97	Syracuse	AHL	43	3	1	4	108	3	0	0	0	6
	AHL	Totals	111	3	3	6	250	19	0	0	0	40

Born; 6/16/75, Saskatoon, Saskatchewan. 6-7, 238. Drafted by Vancouver Canucks (2nd choice, 40th overall) in 1995 Entry Draft.

Kade McAllister — Left Wing

Season	Team	League	GP	G	A	PTS	PIM	GP	G	A	PTS	PIM
95-96	Brantford	CoHL	18	2	3	5	58	—	—	—	—	—
96-97	Brantford	CoHL	51	1	3	4	148	9	0	1	1	12
	CoHL	Totals	69	3	6	9	206	9	0	1	1	12

Born; 12/11/74, Sudbury, Ontario. 5-11, 200.

Chris McAlpine — Defenseman

			Regular Season					Playoffs				
Season	Team	League	GP	G	A	PTS	PIM	GP	G	A	PTS	PIM
94-95	New Jersey	NHL	24	0	3	3	17	—	—	—	—	—
94-95	Albany	AHL	48	4	18	22	49	—	—	—	—	—
95-96	Albany	AHL	57	5	14	19	72	4	0	0	0	13
96-97	Albany	AHL	44	1	9	10	48	—	—	—	—	—
96-97	St. Louis	NHL	15	0	0	0	24	4	0	1	1	0
	NHL	Totals	39	0	3	3	41	4	0	1	1	0
	AHL	Totals	149	10	41	51	169	4	0	0	0	13

Born; 12/1/71, Roseville, Minnesota. 6-0, 190. Drafted by New Jersey Devils (10th choice, 137th overall) in 1990 Entry Draft. Traded to St. Louis Blues by New Jersey with Devils 9th round selection in 1998 Entry Draft for Peter Zezel (2/11/97).

Dustin McArther — Right Wing

			Regular Season					Playoffs				
Season	Team	League	GP	G	A	PTS	PIM	GP	G	A	PTS	PIM
95-96	Detroit	CoHL	7	1	0	1	5	—	—	—	—	—
96-97	Peoria	ECHL	46	11	15	26	106	—	—	—	—	—

Born; 2/21/75, Sarnia, Ontario. 6-0, 188.

Mark McArthur — Goaltender

			Regular Season							Playoffs					
Season	Team	League	GP	W	L	T	MIN	SO	GAVG	GP	W	L	MIN	SO	GAVG
95-96	Utah	IHL	26	12	12	0	1482	0	3.12	—	—	—	—	—	—
96-97	Utah	IHL	56	28	20	6	3112	3	2.99	—	—	—	—	—	—
	IHL	Totals	82	40	32	6	4594	3	3.03	—	—	—	—	—	—

Born; 11/16/75, Peterborough, Ontario. 5-11, 189. Drafted by New York Islanders (5th choice, 112th overall) in 1994 Entry Draft. 1995-96 Shared IHL Best Goaltender Award with Tommy Salo.

Darren McAusland — Left Wing

			Regular Season					Playoffs				
Season	Team	League	GP	G	A	PTS	PIM	GP	G	A	PTS	PIM
92-93	Baltimore	AHL	61	14	14	28	16	—	—	—	—	—
93-94	Portland	AHL	61	6	16	22	17	2	0	0	0	0
94-95	Portland	AHL	46	12	9	21	33	2	0	2	2	2
94-95	Wheeling	ECHL	11	6	1	7	8	—	—	—	—	—
95-96	Portland	AHL	69	7	24	31	39	21	6	5	11	6
96-97	Portland	AHL:	65	9	20	29	32	1	0	0	0	4
	AHL	Totals	302	48	83	131	137	26	6	7	13	12

Born; 3/3/72, Grovedale, Alberta. 5-11, 181. Signed as a free agent by Washington Capitals (7/92). Member of 1993-94 AHL champion Portland Pirates.

Jason McBain — Defenseman

			Regular Season					Playoffs				
Season	Team	League	GP	G	A	PTS	PIM	GP	G	A	PTS	PIM
94-95	Springfield	AHL	77	16	28	44	92	—	—	—	—	—
95-96	Hartford	NHL	3	0	0	0	0	—	—	—	—	—
95-96	Springfield	AHL	73	11	33	44	43	8	1	1	2	2
96-97	Hartford	NHL	6	0	0	0	0	—	—	—	—	—
96-97	Springfield	AHL	58	8	26	34	40	16	0	8	8	12
	NHL	Totals	9	0	0	0	0	—	—	—	—	—
	AHL	Totals	208	35	87	122	175	24	1	9	10	14

Born; 4/12/74, Ilion, New York. 6-3, 210. Drafted by Hartford Whalers (5th choice, 81st overall) in 1992 Entry Draft.

Tony McCabe — Left Wing

			Regular Season					Playoffs				
Season	Team	League	GP	G	A	PTS	PIM	GP	G	A	PTS	PIM
96-97	Amarillo	WPHL	46	26	26	52	28	—	—	—	—	—
96-97	Reno	WCHL	22	11	13	24	25	—	—	—	—	—

Born; 5/25/73, Mississauga, Onatio. 6-2, 200.

Chris McCafferty — Center

			Regular Season					Playoffs				
Season	Team	League	GP	G	A	PTS	PIM	GP	G	A	PTS	PIM
95-96	Utica	CoHL	32	5	6	11	6	—	—	—	—	—
96-97	Nashville	CeHL	66	20	45	65	48	—	—	—	—	—

Born; 6/2/70, Belleville, New Jersey. 5-8, 190.

Rob McCaig — Defenseman

			Regular Season					Playoffs				
Season	Team	League	GP	G	A	PTS	PIM	GP	G	A	PTS	PIM
94-95	Dallas	CeHL	65	5	23	28	*380	—	—	—	—	—
95-96	Louisiana	ECHL	55	3	11	14	*512	5	0	1	1	10
96-97	Louisiana	ECHL	59	4	7	11	383	3	0	0	0	34
	ECHL	Totals	114	7	18	25	895	8	0	1	1	44

Born; 1/5/72, Innisfall, Alberta. 6-3, 205.

Keith McCambridge — Defenseman

			Regular Season					Playoffs				
Season	Team	League	GP	G	A	PTS	PIM	GP	G	A	PTS	PIM
95-96	Saint John	AHL	48	1	3	4	89	16	0	0	0	6
96-97	Saint John	AHL	56	2	1	3	109	—	—	—	—	—
	AHL	Totals	104	3	4	7	198	16	0	0	0	6

Born; 2/1/74, Thompson, Manitoba. 6-2, 205. Drafted by Calgary Flames (10th choice, 201st overall) in 1994 Entry Draft.

Sean McCann — Defenseman

			Regular Season					Playoffs				
Season	Team	League	GP	G	A	PTS	PIM	GP	G	A	PTS	PIM
94-95	Cincinnati	IHL	76	10	12	22	58	10	0	2	2	8
95-96	Carolina	AHL	80	14	33	47	61	—	—	—	—	—
96-97	Grand Rapids	IHL	76	8	26	34	46	5	0	0	0	2
	IHL	Totals	152	18	38	56	104	15	0	2	2	10

Born; 9/18/71, North York, Ontario. 6-0, 195. Drafted by Florida Panthers (1st choice, 1st overall) in 1994 Supplemental Draft.

Brian McCarthy — Center

			Regular Season					Playoffs				
Season	Team	League	GP	G	A	PTS	PIM	GP	G	A	PTS	PIM
94-95	Rochester	AHL	4	0	0	0	5	—	—	—	—	—
94-95	South Carolina	ECHL	21	3	5	8	25	—	—	—	—	—
94-95	Erie	ECHL	16	0	0	0	7	—	—	—	—	—
94-95	Johnstown	ECHL	12	4	4	8	2	5	4	1	5	2
95-96	Bakersfield	WCHL	39	19	17	36	24	—	—	—	—	—
96-97	Bakersfield	WCHL	62	25	46	71	34	4	0	3	3	17
	WCHL	Totals	101	44	63	107	58	4	0	3	3	17
	ECHL	Totals	49	7	9	16	34	5	4	1	5	2

Born; 12/6/71, Salem, Massachusetts. 6-2, 190. Drafted by Buffalo Sabres (2nd choice, 82nd overall) in 1990 Entry Draft.

Alyn McCauley — Center

			Regular Season					Playoffs				
Season	Team	League	GP	G	A	PTS	PIM	GP	G	A	PTS	PIM
96-97	St. John's	AHL	—	—	—	—	—	3	0	1	1	0

Born; 5/29/77, Brockville, Ontario. 5-11, 185. Drafted by New Jersey Devils (5th choice, 79th overall) in 1995 Entry Draft. Traded to Toronto Maple Leafs by New Jersey with Steve Sullivan and Jason Smith and for Doug Gilmour, Dave Ellett, and return of conditional draft pick previously traded to Toronto, (2/25/97).

Bill McCauley — Center

Season	Team	League	GP	G	A	PTS	PIM	GP	G	A	PTS	PIM
95-96	Providence	AHL	62	11	17	28	71	—	—	—	—	—
96-97	Providence	AHL	19	2	3	5	10	—	—	—	—	—
96-97	Charlotte	ECHL	38	8	20	28	39	3	1	1	2	8
	AHL	Totals	81	13	20	33	81	—	—	—	—	—

Born; 4/20/75, Detroit, Michigan. 6-1, 195. Drafted by Florida Panthers (6th choice, 83rd overall) in 1993 Entry Draft. Re-entered Entry Draft, selected by Boston Bruins (4th choice, 73rd overall) in 1995 Entry Draft.

Mike McCormick — Right Wing

Season	Team	League	GP	G	A	PTS	PIM	GP	G	A	PTS	PIM
89-90	Greensboro	ECHL	29	16	3	19	13	11	7	4	11	19
90-91	Greensboro	ECHL	50	18	19	37	90	—	—	—	—	—
91-92	Greensboro	ECHL	31	6	4	10	110	—	—	—	—	—
91-92	Johnstown	ECHL	19	4	9	13	22	5	1	0	1	2
92-93	Fort Worth	CeHL	49	14	16	30	91	—	—	—	—	—
93-94	Fort Worth	CeHL	63	20	15	35	73	—	—	—	—	—
94-95	Fort Worth	CeHL	36	9	10	19	40	—	—	—	—	—
94-95	Wichita	CeHL	16	7	3	10	29	11	3	5	8	9
95-96	N/A											
96-97	Amarillo	WPHL	31	8	5	13	43	—	—	—	—	—
	CeHL	Totals	164	50	44	94	233	11	3	5	8	9
	ECHL	Totals	129	44	35	79	235	16	8	4	12	21

Born; 5/14/68, Lynnwood, Washington. 6-3, 225. Drafted by Chicago Blackhawks (6th choice, 113rd overall) in 1987 Entry Draft. Member of 1989-90 ECHL Champion Greensboro Monarchs. Member of 1994-95 CeHL Champion Wichita Thunder.

Shawn McCosh — Center

Season	Team	League	GP	G	A	PTS	PIM	GP	G	A	PTS	PIM
90-91	New Haven	AHL	66	16	21	37	104	—	—	—	—	—
91-92	Los Angeles	NHL	4	0	0	0	4	—	—	—	—	—
91-92	Phoenix	IHL	71	21	32	53	118	—	—	—	—	—
91-92	New Haven	AHL	—	—	—	—	—	5	0	1	1	0
92-93	New Haven	AHL	46	22	32	54	54	—	—	—	—	—
92-93	Phoenix	IHL	22	9	8	17	36	—	—	—	—	—
93-94	Binghamton	AHL	75	31	44	75	68	—	—	—	—	—
94-95	Rangers	NHL	5	1	0	1	2	—	—	—	—	—
94-95	Binghamton	AHL	67	23	60	83	73	8	3	9	12	6
95-96	Hershey	AHL	71	31	52	83	82	5	1	5	6	8
96-97	Philadelphia	AHL	79	30	51	81	110	10	3	9	12	23
	NHL	Totals	9	1	0	1	6	—	—	—	—	—
	AHL	Totals	404	153	260	413	491	28	7	24	31	37
	IHL	Totals	93	30	40	70	154	—	—	—	—	—

Born; 6/5/69, Oshawa, Ontario. 6-0, 190. Drafted by Detroit Red Wings (5th choice, 95th overall) in 1989 Entry Draft. Traded to Los Angeles Kings by Detroit for Los Angeles' eighth round choice (Justin Krall) in 1992 Entry Draft (8/15/90). Traded to Ottawa Senators by Los Angeles with Bob Kudelski for Marc Fortier and Jim Thomson, (12/19/92). Signed as a free agent by New York Rangers (7/30/93).

Mike McCourt — Defenseman

Season	Team	League	GP	G	A	PTS	PIM	GP	G	A	PTS	PIM
94-95	Thunder Bay	CoHL	65	13	37	50	33	11	3	5	8	6

Season	Team	League	GP	G	A	PTS	PIM	GP	G	A	PTS	PIM
95-96	Thunder Bay	CoHL	13	1	8	9	14	19	1	5	6	18
96-97	Quebec	IHL	11	1	4	5	8	3	0	0	0	0
96-97	Carolina	AHL	7	0	0	0	7	—	—	—	—	—
96-97	Fort Worth	CeHL	50	15	52	67	73	—	—	—	—	—
	CoHL	Totals	78	14	45	59	47	30	4	10	14	24

Born; 7/26/70, Brockville, Ontario. 6-1, 190. Member of 1994-95 CoHL champion Thunder Bay Senators. 1996-97 CeHL Second Team All-Star.

Scott McCrory — Center

Season	Team	League	GP	G	A	PTS	PIM	GP	G	A	PTS	PIM
87-88	Binghamton	AHL	72	18	33	51	29	4	0	1	1	2
88-89	Baltimore	AHL	80	38	51	89	25	—	—	—	—	—
89-90	Rochester	AHL	51	14	41	55	46	13	3	6	9	2
90-91	Rochester	AHL	58	27	25	52	39	2	0	0	0	0
94-95	Kalamazoo	IHL	22	3	12	15	12	—	—	—	—	—
94-95	Houston	IHL	3	1	4	5	0	4	2	2	4	2
95-96	Houston	IHL	25	5	6	11	12	—	—	—	—	—
95-96	San Francisco	IHL	51	13	39	52	24	4	3	1	4	2
96-97	Manitoba	IHL	82	24	47	71	30	—	—	—	—	—
	AHL	Totals	261	97	150	247	139	19	3	7	10	4
	IHL	Totals	183	46	108	154	78	8	5	3	8	6

Born; 2/27/67, Sudbury, Ontario. 5-10, 185. Drafted by Washington Capitals (13th choice, 250th overall) in 1986 Entry Draft. Traded to Buffalo Sabres by Washington for Mark Ferner (6/1/89). Did not play professional hockey in North America from the 1991-92 season until the 1994-95 season.

Hubie McDonough — Center

Season	Team	League	GP	G	A	PTS	PIM	GP	G	A	PTS	PIM
86-87	Flint	IHL	82	27	52	79	59	6	3	2	5	0
87-88	New Haven	AHL	78	30	29	59	43	—	—	—	—	—
88-89	Los Angeles	NHL	4	0	1	1	0	—	—	—	—	—
88-89	New Haven	AHL	74	37	55	92	41	17	10	*21	*31	6
89-90	Los Angeles	NHL	22	3	4	7	10	—	—	—	—	—
89-90	Islanders	NHL	54	18	11	29	26	5	1	0	1	4
90-91	Islanders	NHL	52	6	6	12	10	—	—	—	—	—
90-91	Capital District	AHL	17	9	9	18	4	—	—	—	—	—
91-92	Islanders	NHL	33	7	2	9	15	—	—	—	—	—
91-92	Capital District	AHL	21	11	18	29	14	—	—	—	—	—
92-93	San Jose	NHL	30	6	2	8	6	—	—	—	—	—
92-93	San Diego	IHL	48	26	49	75	26	14	4	7	11	6
93-94	San Diego	IHL	69	31	48	79	61	8	0	7	7	6
94-95	San Diego	IHL	80	43	55	98	10	5	0	1	1	4
95-96	Los Angeles	IHL	11	11	9	20	10	—	—	—	—	—
95-96	Orlando	IHL	58	26	32	58	40	23	7	11	18	10
96-97	Orlando	IHL	68	30	25	55	60	10	5	8	13	6
	NHL	Totals	195	40	26	66	67	5	1	0	1	4
	IHL	Totals	416	194	270	464	266	66	19	36	55	38
	AHL	Totals	190	87	111	198	102	17	10	21	31	6

Born; 7/8/63, Manchester, New Hampshire. 5-9, 180. Signed as a free agent by Los Angeles Kings (4/18/88). Traded to New York Islanders by Los Angeles with Ken Baumgartner for Mikko Makela (11/29/89). Traded to San Jose Sharks for Islanders for cash (8/28/92). 1992-93 IHL Second All-Star Team. 1994-95 IHL Second Team All-Star.

Matt McElwee — Right Wing

Season	Team	League	GP	G	A	PTS	PIM	GP	G	A	PTS	PIM
95-96	Dayton	ECHL	33	5	8	13	110	3	0	0	0	19
96-97	Madison	CoHL	2	1	0	1	2	—	—	—	—	—

Season	Team	League	GP	G	A	PTS	PIM	GP	G	A	PTS	PIM
96-97	Johnstown	ECHL	17	1	1	2	32	—	—	—	—	—
96-97	Toledo	ECHL	31	5	3	8	62	—	—	—	—	—
	ECHL	Totals	81	11	12	23	204	3	0	0	0	19

Born; 7/22/67, Peoria, Illinois. 6-1, 200.

Mark McFarlane — Right Wing

			Regular Season					Playoffs				
Season	Team	League	GP	G	A	PTS	PIM	GP	G	A	PTS	PIM
95-96	Dayton	ECHL	7	1	0	1	34	—	—	—	—	—
95-96	Raleigh	ECHL	3	1	1	2	9	—	—	—	—	—
95-96	Hampton Roads	ECHL	12	1	2	3	89	—	—	—	—	—
95-96	Winston-Salem	SHL	24	14	6	20	131	8	5	5	10	53
96-97	Quad City	CoHL	70	19	28	47	201	6	1	2	3	22
	ECHL	Totals	22	3	3	6	132	—	—	—	—	—

Born; 1/11/70, Amherst, Nova Scotia. 5-10, 185. Member of 1996-97 CoHL Champion Quad City Mallards.

Jim McGeough — Left Wing

			Regular Season					Playoffs				
Season	Team	League	GP	G	A	PTS	PIM	GP	G	A	PTS	PIM
81-82	Washington	NHL	4	0	0	0	0	—	—	—	—	—
82-83	Hershey	AHL	5	1	1	2	10	5	0	2	2	25
83-84	Hershey	AHL	79	40	36	76	108	—	—	—	—	—
84-85	Washington	NHL	11	3	0	3	12	—	—	—	—	—
84-85	Pittsburgh	NHL	14	0	4	4	4	—	—	—	—	—
84-85	Binghamton	AHL	57	32	21	53	26	—	—	—	—	—
85-86	Pittsburgh	NHL	17	3	2	5	8	—	—	—	—	—
85-86	Baltimore	AHL	38	14	13	27	20	—	—	—	—	—
86-87	Pittsburgh	NHL	11	1	4	5	8	—	—	—	—	—
86-87	Baltimore	AHL	45	18	19	37	37	—	—	—	—	—
87-88	Springfield	AHL	30	11	13	24	28	—	—	—	—	—
88-89	N/A											
89-90	Phoenix	IHL	77	35	46	81	90	—	—	—	—	—
90-91	San Diego	IHL	10	2	4	6	4	—	—	—	—	—
90-91	Kalamazoo	IHL	7	0	0	0	2	—	—	—	—	—
90-91	Albany	IHL	12	9	3	12	4	—	—	—	—	—
90-91	Nashville	ECHL	4	2	1	3	0	—	—	—	—	—
91-92	Thunder Bay	CoHL	2	0	1	1	0	—	—	—	—	—
91-92	Richmond	ECHL	24	16	12	28	34	7	0	2	2	8
92-93	Richmond	ECHL	39	14	27	41	66	—	—	—	—	—
93-94	Richmond	ECHL	26	10	8	18	10	—	—	—	—	—
93-94	Dallas	CeHL	28	21	16	37	24	7	3	5	8	8
94-95	Dallas	CeHL	66	50	50	100	38	—	—	—	—	—
95-96	Reno	WCHL	15	4	10	14	4	—	—	—	—	—
95-96	Wichita	CeHL	31	11	20	31	16	—	—	—	—	—
96-97	Wichita	CEHL	21	6	20	26	4	9	9	2	11	8
	NHL	Totals	57	7	10	17	32	—	—	—	—	—
	AHL	Totals	254	116	103	219	237	5	0	2	2	25
	IHL	Totals	106	46	53	99	100	—	—	—	—	—
	CeHL	Totals	146	88	106	194	82	16	12	7	19	16
	ECHL	Totals	89	40	47	87	110	7	0	2	2	8

Born; 4/13/63, Regina, Saskatchewan. 5-10, 180. Drafted by Washington Capitals (6th choice, 110th overall) in 1981 Entry Draft. Traded to Pittsburgh Penguins by Washington for Mark Taylor (3/12/85).

Don McGrath — Defenseman

			Regular Season					Playoffs				
Season	Team	League	GP	G	A	PTS	PIM	GP	G	A	PTS	PIM
87-88	Baltimore	AHL	5	0	0	0	24	—	—	—	—	—
96-97	Central Texas	WPHL	46	2	9	11	141	6	0	1	1	25

Born;

Mike McGready
Defenseman

			Regular Season					Playoffs				
Season	Team	League	GP	G	A	PTS	PIM	GP	G	A	PTS	PIM
96-97	Saginaw	CoHL	36	2	2	4	105	—	—	—	—	—

Born; 4/2/73, Englewood, Colorado. 6-4, 215.

Matt McGuffin
Right Wing

			Regular Season					Playoffs				
Season	Team	League	GP	G	A	PTS	PIM	GP	G	A	PTS	PIM
96-97	Muskegon	CoHL	67	12	15	27	58	2	0	0	0	4

Born; 12/7/66, Brantford, Ontario. 6-0, 210.

Bill McGuigan
Right Wing

			Regular Season					Playoffs				
Season	Team	League	GP	G	A	PTS	PIM	GP	G	A	PTS	PIM
95-96	Detroit	CoHL	14	1	3	4	60	—	—	—	—	—
95-96	Saginaw	CoHL	41	5	6	11	69	—	—	—	—	—
96-97	Fort Worth	CeHL	8	3	3	6	25	—	—	—	—	—
96-97	Alaska	WCHL	47	12	18	30	201	—	—	—	—	—
	CoHL	Totals	55	6	9	15	129	—	—	—	—	—

Born; 5/30/75, Charlottetown, Prince Edward Island. 5-10, 190.

Justin McHugh
Right Wing

			Regular Season					Playoffs				
Season	Team	League	GP	G	A	PTS	PIM	GP	G	A	PTS	PIM
95-96	Jacksonville	ECHL	70	32	36	68	174	18	10	9	19	46
96-97	San Antonio	IHL	25	5	9	14	32	—	—	—	—	—
96-97	Quad City	CoHL	46	28	45	73	70	15	5	8	13	41

Born; 3/19/73, Minnetonka, Minnesota. 5-10, 195. Member of 1996-97 CoHL Champion Quad City Mallards.

Mike McHugh
Left Wing

			Regular Season					Playoffs				
Season	Team	League	GP	G	A	PTS	PIM	GP	G	A	PTS	PIM
88-89	MIN	NHL	3	0	0	0	2	—	—	—	—	—
88-89	KAL	IHL	70	17	29	46	89	6	3	1	4	17
89-90	MIN	NHL	3	0	0	0	0	—	—	—	—	—
89-90	KAL	IHL	73	14	17	31	96	10	0	6	6	16
90-91	MIN	NHL	6	0	0	0	0	—	—	—	—	—
90-91	KAL	IHL	69	27	38	65	82	11	3	8	11	6
91-92	SJ	NHL	8	1	0	1	14	—	—	—	—	—
91-92	SPR	AHL	70	23	31	54	51	11	4	7	11	25
92-93	SPR	AHL	67	19	27	46	111	11	5	2	7	12
93-94	HER	AHL	80	27	43	70	58	11	9	3	12	14
94-95	HER	AHL	68	24	26	50	102	6	3	2	5	6
95-96	HER	AHL	75	15	42	57	118	5	2	2	4	2
96-97	Hershey	AHL	77	23	45	68	135	10	3	9	12	23
	NHL	Totals	20	1	0	1	16	—	—	—	—	—
	AHL	Totals	437	131	214	345	575	54	26	25	51	82
	IHL	Totals	212	58	84	142	267	27	3	15	18	39

Born; 8/16/65, Bowdoin, Maine. 5-10, 190. Drafted by Minnesota North Stars in 1988 Supplemental Draft. Selected by San Jose Sharks in Dispersal Draft (5/30/91). Traded to Hartford Whalers by San Jose for Paul Fenton (10/18/91). Signed as a free agent by Hershey Bears (1993). 1996-97 AHL Playoff MVP. Member of 1996-97 AHL Champion Hershey Bears.

Ian McIntyre — Left Wing

			Regular Season					Playoffs				
Season	Team	League	GP	G	A	PTS	PIM	GP	G	A	PTS	PIM
95-96	Syracuse	AHL	57	6	7	13	108	2	0	0	0	0
96-97	Syracuse	AHL	40	3	12	15	57	—	—	—	—	—
96-97	Wheeling	ECHL	16	1	3	4	16	—	—	—	—	—
	AHL	Totals	97	9	19	28	165	2	0	0	0	0

Born; 2/12/74, Montreal, Quebec. 6-0, 192. Drafted by Quebec Nordiques (5th choice, 76th overall) in 1992 Entry Draft.

Scott McKay — Right Wing

			Regular Season					Playoffs				
Season	Team	League	GP	G	A	PTS	PIM	GP	G	A	PTS	PIM
95-96	Raleigh	ECHL	2	1	0	1	0	—	—	—	—	—
96-97	Carolina	AHL	30	1	9	10	2	—	—	—	—	—
96-97	Port Huron	CoHL	20	9	12	21	28	—	—	—	—	—

Born; 1/26/72, Burlington, Ontario. 5-11, 200.

Steve McKenna — Defenseman

			Regular Season					Playoffs				
Season	Team	League	GP	G	A	PTS	PIM	GP	G	A	PTS	PIM
96-97	Los Angeles	NHL	9	0	0	0	37	—	—	—	—	—
96-97	Phoenix	IHL	66	6	5	11	187	—	—	—	—	—

Born; 8/21/73, Toronto, Ontario. 6-8, 247. Signed as a free agent by Los Angeles Kings (5/23/96).

Sam McKenny — Defenseman

			Regular Season					Playoffs				
Season	Team	League	GP	G	A	PTS	PIM	GP	G	A	PTS	PIM
96-97	Richmond	ECHL	6	0	2	2	6	—	—	—	—	—
96-97	Louisville	ECHL	6	0	1	1	2	—	—	—	—	—
96-97	Dayton	ECHL	29	0	4	4	30	—	—	—	—	—
	ECHL	Totals	41	0	7	7	38	—	—	—	—	—

Born; 6/26/73, Portland, Maine. 6-0, 185.

Rusty McKie — Right Wing

			Regular Season					Playoffs				
Season	Team	League	GP	G	A	PTS	PIM	GP	G	A	PTS	PIM
95-96	Huntsville	SHL	4	0	0	0	17	—	—	—	—	—
96-97	El Paso	WPHL	48	7	9	16	192	11	0	5	5	*74

Born; 10/5/74, Toledo, Ohio. 6-1, 190. Member of 1996-97 WPHL Champion El Paso Buzzards.

Bob McKillop — Right Wing

			Regular Season					Playoffs				
Season	Team	League	GP	G	A	PTS	PIM	GP	G	A	PTS	PIM
91-92	Michigan	CoHL	57	40	39	79	6	2	0	0	0	0
92-93	Detroit	CoHL	57	39	33	72	18	5	2	1	3	0
93-94	Huntsville	ECHL	31	15	23	38	24	—	—	—	—	—
93-94	Detroit	CoHL	15	9	7	16	4	3	4	1	5	12
94-95	Detroit	CoHL	63	32	45	77	37	9	6	2	8	4
95-96	San Diego	WCHL	27	26	17	43	32	—	—	—	—	—
95-96	Detroit	CoHL	37	21	20	41	24	10	5	9	14	6
96-97	Port Huron	CoHL	74	45	43	88	94	5	1	2	3	0
	CoHL	Totals	303	186	187	373	183	34	18	15	33	22

Born; 3/19/70, Kitchener, Ontario. 5-11, 195.

Barry McKinlay — Defenseman

Season	Team	League	GP	G	A	PTS	PIM	GP	G	A	PTS	PIM
91-92	Thunder Bay	CoHL	48	17	28	45	25	13	2	6	8	8
92-93	Thunder Bay	CoHL	55	17	39	56	47	11	2	3	5	11
93-94	Prince Edward Island	AHL	17	2	5	7	6	—	—	—	—	—
93-94	Thunder Bay	CoHL	40	14	43	57	53	9	3	6	9	11
94-95	Prince Edward Island	AHL	8	1	5	6	0	—	—	—	—	—
94-95	Thunder Bay	CoHL	65	26	54	80	100	11	4	13	17	4
95-96	Thunder Bay	CoHL	54	10	43	53	87	19	1	18	19	30
96-97	Thunder Bay	CoHL	65	32	58	90	82	11	6	10	16	16
	AHL	Totals	25	3	10	13	6	—	—	—	—	—
	CoHL	Totals	327	116	265	381	394	74	18	56	74	80

Born; 8/8/67, Edmonton, Alberta. 6-3, 191. Drafted by Montreal Canadiens (12th choice, 206th overall) in 1987 Entry Draft. 1993-94 CoHL Top Defender. 1994-95 CoHL Top Defender. 1993-94 CoHL First Team All-Star. 1994-95 CoHL First Team All-Star. 1996-97 CoHL Defenseman of the Year. 1996-97 CoHL First Team All-Star. Member of 1991-92 CoHL champion Thunder Bay Thunder Hawks. Member of 1993-94 CoHL champion Thunder Bay Senators. Member of 1994-95 CoHL champion Thunder Bay Senators.

Bryan McKinney — Defenseman

Season	Team	League	GP	G	A	PTS	PIM	GP	G	A	PTS	PIM
96-97	Dayton	ECHL	3	0	0	0	2	3	0	0	0	2

Last amateur club; Guelph (OHL).

Kevin McKinnon — Left Wing

Season	Team	League	GP	G	A	PTS	PIM	GP	G	A	PTS	PIM
96-97	Baton Rouge	ECHL	40	7	16	23	16	—	—	—	—	—
96-97	Mississippi	ECHL	13	3	5	8	6	2	0	1	1	0
	ECHL	Totals	53	10	21	31	22	2	0	1	1	0

6-0, 197.

Kevin McKinnon — Left Wing

Season	Team	League	GP	G	A	PTS	PIM	GP	G	A	PTS	PIM
94-95	Erie	ECHL	67	37	48	85	28	—	—	—	—	—
94-95	Minnesota	IHL	1	0	0	0	0	—	—	—	—	—
95-96	N/A											
96-97	Pensacola	ECHL	2	0	0	0	2	—	—	—	—	—
96-97	Nashville	CeHL	52	30	33	63	73	—	—	—	—	—
96-97	Anchorage	WCHL	8	5	1	6	2	2	0	1	1	0
	ECHL	Totals	69	37	48	85	30	—	—	—	—	—

Born; 4/16/71, Fort Erie, Ontario. 5-9, 180. 1994-95 ECHL Rookie of the Year.

Steve McLaren — Defenseman

Season	Team	League	GP	G	A	PTS	PIM	GP	G	A	PTS	PIM
95-96	Indianapolis	IHL	54	1	2	3	170	3	0	0	0	2
96-97	Indianapolis	IHL	63	2	5	7	309	4	0	0	0	10
	IHL	Totals	117	3	7	10	479	7	0	0	0	12

Born; 6-0, 194. Owen Sound, Ontario. 6-0, 194. Drafted by Chicago Blackhawks (3rd choice, 65th overall) in 1994 Entry Draft.

Jim McLarty — Right Wing

Season	Team	League	GP	G	A	PTS	PIM	GP	G	A	PTS	PIM
96-97	Oklahoma City	CeHL	3	0	1	1	12	1	0	0	0	0

Born; 1/29/71, Tisdale, Saskatchewan. 5-11, 190.

Peter McLaughlin — Defenseman

			Regular Season					Playoffs				
Season	Team	League	GP	G	A	PTS	PIM	GP	G	A	PTS	PIM
96-97	Detroit	IHL	18	0	1	1	17	—	—	—	—	—
96-97	Flint	CoHL	14	0	1	1	16	—	—	—	—	—
96-97	Baton Rouge	ECHL	26	1	1	2	14	—	—	—	—	—

Born; 6/29/73, Norwood, Massachusetts. 6-3, 190. Drafted by Pittsburgh Penguins (8th choice, 170th overall) in 1991 Entry Draft.

Greg McLean — Defenseman

			Regular Season					Playoffs				
Season	Team	League	GP	G	A	PTS	PIM	GP	G	A	PTS	PIM
95-96	Wheeling	ECHL	34	0	6	6	54	—	—	—	—	—
96-97	Wheeling	ECHL	19	6	6	12	33	—	—	—	—	—
96-97	Baton Rouge	ECHL	35	4	8	12	54	—	—	—	—	—
	ECHL	Totals	88	10	20	30	141	—	—	—	—	—

Born; 6/29/75, London, Ontario. 6-2, 200.

Jeff McLean — Center

			Regular Season					Playoff				
Season	Team	League	GP	G	A	PTS	PIM	GP	G	A	PTS	PIM
92-93	Kansas City	IHL	60	21	23	44	45	10	3	1	4	2
93-94	Kansas City	IHL	69	27	30	57	44	—	—	—	—	—
93-94	San Jose	NHL	6	1	0	1	0	—	—	—	—	—
94-95	Kansas City	IHL	41	16	18	34	22	4	1	4	5	0
95-96	Kansas City	IHL	71	17	27	44	34	3	0	3	3	2
96-97	Kansas City	IHL	39	8	15	23	14	—	—	—	—	—
96-97	Cincinnati	IHL	9	1	3	4	2	—	—	—	—	—
96-97	Fort Wayne	IHL	6	1	1	2	2	—	—	—	—	—
	IHL	Totals	295	91	117	208	163	17	4	8	12	4

Born; 10/6/69, Port Moody, British Columbia. 5-11, 190. Drafted by San Jose Sharks in Supplemental Draft (6/22/91).

Jamie McLennan — Goaltender

			Regular Season							Playoffs					
Season	Team	League	GP	W	L	T	MIN	SO	GAVG	GP	W	L	MIN	SO	GAVG
91-92	Capital District	AHL	18	4	10	2	952	1	3.78	—	—	—	—	—	—
91-92	Richmond	ECHL	32	16	12	2	1837	0	3.72	—	—	—	—	—	—
92-93	Capital District	AHL	38	17	14	6	2171	1	3.23	1	0	1	20	0	15.00
93-94	Islanders	NHL	22	8	7	6	1287	0	2.84	2	0	1	82	0	4.39
93-94	Salt Lake City	IHL	24	8	12	2	1320	0	3.64	—	—	—	—	—	—
94-95	Islanders	NHL	21	6	11	2	1185	0	3.39	—	—	—	—	—	—
94-95	Denver	IHL	4	3	0	1	239	0	3.00	11	8	2	640	1	*2.15
95-96	Islanders	NHL	13	3	9	1	636	0	3.68	—	—	—	—	—	—
95-96	Worcester	AHL	22	14	7	1	1215	0	2.81	2	0	2	118	0	4.04
95-96	Utah	IHL	14	9	2	2	728	0	2.39	—	—	—	—	—	—
96-97	Worcester	AHL	39	18	13	4	2152	5	2.79	4	2	2	262	0	3.67
	NHL	Totals	56	17	27	9	3108	0	3.22	2	0	1	82	0	4.39
	AHL	Totals	117	53	44	13	6490	2	3.09	7	2	5	400	0	4.35
	IHL	Totals	42	20	14	5	2287	0	3.17	11	8	2	640	1	2.15

Born; 6/30/71, Edmonton, Alberta. 6-0, 190. Drafted by New York Islanders (3rd choice, 48th overall) in 1991 Entry Draft. Signed as a free agent by St. Louis Blues (7/15/96). Member of 1994-95 IHL champion Denver Grizzlies.

Dave McLlwain — Right Wing

			Regular Season					Playoffs				
Season	Team	League	GP	G	A	PTS	PIM	GP	G	A	PTS	PIM
87-88	Pittsburgh	NHL	66	11	8	19	40	—	—	—	—	—
87-88	Muskegon	IHL	9	4	6	10	23	6	2	3	5	8

Season	Team	League	GP	G	A	PTS	PIM	GP	G	A	PTS	PIM
88-89	Pittsburgh	NHL	24	1	2	3	4	3	0	1	1	0
88-89	Muskegon	IHL	46	37	35	72	51	7	8	2	10	6
89-90	Winnipeg	NHL	80	25	26	51	60	7	0	1	1	2
90-91	Winnipeg	NHL	60	14	11	25	46	—	—	—	—	—
91-92	Winnipeg	NHL	3	1	1	2	2	—	—	—	—	—
91-92	Buffalo	NHL	5	0	0	0	2	—	—	—	—	—
91-92	Islanders	NHL	54	8	15	23	28	—	—	—	—	—
91-92	Toronto	NHL	11	1	2	3	4	—	—	—	—	—
92-93	Toronto	NHL	66	14	4	18	30	4	0	0	0	0
93-94	Ottawa	NHL	66	17	26	43	48	—	—	—	—	—
94-95	Ottawa	NHL	43	5	6	11	22	—	—	—	—	—
95-96	Ottawa	NHL	1	0	1	1	2	—	—	—	—	—
95-96	Pittsburgh	NHL	18	2	4	6	4	—	—	—	—	—
95-96	Cleveland	IHL	60	30	45	75	80	—	—	—	—	—
96-97	Cleveland	IHL	63	29	46	75	85	14	8	15	23	6
	NHL	Totals	497	99	106	203	292	14	0	2	2	2
	IHL	Totals	178	100	132	232	239	27	18	20	38	20

Born; 1/9/67, Seaforth, Ontario. 6-0, 185. Drafted by Pittsburgh Penguins (9th choice, 172nd overall) in 1986 Entry Draft. Traded to Winnipeg Jets by Pittsburgh with Randy Cunneyworth and Rick Tabaracci for Jim Kyte, Andrew McBain and Randy Gilhen (6/17/89). Traded to Buffalo Sabres by Winnipeg with Gord Donnelly, Winnipeg's fifth round choice (Yuri Khmylev) in 1992 Entry Draft and future considerations for Darrin Shannon, Mike Hartman and Dean Kennedy (10/11/91). Traded to New York Islanders by Buffalo with Pierre Turgeon, Uwe Krupp and Benoit Hogue for Pat LaFontaine, Randy Hillier, Randy Wood and Islanders fourth round choice (Dean Melanson) in 1992 Entry Draft (10/25/91). Traded to Toronto Maple Leafs with Ken Baumgartner for Daniel Marois and Claude Loiselle (3/10/92). Claimed by Ottawa Senators from Toronto in NHL Waiver Draft (10/3/93). Traded to Pittsburgh by Ottawa for Pittsburgh's eighth round choice (Erich Goldmann) in 1996 Entry Draft. Member of 1988-89 IHL champion Muskegon Lumberjacks.

Jay McNeill — Forward

			Regular Season					Playoffs				
Season	Team	League	GP	G	A	PTS	PIM	GP	G	A	PTS	PIM
96-97	Richmond	ECHL	68	25	29	54	42	8	4	3	7	2

Born; 8/28/72, Powell River, British Columbia. 5-9, 180. Last amateur club; Colorado College (WCHA).

Mike McNeill — Center

			Regular Season					Playoffs				
Season	Team	League	GP	G	A	PTS	PIM	GP	G	A	PTS	PIM
88-89	Fort Wayne	IHL	75	27	35	62	12	11	1	5	6	2
88-89	Moncton	AHL	1	0	0	0	0	—	—	—	—	—
89-90	Indianapolis	IHL	74	17	24	41	15	14	6	4	10	21
90-91	Chicago	NHL	23	3	3	4	6	—	—	—	—	—
90-91	Quebec	NHL	14	2	5	7	4	—	—	—	—	—
90-91	Indianapolis	IHL	33	16	9	25	19	—	—	—	—	—
91-92	Quebec	NHL	26	1	4	5	8	—	—	—	—	—
91-92	Halifax	AHL	30	10	8	18	20	—	—	—	—	—
92-93	Milwaukee	IHL	75	17	17	34	34	6	2	0	2	0
93-94	Milwaukee	IHL	78	21	25	46	40	4	0	1	1	6
94-95	Milwaukee	IHL	80	23	15	38	30	15	2	2	4	14
95-96	Milwaukee	IHL	64	8	9	17	32	5	2	0	2	2
96-97	Milwaukee	IHL	74	18	26	44	24	3	0	1	1	0
	NHL	Totals	63	5	11	16	18	—	—	—	—	—
	IHL	Totals	553	147	160	307	206	58	13	13	267	45
	AHL	Totals	31	10	8	18	20	—	—	—	—	—

Born; 7/22/66, Winona, Minnesota. 6-1, 185. Drafted by St. Louis Blues in supplemental draft (6/10/88). Signed as a free agent by Chicago Blackhawks (9/89). Traded to Quebec Nordiques by Chicago with Ryan McGill for Dan Vincelette and Paul Gillis (3/5/91). 1989-90 IHL Playoff MVP. Member of 1989-90 IHL champion Indianapolis Ice.

Wayne McPhee — Defenseman

			Regular Season					Playoffs				
Season	Team	League	GP	G	A	PTS	PIM	GP	G	A	PTS	PIM
92-93	Brantford	CoHL	57	3	14	17	86	15	0	1	1	32
93-94	Brantford	CoHL	37	1	12	13	19	7	0	1	1	4
94-95	Brantford	CoHL	46	0	10	10	26	—	—	—	—	—
95-96	Brantford	CoHL	74	2	13	15	102	12	1	3	4	8
96-97	Brantford	CoHL	74	2	21	23	52	10	1	4	5	2
	CoHL	Totals	288	8	70	78	285	44	2	9	11	46

Born; 4/1/66, Brantford, Ontario. 6-0, 205. Member of 1992-93 Colonial League champion Brantford Smoke.

Justin McPolin — Left Wing

			Regular Season					Playoffs				
Season	Team	League	GP	G	A	PTS	PIM	GP	G	A	PTS	PIM
96-97	Columbus	ECHL	20	1	0	1	45	3	0	0	0	11

Born; 7/13/76, Toronto, Ontario. 6-2, 220. Last amateur club; London (OHL).

Jason McQuat — Right Wing

			Regular Season					Playoffs				
Season	Team	League	GP	G	A	PTS	PIM	GP	G	A	PTS	PIM
94-95	Wichita	CeHL	7	0	0	0	45	—	—	—	—	—
95-96	Louisiana	ECHL	55	10	8	18	224	4	1	0	1	2
96-97	Manitoba	IHL	2	0	0	0	0	—	—	—	—	—
96-97	Louisiana	ECHL	51	7	5	12	268	12	2	0	2	38
	ECHL	Totals	106	17	13	30	492	16	3	0	3	40

Born; 3/24/74, Oshawa, Ontario. 6-1, 190.

Ken McRae — Right Wing

			Regular Season					Playoffs				
Season	Team	League	GP	G	A	PTS	PIM	GP	G	A	PTS	PIM
87-88	Quebec	NHL	1	0	0	0	0	—	—	—	—	—
87-88	Fredericton	AHL	—	—	—	—	—	3	0	0	0	8
88-89	Quebec	NHL	37	6	11	17	68	—	—	—	—	—
88-89	Halifax	AHL	41	20	21	41	87	—	—	—	—	—
89-90	Quebec	NHL	66	7	8	15	191	—	—	—	—	—
90-91	Quebec	NHL	12	0	0	0	3	—	—	—	—	—
90-91	Halifax	AHL	60	10	36	46	193	—	—	—	—	—
91-92	Quebec	NHL	10	0	1	1	31	—	—	—	—	—
91-92	Halifax	AHL	52	30	41	71	184	—	—	—	—	—
92-93	Toronto	NHL	2	0	0	0	2	—	—	—	—	—
92-93	St. John's	AHL	64	30	44	74	135	9	6	6	12	27
93-94	Toronto	NHL	9	1	1	2	36	6	0	0	0	4
93-94	St. John's	AHL	65	23	41	64	200	—	—	—	—	—
94-95	Detroit	IHL	24	4	9	13	38	—	—	—	—	—
94-95	Phoenix	IHL	2	2	0	2	0	9	3	8	11	21
95-96	Phoenix	IHL	45	11	13	23	65	4	1	0	1	2
96-97	Phoenix	IHL	72	25	28	53	190	—	—	—	—	—
96-97	Providence	AHL	9	5	5	10	26	10	1	3	4	17
	NHL	Totals	137	14	21	35	364	6	0	0	0	4
	AHL	Totals	291	118	188	306	825	22	7	9	16	52
	IHL	Totals	143	42	50	92	293	13	4	8	12	23

Born; 4/23/68, Winchester, Ontario. 6-1, 195. Drafted by Quebec Nordiques (1st choice, 18th overall) in 1986 Entry Draft. Traded to Toronto Maple Leafs by Quebec for Len Esau (7/21/92). Signed as a free agent by Edmonton (9/9/94).

Don McSween — Defenseman

			Regular Season					Playoffs				
Season	Team	League	GP	G	A	PTS	PIM	GP	G	A	PTS	PIM
87-88	Buffalo	NHL	5	0	1	1	6	—	—	—	—	—
87-88	Rochester	AHL	63	9	29	38	18	6	0	1	1	15
88-89	Rochester	AHL	66	7	22	29	45	—	—	—	—	—
89-90	Buffalo	NHL	4	0	0	0	6	—	—	—	—	—
89-90	Rochester	AHL	70	16	43	59	43	17	3	10	13	12
90-91	Rochester	AHL	74	7	44	51	57	15	2	5	7	8
91-92	Rochester	AHL	75	6	32	38	60	16	5	6	11	18
92-93	San Diego	IHL	80	15	40	55	85	14	1	2	3	10
93-94	San Diego	IHL	38	5	13	18	36	—	—	—	—	—
93-94	Anaheim	NHL	32	3	9	12	39	—	—	—	—	—
94-95	Anaheim	NHL	2	0	0	0	0	—	—	—	—	—
95-96	Anaheim	NHL	4	0	0	0	4	—	—	—	—	—
95-96	Baltimore	AHL	12	1	9	10	2	—	—	—	—	—
96-97	Grand Rapids	IHL	75	7	20	27	66	3	0	1	1	8
	NHL	Totals	47	3	10	13	55	—	—	—	—	—
	AHL	Totals	360	46	179	225	225	54	10	22	32	53
	IHL	Totals	193	27	73	100	187	17	1	3	4	18

Born; 6/9/64, Detroit, Michigan. 5-11, 197. Drafted by Buffalo Sabres (10th choice, 154th overall) in 1983 Entry Draft. Singed as a free agent by Anaheim Mighty Ducks (1/12/94). 1989-90 AHL First All-Star Team.

Dale McTavish — Center

			Regular Season					Playoffs				
Season	Team	League	GP	G	A	PTS	PIM	GP	G	A	PTS	PIM
95-96	Saint John	AHL	4	2	3	5	5	15	5	4	9	15
96-97	Calgary	NHL	9	1	2	3	2	—	—	—	—	—
96-97	Saint John	AHL	53	16	21	37	65	3	0	1	1	0
	AHL	Totals	57	18	24	42	70	18	5	5	10	15

Born; 2/28/72, Eganville, Ontario. 6-1, 200.

Jeff Mead — Right Wing

			Regular Space					Playoffs				
Season	Team	League	GP	G	A	PTS	PIM	GP	G	A	PTS	PIM
94-95	Jacksonville	SUN	36	5	10	15	10	—	—	—	—	—
94-95	West Palm Beach	SUN	19	9	10	19	10	5	1	3	4	0
95-96	Johnstown	ECHL	61	15	25	40	31	—	—	—	—	—
96-97	Pensacola	ECHL	37	6	15	21	2	—	—	—	—	—
96-97	Jacksonville	ECHL	27	5	14	19	4	—	—	—	—	—
	ECHL	Totals	115	26	54	80	37	—	—	—	—	—
	SUN	Totals	55	14	20	34	20	5	1	3	4	0

Born; 2/10/71, Arlington, Massachusetts. 5-10, 165. Member of 1994-95 Sunshine League champion West Palm Beach Blaze.

Spencer Meany — Forward

			Regular Season					Playoffs				
Season	Team	League	GP	G	A	PTS	PIM	GP	G	A	PTS	PIM
94-95	Raleigh	ECHL	61	7	18	25	160	—	—	—	—	—
95-96	Raleigh	ECHL	57	11	5	16	129	4	2	1	3	2
96-97	Raleigh	ECHL	37	11	14	25	77	—	—	—	—	—
	ECHL	Totals	155	29	37	66	366	4	2	1	3	2

Born; 4/8/71, Atikokan, Ontario. 6-0, 212

Glen Mears — Defenseman

			Regular Season					Playoffs				
Season	Team	League	GP	G	A	PTS	PIM	GP	G	A	PTS	PIM
93-94	Greensboro	ECHL	25	1	3	4	29	—	—	—	—	—

Season	Team	League	GP	G	A	PTS	PIM	GP	G	A	PTS	PIM
94-95	Flint	CoHL	57	3	10	13	66	3	0	0	0	2
95-96	Toledo	ECHL	62	0	11	11	147	11	0	0	0	17
96-97	Utah	IHL	2	0	0	0	0	—	—	—	—	—
96-97	Port Huron	CoHL	7	0	1	1	11	—	—	—	—	—
96-97	Bakerfield	WCHL	57	8	41	49	190	4	2	5	17	—
	ECHL	Totals	87	1	14	15	176	11	0	0	0	17
	CoHL	Totals	64	3	11	14	77	3	0	0	0	0

Born; 7/14/72, Anchorage, Alaska. 6-3, 215. Drafted by Calgary Flames (5th choice, 62nd overall) in 1990 Entry Draft. 1996-97 WCHL First Team All-Star.

Pat Meehan — Right Wing

			Regular Season					Playoffs				
Season	Team	League	GP	G	A	PTS	PIM	GP	G	A	PTS	PIM
94-95	Dayton	ECHL	10	1	1	2	0	—	—	—	—	—
94-95	Columbus	ECHL	15	6	4	10	14	1	0	0	0	15
96-97	Central Texas	WPHL	39	10	9	19	26	—	—	—	—	—
96-97	Amarillo	WPHL	21	5	9	14	22	—	—	—	—	—
	WPHL	Totals	60	15	18	33	48	—	—	—	—	—
	ECHL	Totals	25	7	5	12	14	1	0	0	0	15

Born; 7/29/73, Prince George, British Columbia. 6-1, 190.

Darren Meek — Defenseman

			Regular Season					Playoffs				
Season	Team	League	GP	G	A	PTS	PIM	GP	G	A	PTS	PIM
96-97	Richmond	ECHL	4	0	1	1	6	—	—	—	—	—
96-97	Huntington	ECHL	56	8	21	29	42	—	—	—	—	—
	ECHL	Totals	60	8	22	30	48	—	—	—	—	—

Born; 9/25/71, Williams Lake, British Columbia. Last amateur club; Alaska-Anchorage (WCHA).

Kevin Meisner — Defenseman

			Regular Season					Playoffs				
Season	Team	League	GP	G	A	PTS	PIM	GP	G	A	PTS	PIM
94-95	Oklahoma City	CeHL	10	2	8	10	11	—	—	—	—	—
95-96	Richmond	ECHL	3	0	2	2	0	—	—	—	—	—
95-96	Louisville	ECHL	53	11	30	41	34	2	0	0	0	2
96-97	Oklahoma City	CeHL	57	10	36	46	51	4	0	1	1	4
	CeHL	Totals	67	12	44	56	62	4	0	1	1	4
	ECHL	Totals	56	11	32	43	34	2	0	0	0	2

Born; 4/2/70, Shawville, Quebec. 6-2, 215.

Dean Melanson — Defenseman

			Regular Season					Playoffs				
Season	Team	League	GP	G	A	PTS	PIM	GP	G	A	PTS	PIM
92-93	Rochester	AHL	8	0	12	1	6	14	1	6	7	18
93-94	Rochester	AHL	80	1	21	22	138	4	0	1	1	2
94-95	Buffalo	NHL	5	0	0	0	4	—	—	—	—	—
94-95	Rochester	AHL	43	4	7	11	84	—	—	—	—	—
95-96	Rochester	AHL	70	3	13	16	204	14	3	3	6	22
96-97	Quebec	IHL	72	3	21	24	95	7	0	2	2	12
	AHL	Totals	201	8	53	61	432	32	4	10	14	42

Born; 11/19/73, Antigonish, Nova Scotia. 5-11, 203. Drafted by Buffalo Sabres (4th choice, 80th overall) in 1992 Entry Draft. Member of 1995-96 AHL champion Rochester Americans.

Rob Melanson — Defenseman

			Regular Season					Playoffs				
Season	Team	League	GP	G	A	PTS	PIM	GP	G	A	PTS	PIM
91-92	Knoxville	ECHL	49	0	11	11	186	—	—	—	—	—

Season	Team	League	GP	G	A	PTS	PIM	GP	G	A	PTS	PIM
91-92	Muskegon	IHL	7	0	2	2	2	1	0	0	0	0
92-93	Cleveland	IHL	27	0	5	5	123	1	0	0	0	0
92-93	Muskegon	CoHL	23	0	7	7	108	7	0	0	0	11
93-94	Rochester	AHL	13	0	1	1	24	—	—	—	—	—
93-94	Muskegon	CoHL	44	2	8	10	184	3	1	1	2	6
94-95	Worcester	AHL	59	0	3	3	210	—	—	—	—	—
95-96	Cornwall	AHL	10	0	0	0	67	—	—	—	—	—
95-96	Muskegon	CoHL	50	2	13	15	260	5	0	0	0	17
96-97	Muskegon	CoHL	63	3	13	16	217	3	0	1	1	16
	CoHL	Totals	180	7	41	48	769	18	1	2	3	50
	AHL	Totals	82	0	4	4	301	—	—	—	—	—
	IHL	Totals	34	0	7	7	125	2	0	0	0	0

Born; 3/5/71, Antigonish, Nova Scotia. 6-1, 202. Drafted by Pittsburgh Penguins (5th choice, 104th overall) in 1991 Entry Draft.

Stan Melanson — Defenseman

Season	Team	League	GP	G	A	PTS	PIM	GP	G	A	PTS	PIM
95-96	Peoria	IHL	4	0	0	0	17	—	—	—	—	—
95-96	Dayton	ECHL	8	1	1	2	35	—	—	—	—	—
95-96	Muskegon	CoHL	45	7	11	18	143	5	0	1	1	10
96-97	Louisiana	ECHL	56	3	8	11	201	17	0	1	1	36
	ECHL	Totals	64	4	9	13	236	17	0	1	1	36

Born; 6/15/72, Antigonish, Nova Scotia. 6-1, 198.

Marek Melanovsky — Center

Season	Team	League	GP	G	A	PTS	PIM	GP	G	A	PTS	PIM
96-97	St. John's	AHL	2	1	2	3	0	2	0	0	0	0

Born; 3/30/77, Humpolec, Czechoslovakia. 5-9, 176. Drafted by Toronto Maple Leafs (5th choice, 171st overall) in 1984 Entry Draft.

Marty Melnychuk — Defenseman

Season	Team	League	GP	G	A	PTS	PIM	GP	G	A	PTS	PIM
96-97	Wichita	CeHL	54	4	8	12	332	8	0	2	2	51

Born; 2/13/75, New Westminster, British Columbia. 6-3, 205.

Taj Melson — Defenseman

Season	Team	League	GP	G	A	PTS	PIM	GP	G	A	PTS	PIM
96-97	San Diego	WCHL	36	8	16	24	47	8	1	5	6	23

Member of 1996-97 WCHL Champion San Diego Gulls. Last amateur club; St. Cloud State (WCHA).

Kelly Melton — Defenseman

Season	Team	League	GP	G	A	PTS	PIM	GP	G	A	PTS	PIM
96-97	Dayton	CoHL	74	4	11	15	56	—	—	—	—	—

Born; 11/3/71, Excelsior, Minnesota. 6-3, 190.

Carl Menard — Right Wing

Season	Team	League	GP	G	A	PTS	PIM	GP	G	A	PTS	PIM
95-96	Memphis	CeHL	60	40	22	62	60	6	1	2	3	4
96-97	Memphis	CeHL	60	20	28	48	43	18	7	5	12	68
	CeHL	Totals	120	60	50	110	103	24	8	7	15	72

Born; 1/19/72, Ottawa, Ontario. 6-0, 200.

Dan Menard — Center

Season	Team	League	GP	G	A	PTS	PIM	GP	G	A	PTS	PIM
			Regular Season					Playoffs				
95-96	Brantford	CoHL	69	12	8	20	64	12	3	3	6	12
96-97	Brantford	CoHL	34	12	15	27	58	—	—	—	—	—
96-97	Utica	CoHL	33	8	13	21	6	3	0	0	0	4
	CoHL	Totals	136	32	36	68	128	15	3	3	6	16

Born; 12/5/73, Ottawa, Ontario. 6-0, 188.

Terry Menard — Center

Season	Team	League	GP	G	A	PTS	PIM	GP	G	A	PTS	PIM
			Regular Season					Playoffs				
89-90	Milwaukee	IHL	22	6	9	15	14	2	0	0	0	0
89-90	Virginia	ECHL	24	14	18	32	28	—	—	—	—	—
90-91	N/A											
91-92	Thunder Bay	CoHL	58	41	57	98	87	12	3	4	7	16
92-93	Thunder Bay	CoHL	36	10	27	37	38	11	4	6	10	36
93-94	Thunder Bay	CoHL	61	41	60	101	111	9	7	9	16	12
94-95	Thunder Bay	CoHL	71	39	60	99	152	11	6	7	13	16
95-96	Thunder Bay	CoHL	58	31	35	66	154	19	6	8	14	55
96-97	Fort Worth	CeHL	63	50	65	115	138	17	8	15	23	46
	CoHL	Totals	284	162	239	401	542	62	26	34	60	131

Born; 2/3/68, Timmins, Ontario. 5-10, 185. 1994-95 CoHL Top Defensive Forward. 1996-97 CeHL First Team All-Star. Member of 1991-92 CoHL champion Thunder Bay Thunder Hawks. Member of 1993-94 CoHL champion Thunder Bay Senators. Member of 1994-95 CoHL champion Thunder Bay Senators. Member of 1996-97 CeHL Champion Fort Worth Fire.

Rob Mencunas — Center

Season	Team	League	GP	G	A	PTS	PIM	GP	G	A	PTS	PIM
			Regular Season					Playoffs				
95-96	Johnstown	ECHL	10	0	1	1	8	—	—	—	—	—
95-96	Winston-Salem	SHL	31	11	14	25	64	—	—	—	—	—
96-97	Columbus	CeHL	2	0	0	0	2	—	—	—	—	—
96-97	Macon	CeHL	35	8	13	21	93	—	—	—	—	—
	CeHL	Totals	37	8	13	21	95	—	—	—	—	—

Born; 11/6/72, Providence, Rhode Island. 6-4, 215.

Tom Menicci — Defenseman

Season	Team	League	GP	G	A	PTS	PIM	GP	G	A	PTS	PIM
			Regular Season					Playoffs				
94-95	Hampton Roads	ECHL	50	11	12	23	47	4	1	0	1	0
95-96	Hampton Roads	ECHL	1	0	0	0	0	—	—	—	—	—
95-96	South Carolina	ECHL	20	1	2	3	14	—	—	—	—	—
95-96	Huntington	ECHL	42	5	7	12	18	—	—	—	—	—
96-97	Huntington	ECHL	70	15	29	44	52	—	—	—	—	—
	ECHL	Totals	183	32	50	82	131	4	1	0	1	0

Born; 7/23/71, Smithtown, New York. 5-10, 190.

Eric Messier — Defenseman

Season	Team	League	GP	G	A	PTS	PIM	GP	G	A	PTS	PIM
			Regular Season					Playoffs				
95-96	Cornwall	AHL	72	5	9	14	111	8	1	1	2	20
96-97	Hershey	AHL	55	16	26	42	69	9	3	8	11	14
96-97	Colorado	NHL	21	0	0	0	4	6	0	0	0	4
	AHL	Totals	127	21	35	56	180	17	4	9	13	34

Born; 10/29/73, Drummondville, Quebec. 6-2, 200. Member of 1996-97 AHL Champion Hershey Bears.

Joby Messier — Defenseman

Season	Team	League	GP	G	A	PTS	PIM	GP	G	A	PTS	PIM
92-93	Rangers	NHL	11	0	0	0	6	—	—	—	—	—
92-93	Binghamton	AHL	60	5	16	21	63	14	1	1	2	6
93-94	Rangers	NHL	4	0	2	2	0	—	—	—	—	—
93-94	Binghamton	AHL	42	6	14	20	58	—	—	—	—	—
94-95	Binghamton	AHL	25	2	9	11	36	1	0	0	0	0
94-95	Rangers	AHL	10	0	2	2	18	—	—	—	—	—
95-96	DNP	Injured										
96-97	Utah	IHL	44	6	20	26	41	7	0	1	1	10
	NHL	Totals	25	0	4	4	24	—	—	—	—	—
	AHL	Totals	137	13	41	54	175	15	1	1	2	6

Born; 3/2/70, Regian, Saskatchewan. 6-0, 200. Drafted by New York Rangers (7th choice, 118th overall) in 1989 Entry Draft. Signed as a free agent by New York Islanders (9/26/95).

Scott Metcalfe — Left Wing

Season	Team	League	GP	G	A	PTS	PIM	GP	G	A	PTS	PIM
87-88	Buffalo	NHL	1	0	1	1	0	—	—	—	—	—
87-88	Edmonton	NHL	2	0	0	0	0	—	—	—	—	—
87-88	Nova Scotia	AHL	43	9	19	28	87	—	—	—	—	—
87-88	Rochester	AHL	22	2	13	15	56	7	1	3	4	24
88-89	Buffalo	NHL	9	1	1	2	13	—	—	—	—	—
88-89	Rochester	AHL	60	20	31	51	241	—	—	—	—	—
89-90	Buffalo	NHL	7	0	0	0	5	—	—	—	—	—
89-90	Rochester	AHL	43	12	17	29	93	2	0	1	1	0
90-91	Rochester	AHL	69	17	22	39	177	14	4	1	5	27
91-92	N/A											
92-93	N/A											
93-94	Rochester	AHL	16	5	7	12	16	4	1	0	1	31
93-94	Knoxville	ECHL	56	25	56	81	136	3	0	1	1	20
94-95	Rochester	AHL	63	19	36	55	216	5	1	1	2	4
95-96	Rochester	AHL	71	21	24	45	228	19	6	8	14	23
96-97	Rochester	AHL	80	32	38	70	205	10	1	3	4	18
	NHL	Totals	19	1	2	3	18	—	—	—	—	—
	AHL	Totals	467	137	207	344	1319	61	14	17	31	127

Born; 1/6/67, Toronto, Ontario. 6-0, 200. Drafted by Edmonton Oilers (1st choice, 20th overall) in 1985 Entry Draft. Traded to Buffalo Sabres by Edmonton for Steve Dykstra (2/88). Member of 1995-96 AHL champion Rochester Americans.

Glen Metropolit — Center

Season	Team	League	GP	G	A	PTS	PIM	GP	G	A	PTS	PIM
95-96	Atlanta	IHL	1	0	0	0	0	—	—	—	—	—
95-96	Nashville	ECHL	58	30	31	61	62	5	3	8	11	2
96-97	Quebec	IHL	22	5	4	9	14	5	0	0	0	2
96-97	Pensacola	ECHL	54	35	47	82	45	12	9	16	25	28
	IHL	Totals	23	5	4	9	14	5	0	0	0	2
	ECHL	Totals	112	65	78	143	107	17	12	24	36	30

Born; 6/25/74, Toronto, Ontario. 6-0, 185.

Andrei Mezin — Goaltender

Season	Team	League	GP	MIN	GAVG	W	L	T	SO	GP	MIN	GAVG	W	L	SO
95-96	Fort Wayne	IHL	1	35	1.72	0	0	0	0	—	—	—	—	—	—
95-96	Flint	CoHL	40	2270	3.49	27	9	2	1	7	410	2.64	5	1	1

Season	Team	League	GP											
96-97	Las Vegas	IHL	10	490	4.04	4	5	0	0	—	—	—	—	—	—
96-97	Flint	CoHL	25	1417	*2.46	19	4	1	2	4	175	4.45	0	2	0
96-97	Rochester	AHL	7	386	4.82	3	3	1	0	—	—	—	—	—	—
	IHL	Totals	11	525	3.89	4	5	0	0	—	—	—	—	—	—
	CoHL	Totals	65	3687	3.09	46	13	3	3	11	585	3.18	5	3	1

Born; 7/8/74, Chelyabinsk, Russia. 6-0, 170. Member of 1995-96 Colonial Cup Champion Flint Generals

Phil Miaskowski — Center

			Regular Season					Playoffs				
Season	Team	League	GP	G	A	PTS	PIM	GP	G	A	PTS	PIM
95-96	Columbus	ECHL	2	0	0	0	6	—	—	—	—	—
95-96	Brantford	CoHL	71	31	25	56	104	12	9	6	15	14
96-97	Brantford	CoHL	61	34	33	67	77	10	8	3	11	8
	CoHL	Totals	132	65	58	123	181	22	17	9	26	22

Born; 4/16/74, Toronto, Ontario. 6-3, 223.

Chad Michalchuk — Left Wing

			Regular Season					Playoffs				
Season	Team	League	GP	G	A	PTS	PIM	GP	G	A	PTS	PIM
96-97	Johnstown	ECHL	4	0	0	0	30	—	—	—	—	—
96-97	Madison	CoHL	36	5	9	14	98	—	—	—	—	—
96-97	Brantford	CoHL	7	1	0	1	23	10	0	2	2	16
	CoHL	Totals	43	6	9	15	121	10	0	2	2	16

Born; 7/10/73, Calgary, Alberta. 5-11, 185.

Dave Michayluk — Left Wing

			Regular Season					Playoffs				
Season	Team	League	GP	G	A	PTS	PIM	GP	G	A	PTS	PIM
81-82	Philadelphia	NHL	1	0	0	0	0	—	—	—	—	—
82-83	Philadelphia	NHL	13	2	6	8	8	—	—	—	—	—
82-83	Maine	AHL	69	32	40	72	16	8	0	2	2	0
83-84	Springfield	AHL	79	18	44	62	37	4	0	0	0	2
84-85	Hershey	AHL	3	0	2	2	2	—	—	—	—	—
84-85	Kalamazoo	IHL	82	*66	33	99	49	11	7	7	14	0
85-86	Nova Scotia	AHL	3	0	1	1	0	—	—	—	—	—
85-86	Muskegon	IHL	77	52	52	104	73	14	6	9	15	12
86-87	Muskegon	IHL	82	47	53	100	69	15	2	14	16	8
87-88	Muskegon	IHL	81	*56	81	137	46	6	2	0	2	18
88-89	Muskegon	IHL	80	50	72	*122	84	13	*9	12	*21	24
89-90	Muskegon	IHL	79	*51	51	102	80	15	8	*14	*22	10
90-91	Muskegon	IHL	83	40	62	102	116	5	2	2	4	4
91-92	Pittsburgh	NHL	—	—	—	—	—	7	1	1	2	0
91-92	Muskegon	IHL	82	39	63	102	154	13	9	8	17	4
92-93	Cleveland	IHL	82	47	65	112	104	4	1	2	3	4
93-94	Cleveland	IHL	81	48	51	99	92	—	—	—	—	—
94-95	Cleveland	IHL	60	19	17	36	22	1	0	0	0	0
95-96	Cleveland	IHL	53	22	21	43	27	3	1	0	1	4
96-97	Cleveland	IHL	46	10	15	25	18	—	—	—	—	—
	NHL	Totals	14	2	6	8	8	7	1	1	2	0
	IHL	Totals	968	547	636	1183	934	100	47	66	113	88
	AHL	Totals	154	50	87	137	55	12	0	2	2	2

Born; 5/18/62, Wakaw, Saskatchewan. 5-10, 185. Drafted by Philadelphia Flyers 95th choice, 65th overall) in 1981 Entry Draft. Signed as a free agent by Pittsburgh Penguins (5/24/89). 1986-87 IHL First Team All-Star. 1987-88 IHL First Team All-Star. 1988-89 IHL First Team All-Star. 1989-90 IHL First Team All-Star. 1984-85 Second Team All-Star. 1991-92 IHL Second Team All-Star. 1992-93 IHL Second Team All-Star. 1988-89 IHL MVP. 1988-89 IHL Playoff MVP. Member of 1991-92 Stanley Cup champion Pittsburgh Penguins. Member of 1985-86 IHL champion Muskegon Lumberjacks. Member of 1988-89 IHL champion Muskegon Lumberjacks.

Max Middendorf — Center

Regular Season / Playoffs

Season	Team	League	GP	G	A	PTS	PIM	GP	G	A	PTS	PIM
86-87	Quebec	NHL	6	1	4	5	4	—	—	—	—	—
87-88	Quebec	NHL	1	0	0	0	0	—	—	—	—	—
87-88	Fredericton	AHL	38	11	13	24	57	12	4	4	8	18
88-89	Halifax	AHL	72	41	39	80	85	4	1	2	3	6
89-90	Quebec	NHL	3	0	0	0	0	—	—	—	—	—
89-90	Halifax	AHL	48	20	17	37	60	—	—	—	—	—
90-91	Edmonton	NHL	3	1	0	1	2	—	—	—	—	—
90-91	Fort Wayne	IHL	15	9	11	20	12	—	—	—	—	—
90-91	Cape Breton	AHL	44	14	21	35	82	4	0	1	1	6
91-92	Cape Breton	AHL	51	20	19	39	108	—	—	—	—	—
91-92	Adirondack	AHL	6	3	5	8	12	5	0	1	1	16
92-93	Fort Wayne	IHL	24	9	13	22	8	—	—	—	—	—
92-93	San Diego	IHL	30	15	11	26	25	8	1	2	3	8
93-94	Fort Wayne	IHL	36	16	20	36	45	9	1	2	3	24
94-95	Fort Wayne	IHL	15	1	4	5	34	—	—	—	—	—
95-96	Winston-Salem	SHL	4	1	5	6	27	—	—	—	—	—
95-96	Bakersfield	WCHL	23	4	12	16	80	—	—	—	—	—
96-97	Huntsville	CeHL	42	14	32	46	79	—	—	—	—	—
NHL	Totals		13	2	4	6	6	—	—	—	—	—
AHL	Totals		259	109	114	223	404	25	5	8	13	46
IHL	Totals		120	50	59	109	122	17	2	4	6	32

Born; 8/18/67, Syracuse, New York. 6-4, 210. Drafted by Quebec Nordiques (3rd choice, 57th overall) in 1985 Entry Draft. Traded to Edmonton Oilers by Quebec for ninth round pick (Brent Brekke) in 1991 Entry Draft (10/10/90). Traded to Detroit Red WIngs by Edmonton for Bill McDougall (2/22/92). Traded to San Diego Gulls by Fort Wayne Komets (1/4/93) to complete deal involving Peter Hankinson (12/17/92). Member of 1991-92 AHL champion Adirondack Red Wings.

Sonny Mignacca — Goaltender

Regular Season / Playoffs

Season	Team	League	GP	W	L	T	MIN	SO	GAVG	GP	W	L	MIN	SO	GAVG
94-95	Syracuse	AHL	19	4	11	2	1097	0	4.65	—	—	—	—	—	—
95-96	Syracuse	AHL	8	2	5	0	377	0	4.14	—	—	—	—	—	—
96-97	Tallahasee	ECHL	38	19	12	5	2027	4	3.23	3	0	2	132	0	3.64
AHL	Totals		27	6	16	2	1474	0	4.52	—	—	—	—	—	—

Born; 1/4/74, Winnipeg, Manitoba. 5-8, 178. Drafted by Vancouver Canucks (10th choice, 213rd overall) in 1992 Entry Draft.

Pat Mikesch — Center

Regular Season / Playoffs

Season	Team	League	GP	G	A	PTS	PIM	GP	G	A	PTS	PIM
95-96	Louisville	ECHL	4	5	0	5	0	3	1	1	2	4
96-97	Kentucky	AHL	77	17	28	45	57	4	1	1	2	2

Born; 4/11/75, Hancock, Michigan. 6-0, 175. Drafted by Detroit Red Wings (8th choice, 231st overall) in 1994 Entry Draft.

Oleg Mikulchik — Defenseman

Regular Season / Playoffs

Season	Team	League	GP	G	A	PTS	PIM	GP	G	A	PTS	PIM
91-92	New Haven	AHL	30	3	3	6	63	4	1	3	4	6
92-93	Moncton	AHL	75	6	20	26	159	5	0	0	0	4
93-94	Winnipeg	NHL	4	0	1	1	17	—	—	—	—	—
93-94	Moncton	AHL	67	9	38	47	121	21	2	10	12	18
94-95	Winnipeg	NHL	25	0	2	2	12	—	—	—	—	—
94-95	Springfield	AHL	50	5	16	21	59	—	—	—	—	—
95-96	Anaheim	NHL	8	0	0	0	4	—	—	—	—	—
95-96	Baltimore	AHL	19	1	7	8	46	12	2	3	5	22
96-97	Long Beach	IHL	16	0	5	5	29	—	—	—	—	—

96-97	Fort Wayne	IHL	51	5	13	18	75	—	—	—	—	—
	NHL	Totals	37	0	3	3	33	—	—	—	—	—
	AHL	Totals	241	23	84	107	448	42	5	16	21	50
	IHL	Totals	67	5	18	23	104	—	—	—	—	—

Born; 6/27/64, Minsk, Russai. 6-2, 200. Signed as a free agent by Winnipeg Jets (7/26/93). Signed as a free agent by Anaheim Mighty Ducks (8/8/95).

Craig Millar — Defenseman

			Regular Season					Playoffs				
Season	Team	League	GP	G	A	PTS	PIM	GP	G	A	PTS	PIM
96-97	Edmonton	NHL	1	0	0	0	2	—	—	—	—	—
96-97	Rochester	AHL	64	7	18	25	65	—	—	—	—	—
96-97	Hamilton	AHL	10	1	3	4	10	22	4	4	8	21
	AHL	Totals	74	8	21	29	75	22	4	4	8	21

Born; 7/12/76, Winnipeg, Manitoba. 6-2, 200. Drafted by Buffalo Sabres (10th choice, 225th overall) in 1994 Entry Draft. Member of 1996-97 AHL All-Rookie Team. Traded to Edmonton Oilers by Buffalo with Barrie Moore for Miroslav Satan (3/18/97).

Kyle Millar — Left Wing

			Regular Season					Playoffs				
Season	Team	League	GP	G	A	PTS	PIM	GP	G	A	PTS	PIM
95-96	Quad City	CoHL	3	0	1	1	0	4	0	2	2	2
96-97	Saginaw	CoHL	32	19	24	43	17	—	—	—	—	—
96-97	Roanoke	ECHL	11	6	5	11	7	—	—	—	—	—
	CoHL	Totals	35	19	25	44	17	4	0	2	2	2

Born; 12/10/73, Winnipeg, Manitoba. 6-2, 195.

Andrew Miller — Center

			Regular Season					Playoffs				
Season	Team	League	GP	G	A	PTS	PIM	GP	G	A	PTS	PIM
95-96	Louisville	ECHL	61	25	34	59	54	3	1	1	2	4
96-97	Memphis	CeHL	54	27	35	62	47	18	5	*18	23	12

Born; 1/20/71, Toronto, Ontario. 6-2, 195. Drafted by Detroit Red Wings (10th choice, 252nd overall) in 1991 Entry Draft.

Brad Miller — Defenseman

			Regular Season					Playoffs				
Season	Team	League	GP	G	A	PTS	PIM	GP	G	A	PTS	PIM
87-88	Rochester	AHL	3	0	0	0	4	2	0	0	0	2
88-89	Buffalo	NHL	7	0	0	0	6	—	—	—	—	—
88-89	Rochester	AHL	3	0	0	0	4	—	—	—	—	—
89-90	Rochester	NHL	1	0	0	0	0	—	—	—	—	—
89-90	Rochester	AHL	60	2	10	12	273	8	1	0	1	52
90-91	Buffalo	NHL	13	0	0	0	67	—	—	—	—	—
90-91	Rochester	AHL	49	0	9	9	248	12	0	4	4	67
91-92	Buffalo	NHL	42	1	4	5	192	—	—	—	—	—
91-92	Rochester	AHL	27	0	4	4	113	11	0	0	0	61
92-93	Ottawa	NHL	11	0	0	0	42	—	—	—	—	—
92-93	New Haven	AHL	41	1	9	10	138	—	—	—	—	—
92-93	St. John's	AHL	20	0	3	3	61	8	0	2	2	10
93-94	Calgary	NHL	8	0	1	1	14	—	—	—	—	—
93-94	Saint John	AHL	36	3	12	15	174	6	1	0	1	21
94-95	Minnesota	IHL	55	1	13	14	181	3	0	0	0	12
95-96	Utah	IHL	1	0	0	0	0	—	—	—	—	—
95-96	Minnesota	IHL	33	0	5	5	170	—	—	—	—	—
95-96	Atlanta	IHL	5	0	0	0	8	—	—	—	—	—
96-97	Quebec	IHL	57	1	7	8	132	4	0	0	0	2
	NHL	Totals	82	1	5	6	321	—	—	—	—	—
	AHL	Totals	239	6	47	53	1015	45	2	6	8	211
	IHL	Totals	151	2	25	27	491	7	0	0	0	14

Born; 7/23/69, Edmonton, Alberta. 6-4, 226. Drafted by Buffalo Sabres (2nd choice, 22nd overall) in 1987 Entry Draft. Selected by Ottawa Senators in NHL expansion draft (6/18/92). Traded to Toronto Maple Leafs by Ottawa for 9th round choice (Pavol Demitra) in 1993 Entry Draft (2/25/93). Traded to Calgary Flames by Toronto with Jeff Perry for Todd Gillingham and Paul Holden (9/3/93).

Colin Miller — Center

			Regular Season					Playoffs				
Season	Team	League	GP	G	A	PTS	PIM	GP	G	A	PTS	PIM
92-93	Atlanta	IHL	76	20	39	59	52	9	2	4	6	22
93-94	Atlanta	IHL	80	13	32	45	48	3	2	3	5	0
94-95	Atlanta	IHL	36	5	14	19	29	—	—	—	—	—
94-95	Las Vegas	IHL	7	0	1	1	2	—	—	—	—	—
94-95	Indianapolis	IHL	13	5	6	11	10	—	—	—	—	—
94-95	Knoxville	ECHL	5	1	2	3	0	—	—	—	—	—
95-96	Dayton	ECHL	69	24	50	74	103	3	0	2	2	8
96-97	Michigan	IHL	1	0	0	0	0	—	—	—	—	—
96-97	Dayton	ECHL	68	20	58	78	60	4	2	2	4	18
	IHL	Totals	213	43	92	135	141	12	4	7	11	22
	ECHL	Totals	142	45	110	155	163	7	2	4	6	26

Born; 8/21/71, Grimsby, Ontario. 6-0, 200. Member of 1993-94 IHL champion Atlanta Knights.

Gary Miller — Defenseman

			Regular Season					Playoffs				
Season	Team	League	GP	G	A	PTS	PIM	GP	G	A	PTS	PIM
92-93	Chatham	CoHL	36	1	8	9	36	—	—	—	—	—
92-93	St. Thomas	CoHL	16	3	8	11	45	15	3	4	7	46
93-94	St. Thomas	CoHL	62	7	30	37	100	3	1	3	4	15
94-95	London	CoHL	4	0	0	0	0	—	—	—	—	—
94-95	Utica	CoHL	63	5	25	30	128	4	0	1	1	32
95-96	St. John's	AHL	1	0	0	0	0	—	—	—	—	—
95-96	Utica	CoHL	74	8	22	30	123	—	—	—	—	—
96-97	Utica	CoHL	44	5	17	22	69	—	—	—	—	—
96-97	Port Huron	CoHL	21	5	7	12	21	5	0	1	1	6
	CoHL	Totals	320	34	117	151	522	27	4	9	13	99

Born; 3/19/72, 6-2, 207. Drafted by Toronto Maple Leafs (11,th choice, 201st overall) in 1991 Entry Draft.

Jason Miller — Center

			Regular Season					Playoffs				
Season	Team	League	GP	G	A	PTS	PIM	GP	G	A	PTS	PIM
90-91	New Jersey	NHL	1	0	0	0	0	—	—	—	—	—
91-92	New Jersey	NHL	3	0	0	0	0	—	—	—	—	—
91-92	Utica	AHL	71	23	32	55	31	4	1	3	4	0
92-93	New Jersey	NHL	2	0	0	0	0	—	—	—	—	—
92-93	Utica	AHL	72	28	42	70	43	5	4	4	8	2
93-94	Albany	AHL	77	22	53	75	65	5	1	1	2	4
94-95	Adirondack	AHL	77	32	33	65	39	4	1	0	1	0
95-96	Peoria	IHL	39	16	22	38	6	11	1	2	3	4
96-97	San Antonio	IHL	76	26	43	69	43	9	1	4	5	6
	NHL	Totals	6	0	0	0	0	—	—	—	—	—
	AHL	Totals	297	105	160	265	178	18	7	8	15	6
	IHL	Totals	115	42	65	107	49	20	2	6	8	10

Born; 3/1/71, Edmonton, Alberta. 6-1, 190. Drafted by New Jersey Devils (2nd choice, 18th overall) in 1989 Entry Draft. Signed as a free agent by Detroit Red Wings (7/28/94).

Kip Miller — Center

			Regular Season					Playoffs				
Season	Team	League	GP	G	A	PTS	PIM	GP	G	A	PTS	PIM
90-91	Quebec	NHL	13	4	3	7	7	—	—	—	—	—
90-91	Halifax	AHL	66	36	33	69	40	—	—	—	—	—

Season	Team	League	GP	G	A	PTS	PIM	GP	G	A	PTS	PIM
91-92	Quebec	NHL	36	5	10	15	12	—	—	—	—	—
91-92	Minnesota	NHL	3	1	2	3	2	—	—	—	—	—
91-92	Halifax	AHL	24	9	17	26	8	—	—	—	—	—
91-92	Kalamazoo	IHL	6	1	8	9	4	12	3	9	12	12
92-93	Kalamazoo	IHL	61	17	39	56	59	—	—	—	—	—
93-94	San Jose	NHL	11	2	2	4	6	—	—	—	—	—
93-94	Kansas City	IHL	71	38	54	92	51	—	—	—	—	—
94-95	Islanders	NHL	8	0	1	1	0	—	—	—	—	—
94-95	Denver	IHL	71	46	60	106	54	17	*15	14	29	8
95-96	Chicago	NHL	10	1	4	5	2	—	—	—	—	—
95-96	Indianapolis	IHL	73	32	59	91	46	5	2	6	8	2
96-97	Chicago	IHL	43	11	41	52	32	—	—	—	—	—
96-97	Indianapolis	IHL	37	17	24	41	18	4	2	2	4	2
	NHL	Totals	81	13	22	35	29	—	—	—	—	—
	IHL	Totals	362	162	285	447	264	38	22	31	53	24
	AHL	Totals	90	45	50	95	48	—	—	—	—	—

Born; 6/11/69, Lansing, Michigan. 5-11, 190. Drafted by Quebec Nordiques (4th choice, 72nd overall) in 1987 Entry Draft. Traded to Minnesota North Stars by Quebec for Steve Maltais (3/8/92). Signed as a free agent by San Jose Sharks (8/10/93). Signed as a free agent by New York Islanders (7/7/94). Signed as a free agent by Chicago Blackhawks (8/7/95). Member of 1994-95 IHL champion Denver Grizzlies.

Kris Miller — Defenseman

			Regular Season					Playoffs				
Season	Team	League	GP	G	A	PTS	PIM	GP	G	A	PTS	PIM
91-92	Raleigh	ECHL	42	12	27	39	78	4	2	3	5	8
91-92	Utica	AHL	1	0	0	0	0	—	—	—	—	—
91-92	Phoenix	IHL	16	1	2	3	17	—	—	—	—	—
92-93	Salt Lake City	IHL	45	4	21	25	45	—	—	—	—	—
92-93	Raleigh	ECHL	30	8	24	32	62	—	—	—	—	—
93-94	Saint John	AHL	58	2	17	19	38	—	—	—	—	—
94-95	Minnesota	IHL	71	4	16	20	61	3	1	0	1	0
95-96	Minnesota	IHL	70	5	10	15	84	—	—	—	—	—
96-97	Orlando	IHL	41	2	3	5	57	10	1	1	2	10
96-97	Raleigh	ECHL	30	3	23	26	61	—	—	—	—	—
	IHL	Totals	243	16	52	68	264	13	2	1	3	10
	AHL	Totals	59	2	17	19	38	—	—	—	—	—
	ECHL	Totals	102	23	74	97	201	4	2	3	5	8

Born; 3/30/69, Bemidji, Minnesota. 6-0, 200. Drafted by Montreal Canadiens (6th choice, 80th overall) in 1987 Entry Draft.

Kurt Miller — Left Wing

			Regular Season					Playoffs				
Season	Team	League	GP	G	A	PTS	PIM	GP	G	A	PTS	PIM
94-95	Adirondack	AHL	78	22	18	40	45	4	1	1	2	2
95-96	Adirondack	AHL	73	26	13	39	46	3	0	0	0	0
95-96	Toledo	ECHL	2	3	3	6	0	—	—	—	—	—
96-97	Hershey	AHL	68	17	25	42	48	15	2	1	3	2
	AHL	Totals	219	65	56	121	139	22	3	2	5	4

Born; 6/1/70, Bemidji, Minnesota. 5-11, 190. Drafted by St. Louis Blues (4th choice, 117th overall) in 1990 Entry Draft. Signed as a free agent by the Detroit Red Wings (8/10/94).

Rod Miller — Defenseman

			Regular Season					Playoffs				
Season	Team	League	GP	G	A	PTS	PIM	GP	G	A	PTS	PIM
94-95	Denver	IHL	47	2	5	7	65	12	1	3	4	11
95-96	Utah	IHL	49	2	1	3	61	—	—	—	—	—
95-96	Atlanta	IHL	21	1	1	2	28	3	0	0	0	2
96-97	Utah	IHL	79	0	12	12	111	6	0	1	1	4
	IHL	Totals	196	5	19	24	265	21	1	4	5	17

Born; 4/2/70, Prince Albert, Saskatchewan. 6-1, 205. Member of 1994-95 IHL champion Denver Grizzlies.

Rob Milliken — Defenseman

Season	Team	League	GP	G	A	PTS	PIM	GP	G	A	PTS	PIM
95-96	Bakersfield	WCHL	28	7	15	22	54	—	—	—	—	—
96-97	Bakersfield	WCHL	64	9	21	30	221	3	0	0	0	12
	WCHL	Totals	92	16	36	52	275	3	0	0	0	12

Born; 10/27/74, Victoria, British Columbia. 6-1, 215.

Craig Mills — Right Wing

Season	Team	League	GP	G	A	PTS	PIM	GP	G	A	PTS	PIM
95-96	Winnipeg	NHL	4	0	2	2	0	1	0	0	0	0
95-96	Springfield	AHL	—	—	—	—	—	2	0	0	0	0
96-97	Indianapolis	IHL	80	12	7	19	199	4	0	0	0	4

Born; 8/27/76, Toronto, Ontario. 5-11, 174. Drafted by Winnipeg Jets (5th choice, 108th overall) in 1994 Entry Draft. Traded to Chicago Blackhawks with Alexei Zhamnov, and Phoenix's first round choice (Ty Jones) for Jeremy Roenick (8/16/96).

Mike Minard — Goaltender

Season	Team	League	GP	W	L	T	MIN	SO	GAVG	GP	W	L	MIN	SO	GAVG
96-97	Hamilton	AHL	3	1	1	0	100	0	4.20	—	—	—	—	—	—
96-97	Wheeling	ECHL	23	3	7	1	899	0	4.60	3	0	2	148	0	6.47

Born; 11/1/76, Owen Sound, Ontario. 6-3, 205. Drafted by Edmonton Oilers (4th choice, 83rd overall) in 1995 Entry Draft.

Darcy Mitani — Center

Season	Team	League	GP	G	A	PTS	PIM	GP	G	A	PTS	PIM
95-96	Charlotte	ECHL	3	0	1	1	2	—	—	—	—	—
96-97	Charlotte	ECHL	44	7	15	22	29	—	—	—	—	—
96-97	Wheeling	ECHL	16	8	10	18	2	3	0	0	0	6
	ECHL	Totals	63	15	26	41	33	3	0	0	0	6

Born; 10/17/73, Dryden, Ontario. 5-9, 185.

Jeff Mitchell — Right Wing

Season	Team	League	GP	G	A	PTS	PIM	GP	G	A	PTS	PIM
95-96	Michigan	IHL	50	5	4	9	119	—	—	—	—	—
96-97	Michigan	IHL	24	0	3	3	40	—	—	—	—	—
96-97	Philadelphia	AHL	31	7	5	12	103	10	1	1	2	20
	IHL	Totals	74	5	7	12	159	—	—	—	—	—

Born; 5/16/75, Wayne, Michigan. 6-1, 190. Drafted by Los Angeles Kings (2nd choice, 68th overall) in 1993 Entry Draft. Rights traded to Dallas Stars by Los Angeles for Vancouver's fifth round choice (previously acquired by Dallas-Los Angeles selected Jason Morgan) in 1995 Entry Draft (6/7/95).

Roy Mitchell — Defenseman

Season	Team	League	GP	G	A	PTS	PIM	GP	G	A	PTS	PIM
89-90	Sherbrooke	AHL	77	5	12	17	98	12	0	2	2	31
90-91	Fredericton	AHL	71	2	15	17	137	9	0	1	1	11
91-92	Kalamazoo	IHL	69	3	26	29	102	11	1	4	5	18
92-93	Minnesota	NHL	3	0	0	0	0	—	—	—	—	—
92-93	Kalamazoo	IHL	79	7	25	32	119	—	—	—	—	—
93-94	Binghamton	AHL	11	1	3	4	18	—	—	—	—	—
93-94	Albany	AHL	42	3	12	15	43	3	0	0	0	0
93-94	Kalamazoo	IHL	13	0	4	4	21	—	—	—	—	—
94-95	Worcester	AHL	80	5	25	30	97	—	—	—	—	—

Season	Team	League	GP	G	A	PTS	PIM	GP	G	A	PTS	PIM
95-96	Worcester	AHL	52	1	3	4	62	4	0	0	0	2
96-97	Central Texas	WPHL	20	1	8	9	12	11	2	7	9	10
	AHL	Totals	333	17	70	87	455	28	0	3	3	44
	IHL	Totals	161	10	55	65	242	11	1	4	5	18

Born; 3/14/69, Edmonton, Alberta. 6-2, 200. Drafted by Montreal Canadiens (9th choice, 188th overall) in 1989 Entry Draft. Signed as a free agent by Minnesota North Stars (7/25/91).

Savo Mitrovic — Center

Season	Team	League	GP	G	A	PTS	PIM	GP	G	A	PTS	PIM
92-93	Detroit	CoHL	46	13	36	49	37	6	3	2	5	24
93-94	Huntsville	ECHL	6	1	3	4	14	—	—	—	—	—
93-94	Greensboro	ECHL	29	3	14	17	12	—	—	—	—	—
93-94	Detroit	CoHL	12	8	10	18	8	3	1	2	3	4
94-95	Detroit	CoHL	68	23	45	68	38	12	5	5	10	21
95-96	Detroit	CoHL	29	5	16	21	20	8	3	8	11	19
96-97	Port Huron	CoHL	38	5	37	42	45	3	0	0	0	0
	CoHL	Totals	193	54	144	198	148	32	12	17	29	68

Born; 2/4/69, Etibicoke, Ontario. 5-11, 200.

Joe Mittelsteadt — Defenseman

Season	Team	League	GP	G	A	PTS	PIM	GP	G	A	PTS	PIM
91-92	Columbus	ECHL	59	7	15	22	296	—	—	—	—	—
92-93	Dallas	CeHL	39	6	21	27	128	7	0	4	4	24
93-94	Dayton	ECHL	2	0	0	0	12	—	—	—	—	—
93-94	Dallas	CeHL	62	10	23	33	220	7	1	3	4	49
94-95	Cape Breton	AHL	37	2	3	5	74	—	—	—	—	—
94-95	Dallas	CeHL	8	1	1	2	29	—	—	—	—	—
95-96	Cape Breton	AHL	19	0	2	2	69	—	—	—	—	—
95-96	Reno	WCHL	31	2	15	17	88	3	0	0	0	9
96-97	Louisiana	ECHL	69	3	20	23	292	17	0	2	2	35
	AHL	Totals	56	2	5	7	143	—	—	—	—	—
	ECHL	Totals	130	10	35	45	600	17	0	2	2	35
	CeHL	Totals	109	17	45	62	377	14	1	7	8	73

Born; 5/23/70, Scarborough, Ontario. 6-1, 220.

Craig Mittelholt — Left Wing

Season	Team	League	GP	G	A	PTS	PIM	GP	G	A	PTS	PIM
94-95	Huntington	ECHL	10	1	1	2	2	—	—	—	—	—
94-95	Jacksonville	SUN	22	9	19	28	6	—	—	—	—	—
95-96	Jacksonville	ECHL	2	0	1	1	2	—	—	—	—	—
95-96	Birmingham	ECHL	2	0	0	0	2	—	—	—	—	—
95-96	Jacksonville	SHL	58	*60	44	104	26	—	—	—	—	—
96-97	Anchorage	WCHL	33	8	8	16	16	—	—	—	—	—
96-97	Thunder Bay	CoHL	14	5	11	16	4	11	4	5	9	4
	ECHL	Totals	14	1	2	3	6	—	—	—	—	—
	SHL	Totals	80	69	63	132	32	—	—	—	—	—

Born; 7/24/74, Ottawa, Ontario. 6-2, 190.

Paul Mitton — Left Wing

Season	Team	League	GP	G	A	PTS	PIM	GP	G	A	PTS	PIM
93-94	Brantford	CoHL	47	6	21	27	93	7	1	0	1	5
94-95	Brantford	CoHL	68	14	12	26	137	—	—	—	—	—
95-96	Brantford	CoHL	67	8	22	30	193	12	1	5	6	28
96-97	Brantford	CoHL	10	3	1	4	22	9	3	1	4	20

| | CoHL | Totals | 192 | 31 | 56 | 87 | 445 | 28 | 5 | 6 | 11 | 53 |

Born; 4/6/70, Hamilton, Ontario. 6-1, 210.

Tim Modreski — Defenseman

Season	Team	League	GP	G	A	PTS	PIM	GP	G	A	PTS	PIM
95-96	Flint	CoHL	18	0	2	2	12	—	—	—	—	—
95-96	Birmingham	ECHL	20	1	6	7	12	—	—	—	—	—
96-97	Saginaw	CoHL	53	0	4	4	44	—	—	—	—	—
96-97	Flint	CoHL	6	0	0	0	0	—	—	—	—	—
	CoHL	Totals	77	0	6	6	66	—	—	—	—	—

Born; 7/21/71, Flint, Michigan. 5-10, 190.

Jaroslav Modry — Defenseman

Season	Team	League	GP	G	A	PTS	PIM	GP	G	A	PTS	PIM
92-93	Utica	AHL	80	7	35	42	62	5	0	2	2	2
93-94	New Jersey	NHL	41	2	15	17	18	—	—	—	—	—
93-94	Albany	AHL	19	1	5	6	25	—	—	—	—	—
94-95	New Jersey	NHL	11	0	0	0	0	—	—	—	—	—
94-95	Albany	AHL	18	5	6	11	14	14	3	3	6	4
95-96	Ottawa	NHL	64	4	14	18	38	—	—	—	—	—
95-96	Los Angeles	NHL	9	0	3	3	6	—	—	—	—	—
96-97	Los Angeles	NHL	30	3	3	6	25	—	—	—	—	—
96-97	Phoenix	IHL	23	3	12	15	17	—	—	—	—	—
96-97	Utah	IHL	11	1	4	5	20	7	0	1	1	6
	NHL	Totals	155	9	35	44	87	—	—	—	—	—
	AHL	Totals	117	13	46	59	101	19	3	5	8	6
	IHL	Totals	34	4	16	20	37	7	0	1	1	6

Born;2/27/71, Ceske-Budejovice, Czechoslovakia. 6-2, 195. Drafted by New Jersey Devils (11th choice, 179th overall) in1990 Entry Draft. Traded to Ottawa Senators for Ottawa's fourth round choice (Alyn McCauley) in 1995 Entry Draft. Traded to Los Angeles by Ottawa with Ottawa's eighth round choice (Stephen Valiquette) in 1996 Entry Draft for Kevin Brown (3/20/96)

Klemen Mohorcic — Goaltender

Season	Team	League	GP	W	L	T	MIN	SO	GAVG	GP	W	L	MIN	SO	GAVG
96-97	Louisville	ECHL	10	0	6	2	468	0	4.74	—	—	—	—	—	—
96-97	Johnstown	ECHL	15	5	5	1	736	0	5.13	—	—	—	—	—	—
	ECHL	Totals	25	5	11	3	1204	0	4.98	—	—	—	—	—	—

Born; 5/25/75, Bled, Slovenia. 5-11, 175.

Michel Mongeau — Center

Season	Team	League	GP	G	A	PTS	PIM	GP	G	A	PTS	PIM
86-87	Saginaw	IHL	76	42	53	95	34	10	3	6	9	6
88-89	Flint	IHL	82	41	76	117	57	—	—	—	—	—
89-90	St. Louis	NHL	7	1	5	6	2	2	0	1	1	0
89-90	Peoria	IHL	73	39	*78	*117	53	5	3	4	7	6
90-91	St. Louis	NHL	7	1	1	2	0	—	—	—	—	—
90-91	Peoria	IHL	73	41	65	106	114	19	10	*16	26	32
91-92	St. Louis	NHL	36	3	12	15	6	—	—	—	—	—
91-92	Peoria	IHL	32	21	34	55	77	10	5	14	19	8
92-93	Tampa Bay	NHL	4	1	1	2	2	—	—	—	—	—
92-93	Milwaukee	IHL	45	24	41	65	69	4	1	4	5	4
92-93	Halifax	AHL	22	13	18	31	10	—	—	—	—	—
93-94	Cornwall	AHL	7	3	11	14	4	—	—	—	—	—

Season	Team	League	GP	G	A	PTS	PIM	GP	G	A	PTS	PIM
93-94	Peoria	IHL	52	29	36	65	50	—	—	—	—	—
94-95	Peoria	IHL	74	30	52	82	72	—	—	—	—	—
95-96	Peoria	IHL	24	5	17	22	24	12	4	11	15	8
96-97	Detroit	IHL	31	12	11	23	30	—	—	—	—	—
96-97	Phoenix	IHL	16	4	10	14	8	—	—	—	—	—
96-97	Milwaukee	IHL	31	6	19	25	29	2	0	1	1	2
	NHL	Totals	54	6	19	25	10	2	0	1	1	0
	IHL	Totals	609	294	492	786	617	62	26	56	82	66
	AHL	Totals	29	16	29	45	14	—	—	—	—	—

Born; 2/9/65, Nun's Island, Quebec. 5-9, 190. Signed as a free agent by St. Louis Blues (8/21/89). Claimed by Tampa Bay Lightning from St. Louis in Expansion Draft (6/18/92). Traded to Quebec Nordiques by Tampa Bay with Martin Simard and Steve Tuttle for Herb Raglan (2/12/93). 1989-90 IHL First Team All-Star. 1989-90 IHL MVP. 1990-91 IHL Second Team All-Star. 1990-91 IHL Playoff MVP. Member of 1990-91 IHL champion Peoria Rivermen.

Eric Montreuil — Center

			Regular Season					Playoffs				
Season	Team	League	GP	G	A	PTS	PIM	GP	G	A	PTS	PIM
95-96	Carolina	AHL	66	7	8	15	81	—	—	—	—	—
96-97	Carolina	AHL	34	4	6	10	39	—	—	—	—	—
96-97	Port Huron	CoHL	3	0	2	2	4	—	—	—	—	—
96-97	Tallahassee	ECHL	3	0	1	1	25	—	—	—	—	—
	AHL	Totals	100	11	14	25	120	—	—	—	—	—

Born; 5/18/75, Verdun, Quebec. 6-1, 177. Drafted by Florida Panthers (13th choice, 265th overall) in 1993 Entry Draft.

James Mooney — Defenseman

			Regular Season					Playoffs				
Season	Team	League	GP	G	A	PTS	PIM	GP	G	A	PTS	PIM
96-97	Jacksonville	ECHL	4	0	1	1	0	—	—	—	—	—
96-97	Johnstown	ECHL	1	0	0	0	0	—	—	—	—	—
96-97	Pensacola	ECHL	15	1	3	4	15	—	—	—	—	—
	ECHL	Totals	20	1	4	5	15	—	—	—	—	—

Born; 7/10/74, 6-1, 235. Calgary, Alberta.

Barrie Moore — Center

			Regular Season					Playoffs				
Season	Team	League	GP	G	A	PTS	PIM	GP	G	A	PTS	PIM
95-96	Buffalo	NHL	3	0	0	0	0	—	—	—	—	—
95-96	Rochester	AHL	64	26	30	56	40	18	3	6	9	18
96-97	Buffalo	NHL	31	2	6	8	18	—	—	—	—	—
96-97	Edmonton	NHL	4	0	0	0	0	—	—	—	—	—
96-97	Rochester	AHL	32	14	15	29	14	—	—	—	—	—
96-97	Hamilton	AHL	9	5	2	7	0	22	2	6	8	15
	NHL	Totals	38	2	6	8	18	—	—	—	—	—
	AHL	Totals	105	45	47	92	54	40	5	12	17	33

Born; 5/22/75, Barrie, Ontario. 5-11, 175. Drafted by Buffalo Sabres (7th choice, 220th overall) in 1993 Entry Draft. Member of 1995-96 AHL champion Rochester Americans.

Blaine Moore — Center

			Regular Season					Playoffs				
Season	Team	League	GP	G	A	PTS	PIM	GP	G	A	PTS	PIM
94-95	Richmond	ECHL	60	30	33	63	181	17	17	17	34	34
95-96	Las Vegas	IHL	67	15	20	35	73	14	2	5	7	24
96-97	Las Vegas	IHL	18	1	3	4	14	—	—	—	—	—
96-97	Port Huron	CoHL	14	6	14	20	10	—	—	—	—	—
	IHL	Totals	85	16	23	39	87	14	2	5	7	24

Born; 10/8/69, Kitimat, British Columbia. 6-0, 185. Member of 1994-95 ECHL champion Richmond Renegades. 1994-95 ECHL Playoff MVP.

David Moore — Defenseman

			Regular Season					Playoffs				
Season	Team	League	GP	G	A	PTS	PIM	GP	G	A	PTS	PIM
91-92	Cincinnati	ECHL	5	0	1	1	2	—	—	—	—	—
91-92	Louisville	ECHL	38	1	15	16	40	13	1	1	2	11
92-93	Louisville	ECHL	2	0	0	0	0	—	—	—	—	—
92-93	Memphis	CeHL	60	18	30	48	114	6	0	2	2	10
93-94	London	CoHL	3	0	0	0	5	—	—	—	—	—
93-94	Memphis	CeHL	53	16	38	54	71	—	—	—	—	—
93-94	Tulsa	CeHL	10	2	2	4	14	11	5	5	10	41
94-95	Tulsa	CeHL	66	20	41	61	127	5	4	3	7	24
95-96	N/A											
96-97	Austin	WPHL	61	10	22	32	84	6	0	1	1	8
	CeHL	Totals	189	56	111	167	326	22	9	10	19	75

Born; 4/26/68, Hampstead, New Hampshire. 6-1, 200. 1993-94 Second Team CeHL All-Star.

Dean Moore — Forward

			Regular Season					Playoffs				
Season	Team	League	GP	G	A	PTS	PIM	GP	G	A	PTS	PIM
95-96	Knoxville	ECHL	34	3	6	9	154	6	0	1	1	13
96-97	Manitoba	IHL	3	0	0	0	7	—	—	—	—	—
96-97	Knoxville	ECHL	56	8	13	21	215	—	—	—	—	—
	ECHL	Totals	90	11	19	30	369	6	0	1	1	13

Born; 7/6/73, Winnipeg, Manitoba. 6-2, 195.

Steve Moore — Center

			Regular Season					Playoffs				
Season	Team	League	GP	G	A	PTS	PIM	GP	G	A	PTS	PIM
95-96	Charlotte	ECHL	6	2	2	4	6	—	—	—	—	—
95-96	Oklahoma City	CeHL	55	26	31	57	84	13	5	7	12	30
96-97	Oklahoma City	CeHL	66	37	28	65	138	4	3	4	7	17
	CeHL	Totals	121	63	59	122	222	17	8	11	19	47

Born; 6/21/71, Gardiner, Maine. 6-0, 200. Member of 1995-96 CeHL champion Oklahoma City Blazers.

Tom Moores — Left Wing

			Regular Season					Playoffs				
Season	Team	League	GP	G	A	PTS	PIM	GP	G	A	PTS	PIM
95-96	Saginaw	CoHL	24	3	4	7	19	5	0	0	0	0
96-97	Saginaw	CoHL	24	2	4	6	34	—	—	—	—	—
	CoHL	Totals	48	5	8	13	53	5	0	0	0	0

Born; 4/14/74, Scarborough, Ontario. 6-1, 210.

Ian Moran — Defenseman

			Regular Season					Playoffs				
Season	Team	League	GP	G	A	PTS	PIM	GP	G	A	PTS	PIM
93-94	Cleveland	IHL	33	5	13	18	39	—	—	—	—	—
94-95	Pittsburgh	NHL	—	—	—	—	—	8	0	0	0	0
94-95	Cleveland	IHL	64	7	31	38	94	4	0	1	1	2
95-96	Pittsburgh	NHL	51	1	1	2	47	—	—	—	—	—
96-97	Pittsburgh	NHL	36	4	5	9	22	5	1	2	3	4
96-97	Cleveland	IHL	36	6	23	29	26	—	—	—	—	—
	NHL	Totals	87	5	6	11	69	13	1	2	3	4
	IHL	Totals	133	18	67	85	159	4	0	1	1	2

Born; 8/24/72, Cleveland, Ohio. 5-11, 195. Drafted by Pittsburgh Penguins (6th choice, 107th overall) in 1990 Entry Draft.

Eric Moreau — Defenseman

Season	Team	League	GP	G	A	PTS	PIM	GP	G	A	PTS	PIM
96-97	Macon	CeHL	66	5	13	18	24	5	0	1	1	2

Born; 12/15/75, Tracy, Quebec. 5-11, 210.

Patrick Moreau — Left Wing

Season	Team	League	GP	G	A	PTS	PIM	GP	G	A	PTS	PIM
95-96	West Palm Beach	SHL	56	10	15	25	127	—	—	—	—	—
96-97	Reno	WCHL	12	0	3	3	20	—	—	—	—	—
96-97	Alaska	WCHL	31	11	9	20	52	—	—	—	—	—
	WCHL	Totals	43	11	12	23	72	—	—	—	—	—

Born; 8/8/74, 5-11, 190.

Jason Morgan — Center

Season	Team	League	GP	G	A	PTS	PIM	GP	G	A	PTS	PIM
96-97	Los Angeles	NHL	3	0	0	0	0	—	—	—	—	—
96-97	Phoenix	IHL	57	3	6	9	29	—	—	—	—	—
96-97	Mississippi	ECHL	6	3	0	3	0	3	1	1	2	6

Born; 10/9/76, St. John's, Newfoundland. 6-1, 185. Drafted by Los Angeles Kings (fifth choice, 118th overall) in 1995 Entry Draft.

Eric Morin — Defenseman

Season	Team	League	GP	G	A	PTS	PIM	GP	G	A	PTS	PIM
96-97	Memphis	CeHL	27	7	11	18	22	17	4	3	7	10

Born; 6/28/72, Saint Constant, Quebec. 6-2, 200.

Stephane Morin — Center

Season	Team	League	GP	G	A	PTS	PIM	GP	G	A	PTS	PIM
89-90	Quebec	NHL	6	0	2	2	2	—	—	—	—	—
89-90	Halifax	AHL	65	28	32	60	60	6	3	4	7	6
90-91	Quebec	NHL	48	13	27	40	30	—	—	—	—	—
90-91	Halifax	AHL	17	8	14	22	18	—	—	—	—	—
91-92	Quebec	NHL	30	2	8	10	14	—	—	—	—	—
91-92	Halifax	AHL	30	17	13	30	29	—	—	—	—	—
92-93	Vancouver	NHL	1	0	1	1	0	—	—	—	—	—
92-93	Hamilton	AHL	70	31	54	85	49	—	—	—	—	—
93-94	Vancouver	NHL	5	1	1	2	6	—	—	—	—	—
93-94	Hamilton	AHL	69	38	71	109	48	4	3	2	5	4
94-95	Minnesota	IHL	81	33	*81	*114	53	2	0	1	1	0
95-96	Minnesota	IHL	80	27	51	78	75	—	—	—	—	—
96-97	Manitoba	IHL	12	3	6	9	4	—	—	—	—	—
96-97	Long Beach	IHL	65	25	57	82	73	18	6	13	19	14
	NHL	Totals	90	16	39	55	52	—	—	—	—	—
	AHL	Totals	251	122	184	306	204	10	6	6	12	10
	IHL	Totals	238	88	195	283	205	20	6	14	20	14

Born; 3/27/69, Montreal, Quebec. 6-1, 175. Drafted by Quebec Nordiques (3rd choice, 43rd overall) in 1989 Entry Draft. Signed as a free agent by Vancouver Canucks (10/5/92). 1993-94 AHL Second Team All-Star. 1994-95 IHL First Team All-Star.

Tim Morin — Right Wing

Season	Team	League	GP	G	A	PTS	PIM	GP	G	A	PTS	PIM
96-97	Hampton Roads	ECHL	2	0	0	0	6	—	—	—	—	—

Season	Team	League	GP	W	L	T	MIN	SO	GAVG	GP	W	L	MIN	SO	GAVG
96-97	Memphis	CeHL	4	2	1	3	0	7	0	0	0	0	0		
96-97	Columbus	CeHL	3	0	0	0	0	—	—	—	—	—			
	CeHL	Totals	7	2	1	3	0	7	0	0	0	0	0		

Born; 5/31/74, Ottawa, Ontario. 6-0, 195.

Alain Morissette — Goaltender

			Regular Season							Playoffs					
Season	Team	League	GP	W	L	T	MIN	SO	GAVG	GP	W	L	MIN	SO	GAVG
90-91	Fredericton	AHL	14	—	—	—	709	0	3.64	2	—	—	17	0	3.53
90-91	Winston-Salem	ECHL	21	—	—	—	1222	0	4.86	—	—	—	—	—	—
91-92	Muskegon	IHL	31	—	—	—	1796	1	3.34	2	—	—	97	0	5.57
91-92	Knoxville	ECHL	1	—	—	—	65	0	4.62	—	—	—	—	—	—
95-96	Louisville	ECHL	48	29	14	4	2744	*2	2.91	3	0	3	179	0	3.36
96-97	Waco	WPHL	14	5	6	2	788	0	3.81	—	—	—	—	—	—
@	ECHL	Totals	70	29	14	4	4031	2	3.53	3	0	3	179	0	3.36

Born; 8/26/69, Rimouski, Quebec. 5-10, 168. Did not play professional hockey in North America between the 1991-92 and 1996-96 seasons. @ ECHL win/loss totals not complete. Signed as a free agent by Montreal Canadiens (9/90). 1995-96 ECHL Best goaltender. 1995-96 ECHL First All-Star Team. Signed as a free agent by the Idaho Steelheads (WCHL), (8/97).

Dave Morissette — Left Wing

			Regular Season					Playoffs			
Season	Team	League	GP	G	A	PTS	PIM	GP	G	A	PTS	PIM
91-92	Bsltimore	AHL	2	0	0	0	6	—	—	—	—	—
91-92	Hampton Roads	ECHL	47	6	10	16	193	13	1	3	4	74
92-93	Hampton Roads	ECHL	54	9	13	22	226	2	0	0	0	2
93-94	Roanoke	ECHL	45	8	10	18	278	2	0	1	1	4
94-95	Minnesota	IHL	50	1	4	5	174	—	—	—	—	—
95-96	Minnesota	IHL	33	3	2	5	104	—	—	—	—	—
96-97	Houston	IHL	59	2	1	3	214	2	0	0	0	0
96-97	Austin	WPHL	5	2	3	5	10	—	—	—	—	—
	IHL	Totals	142	6	7	13	492	2	0	0	0	0
	ECHL	Totals	146	23	33	56	697	17	1	4	5	80

Born; 12/24/71, Quebec City, Quebec. 6-1, 210. Drafted by Washington Capitals (7th choice, 146th overall) in 1991 Entry Draft. Member of 1991-92 ECHL champion Hampton Roads Admirals.

Chris Morque — Defenseman

			Regular Season					Playoffs				
Season	Team	League	GP	G	A	PTS	PIM	GP	G	A	PTS	PIM
94-95	Erie	ECHL	26	3	8	11	83	—	—	—	—	—
94-95	Huntington	ECHL	36	1	9	10	126	—	—	—	—	—
95-96	Quad City	CoHL	2	0	0	0	4	—	—	—	—	—
95-96	Memphis	CeHL	60	9	33	42	235	6	1	2	3	45
96-97	Austin	WPHL	63	5	14	19	126	5	0	2	2	23
	ECHL	Totals	62	4	17	21	209	—	—	—	—	—

Born; 2/16/70, Grand Forks, South Dakota. 6-2, 200.

Derek Morris — Defenseman

			Regular Season					Playoffs				
Season	Team	League	GP	G	A	PTS	PIM	GP	G	A	PTS	PIM
96-97	Saint John	AHL	7	0	3	3	7	5	0	3	3	7

Born; 8/24/76, Edmonton, Alberta. Drafted by Calgary Flames (1st choice, 13th overall) in 1996 Entry Draft.

Keith Morris — Left Wing

			Regular Season					Playoffs				
Season	Team	League	GP	G	A	PTS	PIM	GP	G	A	PTS	PIM
94-95	Peoria	IHL	2	0	1	1	0	—	—	—	—	—
94-95	Columbus	ECHL	62	32	41	73	32	3	1	2	3	2

Season	Team	League	GP	G	A	PTS	PIM	GP	G	A	PTS	PIM
95-96	Detroit	IHL	1	0	0	0	0	—	—	—	—	—
95-96	Columbus	ECHL	66	46	48	94	42	3	1	1	2	0
96-97	Manitoba	IHL	4	0	2	2	0	—	—	—	—	—
96-97	Columbus	ECHL	61	26	47	73	22	6	1	0	1	0
	IHL	Totals	7	0	3	3	0	—	—	—	—	—
	ECHL	Totals	189	104	136	240	96	12	3	3	6	2

Born; 4/24/71, Winnipeg, Manitoba. 6-1, 185. Drafted by Winnipeg Jets (13th choice, 245th overall) in 1990 Entry Draft.

Justin Morrison — Right Wing

			Regular Season					Playoffs				
Season	Team	League	GP	G	A	PTS	PIM	GP	G	A	PTS	PIM
92-93	Toledo	ECHL	13	6	8	14	47	—	—	—	—	—
93-94	Muskegon	CoHL	64	27	33	60	86	3	1	1	2	12
94-95	Muskegon	CoHL	74	32	54	86	224	15	4	15	19	32
95-96	Madison	CoHL	61	21	30	51	179	4	1	6	7	2
96-97	Madison	CoHL	31	13	22	35	61	—	—	—	—	—
96-97	Muskegon	CoHL	41	19	23	42	50	3	0	1	1	17
	CoHL	Totals	271	112	162	274	600	25	6	23	29	63

Born; 2/9/72, Newmarket, Ontario. 5-10, 174. Drafted by Washington Capitals (fourth round, 80th overall) 6/22/91.

Tavis Morrison — Center

			Regular Season					Playoffs				
Season	Team	League	GP	G	A	PTS	PIM	GP	G	A	PTS	PIM
96-97	Dayton	ECHL	23	4	3	7	2	—	—	—	—	—
96-97	Huntington	ECHL	14	7	3	10	2	—	—	—	—	—
	ECHL	Totals	37	11	6	17	4	—	—	—	—	—

Born; 2/14/75, Belleville, Ontario. 6-2, 180.

Mike Morrone — Left Wing

			Regular Season					Playoffs				
Season	Team	League	GP	G	A	PTS	PIM	GP	G	A	PTS	PIM
96-97	Richmond	ECHL	4	0	0	0	9	7	1	1	2	15

Born; 1/3/76, Windsor, Ontario. 5-11, 218.

Scott Morrow — Left Wing

			Regular Season					Playoffs				
Season	Team	League	GP	G	A	PTS	PIM	GP	G	A	PTS	PIM
91-92	Springfield	AHL	2	0	1	1	0	5	0	0	0	9
92-93	Springfield	AHL	70	22	29	51	80	15	6	9	15	21
93-94	Springfield	AHL	30	12	15	27	28	—	—	—	—	—
93-94	Saint John	AHL	8	2	2	4	0	7	2	1	3	10
94-95	Calgary	NHL	4	0	0	0	0	—	—	—	—	—
94-95	Saint John	AHL	64	18	21	39	105	5	2	0	2	4
95-96	Hershey	AHL	79	48	45	93	110	5	2	2	4	6
96-97	Cincinnati	IHL	67	14	23	37	50	—	—	—	—	—
96-97	Providence	AHL	11	3	4	7	15	7	2	1	3	0
	AHL	Totals	264	105	117	222	338	44	14	13	27	50

Born; 6/18/69, Chicago, Illinois. 6-1, 185. Drafted by Hartford Whalers (4th choice, 95th overall) in 1988 Entry Draft. Traded to Calgary Flames by Hartford for Todd Harkins (1/24/94).

Jay Moser — Right Wing

			Regular Season					Playoffs				
Season	Team	League	GP	G	A	PTS	PIM	GP	G	A	PTS	PIM
96-97	Providence	AHL	12	0	2	2	8	—	—	—	—	—
96-97	Rochester	AHL	22	4	9	13	4	9	1	1	2	4
96-97	South Carolina	ECHL	41	19	30	49	32	—	—	—	—	—
	AHL	Totals	34	4	11	15	12	9	1	1	2	4

Born; 12/26/72, Cottage Grove, Minnesota. 6-2, 170. Drafted by Boston Bruins (7th choice, 172nd overall) in 1991 Entry Draft.

Tyler Moss — Goaltender

Season	Team	League	GP	W	L	T	MIN	SO	GAVG	GP	W	L	MIN	SO	GAVG
95-96	Atlanta	IHL	40	11	19	4	2029	1	4.08	3	0	3	213	0	3.10
96-97	Grand Rapids	IHL	15	5	6	1	715	0	2.94	—	—	—	—	—	—
96-97	Adirondack	AHL	11	1	5	2	507	1	4.97	—	—	—	—	—	—
96-97	Saint John	AHL	9	6	1	1	534	0	1.91	5	2	3	242	0	3.72
96-97	Muskegon	CoHL	2	1	1	0	119	0	2.51	—	—	—	—	—	—
	IHL	Totals	55	16	25	5	2744	1	3.78	3	0	3	213	0	3.10
	AHL	Totals	20	7	6	5	1041	1	3.40	5	2	3	242	0	3.72

Born; 6/29/75, Ottawa, Ontario. 6-0, 168. Drafted by Tampa Bay Lightning (2nd choice, 29th overall) in 1993 Entry Draft.

Tom Moulton — Defenseman

Season	Team	League	GP	G	A	PTS	PIM	GP	G	A	PTS	PIM
91-92	St. Thomas	CoHL	2	0	0	0	0	—	—	—	—	—
92-93	St. Thomas	CoHL	35	3	7	10	41	15	3	1	4	21
93-94	Brantford	CoHL	13	4	1	5	10	7	1	0	1	2
94-95	N/A											
95-96	Winston-Salem	SHL	59	5	26	31	200	9	1	1	2	51
96-97	Huntsville	CeHL	66	7	24	31	167	8	0	3	3	38
	CoHL	Totals	50	7	8	15	51	22	4	1	5	23

Born; 3/28/70, London, Ontario. 6-1, 203.

Brian Mueller — Defenseman

Season	Team	League	GP	G	A	PTS	PIM	GP	G	A	PTS	PIM
95-96	Springfield	AHL	51	7	12	19	49	2	0	0	0	0
95-96	Richmond	ECHL	3	1	1	2	2	3	0	2	2	0
96-97	Springfield	AHL	42	7	20	27	28	7	0	2	2	0
96-97	Manitoba	IHL	6	1	1	2	2	—	—	—	—	—
96-97	Quebec	IHL	10	0	0	0	0	—	—	—	—	—
	AHL	Totals	93	14	32	46	77	9	0	2	2	0
	IHL	Totals	16	1	1	2	2	—	—	—	—	—

Born; 6/2/72, Liverpool, New York. 5-11, 225. Drafted by Hartford Whalers (7th choice, 141st overall) in 1991 Entry Draft.

Bryan Muir — Defenseman

Season	Team	League	GP	G	A	PTS	PIM	GP	G	A	PTS	PIM
96-97	Hamilton	AHL	75	8	16	24	80	14	0	5	5	12

Born; 6/8/73, Winnipeg, Manitoba. 6-4, 220. Signed as a free agent by Edmonton Oilers (4/30/96).

Wayne Muir — Right Wing

Season	Team	League	GP	G	A	PTS	PIM	GP	G	A	PTS	PIM
89-90	Virginia	ECHL	1	1	2	3	0	1	0	0	0	0
90-91	Cape Breton	AHL	1	0	0	0	0	—	—	—	—	—
90-91	Roanoke	ECHL	61	31	24	55	239	—	—	—	—	—
91-92	Roanoke	ECHL	46	12	19	31	168	7	1	1	2	36
92-93	Greensboro	ECHL	50	28	24	52	200	—	—	—	—	—
92-93	Dayton	ECHL	6	4	2	6	38	3	1	0	1	16
93-94	Chatham	CoHL	62	29	41	70	269	15	5	4	9	54
94-95	Brantford	CoHL	71	38	46	84	232	—	—	—	—	—
95-96	Brantford	CoHL	74	40	47	87	261	12	8	6	14	31
96-97	Utah	IHL	1	0	0	0	0	—	—	—	—	—
96-97	Brantford	CoHL	73	52	65	117	212	10	5	10	15	27
	CoHL	Totals	280	159	199	358	974	37	18	20	38	112
	ECHL	Totals	164	76	71	147	645	11	2	1	3	52

Born; 1/9/69, Sydney, Nova Scotia. 5-11, 200. 1996-97 CoHL Second Team All-Star.

Ryan Mulhern — Left Wing

			Regular Season					Playoffs				
Season	Team	League	GP	G	A	PTS	PIM	GP	G	A	PTS	PIM
96-97	Portland	AHL	38	19	15	34	16	5	1	1	2	2
96-97	Hampton Roads	ECHL	40	22	16	38	52	—	—	—	—	—

1/11/73, Philadelphia, Pennsylvania. 6-1, 180. Drafted by Calgary Flames (8th choice, 174th overall) in 1992 Entry Draft.

Mike Muller — Defenseman

			Regular Season					Playoffs				
Season	Team	League	GP	G	A	PTS	PIM	GP	G	A	PTS	PIM
93-94	Moncton	AHL	61	2	14	16	88	—	—	—	—	—
94-95	Springfield	AHL	64	2	5	7	61	—	—	—	—	—
95-96	Minnesota	IHL	53	3	7	10	72	—	—	—	—	—
96-97	Grand Rapids	IHL	2	0	0	0	4	—	—	—	—	—
96-97	Mississippi	ECHL	54	15	24	39	36	—	—	—	—	—
96-97	Baton Rouge	ECHL	12	1	10	11	2	—	—	—	—	—
	AHL	Totals	125	4	19	23	149	—	—	—	—	—
	IHL	Totals	55	3	7	10	76	—	—	—	—	—
	ECHL	Totals	66	16	34	50	38	—	—	—	—	—

Born; 9/18/71, Edina, Minnesota. 6-2, 205. Drafted by Winnipeg Jets (2nd choice, 35th overall) in 1990 Entry Draft.

Kory Mullin — Defenseman

			Regular Season					Playoffs				
Season	Team	League	GP	G	A	PTS	PIM	GP	G	A	PTS	PIM
95-96	St. John's	AHL	55	6	4	10	73	2	0	1	1	0
95-96	Brantford	CoHL	1	0	0	0	0	—	—	—	—	—
96-97	St. John's	AHL	29	3	2	5	62	—	—	—	—	—
96-97	Cincinnati	IHL	6	0	0	0	19	—	—	—	—	—
96-97	Birmingham	ECHL	21	5	13	18	102	5	4	1	5	10
	AHL	Totals	84	9	6	15	135	2	0	1	1	0

Born; 5/25/74, Lethbridge, Alberta. 6-2, 185. Signed as a free agent by Toronto Maple Leafs (9/23/93).

Dwight Mullins — Right Wing

			Regular Season					Playoffs				
Season	Team	League	GP	G	A	PTS	PIM	GP	G	A	PTS	PIM
88-89	Flint	IHL	2	0	0	0	15	—	—	—	—	—
94-95	Fort Worth	CeHL	45	10	11	21	197	—	—	—	—	—
95-96	Fort Worth	CeHL	63	15	11	26	235	—	—	—	—	—
96-97	Fort Worth	CeHL	48	12	7	19	301	17	1	4	5	82
	CeHL	Totals	156	37	29	66	733	17	1	4	5	82

Born; 2/28/67, Calgary, Alberta. 5-11, 195. Drafted by Minnesota North Stars (3rd choice, 90th overall) in 1985 Entry Draft. Member of 1996-97 CeHL Champion Fort Worth Fire.

Al Murphy — Defenseman

			Regular Season					Playoffs				
Season	Team	League	GP	G	A	PTS	PIM	GP	G	A	PTS	PIM
89-90	Greensboro	ECHL	3	0	0	0	0	—	—	—	—	—
89-90	Hampton Roads	ECHL	31	3	12	15	105	—	—	—	—	—
90-91	Kansas City	IHL	6	0	0	0	10	—	—	—	—	—
90-91	Hampton Roads	ECHL	33	11	16	27	123	10	3	4	7	34
91-92	Michigan	CoHL	43	10	14	24	85	4	2	0	2	16
92-93	Tulsa	CeHL	34	10	11	21	100	12	3	10	13	48
93-94	Tulsa	CeHL	6	1	3	4	47	—	—	—	—	—
94-95	N/A											
95-96	Reno	WCHL	56	9	25	34	227	3	0	0	0	6

Season	Team	League	GP	G	A	PTS	PIM	GP	G	A	PTS	PIM
96-97	Reno	WCHL	51	10	20	30	277	—	—	—	—	—
	WCHL	Totals	107	19	45	64	504	3	0	0	0	6
	ECHL	Totals	67	14	28	42	228	10	3	4	7	34
	CeHL	Totals	40	11	14	25	147	12	3	10	13	48

Born; 8/8/68, Toronto, Ontario. 6-3, 215. Member of 1990-91 ECHL champion Hamton Roads Admirals. Member of 1992-93 CeHL champion Tulsa Oilers.

Burke Murphy — Right Wing

Season	Team	League	GP	G	A	PTS	PIM	GP	G	A	PTS	PIM
96-97	Saint John	AHL	54	8	18	26	20	—	—	—	—	—

Born; 6/5/73, Gloucester, Ontario. 6-0, 180. Drafted by Calgary Flames (11th choice, 278th overall) in 1993 Entry Draft.

Jay Murphy — Right Wing

Season	Team	League	GP	G	A	PTS	PIM	GP	G	A	PTS	PIM
94-95	Richmond	ECHL	37	24	15	39	78	6	2	3	5	9
95-96	San Francisco	IHL	9	0	3	3	9	—	—	—	—	—
95-96	Richmond	ECHL	52	31	43	74	177	7	4	6	10	18
96-97	Louisiana	ECHL	15	5	5	10	42	17	7	5	12	91
96-97	Alaska	WCHL	28	15	22	37	65	—	—	—	—	—
	ECHL	Totals	104	60	63	123	297	30	13	14	27	118

Born; 1/10/72, Ypsilanti, Michigan. 6-2, 205. Member of 1994-95 ECHL champion Richmond Renegades.

Jodi Murphy — Right Wing

Season	Team	League	GP	G	A	PTS	PIM	GP	G	A	PTS	PIM
93-94	Hamilton	AHL	2	0	0	0	0	—	—	—	—	—
93-94	Richmond	ECHL	3	0	1	1	0	—	—	—	—	—
93-94	Muskegon	CoHL	36	4	1	5	150	1	0	0	0	2
94-95	Saginaw	CoHL	5	0	0	0	29	9	0	0	0	15
94-95	Muskegon	CoHL	39	1	0	1	178	—	—	—	—	—
95-96	Flint	CoHL	35	1	2	3	95	—	—	—	—	—
95-96	Madison	CoHL	17	0	1	1	5	5	0	0	0	7
96-97	Muskegon	CoHL	67	7	0	7	160	1	0	0	0	0
	CoHL	Totals	132	6	4	10	457	15	0	0	0	24

Born; 8/1/73, Halifax, Nova Scotia. 6-5, 235.

Randy Murphy — Forward

Season	Team	League	GP	G	A	PTS	PIM	GP	G	A	PTS	PIM
94-95	Raleigh	ECHL	2	0	0	0	0	—	—	—	—	—
95-96	Lakeland	SHL	60	40	69	109	35	5	1	2	3	4
96-97	Columbus	CeHL	65	36	69	105	42	3	0	3	3	2

Born; 7/25/72, Mississauga, Ontario. 5-7, 170.

Rob Murphy — Center

Season	Team	League	GP	G	A	PTS	PIM	GP	G	A	PTS	PIM
87-88	Vancouver	NHL	5	0	0	0	2	—	—	—	—	—
88-89	Vancouver	NHL	8	0	1	1	2	—	—	—	—	—
88-89	Milwaukee	IHL	8	4	2	6	4	11	3	5	8	34
89-90	Vancouver	NHL	12	1	1	2	0	—	—	—	—	—
89-90	Milwaukee	IHL	64	24	47	71	87	6	2	6	8	12
90-91	Vancouver	NHL	42	5	1	6	90	4	0	0	0	2
90-91	Milwaukee	IHL	23	1	7	8	48	—	—	—	—	—
91-92	Vancouver	NHL	6	0	1	1	6	—	—	—	—	—

Season	Team	League	GP	G	A	PTS	PIM	GP	G	A	PTS	PIM
91-92	Milwaukee	IHL	73	26	38	64	141	5	0	3	3	2
92-93	Ottawa	NHL	44	3	7	10	30	—	—	—	—	—
92-93	New Haven	AHL	26	8	12	20	28	—	—	—	—	—
93-94	Los Angeles	NHL	8	0	1	1	22	—	—	—	—	—
93-94	Phoenix	IHL	72	23	34	57	101	—	—	—	—	—
94-95	Phoenix	IHL	2	0	0	0	10	2	0	1	1	0
95-96	Fort Wayne	IHL	82	24	52	76	107	5	1	2	3	8
96-97	Fort Wayne	IHL	35	9	16	25	40	—	—	—	—	—
	NHL	Totals	125	9	12	21	152	4	0	0	0	2
	IHL	Totals	359	107	196	303	538	29	6	17	23	56

Born; 4/7/69, Hull, Quebec. 6-3, 205. Drafted by Vancouver Canucks (1st choice, 24th overall) in 1987 Entry Draft. Selected by Ottawa Senators in NHL Expansion Draft (6/18/92). Signed as a free agent by Los Angeles Kings (8/2/93). 1989-90 IHL Rookie of the Year.

Greg Murray — Left Wing

Season	Team	League	GP	G	A	PTS	PIM	GP	G	A	PTS	PIM
94-95	Utica	CoHL	6	2	2	4	9	—	—	—	—	—
94-95	Columbus	ECHL	19	8	5	13	4	—	—	—	—	—
95-96	Quad City	CoHL	4	1	1	2	0	—	—	—	—	—
95-96	Jacksonville	SHL	48	38	44	82	53	—	—	—	—	—
96-97	Saginaw	CoHL	10	0	1	1	4	—	—	—	—	—
96-97	Huntsville	CeHL	17	5	9	14	8	—	—	—	—	—
96-97	Nashville	CeHL	17	6	10	16	30	—	—	—	—	—
	CeHL	Totals	34	11	19	30	38	—	—	—	—	—
	CoHL	Totals	20	3	4	7	13	—	—	—	—	—

Born; 10/25/67, Dublin, Ontario. 6-3, 200.

Marty Murray — Center

Season	Team	League	GP	G	A	PTS	PIM	GP	G	A	PTS	PIM
95-96	Calgary	NHL	15	3	3	6	0	—	—	—	—	—
95-96	Saint John	AHL	58	25	31	56	20	14	2	4	6	4
96-97	Calgary	NHL	2	0	0	0	4	—	—	—	—	—
96-97	Saint John	AHL	67	19	39	58	40	5	2	3	5	4
	NHL	Totals	17	3	3	6	4	—	—	—	—	—
	AHL	Totals	125	44	70	114	60	19	4	7	11	8

Born; 2/16/75, Deloraine, Manitoba. 5-9, 170. Drafted by Calgary Flames (5th choice, 96th overall) in 1993 Entry Draft.

Michael P. Murray — Right Wing

Season	Team	League	GP	G	A	PTS	PIM	GP	G	A	PTS	PIM
94-95	Saint John	AHL	65	8	27	35	53	4	0	0	0	6
95-96	Saint John	AHL	32	7	11	18	77	—	—	—	—	—
96-97	Saint John	AHL	17	2	5	7	8	4	1	1	2	12
	AHL	Totals	114	17	43	53	60	4	0	0	0	6

Born; 4/18/71, Cumberland, Rhode Island. Drafted by Calgary Flames (10th choice, 188th overall) in 1990 Entry Draft.

Rob Murray — Center

Season	Team	League	GP	G	A	PTS	PIM	GP	G	A	PTS	PIM
87-88	Fort Wayne	IHL	80	12	21	33	139	6	0	2	2	16
88-89	Baltimore	AHL	80	11	23	34	235	—	—	—	—	—
89-90	Washington	NHL	41	2	7	9	58	9	0	0	0	18
89-90	Baltimore	AHL	23	5	4	9	63	—	—	—	—	—
90-91	Washington	NHL	17	0	3	3	19	—	—	—	—	—
90-91	Baltimore	AHL	48	6	20	26	177	4	0	0	0	12
91-92	Winnipeg	NHL	9	0	1	1	18	—	—	—	—	—

Season	Team	League	GP	G	A	PTS	PIM	GP	G	A	PTS	PIM
91-92	Moncton	AHL	60	16	15	31	247	8	0	1	1	56
92-93	Winnipeg	NHL	10	1	0	1	6	—	—	—	—	—
92-93	Moncton	AHL	56	16	21	37	147	3	0	0	0	6
93-94	Winnipeg	NHL	6	0	0	0	2	—	—	—	—	—
93-94	Moncton	AHL	69	25	32	57	280	21	2	3	5	60
94-95	Winnipeg	NHL	10	0	2	2	2	—	—	—	—	—
94-95	Springfield	AHL	78	16	38	54	373	—	—	—	—	—
95-96	Winnipeg	NHL	1	0	0	0	2	—	—	—	—	—
95-96	Springfield	AHL	74	10	28	38	263	10	1	6	7	32
96-97	Springfield	AHL	78	16	27	43	234	17	2	3	5	66
	NHL	Totals	94	3	13	16	105	9	0	0	0	18
	AHL	Totals	566	121	208	329	2019	63	5	13	18	232

Born; 4/4/67, Toronto, Ontario. 6-0, 180. Drafted by Washington Capitals (3rd choice, 61st overall) in 1985 Entry Draft. Claimed by Minnesota North Stars from Washington in Expansion Draft (5/30/91). Traded to Winnipeg Jets by Minnesota with future considerations for Winnipeg's seventh round draft choice (Geoff Finch) in 1991 Entry Draft and future considerations (5/31/91).

Troy Murray — Center

			Regular Season					Playoffs				
Season	Team	League	GP	G	A	PTS	PIM	GP	G	A	PTS	PIM
81-82	Chicago	NHL	1	0	0	0	0	7	1	0	1	5
82-83	Chicago	NHL	54	8	8	16	27	2	0	0	0	0
83-84	Chicago	NHL	61	15	15	30	45	5	1	0	1	7
84-85	Chicago	NHL	80	26	40	66	82	15	5	14	19	24
85-86	Chicago	NHL	80	45	54	99	94	2	0	0	0	2
86-87	Chicago	NHL	77	28	43	71	59	4	0	0	0	5
87-88	Chicago	NHL	79	22	36	58	96	5	1	0	1	8
88-89	Chicago	NHL	79	21	30	51	113	16	3	6	9	25
89-90	Chicago	NHL	68	17	38	55	86	20	4	4	8	22
90-91	Chicago	NHL	75	14	23	37	74	6	0	1	1	12
91-92	Winnipeg	NHL	74	17	30	47	69	7	0	0	0	2
92-93	Winnipeg	NHL	29	3	4	7	34	—	—	—	—	—
92-93	Chicago	NHL	22	1	3	4	25	4	0	0	0	2
93-94	Chicago	NHL	12	0	1	1	6	—	—	—	—	—
93-94	Ottawa	NHL	15	2	3	5	4	—	—	—	—	—
93-94	Indianapolis	IHL	8	3	3	6	12	—	—	—	—	—
94-95	Ottawa	NHL	33	4	10	14	16	—	—	—	—	—
94-95	Pittsburgh	NHL	13	0	2	2	23	12	2	1	3	12
95-96	Colorado	NHL	63	7	14	21	22	8	0	0	0	19
96-97	Chicago	IHL	81	21	29	50	63	4	0	2	2	2
	NHL	Totals	915	230	354	584	875	113	17	26	43	145
	IHL	Totals	89	24	32	56	75	—	—	—	—	—

Born; 7/31/62, Calgary, Alberta. 6-1, 195. Drafted by Chicago Blackhawks (6th choice, 57th overall) in 1980 Entry Draft. Traded to Winnipeg Jets with Warren Rychel for Bryan Marchment and Chris Norton, (7/22/91). Traded to Chicago by Winnipeg for Steve Bancroft and future considerations. (2/21/93). Traded to Ottawa Senators by Chicago with Chicago's eleventh round choice (Antti Tormanen) in 1994 Entry Draft for Ottawa's eleventh choice (Rob Mara) in 1994 Entry Draft, (3/11/94). Traded to Pittsburgh Penguins by Ottawa with Norm Maciver for Martin Straka (4/7/95). Signed as a free agent by Colorado Avalanche (8/7/95). Won Frank J. Selke Trophy (best defensive forward in NHL) 1985-86. Member of 1995-96 Stanley Cup champion Colorado Avalanche.

Jeremy Mylymok — Defenseman

			Regular Season					Playoffs				
Season	Team	League	GP	G	A	PTS	PIM	GP	G	A	PTS	PIM
95-96	Toledo	ECHL	9	1	0	1	24	8	0	0	0	10
96-97	Quebec	IHL	4	0	0	0	4	4	0	0	0	2
96-97	Toledo	ECHL	18	0	5	5	46	—	—	—	—	—
96-97	Pensacola	ECHL	43	2	13	15	113	11	0	1	1	46
	ECHL	Totals	70	3	18	21	183	19	0	1	1	56

Born; 1/12/72, London, Ontario. 6-0, 200.

Anders Myrvold — Defenseman

Season	Team	League	Regular Season					Playoffs				
			GP	G	A	PTS	PIM	GP	G	A	PTS	PIM
94-95	Cornwall	AHL	—	—	—	—	—	3	0	1	1	2
95-96	Colorado	NHL	4	0	1	1	6	—	—	—	—	—
95-96	Cornwall	AHL	70	5	24	29	125	5	1	0	1	19
96-97	Boston	NHL	9	0	2	2	4	—	—	—	—	—
96-97	Hershey	AHL	20	0	3	3	16	—	—	—	—	—
96-97	Providence	AHL	53	6	15	21	107	10	0	1	1	6
	NHL	Totals	13	0	3	3	10	—	—	—	—	—
	AHL	Totals	143	11	42	53	248	18	1	2	3	27

Born; 8/12/75, Lorenskog, Norway. 6-1, 178. Drafted by Quebec Nordiques (6th choice, 127th overall) in 1993 Entry Draft. Traded to Boston Bruins with Landon Wilson by Colorado for Boston's first round choice in 1998 Entry Draft, (11/22/96).

Chris Nadeau — Defenseman

Season	Team	League	GP	G	A	PTS	PIM	GP	G	A	PTS	PIM
96-97	Huntington	ECHL	66	2	10	12	42	—	—	—	—	—

Born; 4/10/72, Saint John, New Brunswick. 6-0, 200.

Aaron Nagy — Center

Season	Team	League	GP	G	A	PTS	PIM	GP	G	A	PTS	PIM
96-97	Tallahassee	ECHL	18	4	3	7	2	—	—	—	—	—
96-97	Toledo	ECHL	38	10	13	23	27	5	1	0	1	4
	ECHL	Totals	56	14	16	30	29	5	1	0	1	4

Born; 12/29/72, Stratford, Ontario. 6-1, 190.

John Namestnikov — Defenseman

Season	Team	League	GP	G	A	PTS	PIM	GP	G	A	PTS	PIM
93-94	Vancouver	NHL	17	0	5	5	10	—	—	—	—	—
93-94	Hamilton	AHL	59	7	27	34	97	4	0	2	2	19
94-95	Vancouver	NHL	16	0	3	3	4	1	0	0	0	2
94-95	Syracuse	AHL	59	11	22	33	59	—	—	—	—	—
95-96	Vancouver	NHL	—	—	—	—	—	1	0	0	0	0
95-96	Syracuse	AHL	59	13	34	47	85	15	1	8	9	16
96-97	Vancouver	NHL	2	0	0	0	4	—	—	—	—	—
96-97	Syracuse	AHL	55	9	37	46	73	3	2	0	2	0
	NHL	Totals	35	0	8	8	18	2	0	0	0	2
	AHL	Totals	232	40	120	160	314	22	3	10	13	35

Born; 10/9/71, Novgorod, Russia. 5-11, 190. Drafted by Vancouver Canucks (6th choice, 117th overall) in 1991 Entry Draft.

Tyson Nash — Left Wing

Season	Team	League	GP	G	A	PTS	PIM	GP	G	A	PTS	PIM
95-96	Syracuse	AHL	50	4	7	11	58	4	0	0	0	11
95-96	Raleigh	ECHL	6	1	1	2	8	—	—	—	—	—
96-97	Syracuse	AHL	77	17	17	34	105	3	0	2	2	0
	AHL	Totals	127	21	24	45	163	7	0	2	2	11

Born; 3/11/75, Edmonton, Alberta. 6-0, 180. Drafted by Vancouver Canucks (10th choice, 247th overall) in 1994 Entry Draft.

Alain Nasreddine — Defenseman

Season	Team	League	GP	G	A	PTS	PIM	GP	G	A	PTS	PIM
95-96	Carolina	AHL	63	0	5	5	245	—	—	—	—	—
96-97	Carolina	AHL	26	0	4	4	109	—	—	—	—	—
96-97	Indianapolis	IHL	49	0	2	2	248	4	1	1	2	27
	AHL	Totals	89	0	9	9	354	—	—	—	—	—

Born; 7/10/75, Montreal, Quebec. 6-1, 201. Drafted by Florida Panthers (8th choice, 135th overall) in 1993 Entry Draft. Traded to Chicago Blackhawks with a conditional 1998 draft pick by Florida for Ivan Droppa (12/18/96).

Frederik Nasvall — Left Wing

Season	Team	League	GP	G	A	PTS	PIM	GP	G	A	PTS	PIM
95-96	Quad City	CoHL	70	30	28	58	42	4	2	0	2	4
96-97	Quad City	CoHL	74	29	48	77	48	15	8	8	16	22
	CoHL	Totals	144	59	76	135	90	19	10	8	18	26

Born; 11/20/73, Boden, Sweden. 5-8, 171.

Sylvain Naud — Right Wing

			Regular Season					Playoffs				
Season	Team	League	GP	G	A	PTS	PIM	GP	G	A	PTS	PIM
92-93	Tulsa	CeHL	58	39	48	87	114	12	6	13	19	35
93-94	Tulsa	CeHL	24	19	22	41	71	—	—	—	—	—
94-95	Tulsa	CeHL	65	28	36	64	112	7	0	4	4	17
95-96	Tulsa	CeHL	64	32	44	76	107	6	3	1	4	14
96-97	Utah	IHL	8	1	0	1	4	—	—	—	—	—
96-97	New Mexico	WPHL	53	*47	44	91	131	6	1	1	2	12
	CeHL	Totals	211	118	150	268	404	25	9	18	27	66

Born; 3/29/70, LaSalle, Quebec. 5-11, 190. Drafted by Buffalo Sabres (9th choice, 208th overall) in 1990 Entry Draft. 1992-93 CeHL Second Team All-Star. Claimed on waivers by Fort Worth Fire (1993). Traded to Wichita Thunder by Fort Worth for Oleg Santurian and Kevin Stevens (1993). Traded to Tulsa Oilers by Wichita for Dave Doucette and Don Burke (1993). Member of 1992-93 CeHL champion Tulsa Oilers.

Nick Naumenko — Defenseman

			Regular Season					Playoffs				
Season	Team	League	GP	G	A	PTS	PIM	GP	G	A	PTS	PIM
96-97	Worcester	AHL	54	6	22	28	72	1	0	0	0	0

Born; 7/7/74, Chicago, Illinois. Drafted by St. Louis Blues (9th choice, 182nd overall) in 1992 Entry Draft.

Sergei Naumov — Goaltender

			Regular Season							Playoffs				
Season	Team	League	GP	W	L	T	MIN	SO	GAVG	GP	W	L	MIN	SO	GAVG
94-95	Oklahoma City	CeHL	28	13	9	3	1467	0	4.29	1	0	1	60	0	8.00
95-96	San Diego	WCHL	*57	*48	7	2	*3380	*1	3.82	*9	*6	3	*537	0	*2.46
96-97	Las Vegas	IHL	1	1	0	0	60	0	4.00	—	—	—	—	—	—
96-97	San Diego	WCHL	49	*38	8	2	2832	1	*3.14	8	*7	1	465	0	*3.10
	WCHL	Totals	106	86	15	4	6212	2	3.51	17	13	4	1002	0	2.75

Born; 4/4/69, Riga, Latvia. 5-9, 160. 1995-96 WCHL Goaltender of the Year. 1995-96 WCHL Playoff MVP. 1995-96 WCHL First Team All-Star. 1996-97 WCHL Goaltender of the Year. 1996-97 WCHL First Team All-Star. Member of 1995-96 WCHL champion San Diego Gulls. Member of 1996-97 WCHL Champion San Diego Gulls.

Rumun Ndur — Defenseman

			Regular Season					Playoffs				
Season	Team	League	GP	G	A	PTS	PIM	GP	G	A	PTS	PIM
95-96	Rochester	AHL	73	2	12	14	306	17	1	2	3	33
96-97	Buffalo	NHL	2	0	0	0	2	—	—	—	—	—
96-97	Rochester	AHL	68	5	11	16	282	10	3	1	4	21
	AHL	Totals	141	7	23	30	588	27	4	3	7	54

Born; 7/7/75, Zaria, Nigeria. 6-2, 200. Drafted by Buffalo Sabres Sabres (3rd choice, 69th overall) in 1994 Entry Draft. Member of 1995-96 AHL champion Rochester Americans.

Jay Neal — Right Wing

			Regular Season					Playoffs				
Season	Team	League	GP	G	A	PTS	PIM	GP	G	A	PTS	PIM
93-94	Huntinton	ECHL	43	11	15	26	53	—	—	—	—	—
93-94	TOL	ECHL	24	8	10	18	36	14	4	4	8	20
94-95	TOL	ECHL	64	28	34	62	81	4	0	1	1	4
95-96	RAL	ECHL	46	11	23	34	33	4	2	1	3	0
96-97	Amarillo	WPHL	28	13	13	26	45	—	—	—	—	—
96-97	Central Texas	WPHL	25	10	10	20	20	11	4	9	13	6
	ECHL	Totals	177	58	82	140	203	22	6	6	12	24
	WPHL	Totals	53	23	23	46	65	11	4	9	13	6

Born; 6/3/70, Oshawa, Ontario. 6-0, 195. Member of 1993-94 ECHL champion Toledo Storm.

Patrick Neaton — Defenseman

Season	Team	League	GP	G	A	PTS	PIM	GP	G	A	PTS	PIM
93-94	Pittsburgh	NHL	9	1	1	2	12	—	—	—	—	—
93-94	Cleveland	IHL	71	8	24	32	78	—	—	—	—	—
94-95	Cleveland	IHL	2	0	0	0	4	—	—	—	—	—
94-95	San Diego	IHL	71	8	27	35	86	5	0	1	1	0
95-96	Orlando	IHL	77	8	27	35	148	21	3	5	8	34
96-97	Orlando	IHL	81	17	35	52	68	10	0	1	1	13
	IHL	Totals	302	41	113	154	384	36	3	7	10	47

Born; 5/21/71, Detroit, Michigan. 6-0, 180. Drafted by Pittsburgh Penguins (9th choice, 145th overall) in 1990 Entry Draft.

Vaclav Nedomansky — Right Wing

Season	Team	League	GP	G	A	PTS	PIM	GP	G	A	PTS	PIM
92-93	Roanoke	ECHL	22	5	4	9	31	—	—	—	—	—
92-93	Knoxville	ECHL	27	8	11	19	117	—	—	—	—	—
93-94	N/A											
94-95	Phoenix	IHL	41	15	11	26	77	6	0	4	4	23
94-95	Knoxville	ECHL	26	14	9	23	107	—	—	—	—	—
95-96	Phoenix	IHL	3	0	0	0	4	—	—	—	—	—
95-96	Las Vegas	IHL	11	2	4	6	8	2	0	0	0	0
95-96	Knoxville	ECHL	37	32	17	49	160	8	4	4	8	28
96-97	Carolina	AHL	13	4	8	12	8	—	—	—	—	—
96-97	Knoxville	ECHL	45	26	30	56	194	—	—	—	—	—
	IHL	Totals	55	17	15	32	89	8	0	4	4	23
	ECHL	Totals	157	85	71	156	609	8	4	4	48	28

Born; 1/5/71, Bratislavia, Czechoslovakia. 6-1, 210.

Zdenik Nedved — Right Wing

Season	Team	League	GP	G	A	PTS	PIM	GP	G	A	PTS	PIM
94-95	Toronto	NHL	1	0	0	0	2	—	—	—	—	—
95-96	Toronto	NHL	7	1	1	2	6	—	—	—	—	—
95-96	St. John's	AHL	41	13	14	27	22	4	2	0	2	0
96-97	Toronto	NHL	23	3	5	8	6	—	—	—	—	—
96-97	St. John's	AHL	51	9	25	34	34	7	2	2	4	6
	NHL	Totals	31	4	6	10	14	—	—	—	—	—
	AHL	Totals	92	22	39	61	56	11	4	2	6	6

Born; 3/3/75, Lany, Czechoslovakia. 6-0, 180. Drafted by Toronto Maple Leafs (3rd choice, 123rd overall) in 1993 Entry Draft.

David Neilson — Left Wing

Season	Team	League	GP	G	A	PTS	PIM	GP	G	A	PTS	PIM
93-94	Las Vegas	IHL	12	1	3	4	14	—	—	—	—	—
94-95	Las Vegas	IHL	13	0	1	1	51	—	—	—	—	—
94-95	Knoxville	ECHL	33	11	14	25	129	—	—	—	—	—
95-96	Saint John	AHL	13	1	1	2	80	—	—	—	—	—
95-96	Cape Breton	AHL	47	7	10	17	121	—	—	—	—	—
96-97	Knoxville	ECHL	35	12	29	41	98	—	—	—	—	—
96-97	Louisiana	ECHL	30	5	12	17	102	13	1	2	3	38
	AHL	Totals	60	8	11	19	201	—	—	—	—	—
	IHL	Totals	25	1	4	5	65	—	—	—	—	—
	ECHL	Totals	98	28	55	83	329	13	1	2	3	38

Born; 1/25/71, Long Island, New York. 6-3, 215. Drafted by Vancouver Canucks (8th choice, 183rd overall) in 1991 Entry Draft. Signed as a free agent by Las Vegas (3/19/94).

Chad Nelson — Defenseman

			Regular Season					Playoffs				
Season	Team	League	GP	G	A	PTS	PIM	GP	G	A	PTS	PIM
95-96	Charlotte	ECHL	33	5	7	12	162	—	—	—	—	—
95-96	Louisiana	ECHL	19	0	3	3	89	3	0	0	0	27
96-97	Louisiana	ECHL	10	0	3	3	54	—	—	—	—	—
96-97	Wheeling	ECHL	25	1	3	4	79	—	—	—	—	—
96-97	Charlotte	ECHL	21	3	2	5	97	3	0	1	1	6
96-97	San Diego	WCHL	—	—	—	—	—	3	0	1	1	21
	ECHL	Totals	108	9	18	27	481	6	0	1	1	33

Born; 6/3/74, Cranbrook, British Columbia. Member of 1996-97 WCHL Champion San Diego Gulls.

Jeff Nelson — Center

			Regular Season					Playoffs				
Season	Team	League	GP	G	A	PTS	PIM	GP	G	A	PTS	PIM
92-93	Baltimore	AHL	72	14	38	52	12	7	1	3	4	2
93-94	Portland	AHL	80	34	73	107	92	17	10	5	15	20
94-95	Washington	NHL	10	1	0	1	2	—	—	—	—	—
94-95	Portland	AHL	64	33	50	83	57	7	1	4	5	8
95-96	Washington	NHL	33	0	7	7	16	3	0	0	0	4
95-96	Portland	AHL	39	15	32	47	62	—	—	—	—	—
96-97	Grand Rapids	IHL	82	34	55	89	85	5	0	4	4	4
	NHL	Totals	43	1	7	8	18	3	0	0	0	4
	AHL	Totals	255	96	193	289	223	31	12	12	24	30

Born; 12/18/72, Prince Albert, Sakatchewan. 6-0, 180. Drafted by Washington Capitals (4th choice, 36th overall) in 1991 Entry Draft. Member of 1993-94 AHL champion Portland Pirates.

John Nelson — Right Wing

			Regular Season					Playoffs				
Season	Team	League	GP	G	A	PTS	PIM	GP	G	A	PTS	PIM
95-96	St. John's	AHL	3	0	0	0	2	—	—	—	—	—
96-97	Port Huron	CoHL	58	30	39	69	166	5	2	0	2	16

Born; 7/9/69, Scarborough, Ontario. Drafted by Buffalo Sabres (10th choice, 203rd overall) in 1989 Entry Draft.

Todd Nelson — Defenseman

			Regular Season					Playoffs				
Season	Team	League	GP	G	A	PTS	PIM	GP	G	A	PTS	PIM
90-91	Muskegon	IHL	79	4	20	24	32	3	0	0	0	4
91-92	Pittsburgh	NHL	1	0	0	0	0	—	—	—	—	—
91-92	Muskegon	IHL	80	6	35	41	46	14	1	11	12	4
92-93	Cleveland	IHL	76	7	35	42	115	4	0	2	2	4
93-94	Washington	NHL	2	1	0	1	2	4	0	0	0	0
93-94	Portland	AHL	80	11	34	45	69	11	0	6	6	6
94-95	Portland	AHL	75	10	35	45	76	7	0	4	4	6
95-96	Hershey	AHL	70	10	40	50	38	5	1	2	3	8
96-97	Grand Rapids	IHL	81	3	18	21	32	5	1	0	1	0
	NHL	Totals	3	1	0	1	2	4	0	0	0	0
	IHL	Totals	235	17	90	107	193	21	1	13	14	12
	AHL	Totals	225	31	109	140	183	23	1	12	13	20

Born; 5/15/69, Prince Albert, Saskatchewan. 6-0, 200. Drafted by Pittsburgh Penguins (4th choice, 79th overall) in 1989 Entry Draft. Signed as a free agent by Washington Capitals (8/15/93). Member of 1993-94 AHL Champion Portland Pirates. Signed as a free agent by Grand Rapids Griffins (7/96).

Jan Nemecek — Defenseman

Season	Team	League	GP	G	A	PTS	PIM	GP	G	A	PTS	PIM
96-97	Phoenix	IHL	24	1	1	2	2	—	—	—	—	—
96-97	Mississippi	ECHL	20	3	9	12	16	3	0	0	0	4

Born; 2/14/76, Pisek, Czechoslovakia. 6-1, 194. Drafted by Los Angeles Kings (7th choice, 215th overall) in 1994 Entry Draft.

Tom Nemeth — Defenseman

Season	Team	League	GP	G	A	PTS	PIM	GP	G	A	PTS	PIM
92-93	Kalamazoo	IHL	48	6	13	19	24	—	—	—	—	—
92-93	Dayton	ECHL	26	9	28	37	14	—	—	—	—	—
93-94	Dayton	ECHL	66	16	82	98	91	3	1	1	2	16
94-95	Rochester	AHL	56	4	17	21	32	4	2	1	3	4
94-95	South Carolina	ECHL	5	3	3	6	2	—	—	—	—	—
95-96	DNP-injured											
96-97	Dayton	ECHL	23	4	19	23	15	4	2	1	3	2
	ECHL	Totals	120	32	132	164	122	7	3	2	5	18

Born; 1/16/71, St. Catharines, Ontario. Drafted by Minnesota North Stars (8th choice, 206th overall) in 1991 Entry Draft. 1993-94 ECHL First All-Star Team. 1993-94 ECHL Outstanding Defenseman.

Dave Nemirovsky — Right Wing

Season	Team	League	GP	G	A	PTS	PIM	GP	G	A	PTS	PIM
95-96	Florida	NHL	9	0	2	2	0	—	—	—	—	—
95-96	Carolina	AHL	5	1	2	3	0	—	—	—	—	—
96-97	Florida	NHL	39	7	7	14	32	3	1	0	1	0
96-97	Carolina	AHL	34	21	21	42	18	—	—	—	—	—
	NHL	Totals	48	7	9	16	32	3	1	0	1	0
	AHL	Totals	39	22	23	45	18	—	—	—	—	—

Born; 8/1/76, Toronto, Ontario. 6-1, 192. Drafted by Florida Panthers (5th choice, 84th overall) in 1994 Entry Draft.

Mikhail Nemirovsky — Left Wing

Season	Team	League	GP	G	A	PTS	PIM	GP	G	A	PTS	PIM
94-95	Tallahassee	ECHL	6	0	2	2	0	—	—	—	—	—
94-95	Hampton Roads	ECHL	29	6	14	20	33	4	2	0	2	4
95-96	Flint	CoHL	65	29	52	81	121	14	5	10	15	10
96-97	Fredericton	AHL	7	1	0	1	0	—	—	—	—	—
96-97	Fort Wayne	IHL	16	2	4	6	18	—	—	—	—	—
96-97	Madison	CoHL	18	7	15	22	22	—	—	—	—	—
96-97	Flint	CoHL	3	0	5	5	2	9	4	5	9	24
	CoHL	Totals	86	36	72	108	145	23	9	15	24	34
	ECHL	Totals	35	6	16	22	33	4	2	0	2	4

Born; 9/30/74, Moscow, Russia. 6-0, 190. Member of 1995-96 Colonial Cup Champion Flint Generals

Troy Neumeier — Defenseman

Season	Team	League	GP	G	A	PTS	PIM	GP	G	A	PTS	PIM
90-91	Milwaukee	IHL	6	0	0	0	2	—	—	—	—	—
91-92	Milwaukee	IHL	72	1	9	10	55	3	0	0	0	0
92-93	Hamilton	AHL	79	3	11	14	73	—	—	—	—	—
93-94	Hamilton	AHL	44	1	7	8	21	—	—	—	—	—
93-94	Columbus	ECHL	2	0	2	2	2	—	—	—	—	—
94-95	Adirondack	AHL	60	4	17	21	26	4	0	0	0	2
94-95	Toledo	ECHL	10	0	5	5	18	—	—	—	—	—
95-96	Adirondack	AHL	16	0	3	3	10	—	—	—	—	—

Season	Team	League	GP	G	A	PTS	PIM	GP	G	A	PTS	PIM
95-96	Cape Breton	AHL	34	1	3	4	12	—	—	—	—	—
96-97	Hamilton	AHL	63	1	8	9	32	9	1	1	2	4
	AHL	Totals	296	10	49	59	174	13	1	1	2	6
	IHL	Totals	78	1	9	10	57	3	0	0	0	0
	ECHL	Totals	12	0	7	7	20	—	—	—	—	—

Born; 9/3/70, Langenburg, Manitoba. 6-2, 195. Drafted by Vancouver Canucks (9th choice, 191st overall) in 1990 Entry Draft.

Chris Newans — Defenseman

			Regular Season					Playoffs				
Season	Team	League	GP	G	A	PTS	PIM	GP	G	A	PTS	PIM
91-92	Raleigh	ECHL	13	5	4	9	26	—	—	—	—	—
91-92	Dayton	ECHL	23	4	8	12	42	—	—	—	—	—
91-92	Nashville	ECHL	9	6	5	11	16	—	—	—	—	—
91-92	Michigan	CoHL	8	2	6	8	8	—	—	—	—	—
92-93	N/A											
93-94	West Palm Beach	SUN	32	17	25	42	108	5	1	6	7	10
94-95	Saginaw	CoHL	6	4	1	5	27	—	—	—	—	—
94-95	West Palm Beach	SUN	11	4	6	10	33	5	4	4	8	16
95-96	Jacksonville	SHL	26	13	27	40	128	—	—	—	—	—
96-97	Anchorage	WCHL	60	26	57	83	331	9	2	7	9	46
	SHL	Totals	69	34	58	92	269	10	5	10	15	26
	ECHL	Totals	45	15	17	32	84	—	—	—	—	—
	CoHL	Totals	14	6	7	13	35	—	—	—	—	—

Born; 10/6/69, Dauphin, Manitoba. 5-10, 175. WCHL Second Team All-Star. Member of 1993-94 Sunshine champion West Palm Beach Blaze. Member of 1994-95 Sunshine League champion West Palm Beach Blaze.

Ron Newhook — Center

			Regular Season					Playoffs				
Season	Team	League	GP	G	A	PTS	PIM	GP	G	A	PTS	PIM
96-97	Toledo	ECHL	9	1	9	10	2	5	2	0	2	0

Born; 9/8/77, Worth Bay, Ontario. 5-5, 155. Last amateur club; London (OHL).

Todd Newton — Defenseman

			Regular Season					Playoffs				
Season	Team	League	GP	G	A	PTS	PIM	GP	G	A	PTS	PIM
96-97	Quad City	CoHL	69	4	16	20	131	—	—	—	—	—

Born; 12/9/75, St. Catharines, Ontario. 6-1, 220.

Rick Nichol — Goaltender

			Regular Season							Playoffs					
Season	Team	League	GP	W	L	T	MIN	SO	GAVG	GP	W	L	MIN	SO	GAVG
96-97	Oklahoma City	CeHL	23	15	3	1	1216	1	3.11	—	—	—	—	—	—
96-97	Columbus	CeHL	10	4	3	1	460	0	4.95	2	0	1	77	0	4.68
	CeHL	Totals	33	19	6	1	1676	1	3.62	2	0	1	77	0	4.68

Born; 3/13/71, Calgary, Alberta. 5-10, 160.

Scott Nichol — Center

			Regular Season					Playoffs				
Season	Team	League	GP	G	A	PTS	PIM	GP	G	A	PTS	PIM
94-95	Rochester	AHL	71	11	16	27	136	5	0	3	3	14
95-96	Buffalo	NHL	2	0	0	0	10	—	—	—	—	—
95-96	Rochester	AHL	62	14	18	32	170	19	7	6	13	36
96-97	Rochester	AHL	68	22	21	43	133	10	2	1	3	26
	AHL	Totals	201	47	55	102	439	34	9	10	19	76

Born; 12/31/74, Edmonton, Alberta. 5-8, 169. Drafted by Buffalo Sabres (9th choice, 272nd overall) in 1993 Entry Draft. Member of 1995-96 AHL champion Rochester Americans.

Paul Nicolls — Defenseman

			Regular Season					Playoffs				
Season	Team	League	GP	G	A	PTS	PIM	GP	G	A	PTS	PIM
96-97	Port Huron	CoHL	43	2	15	17	33	—	—	—	—	—

Born; 7/5/75, Chilliwack, British Columbia. 6-0, 195.

Barry Nieckar — Left Wing

			Regular Season					Playoffs				
Season	Team	League	GP	G	A	PTS	PIM	GP	G	A	PTS	PIM
91-92	Phoenix	IHL	5	0	0	0	9	—	—	—	—	—
91-92	Raleigh	ECHL	46	10	18	28	229	4	4	0	4	22
92-93	Hartford	NHL	2	0	0	0	2	—	—	—	—	—
92-93	Springfield	AHL	21	2	4	6	65	6	1	0	1	14
93-94	Springfield	AHL	30	0	2	2	67	—	—	—	—	—
93-94	Raleigh	ECHL	18	4	6	10	126	15	5	7	12	51
94-95	Calgary	NHL	3	0	0	0	12	—	—	—	—	—
94-95	Saint John	AHL	65	8	7	15	*491	4	0	0	0	22
95-96	Utah	IHL	53	9	15	24	194	—	—	—	—	—
95-96	Peoria	IHL	10	3	3	6	72	12	4	6	10	48
96-97	Anaheim	NHL	2	0	0	0	5	—	—	—	—	—
96-97	Long Beach	IHL	63	3	10	13	386	5	0	0	0	22
	NHL	Totals	7	0	0	0	19	—	—	—	—	—
	IHL	Totals	131	15	28	43	661	17	4	6	10	70
	AHL	Totals	116	10	13	23	623	10	1	0	1	36
	ECHL	Totals	64	14	24	38	355	19	9	7	16	73

Born; 12/16/67, Rama, Saskatchewan. 6-3, 205. Signed as a free agent by Hartford (9/25/92). Signed as a free agent by Calgary (2/11/95). Signed as a free agent by NY Islanders (8/8/95).

Kirk Nielsen — Right Wing

			Regular Season					Playoffs				
Season	Team	League	GP	G	A	PTS	PIM	GP	G	A	PTS	PIM
96-97	Providence	AHL	68	12	23	35	30	9	2	1	3	2

Born; 10/19/73, Grand Rapids, Minnesota. 6-1, 190. Drafted by Philadelphia Flyers (1st choice, 10th overall) in 1994 Supplemental Draft. Signed as a free agent by Boston Bruins (6/7/96).

Jeff Nielson — Right Wing

			Regular Season					Playoffs				
Season	Team	League	GP	G	A	PTS	PIM	GP	G	A	PTS	PIM
94-95	Binghamton	AHL	76	24	13	37	139	7	0	0	0	22
95-96	Binghamton	AHL	64	22	20	42	56	4	1	1	2	4
96-97	Rangers	NHL	2	0	0	0	2	—	—	—	—	—
96-97	Binghamton	AHL	76	27	26	53	71	4	0	0	0	7
	AHL	Totals	216	73	59	132	266	15	1	1	2	33

Born; 9/20/71, Grand Rapids, Minnesota. 6-0, 175. Drafted by New York Rangers (4rth choice, 69th overall) in 1990 Entry Draft.

Igor Nikulin — Right Wing

			Regular Season					Playoffs				
Season	Team	League	GP	G	A	PTS	PIM	GP	G	A	PTS	PIM
95-96	Baltimore	AHL	4	2	2	4	2	—	—	—	—	—
96-97	Anaheim	NHL	—	—	—	—	—	1	0	0	0	0
96-97	Baltimore	AHL	61	27	25	52	14	3	2	1	3	2
96-97	Fort Wayne	IHL	10	1	2	3	4	—	—	—	—	—
	AHL	Totals	65	29	27	56	16	3	2	1	3	2

Born; 8/26/72, Cherepovets, Russia. 6-1, 190. Drafted by Anaheim Mighty Ducks (4th choice, 107th overall) in 1995 Entry Draft.

Darryl Noren — Center

			Regular Season					Playoffs				
Season	Team	League	GP	G	A	PTS	PIM	GP	G	A	PTS	PIM
90-91	Albany	IHL	7	0	0	0	2	—	—	—	—	—
90-91	Greensboro	ECHL	43	27	23	50	29	13	2	5	7	18
91-92	New Haven	AHL	34	11	9	20	22	—	—	—	—	—
91-92	Halifax	AHL	3	0	0	0	0	—	—	—	—	—
91-92	Greensboro	ECHL	37	36	52	88	48	—	—	—	—	—
92-93	Halifax	AHL	1	0	0	0	0	—	—	—	—	—
92-93	Greensboro	ECHL	61	35	47	82	119	1	1	0	1	0
93-94	Detroit	CoHL	27	18	39	57	22	—	—	—	—	—
93-94	Greensboro	ECHL	26	16	23	39	41	8	1	3	4	20
94-95	Greensboro	ECHL	17	7	16	23	43	—	—	—	—	—
94-95	Charlotte	ECHL	45	39	25	64	63	3	5	1	6	2
95-96	Charlotte	ECHL	70	43	51	94	83	16	7	9	16	37
96-97	San Antonio	IHL	14	1	2	3	23	2	1	1	2	0
96-97	Charlotte	ECHL	57	25	33	58	57	—	—	—	—	—
	AHL	Totals	38	11	9	20	22	—	—	—	—	—
	IHL	Totals	21	1	2	3	25	2	1	1	2	0
	ECHL	Totals	299	203	237	440	426	26	14	13	27	59

Born; 8/7/68, Livonia, Michigan. 5-10, 180. Member of 1995-96 ECHL champion Charlotte Checkers.

Clayton Norris — Right Wing

			Regular Season					Playoffs				
Season	Team	League	GP	G	A	PTS	PIM	GP	G	A	PTS	PIM
92-93	Hershey	AHL	4	0	0	0	5	—	—	—	—	—
92-93	Roanoke	ECHL	4	0	0	0	0	—	—	—	—	—
93-94	Hershey	AHL	62	8	10	18	217	10	1	0	1	18
94-95	Hershey	AHL	76	12	21	33	287	4	0	0	0	8
95-96	Hershey	AHL	57	8	8	16	163	5	0	1	1	4
96-97	Philadelphia	AHL	1	0	0	0	17	—	—	—	—	—
96-97	Orlando	IHL	69	9	9	18	261	10	2	3	5	17
	AHL	Totals	200	28	41	69	689	19	1	1	2	30

Born; 3/8/72, Edmonton, Alberta. 6-2, 205. Drafted by Philadelphia Flyers (6th choice, 116th overall) in 1991 Entry Draft.

Lee Norwood — Defenseman

			Regular Season					Playoffs				
Season	Team	League	GP	G	A	PTS	PIM	GP	G	A	PTS	PIM
80-81	Quebec	NHL	11	1	1	2	9	3	0	0	0	2
80-81	Hershey	AHL	52	11	32	43	78	8	0	4	4	14
81-82	Quebec	NHL	2	0	0	0	2	—	—	—	—	—
81-82	Washington	NHL	26	7	10	17	125	—	—	—	—	—
81-82	Fredericton	AHL	29	6	13	19	74	—	—	—	—	—
82-83	Washington	NHL	8	0	1	1	14	—	—	—	—	—
82-83	Hershey	AHL	67	12	36	48	90	5	0	1	1	2
83-84	St. Catharines	AHL	75	13	46	59	91	7	0	5	5	31
84-85	Peoria	IHL	80	17	60	77	229	18	1	11	12	62
85-86	St. Louis	NHL	71	5	24	29	134	19	2	7	9	64
86-87	Detroit	NHL	57	6	21	27	163	16	1	6	7	31
86-87	Adirondack	AHL	3	0	3	3	0	—	—	—	—	—
87-88	Detroit	NHL	51	9	22	31	131	16	2	6	8	40
88-89	Detroit	NHL	66	10	32	42	100	6	1	2	3	16
89-90	Detroit	NHL	64	8	14	22	95	—	—	—	—	—
90-91	Detroit	NHL	21	3	7	10	50	—	—	—	—	—
90-91	New Jersey	NHL	28	3	2	5	87	4	0	0	0	18
91-92	Hartford	NHL	6	0	0	0	16	—	—	—	—	—
91-92	St. Louis	NHL	44	3	11	14	94	1	0	1	1	0

Season	Team	League	GP	G	A	PTS	PIM	GP	G	A	PTS	PIM
92-93	St. Louis	NHL	32	3	7	10	63	—	—	—	—	—
93-94	Calgary	NHL	16	0	1	1	16	—	—	—	—	—
93-94	San Diego	AHL	4	0	0	0	0	8	0	1	1	11
94-95	DNP-Injured											
95-96	Chicago	IHL	21	2	6	8	26	—	—	—	—	—
95-96	Detroit	IHL	27	3	11	14	26	5	0	3	3	6
96-97	Saginaw	CoHL	12	3	3	6	8	—	—	—	—	—
96-97	San Antonio	IHL	12	0	6	6	10	3	0	0	0	2
	NHL	Totals	503	58	153	211	1099	65	6	22	28	171
	AHL	Totals	226	42	130	172	333	20	0	10	10	47
	IHL	Totals	144	22	83	105	291	34	1	15	16	81

Born; 2/2/60, Trenton, Michigan. 6-1, 198. Selected by Quebec Nordiques (3rd choice, 62nd overall) in 1979 Entry Draft. Traded to Washington Capitals by Quebec for Tim Tookey and seventh round pick (Daniel Poudrier) in 1982 Entry Draft (1/82). Traded to Toronto Maple Leafs by Washington for Dave Shand (10/6/83). Signed as a free agent by St. Louis Blues (8/13/85). Traded to Detroit Red Wings by St. Louis for Larry Trader (8/7/86). Traded to New Jersey Devils by Detroit with future considerations for Paul Ysebaert, Devils received fourth round pick in 1992 (Scott McCabe) to complete deal (11/27/90). Traded to Hartford Whalers by New Jersey for future considerations (10/3/91). Traded to St. Louis by Hartford for future considerations (11/13/91). Released by St. Louis (6/30/93). Signed as a free agent by Calgary Flames (10/20/93). 1984-85 IHL First Team All-Star. 1984-85 IHL Best Defenseman (Governor's Trophy). Member of 1984-85 IHL champion Peoria Rivermen.

Teemu Numminen — Forward

			Regular Season					Playoffs				
Season	Team	League	GP	G	A	PTS	PIM	GP	G	A	PTS	PIM
96-97	Fresno	WCHL	62	31	27	58	41	5	2	1	3	0

Born; 12/23/73, Tampero, Finland. 6-3, 205.

Sean O'Brien — Left Wing

Regular Season / Playoffs

Season	Team	League	GP	G	A	PTS	PIM	GP	G	A	PTS	PIM
94-95	Houston	IHL	13	2	1	3	23	—	—	—	—	—
94-95	Richmond	ECHL	52	5	18	23	147	17	2	5	7	77
95-96	Utah	IHL	7	2	2	4	12	—	—	—	—	—
95-96	Las Vegas	IHL	1	0	0	0	2	—	—	—	—	—
95-96	Houston	IHL	4	0	1	1	12	—	—	—	—	—
95-96	Tallahassee	ECHL	54	9	19	28	179	8	0	2	2	23
96-97	Tallahassee	ECHL	10	7	3	10	29	—	—	—	—	—
96-97	Utah	IHL	50	21	10	31	135	—	—	—	—	—
96-97	Phoenix	IHL	10	3	3	6	20	—	—	—	—	—
	IHL	Totals	85	28	17	45	204	—	—	—	—	—
	ECHL	Totals	116	21	40	61	355	25	2	7	9	100

Born; 2/9/72, Boston, Masachusetts. 6-1, 200. Signed as a free agent by Los Angeles Kings (7/97). Member of 1994-95 ECHL champion Richmond Renegades.

Myles O'Connor — Defenseman

Regular Season / Playoffs

Season	Team	League	GP	G	A	PTS	PIM	GP	G	A	PTS	PIM
88-89	Utica	AHL	1	0	0	0	0	—	—	—	—	—
89-90	Utica	AHL	76	14	33	47	124	5	1	2	3	26
90-91	New Jersey	NHL	22	3	1	4	41	—	—	—	—	—
90-91	Utica	AHL	33	6	17	23	62	—	—	—	—	—
91-92	New Jersey	NHL	9	0	2	2	13	—	—	—	—	—
91-92	Utica	AHL	66	9	39	48	184	—	—	—	—	—
92-93	New Jersey	NHL	7	0	0	0	9	—	—	—	—	—
92-93	Utica	AHL	9	1	5	6	10	—	—	—	—	—
93-94	Anaheim	NHL	5	0	1	1	6	—	—	—	—	—
93-94	San Diego	IHL	39	1	13	14	117	9	1	4	5	83
94-95	San Diego	IHL	16	1	4	5	50	5	0	1	1	0
95-96	Houtson	IHL	80	2	24	26	256	—	—	—	—	—
96-97	Houston	IHL	3	0	0	0	6	—	—	—	—	—
96-97	Cincinnati	IHL	62	0	4	4	241	3	0	0	0	34
	NHL	Totals	43	3	4	7	69	—	—	—	—	—
	IHL	Totals	200	4	45	49	670	17	1	5	6	117
	AHL	Totals	185	30	94	124	380	5	1	2	3	26

Born; 4/2/67, Calgary, Alberta. 5-11, 185. Drafted by New Jersey Devils (4th choice, 45th overall) in 1985 Entry Draft. Signed as a free agent by Anaheim Mighty Ducks (7/22/93).

Matt O'Dette — Defenseman

Regular Season / Playoffs

Season	Team	League	GP	G	A	PTS	PIM	GP	G	A	PTS	PIM
96-97	Roanoke	ECHL	69	6	16	22	139	4	0	0	0	10

Born; 11/9/75, Oshawa, Ontario. 6-5, 220. Drafted by Florida Panthers (7th choice, 157th overall) in 1994 Entry Draft.

Mark O'Donnell — Left Wing

Regular Season / Playoffs

Season	Team	League	GP	G	A	PTS	PIM	GP	G	A	PTS	PIM
96-97	Fort Worth	CeHL	63	35	33	68	24	17	4	7	11	8

Born; 5/3/74, Kanata, Ontario. 6-3, 213. Member of 1996-97 CeHL Champion Fort Worth Fire.

Mike O'Neill — Goaltender

Regular Season / Playoffs

Season	Team	League	GP	W	L	T	MIN	SO	GAVG	GP	W	L	MIN	SO	GAVG
90-91	Fort Wayne	IHL	8	5	2	1	490	0	3.80	—	—	—	—	—	—
90-91	Moncton	AHL	30	13	7	6	1613	0	3.12	8	3	4	435	0	4.00

Season	Team	League	GP	W	L	T	MIN	SO	GAA	GP	W	L	MIN	SO	GAA
91-92	Winnipeg	NHL	1	0	0	0	13	0	4.62	—	—	—	—	—	—
91-92	Fort Wayne	IHL	33	22	6	3	1858	*4	3.13	—	—	—	—	—	—
91-92	Moncton	AHL	32	14	16	2	1902	1	3.41	11	4	7	670	*1	3.85
92-93	Winnipeg	NHL	2	0	0	1	73	0	4.93	—	—	—	—	—	—
92-93	Moncton	AHL	30	13	10	4	1649	1	3.20	—	—	—	—	—	—
93-94	Winnipeg	NHL	17	0	9	1	738	0	4.15	—	—	—	—	—	—
93-94	Moncton	AHL	12	8	4	0	716	1	2.76	—	—	—	—	—	—
93-94	Fort Wayne	IHL	11	4	4	3	642	0	3.55	—	—	—	—	—	—
94-95	Fort Wayne	IHL	28	11	12	4	1603	0	4.08	—	—	—	—	—	—
94-95	Phoenix	IHL	21	13	4	4	1256	1	3.06	9	4	5	535	0	3.70
95-96	Baltimore	AHL	*74	31	*31	7	*4250	2	3.53	12	6	6	689	0	3.75
96-97	Anaheim	NHL	1	0	0	0	31	0	5.81	—	—	—	—	—	—
96-97	Long Beach	IHL	45	26	12	6	2644	1	3.29	1	0	0	7	0	0.00
	NHL	Totals	21	0	9	2	855	0	4.28	—	—	—	—	—	—
	AHL	Totals	178	79	68	19	10130	5	3.33	31	13	17	1794	1	3.85
	IHL	Totals	146	81	40	21	8493	6	3.42	10	4	5	542	0	3.65

Born; 11/3/67, LaSalle, Quebec. 5-7, 160. Drafted by Winnipeg Jets (1st choice, 15th overall) in 1988 Supplemental Draft. Signed as a free agent by Anaheim Mighty Ducks (7/14/95).

Hayden O'Rear — Defenseman

Season	Team	League	GP	G	A	PTS	PIM	GP	G	A	PTS	PIM
92-93	Richmond	ECHL	1	0	0	0	2	—	—	—	—	—
92-93	Knoxville	ECHL	52	4	12	16	45	—	—	—	—	—
93-94	Knoxville	ECHL	61	7	20	27	83	3	0	0	0	0
94-95	Knoxville	ECHL	53	0	11	11	44	—	—	—	—	—
95-96	Winston-Salem	SHL	60	6	34	40	89	8	0	6	6	28
96-97	Anchorage	WCHL	64	8	37	45	70	9	2	4	6	2
	ECHL	Totals	167	11	43	54	174	3	0	0	0	0

Born; 10/8/70, Fairbanks, Alaska. 6-0, 190. Drafted by Vancouver Canucks (9th choice, 218th overall) in 1989 Entry Draft. 1996-97 WCHL Second Team All-Star.

Chris O'Rourke — Defenseman

Season	Team	League	GP	G	A	PTS	PIM	GP	G	A	PTS	PIM
92-93	Detroit	CoHL	51	0	10	10	165	6	0	0	0	10
93-94	Flint	CoHL	47	1	13	14	168	10	0	2	2	56
94-95	Tallahassee	ECHL	15	0	1	1	79	—	—	—	—	—
94-95	Flint	CoHL	34	3	9	12	134	6	0	1	1	25
95-96	West Palm Beach	SHL	7	2	0	2	33	—	—	—	—	—
95-96	Winston-Salem	SHL	39	3	12	15	109	9	0	4	4	37
96-97	Waco	WPHL	29	1	5	6	70	—	—	—	—	—
96-97	Austin	WPHL	15	1	3	4	26	1	0	0	0	12
	CoHL	Totals	132	4	32	36	467	22	0	3	3	91
	SHL	Totals	46	5	12	17	142	9	0	4	4	37
	WPHL	Totals	44	2	8	10	96	1	0	0	0	12

Born; 1/6/71, Calgary, Alberta. 6-2, 195. Drafted by Toronto Maple Leafs (13th choice, 245th overall) in 1991 Entry Draft.

Dan O'Rourke — Left Wing

Season	Team	League	GP	G	A	PTS	PIM	GP	G	A	PTS	PIM
93-94	Erie	ECHL	64	9	21	30	296	—	—	—	—	—
94-95	Tulsa	CeHL	57	12	19	31	180	7	0	1	1	53
95-96	Louisiana	ECHL	40	10	18	28	257	3	0	0	0	9
96-97	Detroit	IHL	1	0	0	0	0	—	—	—	—	—
96-97	Houston	IHL	1	0	0	0	2	—	—	—	—	—
96-97	Louisiana	ECHL	58	28	20	48	160	10	3	1	4	42
	ECHL	Totals	162	47	59	106	713	13	3	1	4	51

Born; 8/31/72, Calgary, Alberta. 6-3, 195.

Tom O'Rourke — Center

			Regular Season					Playoffs				
Season	Team	League	GP	G	A	PTS	PIM	GP	G	A	PTS	PIM
92-93	Detroit	CoHL	41	10	17	27	33	1	0	0	0	2
93-94	Huntsville	ECHL	49	8	16	24	83	3	0	3	3	7
96-97	Waco	WPHL	61	9	19	28	60	—	—	—	—	—

Born; 2/23/70, Calgary, Alberta. 6-0, 197.

Chris O'Sullivan — Defenseman

			Regular Season					Playoffs				
Season	Team	League	GP	G	A	PTS	PIM	GP	G	A	PTS	PIM
96-97	Calgary	NHL	27	2	8	10	2	—	—	—	—	—
96-97	Saint John	AHL	29	3	8	11	17	5	0	4	4	0

Born; 5/15/74, Dorchester, Massachusetts. 6-2, 185. Drafted by Calgary Flames (2nd choice, 30th overall) in 1992 Entry Draft.

Matt Oates — Center

			Regular Season					Playoffs				
Season	Team	League	GP	G	A	PTS	PIM	GP	G	A	PTS	PIM
94-95	Indianapolis	IHL	59	3	6	9	18	—	—	—	—	—
94-95	Columbus	ECHL	11	4	5	9	11	—	—	—	—	—
95-96	Columbus	ECHL	46	12	28	40	63	3	1	0	1	4
96-97	Columbus	ECHL	70	22	43	65	59	8	2	3	5	16
	ECHL	Totals	127	38	76	114	133	11	3	3	6	20

Born; 12/20/72, Evanston, Illinois. 6-3, 208. Drafted by New York Rangers (7th choice, 168th overall) in 1992 Entry Draft. Traded to Chicago Blackhawks by Rangers with Tony Amonte for Stefan Matteau and Brian Noonan (3/21/94).

Jaroslav Obsut — Defenseman

			Regular Season					Playoffs				
Season	Team	League	GP	G	A	PTS	PIM	GP	G	A	PTS	PIM
96-97	Toledo	ECHL	3	1	0	1	0	5	0	1	1	6

Born; 9/3/76, Presov, Czechoslovakia. 6-1, 185. Drafted by Winnipeg Jets (9th choice, 188th overall) in 1995 Entry Draft.

Frederick Oduya — Defenseman

			Regular Season					Playoffs				
Season	Team	League	GP	G	A	PTS	PIM	GP	G	A	PTS	PIM
95-96	Kansas City	IHL	56	2	6	8	235	3	0	0	0	2
96-97	Kentucky	AHL	69	2	9	11	241	—	—	—	—	—

Born; 5/31/75, Stockholm, Sweden. 6-2, 185. Drafted by San Jose Sharks (8th choice, 154th overall) in 1993 Entry Draft.

Simon Olivier — Defenseman

			Regular Season					Playoffs				
Season	Team	League	GP	G	A	PTS	PIM	GP	G	A	PTS	PIM
95-96	Oklahoma City	CeHL	45	17	19	36	136	—	—	—	—	—
96-97	Mississippi	ECHL	67	8	13	21	230	3	1	1	2	12

Born; 2/2/72, Quebec City, Quebec. 5-11, 190.

Krzysztof Oliwa — Left Wing

			Regular Season					Playoffs				
Season	Team	League	GP	G	A	PTS	PIM	GP	G	A	PTS	PIM
93-94	Albany	AHL	33	2	4	6	151	—	—	—	—	—
93-94	Raleigh	ECHL	15	0	2	2	65	9	0	0	0	35
94-95	Albany	AHL	20	1	1	2	77	—	—	—	—	—
94-95	Saint John	AHL	14	1	4	5	79	—	—	—	—	—
94-95	Detroit	IHL	4	0	1	1	24	—	—	—	—	—
94-95	Raleigh	ECHL	5	0	2	2	32	—	—	—	—	—
95-96	Albany	AHL	51	5	11	16	217	—	—	—	—	—
95-96	Raleigh	ECHL	9	1	0	1	53	—	—	—	—	—

Season	Team	League	GP	G	A	PTS	PIM	GP	G	A	PTS	PIM
96-97	New Jersey	NHL	1	0	0	0	5	—	—	—	—	—
96-97	Albany	AHL	60	13	14	27	322	15	7	1	8	49
	AHL	Totals	178	22	34	56	846	15	7	1	8	49
	ECHL	Totals	29	1	4	5	150	9	0	0	0	35

Born; 4/12/73, Tychy, Poland. 6-5, 220. Drafted by New Jersey Devils (4th choice, 65th overall) in 1993 Entry Draft.

Jon Olofson — Defenseman

Regular Season | Playoffs

Season	Team	League	GP	G	A	PTS	PIM	GP	G	A	PTS	PIM
96-97	Waco	WPHL	51	1	12	13	34	—	—	—	—	—

Born; Denver, Colorado. 6-1, 205.

Boyd Olson — Center

Regular Season | Playoffs

Season	Team	League	GP	G	A	PTS	PIM	GP	G	A	PTS	PIM
95-96	Fredericton	AHL	—	—	—	—	—	2	1	0	1	0
96-97	Fredericton	AHL	74	8	12	20	43	—	—	—	—	—
	AHL	Totals	74	8	21	20	43	2	1	0	1	0

Born; 4/4/76, Edmonton, Alberta. 6-1, 170. Drafted by Montreal Canadiens (6th choice, 138th overall) in 1995 Entry Draft.

Sergei Olympiev — Left Wing

Regular Season | Playoffs

Season	Team	League	GP	G	A	PTS	PIM	GP	G	A	PTS	PIM
95-96	Johnstown	ECHL	3	0	1	1	0	—	—	—	—	—
96-97	Alaska	WCHL	56	16	16	32	53	—	—	—	—	—

Born; 1/12/75, 6-4, 220.

Vladimir Orszagh — Right Wing

Regular Season | Playoffs

Season	Team	League	GP	G	A	PTS	PIM	GP	G	A	PTS	PIM
96-97	Utah	IHL	68	12	15	27	30	3	0	1	1	4

Born; 5/24/77, Banska Bystrica, Czechoslovakia. 5-11, 173. Drafted by New York Islanders (4th choice, 106th overall) in 1995 Entry Draft.

Sean Ortiz — Left Wing

Regular Season | Playoffs

Season	Team	League	GP	G	A	PTS	PIM	GP	G	A	PTS	PIM
95-96	Dayton	ECHL	35	4	5	9	29	—	—	—	—	—
95-96	Erie	ECHL	14	0	2	2	17	—	—	—	—	—
96-97	Dayton	CoHL	37	23	13	36	20	—	—	—	—	—
96-97	Utica	CoHL	2	0	1	1	0	—	—	—	—	—
96-97	Flint	CoHL	33	17	16	33	20	13	2	2	4	8
	CoHL	Totals	72	40	30	70	20	13	2	2	4	8
	ECHL	Totals	49	4	7	11	46	—	—	—	—	—

Born; 12/1/71, Peoria, Illinois. 6-0, 200.

Keith Osborne — Right Wing

Regular Season | Playoffs

Season	Team	League	GP	G	A	PTS	PIM	GP	G	A	PTS	PIM
89-90	St. Louis	NHL	5	0	2	2	8	—	—	—	—	—
89-90	Peoria	IHL	56	23	24	47	58	—	—	—	—	—
90-91	Peoria	IHL	54	10	20	30	79	—	—	—	—	—
90-91	Newmarket	AHL	12	0	3	3	6	—	—	—	—	—
91-92	St. John's	AHL	53	11	16	27	21	4	0	1	1	2
92-93	Tampa Bay	NHL	11	1	1	2	8	—	—	—	—	—
92-93	Atlanta	IHL	72	40	49	89	91	8	1	5	6	2
93-94	N/A											
94-95	N/A											
95-96	Peoria	IHL	63	23	28	51	64	9	5	3	8	12

Season	Team	League	GP	G	A	PTS	PIM	GP	G	A	PTS	PIM
96-97	San Antonio	IHL	52	12	13	25	41	—	—	—	—	—
96-97	Utah	IHL	9	3	0	3	4	1	0	0	0	0
	NHL	Totals	16	1	3	4	8	—	—	—	—	—
	IHL	Totals	306	111	134	245	337	18	6	8	14	14
	AHL	Totals	65	11	19	30	27	4	0	1	1	2

Born; 4/2/69, Toronto. 6-1, 180. Drafted by St. Louis Blues (1st choice, 12th overall) in 1987 Entry Draft. Traded to Toronto Maple Leafs by St. Louis for Darren Veitch (3/5/91). Selected by Tampa Bay Lightning in Expansion Draft (6/18/92).

Mark Osborne — Left Wing

			Regular Season					Playoffs				
Season	Team	League	GP	G	A	PTS	PIM	GP	G	A	PTS	PIM
80-81	Adirondack	AHL	—	—	—	—	—	13	2	3	5	2
81-82	Detroit	NHL	80	26	41	67	61	—	—	—	—	—
82-83	Detroit	NHL	80	19	24	43	83	—	—	—	—	—
83-84	Rangers	NHL	73	23	28	51	88	5	0	1	1	7
84-85	Rangers	NHL	23	4	4	8	33	3	0	0	0	4
85-86	Rangers	NHL	62	16	24	40	80	15	2	3	5	26
86-87	Rangers	NHL	58	17	15	32	101	—	—	—	—	—
86-87	Toronto	NHL	16	5	10	15	12	9	1	3	4	6
87-88	Toronto	NHL	79	23	37	60	102	6	1	3	4	16
88-89	Toronto	NHL	75	16	30	46	112	—	—	—	—	—
89-90	Toronto	NHL	78	23	50	73	91	5	2	3	5	12
90-91	Toronto	NHL	18	3	3	6	4	—	—	—	—	—
90-91	Winnipeg	NHL	37	8	8	16	59	—	—	—	—	—
91-92	Winnipeg	NHL	43	4	12	16	65	—	—	—	—	—
91-92	Toronto	NHL	11	3	1	4	8	—	—	—	—	—
92-93	Toronto	NHL	76	12	14	26	89	19	1	1	2	16
93-94	Toronto	NHL	73	9	15	24	145	18	4	2	6	52
94-95	Rangers	NHL	37	1	3	4	19	7	1	0	1	2
95-96	Cleveland	IHL	70	31	38	69	131	3	1	2	3	2
96-97	Cleveland	IHL	59	7	25	32	96	6	1	2	3	14
	NHL	Totals	919	212	319	531	1152	87	12	16	28	141
	IHL	Totals	129	38	63	101	227	9	2	4	6	16

Born; /13/61, Toronto, Ontario. 6-2, 205. Drafted by Detroit Red Wings (2nd choice, 46th overall) in 1980 Entry Draft. Traded to New York Rangers by Detroit with Willie Huber and Mike Blaisdell for Ron Duguay, Eddie Mio and Eddie Johnstone (6/18/83). Traded to Toronto Maple Leafs by Rangers for Jeff Jackson and Toronto's third choice (Rob Zamuner) in 1989 Entry Draft (3/5/87). Traded to Winnipeg Jets by Toronto with Ed Olczyk for Dave Ellett and Paul Fenton (11/10/90). Traded to Toronto by Winnipeg for Lucien DeBlois (3/10/92). Signed as a free agent by Rangers (1/20/95).

Matt Osiecki — Defenseman

			Regular Season					Playoffs				
Season	Team	League	GP	G	A	PTS	PIM	GP	G	A	PTS	PIM
94-95	Tallahassee	ECHL	68	6	27	33	28	13	0	0	0	18
95-96	Tallahassee	ECHL	68	6	24	30	108	12	0	4	4	6
96-97	Tallahassee	ECHL	67	5	21	26	61	3	0	1	1	2
	ECHL	Totals	203	17	72	89	197	28	0	5	5	26

Born; 7/31/72, Burnsville, Minnesota. 6-2, 212.

Frank Ouellette — Goaltender

			Regular Season							Playoffs					
Season	Team	League	GP	W	L	T	MIN	SO	GAVG	GP	W	L	MIN	SO	GAVG
91-92	Flint	CoHL	8	2	4	0	384	0	5.63	—	—	—	—	—	—
91-92	Dayton	ECHL	8	—	—	—	493	0	4.26	2	—	—	111	0	5.41
91-92	Peoria	IHL	12	—	—	—	700	0	3.17	—	—	—	—	—	—
92-93	Wheeling	ECHL	43	24	7	7	2376	2	3.48	9	4	4	560	0	3.54
93-94	South Carolina	ECHL	41	16	15	7	2336	0	4.26	—	—	—	—	—	—
94-95	Erie	ECHL	45	15	28	1	2559	1	4.74	—	—	—	—	—	—
95-96	Anchorage	WCHL	23	9	9	3	1296	1	3.75	—	—	—	—	—	—

96-97	Anchorage	WCHL	51	30	15	5	2959	0	3.85	*9	2	*7	*495	0	4.85
@	ECHL	Totals	137	55	50	15	7764	3	4.18	11	4	4	671	0	3.85
	WCHL	Totals	74	39	24	8	4255	1	3.82	9	2	7	495	0	4.85

Born; 4/16/70, Victoriaville, Quebec. 5-10, 190. @ ECHL win/loss totals are not complete. 1992-93 ECHL First Team All-Star. 1995-96 WCHL Second Team All-Star. 1996-97 WCHL Second Team All-Star.

Mark Ouimet — Center

			Regular Season					Playoffs				
Season	Team	League	GP	G	A	PTS	PIM	GP	G	A	PTS	PIM
92-93	Baltimore	AHL	1	0	1	1	0	—	—	—	—	—
93-94	N/A											
94-95	Worcester	AHL	61	13	29	42	24	—	—	—	—	—
95-96	Adirondack	AHL	59	16	16	32	20	3	0	0	0	2
96-97	Worcester	AHL	2	0	1	1	0	—	—	—	—	—
96-97	Baton Rouge	ECHL	29	9	12	21	7	—	—	—	—	—
	AHL	Totals	123	29	47	76	44	3	0	0	0	2

Born; 10/2/71, London, Ontario. 5-10, 183. Drafted by Washington Capitals (6th choice, 94th overall) in 1990 Entry Draft.

Ronald Ozolinsh — Defenseman

			Regular Season					Playoffs				
Season	Team	League	GP	G	A	PTS	PIM	GP	G	A	PTS	PIM
95-96	Jacksonville	ECHL	36	3	5	8	43	15	1	2	3	27
96-97	San Antonio	IHL	2	0	0	0	0	—	—	—	—	—
96-97	Jacksonville	ECHL	50	1	8	9	41	—	—	—	—	—
	ECHL	Totals	86	4	13	17	84	15	1	2	3	27

Born; 2/7/73, Riga, Latvia. 6-0, 187.

Paul Pachevitch — Right Wing

			Regular Season					Playoffs				
Season	Team	League	GP	G	A	PTS	PIM	GP	G	A	PTS	PIM
93-94	West Palm Beach	SUN	17	9	11	20	17	5	2	0	2	6
94-95	Flint	CoHL	19	4	8	12	19	—	—	—	—	—
94-95	Brantford	CoHL	14	7	5	12	4	—	—	—	—	—
95-96	Detroit	CoHL	19	9	13	22	12	—	—	—	—	—
95-96	Flint	CoHL	5	1	0	1	0	—	—	—	—	—
95-96	Quad City	CoHL	1	0	0	0	0	—	—	—	—	—
96-97	Dayton	ECHL	5	2	3	5	2	—	—	—	—	—
96-97	Reno	WCHL	44	17	20	37	50	—	—	—	—	—
	CoHL	Totals	58	21	26	47	35	—	—	—	—	—

Born; 3/31/67, St. Petersburg, Russia. 6-0, 185. Member of 1993-94 Sunshine League champion West Palm Beach.

Kevin Paden — Center

			Regular Season					Playoffs				
Season	Team	League	GP	G	A	PTS	PIM	GP	G	A	PTS	PIM
95-96	Cape Breton	AHL	1	1	0	1	0	—	—	—	—	—
95-96	Tallahassee	ECHL	23	3	10	13	49	—	—	—	—	—
95-96	Huntington	ECHL	32	4	5	9	52	—	—	—	—	—
96-97	Huntington	ECHL	13	7	5	12	26	—	—	—	—	—
96-97	Nashville	CeHL	23	7	9	16	58	—	—	—	—	—
	ECHL	Totals	68	14	20	34	127	—	—	—	—	—

Born; 2/12/75, Woodhaven, Michigan. 6-4, 200. Drafted by Edmonton Oilers (4th choice, 59th overall) in 1993 Entry Draft.

Jim Paek — Defenseman

			Regular Season					Playoffs				
Season	Team	League	GP	G	A	PTS	PIM	GP	G	A	PTS	PIM
87-88	Muskegon	IHL	82	7	52	59	141	6	0	0	0	29
88-89	Muskegon	IHL	80	3	54	57	96	14	1	10	11	24
89-90	Muskegon	IHL	81	9	41	50	115	15	1	10	11	41
90-91	Canadian	National										
90-91	Pittsburgh	NHL	3	0	0	0	9	8	1	0	1	2
91-92	Pittsburgh	NHL	49	1	7	8	36	19	0	4	4	6
92-93	Pittsburgh	NHL	77	3	15	18	64	—	—	—	—	—
93-94	Pittsburgh	NHL	41	0	4	4	8	—	—	—	—	—
93-94	Los Angeles	NHL	18	1	1	2	10	—	—	—	—	—
94-95	Ottawa	NHL	29	0	2	2	28	—	—	—	—	—
95-96	Houston	IHL	25	2	5	7	20	—	—	—	—	—
95-96	Minnesota	IHL	42	1	11	12	54	—	—	—	—	—
96-97	Manitoba	IHL	9	0	2	2	12	—	—	—	—	—
96-97	Cleveland	IHL	74	3	25	28	36	14	0	1	1	2
	NHL	Totals	217	5	29	34	155	27	1	4	5	8
	IHL	Totals	393	25	190	215	474	49	2	21	23	96

Born; 4/7/67, Weston, Ontario. 6-1, 195. Drafted by Pittsburgh Penguins (9th choice, 170th overall) in 1985 Entry Draft. Traded to Los Angeles Kings by Pittsburgh with Marty McSorley for Tomas Sandstrom and Shawn McEachern (2/16/94). Traded to Ottawa Senators by Los Angeles for Ottawa's seventh round choice (Benoit Larose) in 1995 Entry Draft (6/26/94). Member of 1988-89 IHL champion Muskegon Lumberjacks. Member of 1990-91 Stanley Cup champion Pittsburgh Penguins. Member of 1991-92 Stanley Cup champion Pittsburgh Penguins.

Glenn Painter — Defenseman

			Regular Season					Playoffs				
Season	Team	League	GP	G	A	PTS	PIM	GP	G	A	PTS	PIM
93-94	Memphis	CeHL	53	13	34	47	34	—	—	—	—	—
95-96	Madison	CoHL	72	6	30	36	58	6	1	1	2	11
96-97	Fort Worth	CeHL	64	6	35	41	71	17	1	5	6	18
	CeHL	Totals	117	19	69	88	105	17	1	5	6	18

Born; 3/24/69, Montreal, Quebec. 5-10, 180. Member of 1996-97 CeHL Champion Fort Worth Fire. DNP during 1994-95 season.

Greg Pajor — Right Wing

Season	Team	League	GP	G	A	PTS	PIM	GP	G	A	PTS	PIM
96-97	Brantford	CoHL	55	8	17	25	16	10	1	2	3	4

Born; 9/6/71, Wilsonville, Ontario. 6-0, 180. Last amateur club; Western Ontario University (OUAA).

Drew Palmer — Defenseman

Season	Team	League	GP	G	A	PTS	PIM	GP	G	A	PTS	PIM
96-97	Cleveland	IHL	13	0	0	0	21	—	—	—	—	—
96-97	Kansas City	IHL	26	0	2	2	55	—	—	—	—	—
96-97	Mobile	ECHL	5	0	2	2	25	—	—	—	—	—
	IHL	Totals	39	0	2	2	76	—	—	—	—	—

Born; 1/10/76, Wayzata, Minnesota. 6-3, 210. Last amateur club; Seattle (WHL).

Rod Pamenter — Defenseman

Season	Team	League	GP	G	A	PTS	PIM	GP	G	A	PTS	PIM
96-97	Baton Rouge	ECHL	18	2	4	6	16	—	—	—	—	—
96-97	Raleigh	ECHL	34	2	12	14	26	—	—	—	—	—
	ECHL	Totals	52	4	16	20	42	—	—	—	—	—

Born; 3/22/73, Mississauga, Ontario. 6-0, 205. Last amateur club; Colgate (ECAC).

Greg Pankiewicz — Right Wing

Season	Team	League	GP	G	A	PTS	PIM	GP	G	A	PTS	PIM
91-92	Knoxville	ECHL	59	41	39	80	214	—	—	—	—	—
92-93	New Haven	AHL	62	23	20	43	163	—	—	—	—	—
93-94	Ottawa	NHL	3	0	0	0	2	—	—	—	—	—
93-94	Prince Edward Island	AHL	69	33	29	62	241	—	—	—	—	—
94-95	Prince Edward Island	AHL	75	37	30	67	161	6	1	1	2	24
95-96	Portland	AHL	28	9	12	21	99	—	—	—	—	—
95-96	Chicago	IHL	45	9	16	25	164	5	4	0	4	8
96-97	Chicago	IHL	79	32	34	66	222	—	—	—	—	—
	AHL	Totals	234	102	91	193	664	11	5	1	6	32
	IHL	Totals	124	41	50	91	386	5	4	0	4	8

Born; 10/6/70, Drayton Valley, Alberta. 6-0, 180. Signed as a free agent by Ottawa Senators (5/27/93). Signed as a free agent by Washington Capitals (7/2/95).

Grigori Panteleyev — Left Wing

Season	Team	League	GP	G	A	PTS	PIM	GP	G	A	PTS	PIM
92-93	Boston	NHL	39	8	6	14	12	—	—	—	—	—
92-93	Providence	AHL	39	17	30	47	22	3	0	0	0	10
93-94	Boston	NHL	10	0	0	0	0	—	—	—	—	—
93-94	Providence	AHL	55	24	26	50	20	—	—	—	—	—
94-95	Boston	NHL	1	0	0	0	0	—	—	—	—	—
94-95	Providence	AHL	70	20	23	43	36	13	8	11	19	6
95-96	Utah	IHL	33	11	25	36	18	—	—	—	—	—
95-96	Las Vegas	IHL	29	15	21	36	14	15	4	7	11	2
95-96	Islanders	NHL	4	0	0	0	0	—	—	—	—	—
96-97	San Antonio	IHL	81	25	37	62	41	9	4	2	6	4
	NHL	Totals	54	8	6	14	12	—	—	—	—	—
	AHL	Totals	164	61	79	160	78	16	8	11	19	16
	IHL	Totals	143	51	83	134	73	24	8	9	17	6

Born; 11/13/72, Gastello, Russia. 5-9, 185. Drafted by Boston Bruins (5th choice, 136th overall) in 1992 Entry Draft. Signed as a free agent by New York Islanders (9/20/95).

Perry Pappas — Right Wing

		Regular Season						Playoffs				
Season	Team	League	GP	G	A	PTS	PIM	GP	G	A	PTS	PIM
96-97	Wheeling	ECHL	11	3	1	4	18	—	—	—	—	—
96-97	Baton Rouge	ECHL	39	17	6	23	89	—	—	—	—	—
	ECHL	Totals	50	20	7	27	107	—	—	—	—	—

Born; 11/3/73, Chatham, Ontario. 6-2, 210.

Normand Paquet — Center

		Regular Season						Playoffs				
Season	Team	League	GP	G	A	PTS	PIM	GP	G	A	PTS	PIM
96-97	Thunder Bay	CoHL	74	19	42	61	55	11	2	6	8	4

Born; 7/5/73, Beauport, Quebec. 5-10, 195.

Charles Paquette — Defenseman

		Regular Season						Playoffs				
Season	Team	League	GP	G	A	PTS	PIM	GP	G	A	PTS	PIM
95-96	Providence	AHL	11	0	1	1	8	4	0	1	1	4
95-96	Charlotte	ECHL	45	4	5	9	114	3	0	1	1	6
96-97	Providence	AHL	18	0	3	3	25	6	0	0	0	8
	AHL	Totals	29	0	4	4	33	10	0	1	1	12

Born; 6/17/75, Lachute, Quebec. 6-1, 193. Drafted by Boston Bruins (3rd choice, 88th overall) in 1993 Entry Draft. Member of 1995-96

Darryl Paquette — Goaltender

		Regular Season								Playoffs					
Season	Team	League	GP	W	L	T	MIN	SO	GAVG	GP	W	L	MIN	SO	GAVG
95-96	Portland	AHL	14	2	7	1	616	1	3.12	—	—	—	—	—	—
95-96	Hampton Roads	ECHL	15	7	2	5	785	1	3.06	3	0	3	158	0	7.58
96-97	Hampton Roads	ECHL	60	35	15	5	*3388	4	2.98	9	5	3	504	0	3.21
	ECHL	Totals	75	42	17	10	4173	5	2.99	12	5	6	662	0	4.26

Born; 3/25/71, Sudbury, Ontario. 5-11, 170.

Patrice Paquin — Left Wing

		Regular Season						Playoffs				
Season	Team	League	GP	G	A	PTS	PIM	GP	G	A	PTS	PIM
95-96	Mobile	ECHL	42	15	17	32	73	—	—	—	—	—
96-97	Mobile	ECHL	50	13	13	26	137	—	—	—	—	—
96-97	Birmingham	ECHL	8	0	0	0	6	7	0	1	1	2
	ECHL	Totals	100	28	30	58	216	7	0	1	1	2

Born; 6/26/74, St. Jerome, Quebec. 6-2, 192. Drafted by Philadelphia Flyers (11th choice, 247th overall) in the 1992 Entry Draft.

Jim Paradise — Left Wing

		Regular Season						Playoffs				
Season	Team	League	GP	G	A	PTS	PIM	GP	G	A	PTS	PIM
94-95	Denver	IHL	2	1	0	1	0	—	—	—	—	—
94-95	Tallahassee	ECHL	66	14	16	30	59	—	—	—	—	—
95-96	Tallahassee	ECHL	59	11	18	29	52	12	1	5	6	6
96-97	Tallahassee	ECHL	70	8	27	35	64	3	0	0	0	8
	ECHL	Totals	195	33	61	94	175	15	1	5	6	14

Born; 4/21/70, Mound, Minnesota. 5-10, 185.

Rich Parent — Goaltender

		Regular Season								Playoffs					
Season	Team	League	GP	W	L	T	MIN	SO	GAVG	GP	W	L	MIN	SO	GAVG
94-95	Muskegon	CoHL	35	17	11	3	1867	1	3.60	13	7	4	725	1	3.89
95-96	Rochester	AHL	2	0	1	0	90	0	4.02	—	—	—	—	—	—
95-96	Muskegon	CoHL	36	23	7	4	2087	2	2.44	—	—	—	—	—	—

Season	Team	League	GP											
95-96	Detroit	IHL	19	16	0	1	1040	2	2.77	7	3	3	362	0	3.64
96-97	Detroit	IHL	53	31	13	4	2815	4	2.22	15	8	3	786	1	*1.60
	IHL	Totals	72	47	13	5	3855	6	2.37	22	11	6	1148	1	2.25
	CoHL	Totals	71	40	18	7	3954	3	2.99	13	7	4	725	1	3.89

Born; 3/29/73, Montreal, Quebec. 6-3, 215. Signed as a free agent by St. Louis Blues (8/97). 1995-96 CoHL First Team All-Star. 1995-96 CoHL Best Goaltender. Member of 1996-97 IHL Champion Detroit Vipers.

Sebastien Parent — Forward

			Regular Season					Playoffs				
Season	Team	League	GP	G	A	PTS	PIM	GP	G	A	PTS	PIM
96-97	Memphis	CeHL	10	8	0	8	63	3	2	1	3	4

Richard Park — Center

			Regular Season					Playoffs				
Season	Team	League	GP	G	A	PTS	PIM	GP	G	A	PTS	PIM
94-95	Pittsburgh	NHL	1	0	1	1	2	3	0	0	0	2
95-96	Pittsburgh	NHL	56	4	6	10	36	1	0	0	0	0
96-97	Pittsburgh	NHL	1	0	0	0	0	—	—	—	—	—
96-97	Anaheim	NHL	11	1	1	2	10	11	0	1	1	2
96-97	Cleveland	IHL	50	12	15	27	30	—	—	—	—	—
	NHL	Totals	69	5	8	13	48	15	0	1	1	4

Born; 5/27/76, Seoul, South Korea. 5-11, 190. Drafted by Pittsburgh Penguins (2nd choice, 50th overall) in 1994 Entry Draft. Traded to Anaheim Mighty Ducks by Pittsburgh for Roman Oksiuta, (3/18/97).

Dwight Parrish — Defenseman

			Regular Season					Playoffs				
Season	Team	League	GP	G	A	PTS	PIM	GP	G	A	PTS	PIM
96-97	Michigan	IHL	2	0	0	0	0	—	—	—	—	—
96-97	Fort Wayne	IHL	2	0	0	0	2	—	—	—	—	—
96-97	Dayton	ECHL	57	3	14	17	90	4	0	0	0	28
	IHL	Totals	4	0	0	0	2	—	—	—	—	—

Born; 4/6/72, Farmington, Michigan. 6-0, 195. Last amateur club; Ferris State (CCHA).

Jeff Parrott — Defenseman

			Regular Season					Playoffs				
Season	Team	League	GP	G	A	PTS	PIM	GP	G	A	PTS	PIM
93-94	Cornwall	AHL	52	4	11	15	37	—	—	—	—	—
94-95	Cornwall	AHL	65	2	5	7	99	14	0	1	1	12
95-96	Cornwall	AHL	77	1	11	12	94	8	0	0	0	4
96-97	Detroit	IHL	78	2	8	10	63	18	0	2	2	12
	AHL	Totals	194	7	27	34	230	22	0	1	1	16

Born; 4/6/71, The Pas, Manitoba. Drafted by Quebec Nordiques (4th choice, 106th overall) in 1990 Entry Draft. Member of 1996-97 IHL Champion Detroit Vipers.

Steve Parson — Left Wing

			Regular Season					Playoffs				
Season	Team	League	GP	G	A	PTS	PIM	GP	G	A	PTS	PIM
94-95	Prince Edward Island	AHL	8	2	1	3	0	—	—	—	—	—
94-95	Thunder Bay	CoHL	62	16	29	45	36	—	—	—	—	—
95-96	Thunder Bay	CoHL	66	17	12	29	34	19	8	5	13	23
96-97	Reno	WCHL	7	0	1	1	27	—	—	—	—	—
96-97	South Carolina	ECHL	59	7	16	23	18	18	4	3	7	30
	CoHL	Totals	128	33	41	74	70	19	8	5	13	23

Born; 3/14/73, Elmira, Ontario. 6-0, 180. Signed by Ottawa Senators as a free agent (6/9/94). Member of 1996-97 ECHL Champion South Carolina Stingrays.

Don Parsons — Right Wing

Regular Season | | | | | | | | **Playoffs** | | | | |

Season	Team	League	GP	G	A	PTS	PIM	GP	G	A	PTS	PIM
91-92	Nashville	ECHL	3	0	3	3	0	—	—	—	—	—
92-93	Nashville	ECHL	60	27	34	61	62	9	3	2	5	12
93-94	N/A											
94-95	Tallahassee	ECHL	66	41	35	76	82	13	5	10	15	12
95-96	Johnstown	ECHL	66	50	39	89	104	—	—	—	—	—
96-97	Worcester	AHL	2	1	1	2	4	—	—	—	—	—
96-97	Baton Rouge	ECHL	19	13	14	27	8	—	—	—	—	—
96-97	Louisiana	ECHL	49	28	21	49	94	17	7	9	16	54
	ECHL	Totals	265	159	143	302	350	39	15	21	36	78

Born; 1/17/69, Boston, Massachusetts. 5-10, 190.

Ron Pascucci — Defenseman

Season	Team	League	GP	G	A	PTS	PIM	GP	G	A	PTS	PIM
93-94	Portland	AHL	6	0	0	0	20	—	—	—	—	—
93-94	Hampton Roads	ECHL	58	11	33	44	81	7	0	4	4	14
94-95	Kansas City	IHL	10	0	1	1	8	10	1	1	2	4
94-95	Hampton Roads	ECHL	52	8	37	45	108	—	—	—	—	—
95-96	Portland	AHL	42	2	4	6	49	24	5	5	10	35
95-96	Hampton Roads	ECHL	23	2	9	11	65	—	—	—	—	—
96-97	Portland	AHL	54	2	16	18	29	—	—	—	—	—
	AHL	Totals	102	4	20	24	98	24	5	5	10	35
	ECHL	Totals	133	21	79	100	254	7	0	4	4	14

Born; 6/9/70, Lawrence, Massachusetts. 6-1, 180. Drafted by Washington Capitals (13th choice, 248th overall) in 1988 Entry Draft.

Todd Passini — Defenseman

Season	Team	League	GP	G	A	PTS	PIM	GP	G	A	PTS	PIM
95-96	Lakeland	SHL	60	5	13	18	94	5	0	1	1	12
96-97	Madison	CoHL	74	8	20	28	69	5	0	1	1	7

Born; 7/22/71, Cross Plains, Wisconsin. 6-2, 205.

Steve Passmore — Goaltender

Season	Team	League	GP	W	L	T	MIN	SO	GAVG	GP	W	L	MIN	SO	GAVG
94-95	Cape Breton	AHL	25	8	13	3	1455	0	3.83	—	—	—	—	—	—
95-96	Cape Breton	AHL	2	1	0	0	90	0	1.33	—	—	—	—	—	—
96-97	Cape Breton	AHL	27	12	12	3	1568	1	2.68	22	12	*10	1325	*2	2.76
96-97	Raleigh	ECHL	2	1	1	0	119	0	6.56	—	—	—	—	—	—
	AHL	Totals	54	21	25	6	1545	1	3.28	22	12	10	1325	2	2.76

Born; 1/29/73, Thunder Bay, Ontario. 5-9, 165. 1996-97 AHL Most Sportsmanlike Player. Drafted by Quebec Nordiques (9th choice, 196th overall) in 1992 Entry Draft. Traded to Edmonton Oilers by Quebec for Brad Werenka (3/21/94).

Craig Paterson — Defenseman

Season	Team	League	GP	G	A	PTS	PIM	GP	G	A	PTS	PIM
96-97	Richmond	ECHL	60	1	9	10	147	8	0	0	0	31

Born; 11/6/72, Scarborough, Ontario. 6-2, 208. Last amateur club; Ohio State (CCHA).

Ed Patterson — Right Wing

Season	Team	League	GP	G	A	PTS	PIM	GP	G	A	PTS	PIM
92-93	Cleveland	IHL	63	4	16	20	131	3	1	1	2	2
93-94	Pittsburgh	NHL	27	3	1	4	10	—	—	—	—	—

Season	Team	League	GP	G	A	PTS	PIM	GP	G	A	PTS	PIM
93-94	Cleveland	IHL	55	21	32	53	73	—	—	—	—	—
94-95	Cleveland	IHL	58	13	17	30	93	4	1	2	3	6
95-96	Pittsburgh	NHL	35	0	2	2	38	—	—	—	—	—
96-97	Pittsburgh	NHL	6	0	0	0	8	—	—	—	—	—
96-97	Cleveland	IHL	40	6	12	18	75	13	2	4	6	61
	NHL	Totals	68	3	3	6	56	—	—	—	—	—
	IHL	Totals	216	44	77	121	372	20	4	7	11	69

Born; 11/14/72, Delta, British Columbia. 6-2, 213. Drafted by Pittsburgh Penguins (7th choice, 148th overall) in 1991 Entry Draft.

Rob Pattison — Left Wing

Regular Season / Playoffs

Season	Team	League	GP	G	A	PTS	PIM	GP	G	A	PTS	PIM
95-96	Albany	AHL	5	4	3	7	0	2	0	0	0	0
95-96	Raleigh	ECHL	67	14	23	37	122	4	1	2	3	0
96-97	Albany	AHL	61	24	16	40	31	16	5	1	6	20
96-97	Raleigh	ECHL	20	13	6	19	28	—	—	—	—	—
	AHL	Totals	66	28	19	47	31	18	5	1	6	20
	ECHL	Totals	87	27	29	56	150	4	1	2	3	0

Born; 9/18/71, Sherborn, Massachusetts. 6-0, 195. Signed as a free agent by New Jersey Devils (10/1/95).

Jeff Pawluk — Defenseman

Regular Season / Playoffs

Season	Team	League	GP	G	A	PTS	PIM	GP	G	A	PTS	PIM
93-94	St. Thomas	CoHL	56	8	23	31	23	3	1	0	1	2
94-95	Lakeland	SUN	9	0	2	2	8	—	—	—	—	—
94-95	Huntington	ECHL	7	0	1	1	26	—	—	—	—	—
94-95	Brantford	CoHL	3	0	0	0	0	—	—	—	—	—
95-96	Detroit	CoHL	3	1	0	1	2	—	—	—	—	—
95-96	Wichita	CeHL	23	0	3	3	57	—	—	—	—	—
95-96	Jacksonville	ECHL	26	2	6	8	44	—	—	—	—	—
96-97	Wichita	CeHL	26	3	7	10	26	—	—	—	—	—
96-97	Nashville	CeHL	14	4	5	9	17	—	—	—	—	—
	CeHL	Totals	63	7	15	22	100	—	—	—	—	—
	CoHL	Totals	59	9	23	32	25	3	1	0	1	2
	ECHL	Totals	33	2	7	9	70	—	—	—	—	—

Born; 7/23/73, Windsor, Ontario. 5-11, 212.

Ryan Pawluk — Forward

Regular Season / Playoffs

Season	Team	League	GP	G	A	PTS	PIM	GP	G	A	PTS	PIM
96-97	Toledo	ECHL	4	2	0	2	2	5	2	2	4	0

Born; 3/28/76, Windsor, Ontario. 6-0, 190. Last amateur club; Windsor (OHL).

David Paxton — Defenseman

Regular Season / Playoffs

Season	Team	League	GP	G	A	PTS	PIM	GP	G	A	PTS	PIM
96-97	Thunder Bay	CoHL	2	0	0	0	0	—	—	—	—	—
96-97	Thunder Bay	CoHL	69	7	15	22	41	11	0	1	1	8
	CoHL	Totals	71	7	15	22	41	11	0	1	1	8

Born; 6/6/71, Thunder Bay, Ontario. 6-1, 200.

Davis Payne — Right Wing

Regular Season / Playoffs

Season	Team	League	GP	G	A	PTS	PIM	GP	G	A	PTS	PIM
92-93	Greensboro	ECHL	57	15	20	35	178	1	0	0	0	4
93-94	Phoenix	IHL	22	6	3	9	51	—	—	—	—	—
93-94	Rochester	AHL	2	0	0	0	5	3	0	2	2	0
93-94	Greensboro	ECHL	36	17	17	34	139	8	2	1	3	27

Season	Team	League	GP	G	A	PTS	PIM	GP	G	A	PTS	PIM
94-95	Providence	AHL	2	1	0	1	0	—	—	—	—	—
94-95	Greensboro	ECHL	62	25	36	61	195	17	7	10	17	38
95-96	Boston	NHL	7	0	0	0	7	—	—	—	—	—
95-96	Providence	AHL	51	17	22	39	72	4	1	4	5	2
96-97	Boston	NHL	15	0	1	1	7	—	—	—	—	—
96-97	Providence	AHL	57	18	15	33	104	—	—	—	—	—
	NHL	Totals	22	0	1	1	14	—	—	—	—	—
	AHL	Totals	112	36	37	73	181	7	1	6	7	2
	ECHL	Totals	155	57	73	130	512	26	9	11	20	69

Born; 9/24/70, Port Alberni, British Columbia. 6-2, 205. Drafted by Edmonton Oilers (6th choice, 140th overall) in 1989 Entry Draft. Signed as a free agent by Greensboro Monarchs (1992). Signed as a free agent by Boston Bruins (9/6/95). Signed as a free agent by San Antonio Dragons (8/97).

Jayson Payne — Left Wing

Season	Team	League	GP	G	A	PTS	PIM	GP	G	A	PTS	PIM
95-96	Utica	CoHL	14	0	1	1	85	—	—	—	—	—
96-97	Flint	CoHL	59	4	15	19	224	8	0	0	0	2
96-97	Carolina	AHL	4	1	0	1	5	—	—	—	—	—
96-97	Detroit	IHL	2	0	0	0	0	—	—	—	—	—
96-97	Michigan	IHL	1	0	0	0	5	—	—	—	—	—
	IHL	Totals	3	0	0	0	5	—	—	—	—	—
	CoHL	Totals	73	4	16	20	309	8	0	0	0	2

Born; 9/21/75, Toronto, Ontario. 6-1, 192.

Kent Paynter — Defenseman

Season	Team	League	GP	G	A	PTS	PIM	GP	G	A	PTS	PIM
85-86	Nova Scotia	AHL	23	1	2	3	36	—	—	—	—	—
85-86	Saginaw	IHL	4	0	1	1	2	—	—	—	—	—
86-87	Nova Scotia	AHL	66	2	6	8	57	2	0	0	0	0
87-88	Chicago	NHL	2	0	0	0	2	—	—	—	—	—
87-88	Saginaw	IHL	74	8	20	28	141	10	0	1	1	30
88-89	Chicago	NHL	1	0	0	0	2	—	—	—	—	—
88-89	Saginaw	IHL	69	12	14	26	148	6	2	2	4	17
89-90	Washington	NHL	13	1	2	3	18	3	0	0	0	10
89-90	Baltimore	AHL	60	7	20	27	110	11	5	6	11	34
90-91	Washington	NHL	1	0	0	0	15	1	0	0	0	0
90-91	Baltimore	AHL	43	10	17	27	64	6	2	1	3	8
91-92	Winnipeg	NHL	5	0	0	0	4	—	—	—	—	—
91-92	Moncton	AHL	62	3	30	33	71	11	2	6	8	25
92-93	Ottawa	NHL	6	0	0	0	20	—	—	—	—	—
92-93	New Haven	AHL	48	7	17	24	81	—	—	—	—	—
93-94	Ottawa	NHL	9	0	1	1	8	—	—	—	—	—
93-94	Prince Edward Island	AHL	63	6	20	26	125	—	—	—	—	—
94-95	Milwaukee	IHL	73	3	22	25	104	5	2	3	5	8
95-96	Milwaukee	IHL	79	9	19	28	147	5	0	2	2	10
96-97	Milwaukee	IHL	77	10	28	38	97	3	1	1	2	4
	NHL	Totals	37	1	3	4	69	4	0	0	0	10
	IHL	Totals	376	42	104	146	639	29	5	9	14	69
	AHL	Totals	365	36	112	148	544	33	9	13	22	67

Born; 4/27/65, Summerside, Prince Edward Island. 6-0, 207. Drafted by Chicago Blackhawks (9th choice, 159th overall) in 1983 Entry Draft. Signed as a free agent by Washington Capitals (8/21/89). Traded to Winnipeg Jets by Washington with Bob Joyce and Tyler Larter for Brent Hughes, Simon Wheeldon and Craig Duncanson (5/21/91). Selected by Ottawa Senators in Expansion Draft (6/18/92).

Chris Peach — Left Wing

Season	Team	League	GP	G	A	PTS	PIM	GP	G	A	PTS	PIM
			Regular Season					Playoffs				
96-97	Waco	WPHL	57	21	16	37	58	—	—	—	—	—

Born; 5/18/72, St. John's Newfoundland. 5-9, 175.

Shane Peacock — Defenseman

Season	Team	League	GP	G	A	PTS	PIM	GP	G	A	PTS	PIM
			Regular Season					Playoffs				
94-95	Kalamazoo	IHL	71	13	23	36	42	12	3	5	8	8
95-96	Michigan	IHL	79	24	43	67	26	10	0	4	4	6
96-97	Michigan	IHL	81	9	31	40	49	4	0	2	2	2
	IHL	Totals	231	46	97	143	117	26	3	11	14	16

Born; 7/7/73, Edmonton, Alberta. 5-10, 198. Drafted by Pittsburgh Penguins (3rd choice, 60th overall) in 1991 Entry Draft.

Randy Pearce — Left Wing

Season	Team	League	GP	G	A	PTS	PIM	GP	G	A	PTS	PIM
			Regular Season					Playoffs				
91-92	Baltimore	AHL	12	2	2	4	8	—	—	—	—	—
91-92	Hampton Roads	ECHL	55	32	46	78	134	11	5	9	14	56
92-93	Baltimore	AHL	42	12	5	17	46	—	—	—	—	—
92-93	Hampton Roads	ECHL	16	10	14	24	53	—	—	—	—	—
93-94	Portland	AHL	80	32	36	68	97	17	1	4	5	36
94-95	Phoenix	IHL	14	2	3	4	30	9	3	1	4	8
95-96	Portland	AHL	8	0	2	2	8	—	—	—	—	—
95-96	Phoenix	IHL	48	8	11	19	81	—	—	—	—	—
96-97	Portland	AHL	1	0	0	0	0	—	—	—	—	—
96-97	Hampton Roads	ECHL	70	27	45	72	157	9	1	9	10	27
	AHL	Totals	143	46	45	91	159	17	1	4	5	36
	IHL	Totals	62	10	14	24	111	9	3	1	4	8
	ECHL	Totals	141	69	103	172	344	20	6	18	24	83

Born; 2/23/70, Kitchener, Ontario. 5-11, 203. Drafted by Washington Capitals (4th choice, 72nd overall) in 1990 Entry Draft. Member of 1991-92 ECHL champion Hampton Roads Admirals. Member of 1993-94 AHL champion Portland Pirates.

Rob Pearson — Right Wing

Season	Team	League	GP	G	A	PTS	PIM	GP	G	A	PTS	PIM
			Regular Season					Playoffs				
90-91	Newmarket	AHL	3	0	0	0	29	—	—	—	—	—
91-92	Toronto	NHL	47	14	10	24	58	—	—	—	—	—
91-92	St. John's	AHL	27	15	14	29	107	13	5	4	9	40
92-93	Toronto	NHL	78	23	14	37	211	14	2	2	4	31
93-94	Toronto	NHL	67	12	18	30	189	14	1	0	1	32
94-95	Washington	NHL	32	0	6	6	96	3	1	0	1	17
95-96	St. Louis	NHL	27	6	4	10	54	2	0	0	0	14
95-96	Portland	AHL	44	18	24	42	143	—	—	—	—	—
96-97	St. Louis	NHL	18	1	2	3	37	—	—	—	—	—
96-97	Worcester	AHL	46	11	16	27	199	5	3	0	3	16
	NHL	Totals	269	56	54	110	645	33	4	2	6	94
	AHL	Totals	120	44	54	98	478	18	8	4	12	56

Born; 3/8/71, Oshawa, Ontario. 6-1, 185. Drafted by Toronto Maple Leafs (2nd choice, 12th overall) in 1989 Entry Draft. Traded to Washington Capitals by Toronto with Philadelphia's first round pick (previously acquired by Toronto, Washington selected Nolan Baumgartner) in 1994 Entry Draft for Mike Ridley and St. Louis' first round pick, (previously acquired by Washington, Toronto selected Eric Fichaud) in 1994 Entry Draft (6/28/94).

Scott Pearson — Left Wing

Season	Team	League	GP	G	A	PTS	PIM	GP	G	A	PTS	PIM
88-89	Toronto	NHL	9	0	1	1	2	—	—	—	—	—
89-90	Toronto	NHL	41	5	10	15	90	2	2	0	2	10
89-90	Newmarket	AHL	18	12	11	23	64	—	—	—	—	—
90-91	Toronto	NHL	12	0	0	0	20	—	—	—	—	—
90-91	Quebec	NHL	35	11	4	15	86	—	—	—	—	—
90-91	Halifax	AHL	24	12	15	27	44	—	—	—	—	—
91-92	Quebec	NHL	10	1	2	3	14	—	—	—	—	—
91-92	Halifax	AHL	5	2	1	3	4	—	—	—	—	—
92-93	Quebec	NHL	41	13	1	14	95	3	0	0	0	0
92-93	Halifax	AHL	5	3	1	4	25	—	—	—	—	—
93-94	Edmonton	NHL	72	19	18	37	165	—	—	—	—	—
94-95	Edmonton	NHL	28	1	4	5	54	—	—	—	—	—
94-95	Buffalo	NHL	14	2	1	3	20	5	0	0	0	4
95-96	Buffalo	NHL	27	4	0	4	67	—	—	—	—	—
95-96	Rochester	AHL	26	8	8	16	113	—	—	—	—	—
96-97	Toronto	NHL	1	0	0	0	2	—	—	—	—	—
96-97	St. John's	AHL	14	5	2	7	26	9	5	2	7	14
NHL	Totals		290	56	41	97	615	10	2	0	2	14
AHL	Totals		92	42	38	80	276	9	5	2	7	14

Born; 12/19/69, Cornwall, Ontario. 6-1, 205. Drafted by Toronto Maple Leafs (1st choice, 6th overall) in 1988 Entry Draft. Traded to Quebec Nordiques by Toronto with Toronto's second round choices in 1991 (later traded to Washington-Washington selected Eric Lavigne) and 1992 (Tuomas Gronman) Entry Drafts for Aaron Broten, Lucien DeBlois and Michel Petit. (11/17/90). Traded to Edmonton Oilers by Quebec for Martin Gelinas and Edmonton's sixth round choice (Nicholas Checco) in 1993 Entry Draft (6/20/93). Traded to Buffalo Sabres by Edmonton for Ken Sutton (4/7/95). Singed as a free agent by Toronto Maple Leafs (7/24/96).

Tom Pederson — Defenseman

Season	Team	League	GP	G	A	PTS	PIM	GP	G	A	PTS	PIM
91-92	United States	National										
91-92	Kansas City	IHL	20	6	9	15	16	13	1	6	7	14
92-93	San Jose	NHL	44	7	13	20	31	—	—	—	—	—
92-93	Kansas City	IHL	26	6	15	21	10	12	1	6	7	2
93-94	San Jose	NHL	74	6	19	25	31	14	1	6	7	2
93-94	Kansas City	IHL	7	3	1	4	0	—	—	—	—	—
94-95	San Jose	NHL	47	5	11	16	31	10	0	5	5	8
95-96	San Jose	NHL	60	1	4	5	40	—	—	—	—	—
96-97	Toronto	NHL	15	1	2	3	9	—	—	—	—	—
96-97	St. John's	AHL	1	0	4	4	2	—	—	—	—	—
96-97	Utah	IHL	10	1	2	3	8	7	1	3	4	4
NHL	Totals		240	20	49	69	142	24	1	11	12	10
IHL	Totals		63	16	27	43	34	32	3	15	18	20

Born; 1/14/70, Bloomington, Minnesota. 5-9, 175. Drafted by Minnesota North Stars (12th choice, 217th overall) in 1989 Entry Draft. Claimed by San Jose Sharks from Minnesota in NHL dispersal draft (5/30/91). Signed as a free agent by Toronto Maple Leafs (1997). Member of 1991-92 IHL Champion Kansas City Blades.

Scott Pellerin — Left Wing

Season	Team	League	GP	G	A	PTS	PIM	GP	G	A	PTS	PIM
91-92	Utica	AHL	—	—	—	—	—	3	1	0	1	0
92-93	New Jersey	NHL	45	10	11	21	41	—	—	—	—	—
92-93	Utica	AHL	27	15	18	33	33	2	0	1	1	0
93-94	New Jersey	NHL	1	0	0	0	2	—	—	—	—	—
93-94	Albany	AHL	73	28	46	74	84	5	2	1	3	11
94-95	Albany	AHL	74	23	33	56	95	14	6	4	10	8

Season	Team	League	GP	G	A	PTS	PIM	GP	G	A	PTS	PIM
95-96	New Jersey	NHL	6	2	1	3	0	—	—	—	—	—
95-96	Albany	AHL	75	35	47	82	142	4	0	3	3	10
96-97	St. Louis	NHL	54	8	10	18	35	6	0	0	0	6
96-97	Worcester	AHL	24	10	16	26	37	—	—	—	—	—
	NHL	Totals	100	18	21	39	78	6	0	0	0	6
	AHL	Totals	273	111	160	271	391	28	9	9	18	29

Born; 1/9/70, Shediac, New Brunswick. 5-11, 180. Drafted by New Jersey Devils (4th choice, 47th overall) in 1989 Entry Draft. Signed as a free agent by St. Louis Blues (7/10/96). Member of 1994-95 Calder Cup champion Albany RiverRats.

Ville Peltonen — Left Wing

Season	Team	League	GP	G	A	PTS	PIM	GP	G	A	PTS	PIM
95-95	San Jose	NHL	31	2	11	13	14	—	—	—	—	—
95-96	Kansas City	IHL	29	5	13	18	8	—	—	—	—	—
96-97	San Jose	NHL	28	2	3	5	0	—	—	—	—	—
96-97	Kentucky	AHL	40	22	30	52	21	—	—	—	—	—
	NHL	Totals	59	4	14	18	14	—	—	—	—	—

Born; 5/24/73, Vantaa, Finland. 5-11, 172. Drafted by San Jose Sharks (4th choice, 58th overall) in 1993 Entry Draft.

Darcy Pengelly — Left Wing

Season	Team	League	GP	G	A	PTS	PIM	GP	G	A	PTS	PIM
95-96	Oklahoma City	CeHL	46	17	13	30	161	11	1	1	2	32
96-97	Oklahoma City	CeHL	65	22	16	38	190	4	0	1	1	15
	CeHL	Totals	111	39	29	68	351	15	1	2	3	47

Born; 12/4/74, Reston, Manitoba. 5-11, 177. Member of 1995-96 CeHL champion Oklahoma City Blazers.

Shawn Penn — Forward

Season	Team	League	GP	G	A	PTS	PIM	GP	G	A	PTS	PIM
94-95	Toledo	ECHL	63	14	13	27	208	4	0	0	0	4
95-96	Toledo	ECHL	63	20	16	36	267	10	2	2	4	29
96-97	Chicago	IHL	62	3	7	10	208	4	0	0	0	6
	ECHL	Totals	126	34	29	63	475	14	2	2	4	33

Born; 2/27/71, Madison Heights, Michigan. 6-2, 210.

Darren Perkins — Defenseman

Season	Team	League	GP	G	A	PTS	PIM	GP	G	A	PTS	PIM
92-93	Columbus	ECHL	20	9	4	13	44	—	—	—	—	—
92-93	Erie	ECHL	28	7	17	24	40	—	—	—	—	—
93-94	Adirondack	AHL	2	0	2	2	2	—	—	—	—	—
93-94	Toledo	ECHL	64	23	31	54	160	14	4	8	12	46
94-95	Toledo	ECHL	59	7	29	36	138	4	1	2	3	4
95-96	San Diego	WCHL	54	19	46	65	168	9	5	7	12	25
96-97	Las Vegas	IHL	1	0	0	0	0	—	—	—	—	—
96-97	San Diego	WCHL	50	15	30	45	68	—	—	—	—	—
	ECHL	Totals	171	46	54	100	246	18	5	10	15	50
	WCHL	Totals	104	34	76	110	236	9	5	7	12	25

Born; 12/26/68, Fort Worth, Texas. 5-11, 190. Member of 1993-94 ECHL champion Toledo Storm. Member of 1995-96 WCHL champion San Diego Gulls. 1995-96 WCHL Defenseman of the Year. 1995-96 WCHL First Team All Star.

Kelly Perrault — Defenseman

Season	Team	League	GP	G	A	PTS	PIM	GP	G	A	PTS	PIM
96-97	Chicago	IHL	8	0	3	3	6	4	0	1	1	6

Born; 12/18/73, Fort Saskatchewan, Saskatchewan. 6-1, 195. Last amateur club; Bowling Green State (CCHA).

Sean Perry — Left Wing

			Regular Season					Playoffs				
Season	Team	League	GP	G	A	PTS	PIM	GP	G	A	PTS	PIM
95-96	Johnstown	ECHL	45	5	6	11	96	—	—	—	—	—
96-97	Johnstown	ECHL	31	3	2	5	58	—	—	—	—	—
96-97	Toledo	ECHL	19	1	1	2	20	—	—	—	—	—
	ECHL	Totals	95	9	9	18	174	—	—	—	—	—

Born; 2/9/74, Waltham, Massachusetts. 5-10, 185.

Jim Peters — Defenseman

			Regular Season					Playoffs				
Season	Team	League	GP	G	A	PTS	PIM	GP	G	A	PTS	PIM
92-93	Birmingham	ECHL	21	1	9	10	55	—	—	—	—	—
92-93	Dayton	ECHL	31	1	8	9	74	3	0	0	0	19
93-94	Nashville	ECHL	6	2	2	4	19	2	0	0	0	4
94-95	Utica	CoHL	3	0	0	0	2	—	—	—	—	—
94-95	Wichita	CeHL	11	0	5	5	18	—	—	—	—	—
94-95	Dallas	CeHL	40	7	28	35	56	—	—	—	—	—
95-96	Tulsa	CeHL	31	3	6	9	103	—	—	—	—	—
95-96	Wichita	CeHL	9	1	6	7	4	—	—	—	—	—
96-97	San Antonio	CeHL	19	3	14	17	30	—	—	—	—	—
96-97	Central Texas	WPHL	37	13	18	31	75	7	0	2	2	12
	CeHL	Totals	110	14	59	73	206	—	—	—	—	—
	ECHL	Totals	58	4	19	23	148	5	0	0	0	23

Born; 6/11/69, Barrie, Ontario. 6-2, 190.

Mike Peters — Right Wing

			Regular Season					Playoffs				
Season	Team	League	GP	G	A	PTS	PIM	GP	G	A	PTS	PIM
95-96	Utica	CoHL	7	0	1	1	2	—	—	—	—	—
96-97	Utica	CoHL	71	9	21	30	14	3	0	0	0	0
	CoHL	Totals	78	9	22	31	16	3	0	0	0	0

Born; 5/9/74, Yonkers, New York. 6-2, 205.

Brent Peterson — Left Wing

			Regular Season					Playoffs				
Season	Team	League	GP	G	A	PTS	PIM	GP	G	A	PTS	PIM
95-96	Atlanta	IHL	69	9	19	28	33	3	0	0	0	0
96-97	Tampa Bay	NHL	17	2	0	2	4	—	—	—	—	—
96-97	Adirondack	AHL	52	22	23	45	56	4	3	1	4	2

Born; 7/20/72, Calgary, Alberta. 6-3, 200. Drafted by Tampa Bay Lightning (1st choice, 3rd overall) in 1993 Supplemental Draft.

Cory Peterson — Defenseman

			Regular Season					Playoffs				
Season	Team	League	GP	G	A	PTS	PIM	GP	G	A	PTS	PIM
95-96	Tulsa	CeHL	46	2	9	11	91	3	0	0	0	2
96-97	Raleigh	ECHL	12	0	2	2	4	—	—	—	—	—
96-97	Roanoke	ECHL	30	0	4	4	44	4	0	1	1	2
	ECHL	Totals	42	0	6	6	48	4	0	1	1	2

Born; 6/10/75, Bloomington, Minnesota. 6-1, 205. Drafted by Dallas Stars (10th choice, 269th overall) in 1993 Entry Draft.

Jeff Petruic — Right Wing

			Regular Season					Playoffs				
Season	Team	League	GP	G	A	PTS	PIM	GP	G	A	PTS	PIM
94-95	Peoria	IHL	3	0	1	1	0	—	—	—	—	—
95-96	Providence	AHL	3	1	0	1	2	—	—	—	—	—

Season	Team	League	GP	G	A	PTS	PIM	GP	G	A	PTS	PIM
95-96	Dayton	ECHL	38	13	9	22	26	3	0	1	1	17
96-97	Bakersfield	WCHL	62	36	37	73	50	4	2	1	3	2

Born; 5/19/74, Avonlea, Saskatchewan. 6-1, 202.

Ryan Petz — Forward

	Regular Season							Playoffs				
Season	Team	League	GP	G	A	PTS	PIM	GP	G	A	PTS	PIM
95-96	Columbus	ECHL	28	7	10	17	39	—	—	—	—	—
95-96	Johnstown	ECHL	31	15	13	28	38	—	—	—	—	—
96-97	Johnstown	ECHL	69	25	27	52	90	—	—	—	—	—
	ECHL	Totals	128	47	50	97	167	—	—	—	—	—

Born; 9/9/74, Calgary, Alberta. 5-11, 185.

Chris Phelps — Defenseman

	Regular Season							Playoffs				
Season	Team	League	GP	G	A	PTS	PIM	GP	G	A	PTS	PIM
94-95	Cornwall	AHL	3	0	0	0	0	1	1	0	1	0
94-95	Hampton Roads	ECHL	67	13	39	52	161	4	0	0	0	10
95-96	Utah	IHL	1	0	0	0	0	—	—	—	—	—
95-96	Portland	AHL	1	0	0	0	0	—	—	—	—	—
95-96	Baltimore	AHL	7	0	0	0	4	12	0	2	2	12
95-96	Hampton Roads	ECHL	40	2	22	24	117	3	0	0	0	0
96-97	Portland	AHL	11	0	4	4	10	—	—	—	—	—
96-97	Hampton Roads	ECHL	58	8	37	45	97	6	3	3	6	8
	AHL	Totals	22	0	4	4	14	13	1	2	3	12
	ECHL	Totals	165	23	98	121	380	13	3	3	6	18

Born; 2/21/73, Lapeer, Michigan. 6-0, 195. 1996-97 ECHL First All-Star Team.

Ryan Phillips — Left Wing

	Regular Season							Playoffs				
Season	Team	League	GP	G	A	PTS	PIM	GP	G	A	PTS	PIM
95-96	Wichita	CeHL	18	7	4	11	8	—	—	—	—	—
96-97	Wichita	CeHL	19	3	8	11	49	—	—	—	—	—
96-97	Nashville	CeHL	27	9	14	23	21	—	—	—	—	—
	CeHL	Totals	64	19	26	45	78	—	—	—	—	—

Born; 7/8/75, North Vancouver, British Columbia. 6-0, 185.

Michel Picard — Left Wing

	Regular Season							Playoffs				
Season	Team	League	GP	G	A	PTS	PIM	GP	G	A	PTS	PIM
89-90	Binghamton	AHL	67	16	24	40	98	—	—	—	—	—
90-91	Hartford	NHL	5	1	0	1	2	—	—	—	—	—
90-91	Springfield	AHL	77	*56	40	96	61	18	8	13	21	18
91-92	Hartford	NHL	25	3	5	8	6	—	—	—	—	—
91-92	Springfield	AHL	40	21	17	38	44	11	2	0	2	34
92-93	San Jose	NHL	25	4	0	4	24	—	—	—	—	—
92-93	Kansas City	IHL	33	7	10	17	51	12	3	2	5	20
93-94	Portland	AHL	61	41	44	85	99	17	11	10	21	22
94-95	Ottawa	NHL	24	5	8	13	14	—	—	—	—	—
94-95	Prince Edward Island	AHL	57	32	57	89	58	8	4	4	8	6
95-96	Ottawa	NHL	17	2	6	8	10	—	—	—	—	—
95-96	Prince Edward Island	AHL	55	37	45	82	79	5	5	1	6	2
96-97	Grand Rapids	IHL	82	46	55	101	58	5	2	0	2	10
	NHL	Totals	96	15	19	34	56	—	—	—	—	—
	AHL	Totals	357	203	227	430	439	59	30	28	58	82
	IHL	Totals	115	53	65	118	109	17	5	2	7	30

Born;; 11/7/69, Beauport, Quebec. 5-11, 190. Drafted by Hartford Whalers (8th choice, 178th overall) in 1989 Entry Draft. Traded to San Jose Sharks by Hartford for future considerations (Yvon Corriveau, 1/21/93) 10/9/92. Signed as a free agent by Ottawa Senators (6/16/94). Member of 1990-91 AHL champion Springfield Indians. Member of 1993-94 AHL champion Portland Pirates. 1990-91 AHL First Team All-Star. 1993-94 AHL Second Team All-Star. 1994-95 AHL First Team All-Star. 1996-97 IHL First All-Star Team.

Dennis Pinfold — Left Wing

Season	Team	League	GP	G	A	PTS	PIM	GP	G	A	PTS	PIM
95-96	Saginaw	CoHL	10	0	0	0	45	—	—	—	—	—
96-97	Birmingham	ECHL	57	0	7	7	316	—	—	—	—	—

Born; 2/28/74, Edmonton, Alberta. 6-0, 185.

Jon Pirrong — Defenseman

Season	Team	League	GP	G	A	PTS	PIM	GP	G	A	PTS	PIM
96-97	Johnstown	ECHL	1	0	0	0	0	—	—	—	—	—
96-97	Pensacola	ECHL	33	1	7	8	46	—	—	—	—	—
96-97	Columbus	ECHL	5	0	2	2	10	—	—	—	—	—
	ECHL	Totals	39	1	9	10	56	—	—	—	—	—

Born; 10/10/74, Norfolk, Massachusetts. 6-0, 190. Last amateur club; Rensselaer Polytehcnic Institute (ECAC).

Ryan Pisiak — Right Wing

Season	Team	League	GP	G	A	PTS	PIM	GP	G	A	PTS	PIM
95-96	Wichita	CeHL	24	3	9	12	141	—	—	—	—	—
95-96	San Antonio	CeHL	11	3	0	3	70	13	0	1	1	66
96-97	San Antonio	CeHL	32	12	16	28	*327	—	—	—	—	—
96-97	Memphis	CeHL	13	5	4	9	*85	14	1	4	5	*126
	CeHL	Totals	80	23	29	52	623	27	1	5	6	192

Born; 5/12/75, Swift Current, Saskatchewan. 6-3, 212. Drafted by Los Angeles Kings (7th choice, 231st overall) in 1992 Entry Draft.

Domenic Pittis — Center

Season	Team	League	GP	G	A	PTS	PIM	GP	G	A	PTS	PIM
94-95	Cleveland	IHL	62	18	32	50	66	3	0	2	2	2
95-96	Cleveland	IHL	74	10	28	38	100	3	0	0	0	2
96-97	Pittsburgh	NHL	1	0	0	0	0	—	—	—	—	—
96-97	Long Beach	IHL	65	23	43	66	91	18	5	9	14	26
	IHL	Totals	201	51	103	154	257	24	5	11	16	30

Born; 10/1/74, Calgary, Alberta. 5-11, 180. Drafted by Pittsburgh Penguins (2nd choice, 52nd overall) in 1993 Entry Draft.

Chris Pittman — Center

Season	Team	League	GP	G	A	PTS	PIM	GP	G	A	PTS	PIM
96-97	Baltimore	AHL	2	0	0	0	0	—	—	—	—	—
96-97	Richmond	ECHL	46	10	20	30	127	—	—	—	—	—
96-97	Louisville	ECHL	14	1	1	2	18	—	—	—	—	—
	ECHL	Totals	60	11	21	32	145	—	—	—	—	—

Born; 8/21/76, Stephensville, New Foundland. 6-2, 170. Drafted by Quebec Nordiques (12th choice, 243rd overall) in 1994 Entry Draft.

Kevin Plager — Baton Rouge

Season	Team	League	GP	G	A	PTS	PIM	GP	G	A	PTS	PIM
96-97	Baton Rouge	ECHL	46	10	6	16	54	—	—	—	—	—

Born; 4/27/71, St. Louis, Missouri. 6-1, 210. Drafted by St. Louis Blues (8th choice, 156th overall) in 1989 Entry Draft.

Cam Plante — Defenseman

Regular Season / Playoffs

Season	Team	League	GP	G	A	PTS	PIM	GP	G	A	PTS	PIM
84-85	St. Catharines	AHL	54	5	31	36	42	—	—	—	—	—
84-85	Toronto	NHL	2	0	0	0	0	—	—	—	—	—
85-86	St. Catharines	AHL	49	6	15	21	28	5	0	3	3	2
86-87	Newmarket	AHL	19	3	4	7	14	—	—	—	—	—
86-87	Milwaukee	IHL	56	7	47	54	44	5	2	2	4	4
87-88	Newmarket	AHL	18	2	8	10	14	—	—	—	—	—
88-89	N/A											
89-90	Fort Wayne	IHL	61	7	42	49	45	5	1	6	7	2
90-91	Kansas City	IHL	43	6	14	20	34	—	—	—	—	—
91-92	Thunder Bay	CoHL	54	16	57	73	32	13	0	8	8	6
96-97	Wichita	CeHL	55	12	63	75	74	9	2	7	9	18
	IHL	Totals	160	20	103	123	123	10	3	8	11	6
	AHL	Totals	140	16	58	74	98	5	0	3	3	2

Born; 3/12/64, Brandon, Alberta. 6-0, 185. Drafted by Toronto Maple Leafs (5th choice, 128th overall) in 1983 Entry Draft. Member of 1991-92 CoHL Champion Thunder Bay Thunder Hawks.

Robert Plante — Defenseman

Regular Season / Playoffs

Season	Team	League	GP	G	A	PTS	PIM	GP	G	A	PTS	PIM
96-97	Wichita	CeHL	4	0	0	0	8	—	—	—	—	—
96-97	Alaska	WCHL	18	4	1	5	65	—	—	—	—	—
96-97	Reno	WCHL	8	0	1	1	15	—	—	—	—	—
96-97	El Paso	WPHL	14	0	0	0	75	—	—	—	—	—
96-97	New Mexico	WPHL	5	0	0	0	37	—	—	—	—	—
	WCHL	Totals	26	4	2	6	80	—	—	—	—	—
	WPHL	Totals	19	0	0	0	112	—	—	—	—	—

Born; 12/24/70, Lake Isle, Alberta. 6-1, 225.

Adrien Plavsic — Defenseman

Regular Season / Playoffs

Season	Team	League	GP	G	A	PTS	PIM	GP	G	A	PTS	PIM
89-90	St. Louis	NHL	4	0	1	1	2	—	—	—	—	—
89-90	Vancouver	NHL	11	3	2	5	8	—	—	—	—	—
89-90	Peoria	IHL	51	7	14	21	87	—	—	—	—	—
89-90	Milwaukee	IHL	3	1	2	3	14	6	1	3	4	6
90-91	Vancouver	NHL	48	2	10	12	62	—	—	—	—	—
91-92	Canada	National										
91-92	Vancouver	NHL	16	1	9	10	14	13	1	7	8	4
92-93	Vancouver	NHL	57	6	21	27	53	—	—	—	—	—
93-94	Vancouver	NHL	47	1	9	10	6	—	—	—	—	—
93-94	Hamilton	AHL	2	0	0	0	0	—	—	—	—	—
94-95	Vancouver	NHL	3	0	1	1	4	—	—	—	—	—
94-95	Tampa Bay	NHL	15	2	1	3	4	—	—	—	—	—
95-96	Tampa Bay	NHL	7	1	2	3	6	—	—	—	—	—
95-96	Atlanta	IHL	68	5	34	39	32	3	0	1	1	4
96-97	Anaheim	NHL	6	0	0	0	2	—	—	—	—	—
96-97	Long Beach	IHL	69	7	28	35	86	18	0	9	9	10
	NHL	Totals	214	16	56	72	161	13	1	7	8	4
	IHL	Totals	191	20	78	98	219	27	1	13	14	20

Born; 1/13/70, Montreal, Quebec. 6-1, 200. Drafted by St. Louis Blues (2nd choice, 30th overall) in 1988 Entry Draft. Traded to Vancouver Canucks by St. Louis with Montreal's first round choice (previously acquired by St. Louis, Vancouver selected Shawn Antoski) in 1990 Entry Draft and St. Louis' second round choice (later traded to Montreal, Montreal selected Craig Darby) in 1991 Entry Draft for Rich Sutter, Harold Snepts and St. Louis' second round choice (previously acquired by Vancouver, St. Louis selected Craig Johnson) in 1990 Entry Draft (3/6/90). Traded to Tampa Bay Lightning by Vancouver for Tampa Bay's fifth round choice (David Darguzas) in 1997 Entry Draft (3/23/95). Signed as a free agent by Anaheim Mighty Ducks (8/27/96).

Steve Plouffe — Goaltender

			Regular Season							Playoffs					
Season	Team	League	GP	W	L	T	MIN	SO	GAVG	GP	W	L	MIN	SO	GAVG
95-96	Fort Worth	CeHL	30	10	13	4	1582	0	4.17	—	—	—	—	—	—
96-97	Fort Worth	CeHL	52	*38	9	5	2983	*2	2.88	*17	*11	5	*1022	*1	3.11
	CeHL	Totals	82	48	22	9	4565	2	3.33	17	11	5	1022	1	3.11

Born; 11/23/75, Montreal, Quebec. 6-0, 180. Drafted by Buffalo Sabres (6th choice, 168th overall) in 1994 Entry Draft. 1996-97 CeHL Playoff MVP. 1996-97 CeHL First team All-Star.

Andrew Plumb — Defenseman

			Regular Season					Playoffs				
Season	Team	League	GP	G	A	PTS	PIM	GP	G	A	PTS	PIM
94-95	Utica	CoHL	8	0	1	1	9	—	—	—	—	—
94-95	London	CoHL	45	1	6	7	20	5	0	1	1	18
95-96	Huntsville	SHL	45	3	13	16	74	—	—	—	—	—
95-96	Jacksonville	SHL	8	0	3	3	25	—	—	—	—	—
96-97	Dayton	CoHL	71	2	14	16	71	—	—	—	—	—
	CoHL	Totals	124	3	21	24	100	5	0	1	1	18
	SHL	Totals	53	3	16	19	99	—	—	—	—	—

Born; 2/6/72, Vancouver, British Columbia. 6-2, 205.

Steve Poapst — Defenseman

			Regular Season					Playoffs				
Season	Team	League	GP	G	A	PTS	PIM	GP	G	A	PTS	PIM
91-92	Hampton Roads	ECHL	55	8	20	28	29	14	1	4	5	12
92-93	Baltimore	AHL	7	0	1	1	4	7	0	3	3	6
92-93	Hampton Roads	ECHL	63	10	35	45	57	4	0	1	1	4
93-94	Portland	AHL	78	14	21	35	47	12	0	3	3	8
94-95	Portland	AHL	71	8	22	30	60	7	0	1	1	16
95-96	Washington	NHL	3	1	0	1	0	6	0	0	0	0
95-96	Portland	AHL	70	10	24	34	79	20	2	6	8	16
96-97	Portland	AHL	47	1	20	21	34	5	0	1	1	6
	AHL	Totals	273	33	88	121	224	51	2	14	16	52
	ECHL	Totals	118	18	55	73	86	18	1	5	6	16

Born; 1/3/69, Smith Falls, Ontario. 6-0, 195. Signed as a free agent by Washington Capitals (2/4/95). 1992-93 ECHL First Team All-Star. Member of 1991-92 ECHL champion Hampton Roads Admirals. Member of 1993-94 AHL champion Portland Pirates.

Jason Podollan — Right Wing

			Regular Season					Playoffs				
Season	Team	League	GP	G	A	PTS	PIM	GP	G	A	PTS	PIM
96-97	Florida	NHL	19	1	1	2	4	—	—	—	—	—
96-97	Toronto	NHL	10	0	3	3	6	—	—	—	—	—
96-97	Carolina	AHL	39	21	25	46	36	—	—	—	—	—
96-97	St. John's	AHL	—	—	—	—	—	11	2	3	5	6
	NHL	Totals	29	1	4	5	10	—	—	—	—	—
	AHL	Totals	39	21	25	46	36	11	2	3	5	6

Born; 2/18/76, Vernon, British Columbia. 6-1, 192. Drafted by Florida Panthers (3rd choice, 31st overall) in 1994 Entry Draft. Traded to Toronto Maple Leafs by Florida for Kirk Muller (3/18/97).

Joel Poirer — Left Wing

			Regular Season					Playoffs				
Season	Team	League	GP	G	A	PTS	PIM	GP	G	A	PTS	PIM
96-97	Austin	WPHL	38	2	1	3	18	—	—	—	—	—

Born; 1/21/72, Warwick, Rhode Island. 5-6, 150.

Gaeten Poirier — Left Wing

			Regular Season					Playoffs				
Season	Team	League	GP	G	A	PTS	PIM	GP	G	A	PTS	PIM
96-97	Carolina	AHL	66	5	13	18	66	—	—	—	—	—

Born; 12/28/76, Moncton, New Brunswick. 6-2, 200. Drafted by Florida Panthers (6th choice, 156th overall) in 1996 Entry Draft.

Joel Poirier — Left Wing

			Regular Season					Playoffs				
Season	Team	League	GP	G	A	PTS	PIM	GP	G	A	PTS	PIM
95-96	Portland	AHL	30	5	3	8	34	1	0	0	0	0
95-96	Hampton Roads	ECHL	23	9	8	17	61	—	—	—	—	—
96-97	Hampton Roads	ECHL	70	20	21	41	85	9	1	4	5	4
	ECHL	Totals	93	29	29	58	146	9	1	4	5	4

Born; 1/15/75, Richmond Hill, Ontario. 6-1, 190. Drafted by Washington Capitals (7th choice, 199th overall) in 1993 Entry Draft.

Clark Polglase — Defenseman

			Regular Season					Playoffs				
Season	Team	League	GP	G	A	PTS	PIM	GP	G	A	PTS	PIM
92-93	Detroit	CoHL	38	4	11	15	113	6	0	0	0	15
93-94	Huntsville	ECHL	34	2	14	16	200	—	—	—	—	—
93-94	Detroit	CoHL	10	2	4	6	51	2	1	0	1	46
94-95	Adirondack	AHL	3	0	0	0	7	—	—	—	—	—
94-95	Detroit	IHL	5	1	0	1	7	—	—	—	—	—
94-95	Detroit	CoHL	34	11	13	24	116	12	1	6	7	4
95-96	San Diego	WCHL	49	9	16	25	138	9	3	3	6	8
96-97	San Diego	WCHL	54	8	33	41	123	8	0	1	1	21
	WCHL	Totals	103	17	49	66	261	17	3	4	7	29
	CoHL	Totals	82	17	28	45	429	20	2	6	8	65

Born; 4/7/69, Edmonton, Alberta. 6-2, 200. Member of 1995-96 WCHL Champion San Diego Gulls. Member of 1996-97 WCHL Champion San Diego Gulls.

Paul Polillo — Center

			Regular Season					Playoffs				
Season	Team	League	GP	G	A	PTS	PIM	GP	G	A	PTS	PIM
92-93	Brantford	CoHL	59	33	79	112	18	15	7	13	20	10
93-94	Brantford	CoHL	64	42	*99	*141	37	7	1	9	10	6
94-95	Brantford	CoHL	74	47	*99	*146	48	—	—	—	—	—
94-95	Denver	IHL	1	0	0	0	0	—	—	—	—	—
95-96	Brantford	CoHL	74	*64	*122	*186	62	12	9	16	25	2
96-97	Brantford	CoHL	73	61	*112	*173	49	10	5	19	24	14
	CoHL	Totals	344	247	511	758	214	44	22	57	79	32

Born; 4/24/67, Brantford, Ontario. 5-11, 178. 1992-93 CoHL Second Team All-Star. 1992-93 CoHL sportsmanlike player. 1993-94 CoHL First All-Star team. 1993-94 CoHL sportsmanlike player. 1994-95 CoHL First Team All-Star. 1994-95 CoHL sportsmanlike player. 1994-95 Shared CoHL MVP award with Mark Green. 1995-96 CoHL 1st Team All-Star. 1995-96 CoHL MVP. 1996-97 CoHL MVP. 1996-97 CoHL First All-Star Team. Member of 1992-93 CoHL champion Brantford Smoke.

Mike Pomichter — Center

			Regular Season					Playoffs				
Season	Team	League	GP	G	A	PTS	PIM	GP	G	A	PTS	PIM
94-95	IND	IHL	76	13	9	22	47	—	—	—	—	—
95-96	IND	IHL	4	0	0	0	0	—	—	—	—	—
95-96	POR	AHL	2	0	0	0	0	—	—	—	—	—
95-96	COR	AHL	6	0	1	1	0	—	—	—	—	—
95-96	SJS	AHL	19	2	4	6	4	—	—	—	—	—

Season	Team	League	GP	G	A	PTS	PIM	GP	G	A	PTS	PIM
96-97	Jacksonville	ECHL	61	37	40	77	26	—	—	—	—	—
96-97	Baltimore	AHL	4	2	1	3	4	3	0	0	0	0
96-97	Chicago	IHL	2	0	0	0	0	—	—	—	—	—
	IHL	Totals	82	13	9	22	47	—	—	—	—	—
	AHL	Totals	31	4	6	9	8	3	0	0	0	0

Born; 9/10/73, New Haven, Connecticut. 6-2, 220. Drafted by Chicago Blackhawks (2nd choice, 39th overall) in 1991 Entry Draft. Traded to Toronto Maple Leafs by Chicago for cash (1/29/96).

Jim Popa — Defenseman

			Regular Season					Playoffs				
Season	Team	League	GP	G	A	PTS	PIM	GP	G	A	PTS	PIM
96-97	Alaska	WCHL	1	0	0	0	4	—	—	—	—	—
96-97	Waco	WPHL	36	2	3	5	39	—	—	—	—	—
96-97	San Antonio	CeHL	15	0	2	2	8	—	—	—	—	—

Born; 8/27/72, Massillon, Ohio. 6-2, 205.

Barry Potomski — Left Wing

			Regular Season					Playoffs				
Season	Team	League	GP	G	A	PTS	PIM	GP	G	A	PTS	PIM
92-93	Erie	ECHL	5	1	1	2	31	—	—	—	—	—
92-93	Toledo	ECHL	43	5	18	23	184	14	5	2	7	73
93-94	Toledo	ECHL	13	9	4	13	81	—	—	—	—	—
93-94	Adirondack	AHL	50	9	5	14	224	11	1	1	2	44
94-95	Phoenix	IHL	42	5	6	11	171	—	—	—	—	—
95-96	Los Angeles	NHL	33	3	2	5	104	—	—	—	—	—
95-96	Phoenix	IHL	24	5	2	7	74	3	1	0	1	8
96-97	Los Angeles	NHL	26	3	2	5	93	—	—	—	—	—
96-97	Phoenix	IHL	28	2	11	13	58	—	—	—	—	—
	NHL	Totals	59	6	4	10	197	—	—	—	—	—
	IHL	Totals	94	12	19	31	303	3	1	0	1	8
	ECHL	Totals	61	15	23	38	296	14	5	2	7	73

Born; 11/24/72, Windsor, Ontario. 6-2, 210. Signed as a free agent by Los Angeles Kings (7/7/94). Member of 1992-93 ECHL champion Toledo Storm.

Steve Pottie — Goaltender

			Regular Season							Playoffs					
Season	Team	League	GP	W	L	T	MIN	SO	GAVG	GP	W	L	MIN	SO	GAVG
96-97	Nashville	CeHL	19	4	*7	1	806	0	4.84	—	—	—	—	—	—
96-97	San Antonio	CeHL	27	9	*13	1	1412	0	4.33	—	—	—	—	—	—
	CeHL	Totals	46	13	20	2	2218	0	4.52	—	—	—	—	—	—

Born; 9/28/73, Waverly, Nova Scotia. 6-0, 200.

Marc Potvin — Right Wing

			Regular Season					Playoffs				
Season	Team	League	GP	G	A	PTS	PIM	GP	G	A	PTS	PIM
89-90	Adirondack	AHL	5	2	1	3	9	4	0	1	1	23
90-91	Detroit	NHL	9	0	0	0	55	6	0	0	0	32
90-91	Adirondack	AHL	63	9	13	22	*365	—	—	—	—	—
91-92	Detroit	NHL	5	1	0	1	52	1	0	0	0	0
91-92	Adirondack	AHL	51	13	16	29	314	19	5	4	9	57
92-93	Los Angeles	NHL	20	0	1	1	61	1	0	0	0	0
92-93	Adirondack	AHL	37	8	12	20	109	—	—	—	—	—
93-94	Los Angeles	NHL	3	0	0	0	26	—	—	—	—	—
93-94	Hartford	NHL	51	2	3	5	246	—	—	—	—	—
94-95	Boston	NHL	6	0	1	1	4	—	—	—	—	—
94-95	Providence	AHL	21	4	14	18	84	12	2	4	6	25

Season	Team	League	GP	G	A	PTS	PIM	GP	G	A	PTS	PIM
95-96	Boston	NHL	27	0	0	0	12	5	0	1	1	18
95-96	Providence	AHL	48	9	9	18	118	—	—	—	—	—
96-97	Portland	AHL	71	17	15	32	210	5	0	0	0	12
	NHL	Totals	121	3	5	8	528	13	0	1	1	50
	AHL	Totals	296	62	80	142	1209	40	7	9	16	117

Born; 1/29/67, Ottawa, Ontario. 6-1, 200. Drafted by Detroit Red Wings (9th choice, 169th overall) in 1986 Entry Draft. Traded to Los Angeles Kings by Detroit with Jimmy Carson and Gary Shuchuk for Paul Coffey, Sylvain Couturier and Jim Hiller (1/29/93). Traded to Hartford Whalers by Los Angeles for Doug Houda (11/3/93). Signed as a free agent by Boston Bruins (6/29/94). Member of 1991-92 AHL champion Adirondack Red Wings.

Steve Potvin — Center

Season	Team	League	GP	G	A	PTS	PIM	GP	G	A	PTS	PIM
94-95	Peoria	IHL	2	1	0	1	0	2	0	0	0	0
95-96	Portland	AHL	1	0	0	0	0	—	—	—	—	—
95-96	Raleigh	ECHL	62	15	31	46	175	4	2	2	4	0
96-97	Albany	AHL	16	1	6	7	18	11	0	1	1	16
96-97	Raleigh	ECHL	49	27	39	66	62	—	—	—	—	—
	AHL	Totals	17	1	6	7	18	11	0	1	1	16
	ECHL	Totals	111	42	70	112	237	4	2	2	4	0

Born; 9/26/74, Montreal, Quebec. 5-11, 190.

Jon Pratt — Left Wing

Season	Team	League	GP	G	A	PTS	PIM	GP	G	A	PTS	PIM
94-95	Providence	AHL	44	12	6	18	31	9	1	1	2	8
95-96	Peoria	IHL	45	6	12	18	47	5	1	2	3	6
96-97	Long Beach	IHL	1	0	0	0	0	—	—	—	—	—
96-97	Peoria	ECHL	45	32	25	57	83	2	2	3	5	4
	IHL	Totals	46	6	12	18	47	5	1	2	3	6

Born; 9/25/70, Danvers, Massachusetts. 6-1, 195. Drafted by Minnesota North Stars (9th choice, 154th overall) in 1989 Entry Draft.

Nolan Pratt — Defenseman

Season	Team	League	GP	G	A	PTS	PIM	GP	G	A	PTS	PIM
95-96	Springfield	AHL	62	2	6	8	72	2	0	0	0	0
95-96	Richmond	ECHL	4	1	0	1	2	—	—	—	—	—
96-97	Hartford	NHL	9	0	2	2	6	—	—	—	—	—
96-97	Springfield	AHL	66	1	18	19	127	17	0	3	3	18
	AHL	Totals	128	3	24	27	199	19	0	3	3	18

Born; 8/14/75, Fort McMurray, Alberta. 6-2, 195. Drafted by Hartford Whalers (4th choice, 115th overall) in 1993 Entry Draft.

Jody Praznik — Defenseman

Season	Team	League	GP	G	A	PTS	PIM	GP	G	A	PTS	PIM
89-90	Hampton Roads	ECHL	55	7	35	42	40	5	0	4	4	0
90-91	Hampton Roads	ECHL	64	15	39	54	30	11	0	2	2	10
91-92	Toledo	ECHL	37	3	27	30	26	—	—	—	—	—
91-92	Knoxville	ECHL	19	4	12	16	17	—	—	—	—	—
92-93	Tulsa	CeHL	55	11	33	44	50	12	6	13	19	22
93-94	Tulsa	CeHL	59	5	25	30	52	10	2	2	4	12
94-95	Tulsa	CeHL	60	8	23	31	40	4	1	1	2	2
95-96	Reno	WCHL	57	12	40	52	39	3	0	0	0	0
96-97	New Mexico	WPHL	61	18	52	70	74	6	1	4	5	4
	ECHL	Totals	175	29	113	142	113	16	0	6	6	10
	CeHL	Totals	174	24	81	105	142	26	9	16	25	36

Born; 6/28/69, Winnipeg, Manitoba. 6-1, 200. Drafted by Detroit Red Wings (8th choice, 185th overall) in 1988 Entry Draft. 1996-97 WPHL Defenseman of the Year. Member of 1990-91 ECHL Champion Hampton Roads Admirals. Member of 1992-93 CeHL Champion Tulsa Oilers.

Brad Prefontaine — Defenseman

Regular Season							Playoffs				
Season	Team	League	GP	G	A	PTS	PIM	GP	G	A	PTS	PIM
95-96	Birmingham	ECHL	60	1	7	8	279	—	—	—	—	—
96-97	Columbus	CeHL	63	6	11	17	197	3	0	0	0	30

Born; 7/27/72, Camrose, Alberta. 6-2, 210.

Wayne Presley — Right Wing

Regular Season							Playoffs				
Season	Team	League	GP	G	A	PTS	PIM	GP	G	A	PTS	PIM
84-85	Chicago	NHL	3	0	1	1	0	—	—	—	—	—
85-86	Chicago	NHL	38	7	8	15	38	3	0	0	0	0
85-86	Nova Scotia	AHL	29	6	9	15	22	—	—	—	—	—
86-87	Chicago	NHL	80	32	29	61	114	4	1	0	1	9
87-88	Chicago	NHL	42	12	10	22	52	5	0	0	0	4
88-89	Chicago	NHL	72	21	19	40	100	14	7	5	12	18
89-90	Chicago	NHL	49	6	7	13	69	19	9	6	15	29
90-91	Chicago	NHL	71	15	19	34	122	6	0	1	1	38
91-92	San Jose	NHL	47	8	14	22	76	—	—	—	—	—
91-92	Buffalo	NHL	12	2	2	4	57	7	3	3	6	14
92-93	Buffalo	NHL	79	15	17	32	96	8	1	0	1	6
93-94	Buffalo	NHL	65	17	8	25	103	7	2	1	3	14
94-95	Buffalo	NHL	46	14	5	19	41	5	3	1	4	8
95-96	Rangers	NHL	61	4	6	10	71	—	—	—	—	—
95-96	Toronto	NHL	19	2	2	4	14	5	0	0	0	2
96-97	St. John's	AHL	2	0	0	0	0	—	—	—	—	—
96-97	Detroit	IHL	42	7	16	23	80	18	0	4	4	50
	NHL	Totals	684	155	147	302	953	83	26	17	43	142
	AHL	Totals	31	6	9	15	22	—	—	—	—	—

Born; 3/23/65, Dearborn, Michigan. 5-11, 195. Drafted by Chicago Blackhawks (2nd choice, 39th overall) in 1983 Entry Draft. Traded to San Jose Sharks by Chicago for San Jose's third round choice (Bogdan Savenko) in 1993 Entry Draft, (9/20/91). Traded to Buffalo Sabres by San Jose for Dave Snuggerud, (3/9/92). Signed as a free agent by New York Rangers, (8/31/95). Traded to Toronto Maple Leafs by Rangers for Sergio Momesso (2/29/96). Member of 1996-97 IHL Champion Detroit Vipers.

Wayne Primeau — Center

Regular Season							Playoffs				
Season	Team	League	GP	G	A	PTS	PIM	GP	G	A	PTS	PIM
94-95	Buffalo	NHL	1	1	0	1	0	—	—	—	—	—
95-96	Buffalo	NHL	2	0	0	0	0	—	—	—	—	—
95-96	Rochester	AHL	8	2	3	5	6	17	3	1	4	11
96-97	Buffalo	NHL	45	2	4	6	64	9	0	0	0	6
96-97	Rochester	AHL	24	9	5	14	27	1	0	0	0	0
	NHL	Totals	48	3	4	7	64	9	0	0	0	6
	AHL	Totals	32	11	8	19	33	18	3	1	4	11

Born; 6/4/76, Scarborough, Ontario. 6-3, 193. Drafted by Buffalo Sabres (1st choice, 17th overall) in 1994 Entry Draft. Member of 1995-96 AHL champion Rochester Americans.

Mike Prokopec — Right Wing

Regular Season							Playoffs				
Season	Team	League	GP	G	A	PTS	PIM	GP	G	A	PTS	PIM
94-95	Indianapolis	IHL	70	21	12	33	80	—	—	—	—	—
95-96	Chicago	NHL	9	0	0	0	5	—	—	—	—	—
95-96	Indianapolis	IHL	67	18	22	40	131	5	2	0	2	4
96-97	Chicago	NHL	6	0	0	0	6	—	—	—	—	—
96-97	Indianapolis	IHL	57	13	18	31	143	—	—	—	—	—
96-97	Detroit	IHL	3	2	0	2	4	8	2	1	3	14
	NHL	Totals	15	0	0	0	11	—	—	—	—	—
	IHL	Totals	197	54	52	106	358	13	4	1	5	8

Drafted by Chicago Blackhawks (7th choice, 161st overall) in 1992 Entry Draft.

Sean Pronger — Center

Season	Team	League	Regular Season GP	G	A	PTS	PIM	Playoffs GP	G	A	PTS	PIM
94-95	Sand Diego	IHL	8	0	0	0	2	—	—	—	—	—
94-95	Greensboro	ECHL	2	0	2	2	0	—	—	—	—	—
94-95	Knoxville	ECHL	34	18	23	41	55	—	—	—	—	—
95-96	Anaheim	NHL	7	0	1	1	6	—	—	—	—	—
95-96	Baltimore	AHL	72	16	17	33	61	12	3	7	10	16
96-97	Anaheim	NHL	39	7	7	14	20	9	0	2	2	4
96-97	Baltimore	AHL	41	26	17	43	17	—	—	—	—	—
	NHL	Totals	46	7	8	15	26	9	0	2	2	4
	AHL	Totals	113	42	34	76	78	12	3	7	10	16
	ECHL	Totals	36	18	25	43	55	—	—	—	—	—

Born; 11/30/72, Dryden, Ontario. 6-2, 205. Drafted by Vancouver Canucks (3rd choice, 51st overall) in 1991 Entry Draft. Signed as a free agent by Anaheim Mighty Ducks, (2/14/95).

Vaclav Prospal — Center

Season	Team	League	Regular Season GP	G	A	PTS	PIM	Playoffs GP	G	A	PTS	PIM
93-94	Hershey	AHL	55	14	21	35	38	2	0	0	0	2
94-95	Hershey	AHL	69	13	32	45	36	2	1	0	1	4
95-96	Hershey	AHL	68	15	36	51	59	5	2	4	6	2
96-97	Philadelphia	NHL	63	32	63	95	70	—	—	—	—	—
96-97	Phialdelphia	AHL	18	5	10	15	4	5	1	3	4	4
	AHL	Totals	255	74	152	226	203	9	3	4	7	8

Born; 2/17/75, Ceske-Budejovice, Czechoslovakia. 6-2, 167. Drafted by Philadelphia Flyers (2nd choice, 71st overall) in 1993 Entry Draft. 1996-97 AHL First Team All-Star.

Christian Proulx — Defenseman

Season	Team	League	Regular Season GP	G	A	PTS	PIM	Playoffs GP	G	A	PTS	PIM
92-93	Fredericton	AHL	2	1	0	1	2	4	0	0	0	0
93-94	Montreal	NHL	7	1	2	3	20	—	—	—	—	—
93-94	Fredericton	AHL	70	2	12	14	183	—	—	—	—	—
94-95	Fredericton	AHL	75	1	9	10	184	9	0	1	1	8
95-96	San Francisco	IHL	80	1	15	16	154	4	0	0	0	6
96-97	Milwaukee	IHL	74	3	4	7	145	1	0	0	0	2
	IHL	Totals	154	4	19	23	299	5	0	0	0	8
	AHL	Totals	147	4	11	15	369	13	0	1	1	8

Born; 12/10/73, Coaticook, Quebec. 6-0, 190. Drafted by Montreal Canadiens (7th choice, 164th overall) in 1992 Entry Draft.

Hugo Proulx — Center

Season	Team	League	Regular Season GP	G	A	PTS	PIM	Playoffs GP	G	A	PTS	PIM
94-95	South Carolina	ECHL	10	0	1	1	12	—	—	—	—	—
94-95	Greensboro	ECHL	40	18	28	46	116	18	6	14	20	58
95-96	Saginaw	CoHL	4	2	3	5	14	—	—	—	—	—
95-96	Jacksonville	ECHL	24	11	8	19	43	18	9	9	18	46
96-97	Portland	AHL	2	0	0	0	2	—	—	—	—	—
96-97	Quad City	CoHL	69	48	58	106	82	15	8	11	19	12
	ECHL	Totals	74	29	37	66	171	36	15	23	38	104
	CoHL	Totals	73	50	61	111	96	15	8	11	19	12

Born; 6/8/72, Drummondville, Quebec. 5-11, 185. Member of 1996-97 CoHL Champion Quad City Mallards.

Jimmy Provencher — Right Wing

			Regular Season					Playoffs				
Season	Team	League	GP	G	A	PTS	PIM	GP	G	A	PTS	PIM
96-97	Louisville	ECHL	66	13	24	37	39	—	—	—	—	—

Born; 3/22/75, Kitchener, Ontario. 6-4, 215. Drafted by New Jersey Devils (10th choice, 247th overall) in 1993 Entry Draft.

Tony Prpic — Right Wing

			Regular Season					Playoffs				
Season	Team	League	GP	G	A	PTS	PIM	GP	G	A	PTS	PIM
94-95	Tallahassee	ECHL	20	5	8	13	71	—	—	—	—	—
94-95	Wheeling	ECHL	30	11	16	27	64	3	1	1	2	2
95-96	Fredericton	AHL	26	3	3	6	60	9	2	2	4	18
95-96	Wheeling	ECHL	6	0	2	2	12	—	—	—	—	—
96-97	Fredericton	AHL	16	4	3	7	33	—	—	—	—	—
96-97	Quebec	IHL	3	0	0	0	2	—	—	—	—	—
96-97	Pensacola	ECHL	36	18	11	29	113	11	4	3	7	37
	AHL	Totals	42	7	6	13	93	9	2	2	4	18
	ECHL	Totals	92	34	37	71	260	14	5	4	9	39

Born; 6/16/73, Cleveland, Ohio. 6-4, 222.

Derek Prue — Center

			Regular Season					Playoffs				
Season	Team	League	GP	G	A	PTS	PIM	GP	G	A	PTS	PIM
93-94	Chatham	CoHL	46	13	7	20	18	—	—	—	—	—
93-94	Utica	CoHL	2	0	0	0	0	—	—	—	—	—
93-94	St. Thomas	CoHL	11	2	4	6	2	3	0	0	0	0
96-97	Alaska	WCHL	10	2	2	4	10	—	—	—	—	—
96-97	Tulsa	CeHL	9	4	5	9	6	5	1	1	2	19
	CoHL	Totals	59	15	11	26	20	3	0	0	0	0

Born; 3/24/72, Spruce Grove, Alberta. 6-0, 190. Signed as a free agent by Tucson Gila Monsters (WCHL).

Derek Puppa — Goaltender

			Regular Season						Playoffs					
Season	Team	League	GP	W	L	T	MIN	SO	GAVG	GP	W	L	MIN	SO	GAVG
96-97	Pensacola	ECHL	1	0	1	0	60	0	5.00	—	—	—	—	—	—
96-97	Huntsville	CeHL	25	11	7	3	1219	1	4.87	—	—	—	—	—	—

Born; 2/18/72, Kirkland, Ontario. 5-9, 175.

Brad Purdie — Center

			Regular Season					Playoffs				
Season	Team	League	GP	G	A	PTS	PIM	GP	G	A	PTS	PIM
95-96	Dayton	ECHL	3	1	1	2	0	—	—	—	—	—
95-96	Cornwall	AHL	1	0	0	0	0	—	—	—	—	—
96-97	Chicago	IHL	61	14	22	36	28	4	0	1	1	4
96-97	Peoria	ECHL	11	9	4	13	10	—	—	—	—	—
	ECHL	Totals	14	10	5	15	10	—	—	—	—	—

Born; 9/11/72, Dollard-des-Or, Quebec. 6-0, 195. Last amateur club; Maine (Hockey East).

Dennis Purdie — Right Wing

			Regular Season					Playoffs				
Season	Team	League	GP	G	A	PTS	PIM	GP	G	A	PTS	PIM
92-93	Toledo	ECHL	6	0	0	0	17	—	—	—	—	—
92-93	Johnstown	ECHL	17	10	7	17	38	5	1	3	4	38
93-94	Johnstown	ECHL	57	36	46	82	171	3	3	2	5	8
94-95	Saint John	AHL	12	4	1	5	11	—	—	—	—	—
94-95	Johnstown	ECHL	36	27	33	60	125	5	5	3	8	12
95-96	Minnesota	IHL	2	0	0	0	0	—	—	—	—	—

Season	Team	League	GP	G	A	PTS	PIM	GP	G	A	PTS	PIM
95-96	Toledo	ECHL	48	23	36	59	187	11	9	4	13	24
96-97	Toledo	ECHL	58	37	43	80	169	5	1	3	4	25
	ECHL	Totals	222	133	165	298	707	29	19	14	33	107

Born; 11/27/72, Amherstburg, Ontario. 5-10, 200.

Neal Purdon — Left Wing

Season	Team	League	GP	G	A	PTS	PIM	GP	G	A	PTS	PIM
94-95	Thunder Bay	CoHL	20	2	2	4	4	—	—	—	—	—
95-96	Thunder Bay	CoHL	56	13	9	22	16	13	0	1	1	4
96-97	Thunder Bay	CoHL	69	24	22	46	72	11	3	2	5	6
	CoHL	Totals	145	39	33	72	92	24	3	3	6	10

Born; 2/1/70, Thunder Bay, Ontario. 5-10, 175.

John Purves — Right Wing

Season	Team	League	GP	G	A	PTS	PIM	GP	G	A	PTS	PIM
89-90	Baltimore	AHL	75	29	35	64	12	9	5	7	12	4
90-91	Washington	NHL	7	1	0	1	0	—	—	—	—	—
90-91	Baltimore	AHL	53	22	29	51	27	6	2	3	5	0
91-92	Baltimore	AHL	78	43	46	89	47	—	—	—	—	—
92-93	Germany	N/A										
93-94	Fort Wayne	IHL	69	38	48	86	29	18	10	14	24	12
94-95	Fort Wayne	IHL	60	30	33	63	16	4	4	1	5	6
95-96	San Francisco	IHL	75	56	49	105	32	4	0	3	3	0
96-97	Kansas City	IHL	66	25	47	72	17	3	0	0	0	0
	IHL	Totals	270	149	177	326	94	29	14	18	32	18
	AHL	Totals	206	94	110	204	86	15	7	10	17	4

Born; 2/12/68, Toronto, Ontario. 6-1, 201. Drafted by Washington Capitals (6th choice, 103rd overall) in 1986 Entry Draft. Signed as a free agent by Fort Wayne Komets (10/9/93). Will play for Kansas City Blades during the 1996-97 season after being acquired from the San Francisco franchise. 1995-96 IHL Second Team All-Star.

Bill Pye — Goaltender

Season	Team	League	GP	W	L	T	MIN	SO	GAVG	GP	W	L	MIN	SO	GAVG
91-92	Rochester	AHL	7	0	4	0	272	0	2.87	1	1	0	60	0	2.00
91-92	New Haven	AHL	4	0	3	1	200	0	5.70	—	—	—	—	—	—
91-92	Fort Wayne	IHL	8	5	2	1	451	0	3.86	—	—	—	—	—	—
91-92	Erie	ECHL	5	5	0	0	310	0	4.26	4	1	3	220	0	4.09
92-93	Rochester	AHL	26	9	14	2	1427	0	4.50	—	—	—	—	—	—
93-94	Rochester	AHL	19	7	7	2	980	0	4.29	—	—	—	—	—	—
93-94	South Carolina	ECHL	28	15	10	2	1578	1	3.61	3	1	2	179	0	4.03
94-95	Saginaw	CoHL	13	5	7	0	633	0	4.83	—	—	—	—	—	—
95-96	Columbus	ECHL	25	12	5	1	1227	0	4.50	—	—	—	—	—	—
96-97	Waco	WPHL	46	22	21	2	2620	0	3.64	—	—	—	—	—	—
	AHL	Totals	56	16	28	5	2879	0	4.36	1	1	0	60	0	2.00
	ECHL	Totals	58	32	15	3	3115	1	4.03	7	2	5	399	0	4.06

Born; 4/9/69, Canton, Michigan. Drafted by Buffalo Sabres (5th choice, 107th overall) in 1989 Entry Draft.

Pat Pysz — Right Wing

Season	Team	League	GP	G	A	PTS	PIM	GP	G	A	PTS	PIM
96-97	Columbus	ECHL	36	7	9	16	29	2	0	0	0	0

Born; 1/15/75, Nowy Targ, Poland. 5-11, 187. Drafted by Chicago Blackhawks (6th choice, 102nd overall) in 1993 Entry Draft.

Chad Quenneville — Center

			Regular Season					Playoffs				
Season	Team	League	GP	G	A	PTS	PIM	GP	G	A	PTS	PIM
94-95	Albany	AHL	8	1	5	6	0	—	—	—	—	—
95-96	Atlanta	IHL	6	1	1	2	2	—	—	—	—	—
95-96	Nashville	ECHL	54	16	25	41	24	4	1	2	3	6
96-97	Pensacola	ECHL	70	43	52	95	67	12	6	8	14	10
	ECHL	Totals	124	59	77	136	91	16	7	10	17	16

Born; 5/13/72, South Hadley, Massachusetts. 5-9, 175.

Kevin Quinn — Defenseman

			Regular Season					Playoffs				
Season	Team	League	GP	G	A	PTS	PIM	GP	G	A	PTS	PIM
95-96	Reno	WCHL	2	0	1	1	17	—	—	—	—	—
96-97	Reno	WCHL	29	3	10	13	151	—	—	—	—	—
	WCHL	Totals	31	3	11	14	168	—	—	—	—	—

6-1, 200.

Ken Quinney — Left Wing

			Regular Season					Playoffs				
Season	Team	League	GP	G	A	PTS	PIM	GP	G	A	PTS	PIM
85-86	Fredericton	AHL	61	11	26	37	34	6	2	2	4	9
86-87	Quebec	NHL	25	2	7	9	16	—	—	—	—	—
86-87	Fredericton	AHL	48	14	27	41	20	—	—	—	—	—
87-88	Quebec	NHL	15	2	2	4	5	—	—	—	—	—
87-88	Fredericton	AHL	58	37	39	76	39	13	3	5	8	35
88-89	Halifax	AHL	72	41	49	90	65	4	3	0	3	0
89-90	Halifax	AHL	44	9	16	25	63	2	0	0	0	2
90-91	Quebec	NHL	19	3	4	7	2	—	—	—	—	—
90-91	Halifax	AHL	44	20	20	40	76	—	—	—	—	—
91-92	Adirondack	AHL	63	31	29	60	33	19	7	12	19	9
92-93	Adirondack	AHL	63	32	34	66	15	10	2	9	11	9
93-94	Las Vegas	IHL	79	*55	53	108	52	5	3	3	6	2
94-95	Las Vegas	IHL	78	40	42	82	40	10	3	2	5	9
95-96	Las Vegas	IHL	66	33	36	69	59	9	2	5	7	15
96-97	Las Vegas	IHL	71	27	36	63	39	2	0	0	0	0
	NHL	Totals	59	7	13	20	23	—	—	—	—	—
	AHL	Totals	453	195	240	435	345	54	17	28	45	64
	IHL	Totals	294	155	167	322	190	26	8	10	18	26

Born; 5/23/65, New Westminster, British Columbia. 5-10, 190. Drafted by Quebec Nordiques (9th choice, 203rd overall) in 1984 Entry Draft. Signed as a free agent by DetroitRed Wings (8/12/91). 1993-94 IHL First Team All-Star. Member of 1991-92 AHL champion Adirondack Red Wings.

Deron Quint — Defenseman

			Regular Season					Playoffs				
Season	Team	League	GP	G	A	PTS	PIM	GP	G	A	PTS	PIM
95-96	Winnipeg	NHL	51	5	13	18	22	—	—	—	—	—
95-96	Springfield	AHL	11	2	3	5	4	10	2	3	5	6
96-97	Phoenix	NHL	27	3	11	14	4	7	0	2	2	0
96-97	Springfield	AHL	43	6	18	24	20	12	2	7	9	4
	NHL	Totals	78	8	24	32	26	7	0	2	2	6
	AHL	Totals	54	8	21	29	24	22	4	10	14	10

Born; 3/12/76, Durham, New Hampshire. 6-1, 182. Drafted by Winnipeg Jets (1st choice, 30th overall) in 1994 Entry Draft.

J.F. Quintin — Left Wing

			Regular Season					Playoffs				
Season	Team	League	GP	G	A	PTS	PIM	GP	G	A	PTS	PIM
89-90	Kalamazoo	IHL	68	20	18	38	38	10	8	4	12	14
90-91	Kalamazoo	IHL	78	31	43	74	64	9	1	5	6	11
91-92	San Jose	NHL	8	3	0	3	0	—	—	—	—	—
91-92	Kansas City	IHL	21	4	6	10	29	13	2	10	12	29
92-93	San Jose	NHL	14	2	5	7	4	—	—	—	—	—
92-93	Kansas City	IHL	64	20	29	49	169	11	2	1	3	16
93-94	Kansas City	IHL	41	14	19	33	117	—	—	—	—	—
93-94	Kansas City	IHL	63	23	35	58	130	19	2	9	11	57
95-96	Kansas City	IHL	77	26	35	61	158	5	0	3	3	20
96-97	Kansas City	IHL	21	3	5	8	49	2	0	0	0	2
	NHL	Totals	22	5	5	10	4	—	—	—	—	—
	IHL	Totals	433	141	190	331	754	69	15	28	43	149

Born; 5/28/69, St. Jean, Quebec. 6-1, 180. Drafted by Minnesota North Stars (4th choice, 75th overall) in 1989 Entry Draft. Claimed by San Jose Sharks in Dispersal Draft (5/30/91). Member of 1991-92 IHL champion Kansas City Blades.

Tyler Quiring — Left Wing

			Regular Season					Playoffs				
Season	Team	League	GP	G	A	PTS	PIM	GP	G	A	PTS	PIM
96-97	El Paso	WPHL	26	11	7	18	12	—	—	—	—	—

Born; 1/11/75, Vernon, British Columbia. 5-8, 175.

Mathieu Raby — Defenseman

			Regular Season					Playoffs				
Season	Team	League	GP	G	A	PTS	PIM	GP	G	A	PTS	PIM
95-96	Atlanta	IHL	5	0	0	0	15	—	—	—	—	—
95-96	Nashville	ECHL	62	4	11	15	256	5	0	0	0	28
96-97	Adirondack	AHL	13	0	0	0	28	—	—	—	—	—
96-97	Wheeling	ECHL	39	5	3	8	130	3	0	1	1	6
	ECHL	Totals	101	9	14	23	386	8	0	1	1	34

Born; 1/19/75, Hull, Quebec. 6-2, 204. Drafted by Tampa Bay Lightning (7th choice, 159th overall) in 1993 Entry Draft.

Andre Racicot — Goaltender

			Regular Season							Playoffs					
Season	Team	League	GP	W	L	T	MIN	SO	GAVG	GP	W	L	MIN	SO	GAVG
89-90	Montreal	NHL	1	0	0	0	13	0	13.85	—	—	—	—	—	—
89-90	Sherbrooke	AHL	33	19	11	2	1948	1	2.99	5	0	4	227	0	4.76
90-91	Montreal	NHL	21	7	9	2	975	1	3.20	2	0	1	12	0	10.00
90-91	Fredericton	AHL	22	13	8	1	1252	1	2.88	—	—	—	—	—	—
91-92	Montreal	NHL	9	0	3	3	436	0	3.17	1	0	0	1	0	0.00
91-92	Fredericton	AHL	28	14	8	5	1666	0	3.10	—	—	—	—	—	—
92-93	Montreal	NHL	26	17	5	1	1433	1	3.39	1	0	0	18	0	6.67
93-94	Montreal	NHL	11	2	6	2	500	0	4.44	—	—	—	—	—	—
93-94	Fredericton	AHL	6	1	4	0	292	0	3.28	—	—	—	—	—	—
94-95	Portland	AHL	19	10	7	0	1080	1	2.94	—	—	—	—	—	—
94-95	Phoenix	IHL	3	1	0	0	132	0	3.62	2	0	0	20	0	0.00
95-96	Columbus	ECHL	1	1	0	0	60	0	2.00	—	—	—	—	—	—
95-96	Albany	AHL	2	2	0	0	120	0	2.00	—	—	—	—	—	—
95-96	Indianapolis	IHL	11	3	6	0	547	0	4.71	—	—	—	—	—	—
95-96	Peoria	IHL	4	2	1	1	240	0	3.50	11	6	5	654	1	3.12
96-97	Indianapolis	IHL	2	1	0	1	120	1	1.50	—	—	—	—	—	—
96-97	Kansas City	IHL	6	1	4	0	274	0	4.60	—	—	—	—	—	—
96-97	Las Vegas	IHL	13	6	5	1	760	1	3.16	—	—	—	—	—	—
	NHL	Totals	68	26	23	8	3357	2	3.50	4	0	1	31	0	7.74
	AHL	Totals	110	59	38	8	6358	3	2.98	5	0	4	227	0	4.76
	IHL	Totals	38	14	16	3	2073	2	3.73	13	6	5	674	1	3.03

Born; 6/9/69, Rouyn-Noranda, Quebec. 5-11, 165. Drafted by Montreal Canadiens (5th choice, 83rd overall) in 1989 Entry Draft. Signed as a free agent by Los Angeles (9/22/94). 1989-90 Shared Harry "Hap" Holmes (fewest goals against-AHL) with J.C. Bergeron.

Bruce Racine — Goaltender

			Regular Season							Playoffs					
Season	Team	League	GP	W	L	T	MIN	SO	GAVG	GP	W	L	MIN	SO	GAVG
88-89	Muskegon	IHL	51	*37	11	0	*3039	*3	3.63	5	4	1	300	0	3.00
89-90	Muskegon	IHL	49	29	15	4	2911	1	3.75	9	5	4	566	1	3.34
90-91	Albany	IHL	29	7	18	1	1567	0	3.98	—	—	—	—	—	—
90-91	Muskegon	IHL	9	4	4	1	516	0	4.65	—	—	—	—	—	—
91-92	Muskegon	IHL	27	13	10	3	1559	1	3.50	1	0	1	60	0	6.00
92-93	Cleveland	IHL	35	13	16	6	1949	1	4.31	2	0	0	37	0	3.24
93-94	St. John's	AHL	37	20	9	2	1875	0	3.71	1	0	0	20	0	3.00
94-95	St. John's	AHL	27	11	10	4	1492	1	3.42	2	1	1	119	0	1.51
95-96	St. Louis	NHL	11	0	3	0	230	0	3.13	—	—	—	—	—	—
95-96	Peoria	IHL	22	11	10	1	1228	1	3.37	1	0	1	58	0	3.05
96-97	San Antonio	IHL	44	25	14	2	2426	6	3.02	6	3	2	326	0	3.13
	IHL	Totals	266	139	98	18	15195	13	3.68	24	12	9	1347	1	3.34
	AHL	Totals	64	31	19	6	3367	1	3.58	3	1	1	139	0	1.72

Born; 8/9/66, Cornwall, Ontario. 6-0, 170. Drafted by Pittsburgh Penguins (3rd choice, 58th overall) in 1985 Entry Draft. Signed as a free agent by Toronto Maple Leafs (8/11/93). Signed as a free agent by St. Louis Blues (8/10/95).

Herb Raglan — Right Wing

Regular Season / Playoffs

Season	Team	League	GP	G	A	PTS	PIM	GP	G	A	PTS	PIM
85-86	St. Louis	NHL	7	0	0	0	5	10	1	1	2	24
86-87	St. Louis	NHL	62	6	10	16	159	4	0	0	0	2
87-88	St. Louis	NHL	73	10	15	25	190	10	1	3	4	11
88-89	St. Louis	NHL	50	7	10	17	144	8	1	2	3	13
89-90	St. Louis	NHL	11	0	1	1	21	—	—	—	—	—
90-91	St. Louis	NHL	32	3	3	6	52	—	—	—	—	—
90-91	Quebec	NHL	15	1	3	4	30	—	—	—	—	—
91-92	Quebec	NHL	62	6	14	20	120	—	—	—	—	—
92-93	Tampa Bay	NHL	2	0	0	0	2	—	—	—	—	—
92-93	Halifax	AHL	28	3	9	12	83	—	—	—	—	—
92-93	Atlanta	IHL	24	4	10	14	139	9	3	3	6	32
93-94	Ottawa	NHL	29	0	0	0	52	—	—	—	—	—
93-94	Kalamazoo	IHL	29	6	11	17	112	5	0	0	0	32
94-95	Kalamazoo	IHL	31	4	4	8	94	6	0	0	0	15
95-96	Brantford	CoHL	69	46	38	84	267	12	9	6	15	14
96-97	Brantford	CoHL	11	5	4	9	33	2	3	1	4	4
96-97	Central Texas	WPHL	33	14	18	32	131	10	7	3	10	30
	NHL	Totals	343	33	56	89	775	32	3	6	9	50
	IHL	Totals	84	14	25	39	345	20	3	3	6	79
	CoHL	Totals	80	51	42	93	300	14	12	7	19	18

Born; 8/5/67, Peterborough, Ontario. 6-0, 208. Drafted by St. Louis Blues (1st choice, 37th overall) in 1985 Entry Draft. Traded to Quebec Nordiques by St. Louis with Tony Twist and Andy Rymsha for Darin Kimble (2/4/91). Traded to Tampa Bay Lightning by Quebec for Martin Simard, Michel Mongeau and Steve Tuttle (2/12/93). Signed as a free agent by Ottawa Senators (1/1/94). Loaned to Kalamazoo Wings by Ottawa (3/22/94).

Jamie Ram — Goaltender

Regular Season / Playoffs

Season	Team	League	GP	W	L	T	MIN	SO	GAVG	GP	W	L	MIN	SO	GAVG
94-95	Binghamton	AHL	26	12	10	2	1472	1	3.30	11	6	5	663	1	2.62
95-96	Rangers	NHL	1	0	0	0	27	0	0.00	—	—	—	—	—	—
95-96	Binghamton	AHL	40	18	16	3	2262	1	4.01	1	0	0	34	0	1.75
96-97	Kentucky	AHL	50	25	19	5	2937	4	3.29	1	0	1	60	0	3.00
	AHL	Totals	116	55	45	10	6671	6	3.53	13	6	6	757	1	2.61

Born; 1/18/71, Scarborough, Ontario. 5-11, 175. Drafted by New York Rangers (10th choice, 213th overall) in 1991 Entry Draft.

Bruce Ramsay — Left Wing

Regular Season / Playoffs

Season	Team	League	GP	G	A	PTS	PIM	GP	G	A	PTS	PIM
91-92	Thunder Bay	CoHL	54	7	16	23	*313	12	1	2	3	55
92-93	Thunder Bay	CoHL	52	3	16	19	234	—	—	—	—	—
93-94	Thunder Bay	CoHL	63	9	22	31	313	8	1	2	3	45
94-95	Prince Edward Island	AHL	2	0	1	1	10	1	0	0	0	2
94-95	Thunder Bay	COHL	62	14	29	43	462	11	0	3	3	83
95-96	Milwaukee	IHL	3	0	0	0	5	—	—	—	—	—
95-96	Thunder Bay	CoHL	56	6	15	21	*400	18	2	3	5	*142
96-97	Grand Rapids	IHL	66	3	5	8	306	4	0	0	0	2
96-97	Thunder Bay	CoHL	9	6	4	10	71	—	—	—	—	—
	IHL	Totals	69	3	5	8	311	4	0	0	0	2
	CoHL	Totals	296	45	102	147	1793	50	4	10	14	325

Born; 5/13/69, Dryden, Ontario. 6-0, 178. Signed as a free agent by St. Louis Blues (8/97). Member of 1991-92 CoHL champion Thunder Bay Thunder Hawks. Member of 1993-94 CoHL champion Thunder Bay Senators. Member of 1994-95 CoHL champion Thunder Bay Senators.

Shawn Randall — Right Wing

			Regular Season					Playoffs				
Season	Team	League	GP	G	A	PTS	PIM	GP	G	A	PTS	PIM
96-97	Huntsville	CeHL	48	3	12	15	135	5	0	1	1	4

Born; 11/13/72, Montrose, Michigan. 5-9, 185.

Bob Rapoza — Defenseman

			Regular Season					Playoffs				
Season	Team	League	GP	G	A	PTS	PIM	GP	G	A	PTS	PIM
95-96	Daytona Beach	SHL	5	0	1	1	8	—	—	—	—	—
96-97	Dayton	CoHL	71	6	11	17	56	—	—	—	—	—

Born; 9/29/74, Fall River, Massachusetts. 6-2, 225.

Kevin Rappana — Defenseman

			Regular Season					Playoffs				
Season	Team	League	GP	G	A	PTS	PIM	GP	G	A	PTS	PIM
95-96	Charlotte	ECHL	6	0	0	0	7	3	0	0	0	0
96-97	Worcester	AHL	2	0	1	1	0	—	—	—	—	—
96-97	Charlotte	ECHL	51	3	7	10	123	3	0	0	0	6
	ECHL	Totals	57	3	7	10	130	6	0	0	0	6

Born; 1/24/73, Duluth, Minnesota. 6-2, 190. Drafted by St. Louis Blues (11th choice, 241st overall) in 1991 Entry Draft. Member of 1995-96 ECHL Champion Charlotte Checkers.

Dan Ratushny — Defenseman

			Regular Season					Playoffs				
Season	Team	League	GP	G	A	PTS	PIM	GP	G	A	PTS	PIM
92-93	Vancouver	NHL	1	0	1	1	2	—	—	—	—	—
92-93	Fort Wayne	IHL	63	6	19	25	48	—	—	—	—	—
93-94	Hamilton	AHL	62	8	31	39	22	4	0	0	0	4
94-95	Fort Wayne	IHL	72	3	25	28	46	4	0	1	1	8
95-96	Carolina	AHL	23	5	10	15	28	—	—	—	—	—
95-96	Peoria	IHL	45	7	15	22	45	12	3	4	7	10
96-97	Quebec	IHL	50	14	23	37	34	—	—	—	—	—
	IHL	Totals	230	30	82	112	173	16	3	5	8	18
	AHL	Totals	85	13	41	54	50	4	0	0	0	4

Born; 10/29/70, Nepean, Ontario. 6-1, 210. Drafted by Winnipeg Jets (2nd choice, 25th overall) in 1989 Entry Draft. Traded to Vancouver Canucks by Winnipeg for ninth round pick (Harjis Vitolinsh) in 1993 Entry Draft.

Vern Ray — Defenseman

			Regular Season					Playoffs				
Season	Team	League	GP	G	A	PTS	PIM	GP	G	A	PTS	PIM
91-92	Thunder Bay	CoHL	37	1	7	8	107	7	0	0	0	11
92-93	Thunder Bay	CoHL	47	4	6	10	85	11	1	2	3	13
93-94	Thunder Bay	CoHL	42	4	7	11	45	9	1	2	3	6
94-95	Thunder Bay	CoHL	20	1	6	7	20	11	0	0	0	14
95-96	Fort Worth	CeHL	21	1	5	6	62	—	—	—	—	—
96-97	Fort Worth	CeHL	66	5	5	10	182	17	0	3	3	55
	CoHL	Totals	146	10	26	36	257	38	2	4	6	44
	CeHL	Totals	87	6	10	16	244	17	0	3	3	55

Born; 4/29/70, 6-2, 270. Member of 1991-92 CoHL champion Thunder Bay Thunder Hawks. Member of 1993-94 CoHL champion Thunder Bay Senators. Member of 1994-95 CoHL champion Thunder Bay Senators. Member of 1996-97 CeHL Champion Fort Worth Fire.

Pokey Reddick — Goaltender

			Regular Season							Playoffs					
Season	Team	League	GP	W	L	T	MIN	SO	GAVG	GP	W	L	MIN	SO	GAVG
85-86	Fort Wayne	IHL	29	15	11	0	1674	*3	3.00	—	—	—	—	—	—
86-87	Winnipeg	NHL	48	21	21	4	2762	0	3.24	3	0	2	166	0	3.61

Season	Team	League	GP	W	L	T	MIN	SO	GAVG	GP	W	L	MIN	SO	GAVG
87-88	Winnipeg	NHL	28	9	13	3	1487	0	4.12	—	—	—	—	—	—
87-88	Moncton	AHL	9	2	6	1	545	0	2.86	—	—	—	—	—	—
88-89	Winnipeg	NHL	41	11	17	7	2109	0	4.10	—	—	—	—	—	—
89-90	Edmonton	NHL	11	5	4	2	604	0	3.08	1	0	0	2	0	0.00
89-90	Cape Breton	AHL	15	9	4	1	821	0	3.95	—	—	—	—	—	—
89-90	Phoenix	IHL	3	2	1	0	185	0	2.27	—	—	—	—	—	—
90-91	Edmonton	NHL	2	0	2	0	120	0	4.50	—	—	—	—	—	—
90-91	Cape Breton	AHL	31	19	10	0	1673	2	3.48	2	0	2	124	0	4.84
91-92	Cape Breton	AHL	16	5	3	3	765	0	3.53	—	—	—	—	—	—
91-92	Fort Wayne	IHL	14	6	5	2	787	1	3.05	7	3	4	368	0	2.93
92-93	Fort Wayne	IHL	54	33	16	4	3043	3	3.08	12	*12	0	723	0	*1.49
93-94	Florida	NHL	2	0	1	0	80	0	6.00	—	—	—	—	—	—
93-94	Cincinnati	IHL	54	31	12	6	2894	*2	*3.05	10	6	2	498	*1	2.53
94-95	Las Vegas	IHL	40	23	13	1	2075	*3	3.01	10	4	6	592	0	3.14
95-96	Las Vegas	IHL	47	27	12	4	2636	1	2.94	15	8	6	770	0	3.35
96-97	Grand Rapids	IHL	61	30	14	10	3245	6	2.48	5	2	3	336	0	2.32
	NHL	Notes	132	46	58	16	7163	0	3.71	4	0	2	168	0	3.57
	IHL	Totals	302	167	84	27	16539	19	2.91	59	35	21	3288	1	2.63
	AHL	Totals	71	35	23	5	3804	2	3.50	2	0	2	124	0	4.84

Born; 10/6/64, Halifax, Nova Scotia. 5-8, 170. Signed as a free agent by Winnipeg Jets (9/27/85). Traded to Edmonton Oilers by Winnipeg for future considerations (9/28/89). Signed as a free agent by Florida Panthers (7/12/93). 1985-86 shared James Norris trophy (fewest goals allowed) with Rick St. Croix. 1992-93. 1992-93 IHL playoff MVP. Member of 1992-93 IHL champion Fort Wayne Komets.

Fran Reed — Right Wing

			Regular Season						Playoffs				
Season	Team	League	GP	G	A	PTS	PIM		GP	G	A	PTS	PIM
96-97	Madison	CoHL	23	1	2	3	143		—	—	—	—	—

Born; 2/8/72, West Roxbury, Massachusetts. 6-4, 250.

Jeff Reese — Goaltender

			Regular Season							Playoffs					
Season	Team	League	GP	W	L	T	MIN	SO	GAVG	GP	W	L	MIN	SO	GAVG
86-87	Newmarket	AHL	50	11	29	0	2822	1	4.10	—	—	—	—	—	—
87-88	Toronto	NHL	5	1	2	1	249	0	4.10	—	—	—	—	—	—
87-88	New Market	AHL	28	10	14	3	1587	0	3.89	—	—	—	—	—	—
88-89	Toronto	NHL	10	2	6	1	486	0	4.94	—	—	—	—	—	—
88-89	Newmarket	AHL	37	17	14	3	2072	0	3.82	—	—	—	—	—	—
89-90	Toronto	NHL	21	9	6	3	1101	0	4.41	2	1	1	108	0	3.33
89-90	Newmarket	AHL	7	3	2	2	431	0	4.04	—	—	—	—	—	—
90-91	Toronto	NHL	30	6	13	3	1430	1	3.86	—	—	—	—	—	—
90-91	Newmarket	AHL	3	2	1	0	180	0	2.33	—	—	—	—	—	—
91-92	Toronto	NHL	8	1	5	1	413	1	2.91	—	—	—	—	—	—
91-92	Calgary	NHL	12	3	2	2	587	0	3.78	—	—	—	—	—	—
92-93	Calgary	NHL	26	14	4	1	1311	1	3.20	4	1	3	209	0	4.88
93-94	Calgary	NHL	1	0	0	0	13	0	4.62	—	—	—	—	—	—
93-94	Hartford	NHL	19	5	9	3	1086	1	3.09	—	—	—	—	—	—
94-95	Hartford	NHL	11	2	5	1	477	0	3.27	—	—	—	—	—	—
95-96	Hartford	NHL	7	2	3	0	275	1	3.05	—	—	—	—	—	—
95-96	Tampa Bay	NHL	19	7	7	1	994	0	3.26	5	1	1	198	0	3.64
96-97	New Jersey	NHL	3	0	2	0	139	0	5.61	—	—	—	—	—	—
96-97	Detroit	IHL	32	23	4	3	1763	4	*1.87	11	7	3	519	0	2.55
	NHL	Totals	172	52	64	17	8561	5	3.65	11	3	5	515	0	4.08
	AHL	Totals	125	43	60	8	7092	1	3.93	—	—	—	—	—	—

Born; 3/24/66, Brantford, Ontario. 5-9, 180. Drafted by Toronto Maple Leafs (3rd choice, 67th overall) in 1984 Entry Draft. Traded to Calgary Flames with Craig Berube, Alexander Godynyuk, Gary Leeman and Michel Petit for Doug Gilmour, Jamie Macoun, Ric Nattress, Rick Wamsley and Kent Manderville, (1/2/92). Traded to Hartford Whalers by Calgary for Dan Keczmer, (11/19/93). Traded to Tampa Bay Lightning by Hartford for Tampa Bay's ninth round choice (Ashhat Rakhmatullin) in 1996 Entry Draft (12/1/95). Traded to New Jersey Devils by Tampa Bay with Chicago's second round choice (previosuly acquired by Tampa Bay—New Jersey selected Pierre Dagenais) in 1996 Entry Draft and Tampa Bay's eighth round choice (Jay Bertsch) in 1996 Entry Draft for Corey Schwab, (6/22/96). 1996-97 IHL Second Team All-Star. Member of 1996-97 IHL Champion Detroit Vipers.

Kyle Reeves — Right Wing

Season	Team	League	GP	G	A	PTS	PIM	GP	G	A	PTS	PIM
91-92	Peoria	IHL	60	12	7	19	92	—	—	—	—	—
92-93	Peoria	IHL	50	17	14	31	83	3	0	2	2	2
93-94	Peoria	IHL	3	0	1	1	2	—	—	—	—	—
93-94	Toledo	ECHL	33	12	13	25	75	—	—	—	—	—
94-95	Fort Wayne	IHL	7	0	0	0	17	—	—	—	—	—
94-95	South Carolina	ECHL	2	0	1	1	4	—	—	—	—	—
94-95	Flint	CoHL	36	38	16	54	133	—	—	—	—	—
94-95	Utica	CoHL	13	12	5	17	28	6	2	2	4	12
95-96	Utah	IHL	2	0	0	0	2	—	—	—	—	—
95-96	Fort Worth	CeHL	63	*68	47	115	179	—	—	—	—	—
96-97	Knoxville	ECHL	31	29	22	51	90	—	—	—	—	—
96-97	Baton Rouge	ECHL	24	6	8	14	30	—	—	—	—	—
	IHL	Totals	122	29	22	51	196	3	0	2	2	2
	ECHL	Totals	90	47	44	91	199	—	—	—	—	—
	CoHL	Totals	49	50	21	71	161	6	2	2	4	12

Born; 5/12/71, Swan River, Manitoba. 6-0, 200. Drafted by St. Louis Blues (2nd choice, 64th overall) in 1989 Entry Draft. 1995-96 CeHL First Team All-Star.

Craig Reichert — Right Wing

Season	Team	League	GP	G	A	PTS	PIM	GP	G	A	PTS	PIM
94-95	San Diego	IHL	49	4	12	16	28	—	—	—	—	—
95-96	Baltimore	AHL	68	10	17	27	50	1	0	0	0	0
96-97	Baltimore	AHL	77	22	53	75	54	3	0	2	2	0
96-97	Anaheim	NHL	3	0	0	0	0	—	—	—	—	—
	AHL	Totals	145	32	70	102	104	4	0	2	2	0

Born; 5/11/74, Calgary, Alberta. 6-1, 196. Drafted by Anaheim Mighty Ducks (3rd choice, 67th overall) in 1994 Entry Draft.

Jeff Reid — Center

Season	Team	League	GP	G	A	PTS	PIM	GP	G	A	PTS	PIM
93-94	Las Vegas	IHL	16	2	5	7	10	1	0	0	0	0
93-94	Knoxville	ECHL	57	27	31	58	46	3	0	0	0	2
95-96	Orlando	IHL	18	0	0	0	8	7	0	0	0	6
95-96	Raleigh	ECHL	30	8	18	26	18	4	1	3	4	6
96-97	Raleigh	ECHL	67	17	47	64	49	—	—	—	—	—
	IHL	Totals	34	2	5	7	18	8	0	0	0	6
	ECHL	Totals	154	52	96	148	113	7	1	3	4	8

Born; 9/19/72, Mississauga, Ontario. 5-10, 175.

Ryan Reid — Defenseman

Season	Team	League	GP	G	A	PTS	PIM	GP	G	A	PTS	PIM
95-96	Jacksonville	ECHL	1	0	0	0	19	—	—	—	—	—
95-96	Utica	CoHL	10	0	0	0	29	—	—	—	—	—
95-96	Jacksonville	SHL	21	1	8	9	103	—	—	—	—	—
96-97	Columbus	CeHL	47	1	5	6	142	1	0	0	0	0

Born; 5/2/71, Fort Saskatchewan, Saskatchewan. 6-2, 190.

Scott Reid — Goaltender

Season	Team	League	GP	W	L	T	MIN	SO	GAVG	GP	W	L	MIN	SO	GAVG
96-97	Bakersfield	WCHL	7	3	2	1	358	0	5.02	1	0	0	15	0	8.09

Born; 11/25/76, Grand Prairie, Alberta. 6-3, 185. Last amateur club; Kamloops (WHL).

Shawn Reid — Defenseman

Season	Team	League	GP	G	A	PTS	PIM	GP	G	A	PTS	PIM
94-95	Fort Wayne	IHL	42	4	8	12	28	—	—	—	—	—
94-95	Binghamton	AHL	18	3	4	7	8	9	0	3	3	6
95-96	Binghamton	AHL	45	0	5	5	33	1	0	0	0	0
95-96	Charlotte	ECHL	6	1	5	6	10	—	—	—	—	—
96-97	San Antonio	IHL	39	4	7	11	12	5	0	1	1	2
	IHL	Totals	81	8	15	23	40	5	0	1	1	2
	AHL	Totals	63	3	9	12	41	10	0	3	3	6

Born; 9/21/70, Toronto, Ontario. 6-0, 195. Signed as a free agent by New York Rangers (7/6/94).

Scott Reilly — Left Wing

Season	Team	League	GP	G	A	PTS	PIM	GP	G	A	PTS	PIM
96-97	Saginaw	CoHL	44	1	6	7	79	—	—	—	—	—
96-97	Thunder Bay	CoHL	11	1	4	5	6	—	—	—	—	—
	CoHL	Totals	55	2	10	12	85	—	—	—	—	—

Born; 9/23/71, Scituate, Massachusetts. 5-11, 195.

Dan Reimann — Defenseman

Season	Team	League	GP	G	A	PTS	PIM	GP	G	A	PTS	PIM
96-97	Johnstown	ECHL	33	1	3	4	34	—	—	—	—	—
96-97	Louisville	ECHL	28	0	3	3	19	—	—	—	—	—
	ECHL	Totals	61	1	6	7	53	—	—	—	—	—

Born; 12/17/72, Ramsey, Minnesota. 6-1, 205. Drafted by New Jersey Devils (9th choice, 187th overall) in 1991 Entry Draft.

Todd Reirdon — Defenseman

Season	Team	League	GP	G	A	PTS	PIM	GP	G	A	PTS	PIM
94-95	Raleigh	ECHL	26	2	13	15	33	—	—	—	—	—
94-95	Tallahassee	ECHL	43	5	25	30	61	13	2	5	7	10
95-96	Chicago	IHL	31	0	2	2	39	9	0	2	2	16
95-96	Tallahassee	ECHL	7	1	3	4	10	—	—	—	—	—
95-96	Jacksonville	ECHL	15	1	10	11	41	1	0	2	2	4
96-97	Chicago	IHL	57	3	10	13	108	—	—	—	—	—
96-97	San Antonio	IHL	23	2	5	7	51	9	0	1	1	17
	IHL	Totals	111	5	17	22	198	18	0	3	3	33
	ECHL	Totals	91	9	51	60	145	14	2	7	9	14

Born; 6/25/71, Arlington Heights, Illinois. 6-4, 205. Drafted by New Jersey Devils (14th choice, 242nd overall) in 1990 Entry Draft.

Danny Reja — Left Wing

Season	Team	League	GP	G	A	PTS	PIM	GP	G	A	PTS	PIM
96-97	Hampton Roads	ECHL	7	1	0	1	16	—	—	—	—	—
96-97	Louisville	ECHL	38	11	17	28	43	—	—	—	—	—
	ECHL	Totals	45	12	17	29	59	—	—	—	—	—

Born; 5/16/76, Toronto, Ontario. 6-1, 193. Drafted by Washington Capitals (7th choice, 171st overall) in 1994 Entry Draft.

Chad Remackel — Left Wing

Regular Season / **Playoffs**

Season	Team	League	GP	G	A	PTS	PIM	GP	G	A	PTS	PIM
96-97	Portland	AHL	1	0	0	0	0	—	—	—	—	—
96-97	Grand Rapids	IHL	70	9	18	27	36	1	0	0	0	0

Born; 11/9/71, St. Paul, Minnesota. 6-1, 198. Last amateur club; Colorado College (WCHA).

Jon Rempel — Defenseman

Regular Season / **Playoffs**

Season	Team	League	GP	G	A	PTS	PIM	GP	G	A	PTS	PIM
96-97	Baton Rouge	ECHL	26	1	4	5	63	—	—	—	—	—

Born; 9/11/71, Steinbach, Manitoba. 6-3, 225.

Jason Renard — Right Wing

Regular Season / **Playoffs**

Season	Team	League	GP	G	A	PTS	PIM	GP	G	A	PTS	PIM
93-94	Richmond	ECHL	35	12	12	24	262	—	—	—	—	—
94-95	Fort Wayne	IHL	27	4	2	6	129	3	0	1	1	16
94-95	Saginaw	CoHL	27	6	11	17	117	—	—	—	—	—
95-96	Johnstown	ECHL	10	2	1	3	43	—	—	—	—	—
95-96	South Carolina	ECHL	8	2	2	4	89	—	—	—	—	—
95-96	Saginaw	CoHL	35	7	7	14	187	5	0	2	2	33
96-97	Utica	CoHL	30	9	7	16	152	—	—	—	—	—
96-97	Port Huron	CoHL	35	7	21	28	85	5	4	2	6	30
	CoHL	Totals	127	29	46	75	541	10	4	4	8	63
	ECHL	Totals	53	14	15	29	394	—	—	—	—	—

Born; 4/22/73, Brooks, Alberta. 6-1, 190.

Iannique Renaud — Right Wing

Regular Season / **Playoffs**

Season	Team	League	GP	G	A	PTS	PIM	GP	G	A	PTS	PIM
96-97	Pensacola	ECHL	3	0	0	0	10	—	—	—	—	—
96-97	Anchorage	WCHL	9	0	0	0	52	—	—	—	—	—
96-97	Alaska	WCHL	20	5	5	10	147	—	—	—	—	—
96-97	Bakersfield	WCHL	3	0	3	3	8	3	0	1	1	50
	WCHL	Totals	32	5	8	13	207	3	0	1	1	50

Born; 9/19/75, Winnipeg, Manitoba. 6-3, 215.

Brian Renfrew — Goaltender

Regular Season / **Playoffs**

Season	Team	League	GP	W	L	T	MIN	SO	GAVG	GP	W	L	MIN	SO	GAVG
95-96	Oklahoma City	CeHL	5	2	3	0	269	0	5.13	—	—	—	—	—	—
95-96	Dayton	ECHL	21	6	5	3	912	0	3.09	—	—	—	—	—	—
95-96	Jacksonville	ECHL	8	4	4	0	440	0	4.37	16	9	7	901	0	3.93
96-97	Jacksonville	ECHL	10	0	8	0	517	0	6.15	—	—	—	—	—	—
96-97	Dayton	CoHL	37	7	23	4	2051	0	5.09	—	—	—	—	—	—
	ECHL	Totals	39	10	17	3	1869	0	4.24	16	9	7	901	0	3.93

Born; 5/1/72, Fairbanks, Alaska. 5-9, 165.

Todd Reynolds — Goaltender

Regular Season / **Playoffs**

Season	Team	League	GP	W	L	T	MIN	SO	GAVG	GP	W	L	MIN	SO	GAVG
95-96	Reno	WCHL	5	3	1	0	280	0	3.00	2	0	2	93	0	5.16
96-97	Reno	WCHL	29	6	19	1	1460	0	6.37	—	—	—	—	—	—
96-97	New Mexico	WPHL	4	1	3	0	240	0	7.00	1	0	1	59	0	6.12
	WCHL	Totals	34	9	20	1	1740	0	5.83	2	0	2	93	0	5.16

Born; 9/5/71, Etibicoke, Ontario. 6-2, 187.

Jessie Rezansoff — Right Wing

			Regular Season					Playoffs				
Season	Team	League	GP	G	A	PTS	PIM	GP	G	A	PTS	PIM
96-97	Fredericton	AHL	68	0	8	8	208	—	—	—	—	—

Born; 1/31/76, Regina, Saskatchewan. 6-4, 201. Last amateur club; Calgary (WHL).

Pascal Rheaume — Center

			Regular Season					Playoffs				
Season	Team	League	GP	G	A	PTS	PIM	GP	G	A	PTS	PIM
93-94	Albany	AHL	55	17	18	35	43	5	0	1	1	0
94-95	Albany	AHL	78	19	25	44	46	14	3	6	9	19
95-96	Albany	AHL	68	26	42	68	50	4	1	2	3	2
96-97	New Jersey	NHL	2	1	0	1	0	—	—	—	—	—
96-97	Albany	AHL	51	22	23	45	40	16	2	8	10	16
	AHL	Totals	252	84	108	192	179	39	6	17	23	37

Born; 6/21/73, Quebec City, Quebec. 6-0, 185. Signed as a free agent by New Jersey Devils (10/1/92). Member of 1994-95 Calder Cup champion Albany RiverRats.

Eric Ricard — Defenseman

			Regular Season					Playoffs				
Season	Team	League	GP	G	A	PTS	PIM	GP	G	A	PTS	PIM
89-90	New Haven	AHL	28	1	1	2	55	—	—	—	—	—
90-91	New Haven	AHL	35	1	4	5	65	—	—	—	—	—
90-91	Phoenix	IHL	16	1	3	4	24	—	—	—	—	—
91-92	New Haven	AHL	38	2	9	11	85	2	1	0	1	2
91-92	Louisville	ECHL	23	4	13	17	8	—	—	—	—	—
92-93	Fredericton	AHL	14	0	5	5	18	—	—	—	—	—
93-94	Fort Worth	CeHL	12	0	6	6	14	—	—	—	—	—
94-95	Denver	IHL	1	0	0	0	0	—	—	—	—	—
94-95	Fort Worth	CeHL	60	11	45	56	141	—	—	—	—	—
95-96	Tulsa	CeHL	6	2	3	5	2	6	0	4	4	8
96-97	New Mexico	WPHL	58	13	36	49	131	6	1	1	2	6
	AHL	Totals	115	4	19	23	223	2	1	0	1	2
	IHL	Totals	17	1	3	4	24	—	—	—	—	—
	CeHL	Totals	78	13	54	67	157	6	0	4	4	8

Born; 2/29/69, St. Cesaire, Quebec. 6-4, 235. Drafted by Los Angeles Kings (3rd choice, 102nd overall) in 1989 Entry Draft. 1994-95 CeHL Defenseman of the Year. 1994-95 CeHL First Team All-Star.

Jeff Ricciardi — Defenseman

			Regular Season					Playoffs				
Season	Team	League	GP	G	A	PTS	PIM	GP	G	A	PTS	PIM
92-93	Providence	AHL	3	0	0	0	0	—	—	—	—	—
92-93	Johnstown	ECHL	61	7	29	36	248	5	2	2	4	6
93-94	Indianapolis	IHL	75	3	20	23	307	—	—	—	—	—
94-95	Indianapolis	IHL	60	2	11	13	187	—	—	—	—	—
95-96	Las Vegas	IHL	75	4	13	17	303	15	2	0	2	42
96-97	Manitoba	IHL	81	3	22	25	271	—	—	—	—	—
	IHL	Totals	291	12	66	78	1068	15	2	0	2	42

Born; 6/21/71, Thunder Bay, Ontario. 5-11, 203. Drafted by Winnipeg Jets (8th choice, 159th overall) in 1991 Entry Draft. Traded to Boston Bruins by Winnipeg for future considerations (9/8/92). Signed as a free agent by Chicago Blackhawks (7/28/93).

Chad Richard — Left Wing

			Regular Season					Playoffs				
Season	Team	League	GP	G	A	PTS	PIM	GP	G	A	PTS	PIM
95-96	Anchorage	WCHL	37	3	3	6	*356	—	—	—	—	—
96-97	Anchorage	WCHL	25	7	9	16	313	—	—	—	—	—
96-97	Port Huron	CoHL	15	4	2	6	53	—	—	—	—	—

	WCHL	Totals	62	10	12	22	669	—	—	—	—	—

Born; 6/23/74, Anchorage, Alaska. 6-6, 235.

Marcel Richard — Right Wing

			Regular Season					Playoffs				
Season	Team	League	GP	G	A	PTS	PIM	GP	G	A	PTS	PIM
93-94	Erie	ECHL	1	0	1	1	0	—	—	—	—	—
94-95	London	CoHL	22	7	8	15	2	5	4	2	6	0
95-96	Madison	CoHL	70	24	31	55	48	6	1	2	3	4
96-97	Columbus	CeHL	63	51	58	109	74	3	1	1	2	0
	CoHL	Totals	92	31	39	70	50	11	5	4	9	4

Born; 5/21/69, Kingston, Ontario. 6-0, 200.

Jean-Marc Richard — Defenseman

			Regular Season					Playoffs				
Season	Team	League	GP	G	A	PTS	PIM	GP	G	A	PTS	PIM
87-88	Fredericton	AHL	68	14	42	56	52	7	2	1	3	4
87-88	Quebec	NHL	4	2	1	3	2	—	—	—	—	—
88-89	Halifax	AHL	57	8	25	33	38	4	1	0	1	4
89-90	Quebec	NHL	1	0	0	0	0	—	—	—	—	—
89-90	Halifax	AHL	40	1	24	25	38	—	—	—	—	—
90-91	Halifax	AHL	80	7	41	48	78	—	—	—	—	—
90-91	Fort Wayne	IHL	1	0	0	0	0	19	3	9	12	8
91-92	Fort Wayne	IHL	82	18	68	86	109	7	0	5	5	20
92-93	San Diego	IHL	6	1	0	1	4	—	—	—	—	—
92-93	Fort Wayne	IHL	52	10	33	43	48	12	6	11	17	6
93-94	Las Vegas	IHL	59	15	33	48	44	5	0	3	3	0
94-95	Las Vegas	IHL	81	16	41	57	76	10	0	3	3	4
95-96	Las Vegas	IHL	82	12	40	52	92	15	1	7	8	23
96-97	Quebec	IHL	56	8	26	34	31	9	1	1	2	10
	NHL	Totals	5	2	1	3	2	—	—	—	—	—
	IHL	Totals	419	80	241	321	404	77	11	39	50	71
	AHL	Totals	245	30	132	162	206	11	3	1	4	8

Born; 10/8/66, St. raymond, Quebec. 5-11, 178. Signed as a free agent by Quebec Nordiques (4/87). Loaned to Fort Wayne Komets (3/91). Signed as a free agent by Komets (9/91). Signed as a free agent by Las Vegas Thunder (7/8/93). 1991-92 IHL First Team All-Star. 1993-94 IHL First Team All-Star. 1991-92 IHL best defenseman (Governors Trophy). Member of 1992-93 IHL champion Fort Wayne Komets.

Mark Richards — Goaltender

			Regular Season							Playoffs					
Season	Team	League	GP	W	L	T	MIN	SO	GAVG	GP	W	L	MIN	SO	GAVG
92-93	Moncton	AHL	13	6	6	1	736	0	3.99	4	1	3	231	0	4.94
92-93	Fort Wayne	IHL	3	1	0	0	139	0	4.75	—	—	—	—	—	—
92-93	Toledo	ECHL	11	5	4	1	612	1	2.75	—	—	—	—	—	—
93-94	Moncton	AHL	29	8	16	0	1419	0	4.35	—	—	—	—	—	—
94-95	Tallahassee	ECHL	*59	31	16	7	*3369	0	2.90	13	8	5	760	1	3.16
95-96	Tallahassee	ECHL	50	28	11	5	2627	*2	3.49	9	6	3	537	*2	*2.12
96-97	Baltimore	AHL	1	0	1	0	40	0	4.50	—	—	—	—	—	—
96-97	Tallahassee	ECHL	38	20	11	3	2086	2	3.28	1	0	1	52	0	4.64
	AHL	Totals	43	14	23	1	2195	0	4.24	4	1	3	231	0	4.94
	ECHL	Totals	158	84	42	16	8694	5	3.16	23	14	9	1349	3	2.80

Born; 7/24/69, Abington, Pennsylvania. 5-8, 185.

Steve Richards — Center

			Regular Season					Playoffs				
Season	Team	League	GP	G	A	PTS	PIM	GP	G	A	PTS	PIM
95-96	Hampton Roads	ECHL	60	6	30	36	38	3	1	1	2	2
96-97	Baton Rouge	ECHL	14	0	6	6	4	—	—	—	—	—
96-97	Raleigh	ECHL	11	1	4	5	0	—	—	—	—	—

Season	Team	League	GP	G	A	PTS	PIM	GP	G	A	PTS	PIM
96-97	Tallahassee	ECHL	28	2	3	5	20	3	0	1	1	0
	ECHL	Totals	113	9	43	52	62	6	1	2	3	2

Born; 7/29/71, Abington, Pennsylvania. 5-9, 185.

Todd Richards — Defenseman

			Regular Season					Playoffs				
Season	Team	League	GP	G	A	PTS	PIM	GP	G	A	PTS	PIM
89-90	Sherbrooke	AHL	71	6	18	24	73	5	1	2	3	6
90-91	Hartford	NHL	2	0	4	4	2	6	0	0	0	2
90-91	Fredericton	AHL	3	0	1	1	2	—	—	—	—	—
90-91	Springfield	AHL	71	10	41	51	62	14	2	8	10	2
91-92	Hartford	NHL	6	0	0	0	2	5	0	3	3	4
91-92	Springfield	AHL	43	6	23	29	33	8	0	3	3	2
92-93	Springfield	AHL	78	13	42	55	53	9	1	5	6	2
93-94	Las Vegas	IHL	80	11	35	46	122	5	1	4	5	18
94-95	Las Vegas	IHL	80	12	49	61	130	9	1	2	3	6
95-96	Orlando	IHL	81	19	54	73	59	23	4	9	13	8
96-97	Orlando	IHL	82	9	36	45	134	10	0	1	1	4
	NHL	Totals	8	0	4	4	4	11	0	3	3	6
	IHL	Totals	323	51	174	225	445	47	6	16	22	36
	AHL	Totals	266	35	125	160	223	36	4	18	22	12

Born; 10/20/66, Crystal, Minnesota. 6-0, 194. Drafted by Montreal Canadiens (3rd choice, 33rd overall) in 1985 Entry Draft. Traded to Hartford Whalers by Montreal for future considerations (10/90). Signed as a free agent by Las Vegas Thunder (7/14/93). Signed as a free agent by Orlando Solar Bears (7/10/95). 1993-94 IHL Second Team All-Star. 1994-95 IHL First Team All-Star. 1994-95 IHL Governors Trophy (Best Defenseman). 1995-96 IHL First Team All-Star. Member of 1990-91 AHL champion Springfield Indians.

Travis Richards — Defenseman

			Regular Season					Playoffs				
Season	Team	League	GP	G	A	PTS	PIM	GP	G	A	PTS	PIM
93-94	Kalamazoo	IHL	19	2	10	12	20	4	1	1	2	0
94-95	Dallas	NHL	2	0	0	0	0	—	—	—	—	—
94-95	Kalamazoo	IHL	63	4	16	20	53	15	1	5	6	12
95-96	Dallas	NHL	1	0	0	0	2	—	—	—	—	—
95-96	Michigan	IHL	65	8	15	23	55	9	2	2	4	4
96-97	Grand Rapids	IHL	77	10	13	23	83	5	1	3	4	2
	NHL	Totals	3	0	0	0	2	—	—	—	—	—
	IHL	Totals	224	24	54	78	211	33	5	11	16	18

Born; 3/22/70, Crystal, Minnesota. 6-1, 195. Drafted by Minnesota North Stars (6th choice, 169th overall) in 1988 Entry Draft.

Bryan Richardson — Center

			Regular Season					Playoffs				
Season	Team	League	GP	G	A	PTS	PIM	GP	G	A	PTS	PIM
96-97	Dayton	ECHL	25	5	16	21	28	1	0	0	0	4

Born; 7/28/73, Montreal, Quebec. 5-9, 188. Last amateur club; Rensselaer Polytechnic Institute (ECAC).

Grant Richison — Defenseman

			Regular Season					Playoffs				
Season	Team	League	GP	G	A	PTS	PIM	GP	G	A	PTS	PIM
89-90	Moncton	AHL	50	2	10	12	28	—	—	—	—	—
90-91	Moncton	AHL	49	4	10	14	57	—	—	—	—	—
91-92	Fort Wayne	IHL	48	6	10	16	84	5	0	2	2	9
92-93	Muskegon	CoHL	2	0	1	1	0	—	—	—	—	—
92-93	Fort Wayne	IHL	52	5	18	23	73	12	1	7	8	20
93-94	Fort Wayne	IHL	59	3	17	20	50	17	0	3	3	28
94-95	Fort Wayne	IHL	72	3	16	19	62	4	0	3	3	2
95-96	Fort Wayne	IHL	3	0	1	1	6	—	—	—	—	—
96-97	Fort Wayne	IHL	51	1	7	8	57	—	—	—	—	—
96-97	Quad City	CoHL	6	0	3	3	2	—	—	—	—	—

			GP	G	A	PTS	PIM	GP	G	A	PTS	PIM
	IHL	Totals	285	18	69	87	332	38	1	15	16	59
	AHL	Totals	99	6	20	26	85	—	—	—	—	—
	CoHL	Totals	8	0	4	4	2	—	—	—	—	—

Born; 5/5/67, Detroit, Michigan. 6-2, 205. Member of 1992-93 IHL Champion Fort Wayne Komets.

Barry Richter — Defenseman

Season	Team	League	GP	G	A	PTS	PIM	GP	G	A	PTS	PIM
93-94	Binghamton	AHL	21	0	9	9	12	—	—	—	—	—
94-95	Binghamton	AHL	73	15	41	56	54	11	4	5	9	12
95-96	Rangers	NHL	4	0	1	1	0	—	—	—	—	—
95-96	Binghamton	AHL	69	20	61	81	64	3	0	3	3	0
96-97	Boston	NHL	50	5	13	18	32	—	—	—	—	—
96-97	Providence	AHL	19	2	6	8	4	10	4	4	8	4
	NHL	Totals	54	5	14	19	32	—	—	—	—	—
	AHL	Totals	182	37	117	154	134	24	8	12	20	16

Born; 9/11/70, Madison, Wisconsin. 6-2, 203. Drafted by Hartford Whalers (2nd choice, 32nd overall) in 1988 Entry Draft. Traded to New York Rangers by Hartford with Steve Larmer, Nick Kypreos and Hartford's fourth round choice (Yuri Litvinov) in 1994 Entry Draft for Darren Turcotte and James Patrick (11/2/93). Signed as a free agent by Boston Bruins (7/96). 1995-96 AHL First Team All-Star. 1995-96 Eddie Shore Award (Top defenseman) AHL.

Brian Ridolfi — Left Wing

Season	Team	League	GP	G	A	PTS	PIM	GP	G	A	PTS	PIM
96-97	Dayton	ECHL	67	21	28	49	62	4	0	1	1	8

Born; 10/3/71, Cumberland, Rhode Island. 5-8, 180.

Beau Riedel — Goaltender

Season	Team	League	GP	W	L	T	MIN	SO	GAVG	GP	W	L	MIN	SO	GAVG
96-97	Huntington	ECHL	5	1	3	0	244	0	4.43	—	—	—	—	—	—
96-97	Wheeling	ECHL	4	2	1	1	215	0	4.18	—	—	—	—	—	—
96-97	Johnstown	ECHL	27	9	12	4	1453	0	4.83	—	—	—	—	—	—
	ECHL	Totals	36	12	16	5	1911	0	4.71	—	—	—	—	—	—

Born; 11/19/75, Calgary, Alberta. 6-1, 185.

Vincent Riendeau — Goaltender

Season	Team	League	GP	W	L	T	MIN	SO	GAVG	GP	W	L	MIN	SO	GAVG
86-87	Sherbrooke	AHL	41	25	14	0	2363	2	2.89	13	8	5	742	0	3.80
87-88	Montreal	NHL	1	0	0	0	36	0	8.33	—	—	—	—	—	—
87-88	Sherbrooke	AHL	44	27	13	3	2521	*4	*2.67	2	0	2	127	0	3.31
88-89	St. Louis	NHL	32	11	15	5	1842	0	3.52	—	—	—	—	—	—
89-90	St. Louis	NHL	43	17	19	5	2551	1	3.50	8	3	4	397	0	3.63
90-91	St. Louis	NHL	44	29	9	6	2671	3	3.01	13	6	7	687	*1	3.06
91-92	St. Louis	NHL	3	1	2	0	157	0	4.20	—	—	—	—	—	—
91-92	Detroit	NHL	2	2	0	0	87	0	1.38	2	1	0	73	0	3.29
91-92	Adirondack	AHL	3	2	1	0	179	0	2.68	—	—	—	—	—	—
92-93	Detroit	NHL	22	13	4	2	1193	0	3.22	—	—	—	—	—	—
93-94	Detroit	NHL	8	2	4	0	345	0	4.00	—	—	—	—	—	—
93-94	Adirondack	AHL	10	6	3	0	582	0	3.09	—	—	—	—	—	—
93-94	Boston	NHL	18	7	6	1	976	1	3.07	2	1	1	120	0	4.00
94-95	Boston	NHL	11	3	6	1	565	0	2.87	—	—	—	—	—	—
94-95	Providence	AHL	—	—	—	—	—	—	—	1	1	0	60	0	3.00
96-97	Manitoba	IHL	41	10	18	5	1941	0	3.49	—	—	—	—	—	—
	NHL	Totals	184	85	65	20	10423	5	3.30	25	11	12	1277	1	3.34
	AHL	Totals	98	60	31	3	5645	6	2.81	16	9	7	929	0	3.68

Born; 4/20/66, St. Hyancinthe, Quebec. 5-10, 185. Signed as a free agent by Montreal Canadiens (10/9/85). Traded to St. Louis Blues by Montreal with Sergio Monesso for Jocelyn Lemieux, Darrell May and St. Louis' second round choice (Patrice Brisebois) in 1989 Entry Draft, (8/9/88). Traded to Detroit Red Wings by St. Louis for Rick Zombo (10/18/91). Traded to Boston Bruins by Detroit for Boston's fifth round choice (Chad Wilchynski) in 1995 Entry Draft, (1/17/94). Won Harry "Hap" Holmes Memorial Trophy (fewest goals against-AHL) 1987. Shared Harry "Hap" Holmes Trophy with Jocelyn Perrault, 1988. 1987-88 AHL Second Team All-Star.

Derek Riley — Defenseman

Season	Team	League	GP	G	A	PTS	PIM	GP	G	A	PTS	PIM
96-97	El Paso	WPHL	57	6	11	17	47	8	0	0	0	8

Born; 3/6/75, Thompson, Manitoba. 6-1, 200. Member of 1996-97 WPHL Champion El Paso Buzzards.

Ryan Risidore — Defenseman

Season	Team	League	GP	G	A	PTS	PIM	GP	G	A	PTS	PIM
96-97	Springfield	AHL	63	1	9	10	90	15	0	1	1	12

Born; 4/4/76, Hamilton, Ontario. 6-4, 195. Drafted by Hartford Whalers (3rd choice, 109th overall) in 1994 Entry Draft.

Jaynen Rissling — Defenseman

Season	Team	League	GP	G	A	PTS	PIM	GP	G	A	PTS	PIM
96-97	Johnstown	ECHL	20	2	7	9	23	—	—	—	—	—

Born; 8/4/72, Edmonton, Alberta. 6-1, 200. Last amateur club; Massachusetts (Hockey East).

Darren Ritchie — Right Wing

Season	Team	League	GP	G	A	PTS	PIM	GP	G	A	PTS	PIM
95-96	St. John's	AHL	32	9	5	14	12	—	—	—	—	—
95-96	South Carolina	ECHL	25	6	16	22	4	6	1	2	3	4
96-97	Central Texas	WPHL	14	20	3	23	8	—	—	—	—	—
96-97	Baton Rouge	ECHL	15	8	3	11	4	—	—	—	—	—
	ECHL	Totals	40	14	19	33	8	6	1	2	3	4

Born; 3/10/74, Minnedosa, Manitoba. 5-10, 185.

Jim Ritchie — Right Wing

Season	Team	League	GP	G	A	PTS	PIM	GP	G	A	PTS	PIM
90-91	Nashville	ECHL	58	20	33	53	166	—	—	—	—	—
91-92	Nashville	ECHL	54	20	14	34	39	—	—	—	—	—
91-92	St. Thomas	CoHL	8	4	3	7	17	—	—	—	—	—
92-93	Chatham	CoHL	60	18	39	57	108	—	—	—	—	—
93-94	Chatham	CoHL	55	41	45	86	140	10	5	6	11	27
94-95	Saginaw	CoHL	60	30	43	73	90	11	3	4	7	27
95-96	Saginaw	CoHL	68	28	32	60	103	5	0	1	1	15
96-97	Mobile	ECHL	68	25	25	50	77	3	0	1	1	2
	CoHL	Totals	251	121	162	283	458	26	8	11	19	69
	ECHL	Totals	180	65	72	137	282	3	0	1	1	2

Born; 8/15/70, Chatham, Ontario. 5-11, 190. 1994-95 CoHL First Team All-Star.

J.F. Rivard — Goaltender

Season	Team	League	GP	W	L	T	MIN	SO	GAVG	GP	W	L	MIN	SO	GAVG
96-97	Thunder Bay	CoHL	37	21	12	4	2094	0	3.29	11	5	4	602	0	3.39

Born; 2/10/72, Lorettaville, Quebec. 5-9, 155. Last amateur club; Ottawa (OUAA).

Jamie Rivers — Defenseman

Season	Team	League	GP	G	A	PTS	PIM	GP	G	A	PTS	PIM
95-96	St. Louis	NHL	3	0	0	0	2	—	—	—	—	—
95-96	Worcester	AHL	75	7	45	52	130	4	0	1	1	4
96-97	St. Louis	NHL	15	2	5	7	6	—	—	—	—	—
96-97	Worcester	AHL	63	8	35	43	83	5	1	2	3	14
	NHL	Totals	18	2	5	7	8	—	—	—	—	—
	AHL	Totals	138	15	80	95	213	9	1	3	4	18

Born; 3/16/75, Ottawa, Ontario. 6-0, 190. Drafted by St. Louis Blues (2nd choice, 63rd overall) in 1993 Entry Draft. 1996-97 AHL Second Team All-Star.

Craig Rivet — Defenseman

Season	Team	League	GP	G	A	PTS	PIM	GP	G	A	PTS	PIM
93-94	Fredericton	AHL	4	0	2	2	2	—	—	—	—	—
94-95	Montreal	NHL	5	0	1	1	5	—	—	—	—	—
94-95	Fredericton	AHL	78	5	27	32	126	12	0	4	4	17
95-96	Montreal	NHL	19	1	4	5	54	—	—	—	—	—
95-96	Fredericton	AHL	49	5	18	23	189	6	0	0	0	12
96-97	Montreal	NHL	35	0	4	4	54	5	0	1	1	14
96-97	Fredericton	AHL	23	3	12	15	99	—	—	—	—	—
	NHL	Totals	59	1	9	10	113	5	0	1	1	14
	AHL	Totals	154	13	59	72	416	18	0	4	4	19

Born; 9/13/74, North Bay, Ontario. 6-2, 181. Drafted by Montreal Canadiens (4th choice, 68th overall) in 1992 Entry Draft.

Adam Robbins — Left Wing

Season	Team	League	GP	G	A	PTS	PIM	GP	G	A	PTS	PIM
96-97	Fort Worth	CeHL	58	8	16	24	139	17	5	5	10	25

Born; 1-/17/77, Bancroft, Ontario. 5-11, 195. Member of 1996-97 CeHL Champion Fort Worth Fire. Last amateur club; Belleville, (OHL).

Matt Robbins — Center

Season	Team	League	GP	G	A	PTS	PIM	GP	G	A	PTS	PIM
92-93	Birmingham	ECHL	2	1	1	2	2	—	—	—	—	—
92-93	Johnstown	ECHL	56	23	41	64	37	5	0	5	5	2
93-94	Providence	AHL	9	1	1	2	6	—	—	—	—	—
93-94	Charlotte	ECHL	53	33	56	89	14	3	0	1	1	2
94-95	Charlotte	ECHL	68	28	61	89	20	3	1	6	7	0
95-96	Charlotte	ECHL	67	26	57	83	26	16	5	12	17	6
96-97	Charlotte	ECHL	68	26	53	79	22	3	0	0	0	0
	ECHL	Totals	314	137	269	406	121	30	6	24	30	10

Born; 3/11/70, Westford, Massachusetts. 6-0, 180. Drafted by New York Islanders (11th choice, 170th overall) in 1989 Entry Draft. Member of 1995-96 ECHL champion Charlotte Checkers.

Mario Roberge — Left Wing

Season	Team	League	GP	G	A	PTS	PIM	GP	G	A	PTS	PIM
88-89	Sherbrooke	AHL	58	4	9	13	249	6	0	2	2	8
89-90	Sherbrooke	AHL	73	13	27	40	247	12	5	2	7	53
90-91	Montreal	NHL	5	0	0	0	21	12	0	0	0	24
90-91	Fredericton	AHL	68	12	27	39	*365	2	0	2	2	5
91-92	Montreal	NHL	20	2	1	3	62	—	—	—	—	—
91-92	Fredericton	AHL	6	1	2	3	20	7	0	2	2	20
92-93	Montreal	NHL	50	4	4	8	142	3	0	0	0	0
93-94	Montreal	NHL	28	1	2	3	55	—	—	—	—	—

Season	Team	League	GP	G	A	PTS	PIM	GP	G	A	PTS	PIM
94-95	Montreal	NHL	9	0	0	0	34	—	—	—	—	—
94-95	Fredericton	AHL	28	8	12	20	91	6	1	1	2	6
95-96	Fredericton	AHL	74	9	24	33	205	4	0	2	2	14
96-97	Quebec	IHL	68	8	17	25	256	5	0	1	1	5
	NHL	Totals	112	7	7	14	314	15	0	0	0	24
	AHL	Totals	307	47	101	148	1177	37	6	11	17	106

Born; 1/23/64, Quebec City, Quebec. 5-11, 185. Signed as a free agent by Montreal Canadiens (10/5/88). Member of 1992-93 Stanley Cup champion Montral Canadiens.

Serge Roberge — Right Wing

Season	Team	League	GP	G	A	PTS	PIM	GP	G	A	PTS	PIM
86-87	Virginia	ACHL	49	9	16	25	*353	12	4	2	6	*104
87-88	Sherbrooke	AHL	30	0	1	1	130	5	0	0	0	21
88-89	Sherbrooke	AHL	65	5	7	12	353	6	0	1	1	10
89-90	Sherbrooke	AHL	66	8	5	13	343	12	2	0	2	44
90-91	Quebec	NHL	9	0	0	0	24	—	—	—	—	—
90-91	Halifax	AHL	52	0	5	5	152	—	—	—	—	—
91-92	Halifax	AHL	66	2	8	10	319	—	—	—	—	—
92-93	Halifax	AHL	16	2	2	4	34	—	—	—	—	—
92-93	Utica	AHL	28	0	3	3	85	1	0	0	0	0
93-94	Cape Breton	AHL	51	3	5	8	130	1	0	0	0	0
94-95	Cornwall	AHL	73	0	3	3	342	11	0	0	0	29
95-96	Rochester	AHL	32	0	1	1	42	—	—	—	—	—
95-96	Fredericton	AHL	14	1	1	2	45	7	0	0	0	10
96-97	Quebec	IHL	61	2	4	6	273	—	—	—	—	—
	AHL	Totals	493	21	41	62	1975	43	2	1	3	114

Born; 3/31/65, Quebec City, Quebec. 6-1, 195. Signed as a free agent by Montreal Canadiens (1/25/88). Signed as a free agent by Quebec Nordiques (12/28/90). Member of 1986-87 ACHL champion Virginia Lancers.

Doug Roberts — Left Wing

Season	Team	League	GP	G	A	PTS	PIM	GP	G	A	PTS	PIM
92-93	Raleigh	ECHL	11	0	2	2	6	—	—	—	—	—
92-93	Knoxville	ECHL	44	10	17	27	31	—	—	—	—	—
93-94	Huntington	ECHL	31	12	9	21	4	—	—	—	—	—
93-94	Nashville	ECHL	28	5	7	12	2	—	—	—	—	—
94-95	Dallas	CeHL	60	21	25	46	46	—	—	—	—	—
96-97	New Mexico	WPHL	63	31	37	68	40	6	1	2	3	12
	ECHL	Totals	114	27	35	62	43	—	—	—	—	—

Born; 9/16/68, Detroit, Michigan. 5-10, 185.

Steve Roberts — Right Wing

Season	Team	League	GP	G	A	PTS	PIM	GP	G	A	PTS	PIM
95-96	Dayton	ECHL	41	20	16	36	39	—	—	—	—	—
96-97	Michigan	IHL	2	0	0	0	0	—	—	—	—	—
96-97	Baltimore	AHL	2	0	0	0	0	—	—	—	—	—
96-97	Dayton	ECHL	62	46	26	72	38	4	2	4	6	2
	ECHL	Totals	103	66	42	108	77	4	2	4	6	2

Born; 2/17/74, Saskatoon, Saskatchewan. 5-11, 190.

Chris Robertson — Center

Season	Team	League	GP	G	A	PTS	PIM	GP	G	A	PTS	PIM
89-90	Greensboro	ECHL	59	32	43	75	51	11	5	8	13	7
90-91	Greensboro	ECHL	3	0	1	1	2	—	—	—	—	—
90-91	Richmond	ECHL	21	8	12	20	27	—	—	—	—	—

Season	Team	League	GP	G	A	PTS	PIM	GP	G	A	PTS	PIM
91-92	N/A											
92-93	N/A											
93-94	Tulsa	CeHL	26	23	14	37	24	11	7	4	11	16
94-95	Tulsa	CeHL	17	6	10	16	24	7	5	4	9	6
95-96	Tulsa	CeHL	54	31	55	86	96	3	1	0	1	4
96-97	New Mexico	WPHL	40	29	39	68	60	6	5	5	10	14
	CeHL	Totals	97	60	79	139	144	21	13	8	21	26
	ECHL	Totals	83	40	56	96	80	11	5	8	13	7

Born; 3/28/68, Calgary, Alberta. 6-0, 185. Member of 1989-90 ECHL champion Greensboro Monarchs.

Bert Robertsson — Defenseman

			Regular Season					Playoffs				
Season	Team	League	GP	G	A	PTS	PIM	GP	G	A	PTS	PIM
95-96	Syracuse	AHL	65	1	7	8	109	16	0	1	1	26
96-97	Syracuse	AHL	80	4	9	13	132	3	1	0	1	4
	AHL	Totals	145	5	16	21	241	19	1	1	2	30

Born; 6/30/74, Sodertalje, Sweden. 6-2, 198. Drafted by Vancouver Canucks (8th choice, 254th overall) in 1993 Entry Draft.

Patrice Robitaille — Right Wing

			Regular Season					Playoffs				
Season	Team	League	GP	G	A	PTS	PIM	GP	G	A	PTS	PIM
95-96	Peoria	IHL	69	27	28	55	49	—	—	—	—	—
95-96	Indianapolis	IHL	10	1	1	2	8	—	—	—	—	—
96-97	Milwaukee	IHL	12	1	2	3	4	—	—	—	—	—
96-97	Cincinnati	IHL	20	3	8	11	4	—	—	—	—	—
	IHL	Totals	111	32	39	71	65	—	—	—	—	—

Born; 12/4/70, St. Catharine, Quebec. 6-0, 190.

Dave Roche — Center

			Regular Season					Playoffs				
Season	Team	League	GP	G	A	PTS	PIM	GP	G	A	PTS	PIM
95-96	Pittsburgh	NHL	71	7	7	14	130	16	2	7	9	26
96-97	Pittsburgh	NHL	61	5	5	10	155	—	—	—	—	—
96-97	Cleveland	IHL	18	5	5	10	25	13	6	3	9	*87
	NHL	Totals	132	12	12	24	285	16	2	7	9	26

Born; 6/13/75, Lindsay, Ontario. 6-4, 224. Drafted by Pittsburgh Penguins (3rd choice, 62nd overall) in 1993 Entry Draft.

Normand Rochefort — Defenseman

			Regular Season					Playoffs				
Season	Team	League	GP	G	A	PTS	PIM	GP	G	A	PTS	PIM
80-81	Quebec	NHL	56	3	7	10	51	5	0	0	0	4
81-82	Quebec	NHL	72	4	14	18	115	16	0	2	2	10
82-83	Quebec	NHL	62	6	17	23	40	1	0	0	0	2
83-84	Quebec	NHL	75	2	22	24	47	6	1	0	1	6
84-85	Quebec	NHL	73	3	21	24	74	18	2	1	3	8
85-86	Quebec	NHL	26	5	4	9	30	—	—	—	—	—
86-87	Quebec	NHL	70	6	9	15	46	13	2	1	3	26
87-88	Qubec	NHL	46	3	10	13	49	—	—	—	—	—
88-89	Rangers	NHL	11	1	5	6	18	—	—	—	—	—
89-90	Rangers	NHL	31	3	1	4	24	10	2	1	3	26
89-90	Flint	IHL	7	3	2	5	4	—	—	—	—	—
90-91	Rangers	NHL	44	3	7	10	35	—	—	—	—	—
91-92	Rangers	NHL	26	0	2	2	31	—	—	—	—	—
92-93	Germany											
93-94	Tampa Bay	NHL	6	0	0	0	10	—	—	—	—	—
93-94	Atlanta	IHL	65	5	7	12	43	13	0	2	2	6
94-95	Denver	IHL	77	4	13	17	46	17	1	4	5	12

Season	Team	League	GP	G	A	PTS	PIM	GP	G	A	PTS	PIM
95-96	San Francisco	IHL	77	3	12	15	45	4	0	0	0	2
96-97	Kansas City	IHL	77	7	14	21	28	3	1	0	1	2
	NHL	Totals	598	39	119	158	570	69	7	5	12	82
	IHL	Totals	303	22	48	70	166	37	2	6	8	22

Born; 1/28/61, Trois-Rivieres, Quebec. 6-1, 214. Drafted by Quebec Nordiques (1st choice, 24th overall) in 1980 Entry Draft. Traded to New York Rangers by Quebec with Jason Lafreniere for Bruce Bell, Jari Gronstrand, Walt Poddubny and Rangers' fourth round choice (Eric Dubois) in 1989 Entry Draft (8/1/88). Signed as a free agent by Tampa Bay Lightning. Member of 1993-94 IHL champion Atlanta Knights. Member of 1994-95 IHL champion Denver Grizzlies.

Patrick Rochon — Defenseman

Season	Team	League	GP	G	A	PTS	PIM	GP	G	A	PTS	PIM
96-97	Hershey	AHL	16	1	2	3	8	—	—	—	—	—
96-97	Mississippi	ECHL	54	5	23	28	88	3	0	2	2	26

Born; 4/8/75, Ste. Martins, Quebec. 5-9, 182.

Marc Rodgers — Right Wing

Season	Team	League	GP	G	A	PTS	PIM	GP	G	A	PTS	PIM
92-93	Wheeling	ECHL	64	23	40	63	91	6	1	1	2	8
93-94	Las Vegas	IHL	40	7	7	14	110	4	0	2	2	17
93-94	Knoxville	ECHL	27	12	18	30	83	—	—	—	—	—
94-95	Las Vegas	IHL	58	17	19	36	131	10	2	6	8	16
95-96	Las Vegas	IHL	51	13	16	29	65	—	—	—	—	—
95-96	Utah	IHL	31	6	14	20	51	21	4	4	8	16
96-97	Utah	IHL	5	2	2	4	10	—	—	—	—	—
96-97	Quebec	IHL	70	25	42	67	115	9	1	9	10	14
	IHL	Totals	255	70	100	170	472	44	7	21	28	63
	ECHL	Totals	91	35	58	93	174	6	1	1	2	8

Born; 3/16/72, Bryson, Quebec. 5-10, 185. Member of 1995-96 IHL champion Utah Grizzlies.

Dmitri Rodine — Defenseman

Season	Team	League	GP	G	A	PTS	PIM	GP	G	A	PTS	PIM
96-97	Utah	IHL	3	0	0	0	4	—	—	—	—	—
96-97	Detroit	IHL	10	0	0	0	4	—	—	—	—	—
96-97	Flint	CoHL	58	7	25	32	35	11	0	0	0	6
	IHL	Totals	13	0	0	0	8	—	—	—	—	—

Born; 2/25/75, Tallinn, Russia. 6-1, 205. Member of 1996-97 CoHL All-Rookie Team.

Jacque Rodrique — Defenseman

Season	Team	League	GP	G	A	PTS	PIM	GP	G	A	PTS	PIM
94-95	Syracuse	AHL	2	0	1	1	0	—	—	—	—	—
95-96	Dayton	ECHL	30	1	10	11	31	—	—	—	—	—
95-96	Richmond	ECHL	5	2	2	4	10	—	—	—	—	—
95-96	Columbus	ECHL	13	4	9	13	12	3	0	1	1	12
96-97	Fort Wayne	IHL	1	0	0	0	0	—	—	—	—	—
96-97	Utica	CoHL	37	9	20	29	28	—	—	—	—	—
96-97	Dayton	CoHL	35	6	24	30	36	—	—	—	—	—
	CoHL	Totals	72	15	44	59	64	—	—	—	—	—
	ECHL	Totals	48	7	21	28	53	3	0	1	1	12

Born; 5/7/71, Nashua, New Hampshire. 6-0, 195.

Sylvain Rodrique — Goaltender

Season	Team	League	GP	W	L	T	MIN	SO	GAVG	GP	W	L	MIN	SO	GAVG
96-97	Hershey	AHL	—	—	—	—	—	—	—	1	0	0	26	0	2.31

Stacy Roest — Center

			Regular Season					Playoffs				
Season	Team	League	GP	G	A	PTS	PIM	GP	G	A	PTS	PIM
94-95	Adirondack	AHL	3	0	0	0	0	—	—	—	—	—
95-96	Adirondack	AHL	76	16	39	55	40	3	0	0	0	2
96-97	Adirondack	AHL	78	25	41	66	30	4	1	1	2	0
	AHL	Totals	157	41	80	121	70	7	1	1	2	2

Born; 3/15/74, Lethbridge, Alberta. 5-9, 191.

Jeff Rohlicek — Center

			Regular Season					Playoffs				
Season	Team	League	GP	G	A	PTS	PIM	GP	G	A	PTS	PIM
86-87	Fredericton	AHL	70	19	37	56	22	—	—	—	—	—
87-88	Vancouver	NHL	7	0	0	0	4	—	—	—	—	—
87-88	Fredericton	AHL	65	26	31	57	50	—	—	—	—	—
88-89	Vancouver	NHL	2	0	0	0	4	—	—	—	—	—
88-89	Milwaukee	IHL	78	47	63	110	106	11	6	6	12	8
89-90	Springfield	AHL	12	1	2	3	4	7	3	2	5	6
89-90	Milwaukee	IHL	53	22	26	48	37	—	—	—	—	—
90-91	New Haven	AHL	4	1	1	2	6	—	—	—	—	—
90-91	Phoenix	IHL	74	29	31	60	67	10	7	6	13	12
91-92	Phoenix	IHL	23	5	11	16	32	—	—	—	—	—
91-92	Indianapolis	IHL	59	25	32	57	28	—	—	—	—	—
92-93	Milwaukee	IHL	11	1	1	2	8	—	—	—	—	—
92-93	Adirondack	AHL	29	6	16	22	20	11	4	5	9	10
92-93	Toledo	ECHL	8	5	8	13	14	—	—	—	—	—
93-94	Toledo	ECHL	57	28	54	82	36	—	—	—	—	—
93-94	Nashville	ECHL	4	1	1	2	4	2	1	0	1	2
94-95	Chicago	IHL	18	4	4	8	13	—	—	—	—	—
94-95	Fort Wayne	IHL	22	9	14	23	8	4	1	2	3	4
95-96	Fort Wayne	IHL	38	8	12	20	34	—	—	—	—	—
96-97	Mississippi	ECHL	69	34	56	90	34	3	1	3	4	4
	NHL	Totals	9	0	0	0	8	—	—	—	—	—
	IHL	Totals	405	150	194	344	333	25	14	14	28	24
	AHL	Totals	180	53	87	140	102	18	7	7	14	16
	ECHL	Totals	138	68	119	187	132	5	2	3	5	6

Born; 1/27/66, Park Ridge, Illinois. 6-0, 190. Drafted by Vancouver Canucks (2nd choice, 31st overall) in 1984 Entry Draft. Traded to New York Islanders by Vancouver for Jack Capuano (3/6/90). Released by Islanders (9/10/90). Signed as a free agent by Los Angeles Kings (10/90). Traded to Chicago Blackhawks by Los Angeles for Rick Lanz (12/2/91). 1988-89 IHL First Team All-Star. Member of 1989-90 AHL champion Springfield Indians.

Layne Roland — Right Wing

			Regular Season					Playoffs				
Season	Team	League	GP	G	A	PTS	PIM	GP	G	A	PTS	PIM
95-96	Dayton	ECHL	3	0	2	2	2	—	—	—	—	—
95-96	Erie	ECHL	64	27	33	60	40	—	—	—	—	—
96-97	Amarillo	WPHL	28	16	12	28	23	—	—	—	—	—
96-97	Central Texas	WPHL	22	8	7	15	6	11	7	10	17	14
	ECHL	Totals	67	27	35	62	42	—	—	—	—	—
	WPHL	Totals	50	24	19	43	29	11	7	10	17	14

Born; 2/6/74, Vernon, British Columbia. 6-2, 205. Drafted by Chicago Blackhawks (8th choice, 185th overall) in 1992 Entry Draft.

Russ Romaniuk — Left Wing

			Regular Season					Playoffs				
Season	Team	League	GP	G	A	PTS	PIM	GP	G	A	PTS	PIM
91-92	Winnipeg	NHL	27	3	5	8	18	—	—	—	—	—
91-92	Moncton	AHL	45	16	15	31	25	10	5	4	9	19
92-93	Winnipeg	NHL	28	3	1	4	22	1	0	0	0	0

Season	Team	League	GP	G	A	PTS	PIM	GP	G	A	PTS	PIM
92-93	Moncton	AHL	28	18	8	26	40	5	0	4	4	2
92-93	Fort Wayne	IHL	4	2	0	2	7	—	—	—	—	—
93-94	Winnipeg	NHL	24	4	8	12	6	—	—	—	—	—
93-94	Moncton	AHL	18	16	8	24	24	17	2	6	8	30
94-95	Winnipeg	NHL	6	0	0	0	0	—	—	—	—	—
94-95	Springfield	AHL	17	5	7	12	29	—	—	—	—	—
95-96	Philadelphia	NHL	17	3	0	3	17	1	0	0	0	0
95-96	Hershey	AHL	27	19	10	29	43	—	—	—	—	—
96-97	Manitoba	IHL	46	14	13	27	43	—	—	—	—	—
	NHL	Totals	102	13	14	27	63	2	0	0	0	0
	AHL	Totals	135	74	48	122	161	32	7	14	21	51
	IHL	Totals	50	16	13	29	50	—	—	—	—	—

Born; 5/9/70, Winnipeg, Manitoba. 6-0, 185. Drafted by Winnipeg Jets (2nd choice, 31st overall) in 1988 Entry Draft. Traded to Philadelphia Flyers by Winnipeg for Jeff Finley (6/27/95).

Jeff Romfo — Right Wing

Season	Team	League	GP	G	A	PTS	PIM	GP	G	A	PTS	PIM
96-97	South Carolina	ECHL	51	15	33	48	36	15	4	4	8	10

Born; 2/9/74, Blaine, Minnesota. 5-11, 195. Drafted by Minnesota North Stars (8th choice, 226th overall) in 1992 Entry Draft. Member of 1996-97 ECHL Champion South Carolina Stingrays.

Ed Ronan — Right Wing

Season	Team	League	GP	G	A	PTS	PIM	GP	G	A	PTS	PIM
91-92	Montreal	NHL	3	0	0	0	0	—	—	—	—	—
91-92	Fredericton	AHL	78	25	34	59	82	7	5	1	6	6
92-93	Montreal	NHL	53	5	7	12	20	14	2	3	5	10
92-93	Fredericton	AHL	16	10	5	15	15	5	2	4	6	6
93-94	Montreal	NHL	61	6	8	14	42	7	1	0	1	0
94-95	Montreal	NHL	30	1	4	5	12	—	—	—	—	—
95-96	Winnipeg	NHL	17	0	0	0	16	—	—	—	—	—
95-96	Springfield	AHL	31	8	16	24	50	10	7	6	13	4
96-97	Buffalo	NHL	18	1	4	5	11	6	1	0	1	6
96-97	Rochester	AHL	47	13	21	34	62	—	—	—	—	—
	NHL	Totals	182	13	23	36	101	27	4	3	7	16
	AHL	Totals	172	56	76	132	209	22	14	11	25	16

Born; 3/21/68, Quincy, Massachusetts. 6-0, 197. Drafted by Montreal Canadiens (13th choice, 227th overall) in 1987 Entry Draft. Signed as a free agent by Winnipeg Jets (10/13/95). Member of 1992-93 Stanley Cup champion Montreal Canadiens.

Al Rooney — Goaltender

Season	Team	League	GP	W	L	T	MIN	SO	GAVG	GP	W	L	MIN	SO	GAVG
96-97	Nashville	CeHL	17	3	13	0	918	0	4.44	—	—	—	—	—	—
96-97	Port Huron	CoHL	9	3	3	0	394	0	4.27	—	—	—	—	—	—

Born; 12/28/72, North Babylon, New York. 5-10, 175.

Jason Rose — Defenseman

Season	Team	League	GP	G	A	PTS	PIM	GP	G	A	PTS	PIM
96-97	El Paso	WPHL	60	6	14	20	103	9	1	4	5	15

Born; 1/12/75, Martensville, Saskatchewan. 6-0, 180. Member of 1996-97 WPHL Champion El Paso Buzzards.

Howie Rosenblatt — Right Wing

Season	Team	League	GP	G	A	PTS	PIM	GP	G	A	PTS	PIM
91-92	Maine	AHL	2	0	0	0	9	—	—	—	—	—
91-92	Cincinnati	ECHL	50	26	16	42	235	9	3	8	11	55

Season	Team	League	GP	G	A	PTS	PIM	GP	G	A	PTS	PIM
92-93	Cincinnati	IHL	45	10	7	17	201	—	—	—	—	—
92-93	Birmingham	ECHL	6	4	3	7	23	—	—	—	—	—
93-94	Providence	AHL	19	6	4	10	59	—	—	—	—	—
93-94	Charlotte	ECHL	44	21	17	38	173	3	3	3	6	2
94-95	Providence	AHL	3	0	0	0	7	1	0	0	0	0
94-95	Charlotte	ECHL	5	1	1	2	38	—	—	—	—	—
94-95	Greensboro	ECHL	41	12	34	46	245	14	5	1	6	76
95-96	Raleigh	ECHL	25	4	13	17	109	—	—	—	—	—
95-96	Dayton	ECHL	7	2	2	4	27	—	—	—	—	—
96-97	San Antonio	IHL	15	2	4	6	26	—	—	—	—	—
96-97	Quad City	CoHL	40	13	32	45	123	14	3	9	12	*58
	IHL	Totals	60	12	11	23	227	—	—	—	—	—
	AHL	Totals	24	6	4	10	75	1	0	0	0	0
	ECHL	Totals	178	70	86	156	850	26	11	12	23	133

Born; 1/3/69, Philadelphia, Pennsylvania. 6-0, 205. Member of 1996-97 CoHL Champion Quad City Mallards.

Andy Ross — Left Wing

			Regular Season					Playoffs				
Season	Team	League	GP	G	A	PTS	PIM	GP	G	A	PTS	PIM
90-91	Erie	ECHL	54	10	19	29	96	1	0	0	0	0
91-92	Knoxville	ECHL	9	2	3	5	2	—	—	—	—	—
91-92	Erie	ECHL	36	13	16	29	53	—	—	—	—	—
92-93	Memphis	CeHL	50	23	24	47	130	6	1	1	2	11
93-94	Memphis	CeHL	55	18	21	39	56	—	—	—	—	—
94-95	Memphis	CeHL	47	18	17	35	55	—	—	—	—	—
94-95	Tulsa	CeHL	17	4	6	10	12	—	—	—	—	—
95-96	Memphis	CeHL	62	12	20	32	118	5	1	0	1	0
96-97	Austin	WPHL	61	35	34	69	34	6	3	0	3	10
	CeHL	Totals	231	75	88	163	371	11	2	1	3	11
	ECHL	Totals	99	25	38	63	151	1	0	0	0	0

Born; 5/24/70, Philadelphia, Pennsylvania. 6-3, 215.

Mike Ross — Center

			Regular Season					Playoffs				
Season	Team	League	GP	G	A	PTS	PIM	GP	G	A	PTS	PIM
93-94	Columbus	ECHL	64	34	35	69	32	6	5	1	6	2
94-95	Columbus	ECHL	67	24	37	61	44	—	—	—	—	—
95-96	South Carolina	ECHL	68	33	38	71	56	8	4	4	8	4
96-97	South Carolina	ECHL	70	50	60	*110	35	18	11	14	25	8
	ECHL	Totals	269	141	170	311	167	32	20	19	39	14

Born; 6/7/67, Grand Rapids, Michigan. 5-10, 175. 1996-97 ECHL MVP. 1996-97 ECHL Most Sportsmanlike Player. 1996-97 ECHL First All-Star Team. Member of 1996-97 ECHL Champion South Carolina Stingrays.

Dominic Roussel — Goaltenders

			Regular Season							Playoffs					
Season	Team	League	GP	W	L	T	MIN	SO	GAVG	GP	W	L	MIN	SO	GAVG
90-91	Hershey	AHL	45	20	14	7	2507	1	3.61	7	3	4	366	0	3.44
91-92	Philadelphia	NHL	17	7	8	2	922	1	2.60	—	—	—	—	—	—
91-92	Hershey	AHL	35	15	11	6	2040	1	3.56	—	—	—	—	—	—
92-93	Philadelphia	NHL	34	13	11	5	1769	1	3.76	—	—	—	—	—	—
92-93	Hershey	AHL	6	0	3	3	372	0	3.71	—	—	—	—	—	—
93-94	Philadelphia	NHL	60	29	20	5	3285	1	3.34	—	—	—	—	—	—
94-95	Philadelphia	NHL	19	11	7	0	1075	1	2.34	1	0	0	23	0	0.00
94-95	Hershey	AHL	1	0	1	0	59	0	5.07	—	—	—	—	—	—
95-96	Philadelphia	NHL	9	2	3	2	456	1	2.89	—	—	—	—	—	—
95-96	Winnipeg	NHL	7	2	2	0	285	0	3.37	—	—	—	—	—	—
95-96	Hershey	AHL	12	4	4	3	690	0	2.78	—	—	—	—	—	—
96-97	Philadelphia	AHL	36	18	9	3	1852	2	2.66	1	0	0	26	0	6.93

	NHL	Totals	146	64	51	14	7792	5	3.19	1	0	0	23	0	0.00
	AHL	Totals	135	57	42	22	7520	4	3.30	8	3	4	392	0	3.68

Born; 2/22/70, Hull, Quebec. 6-1, 191. Drafted by Philadelphia Flyers (4th choice, 63rd overall) in 1988 Entry Draft. Traded to Winnipeg Jets by Philadelphia for Tim Cheveldae and Winnipeg's third round choice (Chester Gallant) in 1996 Entry Draft, (2/27/96). Signed as a free agent by Philadelphia, (7/3/96).

Jon Rowe — Defenseman

Season	Team	League	GP	G	A	PTS	PIM	GP	G	A	PTS	PIM
96-97	Columbus	CeHL	47	5	11	16	86	1	0	1	1	0

Born; Westwood, Massachusetts. 5-10, 185. Last amateur club; Providence (Hockey East).

Sean Rowe — Right Wing

Season	Team	League	GP	G	A	PTS	PIM	GP	G	A	PTS	PIM
93-94	Fort Worth	CeHL	61	22	35	57	43	—	—	—	—	—
94-95	Fort Worth	CeHL	56	22	40	62	19	—	—	—	—	—
95-96	Louisiana	ECHL	47	24	22	46	28	—	—	—	—	—
95-96	Columbus	ECHL	13	14	10	24	8	3	0	2	2	0
96-97	Anchorage	WCHL	58	43	53	96	40	9	5	6	11	6
	CeHL	Totals	117	44	75	119	62	—	—	—	—	—
	ECHL	Totals	60	38	32	70	36	3	0	2	2	0

Born; 12/17/70, Montreal, Quebec. 6-1, 200. 1996-97 ECHL Second Team All-Star.

Chris Rowland — Right Wing

Season	Team	League	GP	G	A	PTS	PIM	GP	G	A	PTS	PIM
92-93	Prince Edward Island	AHL	34	4	4	8	65	—	—	—	—	—
92-93	Thunder Bay	CoHL	22	5	3	8	65	11	3	4	7	44
93-94	Prince Edward Island	AHL	40	6	2	8	122	—	—	—	—	—
93-94	Thunder Bay	CoHL	14	4	6	10	13	9	3	2	5	31
94-95	Fort Wayne	IHL	5	0	1	1	14	—	—	—	—	—
94-95	Prince Edward Island	AHL	8	1	0	1	5	—	—	—	—	—
94-95	Thunder Bay	CoHL	64	30	44	74	255	11	7	7	14	34
95-96	Fort Wayne	IHL	1	0	0	0	2	—	—	—	—	—
95-96	Louisville	ECHL	65	28	23	51	373	1	0	0	0	10
96-97	Baltimore	AHL	5	0	1	1	15	—	—	—	—	—
96-97	Louisville	ECHL	46	9	25	34	256	—	—	—	—	—
96-97	South Carolina	ECHL	14	4	6	10	69	18	5	5	10	39
	AHL	Totals	87	11	7	18	197	—	—	—	—	—
	IHL	Totals	6	0	1	1	16	—	—	—	—	—
	ECHL	Totals	125	41	54	95	698	19	5	5	10	49
	CoHL	Totals	100	39	53	92	333	31	13	13	26	109

Born; 3/30/71, Sylvan Lake, Manitoba. 6-1, 195. Member of 1993-94 CoHL champion Thunder Bay Senators. Member of 1994-95 CoHL champion Thunder Bay Senators. Member of 1996-97 ECHL Champion South Carolina Stingrays.

Andre Roy — Left Wing

Season	Team	League	GP	G	A	PTS	PIM	GP	G	A	PTS	PIM
95-96	Boston	NHL	3	0	0	0	0	—	—	—	—	—
95-96	Providence	AHL	58	7	8	15	167	1	0	0	0	10
96-97	Boston	NHL	10	0	2	2	12	—	—	—	—	—
96-97	Providence	AHL	50	17	11	28	234	—	—	—	—	—
	NHL	Totals	13	0	2	2	12	—	—	—	—	—
	AHL	Totals	108	24	19	43	401	1	0	0	0	10

Born; 2/8/75, Port Chester, New York. 6-3, 178. Drafted by Boston Bruins (5th choice, 151st overall) in 1994 Entry Draft.

Jean Yves-Roy — Right Wing

			Regular Season					Playoffs				
Season	Team	League	GP	G	A	PTS	PIM	GP	G	A	PTS	PIM
92-93	Binghamton	AHL	49	13	15	28	21	14	5	2	7	4
92-93	Canada	National										
93-94	Binghamton	AHL	65	41	24	65	33	—	—	—	—	—
93-94	Canada	National										
94-95	Rangers	NHL	3	1	0	1	2	—	—	—	—	—
94-95	Binghamton	AHL	67	41	36	77	28	11	4	6	10	12
95-96	Ottawa	NHL	4	1	1	2	2	—	—	—	—	—
95-96	Prince Edward Island	AHL	67	40	55	95	64	5	4	8	12	6
96-97	Boston	NHL	52	10	15	25	22	—	—	—	—	—
96-97	Providence	AHL	27	9	16	25	30	10	2	7	9	2
	NHL	Totals	59	12	16	28	26	—	—	—	—	—
	AHL	Totals	275	144	146	290	176	40	15	23	38	24

Born; 2/17/69, Rosemere, Quebec. 5-10, 180. Signed as a free agent by the New York Rangers (7/20/92). Traded to Ottawa Senators by Rangers for Steve Larouche (10/5/92). Signed as a free agent by Boston Bruins (7/96).

Martin Roy — Defenseman

			Regular Season					Playoffs				
Season	Team	League	GP	G	A	PTS	PIM	GP	G	A	PTS	PIM
95-96	Richmond	ECHL	57	6	9	15	278	7	0	4	4	16
96-97	Manitoba	IHL	22	0	1	1	48	—	—	—	—	—
96-97	Richmond	ECHL	25	2	5	7	105	5	0	0	0	10
	ECHL	Totals	82	8	14	22	383	12	0	4	4	26

Born; 11/25/72, Lauzon, Quebec. 6-1, 210.

Serge Roy — Defenseman

			Regular Season					Playoffs				
Season	Team	League	GP	G	A	PTS	PIM	GP	G	A	PTS	PIM
89-90	Fort Wayne	IHL	19	1	4	5	13	—	—	—	—	—
90-91	Phoenix	IHL	7	1	4	5	25	—	—	—	—	—
90-91	New Haven	AHL	46	3	12	15	25	—	—	—	—	—
91-92	Brantford	CoHL	11	2	9	11	16	—	—	—	—	—
95-96	San Diego	WCHL	53	9	46	55	61	8	0	2	2	14
96-97	San Diego	WCHL	45	8	22	30	48	6	1	1	2	4
	IHL	Totals	26	2	8	10	38	—	—	—	—	—
	WCHL	Totals	98	17	68	85	109	14	1	3	4	18

Born; 6/25/62, Sept-Iles, Quebec. 5-9, 190. 1995-96 WCHL First Team All-Star. Member of 1995-96 WCHL champion San Diego Gulls. Member of 1996-97 WCHL Champion San Diego Gulls.

Stephane Roy — Left Wing/Defenseman

			Regular Season					Playoffs				
Season	Team	League	GP	G	A	PTS	PIM	GP	G	A	PTS	PIM
87-88	Minnesota	NHL	12	1	0	1	0	—	—	—	—	—
87-88	Kalamazoo	IHL	58	21	12	33	52	5	1	2	3	11
88-89	Kalamazoo	IHL	20	5	4	9	27	—	—	—	—	—
88-89	Halifax	AHL	42	8	16	24	28	1	0	0	0	0
95-96	Memphis	CeHL	60	18	44	62	33	6	1	2	3	8
96-97	Memphis	CeHL	38	16	28	44	25	—	—	—	—	—
96-97	Anchorage	WCHL	22	3	12	15	27	2	1	2	3	0
	IHL	Totals	78	26	16	42	79	5	1	2	3	11
	CeHL	Totals	98	34	72	106	58	6	1	2	3	8

Born; 6/29/67, Quebec City, Quebec. 6-0, 195. Drafted by Minnesota North Stars (1st choice, 51st overall) in 1985 Draft. Traded to Quebec Nordiques by Minnesota for future considerations (12/15/88). Did not play professional hockey in North America between the 1989-90 and 1995-96 seasons.

Stephane Roy — Center

			Regular Season					Playoffs				
Season	Team	League	GP	G	A	PTS	PIM	GP	G	A	PTS	PIM
95-96	Worcester	AHL	1	0	0	0	2	—	—	—	—	—
96-97	Worcester	AHL	66	24	23	47	57	5	2	0	2	4
	AHL	Totals	67	24	23	47	59	5	2	0	2	4

Born; 1/26/76, Ste-Martine, Quebec. 5-10, 173. Drafted by St. Louis Blues (1st choice, 68th overall) in 1994 Entry Draft.

Eric Royal — Center

			Regular Season					Playoffs				
Season	Team	League	GP	G	A	PTS	PIM	GP	G	A	PTS	PIM
95-96	Wheeling	ECHL	30	5	9	14	34	—	—	—	—	—
96-97	Wheeling	ECHL	70	31	61	92	68	3	0	0	0	0
	ECHL	Totals	100	36	70	106	102	3	0	0	0	0

Born; 2/16/72, Rochester, New Hampshire. 6-0, 185.

Gaetan Royer — Right Wing

			Regular Season					Playoffs				
Season	Team	League	GP	G	A	PTS	PIM	GP	G	A	PTS	PIM
96-97	Indianapolis	IHL	29	2	4	6	60	—	—	—	—	—
96-97	Jacksonville	ECHL	28	7	8	15	149	—	—	—	—	—

Born; 3/13/76, Donnacona, Quebec. 6-3, 193. Signed as a free agent by Chicago Blackhawks (9/9/94).

Matt Ruchty — Left Wing

			Regular Season					Playoffs				
Season	Team	League	GP	G	A	PTS	PIM	GP	G	A	PTS	PIM
91-92	Utica	AHL	73	9	14	23	250	4	0	0	0	25
92-93	Utica	AHL	74	4	14	18	253	4	0	2	2	15
93-94	Albany	AHL	68	11	11	22	303	5	0	1	1	18
94-95	Albany	AHL	78	26	23	49	348	12	5	10	15	43
95-96	Syracuse	AHL	68	12	16	28	321	—	—	—	—	—
95-96	Atlanta	IHL	12	3	4	7	38	3	1	1	2	36
96-97	Grand Rapids	IHL	63	14	20	34	364	5	0	1	1	23
96-97	Utica	CoHL	10	2	3	5	45	—	—	—	—	—
	AHL	Totals	361	62	78	140	1127	25	5	13	18	101
	IHL	Totals	75	17	24	41	402	8	1	2	3	59

Born; 11/27/69, Kitchener, Ontario. 6-1, 225. Drafted by New Jersey Devils (4th choice, 65th overall) in 1988 Entry Draft. Member of 1994-95 AHL champion Albany RiverRats.

Mike Rucinski — Defenseman

			Reuglar Season					Playoffs				
Season	Team	League	GP	G	A	PTS	PIM	GP	G	A	PTS	PIM
96-97	Springfield	AHL	6	0	1	1	0	—	—	—	—	—
96-97	Raleigh	ECHL	61	20	23	43	85	—	—	—	—	—

Born; 3/30/75, Trenton, Michigan. 5-11, 179. Drafted by Hartford Whalers (8th choice, 217th overall) in 1995 Entry Draft.

Ken Ruddik — Defenseman

			Regular Season					Playoffs				
Season	Team	League	GP	G	A	PTS	PIM	GP	G	A	PTS	PIM
96-97	Louisiana	ECHL	56	7	4	11	93	—	—	—	—	—

Born; 8/15/72, Hamilton, Ontario. 6-1, 205. Last amateur club; St. Lawrence (ECAC).

Jason Ruff — Left Wing

			Regular Season					Playoffs				
Season	Team	League	GP	G	A	PTS	PIM	GP	G	A	PTS	PIM
90-91	Peoria	IHL	—	—	—	—	—	5	0	0	0	2
91-92	Peoria	IHL	67	27	45	72	148	10	7	7	14	19

Season	Team	League	GP	G	A	PTS	PIM	GP	G	A	PTS	PIM
92-93	St. Louis	NHL	7	2	1	3	8	—	—	—	—	—
92-93	Tampa Bay	NHL	1	0	0	0	0	—	—	—	—	—
92-93	Peoria	IHL	40	22	21	43	81	—	—	—	—	—
92-93	Atlanta	IHL	26	11	14	25	90	7	2	1	3	26
93-94	Tampa Bay	NHL	6	1	2	3	2	—	—	—	—	—
93-94	Atlanta	IHL	71	24	25	49	122	14	6	*17	23	41
94-95	Atlanta	IHL	64	42	34	76	161	3	3	1	4	10
95-96	Atlanta	IHL	59	39	33	72	135	2	0	0	0	16
96-97	Quebec	IHL	80	35	50	85	93	9	8	5	13	10
	NHL	Totals	14	3	3	6	10	—	—	—	—	—
	IHL	Totals	407	200	222	422	830	50	26	31	57	124

Born; 1/27/70, Kelkowna, British Columbia. 6-2, 205. Drafted by St. Louis Blues (3rd choice, 96th overall) in 1990 Entry Draft. Traded to Tampa Bay Lightning by St. Louis with future considerations for Doug Crossman, Basil McRae and fourth round choice (A. Petrakov) in 1996 Entry Draft (1/28/93). Member of 1990-91 IHL champion Peoria Rivermen. Member of 1993-94 IHL champion Atlanta Knights.

Darren Rumble — Defenseman

Season	Team	League	GP	G	A	PTS	PIM	GP	G	A	PTS	PIM
89-90	Hershey	AHL	57	2	13	15	31	—	—	—	—	—
90-91	Philadelphia	NHL	3	1	0	1	0	—	—	—	—	—
90-91	Hershey	AHL	73	6	35	41	48	3	0	5	5	2
91-92	Hershey	AHL	79	12	54	66	118	6	0	3	3	2
92-93	Ottawa	NHL	69	3	13	16	61	—	—	—	—	—
92-93	New Haven	AHL	2	1	0	1	0	—	—	—	—	—
93-94	Ottawa	NHL	70	6	9	15	116	—	—	—	—	—
93-94	Prince Edward Island	AHL	3	2	0	2	0	—	—	—	—	—
94-95	Prince Edward Island	AHL	70	7	46	53	77	11	0	6	6	4
95-96	Philadelphia	NHL	5	0	0	0	4	—	—	—	—	—
95-96	Hershey	AHL	58	13	37	50	83	5	0	0	0	6
96-97	Philadelphia	NHL	10	0	0	0	0	—	—	—	—	—
96-97	Philadelphia	AHL	72	18	44	62	83	7	0	3	3	19
	NHL	Totals	157	10	22	32	181	—	—	—	—	—
	AHL	Totals	414	60	229	289	440	32	0	17	17	33

Born; 1/23/69, Barrie, Ontario. 6-1, 200. Drafted by Philadelphia Flyers (1st choice, 20th overall) in 1987 Entry Draft. Claimed by Ottawa Senators from Philadelphia in Expansion Draft (6/18/92). Signed as a free agent by Philadelphia (7/31/95). 1994-95 AHL Second Team All-Star. 1996-97 AHL First Team All-Star. 1996-97 AHL Outstanding Defenseman.

Daniel Ruoho — Left Wing

Season	Team	League	GP	G	A	PTS	PIM	GP	G	A	PTS	PIM
93-94	South Carolina	ECHL	56	7	22	29	106	3	0	2	2	2
94-95	South Carolina	ECHL	22	7	6	13	25	—	—	—	—	—
94-95	Charlotte	ECHL	28	8	6	14	41	3	0	1	1	2
95-96	Madison	CoHL	72	9	30	39	46	6	3	1	4	9
96-97	Madison	CoHL	62	14	33	47	61	5	0	1	1	6
	CoHL	Totals	134	23	63	86	107	11	3	2	5	15
	ECHL	Totals	106	22	34	56	172	6	0	3	3	4

Born; 6/22/70, Madison, Wisconsin. 6-4, 215. Drafted by Buffalo Sabres (9th choice 160th overall) in 1988 Entry Draft.

Mark Rupnow — Left Wing

Season	Team	League	GP	G	A	PTS	PIM	GP	G	A	PTS	PIM
95-96	South Carolina	ECHL	59	12	14	26	35	—	—	—	—	—
96-97	Mississippi	ECHL	30	11	7	18	17	—	—	—	—	—
	ECHL	Totals	89	23	21	44	52	—	—	—	—	—

Born; 2/21/70, Belleville, Ontario. 5-11, 200.

Paul Rushforth — Center

			Regular Season					Playoffs				
Season	Team	League	GP	G	A	PTS	PIM	GP	G	A	PTS	PIM
94-95	Rochester	AHL	25	8	6	14	10	2	0	0	0	0
94-95	South Carolina	ECHL	41	6	8	14	130	—	—	—	—	—
95-96	South Carolina	ECHL	56	20	26	46	141	7	1	0	1	8
96-97	Rochester	AHL	7	0	2	2	4	1	0	0	0	0
96-97	Birmingham	ECHL	17	7	8	15	52	8	3	9	12	34
	AHL	Totals	32	8	8	16	14	3	0	0	0	0
	ECHL	Totals	114	33	42	75	323	15	4	9	13	42

Born; 4/22/74, Prince Geroge, British Columbia. 6-0, 189. Drafted by Buffalo Sabres (8th choice, 131st overall) in 1992 Entry Draft.

Jason Rushton — Right Wing

			Regular Season					Playoffs				
Season	Team	League	GP	G	A	PTS	PIM	GP	G	A	PTS	PIM
94-95	Chicago	IHL	2	0	0	0	10	—	—	—	—	—
95-96	Jacksonville	SHL	8	3	6	9	24	—	—	—	—	—
95-96	Wichita	CeHL	44	17	13	30	263	—	—	—	—	—
96-97	Tulsa	CeHL	64	37	29	66	341	5	5	4	9	22
96-97	Syracuse	AHL	3	3	0	3	7	2	0	0	0	5
	CeHL	Totals	108	54	42	96	604	5	5	4	9	22

Born; 12/12/74, Victoria, British Columbia. 5-11, 205.

Mike Rusk — Defenseman

			Regular Season					Playoffs				
Season	Team	League	GP	G	A	PTS	PIM	GP	G	A	PTS	PIM
95-96	Columbus	ECHL	47	3	13	16	63	3	1	0	1	2
96-97	Columbus	ECHL	59	4	26	30	80	4	0	0	0	2
	ECHL	Totals	106	7	39	46	143	7	1	0	1	4

Born; 4/26/75, Milton, Ontario. 6-1, 175. Drafted by Chicago Blackhawks (10th choice, 232nd overall) in 1993 Entry Draft.

Ted Russell — Defenseman

			Regular Season					Playoffs				
Season	Team	League	GP	G	A	PTS	PIM	GP	G	A	PTS	PIM
95-96	Dayton	ECHL	43	4	14	18	40	—	—	—	—	—
95-96	Johnstown	ECHL	18	2	6	8	4	—	—	—	—	—
96-97	Johnstown	ECHL	64	9	41	50	92	—	—	—	—	—
	ECHL	Totals	125	15	61	76	136	—	—	—	—	—

Born; 5/7/71, Saint John, Newfoundland. 5-10, 190.

Yevgeni Ryabchikov — Goaltender

			Regular Season							Playoffs					
Season	Team	League	GP	W	L	T	MIN	SO	GAVG	GP	W	L	MIN	SO	GAVG
94-95	Providence	AHL	14	6	3	1	721	0	3.49	—	—	—	—	—	—
95-96	Providence	AHL	1	0	0	0	40	0	3.00	—	—	—	—	—	—
95-96	Charlotte	ECHL	1	0	1	0	29	0	8.24	—	—	—	—	—	—
95-96	Huntington	ECHL	8	3	3	0	360	0	4.17	—	—	—	—	—	—
95-96	Erie	ECHL	16	2	7	1	858	0	3.50	—	—	—	—	—	—
96-97	Providence	AHL	1	0	0	0	20	0	6.00	—	—	—	—	—	—
96-97	Charlotte	ECHL	14	5	6	2	734	1	3.84	—	—	—	—	—	—
96-97	Dayton	ECHL	15	6	4	3	842	0	4.28	—	—	—	—	—	—
	AHL	Totals	16	6	3	1	781	0	3.53	—	—	—	—	—	—
	ECHL	Totals	54	16	21	6	2823	1	3.95	—	—	—	—	—	—

Born; 1/16/74, Yaroslavl, Soviet Union. 5-11, 167. Drafted by Boston Bruins (1st choice, 21st overall) in 1994 Entry Draft.

Dan Ryder
Goaltender

			Regular Season							Playoffs					
Season	Team	League	GP	MIN	GAVG	W	L	T	SO	GP	MIN	GAVG	W	L	SO
92-93	Kansas City	IHL	10	514	4.09	3	3	2	0	—	—	—	—	—	—
92-93	Johnstown	ECHL	4	214	4.21	1	1	1	0	—	—	—	—	—	—
92-93	Columbus	ECHL	1	60	6.00	0	1	0	0	—	—	—	—	—	—
93-94	Kansas City	IHL	3	139	4.73	1	1	0	0	—	—	—	—	—	—
93-94	Roanoke	ECHL	42	1947	3.98	22	13	0	0	—	—	—	—	—	—
94-95	Kansas City	IHL	3	140	4.71	1	2	0	0	—	—	—	—	—	—
94-95	Roanoke	ECHL	21	1008	3.93	7	6	2	1	1	20	3.00	0	0	0
95-96	Detroit	CoHL	28	1425	3.66	11	12	1	0	5	247	3.89	3	1	0
96-97	Port Huron	CoHL	1	60	8.00	0	1	0	0	—	—	—	—	—	—
96-97	Saginaw	CoHL	46	2273	4.91	12	*24	3	0	—	—	—	—	—	—
	IHL	Totals	16	793	4.31	5	6	2	0	—	—	—	—	—	—
	CoHL	Totals	75	3758	4.49	23	37	4	0	5	247	3.89	3	1	0
	ECHL	Totals	68	3229	4.01	30	21	3	1	1	20	3.00	0	0	0

Born; 10/24/72, Kitchener, Ontario. 6-1, 200. Drafted by San Jose Sharks (6th choice, 89th overall) in 1991 Entry Draft.

Steve Simoni's hard work and determination has opened the door for an opportunity for full-time IHL play.   Photo courtesy of OKC Blazers

Jason Saal — Goaltender

			Regular Season							Playoffs					
Season	Team	League	GP	W	L	T	MIN	SO	GAVG	GP	W	L	MIN	SO	GAVG
95-96	St. John's	AHL	24	9	8	1	1083	0	3.76	1	0	0	13	0	0.00
95-96	South Carolina	ECHL	8	5	3	0	428	0	3.51	—	—	—	—	—	—
96-97	St. John's	AHL	12	2	5	2	569	0	4.11	—	—	—	—	—	—
96-97	Peoria	ECHL	17	8	6	1	924	1	2.79	—	—	—	—	—	—
	AHL	Totals	36	11	13	3	1652	0	3.89	1	0	0	13	0	0.00
	ECHL	Totals	25	13	9	1	1352	1	3.02	—	—	—	—	—	—

Born; 2/1/75, Sterling Heights, Michigan. 5-11, 175. Drafted by Los Angeles Kings (5th choice, 117th overall) in 1993 Entry Draft. Signed as a free agent by Toronto Maple Leafs (8/3/95).

Ken Sabourin — Defenseman

			Regular Season					Playoffs				
Season	Team	League	GP	G	A	PTS	PIM	GP	G	A	PTS	PIM
85-86	Moncton	AHL	3	0	0	0	0	6	0	1	1	2
86-87	Moncton	AHL	75	1	10	11	166	6	0	1	1	27
87-88	Salt Lake City	IHL	71	2	8	10	186	16	1	6	7	57
88-89	Calgary	NHL	6	0	1	1	26	1	0	0	0	0
88-89	Salt Lake City	IHL	74	2	18	20	197	11	0	1	1	26
89-90	Calgary	NHL	5	0	0	0	10	—	—	—	—	—
89-90	Salt Lake City	IHL	76	5	19	24	336	11	0	2	2	40
90-91	Calgary	NHL	16	1	3	4	36	—	—	—	—	—
90-91	Washington	NHL	28	1	4	5	81	11	0	0	0	34
90-91	Salt Lake City	IHL	28	2	15	17	77	—	—	—	—	—
91-92	Washington	NHL	19	0	0	0	48	—	—	—	—	—
91-92	Baltimore	AHL	30	3	8	11	106	—	—	—	—	—
92-93	Baltimore	AHL	30	5	14	19	68	—	—	—	—	—
92-93	Salt Lake City	IHL	52	2	11	13	140	—	—	—	—	—
93-94	Milwaukee	IHL	81	6	13	19	279	4	0	0	0	10
94-95	Milwaukee	IHL	75	3	16	19	297	15	1	1	2	69
95-96	Milwaukee	IHL	82	2	8	10	252	5	0	1	1	24
96-97	Milwaukee	IHL	81	2	9	11	233	3	0	0	0	2
	NHL	Totals	74	2	8	10	201	12	0	0	0	34
	IHL	Totals	620	26	117	143	1997	65	2	11	13	228
	AHL	Totals	138	8	35	43	340	12	0	2	2	29

Born; 4/28/66, Scarbrough, Ontario. 6-3, 205. Drafted by Calgary Flames (2nd choice, 33rd overall) in 1984 Entry Draft. Traded to Washington Capitals for Paul Fenton (1/24/91). Traded to Calgary by Washington for future considerations (12/16/92). Member of 1987-88 IHL champion Salt Lake City Golden Eagles.

David Sacco — Right Wing

			Regular Season					Playoffs				
Season	Team	League	GP	G	A	PTS	PIM	GP	G	A	PTS	PIM
93-94	United States	National										
93-94	Toronto	NHL	4	1	1	2	4	—	—	—	—	—
93-94	St. John's	AHL	5	3	1	4	2	—	—	—	—	—
94-95	Anaheim	NHL	8	0	2	2	0	—	—	—	—	—
94-95	San Diego	IHL	45	11	25	36	57	4	3	1	4	0
95-96	Anaheim	NHL	23	4	10	14	18	—	—	—	—	—
95-96	Baltimore	AHL	25	14	16	30	18	2	0	1	1	4
96-97	Baltimore	AHL	51	18	38	56	30	1	0	2	2	0
	NHL	Totals	35	5	13	18	22	—	—	—	—	—
	AHL	Totals	81	35	55	90	50	1	0	2	2	0

Born; 7/31/71, Malden, Massachusetts. 6-1, 190. Drafted by Toronto Maple Leafs (9th choice, 195th overall) in 1988 Entry Draft. Traded by Toronto to Anaheim Mighty Ducks for Terry Yake (9/28/94).

Mark Sakala — Forward

			Regular Season					Playoffs				
Season	Team	League	GP	G	A	PTS	PIM	GP	G	A	PTS	PIM
96-97	Louisiana	ECHL	7	0	1	1	10	—	—	—	—	—
96-97	Knoxville	ECHL	26	0	3	3	16	—	—	—	—	—
	ECHL	Totals	33	0	4	4	26	—	—	—	—	—

Born; 2/7/72, Grosse Isle, Michigan. 6-0, 195. Last amateur club; Michigan (CCHA).

Brian Sakic — Center

			Regular Season					Playoffs				
Season	Team	League	GP	G	A	PTS	PIM	GP	G	A	PTS	PIM
92-93	Erie	ECHL	51	18	33	51	22	—	—	—	—	—
93-94	Flint	CoHL	64	39	86	125	30	10	6	7	13	2
94-95	Flint	CoHL	62	38	85	113	22	6	1	5	6	0
95-96	Flint	CoHL	74	30	66	96	30	15	8	12	20	0
96-97	Austin	WPHL	16	2	8	10	23	—	—	—	—	—
96-97	Flint	CoHL	53	19	47	66	4	13	5	15	20	4
	CoHL	Totals	253	116	284	400	86	44	20	39	59	6

Born; 9/4/71, Burnaby, British Columbia. 5-10, 179. Drafted by Washington Capitals (5th round, 93rd overall) 6/16/90. Signed by New York Rangers as a free agent 8/13/92. Member of 1995-96 Colonial Cup Champion Flint Generals.

Jeff Salajko — Goaltender

			Regular Season						Playoffs					
Season	Team	League	GP	W	L	T	MIN	SO	GAVG	GP	W	L	MIN	SO	GAVG
96-97	Indianapolis	IHL	1	1	0	0	60	0	1.00	—	—	—	—	—	—
96-97	Columbus	ECHL	54	35	14	3	3085	1	3.35	8	3	5	516	0	2.79

Last amateur club; Sarnia (OHL). Drafted by San Jose Sharks (12th choice, 236th overall) in 1993 Entry Draft.

Ruslan Salei — Defenseman

			Regular Season					Playoffs				
Season	Team	League	GP	G	A	PTS	PIM	GP	G	A	PTS	PIM
95-96	Las Vegas	IHL	76	7	23	30	123	15	3	7	10	18
96-97	Anaheim	NHL	30	0	1	1	37	—	—	—	—	—
96-97	Las Vegas	IHL	8	0	2	2	24	3	2	1	3	6
96-97	Baltimore	AHL	12	1	4	5	12	—	—	—	—	—
	IHL	Totals	84	7	25	32	147	18	5	8	13	24

Born; 11/2/74, Minsk, Belarus. 6-1, 200. Drafted by Anaheim Mighty Ducks (1st choice, 9th overall) 1996 Entry Draft.

Jamie Salera — Center

			Regular Season					Playoffs				
Season	Team	League	GP	G	A	PTS	PIM	GP	G	A	PTS	PIM
95-96	Huntsville	SHL	3	3	1	4	4	—	—	—	—	—
96-97	Saginaw	CoHL	12	2	0	2	2	—	—	—	—	—
96-97	Nashville	CeHL	24	6	10	16	21	—	—	—	—	—

Born; 8/10/73, Providence, Rhode Island. 5-11, 190.

Steve Salhany — Left Wing

			Regular Season					Playoffs				
Season	Team	League	GP	G	A	PTS	PIM	GP	G	A	PTS	PIM
96-97	El Paso	WPHL	45	9	15	24	53	11	2	2	4	20
96-97	Roanoke	ECHL	4	0	1	1	2	—	—	—	—	—

Born; Montreal, Quebec. 6-2, 190. Member of 1996-97 WPHL Champion El Paso Buzzards.

Sergei Samsonov — Left Wing

Season	Team	League	Regular Season GP	G	A	PTS	PIM	Playoffs GP	G	A	PTS	PIM
96-97	Detroit	IHL	73	29	35	64	18	19	8	4	12	12

Born; 10/27/78, Moscow, Russia. 5-10, 190. Drafted by Boston Bruins (2nd choice, 8th overall) in 1997 Entry Draft. 1996-97 IHL Rookie of the Year. Member of 1996-97 IHL Champion Detroit Vipers.

Mike Sancimino — Center

Season	Team	League	Regular Season GP	G	A	PTS	PIM	Playoffs GP	G	A	PTS	PIM
96-97	Louisville	ECHL	70	28	33	61	58	—	—	—	—	—

Born; 2/15/74, Warren, Michigan. 6-2, 205. Last amateur club; Cornell (ECAC).

Mike Sanderson — Center

Season	Team	League	Regular Season GP	G	A	PTS	PIM	Playoffs GP	G	A	PTS	PIM
91-92	Nashville	ECHL	4	2	1	3	2	—	—	—	—	—
91-92	Johnstown	ECHL	6	1	2	3	4	—	—	—	—	—
92-93	Fort Worth	CeHL	60	37	31	68	33	—	—	—	—	—
93-94	Fort Worth	CeHL	63	27	34	61	37	—	—	—	—	—
94-95	Dallas	CeHL	3	0	0	0	2	—	—	—	—	—
94-95	Tulsa	CeHL	25	18	14	32	10	7	2	3	5	2
95-96	Bakersfield	WCHL	57	19	27	46	22	—	—	—	—	—
96-97	Fort Worth	CeHL	56	16	32	48	16	15	6	3	9	8
	CeHL	Totals	207	98	111	209	98	22	8	6	14	10
	ECHL	Totals	10	3	3	6	6	—	—	—	—	—

Born; 5/31/70, Moose Jaw, Saskatchewan. 5-11, 185. Member of 1996-97 CeHL Champion Fort Worth Fire.

Terran Sandwith — Defenseman

Season	Team	League	Regular Season GP	G	A	PTS	PIM	Playoffs GP	G	A	PTS	PIM
92-93	Hershey	AHL	61	1	12	13	140	—	—	—	—	—
93-94	Hershey	AHL	62	3	5	8	169	2	0	1	1	4
94-95	Hershey	AHL	11	1	1	2	32	—	—	—	—	—
95-96	Hamilton	AHL	5	0	2	2	4	—	—	—	—	—
96-97	Hamilton	AHL	78	3	6	9	213	22	0	2	2	27
	AHL	Totals	217	8	26	34	558	24	0	3	3	31

Born; 4/17/72, Stoney Plain, Alberta. 6-4, 210. Drafted by Philadelphia Flyers (4th choice, 42nd overall) in 1990 Entry Draft.

Steve Sangermano — Center

Season	Team	League	Regular Season GP	G	A	PTS	PIM	Playoffs GP	G	A	PTS	PIM
93-94	Johnstown	ECHL	2	1	0	1	0	—	—	—	—	—
93-94	South Carolina	ECHL	2	0	0	0	0	—	—	—	—	—
94-95	Dallas	CeHL	3	0	0	0	0	—	—	—	—	—
94-95	Jacksonville	SUN	6	0	3	3	2	—	—	—	—	—
95-96	Jacksonville	ECHL	1	0	1	1	0	—	—	—	—	—
95-96	Daytona Beach	SHL	53	34	*60	94	148	4	1	1	2	23
96-97	Adirondack	AHL	11	5	0	5	4	—	—	—	—	—
96-97	Quad City	CoHL	54	25	57	82	82	15	10	10	20	16
	ECHL	Totals	5	1	1	2	0	—	—	—	—	—
	SHL	Totals	59	34	63	97	150	4	1	1	2	23

Born; 10/11/72, Burrillville, Rhode Island. 5-11, 170. Member of 1996-97 CoHL Champion Quad City Mallards.

Gino Santerre — Defenseman

			Regular Season					Playoffs				
Season	Team	League	GP	G	A	PTS	PIM	GP	G	A	PTS	PIM
95-96	Louisville	ECHL	59	10	37	47	49	3	0	0	0	0
96-97	Louisville	ECHL	42	8	30	38	18	—	—	—	—	—
	ECHL	Totals	101	18	67	85	67	3	0	0	0	0

Born; 7/22/70, Ste. Foy, Quebec. 5-10, 180.

Art Saran — Defenseman

			Regular Season					Playoffs				
Season	Team	League	GP	G	A	PTS	PIM	GP	G	A	PTS	PIM
94-95	Jacksonville	SUN	4	0	2	2	2	—	—	—	—	—
95-96	Wichita	CeHL	35	4	7	11	45	—	—	—	—	—
96-97	Saginaw	CoHL	56	1	8	9	75	—	—	—	—	—

Born; 1/23/75, Harrisville, Rhode Island. 5-11, 185.

Geoff Sarjeant — Goaltender

			Regular Season							Playoffs					
Season	Team	League	GP	W	L	T	MIN	SO	GAVG	GP	W	L	MIN	SO	GAVG
92-93	Peoria	IHL	41	22	14	3	2356	0	3.31	3	0	3	179	0	4.36
93-94	Peoria	IHL	41	25	9	2	2275	*2	*2.45	4	2	2	211	0	3.69
94-95	St. Louis	NHL	4	1	0	0	120	0	3.00	—	—	—	—	—	—
94-95	Peoria	IHL	55	32	12	8	3146	0	3.01	4	0	3	206	0	5.81
95-96	San Jose	NHL	4	0	2	1	171	0	4.91	—	—	—	—	—	—
95-96	Kansas City	IHL	41	18	18	1	2166	1	3.88	2	0	1	99	0	1.82
96-97	Cincinnati	IHL	59	32	20	5	3287	1	2.87	3	0	3	158	0	4.55
	NHL	Totals	8	1	2	1	291	0	4.12	—	—	—	—	—	—
	IHL	Totals	237	129	73	19	13230	4	3.07	16	2	12	853	0	4.29

Born; 11/30/69, Newmarket, Ontario. 5-9, 180. Drafted by St. Louis Blues (1st choice, 17th overall) in 1990 Supplemental Draft. Signed as a free agent by San Jose Sharks (9/23/95). 1993-94 IHL First Team All-Star.

Hardy Sauter — Defenseman

			Regular Season					Playoffs				
Season	Team	League	GP	G	A	PTS	PIM	GP	G	A	PTS	PIM
95-96	Tallahassee	ECHL	63	16	32	48	44	12	1	6	7	8
96-97	Houston	IHL	1	0	0	0	0	—	—	—	—	—
96-97	Oklahoma City	CeHL	66	32	69	101	54	4	3	2	5	12

Born; 2/25/71, Dayton, Ohio. 5-10, 180. 1996-97 CeHL First Team All-Star. 1996-97 CeHL Defenseman of the Year.

Alain Savage — Forward

			Regular Season					Playoffs				
Season	Team	League	GP	G	A	PTS	PIM	GP	G	A	PTS	PIM
96-97	Cleveland	IHL	3	0	0	0	0	—	—	—	—	—
96-97	Hampton Roads	ECHL	64	26	25	51	147	9	5	4	9	2

Born; 11/13/74, Montreal, Quebec. 5-7, 190.

Reggie Savage — Center

			Regular Season					Playoffs				
Season	Team	League	GP	G	A	PTS	PIM	GP	G	A	PTS	PIM
90-91	Washington	NHL	1	0	0	0	0	—	—	—	—	—
90-91	Baltimore	AHL	62	32	29	61	10	6	1	1	2	6
91-92	Baltimore	AHL	77	42	28	70	51	—	—	—	—	—
92-93	Washington	NHL	16	2	3	5	12	—	—	—	—	—
92-93	Baltimore	AHL	40	37	18	55	28	—	—	—	—	—
93-94	Quebec	NHL	17	3	4	7	16	—	—	—	—	—
93-94	Cornwall	AHL	33	21	13	34	56	—	—	—	—	—
94-95	Cornwall	AHL	34	13	7	20	56	14	5	6	11	40

Season	Team	League	GP	G	A	PTS	PIM	GP	G	A	PTS	PIM
95-96	Atlanta	IHL	66	22	14	36	118	—	—	—	—	—
95-96	Syracuse	AHL	10	9	5	14	28	16	9	6	15	54
96-97	Springfield	AHL	68	32	25	57	103	17	6	7	13	24
	NHL	Totals	34	5	7	12	28	—	—	—	—	—
	AHL	Totals	324	186	125	311	332	53	21	20	41	124

Born; 5/1/70, Montreal, Quebec. 5-10, 187. Drafted by Washington Capitals (1st choice, 15th overall) in 1988 Entry Draft. Traded to Quebec Nordiques by Washington with Paul MacDermid for Mike Hough (6/20/93). Signed as a free agent by Phoenix Coyotes (8/28/96).

Bogden Savenko — Right Wing

			Regular Season					Playoffs				
Season	Team	League	GP	G	A	PTS	PIM	GP	G	A	PTS	PIM
94-95	Indianapolis	IHL	62	18	17	35	49	—	—	—	—	—
95-96	Syracuse	AHL	69	16	20	36	68	14	2	4	6	20
96-97	Syracuse	AHL	38	7	9	16	24	—	—	—	—	—
96-97	Quebec	IHL	14	2	1	3	4	9	2	0	2	0
	AHL	Totals	107	23	29	52	92	14	2	4	6	20
	IHL	Totals	76	20	18	38	53	9	2	0	2	0

Born;11/20/74, Kiev, Russia. 6-1, 192. Drafted by Chicago Blackhawks (3rd choice, 54th overall). Traded to Vancouver by Chicago with Hartford's third round choice (previously acquired by Chicago, Vancouver selected Larry Courville) in 1995 Entry Draft for Gerald Diduck (4/7/95).

Ryan Savoia — Center

			Regular Season					Playoffs				
Season	Team	League	GP	G	A	PTS	PIM	GP	G	A	PTS	PIM
94-95	Cleveland	IHL	1	0	0	0	0	—	—	—	—	—
95-96	Cleveland	IHL	49	6	7	13	31	—	—	—	—	—
96-97	Cleveland	IHL	4	1	0	1	2	—	—	—	—	—
96-97	Fort Wayne	IHL	8	0	2	2	2	—	—	—	—	—
96-97	Johnstown	ECHL	60	35	44	79	100	—	—	—	—	—
	IHL	Totals	62	7	9	16	31	—	—	—	—	—

Born; 5/6/73, Thorold, Ontario. 6-1, 205. Signed as a free agent by Pittsburgh Penguins (4/7/95).

Kevin Sawyer — Right Wing

			Regular Season					Playoffs				
Season	Team	League	GP	G	A	PTS	PIM	GP	G	A	PTS	PIM
95-96	Boston	NHL	2	0	0	0	5	—	—	—	—	—
95-96	St. Louis	NHL	6	0	0	0	23	—	—	—	—	—
95-96	Providence	AHL	4	0	0	0	29	4	0	1	1	9
95-96	Worcester	AHL	41	3	4	7	268	—	—	—	—	—
96-97	Boston	NHL	2	0	0	0	0	—	—	—	—	—
96-97	Providence	AHL	60	8	9	17	367	6	0	0	0	32
	NHL	Totals	10	0	0	0	28	—	—	—	—	—
	AHL	Totals	105	11	13	24	664	6	0	0	0	32

Born; 2/21/74, Christina Lake, British Columbia. 6-2, 205. Signed as a free agent by St. Louis Blues (2/28/95). Traded to Boston Bruins by St. Louis with Steve Staois for Steve Leach (3/8/96). Signed as a free agent by Dallas Stars (7/97).

Curtis Sayler — Right Wing

			Regular Season					Playoffs				
Season	Team	League	GP	G	A	PTS	PIM	GP	G	A	PTS	PIM
96-97	Central Texas	WPHL	1	0	0	0	0	—	—	—	—	—
96-97	San Antonio	CeHL	25	2	4	6	120	—	—	—	—	—
96-97	Port Huron	CoHL	38	4	3	7	176	5	0	0	0	10

Born; 3/30/75, Beauvallon, Alberta. 5-11, 200.

Chris Sbrocca — Center

Season	Team	League	GP	G	A	PTS	PIM	GP	G	A	PTS	PIM
96-97	Quebec	IHL	6	1	2	3	8	—	—	—	—	—
96-97	Pensacola	ECHL	65	25	46	71	201	12	4	5	9	26

Born; 1/22/74, Montreal, Quebec. 5-10, 185. Last amateur club; Lowell (Hockey East).

Dave Scatchard — Right Wing

Season	Team	League	GP	G	A	PTS	PIM	GP	G	A	PTS	PIM
95-96	Syracuse	AHL	1	0	0	0	0	15	5	2	7	29
96-97	Syracuse	AHL	26	8	7	15	65	—	—	—	—	—
	AHL	Totals	27	8	7	15	65	15	5	2	7	29

Born; 2/20/76, Hinton, Alberta. 6-2, 185. Drafted by Vancouver Canucks (3rd choice, 42 overall) in 1994 Entry Draft.

Trent Schachle — Center

Season	Team	League	GP	G	A	PTS	PIM	GP	G	A	PTS	PIM
96-97	Dayton	ECHL	61	10	25	35	109	4	0	3	3	8

Born; 8/31/72, Wasilla, Alaska.

Peter Schaefer — Left Wing

Season	Team	League	GP	G	A	PTS	PIM	GP	G	A	PTS	PIM
96-97	Syracuse	AHL	5	0	3	3	0	3	1	3	4	14

Born; 7/12/77, Yellow Grass, Saskatchewan. 5-11, 187. Drafted by Vancouver Canucks (3rd choice, 66th overall) in 1995 Entry Draft.

Paxton Schafer — Goaltender

Season	Team	League	GP	W	L	T	MIN	SO	GAVG	GP	W	L	MIN	SO	GAVG
96-97	Boston	NHL	3	0	0	0	77	0	4.68	—	—	—	—	—	—
96-97	Providence	AHL	22	9	10	0	1206	1	3.73	—	—	—	—	—	—
96-97	Charlotte	ECHL	4	3	1	0	239	0	1.75	—	—	—	—	—	—

Born; 2/26/76, Medicine Hat, Alberta. 5-9, 152. Drafted by Boston Bruins (3rd choice, 47th overall) in 1995 Entry Draft.

Pasi Schalin — Left Wing

Season	Team	League	GP	G	A	PTS	PIM	GP	G	A	PTS	PIM
91-92	Maine	AHL	5	0	0	0	0	—	—	—	—	—
92-93	N/A											
93-94	West Palm Beach	SUN	22	6	8	14	6	—	—	—	—	—
93-94	Daytona Beach	SUN	29	21	19	40	29	2	0	1	1	0
93-94	Nashville	ECHL	4	0	2	2	0	—	—	—	—	—
94-95	Daytona Beach	SUN	15	7	13	20	6	—	—	—	—	—
95-96	N/A											
96-97	San Diego	WCHL	38	14	18	32	6	—	—	—	—	—
96-97	Alaska	WCHL	4	2	0	2	7	—	—	—	—	—
	SUN	Totals	66	34	40	74	41	2	0	1	1	0
	WCHL	Totals	42	16	18	34	13	—	—	—	—	—

Born; 2/8/68, Imatra, Finland. 5-11, 185.

Jeff Scharf — Center

Season	Team	League	GP	G	A	PTS	PIM	GP	G	A	PTS	PIM
96-97	Charlotte	ECHL	6	0	1	1	23	2	0	0	0	0

Born; 3/6/77, Sudbury, Ontario. 6-1, 190.

Lee Schill — Goaltender

Regular Season / Playoffs

Season	Team	League	GP	W	L	T	MIN	SO	GAVG	GP	W	L	MIN	SO	GAVG
95-96	Bakersfield	WCHL	26	12	11	0	1360	0	4.85	—	—	—	—	—	—
96-97	Bakersfield	WCHL	*55	27	*22	3	*3034	*2	4.81	4	1	3	224	0	4.28
	WCHL	Totals	81	39	33	3	4394	2	4.82	4	1	3	224	0	4.28

Born; 5/12/71, Vancouver, British Columbia. 5-10, 190.

Chris Schmidt — Center

Regular Season / Playoffs

Season	Team	League	GP	G	A	PTS	PIM	GP	G	A	PTS	PIM
96-97	Phoenix	IHL	37	3	6	9	60	—	—	—	—	—
96-97	Mississippi	ECHL	18	7	7	14	35	—	—	—	—	—

Born; 3/1/76, Beaverlodge, ALberta. 6-3, 200. Drafted by Los Angeles Kings (4th choice, 111th overall) in 1994 Entry Draft.

Colin Schmidt — Left Wing

Regular Season / Playoffs

Season	Team	League	GP	G	A	PTS	PIM	GP	G	A	PTS	PIM
96-97	Hamilton	AHL	15	2	2	4	2	—	—	—	—	—
96-97	Wheeling	ECHL	37	9	19	28	25	—	—	—	—	—

Born; 2/3/74, Regina, Saskatchewan. 5-11, 185. Drafted by Edmonton Oilers (9th choice, 190th overall) in 1992 Entry Draft.

Ryan Schmidt — Defenseman

Regular Season / Playoffs

Season	Team	League	GP	G	A	PTS	PIM	GP	G	A	PTS	PIM
93-94	Dallas	CeHL	6	0	0	0	9	—	—	—	—	—
94-95	Roanoke	ECHL	4	0	0	0	0	—	—	—	—	—
94-95	Utica	CoHL	11	1	0	1	6	—	—	—	—	—
94-95	Detroit	CoHL	19	2	3	5	50	—	—	—	—	—
95-96	West Palm Beach	SHL	8	0	0	0	28	—	—	—	—	—
95-96	Wichita	CeHL	26	2	5	7	66	—	—	—	—	—
96-97	Dayton	CeHL	3	0	1	1	0	—	—	—	—	—
96-97	Amarillo	WPHL	39	0	4	4	81	—	—	—	—	—
	CoHL	Totals	33	3	4	7	56	—	—	—	—	—
	CeHL	Totals	32	2	5	7	75	—	—	—	—	—

Born; 5/23/73, Grosse Ile, Michigan. 6-1, 215.

Andy Schneider — Left Wing

Regular Season / Playoffs

Season	Team	League	GP	G	A	PTS	PIM	GP	G	A	PTS	PIM
92-93	New Haven	AHL	19	2	2	4	13	—	—	—	—	—
93-94	Ottawa	NHL	10	0	0	0	15	—	—	—	—	—
93-94	Prince Edward Island	AHL	61	15	46	61	119	—	—	—	—	—
94-95	Sweden											
94-95	Canada	National										
94-95	Prince Edward Island	AHL	10	1	5	6	25	11	5	5	10	11
95-96	Minnesota	IHL	81	12	28	40	85	—	—	—	—	—
96-97	Manitoba	IHL	79	14	37	51	142	—	—	—	—	—
	IHL	Totals	160	26	65	91	227	—	—	—	—	—
	AHL	Totals	90	18	53	71	157	11	5	5	10	11

Born; 3/29/72, Edmonton, Alberta. 5-9, 170. Signed as a free agent by Ottawa Senators (10/9/92).

Bryan Schoen — Goaltender

Regular Season / Playoffs

Season	Team	League	GP	W	L	T	MIN	SO	GAVG	GP	W	L	MIN	SO	GAVG
93-94	Roanoke	ECHL	6	1	4	0	279	0	4.94	—	—	—	—	—	—
93-94	Louisville	ECHL	11	3	7	0	576	0	4.48	6	2	4	351	*1	4.62

Season	Team	League	GP	G	A	PTS	PIM		GP	G	A	PTS	PIM
93-94	Fort Worth	CeHL	4	2	1	0	211	0	3.98	—	—	—	—	—
94-95	Fort Worth	CeHL	32	11	10	2	1503	0	4.43	—	—	—	—	—
95-96	Los Angeles	IHL	2	0	1	1	110	0	4.36	—	—	—	—	—
95-96	Louisiana	ECHL	11	5	3	2	605	1	3.07	—	—	—	—	—
95-96	Louisville	ECHL	26	18	4	2	1418	0	3.34	—	—	—	—	—
96-97	Louisiana	ECHL	13	6	2	0	552	0	3.91	7	3	1	307	0	3.52
	ECHL	Totals	67	33	20	4	3430	1	3.71	13	5	5	658	1	4.10
	CeHL	Totals	36	13	11	2	1714	0	4.38	—	—	—	—	—

Born; 9/9/71, Minneapolis, Minnesota. 6-2, 195. Drafted by Minnesota North Stars (6th choice, 91st overall) in 1989 Entry Draft.

Paxton Schulte — Left Wing

			Regular Season					Playoffs				
Season	Team	League	GP	G	A	PTS	PIM	GP	G	A	PTS	PIM
93-94	Quebec	NHL	1	0	0	0	2	—	—	—	—	—
93-94	Cornwall	AHL	56	15	15	30	102	—	—	—	—	—
94-95	Cornwall	AHL	74	14	22	36	217	14	3	3	6	29
95-96	Cornwall	AHL	*69	25	31	56	171	—	—	—	—	—
95-96	Saint John	AHL	*14	4	5	9	25	14	4	7	11	40
96-97	Calgary	NHL	1	0	0	0	2	—	—	—	—	—
96-97	Saint John	AHL	71	14	23	37	274	4	2	0	2	35
	NHL	Totals	2	0	0	0	4	—	—	—	—	—
	AHL	Totals	274	72	96	168	789	32	9	10	19	104

Born; 7/16/72, Ionaway, Alberta. 6-2, 210. Drafted by Quebec Nordiques (7th choice, 124th ovwerall) in 1992 Entry Draft. Traded to Calgary Flames by Quebec for Vesa Viitakoski (3/19/96). *Because of that trade Schulte appeared in 83 games during the 1995-96 season.

Bobby Schwark — Defenseman

			Regular Season					Playoffs				
Season	Team	League	GP	G	A	PTS	PIM	GP	G	A	PTS	PIM
96-97	Reno	WCHL	3	0	0	0	6	—	—	—	—	—
96-97	Alaska	WCHL	38	0	8	8	124	—	—	—	—	—
96-97	Memphis	CeHL	8	0	0	0	4	—	—	—	—	—
	WCHL	Totals	41	0	8	8	130	—	—	—	—	—

Born; 2/1/72, Ardworth, Saskatchewan. 6-3, 210. Last amateur club; Alaska-Fairbanks (CCHA).

Blair Scott — Defenseman

			Regular Season					Playoffs				
Season	Team	League	GP	G	A	PTS	PIM	GP	G	A	PTS	PIM
93-94	Cornwall	AHL	19	1	2	3	13	—	—	—	—	—
94-95	Cornwall	AHL	56	8	16	24	108	14	3	5	8	12
95-96	Chicago	IHL	14	0	2	2	32	—	—	—	—	—
95-96	Atlanta	IHL	19	1	1	2	38	—	—	—	—	—
95-96	Cape Breton	AHL	30	4	4	8	42	—	—	—	—	—
96-97	Hershey	AHL	47	2	12	14	100	—	—	—	—	—
	AHL	Totals	152	15	34	49	273	14	3	5	8	12
	IHL	Totals	33	1	3	4	70	—	—	—	—	—

Born; 2/25/72, Winnipeg, Manitoba. 6-0, 194. Signed as a free agent by Quebec Nordiques (7/6/93).

Brent Scott — Right Wing

			Regular Season					Playoffs				
Season	Team	League	GP	G	A	PTS	PIM	GP	G	A	PTS	PIM
95-96	Bakersfield	WCHL	54	29	42	71	251	—	—	—	—	—
96-97	El Paso	WPHL	60	19	31	50	235	9	4	2	6	44

Born; 9/9/66, Calgary, Alberta. 5-10, 200. Member of 1996-97 WPHL Champion El Paso Buzzards.

Fred Scott — Center

Season	Team	League	GP	G	A	PTS	PIM	GP	G	A	PTS	PIM
96-97	Dayton	CoHL	59	18	12	30	51	—	—	—	—	—

Born; 1/10/73, Cambridge, Ohio. 5-11, 195. Last amateur club; Alaska-Fairbanks (CCHA).

Travis Scott — Goaltender

Season	Team	League	GP	W	L	T	MIN	SO	GAVG	GP	W	L	MIN	SO	GAVG
96-97	Worcester	AHL	29	14	10	1	1482	1	3.04	—	—	—	—	—	—
96-97	Baton Rouge	ECHL	10	5	2	1	501	0	2.63	—	—	—	—	—	—

Born; 9/14/75, Kanata, Ontario. 6-2, 185. Last amateur club; Ottawa (OHL).

Chris Scourletis — Defenseman

Season	Team	League	GP	G	A	PTS	PIM	GP	G	A	PTS	PIM
94-95	Raleigh	ECHL	4	0	1	1	2	—	—	—	—	—
95-96	Detroit	CoHL	74	0	8	8	206	10	0	0	0	70
96-97	Michigan	IHL	3	0	0	0	12	—	—	—	—	—
96-97	Port Huron	CoHL	68	5	18	23	333	5	0	0	0	15
	CoHL	Totals	142	5	26	31	539	15	0	0	0	85

Born; 8/4/71, Gloucester, Massachusetts. 5-11, 197.

Claudio Scremin — Defenseman

Season	Team	League	GP	G	A	PTS	PIM	GP	G	A	PTS	PIM
90-91	Kansas City	IHL	77	7	14	21	60	—	—	—	—	—
91-92	Kansas City	IHL	70	5	23	28	44	15	1	6	7	14
91-92	San Jose	NHL	13	0	0	0	25	—	—	—	—	—
92-93	San Jose	NHL	4	0	1	1	4	—	—	—	—	—
92-93	Kansas City	IHL	75	10	22	32	93	12	0	5	5	18
93-94	Kansas City	IHL	38	7	17	24	39	—	—	—	—	—
94-95	Kansas City	IHL	61	8	30	38	29	20	8	12	20	14
95-96	Kansas City	IHL	79	6	47	53	83	5	0	1	1	6
96-97	Kansas City	IHL	69	7	25	32	71	3	1	1	2	2
	NHL	Totals	17	0	1	1	29	—	—	—	—	—
	IHL	Totals	469	50	178	228	419	55	10	25	35	54

Born; 5/28/68, Burnaby, British Columbia. 6-2, 205. Drafted by Washington Capitals (12th choice, 204th overall) in 1988 Entry Draft. Traded to Minnesota North Stars by Washington for Don Beaupre (11/1/88). Signed as a free agent by San Jose Sharks (9/3/91). Member of 1991-92 IHL champion Kansas City Blades.

Glen Seabury — Center

Season	Team	League	GP	G	A	PTS	PIM	GP	G	A	PTS	PIM
95-96	Detroit	CoHL	38	4	10	14	41	5	0	0	0	4
96-97	Port Huron	CoHL	50	2	13	15	34	—	—	—	—	—
96-97	Saginaw	CoHL	18	0	10	10	10	—	—	—	—	—
	CoHL	Totals	106	6	33	39	85	5	0	0	0	4

Born; 8/30/70, Stoneham, Massachusetts. 6-2, 210.

Doug Searle — Defenseman

Season	Team	League	GP	G	A	PTS	PIM	GP	G	A	PTS	PIM
93-94	Las Vegas	IHL	1	0	0	0	0	—	—	—	—	—
93-94	Knoxville	ECHL	65	6	12	18	154	3	0	1	1	4
94-95	Las Vegas	IHL	7	0	1	1	18	—	—	—	—	—
94-95	Knoxville	ECHL	56	7	11	18	205	4	0	0	0	15

Season	Team	League	GP	G	A	PTS	PIM	GP	G	A	PTS	PIM
95-96	Phoenix	IHL	4	0	0	0	17	—	—	—	—	—
95-96	Knoxville	ECHL	58	4	30	34	261	7	1	1	2	31
96-97	Roanoke	ECHL	70	4	8	12	102	4	0	1	1	0
	IHL	Totals	12	0	1	1	35	—	—	—	—	—
	ECHL	Totals	249	21	61	82	722	18	1	4	5	50

Born; 3/21/72, Toronto, Ontario. 6-4, 220.

Sverre Sears — Defenseman

			Regular Season					Playoffs				
Season	Team	League	GP	G	A	PTS	PIM	GP	G	A	PTS	PIM
93-94	Greensboro	ECHL	63	6	17	23	158	7	1	0	1	4
94-95	Detroit	IHL	15	0	3	3	15	3	0	0	0	2
94-95	Erie	ECHL	21	0	8	8	83	—	—	—	—	—
94-95	Greensboro	ECHL	9	0	0	0	14	—	—	—	—	—
95-96	Detroit	IHL	18	0	1	1	21	—	—	—	—	—
95-96	Minnesota	IHL	1	0	0	0	0	—	—	—	—	—
95-96	Los Angeles	IHL	12	0	0	0	19	—	—	—	—	—
95-96	Flint	CoHL	44	6	16	22	218	11	2	2	4	52
96-97	Houston	IHL	15	0	0	0	15	—	—	—	—	—
96-97	Baton Rouge	ECHL	25	1	10	11	91	—	—	—	—	—
96-97	Knoxville	ECHL	26	1	10	11	94	—	—	—	—	—
	IHL	Totals	61	0	4	4	70	3	0	0	0	2
	ECHL	Totals	144	8	45	53	440	7	1	0	1	4

Born; 10/18/70, Dover, Massachusetts. 6-1, 195. Drafted by Philadelphia Flyers (6th choice, 159th overall) in 1989 Entry Draft. Member of 1995-96 Colonial Cup Champion Flint Generals.

Brian Secord — Center

			Regular Season					Playoffs				
Season	Team	League	GP	G	A	PTS	PIM	GP	G	A	PTS	PIM
95-96	Springfield	AHL	1	0	0	0	0	—	—	—	—	—
96-97	Springfield	AHL	6	1	2	3	2	—	—	—	—	—
96-97	Hamilton	AHL	3	1	1	2	0	—	—	—	—	—
96-97	Quebec	IHL	3	1	0	1	4	—	—	—	—	—
96-97	Richmond	ECHL	31	14	8	22	58	—	—	—	—	—
96-97	Pensacola	ECHL	19	5	9	14	20	12	2	3	5	14
	AHL	Totals	10	2	3	5	2	—	—	—	—	—
	ECHL	Totals	50	19	17	36	78	12	2	3	5	14

Born; 1/19/75, Ridgetown, Ontario. 5-11, 180. Signed as a free agent by Hartford Whalers (9/27/95).

Brett Seguin — Center

			Regular Season					Playoffs				
Season	Team	League	GP	G	A	PTS	PIM	GP	G	A	PTS	PIM
92-93	Muskegon	CoHL	49	24	40	64	48	7	6	8	14	20
92-93	Phoenix	IHL	16	2	7	9	8	—	—	—	—	—
93-94	Fort Wayne	IHL	6	0	0	0	4	—	—	—	—	—
93-94	Muskegon	CoHL	46	24	50	74	105	3	1	3	4	8
94-95	Phoenix	IHL	2	0	2	2	0	—	—	—	—	—
94-95	Muskegon	CoHL	74	55	67	122	74	17	13	20	33	10
95-96	Detroit	IHL	3	0	0	0	0	—	—	—	—	—
95-96	Muskegon	CoHL	62	31	75	106	70	5	4	3	7	28
96-97	Austin	WPHL	53	35	54	89	26	6	1	5	6	2
	CoHL	Totals	231	134	232	366	297	32	24	34	58	66
	IHL	Totals	27	2	9	11	12	—	—	—	—	—

Drafted by Los Angeles Kings (6th round, 130th overall) 6/6/22/91. 1994-95 CoHL Second Team All-Star.

Kurt Seher — Defenseman

Season	Team	League	GP	G	A	PTS	PIM	GP	G	A	PTS	PIM
92-93	Providence	AHL	2	0	0	0	2	3	0	0	0	2
93-94	Providence	AHL	8	0	0	0	8	—	—	—	—	—
93-94	Charlotte	ECHL	51	6	21	27	54	3	0	0	0	2
94-95	Providence	AHL	15	0	3	3	4	6	0	0	0	2
94-95	Charlotte	ECHL	49	8	13	21	51	1	1	0	1	0
95-96	Charlotte	ECHL	68	10	37	47	71	16	3	10	13	14
96-97	Utah	IHL	16	0	5	5	4	—	—	—	—	—
96-97	Manitoba	IHL	3	0	1	1	2	—	—	—	—	—
96-97	Charlotte	ECHL	28	4	10	14	24	3	0	1	1	18
	AHL	Totals	25	0	3	3	14	9	0	0	0	4
	IHL	Totals	19	0	6	6	6	—	—	—	—	—
	ECHL	Totals	196	28	81	109	200	23	4	11	15	34

Born; 4/15/73, Lethbridge, Alberta. 6-2, 200. Drafted by Boston Bruins (6th choice, 184th overall) in 1993 Entry Draft. Member of 1995-96 ECHL champion Charlotte Checkers.

Troy Seibel — Goaltender

Season	Team	League	GP	W	L	T	MIN	SO	GAVG	GP	W	L	MIN	SO	GAVG
95-96	Huntsville	SHL	30	15	14	0	1719	1	4.40	10	7	2	584	0	3.91
96-97	Huntsville	CeHL	49	28	17	0	2710	0	4.12	9	5	4	545	0	3.75

Born; 6/16/70, Drumheller, Alberta. 6-2, 198. Member of 1995-96 SHL champion Huntsville Channel Cats.

Dave Seitz — Center

Season	Team	League	GP	G	A	PTS	PIM	GP	G	A	PTS	PIM
96-97	Rochester	AHL	13	0	2	2	4	—	—	—	—	—
96-97	South Carolina	ECHL	58	43	54	97	48	17	9	15	24	30

Born; 2/2/74, Buffalo, New York. 5-10, 180.

Marc Seliger — Goaltender

Season	Team	League	GP	W	L	T	MIN	SO	GAVG	GP	W	L	MIN	SO	GAVG
96-97	Portland	AHL	6	0	3	1	253	0	4.98	—	—	—	—	—	—
96-97	Hampton Roads	ECHL	16	10	3	1	723	0	3.40	2	0	1	90	0	4.68

Born; 5/1/74, Rosenheim, Germany. 5-11, 165. Drafted by Washington Capitals (9th choice, 251st overall) in 1993 Entry Draft.

Alexander Semak — Center

Season	Team	League	GP	G	A	PTS	PIM	GP	G	A	PTS	PIM
91-92	New Jersey	AHL	25	5	6	11	0	1	0	0	0	0
91-92	Utica	AHL	7	3	2	5	0	—	—	—	—	—
92-93	New Jersey	NHL	82	37	42	79	70	5	1	1	2	0
93-94	New Jersey	NHL	54	12	17	29	22	2	0	0	0	0
94-95	New Jersey	NHL	19	2	6	8	13	—	—	—	—	—
94-95	Tampa Bay	NHL	22	5	5	10	12	—	—	—	—	—
95-96	Islanders	NHL	69	20	14	34	68	—	—	—	—	—
96-97	Vancouver	NHL	18	2	1	3	2	—	—	—	—	—
96-97	Syracuse	AHL	23	10	14	24	12	—	—	—	—	—
96-97	Las Vegas	IHL	13	11	13	24	10	3	0	4	4	4
	NHL	Totals	289	83	91	174	187	8	1	1	2	0
	AHL	Totals	55	18	22	40	12	1	0	0	0	0

Born; 2/11/66, Ufa, Russia. 5-10, 185. Drafted by New Jersey Devils (12th choice, 207th overall) in 1988 Entry Draft. Traded to Tampa Bay Lightning by New Jersey with Ben Hankinson for Shawn Chambers and Danton Cole, (3/14/95). Traded to New York Islanders by Tampa Bay for Islanders fifth round choice (Karel Betik) in 1997 Entry Draft (9/14/95).

Brandy Semchuk — Right Wing

Season	Team	League	Regular Season GP	G	A	PTS	PIM	Playoffs GP	G	A	PTS	PIM
90-91	New Haven	AHL	21	1	4	5	6	—	—	—	—	—
91-92	Phoenix	IHL	15	1	5	6	6	—	—	—	—	—
91-92	Raleigh	ECHL	5	1	2	3	16	2	1	0	1	4
92-93	Phoenix	IHL	56	13	12	25	58	—	—	—	—	—
92-93	Los Angeles	NHL	1	0	0	0	2	—	—	—	—	—
93-94	Phoenix	IHL	2	0	0	0	6	—	—	—	—	—
93-94	Erie	ECHL	44	17	15	32	37	—	—	—	—	—
94-95	Nashville	ECHL	9	3	2	5	2	—	—	—	—	—
94-95	San Antonio	CeHL	29	17	16	33	34	13	1	5	6	33
95-96	San Antonio	CeHL	12	5	2	7	43	—	—	—	—	—
96-97	San Antonio	CeHL	10	4	6	10	2	—	—	—	—	—
96-97	Columbus	CeHL	13	5	5	10	8	3	0	1	1	12
	IHL	Totals	73	14	17	31	70	—	—	—	—	—
	CeHL	Totals	64	31	29	60	87	16	1	6	7	45
	ECHL	Totals	58	21	19	40	55	2	1	0	1	4

Born; 9/22/71, Calgary, Alberta. 6-1, 215. Drafted by Los Angeles Kings (2nd choice, 28th overall) in 1990 Entry Draft.

Trevor Senn — Right Wing

Season	Team	League	Regular Season GP	G	A	PTS	PIM	Playoffs GP	G	A	PTS	PIM
91-92	Winston-Salem	ECHL	41	16	25	41	196	4	0	0	0	60
92-93	Wheeling	ECHL	53	14	21	35	301	14	3	2	5	89
93-94	Greensboro	ECHL	4	2	3	5	50	8	0	2	2	37
94-95	Greensboro	ECHL	15	5	3	8	141	—	—	—	—	—
94-95	South Carolina	ECHL	15	2	1	3	139	—	—	—	—	—
94-95	Richmond	ECHL	9	1	0	1	98	16	5	8	13	*138
95-96	Houston	IHL	2	0	0	0	22	—	—	—	—	—
95-96	Richmond	ECHL	57	18	31	49	507	7	3	3	6	21
96-97	Baltimore	AHL	27	4	5	9	167	—	—	—	—	—
96-97	Richmond	ECHL	28	8	14	22	211	8	2	5	7	58
	ECHL	Totals	222	66	98	164	1643	57	13	20	33	403

Born; 4/7/70, Saskatoon, Saskatchewan. 5-9, 185. Member of 1994-95 ECHL Champion Richmond Renegades.

Jeff Serowik — Defenseman

Season	Team	League	Regular Season GP	G	A	PTS	PIM	Playoffs GP	G	A	PTS	PIM
90-91	Toronto	NHL	1	0	0	0	0	—	—	—	—	—
90-91	Newmarket	AHL	60	8	15	23	45	—	—	—	—	—
91-92	St. John's	AHL	78	11	34	45	60	16	4	9	13	22
92-93	St. John's	AHL	77	19	35	54	92	9	1	5	6	8
93-94	Cincinnati	IHL	79	6	21	27	98	7	0	1	1	8
94-95	Boston	NHL	1	0	0	0	0	—	—	—	—	—
94-95	Providence	AHL	78	28	34	62	10	13	4	6	10	10
95-96	Indianapolis	IHL	69	20	23	43	86	—	—	—	—	—
95-96	Las Vegas	IHL	13	7	6	13	18	15	6	5	11	16
96-97	Las Vegas	IHL	42	5	19	24	34	3	0	0	0	4
	NHL	Totals	2	0	0	0	0	—	—	—	—	—
	AHL	Totals	293	66	139	205	299	38	9	20	29	40
	IHL	Totals	203	38	69	107	236	25	6	6	12	28

Born; 1/10/67, Manchester, New Hampshire. 6-0, 190. Drafted by Toronto Maple Leafs (5th choice, 85th overall) in 1985 Entry Draft. Signed as a free agent by Florida Panthers (7/20/93). Signed as a free agent by Boston Bruins (6/29/94). Signed as a free agent by Chicago Blackhawks (8/10/95). 1992-93 AHL Second Team All-Star. 1994-95 AHL best defensman (Eddie Shore Plaque). 1994-95 AHL First Team All-Star.

Pierre Sevigny — Left Wing

Season	Team	League	GP	G	A	PTS	PIM	GP	G	A	PTS	PIM
91-92	Fredericton	AHL	74	22	37	59	145	7	1	1	2	26
92-93	Fredericton	AHL	80	36	40	76	113	5	1	1	2	2
93-94	Montreal	NHL	43	4	5	9	42	3	0	1	1	0
94-95	Montreal	NHL	19	0	0	0	15	—	—	—	—	—
95-96	Fredericton	AHL	76	39	42	81	188	10	5	9	14	20
96-97	Montreal	NHL	13	0	0	0	5	—	—	—	—	—
96-97	Fredericton	AHL	32	9	17	26	58	—	—	—	—	—
	NHL	Totals	75	4	5	9	72	3	0	1	1	0
	AHL	Totals	262	106	136	242	504	22	7	11	18	48

Born; 8/9/71, Trois-Rivieries, Quebec. 6-0, 189. Drafted by Montreal Canadiens (4th choice, 51st overall) in 1989 Entry Draft.

Dean Seymour — Center

Season	Team	League	GP	G	A	PTS	PIM	GP	G	A	PTS	PIM
95-96	Fresno	WCHL	5	4	5	9	2	7	0	2	2	0
96-97	Louisiana	ECHL	23	4	12	16	30	—	—	—	—	—
96-97	Louisville	ECHL	39	15	32	47	27	—	—	—	—	—
	ECHL	Totals	62	19	44	63	57	—	—	—	—	—

Born; 12/8/71, Saskatoon, Saskatchewan. 5-11, 188. Last amateur club; Northern Michigan (WCHA).

Konstantin Shafranov — Right Wing

Season	Team	League	GP	G	A	PTS	PIM	GP	G	A	PTS	PIM
93-94	Detroit	CoHL	4	3	2	5	0	—	—	—	—	—
94-95	N/A											
95-96	Fort Wayne	IHL	74	46	28	74	26	5	1	2	3	4
96-97	St. Louis	NHL	5	2	1	3	0	—	—	—	—	—
96-97	Worcester	AHL	62	23	25	48	16	5	0	2	2	0

Born; 9/11/68, Ust-Kamenogorak, Russia. 5-11, 176. Drafted by St. Louis Blues (10th choice, 229th overall) in 1996 Entry Draft.

Yevgeny Shaldybin — Defenseman

Season	Team	League	GP	G	A	PTS	PIM	GP	G	A	PTS	PIM
96-97	Boston	NHL	3	1	0	1	0	—	—	—	—	—
96-97	Providence	AHL	65	4	13	17	28	3	0	0	0	0

Born; 7/29/75, Novosibirsk, Russia. 6-1, 198. Drafted by Boston Bruins (6th choice, 151st overall) in 1995 Entry Draft.

Ryan Shanahan — Right Wing

Season	Team	League	GP	G	A	PTS	PIM	GP	G	A	PTS	PIM
95-96	Louisiana	ECHL	4	3	2	5	2	5	2	0	2	20
96-97	Louisiana	ECHL	11	4	3	7	66	—	—	—	—	—
96-97	Wheeling	ECHL	39	6	21	27	101	3	0	0	0	0
	ECHL	Totals	54	13	26	39	169	8	2	0	2	20

Born; 4/3/75, Buffalo, New York. 6-1, 195. Drafted by Detroit Red Wings (10th choice, 230th overall) in 1993 Entry Draft.

Daniel Shank — Right Wing

Season	Team	League	GP	G	A	PTS	PIM	GP	G	A	PTS	PIM
88-89	Adirondack	AHL	42	5	20	25	113	17	11	8	19	102
89-90	Detroit	NHL	57	11	13	24	143	—	—	—	—	—
89-90	Adirondack	AHL	14	8	8	16	36	—	—	—	—	—
90-91	Detroit	NHL	7	0	1	1	14	—	—	—	—	—
90-91	Adirondack	AHL	60	26	49	75	278	—	—	—	—	—
91-92	Hartford	NHL	13	2	0	2	18	5	0	0	0	22

Season	Team	League	GP	G	A	PTS	PIM	GP	G	A	PTS	PIM
91-92	Adirondack	AHL	27	13	21	34	112	—	—	—	—	—
91-92	Srpringfield	AHL	31	9	19	28	83	8	8	0	8	48
92-93	San Diego	IHL	77	39	53	92	*495	14	5	10	15	*131
93-94	San Diego	IHL	63	27	36	63	273	—	—	—	—	—
93-94	Phoenix	IHL	7	4	6	10	26	—	—	—	—	—
94-95	Minnesota	IHL	19	4	11	15	30	—	—	—	—	—
94-95	Detroit	IHL	54	44	27	71	142	5	2	2	4	6
95-96	Las Vegas	IHL	49	36	29	65	191	—	—	—	—	—
95-96	Detroit	IHL	29	14	19	33	96	12	4	5	9	38
96-97	San Antonio	IHL	81	33	58	91	293	9	3	3	6	32
	NHL	Totals	77	13	14	27	175	5	0	0	0	22
	IHL	Totals	379	201	239	440	1546	40	14	20	34	207
	AHL	Totals	174	61	117	168	622	25	19	8	27	150

Born; 5/12/67, Montreal, Quebec. 5-11, 200. Signed as a free agent by Detroit Red Wings (5/26/89). Traded to Hartford Whalers by Detroit for Chris Tancill (12/18/91). 1992-93 IHL First Team All-Star. Member of 1988-89 AHL champion Adirondack Red Wings.

Brian Shantz — Center

			Regular Season					Playoffs				
Season	Team	League	GP	G	A	PTS	PIM	GP	G	A	PTS	PIM
92-93	Erie	ECHL	38	14	26	40	44	5	2	3	4	23
93-94	Tulsa	CeHL	4	0	1	1	0	—	—	—	—	—
93-94	Erie	ECHL	54	25	43	68	58	—	—	—	—	—
94-95	San Antonio	CeHL	66	39	*80	*119	125	13	10	17	27	27
95-96	San Antonio	CeHL	64	54	*85	*139	90	12	3	11	14	22
96-97	San Antonio	IHL	26	2	9	11	21	—	—	—	—	—
96-97	Fort Wayne	IHL	18	2	5	7	4	—	—	—	—	—
96-97	Quad City	CoHL	9	1	13	14	2	—	—	—	—	—
	IHL	Totals	44	4	14	18	25	—	—	—	—	—
	CeHL	Totals	134	93	166	259	215	25	13	28	41	49
	ECHL	Totals	92	39	69	108	102	5	2	3	5	23

Born; 5/15/70, Edmonton, Alberta. 5-9, 180. 1995-96 CeHL MVP. 1995-96 CeHL First Team All-Star.

Vadim Sharifijanov — Right Wing

			Regular Season					Playoffs				
Season	Team	League	GP	G	A	PTS	PIM	GP	G	A	PTS	PIM
94-95	Albany	AHL	1	1	1	2	0	9	3	3	6	10
95-96	Albany	AHL	69	14	28	42	28	—	—	—	—	—
96-97	New Jersey	NHL	2	0	0	0	0	—	—	—	—	—
96-97	Albany	AHL	70	14	27	41	89	10	3	3	6	6
	AHL	Totals	140	29	56	85	117	19	6	6	12	16

Born; 12/23/75, Ufa, Russia. 5-11, 210. Drafted by New Jersey Devils (1st choice, 25th overall) in 1994 Entry Draft. Member of 1994-95 Calder Cup champion Alabany RiverRats.

Jeff Sharples — Defenseman

			Regular Season					Playoffs				
Season	Team	League	GP	G	A	PTS	PIM	GP	G	A	PTS	PIM
86-87	Detroit	NHL	3	0	1	1	2	2	0	0	0	2
87-88	Detroit	NHL	56	10	25	35	42	4	0	3	3	4
87-88	Adirondack	AHL	4	2	1	3	4	—	—	—	—	—
88-89	Detroit	NHL	46	4	9	13	26	1	0	0	0	0
88-89	Adirondack	AHL	10	0	4	4	8	—	—	—	—	—
89-90	Adirondack	AHL	9	2	5	7	6	—	—	—	—	—
89-90	Cape Breton	AHL	38	4	13	17	28	—	—	—	—	—
89-90	Utica	AHL	13	2	5	7	19	5	1	2	3	15
90-91	Utica	AHL	64	16	29	45	42	—	—	—	—	—
91-92	Capital District	AHL	31	3	12	15	18	7	6	5	11	4
92-93	Kansas City	IHL	39	5	21	26	43	8	0	0	0	6

Season	Team	League	GP	G	A	PTS	PIM	GP	G	A	PTS	PIM
93-94	Las Vegas	IHL	68	18	32	50	68	5	2	1	3	6
94-95	Las Vegas	IHL	72	20	33	53	63	10	4	4	8	16
95-96	Las Vegas	IHL	41	6	14	20	56	—	—	—	—	—
95-96	Utah	IHL	31	2	15	17	18	21	3	10	13	16
96-97	Utah	IHL	49	9	26	35	54	7	0	2	2	10
	NHL	Totals	105	14	35	49	70	7	0	3	3	6
	IHL	Totals	300	60	141	201	302	51	9	17	26	56
	AHL	Totals	169	29	69	98	125	12	7	7	14	19

Born; 7/28/67, Terrace, British Columbia. 6-1, 195. Drafted by Detroit Red Wings (2nd choice, 29th overall) in 1985 Entry Draft. Traded to Edmonton Oilers by Detroit with Petr Klima, Joe Murphy and Adam Graves for Jimmy Carson, Kevin McClelland and Edmonton's fifth round choice (later traded to Montreal-Montreal selected Brad Layzell) in 1991 Entry Draft (11/2/89). Traded to New Jersey Devils by Edmonton for Reijo Ruotsalainen (3/6/90). Member of 1995-96 IHL champion Utah Grizzlies.

Scott Shaunessy — Defenseman

			Regular Season					Playoffs				
Season	Team	League	GP	G	A	PTS	PIM	GP	G	A	PTS	PIM
86-87	Quebec	NHL	3	0	0	0	7	—	—	—	—	—
87-88	Fredericton	AHL	60	0	9	9	257	1	0	0	0	2
88-89	Quebec	NHL	4	0	0	0	16	—	—	—	—	—
88-89	Halifax	AHL	41	3	10	13	106	—	—	—	—	—
89-90	Halifax	AHL	27	3	5	8	105	—	—	—	—	—
89-90	Fort Wayne	IHL	45	3	9	12	267	5	0	1	1	31
90-91	Albany	IHL	34	3	9	12	126	—	—	—	—	—
90-91	Muskegon	IHL	23	1	4	5	104	5	0	0	0	21
91-92	Fort Wayne	IHL	53	3	8	11	243	7	0	1	1	27
92-93	Cincinnati	IHL	71	2	7	9	222	—	—	—	—	—
96-97	Austin	WPHL	32	3	4	7	138	6	3	0	3	22
	NHL	Totals	7	0	0	0	23	—	—	—	—	—
	IHL	Totals	226	12	37	49	962	17	0	2	2	79
	AHL	Totals	128	6	24	30	468	1	0	0	0	2

Born; 1/22/64, Newport, Rhode Island. 6-4, 220. Drafted by Quebec Nordiques (9th choice, 192nd overall) in 1983 Entry Draft.

Brad Shaw — Defenseman

			Regular Season					Playoffs				
Season	Team	League	GP	G	A	PTS	PIM	GP	G	A	PTS	PIM
84-85	Binghamton	AHL	24	1	10	11	4	8	1	8	9	6
84-85	Salt Lake City	IHL	44	3	29	32	25	—	—	—	—	—
85-86	Hartford	NHL	8	0	2	2	4	—	—	—	—	—
85-86	Binghamton	AHL	64	10	44	54	33	5	0	2	2	6
86-87	Hartford	NHL	2	0	0	0	0	—	—	—	—	—
86-87	Binghamton	AHL	77	9	30	39	43	12	1	8	9	2
87-88	Hartford	NHL	1	0	0	0	0	—	—	—	—	—
87-88	Binghamton	AHL	73	12	50	62	50	4	0	5	5	4
88-89	Hartford	NHL	3	1	0	1	0	3	1	0	1	0
88-89	Canada	National										
89-90	Hartford	NHL	64	3	32	35	30	7	2	5	7	0
90-91	Hartford	NHL	72	4	28	32	29	6	1	2	3	2
91-92	Hartford	NHL	62	3	22	25	44	3	0	1	1	4
92-93	Ottawa	NHL	81	7	34	41	34	—	—	—	—	—
93-94	Ottawa	NHL	66	4	19	23	59	—	—	—	—	—
94-95	Ottawa	NHL	2	0	0	0	0	—	—	—	—	—
94-95	Atlanta	IHL	26	1	18	19	17	5	3	4	7	9
95-96	Detroit	IHL	79	7	54	61	46	8	2	3	5	8
96-97	Detroit	IHL	59	6	32	38	30	21	2	9	11	10
	NHL	Totals	361	22	137	159	200	19	4	8	12	6
	AHL	Totals	238	32	134	166	130	29	2	23	25	18
	IHL	Totals	208	17	133	150	118	34	7	16	23	27

Born; 4/28/64, Mississauga, Ontario. 6-0, 190. Drafted by Detroit Red Wings (5th choice, 86th overall) in 1982 Entry Draft. Rigths traded to Hartford Whalers by Detroit for Hartford's eighth round choice (Urban Nordin) in 1984 Entry Draft (5/29/84). Traded to New Jersey Devils by Hartford for cash (6/13/92). Claimed by Ottawa Senators from New Jersey in Expansion Draft (6/18/92). 1986-87 AHL First Team All-Star. 1987-88 AHL First Team All-Star. 1986-87 AHL Best Defenseman (Eddie Shore Plaque). 1996-97 IHL First Team All-Star. Member of 1996-97 IHL Champion Detroit Vipers.

Rob Shearer — Center

Season	Team	League	GP	G	A	PTS	PIM	GP	G	A	PTS	PIM
96-97	Hershey	AHL	78	12	16	28	88	23	0	4	4	9

Born; 10/19/76, Kitchener, Ontario. 5-10, 190. Member of 1996-97 AHL Champion Hershey Bears. Last amateur club; Windsor (OHL).

Ken Shepard — Goaltender

Season	Team	League	GP	W	L	T	MIN	SO	GAVG	GP	W	L	MIN	SO	GAVG
95-96	Binghamton	AHL	14	6	4	2	726	1	3.14	1	0	0	38	0	3.13
95-96	Charlotte	ECHL	17	10	4	1	952	0	3.15	8	6	1	374	0	2.89
96-97	Binghamton	AHL	14	3	7	2	747	0	3.78	—	—	—	—	—	—
96-97	Charlotte	ECHL	21	7	11	1	1185	0	4.45	—	—	—	—	—	—
	AHL	Totals	28	9	11	4	1473	1	3.46	1	0	0	38	0	3.13
	ECHL	Totals	38	17	15	2	2137	0	3.87	8	6	1	374	0	2.89

Born; 1/20/74, Toronto, Ontario. 5-10, 192. Drafted by New York Rangers (10th choice, 216th overall) in 1993 Entry Draft. Member of 1995-96 ECHL champion Charlotte Checkers.

Andrew Sherman — Right Wing

Season	Team	League	GP	G	A	PTS	PIM	GP	G	A	PTS	PIM
95-96	Lakeland	SHL	59	16	31	47	125	5	3	2	5	11
96-97	Columbus	CoHL	30	4	10	14	103	—	—	—	—	—

Born; 11/8/70, Schenectady, New York. 6-2, 200.

Dan Shermerhorn — Center

Season	Team	League	GP	G	A	PTS	PIM	GP	G	A	PTS	PIM
96-97	Hampton Roads	ECHL	12	2	5	7	6	9	2	2	4	6

Born; 7/15/73, Calgary, Alberta. 5-11, 200.

Todd Sheshtok — Goaltender

Season	Team	League	GP	W	L	T	MIN	SO	GAVG	GP	W	L	MIN	SO	GAVG
96-97	Fresno	WCHL	18	12	2	0	935	1	3.59	2	0	0	12	0	5.16

Born; 8/28/74, Westford, Massachusetts. 5-10, 165.

Jeff Shevalier — Left Wing

Season	Team	League	GP	G	A	PTS	PIM	GP	G	A	PTS	PIM
94-95	Los Angeles	NHL	1	1	0	1	0	—	—	—	—	—
94-95	Phoenix	IHL	68	31	39	70	44	9	5	4	9	0
95-96	Phoenix	IHL	79	29	38	67	72	4	2	2	4	2
96-97	Los Angeles	NHL	26	4	9	13	6	—	—	—	—	—
96-97	Phoenix	IHL	46	16	21	37	26	—	—	—	—	—
	NHL	Totals	27	5	9	14	6	—	—	—	—	—
	IHL	Totals	147	60	77	137	116	13	7	6	13	2

Born; 3/14/74, Mississauga, Ontario. 5-11, 185. Drafted by Los Angeles Kings (4th choice, 111th overall) in 1992 Entry Draft.

Jordan Shields — Left Wing

			Regular Season					Playoffs				
Season	Team	League	GP	G	A	PTS	PIM	GP	G	A	PTS	PIM
96-97	Dayton	ECHL	45	18	21	39	8	—	—	—	—	—

Born; 4/27/72, Gloucester, Ontario. 5-10, 180.

Steve Shields — Goaltender

			Regular Season							Playoffs					
Season	Team	League	GP	W	L	T	MIN	SO	GAVG	GP	W	L	MIN	SO	GAVG
94-95	Rochester	AHL	13	3	8	0	673	0	4.72	1	0	0	20	0	9.00
94-95	South Carolina	ECHL	21	11	5	2	1157	2	2.69	3	0	2	144	0	4.58
95-96	Buffalo	NHL	2	1	0	0	75	0	3.20	—	—	—	—	—	—
95-96	Rochester	AHL	43	20	17	2	2356	1	3.56	*19	*15	3	*1126	0	2.50
96-97	Buffalo	NHL	13	3	8	2	789	0	2.97	10	4	6	570	1	2.74
96-97	Rochester	AHL	23	14	6	2	1331	1	2.70	—	—	—	—	—	—
	NHL	Totals	15	4	8	2	864	0	2.99	10	4	6	570	1	2.74
	AHL	Totals	79	37	31	4	4260	2	3.56	20	15	3	1146	0	2.62

Born; 7/19/72, Toronto, Ontario. 6-3, 210. Drafted by Buffalo Sabres (5th choice, 101st overall) in 1991 Entry Draft. Member of 1995-96 AHL champion Rochester Americans.

Andrew Shier — Right Wing

			Regular Season					Playoffs				
Season	Team	League	GP	G	A	PTS	PIM	GP	G	A	PTS	PIM
94-95	Richmond	ECHL	64	28	37	65	126	17	8	19	27	33
95-96	Milwaukee	IHL	39	2	1	3	8	—	—	—	—	—
95-96	Madison	CoHL	2	2	2	4	0	—	—	—	—	—
95-96	Richmond	ECHL	4	3	1	4	6	7	7	7	14	2
96-97	Baltimore	AHL	3	1	0	1	0	—	—	—	—	—
96-97	Richmond	ECHL	52	29	39	68	127	8	7	6	13	28
	ECHL	Totals	120	60	77	137	259	32	22	32	54	63

Born; 8/15/71, Lansing, Michigan. 5-11, 165. Member of 1994-95 ECHL champion Richmond Renegades.

Dean Shmyr — Right Wing

			Regular Season					Playoffs				
Season	Team	League	GP	G	A	PTS	PIM	GP	G	A	PTS	PIM
92-93	Dallas	CeHL	57	5	18	23	163	7	0	1	1	12
93-94	Dallas	CeHL	50	2	12	14	96	7	0	3	3	35
94-95	San Antonio	CeHL	60	3	29	32	225	12	0	1	1	30
95-96	Quad City	CoHL	72	3	20	23	195	4	0	3	3	6
96-97	Utah	IHL	9	0	0	0	31	—	—	—	—	—
96-97	New Mexico	WPHL	44	7	6	13	240	1	0	0	0	0
	CeHL	Totals	167	10	59	69	484	26	0	5	5	77

Born; 4/29/71, Vancouver, British Columbia. 6-0, 170.

Jason Shmyr — Left Wing

			Regular Season					Playoffs				
Season	Team	League	GP	G	A	PTS	PIM	GP	G	A	PTS	PIM
96-97	Pensacola	ECHL	1	0	0	0	2	—	—	—	—	—
96-97	Anchorage	WCHL	51	8	12	20	388	9	1	1	2	50

Born; 7/27/75, Fairview, Alberta. 6-4, 215.

Bruce Shoebottom — Defenseman

			Regular Season					Playoffs				
Season	Team	League	GP	G	A	PTS	PIM	GP	G	A	PTS	PIM
85-86	New Haven	AHL	6	2	0	2	12	—	—	—	—	—
85-86	Binghamton	AHL	62	7	5	12	249	—	—	—	—	—

Season	Team	League	GP	G	A	PTS	PIM	GP	G	A	PTS	PIM
86-87	Fort Wayne	IHL	75	2	10	12	309	10	0	0	0	31
87-88	Boston	NHL	3	0	1	1	0	4	1	0	1	42
87-88	Maine	AHL	70	2	12	14	138	—	—	—	—	—
88-89	Boston	NHL	29	1	3	4	44	10	0	2	2	35
88-89	Maine	AHL	44	0	8	8	265	—	—	—	—	—
89-90	Boston	NHL	2	0	0	0	4	—	—	—	—	—
89-90	Maine	AHL	66	3	11	14	228	—	—	—	—	—
90-91	Boston	NHL	1	0	0	0	5	—	—	—	—	—
90-91	Maine	AHL	71	2	8	10	238	1	0	0	0	14
91-92	Peoria	IHL	79	4	12	16	234	10	0	0	0	33
92-93	Rochester	AHL	65	7	5	12	253	14	0	0	0	19
93-94	Oklahoma City	CeHL	43	4	11	15	236	1	0	0	0	14
94-95	Rochester	AHL	1	0	0	0	0	—	—	—	—	—
95-96	San Diego	WCHL	22	1	7	8	102	9	0	2	2	17
96-97	San Diego	WCHL	38	6	6	12	288	2	0	0	0	24
	NHL	Totals	35	1	4	5	53	14	1	2	3	77
	AHL	Totals	385	23	49	72	1383	15	0	0	0	33
	IHL	Totals	154	6	22	28	543	20	0	0	0	64
	WCHL	Totals	60	7	13	20	390	11	0	2	2	41

Born; 8/20/65, Windsor, Ontario. 6-3, 215. Drafted by Los Angeles Kings (1st choice, 47th overall) in 1983 Entry Draft. Traded to Washington Capitals by Los Angeles for Bryan Erickson (10/31/85). Signed as a free agent by Boston Bruins (7/20/87). Member of 1995-96 WCHL champion San Diego Gulls. Member of 1996-97 WCHL Champion San Diego Gulls.

Terry Shook — Defenseman

			Regular Season					Playoffs				
Season	Team	League	GP	G	A	PTS	PIM	GP	G	A	PTS	PIM
84-85	Erie	ACHL	54	3	31	34	67	12	1	2	3	18
85-86	Erie	ACHL	60	3	41	44	194	10	0	3	3	40
95-96	Detroit	CoHL	29	1	7	8	92	3	0	1	1	20
96-97	Saginaw	CoHL	38	2	5	7	46	—	—	—	—	—
	ACHL	Totals	114	6	72	78	261	22	1	5	6	58
	CoHL	Totals	67	3	12	15	138	3	0	1	1	20

Born; 3/15/64, Grosse Pointe, Michigan. 6-2, 198.

Gary Shuchuk — Center

			Regular Season					Playoffs				
Season	Team	League	GP	G	A	PTS	PIM	GP	G	A	PTS	PIM
90-91	Detroit	NHL	6	1	2	3	6	3	0	0	0	0
90-91	Adirondack	AHL	59	23	24	47	32	—	—	—	—	—
91-92	Adirondack	AHL	79	32	48	80	48	19	4	9	13	18
92-93	Adirondack	AHL	47	24	53	77	66	—	—	—	—	—
92-93	Los Angeles	NHL	25	2	4	6	16	17	2	2	4	12
93-94	Los Angeles	NHL	56	3	4	7	30	—	—	—	—	—
94-95	Los Angeles	NHL	22	3	6	9	6	—	—	—	—	—
94-95	Phoenix	IHL	13	8	7	15	12	—	—	—	—	—
95-96	Los Angeles	NHL	33	4	10	14	12	—	—	—	—	—
95-96	Phoenix	IHL	33	8	21	29	76	4	1	0	1	4
96-97	Houston	IHL	55	18	23	41	48	13	5	2	7	18
	NHL	Totals	142	13	26	39	70	20	2	2	4	12
	AHL	Totals	185	79	125	204	146	19	4	9	13	18
	IHL	Totals	101	34	51	85	136	17	6	2	8	22

Born; 2/17/67, Edmonton, Alberta. 5-10, 190. Drafted by Detroit Red Wings (1st choice, 22nd overall) in 1988 Supplemental Draft. Traded to Los Angeles Kings by Detroit with Jimmy Carson and Marc Potvin for Paul Coffey, Sylvain Couturier and Jim Hiller (1/29/93). Member of 1991-92 AHL champion Adirondack Red Wings.

Rich Shulmistra — Goaltender

Season	Team	League	GP	W	L	T	MIN	SO	GAVG	GP	W	L	MIN	SO	GAVG
94-95	Cornwall	AHL	20	4	9	2	937	0	3.71	8	4	3	446	0	2.95
95-96	Cornwall	AHL	36	9	18	2	1844	0	3.25	1	0	0	8	0	6.75
96-97	Albany	AHL	23	5	9	2	1062	2	2.43	2	1	0	77	0	1.56
	AHL	Totals	79	18	36	6	3843	2	3.14	11	5	3	531	0	2.82

Regular Season / Playoffs

Born; 4/1/71, Sudbury, Ontario. 6-2, 186. Drafted by Quebec Nordiques (1st choice, 4th overall) in 1992 Supplemental Draft.

David Shute — Left Wing

Season	Team	League	GP	G	A	PTS	PIM	GP	G	A	PTS	PIM
91-92	Muskegon	IHL	7	1	2	3	6	—	—	—	—	—
91-92	Knoxville	ECHL	57	18	35	53	91	—	—	—	—	—
92-93	Chatham	CoHL	15	4	9	13	10	—	—	—	—	—
93-94	Raleigh	ECHL	27	10	13	23	21	—	—	—	—	—
93-94	Hampton Roads	ECHL	8	2	4	6	6	5	0	2	2	2
94-95	San Antonio	CeHL	53	22	31	53	68	13	11	5	16	12
95-96	San Antonio	CeHL	17	7	6	13	41	—	—	—	—	—
95-96	Wichita	CeHL	46	42	27	69	42	—	—	—	—	—
96-97	Waco	WPHL	5	3	0	3	2	—	—	—	—	—
96-97	Wichita	CeHL	16	8	2	10	29	—	—	—	—	—
96-97	Oklahoma City	CeHL	32	15	15	30	51	—	—	—	—	—
	CeHL	Totals	164	94	81	175	251	13	11	5	16	12
	ECHL	Totals	92	30	52	82	118	5	0	2	2	2

Born; 2/10/71, Carlyle, Pennsylvania. 6-0. 190. Drafted by Pittsburgh Penguins (9th choice, 163rd overall) in 1989 Entry Draft. Traded to Wichita Thunder by San Antonio Iguanas for Rob Weingartner. 1995-96 CeHL First Team All-Star.

Derek Shybunka — Goaltender

Season	Team	League	GP	W	L	T	MIN	SO	GAVG	GP	W	L	MIN	SO	GAVG
96-97	Tulsa	CeHL	45	17	*20	3	2451	0	4.23	1	0	0	7	0	0.00

Born; 9/25/70, Edmonton, Alberta. 5-9, 175.

Peter Sidorkiewicz — Goaltender

Season	Team	League	GP	W	L	T	MIN	SO	AVG	GP	W	L	MIN	SO	AVG
84-85	Binghamton	AHL	45	31	9	5	2691	3	3.05	8	4	4	481	0	3.87
84-85	Fort Wayne	IHL	10	4	4	2	590	0	4.37	—	—	—	—	—	—
85-86	Binghamton	AHL	49	21	22	3	2819	2	*3.19	4	1	3	235	0	3.06
86-87	Binghamton	AHL	57	23	16	0	3304	4	2.92	13	6	7	794	0	*2.72
87-88	Hartford	NHL	1	0	1	0	60	0	6.00	—	—	—	—	—	—
87-88	Binghamton	AHL	42	19	17	3	2345	0	3.68	3	0	2	147	0	3.27
88-89	Hartford	NHL	44	22	18	4	2635	4	3.03	2	0	2	124	0	3.87
89-90	Hartford	NHL	46	19	19	7	2703	1	3.57	7	3	4	429	0	3.22
90-91	Hartford	NHL	52	21	22	7	2953	1	3.33	6	2	4	359	0	4.01
91-92	Hartford	NHL	35	9	19	6	1995	2	3.34	—	—	—	—	—	—
92-93	Ottawa	NHL	64	8	46	3	3388	0	4.43	—	—	—	—	—	—
93-94	New Jersey	NHL	3	0	3	0	130	0	2.77	—	—	—	—	—	—
93-94	Albany	AHL	15	6	7	2	907	0	3.97	—	—	—	—	—	—
93-94	Fort Wayne	IHL	11	6	3	0	591	*2	2.74	*18	10	8	*1054	*1	3.36
94-95	Fort Wayne	IHL	16	8	6	1	941	1	3.70	3	1	2	144	0	5.00
95-96	Albany	AHL	32	19	7	5	1809	3	2.95	1	0	1	58	0	3.06
96-97	Albany	AHL	62	31	23	6	3539	2	2.90	16	7	8	920	0	3.13
	NHL	Totals	245	79	128	27	13864	8	3.60	15	5	10	912	0	3.62
	AHL	Totals	302	150	101	24	17414	14	3.14	45	18	25	2635	0	3.14
	IHL	Totals	37	18	13	3	2122	3	3.62	21	11	10	1198	1	3.56

Born; 6/29/63, Dabrowa Bialostocka, Poland. 5-9, 180. Drafted by Washington Capitals (5th choice, 91st overall) in 1981 Entry Draft. Traded to Hartford Whalers by Washington with Dean Evason for David Jensen (3/12/85). Claimed by Ottawa Senators from Hartford in Expansion Draft (6/18/92). Traded to New Jersey Devils with future considerations (Mike Peluso 6/26/93) for Craig Billington, Troy Mallette and New Jersey's fourth round choice (Cosmo DuPaul) in 1993 Entry Draft (6/20/93). 1987 AHL Second Team All-Star.

Marc Siegel — Goaltender

			Regular Season							Playoffs				
Season	Team	League	GP	W	L	T	MIN	SO	AVG	GP	W	L	MIN	SO	AVG
96-97	Johnstown	ECHL	10	0	6	0	440	0	5.31	—	—	—	—	—	—
96-97	Toledo	ECHL	8	4	3	1	462	0	4.16	—	—	—	—	—	—
	ECHL	Totals	18	4	9	1	902	0	4.72	—	—	—	—	—	—

Born; 12/23/73, Pompano Beach, Florida. 6-2, 185.

Zdenik Sikl — Left Wing

			Regular Season					Playoffs				
Season	Team	League	GP	G	A	PTS	PIM	GP	G	A	PTS	PIM
96-97	Flint	CoHL	21	3	0	3	2	—	—	—	—	—
96-97	Utica	CoHL	1	0	0	0	0	—	—	—	—	—
96-97	Muskegon	CoHL	6	3	5	8	0	1	0	0	0	0
	CoHL	Totals	28	6	5	11	2	1	0	0	0	0

Born; 6/20/71, Most, Czechoslovakia. 6-0, 196.

Andy Silverman — Defenseman

			Regular Season					Playoffs				
Season	Team	League	GP	G	A	PTS	PIM	GP	G	A	PTS	PIM
94-95	Binghamton	AHL	5	0	1	1	2	—	—	—	—	—
94-95	Charlotte	ECHL	64	3	11	14	57	3	0	0	0	2
95-96	Binghamton	AHL	75	5	15	20	92	4	0	0	0	6
96-97	Binghamton	AHL	20	0	1	1	28	—	—	—	—	—
96-97	Baltimore	AHL	42	2	1	3	24	1	0	0	0	0
	AHL	Totals	142	7	18	25	146	5	0	0	0	6

Born; 8/23/72, Beverly, Massachusetts. 6-3, 210. Drafted by New York Rangers (11th choice, 181st overall) in 1990 Entry Draft.

Trevor Sim — Center

			Regular Season					Playoffs				
Season	Team	League	GP	G	A	PTS	PIM	GP	G	A	PTS	PIM
89-90	Edmonton	NHL	3	0	1	1	2	—	—	—	—	—
90-91	Cape Breton	AHL	62	20	9	29	39	2	0	0	0	0
91-92	Cape Breton	AHL	2	0	1	1	0	—	—	—	—	—
91-92	Wheeling	ECHL	53	25	29	54	110	5	7	2	9	4
92-93	N/A											
93-94	Milwaukee	IHL	32	7	13	20	10	4	1	0	1	0
94-95	Milwaukee	IHL	37	9	10	19	26	7	1	2	3	4
94-95	Syracuse	AHL	3	2	0	2	0	—	—	—	—	—
95-96	Milwaukee	IHL	7	0	0	0	0	—	—	—	—	—
95-96	Raleigh	ECHL	28	11	17	28	26	4	0	0	0	0
96-97	Orlando	IHL	58	9	21	30	32	2	0	1	1	0
	IHL	Totals	134	25	44	69	68	13	2	3	5	4
	AHL	Totals	67	22	10	32	39	2	0	0	0	0
	ECHL	Totals	81	36	46	82	136	9	7	2	9	4

Born; 6/9/70, Calgary, Alberta. 6-2, 192. Drafted by Edmonton Oilers (3rd choice, 53rd overall) in 1988 Entry Draft.

Martin Simard — Right Wing

			Regular Season					Playoffs				
Season	Team	League	GP	G	A	PTS	PIM	GP	G	A	PTS	PIM
87-88	Salt Lake City	IHL	82	8	23	31	281	19	6	3	9	100
88-89	Salt Lake City	IHL	71	13	15	28	221	14	4	0	4	45
89-90	Salt Lake City	IHL	59	22	23	45	151	11	5	8	13	10

Season	Team	League	GP	G	A	PTS	PIM	GP	G	A	PTS	PIM
90-91	Calgary	NHL	16	0	2	2	53	—	—	—	—	—
90-91	Salt Lake City	IHL	54	24	25	49	114	4	3	0	3	20
91-92	Calgary	NHL	21	1	3	4	119	—	—	—	—	—
91-92	Salt Lake City	IHL	11	3	7	10	51	—	—	—	—	—
91-92	Halifax	AHL	10	5	3	8	26	—	—	—	—	—
92-93	Tampa Bay	NHL	7	0	0	0	11	—	—	—	—	—
92-93	Atlanta	IHL	19	5	5	10	77	—	—	—	—	—
92-93	Halifax	AHL	13	3	4	7	17	—	—	—	—	—
93-94	Cornwall	AHL	57	10	10	20	152	7	3	1	4	7
94-95	Milwaukee	IHL	57	7	5	12	100	5	0	0	0	2
95-96	Providence	AHL	78	26	27	53	184	4	1	1	2	6
96-97	Providence	AHL	69	13	25	38	137	9	1	0	1	10
	NHL	Totals	44	1	5	6	183	—	—	—	—	—
	IHL	Totals	353	82	103	185	994	53	18	11	29	177
	AHL	Totals	227	57	69	126	516	20	5	2	7	23

Born; 6/25/66, Montreal, Quebec. 6-3, 215. Signed as a free agent by Calgary Flames (5/19/87). Traded to Quebec Nordiques by Calgary for Greg Smyth (3/10/92). Traded to Tampa Bay Lightning by Quebec to complete an earlier deal which sent Tim Hunter to Quebec (6/22/92). Traded to Quebec by Tampa Bay with Michel Mongeau and Steve Tuttle for Herb Raglan (2/12/93). Signed as a free agent by Phoenix Coyotes (7/97).

Darcy Simon — Defenseman

			Regular Season					Playoffs				
Season	Team	League	GP	G	A	PTS	PIM	GP	G	A	PTS	PIM
90-91	Fredericton	AHL	29	0	3	3	18	9	2	0	2	45
91-92	Fredericton	AHL	58	9	11	20	308	4	0	0	0	13
92-93	Fredericton	AHL	57	2	7	9	257	2	0	0	0	6
92-93	Wheeling	ECHL	3	0	1	1	26	—	—	—	—	—
93-94	Prince Edward Island	AHL	45	1	5	6	263	—	—	—	—	—
94-95	Prince Edward Island	AHL	65	4	10	14	220	11	1	4	5	38
95-96	Prince Edward Island	AHL	79	3	13	16	314	2	0	0	0	2
96-97	Grand Rapids	IHL	71	4	12	16	327	5	1	2	3	35
	AHL	Totals	333	19	49	68	1380	28	3	4	7	104

Born; 1/21/70, North Battleford, Saskatchewan. 6-1, 200. Signed as a free agent by Montreal Canadiens (10/3/90).

Jason Simon — Left Wing

			Regular Season					Playoffs				
Season	Team	League	GP	G	A	PTS	PIM	GP	G	A	PTS	PIM
89-90	Utica	AHL	16	3	4	7	28	2	0	0	0	12
89-90	Nashville	ECHL	13	4	3	7	81	5	1	3	4	17
90-91	Utica	AHL	50	2	12	14	189	—	—	—	—	—
90-91	Johnstown	ECHL	22	11	9	20	55	—	—	—	—	—
91-92	Utica	AHL	1	0	0	0	12	—	—	—	—	—
91-92	San Diego	IHL	13	1	4	5	45	3	0	1	1	9
91-92	Flint	CoHL	33	9	33	42	261	—	—	—	—	—
92-93	Detroit	CoHL	11	7	13	20	38	—	—	—	—	—
92-93	Flint	CoHL	44	17	32	49	202	—	—	—	—	—
93-94	Islanders	NHL	4	0	0	0	34	—	—	—	—	—
93-94	Salt Lake City	IHL	50	7	7	14	*323	—	—	—	—	—
93-94	Detroit	CoHL	13	9	16	25	87	—	—	—	—	—
94-95	Denver	IHL	61	3	6	9	300	1	0	0	0	12
95-96	Springfield	AHL	18	2	2	4	90	7	1	0	1	26
96-97	Phoenix	NHL	1	0	0	0	0	—	—	—	—	—
96-97	Las Vegas	IHL	64	4	3	7	402	3	0	0	0	0
	NHL	Totals	5	0	0	0	34	—	—	—	—	—
	IHL	Totals	188	15	20	35	1070	7	0	1	1	21
	AHL	Totals	85	7	18	25	319	9	1	0	1	38
	CoHL	Totals	101	42	94	136	588	—	—	—	—	—
	ECHL	Totals	35	15	12	27	136	5	1	3	4	17

Born; 3/21/69, Sarnia Reserve, Ontario. 6-1, 210. Drafted by New Jersey Devils (9th choice, 215th overall) in 1989 Entry Draft. Signed as a free agent by New York Islanders (1/6/94). Signed as a free agent by Winnipeg Jets (8/9/95). Member of 1994-95 IHL champion Denver Grizzlies.

Todd Simon — Center

			Regular Season					Playoffs				
Season	Team	League	GP	G	A	PTS	PIM	GP	G	A	PTS	PIM
92-93	Rochester	AHL	67	27	66	93	54	12	3	14	17	15
93-94	Buffalo	NHL	15	0	1	1	0	5	1	0	1	0
93-94	Rochester	AHL	55	33	52	85	79	—	—	—	—	—
94-95	Rochester	AHL	69	25	65	90	78	5	0	2	2	21
95-96	Las Vegas	IHL	52	26	48	74	48	—	—	—	—	—
95-96	Detroit	IHL	29	19	16	35	20	12	2	12	14	6
96-97	Detroit	IHL	80	21	51	72	46	18	4	6	10	12
	AHL	Totals	191	85	183	268	211	17	3	16	19	36
	IHL	Totals	161	66	115	181	114	30	6	18	24	18

Born; 4/21/72, Toronto, Ontario. 5-10, 187. Drafted by Buffalo Sabres (9th choice, 203rd overall) in 1992 Entry Draft. 1995-96 IHL First Team All-Star. Member of 1996-97 IHL Champion Detroit Vipers.

Steve Simoni — Right Wing

			Regular Season					Playoffs				
Season	Team	League	GP	G	A	PTS	PIM	GP	G	A	PTS	PIM
92-93	Oklahoma City	CeHL	56	33	28	61	35	11	4	5	9	12
93-94	Oklahoma City	CeHL	63	34	27	61	53	7	1	4	5	4
94-95	Oklahoma City	CeHL	57	23	18	41	80	5	0	2	2	2
95-96	Oklahoma City	CeHL	64	39	26	65	106	13	5	2	7	25
96-97	Houston	IHL	18	3	3	6	14	—	—	—	—	—
96-97	Oklahoma City	CeHL	41	20	13	33	96	4	0	0	0	16
	CeHL	Totals	281	149	112	261	423	40	10	13	23	59

Born; 1/25/67, Haileybury, Ontario. 6-2, 225. Member of 1995-96 CeHL champion Oklahoma City Blazers.

Darren Sinclair — Left Wing

			Regular Season					Playoffs				
Season	Team	League	GP	G	A	PTS	PIM	GP	G	A	PTS	PIM
96-97	Syracuse	AHL	68	12	16	28	32	3	0	2	2	0

Born; 11/24/76, Brooks, Alberta. 6-0, 200. Last amateur club; Spokane (WHL).

Jeff Sirkka — Defenseman

			Regular Season					Playoffs				
Season	Team	League	GP	G	A	PTS	PIM	GP	G	A	PTS	PIM
89-90	Maine	AHL	56	0	9	9	110	—	—	—	—	—
89-90	Binghamton	AHL	16	0	1	1	38	—	—	—	—	—
90-91	Indianapolis	IHL	69	6	12	18	203	6	0	0	0	6
91-92	Indianapolis	IHL	71	3	17	20	146	—	—	—	—	—
92-93	Rochester	AHL	59	6	11	17	132	3	0	0	0	7
93-94	Portland	AHL	76	6	18	24	113	15	2	6	8	47
94-95	Denver	IHL	58	4	18	22	86	5	0	1	1	19
95-96	Orlando	IHL	47	2	15	17	122	—	—	—	—	—
95-96	Kansas City	IHL	25	1	2	3	41	4	0	0	0	10
96-97	Kansas City	IHL	5	0	0	0	9	—	—	—	—	—
96-97	Long Beach	IHL	45	3	3	6	44	—	—	—	—	—
96-97	Utah	IHL	6	0	0	0	12	1	0	1	1	0
	IHL	Totals	326	19	67	86	663	16	0	2	2	35
	AHL	Totals	207	12	39	51	393	18	2	6	8	54

Born; 6/17/68, Sudbury, Ontario. 6-0, 193. Signed as a free agent by Boston Bruins (9/89). Traded to Hartford Whalers by Boston for Steve Dykstra (3/3/90). Signed as a free agent by Chicago Blackhawks (9/90). Member of 1993-94 AHL champion Portland Pirates. Member of 1994-95 IHL champion Denver Grizzlies.

Alain Sirois — Center

			Regular Season					Playoffs				
Season	Team	League	GP	G	A	PTS	PIM	GP	G	A	PTS	PIM
95-96	Worcester	AHL	2	1	0	1	0	—	—	—	—	—
96-97	Worcester	AHL	2	0	0	0	0	—	—	—	—	—
96-97	Baton Rouge	ECHL	62	29	29	58	64	—	—	—	—	—
	AHL	Totals	4	1	0	1	0	—	—	—	—	—

Born; 2/19/75, Riviere du Loup, Quebec. 6-0, 195. Last amateur club; Rimouski (QMJHL).

Ryan Sittler — Left Wing

			Regular Season					Playoffs				
Season	Team	League	GP	G	A	PTS	PIM	GP	G	A	PTS	PIM
94-95	Hershey	AHL	42	2	7	9	48	—	—	—	—	—
94-95	Johnstown	ECHL	1	1	1	2	0	—	—	—	—	—
95-96	Hershey	AHL	7	0	1	1	6	—	—	—	—	—
95-96	St. John's	AHL	6	1	2	3	18	4	0	0	0	4
95-96	Raleigh	ECHL	12	2	8	10	8	—	—	—	—	—
95-96	Mobile	ECHL	21	3	11	14	30	—	—	—	—	—
96-97	Baltimore	AHL	66	4	22	26	167	3	1	0	1	0
	AHL	Totals	121	7	32	39	239	7	1	0	1	4
	ECHL	Totals	34	6	20	26	38	—	—	—	—	—

Born; 1/28/74, London, Ontario. 6-2, 195. Drafted by Philadelphia Flyers (1st choice, 7th overall) in 1992 Entry Draft.

Chris Sittlow — Forward

			Regular Season					Playoffs				
Season	Team	League	GP	G	A	PTS	PIM	GP	G	A	PTS	PIM
96-97	Bakersfield	WCHL	37	11	16	27	25	—	—	—	—	—

Born; 2/16/71, Baldwin, Wisconsin. 5-10, 180.

Grant Sjerven — Goaltender

			Regular Season							Playoffs					
Season	Team	League	GP	W	L	T	MIN	SO	GAVG	GP	W	L	MIN	SO	GAVG
94-95	Chicago	IHL	7	0	3	1	252	0	4.29	—	—	—	—	—	—
94-95	Richmond	ECHL	26	17	6	2	1438	1	3.01	—	—	—	—	—	—
95-96	Houston	IHL	12	4	6	1	628	0	3.63	—	—	—	—	—	—
95-96	Richmond	ECHL	22	15	2	4	1292	0	*2.65	5	2	3	328	0	4.40
96-97	Richmond	ECHL	33	19	9	3	1854	0	3.40	7	3	4	419	0	3.87
	IHL	Totals	19	4	9	2	880	0	3.82	—	—	—	—	—	—
	ECHL	Totals	81	51	17	9	4584	1	3.06	12	5	7	747	0	4.10

Born; 3/13/70, Brandon, Manitoba. 6-0, 195.

Jarrod Skalde — Center

			Regular Season					Playoffs				
Season	Team	League	GP	G	A	PTS	PIM	GP	G	A	PTS	PIM
90-91	New Jersey	NHL	1	0	1	1	0	—	—	—	—	—
90-91	Utica	AHL	3	3	2	5	0	—	—	—	—	—
91-92	New Jersey	NHL	15	2	4	6	4	—	—	—	—	—
91-92	Utica	AHL	62	20	20	40	56	4	3	1	4	8
92-93	New Jersey	NHL	11	0	2	2	4	—	—	—	—	—
92-93	Utica	AHL	59	21	39	60	76	5	0	2	2	19
92-93	Cincinnati	IHL	4	1	2	3	4	—	—	—	—	—
93-94	Anaheim	NHL	20	5	4	9	10	—	—	—	—	—
93-94	San Diego	IHL	57	25	38	63	73	9	3	12	15	10
94-95	Las Vegas	IHL	74	34	41	75	103	9	2	4	6	8
95-96	Calgary	NHL	1	0	0	0	0	—	—	—	—	—
95-96	Baltimore	AHL	11	2	6	8	55	—	—	—	—	—
95-96	Saint John	AHL	68	27	40	67	98	16	4	9	13	6

Season	Team	League	GP	G	A	PTS	PIM	GP	G	A	PTS	PIM
96-97	Saint John	AHL	65	32	36	68	94	3	0	0	0	14
	NHL	Totals	48	7	11	18	18	—	—	—	—	—
	AHL	Totals	268	105	143	248	379	28	7	12	19	47
	IHL	Totals	135	60	81	141	180	18	5	16	21	18

Born; 2/26/71, Niagara Falls, Ontario. 6-0, 180. Drafted by New Jersey Devils (3rd choice, 26th overall) in 1989 Entry Draft. Claimed by Anaheim Mighty Ducks from New Jersey in Expansion Draft (6/24/93). Signed as a free agent by Anaheim (5/31/95). Traded to Calgary Flames by Anaheim for Bobby Marshall (10/30/95). Signed as a free agent by San Jose Sharks (8/97).

Ray Skinner — Center

Season	Team	League	GP	G	A	PTS	PIM	GP	G	A	PTS	PIM
96-97	Thunder Bay	CoHL	30	2	6	8	61	8	0	0	0	23

Born;

Zdenek Skorepa — Left Wing

Season	Team	League	GP	G	A	PTS	PIM	GP	G	A	PTS	PIM
96-97	Albany	AHL	60	12	12	24	38	13	3	2	5	14

Born; 8/10/76, Duchcov, Czechoslovakia. 6-0, 185. Drafted by New Jersey Devils (4th choice, 103rd overall) in 1994 Entry Draft.

Peter Skudra — Goaltender

Season	Team	League	GP	W	L	T	MIN	SO	GAVG	GP	W	L	MIN	SO	GAVG
94-95	Memphis	CeHL	2	0	1	0	80	0	6.00	—	—	—	—	—	—
94-95	Greensboro	ECHL	33	13	9	5	1613	0	4.20	6	2	3	342	0	4.92
95-96	Erie	ECHL	12	3	8	1	681	0	4.14	—	—	—	—	—	—
95-96	Johnstown	ECHL	30	12	11	4	1657	0	3.55	—	—	—	—	—	—
96-97	Hamilton	AHL	32	8	16	2	1616	0	3.75	—	—	—	—	—	—
96-97	Johnstown	ECHL	4	2	1	1	200	0	3.30	—	—	—	—	—	—
	ECHL	Totals	79	30	29	11	4151	0	3.89	6	2	3	342	0	4.92

Born; 4/24/73, Riga, Latvia. 6-1, 177.

John Slaney — Defenseman

Season	Team	League	GP	G	A	PTS	PIM	GP	G	A	PTS	PIM
91-92	Baltimore	AHL	6	2	4	6	0	—	—	—	—	—
92-93	Baltimore	AHL	79	20	46	66	60	7	0	7	7	8
93-94	Washington	NHL	47	7	9	16	27	11	1	1	2	2
93-94	Portland	AHL	29	14	13	27	17	—	—	—	—	—
94-95	Washington	NHL	16	0	3	3	6	—	—	—	—	—
94-95	Portland	AHL	8	3	10	13	4	7	1	3	4	4
95-96	Colorado	NHL	7	0	3	3	4	—	—	—	—	—
95-96	Cornwall	AHL	5	0	4	4	2	—	—	—	—	—
95-96	Los Angeles	NHL	31	6	11	17	10	—	—	—	—	—
96-97	Los Angeles	NHL	32	3	11	14	4	—	—	—	—	—
96-97	Phoenix	IHL	35	9	25	34	8	—	—	—	—	—
	NHL	Totals	133	16	37	53	51	11	1	1	2	2
	AHL	Totals	127	39	77	116	83	14	1	10	11	12

Born; 2/7/72, St. John's Newfoundland. 6-0, 185. Drafted by Washington Capitals (1st choice, 9th overall) in 1990 Entry Draft. Traded to Colorado Avalanche by Washington for Philadelphia's third round choice (previously acquired by Colorado—Washington selected Shawn McNeil) in 1996 Entry Draft, (7/12/95). Traded to Los Angeles Kings by Colorado for Winnipeg's sixth round choice (previosuly acquired by Los Angeles—Colorado selected Brian Willsie) in 1996 Entry Draft, (12/28/95). Signed as a free agent by Phoenix Coyotes (8/18/97).

Jan Slavik — Defenseman

Season	Team	League	GP	G	A	PTS	PIM	GP	G	A	PTS	PIM
96-97	Peoria	ECHL	29	1	3	4	25	1	0	0	0	4

Born;

Lukas Smital — Right Wing

Season	Team	League	GP	G	A	PTS	PIM	GP	G	A	PTS	PIM
96-97	Johnstown	ECHL	68	19	29	48	62	—	—	—	—	—

Born; 8/15/74, Brno, Czech Republic. 6-1, 200.

Adam Smith — Defenseman

Season	Team	League	GP	G	A	PTS	PIM	GP	G	A	PTS	PIM
96-97	Binghamton	AHL	56	0	8	8	59	2	0	0	0	0

Born; 5/24/76, Digby, Nova Scotia. 6-0, 190. Drafted by New York Rangers (3rd choice, 78th overall) in 1994 Entry Draft.

Brandon Smith — Defense

Season	Team	League	GP	G	A	PTS	PIM	GP	G	A	PTS	PIM
94-95	Adirondack	AHL	14	1	2	3	7	3	0	0	0	2
94-95	Minnesota	IHL	1	0	0	0	0	—	—	—	—	—
94-95	Dayton	ECHL	60	16	49	65	57	4	2	3	5	0
95-96	Adirondack	AHL	48	4	13	17	22	3	0	1	1	2
96-97	Adirondack	AHL	80	8	26	34	30	4	0	0	0	0
	AHL	Totals	142	13	41	54	59	10	0	1	1	4

Born; 2/25/73, Prince George, British Columbia. 6-0, 195. 1994-95 ECHL Defenseman of the Year. First Team ECHL All-Star 1994-95.

Chris Smith — Defenseman

Season	Team	League	GP	G	A	PTS	PIM	GP	G	A	PTS	PIM
96-97	Tulsa	CeHL	66	13	29	42	117	5	0	1	1	4

Born; 1/19/73, Hamburg, Michigan. 5-10, 190. Last amateur club; Michigan State (CCHA).

D.J. Smith — Defenseman

Season	Team	League	GP	G	A	PTS	PIM	GP	G	A	PTS	PIM
95-96	St. John's	AHL	1	0	0	0	0	—	—	—	—	—
96-97	Toronto	NHL	8	0	1	1	7	—	—	—	—	—
96-97	St. John's	AHL	—	—	—	—	—	1	0	0	0	0
	AHL	Totals	1	0	0	0	0	1	0	0	0	0

Born; 5/13/77, Windsor, Ontario. 6-1, 200. Drafted by New York Islanders (3rd choice, 41st overall) in 1995 Entry Draft. Traded to Toronto Maple Leafs by Islanders with Wendel Clark and Mathieu Schneider for Darby Hendrickson, Kenny Jonsson, Sean Haggerty and Toronto's first round choice (Roberto Luongo) in the 1997 Entry Draft (3/13/96).

Darin Smith — Left Wing

Season	Team	League	GP	G	A	PTS	PIM	GP	G	A	PTS	PIM
87-88	Peoria	IHL	81	21	23	44	144	7	1	2	3	16
88-89	Peoria	IHL	62	13	17	30	127	4	1	0	1	7
89-90	Peoria	IHL	76	16	13	29	147	5	1	0	1	2
90-91	Kansas City	IHL	78	22	38	60	161	—	—	—	—	—
91-92	Fort Wayne	IHL	61	11	22	33	165	5	0	2	2	8
92-93	St. Thomas	CoHL	57	*57	50	107	129	14	4	17	21	55
93-94	Fort Wayne	IHL	42	21	14	35	53	18	7	5	12	37
93-94	Brantford	CoHL	6	9	5	14	7	—	—	—	—	—
93-94	St. Thomas	CoHL	28	8	30	38	39	—	—	—	—	—
94-95	Fort Wayne	IHL	53	16	23	39	77	4	1	1	2	8
94-95	London	CoHL	24	14	21	35	38	—	—	—	—	—
95-96	Fort Wayne	IHL	63	16	15	31	105	—	—	—	—	—
95-96	Orlando	IHL	16	1	7	8	38	18	1	4	5	44

Season	Team	League	GP	G	A	PTS	PIM	GP	G	A	PTS	PIM
96-97	Grand Rapids	IHL	14	2	1	3	23	—	—	—	—	—
96-97	Las Vegas	IHL	59	13	17	30	74	3	0	0	0	2
	IHL	Totals	605	152	190	342	1114	64	12	14	26	124
	CoHL	Totals	115	88	106	194	213	14	4	17	21	55

Born; 2/20/67, St. Catharines, Ontario. 6-2, 205. Drafted by St. Louis Blues (4th choice, 75th overall) in 1987 Entry Draft. 1992-93 CoHL First Team All-Star.

Dan Smith — Defenseman

Season	Team	League	GP	G	A	PTS	PIM	GP	G	A	PTS	PIM
96-97	Hershey	AHL	8	0	1	1	6	15	0	1	1	25

Born; 5/2/76, Vernon, British Columbia. 5-11, 180. Drafted by Colorado Avalanche (7th choice, 181st overall) in 1995 Entry Draft. Member of 1996-97 AHL Champion Hershey Bears.

Dave Smith — Center

Season	Team	League	GP	G	A	PTS	PIM	GP	G	A	PTS	PIM
92-93	Dayton	ECHL	49	22	29	51	183	3	0	0	0	26
92-93	Fort Wayne	IHL	25	7	6	13	77	10	4	5	9	46
93-94	Fort Wayne	IHL	65	22	22	44	196	18	2	6	8	68
94-95	Binghamton	AHL	77	20	40	60	225	8	2	4	6	38
95-96	Detroit	IHL	24	6	9	15	81	—	—	—	—	—
95-96	Los Angeles	IHL	53	21	37	58	150	—	—	—	—	—
96-97	Long Beach	IHL	61	17	17	34	175	—	—	—	—	—
96-97	Orlando	IHL	15	4	3	7	54	10	2	3	5	53
	IHL	Totals	243	77	94	171	733	38	8	14	22	167

Born; 11/21/68, Arthur, Ontario. 6-0, 191.

Dennis Smith — Defenseman

Season	Team	League	GP	G	A	PTS	PIM	GP	G	A	PTS	PIM
84-85	Erie	ACHL	19	5	20	25	67	—	—	—	—	—
85-86	Peoria	IHL	70	5	15	20	102	10	0	2	2	18
86-87	Adirondack	AHL	64	4	24	28	120	6	0	0	0	8
87-88	Adirondack	AHL	75	6	24	30	213	11	2	2	4	47
88-89	Adirondack	AHL	75	5	35	40	176	17	1	6	7	47
89-90	Washington	NHL	4	0	0	0	0	—	—	—	—	—
89-90	Baltimore	AHL	74	8	25	33	103	12	0	3	3	65
90-91	Los Angeles	NHL	4	0	0	0	4	—	—	—	—	—
90-91	New Haven	AHL	61	7	25	32	148	—	—	—	—	—
91-92	Maine	AHL	59	2	32	34	63	—	—	—	—	—
91-92	Baltimore	AHL	17	1	4	5	23	—	—	—	—	—
92-93	N/A											
93-94	Providence	AHL	58	2	22	24	89	—	—	—	—	—
94-95	Detroit	IHL	8	2	0	2	12	—	—	—	—	—
94-95	Kalamazoo	IHL	31	2	1	3	41	13	0	2	2	33
95-96	Michigan	IHL	49	0	10	10	62	10	0	0	0	6
96-97	Michigan	IHL	62	2	7	9	60	3	0	0	0	6
	NHL	Totals	8	0	0	0	4	—	—	—	—	—
	AHL	Totals	483	35	191	226	935	46	3	11	14	167
	IHL	Totals	220	11	33	44	277	36	0	4	4	63

Born; 5/27/64, Livonia, Michigan. 5-11, 190. Signed as a free agent by Detroit Red Wings (9/86). Signed as a free agent by Washington Capitals (6/29/89). Signed as a free agent by Los Angeles Kings (7/11/90). Signed as a free agent by Boston Bruins (8/2/91). Traded to Washington by Boston with John Byce for Brent Hughes and future considerations (1/24/92). 1989-90 AHL Second Team All-Star. Member of 1988-89 AHL champion Adirondack Red Wings.

Derrick Smith — Left Wing

			Regular Season					Playoffs				
Season	Team	League	GP	G	A	PTS	PIM	GP	G	A	PTS	PIM
84-85	Philadelphia	NHL	77	17	22	39	31	19	2	5	7	16
85-86	Philadelphia	NHL	69	6	6	12	57	4	0	0	0	10
86-87	Philadelphia	NHL	71	11	21	32	34	26	6	4	10	26
87-88	Philadelphia	NHL	76	16	8	24	104	7	0	0	0	6
88-89	Philadelphia	NHL	74	16	14	30	43	19	5	2	7	12
89-90	Philadelphia	NHL	55	3	6	9	32	—	—	—	—	—
90-91	Philadelphia	NHL	72	11	10	21	37	—	—	—	—	—
91-92	Minnesota	NHL	33	2	4	6	33	7	1	0	1	9
91-92	Kalamazoo	IHL	6	1	5	6	4	—	—	—	—	—
92-93	Minnesota	NHL	9	0	1	1	2	—	—	—	—	—
92-93	Kalamazoo	IHL	52	22	13	35	43	—	—	—	—	—
93-94	Dallas	NHL	1	0	0	0	0	—	—	—	—	—
93-94	Kalamazoo	IHL	77	44	37	81	90	5	0	0	0	18
94-95	Kalamazoo	IHL	68	30	21	51	103	16	3	8	11	8
95-96	Kalamazoo	IHL	69	15	26	41	79	10	4	3	7	16
96-97	Kalamazoo	IHL	68	8	21	29	55	4	1	0	1	16
	NHL	Totals	537	82	92	175	373	82	14	11	25	79
	IHL	Totals	340	120	123	243	374	35	8	11	19	58

Born; 1/22/65, Scarborough, Ontario. 6-2, 215. Drafted by Philadelphia Flyers (2nd choice, 44th overall) in 1983 Entry Draft. Claimed on waivers by Minnesota North Stars from Philadelphia (10/26/91).

Doug Smith — Right Wing

			Regular Season					Playoffs				
Season	Team	League	GP	G	A	PTS	PIM	GP	G	A	PTS	PIM
95-96	Erie	ECHL	2	0	0	0	12	—	—	—	—	—
95-96	Saginaw	CoHL	3	0	2	2	0	—	—	—	—	—
95-96	Detroit	CoHL	53	25	33	58	32	8	1	4	5	8
96-97	Central Texas	WPHL	63	31	40	71	105	10	3	3	6	19
	CoHL	Totals	56	25	35	60	32	8	1	4	5	8

Born; 3/5/70, East Lansing, Michigan. 5-9, 170.

Gairin Smith — Left Wing

			Regular Season					Playoffs				
Season	Team	League	GP	G	A	PTS	PIM	GP	G	A	PTS	PIM
93-94	Charlotte	ECHL	17	5	2	7	77	—	—	—	—	—
93-94	Roanoke	ECHL	38	6	11	17	137	2	1	1	2	0
94-95	Cape Breton	AHL	6	0	1	1	16	—	—	—	—	—
94-95	Saginaw	CoHL	1	0	0	0	0	—	—	—	—	—
94-95	Wheeling	ECHL	48	8	11	19	195	—	—	—	—	—
95-96	Wheeling	ECHL	67	13	23	36	239	7	3	1	4	10
96-97	Carolina	AHL	6	0	0	0	30	—	—	—	—	—
96-97	Port Huron	CoHL	19	16	9	25	101	—	—	—	—	—
	AHL	Totals	12	0	1	1	46	—	—	—	—	—
	ECHL	Totals	170	32	47	79	648	9	4	2	6	10
	CoHL	Totals	20	16	9	25	101	—	—	—	—	—

Born; 4/15/72, Tillsonburg, Ontario. 6-0, 195.

Geoff Smith — Defenseman

			Regular Season					Playoffs				
Season	Team	League	GP	G	A	PTS	PIM	GP	G	A	PTS	PIM
89-90	Edmonton	NHL	74	4	11	15	52	3	0	0	0	0
90-91	Edmonton	NHL	59	1	12	13	55	4	0	0	0	0
91-92	Edmonton	NHL	74	2	16	18	43	5	0	1	1	6
92-93	Edmonton	NHL	78	4	14	18	30	—	—	—	—	—

Season	Team	League	GP	G	A	PTS	PIM	GP	G	A	PTS	PIM
93-94	Edmonton	NHL	21	0	3	3	12	—	—	—	—	—
93-94	Florida	NHL	56	1	5	6	38	—	—	—	—	—
94-95	Florida	NHL	47	2	4	6	22	—	—	—	—	—
95-96	Florida	NHL	31	3	7	10	20	1	0	0	0	2
96-97	Florida	NHL	3	0	0	0	2	—	—	—	—	—
96-97	Carolina	AHL	27	3	4	7	20	—	—	—	—	—
	NHL	Totals	443	17	72	89	274	13	0	1	1	8

Born; 3/7/69, Edmonton, Alberta. 6-3, 194. Drafted by Edmonton Oilers (3rd choice, 67th overall) in 1987 Entry Draft. Traded to Florida Panthers by Edmonton with Edmonton's fourth round choice (David Nemirovsky) in 1994 Entry Draft for Florida's third round choice (Corey Neilson) in 1994 Entry Draft and St. Louis' sixth round choice (previosuly acquired by Florida—later traded to Winnipeg—Winnipeg selected Chris Kibermanis) in 1994 Entry Draft, (12/6/93) Member of 1989-90 Stanley Cup Champion Edmonton Oilers.

Greg Smith — Goaltender

			Regular Season							Playoffs				
Season	Team	League	GP	W	L	T	MIN	SO	GAVG	GP	W	L	MIN	SO	GAVG
92-93	Dallas	CeHL	21	7	11	2	1243	0	4.15	1	0	0	8	0	15.00
93-94	Dallas	CeHL	33	12	13	6	1860	0	5.06	—	—	—	—	—	—
93-94	Wichita	CeHL	5	1	2	0	210	0	6.01	2	0	1	67	0	3.58
94-95	Wichita	CeHL	29	17	8	2	1515	1	4.08	5	2	0	183	0	*2.30
95-96	Wichita	CeHL	12	2	9	0	608	0	5.82	—	—	—	—	—	—
95-96	Bakersfield	WCHL	19	5	8	4	1037	0	5.56	—	—	—	—	—	—
96-97	Knoxville	ECHL	6	4	2	0	331	0	4.53	—	—	—	—	—	—
96-97	Nashville	CeHL	26	4	18	0	1365	0	5.32	—	—	—	—	—	—
	CeHL	Totals	126	43	61	10	6801	1	4.83	8	2	1	258	0	3.02

Born; 8/11/71, Southgate, Michigan. 6-0, 190. Member of 1993-94 CeHL champion Wichita Thunder. Member of 1994-95 CeHL champion Wichita Thunder.

Jason Smith — Defenseman

Season	Team	League	GP	G	A	PTS	PIM	GP	G	A	PTS	PIM
96-97	Saint John	AHL	25	0	0	0	21	—	—	—	—	—
96-97	Roanoke	ECHL	17	0	1	1	39	—	—	—	—	—

Born; 11/19/74, Calgary, Alberta. 6-4, 210. Drafted by Calgary Flames (4th choice, 95th overall) in 1993 Entry Draft.

Jason Smith — Defenseman

Season	Team	League	GP	G	A	PTS	PIM	GP	G	A	PTS	PIM
92-93	Erie	ECHL	22	3	8	11	2	5	1	1	2	2
93-94	Erie	ECHL	68	22	37	59	44	—	—	—	—	—
94-95	Erie	ECHL	56	7	34	41	38	—	—	—	—	—
94-95	Utica	CoHL	1	0	1	1	2	—	—	—	—	—
95-96	Utica	COHL	74	23	64	87	38	—	—	—	—	—
96-97	Mobile	ECHL	19	4	5	9	7	—	—	—	—	—
96-97	Austin	WPHL	31	3	16	19	10	6	0	2	2	2
	ECHL	Totals	165	36	84	120	91	5	1	1	2	2
	CoHL	Totals	75	23	65	88	40	—	—	—	—	—

Born; 5/21/72, Winnipeg, Manitoba. 5-10, 200. 1995-96 CoHL Second Team All-Star.

Jeff Smith — Defenseman

Season	Team	League	GP	G	A	PTS	PIM	GP	G	A	PTS	PIM
96-97	Amarillo	WPHL	30	7	9	16	74	—	—	—	—	—
96-97	Mobile	ECHL	18	0	5	5	12	—	—	—	—	—

Born; 5/3/74, Belleville, Ontario. 6-0, 200.

Michael Smith — Defenseman

			Regular Season					Playoffs				
Season	Team	League	GP	G	A	PTS	PIM	GP	G	A	PTS	PIM
92-93	Rochester	AHL	2	0	1	1	0	—	—	—	—	—
93-94	Roanoke	ECHL	67	5	57	62	62	2	0	0	0	2
94-95	Minnesota	IHL	13	0	2	2	0	—	—	—	—	—
94-95	Roanoke	ECHL	57	6	40	46	59	8	4	2	6	8
95-96	Roanoke	ECHL	69	10	38	48	41	3	0	0	0	4
96-97	Saint John	AHL	12	0	5	5	12	—	—	—	—	—
96-97	Roanoke	ECHL	57	6	35	41	25	—	—	—	—	—
	AHL	Totals	14	0	6	6	12	—	—	—	—	—
	ECHL	Totals	250	27	170	197	187	13	4	2	6	14

Born; 1/17/71, Winnipeg, Manitoba. 6-0, 185. Drafted by Buffalo Sabres (13th choice, 255th overall) in 1991 Entry Draft.

Greg Smyth — Defenseman

			Regular Season					Playoffs				
Season	Team	League	GP	G	A	PTS	PIM	GP	G	A	PTS	PIM
85-86	Hershey	AHL	2	0	1	1	5	8	0	0	0	60
86-87	Philadelphia	NHL	1	0	0	0	0	1	0	0	0	2
86-87	Hershey	AHL	35	0	2	2	158	2	0	0	0	19
87-88	Philadelphia	NHL	48	1	6	7	192	5	0	0	0	38
87-88	Hershey	AHL	21	0	10	10	102	—	—	—	—	—
88-89	Quebec	NHL	10	0	1	1	70	—	—	—	—	—
88-89	Halifax	AHL	43	3	9	12	310	4	0	1	1	35
89-90	Quebec	NHL	13	0	0	0	57	—	—	—	—	—
89-90	Halifax	AHL	49	5	14	19	235	6	1	0	1	52
90-91	Quebec	NHL	1	0	0	0	0	—	—	—	—	—
90-91	Halifax	AHL	56	6	23	29	340	—	—	—	—	—
91-92	Quebec	NHL	29	0	2	2	138	—	—	—	—	—
91-92	Calgary	NHL	7	1	1	2	15	—	—	—	—	—
91-92	Halifax	AHL	9	1	3	4	35	—	—	—	—	—
92-93	Calgary	NHL	35	1	2	3	95	—	—	—	—	—
92-93	Salt Lake City	IHL	5	0	1	1	31	—	—	—	—	—
93-94	Florida	NHL	12	1	0	1	37	—	—	—	—	—
93-94	Toronto	NHL	11	0	1	1	38	—	—	—	—	—
93-94	Chicago	NHL	38	0	0	0	108	6	0	0	0	0
94-95	Chicago	NHL	22	0	3	3	33	—	—	—	—	—
94-95	Indianapolis	IHL	2	0	0	0	0	—	—	—	—	—
95-96	Chicago	IHL	15	1	3	4	53	—	—	—	—	—
95-96	Los Angeles	IHL	41	2	7	9	231	—	—	—	—	—
96-97	St. John's	AHL	43	2	4	6	273	5	0	1	1	14
	NHL	Totals	227	4	16	20	783	12	0	0	0	40
	AHL	Totals	258	17	65	82	1453	17	1	2	3	120
	IHL	Totals	63	3	11	14	315	—	—	—	—	—

Born; 4/23/66, Oakville, Ontario. 6-3, 212. Drafted by Philadelphia Flyers (1st choice, 22nd overall) in 1984 Entry Draft. traded to Quebec Nordiques by Philadelphia with Philadelphia's third round choice (John Tanner) in the 1989 Entry Draft for Terry Carkner (7/25/88). Traded to Calgary Flames by Quebec for Martin Simard (3/10/92). Signed as a free agent by Florida Panthers (8/10/93). Traded to Toronto Maple Leafs by Florida for cash (12/7/93). Claimed on waivers by Chicago Blackhawks from Toronto (1/8/94).

Kevin Smyth — Left Wing

			Regular Season					Playoffs				
Season	Team	League	GP	G	A	PTS	PIM	GP	G	A	PTS	PIM
93-94	Hartford	NHL	21	3	2	5	10	—	—	—	—	—
93-94	Springfield	AHL	42	22	27	49	72	6	4	5	9	0
94-95	Hartford	NHL	16	1	5	6	13	—	—	—	—	—
94-95	Springfield	AHL	57	17	22	39	72	—	—	—	—	—
95-96	Hartford	NHL	21	2	1	3	8	—	—	—	—	—

Season	Team	League	GP	G	A	PTS	PIM	GP	G	A	PTS	PIM
95-96	Springfield	AHL	47	15	33	48	87	10	5	5	10	8
96-97	Orlando	IHL	38	14	17	31	49	10	1	2	3	6
	NHL	Totals	58	6	8	14	31	—	—	—	—	—
	AHL	Totals	146	54	82	136	231	16	9	10	19	8

Born; 11/22/73, Banff, Alberta. 6-2, 220. Drafted by Hartford Whalers (4th choice, 79th overall) in 1992 Entry Draft.

Chris Snell — Defenseman

			Regular Season					Playoffs				
Season	Team	League	GP	G	A	PTS	PIM	GP	G	A	PTS	PIM
91-92	Rochester	AHL	65	5	27	32	66	10	2	1	3	6
92-93	Rochester	AHL	76	14	57	71	83	17	5	8	13	39
93-94	Toronto	NHL	2	0	0	0	2	—	—	—	—	—
93-94	St. John's	AHL	75	22	74	96	92	11	1	15	16	10
94-95	Los Angeles	NHL	32	2	7	9	22	—	—	—	—	—
94-95	Phoenix	IHL	57	15	49	64	122	—	—	—	—	—
95-96	Phoenix	IHL	40	9	22	31	113	—	—	—	—	—
95-96	Binghamton	AHL	32	7	25	32	48	4	2	2	4	6
96-97	Indianapolis	IHL	73	22	45	67	130	2	0	0	0	2
	NHL	Totals	34	2	7	9	24	—	—	—	—	—
	AHL	Totals	248	48	183	231	289	42	10	26	36	61
	IHL	Totals	170	46	116	162	365	2	0	0	0	2

Born; 7/12/71, Regina, Saskatchewan. 5-11, 184. Drafted by Buffalo Sabres (8th choice, 145th overall) in 1991 Entry Draft. Signed as a free agent by Toronto Maple Leafs (8/3/93). Traded to Los Angeles Kings by Toronto with Eric Lacroix and Toronto's fourth round choice (Eric Belanger) in 1996 Entry Draft for Dixon Ward, Guy Leveque and Kelly Fairchild (10/3/94). Traded to New York Rangers by Los Angeles for Steve Larouche (1/14/96). Signed as a free agent by Chicago Blackhawks (7/96). 1994 AHL First Team All-Star. Won Eddie Shore Plaque (Top defenseman in AHL) 1994. 1995 IHL First Team All-Star. 1996-97 IHL Second Team All-Star.

Gary Socha — Center

			Regular Season					Playoffs				
Season	Team	League	GP	G	A	PTS	PIM	GP	G	A	PTS	PIM
92-93	Salt Lake City	IHL	4	0	0	0	0	—	—	—	—	—
93-94	South Carolina	ECHL	64	23	37	60	60	3	2	0	2	0
93-94	Saint John	AHL	3	0	1	1	0	—	—	—	—	—
94-95	South Carolina	ECHL	68	33	37	70	80	9	3	5	8	4
95-96	South Carolina	ECHL	2	1	1	2	17	—	—	—	—	—
96-97	Tallahassee	ECHL	22	9	6	15	20	3	0	1	1	2
	ECHL	Totals	156	66	81	147	177	15	5	6	11	6

Born; 12/30/69, Attleboro, Massachusetts. 6-4, 185. Drafted by Calgary Flames (3rd choice, 84th overall) in 1988 Entry Draft.

Tommy Soderstrom — Goaltender

			Regular Season						Playoffs				
Season	Team	League	GP	W	L	T	MIN	SO	AVG	GP	W	L	MIN	SO	AVG
92-93	Philadelphia	NHL	44	20	17	6	2512	5	3.42	—	—	—	—	—	—
92-93	Hershey	AHL	7	4	1	0	373	0	2.41	—	—	—	—	—	—
93-94	Philadelphia	NHL	34	6	18	4	1736	2	4.01	—	—	—	—	—	—
93-94	Hershey	AHL	9	3	4	1	461	0	4.81	—	—	—	—	—	—
94-95	Islanders	NHL	26	8	12	3	1350	1	3.11	—	—	—	—	—	—
95-96	Islanders	NHL	51	11	22	6	2590	2	3.87	—	—	—	—	—	—
96-97	Rochester	AHL	2	2	0	0	120	0	4.00	—	—	—	—	—	—
96-97	Utah	IHL	26	12	11	0	1463	0	3.12	—	—	—	—	—	—
	NHL	Totals	155	45	69	19	8188	10	3.63	—	—	—	—	—	—
	AHL	Totals	18	9	5	1	954	0	3.77	—	—	—	—	—	—

Born; 7/17/69, Stockholm, Sweden. 5-7, 157. Drafted by Philadelphia Flyers (14th choice, 214th overall) in 1990 Entry Draft.

Kevin Solari — Left Wing

			Regular Season					Playoffs				
Season	Team	League	GP	G	A	PTS	PIM	GP	G	A	PTS	PIM
94-95	Columbus	ECHL	11	1	1	2	25	—	—	—	—	—
95-96	N/A											

Season	Team	League	GP	G	A	PTS	PIM	GP	G	A	PTS	PIM
96-97	Grand Rapids	IHL	1	0	0	0	2	—	—	—	—	—
96-97	Muskegon	CoHL	48	14	12	26	65	—	—	—	—	—
96-97	Utica	CoHL	21	6	5	11	39	3	0	1	1	0
	CoHL	Totals	69	20	17	37	104	3	0	1	1	0

Born; 3/7/74, Hamilton, Ontario. 6-0, 203.

Brent Sopel — Defenseman

Season	Team	League	GP	G	A	PTS	PIM	GP	G	A	PTS	PIM
95-96	Syracuse	AHL	1	0	0	0	0	—	—	—	—	—
96-97	Syracuse	AHL	2	0	0	0	0	3	0	0	0	0
	AHL	Totals	3	0	0	0	0	3	0	0	0	0

Born; 1/7/77, Calgary, Alberta. 6-1, 185. Drafted by Vancouver Canucks (6th choice, 144th overall) in 1995 Entry Draft.

Lee Sorochan — Defenseman

Season	Team	League	GP	G	A	PTS	PIM	GP	G	A	PTS	PIM
94-95	Binghamton	AHL	—	—	—	—	—	8	0	0	0	11
95-96	Binghamton	AHL	45	2	8	10	26	1	0	0	0	0
96-97	Binghamton	AHL	77	4	27	31	160	4	0	2	2	18
	AHL	Totals	122	6	35	41	186	13	0	2	2	29

Born; 9/9/75, Edmonton, Alberta. 6-1, 210. Drafted by New York Rangers (2nd choice, 34th overall) in 1993 Entry Draft.

Oleg Sorokins — Defenseman

Season	Team	League	GP	G	A	PTS	PIM	GP	G	A	PTS	PIM
96-97	Jacksonville	ECHL	2	0	0	0	2	—	—	—	—	—
96-97	Roanoke	ECHL	3	0	1	1	0	—	—	—	—	—
96-97	Quad City	CoHL	39	2	18	20	10	—	—	—	—	—
96-97	Utica	CoHL	8	0	6	6	2	—	—	—	—	—
	CoHL	Totals	47	2	24	26	12	—	—	—	—	—
	ECHL	Totals	5	0	1	1	2	—	—	—	—	—

Born; 1/4/74, Riga, Latvia. 5-10, 180.

Christian Soucy — Goaltender

Season	Team	League	GP	W	L	T	MIN	SO	GAVG	GP	W	L	MIN	SO	GAVG
93-94	Chicago	NHL	1	0	0	0	3	0	0.00	—	—	—	—	—	—
93-94	Indianapolis	IHL	46	14	25	1	2302	1	4.14	—	—	—	—	—	—
94-95	Indianapolis	IHL	42	15	17	5	2216	0	4.01	—	—	—	—	—	—
95-96	Indianapolis	IHL	22	12	9	0	1197	0	3.11	—	—	—	—	—	—
96-97	Kentucky	AHL	3	0	2	0	138	0	4.77	—	—	—	—	—	—
96-97	Baton Rouge	ECHL	46	18	20	1	2421	3	3.17	—	—	—	—	—	—
	IHL	Totals	110	41	51	6	5715	1	3.87	—	—	—	—	—	—

Born; 9/14/70, Gatineau, Quebec. 5-11, 160. Signed as a free agent by Chicago Blackhawks (6/21/93).

Stephen Soulliere — Left Wing

Season	Team	League	GP	G	A	PTS	PIM	GP	G	A	PTS	PIM
95-96	Phoenix	IHL	5	0	0	0	2	—	—	—	—	—
95-96	Knoxville	ECHL	59	26	26	52	124	5	0	2	2	16
96-97	Phoenix	IHL	6	0	1	1	2	—	—	—	—	—
96-97	Knoxville	ECHL	58	25	42	67	63	—	—	—	—	—
	IHL	Totals	11	0	1	1	4	—	—	—	—	—
	ECHL	Totals	117	51	68	119	187	5	0	2	2	16

Born; 5/30/75, Greenfield Park, Quebec. 5-11, 180. Signed as a free agent by Los Angeles Kings (7/1/94).

Sheldon Souray — Defenseman

			Regular Season					Playoffs				
Season	Team	League	GP	G	A	PTS	PIM	GP	G	A	PTS	PIM
94-95	Albany	AHL	7	0	2	2	8	—	—	—	—	—
95-96	Albany	AHL	6	0	2	2	12	4	0	1	1	4
96-97	Albany	AHL	70	2	11	13	160	16	2	3	5	47
	AHL	Totals	83	2	15	17	180	20	2	4	6	51

Born; 7/13/76, Elk Point, Alberta. 6-2, 210. Drafted by New Jersey Devils (3rd choice, 71st overall) in 1994 Entry Draft.

Ken Spangler — Defenseman

			Regular Season					Playoffs				
Season	Team	League	GP	G	A	PTS	PIM	GP	G	A	PTS	PIM
87-88	Newmarket	AHL	64	3	6	9	128	—	—	—	—	—
88-89	Flint	IHL	37	4	15	19	97	—	—	—	—	—
88-89	Baltimore	AHL	12	0	3	3	33	—	—	—	—	—
89-90	Phoenix	IHL	58	3	16	19	156	—	—	—	—	—
90-91	Nashville	ECHL	45	9	25	34	226	—	—	—	—	—
91-92	Flint	CoHL	53	13	34	47	233	—	—	—	—	—
92-93	Flint	CoHL	41	3	13	16	128	6	0	0	0	29
93-94	Flint	CoHL	45	2	15	17	256	9	1	3	4	78
94-95	Flint	CoHL	55	6	20	26	135	6	0	1	1	20
95-96	Flint	CoHL	3	0	0	0	2	—	—	—	—	—
96-97	Flint	CoHL	65	9	27	36	170	10	0	1	1	10
	IHL	Totals	95	7	31	38	253	—	—	—	—	—
	AHL	Totals	76	3	9	12	161	—	—	—	—	—
	CoHL	Totals	262	33	109	142	924	31	1	5	6	137

Born; 5/2/67, Edmonton, Alberta. 6-0, 200. Drafted by Toronto Maple Leafs (2nd choice, 22nd overall) in 1985 Entry Draft.

Todd Sparks — Left Wing

			Regular Season					Playoffs				
Season	Team	League	GP	G	A	PTS	PIM	GP	G	A	PTS	PIM
95-96	Springfield	AHL	3	0	0	0	2	—	—	—	—	—
95-96	Richmond	ECHL	49	17	26	43	100	6	1	5	6	6
96-97	Fredericton	AHL	67	17	23	40	83	—	—	—	—	—
	AHL	Totals	70	17	23	40	85	—	—	—	—	—

Born; 6/9/71, Edmunston, New Brunswick. 6-0, 190. Drafted by New York Islanders (8th choice, 158th overall) in 1991 Entry Draft.

Jamie Spencer — Left Wing

			Regular Season					Playoffs				
Season	Team	League	GP	G	A	PTS	PIM	GP	G	A	PTS	PIM
95-96	Indianapolis	IHL	1	0	0	0	0	—	—	—	—	—
95-96	Columbus	ECHL	70	23	23	46	45	3	0	1	1	2
96-97	Baltimore	AHL	65	7	14	21	25	2	1	0	1	0

Born; 8/11/73, Carmel, Indiana. 5-11, 190.

Greg Spenrath — Left Wing

			Regular Season					Playoffs				
Season	Team	League	GP	G	A	PTS	PIM	GP	G	A	PTS	PIM
90-91	Binghamton	AHL	2	0	0	0	14	—	—	—	—	—
90-91	Erie	ECHL	61	29	36	65	*407	4	1	2	3	46
91-92	Kalamazoo	IHL	69	4	7	11	237	—	—	—	—	—
92-93	Indianapolis	IHL	9	0	1	1	68	1	0	0	0	5
92-93	Binghamton	AHL	1	0	0	0	2	—	—	—	—	—
92-93	Erie	ECHL	55	17	28	45	344	3	1	0	1	77
93-94	Las Vegas	IHL	43	2	0	2	222	—	—	—	—	—
94-95	Prince Edward Island	AHL	58	3	5	8	216	9	0	2	2	28
95-96	Fresno	WCHL	57	20	35	55	206	7	4	5	9	16

Season	Team	League	GP	G	A	PTS	PIM	GP	G	A	PTS	PIM
96-97	Utah	IHL	2	0	1	1	8	—	—	—	—	—
96-97	Fresno	WCHL	61	14	32	46	375	5	0	4	4	53
	IHL	Totals	122	6	9	15	535	1	0	0	0	5
	AHL	Totals	61	3	5	8	232	9	0	2	2	28
	WCHL	Totals	118	34	67	101	581	12	4	9	13	69
	ECHL	Totals	116	46	64	110	751	7	2	2	4	123

Born; 9/27/69, Edmonton, Alberta. 6-3, 225. Drafted by New York Rangers (9th choice, 160th overall) in 1989 Entry Draft. Signed as a free agent by Minnesota North Stars (7/25/91).

Kevin Spero — Defenseman

Season	Team	League	GP	G	A	PTS	PIM	GP	G	A	PTS	PIM
96-97	Amarillo	WPHL	29	1	2	3	17	—	—	—	—	—
96-97	Waco	WPHL	19	0	3	3	6	—	—	—	—	—
	WPHL	Totals	48	1	5	6	23	—	—	—	—	—

Born; 2/20/73, Prescott, Ontario. 6-0, 195.

John Spoltore — Center

Season	Team	League	GP	G	A	PTS	PIM	GP	G	A	PTS	PIM
95-96	Louisiana	ECHL	70	33	68	101	99	5	4	4	8	2
96-97	Louisiana	ECHL	9	0	8	8	8	17	10	13	23	20
	ECHL	Totals	79	33	76	109	107	22	14	17	31	22

Born; 8/25/71, Bridgeton, New Jersey. 5-10, 195.

Corey Spring — Right Wing

Season	Team	League	GP	G	A	PTS	PIM	GP	G	A	PTS	PIM
95-96	Atlanta	IHL	73	14	14	28	104	2	0	0	0	0
95-96	Adirondack	AHL	69	20	26	46	118	4	0	0	0	14

Born; 5/31/71, Cranbrook, British Columbia. 6-4, 214. Signed as a free agent by Tampa Bay Lightning (7/24/95).

Jim Sprott — Defenseman

Season	Team	League	GP	G	A	PTS	PIM	GP	G	A	PTS	PIM
89-90	Halifax	AHL	22	2	1	3	103	—	—	—	—	—
90-91	Halifax	AHL	9	0	2	2	17	—	—	—	—	—
90-91	Fort Wayne	IHL	19	0	1	1	67	—	—	—	—	—
90-91	Peoria	IHL	31	2	5	7	92	—	—	—	—	—
90-91	Greensboro	ECHL	3	0	0	0	31	—	—	—	—	—
91-92	New Haven	AHL	54	4	11	15	140	3	0	0	0	17
92-93	Halifax	AHL	77	6	21	27	180	—	—	—	—	—
93-94	St. John's	AHL	9	1	0	1	35	—	—	—	—	—
93-94	South Carolina	ECHL	46	8	25	33	221	3	0	0	0	5
93-94	Brantford	CoHL	12	1	3	4	55	—	—	—	—	—
94-95	South Carolina	ECHL	21	1	6	7	100	—	—	—	—	—
95-96	South Carolina	ECHL	2	0	0	0	24	—	—	—	—	—
95-96	San Antonio	CeHL	51	11	33	44	220	13	2	8	10	51
96-97	San Antonio	CeHL	64	15	42	57	209	—	—	—	—	—
	AHL	Totals	171	13	35	48	475	3	0	0	0	17
	IHL	Totals	50	2	6	8	159	—	—	—	—	—
	CeHL	Totals	115	26	75	101	429	13	2	8	10	51
	ECHL	Totals	72	9	31	40	376	3	0	0	0	5

Born; 4/11/69, Hanover, Ontario. 6-2, 220. Drafted by Quebec Nordiques (3rd choice, 51st overall) in 1987 Entry Draft.

Andrei Srubko — Defenseman

Regular Season / Playoffs

Season	Team	League	GP	G	A	PTS	PIM	GP	G	A	PTS	PIM
96-97	Toledo	ECHL	62	0	8	8	238	5	0	0	0	4

Born;

Martin St. Amour — Left Wing

Regular Season / Playoffs

Season	Team	League	GP	G	A	PTS	PIM	GP	G	A	PTS	PIM
90-91	Fredericton	AHL	45	13	16	29	51	1	0	0	0	0
91-92	Cincinnati	ECHL	60	44	44	88	183	9	4	9	13	18
92-93	New Haven	AHL	71	21	39	60	78	—	—	—	—	—
93-94	Prince Edward Island	AHL	37	13	12	25	65	—	—	—	—	—
93-94	Providence	AHL	12	0	3	3	22	—	—	—	—	—
94-95	N/A											
95-96	San Francisco	IHL	4	0	2	2	6	—	—	—	—	—
95-96	Los Angeles	IHL	1	0	0	0	0	—	—	—	—	—
95-96	San Diego	WCHL	53	*61	48	*109	182	9	6	7	13	10
96-97	San Diego	WCHL	59	*60	67	*127	170	8	*8	4	12	23
	AHL	Totals	165	47	70	117	226	1	0	0	0	0
	IHL	Totals	5	0	2	2	6	—	—	—	—	—
	WCHL	Totals	112	121	115	236	352	17	14	11	25	33

Born; 1/30/70, Montreal, Quebec. 6-3, 195. Drafted by Montreal Canadiens (2nd choice, 34th overall) in 1988 Entry Draft. 1995-96 WCHL First Team All-Star. 1996-97 WCHL MVP. 1996-97 WCHL First Team All-Star. Member of 1995-96 WCHL champion San Diego Gulls. Member of 1996-97 WCHL Champion San Diego Gulls.

Stephane St. Amour — Right Wing

Regular Season / Playoffs

Season	Team	League	GP	G	A	PTS	PIM	GP	G	A	PTS	PIM
95-96	Raleigh	ECHL	3	0	0	0	0	—	—	—	—	—
95-96	Jacksonville	ECHL	32	14	11	25	43	—	—	—	—	—
95-96	San Diego	WCHL	17	12	7	19	32	9	2	2	4	8
96-97	San Diego	WCHL	61	56	51	107	167	4	0	2	2	6
	WCHL	Totals	78	68	58	126	199	13	2	4	6	14
	ECHL	Totals	35	14	11	25	43	—	—	—	—	—

Born; 1/20/74, St. Hippolyte, Quebec. 5-11, 190. Member of 1995-96 WCHL champion San Diego Gulls. 1996-97 WCHL Second Team All-Star. Member of 1996-97 WCHL Champion San Diego Gulls.

Kevin St. Jacques — Left Wing

Regular Season / Playoffs

Season	Team	League	GP	G	A	PTS	PIM	GP	G	A	PTS	PIM
92-93	Indianapolis	IHL	71	10	21	31	93	4	0	0	0	0
93-94	Indianapolis	IHL	49	5	23	28	91	—	—	—	—	—
93-94	Flint	CoHL	10	5	13	18	2	10	4	14	18	19
94-95	Indianapolis	IHL	12	4	5	9	10	—	—	—	—	—
94-95	Columbus	ECHL	46	14	38	52	88	—	—	—	—	—
95-96	Detroit	CoHL	21	11	10	21	32	—	—	—	—	—
95-96	Saginaw	CoHL	—	—	—	—	—	5	1	2	3	4
96-97	Las Vegas	IHL	7	2	2	4	4	—	—	—	—	—
96-97	San Diego	WCHL	57	41	62	103	148	8	4	8	12	31
	IHL	Totals	139	21	51	72	198	4	0	0	0	0
	CoHL	Totals	31	16	23	39	34	15	5	16	21	23

Born; 2/25/71, Edmonton, Alberta. 5-11, 190. Selected by Chicago Blackhawks (8th choice, 112th overall) 1991 Entry Draft. Member of 1996-97 WCHL Champion San Diego Gulls.

Kevin St. Pierre — Goaltender

Season	Team	League	GP	W	L	T	MIN	SO	GAVG	GP	W	L	MIN	SO	GAVG
95-96	Wichita	CeHL	14	6	5	1	661	0	4.54	—	—	—	—	—	—
96-97	Wichita	CeHL	16	7	8	1	899	0	4.14	—	—	—	—	—	—
96-97	Nashville	CeHL	3	0	2	0	91	0	5.95	—	—	—	—	—	—
96-97	San Antonio	CeHL	12	9	3	0	664	0	3.34	—	—	—	—	—	—
	CeHL	Totals	45	22	18	2	2315	0	4.10	—	—	—	—	—	—

Born; 4/7/75, Sherbrooke, Quebec. 6-3, 205. Selected by Wichita Thunder in San Antonio Dispersal Draft (6/10/97).

Brian Stacey — Defenseman

Season	Team	League	GP	G	A	PTS	PIM	GP	G	A	PTS	PIM
96-97	Kansas City	IHL	53	2	8	10	43	1	0	0	0	2
96-97	Mobile	ECHL	5	2	2	4	6	—	—	—	—	—

Born; 6/28/75, East York, Ontario. 6-3, 200. Last amateru club; Sault Ste. Marie (OHL).

Nick Stajduhar — Defenseman

Season	Team	League	GP	G	A	PTS	PIM	GP	G	A	PTS	PIM
94-95	Cape Breton	AHL	54	12	26	38	55	—	—	—	—	—
95-96	Edmonton	NHL	2	0	0	0	4	—	—	—	—	—
95-96	Cape Breton	AHL	8	2	0	2	11	—	—	—	—	—
95-96	Canadian	National										
96-97	Hamilton	AHL	11	1	2	3	2	—	—	—	—	—
96-97	Quebec	IHL	7	1	3	4	2	—	—	—	—	—
96-97	Pensacola	ECHL	30	9	15	24	32	12	1	6	7	34
	AHL	Totals	73	15	28	43	68	—	—	—	—	—

Born; 12/6/74, Kitchener, Ontario. 6-3, 206. Drafted by Edmonton Oilers (2nd choice, 16th overall) in 1993 Entry Draft.

Jeff Staples — Defenseman

Season	Team	League	GP	G	A	PTS	PIM	GP	G	A	PTS	PIM
95-96	Hershey	AHL	61	7	3	10	100	5	0	1	1	0
96-97	Philadelphia	AHL	74	4	11	15	157	8	0	2	2	10
	AHL	Totals	135	11	14	25	257	13	0	3	3	10

Born; 3/4/75, Kitimat, British Columbia. 6-2, 207. Drafted by Philadelphia Flyers (10th choice, 244th overall) in 1993 Entry Draft.

Sergei Stas — Defenseman

Season	Team	League	GP	G	A	PTS	PIM	GP	G	A	PTS	PIM
93-94	Erie	ECHL	2	1	2	3	4	—	—	—	—	—
94-95	Erie	ECHL	35	1	15	16	108	—	—	—	—	—
95-96	Fort Wayne	IHL	38	1	2	3	90	—	—	—	—	—
95-96	Phoenix	IHL	3	0	0	0	6	—	—	—	—	—
95-96	Quad City	CoHL	15	2	7	9	30	4	0	1	1	4
96-97	Las Vegas	IHL	12	0	1	1	39	—	—	—	—	—
96-97	San Antonio	IHL	9	1	1	2	40	—	—	—	—	—
96-97	Fort Wayne	IHL	14	1	3	4	23	—	—	—	—	—
96-97	Saginaw	CoHL	29	5	17	22	63	—	—	—	—	—
	IHL	Totals	76	3	7	10	198	—	—	—	—	—
	CoHL	Totals	44	7	24	31	93	4	0	1	1	4
	ECHL	Totals	37	2	17	19	112	—	—	—	—	—

Born; 4/28/74, Rlinsk, Russia. 6-0, 190.

Robb Stauber — Goaltender

			Regular Season							Playoffs					
Season	Team	League	GP	W	L	T	MIN	SO	GAVG	GP	W	L	MIN	SO	GAVG
89-90	Los Angeles	NHL	2	0	1	0	83	0	7.95	—	—	—	—	—	—
89-90	New Haven	AHL	14	6	6	2	851	0	3.03	5	2	3	302	0	4.77
90-91	New Haven	AHL	33	13	16	4	1882	1	3.67	—	—	—	—	—	—
90-91	Phoenix	IHL	4	1	2	0	160	0	4.13	—	—	—	—	—	—
91-92	Phoenix	IHL	22	8	12	1	1242	0	3.86	—	—	—	—	—	—
92-93	Los Angeles	NHL	31	15	8	4	1735	0	3.84	4	3	1	240	0	4.00
93-94	Los Angeles	NHL	22	4	11	5	1144	1	3.41	—	—	—	—	—	—
93-94	Phoenix	IHL	3	1	1	0	121	0	6.42	—	—	—	—	—	—
94-95	Los Angeles	NHL	1	0	0	0	16	0	7.50	—	—	—	—	—	—
94-95	Buffalo	NHL	6	2	3	0	317	0	3.79	—	—	—	—	—	—
95-96	Rochester	AHL	16	6	7	1	833	0	3.53	—	—	—	—	—	—
96-97	Portland	AHL	30	13	13	2	1606	0	3.06	—	—	—	—	—	—
	NHL	Totals	62	21	23	9	3295	1	3.81	4	3	1	240	0	4.00
	AHL	Totals	93	38	42	9	5172	1	3.35	5	2	3	302	0	4.77
	IHL	Totals	29	10	15	1	1523	0	4.10	—	—	—	—	—	—

Born; 11/25/67, Duluth, Minnesota. 5-11, 180. Drafted by Los Angeles Kings (5th choice, 107th overall) in 1986 Entry Draft. Traded to Buffalo Sabres by Los Angeles with Alexei Zhitnik, Charlie Huddy and Los Angeles' fifth round choice (Marian Menhart) in 1996 Entry Draft for Philippe Boucher, Denis Tsygurov and Grant Fuhr (2/14/95). Signed as a free agent by Washington Capitals (8/20/96).

Mike Steckler — Center

			Regular Season					Playoffs				
Season	Team	League	GP	G	A	PTS	PIM	GP	G	A	PTS	PIM
94-95	Utica	CoHL	52	13	28	41	52	6	2	0	2	4
95-96	Utica	CoHL	74	15	20	35	49	—	—	—	—	—
96-97	Utica	CoHL	23	4	2	6	17	—	—	—	—	—
	CoHL	Totals	149	32	50	82	118	6	2	0	2	4

Born; 9/13/66, New Hartford, New York. 6-1, 215.

Troy Stephens — Center

			Regular Season					Playoffs				
Season	Team	League	GP	G	A	PTS	PIM	GP	G	A	PTS	PIM
94-95	Saginaw	CoHL	37	15	18	33	24	11	4	8	12	12
95-96	Fort Worth	CeHL	63	20	40	60	129	—	—	—	—	—
96-97	Utica	CoHL	69	41	48	89	78	3	0	1	1	2
	CoHL	Totals	106	56	66	122	102	14	4	9	13	14

Born; 2/28/71, Mississauga, Ontario. 5-8, 170.

John Stevens — Defenseman

			Regular Season					Playoffs				
Season	Team	League	GP	G	A	PTS	PIM	GP	G	A	PTS	PIM
84-85	Hershey	AHL	3	0	0	0	0	—	—	—	—	—
85-86	Kalamazoo	IHL	6	0	1	1	8	6	0	3	3	9
86-87	Philadelphia	NHL	6	0	2	2	14	—	—	—	—	—
86-87	Hershey	AHL	63	1	15	16	131	3	0	0	0	7
87-88	Philadelphia	NHL	3	0	0	0	0	—	—	—	—	—
87-88	Hershey	AHL	59	1	15	16	108	—	—	—	—	—
88-89	Hershey	AHL	78	3	13	16	129	12	1	1	2	29
89-90	Hershey	AHL	79	3	10	13	193	—	—	—	—	—
90-91	Hartford	NHL	14	0	1	1	11	—	—	—	—	—
90-91	Springfield	AHL	65	0	12	12	139	18	0	6	6	35
91-92	Hartford	NHL	21	0	4	4	19	—	—	—	—	—
91-92	Springfield	AHL	45	1	12	13	73	11	1	3	4	27
92-93	Springfield	AHL	74	1	19	20	111	15	0	1	1	18

Season	Team	League	GP	G	A	PTS	PIM	GP	G	A	PTS	PIM
93-94	Hartford	NHL	9	0	3	3	4	—	—	—	—	—
93-94	Springfield	AHL	71	3	9	12	85	3	0	0	0	0
94-95	Springfield	AHL	79	5	15	20	122	—	—	—	—	—
95-96	Springfield	AHL	69	0	19	19	95	10	0	1	1	31
96-97	Philadelphia	AHL	74	2	18	20	116	10	0	2	2	8
	NHL	Totals	53	0	10	10	48	—	—	—	—	—
	AHL	Totals	759	20	157	177	1302	82	2	14	16	155

Born; 5/4/66, Campbellton, New Brunswick. 6-1, 195. Drafted by Philadelphia Flyers (5th choice, 47th overall) in 1984 Entry Draft. Signed as a free agent by Hartford (7/30/90). Signed as a free agent by Philadelphia (8/6/96). Member of 1990-91 AHL champion Springfield Indians.

Mike Stevens — Left Wing

			Regular Season					Playoffs				
Season	Team	League	GP	G	A	PTS	PIM	GP	G	A	PTS	PIM
84-85	Vancouver	NHL	6	0	3	3	6	—	—	—	—	—
85-86	Fredericton	AHL	79	12	19	31	208	6	1	1	2	35
86-87	Fredericton	AHL	71	7	18	25	258	—	—	—	—	—
87-88	Boston	NHL	7	0	1	1	9	—	—	—	—	—
87-88	Maine	AHL	63	30	25	55	265	7	1	2	3	37
88-89	Islanders	NHL	9	1	0	1	14	—	—	—	—	—
88-89	Springfield	AHL	42	17	13	30	120	—	—	—	—	—
89-90	Toronto	NHL	1	0	0	0	0	—	—	—	—	—
89-90	Springfield	AHL	28	12	10	22	75	—	—	—	—	—
89-90	Newmarket	AHL	46	16	28	44	86	—	—	—	—	—
90-91	Newmarket	AHL	68	24	23	47	229	—	—	—	—	—
91-92	St. John's	AHL	30	13	11	24	65	—	—	—	—	—
91-92	Binghamton	AHL	44	15	15	30	87	11	7	6	13	45
92-93	Binghamton	AHL	68	31	61	92	230	14	5	5	10	63
93-94	Saint John	AHL	79	20	37	57	293	6	1	3	4	34
94-95	Cincinnati	IHL	80	34	43	77	274	10	6	3	9	16
95-96	Cleveland	IHL	81	31	43	74	252	3	1	0	1	8
96-97	Cleveland	IHL	6	1	4	5	32	—	—	—	—	—
96-97	Manitoba	IHL	22	8	4	12	54	—	—	—	—	—
96-97	Cincinnati	IHL	46	16	18	34	140	3	0	2	2	8
	NHL	Totals	23	1	4	5	29	—	—	—	—	—
	AHL	Totals	618	197	260	457	1916	44	15	17	32	214
	IHL	Totals	235	90	112	202	752	16	7	5	12	32

Born; 12/30/65, Kitchener, Ontario. 5-11, 195. Drafted by Vancouver Canucks (5th choice, 58th overall) in 1984 Entry Draft. Traded to Boston Bruins by Vancouver for cash (10/6/87). Signed as a free agent by New York Islanders (8/20/88). Traded to Toronto Maple Leafs by Islanders with Gilles Thibaudeau for Jack Capuano, Paul Gagne and Derek Laxdal (12/20/89). Traded to New York Rangers by Toronto for Guy Larose (12/26/91). Signed as a free agent by Calgary Flames (8/10/93)

Randy Stevens — Forward

			Regular Season					Playoffs				
Season	Team	League	GP	G	A	PTS	PIM	GP	G	A	PTS	PIM
95-96	Las Vegas	IHL	2	0	0	0	2	—	—	—	—	—
95-96	Knoxville	ECHL	47	5	17	22	28	4	0	0	0	6
96-97	Kentucky	AHL	26	3	2	5	25	—	—	—	—	—
96-97	Louisville	ECHL	38	7	14	21	35	—	—	—	—	—
	ECHL	Totals	85	12	31	43	63	4	0	0	0	6

Born; 8/9/73, Sault Ste. Marie, Michigan. 6-0, 195.

Rod Stevens — Center

			Regular Season					Playoffs				
Season	Team	League	GP	G	A	PTS	PIM	GP	G	A	PTS	PIM
94-95	Syracuse	AHL	78	21	21	42	63	—	—	—	—	—
95-96	Syracuse	AHL	60	13	17	30	30	16	3	4	7	14

Season	Team	League	GP	G	A	PTS	PIM	GP	G	A	PTS	PIM
96-97	Syracuse	AHL	74	20	9	29	26	—	—	—	—	—
	AHL	Totals	212	54	47	101	119	16	3	4	7	14

Born; 4/5/74, Fort St. John, British Columbia. 5-10, 175. Signed as a free agent by Vancouver Canucks (10/4/93).

Troy Stevens — Center

			Regular Season					Playoffs				
Season	Team	League	GP	G	A	PTS	PIM	GP	G	A	PTS	PIM
94-95	Nashville	ECHL	25	5	16	21	23	12	4	1	5	8
95-96	Nashville	ECHL	4	0	0	0	5	—	—	—	—	—
95-96	South Carolina	ECHL	6	0	1	1	4	—	—	—	—	—
95-96	Raleigh	ECHL	13	2	6	8	16	—	—	—	—	—
95-96	Muskegon	CoHL	29	3	2	5	15	4	0	1	1	0
96-97	Utica	CoHL	47	9	31	40	25	—	—	—	—	—
	CoHL	Totals	76	12	33	45	40	4	0	1	1	0
	ECHL	Totals	48	7	23	30	48	12	4	1	5	8

Born; 9/3/72, Phoenix, Arizona. 5-10, 180.

Jeremy Stevenson — Left Wing

			Regular Season					Playoffs				
Season	Team	League	GP	G	A	PTS	PIM	GP	G	A	PTS	PIM
94-95	Greensboro	ECHL	43	14	13	27	231	17	6	11	17	64
95-96	Anaheim	NHL	3	0	1	1	12	—	—	—	—	—
95-96	Baltimore	AHL	60	11	10	21	295	12	4	2	6	23
96-97	Anaheim	NHL	5	0	0	0	14	—	—	—	—	—
96-97	Baltimore	AHL	25	8	8	16	125	3	0	0	0	8
	NHL	Totals	8	0	1	1	26	—	—	—	—	—
	AHL	Totals	85	19	18	37	420	15	4	2	6	31

Born; 7/28/74, Elliot Lake, Ontario. 6-2, 215. Drafted by Winnipeg Jets (3rd choice, 60th overall) in 1992 Entry Draft. Re-entered Entry Draft, Anaheim's 10th choice, 262nd overall in 1994 Entry Draft.

Shayne Stevenson — Center

			Regular Season					Playoffs				
Season	Team	League	GP	G	A	PTS	PIM	GP	G	A	PTS	PIM
90-91	Boston	NHL	14	0	0	0	26	—	—	—	—	—
90-91	Maine	AHL	58	22	28	50	112	—	—	—	—	—
91-92	Boston	NHL	5	0	1	1	2	—	—	—	—	—
91-92	Maine	AHL	54	10	23	33	150	—	—	—	—	—
92-93	Tampa Bay	NHL	8	0	1	1	7	—	—	—	—	—
92-93	Atlanta	IHL	53	17	17	34	160	6	0	2	2	2
93-94	Fort Wayne	IHL	22	3	5	8	116	—	—	—	—	—
93-94	Muskegon	CoHL	1	2	0	2	0	—	—	—	—	—
93-94	St. Thomas	CoHL	6	3	3	6	15	2	0	2	2	9
94-95	Utica	COHL	43	17	40	57	37	6	0	3	3	14
95-96	Utica	COHL	27	11	21	32	72	—	—	—	—	—
96-97	Utica	CoHL	10	2	6	8	18	—	—	—	—	—
96-97	Saginaw	CoHL	17	2	23	25	30	—	—	—	—	—
96-97	Brantford	CoHL	10	3	9	12	25	6	5	3	8	24
	NHL	Totals	27	0	2	2	35	—	—	—	—	—
	AHL	Totals	112	32	51	83	262	—	—	—	—	—
	IHL	Totals	75	20	22	42	276	6	0	2	2	2
	CoHL	Totals	114	40	102	142	197	14	5	8	13	47

Born; 10/26/70, Aurora, Ontario. 6-1, 190. Drafted by Boston Bruins (1st choice, 17th overall) in 1989 Entry Draft. Selected by Tampa Bay Lightning in NHL Expansion Draft (6/18/92).

Brad Stewart — Defenseman

Season	Team	League	GP	G	A	PTS	PIM	GP	G	A	PTS	PIM
96-97	Louisville	ECHL	1	0	0	0	0	—	—	—	—	—
96-97	Amarillo	WPHL	60	3	23	26	36	—	—	—	—	—

Born; 5/10/72, St. Catharines, Ontario. 6-0, 190.

Cam Stewart — Left Wing

Season	Team	League	GP	G	A	PTS	PIM	GP	G	A	PTS	PIM
93-94	Boston	NHL	57	3	6	9	66	8	0	3	3	7
93-94	Providence	AHL	14	3	2	5	5	—	—	—	—	—
94-95	Boston	NHL	5	0	0	0	2	—	—	—	—	—
94-95	Providence	AHL	31	13	11	24	38	9	2	5	7	0
95-96	Boston	NHL	6	0	0	0	0	5	1	0	1	2
95-96	Providence	AHL	54	17	25	42	39	—	—	—	—	—
96-97	Boston	NHL	15	0	1	1	4	—	—	—	—	—
96-97	Providence	AHL	18	4	3	7	37	—	—	—	—	—
96-97	Cincinnati	IHL	7	3	2	5	8	1	0	0	0	0
	NHL	Totals	83	3	7	10	72	13	1	3	4	9
	AHL	Totals	117	37	41	78	119	9	2	5	7	0

Born; 9/18/71, Kitchener, Ontario. 5-11, 196. Drafted by Boston Bruins (2nd choice, 63rd overall) in 1990 Entry Draft.

Dave Stewart — Defenseman

Season	Team	League	GP	G	A	PTS	PIM	GP	G	A	PTS	PIM
91-92	Toledo	ECHL	3	0	2	2	2	—	—	—	—	—
92-93	Muskegon	CoHL	17	3	11	14	35	2	0	0	0	0
93-94	Flint	CoHL	8	1	14	15	8	—	—	—	—	—
94-95	Roanoke	ECHL	68	14	46	60	200	8	2	1	3	20
95-96	Roanoke	ECHL	65	13	28	41	239	3	0	1	1	4
96-97	Roanoke	ECHL	57	9	30	39	168	4	0	1	1	4
	ECHL	Totals	193	36	106	142	609	15	2	3	5	28
	CoHL	Totals	25	4	25	29	43	2	0	0	0	0

Born; 1/11/72, Norwood, Ontario. 6-1, 205.

Glen Stewart — Left Wing

Season	Team	League	GP	G	A	PTS	PIM	GP	G	A	PTS	PIM
94-95	Greensboro	ECHL	57	33	45	78	51	6	2	5	7	27
95-96	Erie	ECHL	69	41	51	92	145	—	—	—	—	—
96-97	Utah	IHL	1	0	0	0	0	—	—	—	—	—
96-97	Fort Wayne	IHL	8	0	0	0	2	—	—	—	—	—
96-97	Quad City	CoHL	65	66	69	135	30	14	6	12	16	10
	IHL	Totals	9	0	0	0	2	—	—	—	—	—
	ECHL	Totals	126	74	96	170	196	6	2	5	7	27

Born; 7/30/70, Scarborough, Ontario. 6-0, 185. 1995-96 ECHL First Team All-Star. 1996-97 CoHL First Team All-Star. Member of 1996-97 CoHL Champion Quad City Mallards.

Michael Stewart — Defenseman

Season	Team	League	GP	G	A	PTS	PIM	GP	G	A	PTS	PIM
92-93	Binghamton	AHL	68	2	10	12	71	1	0	0	0	0
93-94	Binghamton	AHL	79	8	42	50	75	—	—	—	—	—
94-95	Binghamton	AHL	68	6	21	27	83	—	—	—	—	—
94-95	Springfield	AHL	7	0	3	3	21	—	—	—	—	—
95-96	Detroit	IHL	41	6	6	12	95	—	—	—	—	—

Season	Team	League	GP	G	A	PTS	PIM	GP	G	A	PTS	PIM
95-96	Springfield	AHL	29	2	6	8	44	10	1	3	4	22
96-97	Rochester	AHL	4	0	0	0	0	9	1	3	4	23
	AHL	Totals	255	18	82	100	294	20	2	6	8	45

Born; 5/30/72, Calgary, Alberta. 6-2, 210. Drafted by New York Rangers (1st choice, 13th overall) in 1990 Entry Draft. Traded to Hartford Whalers by Rangers with Glen Featherstone, NY Rangers' first round choice (Jean-Sebastien Giguere) in 1995 Entry Draft and fourth round choice (Steve Wasylko) in 1996 Entry Draft for Pat Verbeek (3/23/95).

Thomas Stewart — Center

			Regular Season					Playoffs				
Season	Team	League	GP	G	A	PTS	PIM	GP	G	A	PTS	PIM
96-97	Macon	CeHL	64	24	27	51	164	5	0	1	1	17

Born; Brampton, Ontario.

Mark Stitt — Forward

			Regular Season					Playoff				
Season	Team	League	GP	G	A	PTS	PIM	GP	G	A	PTS	PIM
95-96	Toledo	ECHL	67	15	36	51	86	11	1	6	7	12
96-97	San Diego	WCHL	63	31	75	106	99	8	2	6	8	8

Member of 1996-97 WCHL Champion San Diego Gulls.

Darren Stolk — Defenseman

			Regular Season					Playoffs				
Season	Team	League	GP	G	A	PTS	PIM	GP	G	A	PTS	PIM
89-90	Muskegon	IHL	65	3	3	6	59	6	1	0	1	2
90-91	Muskegon	IHL	47	2	8	10	40	—	—	—	—	—
90-91	Kansas City	IHL	23	2	10	12	36	—	—	—	—	—
91-92	Salt Lake City	IHL	65	2	8	10	68	5	0	0	0	2
92-93	Salt Lake City	IHL	64	4	5	9	65	—	—	—	—	—
93-94	Providence	AHL	57	4	10	14	56	—	—	—	—	—
94-95	Providence	AHL	23	3	6	9	13	4	0	1	1	4
95-96	Fresno	WCHL	29	4	14	18	58	2	0	0	0	0
96-97	Fresno	WCHL	32	3	16	19	50	5	2	2	4	31
	IHL	Totals	264	13	34	47	268	11	1	0	1	4
	AHL	Totals	80	7	16	23	121	4	0	1	1	4
	WCHL	Totals	61	7	30	37	108	7	2	2	4	31

Born; 7/22/68, Taber, Alberta. 6-4, 225. Drafted by Pittsburgh Penguins (11th choice, 235th overall) in 1988 Entry Draft.

Mike Stone — Center

			Regular Season					Playoffs				
Season	Team	League	GP	G	A	PTS	PIM	GP	G	A	PTS	PIM
94-95	Huntington	ECHL	68	27	30	57	18	4	1	2	3	0
95-96	Worcester	AHL	2	0	0	0	0	—	—	—	—	—
95-96	Huntington	ECHL	57	14	30	44	24	—	—	—	—	—
96-97	Huntington	ECHL	67	27	51	78	30	—	—	—	—	—
	ECHL	Totals	189	68	111	179	72	4	1	2	3	0

Born; 7/13/72, Detroit, Michigan.

Jim Storm — Left Wing

			Regular Season					Playoffs				
Season	Team	League	GP	G	A	PTS	PIM	GP	G	A	PTS	PIM
93-94	Hartford	NHL	68	6	10	16	27	—	—	—	—	—
94-95	Hartford	NHL	6	0	3	3	0	—	—	—	—	—
94-95	Springfield	AHL	33	11	11	22	29	—	—	—	—	—
95-96	Dallas	NHL	10	1	2	3	17	—	—	—	—	—
95-96	Michigan	IHL	60	18	33	51	27	10	4	8	12	2

Season	Team	League	GP	G	A	PTS	PIM	GP	G	A	PTS	PIM
96-97	Michigan	IHL	75	25	24	49	27	4	0	1	1	4
	NHL	Totals	84	7	15	22	44	—	—	—	—	—
	IHL	Totals	135	43	57	100	54	14	4	9	13	6

Born; 2/5/71, Milford, Michigan 6-2, 200. Drafted by Hartford Whalers (5th choice, 75th overall) in 1991 Entry Draft.

Jamie Storr — Goaltender

			Regular Season							Playoffs				
Season	Team	League	GP	W	L	T	MIN	SO	GAVG	GP	W	L	MIN	SO	GAVG
94-95	Los Angeles	NHL	5	1	3	1	263	0	3.88	—	—	—	—	—	—
95-96	Los Angeles	NHL	5	3	1	0	262	0	2.75	—	—	—	—	—	—
95-96	Phoenix	IHL	48	22	20	4	2710	2	3.08	2	1	1	118	1	2.03
96-97	Los Angeles	NHL	5	2	1	1	265	0	2.49	—	—	—	—	—	—
96-97	Phoenix	IHL	44	16	22	4	2442	0	3.61	—	—	—	—	—	—
	NHL	Totals	15	6	5	2	790	0	3.04	—	—	—	—	—	—
	IHL	Totals	92	38	42	8	5152	2	3.33	2	1	1	118	1	2.03

Born; 12/28/75, Brampton, Ontario. 6-0, 170. Drafted by Los Angeles Kings (1st choice, 7th overall) in 1994 Entry Draft.

Shannon Storr — Defenseman

Season	Team	League	GP	G	A	PTS	PIM	GP	G	A	PTS	PIM
96-97	Reno	WCHL	15	3	0	3	14	—	—	—	—	—
96-97	Amarillo	WPHL	8	0	1	1	11	—	—	—	—	—

Born; 5/17/71, Brampton, Ontario. 6-0, 185.

Wayne Strachan — Center

Season	Team	League	GP	G	A	PTS	PIM	GP	G	A	PTS	PIM
95-96	Los Angeles	IHL	75	19	30	49	55	—	—	—	—	—
96-97	Long Beach	IHL	6	3	0	3	2	—	—	—	—	—
96-97	Manitoba	IHL	25	3	10	13	24	—	—	—	—	—
96-97	Roanoke	ECHL	25	19	13	32	23	—	—	—	—	—
96-97	Thunder Bay	CoHL	8	4	6	10	2	4	3	3	6	10
	IHL	Totals	106	25	40	65	81	—	—	—	—	—

Born; 12/12/72, Fort Francis, Ontario. 5-9, 185. Selected by New York Rangers in 1993 Supplemental Draft.

Keith Street — Center

Season	Team	League	GP	G	A	PTS	PIM	GP	G	A	PTS	PIM
88-89	Milwaukee	IHL	40	10	11	21	22	—	—	—	—	—
89-90	Milwaukee	IHL	55	5	13	18	25	—	—	—	—	—
95-96	Anchorage	WCHL	54	44	40	84	68	—	—	—	—	—
96-97	Anchorage	WCHL	64	44	70	114	61	6	4	2	6	4
	IHL	Totals	95	15	24	39	47	—	—	—	—	—
	WCHL	Totals	118	88	110	198	129	6	4	2	6	4

Born; 3/18/65, Moose Jaw, Saskatchewan. 6-0, 175. Did not play professional hockey in North America between the 1989-90 and 1995-96 seasons. Signed as a free agent by Vancouver Canucks (7/22/88)

Rob Striar — Defenseman

Season	Team	League	GP	G	A	PTS	PIM	GP	G	A	PTS	PIM
93-94	Jacksonville	SUN	28	2	5	7	30	—	—	—	—	—
93-94	Daytona Beach	SUN	4	0	0	0	2	—	—	—	—	—
93-94	Fort Worth	CeHL	8	0	4	4	34	—	—	—	—	—
94-95	N/A											
95-96	Utica	CoHL	1	0	0	0	0	—	—	—	—	—
95-96	Erie	ECHL	10	0	0	0	26	—	—	—	—	—
95-96	Hamtpn Roads	ECHL	2	0	0	0	2	—	—	—	—	—

96-97	Saginaw	CoHL	71	3	8	11	115	—	—	—	—	—
	CoHL	Totals	72	3	8	11	115	—	—	—	—	—
	SUN	Totals	32	2	5	7	32	—	—	—	—	—
	ECHL	Totals	12	0	0	0	28	—	—	—	—	—

Born; 8/24/72, New York, New York. 6-0, 200.

Mark Strobel — Defenseman

			Regular Season					Playoffs				
Season	Team	League	GP	G	A	PTS	PIM	GP	G	A	PTS	PIM
95-96	Albany	AHL	28	1	1	2	2	—	—	—	—	—
95-96	Raleigh	ECHL	26	1	5	6	18	—	—	—	—	—
96-97	Albany	AHL	60	3	10	13	65	8	1	1	2	2
	AHL	Totals	88	4	11	15	67	8	1	1	2	2

Born; 8/15/73, St. Paul, Minnesota. 6-0, 200.

Mark Strohack — Defenseman

			Regular Season					Playoffs				
Season	Team	League	GP	G	A	PTS	PIM	GP	G	A	PTS	PIM
96-97	Utica	CoHL	1	0	0	0	0	—	—	—	—	—
96-97	Fort Worth	CeHL	66	13	38	51	79	17	2	13	15	14

Born; 2/12/71, Waterloo, Ontario. 6-1, 215. Member of 1996-97 CeHL Champion Fort Worth Fire.

Doug Stromback — Right Wing

			Regular Season					Playoffs				
Season	Team	League	GP	G	A	PTS	PIM	GP	G	A	PTS	PIM
88-89	Flint	IHL	2	0	0	0	0	—	—	—	—	—
88-89	Johnstown	ECHL	3	0	2	2	0	—	—	—	—	—
88-89	Erie	ECHL	50	40	43	83	77	4	0	2	2	0
89-90	Erie	ECHL	53	23	43	66	16	7	4	5	9	0
90-91	Erie	ECHL	24	14	15	29	25	5	4	2	6	0
91-92	N/A											
92-93	N/A											
93-94	Huntington	ECHL	23	2	4	6	30	—	—	—	—	—
93-94	Muskegon	CoHL	39	13	12	25	19	—	—	—	—	—
94-95	Utica	CoHL	6	2	3	5	8	—	—	—	—	—
94-95	Tulsa	CeHL	27	9	10	19	19	—	—	—	—	—
94-95	Memphis	CeHL	6	5	4	9	6	—	—	—	—	—
95-96	Memphis	CeHL	60	26	38	64	41	6	0	1	1	6
96-97	Memphis	CeHL	58	21	31	52	53	—	—	—	—	—
96-97	Tulsa	CeHL	7	3	6	9	6	5	0	2	2	0
	CeHL	Totals	158	64	89	153	125	11	0	3	3	6
	ECHL	Totals	153	79	107	186	148	16	8	9	17	0
	CoHL	Totals	45	15	15	30	27	—	—	—	—	—

Born; 3/2/67, Farmington, Michigan. 6-1, 200. Drafted by Washington Capitals (7th choice, 124th overall) 1985 Entry Draft.

Brett Strot — Right Wing

			Regular Season					Playoffs				
Season	Team	League	GP	G	A	PTS	PIM	GP	G	A	PTS	PIM
90-91	Knoxville	ECHL	55	36	28	64	36	3	0	0	0	4
91-92	Michigan	CoHL	54	38	40	78	29	4	0	4	4	7
92-93	Birmingham	ECHL	43	15	21	36	37	—	—	—	—	—
92-93	Detroit	CoHL	7	3	2	5	6	—	—	—	—	—
93-94	Flint	CoHL	53	36	71	107	37	10	10	10	20	2
94-95	Dayton	ECHL	4	1	3	4	0	—	—	—	—	—
94-95	Tallahassee	ECHL	7	2	6	8	4	—	—	—	—	—
94-95	Flint	CoHL	32	16	28	44	28	6	4	3	7	6
95-96	Minnesota	IHL	1	0	0	0	0	—	—	—	—	—
95-96	Quad City	CoHL	51	34	29	63	79	1	0	1	1	0

96-97	San Diego	WCHL	9	0	3	3	2	—	—	—	—	—
96-97	Quad City	CoHL	44	20	35	55	17	—	—	—	—	—
96-97	Madison	CoHL	—	—	—	—	—	5	0	2	2	0
	CoHL	Totals	241	147	205	352	196	26	14	19	33	15
	ECHL	Totals	109	54	58	112	77	3	0	0	0	4

Born; 7/11/67, Maple Grove, Minnesota. 6-0, 188.

Jason Strudwick — Defenseman

			Regular Season					Playoffs				
Season	Team	League	GP	G	A	PTS	PIM	GP	G	A	PTS	PIM
95-96	Islanders	NHL	1	0	0	0	7	—	—	—	—	—
95-96	Worcester	AHL	60	2	7	9	119	4	0	1	1	0
96-97	Kentucky	AHL	80	1	9	10	198	4	0	0	0	0
	AHL	Totals	140	3	16	19	317	8	0	1	1	0

Born; otn, Alberta. 6-3, 210. Drafted by New York Islanders (3rd choice, 63rd overall) in 1994 Entry Draft.

Steve Strunk — Center

			Regular Season					Playoffs				
Season	Team	League	GP	G	A	PTS	PIM	GP	G	A	PTS	PIM
92-93	Milwaukee	IHL	15	4	5	9	6	3	1	0	1	4
92-93	Columbus	ECHL	62	32	28	60	61	—	—	—	—	—
93-94	Milwaukee	IHL	31	8	8	16	28	—	—	—	—	—
93-94	Phoenix	IHL	12	3	8	11	18	—	—	—	—	—
94-95	Detroit	IHL	57	6	16	22	48	5	0	0	0	0
95-96	Prince Edward Island	AHL	55	8	20	28	70	4	0	1	1	4
96-97	Detroit	IHL	1	0	1	1	2	—	—	—	—	—
96-97	Milwaukee	IHL	71	10	9	19	54	2	0	0	0	4
	IHL	Totals	187	31	47	78	156	10	1	1	2	8

Born; 8/1/68, Wausau, Wisconsin. 5-8, 175.

Joe Suk — Center

			Regular Season					Playoffs				
Season	Team	League	GP	G	A	PTS	PIM	GP	G	A	PTS	PIM
95-96	Louisville	ECHL	67	19	37	56	63	3	0	1	1	2
96-97	Macon	CeHL	65	21	37	58	71	5	2	0	2	2

Born; 2/26/70, Chicago, Illinois. 5-11, 200.

Steve Suk — Center

			Regular Season					Playoffs				
Season	Team	League	GP	G	A	PTS	PIM	GP	G	A	PTS	PIM
95-96	Louisville	ECHL	31	10	19	29	22	—	—	—	—	—
95-96	Mobile	ECHL	39	11	28	39	22	—	—	—	—	—
96-97	Mobile	ECHL	59	19	44	63	60	3	0	4	4	0
	ECHL	Totals	129	40	91	131	104	3	0	4	4	0

Born; 3/21/73, Highland Park, Illinois. 5-11, 185.

Brian Sullivan — Right Wing

			Regular Season					Playoffs				
Season	Team	League	GP	G	A	PTS	PIM	GP	G	A	PTS	PIM
91-92	Utica	AHL	70	23	24	47	58	4	0	4	4	6
92-93	Utica	AHL	75	30	27	57	88	5	0	0	0	12
92-93	New Jersey	NHL	2	0	1	1	0	—	—	—	—	—
93-94	Albany	AHL	77	31	30	61	140	5	1	1	2	18
94-95	San Diego	IHL	74	24	23	47	97	5	0	1	1	7
95-96	N/A											
96-97	San Antonio	IHL	77	22	24	46	115	9	1	2	3	11
	AHL	Totals	222	84	81	165	286	14	1	5	6	36
	IHL	Totals	151	46	47	93	212	14	1	3	4	18

Born; 4/23/69, South Windsor, Connecticut. 6-4, 215. Drafted by New Jersey Devils (3rd choice, 65th overall) in 1987 Entry Draft. Signed as a free agent by Anaheim Mighty Ducks (9/2/74).

Chris Sullivan — Defenseman

			Regular Season					Playoffs				
Season	Team	League	GP	G	A	PTS	PIM	GP	G	A	PTS	PIM
95-96	Nashville	ECHL	59	4	16	20	41	5	0	0	0	4
96-97	Dayton	ECHL	68	4	17	21	78	4	0	1	1	2
	ECHL	Totals	127	8	33	41	119	9	0	1	1	6

Born; 3/30/72, Hull, Massachusetts. 6-2, 218.

Mike Sullivan — Center

			Regular Season					Playoffs				
Season	Team	League	GP	G	A	PTS	PIM	GP	G	A	PTS	PIM
96-97	Adirondack	AHL	17	1	3	4	2	—	—	—	—	—
96-97	Toledo	ECHL	36	9	23	32	18	5	0	3	3	4

Born; 10/16/73, Woburn, Massachusetts. 6-0, 190. Drafted by Detroit Red Wings (4th choice, 118th overall) in 1992 Entry Draft.

Tim Sullivan — Right Wing

			Regular Season					Playoffs				
Season	Team	League	GP	G	A	PTS	PIM	GP	G	A	PTS	PIM
93-94	Nashville	ECHL	65	33	33	66	141	2	0	1	1	7
94-95	Nashville	ECHL	55	16	15	31	133	11	2	5	7	32
95-96	Utica	CoHL	21	4	11	15	18	—	—	—	—	—
95-96	Oklahoma City	CeHL	29	15	18	33	113	10	4	2	6	33
96-97	Oklahoma City	CeHL	46	15	26	41	156	—	—	—	—	—
	ECHL	Totals	120	49	48	97	274	13	2	6	8	39
	CeHL	Totals	75	30	44	74	269	10	4	2	6	33

Born; 8/1/70, Boston, Massachusetts. 5-11, 185. Member of 1995-96 CeHL champion Oklahoma City Blazers.

Olie Sundstrom — Goaltender

			Regular Season							Playoffs					
Season	Team	League	GP	W	L	T	MIN	SO	GAVG	GP	W	L	MIN	SO	GAVG
92-93	Columbus	ECHL	8	4	3	0	416	0	4.04	—	—	—	—	—	—
92-93	Nashville	ECHL	21	8	7	0	1087	0	5.46	—	—	—	—	—	—
93-94	Cleveland	IHL	46	20	19	4	2521	0	4.09	—	—	—	—	—	—
94-95	Cleveland	IHL	23	3	17	1	1235	0	5.05	—	—	—	—	—	—
95-96	Erie	ECHL	47	20	22	3	2430	0	4.07	—	—	—	—	—	—
96-97	Johnstown	ECHL	*24	8	*15	1	1349	0	4.89	—	—	—	—	—	—
96-97	Wheeling	ECHL	*37	23	*11	2	2011	0	3.82	1	0	1	31	0	13.43
	IHL	Totals	69	23	36	5	3756	0	4.41	—	—	—	—	—	—
	ECHL	Totals	137	63	58	6	7293	0	4.36	1	0	1	31	0	13.43

Born; 4/2/68, Ange, Sweden. 6-0, 180.

Ken Sutton — Defenseman

			Regular Season					Playoffs				
Season	Team	League	GP	G	A	PTS	PIM	GP	G	A	PTS	PIM
89-90	Rochester	AHL	57	5	14	19	83	11	1	6	7	15
90-91	Buffalo	NHL	15	3	6	9	13	6	0	1	1	2
90-91	Rochester	AHL	62	7	24	31	65	3	1	1	2	14
91-92	Buffalo	NHL	64	2	18	20	71	7	0	2	2	4
92-93	Buffalo	NHL	63	8	14	22	30	8	3	1	4	8
93-94	Buffalo	NHL	78	4	20	24	71	4	0	0	0	2
94-95	Buffalo	NHL	12	1	2	3	30	—	—	—	—	—
94-95	Edmonton	NHL	12	3	1	4	12	—	—	—	—	—
95-96	Edmonton	NHL	32	0	8	8	43	—	—	—	—	—
95-96	St. Louis	NHL	6	0	0	0	4	1	0	0	0	0
95-96	Worcester	AHL	32	4	16	20	60	4	0	2	2	21

Season	Team	League	GP	G	A	PTS	PIM	GP	G	A	PTS	PIM
96-97	Manitoba	IHL	20	3	10	13	48	—	—	—	—	—
96-97	Albany	AHL	61	6	13	19	79	16	4	8	12	55
	NHL	Totals	282	21	69	90	274	26	3	4	7	16
	AHL	Totals	212	22	67	89	287	34	6	17	23	105

Born; 5/11/69, Edmonton, Alberta. 6-0, 198. Drafted by Buffalo Sabres (4th choice, 98th overall) in 1989 Entry Draft. Traded to Edmonton Oilers by Buffalo for Scott Pearson (4/7/95). Traded to St. Louis Blues by Edmonton with Igor Kravchuk for Jeff Norton and Donald Dufresne (1/4/96). Traded to New Jersey Devils with St. Louis' second round choice in the 1999 Entry Draft for Ricard Persson and Mike Peluso, (11/26/96).

Jaroslav Svejkovsky — Right Wing

Season	Team	League	GP	G	A	PTS	PIM	GP	G	A	PTS	PIM
96-97	Washington	NHL	19	7	3	10	4	—	—	—	—	—
96-97	Portland	AHL	54	38	28	66	56	5	2	0	2	6

Born; 10/1/76, Plzen, Czechoslovakia. 5-11, 185. Drafted by Washington Capitals (2nd choice, 17th overall) in 1996 Entry Draft. 1996-97 AHL Outstanding Rookie. Member of 1996-97 AHL All-Rookie Team.

Bob Sweeney — Center

Season	Team	League	GP	G	A	PTS	PIM	GP	G	A	PTS	PIM
86-87	Boston	NHL	14	2	4	6	21	3	0	0	0	0
86-87	Moncton	AHL	58	29	26	55	81	4	0	2	2	13
87-88	Boston	NHL	80	22	23	45	73	23	6	8	14	66
88-89	Boston	NHL	75	14	14	28	99	10	2	4	6	19
89-90	Boston	NHL	70	22	24	46	93	20	0	2	2	30
90-91	Boston	NHL	80	15	33	48	115	17	4	2	6	45
91-92	Boston	NHL	63	6	14	20	103	14	1	0	1	25
91-92	Maine	AHL	1	1	0	1	0	—	—	—	—	—
92-93	Buffalo	NHL	80	21	26	47	118	8	2	2	4	8
93-94	Buffalo	NHL	60	11	14	25	94	1	0	0	0	0
94-95	Buffalo	NHL	45	5	4	9	18	5	0	0	0	4
95-96	Islanders	NHL	66	6	6	12	59	—	—	—	—	—
95-96	Calgary	NHL	6	1	1	2	6	2	0	0	0	0
96-97	Quebec	IHL	69	10	21	31	120	9	2	0	2	8
	NHL	Totals	639	125	163	288	799	103	15	18	33	197
	AHL	Totals	59	30	26	56	81	4	0	2	2	13

Born; 1/25/64, Concord, Massachusetts. 6-3, 200. Drafted by Boston Bruins (6th choice, 123rd overall) in 1982 Entry Draft. Claimed on waivers by Buffalo Sabres from Boston, (10/9/92). Claimed on waivers by New York Islanders from Buffalo in NHL Waiver Draft, (10/2/95). Traded to calgary Flames by Islanders for Pat Concaher and Calgary's sixth round choice (Ilja Demidov) in 1997 Entry Draft., (3/20/96).

Tim Sweeney — Left Wing

Season	Team	League	GP	G	A	PTS	PIM	GP	G	A	PTS	PIM
89-90	Salt Lake City	IHL	81	46	51	97	32	11	5	4	9	4
90-91	Calgary	NHL	42	7	9	16	8	—	—	—	—	—
90-91	Salt Lake City	IHL	31	19	16	35	8	4	3	3	6	0
91-92	United States	National										
91-92	Calgary	NHL	11	1	2	3	4	—	—	—	—	—
92-93	Boston	NHL	14	1	7	8	6	3	0	0	0	0
92-93	Providence	AHL	60	41	55	96	32	3	2	2	4	0
93-94	Anaheim	NHL	78	16	27	43	49	—	—	—	—	—
94-95	Anaheim	NHL	13	1	1	2	2	—	—	—	—	—
94-95	Providence	AHL	2	2	2	4	0	13	8	*17	*25	6
95-96	Boston	NHL	41	8	8	16	14	1	0	0	0	2
95-96	Providence	AHL	34	17	22	39	12	—	—	—	—	—

Season	Team	League	GP	G	A	PTS	PIM	GP	G	A	PTS	PIM
96-97	Boston	NHL	36	10	11	21	14	—	—	—	—	—
96-97	Providence	AHL	23	11	22	33	6	—	—	—	—	—
	NHL	Totals	235	44	65	109	97	4	0	0	0	2
	AHL	Totals	119	71	101	172	50	16	10	19	29	6
	IHL	Totals	112	65	67	132	40	15	8	7	15	4

Born; 4/12/67, Boston, Massachusetts. 5-11, 185. Drafted by Calgary Flames (7th choice, 122nd overall) in 1985 Entry Draft. Signed as a free agent by Boston Bruins (9/16/92). Claimed by Anaheim Mighty Ducks from Boston in Expansion Draft (6/24/93). Signed as a free agent by Boston (8/9/95). 1989-90 IHL Second Team All-Star. 1992-93 AHL Second Team All-Star.

Wes Swinson — Defenseman

Season	Team	League	GP	G	A	PTS	PIM	GP	G	A	PTS	PIM
96-97	Carolina	AHL	10	0	0	0	10	—	—	—	—	—
96-97	Tallahassee	ECHL	17	3	9	12	28	3	0	1	1	4

Born; 5/26/75, Peterborough, Ontario. Drafted by Hartford Whalers (7th choice, 240th overall) in 1993 Entry Draft.

Petr Sykora — Center

Season	Team	League	GP	G	A	PTS	PIM	GP	G	A	PTS	PIM
93-94	Cleveland	IHL	13	4	5	9	8	—	—	—	—	—
94-95	Detroit	IHL	29	12	17	29	16	—	—	—	—	—
95-96	New Jersey	NHL	63	18	24	42	32	—	—	—	—	—
95-96	Albany	AHL	5	4	1	5	0	—	—	—	—	—
96-97	New Jersey	NHL	19	1	2	3	4	2	0	0	0	2
96-97	Albany	AHL	43	20	25	45	48	4	1	4	5	2
	NHL	Totals	82	19	26	45	36	2	0	0	0	2
	AHL	Totals	48	24	26	50	48	4	1	4	5	2
	IHL	Totals	42	16	22	38	24	—	—	—	—	—

Born; 11/19/76, Plzen, Czechoslovakia. 5-11, 185. Drafted by New Jersey Devils (1st choice, 18th overall) in 1995 Entry Draft.

Dean Sylvester — Right Wing

Season	Team	League	GP	G	A	PTS	PIM	GP	G	A	PTS	PIM
95-96	Kansas City	IHL	36	11	10	21	15	4	0	0	0	2
95-96	Mobile	ECHL	44	24	27	51	35	—	—	—	—	—
96-97	Kansas City	IHL	77	23	22	45	47	3	1	1	2	0
	IHL	Totals	113	34	32	66	62	7	1	1	2	2

Born; 12/30/72, Weymouth, Massachusetts. 6-2, 200.

Brad Symes — Defenseman

Season	Team	League	GP	G	A	PTS	PIM	GP	G	A	PTS	PIM
96-97	Hamilton	AHL	5	0	0	0	7	—	—	—	—	—
96-97	Wheeling	ECHL	51	6	17	23	63	1	0	0	0	0

Born; 4/26/76, Edmonton, Alberta. 6-2, 210. Drafted by Edmonton Oilers (5th choice, 60th overall) in 1994 Entry Draft.

Gerv Sytnyk — Center

Season	Team	League	GP	G	A	PTS	PIM	GP	G	A	PTS	PIM
96-97	Alaska	WCHL	24	9	8	17	16	—	—	—	—	—

Born; 12/15/75, Oshawa, Ontario. 5-9, 175.

Mike Szoke — Forward

Season	Team	League	GP	G	A	PTS	PIM	GP	G	A	PTS	PIM
96-97	Fresno	WCHL	31	11	11	22	21	—	—	—	—	—
96-97	Reno	WCHL	4	2	2	4	0	—	—	—	—	—

Born; 8/12/74, High Level, Alberta. 5-10, 175. Drafted by Tampa Bay Lightning (11th choice, 263rd overall) in 1993 Entry Draft.

Sean Tallaire — Right Wing

			Regular Season					Playoffs				
Season	Team	League	GP	G	A	PTS	PIM	GP	G	A	PTS	PIM
96-97	Manitoba	IHL	74	21	29	50	67	—	—	—	—	—

10/3/73, Steinbahc, Minnesota. 5-10, 185. Drafted by Vancouver Canucks (7th choice, 202nd overall) in 1993 Entry Draft.

Rob Tallas — Goaltender

			Regular Season							Playoffs					
Season	Team	League	GP	W	L	T	MIN	SO	GAVG	GP	W	L	MIN	SO	GAVG
94-95	Providence	AHL	2	1	0	0	82	1	2.90	—	—	—	—	—	—
94-95	Charlotte	ECHL	36	21	9	3	2011	0	3.40	—	—	—	—	—	—
95-96	Boston	NHL	1	1	0	0	60	0	3.00	—	—	—	—	—	—
95-96	Providence	AHL	37	12	16	7	2136	1	3.29	2	0	2	135	0	4.01
96-97	Boston	NHL	28	8	12	1	1244	1	3.33	—	—	—	—	—	—
96-97	Providence	AHL	24	9	14	1	1424	0	3.50	—	—	—	—	—	—
	NHL	Totals	29	9	12	1	1304	1	3.31	—	—	—	—	—	—
	AHL	Totals	63	22	30	8	3642	2	3.36	2	0	2	135	0	4.01

Born; 3/20/73, Edmonton, Alberta. 6-0, 178. Signed as a free agent by Boston (9/13/95).

Mike Tamburro — Goaltender

			Regular Season							Playoffs					
Season	Team	League	GP	W	L	T	MIN	SO	GAVG	GP	W	L	MIN	SO	GAVG
96-97	Cleveland	IHL	26	13	8	2	1326	1	2.99	1	0	0	12	0	0.00
96-97	Louisville	ECHL	1	0	1	0	60	0	6.00	—	—	—	—	—	—

Born; 3/26/73, Toronto, Ontario. 5-8, 170. Last amateur club; Rennsalaer Polytechnic Institute (ECAC).

Chris Tancill — Center

			Regular Season					Playoffs				
Season	Team	League	GP	G	A	PTS	PIM	GP	G	A	PTS	PIM
90-91	Hartford	NHL	9	1	1	2	4	—	—	—	—	—
90-91	Springfield	AHL	72	37	35	72	46	17	8	4	12	32
91-92	Hartford	NHL	10	0	0	0	2	—	—	—	—	—
91-92	Detroit	NHL	1	0	0	0	0	—	—	—	—	—
91-92	Springfield	AHL	17	12	7	19	20	—	—	—	—	—
91-92	Adirondack	AHL	50	36	34	70	42	19	7	9	16	31
92-93	Detroit	NHL	4	1	0	1	2	—	—	—	—	—
92-93	Adirondack	AHL	68	*59	43	102	62	10	7	7	14	10
93-94	Dallas	NHL	12	1	3	4	8	—	—	—	—	—
93-94	Kalamazoo	IHL	60	41	54	95	55	5	0	2	2	8
94-95	San Jose	NHL	26	3	11	14	10	11	1	1	2	8
94-95	Kansas City	IHL	64	31	28	59	40	—	—	—	—	—
95-96	San Jose	NHL	45	7	16	23	20	—	—	—	—	—
95-96	Kansas City	IHL	27	12	16	28	18	—	—	—	—	—
96-97	San Jose	NHL	25	4	0	4	8	—	—	—	—	—
96-97	Kentucky	AHL	42	19	26	45	31	4	2	0	2	2
	NHL	Totals	114	22	31	53	54	11	1	1	2	8
	AHL	Totals	249	163	145	308	201	50	24	20	44	75
	IHL	Totals	151	84	98	182	113	5	0	2	2	8

Born; 2/7/68, Livonia, Michigan. 5-10, 185. Drafted by Hartford Whalers (1st choice, 15th overall) in 1989 Supplemental Draft. Traded to Detroit Red Wings to Hartford for daniel Shank (12/18/91). Signed as a free agent by Dallas Stars (8/28/93). Signed as a free agent by San Jose Sharks (8/24/94). Member of 1990-91 AHL champion Springfield Indians. Member of 1991-92 AHL champion Adirondack Red Wings.

Martin Tanguay — Center

			Regular Season					Playoffs				
Season	Team	League	GP	G	A	PTS	PIM	GP	G	A	PTS	PIM
96-97	Knoxville	ECHL	41	9	16	25	47	—	—	—	—	—

Born; 1/12/73, Ste. Julie, Quebec. 5-11, 185.

John Tanner — Goaltender

Regular Season | **Playoffs**

Season	Team	League	GP	W	L	T	MIN	SO	GAVG	GP	W	L	MIN	SO	GAVG
89-90	Quebec	NHL	1	0	1	0	60	0	3.00	—	—	—	—	—	—
90-91	Quebec	NHL	6	1	3	1	228	0	4.21	—	—	—	—	—	—
91-92	Quebec	NHL	14	1	7	4	796	1	3.47	—	—	—	—	—	—
91-92	Halifax	AHL	12	6	5	1	672	2	2.59	—	—	—	—	—	—
91-92	New Haven	AHL	16	7	6	2	908	0	3.77	—	—	—	—	—	—
92-93	Halifax	AHL	51	20	18	7	2852	0	4.19	—	—	—	—	—	—
93-94	Cornwall	AHL	38	14	15	4	2035	1	3.63	—	—	—	—	—	—
93-94	San Diego	IHL	13	5	3	2	629	0	3.53	3	0	1	118	0	2.53
94-95	Greensboro	ECHL	6	0	4	1	342	0	4.73	—	—	—	—	—	—
94-95	San Diego	IHL	8	1	3	1	344	0	4.87	—	—	—	—	—	—
95-96	Detroit	CoHL	2	1	0	0	112	0	4.27	—	—	—	—	—	—
95-96	Muskegon	CoHL	2	0	2	0	89	0	5.38	—	—	—	—	—	—
95-96	Rochester	AHL	10	3	6	1	579	0	3.94	—	—	—	—	—	—
96-97	Wheeling	ECHL	19	7	10	1	940	0	3.76	—	—	—	—	—	—
	NHL	Totals	21	2	11	5	1084	1	3.60	—	—	—	—	—	—
	AHL	Totals	127	50	50	15	7046	3	3.80	—	—	—	—	—	—
	IHL	Totals	21	6	6	3	973	0	4.01	3	0	1	118	0	2.53
	ECHL	Totals	25	7	14	2	1282	0	4.02	—	—	—	—	—	—
	CoHL	Totals	4	1	2	0	201	0	4.78	—	—	—	—	—	—

Born; 3/17/71, Cambridge, Ontario. 6-3, 182. Drafted by Quebec Nordiques (4th choice, 54th overall) in 1989 Entry Draft. Traded to Anaheim Mighty Ducks by Quebec for Anaheim's fourth round choice (Tomi Kallio) in 1995 Entry Draft (2/20/94).

Marc Tardif — Left Wing

Regular Season | **Playoffs**

Season	Team	League	GP	G	A	PTS	PIM	GP	G	A	PTS	PIM
93-94	Atlanta	IHL	65	9	13	22	154	—	—	—	—	—
94-95	Atlanta	IHL	5	0	0	0	2	—	—	—	—	—
94-95	Nashville	ECHL	54	16	26	42	263	8	1	0	1	30
95-96	Worcester	AHL	3	0	0	0	0	—	—	—	—	—
95-96	South Carolina	ECHL	52	25	18	43	206	8	3	4	7	41
96-97	Rochester	AHL	1	0	0	0	0	—	—	—	—	—
96-97	South Carolina	ECHL	56	15	22	37	187	18	4	12	16	*114
	IHL	Totals	70	9	13	22	156	—	—	—	—	—
	AHL	Totals	4	0	0	0	0	—	—	—	—	—
	ECHL	Totals	162	56	66	122	656	34	8	16	24	185

Born; 1/6/73, Montreal, Quebec. 6-1, 190. Drafted by Tampa Bay Lightning (10th choice, 218th overall) in 1992 Entry Draft. Member of 1996-97 ECHL Champion South Carolina Stingrays.

Patrice Tardif — Center

Regular Season | **Playoffs**

Season	Team	League	GP	G	A	PTS	PIM	GP	G	A	PTS	PIM
93-94	Peoria	IHL	11	4	4	8	21	4	2	0	2	4
94-95	St. Louis	NHL	27	3	10	13	29	—	—	—	—	—
94-95	Peoria	IHL	53	27	18	45	83	—	—	—	—	—
95-96	Los Angeles	NHL	15	1	1	2	37	—	—	—	—	—
95-96	St. Louis	NHL	23	3	0	3	12	—	—	—	—	—
95-96	Worcester	AHL	30	13	13	26	69	—	—	—	—	—
96-97	Phoenix	IHL	9	0	3	3	13	—	—	—	—	—
96-97	Detroit	IHL	66	24	23	47	70	11	0	1	1	8
	NHL	Totals	65	7	11	18	78	—	—	—	—	—
	IHL	Totals	139	55	48	103	187	15	2	1	3	12

Born; 10/30/70, Thetford Mines, Quebec. Drafted by St. Louis Blues (2nd choice, 54th overall) in 1990 Entry Draft. Traded to Los Angeles Kings with Craig Johnson, Roman Vopat, St. Louis first round pick (Matt Zultek) in 1997 Entry Draft and fifth round pick (Peter Hogan) in 1996 Entry Draft for Wayne Gretzky (2/27/96). Member of 1996-97 IHL Champion Detroit Vipers.

Chris Taylor — Center

Season	Team	League	GP	G	A	PTS	PIM	GP	G	A	PTS	PIM
92-93	Capital District	AHL	77	19	43	62	32	4	0	1	1	2
93-94	Salt Lake City	IHL	79	21	20	41	38	—	—	—	—	—
94-95	Islanders	NHL	10	0	3	3	2	—	—	—	—	—
94-95	Denver	IHL	78	38	48	86	47	14	7	6	13	10
95-96	Islanders	NHL	11	0	1	1	2	—	—	—	—	—
95-96	Utah	IHL	50	18	23	41	60	22	5	11	16	26
96-97	Islanders	NHL	1	0	0	0	0	—	—	—	—	—
96-97	Utah	IHL	71	27	40	67	24	7	1	2	3	0
	NHL	Totals	22	0	4	4	4	—	—	—	—	—
	IHL	Totals	278	104	131	235	169	43	13	19	32	36

Born; 3/6/72, Stratford, Ontario. 6-1, 196. Drafted by New York Islanders (2nd choice, 27th overall) in 1990 Entry Draft. Signed as a free agent by Los Angeles Kings (8/97). Member of 1994-95 IHL champion Denver Grizzlies. Member of 1995-96 IHL champion Utah Grizzlies.

Jason Taylor — Right Wing

Season	Team	League	GP	G	A	PTS	PIM	GP	G	A	PTS	PIM
91-92	Columbus	ECHL	21	7	9	16	147	—	—	—	—	—
92-93	Dallas	CeHL	60	38	32	70	210	7	1	2	3	23
93-94	Brantford	CoHL	43	4	6	10	176	5	0	0	0	22
94-95	Dallas	CeHL	26	6	12	18	118	—	—	—	—	—
94-95	London	CoHL	18	1	3	4	165	—	—	—	—	—
94-95	Brantford	CoHL	13	1	3	4	36	—	—	—	—	—
95-96	Detroit	CoHL	30	10	18	28	66	8	0	2	2	35
96-97	Central Texas	WPHL	44	10	31	41	250	11	4	7	11	12
	CoHL	Totals	104	16	30	46	443	13	0	2	2	57
	CeHL	Totals	86	44	44	88	328	7	1	2	3	23

Born; 7/19/67, Oak Lake, Manitoba. 5-10, 188.

Mike Taylor — Center

Season	Team	League	GP	G	A	PTS	PIM	GP	G	A	PTS	PIM
94-95	St. John's	AHL	4	0	1	1	0	—	—	—	—	—
94-95	Cornwall	AHL	3	0	0	0	2	—	—	—	—	—
94-95	Richmond	ECHL	42	7	21	28	90	17	3	14	17	23
95-96	Springfield	AHL	2	1	1	2	2	—	—	—	—	—
95-96	Portland	AHL	1	0	0	0	2	—	—	—	—	—
95-96	Richmond	ECHL	65	27	48	75	261	7	1	6	7	21
96-97	Orlando	IHL	2	0	0	0	2	—	—	—	—	—
96-97	Chicago	IHL	43	8	16	24	60	4	0	2	2	0
96-97	Baltimore	AHL	5	0	1	1	4	—	—	—	—	—
96-97	Richmond	ECHL	28	16	19	35	43	—	—	—	—	—
	IHL	Totals	45	8	16	24	62	4	0	2	2	0
	AHL	Totals	10	1	2	3	6	—	—	—	—	—
	ECHL	Totals	135	50	88	138	394	24	4	20	24	44

Born; 8/18/71, Kingston, Ontario. 5-9, 180. Member of 1994-95 ECHL champion Richmond Renegades.

Paul Taylor — Goaltender

Season	Team	League	GP	W	L	T	MIN	SO	GAVG	GP	W	L	MIN	SO	GAVG
94-95	Dayton	ECHL	32	18	11	2	1685	3	3.45	2	0	1	108	0	1.67
94-95	Peoria	IHL	2	2	0	0	120	0	2.50	—	—	—	—	—	—
95-96	Peoria	IHL	16	5	8	1	913	0	4.34	1	0	0	20	0	3.00
95-96	Dayton	ECHL	5	3	1	0	260	0	4.62	—	—	—	—	—	—

96-97	Saint John	AHL	4	0	4	0	238	0	5.04	—	—	—	—	—	—
96-97	Fort Wayne	IHL	1	1	0	0	60	0	3.00	—	—	—	—	—	—
96-97	Roanoke	ECHL	2	1	1	0	120	0	2.50	—	—	—	—	—	—
	IHL	Totals	19	8	8	1	1093	0	4.06	1	0	0	20	0	3.00
	ECHL	Totals	39	22	13	3	2065	3	3.54	2	0	1	108	0	1.67

Born; 8/20/71, Vancouver, British Columbia. 6-1, 190.

Rod Taylor — Left Wing

			Regular Season					Playoffs				
Season	Team	League	GP	G	A	PTS	PIM	GP	G	A	PTS	PIM
91-92	Hampton Roads	ECHL	40	26	24	50	29	14	*16	10	*26	26
92-93	Baltimore	AHL	18	3	4	7	2	4	0	0	0	10
92-93	Hampton Roads	ECHL	37	30	22	52	63	2	3	0	3	10
93-94	Hampton Roads	ECHL	65	54	34	88	133	7	1	5	6	24
94-95	Hampton Roads	ECHL	68	38	40	78	118	4	2	1	3	6
95-96	Hampton Roads	ECHL	62	40	17	57	102	3	2	1	3	8
96-97	Hampton Roads	ECHL	68	33	33	66	137	9	3	1	4	6
	ECHL	Totals	340	221	170	391	582	39	27	18	45	80

Born; 12/1/66, Lake Orion, Michigan. 5-10, 185. Member of 1991-92 ECHL Champion Hampton Roads Admirals.

Marc Terris — Right Wing

			Regular Season					Playoffs				
Season	Team	League	GP	G	A	PTS	PIM	GP	G	A	PTS	PIM
95-96	Mobile	ECHL	30	6	13	19	18	—	—	—	—	—
95-96	Louisville	ECHL	2	0	1	1	0	—	—	—	—	—
95-96	Huntington	ECHL	31	7	10	17	4	—	—	—	—	—
96-97	Peoria	ECHL	68	20	31	51	19	10	3	7	10	2
	ECHL	Totals	131	33	55	88	41	10	3	7	10	2

Born; 9/2/72, Edmonton, Alberta. 6-1, 190.

Jose Theodore — Goaltender

			Regular Season							Playoffs				
Season	Team	League	GP	W	L	T	MIN	SO	GAVG	GP	W	L	MIN	SO	GAVG
94-95	Fredericton	AHL	—	—	—	—	—	—	—	1	0	1	60	0	3.00
95-96	Montreal	NHL	1	0	0	0	9	0	6.67	—	—	—	—	—	—
96-97	Montreal	NHL	16	5	6	2	821	0	3.87	2	1	1	168	0	2.50
96-97	Fredericton	AHL	26	12	12	0	1469	0	3.55	—	—	—	—	—	—
	NHL	Totals	17	5	6	2	830	0	3.90	2	1	1	168	0	2.50
	AHL	Totals	26	12	12	0	1469	0	3.55	1	0	1	60	0	3.00

Born; 9/13/76, Laval, Quebec. 5-11, 180. Drafted by Montreal Canadiens (2nd choice, 44th overall) in 1994 Entry Draft.

Joel Theriault — Defenseman

			Regular Season					Playoffs				
Season	Team	League	GP	G	A	PTS	PIM	GP	G	A	PTS	PIM
96-97	Hampton Roads	ECHL	50	2	4	6	206	6	0	0	0	10

Born; 10/30/76, Montreal, Quebec. 6-3, 201. Drafted by Washington Capitals (5th choice, 95th overall) in 1995 Entry Draft.

Christian Therrien — Center

			Regular Season					Playoffs				
Season	Team	League	GP	G	A	PTS	PIM	GP	G	A	PTS	PIM
96-97	Macon	CeHL	50	11	24	35	20	—	—	—	—	—

Born;

Mario Therrien — Left Wing

			Regular Season					Playoffs				
Season	Team	League	GP	G	A	PTS	PIM	GP	G	A	PTS	PIM
96-97	Macon	CeHL	66	30	22	52	96	5	0	3	3	32

Born; 5/18/72, Ste. Anne Des Plaines, Quebec. 6-3, 225.

Travis Thiessen — Defenseman

Season	Team	League	GP	G	A	PTS	PIM	GP	G	A	PTS	PIM
92-93	Cleveland	IHL	64	3	7	0	69	4	0	0	0	16
93-94	Cleveland	IHL	74	2	13	15	75	—	—	—	—	—
94-95	Indianapolis	IHL	41	2	3	5	36	—	—	—	—	—
94-95	Saint John	AHL	9	1	2	3	12	5	0	1	1	0
94-95	Flint	CoHL	5	0	1	1	2	—	—	—	—	—
95-96	Indianapolis	IHL	4	0	1	1	8	—	—	—	—	—
95-96	Peoria	IHL	63	3	12	15	102	12	1	4	5	8
96-97	Indianapolis	IHL	8	0	3	3	8	—	—	—	—	—
96-97	Manitoba	IHL	25	0	8	8	28	—	—	—	—	—
96-97	Peoria	ECHL	14	1	6	7	12	10	0	6	6	12
	IHL	Totals	279	10	47	57	326	16	1	4	5	24

Born; 7/11/72, North Battleford, Saskatchewan. 6-3, 202. Drafted by Pittsburgh Penguins (3rd choice, 67th overall) in 1992 Entry Draft. Signed as a free agent by Chicago Blackhawks (6/9/94)

Mike Thomas — Goaltender

Season	Team	League	GP	W	L	T	MIN	SO	GAVG	GP	W	L	MIN	SO	GAVG
96-97	El Paso	WPHL	27	7	5	3	1072	0	4.08	2	0	0	28	0	8.57

Born; 4/6/71, Thompson, Manitoba. 5-10, 200. Member of 1996-97 WPHL Champion El Paso Buzzards.

Kahlil Thomas — Center

Season	Team	League	GP	G	A	PTS	PIM	GP	G	A	PTS	PIM
96-97	Columbus	CeHL	1	0	0	0	0	—	—	—	—	—
96-97	Detroit	IHL	1	1	0	1	0	—	—	—	—	—
96-97	Pensacola	ECHL	5	0	1	1	0	—	—	—	—	—
96-97	Flint	CoHL	50	26	26	52	51	14	4	4	8	6

Born; 12/22/75, Toronto, Ontario. 5-9, 190.

Scott Thomas — Right Wing

Season	Team	League	GP	G	A	PTS	PIM	GP	G	A	PTS	PIM
91-92	Rochester	AHL	—	—	—	—	—	9	0	1	1	17
92-93	Buffalo	NHL	7	1	1	2	15	—	—	—	—	—
92-93	Rochester	AHL	65	32	27	59	38	17	8	5	13	6
93-94	Buffalo	NHL	32	2	2	4	8	—	—	—	—	—
93-94	Rochester	AHL	11	4	5	9	0	—	—	—	—	—
94-95	Rochester	AHL	55	21	25	46	115	5	4	0	4	4
95-96	Cincinnati	IHL	78	32	28	60	54	17	13	2	15	4
96-97	Cincinnati	IHL	71	32	29	61	46	3	0	0	0	0
	NHL	Totals	39	3	3	6	23	—	—	—	—	—
	IHL	Totals	149	64	57	121	100	20	13	2	15	4
	AHL	Totals	131	57	57	114	153	31	12	6	18	27

Born; 1/18/70, Buffalo, New York. 6-2, 202. Drafted by Buffalo Sabres (2nd choice, 56th overall) in 1989 Entry Draft.

Dave Thomlinson — Left Wing

Season	Team	League	GP	G	A	PTS	PIM	GP	G	A	PTS	PIM
87-88	Peoria	IHL	74	27	30	57	56	7	4	3	7	11
88-89	Peoria	IHL	64	27	29	56	154	3	0	1	1	8
89-90	St. Louis	NHL	19	1	2	3	12	—	—	—	—	—
89-90	Peoria	IHL	59	27	40	67	87	5	1	1	2	15
90-91	St. Louis	NHL	3	0	0	0	0	9	3	1	4	4
90-91	Peoria	IHL	80	53	54	107	107	11	6	7	13	28

Season	Team	League	GP	G	A	PTS	PIM	GP	G	A	PTS	PIM
91-92	Boston	NHL	12	0	1	1	17	—	—	—	—	—
91-92	Maine	AHL	25	9	11	20	36	—	—	—	—	—
92-93	Binghamton	AHL	54	25	35	60	61	12	2	5	7	8
93-94	Los Angeles	NHL	7	0	0	0	21	—	—	—	—	—
93-94	Phoenix	IHL	39	10	15	25	70	—	—	—	—	—
94-95	Los Angeles	NHL	1	0	0	0	0	—	—	—	—	—
94-95	Phoenix	IHL	77	30	40	70	87	9	5	3	8	8
95-96	Phoenix	IHL	48	10	13	23	65	4	1	0	1	2
96-97	Phoenix	IHL	67	16	24	40	40	—	—	—	—	—
	NHL	Totals	42	1	3	4	50	9	3	1	4	4
	IHL	Totals	508	200	245	445	651	39	17	15	32	72
	AHL	Totals	79	34	46	80	97	12	2	5	7	8

Born; 10/22/66, Edmonton, Alberta. 6-1, 215. Drafted by Toronto Maple Leafs (3rd choice, 43rd overall) in 1985 Entry Draft. Signed as a free agent by St. Louis Blues (6/4/87). Signed as a free agent by Boston Bruins (7/30/91). Signed as a free agent by New York Rangers (9/4/92). Signed as a free agent by Los Angeles Kings (7/22/93). Member of 1990-91 IHL champion Peoria Rivermen.

Brent Thompson — Defenseman

			Regular Season					Playoffs				
Season	Team	League	GP	G	A	PTS	PIM	GP	G	A	PTS	PIM
90-91	Phoenix	IHL	—	—	—	—	—	4	0	1	1	6
91-92	Los Angeles	NHL	27	0	5	5	89	4	0	0	0	4
91-92	Phoenix	IHL	42	4	13	17	139	—	—	—	—	—
92-93	Los Angeles	NHL	30	0	4	4	76	—	—	—	—	—
92-93	Phoenix	IHL	22	0	5	5	112	—	—	—	—	—
93-94	Los Angeles	NHL	24	1	0	1	81	—	—	—	—	—
93-94	Phoenix	IHL	26	1	11	12	118	—	—	—	—	—
94-95	Winnipeg	NHL	29	0	0	0	78	—	—	—	—	—
95-96	Winnipeg	NHL	10	0	1	1	21	—	—	—	—	—
95-96	Springfield	AHL	58	2	10	12	203	10	1	4	5	*55
96-97	Phoenix	NHL	1	0	0	0	7	—	—	—	—	—
96-97	Phoenix	IHL	12	0	1	1	67	—	—	—	—	—
96-97	Springfield	AHL	64	2	15	17	215	17	0	2	2	31
	NHL	Totals	121	1	10	11	352	4	0	0	0	4
	AHL	Totals	122	4	25	29	418	27	1	6	7	86
	IHL	Totals	102	5	30	35	436	4	0	1	1	6

Born; 1/9/71, Calgary, Alberta. 6-2, 190. Drafted by Los Angeles Kings (1st choice, 39th overall) in 1989 Entry Draft. Traded to Winnipeg Jets by Los Angeles with future considerations for the rights to Ruslan Batyrshin and Phoenix Coyotes' second round choice (Marian Cisar) in 1986 Entry Draft (8/8/94). Signed as a free agent by New York Rangers (8/26/97).

Jeremy Thompson — Forward

			Regular Season					Playoffs				
Season	Team	League	GP	G	A	PTS	PIM	GP	G	A	PTS	PIM
95-96	Nashville	CeHL	3	2	0	2	6	5	2	0	2	5
96-97	Austin	WPHL	8	4	3	7	20	6	3	1	4	31
96-97	Reno	WCHL	48	11	18	29	150	—	—	—	—	—

Born; 4/8/75, Whitecourt, Alberta. 5-11, 190.

Jamie Thompson — Center

			Regular Season					Playoffs				
Season	Team	League	GP	G	A	PTS	PIM	GP	G	A	PTS	PIM
96-97	El Paso	WPHL	50	34	28	62	65	9	4	8	12	12

Member of 1996-97 WPHL Champion El Paso Buzzards. Last amateur club; Maine (Hockey East).

Glen Thornborough — Forward

			Regular Season					Playoffs				
Season	Team	League	GP	G	A	PTS	PIM	GP	G	A	PTS	PIM
96-97	Louisville	ECHL	1	0	0	0	0	—	—	—	—	—
96-97	Memphis	CeHL	40	5	5	10	12	5	1	0	1	15

Born; 2/1/72, Glenboro, Alberta. 6-3, 210. Last amateur club; Alaska-Anchorage (WCHA).

Bob Thornton — Forward

			Regular Season					Playoffs				
Season	Team	League	GP	G	A	PTS	PIM	GP	G	A	PTS	PIM
96-97	San Diego	WCHL	7	0	0	0	0	—	—	—	—	—
96-97	Alaska	WCHL	23	5	13	18	8	—	—	—	—	—
	WCHL	Totals	30	5	13	18	8	—	—	—	—	—

Born;

Rob Thorpe — Left Wing

			Regular Season					Playoffs				
Season	Team	League	GP	G	A	PTS	PIM	GP	G	A	PTS	PIM
96-97	Michigan	IHL	1	0	0	0	0	—	—	—	—	—
96-97	Toledo	ECHL	68	47	28	75	64	2	1	1	2	0

Born; 7/22/73, Hamilton, Ontario. 6-0, 200.

Steve Thorpe — Goaltender

			Regular Season							Playoffs					
Season	Team	League	GP	W	L	T	MIN	SO	GAVG	GP	W	L	MIN	SO	GAVG
95-96	Nashville	ECHL	23	10	7	0	1079	0	4.84	2	0	0	56	0	2.14
96-97	Memphis	CeHL	35	17	11	1	1738	1	3.69	15	9	*6	915	*1	3.28

Born; 7/6/74, Toronto, Ontario. 5-10, 165.

Chuck Thuss — Goaltender

			Regular Season							Playoffs					
Season	Team	League	GP	W	L	T	MIN	SO	GAVG	GP	W	L	MIN	SO	GAVG
95-96	Los Angeles	IHL	22	5	10	1	976	0	3.93	—	—	—	—	—	—
95-96	Louisiana	ECHL	15	6	4	1	686	0	3.67	3	2	1	143	0	4.62
96-97	Birmingham	ECHL	27	10	8	5	1435	1	4.31	—	—	—	—	—	—
96-97	Mobile	ECHL	9	4	3	1	442	0	3.12	2	0	2	119	0	4.04
	ECHL	Totals	51	20	15	7	2563	1	3.93	5	2	3	262	0	4.35

Born; 2/15/72, Arkona, Ontario. 6-1, 193

Brad Tiley — Defenseman

			Regular Season					Playoffs				
Season	Team	League	GP	G	A	PTS	PIM	GP	G	A	PTS	PIM
91-92	Maine	AHL	62	7	22	29	36	—	—	—	—	—
92-93	Binghamton	AHL	26	6	10	16	19	8	0	1	1	2
92-93	Phoenix	IHL	46	11	27	38	35	—	—	—	—	—
93-94	Binghamton	AHL	29	6	10	16	6	—	—	—	—	—
93-94	Phoenix	IHL	35	8	15	23	21	—	—	—	—	—
94-95	Detroit	IHL	56	7	19	26	32	—	—	—	—	—
94-95	Fort Wayne	IHL	14	1	6	7	2	3	1	2	3	0
95-96	Orlando	IHL	69	11	23	34	82	23	2	4	6	16
96-97	Long Beach	IHL	3	1	0	1	2	—	—	—	—	—
96-97	Phoenix	IHL	66	8	28	36	34	—	—	—	—	—
	IHL	Totals	289	47	118	165	208	26	3	6	9	16
	AHL	Totals	117	19	42	61	61	8	0	1	1	2

Born; 7/5/71, Markdale, Ontario. 6-1, 190. Drafted by Boston Bruins (fourth choice, 84th overall) in 1991 Entry Draft. Signed as a free agent by New York Rangers (9/4/92).

Tom Tilley — Defenseman

			Regular Season					Playoffs				
Season	Team	League	GP	G	A	PTS	PIM	GP	G	A	PTS	PIM
88-89	St. Louis	NHL	70	1	22	23	47	10	1	2	3	17
89-90	St. Louis	NHL	34	0	5	5	6	—	—	—	—	—
89-90	Peoria	IHL	22	1	8	9	13	—	—	—	—	—
90-91	St. Louis	NHL	22	2	4	6	4	—	—	—	—	—
90-91	Peoria	IHL	48	7	38	45	53	13	2	9	11	25
91-92	Italy											
91-92	Canadian	National										
92-93	Italy											
93-94	St. Louis	NHL	48	1	7	8	32	4	0	1	1	2
94-95	Atlanta	IHL	10	2	6	8	14	—	—	—	—	—
94-95	Indianapolis	IHL	25	2	13	15	19	—	—	—	—	—
95-96	Milwaukee	IHL	80	11	68	79	58	4	2	2	4	4
96-97	Milwaukee	IHL	25	1	10	11	8	3	0	1	1	0
	NHL	Totals	174	4	38	42	89	14	1	3	4	19
	IHL	Totals	210	24	143	167	165	20	4	12	16	29

Born; 3/28/65, Trenton, Ontario. 6-0, 190. Drafted by St. Louis Blues (13th choice, 196th overall) in 1984 Entry Draft. Traded to Tampa Bay Lightning by St. Louis for Adam Creighton (10/6/94). Traded to Chicago Blackhawks by Tampa Bay with Jim Cummins and Jeff Buchanan for Paul Ysebaert and Rich Sutter(2/22/95). 1990-91 IHL Second Team All-Star. 1995-96 IHL Second Team All-Star. Member of 1990-91 IHL champion Peoria Rivermen.

Mattias Timander — Defenseman

			Regular Season					Playoffs				
Season	Team	League	GP	G	A	PTS	PIM	GP	G	A	PTS	PIM
96-97	Boston	NHL	41	1	8	9	14	—	—	—	—	—
96-97	Providence	AHL	32	3	11	14	20	10	1	1	2	12

Born; 4/16/74, Solleftea, Sweden. 6-1, 194. Drafted by Boston Bruins (7th choice, 208th overall) in 1992 Entry Draft.

Sergei Tkachenko — Goaltender

			Regular Season							Playoffs					
Season	Team	League	GP	W	L	T	MIN	SO	GAVG	GP	W	L	MIN	SO	GAVG
92-93	Hamilton	AHL	1	1	0	0	60	0	3.00	—	—	—	—	—	—
92-93	Brantford	CoHL	4	0	1	0	96	0	6.88	—	—	—	—	—	—
93-94	Hamilton	AHL	2	0	1	1	125	0	4.32	—	—	—	—	—	—
93-94	Columbus	ECHL	34	18	7	4	1884	0	4.11	4	1	2	182	0	5.27
94-95	Syracuse	AHL	2	0	2	0	118	0	4.57	—	—	—	—	—	—
94-95	South Carolina	ECHL	16	7	7	1	868	0	3.25	—	—	—	—	—	—
94-95	Birmingham	ECHL	6	2	4	0	359	0	4.17	—	—	—	—	—	—
95-96	Syracuse	AHL	14	2	8	1	733	2	4.26	1	0	1	60	0	5.00
95-96	Oklahoma City	CeHL	16	12	3	1	944	1	2.35	1	0	1	63	0	4.73
95-96	Raleigh	ECHL	3	0	2	1	179	0	4.69	—	—	—	—	—	—
96-97	Louisiana	ECHL	10	5	3	1	524	0	4.46	—	—	—	—	—	—
96-97	Knoxville	ECHL	22	6	14	0	1234	0	3.79	—	—	—	—	—	—
96-97	Utica	CoHL	—	—	—	—	—	—	—	3	0	3	178	0	4.73
	AHL	Totals	19	3	11	2	1036	2	4.23	1	0	1	60	0	5.00
	ECHL	Totals	91	38	37	7	5049	0	3.95	4	1	2	182	0	5.27
	CoHL	Totals	4	0	1	0	96	0	6.88	3	0	3	178	0	4.73

Born; 6/6/71, Kiev, USSR. 6-2, 198. Drafted by Vancouver Canucks (9th choice, 280th overall) in 1993 Entry Draft. Member of 1995-96 CeHL champion Oklahoma City Blazers.

Stas Tkatch — Left Wing

			Regular Season					Playoffs				
Season	Team	League	GP	G	A	PTS	PIM	GP	G	A	PTS	PIM
92-93	Nashville	ECHL	52	13	18	31	96	8	2	1	3	15
93-94	Nashville	ECHL	67	36	35	71	143	2	0	0	0	5

			GP	G	A	PTS	PIM					
94-95	Detroit	CoHL	74	39	45	84	72	12	0	2	2	6
95-96	Madison	CoHL	68	39	23	62	117	6	0	2	2	4
96-97	Madison	CoHL	46	23	33	56	53	—	—	—	—	—
96-97	Quad City	CoHL	23	13	18	31	36	15	3	7	10	24
	CoHL	Totals	142	78	68	146	189	18	0	4	4	10
	ECHL	Totals	119	49	53	102	239	10	2	1	3	20

Born; 7/12/71, Moscow, Russia. 6-1, 183. Member of 1996-97 CoHL Champion Quad City Mallards.

Mike Tobin — Left Wing

Season	Team	League	GP	G	A	PTS	PIM	GP	G	A	PTS	PIM
96-97	Brantford	CoHL	1	0	0	0	0	—	—	—	—	—
96-97	El Paso	WPHL	24	1	3	4	66	10	0	0	0	12

Member of 1996-97 WPHL Champion El Paso Buzzards.

Lorne Toews — Left Wing

Season	Team	League	GP	G	A	PTS	PIM	GP	G	A	PTS	PIM
94-95	Wheeling	ECHL	54	8	11	19	71	3	0	1	1	2
95-96	Wheeling	ECHL	35	3	7	10	88	—	—	—	—	—
95-96	Columbus	ECHL	16	3	6	9	65	3	2	1	3	4
96-97	Baltimore	AHL	1	0	0	0	0	—	—	—	—	—
96-97	Columbus	ECHL	70	25	25	50	198	8	1	5	6	14
	ECHL	Totals	105	14	24	38	224	6	2	2	4	6

Born; 6/17/73, Winnipeg, Manitoba. 6-0, 195.

Chris Tok — Defenseman

Season	Team	League	GP	G	A	PTS	PIM	GP	G	A	PTS	PIM
95-96	Jacksonville	ECHL	8	1	3	4	21	—	—	—	—	—
95-96	Fort Wayne	IHL	60	2	4	6	120	4	0	0	0	19
96-97	Fort Wayne	IHL	19	1	3	4	35	—	—	—	—	—
96-97	Manitoba	IHL	48	0	4	4	74	—	—	—	—	—
	IHL	Totals	127	3	11	14	229	4	0	0	0	19

Born; 3/19/73, Grand Rapids, Michigan. 6-1, 185. Drafted by Pittsburgh Penguins (10th choice, 214th overall) in 1991 Entry Draft.

Janis Tomans — Left Wing

Season	Team	League	GP	G	A	PTS	PIM	GP	G	A	PTS	PIM
95-96	Jacksonville	ECHL	32	17	18	35	35	18	6	7	13	21
96-97	San Antonio	IHL	8	1	2	3	6	—	—	—	—	—
96-97	Madison	CoHL	37	24	33	57	44	5	4	1	5	6

Born; 2/5/75, Riga, Latvia. 6-1, 200.

Justin Tomberlin — Forward

Season	Team	League	GP	G	A	PTS	PIM	GP	G	A	PTS	PIM
94-95	Raleigh	ECHL	53	11	18	29	17	—	—	—	—	—
95-96	Quad City	CoHL	8	1	1	2	2	—	—	—	—	—
95-96	Lakeland	SHL	46	46	48	94	42	5	4	5	9	0
96-97	Columbus	CeHL	51	24	27	51	61	3	1	2	3	0

Born; 11/15/70, Grand Rapids, Michigan. 6-1, 195. Drafted by Toronto Maple Leafs (11th choice, 192nd overall) in 1989 Entry Draft.

Mike Tomlak — Center

Season	Team	League	GP	G	A	PTS	PIM	GP	G	A	PTS	PIM
89-90	Hartford	NHL	70	7	14	21	48	7	0	1	1	2
90-91	Hartford	NHL	64	8	8	16	55	3	0	0	0	2

Season	Team	League	GP	G	A	PTS	PIM	GP	G	A	PTS	PIM
90-91	Springfield	AHL	15	4	9	13	15	—	—	—	—	—
91-92	Hartford	NHL	6	0	0	0	0	—	—	—	—	—
91-92	Springfield	AHL	39	16	21	37	24	—	—	—	—	—
92-93	Springfield	AHL	38	16	21	37	56	5	1	1	2	2
93-94	Hartford	NHL	1	0	0	0	0	—	—	—	—	—
93-94	Springfield	AHL	79	44	56	100	53	4	2	5	7	4
94-95	Milwaukee	IHL	63	27	41	68	54	15	4	5	9	8
95-96	Milwaukee	IHL	82	11	32	43	68	5	0	2	2	6
96-97	Milwaukee	IHL	47	8	23	31	44	—	—	—	—	—
	NHL	Totals	141	15	22	37	103	10	0	1	1	4
	IHL	Totals	192	46	96	142	166	20	4	7	11	14
	AHL	Totals	171	80	107	187	148	9	3	6	9	6

Born; 10/17/65, Thunder Bay, Ontario. 6-3, 205. Drafted by Toronto Maple Leafs (10th choice, 208th overall) in 1983 Entry Draft. Signed as a free agent by Hartford Whalers (11/14/88).

Mike Tomlinson — Center

			Regular Season					Playoffs				
Season	Team	League	GP	G	A	PTS	PIM	GP	G	A	PTS	PIM
92-93	Chatham	CoHL	48	14	27	41	58	—	—	—	—	—
92-93	Brantford	CoHL	3	0	0	0	2	—	—	—	—	—
93-94	Utica	CoHL	63	24	31	55	148	—	—	—	—	—
94-95	Utica	CoHL	52	16	20	36	128	6	0	2	2	16
95-96	Utica	CoHL	74	21	41	62	203	—	—	—	—	—
96-97	New Mexico	WPHL	58	32	45	77	143	6	1	3	4	2
	CoHL	Totals	240	75	119	194	539	6	0	2	2	16

Born; 3/23/71, Peterborough, Ontario. 6-0, 183.

Shayne Tomlinson — Defenseman

			Regular Season					Playoffs				
Season	Team	League	GP	G	A	PTS	PIM	GP	G	A	PTS	PIM
96-97	Richmond	ECHL	6	1	1	2	2	3	0	2	2	0

Last amateur club; Northern Michigan (WCHA).

Jeff Toms — Left Wing

			Regular Season					Playoffs				
Season	Team	League	GP	G	A	PTS	PIM	GP	G	A	PTS	PIM
94-95	Atlanta	IHL	40	7	8	15	10	4	0	0	0	4
95-96	Tampa Bay	NHL	1	0	0	0	0	—	—	—	—	—
95-96	Atlanta	IHL	68	16	18	34	18	1	0	0	0	0
96-97	Tampa Bay	NHL	34	2	8	10	10	—	—	—	—	—
96-97	Adirondack	AHL	37	11	16	27	8	4	1	2	3	0
	NHL	Totals	35	2	8	10	10	—	—	—	—	—
	IHL	Totals	108	23	26	49	28	5	0	0	0	4

Born; 6/4/74, Swift Current, Saskatchewan. 6-3, 180. Drafted by New Jersey Devils (9th choice, 210th overall) in 1992 Entry Draft. Traded to Tampa Bay Lightning by New Jersey for Vancouver's fourth round choice (previously acquired from Vancouver, later traded to Calgary, Flames selected Ryan Duthie) in 1994 Entry Draft (5/31/94).

Brad Toporowski — Defenseman

			Regular Season					Playoffs				
Season	Team	League	GP	G	A	PTS	PIM	GP	G	A	PTS	PIM
95-96	Erie	ECHL	65	5	12	17	154	—	—	—	—	—
96-97	Thunder Bay	CoHL	71	6	32	38	117	11	0	0	0	22

Born; 6/30/73, Paddockwood, Saskatchewan. 6-1, 200.

Kerry Toporowski — Defense

			Regular Season					Playoffs				
Season	Team	League	GP	G	A	PTS	PIM	GP	G	A	PTS	PIM
91-92	Indianapolis	IHL	18	1	2	3	206	—	—	—	—	—
92-93	Indianapolis	IHL	17	0	0	0	57	—	—	—	—	—
93-94	Indianapolis	IHL	32	1	4	5	126	—	—	—	—	—
93-94	Las Vegas	IHL	13	1	0	1	129	2	0	0	0	31
94-95	Las Vegas	IHL	37	1	4	5	300	5	0	1	1	69
95-96	Adirondack	AHL	53	1	5	6	283	—	—	—	—	—
96-97	Chicago	IHL	51	1	4	5	231	1	0	0	0	29
	IHL	Totals	117	4	10	11	818	7	0	1	1	100

Born; 4/9/71, Prince Albert, Saskatchewan. 6-2, 212. Drafted by San Jose Sharks (5th choice, 67th overall) in 1991 Entry Draft. Traded to Chicago Blackhawks by San Jose with San Jose's second choice (later traded to Winnipeg) in 1992 Entry Draft for Doug Wilson (9/6/91).

Shayne Toporowski — Right Wing

			Regular Season					Playoffs				
Season	Team	League	GP	G	A	PTS	PIM	GP	G	A	PTS	PIM
95-96	St. John's	AHL	72	11	26	37	216	4	1	1	2	4
96-97	Toronto	NHL	3	0	0	0	7	—	—	—	—	—
96-97	St. John's	AHL	72	20	17	37	210	11	3	2	5	16
	AHL	Totals	144	31	43	74	426	15	4	3	7	20

Born; 8/6/75, Paddockwood, Saskatchewan. 6-2, 216. Drafted by Los Angeles Kings (1st choice, 42nd overall) in 1993 Entry Draft. Traded to Toronto Maple Leafs by Los Angeles with Dixon Ward, Guy Leveque and Kelly Fairchild for Eric Lacroix, Chris Snell and Toronto's fourth round choice (Eric Belanger) in the 1996 Entry Draft.

Mike Torchia — Goaltender

			Regular Season							Playoffs					
Season	Team	League	GP	W	L	T	MIN	SO	GAVG	GP	W	L	MIN	SO	GAVG
92-93	Canada	National													
92-93	Kalamazoo	IHL	48	19	17	9	2729	0	3.80	—	—	—	—	—	—
93-94	Kalamazoo	IHL	43	23	12	2	2168	0	3.68	4	1	3	221	*1	3.80
94-95	Dallas	NHL	6	3	2	1	327	0	3.30	—	—	—	—	—	—
94-95	Kalamazoo	IHL	41	19	14	5	2140	*3	2.97	6	0	4	257	0	3.97
95-96	Michigan	IHL	1	1	0	0	60	0	1.00	—	—	—	—	—	—
95-96	Orlando	IHL	7	3	1	1	341	0	2.99	—	—	—	—	—	—
95-96	Portland	AHL	12	2	6	2	577	0	4.79	—	—	—	—	—	—
95-96	Baltimore	AHL	5	2	1	1	257	0	4.61	1	0	0	40	0	0.00
95-96	Hampton Roads	ECHL	5	2	2	0	260	0	3.92	—	—	—	—	—	—
96-97	Fort Wayne	IHL	57	20	*31	3	2971	1	3.47	—	—	—	—	—	—
96-97	Baltimore	AHL	—	—	—	—	—	—	—	1	0	0	40	0	6.00
	IHL	Totals	197	85	75	20	10409	4	3.47	10	1	7	478	1	3.89
	AHL	Totals	17	4	7	3	833	0	4.61	2	0	0	80	0	3.01

Born; 2/23/72, Toronto, Ontario. 5-11, 215. Drafted by Minnesota North Stars (2nd choice, 74th overall) in 1991 Entry Draft. Traded to Washington Capitals by Dallas for future considerations (7/14/95). Traded to Anaheim Mighty Ducks by Washington for Todd Krygier.

Doug Torrell — Forward

			Regular Season					Playoffs				
Season	Team	League	GP	G	A	PTS	PIM	GP	G	A	PTS	PIM
92-93	Hamilton	AHL	75	16	28	44	24	—	—	—	—	—
93-94	Hamilton	AHL	75	18	26	44	43	4	0	0	0	2
94-95	Minnesota	IHL	4	0	1	1	0	—	—	—	—	—
95-96	San Diego	WCHL	20	13	10	23	29	9	*8	5	13	13

Season	Team	League	GP	G	A	PTS	PIM	GP	G	A	PTS	PIM
96-97	Utah	IHL	2	0	0	0	2	—	—	—	—	—
96-97	Phoenix	IHL	1	0	0	0	0	—	—	—	—	—
96-97	Orlando	IHL	2	1	0	1	5	—	—	—	—	—
96-97	Las Beach	IHL	9	2	1	3	2	1	0	0	0	0
96-97	San Diego	WCHL	41	29	31	60	65	8	7	6	13	24
	AHL	Totals	150	34	54	88	67	4	0	0	0	2
	IHL	Totals	18	3	2	5	9	1	0	0	0	0
	WCHL	Totals	61	42	41	83	94	17	15	11	26	37

Born; 4/29/69, Hibbing, Minnesota. 6-2, 200. Drafted by Vancouver Canucks (3rd choice, 66th overall) in 1987 Entry Draft. Member of 1995-96 WCHL champion San Diego Gulls. Member of 1996-97 WCHL Champion San Diego Gulls.

Jeff Tory — Defenseman

			Regular Season					Playoffs				
Season	Team	League	GP	G	A	PTS	PIM	GP	G	A	PTS	PIM
96-97	Kentucky	AHL	3	0	2	2	0	4	0	0	0	2

Born; 5/9/73, Burnaby, British Columbia. 5-11, 195. Last amateur club; Maine (Hockey East).

Graeme Townshend — Right Wing

			Regular Season					Playoffs				
Season	Team	League	GP	G	A	PTS	PIM	GP	G	A	PTS	PIM
88-89	Maine	AHL	5	2	1	3	11	—	—	—	—	—
89-90	Boston	NHL	4	0	0	0	7	—	—	—	—	—
89-90	Maine	AHL	64	15	13	28	162	—	—	—	—	—
90-91	Boston	NHL	18	2	5	7	12	—	—	—	—	—
90-91	Maine	AHL	46	16	10	26	119	2	2	0	2	4
91-92	Islanders	NHL	7	1	2	3	0	—	—	—	—	—
91-92	Capital District	AHL	61	14	23	37	94	4	0	2	2	0
92-93	Islanders	NHL	2	0	0	0	0	—	—	—	—	—
92-93	Capital District	AHL	67	29	21	50	45	2	0	0	0	0
93-94	Ottawa	NHL	14	0	0	0	9	—	—	—	—	—
93-94	Prince Edward Island	AHL	56	16	13	29	107	—	—	—	—	—
94-95	Houston	IHL	71	19	21	40	204	4	0	2	2	22
95-96	Minnesota	IHL	3	0	0	0	0	—	—	—	—	—
95-96	Houston	IHL	63	21	11	32	97	—	—	—	—	—
96-97	Houston	IHL	74	21	15	36	68	3	0	0	0	2
	NHL	Totals	45	3	7	10	28	—	—	—	—	—
	AHL	Totals	299	92	81	173	538	8	2	2	4	4
	IHL	Totals	211	61	47	108	369	7	0	2	2	24

Born; 10/23/65, Kingston, Jamaica. 6-2, 215. Signed as a free agent by Boston Bruins (5/12/89). Signed as a free agent by New York Islanders (9/3/91). Signed as a free agent by Ottawa Senators (8/24/93).

Randy Toye — Left Wing

			Regular Season					Playoffs				
Season	Team	League	GP	G	A	PTS	PIM	GP	G	A	PTS	PIM
96-97	Nashville	CeHL	2	1	1	2	0	—	—	—	—	—
96-97	Central Texas	WPHL	25	7	9	16	22	—	—	—	—	—
96-97	Amarillo	WPHL	27	4	11	15	12	—	—	—	—	—
	WPHL	Totals	52	11	20	31	34	—	—	—	—	—

Born; 1/28/75, Carr Landing, British Columbia. 6-2, 210.

Tripp Tracy — Goaltender

			Regular Season							Playoffs					
Season	Team	League	GP	W	L	T	MIN	SO	GAVG	GP	W	L	MIN	SO	GAVG
96-97	Springfield	ECHL	2	1	1	0	119	0	3.53	—	—	—	—	—	—
96-97	Richmond	ECHL	35	18	15	1	2040	1	3.21	1	1	0	60	0	2.00

Born; 12/20/73, Detroit, Michigan. 5-10, 175. Last amateur club; Harvard (ECAC).

Patrick Traverse — Defenseman

			Regular Season					Playoffs				
Season	Team	League	GP	G	A	PTS	PIM	GP	G	A	PTS	PIM
92-93	New Haven	AHL	2	0	0	0	2	—	—	—	—	—
93-94	Prince Edward Island	AHL	3	0	1	1	2	—	—	—	—	—
94-95	Prince Edward Island	AHL	70	5	13	18	19	7	0	2	2	0
95-96	Ottawa	NHL	5	0	0	0	2	—	—	—	—	—
95-96	Prince Edward Island	AHL	55	4	21	25	32	5	1	2	3	2
96-97	Worcester	AHL	24	0	4	4	23	—	—	—	—	—
96-97	Grand Rapids	IHL	10	2	1	3	10	2	0	1	1	2
	AHL	Totals	154	9	39	48	78	12	1	4	5	2

Born; 3/14/74, Montreal, Quebec. 6-3, 173. Drafted by Ottawa Senators (3rd choice, 50th overall) in 1992 Entry Draft.

Dean Trboyevich — Defenseman

			Regular Season					Playoffs				
Season	Team	League	GP	G	A	PTS	PIM	GP	G	A	PTS	PIM
91-92	Capital District	AHL	22	0	3	3	65	—	—	—	—	—
91-92	Richmond	ECHL	23	1	6	7	100	—	—	—	—	—
91-92	Salt Lake City	IHL	5	0	1	1	7	—	—	—	—	—
95-96	Detroit	IHL	—	—	—	—	—	1	0	0	0	2
95-96	Anchorage	WCHL	31	5	12	17	121	—	—	—	—	—
95-96	Detroit	CoHL	25	2	6	8	136	10	3	3	6	53
96-97	Grand Rapids	IHL	30	1	1	2	73	5	0	1	1	14
96-97	Anchorage	WCHL	38	6	18	24	118	—	—	—	—	—
	IHL	Totals	35	1	2	3	80	6	0	1	1	16
	WCHL	Totals	69	11	30	41	239	—	—	—	—	—

Born; 6/6/68, Bovey, Minnesota. 6-1, 200. Did not play professional hockey in North America between the seasons of 1991-92 and 1995-96.

Dan Trebil — Defenseman

			Regular Season					Playoffs				
Season	Team	League	GP	G	A	PTS	PIM	GP	G	A	PTS	PIM
96-97	Anaheim	NHL	29	3	3	6	23	9	0	1	1	6
96-97	Baltimore	AHL	49	4	20	24	38	—	—	—	—	—

Born; 4/10/74, Edina, Minnesota. 6-3, 185. Drafted by New Jersey Devils (7th choice, 138th overall) in 1992 Entry Draft. Signed as a free agent by Anaheim Mighty Ducks (5/30/96). Last amateur club; Minnesota (WCHA).

J.F. Tremblay — Forward

Season	Team	League	GP	G	A	PTS	PIM	GP	G	A	PTS	PIM
96-97	Roanoke	ECHL	36	6	7	13	140	4	0	1	1	4

Born; 4/3/75, Montreal, Quebec. 5-11, 185.

Yannick Tremblay — Defenseman

			Regular Season					Playoffs				
Season	Team	League	GP	G	A	PTS	PIM	GP	G	A	PTS	PIM
96-97	Toronto	NHL	5	0	0	0	0	—	—	—	—	—
96-97	St. John's	AHL	67	7	25	32	34	11	2	9	11	0

Born; 11/15/75, Pointe-aux-Trembles, Quebec. 6-2, 185. Drafted by Toronto Maple Leafs (4th choice, 145th overall) in 1995 Entry Draft.

Pascal Trepanier — Defenseman

			Regular Season					Playoffs				
Season	Team	League	GP	G	A	PTS	PIM	GP	G	A	PTS	PIM
94-95	Kalamazoo	IHL	14	1	2	3	47	—	—	—	—	—
94-95	Cornwall	AHL	4	0	0	0	9	14	2	7	9	32
94-95	Dayton	ECHL	36	16	28	44	133	9	2	4	6	20
95-96	Cornwall	AHL	70	13	20	33	142	8	1	2	3	24
96-97	Hershey	AHL	73	14	39	53	151	23	6	13	19	59
	AHL	Totals	147	27	59	86	302	45	9	22	31	115

Born; 9/4/73, Garpe, Quebec. 6-0, 202. 1996-97 AHL Second Team All-Star. Member of 1996-97 AHL Champion Hershey Bears.

Bill Trew — Center

			Regular Season					Playoffs				
Season	Team	League	GP	G	A	PTS	PIM	GP	G	A	PTS	PIM
96-97	El Paso	WPHL	62	33	29	62	18	11	6	7	13	0

Born; 1/1/74, Garden Hill, Ontario. 5-11, 175.

Jeff Triano — Defenseman

			Regular Season					Playoffs				
Season	Team	League	GP	G	A	PTS	PIM	GP	G	A	PTS	PIM
82-83	St. Catharines	AHL	4	0	0	0	2	—	—	—	—	—
84-85	St. Catharines	AHL	3	0	0	0	0	—	—	—	—	—
96-97	Amarillo	WPHL	52	4	27	31	40	—	—	—	—	—
	AHL	Totals	7	0	0	0	2	—	—	—	—	—

Born; 11/4/64, Niagara Falls, Ontario. 6-1, 195. Drafted by Toronto Maple Leafs (11th choice, 139th overall) in 1982 Entry Draft.

Jeff Trigg — Goaltender

			Regular Season							Playoffs					
Season	Team	League	GP	W	L	T	MIN	SO	GAVG	GP	W	L	MIN	SO	GAVG
96-97	Anchorage	WCHL	17	11	3	0	871	1	4.14	3	0	0	42	0	9.96

Born; 10/3/69, Saskatoon, Saskatchewan. 6-0, 177.

Pavel Trnka — Defenseman

			Regular Season					Playoffs				
Season	Team	League	GP	G	A	PTS	PIM	GP	G	A	PTS	PIM
95-96	Baltimore	AHL	69	2	6	8	44	6	0	0	0	2
96-97	Baltimore	AHL	69	6	14	20	86	3	0	0	0	2
	AHL	Totals	138	8	20	28	130	9	0	0	0	4

Born; 7/27/76, Pizen, Czechoslovakia. 6-3, 190. Drafted by Anaheim Mighty Ducks (5th choice, 106th overall) in 1994 Entry Draft.

Rhett Trombley — Right Wing

			Regular Season					Playoffs				
Season	Team	League	GP	G	A	PTS	PIM	GP	G	A	PTS	PIM
94-95	Las Vegas	IHL	30	4	0	4	141	3	0	0	0	10
94-95	Toledo	ECHL	13	0	2	2	80	—	—	—	—	—
95-96	Las Vegas	IHL	15	0	2	2	56	—	—	—	—	—
95-96	Carolina	AHL	34	2	2	4	163	—	—	—	—	—
96-97	Syracuse	AHL	10	0	0	0	30	1	0	0	0	2
96-97	Las Vegas	IHL	44	4	3	7	199	1	0	0	0	2
96-97	Toledo	ECHL	4	0	1	1	25	—	—	—	—	—
	IHL	Totals	89	8	3	11	396	4	0	0	0	12
	AHL	Totals	44	2	2	4	193	1	0	0	0	2

Born; 12/9/74, New Westminster, British Columbia. 6-3, 225. Signed as a free agent by Florida (4/5/95).

Jean Guy-Trudel — Center

			Regular Season					Playoffs				
Season	Team	League	GP	G	A	PTS	PIM	GP	G	A	PTS	PIM
96-97	Peoria	ECHL	37	25	29	54	47	9	9	10	19	22
96-97	Quad City	CoHL	5	8	7	15	4	—	—	—	—	—
96-97	San Antonio	IHL	12	1	5	6	4	—	—	—	—	—
96-97	Chicago	IHL	6	1	2	3	2	—	—	—	—	—
	IHL	Totals	18	2	7	9	6	—	—	—	—	—

Born; 10/18/75, Sudbury, Ontario. 6-0, 194. Last amateur club; Hull (QMJHL).

Rob Trumbley — Right Wing

			Regular Season					Playoffs				
Season	Team	League	GP	G	A	PTS	PIM	GP	G	A	PTS	PIM
95-96	Cape Breton	AHL	11	1	2	3	31	—	—	—	—	—
95-96	Wheeling	ECHL	51	8	10	18	321	7	0	2	2	44
96-97	Hamilton	AHL	25	2	3	5	97	—	—	—	—	—
96-97	Wheeling	ECHL	34	15	22	37	164	2	1	0	1	14
	AHL	Totals	36	3	5	8	128	—	—	—	—	—
	ECHL	Totals	85	23	32	55	485	9	1	2	3	58

Born; 8/9/74, Regina, Saskatchewan. 5-10, 180. Drafted by Vancouver Canucks (8th choice, 195th overall) in 1994 Entry Draft.

Jason Trzcinski — Center

			Regular Season					Playoffs				
Season	Team	League	GP	G	A	PTS	PIM	GP	G	A	PTS	PIM
96-97	Tallahassee	ECHL	32	3	2	5	14	—	—	—	—	—
96-97	Louisville	ECHL	15	2	5	7	9	—	—	—	—	—
	ECHL	Totals	47	5	7	12	23	—	—	—	—	—

Born; 12/2/72, Livonia, Michigan. 6-2, 195. Last amateur club; Lake Superior (CCHA).

Gatis Tseplis — Defenseman

			Regular Season					Playoffs				
Season	Team	League	GP	G	A	PTS	PIM	GP	G	A	PTS	PIM
96-97	Huntsville	CeHL	10	1	0	1	4	—	—	—	—	—
96-97	San Antonio	CeHL	21	5	12	17	10	—	—	—	—	—
96-97	Nashville	CeHL	12	2	4	6	6	—	—	—	—	—
	CeHL	Totals	43	8	16	24	20	—	—	—	—	—

Born; 5/1/71, Riga, Latvia. 6-1, 195.

Nikolai Tsulygin — Defenseman

			Regular Season					Playoffs				
Season	Team	League	GP	G	A	PTS	PIM	GP	G	A	PTS	PIM
95-96	Baltimore	AHL	78	3	18	21	109	12	0	5	5	18
96-97	Anaheim	NHL	22	0	1	1	8	—	—	—	—	—
96-97	Fort Wayne	IHL	5	2	1	3	8	—	—	—	—	—
96-97	Baltimore	AHL	17	4	13	17	8	3	0	0	0	0
	AHL	Totals	95	7	31	38	117	15	0	5	5	18

Born; 6/29/75, Ufa, USSR. 6-4, 205. Drafted by Anaheim Mighty Ducks (2nd choice, 30th overall) in 1993 Entry Draft.

Travis Tucker — Defenseman

			Regular Season					Playoffs				
Season	Team	League	GP	G	A	PTS	PIM	GP	G	A	PTS	PIM
94-95	Syracuse	AHL	2	0	0	0	2	—	—	—	—	—
94-95	Charlotte	ECHL	62	5	11	16	250	3	1	0	1	6
95-96	Louisville	ECHL	62	17	23	40	211	3	0	0	0	14
96-97	Portland	AHL	2	0	0	0	4	—	—	—	—	—
96-97	Kansas City	IHL	2	0	0	0	5	—	—	—	—	—
96-97	Quad City	CoHL	68	15	27	42	163	15	0	1	1	22
	AHL	Totals	4	0	0	0	6	—	—	—	—	—
	ECHL	Totals	124	22	34	56	461	6	1	0	1	20

Born; 3/15/71, Hartford, Connecticut. 6-3, 220. Drafted by Detroit Red Wings (9th choice, 192nd overall) in 1990 Entry Draft. Member of 1996-97 CoHL Champion Quad City Mallards.

Wade Tulk — Left Wing

			Regular Season					Playoffs				
Season	Team	League	GP	G	A	PTS	PIM	GP	G	A	PTS	PIM
96-97	Nashville	CeHL	38	9	15	24	42	—	—	—	—	—
96-97	Huntsville	CeHL	8	2	1	3	9	—	—	—	—	—

Born; 9/13/71, St. Catharines, Ontario. 5-9, 190.

Brent Tully — Defenseman

			Regular Season					Playoffs				
Season	Team	League	GP	G	A	PTS	PIM	GP	G	A	PTS	PIM
93-94	Hamilton	AHL	1	0	0	0	0	1	1	0	1	0
93-94	Canada	NATL										
94-95	Syracuse	AHL	63	6	3	9	106	—	—	—	—	—
95-96	Syracuse	AHL	52	3	13	16	114	—	—	—	—	—
96-97	Syracuse	AHL	26	4	2	6	19	—	—	—	—	—
	AHL	Totals	142	13	18	31	239	1	1	0	1	0

Born; 3/26/74, Peterborough, Ontario. 6-3, 190. Drafted by Vancouver Canucks (5th choice, 93rd overall) in 1992 Entry Draft.

Marko Tuomainen — Right Wing

			Regular Season					Playoffs				
Season	Team	League	GP	G	A	PTS	PIM	GP	G	A	PTS	PIM
94-95	Edmonton	NHL	4	0	0	0	0	—	—	—	—	—
95-96	Cape Breton	AHL	58	25	35	60	71	—	—	—	—	—
96-97	Hamilton	AHL	79	31	21	52	130	22	7	5	12	4
	AHL	Totals	137	56	56	112	201	22	7	5	12	4

Born; 4/25/72, Kuopio, Finland. 6-3, 203. Drafted by Edmonton Oilers (10th choice, 205th overall) in 1992 Entry Draft.

Matt Turek — Center

			Regular Season					Playoffs				
Season	Team	League	GP	G	A	PTS	PIM	GP	G	A	PTS	PIM
96-97	Knoxville	ECHL	62	11	20	31	62	—	—	—	—	—

Born; 2/14/73, Toronto, Ontario. 5-11, 190.

Roman Turek — Goaltender

			Regular Season						Playoffs					
Season	Team	League	GP	W	L	T	MIN	SO	GAVG	GP	W	L	MIN	SO	GAVG
96-97	Dallas	NHL	6	3	1	0	263	0	2.05	—	—	—	—	—	—
96-97	Michigan	IHL	29	8	13	4	1556	0	2.97	—	—	—	—	—	—

Born; 5/21/70, Pisek, Czechoslovakia. 6-3, 193. Drafted by Minnesota North Stars (6th choice, 113th overall) in 1990 Entry Draft.

Mark Turner — Center

			Regular Season					Playoffs				
Season	Team	League	GP	G	A	PTS	PIM	GP	G	A	PTS	PIM
90-91	Cincinnati	ECHL	54	25	27	52	89	4	0	1	1	13
90-91	Fort Wayne	IHL	20	6	6	12	21	4	0	0	0	2
91-92	Fort Wayne	IHL	49	8	10	18	68	5	2	0	2	6
92-93	Muskegon	CoHL	37	25	33	58	33	2	2	1	3	4
92-93	Chatham	CoHL	15	9	10	19	30	—	—	—	—	—
93-94	Muskegon	CoHL	61	46	58	104	57	2	0	0	0	0
94-95	Muskegon	CoHL	20	7	13	20	48	—	—	—	—	—
94-95	Utica	CoHL	18	6	10	16	28	—	—	—	—	—
94-95	Flint	CoHL	10	1	11	12	16	6	2	2	4	33
95-96	Muskegon	CoHL	67	32	69	101	99	1	1	1	2	0
96-97	Columbus	ECHL	55	20	48	68	81	8	3	5	8	6
	IHL	Totals	69	14	16	30	89	9	2	0	2	8
	CoHL	Totals	228	126	204	330	311	11	5	4	9	37
	ECHL	Totals	109	45	75	120	170	12	3	6	9	19

Born; 5/9/68, Windsor, Ontario. 5-10, 185.

Steve Tuttle — Right Wing

Season	Team	League	GP	G	A	PTS	PIM	GP	G	A	PTS	PIM
88-89	St. Louis	NHL	53	13	12	25	6	6	1	2	3	0
89-90	St. Louis	NHL	71	12	10	22	4	5	0	1	1	2
90-91	St. Louis	NHL	20	3	6	9	2	6	0	3	3	0
90-91	Peoria	IHL	42	24	32	56	8	—	—	—	—	—
91-92	Peoria	IHL	71	43	46	89	22	10	4	8	12	4
92-93	Milwaukee	IHL	51	27	34	61	12	4	0	2	2	2
92-93	Halifax	AHL	22	11	17	28	2	—	—	—	—	—
93-94	Milwaukee	IHL	78	27	44	71	34	4	0	2	2	4
94-95	Peoria	IHL	38	14	13	27	14	—	—	—	—	—
94-95	Milwaukee	IHL	21	3	1	4	8	—	—	—	—	—
95-96	Milwaukee	IHL	81	32	35	67	36	5	1	2	3	0
96-97	Milwaukee	IHL	71	25	19	44	20	3	1	1	2	2
	NHL	Totals	144	28	28	56	12	17	1	6	7	2
	IHL	Totals	453	195	224	419	154	26	6	15	21	12

Born; 1/5/66, Vancouver, British Columbia. 6-1, 197. Drafted by St. Louis Blues (8th choice, 113th overall) in 1984 Entry Draft. Traded to Tampa Bay Lightning by St. Louis with Rob Robinson, Darin Kimble and Pat Jablonski for future considerations (6/19/92). Loaned to Milwaukee Admirals at beginning of 1992-93 season. Traded to Quebec Nordiques by Tampa Bay with Martin Simard and Michel Mongeau for Herb Raglan. (2/12/93). Signed as a free agent by Milwaukee (9/2/93). 1991-92 IHL First All-Star team.

Paul Tzountzouris — Defenseman

Season	Team	League	GP	G	A	PTS	PIM	GP	G	A	PTS	PIM
95-96	Quad City	CoHL	1	0	0	0	0	—	—	—	—	—
95-96	Winston-Salem	SHL	9	0	2	2	17	—	—	—	—	—
95-96	Daytona Beach	SHL	17	2	3	5	52	—	—	—	—	—
96-97	Flint	CoHL	21	2	5	7	29	—	—	—	—	—
96-97	Madison	CoHL	7	2	1	3	2	3	0	0	0	2
	CoHL	Totals	29	4	6	10	31	3	0	0	0	2
	SHL	Totals	26	2	5	7	69	—	—	—	—	—

Born; 8/25/74, Toronto, Ontario. 6-2, 201.

Shawn Ulrich — Center

Season	Team	League	GP	G	A	PTS	PIM	GP	G	A	PTS	PIM
95-96	Alaska	WCHL	58	34	64	98	62	5	3	6	9	2
96-97	Alaska	WCHL	53	30	36	66	30	—	—	—	—	—
96-97	Anchorage	WCHL	16	5	7	12	32	9	3	2	5	10
	WCHL	Totals	127	69	107	176	124	14	6	8	14	12

Born; 10/31/69. 5-8, 190.

Stefan Ustorf — Center

Season	Team	League	GP	G	A	PTS	PIM	GP	G	A	PTS	PIM
94-95	Portland	AHL	63	21	38	59	51	7	1	6	7	7
95-96	Washington	NHL	48	7	10	17	14	5	0	0	0	0
95-96	Portland	AHL	8	1	4	5	6	—	—	—	—	—
96-97	Washington	NHL	6	0	0	0	2	—	—	—	—	—
96-97	Portland	AHL	36	7	17	24	27	—	—	—	—	—
	NHL	Totals	54	7	10	17	16	5	0	0	0	0
	AHL	Totals	107	29	59	88	84	7	1	6	7	7

Born; 1/3/74, Kaufbeuren, Germany. 6-0, 185. Drafted by Washington Capitals (3rd choice, 53rd overall) in 1992 Entry Draft.

Marc Vachon — Defenseman

			Regular Season					Playoffs				
Season	Team	League	GP	G	A	PTS	PIM	GP	G	A	PTS	PIM
89-90	Johnstown	ECHL	58	18	21	39	30	—	—	—	—	—
89-90	Hampton Roads	ECHL	1	0	0	0	0	4	1	1	2	13
91-92	Thunder Bay	CoHL	45	17	28	45	42	—	—	—	—	—
91-92	Michigan	CoHL	4	1	2	3	4	4	1	1	2	4
92-93	Muskegon	CoHL	55	12	20	32	60	7	1	0	1	0
93-94	Flint	CoHL	56	16	16	32	30	—	—	—	—	—
93-94	St. Thomas	CoHL	6	2	4	6	0	3	3	0	3	0
94-95	Utica	CoHL	9	1	3	4	11	—	—	—	—	—
95-96	Quad City	CoHL	2	0	0	0	0	—	—	—	—	—
95-96	Huntsville	SHL	41	9	24	33	150	10	1	5	6	45
96-97	Huntsville	CeHL	57	9	18	27	100	9	1	2	3	12
	CoHL	Totals	177	49	73	122	147	14	5	1	6	4
	ECHL	Totals	59	18	21	39	30	4	1	1	2	13

Born; 10/5/65, Hawksbury, Ontario. 6-0, 190. Member of 1995-96 SHL champion Huntsville Channel Cats.

Nicholas Vachon — Center

			Regular Season					Playoffs				
Season	Team	League	GP	G	A	PTS	PIM	GP	G	A	PTS	PIM
93-94	Atlanta	IHL	3	1	1	2	0	—	—	—	—	—
93-94	Knoxville	ECHL	61	29	57	86	139	3	0	0	0	2
94-95	Phoenix	IHL	64	13	26	39	137	9	1	2	3	24
95-96	Phoenix	IHL	73	13	17	30	168	1	0	0	0	2
96-97	Islanders	NHL	1	0	0	0	0	—	—	—	—	—
96-97	Phoenix	IHL	16	3	3	6	18	—	—	—	—	—
96-97	Utah	IHL	33	3	5	8	110	—	—	—	—	—
96-97	Long Beach	IHL	13	1	2	3	42	18	1	2	3	43
	IHL	Totals	202	34	54	88	475	28	2	4	6	69

Born; 7/20/72, Montreal, Quebec. 5-10, 185. Drafted by Toronto Maple Leafs (11th choice, 241st overall) in 1990 Entry Draft. Signed as a free agent by Los Angeles Kings, (9/12/95). Traded to New York Islanders by Los Angeles for Chris Marinucci, (11/19/96). Signed as a free agent by Long Beach Ice Dogs, (8/97).

Chris Valicevic — Defenseman

			Regular Season					Playoffs				
Season	Team	League	GP	G	A	PTS	PIM	GP	G	A	PTS	PIM
93-94	Cornwall	AHL	6	0	0	0	0	—	—	—	—	—
93-94	Greensboro	ECHL	59	14	38	52	73	8	0	2	2	6
94-95	Worcester	AHL	3	0	1	1	2	—	—	—	—	—
94-95	Greensboro	ECHL	37	5	28	33	39	—	—	—	—	—
95-96	Louisiana	ECHL	70	24	70	94	109	5	0	5	5	10
96-97	Louisiana	ECHL	70	18	51	69	75	17	7	10	17	18
	AHL	Totals	9	0	1	1	2					

Born; 4/25/68, Mt. Clemens, Michigan. 6-0, 200. 1995-96 ECHL Best Defenseman. 1995-96 ECHL First All-Star Team. 1996-97 ECHL Best Defenseman. 1996-97 ECHL First Team All-Star.

Rob Valicevic — Right Wing

			Regular Season					Playoffs				
Season	Team	League	GP	G	A	PTS	PIM	GP	G	A	PTS	PIM
95-96	Springfield	AHL	2	0	0	0	2	—	—	—	—	—
95-96	Louisiana	ECHL	60	42	20	62	85	5	2	3	5	8
96-97	Houston	IHL	58	11	12	23	42	12	1	3	4	11
96-97	Louisiana	ECHL	8	7	2	9	21	—	—	—	—	—
	ECHL	Totals	68	49	22	71	106	5	2	3	5	8

Born; 1/6/71, Detroit, Michigan. 6-1, 195. Drafted by New York Islanders (6th choice, 114th overall) in 1991 Entry Draft.

Carl Valimont
Defenseman

			Regular Season					Playoffs				
Season	Team	League	GP	G	A	PTS	PIM	GP	G	A	PTS	PIM
88-89	Milwaukee	IHL	79	4	33	37	56	11	2	8	10	12
89-90	Milwaukee	IHL	78	13	28	41	48	3	0	1	1	6
90-91	Milwaukee	IHL	80	10	21	31	66	6	2	1	3	2
91-92	Milwaukee	IHL	71	14	31	45	81	5	0	2	2	4
92-93	Milwaukee	IHL	59	4	18	22	52	4	0	1	1	2
93-94	Milwaukee	IHL	14	1	7	8	20	—	—	—	—	—
94-95	Houston	IHL	69	5	18	23	66	2	0	0	0	0
95-96	Cincinnati	IHL	4	0	0	0	2	—	—	—	—	—
95-96	Houston	IHL	54	4	17	21	44	—	—	—	—	—
96-97	Milwaukee	IHL	12	0	2	2	6	—	—	—	—	—
96-97	Houston	IHL	59	4	10	14	28	13	0	2	2	2
	IHL	Totals	579	59	185	244	469	44	4	15	19	28

Born; 3/1/66, Southington, Connecticut. 6-0, 196. Drafted by Vancouver Canucks (10th choice, 193rd overall) in 1985 Entry Draft.

Steve Valiquette
Goaltender

			Regular Season						Playoffs					
Season	Team	League	GP	W	L	T	MIN	SO	GAVG	GP	W	L	MIN	SO	GAVG
96-97	Dayton	ECHL	3	1	0	0	89	0	4.03	2	1	1	119	0	2.54

Last amateur club; Sudbury (OHL). Drafted by Los Angeles Kings (8th choice, 190th overall) in 1996 Entry Draft.

Lindsay Vallis
Right Wing

			Regular Season					Playoffs				
Season	Team	League	GP	G	A	PTS	PIM	GP	G	A	PTS	PIM
90-91	Fredericton	AHL	—	—	—	—	—	7	0	0	0	6
91-92	Fredericton	AHL	71	10	19	29	84	4	0	1	1	7
92-93	Fredericton	AHL	65	18	16	34	38	5	0	2	2	10
93-94	Montreal	NHL	1	0	0	0	0	—	—	—	—	—
93-94	Fredericton	AHL	75	9	30	39	103	—	—	—	—	—
94-95	Worcester	AHL	14	0	7	7	28	—	—	—	—	—
95-96	Worcester	AHL	65	9	19	28	81	4	0	2	2	4
96-97	Fresno	WCHL	58	26	65	91	82	4	0	3	3	0
	AHL	Totals	290	46	91	137	334	20	0	5	5	27

Born; 1/12/71, Calgary, Alberta. Drafted by Montreal Canadiens 1rst choice, 13th overall) in 1989 Entry Draft. 1996-97 WCHL Second All-Star Team.

Quinton Van Horlick
Right Wing

			Regular Season					Playoffs				
Season	Team	League	GP	G	A	PTS	PIM	GP	G	A	PTS	PIM
95-96	Erie	ECHL	1	0	0	0	5	—	—	—	—	—
96-97	Waco	WPHL	24	1	3	4	94	—	—	—	—	—
96-97	Amarillo	APHL	12	0	1	1	17	—	—	—	—	—
	WPHL	Totals	36	1	4	5	111	—	—	—	—	—

Born;

Colby Van Tassel
Defenseman

			Regular Season					Playoffs				
Season	Team	League	GP	G	A	PTS	PIM	GP	G	A	PTS	PIM
96-97	Madison	CoHL	44	2	7	9	161	—	—	—	—	—
96-97	Muskegon	CoHL	21	1	5	6	38	3	0	0	0	11
	CoHL	Totals	65	3	12	15	199	3	0	0	0	11

Born; 3/25/72, Kansas City, Missouri. 6-2, 220.

Mike Vandenberghe — Defenseman

			Regular Season					Playoffs				
Season	Team	League	GP	G	A	PTS	PIM	GP	G	A	PTS	PIM
93-94	Richmond	ECHL	28	5	5	10	135	—	—	—	—	—
93-94	Dayton	ECHL	37	6	14	20	85	3	0	1	1	4
94-95	Dayton	ECHL	24	1	9	10	75	—	—	—	—	—
94-95	Richmond	ECHL	6	1	0	1	32	—	—	—	—	—
94-95	Knoxville	ECHL	20	3	9	12	99	4	1	0	1	4
95-96	Knoxville	ECHL	65	1	13	14	162	8	0	0	0	13
96-97	Knoxville	ECHL	62	3	15	18	129	—	—	—	—	—
	ECHL	Totals	242	20	65	85	717	15	1	1	2	21

Born; 3/11/72, Reston, Manitoba. 6-0, 215.

Ryan VandenBussche — Right Wing

			Regular Season					Playoffs				
Season	Team	League	GP	G	A	PTS	PIM	GP	G	A	PTS	PIM
92-93	St. John's	AHL	1	0	0	0	0	—	—	—	—	—
93-94	St. John's	AHL	44	4	10	14	124	—	—	—	—	—
93-94	Springfield	AHL	9	1	2	3	29	5	0	0	0	16
94-95	St. John's	AHL	53	2	13	15	239	—	—	—	—	—
95-96	Binghamton	AHL	68	3	17	20	240	4	0	0	0	9
96-97	Rangers	NHL	11	1	0	1	30	—	—	—	—	—
96-97	Binghamton	AHL	38	8	11	19	133	—	—	—	—	—
	AHL	Totals	213	18	53	71	765	9	0	0	0	25

Born; 2/28/73, Simcoe, Ontario. 5-11, 185. Drafted by Toronto Maple Leafs (8th choice, 173 overall) in 1992 Entry Draft. Signed as a free agent by New York Rangers (7/10/95).

Pete Vandermeer — Forward

			Regular Season					Playoffs				
Season	Team	League	GP	G	A	PTS	PIM	GP	G	A	PTS	PIM
96-97	Columbus	ECHL	30	6	11	17	195	7	2	1	3	26

Last amateur club; Red Deer (WHL).

Vaclav Varada — Right Wing

			Regular Season					Playoffs				
Season	Team	League	GP	G	A	PTS	PIM	GP	G	A	PTS	PIM
95-96	Buffalo	NHL	1	0	0	0	0	—	—	—	—	—
95-96	Rochester	AHL	5	3	0	3	4	—	—	—	—	—
96-97	Buffalo	NHL	5	0	0	0	2	—	—	—	—	—
96-97	Rochester	AHL	53	23	25	48	81	10	1	6	7	27
	NHL	Totals	6	0	0	0	2	—	—	—	—	—
	AHL	Totals	58	26	25	51	85	10	1	6	7	27

Born; 4/26/76, Vsetin, Czechoslovakia. 6-0, 200. Drafted by San Jose Sharks (4th choice, 89th overall) in 1994 Entry Draft. Traded to Buffalo Sabres by San Jose with Martin Spahnel, an optional first round choice in 1996 Entry Draft and Philadelphia's fourth round choice (previously acquired by San Jose—Buffalo selcted Mike Martone) in 1996 Entry Draft for Doug Bodger, (11/16/95).

John Varga — Left Wing

			Regular Season					Playoffs				
Season	Team	League	GP	G	A	PTS	PIM	GP	G	A	PTS	PIM
94-95	Portland	AHL	2	0	1	1	0	—	—	—	—	—
94-95	Milwaukee	IHL	1	0	0	0	0	—	—	—	—	—
95-96	Cornwall	AHL	10	1	0	1	6	—	—	—	—	—
95-96	Columbus	ECHL	33	19	17	36	38	—	—	—	—	—
95-96	Wheeling	ECHL	17	10	6	16	13	7	1	3	4	16
96-97	Wheeling	ECHL	66	*56	45	101	84	3	0	1	1	6
	AHL	Totals	12	1	1	2	6	—	—	—	—	—
	ECHL	Totals	116	85	68	153	135	10	1	4	5	22

Born; 1/31/74, Chicago, Illinois. 5-10, 180. Drafted by Washington Capitals (5th choice, 119th overall) in 1992 Entry Draft.

John Vary — Defenseman

			Regular Season					Playoffs				
Season	Team	League	GP	G	A	PTS	PIM	GP	G	A	PTS	PIM
91-92	Binghamton	AHL	1	0	0	0	0	—	—	—	—	—
92-93	Binghamton	AHL	12	0	2	2	8	—	—	—	—	—
92-93	Phoenix	IHL	9	0	6	6	10	—	—	—	—	—
92-93	Erie	ECHL	46	15	31	46	158	5	1	2	3	20
93-94	Erie	ECHL	55	10	29	39	129	—	—	—	—	—
94-95	Wichita	CeHL	63	12	38	50	163	11	3	5	8	16
95-96	Louisiana	ECHL	70	2	27	29	174	5	1	3	4	10
96-97	Muskegon	CoHL	74	14	54	68	106	3	1	2	3	2
	AHL	Totals	13	0	2	2	8	—	—	—	—	—
	ECHL	Totals	171	27	87	114	461	10	2	5	7	30

Born; 2/1/72, Owen Sound, Ontario. 6-1, 207. Drafted by New York Rangers (3rd choice, 55th overall) in 1990 Entry Draft. Member of 1994-95 CeHL champion Wichita Thunder.

Alex Vasilevski — Rigth Wing

			Regular Season					Playoffs				
Season	Team	League	GP	G	A	PTS	PIM	GP	G	A	PTS	PIM
95-96	St. Louis	NHL	1	0	0	0	0	—	—	—	—	—
95-96	Worcester	AHL	69	18	21	39	112	4	2	1	3	10
96-97	St. Louis	NHL	3	0	0	0	2	—	—	—	—	—
96-97	Worcester	AHL	61	9	23	32	100	—	—	—	—	—
96-97	Grand Rapids	IHL	10	1	5	6	43	5	0	1	1	19
	NHL	Totals	4	0	0	0	2	—	—	—	—	—
	AHL	Totals	130	27	44	71	212	4	2	1	3	10

Born; 1/8/75, Kiev, USSR. 5-11, 190. Drafted by St. Louis Blues (9th choice, 271st overall) in 1993 Entry Draft.

Andrey Vasiliev — Left Wing

			Regular Season					Playoffs				
Season	Team	League	GP	G	A	PTS	PIM	GP	G	A	PTS	PIM
94-95	Denver	IHL	74	28	37	65	48	13	9	4	13	22
94-95	Islanders	NHL	2	0	0	0	2	—	—	—	—	—
95-96	Islanders	NHL	10	2	5	7	2	—	—	—	—	—
95-96	Utah	IHL	43	26	20	46	34	22	12	4	16	18
96-97	Islanders	NHL	3	0	0	0	2	—	—	—	—	—
96-97	Utah	IHL	56	16	18	34	42	7	4	1	5	0
	NHL	Totals	15	2	5	7	6	—	—	—	—	—
	IHL	Totals	173	70	75	145	124	42	25	9	34	40

Born; 3/30/72, Voskresensk, Russia. 5-8, 176. Drafted by New York Islanders (11th choice, 248th overall) in 1992 Entry Draft. Member of 1994-95 IHL champion Denver Grizzlies. 1995-96 IHL champion Utah Grizzlies.

Herbert Vasiljevs — Center

			Regular Season					Playoffs				
Season	Team	League	GP	G	A	PTS	PIM	GP	G	A	PTS	PIM
96-97	Carolina	AHL	54	13	18	31	30	—	—	—	—	—
96-97	Port Huron	CoHL	3	3	2	5	4	—	—	—	—	—
96-97	Knoxville	ECHL	3	1	1	2	0	—	—	—	—	—

Born; 5/27/76, Riga, Latvia. 5-11, 170.

Kevin Vaughn — Defenseman

			Regular Season					Playoffs				
Season	Team	League	GP	G	A	PTS	PIM	GP	G	A	PTS	PIM
96-97	Columbus	ECHL	53	0	2	2	31	—	—	—	—	—

John Vecchiarelli — Center

Regular Season / **Playoffs**

Season	Team	League	GP	G	A	PTS	PIM	GP	G	A	PTS	PIM
85-86	Flint	IHL	81	40	52	92	89	—	—	—	—	—
86-87	Flint	IHL	12	4	3	7	23	—	—	—	—	—
86-87	Peoria	IHL	65	18	34	52	91	—	—	—	—	—
93-94	Dallas	CeHL	6	4	3	7	14	—	—	—	—	—
93-94	Chatham	CoHL	48	45	64	109	105	15	10	*18	*28	41
94-95	Saginaw	CoHL	40	33	46	79	155	11	8	13	21	22
95-96	Las Vegas	IHL	2	0	1	1	4	—	—	—	—	—
95-96	Utica	CoHL	58	32	50	82	165	—	—	—	—	—
96-97	Utica	CoHL	73	56	50	106	153	3	3	1	4	8
	IHL	Totals	158	62	89	151	203	—	—	—	—	—
	CoHL	Totals	219	166	210	376	575	29	21	32	53	71

Born; 7/24/64, Toronto, Ontario. 6-0, 190. Did not play professionally in North America between the 1987-88 and 1993-94 seasons. 1993-94 CoHL First All-Star Team.

Eric Veilleux — Center

Regular Season / **Playoffs**

Season	Team	League	GP	G	A	PTS	PIM	GP	G	A	PTS	PIM
93-94	Cornwall	AHL	77	8	19	27	69	13	1	7	8	20
94-95	Cornwall	AHL	70	13	23	36	93	13	1	1	2	20
95-96	Cornwall	AHL	71	25	35	60	119	8	2	6	8	2
96-97	Hershey	AHL	68	28	33	61	118	23	*11	10	21	14
	AHL	Totals	286	74	110	184	399	57	15	24	39	56

Born; 2/20/72, Quebec City, Quebec. 5-7, 148. Signed as a free agent by Quebec Nordiques (10/6/93). Member of 1996-97 AHL Champion Hersey Bears.

Mike Veisor — Goaltender

Regular Season / **Playoffs**

Season	Team	League	GP	W	L	T	MIN	SO	GAVG	GP	W	L	MIN	SO	GAVG
96-97	Baton Rouge	ECHL	26	6	11	2	1144	1	3.30	—	—	—	—	—	—

Born; 12/7/72, Dallas, Texas. 6-2, 195. Drafted by St. Louis Blues (12th choice, 263rd overall) in 1991 Enrty Draft.

Scott Vettraino — Goaltender

Regular Season / **Playoffs**

Season	Team	League	GP	W	L	T	MIN	SO	GAVG	GP	W	L	MIN	SO	GAVG
96-97	Toledo	ECHL	1	0	1	0	27	0	8.88	—	—	—	—	—	—
96-97	Dayton	CoHL	35	4	20	4	1643	0	5.59	—	—	—	—	—	—

7/24/71, Southfield, Michigan. 5-10, 180.

Steve Vezina — Goaltender

Regular Season / **Playoffs**

Season	Team	League	GP	W	L	T	MIN	SO	GAVG	GP	W	L	MIN	SO	GAVG
95-96	Saginaw	CoHL	43	17	19	4	2158	0	4.67	—	—	—	—	—	—
96-97	Binghamton	AHL	1	0	0	0	20	0	6.00	—	—	—	—	—	—
96-97	Jacksonville	ECHL	44	14	19	8	2440	0	3.54	—	—	—	—	—	—

Born; 10/25/75, Montreal, Quebec. 5-11, 175. Drafted by Winnipeg Jets (6th choice, 44 overall) in 1994 Entry Draft.

Bruno Villenueve — Right Wing

Regular Season / **Playoffs**

Season	Team	League	GP	G	A	PTS	PIM	GP	G	A	PTS	PIM
91-92	Knoxville	ECHL	48	38	35	72	12	—	—	—	—	—
91-92	Raleigh	ECHL	8	5	2	7	9	4	0	2	2	2
92-93	Raleigh	ECHL	54	30	19	49	47	10	3	5	8	2
93-94	Knoxville	ECHL	48	27	29	56	65	3	2	0	2	2
94-95	Brantford	CoHL	10	3	2	5	0	—	—	—	—	—

Season	Team	League	GP	G	A	PTS	PIM	GP	G	A	PTS	PIM
94-95	Utica	CoHL	49	22	25	47	30	6	2	0	2	2
95-96	Winston-Salem	SHL	60	23	33	56	82	9	3	2	5	0
96-97	Macon	CeHL	66	49	46	95	14	5	1	4	5	0
	ECHL	Totals	158	100	85	185	133	17	5	7	12	6
	CoHL	Totals	59	25	27	52	30	6	2	0	2	2

Born; 7/4/70, Hull, Quebec. 5-11, 187.

Daniel Villeneuve — Defenseman

Season	Team	League	GP	G	A	PTS	PIM	GP	G	A	PTS	PIM
96-97	Saginaw	CoHL	8	0	0	0	43	—	—	—	—	—
96-97	San Antonio	CeHL	60	3	8	11	334	—	—	—	—	—

Born; 3/21/75, Buckingham, Quebec. 6-2, 200.

Mark Vilneff — Defenseman

Season	Team	League	GP	G	A	PTS	PIM	GP	G	A	PTS	PIM
94-95	Muskegon	CoHL	71	1	10	11	60	14	1	3	4	6
95-96	Muskegon	CoHL	69	3	3	6	27	5	0	1	1	0
96-97	Muskegon	CoHL	66	1	10	11	38	3	0	0	0	4
	CoHL	Totals	206	5	23	28	125	22	1	4	5	10

Born; 11/28/73, Cobourg, Ontario. 6-2, 195.

Paul Vincent — Center

Season	Team	League	GP	G	A	PTS	PIM	GP	G	A	PTS	PIM
94-95	St. John's	AHL	2	0	2	2	0	—	—	—	—	—
95-96	St. John's	AHL	16	2	3	5	2	1	0	0	0	2
95-96	Raleigh	ECHL	30	12	9	21	29	—	—	—	—	—
96-97	St. John's	AHL	3	0	2	2	12	—	—	—	—	—
96-97	Peoria	ECHL	45	31	29	60	72	10	7	8	15	8
	AHL	Totals	21	2	7	9	14	1	0	0	0	2
	ECHL	Totals	75	43	38	81	101	10	7	8	15	8

Born; 1/4/75, Utica, New York. 6-4, 200. Drafted by Toronto Maple Leafs (4th choice, 149th overall) in 1993 Entry Draft.

Terry Virtue — Defenseman

Season	Team	League	GP	G	A	PTS	PIM	GP	G	A	PTS	PIM
91-92	Roanoke	ECHL	38	4	22	26	165	—	—	—	—	—
91-92	Louisville	ECHL	23	1	15	16	58	13	0	8	8	49
92-93	Louisville	ECHL	28	0	17	17	84	—	—	—	—	—
92-93	Wheeling	ECHL	31	3	15	18	86	16	3	5	8	18
93-94	Cape Breton	AHL	26	4	6	10	10	—	—	—	—	—
93-94	Wheeling	ECHL	34	5	28	33	61	6	2	2	4	4
94-95	Atlanta	IHL	1	0	0	0	2	—	—	—	—	—
94-95	Worcester	AHL	73	14	25	39	186	—	—	—	—	—
95-96	Worcester	AHL	76	7	31	38	234	4	0	0	0	4
96-97	Worcester	AHL	80	16	26	42	220	5	0	4	4	8
	AHL	Totals	255	41	88	129	650	9	0	4	4	12
	ECHL	Totals	154	13	97	110	454	35	5	15	20	71

Born; 8/12/70, Scarborough, Ontario. 6-0, 200. Signed as a free agent by St. Louis Blues (1/29/96).

Mark Visheau — Defenseman

Season	Team	League	GP	G	A	PTS	PIM	GP	G	A	PTS	PIM
93-94	Winnipeg	NHL	1	0	0	0	0	—	—	—	—	—
93-94	Moncton	AHL	48	4	5	9	58	—	—	—	—	—

Season	Team	League	GP	G	A	PTS	PIM	GP	G	A	PTS	PIM
94-95	Springfield	AHL	35	0	4	4	94	—	—	—	—	—
95-96	Minnesota	IHL	10	0	0	0	25	—	—	—	—	—
95-96	Cape Breton	AHL	8	0	0	0	38	—	—	—	—	—
95-96	Wheeling	ECHL	7	1	2	3	14	7	0	3	3	4
96-97	Quebec	IHL	64	3	10	13	173	9	1	1	2	11
96-97	Raleigh	ECHL	15	1	5	6	61	—	—	—	—	—
	AHL	Totals	91	4	9	13	190	—	—	—	—	—
	IHL	Totals	74	3	10	13	198	9	1	1	2	11
	ECHL	Totals	22	2	7	9	75	7	0	3	3	4

Born; 6/27/73, Burlington, Ontario. 6-6, 210. Drafted by Winnipeg Jets (4th choice, 84th overall) in 1992 Entry Draft.

Nick Vitucci — Goaltender

			Regular Season							Playoffs				
Season	Team	League	GP	W	L	T	MIN	SO	GAVG	GP	W	L	MIN	SO	GAVG
88-89	Carolina	ECHL	22	11	9	0	1238	1	4.65	10	*8	2	592	0	3.55
89-90	Winston-Salem	ECHL	6	—	—	—	360	0	4.67	—	—	—	—	—	—
89-90	Greensboro	ECHL	28	10	9	5	1496	0	4.57	3	1	1	153	0	2.75
90-91	Greensboro	ECHL	41	22	16	2	2225	1	3.82	*13	8	5	*813	0	3.17
91-92	Hershey	AHL	4	—	—	—	191	0	4.71	—	—	—	—	—	—
91-92	Maine	AHL	1	—	—	—	65	0	2.77	—	—	—	—	—	—
91-92	Greensboro	ECHL	42	28	8	2	2358	1	3.46	11	5	6	673	0	2.67
92-93	Peoria	IHL	8	3	4	1	479	0	3.38	—	—	—	—	—	—
92-93	Hampton Roads	ECHL	29	17	7	3	1669	1	*3.06	3	1	2	206	0	2.33
93-94	Peoria	IHL	11	3	4	1	422	0	4.98	—	—	—	—	—	—
93-94	Toledo	ECHL	27	15	6	4	1532	0	3.64	—	—	—	—	—	—
94-95	Toledo	ECHL	56	*35	16	3	3273	*3	3.23	4	1	3	239	0	3.01
95-96	Charlotte	ECHL	48	*32	13	3	2794	0	3.52	11	7	2	585	1	2.46
96-97	Binghamton	AHL	2	0	0	2	129	0	4.17	—	—	—	—	—	—
96-97	Charlotte	ECHL	36	20	10	4	2029	0	3.46	3	0	3	178	0	3.37
	IHL	Totals	19	6	8	2	901	0	4.13	—	—	—	—	—	—
%	AHL	Totals	7	0	0	2	385	0	4.21	—	—	—	—	—	—
^	ECHL	Totals	335	190	94	26	18974	7	3.64	58	31	24	3439	1	2.95

Born; 6/16/67, Welland, Ontario. 5-9, 175. % AHL win/loss records not complete. ^ ECHL win/loss records not complete. 1989-90 ECHL playoff MVP. 1995-96 ECHL playoff MVP. 1991-92 ECHL First All-Star Team. 1992-93 ECHL Top Goaltender. Member of 1988-89 ECHL champion Carolina Thunderbirds. Member of 1989-90 ECHL champion Greensboro Monarchs. Back-up goaltender for 1993-94 ECHL champion Toledo Storm. Member of 1995-96 ECHL champion Charlotte Checkers.

Jan Vodrazka — Defenseman

			Regular Season					Playoffs				
Season	Team	League	GP	G	A	PTS	PIM	GP	G	A	PTS	PIM
96-97	Richmond	ECHL	4	0	0	0	12	7	0	1	1	36

Born; 11/10/76, Pizen, Czechoslovakia. 6-1, 200. Last amateur club; Detroit (OHL).

Tomas Vokoun — Goaltender

			Regular Season							Playoffs					
Season	Team	League	GP	W	L	T	MIN	SO	GAVG	GP	W	L	MIN	SO	GAVG
95-96	Fredericton	AHL	—	—	—	—	—	—	—	1	0	1	59	0	4.09
95-96	Wheeling	ECHL	35	20	10	2	1912	0	3.67	7	4	3	436	0	2.61
96-97	Montreal	NHL	1	0	0	0	20	0	12.00	—	—	—	—	—	—
96-97	Fredericton	AHL	47	12	26	7	2645	2	3.49	—	—	—	—	—	—
	AHL	Totals	47	12	26	7	2645	2	3.49	1	0	1	59	0	4.09

Born; 7/2/76, Karlovy Vary, Czechoslovakia. 5-11, 180. Drafted by Montreal Canadiens (11th choice, 226th overall) in 1994 Entry Draft.

Alexander Volchkov — Left Wing

			Regular Season					Playoffs				
Season	Team	League	GP	G	A	PTS	PIM	GP	G	A	PTS	PIM
96-97	Portland	AHL	—	—	—	—	—	4	0	0	0	0

Born; 9/25/77, Moscow, Russia. 6-1, 194. Drafted by Washington Capitals (1st choice, 4th overall) in 1996 Entry Draft.

Phil von Steffenelli — Defenseman

Season	Team	League	GP	G	A	PTS	PIM	GP	G	A	PTS	PIM
91-92	Milwaukee	IHL	80	2	34	36	40	5	1	2	3	2
92-93	Hamilton	AHL	78	11	20	31	75	—	—	—	—	—
93-94	Hamilton	AHL	80	10	31	41	89	4	1	0	1	2
94-95	Providence	AHL	75	6	13	19	93	11	2	4	6	6
95-96	Boston	NHL	27	0	4	4	16	—	—	—	—	—
95-96	Providence	AHL	42	9	21	30	52	—	—	—	—	—
96-97	Ottawa	NHL	6	0	1	1	7	—	—	—	—	—
96-97	Detroit	IHL	67	14	26	40	86	21	2	4	6	20
	NHL	Totals	33	0	5	5	23	—	—	—	—	—
	AHL	Totals	275	36	85	121	309	15	3	4	7	8
	IHL	Totals	147	16	60	76	126	26	3	6	9	22

Born; 4/10/69, Vancouver, British Columbia. 6-1, 200. Drafted by Vancouver Canucks (5th choice, 122nd overall) in 1988 Entry Draft. Signed as a free agent by Boston Bruins (9/10/94). Signed as a free agent by Ottawa Seantors (7/96).

Roman Vopat — Center

Season	Team	League	GP	G	A	PTS	PIM	GP	G	A	PTS	PIM
95-96	St. Louis	NHL	25	2	3	5	48	—	—	—	—	—
95-96	Worcester	AHL	5	2	0	2	14	—	—	—	—	—
96-97	Los Angeles	NHL	29	4	5	9	60	—	—	—	—	—
96-97	Phoenix	IHL	50	8	8	16	139	—	—	—	—	—
	NHL	Totals	54	6	8	14	108	—	—	—	—	—

Born; 4/21/76, Litvinov, Czechoslovakia. 6-3, 216. Drafted by St. Louis Blues (4th choice, 172nd overall) in 1994 Entry Draft. Traded to Los Angeles Kings by St. Louis with Craig Johnson, Patrice Tardif, St. Louis' fifth round draft choice (Peter Hogan) and St. Louis' first round draft choice (Matt Zultek) in 1997 Entry Draft for Wayne Gretzky, (2/27/96).

Vladimir Vorobiev — Left Wing

Season	Team	League	GP	G	A	PTS	PIM	GP	G	A	PTS	PIM
96-97	Rangers	NHL	16	5	5	10	6	—	—	—	—	—
96-97	Binghamton	AHL	61	22	27	49	6	4	1	1	2	2

Born; 10/2/72, Cherepovets, Russia. 5-11, 185. Drafted by New York Rangers (10th choice, 240th overall) in 1992 Entry Draft.

Sergei Voronov — Defenseman

Season	Team	League	GP	G	A	PTS	PIM	GP	G	A	PTS	PIM
95-96	Cleveland	IHL	2	0	0	0	4	—	—	—	—	—
95-96	Hampton Roads	ECHL	57	6	23	29	241	2	0	0	0	6
96-97	Las Vegas	IHL	40	2	4	6	99	—	—	—	—	—
	IHL	Totals	42	2	4	6	103	—	—	—	—	—

Born; 2/5/71, Moscow, Russia. 6-2, 200. Drafted by Pittsburgh Penguins (7th choice, 206th overall) in 1995 Entry Draft.

Nick Vukota — Right Wing

			Regular Season					Playoffs				
Season	Team	League	GP	G	A	PTS	PIM	GP	G	A	PTS	PIM
87-88	Islanders	NHL	17	1	0	1	82	2	0	0	0	23
87-88	Springfield	AHL	52	7	9	16	375	—	—	—	—	—
88-89	Islanders	NHL	48	2	2	4	237	—	—	—	—	—
88-89	Springfield	AHL	3	1	0	1	33	—	—	—	—	—
89-90	Islanders	NHL	76	4	8	12	290	1	0	0	0	17
90-91	Islanders	NHL	60	2	4	6	238	—	—	—	—	—
90-91	Capital District	AHL	2	0	0	0	9	—	—	—	—	—
91-92	Islanders	NHL	74	0	6	6	293	—	—	—	—	—
92-93	Islanders	NHL	74	2	5	7	216	15	0	0	0	16
93-94	Islanders	NHL	72	3	1	4	237	4	0	0	0	17
94-95	Islanders	NHL	40	0	2	2	109	—	—	—	—	—
95-96	Islanders	NHL	32	1	1	2	106	—	—	—	—	—
96-97	Islanders	NHL	17	1	0	1	71	—	—	—	—	—
96-97	Utah	IHL	43	11	11	22	185	7	1	2	3	20
	NHL	Totals	510	16	29	45	1879	22	0	0	0	73
	AHL	Totals	57	8	9	17	417	—	—	—	—	—

Born; 9/14/66, Saskatoon, Saskatchewan. 6-1, 225. Signed as a free agent by New York Islanders (3/2/87).

Sergei Vyshedkevich — Defenseman

			Regular Season					Playoffs				
Season	Team	League	GP	G	A	PTS	PIM	GP	G	A	PTS	PIM
96-97	Albany	AHL	65	8	27	35	16	12	0	6	6	0

Born; 1/3/75, Dedovsk, Russia. 6-0, 185. Drafted by New Jersey Devils (3rd choice, 70th overall) in 1995 Entry Draft.

Binghamton's Chris Ferraro tucks the puck behind Albany's Mike Dunham. Both players played in the NHL last season. Photo by Just Sports

Chad Wagner — Defenseman

			Regular Season					Playoffs				
Season	Team	League	GP	G	A	PTS	PIM	GP	G	A	PTS	PIM
95-96	San Diego	WCHL	45	5	12	17	289	2	0	0	0	29
96-97	San Diego	WCHL	45	6	10	16	*503	5	2	1	3	*80
	WCHL	Totals	90	11	22	33	792	7	2	1	3	109

Born; 11/12/74, Calgary, Alberta. 6-5, 225. Member of 1995-96 WCHL Champion San Diego Gulls. Member of 1996-97 WCHL Champion San Diego Gulls

Jimmy Waite — Goaltender

			Regular Season							Playoffs					
Season	Team	League	GP	W	L	T	MIN	SO	GAVG	GP	W	L	MIN	SO	GAVG
88-89	Chicago	NHL	11	0	7	1	494	0	5.22	—	—	—	—	—	—
88-89	Saginaw	IHL	5	3	1	0	304	0	1.97	—	—	—	—	—	—
89-90	Chicago	NHL	4	2	0	0	183	0	4.59	—	—	—	—	—	—
89-90	Indianapolis	IHL	54	*34	14	5	*3207	*5	*2.53	*10	*9	1	*602	*1	*1.89
90-91	Chicago	NHL	1	1	0	0	60	0	2.00	—	—	—	—	—	—
90-91	Indianapolis	IHL	49	*26	18	4	2888	3	3.47	6	2	4	369	0	3.25
91-92	Chicago	NHL	17	4	7	4	877	0	3.69	—	—	—	—	—	—
91-92	Indianapolis	IHL	13	4	7	1	702	0	4.53	—	—	—	—	—	—
91-92	Hershey	AHL	11	6	4	1	631	0	4.18	6	2	4	360	0	3.17
92-93	Chicago	NHL	20	6	7	1	996	2	2.95	—	—	—	—	—	—
93-94	San Jose	NHL	15	3	7	0	697	0	4.30	2	0	0	40	0	4.50
94-95	Chicago	NHL	2	1	1	0	119	0	2.52	—	—	—	—	—	—
94-95	Indianapolis	IHL	4	2	1	1	239	0	3.25	—	—	—	—	—	—
95-96	Chicago	NHL	1	0	0	0	31	0	0.00	—	—	—	—	—	—
95-96	Indianapolis	IHL	56	28	18	6	3157	0	3.40	5	2	3	297	1	3.02
96-97	Chicago	NHL	2	0	1	1	105	0	4.00	—	—	—	—	—	—
96-97	Indianapolis	IHL	41	22	15	4	2451	4	2.74	4	1	3	223	0	3.51
	NHL	Totals	73	17	30	7	3562	2	3.77	2	0	0	40	0	4.50
	IHL	Totals	222	119	74	21	12948	12	3.10	25	14	11	1491	2	2.70

Born; 4/15/69, Sherbrooke, Ontario. 6-1, 180. Drafted by Chicago Blackhawks (1st choice, 8th overall) in 1987 Entry Draft. Traded to San Jose Sharks by Chicago for future considerations (Neil Wilkinson, 7/9/93) (6/19/93). Traded to Chicago by San Jose for a conditional draft choice in 1997 Entry Draft. 1989-90 IHL First Team All-Star. 1989-90 Won James Norris Trophy (fewest goals against-IHL). Member of 1989-90 IHL champion Indianapolis Ice.

Steffon Walby — Right Wing

			Regular Season					Playoffs				
Season	Team	League	GP	G	A	PTS	PIM	GP	G	A	PTS	PIM
93-94	St. John's	AHL	63	15	22	37	79	2	0	0	0	2
94-95	St. John's	AHL	70	23	23	46	30	5	1	1	2	4
95-96	St. John's	AHL	57	23	31	54	61	4	2	2	4	17
96-97	Hershey	AHL	74	24	23	47	61	23	9	5	14	38
	AHL	Totals	264	85	99	184	231	34	12	8	20	61

Born; 11/22/72, Madison, Wisconsin. 6-1, 198. Signed as a free agent by Toronto Maple Leafs (8/20/93). Member of 1996-97 AHL Champion Hershey Bears.

Richie Walcott — Right Wing

			Regular Season					Playoffs				
Season	Team	League	GP	G	A	PTS	PIM	GP	G	A	PTS	PIM
91-92	Baltimore	AHL	51	1	1	2	277	—	—	—	—	—
91-92	Hampton Roads	ECHL	7	1	0	1	23	—	—	—	—	—
92-93	Hampton Roads	ECHL	14	1	1	2	116	—	—	—	—	—
92-93	Wheeling	ECHL	8	0	0	0	46	—	—	—	—	—
93-94	Rochester	AHL	17	1	0	1	66	—	—	—	—	—
93-94	Hampton Roads	ECHL	41	2	1	3	143	—	—	—	—	—
94-95	Utica	CoHL	61	6	9	15	309	6	0	0	0	16

Season	Team	League	GP	G	A	PTS	PIM	GP	G	A	PTS	PIM
95-96	Dayton	ECHL	3	1	1	2	40	—	—	—	—	—
95-96	Birmingham	ECHL	17	2	1	3	78	—	—	—	—	—
95-96	Utica	CoHL	23	1	0	1	99	—	—	—	—	—
96-97	Brantford	CoHL	41	4	5	9	86	—	—	—	—	—
96-97	Madison	CoHL	5	0	2	2	21	5	0	1	1	11
	AHL	Totals	68	1	1	2	323	—	—	—	—	—
	CoHL	Totals	130	11	16	27	515	11	0	1	1	27
	ECHL	Totals	90	7	4	11	446	—	—	—	—	—

Born; 5/17/70, Grand Cache, Alberta. 6-2, 225.

Steve Walker — Left Wing

			Regular Season					Playoffs				
Season	Team	League	GP	G	A	PTS	PIM	GP	G	A	PTS	PIM
93-94	Wheeling	ECHL	9	1	0	1	2	—	—	—	—	—
94-95	Muskegon	CoHL	56	18	28	46	35	17	4	1	5	19
95-96	Muskegon	CoHL	69	43	57	100	121	5	2	3	6	0
96-97	Detroit	IHL	54	12	12	24	27	20	10	9	19	8
96-97	Rochester	AHL	3	0	0	0	17	—	—	—	—	—
97-97	Flint	CoHL	16	13	16	29	34	—	—	—	—	—
	CoHL	Totals	141	74	101	175	190	22	6	4	10	19

Born; 1/12/73, Collingwood, Ontario. 6-0, 190. 1995-96 CoHL Second Team All-Star. Member of 1996-97 IHL Champion Detroit Vipers.

Sinhue Wallinheimo — Goaltender

			Regular Season						Playoffs					
Season	Team	League	GP	W	L	T	MIN	SO	GAVG	GP	W	L	MIN	SO	GAVG
96-97	Hershey	AHL	13	5	4	1	581	0	3.30	2	0	0	4	0	16.14
96-97	Mobile	ECHL	26	14	9	1	1453	0	3.26	—	—	—	—	—	—

Born; 3/9/72, Jyvasklya, Finland. 6-2, 200. Member of 1996-97 AHL Champion Hershey Bears. Last amateur club; Denver (WCHA).

Bobby Wallwork — Right Wing

			Regular Season					Playoffs				
Season	Team	League	GP	G	A	PTS	PIM	GP	G	A	PTS	PIM
90-91	Cincinnati	ECHL	18	7	11	18	18	2	0	0	0	0
91-92	Cincinnati	ECHL	63	22	46	68	48	9	5	7	12	6
92-93	Italy											
93-94	Memphis	CeHL	64	43	40	83	83	—	—	—	—	—
94-95	Memphis	CeHL	64	42	50	92	66	—	—	—	—	—
95-96	Muskegon	CoHL	71	40	39	79	61	5	3	5	8	2
96-97	Austin	WPHL	61	42	53	95	80	6	2	2	4	12
	CeHL	Totals	128	85	90	175	149	—	—	—	—	—
	ECHL	Totals	81	29	57	86	66	11	5	7	12	6

Born; 3/15/68, Boston, Massachusetts. 5-9, 185. Drafted by Buffalo Sabres (12th round, 244th overall) 6/11/88. 1993-94 CeHL First Team All-Star. 1994-95 CeHL Second Team All-Star.

Kurt Walsten — Defenseman

			Regular Season					Playoffs				
Season	Team	League	GP	G	A	PTS	PIM	GP	G	A	PTS	PIM
93-94	Huntsville	ECHL	13	1	2	3	107	—	—	—	—	—
94-95	Dallas	CeHL	2	0	1	1	2	—	—	—	—	—
95-96	N/A											
96-97	Fresno	WCHL	23	0	1	1	112	—	—	—	—	—
96-97	Anchorage	WCHL	32	6	10	16	60	—	—	—	—	—
	WCHL	Totals	55	6	11	17	172	—	—	—	—	—

Born; 5/5/68, Kenora, Ontario.

Greg Walters — Left Wing

Season	Team	League	GP	G	A	PTS	PIM	GP	G	A	PTS	PIM
			Regular Season					Playoffs				
90-91	Newmarket	AHL	54	7	14	21	58	—	—	—	—	—
91-92	St. John's	AHL	10	0	2	2	20	—	—	—	—	—
91-92	Raleigh	ECHL	18	9	13	22	30	4	1	2	3	8
92-93	St. John's	AHL	27	4	5	9	82	1	0	1	1	4
92-93	Brantford	CoHL	26	14	19	33	44	10	11	8	19	20
93-94	St. John's	AHL	13	0	2	2	67	—	—	—	—	—
93-94	Brantford	CoHL	42	42	62	104	88	7	5	3	8	8
94-95	Fort Wayne	IHL	44	4	9	13	142	—	—	—	—	—
94-95	Chicago	IHL	18	1	4	5	110	2	0	0	0	0
95-96	Chicago	IHL	50	4	7	11	254	5	0	0	0	12
96-97	Rochester	AHL	55	5	10	15	247	10	3	6	9	20
	AHL	Totals	159	16	33	49	474	11	3	7	10	24
	IHL	Totals	112	9	22	31	506	7	0	0	0	12
	CoHL	Totals	68	56	81	137	132	17	16	11	27	28

Born; 8/12/70, Calgary, Alberta. 6-1, 195. Drafted by Toronto Maple Leafs (3rd pick, 80th overall) in 1990 Entry Draft. 1993-94 CoHL Second Team All-Star. Member of 1992-93 CoHL champion Brantford Smoke.

Ed Ward — Right Wing

Season	Team	League	GP	G	A	PTS	PIM	GP	G	A	PTS	PIM
			Regular Season					Playoffs				
91-92	Halifax	AHL	51	7	11	18	65	—	—	—	—	—
91-92	Greensboro	ECHL	12	4	8	12	21	—	—	—	—	—
92-93	Halifax	AHL	70	13	19	32	56	—	—	—	—	—
93-94	Quebec	NHL	7	1	0	1	5	—	—	—	—	—
93-94	Cornwall	AHL	60	12	30	42	65	12	1	3	4	14
94-95	Calgary	NHL	2	1	1	2	2	—	—	—	—	—
94-95	Cornwall	AHL	56	10	14	24	118	—	—	—	—	—
94-95	Saint John	AHL	11	4	5	9	20	5	1	0	1	10
95-96	Calgary	NHL	41	3	5	8	44	—	—	—	—	—
95-96	Saint John	AHL	12	1	2	3	45	16	4	4	8	27
96-97	Calgary	NHL	40	5	8	13	49	—	—	—	—	—
96-97	Saint John	AHL	1	0	0	0	0	—	—	—	—	—
96-97	Detroit	IHL	31	7	6	13	45	—	—	—	—	—
	NHL	Totals	90	10	14	24	100	—	—	—	—	—
	AHL	Totals	261	47	81	128	369	33	6	7	13	51

Born; 11/10/69, Edmonton, Alberta. 6-3, 190. Drafted by Quebec Nordiques (7th choice, 108th overall) in 1988 Entry Draft. Traded to Calgary Flames by Quebec for Francois Groleau (3/23/95).

Steve Washburn — Center

Season	Team	League	GP	G	A	PTS	PIM	GP	G	A	PTS	PIM
			Regular Season					Playoffs				
94-95	Cincinnati	IHL	6	3	1	4	0	9	1	3	4	4
95-96	Florida	NHL	1	0	1	1	0	1	0	1	1	0
95-96	Carolina	AHL	78	29	54	83	45	—	—	—	—	—
96-97	Florida	NHL	18	3	6	9	4	—	—	—	—	—
96-97	Carolina	AHL	60	23	40	63	66	—	—	—	—	—
	NHL	Totals	19	3	7	10	4	1	0	1	1	0
	AHL	Totals	138	52	94	146	111	—	—	—	—	—

Born; 4/10/75, Ottawa, Ontario. 6-2, 191. Drafted by Florida Panthers (5th choice, 78th overall) in 1993 Entry Draft.

Joakim Wassberger — Right Wing

			Regular Season					Playoffs				
Season	Team	League	GP	G	A	PTS	PIM	GP	G	A	PTS	PIM
94-95	Oklahoma City	CeHL	4	1	1	2	2	—	—	—	—	—
94-95	Daytona Beach	SUN	2	0	0	0	0	—	—	—	—	—
95-96	Quad City	CoHL	73	24	48	72	34	4	2	0	2	2
96-97	Mississippi	ECHL	26	6	9	15	6	—	—	—	—	—
96-97	Raleigh	ECHL	35	9	17	26	17	—	—	—	—	—
	ECHL	Totals	61	15	26	41	23	—	—	—	—	—

Born; 3/12/70, Stockholm, Sweden. 5-10, 183.

Steve Webb — Right Wing

			Regular Season					Playoffs				
Season	Team	League	GP	G	A	PTS	PIM	GP	G	A	PTS	PIM
95-96	Detroit	IHL	4	0	0	0	24	—	—	—	—	—
95-96	Muskegon	CoHL	58	18	24	42	263	5	1	2	3	22
96-97	Islanders	NHL	41	1	4	5	144	—	—	—	—	—
96-97	Kentucky	AHL	25	6	6	12	103	2	0	0	0	19

Born; 4/30/75, Peterborough, Ontario. 4/30/75. Drafted by Buffalo Sabres (8th choice, 176th overall) in 1994 Entry Draft.

Matt Weder — Goaltender

			Regular Season						Playoffs					
Season	Team	League	GP	W	L	T	MIN	SO	GAVG	GP	W	L	MIN	SO	GAVG
96-97	Detroit	IHL	1	0	0	0	40	0	4.50	—	—	—	—	—	—
96-97	Flint	CoHL	13	2	4	0	424	0	3.54	—	—	—	—	—	—
96-97	Saginaw	CoHL	5	0	2	1	170	0	8.47	—	—	—	—	—	—
	CoHL	Totals	18	2	6	1	594	0	4.95	—	—	—	—	—	—

Born; 6/14/72, Flint, Michigan. 6-1, 195. Last amateur club; Colgate (ECAC).

Kevin Weekes — Goaltender

			Regular Season						Playoffs					
Season	Team	League	GP	W	L	T	MIN	SO	GAVG	GP	W	L	MIN	SO	GAVG
95-96	Carolina	AHL	60	24	25	8	3403	2	4.04	—	—	—	—	—	—
96-97	Carolina	AHL	51	17	*28	4	2899	1	3.56	—	—	—	—	—	—
	AHL	Totals	111	41	53	12	6302	3	3.82	—	—	—	—	—	—

Born; 4/4/75, Toronto, Ontario. 6-0, 158. Drafted by Florida Panthers (2nd choice, 41st overall) in 1993 Entry Draft.

Andy Weidenbach — Center

			Regular Season					Playoffs				
Season	Team	League	GP	G	A	PTS	PIM	GP	G	A	PTS	PIM
96-97	Cleveland	IHL	9	1	1	2	2	—	—	—	—	—
96-97	Hampton Roads	ECHL	59	23	26	49	55	7	1	1	2	10

Born; 5/28/71, Lincoln Park, Michigan. 5-8, 175.

Rob Weingartner — Right Wing

			Regular Season					Playoffs				
Season	Team	League	GP	G	A	PTS	PIM	GP	G	A	PTS	PIM
92-93	Wichita	CeHL	35	10	4	14	71	—	—	—	—	—
93-94	Wichita	CeHL	50	16	17	33	150	11	1	4	5	49
94-95	Wichita	CeHL	49	20	11	31	274	11	4	6	10	30
95-96	Wichita	CeHL	15	1	6	7	69	—	—	—	—	—
95-96	San Antonio	CeHL	45	20	30	50	184	13	5	10	15	45
96-97	Manitoba	IHL	4	0	1	1	11	—	—	—	—	—
96-97	Louisiana	ECHL	59	20	15	35	334	17	5	10	15	46
	CeHL	Totals	194	67	68	135	748	35	10	20	30	124

Born; 10/22/71, Lake Ronkonkoma, New York. 5-10, 190. Member of 1993-94 CeHL champion Wichita Thunder. Member of 1994-95 CeHL champion Wichita Thunder.

Jason Welch — Center

			Regular Season					Playoffs				
Season	Team	League	GP	G	A	PTS	PIM	GP	G	A	PTS	PIM
96-97	El Paso	WPHL	51	27	31	58	30	11	5	9	14	12

Member of 1996-97 WPHL Champion El Paso Buzzards. Last amateur club; Northern Michigan (WCHA).

Jeff Wells — Defenseman

			Regular Season					Playoffs				
Season	Team	League	GP	G	A	PTS	PIM	GP	G	A	PTS	PIM
94-95	Providence	AHL	51	3	11	14	23	9	2	1	3	0
95-96	Cincinnati	IHL	62	10	19	29	46	17	2	4	6	8
95-96	Birmingham	ECHL	3	1	2	3	4	—	—	—	—	—
96-97	Cincinnati	IHL	79	10	11	21	41	3	0	0	0	4
	IHL	Totals	161	20	30	50	87	20	2	4	6	12

Born; 3/19/70, Brockville, Ontario. 6-0, 195.

Marty Wells — Left Wing

			Regular Season					Playoffs				
Season	Team	League	GP	G	A	PTS	PIM	GP	G	A	PTS	PIM
93-94	Chatham	CoHL	49	21	24	45	28	15	9	8	17	11
94-95	Thunder Bay	CoHL	11	0	3	3	4	—	—	—	—	—
95-96	Alaska	WCHL	10	4	7	11	2	—	—	—	—	—
95-96	Bakersfield	WCHL	17	8	5	13	24	—	—	—	—	—
95-96	Anchorage	WCHL	7	1	2	3	13	—	—	—	—	—
96-97	Quad City	CoHL	2	1	0	1	6	—	—	—	—	—
96-97	Saginaw	CoHL	27	8	6	14	30	—	—	—	—	—
96-97	Dayton	CoHL	27	9	6	15	6	—	—	—	—	—
	CoHL	Totals	116	39	39	78	74	15	9	8	17	11
	WCHL	Totals	34	13	14	27	39	—	—	—	—	—

Born; 11/3/72, Toronto, Ontario. 5-8, 200.

Wade Welte — Left Wing

			Regular Season					Playoffs				
Season	Team	League	GP	G	A	PTS	PIM	GP	G	A	PTS	PIM
94-95	West Palm Beach	SUN	52	25	18	43	163	5	1	1	2	20
95-96	Jacksonville	SHL	8	0	0	0	26	—	—	—	—	—
95-96	Fresno	WCHL	12	5	2	7	35	—	—	—	—	—
95-96	Bakersfield	WCHL	32	16	16	32	84	—	—	—	—	—
96-97	Bakersfield	WCHL	61	28	21	49	280	4	0	2	2	58
	WCHL	Totals	105	49	39	88	399	4	0	2	2	58
	SHL	Totals	60	25	18	43	189	5	1	1	2	20

Born; 5/24/73, Richmond, Saskatoon. 5-8, 190.

Brad Werenka — Defenseman

			Regular Season					Playoffs				
Season	Team	League	GP	G	A	PTS	PIM	GP	G	A	PTS	PIM
91-92	Cape Breton	AHL	66	6	21	27	95	5	0	3	3	6
92-93	Edmonton	NHL	27	5	3	8	24	—	—	—	—	—
92-93	Cape Breton	AHL	4	1	1	2	4	16	4	17	21	12
92-93	Canada	National										
93-94	Edmonton	NHL	15	0	4	4	14	—	—	—	—	—
93-94	Quebec	NHL	11	0	7	7	8	—	—	—	—	—
93-94	Cape Breton	AHL	25	6	17	23	19	—	—	—	—	—
93-94	Cornwall	AHL	—	—	—	—	—	12	2	10	12	22
93-94	Canada	National										
94-95	Milwaukee	IHL	80	8	45	53	161	15	3	10	13	36
95-96	Chicago	NHL	9	0	0	0	8	—	—	—	—	—

Season	Team	League	GP	G	A	PTS	PIM	GP	G	A	PTS	PIM
95-96	Indianapolis	IHL	73	15	42	57	85	5	1	3	4	8
96-97	Indianapolis	IHL	82	20	56	76	83	4	1	4	5	6
	NHL	Totals	62	5	14	19	54	—	—	—	—	—
	IHL	Totals	235	43	143	186	329	24	5	17	22	50
	AHL	Totals	95	13	39	52	118	33	6	30	36	40

Born; 2/12/69, Two Hills, Alberta. 6-2, 205. Drafted by Edmonton Oilers (2nd choice, 42nd overall) in 1987 Entry Draft. Traded to Quebec Nordiques by Edmonton for Steve Passmore (3/21/94). Signed as a free agent by Chicago Blackhawks (8/7/95). Member of 1992-93 AHL champion Cape Breton Oilers. 1996-97 IHL Governor's Trophy (Best Defenseman). 1996-97 IHL First Team All-Star.

Darcy Werenka — Defenseman

Season	Team	League	GP	G	A	PTS	PIM	GP	G	A	PTS	PIM
92-93	Binghamton	AHL	3	0	1	1	2	3	0	0	0	0
93-94	Binghamton	AHL	53	5	22	27	10	—	—	—	—	—
94-95	Binghamton	AHL	73	17	29	46	12	11	4	3	7	2
95-96	Chicago	IHL	12	2	5	7	10	—	—	—	—	—
95-96	Atlanta	IHL	58	6	20	27	22	—	—	—	—	—
96-97	Quebec	IHL	5	1	1	2	2	—	—	—	—	—
96-97	Houston	IHL	74	12	20	32	31	13	2	1	3	2
	IHL	Totals	149	21	46	67	89	13	2	1	3	2
	AHL	Totals	129	22	52	74	24	14	4	3	7	4

Born; 5/13/73, Edmonton, Alberta. 6-1, 210. Drafted by New York Rangers (2nd choice, 37th overall) in 1991 Entry Draft.

Bob Westerby — Left Wing

Season	Team	League	GP	G	A	PTS	PIM	GP	G	A	PTS	PIM
95-96	Rochester	AHL	40	2	6	8	155	—	—	—	—	—
96-97	Baton Rouge	ECHL	54	6	14	20	310	—	—	—	—	—

Born; 10/29/75, Kelowna, British Columbia. 6-1, 195. Drafted by Buffalo Sabres (9th choice, 199th overall) in 1994 Entry Draft.

Darren Wetherill — Defenseman

Season	Team	League	GP	G	A	PTS	PIM	GP	G	A	PTS	PIM
94-95	Richmond	ECHL	56	6	12	18	114	17	1	2	3	41
94-95	Cornwall	AHL	3	0	0	0	12	—	—	—	—	—
95-96	Orlando	IHL	14	1	1	2	15	10	0	0	0	11
95-96	Baltimore	AHL	2	0	0	0	2	—	—	—	—	—
95-96	Richmond	ECHL	63	6	19	25	166	—	—	—	—	—
96-97	Orlando	IHL	32	0	0	0	43	8	0	1	1	25
	IHL	Totals	46	1	1	2	58	18	0	1	1	36
	AHL	Totals	5	0	0	0	14	—	—	—	—	—
	ECHL	Totals	119	12	31	43	280	17	1	2	3	41

Born; 1/28/70, Regina, Saskatchewan. 6-0, 185. Drafted by Boston Bruins (8th choice, 189th overall) in 1990 Entry Draft. Signed as a free agent by Orlando Solar Bears (8/96). Member of 1994-95 ECHL champion Richmond Renegades.

Ben White — Defenseman

Season	Team	League	GP	G	A	PTS	PIM	GP	G	A	PTS	PIM
96-97	Utica	CoHL	17	0	5	5	11	3	0	0	0	4

Born; Sudbury, Ontario. 6-3, 215.

Kam White — Defenseman

Season	Team	League	GP	G	A	PTS	PIM	GP	G	A	PTS	PIM
95-96	South Carolina	ECHL	6	0	1	1	10	—	—	—	—	—
96-97	Mississippi	ECHL	3	0	0	0	4	—	—	—	—	—
96-97	Johnstown	ECHL	47	0	5	5	261	—	—	—	—	—

Born; 2/13/76, Toronto, Ontario. 6-3, 217. Drafted by Toronto Maple Leafs (5th choice, 152nd overall) in 1994 Entry Draft.

Peter White — Center
Regular Season / **Playoffs**

Season	Team	League	GP	G	A	PTS	PIM	GP	G	A	PTS	PIM
92-93	Cape Breton	AHL	64	12	28	40	10	16	3	3	6	12
93-94	Edmonton	NHL	26	3	5	8	2	—	—	—	—	—
93-94	Cape Breton	AHL	45	21	49	70	12	5	2	3	5	2
94-95	Edmonton	NHL	9	2	4	6	0	—	—	—	—	—
94-95	Cape Breton	AHL	65	36	*69	*105	30	—	—	—	—	—
95-96	Edmonton	NHL	26	5	3	8	0	—	—	—	—	—
95-96	Toronto	NHL	1	0	0	0	0	—	—	—	—	—
95-96	St. John's	AHL	17	6	7	13	6	—	—	—	—	—
95-96	Atlanta	IHL	36	21	20	41	4	3	0	3	3	2
96-97	Philadelphia	AHL	80	*44	61	*105	28	10	6	8	14	6
	NHL	Totals	62	10	12	22	2	—	—	—	—	—
	AHL	Totals	271	119	214	333	86	31	11	17	28	32

Born; 3/15/69, Montreal, Quebec. 5-11, 195. Drafted by Edmonton Oilers' (4rth choice, 92 overall) in 1989 Entry Draft. 1994-95 AHL Second Team All-Star. 1996-97 AHL Second Team All-Star. Traded to Toronto Maple Leafs by Edmonton with Edmonton's fourth round choice (Jason Sessa) in 1996 Entry Draft for Kent Manderville (12/4/95). Signed as a free agent by Philadelphia Flyers (8/19/96).

Tim White — Right Wing
Regular Season / **Playoffs**

Season	Team	League	GP	G	A	PTS	PIM	GP	G	A	PTS	PIM
96-97	Dayton	CoHL	32	8	17	25	39	—	—	—	—	—

Born; 9/26/74, Lincoln Park, Michigan. 6-2, 215.

Keith Whitmore — Defenseman
Regular Season / **Playoffs**

Season	Team	League	GP	G	A	PTS	PIM	GP	G	A	PTS	PIM
91-92	Hampton Roads	ECHL	45	10	20	30	70	14	1	5	6	12
92-93	Hampton Roads	ECHL	7	1	3	4	10	—	—	—	—	—
92-93	Knoxville	ECHL	50	8	27	35	86	—	—	—	—	—
93-94	Flint	CoHL	55	19	59	78	131	10	4	7	11	4
94-95	Flint	CoHL	45	6	29	35	50	6	2	2	4	8
95-96	Detroit	CoHL	47	9	28	37	64	—	—	—	—	—
96-97	Saginaw	CoHL	72	11	66	77	110	—	—	—	—	—
	CoHL	Totals	219	45	182	227	355	16	6	9	15	12
	ECHL	Totals	102	19	50	69	166	14	1	5	6	12

Born; 11/24/70, Sudbury, Ontario. 5-10, 187. Member of 1991-92 ECHL Champion Hampton Roads Admirals. 1993-94 CoHL Second Team All-Star.

Dean Whitney — Goaltender
Regular Season / **Playoffs**

Season	Team	League	GP	W	L	T	MIN	SO	GAVG	GP	W	L	MIN	SO	GAVG
95-96	Mobile	ECHL	25	4	9	3	1210	0	4.41	—	—	—	—	—	—
96-97	Wichita	CeHL	21	6	9	3	942	0	5.35	—	—	—	—	—	—

Born; 12/8/74, Edmonton, Alberta. 5-9, 155.

Ray Whitney — Center
Regular Season / **Playoffs**

Season	Team	League	GP	G	A	PTS	PIM	GP	G	A	PTS	PIM
91-92	San Diego	IHL	63	36	54	90	12	4	0	0	0	0
91-92	San Jose	NHL	2	0	3	3	0	—	—	—	—	—
92-93	San Jose	NHL	26	4	6	10	4	—	—	—	—	—
92-93	Kansas City	IHL	46	20	33	53	14	12	5	7	12	2
93-94	San Jose	NHL	61	14	26	40	14	14	0	4	4	8
94-95	San Jose	NHL	39	13	12	25	14	11	4	4	8	2
95-96	San Jose	NHL	60	17	24	41	16	—	—	—	—	—

Season	Team	League	GP	G	A	PTS	PIM	GP	G	A	PTS	PIM
96-97	San Jose	NHL	12	0	2	2	4	—	—	—	—	—
96-97	Utah	IHL	43	13	35	48	34	7	3	1	4	6
96-97	Kentucky	AHL	9	1	7	8	2	—	—	—	—	—
	NHL	Totals	200	48	73	121	52	25	4	8	12	10
	IHL	Totals	152	69	122	191	60	23	8	8	16	8

Born; 5/8/72, Fort Saskatchewan, Alberta. 5-9, 160. Drafted by San Jose Sharks (2nd choice, 23rd overall) in 1991 Entry Draft.

Jeff Whittle — Right Wing

Season	Team	League	GP	G	A	PTS	PIM	GP	G	A	PTS	PIM
92-93	Hampton Roads	ECHL	5	1	0	1	19	—	—	—	—	—
92-93	Erie	ECHL	45	9	16	25	133	—	—	—	—	—
93-94	Erie	ECHL	67	47	42	89	126	—	—	—	—	—
94-95	Fort Wayne	IHL	2	2	0	2	0	—	—	—	—	—
94-95	Flint	CoHL	58	31	44	75	133	6	2	2	4	15
95-96	Detroit	IHL	1	0	0	0	0	—	—	—	—	—
95-96	Flint	CoHL	54	24	31	55	98	—	—	—	—	—
95-96	Utica	CoHL	15	6	6	12	26	—	—	—	—	—
96-97	Detroit	IHL	1	0	0	0	0	—	—	—	—	—
96-97	Flint	CoHL	74	28	55	83	111	14	*12	12	24	14
	IHL	Totals	4	2	0	2	0	—	—	—	—	—
	CoHL	Totals	201	89	136	225	368	20	14	14	28	29
	ECHL	Totals	117	57	58	115	278	—	—	—	—	—

Born; 3/22/71, Toronto, Ontario. 5-9, 187.

Mike Whitton — Left Wing

Season	Team	League	GP	G	A	PTS	PIM	GP	G	A	PTS	PIM
95-96	Toledo	ECHL	29	7	13	20	41	—	—	—	—	—
95-96	Birmingham	ECHL	6	1	0	1	0	—	—	—	—	—
96-97	Toledo	ECHL	45	12	8	20	98	—	—	—	—	—
	ECHL	Totals	80	20	21	41	139	—	—	—	—	—

Born; 9/3/70, Toronto, Ontario. 6-2, 215.

Sean Whyte — Right Wing

Season	Team	League	GP	G	A	PTS	PIM	GP	G	A	PTS	PIM
90-91	Phoenix	IHL	60	18	17	35	61	4	1	0	1	2
91-92	Los Angeles	NHL	3	0	0	0	0	—	—	—	—	—
91-92	Phoenix	IHL	72	24	30	54	113	—	—	—	—	—
92-93	Los Angeles	NHL	18	0	2	2	12	—	—	—	—	—
92-93	Phoenix	IHL	51	11	35	46	65	—	—	—	—	—
93-94	Cornwall	AHL	18	6	9	15	16	9	1	2	3	2
93-94	Tulsa	CeHL	50	42	29	71	93	—	—	—	—	—
94-95	Worcester	AHL	59	13	8	21	76	—	—	—	—	—
95-96	Phoenix	IHL	11	0	2	2	4	—	—	—	—	—
95-96	Fort Wayne	CeHL	51	15	37	52	94	—	—	—	—	—
96-97	El Paso	WPHL	60	21	39	60	105	11	2	*14	16	36
	IHL	Totals	194	53	84	137	243	4	1	0	1	2
	AHL	Totals	77	19	17	36	92	9	1	2	3	2
	CeHL	Totals	101	57	66	123	187	—	—	—	—	—

Born; 5/4/70, Sudbury, Ontario. Drafted by Los Angeles Kings (7th choice, 165th overall) in 1989 Entry Draft. Member of 1996-97 WPHL Champion El Paso Buzzards.

Joakim Wiberg — Goaltender

Season	Team	League	GP	W	L	T	MIN	SO	GAVG	GP	W	L	MIN	SO	GAVG
95-96	West Palm Beach	SHL	12	2	3	0	437	0	6.18	—	—	—	—	—	—
95-96	Johnstown	ECHL	1	0	0	0	60	0	4.00	—	—	—	—	—	—
96-97	Madison	CoHL	13	4	2	1	537	0	3.46	—	—	—	—	—	—
96-97	Utica	CoHL	4	0	3	0	133	0	6.29	—	—	—	—	—	—
96-97	Quad City	CoHL	1	0	0	0	7	0	8.33	—	—	—	—	—	—
	CoHL	Totals	18	4	5	1	678	0	4.07	—	—	—	—	—	—

Born; 10/23/72, Salem, Sweden. 6-1, 185.

Kurt Wickenheiser — Center

Season	Team	League	GP	G	A	PTS	PIM	GP	G	A	PTS	PIM
96-97	New Mexico	WPHL	55	46	28	74	62	6	6	3	9	4

Born; 8/24/64, Regina, Saskatchewan. 5-11, 183.

Jason Widmer — Defenseman

Season	Team	League	GP	G	A	PTS	PIM	GP	G	A	PTS	PIM
92-93	Capital District	AHL	4	0	0	0	2	—	—	—	—	—
94-95	Islanders	NHL	1	0	0	0	0	—	—	—	—	—
94-95	Worcester	AHL	73	8	26	34	136	—	—	—	—	—
94-95	Canada	National										
95-96	Islanders	NHL	4	0	0	0	7	—	—	—	—	—
95-96	Worcester	AHL	76	6	21	27	129	4	2	0	2	9
96-97	Kentucky	AHL	76	4	24	28	105	4	0	0	0	8
	NHL	Totals	5	0	0	0	7	—	—	—	—	—
	AHL	Totals	229	18	71	89	372	8	2	0	2	17

Born; 8/1/73, Calgary, Alberta. 6-0, 205. Drafted by New York Islanders (8th choice, 176th overall) in 1992 Entry Draft.

Adam Wiesel — Defenseman

Season	Team	League	GP	G	A	PTS	PIM	GP	G	A	PTS	PIM
95-96	Fredericton	AHL	69	6	13	19	12	2	0	0	0	0
96-97	Fredericton	AHL	65	4	7	11	14	—	—	—	—	—
	AHL	Totals	134	10	20	30	26	2	0	0	0	0

Born; 1/25/75, South Hadley, Massachusetts. 6-3, 210. Drafted by Montreal Canadiens (4th choice, 85th overall) in 1993 Entry Draft.

George Wilcox — Center

Season	Team	League	GP	G	A	PTS	PIM	GP	G	A	PTS	PIM
95-96	Louisville	ECHL	62	25	29	54	151	1	0	0	0	12
96-97	Anchorage	WCHL	52	18	30	48	165	9	3	4	7	42

Born; 2/16/70, Sept Isles, Quebec. 6-1, 190.

Derek Wilkinson — Goaltender

Season	Team	League	GP	W	L	T	MIN	SO	GAVG	GP	W	L	MIN	SO	GAVG
94-95	Atlanta	IHL	46	22	17	2	2414	1	3.01	4	2	1	197	0	2.43
95-96	Tampa Bay	NHL	4	0	3	0	200	0	4.50	—	—	—	—	—	—
95-96	Atlanta	IHL	28	11	11	2	1432	1	4.10	—	—	—	—	—	—
96-97	Tampa Bay	NHL	5	0	2	1	169	0	4.26	—	—	—	—	—	—
96-97	Cleveland	IHL	46	20	17	6	2595	1	3.19	14	8	*6	893	0	2.95
	NHL	Totals	9	0	5	1	369	0	4.39	—	—	—	—	—	—
	IHL	Totals	120	53	45	10	6441	3	3.33	18	10	7	1090	0	2.86

Born; 7/29/74, Lasalle, Quebec. 6-0, 170. Drafted by Tampa Bay Lightning (7th choice, 145th overall) in 1992 Entry Draft.

Craig Willard — Defenseman

Season	Team	League	GP	G	A	PTS	PIM	GP	G	A	PTS	PIM
96-97	Macon	CeHL	55	4	5	9	116	—	—	—	—	—

Born; 8/22/71, St. Charles, Illinois. 6-1, 190.

Paul Willett — Center

Season	Team	League	GP	G	A	PTS	PIM	GP	G	A	PTS	PIM
89-90	Sherbrooke	AHL	2	0	1	1	2	—	—	—	—	—
90-91	Roanoke	ECHL	29	21	29	50	26	—	—	—	—	—
90-91	New Haven	AHL	42	11	19	30	18	—	—	—	—	—
91-92	New Haven	AHL	69	29	51	80	68	5	3	1	4	2
92-93	Fort Wayne	IHL	74	33	52	85	109	10	7	6	13	22
93-94	Greensboro	ECHL	2	1	0	1	4	—	—	—	—	—
93-94	Cornwall	AHL	56	24	34	58	60	13	2	10	12	0
94-95	Fort Wayne	IHL	80	26	47	73	74	1	0	1	1	0
95-96	Fort Wayne	IHL	81	24	37	61	118	5	2	1	3	4
96-97	Fort Wayne	IHL	36	7	10	17	50	—	—	—	—	—
IHL	Totals		271	90	146	236	351	16	9	8	17	26
AHL	Totals		169	64	105	169	148	18	5	11	16	2
ECHL	Totals		31	22	29	51	30					

Born; 10/15/69, New Richmond, Quebec. 5-10, 180. Member of 1992-93 IHL champion Fort Wayne Komets.

Darryl Williams — Left Wing

Season	Team	League	GP	G	A	PTS	PIM	GP	G	A	PTS	PIM
88-89	New Haven	AHL	15	5	5	10	24	—	—	—	—	—
89-90	New Haven	AHL	51	9	13	22	124	—	—	—	—	—
90-91	New Haven	AHL	57	14	11	25	278	—	—	—	—	—
90-91	Phoenix	IHL	12	2	1	3	53	7	1	0	1	12
91-92	New Haven	AHL	13	0	2	2	69	—	—	—	—	—
91-92	Phoenix	IHL	48	8	19	27	219	—	—	—	—	—
92-93	Los Angeles	NHL	2	0	0	0	10	—	—	—	—	—
92-93	Phoenix	IHL	61	18	7	25	314	—	—	—	—	—
93-94	Phoenix	IHL	52	11	18	29	237	—	—	—	—	—
94-95	Detroit	IHL	66	10	12	22	268	4	0	0	0	14
95-96	Detroit	IHL	72	8	19	27	294	12	0	3	3	30
96-97	Long Beach	IHL	82	13	17	30	285	14	2	2	4	26
IHL	Totals		393	70	93	163	1670	37	3	5	8	82
AHL	Totals		136	28	31	59	495	—	—	—	—	—

Born; 2/29/68, Mt. Pearl, Newfoundland. 5-11, 190. Signed as a free agent by Los Angeles Kings (9/89).

David Williams — Defenseman

Season	Team	League	GP	G	A	PTS	PIM	GP	G	A	PTS	PIM
90-91	Muskegon	IHL	14	1	2	3	4	—	—	—	—	—
90-91	Knoxville	ECHL	38	12	15	27	40	3	0	0	0	4
91-92	San Jose	NHL	56	3	25	28	40	—	—	—	—	—
91-92	Kansas City	IHL	18	2	3	5	22	—	—	—	—	—
92-93	San Jose	NHL	40	1	11	12	49	—	—	—	—	—
92-93	Kansas City	IHL	31	1	11	12	28	—	—	—	—	—
93-94	Anaheim	NHL	56	5	15	20	42	—	—	—	—	—
93-94	San Diego	IHL	16	1	6	7	17	—	—	—	—	—
94-95	Anaheim	NHL	21	2	2	4	26	—	—	—	—	—
94-95	San Diego	IHL	2	0	1	1	0	5	1	0	1	0
95-96	Detroit	IHL	81	5	14	19	81	11	1	3	4	6

Season	Team	League	GP	G	A	PTS	PIM	GP	G	A	PTS	PIM
96-97	Worcester	AHL	72	3	17	20	89	5	1	1	2	0
	NHL	Totals	173	11	53	64	157	—	—	—	—	—
	IHL	Totals	162	10	37	47	152	16	2	3	5	6

Born; 8/25/67, Plainfield, New Jersey. 6-2, 195. Drafted by New Jersey Devils (12th choice, 234th overall) in 1985 Entry Draft. Signed as a free agent by San Jose Sharks, (8/9/91). Claimed by Anaheim Mighty Ducks from San Jose in Expansion Draft (6/24/93). Signed as a free agent by Hartford Whalers, (8/25/95). Signed as a free agent by St. Louis Blues, (7/29/96).

Jack Williams — Left Wing

			Regular Season					Playoffs				
Season	Team	League	GP	G	A	PTS	PIM	GP	G	A	PTS	PIM
92-93	Roanoke Valley	ECHL	43	19	26	45	28	—	—	—	—	—
93-94	Wichita	CeHL	64	17	32	49	104	11	3	2	5	4
94-95	Wichita	CeHL	53	16	20	36	58	11	2	3	5	20
95-96	Reno	WCHL	3	1	1	2	14	—	—	—	—	—
95-96	Wichita	CeHL	46	18	27	45	45	—	—	—	—	—
96-97	Austin	WPHL	2	0	0	0	0	—	—	—	—	—
96-97	Louisiana	ECHL	49	10	10	20	124	17	4	4	8	35
	CeHL	Totals	163	51	79	130	207	22	5	5	10	24
	ECHL	Totals	92	29	36	65	152	17	4	4	8	35

Born; 2/12/72, Providence, Rhode Island. 6-0, 185. Member of 1993-94 CeHL champion Wichita Thunder. Member of 1994-95 CeHL champion Wichita Thunder.

Jeff Williams — Left Wing

			Regular Season					Playoffs				
Season	Team	League	GP	G	A	PTS	PIM	GP	G	A	PTS	PIM
96-97	Albany	AHL	46	13	21	34	12	15	1	2	3	15
96-97	Raleigh	ECHL	20	4	8	12	8	—	—	—	—	—

Born; 2/11/76, Pinte-Claire, Quebec. 6-0, 175. Drafted by New Jersey Devils (8th choice, 181st overall) in 1994 Entry Draft.

Max Williams — Center

			Regular Season					Playoffs				
Season	Team	League	GP	G	A	PTS	PIM	GP	G	A	PTS	PIM
96-97	Charlotte	ECHL	6	0	2	2	2	—	—	—	—	—
96-97	Birmingham	ECHL	43	4	16	20	8	—	—	—	—	—
96-97	Peoria	ECHL	17	9	10	19	2	10	0	3	3	4
	ECHL	Totals	66	13	28	41	12	10	0	3	3	4

Born; 5/22/73, Mahwah, New Jersey. 5-9, 155. Last amateur club; Wisconsin (WCHA).

Mike Williams — Goaltender

			Regular Season							Playoffs				
Season	Team	League	GP	W	L	T	MIN	SO	GAVG	GP	W	L	MIN	SO	GAVG
90-91	Cincinnati	ECHL	12	—	—	—	671	0	5.18	—	—	—	—	—	—
90-91	Nashville	ECHL	3	—	—	—	121	0	5.95	—	—	—	—	—	—
91-92	Toledo	ECHL	44	—	—	—	2490	0	3.81	1	—	—	59	0	6.10
92-93	Toledo	ECHL	8	2	1	2	376	0	4.47	—	—	—	—	—	—
92-93	Knoxville	ECHL	21	3	13	2	1145	0	4.98	—	—	—	—	—	—
93-94	Oklahoma City	CeHL	41	20	12	4	2350	1	3.75	7	3	3	422	0	3.69
94-95	San Antonio	CeHL	38	15	12	4	2000	0	4.17	4	1	1	144	0	2.91
95-96	San Antonio	CeHL	48	27	10	5	2481	*3	3.60	13	7	6	749	0	3.45
96-97	Oklahoma City	CeHL	11	7	0	1	552	1	2.94	4	1	3	241	0	3.49
	CeHL	Totals	138	69	34	14	7383	5	3.75	28	12	13	1556	0	3.47
*	ECHL	Totals	88	5	14	4	4803	0	4.38	1	—	—	59	0	6.10

Born; 4/16/67, Brownstown, Michigan. 6-0, 200. Drafted by Quebec Nordiques (12th choice, 219th overall) in 1987 Entry Draft. * ECHL Goaltending won/loss record is incomplete.

Paul Williams — Center

Season	Team	League	GP	G	A	PTS	PIM	GP	G	A	PTS	PIM
95-96	Anchorage	WCHL	48	27	23	50	10	—	—	—	—	—
96-97	Anchorage	WCHL	62	41	35	76	8	9	3	1	4	12
	WCHL	Totals	110	68	58	126	18	9	3	1	4	12

Born; 11/16/70, Anchorage, Alaska. 6-0, 205.

Rick Willis — Left Wing

Season	Team	League	GP	G	A	PTS	PIM	GP	G	A	PTS	PIM
95-96	Binghamton	AHL	39	3	2	5	62	2	0	0	0	0
95-96	Charlotte	ECHL	11	3	1	4	49	—	—	—	—	—
96-97	Binghamton	AHL	74	5	9	14	78	4	1	1	2	21
	AHL	Totals	113	8	11	19	140	6	1	1	2	21

Born; 1/12/72, Lynn, Massachusetts. 6-0, 190. Drafted by New York Rangers (5th choice, 76th overall) in 1990 Entry Draft.

Clarke Wilm — Center

Season	Team	League	GP	G	A	PTS	PIM	GP	G	A	PTS	PIM
96-97	Saint John	AHL	62	9	19	28	107	5	2	0	2	15

Born; 10/24/76, Central Butte, Saskatchewan. 6-0, 202. Drafted by Calgary Flames (5th choice, 150th overall) in 1995 Entry Draft.

Landon Wilson — Right Wing

Season	Team	League	GP	G	A	PTS	PIM	GP	G	A	PTS	PIM
94-95	Cornwall	AHL	8	4	4	8	25	13	3	4	7	68
95-96	Colorado	NHL	7	1	0	1	6	—	—	—	—	—
95-96	Cornwall	AHL	53	21	13	34	154	8	1	3	4	22
96-97	Colorado	NHL	9	1	2	3	23	—	—	—	—	—
96-97	Boston	NHL	40	7	10	17	49	—	—	—	—	—
96-97	Providence	AHL	2	2	1	3	2	10	3	4	7	16
	NHL	Totals	56	9	12	21	78	—	—	—	—	—
	AHL	Totals	63	27	18	45	181	31	7	11	18	106

Drafted by Toronto Maple Leafs (2nd choice, 19th overall) in 1993 Entry Draft. Traded to Quebec Nordiques by Toronto with Wendel Clark, Sylvain Lefebvre and Toronto's first round choice (Jeff Kealty) in 1994 Entry Draft for Garth Butcher, Todd Warriner, Mats Sundin and Philadelphia's first round choice-later traded to Washington (Capitals selected Nolan Baumgartner) in 1994 Entry Draft (6/28/94). Traded to Boston Bruins with Anders Myrvold by Colorado for Boston's first round choice in the 1998 Entry Draft., (11/22/96).

Ross Wilson — Right Wing

Season	Team	League	GP	G	A	PTS	PIM	GP	G	A	PTS	PIM
89-90	New Haven	AHL	61	19	14	33	39	—	—	—	—	—
90-91	New Haven	AHL	68	29	17	46	28	—	—	—	—	—
91-92	Phoenix	IHL	28	9	9	18	81	—	—	—	—	—
91-92	Kalamazoo	IHL	31	18	6	24	38	11	9	1	10	6
92-93	Kalamazoo	IHL	58	15	14	29	49	—	—	—	—	—
93-94	Moncton	AHL	75	29	38	67	49	21	10	9	19	18
94-95	Minnesota	IHL	2	0	1	1	0	—	—	—	—	—
94-95	Worcester	AHL	70	17	24	41	82	—	—	—	—	—
95-96	Saginaw	CoHL	42	38	30	68	68	—	—	—	—	—
95-96	Portland	AHL	14	5	2	7	14	—	—	—	—	—
95-96	Fort Wayne	IHL	21	3	8	11	10	5	1	1	2	0
96-97	Detroit	IHL	2	0	0	0	0	—	—	—	—	—
96-97	Fort Wayne	IHL	5	0	1	1	4	—	—	—	—	—
96-97	Flint	CoHL	68	53	56	109	47	14	9	11	20	10

	AHL	Totals	288	99	95	194	212	21	10	9	19	18
	IHL	Totals	140	45	38	83	178	16	10	2	12	6
	CoHL	Totals	110	91	86	177	115	14	9	11	20	10

Born; 6/26/69, The Pas, Manitoba. 6-3, 210. Drafted by Los Angeles Kings (3rd choice, 43rd overall) in 1987 Entry Draft.

Steve Wilson — Defenseman

Season	Team	League	GP	G	A	PTS	PIM	GP	G	A	PTS	PIM
92-93	Dayton	ECHL	63	11	18	29	49	3	0	0	0	7
93-94	Dayton	ECHL	60	13	26	39	134	3	1	0	1	2
93-94	Kalamazoo	IHL	3	0	0	0	2	—	—	—	—	—
93-94	Peoria	IHL	1	0	0	0	0	—	—	—	—	—
93-94	Salt Lake City	IHL	2	0	0	0	0	—	—	—	—	—
94-95	Dayton	ECHL	16	12	9	21	30	—	—	—	—	—
94-95	Phoenix	IHL	54	3	6	9	61	9	0	6	6	0
95-96	Phoenix	IHL	22	1	0	1	18	—	—	—	—	—
95-96	Peoria	IHL	54	5	15	20	44	12	0	2	2	8
96-97	Manitoba	IHL	81	4	10	14	75	—	—	—	—	—
	IHL	Totals	217	13	31	44	200	21	0	8	8	8
	ECHL	Totals	139	36	53	89	213	6	1	0	1	9

Born; 9/3/68, Kingston, Ontario. 6-2, 205.

Tom Wilson — Defenseman

Season	Team	League	GP	G	A	PTS	PIM	GP	G	A	PTS	PIM
94-95	Lakeland	SUN	44	2	8	10	156	—	—	—	—	—
95-96	Mobile	ECHL	2	0	0	0	11	—	—	—	—	—
95-96	Lakeland	SHL	51	2	10	12	160	5	0	3	3	15
96-97	Columbus	CeHL	55	7	8	15	218	2	0	0	0	2
	SHL	Totals	95	4	18	22	316	5	0	3	3	15

Born; 1/14/73, Toronto, Ontario. 6-1, 205.

Brad Wingfield — Left Wing

Season	Team	League	GP	G	A	PTS	PIM	GP	G	A	PTS	PIM
96-97	Central Texas	WPHL	35	4	4	8	176	2	0	0	0	0

Born; 6/24/75, Vancouver, British Columbia. 6-0, 212.

Jeff Winter — Defenseman

Season	Team	League	GP	G	A	PTS	PIM	GP	G	A	PTS	PIM
96-97	Madison	CoHL	73	7	19	26	73	5	2	2	4	2

Born; 2/26/72, New Milford, Connecticut. 6-4, 210. Member of 1996-97 CoHL All-Rookie Team.

Brian Wiseman — Center

Season	Team	League	GP	G	A	PTS	PIM	GP	G	A	PTS	PIM
94-95	Chicago	IHL	75	17	55	72	52	3	1	1	2	4
95-96	Chicago	IHL	73	33	55	88	117	—	—	—	—	—
96-97	Toronto	NHL	3	0	0	0	0	—	—	—	—	—
96-97	St. John's	AHL	71	33	62	95	83	7	5	4	9	8
	IHL	Totals	148	50	110	160	169	3	1	1	2	4

Born; 7/13/71, Chatham, Ontario. 5-7, 185. Drafted by New York Rangers (11th choice, 257th overall) in 1991 Entry Draft.

Brendan Witt — Defenseman

Season	Team	League	GP	G	A	PTS	PIM	GP	G	A	PTS	PIM
95-96	Washington	NHL	48	2	3	5	85	—	—	—	—	—

Season	Team	League	GP	G	A	PTS	PIM	GP	G	A	PTS	PIM
96-97	Washington	NHL	44	3	2	5	88	—	—	—	—	—
96-97	Portland	AHL	30	2	4	6	56	5	1	0	1	30
	NHL	Totals	92	5	5	10	173	—	—	—	—	—

Born; 2/20/75, Humboldt, Saskatchewan. 6-1, 205. Drafted by Washington Capitals (1st choice, 11th overall) in 1993 Entry Draft.

Derek Wood — Forward

			Regular Season					Playoffs				
Season	Team	League	GP	G	A	PTS	PIM	GP	G	A	PTS	PIM
96-97	Columbus	ECHL	66	27	30	57	181	8	1	2	3	35

Last amateur club; Medicine Hat (WHL).

Doug Wood — Defenseman

			Regular Season					Playoffs				
Season	Team	League	GP	G	A	PTS	PIM	GP	G	A	PTS	PIM
96-97	Syracuse	AHL	19	1	3	4	16	1	0	0	0	0
96-97	South Carolina	ECHL	43	1	14	15	65	—	—	—	—	—
96-97	Raleigh	ECHL	6	0	1	1	14	—	—	—	—	—
	ECHL	Totals	49	1	15	16	79	—	—	—	—	—

Born; 1/7/74, Waltham, Massachusetts. 6-2, 215. Last amateur club; Boston University (Hockey East).

Peter Wood — Goaltender

			Regular Season						Playoffs					
Season	Team	League	GP	W	L	T	MIN	SO	GAVG	GP	W	L	MIN	SO	GAVG
96-97	Saginaw	CoHL	1	0	1	0	15	0	12.22	—	—	—	—	—	—
96-97	Nashville	CeHL	12	1	7	0	530	0	6.45	—	—	—	—	—	—

Born; 9/4/70, Owen Sound, Ontario. 5-10, 160.

Bob Woods — Defenseman/Right Wing

			Regular Season					Playoffs				
Season	Team	League	GP	G	A	PTS	PIM	GP	G	A	PTS	PIM
88-89	Utica	AHL	11	0	1	1	2	4	0	0	0	2
89-90	Utica	AHL	58	2	12	14	30	5	0	0	0	6
90-91	Utica	AHL	33	4	6	10	21	—	—	—	—	—
90-91	Johnstown	ECHL	23	12	25	37	32	—	—	—	—	—
91-92	Johnstown	ECHL	63	18	43	61	44	6	4	1	5	14
92-93	Johnstown	ECHL	61	11	36	47	72	5	1	1	2	8
93-94	Hershey	AHL	28	2	9	11	21	11	2	4	6	8
93-94	Johnstown	ECHL	43	18	37	55	57	3	1	3	4	4
94-95	Utica	CoHL	1	0	0	0	0	—	—	—	—	—
95-96	Portland	AHL	5	0	1	1	2	2	0	0	0	9
95-96	Hampton Roads	ECHL	66	3	26	29	106	3	1	2	3	17
96-97	Hershey	AHL	6	1	0	1	2	16	0	1	1	4
96-97	Mobile	ECHL	69	19	50	69	68	3	1	0	1	2
	AHL	Totals	141	9	29	38	78	38	2	5	7	29
	ECHL	Totals	325	81	217	298	379	20	8	7	15	45

Born; 1/24/68, LeRoy, Saskatchewan. 6-1, 192. Drafted by New Jersey Devils (11th choice, 201st overall) in 1988 Entry Draft. 1996-97 ECHL Second Team All-Star. Member of 1996-97 ECHL Champion Hershey Bears.

Martin Woods — Defenseman

			Regular Season					Playoffs				
Season	Team	League	GP	G	A	PTS	PIM	GP	G	A	PTS	PIM
95-96	Hampton Roads	ECHL	7	0	1	1	14	—	—	—	—	—
95-96	Jacksonville	ECHL	33	6	12	18	80	—	—	—	—	—
95-96	Johnstown	ECHL	22	4	8	12	95	—	—	—	—	—
96-97	Philadelphia	AHL	1	0	0	0	0	—	—	—	—	—
96-97	Johnstown	ECHL	67	16	34	50	233	—	—	—	—	—
	ECHL	Totals	129	26	55	81	422	—	—	—	—	—

Born; 5/14/75, Hull, Quebec. 6-1, 200. Drafted by Winnipeg Jets (8th choice, 171st overall) in 1993 Entry Draft.

Mark Wotton — Defenseman

Season	Team	League	Regular Season GP	G	A	PTS	PIM	Playoffs GP	G	A	PTS	PIM
94-95	Vancouver	NHL	1	0	0	0	0	5	0	0	0	4
94-95	Syracuse	AHL	75	12	29	41	50	—	—	—	—	—
95-96	Syracuse	AHL	80	10	35	45	96	15	1	12	13	20
96-97	Vancouver	NHL	36	3	6	9	19	—	—	—	—	—
96-97	Syracuse	AHL	27	2	8	10	25	2	0	0	0	4
	NHL	Totals	37	3	6	9	19	5	0	0	0	4
	AHL	Totals	182	24	72	96	171	17	1	12	13	24

Born; 11/16/73, Foxwarren, Manitoba. 5-11, 187. Drafted by Vancouver Canucks (11th choice, 237th overall) in 1992 Entry Draft.

Bob Wren — Left Wing

Season	Team	League	Regular Season GP	G	A	PTS	PIM	Playoffs GP	G	A	PTS	PIM
94-95	Springfield	AHL	61	16	15	31	118	—	—	—	—	—
94-95	Richmond	ECHL	2	0	1	1	0	—	—	—	—	—
95-96	Detroit	IHL	1	0	0	0	0	—	—	—	—	—
95-96	Knoxville	ECHL	50	21	35	56	257	8	4	11	15	32
96-97	Baltimore	AHL	73	23	36	59	97	3	1	1	2	0
	AHL	Totals	134	39	51	90	215	3	1	1	2	0
	ECHL	Totals	52	21	36	57	257	8	4	11	15	32

Born; 9/16/74, Preston, Ontario. 5-10, 185. Drafted by Los Angeles Kings (3rd choice, 94th overall) in 1993 Entry Draft. Signed as a free agent by Hartford Whalers (9/6/94).

Jamie Wright — Left Wing

Season	Team	League	Regular Season GP	G	A	PTS	PIM	Playoffs GP	G	A	PTS	PIM
96-97	Michigan	IHL	60	6	8	14	34	1	0	0	0	0

Born; 5/13/76, Kitchener, Ontario. 6-0, 172. Drafted by Dallas Stars (3rd choice, 98th overall) in 1994 Entry Draft.

Jason Wright — Defenseman

Season	Team	League	Regular Season GP	G	A	PTS	PIM	Playoffs GP	G	A	PTS	PIM
95-96	Richmond	ECHL	3	0	1	1	2	—	—	—	—	—
96-97	Richmond	ECHL	67	6	14	20	84	4	0	1	1	2
	ECHL	Totals	70	6	15	21	86	4	0	1	1	2

Born; 7/6/72, Thunder Bay, Ontario. 6-0, 195.

Shayne Wright — Defenseman

Season	Team	League	Regular Season GP	G	A	PTS	PIM	Playoffs GP	G	A	PTS	PIM
95-96	Rochester	AHL	48	0	7	7	99	5	0	1	1	8
96-97	Rochester	AHL	80	7	30	37	124	10	2	3	5	6
	AHL	Totals	128	7	37	44	223	15	2	4	6	14

Born; 6/30/75, Welland, Ontario. 6-0, 189. Drafted by Buffalo Sabres (12th choice, 277th overall) in 1994 Entry Draft. Member of 1995-96 AHL champion Rochester Americans.

Tyler Wright — Center

			Regular Season					Playoffs				
Season	Team	League	GP	G	A	PTS	PIM	GP	G	A	PTS	PIM
92-93	Edmonton	NHL	7	1	1	2	19	—	—	—	—	—
93-94	Edmonton	NHL	5	0	0	0	4	—	—	—	—	—
93-94	Cape Breton	AHL	65	14	27	41	160	5	2	0	2	11
94-95	Edmonton	NHL	6	1	0	1	14	—	—	—	—	—
94-95	Cape Breton	AHL	70	16	15	31	184	—	—	—	—	—
95-96	Edmonton	NHL	23	1	0	1	33	—	—	—	—	—
95-96	Cape Breton	AHL	31	6	12	18	158	—	—	—	—	—
96-97	Pittsburgh	NHL	45	2	2	4	70	—	—	—	—	—
96-97	Cleveland	IHL	10	4	3	7	34	14	4	2	6	44
	NHL	Totals	41	3	1	4	70	—	—	—	—	—
	AHL	Totals	166	36	54	90	502	5	2	0	2	11

Born; 4/6/73, Canora, Saskatchewan. 5-11, 185. Drafted by Edmonton Oilers (1st choice, 12th overall) in 1991 Entry Draft. Traded to Pittsburgh Penguins by Edmonton for Pittsburgh's seventh round choice (Brandon Lafrance) in 1996 Entry Draft, (6/22/96).

Bakersfield's Lee Schill appeared in 55 games for the Fog last season.

Photo by Heidi Bauer

Terry Yake — Center

Season	Team	League	GP	G	A	PTS	PIM	GP	G	A	PTS	PIM
88-89	Hartford	NHL	2	0	0	0	0	—	—	—	—	—
88-89	Binghamton	AHL	75	39	56	95	57	—	—	—	—	—
89-90	Hartford	NHL	2	0	1	1	0	—	—	—	—	—
89-90	Binghamton	AHL	77	13	42	55	37	—	—	—	—	—
90-91	Hartford	NHL	19	1	4	5	10	6	1	1	2	16
90-91	Springfield	AHL	60	35	42	77	56	15	9	9	18	10
91-92	Hartford	NHL	15	1	1	2	4	—	—	—	—	—
91-92	Springfield	AHL	53	21	34	55	63	8	3	4	7	2
92-93	Hartford	NHL	66	22	31	53	46	—	—	—	—	—
92-93	Springfield	AHL	16	8	14	22	27	—	—	—	—	—
93-94	Anaheim	NHL	82	21	31	52	44	—	—	—	—	—
94-95	Toronto	NHL	19	3	2	5	2	—	—	—	—	—
94-95	Denver	IHL	2	0	3	3	2	17	4	11	15	16
95-96	Milwaukee	IHL	70	32	56	88	70	5	3	6	9	4
96-97	Rochester	AHL	78	34	*67	101	77	10	8	8	16	2
	NHL	Totals	205	48	70	118	106	6	1	1	2	16
	AHL	Totals	359	150	255	405	317	33	20	21	41	14
	IHL	Totals	72	32	59	91	72	22	7	17	24	20

Born; 10/22/68, New Westminster, British Columbia. 5-11, 185. Drafted by Hartford Whalers (3rd choice, 81st overall) in 1987 Entry Draft. Claimed by Anaheim from Hartford in Expansion Draft (6/24/93). Traded to Toronto Maple Leafs by Anaheim for David Sacco (9/28/94). Member of 1990-91 AHL champion Springfield Indians. Member of 1994-95 IHL champion Denver Grizzlies.

Shawn Yakimishyn — Center

Season	Team	League	GP	G	A	PTS	PIM	GP	G	A	PTS	PIM
93-94	Columbus	ECHL	7	1	4	5	25	6	0	1	1	18
94-95	Columbus	ECHL	6	0	1	1	24	—	—	—	—	—
94-95	Tallahassee	ECHL	1	0	0	0	0	—	—	—	—	—
94-95	Saginaw	CoHL	33	3	8	11	16	11	5	3	8	55
95-96	Saginaw	CoHL	69	13	23	36	184	3	1	0	1	2
96-97	Utica	CoHL	72	21	26	47	144	3	0	1	1	6
	CoHL	Totals	174	37	57	94	344	17	6	4	10	63
	ECHL	Totals	14	1	5	6	49	6	0	1	1	18

Born; 2/15/72, Roblin, Manitoba. 5-9, 180.

Ravil Yakubov — Center

Season	Team	League	GP	G	A	PTS	PIM	GP	G	A	PTS	PIM
96-97	Saint John	AHL	24	3	5	8	18	—	—	—	—	—
96-97	Fort Wayne	IHL	6	0	2	2	2	—	—	—	—	—
96-97	Utah	IHL	13	3	8	11	8	7	3	0	3	0
	IHL	Totals	19	3	10	13	10	7	3	0	3	0

Born; 7/26/70, Moscow, Russia. 6-1, 190. Drafted by Calgary Flames (6th choice, 126th overall) in 1992 Entry Draft.

Igor Yankovitch — Defenseman

Season	Team	League	GP	G	A	PTS	PIM	GP	G	A	PTS	PIM
95-96	Flint	CoHL	6	0	0	0	6	—	—	—	—	—
95-96	Saginaw	CoHL	51	2	11	13	101	—	—	—	—	—
95-96	Utica	CoHL	6	0	1	1	12	—	—	—	—	—
96-97	Muskegon	CoHL	52	5	15	20	65	—	—	—	—	—
96-97	Port Huron	CoHL	22	0	7	7	20	5	1	2	3	6
	CoHL	Totals	137	7	34	41	204	5	1	2	3	6

Born; 2/26/75, Kiev, Russia. 6-4, 205.

Mark Yannetti — Defenseman

			Regular Season					Playoffs				
Season	Team	League	GP	G	A	PTS	PIM	GP	G	A	PTS	PIM
94-95	San Antonio	CeHL	48	2	11	13	47	13	0	2	2	14
95-96	San Antonio	CeHL	64	2	16	18	68	13	1	1	2	11
96-97	San Antonio	CeHL	66	8	16	24	51	—	—	—	—	—
	CeHL	Totals	178	12	43	55	166	26	1	3	4	25

Born; 6/7/71, Bayford, Massachusetts. 5-11, 195.

Brendan Yarema — Center

			Regular Season					Playoffs				
Season	Team	League	GP	G	A	PTS	PIM	GP	G	A	PTS	PIM
96-97	St. John's	AHL	9	1	4	5	8	—	—	—	—	—
96-97	South Carolina	ECHL	12	3	6	9	28	9	1	0	1	38

Born; 7/16/76, Sault Ste. Marie, Ontario. 6-0, 195. Member of 1996-97 ECHL Champion South Carolina Stingrays.

Alexei Yegerov — Center

			Regular Season					Playoffs				
Season	Team	League	GP	G	A	PTS	PIM	GP	G	A	PTS	PIM
94-95	Fort Worth	CeHL	18	4	10	14	15	—	—	—	—	—
95-96	San Jose	NHL	9	3	2	5	2	—	—	—	—	—
95-96	Kansas City	IHL	65	31	25	56	84	5	2	0	2	8
96-97	San Jose	NHL	2	0	1	1	0	—	—	—	—	—
96-97	Kentucky	AHL	75	26	32	58	59	4	0	1	1	2
	NHL	Totals	11	3	3	6	2	—	—	—	—	—

Born; 5/21/75, St. Petersburg, Russia. 5-11, 185. Drafted by San Jose Sharks (3rd choice, 66th overall) in 1994 Entry Draft.

Mike Yeo — Left Wing

			Regular Season					Playoffs				
Season	Team	League	GP	G	A	PTS	PIM	GP	G	A	PTS	PIM
94-95	Houston	IHL	63	5	12	17	100	—	—	—	—	—
95-96	Houston	IHL	69	14	16	30	113	—	—	—	—	—
96-97	Houston	IHL	56	10	11	21	105	13	2	3	5	2
	IHL	Totals	188	29	39	68	318	13	2	3	5	2

Born; 7/31/73, Thunder Bay, Ontario. 6-1, 190.

Sergei Yerkovich — Defenseman

			Regular Season					Playoffs				
Season	Team	League	GP	G	A	PTS	PIM	GP	G	A	PTS	PIM
96-97	Las Vegas	IHL	76	6	19	25	167	—	—	—	—	—

Born; 3/9/74, Minsk, Russia. 6-3, 210. Drafted by Edmonton Oilers (3rd choice, 68th overall) in 1997 Entry Draft.

Juha Ylonen — Center

			Regular Season					Playoffs				
Season	Team	League	GP	G	A	PTS	PIM	GP	G	A	PTS	PIM
96-97	Phoenix	NHL	2	0	0	0	0	—	—	—	—	—
96-97	Springfield	AHL	70	20	41	61	6	17	5	*16	21	4

Born; 2/13/72, Helsinki, Finland. 6-0, 180. Drafted by Winnipeg Jets (5th choice, 91st overall) in 1991 Entry Draft.

Fujusawa Yoshifumi — Left Wing

			Regular Season					Playoffs				
Season	Team	League	GP	G	A	PTS	PIM	GP	G	A	PTS	PIM
96-97	Alaska	WCHL	34	9	10	19	0	—	—	—	—	—

Adam Young — Defenseman

Season	Team	League	GP	G	A	PTS	PIM	GP	G	A	PTS	PIM
			Regular Season					Playoffs				
96-97	Louisville	ECHL	55	3	3	6	269	—	—	—	—	—

Born; 1/15/75, Toronto, Ontario. 6-4, 222. Drafted by New Jersey Devils (8th choice, 148th overall) in 1995 Entry Draft.

Kevin Young — Center

Season	Team	League	GP	G	A	PTS	PIM	GP	G	A	PTS	PIM
			Regular Season					Playoffs				
96-97	Dayton	CoHL	51	13	14	27	26	—	—	—	—	—
96-97	Waco	WPHL	17	5	1	6	2	—	—	—	—	—

Born; 4/24/76, Alexandria, Indiana. 6-0, 185.

Wendell Young — Goaltender

Season	Team	League	GP	W	L	T	MIN	SO	GAVG	GP	W	L	MIN	SO	GAVG
			Regular Season							Playoffs					
83-84	Fredericton	AHL	11	7	3	0	569	1	4.11	—	—	—	—	—	—
83-84	Milwaukee	IHL	6	4	1	1	339	0	3.01	—	—	—	—	—	—
83-84	Salt Lake City	CHL	20	11	6	0	1094	0	4.39	4	0	2	122	0	5.42
84-85	Fresno	AHL	22	7	11	3	1242	0	4.01	—	—	—	—	—	—
85-86	Vancouver	NHL	22	4	9	3	1023	0	3.58	1	0	1	60	0	5.00
85-86	Fredericton	AHL	24	12	8	4	1457	0	3.21	—	—	—	—	—	—
86-87	Vancouver	NHL	8	1	6	1	420	0	5.00	—	—	—	—	—	—
86-87	Fredericton	AHL	30	11	16	0	1676	0	4.22	—	—	—	—	—	—
87-88	Philadelphia	NHL	6	3	2	0	320	0	3.75	—	—	—	—	—	—
87-88	Hershey	AHL	51	*33	15	1	2922	1	2.77	12	*12	0	*767	*1	*2.19
88-89	Pittsburgh	NHL	22	12	9	0	1150	0	4.80	1	0	0	39	0	1.54
88-89	Muskegon	IHL	2	1	0	1	125	0	3.36	—	—	—	—	—	—
89-90	Pittsburgh	NHL	43	16	20	3	2318	1	4.17	—	—	—	—	—	—
90-91	Pittsburgh	NHL	18	4	6	2	773	0	4.04	—	—	—	—	—	—
91-92	Pittsburgh	NHL	18	7	6	0	838	0	3.79	—	—	—	—	—	—
92-93	Tampa Bay	NHL	31	7	19	2	1591	0	3.66	—	—	—	—	—	—
92-93	Atlanta	IHL	3	3	0	0	183	0	2.62	—	—	—	—	—	—
93-94	Tampa Bay	NHL	9	2	3	1	480	1	2.50	—	—	—	—	—	—
93-94	Atlanta	IHL	2	2	0	0	120	0	3.00	—	—	—	—	—	—
94-95	Pittsburgh	NHL	10	3	6	0	497	0	3.26	—	—	—	—	—	—
94-95	Chicago	IHL	37	14	11	7	1882	0	3.57	—	—	—	—	—	—
95-96	Chicago	IHL	61	30	20	6	3285	1	3.63	9	4	5	540	0	3.33
96-97	Chicago	IHL	52	25	21	4	2931	1	3.48	4	1	3	257	0	3.04
NHL	Totals		187	59	86	12	9410	2	3.94	2	0	1	99	0	3.64
AHL	Totals		138	70	50	8	7866	1	3.16	12	12	0	767	1	2.19
IHL	Totals		163	79	53	19	8865	2	3.51	13	5	8	797	0	3.24

Born; 8/1/63, Haifax, Nova Scotia. 5-9, 181. Drafted by Vancouver Canucks (3rd choice, 73rd overall) in 1981 Entry Draft. Traded to Philadelphia Flyers by Vancouver with Vancouver's third round choice (Kimbi Daniels) in 1990 Entry Draft for Darren Jensen and Darryl Stanley (8/28/87). Traded to Pittsburgh Penguins by Philadelphia with Philadelphia's seventh round choice (Mika Valila) in 1990 Entry Draft for Pittsburgh's third round choice (Chris Therien) in 1990 Entry Draft (9/1/88). Claimed by Tampa Bay Lightning from Pittsburgh in Expansion Draft (6/18/92). Traded to Pittsburgh by Tampa Bay for future considerations (2/16/95). 1987-88 AHL First Team All-Star. 1987-88 AHL Top Goaltender. 1987-88 AHL Playoff MVP. Member of 1987-88 AHL champion Hershey Bears.

Ildar Yubin — Defenseman

Season	Team	League	GP	G	A	PTS	PIM	GP	G	A	PTS	PIM
			Regular Season					Playoffs				
96-97	Dayton	ECHL	38	4	10	14	98	3	0	0	0	4

Born; 6/8/74, Yaroslav, Russia. 5-9, 180.

Steve Yule — Defenseman

			Regular Season					Playoffs				
Season	Team	League	GP	G	A	PTS	PIM	GP	G	A	PTS	PIM
92-93	Springfield	AHL	38	0	4	4	52	—	—	—	—	—
93-94	Springfield	AHL	61	4	13	17	133	5	0	4	4	8
94-95	Springfield	AHL	61	1	10	11	143	—	—	—	—	—
95-96	N/A											
96-97	Grand Rapids	IHL	3	0	1	1	9	—	—	—	—	—
96-97	Mississippi	ECHL	62	3	13	16	209	3	1	0	1	2
	AHL	Totals	160	5	27	32	328	5	0	4	4	8

Born; 5/27/72, Gleichen, Alberta. 6-1, 210. Drafted by Hartford Whalers (8th choice, 163rd overall) in 1991 Entry Draft.

Shoe! Bruce Shoebottom has been a fan favorite everywhere that he has played.

Photo by Heidi Bauer

Libor Zabransky — Defenseman

Season	Team	League	GP	G	A	PTS	PIM	GP	G	A	PTS	PIM
96-97	St. Louis	NHL	34	1	5	6	44	—	—	—	—	—
96-97	Worcester	AHL	23	3	6	9	24	5	2	4	5	76

Born; 11/25/73, Brno, Czechoslovakia. 6-3, 196. Drafted by St. Louis Blues (7th choice, 209th overall) in 1995 Entry Draft.

Dean Zayonce — Defenseman

Season	Team	League	GP	G	A	PTS	PIM	GP	G	A	PTS	PIM
91-92	Greensboro	ECHL	26	2	7	9	151	—	—	—	—	—
91-92	Halifax	AHL	24	0	3	3	26	—	—	—	—	—
92-93	Greensboro	ECHL	26	1	9	10	73	1	0	0	0	0
92-93	Halifax	AHL	22	0	1	1	6	—	—	—	—	—
93-94	Greensboro	ECHL	56	11	16	27	260	8	0	0	0	14
94-95	Greensboro	ECHL	60	2	14	16	245	17	0	2	2	54
95-96	Atlanta	IHL	24	0	5	5	58	—	—	—	—	—
95-96	San Antonio	CeHL	49	7	14	21	140	—	—	—	—	—
96-97	Carolina	AHL	32	0	0	0	49	—	—	—	—	—
96-97	Tallahassee	ECHL	6	2	5	7	2	—	—	—	—	—
	AHL	Totals	78	0	4	4	81	—	—	—	—	—
	ECHL	Totals	174	18	51	69	731	26	0	2	2	68

Born; 10/28/70, Kelowna, British Columbia. 6-0, 192.

Richard Zednik — Left Wing

Season	Team	League	GP	G	A	PTS	PIM	GP	G	A	PTS	PIM
95-96	Washington	NHL	1	0	0	0	0	—	—	—	—	—
95-96	Portland	AHL	1	0	0	0	0	21	4	5	9	26
96-97	Washington	NHL	11	2	1	3	4	—	—	—	—	—
96-97	Portland	AHL	56	15	20	35	70	5	1	0	1	6
	NHL	Totals	12	2	1	3	4	—	—	—	—	—
	AHL	Totals	57	15	20	35	70	26	5	5	10	32

Born; 1/6/76, Bystrica, Czechoslovakia. 5-11, 172. Drafted by Washington Capitals (10th choice, 249th overall) in 1994 Entry Draft.

Jason Zent — Left Wing

Season	Team	League	GP	G	A	PTS	PIM	GP	G	A	PTS	PIM
94-95	Prince Edward Island	AHL	55	15	11	26	46	9	6	1	7	6
95-96	Prince Edward Island	AHL	68	14	5	19	61	5	2	1	3	4
96-97	Ottawa	NHL	22	3	3	6	9	—	—	—	—	—
96-97	Worcester	NHL	45	14	10	24	45	5	3	4	7	4
	AHL	Totals	168	43	26	69	152	19	11	6	17	14

Born; 4/15/71, Buffalo, New York. 5-11, 180. Drafted by New York Islanders (3rd choice, 44th overall) in 1989 Entry Draft. Traded to Ottawa Senators by Islanders for fifth round choice in 1996 (Andrew Berenzweig) (10/15/94).

Rob Zettler — Defenseman

Season	Team	League	GP	G	A	PTS	PIM	GP	G	A	PTS	PIM
87-88	Kalamazoo	IHL	2	0	1	1	0	7	0	2	2	2
88-89	Minnesota	NHL	2	0	0	0	0	—	—	—	—	—
88-89	Kalamazoo	IHL	80	5	21	26	79	6	0	1	1	26
89-90	Minnesota	NHL	31	0	8	8	45	—	—	—	—	—
89-90	Kalamazoo	IHL	41	6	10	16	64	7	0	0	0	6
90-91	Minnesota	NHL	47	1	4	5	119	—	—	—	—	—
90-91	Kalamazoo	IHL	1	0	0	0	2	—	—	—	—	—
91-92	San Jose	NHL	74	1	8	9	99	—	—	—	—	—

Season	Team	League	GP	G	A	PTS	PIM	GP	G	A	PTS	PIM
92-93	San Jose	NHL	80	0	7	7	150	—	—	—	—	—
93-94	San Jose	NHL	42	0	3	3	65	—	—	—	—	—
93-94	Philadelphia	NHL	33	0	4	4	69	—	—	—	—	—
94-95	Philadelphia	NHL	32	0	1	1	34	1	0	0	0	2
95-96	Toronto	NHL	29	0	1	1	48	2	0	0	0	0
96-97	Utah	IHL	30	0	10	10	60	—	—	—	—	—
	NHL	Totals	370	2	36	38	629	3	0	0	0	2
	IHL	Totals	154	11	42	53	205	20	0	3	3	34

Born; 3/8/68, Sept Iles, Quebec. 6-3, 200. Drafted by Minnesota North Stars (5th choice, 55th overall) in 1986 Entry Draft. Claimed by San Jose Sharks from Minnesota in Dispersal Draft (5/30/91). Traded to Philadelphia Flyers by San Jose for Viacheslav Butsayev, (2/1/94). Traded to Toronto Maple Leafs by Philadelphia for Toronto's fifth round choice (Per-Ragna Bergqvist) in 1996 Entry Draft, (7/8/95).

Alexander Zhurik — Defenseman

Season	Team	League	GP	G	A	PTS	PIM	GP	G	A	PTS	PIM
95-96	Cape Breton	AHL	80	5	36	41	85	—	—	—	—	—
96-97	Hamilton	AHL	72	5	16	21	49	22	2	11	13	14
	AHL	Totals	152	10	52	62	134	22	2	11	13	14

Born; 5/29/75, Minsk, Russia. 6-3, 195. Drafted by Edmonton Oilers (7th choice, 163rd overall) in 1993 Entry Draft.

Rick Zombo — Defenseman

Season	Team	League	GP	G	A	PTS	PIM	GP	G	A	PTS	PIM
84-85	Detroit	NHL	1	0	0	0	0	—	—	—	—	—
84-85	Adirondack	AHL	56	3	32	35	70	—	—	—	—	—
85-86	Detroit	NHL	14	0	1	1	16	—	—	—	—	—
85-86	Adirondack	AHL	69	7	34	41	94	17	0	4	4	40
86-87	Detroit	NHL	44	1	4	5	59	7	0	1	1	9
86-87	Adirondack	AHL	25	0	6	6	22	—	—	—	—	—
87-88	Detroit	NHL	62	3	14	17	96	16	0	6	6	55
88-89	Detroit	NHL	75	1	20	21	106	6	0	1	1	16
89-90	Detroit	NHL	77	5	20	25	95	—	—	—	—	—
90-91	Detroit	NHL	77	4	19	23	55	7	1	0	1	10
91-92	Detroit	NHL	3	0	0	0	15	—	—	—	—	—
91-92	St. Louis	NHL	64	3	15	18	46	6	0	2	2	12
92-93	St. Louis	NHL	71	0	15	15	78	11	0	1	1	12
93-94	St. Louis	NHL	74	2	8	10	85	4	0	0	0	11
94-95	St. Louis	NHL	23	1	4	5	24	3	0	0	0	2
95-96	Boston	NHL	67	4	10	14	53	—	—	—	—	—
96-97	Phoenix	IHL	23	0	6	6	22	—	—	—	—	—
	NHL	Totals	652	24	130	154	728	60	1	11	12	127
	AHL	Totals	150	10	72	82	186	17	0	4	4	40

Born; 5/8/63, Des Plaines, Michigan. 6-1, 202. Drafted by Detroit Red Wings (6th chioce, 149th overall) in 1981 Entry Draft. Traded to St. Louis Blues for Vincent Riendeau (10/18/91). Traded to Boston Bruins by St. Louis for Fred Knipscheer, (10/2/95).

Jarrett Zukiwsky — Right Wing

Season	Team	League	GP	G	A	PTS	PIM	GP	G	A	PTS	PIM
96-97	Mobile	ECHL	5	2	1	3	14	2	1	0	1	2

Born; 12/7/72, Pincher Creek, Alberta. 5-11, 200. Last amateur club; Lethbridge (CWUHA).

Peter Zurba
Right Wing

			Regular Season					Playoffs				
Season	Team	League	GP	G	A	PTS	PIM	GP	G	A	PTS	PIM
95-96	Huntsville	SHL	27	2	18	20	168	10	1	1	2	23
96-97	Utah	IHL	4	0	0	0	37	—	—	—	—	—
96-97	Central Texas	WPHL	44	10	7	17	*291	11	3	3	6	52

Born; 11/15/74, Thompson, Manitoba. 5-11, 174. Member of 1995-96 SHL champion Huntsville Channel Cats.

Sergei Zvyagin
Goaltender

			Regular Season							Playoffs					
Season	Team	League	GP	W	L	T	MIN	SO	GAVG	GP	W	L	MIN	SO	GAVG
94-95	Detroit	CoHL	32	12	15	2	1705	0	4.36	8	4	3	407	0	3.24
95-96	Detroit	CoHL	40	14	13	6	1873	1	3.62	—	—	—	—	—	—
95-96	Quad City	CoHL	9	6	3	0	538	0	2.90	3	0	3	179	0	6.69
96-97	Michigan	IHL	2	1	1	0	79	0	3.03	—	—	—	—	—	—
96-97	Quad City	CoHL	*60	*42	15	2	*3475	1	2.99	*15	*11	3	*912	0	3.22
	CoHL	Totals	141	74	46	10	7591	2	3.45	26	15	9	1498	0	3.64

Born; 2/17/71, Moscow, Russia. 5-8, 167. 1996-97 CoHL Outstanding Netminder. 1996-97 Playoff MVP. 1996-97 CoHL First Team All-Star. Member of 1996-97 CoHL Champion Quad City Mallards.

The following is a list of players whom either did not play 20 games this season or appear in the playoffs. Next to each player you will see the team(s) he played with, the league and his statistics. Goaltenders and skaters have been broken up in this section. Unless noted all statistics are regular season statistics.

Last Name	First Name	Team	League	Position	GP	G	A	PTS	PIM
Adams	Matt	Pensacola	ECHL	Forward	7	0	0	0	0
Allen	Scott	Johnstown	ECHL	Center	1	0	0	0	0
Anderson	Kent	Oklahoma City	CeHL	Defenseman	4	1	1	2	2
Ashley	Don	Nashville	CeHL	Defenseman	5	1	0	1	4
"	"	Macon	CeHL	Defenseman	1	0	0	0	0
Aubrey	Ron	Nashville	CeHL	Left Wing	7	3	2	5	110
"	"	San Antonio	CeHL	Left Wing	7	0	2	2	65
"	"	Reno	WCHL	Left Wing	3	0	0	0	18
"	"	Waco	WCHL	Left Wing	1	0	0	0	2
Badelt	Michael	Tulsa	CeHL	Defenseman	2	0	0	0	0
Baker	Jeremy	Columbus	CeHL	Right Wing	8	1	0	1	2
"	"	Waco	WPHL	Forward	6	2	1	3	5
Baliar	Brano	Saginaw	CoHL	Left Wing	1	0	0	0	0
Barica	Dusan	Alaska	WCHL	Forward	1	0	0	0	0
Barton	Pat	Dayton	CoHL	Right Wing	7	1	0	1	11
Bear	Rob	Wichita	CeHL	Defenseman	8	1	3	4	39
Beaudin	Jeff	Knoxville	ECHL	Left Wing	3	0	1	1	7
"	"	Central Texas	WPHL	Left Wing	11	1	1	2	28
Beaulieu	Corey	Manitoba	IHL	Defenseman	6	0	0	0	14
Beauregard	David	Kentcuky	AHL	Left Wing	5	0	3	3	0
Belov	Oleg	Long Beach	IHL	Center	7	0	1	1	8
Berrington	Paul	Huntsville	CeHL	Center	3	1	0	1	7
Bertuzzi	Todd	Utah	IHL	Center	13	5	5	10	16
Bibeau	Matt	San Diego	WCHL		2	0	0	0	0
Bogden	Shane	Wheeling	ECHL	Left Wing	3	0	0	0	18
Bognar	Derby	Alaska	WCHL	Defenseman	2	0	0	0	4
Bonneau	Rob	Portland	AHL	Forward	1	1	1	2	0
Bordelcau	Paulin	Fredericton	AHL	Center	3	1	3	4	2
Borggaard	Andy	Knoxville	ECHL	Left Wing	1	0	0	0	2
Borgo	Richard	Dayton	CoHL	Right Wing	4	0	3	3	38
Borisychev	Ilya	Reno	WCHL	Defenseman	15	1	4	5	16
Brackett	Griff	Nashville	CeHL	Left Wing	5	1	0	1	5
"	"	Waco	CeHL	Left Wing	5	1	1	2	0
Bradley	Matt	Kentucky	AHL	Right Wing	1	0	1	1	0
Brandon	Bob	Peoria	ECHL	Left Wing	3	0	0	0	7
Brezeault	Reggie	Port Huron	CoHL	Center	11	1	3	4	10
"	"	Macon	CeHL	Center	3	0	0	0	9
Brickley	Andy	Utah	IHL	Left Wing	1	1	0	1	0
Briese	Corey	Port Huron	CoHL	Left Wing	1	0	1	1	2
Broten	Neal	Phoenix	IHL	Center	11	3	3	6	4
Brown	Tom	Charlotte	ECHL	Defenseman	3	0	1	1	0
Brymer	John	Port Huron	CoHL		1	0	1	1	0
Burkett	Mike	Worcester	AHL	Left Wing	3	0	0	0	2
Byrne	Chris	Pensacola	ECHL	Defenseman	7	0	1	1	31
Cabana	Clint	Syracuse	AHL	Defenseman	2	0	0	0	0
Cahill	Chris	Alaska	WCHL	Center	11	2	6	8	12
Cahill	Darcy	San Antonio	CeHL	Center	3	0	1	1	4
"	"	Nashville	CeHL	Center	8	3	7	10	14
Cain	Aaron	Richmond	ECHL	Left Wing	5	0	0	0	23
Cairns	Eric	Binghamton	AHL	Defenseman	10	1	1	2	96
Caley	Troy	Utica	CoHL	Center	2	0	0	0	0
"	"	Muskegon	CoHL	Center	2	0	0	0	0
"	"	Saginaw	CoHL	Center	7	0	0	0	2

Last Name	First Name	Team	League	Position	GP	G	A	PTS	PIM
Cardinal	Curtis	El Paso	WPHL	Left Wing	7	0	0	0	5
Caron	Michael	Quebec	IHL	Defenseman	1	0	0	0	0
Cassidy	Bruce	Indianapolis	IHL	Defenseman	10	0	4	4	11
Cavanagh	Pat	Dayton	ECHL	Right Wing	1	0	0	0	5
Chartier	Scott	Jacksonville	ECHL	Defenseman	10	1	7	8	26
Charland	Carl	Quebec	IHL	Right Wing	5	1	0	1	0
Chynoweth	Dean	Providence	AHL	Defenseman	2	0	0	0	13
Clouston	Shaun	Reno	WCHL	Center	1	0	0	0	4
Coe	Jeremy	Huntington	ECHL	Defenseman	2	0	0	0	0
Colicito	Danny	Anchorage	WCHL	Right Wing	2	0	0	0	0
Collins	Mike	Amarillo	WPHL	Center	2	0	1	1	0
Collins	Sean	Reno	WCHL	Defenseman	8	0	1	1	10
Connolly	Jeff	Charlotte	ECHL	Right Wing	8	0	2	2	10
Conroy	Craig	Fredericton	AHL	Center	9	10	6	16	10
"	"	Worcester	AHL	Center	5	5	6	11	2
Conte	D.J.	Fresno	WCHL	Defenseman	2	0	0	0	0
Corbin	Yvon	Mississippi	ECHL	Left Wing	6	1	5	6	2
Costa	Tom	Pensacola	ECHL	Defenseman	17	0	3	3	47
Cote	Alain	Charlotte	ECHL	Defenseman	13	0	2	2	4
Coupal	Gary	Columbus	ECHL	Left Wing	10	0	0	0	67
Creighton	Adam	Indianapolis	IHL	Center	6	1	7	8	11
Cronin	Shawn	Fort Wayne	IHL	Defenseman	13	0	1	1	27
Crowder	Troy	Syracuse	AHL	Right Wing	2	0	0	0	0
Cubin	Rich	Nashville	CeHL		3	0	0	0	2
Culic	Chet	Louisville	ECHL	Forward	5	0	3	3	0
Cullen	Scott	Amarillo	WPHL	Left Wing	1	0	0	0	0
Curran	Brian	Philadelphia	AHL	Defenseman	3	0	0	0	8
Daley	Gerry	Charlotte	ECHL	Right Wing	4	1	2	3	0
Daly	Joe	Alaska	WCHL	Defenseman	4	0	0	0	23
Dame	Brad	Nashville	CeHL	Defenseman	4	0	0	0	4
Davis	Bob	Pensacola	ECHL	Defenseman	3	0	0	0	6
Davis	Shawn	Pensacola	ECHL	Defenseman	5	0	1	1	2
"	"	Amarillo	WPHL	Defenseman	12	0	1	1	8
Dean	Kevin	Albany	AHL	Defenseman	2	0	1	1	4
Delmore	Andy	Fredericton	AHL	Defenseman	4	0	1	1	0
Dent	Ted	Toledo	ECHL	Center	4	2	0	2	6
Derungs	Thomas	Oklahoma City	CeHL	Defenseman	2	0	0	0	2
Dobrescu	Aaron	Central Texas	WPHL	Defenseman	1	0	0	0	2
Domonsky	Brad	Dayton	ECHL	Right Wing	6	0	0	0	40
Donovan	Larry	Oklahoma City	CeHL	Right Wing	3	0	0	0	0
Donovan	Shean	Kentucky	AHL	Right Wing	3	1	3	4	18
Dottori	Mark	Port Huron	CoHL	Right Wing	4	0	0	0	0
Dubuc	Dave	Waco	WPHL	Defenseman	2	0	0	0	0
Duguay	Ron	San Diego	WCHL	Center	2	1	1	2	0
Duncan	Iain	Nashville	CeHL	Left Wing	12	7	11	18	68
Dupas	Dave	Fresno	WCHL	Defenseman	19	0	8	8	21
DuPaul	Cosmo	Raleigh	ECHL	Center	14	4	6	10	6
Duthie	Ryan	Manitoba	IHL	Center	4	0	0	0	2
Dutiame	Mark	Rochester	AHL	Left Wing	6	1	1	2	0
Dwyer	Don	San Antonio	CeHL	Defenseman	3	0	0	0	2
"	"	Amarillo	WPHL	Left Wing	2	0	0	0	0
Edgerly	Derek	Saginaw	CoHL	Center	6	1	3	4	2
Ensom	Jim	Quad City	CoHL	Left Wing	7	0	4	4	22
Esposito	Phil	Mobile	ECHL	Left Wing	19	2	1	3	65

Last Name	First Name	Team	League	Position	GP	G	A	PTS	PIM
Fagan	Andrew	Quad City	CoHL	Left Wing	5	0	2	2	20
Fedotov	Sergei	Springfield	AHL	Defenseman	2	0	0	0	2
Fedyk	Brent	Michiagn	IHL	Right Wing	9	1	2	3	4
Findlay	Tim	Syracuse	AHL	Right Wing	2	0	0	0	0
Fisher	Pat	Saginaw	CoHL	Defenseman	3	0	0	0	0
Focht	Dan	Springfield	AHL	Defenseman	1	0	0	0	2
Fournel	Dan	South Carolina	ECHL	Right Wing	4	1	0	1	31
Fry	Curtis	Syracuse	AHL	Center	5	0	0	0	4
Fukami	Scott	Reno	WCHL	Forward	12	3	6	9	6
Gaffney	Charlie	Birmingham	ECHL	Center	11	1	2	3	2
Gagnon	Andrew	Utica	CoHL	Defenseman	2	0	0	0	0
"	"	San Antonio	CeHL	Defenseman	5	0	2	2	8
Gallagher	Ernie	Amarillo	WPHL		14	1	6	7	17
Gallardi	Chris	Alaska	WCHL	Defenseman	17	1	5	6	54
Gardner	Paul	Portland	AHL	Forward	1	0	1	1	0
Gareau	Marty	Fresno	WCHL	Right Wing	8	1	0	1	18
Gauthier	Luc	Fredericton	AHL	Defenseman	2	0	0	0	0
George	Chris	Hershey	AHL	Right Wing	2	0	0	0	2
Gervais	Andre	Macon	CeHL	Center	2	0	0	0	2
Gignac	Chris	Dayton	CoHL	Center	1	0	0	0	0
Gladu	Patrick	Amarillo	WPHL	Left Wing	5	0	1	1	35
Golden	Ryan	Saginaw	CoHL	Left Wing	16	4	3	7	6
Gorman	Harry	Utica	CoHL	Left Wing	1	0	0	0	0
Gorokhov	Ilja	Las Vegas	IHL	Defenseman	1	0	0	0	0
Green	Brian	Muskegon	CoHL	Right Wing	5	0	0	0	0
"	"	Flint	CoHL	Right Wing	7	1	1	2	23
Gregoire	J.F.	Fredericton	AHL	Left Wing	15	1	3	4	0
Gudzik	Sergei	Waco	WPHL	Forward	1	0	0	0	0
Guzzo	Ange	Port Huron	CoHL	Defenseman	8	0	1	1	4
Hachborn	Len	Grand Rapids	IHL	Center	19	2	2	4	6
Hall	Maurice	Bakersfield	WCHL	Forward	2	0	0	0	0
Hall	Shaun (Sean)	Alaska	WCHL	Defenseman	5	0	0	0	4
"	"	San Antonio	CeHL	Defenseman	2	0	0	0	0
Hanley	Tim	El Paso	WPHL	Defenseman	15	0	6	6	2
Harper	Jeff	Richmond	ECHL	Forward	14	1	2	3	12
Harrell	Rob	Madison	CoHL	Defenseman	2	0	0	0	2
Hartje	Tod	Dayton	ECHL	Center	4	2	1	3	6
Heistad	Jeramie	Johnstown	ECHL	Defenseman	16	1	5	6	42
Helesic	Peter	Thunder Bay	CoHL	Right Wing	2	0	1	1	0
Hendrickson	Darby	St. John's	AHL	Center	12	5	4	9	21
Henry	Shane	Waco	WPHL	Center	12	3	2	5	2
Hideji	Tsuchida	Dayton	ECHL	Left Wing	5	0	0	0	2
Hill	Kevin	Muskegon	CoHL	Right Wing	2	0	0	0	0
Hitchings	Jason	Waco	WPHL		1	0	0	0	0
Hollingshead	Kelly	Knoxville	ECHL	Defenseman	8	2	5	7	11
Holmes	Dan	Alaska	WCHL	Right Wing	4	0	0	0	0
Holmstrom	Tomas	Adirondack	AHL	Left Wing	6	3	1	4	7
Holowatiuk	Bill	Roanoke	ECHL	Defenseman	3	0	0	0	2
Houda	Doug	Utah	IHL	Defenseman	3	0	0	0	7
Hughes	Brent	Utah	IHL	Left Wing	5	2	2	4	11
Huiatt	Roger	Saginaw	CoHL	Center	4	0	0	0	0
Hutchings	Steve	Alaska	WCHL	Center	1	0	0	0	0
Hutten	Ethan	Amarillo	WPHL	Defenseman	1	0	0	0	0
Jackopin	John	Adirondack	AHL	Defenseman	3	0	0	0	9
Jette	Luc	Macon	CeHL	Defenseman	16	4	0	4	20
Johansson	Tobias	Reno	WCHL	Defenseman	3	0	0	0	0

Last Name	First Name	Team	League	Position	GP	G	A	PTS	PIM
Johnson	Jay	Fresno	WCHL	Center	1	0	1	1	2
"	"	New Mexico	WPHL	Center	6	1	0	1	2
Johnson	Karl	Amarillo	WPHL	Defenseman	5	0	0	0	9
"	"	Knoxville	ECHL	Defenseman	3	0	0	0	4
Johnston	Ryan	Huntington	ECHL	Defenseman	5	0	0	0	2
Joseph	Derek	El Paso	WPHL	Left Wing	8	1	1	2	2
Kalmikov	Konstantin	St. John's	AHL	Center	2	0	0	0	0
Kalverda	Gord	Quad City	CoHL		4	1	0	1	4
"	"	Macon	CeHL	Center	8	1	2	3	12
Karmanos	Jason	Raleigh	ECHL	Forward	16	3	5	8	2
Keegen	Robert	Macon	CeHL	Left Wing	3	0	0	0	2
Kelley	Jonathan	Tallahassee	ECHL	Center	1	0	1	1	2
Kelley	Matt	Nashville	CeHL	Defenseman	6	1	3	4	2
"	"	El Paso	WPHL	Defenseman	1	0	0	0	0
Kelly	Matt	Peoria	ECHL	Defenseman	13	0	0	0	6
Kelly	Mike R.	Madison	CoHL	Center	1	0	0	0	2
Kennedy	Mike	Michigan	IHL	Center	2	0	1	1	2
Kennedy	Sheldon	Providence	AHL	Right Wing	3	0	1	1	2
Kissock	Darin	Reno	WCHL	Defenseman	6	0	1	1	2
Klima	Petr	Cleveland	IHL	Left Wing	19	7	14	21	6
Kocur	Joey	San Antonio	IHL	Right Wing	5	1	1	2	24
Koen	Bayne	Alaska	WCHL	Defenseman	2	1	0	1	5
Koftinoff	Joe	Reno	WCHL	Forward	8	1	0	1	33
Korolev	Igor	Michigan	IHL	Right Wing	4	2	2	4	0
"	"	Phoenix	IHL	Right Wing	4	2	6	8	4
Kourilin	Evgeny	Nashville	CeHL	Center	6	0	0	0	0
Kroseberg	Gunnar	Madison	CoHL	Defenseman	4	0	0	0	2
"	"	Alaska	WCHL	Defenseman	4	0	0	0	7
Kroupa	Vlastimil	Kentucky	AHL	Defenseman	5	0	3	3	0
Kudrna	Jaroslav	Kentucky	AHL	Left Wing	7	0	0	0	4
Kulmanovsky	Dima	Alaska	WCHL	Forward	1	0	0	0	0
Kypreos	Nick	St. John's	AHL	Left WIng	4	0	0	0	4
LaBonte	Christian	Utica	CoHL	Center	2	0	0	0	0
"	"	Memphis	CeHL	Center	8	4	1	5	21
"	"	Waco	WPHL	Forward	5	0	0	0	2
Lacroix	Rick	Birminghan	ECHL	Defenseman	12	2	4	6	19
Lafreniere	Jason	Michigan	IHL	Center	17	2	4	6	18
Laing	Jim	Brantford	CoHL	Defenseman	5	0	0	0	4
Lalonde	Christian	San Diego	WCHL	Defenseman	1	0	0	0	0
Lamontange	Mark	Tulsa	CeHL		16	3	3	6	8
Landmesser	Derek	Thunder Bay	CoHL	Defenseman	17	0	3	3	11
Langkow	Daymond	Adirondack	AHL	Center	2	1	1	2	0
Lapointe	Claude	Utah	IHL	Center	9	7	6	13	14
LaRocque	Matt	El Paso	WPHL	Left Wing	4	1	0	1	9
LaRose	Patrick	San Antonio	CeHL	Defenseman	12	1	0	1	73
Lee	Tim	Alaska	WCHL	Forward	8	1	1	2	0
Lee	Darin	Dayton	CoHL	Center	4	1	0	1	2
Legault	Aaron	Madison	CoHL	Right Wing	3	0	1	1	0
"	"	Saginaw	CoHL	Right Wing	16	1	2	3	32
Leveque	Guy	San Antonio	IHL	Center	3	0	1	1	0
Lindgren	Mats	Hamilton	AHL	Left Wing	9	6	7	13	6
Littleton	Tom	Dayton	CoHL	Center	9	0	0	0	2
Lopatka	Geoff	Louisville	ECHL	Left Wing	1	0	0	0	0
Lorenz	Terry	Charlotte	ECHL	Center	3	1	1	2	0
Lowe	Ed	Richmond	ECHL	Right Wing	2	0	1	1	0
"	"	Dayton	ECHL	Right Wing	2	0	0	0	0

Last Name	First Name	Team	League	Position	GP	G	A	PTS	PIM
MacCormick	Roddy	South Carolina	ECHL	Right Wing	2	0	1	1	0
MacDonald	Bruce	Toledo	ECHL	Right WIng	7	0	2	2	4
MacLean	Paul	Toledo	ECHL	Left Wing	10	0	1	1	2
MacLean	Terry	El Paso	WPHL	Center	1	0	0	0	0
"	"	Alaska	WCHL	Center	3	0	1	1	0
Madia	Rob	San Diego	WCHL	Center	1	1	0	1	0
Maki	Bryan	Amarillo	WPHL	Left Wing	16	0	1	1	20
Malik	Marek	Springfield	AHL	Defenseman	3	0	3	3	4
Malkoc	Dean	Providence	AHL	Defenseman	4	0	2	2	28
Mannetta	Vince	Nashville	CeHL	Right Wing	13	4	3	7	4
Mansoff	Jason	Portland	AHL	Defenseman	7	0	0	0	0
Mark	Gord	Providence	AHL	Defenseman	7	0	1	1	36
"	"	Utah	IHL	Defenseman	12	1	2	3	11
Markstrom	Chris	Madison	CoHL	Left Wing	13	1	1	2	2
Martin	Matt	St. John's	AHL	Defenseman	12	1	3	4	4
Marziale	Ralph	Utica	CoHL	Center	2	0	0	0	0
Matteson	Doug	Saginaw	CoHL	Defenseman	1	0	0	0	0
Matthews	Dave	Waco	WPHL		3	0	0	0	0
McArthur	Jeff	El Paso	WPHL	Defenseman	4	0	0	0	10
McGee	Tony	El Paso	WPHL	Left Wing	2	0	0	0	18
McGhan	Mike	Toledo	ECHL	Left Wing	9	1	2	3	14
"	"	Louisville	ECHL	Left Wing	1	0	1	1	0
McGrath	Mike	Fresno	WCHL	Defenseman	1	0	0	0	0
McGroarty	Jim	Fresno	WCHL	Left WIng	4	1	3	4	2
McInnis	Paul	Waco	WPHL	Left WIng	15	0	0	0	89
McKee	Jay	Rochester	AHL	Defenseman	7	2	5	7	4
McLaughlin	Mike	Jacksonville	ECHL	Left Wing	8	4	8	12	4
Mikhalev	Andrei	Nashville	CeHL	Right Wing	3	2	0	2	0
Mildengren	Jack	Fresno	WCHL	Forward	2	0	0	0	0
Miller	Bill	El Paso	WPHL	Forward	19	1	5	6	41
Moger	Sandy	Providence	AHL	Right Wing	3	0	2	2	19
Moore	Skeeter	Amarillo	WPHL	Right Wing	7	5	12	17	18
Morden	Steve	Brantford	CoHL	Right Wing	9	1	1	2	2
Morel	Kelly	Jacksonville	ECHL	Defenseman	7	0	0	0	4
Mulford	Greg	Central Texas	WPHL	Left Wing	2	0	0	0	2
Murray	Scott	Oklahoma City	CeHL	Defenseman	3	0	0	0	2
Murray	Tim	Detroit	IHL	Defenseman	5	0	4	4	2
Mychalshyn	Mike	San Antonio	CeHL	Defenseman	17	1	3	4	12
Myhres	Brantt	San Antonio	IHL	Left Wing	12	0	0	0	98
Nabokov	Dmitri	Indianapolis	IHL	Center	2	0	0	0	0
Nazarov	Andrei	Kentcuky	AHL	Left WIng	3	1	2	3	4
Nelson	Ben	Charlotte	ECHL	Defenseman	3	0	0	0	2
Nordberg	Robert	Utah	IHL	Right Wing	16	3	6	9	12
Nordstrom	Carlin	Fort Wayne	IHL	Right WIng	9	1	1	2	24
Norris	Warren	St. John's	AHL	Center	9	1	0	1	4
O'Brien	Thomas	Port Huron	CoHL	Right Wing	6	1	0	1	2
"	"	Dayton	CoHL	Right Wing	11	1	4	5	0
O'Neill	Jeff	Springfield	AHL	Center	1	0	0	0	0
Oakenfold	Kevin	Alaska	WCHL	Forward	6	0	0	0	0
Olsson	Christer	Worcester	AHL	Defenseman	2	0	0	0	0
Pagnutti	Matthew	Carolina	AHL	Defenseman	1	0	0	0	0
Paleczny	Ron	Knoxville	ECHL	Defenseman	13	0	1	1	2
"	"	Columbus	ECHL	Defenseman	1	0	0	0	0
Pandolfo	Jay	Albany	AHL	Left Wing	12	3	9	12	0
Paolucci	Dan	Port Huron	CoHL	Left Wing	1	0	0	0	0
Parker	Troy	Quad City	CoHL		1	0	0	0	0

Last Name	First Name	Team	League	Position	GP	G	A	PTS	PIM
Patterson	Alan	El Paso	WPHL	Center	11	2	1	3	2
Patton	Kirk	Alaska	WCHL	Defenseman	13	1	1	2	45
Pawlaczyk	Dan	Toledo	ECHL	Center	13	1	5	6	11
Peake	Pat	Portland	AHL	Right Wing	3	0	2	2	0
Pederson	Denis	Albany	AHL	Center	3	1	3	4	7
Peregudov	Konstantin	Las Vegas	IHL	Left Wing	1	0	0	0	2
Perna	Mike	Huntington	ECHL	Defenseman	16	1	0	1	59
Persson	Richard	Albany	AHL	Defenseman	13	1	4	5	8
Petersen	Eric	Jacksonville	ECHL	Forward	10	0	5	5	4
Peterson	Chris	Bakersfield	WCHL	Forward	10	2	3	5	15
Petrovicky	Robert	Worcester	AHL	Center	12	5	4	9	19
Phillips	Stephen	Columbus	CeHL	Defenseman	1	0	0	0	2
Phillips	Steve	San Antonio	CeHL	Center	3	1	0	1	7
"	"	Madison	CoHL	Center	2	1	2	3	4
Picklyk	Derek	Alaska	WCHL	Forwrad	5	1	0	1	0
Piirto	Dave	Waco	WPHL	Defenseman	15	0	0	0	36
Pivetz	Marc	Hershey	AHL	Defenseman	5	0	0	0	4
Pluck	David	Macon	CeHL	Defenseman	2	0	0	0	2
Podalinski	Alex	Nashville	CeHL	Left Wing	7	2	3	5	4
Posmyk	Marek	St. John's	AHL	Defenseman	2	0	0	0	2
Power	Chad	Detroit	IHL	Left Wing	7	0	1	1	11
Pozzo	Kevin	Kansas City	IHL	Defenseman	1	0	0	0	2
"	"	Las Vegas	IHL	Defenseman	7	0	1	1	6
"	"	Tallahassee	ECHL	Defenseman	8	1	2	3	15
Proffitt	Rob	Alaska	WCHL	Center	4	1	1	2	9
Puhlaksi	Greg	Toledo	ECHL	Center	1	0	0	0	0
Quigley	Ryan	Nashville	CeHL	Defenseman	3	0	1	1	0
Quinn	Brian	Amarillo	WPHL	Center	3	0	0	0	0
Racine	Yves	Quebec	IHL	Defenseman	6	0	4	4	4
"	"	Kentucky	AHL	Defenseman	4	0	1	1	2
Rajsek (Rojsek)	Rok	Madison	CoHL	Left Wing	10	1	2	3	4
"	"	Dayton	CoHL	Forward	6	0	0	0	0
"	"	Johnstown	ECHL	Right Wing	1	0	0	0	0
Ralph	Jason	Flint	CoHL	Right Wing	7	1	0	1	0
Recunyk	Rick	Alaska	WCHL	Left Wing	11	3	1	4	40
Reier	Mike	Reno	WCHL	Center	3	2	1	3	0
Reis	Mike	Anchorage	WCHL	Defenseman	3	1	1	2	0
Ricci	Angelo	Amarillo	WPHL	Forward	16	2	10	12	43
Richard (s)	Jason	Johnstown	ECHL	Defenseman	6	0	0	0	6
"	"	Madison	CoHL	Defenseman	2	0	1	1	0
Riga	Bill	El Paso	WPHL	Left Wing	7	1	1	2	0
Robinson	Mark	Raleigh	ECHL	Forward	4	0	0	0	2
Roed	Peter	Louisville	ECHL	Left Wing	7	1	0	1	4
Roenick	Trevor	Springfield	AHL	Right Wing	7	1	1	2	8
"	"	Phoenix	IHL	Right Wing	8	2	2	4	22
Roesler	Richard	Amarillo	WPHL	Defenseman	2	0	0	0	9
Rohloff	Jon	Providence	AHL	Defenseman	3	1	1	2	0
Rohovich	Tyson	Flint	CoHL	Defenseman	6	0	0	0	4
"	"	Huntington	ECHL	Defenseman	6	0	0	0	6
Rowe	David	Madison	CoHL	Defenseman	16	0	0	0	8
Royer	Remi	Indianapolis	IHL	Defenseman	10	0	1	1	17
Rublein	Dan	Mobile	ECHL	Defenseman	4	0	1	1	6
"	"	Waco	WPHL	Defenseman	2	0	0	0	2
Rybovic	Lubomir	Grand Rapids	IHL	Left Wing	1	0	0	0	0
Saglo	Rotislav	Pensacola	ECHL	Forward	11	0	1	1	4
Sailfullin	Ramil	Quebec	IHL	Center	1	0	0	0	0

Last Name	First Name	Team	League	Position	GP	G	A	PTS	PIM
Salsman	Marc	Jacksonville	ECHL	Forward	7	1	1	2	9
Sarault	Yves	Hershey	AHL	Left Wing	6	2	3	5	8
Saterdalen	Jeff	Port Huron	CoHL	Right Wing	2	0	0	0	0
"	"	Saginaw	CoHL	Right Wing	11	1	1	2	23
Scanzano	Jason	Utica	CoHL	Left Wing	6	0	2	2	2
Schooley	Derek	Pensacola	ECHL	Defenseman	3	0	0	0	9
"	"	Peoria	ECHL	Defenseman	1	0	1	1	0
Schriner	Rob	Waco	WPHL	Center	15	10	7	17	6
Schuhwerk	Rick	Hershey	AHL	Defenseman	6	0	0	0	2
Scott	Brian	Johnstown	ECHL	Forward	7	2	1	3	4
Seamone	Mark	El Paso	WPHL	Right Wing	6	0	1	1	6
Seibel	Chad	Reno	WCHL	Defenseman	9	2	3	5	6
Sellars	Joe	Tulsa	CeHL	Left Wing	10	2	1	3	7
Selmser	Sean	Manitoba	IHL	Left Wing	4	0	2	2	12
Senior	Mike	Nashville	CeHL	Center	9	1	5	6	9
Shargorodsky	Oleg	Detroit	IHL	Defenseman	3	0	3	3	4
Shedden	Darryl	Louisiana	ECHL	Right Wing	1	0	0	0	10
"	"	Hampton Roads	ECHL	Right Wing	10	0	2	2	4
Shewan	Mike	Brantford	CoHL	Defenseman	2	1	0	1	0
Shilov	Sergei	Saginaw	CoHL	Right Wing	10	2	2	4	4
Short	Kayle	Portland	AHL	Defenseman	1	0	1	1	0
Simerson	T.J.	Saginaw	CoHL	Right Wing	1	0	0	0	0
Simms	Chris	Alaska	WCHL	Forward	18	3	7	10	8
Simpson	Bob	Saginaw	CoHL	Left Wing	13	3	2	5	4
Simpson	Reid	Albany	AHL	Left Wing	3	0	0	0	10
Skolnik	Jarred	Wichita	CeHL	Right Wing	3	0	0	0	24
Smolinski	Bryan	Detroit	IHL	Center	6	5	7	12	10
Smyth	Brad	Phoenix	IHL	Right Wing	3	5	2	7	0
Sorenson	Kelly	Hampton Roads	ECHL	Right Wing	5	1	0	1	0
Srochenski	Darren	Reno	WCHL	Defensman	7	0	1	1	24
St. Cyr	Gerry	Reno	WCHL	Left Wing	9	2	4	6	6
Stahl	Craig	Charlotte	ECHL	Left Wing	5	0	1	1	12
Stephenson	Travis	Reno	WCHL	Forward	6	1	4	5	4
Stone	Shawn	El Paso	WPHL	Right Wing	7	2	1	3	0
Stoughton	Gerald	Austin	WPHL	Left Wing	5	0	0	0	12
Straub	Brian	Houston	IHL	Defenseman	7	0	3	3	11
Strutch	David	Waco	WPHL	Center	11	4	7	11	0
Suhy	Andy	Toledo	ECHL	Defenseman	3	0	3	3	20
Sullivan	Steve	Albany	AHL	Center	15	8	7	15	16
Svindle	Libor	El Paso	WPHL	Defenseman	11	0	2	2	8
Svoboda	Valeriy	Roanoke	ECHL	Forward	5	0	3	3	0
Sylvester	Derek	El Paso	WPHL	Defenseman	3	0	0	0	0
Tansy	Ryan	Reno	WCHL	Right Wing	5	0	0	0	13
Tarsha	Chris	Toledo	ECHL	Forward	1	0	0	0	0
Thibeault	David	Kentucky	AHL	Left Wing	1	0	0	0	0
Tobin	Jim	Anchorage	WCHL	Forward	5	3	1	4	24
Toll	Steven	Raleigh	ECHL	Right Wing	7	1	3	4	2
Tompkins	Dan	Roanoke	ECHL	Forward	5	1	2	3	2
Torgajev	Pavel	Saint John	AHL	Center	5	1	2	3	4
Trakosas	George	Nashville	CeHL	Center	3	1	0	1	0
Uniac	John	Tallahassee	ECHL	Defenseman	9	0	4	4	13
Varlamov	Sergei	Saint John	AHL	Left Wing	1	0	0	0	2
Venedam	Sean	Adirondack	AHL	Center	13	0	1	1	4
Venema	Dwayne	Port Huron	CoHL	Defenseman	6	1	0	1	29
Venis	Ken	Reno	WCHL	Defenseman	13	0	5	5	16
Vinze	Boris	Reno	WCHL	Right Wing	7	0	0	0	4
"	"	Waco	WPHL		3	0	0	0	2

Last Name	First Name	Team	League	Position	GP	G	A	PTS	PIM
Vipond	Kelly	San Diego	WCHL	Right Wing	8	1	5	6	41
Vlastelic	Tony	Tulsa	CeHL	Left Wing	6	2	0	2	0
"	"	Wichita	CeHL	Left Wing	3	0	0	0	2
Vopat	Jan	Phoenix	IHL	Defenseman	4	0	6	6	6
Voth	Curtis	Amarillo	WPHL	Right Wing	11	2	1	3	40
Walker	Bryan	Madison	CoHL	Defenseman	15	0	4	4	6
Ware	Mike	St. John's	AHL	Right Wing	5	1	0	1	14
Wassilyn	Joe	Brantford	CoHL	Center	7	0	1	1	4
"	"	Nashville	CeHL	Center	5	0	0	0	6
Wasyluk	Trevor	Springfield	AHL	Left Wing	1	0	0	0	0
Wells	Chris	Cleveland	IHL	Center	15	4	6	10	9
Wheeler	Shawn	Charlotte	ECHL	Left Wing	11	3	5	8	40
Wiemer	Jason	Adirondack	AHL	Center	4	1	0	1	7
Wilkinson	Neil	Cleveland	IHL	Defenseman	2	0	1	1	0
Williams	Pat	Alaska	WCHL	Forward	2	2	0	2	0
Wilmert	Sean	Reno	WCHL	Defenseman	11	2	0	2	39
"	"	Columbus	CeHL	Defenseman	3	0	0	0	2
"	"	Nashville	CeHL	Defenseman	2	0	0	0	7
"	"	Amarillo	WPHL	Defenseman	1	0	0	0	0
Wilson	Carey	Manitoba	IHL	Center	7	0	4	4	2
Wilson	Robb	San Antonio	CeHL	Defenseman	5	0	2	2	6
"	"	Nashville	CeHL	Defenseman	8	0	2	2	10
"	"	Columbus	CeHL	Defenseman	1	0	0	0	2
Winnes	Chris	Utah	IHL	Right Wing	5	0	0	0	0
Wismer	Chris	Roanoke	ECHL	Defenseman	3	0	0	0	2
Wolgemuth	Lance	Nashville	CeHL	Defenseman	9	0	1	1	38
Wood	Dody	Kansas City	IHL	Left Wing	6	3	6	9	35
Wood	Russ	Toledo	ECHL	Defenseman	2	0	0	0	0
"	"	Brantford	CoHL	Defenseman	8	0	0	0	17
Woods	Brock	Huntington	ECHL	Defenseman	5	0	0	0	2
Woods	Darren	Huntington	ECHL	Defenseman	1	0	0	0	0
Wright	Dennis	Worcester	AHL	Left Wing	2	0	0	0	12
Yakabuski	Marc	Jacksonville	ECHL	Defenseman	4	2	1	3	4
Yoshinori	Ishioka	Alaska	WCHL	Right Wing	2	0	0	0	0
Zholtok	Sergei	Las Vegas	IHL	Center	19	13	14	27	20
Ziegler	Rolf	Raleigh	ECHL	Defenseman	6	0	0	0	2

Goaltenders

Last Name	First Name	Team	League	Games	Minutes	AVG	W	L	T	SO
Adams ***	Andy	South Carolina	ECHL	2	87:34	5.48	0	1	0	0
Allison	Blair	Orlando	IHL	1	40:39	7.38	0	1	0	0
Beedon	Roger	Port Huron	CoHL	5	140:55	4.26	0	0	1	0
Black	Chad	Utica	CoHL	1	4:27	0.00	0	0	0	0
Careau	Sylvain	Roanoke	ECHL	1	18:02	0.00	0	0	0	0
Casey	Jon	Worcester	AHL	4	244:50	2.45	2	1	1	0
Charbonneau	Vince	Flint	CoHL	1	19:25	9.27	0	0	0	0
Christians	Derek	Reno	WCHL	3	129:23	8.81	0	1	0	0
Chung	Khang	New Mexico	WPHL	1	12:28	0.00	0	0	0	0
Condon	Sean	Tulsa	CeHL	10	434:38	4.69	3	5	0	0
Conley	Mark	Macon	CeHL	1	2:11	0.00	0	0	0	0
Convery	Brent	San Antonio	CeHL	9	445:57	5.79	1	5	1	0
Cook	Robin	Columbus	CeHL	1	40:00	6.00	0	1	0	0
Cooper	Kory	Portland	AHL	3	50:58	5.89	1	0	0	0
Crowe	Craig	Reno	WCHL	7	272:48	6.16	0	3	1	0
"	"	Bakersfield	WCHL	5	112:01	6.43	1	0	0	0
Donaldson	Scott	Saginaw	CoHL	1	45:11	5.31	0	0	0	0
Dunham	Mike	Albany	AHL	3	184:01	3.91	1	1	1	0
Dunne	Adam	Saginaw	CoHL	1	44:48	9.38	0	1	0	0
Duval	Brett	Louisville	ECHL	1	40:00	9.00	0	0	0	0
Economou	Chris	Brantford	CoHL	2	74:17	8.08	1	0	0	0
"	"	Waco	WPHL	2	39:01	9.23	0	0	0	0
Foster	Darryl	Dayton	CoHL	9	376:01	6.06	1	6	0	0
Germain	Lou	Utica	CoHL	2	47:30	3.79	0	0	1	0
Grobins	Nathan	Macon	CeHL	2	21:11	2.83	1	0	0	0
"	"	Waco	WPHL	9	381:09	3.15	3	3	0	1
Haltia	Patrik	Saint John	AHL	3	178:26	5.72	0	3	0	0
Hamilton	Brian	Peoria	ECHL	2	67:20	1.78	1	0	0	0
Henry	Frederic	Albany	AHL	1	60:00	3.00	1	0	0	0
Hodson	Kevin	Quebec	IHL	2	118:44	3.54	1	1	0	0
Ivankovic	Frank	Columbus	CeHL	2	120:00	4.50	1	1	0	0
Izzi	Chris	Saginaw	CoHL	4	51:26	8.16	0	1	0	0
Jensen	James	Jacksonville	ECHL	4	199:25	4.81	1	1	1	0
Karitisiotis	Angelo	Bakersfield	WCHL	7	326:52	4.96	2	2	1	0
Konte	Jim	Louisville	ECHL	5	271:54	6.18	0	3	1	0
Kreutzer	Kevin	Jacksonville	ECHL	5	298:18	3.62	0	4	1	0
Lacher	Blaine	Grand Rapids	IHL	11	510:41	3.76	1	8	1	0
Lalime	Patrick	Cleveland	IHL	14	834:15	3.24	6	6	2	1
Lovell	Greg	Huntsville	CeHL	2	16:54	14.20	0	0	0	0
MacLeod	Chad	Flint	CoHL	4	37:27	4.81	0	0	0	0
Malarchuk	Grant	Las Vegas	IHL	3	63:55	5.63	1	1	0	0
Matwijw	Stan	Saginaw	CoHL	1	3:47	0.00	0	0	0	0
"	"	Huntsville	CeHL	5	178:29	7.40	0	4	1	0
McDonald	Dave	Brantford	CoHL	10	496:41	4.71	3	5	1	0
McKersie	John	South Carolina	ECHL	3	96:26	5.60	1	0	0	0
McLeod	Billy	Central Texas	WPHL	2	80:00	6.00	0	1	0	0
Mewhort	John	Toledo	ECHL	1	1:26	0.00	0	0	0	0
Moberg	Larry	Roanoke	ECHL	13	515:37	4.54	2	6	0	1
Pavlat	Travis	Saginaw	CoHL	1	40:00	6.00	0	0	0	0
Perno	Len	Binghamton	AHL	1	6:03	0.00	0	0	0	0
"	"	Rochester	AHL	2	37:31	1.60	0	0	0	0
"	"	Utica	CoHL	3	126:34	5.21	0	2	0	0
"	"	Knoxville	ECHL	1	59:11	7.10	0	1	0	0

*** Playoff Statistics

Last Name	First Name	Team	League	Games	Minutes	AVG	W	L	T	SO
Petroni	Jayson	Saginaw	CoHL	1	50:05	3.59	0	1	0	0
Puppa	Daren	Adirondack	AHL	1	62:08	2.90	1	0	0	0
Rheaume	Manon	Reno	WCHL	11	424:46	5.65	2	3	1	0
Robus	Rick	Knoxville	ECHL	1	20:00	3.00	0	0	0	0
Roloson	Dwayne	Saint John	AHL	8	480:39	2.75	6	2	0	1
Shocket	Ari	Peoria	ECHL	2	119:37	5.52	0	2	0	0
Simpson	Kevin	New Mexico	WPHL	6	62:33	6.71	0	0	0	0
Soltys	Eric	New Mexico	WPHL	4	152:49	5.89	1	1	1	0
Thompkins	Paul	San Antonio	CeHL	4	64:14	8.41	0	1	0	0
Villenueve	Martin	Fredericton	AHL	3	113:40	2.11	1	1	0	0
Wachter	Steve	Mississippi	ECHL	1	18:44	0.00	0	0	1	0
Willis	Jordan	Dayton	ECHL	8	429:07	3.50	4	4	0	0
"	"	Kalamazoo	IHL	2	102:09	4.70	0	2	0	0

Duane Derksen made the CoHL Second All-Star Team after the 1996-97 season.   Photo courtesy of Madison Monsters.

The Leagues
The Teams

The following section contains final regular season and playoff results from the seven minor-pro leagues functioning during the 1996-97 hockey season.

Included are final standings, playoff results, league directories and statistical leaders from both the past season and from all-time.

The only thing that could stop the Philadelphia Phantoms Vaclav Prospal last season was a call-up to the Flyers.   Photo by Just Sports

American Hockey League

1996-97 Final Standings
Northern Conference
Canadian Division

	GP	W	L	OTL	T	GF	GA	PTS
St. John's	80	36	28	6	10	265	264	88
Saint John	80	28	36	3	13	237	269	72
Hamilton	80	28	39	4	9	220	276	69
Fredericton	80	26	44	4	9	234	283	69

Empire State Division

	GP	W	L	OTL	T	GF	GA	PTS
Rochester	80	40	30	1	9	298	257	90
Adirondack	80	38	28	2	12	258	249	90
Albany	80	38	28	5	9	269	231	90
Syracuse	80	32	38	0	10	241	265	74
Binghamton	80	27	38	2	13	245	300	69

Southern Conference
New England Division

	GP	W	L	OTL	T	GF	GA	PTS
Worcester	80	43	23	5	9	256	234	100
Springfield	80	41	25	2	12	268	229	96
Portland	80	37	26	7	10	279	264	83
Providence	80	35	40	2	3	262	289	75

Mid-Atlantic Division

	GP	W	L	OTL	T	GF	GA	PTS
Philadelphia	80	49	18	3	10	325	230	111
Hershey	80	43	22	5	10	273	220	101
Kentucky	80	36	35	0	9	278	284	81
Baltimore	80	30	37	3	10	251	285	73
Carolina	80	28	43	5	4	273	303	65

Teams awarded one point for an overtime loss

1997 Playoffs
First Round
St. John's defeated Binghamton 3-1
Hamilton defeated Saint John 3-2
Rochester defeated Syracuse 3-0
Albany defeated Adirondack 3-1
Providence defeated Worcester 3-2
Springfield defeated Portland 3-2
Philadelphia defeated Baltimore 3-0
Hersehy defeated Kentucky 3-1

Second Round
Hamilton defeated St. John's 4-3
Albany defeated Rochester 4-3
Springfield defeated Providence 4-1
Hershey defeated Philadelphia 4-3

Third Round
Hamilton defeated Albany 4-1
Hershey defeated Springfield 4-3

Calder Cup Championship
Hershey defeated Hamilton 4-1

Hershey wins eighth Calder Cup in franchise history

1996-97 Top 15 Scorers

Player		Team	Games	Goals	Assists	Points	PIM
Peter	White	Philadelphia	80	44	61	105	28
Terry	Yake	Rochester	78	34	67	101	77
Brian	Wiseman	St. John's	71	33	62	95	83
Vaclav	Prospal	Philadelphia	63	32	63	95	70
Patrik	Juhlin	Philadelphia	78	31	60	91	24
Alexei	Lojkin	Fredericton	79	33	56	89	41
Gilbert	Dionne	Carolina	72	41	47	88	69
Blair	Atcheynum	Hershey	77	42	45	87	57
Jan	Calhoun	Kentucky	66	43	43	86	68
Shawn	McCosh	Philadelphia	79	30	51	81	110
Bruce	Coles	Philadelphia	79	31	49	80	152
Peter	Ferraro	Binghamton	75	38	39	77	171
Ralph	Intranuovo	Hamilton	68	36	40	76	88
Steve	Brule	Albany	79	28	48	76	27
Craig	Reichart	Baltimore	77	22	53	75	54

Goals

Player	Team	Goals
White	Philadelphia	44
Calhoun	Kentucky	43
Atcheynum	Hershey	42
Dionne	Carolina	41
Several Tied At		38

Assists

Player	Team	Assists
Yake	Rochester	67
Prospal	Philadelphia	63
Wiseman	St. John's	62
White	Philadelphia	61
Juhlin	Philadelphia	60

Penalty Minutes

Player	Team	PIM
Bonvie	Hamilton	522
Brown, Brad	Fredericton	368
Sawyer	Providence	367
Oliwa	Albany	322
Belak	Hershey	320

Top Goaltenders

Player	Team	GP	MIN	AVG	W	L	T	SO	GA	SAVES	SPCT
Labbe	Hershey	66	3811	2.52	34	22	9	6	160	1707	.914
Langkow	Springfield	33	1929	2.64	15	9	7	0	85	875	.911
Roussel	Philadelphia	36	1852	2.66	18	9	3	2	82	892	.916
Passmore	Hamilton	27	1568	2.68	12	12	3	1	70	637	.901
Maracle	Adirondack	68	3843	2.70	34	22	9	5	173	1889	.916
McLennan	Worcester	39	2152	2.79	18	13	4	2	100	935	.903
Deschenes	Rochester	38	1898	2.85	15	13	3	2	90	863	.906
Little	Philadelphia	54	3007	2.89	31	12	7	0	145	1457	.909
Sidorkiewicz	Albany	62	3539	2.90	31	23	6	2	171	1559	.901

Wins

Player	Team	Wins
Labbe	Hershey	34
Maracle	Adirondack	34
Sidorkiewicz	Albany	31
Little	Philadelphia	31
Ram	Kentucky	25

Minutes

Player	Team	Min
Maracle	Adirondack	3843
Labbe	Hershey	3810
Sidorkiewicz	Albany	3539
Cloutier	Binghamton	3366
Cassivi	Syracuse	3069

Save Percentage

Player	Team	SPCT
Daigle	Springfield	.940
Buzak	Worcester	.918
Maracle	Adirondack	.916
Roussel	Philadelphia	.916
Shulmistra	Albany	.916

AHL Regular Season Awards

First Team	Position	Second Team
Jean-Francois Labbe, Hershey	Goaltender	Norm Maracle, Adirondack
Darren Rumble, Philadelphia	Defenseman	Jamie Rivers, Worcester
Terry Hollinger, Rochester	Defenseman	Pascal Trepanier, Hershey
Vaclav Prospal, Philadelphia	Center	Peter White, Philadelphia
Blair Atcheynum, Hershey	Right Wing	Jan Calhoun, Kentucky
Patrik Juhlin, Philadelphia	Left Wing	Ralph Intranuovo, Hamilton

Les Cunningham (MVP) — Jean-Francois Labbe, Hershey
Eddie Shore (Defenseman) — Darren Rumble, Philadelphia
Fred T. Hunt (sportmanship, determination, dedication) — Steve Passmore, Hamilton
"Red" Garrett (rookie) — Jaroslav Svejkovsky, Portland
"Baz" Bastien (Goalie) — Jean-Francois Labbe, Hershey
Louis Pieri (Coach) — Greg Gilbert, Worcester
Calder Cup (AHL Champions) — Hershey Bears
Jack Butterfield (Playoff MVP) — Mike McHugh, Hershey

AHL Regular Season All-Time Leaders

Games Played

Willie Marshall	1,205
Fred Glover	1,201
Harold Pidhirny	1,071
Mike Nykoluk	1,069
Jody Gage	1,035

Goals

Willie Marshall	523
Fred Glover	520
Jody Gage	504
Dick Gamble	468
Jimmy Anderson	426

Assists

Willie Marshall	852
Fred Glover	814
Mike Nykoluk	686
Tim Tookey	621
Art Stratton	555

Points

Willie Marshall	1,375
Fred Glover	1,334
Jody Gage	1,048
Tim Tookey	974
Dick Gamble	892

Penalty Minutes

Fred Glover	2,402
*Rob Murray	2,019
Mike Stevens	1,915
Serge Roberge	1,887
Mike Stothers	1,840

Wins

Sam St. Laurent	164
* Peter Sidorkiewicz	158
Ken Holland	143
Jacques Cloutier	126
Mark LaForest	123

All-Time Calder Cup Wins (Active Clubs Only)

Hershey	8
Springfield	7
Rochester	6
Adirondack	4
Providence	4
Cape Breton, Portland and Albany	1

* Active in AHL Last Season

American Hockey League

American Hockey League
425 Union Street
West Springfield, MA 01089
Phone: (413) 781-2030
Fax: (413) 733-4767

Adirondack Red Wings
1 Civic Center Plaza
Glen Falls, New York 12801
Phone: (518) 798-0366
Fax: (518) 798-0816
Dir. of Opr. Don Ostrom
Coach: Glenn Merkosky
Division: Empire State
Affilations: Detroit
and Tampa Bay

Albany RiverRats
51 South Pearl St.
Albany, New York 12207
Phone: (518) 487-2244
Fax: (518) 487-2248
President: Doug Burch
Coach: John Cunniff
Division: Empire State
Affiliation: New Jersey

Cincinnati Mighty Ducks
2250 Seymour Avenue
Cincinnati, Ohio 45212
Phone: (513) 351-3999
Fax: (513) 351-5898
GM: Peter Robinson
Coach: Moe Mantha
Division: Mid-Atlantic
Affiliation: Anaheim

Fredericton Canadiens
P.O. Box HABS
Fredericton, NB E3B 4Y2
Phone: (506) 459-4227
Fax: (506) 457-4250
Dir. of Opr: Wayne Gamble
Coach: Michel Therrien
Division: Atlantic
Affiliation: Montreal and
Los Angeles

Hamilton Bulldogs
85 York Blvd.
Hamilton, Ontario L8R 3L4
Phone: (905) 529-8500
Fax: (905) 529-1188
GM: Scott Howson
Coach: Lorne Molleken
Division: Empire State
Affiliation: Edmonton

Hartford Wolf Pack
196 Trumbull Street
3rd Floor
Hartford, Connecticut 06103
Phone: (860) 246-7825
Fax: (860) 240-7618
V.P. Tom Mitchell
Coach: E. J. McGuire
Division: New England
Affiliation: New York Rangers

Hershey Bears
P.O. Box 866
Hershey, Pennsylvania 17033
Phone: (717) 534-3380
Fax: (717) 534-3383
GM: Doug Yingst
Coach: Bob Hartley
Division: Mid-Atlantic
Affiliation: Colorado

Kentucky Thoroughblades
410 West Vine Street
Lexington, Kentucky 40507
Phone: (606) 259-1996
Fax: (606) 252-3684
CEO: Ron DeGregorio
Coach: Jim Wiley
Division: Mid-Atlantic
Affiliation: San Jose
and New York Islanders

Best of New Haven
275 South Orange Street
New Haven, Connecticut 06510
Phone: (203) 777-7878
Fax: (203) 777-6667
GM: Dave Gregory
Coach: Kevin McCarthy
Division: New England
Affiliation; Carolina Hurricanes
and Florida Panthers

Philadelphia Phantoms
The CoreStates Spectrum
1 CoreStates Complex
Philadelphia, PA 19148
Phone: (215) 465-4522
Fax: (215) 952-5245
C.O.O. Frank Miceli
Coach: Bill Barber
Division: Mid-Atlantic
Affiliation: Philadelphia Flyers

Portland Pirates
85 Free Street
Portland, Maine 04101
Phone: (207) 828-4665
Fax: (207) 773-3278
GM: Dave Fisher
Coach: Bryan Trottier
Division: Atlantic
Affiliation: Washington

Providence Bruins
1 LaSalle Square
Providence, RI 02903
Phone: (401) 273-5000
Fax: (401) 273-5004
CEO: Ed Anderson
Coach: Tom McVie
Division: New England
Affilation: Boston

Rochester Americans
50 South Avenue
Rochester, New York 14604
Phone: (716) 454-5335
Fax: (716) 454-3954
GM: Jody Gage
Coach: Brian McCutcheon
Division: Empire State
Affilation: Buffalo

Saint John Flames
P.O. Box 4040, Station B
Saint John, NB E2M 5E6
Phone: (506) 635-2637
Fax: (506) 633-4625
President: Gord Thorne
Coach: Bill Stewart
Division: Atlantic
Affiliation: Calgary

Springfield Falcons
P.O. Box 3190
Springfield, MA 01101
Phone: (413) 739-3344
Fax: (413) 739-3389
President: Bruce Landon
Coach: Dave Farrish
Division: New England
Affiliations: Phoenix

St. John's Maple Leafs
6 Logy Bay Road
St. John's NFLD A1A 1J3
Phone: (709) 726-1010
Fax: (709) 726-1511
GM: Glenn Stanford
Coach: Al MacAdam
Division: Atlantic
Affiliation: Toronto

Syracuse Crunch
800 South State Street
Syracuse, New York 13202
Phone: (315) 473-4444
Fax: (315) 473-4449
GM: Vance Lederman
Coach: Jack McIlhargey
Division: Empire State
Affiliation: Vancouver
and Pittsburgh

Worcester IceCats
303 Main Street
Worcester, Massachusetts 01608
Phone (508) 798-5400
Fax: (508) 799-5267
Vice President: Peter Ricciardi
Coach: Greg Gilbert
Division: New England
Affiliations: St. Louis
and Ottawa

Lowell Lock Monsters
440 Middlesex Road
Suite 107
Tyngsboro, Massachusetts 01879
Phone: (508) 649-8744
Fax: (508) 649-9142
G.M. Tom Rowe
To begin play during the 1998-99 season.

International Hockey League

1996-97 Final Standings
Eastern Conference
Northeast Division

	GP	W	L	SOL	GF	GA	PTS
Detroit	82	57	17	8	280	188	122
Orlando	82	53	24	5	305	232	111
Cincinnati	82	43	29	10	254	248	96
Quebec	82	41	30	11	267	248	93
Grand Rapids	82	40	30	12	244	246	92

Central Division

	GP	W	L	SOL	GF	GA	PTS
Indianapolis	82	44	29	9	289	230	97
Cleveland	82	40	32	10	286	280	90
Michigan	82	31	44	7	208	272	69
Fort Wayne	82	28	47	7	223	318	63

Western Conference
Midwest Division

	GP	W	L	SOL	GF	GA	PTS
San Antonio	82	45	30	7	276	278	97
Kansas City	82	38	29	15	271	270	91
Chicago	82	40	36	6	276	290	86
Milwaukee	82	38	36	8	253	298	84
Manitoba	82	32	40	10	262	300	74

Southwest Division

	GP	W	L	SOL	GF	GA	PTS
Long Beach	82	54	19	9	309	247	117
Houston	82	44	30	8	247	228	96
Utah	82	43	33	6	259	254	92
Las Vegas	82	41	34	7	287	299	89
Phoenix	82	27	42	13	239	309	67

1997 Playoffs
First Round
Detroit defeated Kalamazoo 3-1
Quebec defeated Cincinnati 3-0
Orlando defeated Grand Rapids 3-2
Cleveland defeated Indianapolis 3-1
Long Beach defeated Milwaukee 3-0
Utah defeated Kansas City 3-0
Houston defeated Las Vegas 3-0
San Antonio defeated Chicago 3-1
Second Round
Detroit defeated Quebec 4-2
Cleveland defeated Orlando 4-1
Long Beach defeated Utah 4-0
Houston defeated San Antonio 4-1
Third Round
Detroit defeated Cleveland 4-1
Long Beach defeated Houston 4-1
Turner Cup Championship
Detroit defeated Long Beach 4-2

Detoit Vipers win first ever Turner Cup

1995-96 Top 15 Scorers

Player		Team	Games	Goals	Assists	Points	PIM
Rob	Brown	Chicago	76	37	80	117	98
Steve	Maltais	Chicago	81	60	54	114	62
Steve	Larouche	Quebec	79	49	53	102	78
Michel	Picard	Grand Rapids	82	46	55	101	58
Patrice	Lefebvre	Las Vegas	82	21	73	94	94
Kip	Miller	Indianapolis	80	28	65	93	50
Daniel	Shank	San Antonio	81	33	58	91	293
Stephane	Morin	Long Beach	77	28	63	91	77
Mark	Beaufait	Orlando	80	26	65	91	63
Martin	Gendron	Las Vegas	81	51	39	90	20
Jeff	Nelson	Grand Rapids	82	34	55	89	85
Tony	Hrkac	Milwaukee	81	27	61	88	20
Patrik	Augusta	Long Beach	82	45	42	87	96
Jason	Ruff	Quebec	80	35	50	85	93
Jeff	Christian	Cleveland	69	40	40	80	262

Goals

Player	Team	Goals
Maltais	Chicago	60
Gendron	Las Vegas	51
Larouche	Quebec	49
Picard	Grand Rapids	46
Several Tied	@	45

Assists

Player	Team	Assists
Brown	Chicago	80
Lefebvre	Las Vegas	79
Miller	Indianapolis	65
Beaufait	Orlando	65
Morin	Long Beach	63

Penalty Minutes

Player	Team	PIM
Gagnon	Fort Wayne	457
Simon	Las Vegas	402
Dreger	Orlando	387
Nieckar	Long Beach	386
Ruchty	Grand Rapids	364

Top Goaltenders

Player	Team	GP	MIN	AVG	W	L	SOL	SO	GA	SAVES	SPCT
Reese	Detroit	32	1763	1.87	23	4	3	4	55	693	.926
Parent	Detroit	53	2815	2.22	31	13	4	4	104	1188	.920
Draper	Long Beach	39	2267	2.30	28	7	3	2	87	870	.909
Reddick	Grand Rapids	61	3245	2.48	30	14	10	6	134	1436	.915
Chabot	Houston	72	4265	2.53	39	26	7	7	180	2063	.920
Bester	Orlando	61	3115	2.54	37	13	3	2	132	1226	.903
Lamothe	Indianapolis	38	2271	2.64	20	14	4	1	100	1116	.918
Beauregard	Quebec	67	3946	2.65	35	20	11	4	174	1686	.906
MacDonald	Cincinnati	31	1617	2.71	11	9	5	2	73	736	.910

Wins

Player	Team	Wins
Chabot	Houston	39
Bester	Orlando	37
Beauregard	Quebec	35
Lorenz	Milwaukee	33
Sarjeant	Cincinnati	32

Minutes

Player	Team	Min
Chabot	Houston	4265
Beauregard	Quebec	3945
Lorenz	Milwaukee	3903
Sarjeant	Cincinnati	3287
Duffus	Las Vegas	3266

Save Percentage

Player	Team	SPCT
Reese	Detroit	.926
Chabot	Houston	.920
Parent	Detroit	.920
Sarjeant	Cincinnati	.919
Lamothe	Indianapolis	.918

IHL Regular Season Awards

First Team	Position	Second Team
Frederic Chabot, Houston	Goaltender	Jeff Reese, Detroit
Brad Werenka, Indianapolis	Defenseman	Victor Ignatjev, Long Beach
Brad Shaw, Detroit	Defenseman	Chris Snell, Indianapolis
Michel Picard, Grand Rapids	Forward	Mark Beaufait, Orlando
Rob Brown, Chicago	Forward	Patrick Augusta, Long Beach
Steve Larouche, Quebec	Forward	Steve Maltais, Chicago

James Gatschene Memorial (MVP) — Frederic Chabot, Houston
Governors' Trophy (Defenseman) — Brad Werenka, Indianapolis
Ironman Award (offense, defense and all games played) — Brad Werenka, Indianapolis
U.S. Born Rookie of the Year — Brian Felsner, Orlando
James Norris (Lowest goals against per team) — Rich Parent and Jeff Reese, Detroit
Rookie-of-the-Year — Sergei Samsanov, Detroit
Turner Cup (IHL Champions) — Detroit Vipers
Bud Poile (Playoff MVP) — Peter Ciavaglia, Detroit

IHL Regular Season All-Time Leaders

Goals

* Dave Michayluk	547
Scott Gruhl	532
Joe Kastelic	526
Bryan McLay	474
Len Thornson	426

Assists

Len Thornson	826
Chick Chalmers	791
* Jock Callander	679
* Dave Michayluk	636
Bryan McLay	626

Points

Len Thornson	1,252
* Dave Michayluk	1,183
Chick Chalmers	1,154
Scott Gruhl	1,144
Bryan McLay	1,100

Penalty Minutes

Kevin Evans	3,085
* Rick Hayward	2,413
Gord Malinoski	2,175
Paul Tantardini	2,150
Mike Rusin	2,045

Turner Cup Championships by Active Franchise

Cleveland	4
Fort Wayne	4
Michigan	2
San Antonio	2
Utah	2
Detroit	1
Indianapolis	1
Kansas City	1
Quebec	1

International Hockey League

International Hockey League
1577 N. Woodward Avenue, Suite 212
Bloomfield Hills, MI 48304
Phone: (810) 258-0940
Fax: (810) 258-0940

Chicago Wolves
10550 Lunt Avenue
Rosemont, Illinois, 60018
Phone: (847) 390-0404
Fax: (847) 390-9792
GM: Gene Ubriaco
Coach: Alpo Suhonen

Houston Aeros
24 Greenway Plaza, Suite 800
Houston, Texas 77046
Phone: (713) 621-2842
Fax: (713) 627-0397
GM: Steve Patterson
Coach: Dave Tippett

Cincinnati Cyclones
537 E. Pete Rose Way 2nd Floor
Cincinnati, Ohio 45202
Phone: (513) 421-7825
Fax: (513) 421-1210
GM: Ron Smith
Coach: Ron Smith

Indianapolis Ice
222 E. Ohio Street, #810
Indianapolis, Indiana 46204
Phone: (317) 266-1234
Fax: (317) 266-1233
GM: Ray Compton
Coach: Bob Ferguson

Michigan K-Wings
3620 Van Rick Drive
Kalamazoo, MI 49002
Phone: (616) 349-9772
Fax: (616) 345-6584
GM: Bill Inglis
Coach: Claude Noel

Cleveland Lumberjacks
One Center Ice, 200 Huron Road
Cleveland, Ohio 44115
Phone: (216) 420-0000
Fax: (216) 420-2500
GM: Larry Gordon
Coach: Perry Ganchar

Kansas City Blades
1800 Genesee
Kansas City, MO 64102
Phone: (816) 842-5233
Fax: (816) 842-5610
GM: Doug Soetaert
Coach: Paul MacLean

Milwaukee Admirals
1001 N. 4rth Street
Milwaukee, WI 53203
Phone: (414) 227-0550
Fax: (414) 227-0568
GM: Phil Wittliff
Coach: Al Sims

Detroit Vipers
2 Championship Drive
Auburn Hills, Michigan 48326
Phone: (810) 377-8613
Fax: (810) 377-2695
GM: Rick Dudley
Coach: Steve Ludzik

Las Vegas Thunder
P.O. Box 70065
Las Vegas, Nevada 89170-0065
Phone: (702) 798-7825
Fax: (702) 798-9464
GM: Bob Strumm
Coach: Chris McSorley

Orlando Solar Bears
1200 Edgewater Drive
Orlando, FL 32801
Phone: (407) 428-6600
Fax: (407) 841-6383
GM: Don Waddell
Coach: Curt Fraser

Fort Wayne Komets
1010 Memorial Way, Suite 100
Fort Wayne, Indiana 46805
Phone: (219) 483-0011
Fax: (219) 483-3899
GM: David Franke
Coach: John Torchetti

Long Beach Ice Dogs
300 E. Ocean Blvd.
Long Beach, CA 90802
Phone: (310) 423-3647
Fax: (310) 437-5116
GM: John Van Boxmeer
Coach: John Van Boxmeer

Phoenix Roadrunners
1826 W. McDowell Road
Phoenix, Arizona 85007
Phone: (602) 340-0001
Fax: (602) 340-0041
GM: Adam Keller
Suspended play for 1997-98

Grand Rapids Griffins
130 West Fulton
Van Andel Arena
Grand Rapids, Michigan 49503
Phone: (616) 774-4585
Fax: (616) 336-5464
GM: Bob McNamara
Coach: Dave Allison

San Francisco Spiders
885 Island Drive, Suite 202
Alameda, California 94502
Phone (510) 523-9900
Fax (510) 523-9987
PR Director: Kevin Gallant
Suspended play for 1997-98 season

Manitoba Moose
1430 Maroons Road

Winnipeg, Manitoba R3G 0L5
Phone: (204) 987-7825
Fax: (204) 896-6673
GM: Randy Carlyle
Coach: Randy Carlyle

San Antonio Dragons
600 East Market Street, Suite 103-B
San Antonio, Texas 78205
Phone: (210) 737-7825
Fax: (210) 212-8121
GM: Jeff Brubaker
Coach: Jeff Brubaker

Quebec Rafales
2205 Ave. Du Colisee'

Quebec, Quebec G1L 4W7
Phone: (418) 522-3000
Fax: (418) 522-5757
GM: Joe Bucchino
Coach: Jean Pronovost

Utah Grizzlies
301 South West Temple
Salt Lake City, UT 84101
Phone: (801) 325-7825
Fax: (801) 325-7820
GM: Butch Goring
Coach: Butch Goring

Divisional Alignment

Eastern Conference

Northeast Division
Detroit Vipers
Grand Rapids Griffins
Orlando Solar Bears
Quebec Rafales

Central Division
Cincinnati Cyclones
Cleveland Lumberjacks
Fort Wayne Komets
Indianapolis Ice
Michigan K-Wings

Western Conference

Midwest Division
Chicago Wolves
Kansas City Blades
Manitoba Moose
Milwaukee Admirals

Southwest Division
Houston Aeros
Las Vegas Thunder
Long Beach Ice Dogs
San Antonio Dragons
Utah Grizzlies

Central Hockey League
1996-97 Final Standings

Eastern Division

	GP	W	L	OTL	GF	GA	PTS
Huntsville	66	39	24	3	311	297	81
Macon	66	38	24	4	276	237	80
Memphis	66	35	27	4	278	260	74
Columbus	66	32	28	6	292	291	70
Nashville	66	12	52	2	219	359	26

Western Division

	GP	W	L	OTL	GF	GA	PTS
Oklahoma City	66	48	12	6	307	200	102
Fort Worth	66	45	16	5	279	210	95
Tulsa	66	30	32	4	286	284	64
Wichita	66	25	31	10	279	324	60
San Antonio	66	26	36	4	261	326	56

1997 Playoffs
First Round
Huntsville defeated Columbus 3-0
Memphis defeated Macon 3-2
Fort Worth defeated Tulsa 3-2
Wichita defeated Oklahoma City 3-1

Second Round
Fort Worth defeated Wichita 4-1
Memphis defeated Huntsville 4-2

Levins Trophy Championship
Fort Worth defeated Memphis 4-3

Fort Worth wins first Levins Trophy Championship

1996-97 Top 15 Scorers

Player		Team	Games	Goals	Assists	Points	PIM
Trevor	Jobe	Columbus	61	61	73	134	147
Doug	Lawrence	Tulsa	66	27	100	127	250
Terry	Menard	Fort Worth	63	50	65	115	138
Marcel	Richard	Columbus	63	51	58	109	74
Hardy	Sauter	Oklahoma City	66	32	69	101	54
Luc	Beausoleil	Tulsa	62	60	35	95	57
Bruno	Villeneuve	Macon	66	49	46	95	14
Alex	Kholomeyev	Huntsville	57	37	58	96	90
Joe	Burton	Oklahoma City	66	53	41	94	39
Alexei	Deev	Macon	66	38	54	92	28
Igor	Bonderev	Huntsville	60	38	53	91	26
George	Dupont	Oklahoma City	63	31	60	91	328
Paul	Jackson	San Antonio	61	44	46	90	391
Craig	Coxe	Tulsa	64	29	59	88	95
Bob	Berg	Wichita	56	36	49	85	105

Goals

Player	Team	Goals
Jobe	Columbus	61
Beausoleil	Tulsa	60
Burton	Oklahoma City	54
Richard	Columbus	51
Menard	Fort Worth	50

Assists

Player	Team	Assists
Lawrence	Tulsa	100
Jobe	Columbus	73
Murphy	Columbus	69
Sauter	Oklahoma City	57
Menard	Fort Worth	65

Penalty Minutes

Player	Team	PIM
Pisiak	Memphis	412
Jackson	San Antonio	391
Kopec	Wichita	365
Larocque	Fort Worth	354
Rushton	Tulsa	341

Top Goaltenders

Player	Team	GP	MIN	AVG	W	L	SOL	SO	GA	SAVES	SPCT
Filiatrault	Oklahoma City	41	2186	2.80	26	9	4	1	102	845	.892
Plouffe	Fort Worth	52	2983	2.88	38	9	5	2	143	1429	.909
Gagnon	Macon	57	3155	3.27	33	18	2	1	172	1609	.903
Nichol	Columbus	33	1676	3.62	19	6	2	1	101	684	.871
Thorpe	Memphis	35	1738	3.69	17	11	1	1	107	858	.889
Hamelin	Wichita	40	2215	3.76	18	16	3	0	139	1087	.887
Branch	Tulsa	18	1054	3.76	10	7	1	0	66	473	.877
Delormiere	Fort Worth	17	970	3.84	7	7	0	0	62	427	.873
Gregga	Wichita	16	714	3.87	4	5	2	0	46	368	.889

Wins

Player	Team	Wins
Plpouffe	Fort Worth	38
Gagnon	Macon	33
Seibel	Huntsville	28
Filiatrault	Oklahoma City	26
Nichol	Columbus	19

Minutes

Player	Team	Min
Gagnon	Macon	3155
Plouffe	Fort Worth	2983
Seibel	Huntsville	2709
Shybunka	Tulsa	2451
Pottie	San Antonio	2218

Save Percentage

Player	Team	SPCT
Plouffe	Fort Worth	.909
Gagnon	Macon	.903
Filiatrault	Oklahoma City	.892
St. Pierre	San Antonio	.889
Thorpe	Memphis	.889

CeHL Regular Season Award Winners

First Team	Position	Second Team
Steve Plouffe, Fort Worth	Goaltender	Jean-ian Filiatrault, OKC
Hardy Sauter, Oklahoma City	Defenseman	Dan Brown, Memphis
Igor Bonderev, Huntsville	Defenseman	Mike McCourt, Ft. Worth
Terry Menard, Fort Worth	Center	Trevor Jobe, Columbus
Joe Burton, Oklahoma City	Right Wing	Luc Beausoleil, Tulsa
Doug Lawrence, Tulsa	Left Wing	Bob Berg, Wichita

Most Valuable Player — Trevor Jobe, Columbus
Defenseman of the Year — Hardy Sauter, Oklahoma City
Rookie of the Year — Cory Dasdall, Wichita
Goaltender of the Year — Jean-ian Filiatrault, Oklahoma City
Coach of the Year — Bill McDonald, Fort Worth
Levins Trophy (CeHL Champions) — Fort Worth
President's Trophy (Playoff MVP) — Steve Plouffe, Fort Worth

Central League All-Time Leaders

Goals

*Joe Burton	245
*Paul Jackson	216
*Steve Simoni	149
*Luc Beausoleil	148
Taylor Hall	124

Assists

*Doug Lawrence	334
*Paul Jackson	224
*George Dupont	221
Dave Doucette	207
Brian Shantz	165

Points

*Paul Jackson	440
*Doug Lawrence	422
*Joe Burton	406
*George Dupont	311
*Bob Berg	287

Penalty Minutes

*Paul Jackson	1,041
*Doug Lawrence	996
*George Dupont	879
Greg Neish	874
Rob Weingartner	748

Wins

Tony Martino	100
*Mike Williams	69
Alan Perry	61
Bobby Desjardins	59
*Jean-ian Filiatrault	56

All-Time Levins Trophy Winners (Franchise Records)

Wichita	2
Tulsa	1
Oklahoma City	1
Fort Worth	1

Central Hockey League
222 East Ohio Street, Suite 820
Indianapolis, Indiana 46204
Phone: (317) 916-0555
Fax: (317) 916-0563

Western Division
Fort Worth Fire
University Centre
1300 S. University, Suite 515
Fort Worth, Texas 76107
Phone: (817) 336-1992
Fax: (817) 336-1997
GM: Matt van Hala
Coach: TBA

Memphis RiverKings
Mid-South Coliseum
The Fairgrounds
Memphis, Tennessee 38104
Phone (901) 278-9009
Fax (901) 274-3209
GM: Jim Riggs
Coach: Herb Boxer

Oklahoma City Blazers
119 N. Robinson, Suite 230
Oklahoma City, OK 73102
Phone: (405) 235-7825
Fax: (405) 272-9876
GM: Brad Lund
Coach: Doug Sauter

Tulsa Oilers
6413 S, Mingo, Suite 200
Tulsa, Oklahoma 74133
Phone: (918) 252-7825
Fax: (918) 249-5977
GM: Jeff Lund
Coach: Ric Seiling

Wichita Thunder
505 W. Maple, Suite 100

Wichita, Kansas 67213
Phone (316) 264-4625
Fax: (316) 264-3037
GM: Bill Shuck
 Coach: Bryan Wells

East Division
Columbus Cottonmouths
P.O. Box 1886
Columbus Civic Center, 400 Fourth
Columbus, Georgia 31902-1886
Phone: (706) 571-0086
Fax: (706) 571-0080
GM: Phil Roberto
Coach: Bruce Garber

Fayetteville Force
121 E. Mountain Drive
Room 22B
Fayetteville, North Carolina 28306
Phone (910) 438-9000
Fax (910) 438-9004
President: Alan May
Coach: Alan May

Huntsville Channel Cats
700 Monroe Street
Huntsville, Alabama 35801
Phone: (205) 551-2383
Fax: (205) 551-2382
GM: Conredge Holloway
Coach: Larry Floyd

Macon Whoopee
200 Coliseum Drive
Macon, Georgia 31217
Phone: (912) 741-1000
Fax: (912) 741-0089
GM: Pat Nugent
Coach: John Paris Jr.

Nashville Ice Flyers
P.O. Box 190595
417 4th Avenue North
Nashville, TN 37219
Phone: (615) 259-4625
Fax: (615) 259-2429
GM/Coach: David Lohrei
Assist GM/Dir. of Ops : Kim Jump

East Coast Hockey League

1996-97 Final Standings

East Division

	GP	W	L	SOL	GF	GA	PTS
South Carolina	70	45	15	10	345	253	100
Hampton Roads	70	46	19	5	286	223	97
Richmond	70	41	25	4	252	235	86
Roanoke	70	38	26	6	262	250	82
Charlotte	70	35	28	7	271	267	77
Raleigh	70	30	33	7	256	293	67
Knoxville	70	24	43	3	260	343	51

North Division

	GP	W	L	SOL	GF	GA	PTS
Columbus	70	44	21	5	303	257	93
Peoria	70	43	21	6	308	219	92
Dayton	70	36	26	8	253	258	80
Wheeling	70	36	29	5	298	291	77
Toledo	70	32	28	10	258	248	74
Huntington	70	33	33	4	273	296	70
Louisville	70	29	31	10	234	290	68
Johnstown	70	24	39	7	253	354	55

South Division

	GP	W	L	SOL	GF	GA	PTS
Tallahassee	70	39	23	8	263	236	86
Birmingham	70	36	25	9	291	296	81
Louisiana	70	38	28	4	292	244	80
Mobile	70	34	25	11	257	263	79
Mississippi	70	34	26	10	241	245	78
Pensacola	70	36	31	3	275	275	75
Baton Rouge	70	31	33	6	222	238	68
Jacksonville	70	21	37	12	220	299	54

1997 Playoffs
First Round
South Carolina defeated Charlotte 3-0
Hampton Roads defeated Roanoke 3-1
Richmond defeated Dayton 3-1
Columbus defeated Toledo 3-2
Peoria defeated Wheeling 3-0
Pensacola defeated Tallahassee 3-0
Birmingham defeated Mississippi 3-0
Louisiana defeated Mobile 3-0

Second Round
South Carolina defeated Hampton Roads 3-2
Peoria defeated Columbus 3-0
Pensacola defeated Richmond 3-1
Louisiana defeated Birmingham 3-2

Third Round
South Carolina defeated Pensacola 3-2
Louisiana defeated Peoria 3-1

Riley Cup Championship
South Carolina defeated Louisiana 4-1

South Carolina wins first ever Riley Cup

1995-96 Top 15 Scorers

Player		Team	Games	Goals	Assists	Points	PIM
Ed	Courtenay	South Carolina	68	54	56	110	70
Mike	Ross	South Carolina	70	50	60	110	35
Dany	Bousquet	Birmingham	68	54	53	107	39
John	Varga	Wheeling	66	56	45	101	84
Darren	Colbourne	Raleigh	69	53	48	101	32
Ron	Handy	Louisiana	66	33	67	100	58
Dave	Seitz	South Carolina	58	43	54	97	48
Dominic	Maltais	Hampton Roads	68	42	55	97	211
Jeff	Jablonski	Roanoke	68	52	44	96	30
Chad	Quenneville	Pensacola	70	43	52	95	67
Van	Burgess	Huntington	70	47	47	94	50
Scott	Burfoot	Richmond	62	32	62	94	37
Jim	Brown	Knoxville	64	44	48	92	66
Cal	Ingraham	Tallahassee	70	34	58	92	54
Alexsander	Chunchukov	Johnstown	70	34	58	92	75

Goals

Player	Team	Goals
Varga	Wheeling	56
Courtenay	South Carolina	54
Bousquet	Birmingham	54
Colbourne	Raleigh	53
Jablonski	Roanoke	52

Assists

Player	Team	Assists
Handy	Louisiana	67
De Pourcq	Louisiana	63
Burfoot	Richmond	62
Royal	Wheeling	61
Ling	Mobile	61

Penalty Minutes

Player	Team	PIM
Evans	Mississippi	505
Charbonneau	Wheeling	400
Jutras	Knoxville	399
McCaig	Louisiana	383
Gulash	Birmingham	363

Top Goaltenders

Player	Team	GP	MIN	AVG	W	L	SOL	SO	GA	SAVES	SPCT
Hillebrandt	Peoria	26	1487	2.82	18	4	1	2	70	667	.905
Herlofsky	Dayton	26	1549	2.87	17	4	4	1	74	716	.906
Bonner	Peoria	23	1315	2.87	13	8	1	1	63	567	.900
Goverde	Toledo	44	2554	2.96	23	14	6	5	126	1356	.915
Paquette	Hampton Roads	60	3388	2.98	35	15	5	4	168	1429	.895
Delorme	Louisiana	56	3115	3.06	36	14	3	2	159	1522	.905
Daigle	Mississippi	34	1951	3.08	20	8	5	2	100	1063	.914
Soucy	Baton Rouge	46	2421	3.17	18	20	3	3	128	1208	.904
Lendzyk	South Carolina	47	2590	3.20	28	10	7	0	138	1118	.890

Wins

Player	Team	Wins
Delorme	Louisiana	36
Salajko	Columbus	35
Paquette	Hampton Roads	35
Gagnon	Roanoke	34
Sundstrom	Wheeling	31

Minutes

Player	Team	Min
Paquette	Hampton Roads	3387
Gagnon	Roanoke	3386
Sundstrom	Wheeling	3360
Laurie	Huntington	3197
Delorme	Louisiana	3114

Save Percentage

Player	Team	SPCT
Scott	Baton Rouge	.917
Goverde	Toledo	.915
Daigle	Mississippi	.914
Herlofsky	Dayton	.906
Salajko	Columbus	.906

ECHL Regular Season Awards

First Team	Position	Second Team
Marc Delorme, Louisiana	Goaltender	David Goverde, Toledo
Chris Valicevic, Louisiana	Defenseman	Chris Hynnes, South Carolina
Chris Phelps, Hampton Roads	Defenseman	Bob Woods, Mobile
Mike Ross, South Carolina	Center	Dany Bousquet, Birmingham
Ed Courtenay, South Carolina	Right Wing	Dominic Maltais, HRD
Jeff Jablonski, Roanoke	Left Wing	Jason Elders, Mobile

Most Valuable Player — Mike Ross, South Carolina
Best Defenseman — Chris Valicevic, Louisiana
Rookie of the Year — Dany Bousquet, Birmingham
Best Goalie — Marc Delorme, Louisiana
Best Coach — Brian McCutcheon, Columbus
Riley Cup (ECHL Champions) — South Carolina Stingrays
Playoff MVP — Jason Fitzsimmons, South Carolina

ECHL All-Time Leaders

Games Played

Darren Schwartz	422
*Rob Dumas	362
*Phil Berger	360
*David Craievich	359
Perry Florio	358

Goals

Trevor Jobe	313
Darren Schwartz	286
*Darren Colbourne	263
*Phil Berger	251
*Sheldon Gorski	239

Assists

*Phil Berger	348
Trevor Jobe	298
*Darryl Noren	270
*Matt Robbins	269
*Victor Gervais	250

Points

Trevor Jobe	611
*Phil Berger	599
Darren Schwartz	515
*Darryl Noren	498
*Sheldon Gorski	474

Penalty Minutes

*Trevor Senn	1,643
Darren Schwartz	1,591
Jerome Bechard	1,361
Brock Kelly	1,203
*Cam Brown	1,200

Wins

*Nick Vitucci	194
*Rob Laurie	94
*Mark Richards	84
*Cory Cadden	83
Mark Bernard	82

Riley Cup Winners by Franchise

Hampton Roads	2
Toledo	2
South Carolina	1
Wheeling	1
Richmond	1
Charlotte	1

East Coast Hockey League
125 Village Boulevard, Suite 210
Princeton, New Jersey 08540
Phone (609) 452-0770
Fax: (609) 452-7147

Baton Rouge Kingfish
PO Box 2142
Baton Rouge, LA 70821
Phone: (504) 336-4625
Fax: (504) 336-4011
GM: Ron Hansis
Coach: Dave Schultz

Birmingham Bulls
PO Box 1506
Birmingham, AL 35201
Phone: (205) 458-8833
Fax: (205) 458-8489
GM: Art Clarkson
Coach: Dennis Desrosiers

Charlotte Checkers
2700 E. Independance Blvd.
Charlotte, NC 28205
Phone: (704) 342-4423
Fax: (704) 377-4595
GM: Fred Creighton
GM: John Marks

Columbus Chill
7001 Dublin Park Drive
Dublin, Ohio 43016
Phone: (614) 791-9999
Fax: (614) 791-9302
GM: David Paitson
Coach: TBA

Dayton Bombers
3640 Colonel Glenn Hwy. #417
Dayton, Ohio 43435
Phone: (937) 775-4747
Fax: (937) 775-4749
GM: Stephane Boutin
Coach: Mark Kumpel

Hampton Roads Admirals
PO Box 299
Norfolk, Virginia 23501
Phone: (757) 640-1212
Fax: (757) 640-8447
GM: Al MacIssac
GM: John Brophy

Huntington Blizzard
763 Third Avenue
Huntington, WV 25701
Phone: (304) 697-7825
Fax: (304) 697-7832
GM: Morris Jeffreys
Coach: Charlie Huddy

Jacksonville Lizard Kings
5569-7 Bowden Road
Jacksonville, FL 32216
Phone: (904) 448-8800
Fax: (904) 733-4413
GM: Larry Lane
Coach: Bruce Cassidy

Johnstown Chiefs
326 Napoleon Street
Johnstown, PA 15901
Phone: (814) 539-1799
Fax: (814) 536-1316
GM: Toby O'Brien
Coach: Nick Fotiu

Louisiana IceGators
444 Cajundome Blvd.
Lafayette, LA 70506
Phone: (318) 234-4423
Fax: (318) 232-1254
GM: Dave Berryman
Coach: Doug Shedden

Louisville RiverFrogs
PO Box 36407
Louisville, KY 40233
Phone: (502) 367-9121
Fax: (502) 368-5120
GM: Dale Owens
Coach: Warren Young

Mississippi Sea Wolves
2350 Beach Blvd.
Biloxi, MS 39531
Phone: (601) 388-6151
Fax: (601) 388-5848
GM: John Gagnon
Coach: Bruce Boudreau

Mobile Mysticks
PO Box 263
Mobile, Alabama 36601-0263
Phone: (334) 434-7932
Fax: (334) 434-7931
GM: Steve Chapman
Coach: Matt Shaw

New Orleans Brass
400 Poydros Street, #2450
New Orleans, Louisiana 70130
Phone (504) 522-7825
Fax: (504) 527-5436
GM: Larry Kish
Coach: Ted Sator

Pensacola Ice Pilots
Civic Center/E. Gregory St.-Rear
Pensacola, Florida 32501-4956
Phone: (850) 432-7825
Fax: (850) 432-1929
Hockey Ops: Joe Bucchino
Coach: Al Pederson

Peoria Rivermen
201 SW Jefferson
Peoria, Illinois 61602
Phone: (309) 676-1040
Fax: (309) 676-2488
GM: TBA
Coach: Mark Reeds

Raleigh IceCaps
4000 West Chase Blvd, Suite 110
Raleigh, NC 27607
Phone: (919) 755-1427
Fax: (919) 755-0899
GM: Frank Milne
Coach: Dan Wiebe

Richmond Renegades
601 E. Leigh Street
Richmond, VA 23219
Phone: (804) 643-7865
Fax: (804) 649-0651
Pres./Hockey Ops: Craig Laughlin
Coach: Scott Gruhl

Roanoke Express
4502 Starkey Rd. SW Suite 211
Roanoke, VA 24014
Phone: (540) 989-4625
Fax: (540) 989-8681
GM: Pierre Paiement
Coach: Frank Anzalone

South Carolina Stingrays
3107 Firestone Road
North Charleston, SC 29418
Phone: (803) 744-2248
Fax: (803) 744-2898
Hockey Ops: Rick Vaive
Coach: Rick Vaive

Tallahassee Tiger Sharks
133 North Monroe Street
Tallahassee, FL 32301
Phone: (850) 224-7700
Fax: (850) 224-6300
GM: TBA
Coach: Terry Christensen

Toledo Storm
One Main Street
Toledo, Ohio 43605
Phone: (419) 691-0200
Fax: (419) 698-8998
GM: Pat Pylypuik
Coach: Greg Puhalski

Wheeling Nailers
PO Box 6563
Wheeling, WV 26003-0815
Phone: (304) 234-4625
Fax: (304) 233-4846
GM: Marty Nash
Coach: Peter Laviolette

Chesapeake Icebreakers
14450 Old Mill Road, Suite 201
Upper Marlboro, Maryland 20772
Phone: (301) 952-0300
Fax: (301) 952-6875
Dir/Hockey Ops: Mike Mudd
Coach: Rick Paterson

Greenville Hockey (1998-99)
650 Academy Street
Greenville, South Carolina 29601
Phone (864) 241-3831
Fax: (864) 241-3872
GM Carl Scheer
Coach TBA

Pee Dee Pride
One Civic Center Plaza
3300 West Radio Drive
Florence, South Carolina, 29501
Phone: (803) 669-7825
Phone: (803) 669-7149
GM: Shawn Jones
Coach: Jack Capuano

Divisional Alignments

Northeast Division	Northwest Division	Southeast Division	Southwest Division
Chesapeake Icebreakers	Columbus Chill	Charlotte Checkers	Baton Rouge Kingfish
Hampton Roads Admirals	Dayton Bombers	Jacksonville Lizard Kings	Birmingham Bulls
Johnstown Chiefs	Huntington Blizzard	Pee Dee Pride	Louisiana IceGators
Richmond Renegades	Louisville River Frogs	Raleigh IceCaps	Mississippi Sea Wolves
Roanoke Express	Peoria Rivermen	South Carolina Stingrays	Mobile Mysticks
Wheeling Nailers	Toledo Storm	Tallahassee Tiger Sharks	New Orleans Brass
			Pensacola Ice Pilots

Colonial Hockey League

(Starting with the 1997-98 Season the Colonial League will be known as the United Hockey League)

1996-97 Final Standings
East Division

	GP	W	L	OTL	GF	GA	PTS
Flint	74	55	18	1	371	232	111
Brantford	74	42	25	7	321	286	91
Port Huron	74	38	31	5	280	288	81
Utica	74	22	42	10	278	385	54
Saginaw	74	21	48	5	263	399	47

West Division

	GP	W	L	T	GF	GA	PTS
Quad City	74	51	20	3	384	245	105
Madison	74	46	21	7	315	259	99
Thunder Bay	74	43	23	8	333	266	94
Muskegon	74	39	29	6	268	257	84
Dayton	74	13	53	8	216	412	34

1996 Playoffs
First Round
Flint defeated Utica 3-0
Brantford defeated Port Huron 3-2
Quad City defeated Muskegon 3-0
Thunder Bay defeated Madison 3-2

Second Round
Flint defeated Brantford 4-1
Quad City defeated Thunder Bay 4-3

Colonial Cup Championship
Quad City defeated Flint 4-2

Quad City wins their first Colonial Cup in franchise history

1996-97 Top 15 Scorers

Player		Team	Games	Goals	Assists	Points	PIM
Paul	Polillo	Brantford	73	61	112	173	49
Mark	Green	Saginaw	72	80	65	145	85
Glenn	Stewart	Quad City	65	66	69	135	30
Kevin	Kerr	Flint	68	72	53	125	200
Mike	Maurice	Brantford	60	48	76	124	48
Jason	Firth	Thunder Bay	56	37	83	120	22
Wayne	Muir	Brantford	73	52	65	117	212
Ross	Wilson	Flint	68	53	56	109	47
John	Vecchiarelli	Utica	73	56	50	106	153
Hugo	Proulx	Quad City	69	48	58	106	82
Kent	Hawley	Madison	72	28	77	105	48
Matt	Loen	Madison	73	47	56	103	16
Forbes	MacPherson	Thunder Bay	72	42	61	103	68
Brant	Blackned	Thunder Bay	70	49	51	100	79

Goals

Player	Team	Goals
Green	Saginaw	80
Kerr	Flint	72
Stewart	Quad City	66
Polillo	Brantford	61
Vecchiarelli	Utica	56

Assists

Player	Team	Assists
Polillo	Brantford	112
Firth	Thunder Bay	83
Hawley	Madison	77
Maurice	Brantford	76
Stewart	Quad City	69

Penalty Minutes

Player	Team	PIM
Davidson	Saginaw	440
Angelstad	Thunder Bay	422
Holliday	Thunder Bay	403
Scourletis	Port Huron	333
Eaton	Saginaw	301

Top Goaltenders

Player	Team	GP	MIN	AVG	W	L	SOL	SO	GA	SAVES	SPCT
Mezin	Flint	25	1417	2.46	19	4	1	2	58	531	.902
Zvyagin	Quad City	60	3475	2.99	42	15	2	1	173	1620	.904
Mazzoli	Muskegon	25	1429	3.02	13	10	2	1	72	650	.900
Rivard	Thunder Bay	37	2094	3.29	21	12	4	0	115	1067	.903
Derksen	Madison	59	3365	3.39	36	17	5	0	190	1686	.899
Krake	Brantford	52	2996	3.40	29	16	4	3	170	1591	.903
Galkin	Flint	42	2351	3.42	31	10	0	1	134	975	.879
Bell	Thunder Bay	41	2340	3.49	22	11	4	0	136	1170	.896
Karpenko	Port Huron	23	1149	3.50	9	9	1	0	67	540	.890
Greer	Muskegon	30	1595	3.54	15	10	2	0	94	813	.896
Caley	Muskegon	23	1284	3.55	10	8	2	0	76	605	.888
Butt	Port Huron	46	2451	3.72	25	15	3	0	152	1169	.885
Fletcher	Quad City	19	941	4.02	9	5	1	0	63	413	.868

Wins			Minutes			Save Percentage		
Player	Team	Wins	Player	Team	Min	Player	Team	SPCT
Zvyagin	Quad City	42	Zvyagin	Quad City	3474	Franek	Brantford	.930
Derksen	Madison	36	Derksen	Madison	3364	Zvyagin	Quad City	.904
Galkin	Flint	31	Krake	Brantford	2995	Krake	Brantford	.903
Krake	Brantford	29	Butt	Port Huron	2451	Rivard	Thunder Bay	.903
Butt	Port Huron	25	Galkin	Flint	2350	Mezin	Flint	.902

CoHL Regular Season Awards

First Team	Position	Second Team
Sergei Zvyagin, Quad City	Goaltender	Duane Derksen, Madison
Brett MacDonald, Flint	Defenseman	John Batten, Quad City
Barry McKinlay, Thunder Bay	Defenseman	Bernie John, Brantford
Paul Polillo, Brantford	Center	Jason Firth, Thunder Bay
Kevin Kerr, Flint	Right Wing	Mike Maurice, Brantford
Glenn Stewart, Quad City	Left Wing	Wayne Muir, Brantford

(MVP) Paul Polillo, Brantford
(Defenseman) Barry McKinlay, Thunder Bay
(Sportmanship) Kent Hawley, Madison
(Rookie) Forbes MacPherson, Thunder Bay
(Goalie) Sergei Zvyagin, Quad City
(Best Defenseive Forward) Brian Downey, Madison
Colonial Cup (CoHL Champions) Quad City Mallards
(Playoff MVP) Sergei Zvyagin, Quad City Mallards

UHL All-Time Leaders

Games Played		Goals		Assists	
*Kent Hawley	363	*Paul Polillo	247	*Paul Polillo	511
*Brett MacDonald	357	*Kevin Kerr	245	*Kent Hawley	346
*Paul Polillo	344	*Mark Green	202	*Jason Firth	322
*Barry McKinlay	327	*Bob McKillop	186	*Brian Sakic	284
*Steve Beadle	324	*Kent Hawley	167	*Barry McKinlay	265

Points		Penalty Minutes		Wins	
*Paul Polillo	758	*Bruce Ramsay	1,793	*Kevin Butt	123
*Kent Hawley	513	*Mel Angelstad	1,704	*Sergei Zvyagin	74
*Jason Firth	473	Jacques Mailhot	1,302	Pat Szturm	61
*Kevin Kerr	456	Andy Bezeau	1,072	*Ron Bertrand	60
Terry Menard	401	*Kevin Kerr	987	*Duane Derksen	55

All-Time Colonial Cups By Franchise
Thunder Bay 3
Quad City 1
Flint 1
Brantford 1

United Hockey League
1301 Edgewater Point Suite 301
Lake St. Louis, Missouri 63367
Phone: (314) 625-6011
Fax: (314) 625-2009

Brantford Smoke
69-79 Market Street South
Brantford, Ontario, N3T 5R7
Phone (519) 751-9467
Fax: (519) 751-2366
GM: Larry Trader
Coach: Larry Trader

B.C. Icemen
One Stuart Street
Binghamton, New York 13901
Phone: (607) 772-9300
Fax: (607) 772-0707
GM: Patrick Snyder
Coach: Al Hill

Flint Generals
3501 Lapeer Road
Flint, Michigan 48503
Phone: (810) 742-9422
Fax: (810) 742-5892
GM: Robbie Nicholls
Coach: Robbie Nicholls

Madison Monsters
Dane County Exposition Center
1881 Expo Mall East
Madison, WI 53713
Phone: (608) 251-2884
Fax: (608) 251-2923
VP Operations: TBA
Coach: Kent Hawley

Muskegon Fury
470 West Western Avenue
Muskegon, MI 49440
Phone: (616) 726-5058
Fax: (616) 728-0428
GM: Tony Lisman
Coach: Paul Kelly

Port Huron Border Cats
215 Huron Avenue
Port Huron, MI 48060
Phone: (810) 982-2287
Fax: (810) 982-9838
GM: Costa Papista
Coach: Doug Crossman

Quad City Mallards
501 15th Street, Suite 900
Moline, Illinois 61265
Phone: (309) 764-7825
Fax: (309) 764-7858
GM: Howard Cornfield
Coach: TBA

Saginaw Lumber Kings
4855 State Street, Suite 3
Saginaw, MI 48603
Phone: (517) 790-3771
Fax: (517) 790-7161
GM: John Blum
Coach: John Blum

Thunder Bay Thunder Cats
901 Miles Street East
Thunder Bay, Ontario P7C 1J9
Phone: (807) 623-7121
Fax: (807) 622-3306
GM: Gary Cook
Coach: Kevin Devine

Winston-Salem IceHawks
300 Deacon Boulevard
Winston-Salem, NC 27015
Phone: (910) 748-9111
Fax: (910) 748-8002
GM: Jeff Croop
Coach: Robert Dirk

Divisional Alignment

East Division
B.C. Icemen
Brantford Smoke
Flint Generals
Port Huron Border Cats
Saginaw Lumber Kings

West Division
Madison Monsters
Muskegon Fury
Quad City Mallards
Thunder Bay Thunder Cats
Winston-Salem IceHawks

West Coast Hockey League
1996-97 Final Standings

	GP	W	L	OTL	GF	GA	PTS
San Diego	64	50	12	2	400	210	102
Anchorage	64	41	18	5	349	260	87
Fresno	64	38	20	6	313	254	82
Bakersfield	64	33	26	5	345	325	71
Reno	64	16	43	5	252	418	37
Alaska	64	13	47	4	230	423	30

1997 Playoffs
First Round
San Diego defeated Bakersfield 3-1
Anchorage defeated Fresno 3-2
Championship
San Diego defeated Anchorage 4-0

San Diego wins second consecutive Taylor Cup

1999-97 Top 15 Scorers

Player		Team	Games	Goals	Assists	Points	PIM
Martin	St. Amour	San Diego	59	60	67	127	182
Steve	Dowhy	Bakersfield	63	51	78	124	84
Keith	Street	Anchorage	64	44	70	114	61
Criag	Lyons	Fresno	61	51	60	111	108
Glen	Gulutzan	Fresno	60	30	80	110	52
Dean	Larson	Anchorage	58	29	79	108	54
Stephane	St. Amour	San Diego	61	56	51	107	167
Mark	Stitt	San Diego	63	31	75	106	99
Kevin	St. Jacques	San Diego	57	41	62	103	148
Derek	Donald	Anchorage	57	51	47	98	52
Sean	Rowe	Anchorage	58	43	53	96	40
Lindsay	Vallis	Bakersfield	58	26	65	91	82
Brad	Belland	San Diego	54	22	68	90	132
Carl	Boudreau	Reno	55	32	53	85	57
Chris	Newans	Anchorage	60	26	57	83	331

Goals			Assists			Penalty Minutes		
Player	Team	Goals	Player	Team	Assists	Player	Team	PIM
Martin St. Amour	San Diego	60	Gulutzan	Fresno	80	Wagner	San Diego	503
Stephane St. Amour	San Diego	56	Larson	Anchorage	79	Shmyr	Anchorage	388
Donald	Anchorage	51	Stitt	San Diego	75	Spenrath	Fresno	375
Dowhy	Bakersfield	51	Dowhy	Bakersfield	73	Newans	Anchorage	331
Craig Lyons	Fresno	51	Street	Anchorage	70	Richard	Anchorage	313

Top Goaltenders

Player	Team	GP	MIN	AVG	W	L	SOL	SO	GA	SAVES	SPCT
Naumov	San Diego	49	2832	3.14	38	8	2	1	148	1303	.898
Laviolette	San Diego	19	995	3.44	12	4	0	0	57	450	.888
Shestok	Fresno	18	935	3.59	12	2	0	1	56	409	.879
Ouellette	Anchorage	51	2959	3.85	30	15	5	0	190	1372	.878
Ferguson	Fresno	51	2895	3.92	26	18	6	0	189	1413	.882
Trigg	Anchorage	17	871	4.14	11	3	0	1	60	434	.878
Schill	Bakersfield	55	3034	4.81	27	22	3	2	243	1675	.873
French	Alaska	35	1770	6.27	5	21	2	0	185	975	.841
Reynolds	Reno	29	1460	6.37	6	19	1	0	155	924	.856

Wins			Minutes			Save Percentage		
Player	Team	Wins	Player	Team	Min	Player	Team	SPCT
Naumov	San Diego	38	Schill	Bakersfield	3033	Naumov	San Diego	.898
Ouellette	Anchorage	30	Ouellette	Anchorage	2959	Laviolette	San Diego	.888
Schill	Bakersfield	27	Ferguson	Fresno	2894	Ferguson	Fresno	.882
Ferguson	Fresno	26	Naumov	San Diego	2831	Shestok	Fresno	.879
Several	@	12	French	Alaska	1770	Trigg	Anchorage	.878

WCHL Awards

First Team	Position	Second Team
Sergei Naumov, San Diego	Goaltender	Francis Ouellette, Anchorage
		(tie) Jeff Ferguson, Fresno
Alan Leggett, San Diego	Defenseman	Chris Newans, Anchorage
Glen Mears, Bakersfield	Defenseman	Hayden O'Rear, Anchorage
Steve Dowhy, Bakersfield	Center	Dean Larson, Anchorage
Martin St. Amour, San Diego	Left Wing	Sean Rowe, Anchorage
Craig Lyons, Fresno	Right Wing	Stephane St. Amour, SD
		(tie) Lindsay Vallis, BFD

(MVP) Martin St. Amour, San Diego
(Defenseman) Alan Leggett, San Diego
(Goalie) Sergei Naumov, San Diego
Taylor Cup (WCHL Champions) San Diego Gulls
(Playoff MVP) Alan Leggett, San Diego

WCHL All-Time Leaders

Games Played			Goals			Assists		
*Shawn Ulrich	127		*Martin St. Amour	121		*Brad Belland	140	
*Steve Dowhy	121		*Derek Donald	89		*Dean Larson	140	
*Greg Spenrath	118		*Keith Street	88		*Steve Dowhy	126	
*Keith Street	118		*Steve Dowhy	87		*Martin St. Amour	115	
*Jamie Adams	116		*Shawn Ulrich	69		* Keith Street	110	
Points			Penalty Minutes			Wins		
*Martin St. Amour	236		*Chad Wagner	792		*Sergei Naumov	86	
*Steve Dowhy	213		*Chad Richard	669		*Jeff Ferguson	48	
*Dean Larson	200		*Greg Spenrath	581		*Lee Schill	40	
*Keith Street	198		*Al Murphy	504		*Frank Ouellette	39	
*Brad Belland	192		*Mark Kuntz	454		*Todd Henderson	20	

All-Time Taylor Cups by Franchise

San Diego 2

Alaska Gold Kings
529 4th Avenue
Fairbanks, Alaska 99701
Phone: (907) 456-7825
Fax: (907) 452-4020
President/CEO: John Rosie
Franchise Suspended for 97-98

Bakersfield Fog
5301 Office Park Drive Suite 400
Bakersfield, California 93309
Phone (805) 324-7825
Fax: (805) 324-6929
G.M. Jay Brazeau
Coach: Keith Gretzky

Phoenix Mustangs
1826 West McDowell Road
Phoenix, Arizona, 85007
Phone: (602) 340-0001
Fax: (602) 340-0041
GM: Adam Keller
Coach: Brad McCaughey

Tucson Gila Monsters
110 South Church Ave. Suite 7184 A
Tucson, AZ 85701
Phone: (520) 903-9000
Fax: (520) 903-9002
GM: JD Lash
Coach: Martin Raymond

Anchorage Aces
245 West 5th Avenue, Suite 128
Anchorage, Alaska 99501
Phone: (907) 258-2237
Fax: (907) 278-4297
G.M. Walt Edwards
Coach: Walt Poddubny

Reno Rage
4590 S. Virginia Street
Reno, Nevada 89502
Phone: (702) 828-3400
Fax: (702) 828-6093
GM: Tom O'Gorman
Coach: Ron Flockhart

San Diego Gulls
3500 Sports Arena Blvd.
San Diego, California 92110
Phone: (619) 225-9813
Fax (619) 224-3010
G.M. Steve Ferguson
Coach: Steve Martinson

North Division
Anchorage Aces
Idaho Steelheads
Reno Rage
Tacoma Sabrecats

Fresno's Fighting Falcons
PO Box 26916
Fresno, CA 93729-6916
Phone: (209) 650-4000
Fax: (209) 438-5691
G.M. Dean Hargrove
Coach: Guy Gadowsky

Idaho Steelheads
290 Bobwhite Court, Suite 300
Boise, Idaho, 83706
Phone: (208) 383-0080
Fax: (208) 383-0194
GM: Matt Loughran
Head Coach: Dave Langevin

Tacoma Sabrecats
1111 South Fawcett Ave., Suite 204
Tacoma, WA 98402
Phone: (253) 627-2673
Fax: (253) 573-1009
GM: John Olver
Coach: John Olver

West Coast Hockey League
63 Keystone Avenue, Suite 201
Reno, Nevada 89503
Phone (702) 329-7666
Fax: (702) 329-3048

South Division
Bakersfield Fog
Fresno's Fighting Falcons
Phoenix Mustangs
San Diego Gulls
Tucson Gila Monsters

Western Professional Hockey League
1996-97 Final Standings

	GP	W	L	OTL	GF	GA	PTS
New Mexico	64	42	20	2	323	258	86
Austin	64	35	22	7	271	249	77
El Paso	64	33	23	8	284	272	74
Central Texas	64	35	27	2	243	229	72
Waco	64	30	30	4	220	249	64
Amarillo	64	17	39	8	239	323	42

1997 Playoffs
First Round
Central Texas defeated New Mexico 4-2
El Paso defeated Austin 4-2
Championship
El Paso defeated Central Texas 4-1

El Paso wins inaugural WPHL Championship

1999-97 Top 15 Scorers

Player		Team	Games	Goals	Assists	Points	PIM
Chris	Brooks	Amarillo	64	45	65	110	34
Bobby	Wallwork	Austin	61	42	53	95	80
Sylvain	Naud	New Mexico	53	47	44	91	131
Brett	Seguin	Austin	53	35	54	89	26
Rob	Hartnell	Waco	67	31	55	86	94
Chris	MacKenzie	El Paso	55	29	55	84	50
Mike	Tomlinson	New Mexico	58	32	45	77	143
Kurt	Wickenheiser	New Mexico	55	46	28	74	62
Doug	Smith	Central Texas	63	31	40	71	105
Jody	Praznik	New Mexico	61	18	52	70	74
Andy	Ross	Austin	61	35	34	69	34
Mark	Karpen	Amarillo	57	32	36	68	38
Doug	Roberts	New Mexico	63	31	37	68	40
Chris	Robertson	New Mexico	40	29	39	68	60
Jim	Burton	Austin	52	21	47	68	65

Goals

Player	Team	Goals
Naud	New Mexico	47
Wickenheiser	New Mexico	46
Brooks	Amarillo	45
Wallwork	Austin	42
Several Tied	@	35

Assists

Player	Team	Assists
Brooks	Amarillo	65
Hartnell	Waco	55
MacKenzie	El Paso	55
Seguin	Austin	54
Wallwork	Austin	53

Penalty Minutes

Player	Team	PIM
Zurba	Central Texas	291
Boucher	New Mexico	263
Taylor	Central Texas	250
Mailhot	Central Texas	247
Shmyr	New Mexico	240

Top Goaltenders

Player	Team	GP	MIN	AVG	W	L	SOL	SO	GA	SAVES	SPCT
Berthiaume	Central Texas	54	3034	3.38	30	20	0	2	171	1533	.900
Blue	Austin	33	1955	3.47	17	11	5	1	113	1095	.906
Martino	New Mexico	51	2846	3.50	33	13	1	1	166	1458	.898
Pye	Waco	46	2620	3.64	22	21	2	0	159	1226	.885
Erickson	Austin	32	1875	3.90	18	11	2	0	122	1138	.903
Gordon	El Paso	50	2762	4.06	26	18	5	0	187	1356	.879
Thomas	El Paso	27	1072	4.08	7	5	3	0	73	497	.872
DelGuidice	Amarillo	49	2620	4.42	13	26	7	0	193	1475	.884
Laurin	Amarillo	25	1200	5.40	4	13	1	0	108	685	.864

Wins

Player	Team	Wins
Martino	New Mexico	33
Berthiaume	Austin	30
Gordon	El Paso	26
Pye	Waco	22
Erickson	Austin	18

Minutes

Player	Team	Min
Berthiaume	Central Texas	3033
Martino	New Mexico	2845
Gordon	El Paso	2761
DelGuidice	Amarillo	2619
Pye	Waco	2619

Save Percentage

Player	Team	SPCT
Blue	Austin	.906
Grobins	Waco	.904
Erickson	Austin	.903
Berthiaume	Central Texas	.900
Martino	New Mexico	.898

WPHL Awards

(MVP)	Chris Brooks, Amarillo
(Defenseman)	Jody Praznik, New Mexico
(Goalie)	Daniel Berthiaume, Central Texas
President's Cup (WPHL Champions)	El Paso Buzzards
(Playoff MVP)	Chris MacKenzie, El Paso

Western Professional Hockey League
14040 North Cave Creek Road, Suite #100
Phoenix, Arizona
Phone (602) 485-9399
Fax: (602) 485-9449

Amarillo Rattlers
320 South Polk St., Suite #800
Amarillo, Texas 79101
Phone: (806) 374-7825
Fax: (806) 374-7835
Contact: Mark Adams
Coach: Mike Collins

Austin Ice Bats
7311 Decker Lane
Austin, Texas 78724
Phone: (512) 927-7825
Fax: (512) 927-7828
Contact: Scott Shaunessy
Coach: Jim Burton

Central Texas Stampede
600 Forest Drive
Belton, Texas 76513
Phone (254) 933-3500
Fax: (254) 933-9490
Contact: John Jordan
Coach: TBA

Odessa Jackalopes
PO Box 51187
Midland, Texas 79710
Phone: (915) 552-7825
Fax: (915) 550-6670
Contact: Monty Hoppel
Coach: Joe Clark

El Paso Buzzards
4100 East Paisano Drive
El Paso, Texas 79905
Phone: (915) 534-7825
Fax: (915) 534-7876
Contact: Kimm Neff
Coach: Todd Brost

New Mexico Scorpions
1101 Cardenas Plaza, Suite 201
Albuquerque, NM 87110
Phone: (505) 232-7825
Fax: (505) 232-7829
Contact: Steve Thayer
Coach: Garry Unger

Waco Wizards
2040 North Valley Mills Drive
Waco, Texas 79710
Phone: (915) 399-9300
Fax (915) 399-9100
Contact: Deb Baize
Coach: Coach: Rob Schriner

San Angelo Outlaws
3260 Sherwood Way
San Angelo, Texas 76901
Phone: (915) 949-7825
Fax: (915) 223-0999
Contact: Dick Moore
Coach: Shaun Clouston

Fort Worth Bulls
819 Penn Street
Fort Worth, Texas 76102
Phone: (817) 335-7825
Fax: (817) 882-9393
Contact: Ernie Horn
Coach: Bill McDonald

Lake Charles Ice Pilots
900 Lakeshore Drive
Civic Center 2nd Floor
Lake Charles, LA 70602
Phone: (318) 436-0055
Fax: (318) 436-0054
Contact: Thom Hager
Coach: Dennis Maruk

Monroe Moccasins
2102 Louisville Avenue
Monroe. LA 71201
Phone: (318) 398-9434
Fax: (318) 398-9992
Contact: Ray Delia
Coach: Rob Bremner

Shreveport Mudbugs
3701 Hudson Street, 2nd Floor
Shreveport, Louisiana 71109
Phone: (318) 636-2847
Fax: (318) 636-2280
Contact: Dan Heisserer
Coach: Jean Laforest

East Division
Austin Ice Bats
Central Texas Stampede
Fort Worth Bulls
Lake Charles Ice Pilots
Monroe Moccasins
Shreveport Mudbugs
Waco Wizards

West Division
Amarillo Rattlers
El Paso Buzzards
New Mexico Scorpions
Odessa Jackalopes
San Angelo Outlaws

Workhorse Goaltenders

Port Huron netminder Kevin Butt leads the United League in all-time wins.

Photo courtesy of Border Cats

Norm Maracle was amongst the AHL leaders in several categories, including wins, minutes and save percentage. Photo by Just Sports

Double the Teams, Double the Noise!

WPHL
WESTERN PROFESSIONAL HOCKEY LEAGUE

Merchandise 1-800-882-8852
All 12 teams including t-shirts for the 1998-99 Corpus Christi expansion club

New Mexico's Sylvain Naud was one of the top stars during the WPHL's inaugural season.   Photo provided by WPHL.

searching for minor pro news

on the internet??

your search is over

http://www.inthecrease.com

In the Crease
Professional Hockey Journal

"The world revolves around hockey"

Titles by Athletic Guide Publishing

Ice Pages Minor Professional Hockey Guide

How To Market Your Student Athlete

College Basketball Guide

College Volleyball Guide

College Hockey Guide

Junior Hockey Hockey Guide

Prep School Hockey Guide

Pro Hockey Guide

Hockey Camp Guide

Hockey DeskTop Reference

For a catalog call

800-255-1050

or write

Athletic Guide Publishing
P. O. Box 1050
Flagler Beach, FL 32136-1050